Stanley Gibbons
Stamp Catalogue

Middle East

(including Iraq, Israel, Jordan, Lebanon,
Palestinian Authority and Syria)

1st Edition 2018

STANLEY GIBBONS LTD
London and Ringwood

By Appointment to
Her Majesty The Queen
Philatelists
Stanley Gibbons Ltd,
London

1st edition – 2018

Published by Stanley Gibbons Ltd
Editorial, Publications Sales Offices
7 Parkside, Christchurch Road, Ringwood,
Hants BH24 3SH

British Library Cataloguing in
Publication Data.
A catalogue record for this book is available
from the British Library.

Errors and omissions excepted. The colour reproduction of stamps is only as accurate as the printing process will allow.

ISBN-13: 978-1-911304-26-5

Item No. R 1420-18

Printed by
Cambrian Printers, Wales

Stanley Gibbons Foreign Catalogue

ABOUT THIS EDITION

It is over 35 years since the present split into 'Parts 2 to 22' was announced, dividing up what had up to then been an alphabetical listing of European and Overseas countries over seven large volumes into handy-sized catalogues, bringing together countries or groups of countries, generally united by geography or political affiliations.

Back in 1979 the new 'Parts' catalogues proved to be very popular with collectors, but over time these volumes have grown in size, with the ever increasing numbers of new issues.

In 2015 Stanley Gibbons celebrated 150 years of catalogue production and it seemed the right time to take a look at the structure and break down of our Foreign catalogue range.

This is the second part of our Middle East catalogue.

- Prices have been thoroughly revised and brought up to date, by leading experts in the field.
- Specimen stamps have been included for the first time.
- New varieties have been added to this catalogue; see the next page for a detailed list.
- Other areas of interest covered in this catalogue include; Gaza and Palestine.

New issue listings have been updated:

- Iraq – listed to December 2017
- Israel – December 2017
- Jordan – December 2017
- Lebanon – December 2017
- Palestinian Authority – December 2017
- Syria – August 2017

Addresses for specialist societies for this area are on page iv.

The first supplement to this catalogue appeared in *Gibbons Stamp Monthly* for December 2018.

We would like to thank James Bendon for all his advice with the listing of specimen stamps in this catalogue and also Norayr Agopian for his advice.

Hugh Jefferies, Editor
Clare de la Feuillade, Deputy Editor
Sue Price, New Issues Listings
Barbara Hawkins, Pricing Assistant
Emma Fletcher, Designer and page layout

STAMPS ADDED

IRAQ
Z54
Z197
Z206
Z207
Z230
2b
19b
107e
2516a

II. Issues for Baghdad
4a
11a
20ab
20ac

III. Issues for Mosul
5a

ISRAEL
619a
1482a
1572a
MS1772*a*
1803a
1892*a*/1892*c*
1892*d*/1892*i*
1918*a*/1918*c*
MS1979*a*
2011c
2063b
2073b
2101a
SB42*a*
SB42*b*

LEBANON
1358*a*
MS1445*a*

PALESTINIAN AUTHORITY
PA73b
PA237a
PA369a
PA371a

SYRIA
2075a
2075*b*
2338a
2346a

JORDAN
4a
12a
67a
O117b

NUMBERS ALTERED

IRAQ

OLD	NEW
10a	10ab
10b	10a
2242a	2242b
2243a	2243b
2244a	2244b

ISRAEL

OLD	NEW
1482a	1482b
1666a	1668
1668	1669
1669	1670
1670	1671
1671	1672
1672	1673
1672a	1674
1673	1675
1674	1676

SYRIA

OLD	NEW
1777a	1778
1778	1779
1779	1780
1780	1781
1781	1782
1782	1783
1783	1784
1784	1785

SPECIALIST SOCIETIES

Arabian Philatelic Association
Contact: David Jessich
3600 Avendale Drive
Austin
Texas
78738-5026
USA

Email: jessich@hotmail.com

Society of Israel Philatelists
Website: www.israelstamps.com
Email: israelstamps@gmail.com

Holyland Philatelic Society
Secretary: D. Smith
25 Matford Avenue
Exeter
EX2 4PL

Email: holylandphilatelicsociety@yahoo.com

Contents

Stanley Gibbons Holdings Plc

Stanley Gibbons Limited,
Stanley Gibbons Auctions
399 Strand, London WC2R 0LX
Tel: +44 (0)207 836 8444
Fax: +44 (0)207 836 7342
E-mail: help@stanleygibbons.com
Website: www.stanleygibbons.com
for all departments, Auction and Specialist Stamp Departments.
Open Monday–Friday 9.30 a.m. to 5 p.m.
Shop. Open Monday–Friday 9 a.m. to 5.30 p.m. and Saturday 9.30 a.m. to 5.30 p.m.

Stanley Gibbons Publications,
Gibbons Stamp Monthly and Philatelic Exporter
7 Parkside, Christchurch Road, Ringwood, Hampshire BH24 3SH.
Tel: +44 (0)1425 472363
Fax: +44 (0)1425 470247
E-mail: help@stanleygibbons.com
Publications Mail Order.
FREEPHONE 0800 611622
Monday–Friday 8.30 a.m. to 5 p.m.

Stanley Gibbons (Asia) Limited
12/F, 100 Queen's Road Central
Central Hong Kong
Tel: +852 3180 9370
E-mail: elee@stanleygibbons.com

Stanley Gibbons Publications Overseas Representation
Stanley Gibbons Publications are represented overseas by the following

Australia
Renniks Publications PTY LTD
Unit 3 37-39 Green Street,
Banksmeadow, NSW 2019, Australia
Tel: +612 9695 7055
Website: www.renniks.com

Canada
Unitrade Associates
99 Floral Parkway, Toronto,
Ontario M6L 2C4, Canada
Tel: +1 416 242 5900
Website: www.unitradeassoc.com

Germany
Schaubek Verlag Leipzig
Am Glaeschen 23, D-04420
Markranstaedt, Germany
Tel: +49 34 205 67823
Website: www.schaubek.de

Italy
Ernesto Marini S.R.L.
V. Struppa, 300, Genova, 16165, Italy
Tel: +3901 0247-3530
Website: www.ernestomarini.it

Japan
Japan Philatelic
PO Box 2, Suginami-Minami,
Tokyo 168-8081, Japan
Tel: +81 3330 41641
Website: www.yushu.co.jp

Netherlands (also covers Belgium Denmark, Finland & France)
Uitgeverij Davo BV
PO Box 411, Ak Deventer, 7400
Netherlands
Tel: +315 7050 2700
Website: www.davo.nl

New Zealand
House of Stamps
PO Box 12, Paraparaumu,
New Zealand
Tel: +61 6364 8270
Website: www.houseofstamps.co.nz

Philatelic Distributors
PO Box 863
15 Mount Edgecumbe Street
New Plymouth 4615, New Zealand
Tel: +6 46 758 65 68
Website: www.stampcollecta.com

Norway
SKANFIL A/S
SPANAV. 52 / BOKS 2030
N-5504 HAUGESUND, Norway
Tel: +47-52703940
E-mail: magne@skanfil.no

Singapore
C S Philatelic Agency
Peninsula Shopping Centre #04-29
3 Coleman Street, 179804, Singapore
Tel: +65 6337-1859
Website: www.cs.com.sg

South Africa
Peter Bale Philatelics
P.O. Box 3719
Honeydew 2040
Gauteng
South Africa
Tel: +27 11 462 2463
E-mail: balep@iafrica.com

Sweden
Chr Winther Sorensen AB
Box 43, S-310 20 Knaered, Sweden
Tel: +46 43050743
Website: www.collectia.se

General Philatelic Information and Guidelines to the Scope of Stanley Gibbons Foreign Catalogues

These notes reflect current practice in compiling the Foreign Catalogue.

The *Stanley Gibbons Stamp Catalogue* has a very long history and the vast quantity of information it contains has been carefully built up by successive generations through the work of countless individuals. Philately itself is never static and the Catalogue has evolved and developed during this long time-span. These notes apply to current policy – some of the older listings were prepared using slightly different criteria – and we hope you find them useful in using the catalogue.

THE CATALOGUE IN GENERAL

Contents. The Catalogue is confined to adhesive postage stamps, including miniature sheets. For particular categories the rules are:

(a) Revenue (fiscal) stamps or telegraph stamps are listed only where they have been expressly authorised for postal duty.

(b) Stamps issued only precancelled are included, but normally issued stamps available additionally with precancel have no separate precancel listing unless the face value is changed.

(c) Stamps prepared for use but not issued, hitherto accorded full listing, are nowadays footnoted with a price (where possible).

(d) Bisects (trisects, etc.) are only listed where such usage was officially authorised.

(e) Stamps issued only on first day covers and not available separately are not listed but priced (on the cover) in a footnote.

(f) New printings, as such, are not listed, though stamps from them may qualify under another category, e.g. when a prominent new shade results.

(g) Official and unofficial reprints are dealt with by footnote.

(h) Stamps from imperforate printings of modern issues which also occur perforated are covered by footnotes or general notes, but are listed where widely available for postal use.

Exclusions. The following are excluded:

(a) non-postal revenue or fiscal stamps;

(b) postage stamps used fiscally;

(c) local carriage labels and private local issues;

(d) telegraph stamps;

(e) bogus or phantom stamps;

(f) railway or airline letter fee stamps, bus or road transport company labels;

(g) cut-outs;

(h) all types of non-postal labels;

(i) documentary labels for the postal service, e.g. registration, recorded delivery, airmail etiquettes, etc.;

(j) privately applied embellishments to official issues and privately commissioned items generally;

(k) stamps for training postal officers;

(l) specimen stamps. (except those distributed by the UPU)

Full listing. 'Full listing' confers our recognition and implies allotting a catalogue number and (wherever possible) a price quotation.

In judging status for inclusion in the catalogue broad considerations are applied to stamps. They must be issued by a legitimate postal authority, recognised by the government concerned, and must be adhesives valid for proper postal use in the class of service for which they are inscribed. Stamps, with the exception of such categories as postage dues and officials, must be available to the general public, at face value, in reasonable quantities without any artificial restrictions being imposed on their distribution.

We record as abbreviated Appendix entries, without catalogue numbers or prices, stamps from countries which either persist in having far more issues than can be justified by postal need or have failed to maintain control over their distribution so that they have not been available to the public in reasonable quantities at face value. Miniature sheets and imperforate stamps are not mentioned in these entries.

The publishers of this catalogue have observed, with concern, the proliferation of 'artificial' stamp-issuing territories. On several occasions this has resulted in separately inscribed issues for various component parts of otherwise united states or territories.

Stanley Gibbons Publications have decided that where such circumstances occur, they will not, in the future, list these items in the SG catalogue without first satisfying themselves that the stamps represent a genuine political, historical or postal division within the country concerned. Any such issues which do not fulfil this stipulation will be recorded in the Catalogue Appendix only.

For errors and varieties the criterion is legitimate (albeit inadvertent) sale over a post office counter in the normal course of business. Details of provenance are always important; printers' waste and fraudulently manufactured material is excluded.

Certificates. In assessing unlisted items due weight is given to Certificates from recognised Expert Committees and, where appropriate, we will usually ask to see them.

New issues. New issues are listed regularly in the Catalogue Supplement in *Gibbons Stamp Monthly*, then consolidated into the next available edition of the Catalogue.

Date of issue. Where local issue dates differ from dates of release by agencies, 'date of issue' is the local date. Fortuitous stray usage before the officially intended date is disregarded in listing.

Catalogue numbers. Stamps of each country are catalogued chronologically by date of issue. Subsidiary classes (e.g. postage due stamps) are integrated into one list with postage and commemorative stamps and distinguished by a letter prefix to the catalogue number.

The catalogue number appears in the extreme left column. The boldface type numbers in the next column are merely cross-references to illustrations. Catalogue numbers in the *Gibbons Stamp Monthly* Supplement are provisional only and may need to be altered when the lists are consolidated. Miniature sheets only purchasable intact at a post office have a single MS number; sheetlets – individual stamps available – number each stamp separately. The catalogue no longer gives full listing to designs originally issued in normal sheets, which subsequently appear in sheetlets showing changes of colour, perforation, printing process or face value. Such stamps will be covered by footnotes.

Once published in the Catalogue, numbers are changed as little as possible; really serious renumbering is reserved for the occasions when a complete country or an entire issue is being rewritten. The edition first affected includes cross-reference tables of old and new numbers.

Our catalogue numbers are universally recognised in specifying stamps and as a hallmark of status.

Illustrations. Stamps are illustrated at three-quarters linear size. Stamps not illustrated are the same size and format as the value shown unless otherwise indicated. Stamps issued only as miniature sheets have the stamp alone illustrated but sheet size is also quoted. Overprints, surcharges, watermarks and postmarks are normally actual size. Illustrations of varieties are often enlarged to show the detail.

CONTACTING THE CATALOGUE EDITOR

The editor is always interested in hearing from people who have new information which will improve or correct the Catalogue. As a general rule he must see and examine the actual stamps before they can be considered for listing; photographs or photocopies are insufficient evidence. Neither he nor his staff give opinions as to the genuineness of stamps.

Submissions should be made in writing to the Catalogue Editor, Stanley Gibbons Publications, 7 Parkside, Christchurch Road, Ringwood, Hants BH24 3SH. The cost of return postage for items submitted is appreciated, and this should include the registration fee if required.

Where information is solicited purely for the benefit of the enquirer, the editor cannot undertake to reply if the answer is already contained in these published notes or if return postage is omitted. Written communications are greatly preferred to enquiries by telephone or e-mail and the editor regrets that he or his staff cannot see personal callers without a prior appointment being made.

The editor welcomes close contact with study circles and is interested, too, in finding local correspondents who will verify and supplement official information in overseas countries where this is deficient.

We regret we do not give opinions as to the genuineness of stamps, nor do we identify stamps or number them by our Catalogue.

TECHNICAL MATTERS

The meanings of the technical terms used in the Catalogue will be found in *Philatelic Terms Illustrated*, published by Stanley Gibbons (Price £14.95 plus postage).

1. Printing

Printing errors. Errors in printing are of major interest to the Catalogue. Authenticated items meriting consideration would include background, centre or frame inverted or omitted; centre or subject transposed; error of colour; error or omission of value; double prints and impressions; printed both sides; and so on. Designs *tête-bêche*, whether intentionally or by accident, are listable. *Se-tenant* arrangements of stamps are recognised in the listings or footnotes. Gutter pairs (a pair of stamps separated by blank margin) are excluded unless they have some philatelic importance. Colours only partially omitted are not listed, neither are stamps printed on the gummed side.

Printing varieties. Listing is accorded to major changes in the printing base which lead to completely new types. In recess-printing this could be a design re-engraved, in photogravure or photolithography a screen altered in whole or in part. It can also encompass flat-bed and rotary printing if the results are readily distinguishable.

To be considered at all, varieties must be constant.

Early stamps, produced by primitive methods, were prone to numerous imperfections; the lists reflect this, recognising re-entries, retouches, broken frames, misshapen letters, and so on. Printing technology has, however, radically improved over the years, during which time photogravure and lithography have become predominant. Varieties nowadays are more in the nature of flaws and these, being too specialised for a general catalogue, are almost always outside the scope. We therefore do not list such items as dry prints, kiss prints, doctor-blade flaws, blanket set-offs, doubling through blanket stretch, plate cracks and scratches, registration flaws (leading to colour shifts), lithographic ring flaws, and so on. Neither do we recognise fortuitous happenings like paper creases or confetti flaws.

Overprints (and surcharges). Overprints of different types qualify for separate listing. These include overprints in different colours; overprints from different printing processes such as litho and typo; overprints in totally different typefaces, etc.

Overprint errors and varieties. Major errors in machine-printed overprints are important and listable. They include overprint inverted or omitted; overprint double (treble, etc.); overprint diagonal; overprint double, one inverted; pairs with one overprint omitted, e.g. from a radical shift to an adjoining stamp; error of colour; error of type fount; letters inverted or omitted, etc. If the overprint is handstamped, few of these would qualify and a distinction is drawn.

Varieties occurring in overprints will often take the form of broken letters, slight differences in spacing, rising spacers, etc. Only the most important would be considered for footnote mention.

Sheet positions. If space permits we quote sheet positions of listed varieties and authenticated data is solicited for this purpose.

2. Paper

All stamps listed are deemed to be on 'ordinary' paper of the wove type and white in colour; only departures from this are mentioned.

Types. Where classification so requires we distinguish such other types of paper as, for example, vertically and horizontally laid; wove and laid bâtonné; card(board); carton; cartridge, enamelled; glazed; GC (Grande Consommation); granite; native; pelure; porous; quadrillé; ribbed; rice; and silk thread.

The 'traditional' method of indentifying chalk-surfaced papers has been that, when touched with a silver wire, a black mark is left on the paper, and the listings in this catalogue are based on that test. However, the test itself is now largely discredited, for, although the mark can be removed by a soft rubber, some damage to the stamp will result from its use.

The difference between chalk-surfaced and pre-war ordinary papers is fairly clear: chalk-surfaced papers being smoother to the touch and showing a characteristic sheen when light is reflected off their surface. Under good magnification tiny bubbles or pock marks can be seen on the surface of the stamp and at the tips of the perforations the surfacing appears 'broken'. Traces of paper fibres are evident on the surface of ordinary paper and the ink shows a degree of absorption into it.

The various makeshifts for normal paper are listed as appropriate. They include printing on: unfinished banknotes, war maps, ruled paper, Post Office forms, and the unprinted side of glossy magazines. The varieties of double paper and joined paper are recognised.

Descriptive terms. The fact that a paper is hand-made (and thus probably of uneven thickness) is mentioned where necessary. Such descriptive terms as 'hard' and 'soft'; 'smooth' and 'rough'; 'thick', 'medium' and 'thin' are applied where there is philatelic merit in classifying papers.

Coloured, very white and toned papers. A coloured paper is one that is coloured right through (front and back of the stamp). In the Catalogue the colour of the paper is given in italics, thus

black/*rose* = black design on rose paper.

Papers have been made specially white in recent years by, for example, a very heavy coating of chalk. We do not classify shades of whiteness of paper as distinct varieties. There does exist, however, a type of paper from early days called toned. This is off-white, often brownish or buffish, but it cannot be assigned a definite colour. A toning effect brought on by climate, incorrect storage or gum staining is disregarded here, as this was not the state of the paper when issued.

Safety devices. The Catalogue takes account of such safety devices as varnish lines, grills, burelage or imprinted patterns on the front or moiré on the back of stamps.

Modern developments. Two modern developments also affect the listings, printing on self-adhesive paper and the tendency, philatelic in origin, for conventional paper to be reinforced or replaced by different materials. Some examples are the use of foils in gold, silver, aluminium, palladium and steel; application of an imitation wood veneer; printing on plastic moulded in relief; and use of a plastic laminate to give a three-dimensional effect. Examples also occur of stamps impregnated with scent; printed on silk; and incorporating miniature gramophone records.

3. Perforation and Rouletting

Perforation gauge. The gauge of a perforation is the number of holes in a length of 2 cm. For correct classification the size of the holes (large or small) may need to be distinguished; in a few cases the actual number of holes on each edge of the stamp needs to be quoted.

Measurement. The Gibbons Instanta gauge is the standard for measuring perforations. The stamp is viewed against a dark background with the transparent gauge put on top of it. Though the gauge measures to decimal accuracy, perforations read from it are generally quoted in the Catalogue to the nearest half. For example:

Just over perf.
12¾ to just under perf. 13¼ = perf. 13
Perf. 13¼ exactly, rounded up = perf. 13½
Just over perf.
13¼ to just under perf. 13¾ = perf. 13½
Perf. 13¾ exactly, rounded up = perf. 14

However, where classification depends on it, actual quarter-perforations are quoted.

Notation. Where no perforation is quoted for an issue it is imperforate. Perforations are usually abbreviated (and spoken) as follows, though sometimes they may be spelled out for clarity. This notation for rectangular stamps (the majority) applies to diamond shapes if 'top' is read as the edge to the top right.

P 14: perforated alike on all sides (read: 'perf. 14').

P 14×15: the first figure refers to top and bottom, the second to left and right sides (read: 'perf. 14 by 15'). This is a compound perforation. For an upright triangular stamp the first figure refers to the two sloping sides and the second to the base. In inverted triangulars the base is first and the second figure refers to the sloping sides.

P 14-15: perforation measuring anything between 14 and 15: the holes are irregularly spaced, thus the gauge may vary along a single line or even along a single edge of the stamp (read: 'perf. 14 to 15').

P 14 irregular. perforated 14 from a worn perforator, giving badly aligned holes irregular spaced (read 'irregular perf. 14').

P *comp(ound)* 14×15: two gauges in use but not necessarily on opposite sides of the stamp. It could be one side in one gauge and three in the other, or two adjacent sides with the same gauge (Read: 'perf. compound of 14 and 15'). For three gauges or more, abbreviated as 'P 14, 14½, 15 or compound' for example.

P 14, 14½: perforated approximately 14¼ (read: 'perf. 14 or 14½'). It does not mean two stamps, one perf. 14 and the other perf. 14½. This obsolescent notation is gradually being replaced in the Catalogue.

Imperf: imperforate (not perforated).

Imperf × P 14: imperforate at top and bottom and perf 14 at sides.

P 14 × *imperf* = perf 14 at top and bottom and imperforate at sides.

Such headings as 'P 13 × 14 (vert) and P 14 × 13 (horiz)' indicate which perforations apply to which stamp format – vertical or horizontal.

Some stamps are additionally perforated so that a label or tab is detachable; others have been perforated suitably for use as two halves. Listings are normally for whole stamps, unless stated otherwise.

Other terms. Perforation almost always gives circular holes; where other shapes have been used they are specified, e.g. square holes; lozenge perf. Interrupted perfs are brought about by the omission of pins at regular intervals. Perforations have occasionally been simulated by being printed as part of the design. With few exceptions, privately applied perforations are not listed.

Perforation errors and varieties. Authenticated errors, where a stamp normally perforated is accidentally issued imperforate, are listed provided no traces of perforation (blind holes or indentations) remain. They must be provided as pairs, both stamps wholly imperforate, and are only priced in that form.

Stamps merely imperforate between stamp and margin (fantails) are not listed.

Imperforate-between varieties are recognised, where one row of perfs has been missed. They are listed and priced in pairs:

Imperf between (horiz pair): a horizontal pair of stamps with perfs all around the edges but none between the stamps.

Imperf between (vert pair): a vertical pair of stamps with perfs all around the edges but none between the stamps.

Where several of the rows have escaped perforation the resulting varieties are listable. Thus:

Imperf vert (horiz pair): a horizontal pair of stamps perforated top and bottom; all three vertical directions are imperf – the two outer edges and between the stamps.

Imperf horiz (vert pair): a vertical pair perforated at left and right edges; all three horizontal directions are imperf – the top, bottom and between the stamps.

Straight edges. Large sheets cut up before issue to post offices can cause stamps with straight edges, i.e. imperf on one side or on two sides at right angles. They are not usually listable in this condition and are worth less than corresponding stamps properly perforated all round. This does not, however, apply to certain stamps, mainly from coils and booklets, where straight edges on various sides are the manufacturing norm affecting every stamp. The listings and notes make clear which sides are correctly imperf.

Malfunction. Varieties of double, misplaced or partial perforation caused by error or machine malfunction are not listable, neither are freaks, such as perforations placed diagonally from paper folds. Likewise disregarded are missing holes caused by broken pins, and perforations 'fading out' down a sheet, the machinery progressively disengaging to leave blind perfs and indentations to the paper.

Centering. Well-centred stamps have designs surrounded by equal opposite margins. Where this condition affects the price the fact is stated.

Type of perforating. Where necessary for classification, perforation types are distinguished. These include:

Line perforation from one line of pins punching single rows of holes at a time.

Comb perforation from pins disposed across the sheet in comb formation, punching out holes at three sides of the stamp a row at a time.

Harrow perforation applied to a whole pane or sheet at one stroke.

Rotary perforation from the toothed wheels operating across a sheet, then crosswise.

Sewing-machine perforation. The resultant condition, clean-cut or rough, is distinguished where required.

Pin-perforation is the commonly applied term for pin-roulette in which, instead of being punched out, round holes are pricked by sharp-pointed pins and no paper is removed.

Punctured stamps. Perforation holes can be punched into the face of the stamp. Patterns of small holes, often in the shape of initial letters, are privately applied devices against pilferage. These 'perfins' are outside the scope. Identification devices, when officially inspired, are listed or noted; they can be shapes, or letters or words formed from holes, sometimes converting one class of stamp into another.

Rouletting. In rouletting the paper is cut, for ease of separation, but none is removed. The gauge is measured, when needed, as for perforations. Traditional French terms descriptive of the type of cut are often used and types include:

Arc roulette (percé en arc). Cuts are minute, spaced arcs, each roughly a semicircle.

Cross roulette (percé en croix). Cuts are tiny diagonal crosses.

Line roulette (parcé en ligne or en ligne droite). Short straight cuts parallel to the frame of the stamp. The commonest basic roulette. Where not further described, 'roulette' means this type.

Rouletted in colour or coloured roulette (percé en lignes colorees or en lignes de coleur). Cuts with coloured edges, arising from notched rule inked simultaneously with the printing plate.

Saw-tooth roulette (percé en scie). Cuts applied zigzag fashion to resemble the teeth of a saw.

Serpentine roulette (percé en serpentin). Cuts as sharply wavy lines.

Zigzag roulettes (percé en zigzags). Short straight cuts at angles in alternate directions, producing sharp points on separation. US usage favours 'serrate(d) roulette' for this type.

Pin-roulette (originally *percé en points* and now *perforés trous d'epingle)* is commonly called pin-perforation in English.

4. Gum

All stamps listed are assumed to have gum of some kind; if they were issued without gum this is stated. Original gum (o.g.) means that which was present on the stamp as issued to the public. Deleterious climates and the presence of certain chemicals can cause gum to crack and, with early stamps, even make the paper deteriorate. Unscrupulous fakers are adept in removing it and regumming the stamp to meet the unreasoning demand often made for 'full o.g.' in cases where such a thing is virtually impossible.

Until recent times the gum used for stamps has been gum arabic, but various synthetic adhesives – tinted or invisible-looking – have been in use since the 1960s. Stamps existing with more than one type of gum are not normally listed separately, though the fact is noted where it is of philatelic significance, e.g. in distinguishing reprints or new printings.

The distinct variety of grilled gum is, however, recognised. In this the paper is passed through a gum breaker prior to printing to prevent subsequent curling. As the patterned rollers were sufficient to impress a grill into the paper beneath the gum we can quote prices for both unused and used examples.

Self-adhesive stamps are issued on backing paper from which they are peeled before affixing to mail. Unused examples are priced as for backing paper intact. Used examples are best kept on cover or on piece.

5. Watermarks

Stamps are on unwatermarked paper except where the heading to the set says otherwise.

Detection. Watermarks are detected for Catalogue description by one of four methods:

(1) holding stamps to the light;

(2) laying stamps face down on a dark background;

(3) adding a few drops of petroleum ether 40/60 to the stamp laid face down in a watermark tray; or

(4) by use of the Stanley Gibbons Detectamark, or other equipment, which works by revealing the thinning of the paper at the watermark. (Note that petroleum ether is highly inflammable in use and can damage photogravure stamps.)

Listable types. Stamps occurring on both watermarked and unwatermarked papers are different types and both receive full listing.

Single watermarks (devices occurring once on every stamp) can be modified in size and shape as between different issues; the types are noted but not usually separately listed. Fortuitous absence of watermark from a single stamp or its gross displacement would not be listable.

To overcome registration difficulties the device may be repeated at close intervals (a **multiple watermark**), single stamps thus showing parts of several devices. Similarly a large **sheet watermark** (or all-over watermark) covering numerous stamps can be used. We give informative notes and illustrations for them. The designs may be such that numbers of stamps in the sheet automatically lack watermark; this is not a listable variety. Multiple and all-over watermarks sometimes undergo modifications, but if the various types are difficult to distinguish from single stamps notes are given but not separate listings.

Papermakers' watermarks are noted where known but not listed separately, since most stamps in the sheet will lack them. Sheet watermarks which are nothing more than officially adopted papermakers' watermarks are, however, given normal listing.

Marginal watermarks, falling outside the pane of stamps, are ignored except where misplacement causes the adjoining row to be affected, in which case they may be footnoted.

Watermark errors and varieties. Watermark errors are recognised as of major importance. They comprise stamps intended to be on unwatermarked paper but issued watermarked by mistake, or stamps printed on paper with the wrong watermark. Watermark varieties, on the other hand, such as broken or deformed bits on the dandy roll, are not listable.

Watermark positions. Paper has a side intended for printing and watermarks are usually impressed so that they read normally when looked through from that printed side.

Illustrations in the Catalogue are of watermarks in normal positions (from the front of the stamps) and are actual size where possible.

Differences in watermark position are collectable as distinct varieties. In this Catalogue, however, only normal sideways watermarks are listed (and 'sideways inverted' is treated as 'sideways'). Inverted and reversed watermarks have always been outside its scope: in the early days of flat-bed printing, sheets of watermarked paper were fed indiscriminately through the press and the resulting watermark positions had no particular philatelic significance. Similarly, the special make-up of sheets for booklets can in some cases give equal quantities of normal and inverted watermarks.

6. Colours

Stamps in two or three colours have these named in order of appearance, from the centre moving outwards.

Four colours or more are usually listed as multicoloured.

In compound colour names the second is the predominant one, thus:

orange-red = a red tending towards orange;
red-orange = an orange containing more red than usual.

Standard colours used. The 200 colours most used for stamp identification are given in the Stanley Gibbons Colour Key. The Catalogue has used the Key as a standard for describing new issues for some years. The names are also introduced as lists are rewritten, though exceptions are made for those early issues where traditional names have become universally established.

Determining colours. When comparing actual stamps with colour samples in the Key, view in a good north daylight (or its best substitute: fluorescent 'colour-matching' light). Sunshine is not recommended. Choose a solid portion of the stamp design; if available, marginal markings such as solid bars of colour or colour check dots are helpful. Shading lines in the design can be misleading as they appear lighter than solid colour. Postmarked portions of a stamp appear darker than normal. If more than one colour is present, mask off the extraneous ones as the eye tends to mix them.

Errors of colour. Major colour errors in stamps or overprints which qualify for listing are: wrong colours; one colour inverted in relation to the rest; albinos (colourless impressions), where these have Expert Committee certificates; colours completely omitted, but only on unused stamps (if found on used stamps the information is footnoted).

Colours only partially omitted are not recognised.

Colour shifts, however spectacular, are not listed.

Shades. Shades in philately refer to variations in the intensity of a colour or the presence of differing amounts of other colours. They are particularly significant when they can be linked to specific printings. In general, shades need to be quite marked to fall within the scope of this Catalogue; it does not favour nowadays listing the often numerous shades of a stamp, but chooses a single applicable colour name which will indicate particular groups of outstanding shades. Furthermore, the listings refer to colours as issued: they may deteriorate into something different through the passage of time.

Modern colour printing by lithography is prone to marked differences of shade, even within a single run, and variations can occur within the same sheet. Such shades are not listed.

Aniline colours. An aniline colour meant originally one derived from coal-tar; it now refers more widely to colour of a particular brightness suffused on the surface of a stamp and showing through clearly on the back.

Colours of overprints and surcharges. All overprints and surcharges are in black unless otherwise in the heading or after the description of the stamp.

7. Luminescence

Machines which sort mail electronically have been introduced in recent years. In consequence some countries have issued stamps on fluorescent or phosphorescent papers, while others have marked their stamps with phosphor bands.

The various papers can only be distinguished by ultraviolet lamps emitting particular wavelengths. They are separately listed only when the stamps have some other means of distinguishing them, visible without the use of these lamps. Where this is not so, the papers are recorded in footnotes or headings. (Collectors using the lamps should exercise great care in their use as exposure to their light is extremely dangerous to the eyes).

Phosphor bands are listable, since they are visible to the naked eye (by holding stamps at an angle to the light and looking along them, the bands appear dark). Stamps existing with and without phosphor bands or with differing numbers of bands are given separate listings. Varieties such as double bands, misplaced or omitted bands, bands printed on the wrong side, are not listed.

8. Coil Stamps

Stamps issued only in coil form are given full listing. If stamps are issued in both sheets and coils the coil stamps are listed separately only where there is some feature (e.g. perforation) by which singles can be distinguished. Coil strips containing different stamps *se-tenant* are also listed.

Coil join pairs are too random and too easily faked to permit of listing; similarly ignored are coil stamps which have accidentally suffered an extra row of perforations from the claw mechanism in a malfunctioning vending machine.

9. Booklet Stamps

Single stamps from booklets are listed if they are distinguishable in some way (such as watermark or perforation) from similar sheet stamps. Booklet panes, provided they are distinguishable from blocks of sheet stamps, are listed for most countries; booklet panes containing more than one value *se-tenant* are listed under the lowest of the values concerned.

Lists of stamp booklets are given for certain countries and it is intended to extend this generally.

10. Forgeries and Fakes

Forgeries. Where space permits, notes are considered if they can give a concise description that will permit unequivocal detection of a forgery. Generalised warnings, lacking detail, are not nowadays inserted since their value to the collector is problematic.

Fakes. Unwitting fakes are numerous, particularly 'new shades' which are colour changelings brought about by exposure to sunlight, soaking in water contaminated with dyes from adherent paper, contact with oil and dirt from a pocketbook, and so on. Fraudulent operators, in addition, can offer to arrange: removal of hinge marks; repairs of thins on white or coloured papers; replacement of missing margins or perforations; reperforating in true or false gauges; removal of fiscal cancellations; rejoining of severed pairs, strips and blocks; and (a major hazard) regumming. Collectors can only be urged to purchase from reputable sources and to insist upon Expert Committee certification where there is any doubt.

The Catalogue can consider footnotes about fakes where these are specific enough to assist in detection.

PRICES

Prices quoted in this Catalogue are the selling prices of Stanley Gibbons Ltd at the time when the book went to press. They are for stamps in fine condition for the issue concerned; in issues where condition varies they may ask more for the superb and less for the sub-standard.

All prices are subject to change without prior notice and Stanley Gibbons Ltd may from time to time offer stamps at other than catalogue prices in consequence of special purchases or particular promotions.

No guarantee is given to supply all stamps priced, since it is not possible to keep every catalogued item in stock. Commemorative issues may, at times, only be available in complete sets and not as individual values.

Quotations of prices. The prices in the left-hand column are for unused stamps and those in the right-hand column are for used.

Prices are expressed in pounds and pence sterling. One pound comprises 100 pence (£1 = 100p).

The method of notation is as follows: pence in numerals (e.g. 10 denotes ten pence); pounds and pence up to £100, in numerals (e.g. 4·25 denotes four pounds and twenty-five pence); prices above £100 expressed in whole pounds with the '£' sign shown.

Unused stamps. Prices for stamps issued up to the end of the Second World War (1945) are for lightly hinged examples and more may be asked if they are in unmounted mint condition. Prices for all later unused stamps are for unmounted mint. Where not available in this condition, lightly hinged stamps are often available at a lower price.

Used stamps. The used prices are normally for stamps postally used but may be for stamps cancelled-to-order where this practice exists.

A pen-cancellation on early issues can sometimes correctly denote postal use. Instances are individually noted in the Catalogue in explanation of the used price given.

Prices quoted for bisects on cover or on large piece are for those dated during the period officially authorised.

Stamps not sold unused to the public but affixed by postal officials before use (e.g. some parcel post stamps) are priced used only.

Minimum price. The minimum catalogue price quoted is 10p. For individual stamps prices between 10p and 95p are provided as a guide for catalogue users. The lowest price charged for individual stamps purchased from Stanley Gibbons Ltd. is £1.

Set prices. Set prices are generally for one of each value, excluding shades and varieties, but including major colour changes. Where there are alternative shades, etc, the cheapest is usually included. The number of stamps in the set is always stated for clarity.

Where prices are given for *se-tenant* blocks or strips any mint price quoted is for the complete *se-tenant* strip or block. Mint and used set prices are always for a set of single stamps.

Repricing. Collectors will be aware that the market factors of supply and demand directly influence the prices quoted in this Catalogue. Whatever the scarcity of a particular stamp, if there is no one in the market who wishes to buy it it cannot be expected to achieve a high price. Conversely, the same item actively sought by numerous potential buyers may cause the price to rise.

All the prices in this Catalogue are examined during the preparation of each new edition by expert staff of Stanley Gibbons and repriced as necessary. They take many factors into account, including supply and demand, and are in close touch with the international stamp market and the auction world.

GUARANTEE

All stamps are guaranteed genuine originals in the following terms:

If not as described, and returned by the purchaser, we undertake to refund the price paid to us in the original transaction. If any stamp is certified as genuine by the Expert Committee of the Royal Philatelic Society, London, or by B.P.A. Expertising Ltd, the purchaser shall not be entitled to make claim against us for any error, omission or mistake in such certificate. Consumers' statutory rights are not affected by this guarantee.

The establishment Expert Committees in this country are those of the Royal Philatelic Society, 41 Devonshire Place, London W19 6JY, and B.P.A. Expertising Ltd, P.O. Box 1141, Guildford, Surrey GU5 0WR. They do not undertake valuations under any circumstances and fees are payable for their services.

Abbreviations

Printers

A.B.N. Co.	American Bank Note Co, New York.
B.A.B.N.	British American Bank Note Co. Ottawa
B.D.T.	B.D.T. International Security Printing Ltd, Dublin, Ireland
B.W.	Bradbury Wilkinson & Co, Ltd.
Cartor	Cartor S.A., La Loupe, France
C.B.N.	Canadian Bank Note Co, Ottawa.
Continental	Continental Bank Note Co. B.N. Co.
Courvoisier	Imprimerie Courvoisier S.A., La-Chaux-de-Fonds, Switzerland.
D.L.R.	De La Rue & Co, Ltd, London.
Enschedé	Joh. Enschedé en Zonen, Haarlem, Netherlands.
Format	Format International Security Printers Ltd., London
Harrison	Harrison & Sons, Ltd. London
J.W.	John Waddington Security Print Ltd., Leeds
P.B.	Perkins Bacon Ltd, London.
Questa	Questa Colour Security Printers Ltd, London
Walsall	Walsall Security Printers Ltd
Waterlow	Waterlow & Sons, Ltd, London.

General Abbreviations

Alph	Alphabet
Anniv	Anniversary
Comp	Compound (perforation)
Des	Designer; designed
Diag	Diagonal; diagonally
Eng	Engraver; engraved
F.C.	Fiscal Cancellation
H/S	Handstamped
Horiz	Horizontal; horizontally
Imp, Imperf	Imperforate
Inscr	Inscribed
L	Left
Litho	Lithographed
mm	Millimetres
MS	Miniature sheet
N.Y.	New York
Opt(d)	Overprint(ed)
P or P-c	Pen-cancelled
P, Pf or Perf	Perforated
Photo	Photogravure
Pl	Plate
Pr	Pair
Ptd	Printed
Ptg	Printing
R	Right
R.	Row
Recess	Recess-printed
Roto	Rotogravure
Roul	Rouletted
S	Specimen (overprint)
Surch	Surcharge(d)
T.C.	Telegraph Cancellation
T	Type
Typo	Typographed
Un	Unused
Us	Used
Vert	Vertical; vertically
W or wmk	Watermark
Wmk s	Watermark sideways

(†) = Does not exist

(–) (or blank price column) = Exists, or may exist, but no market price is known.

/ between colours means 'on' and the colour following is that of the paper on which the stamp is printed.

Colours of Stamps

Bl (blue); blk (black); brn (brown); car, carm (carmine); choc (chocolate); clar (claret); emer (emerald); grn (green); ind (indigo); mag (magenta); mar (maroon); mult (multicoloured); mve (mauve); ol (olive); orge (orange); pk (pink); pur (purple); scar (scarlet); sep (sepia); turq (turquoise); ultram (ultramarine); verm (vermilion); vio (violet); yell (yellow).

Colour of Overprints and Surcharges

(B.) = blue, (Blk.) = black, (Br.) = brown, (C.) = carmine, (G.) = green, (Mag.) = magenta, (Mve.) = mauve, (Ol.) = olive, (O.) = orange, (P.) = purple, (Pk.) = pink, (R.) = red, (Sil.) = silver, (V.) = violet, (Vm.) or (Verm.) = vermilion, (W.) = white, (Y.) = yellow.

Arabic Numerals

As in the case of European figures, the details of the Arabic numerals vary in different stamp designs, but they should be readily recognised with the aid of this illustration.

٠	١	٢	٣	٤	٥	٦	٧	٨	٩
0	1	2	3	4	5	6	7	8	9

International Philatelic Glossary

Arabia	*English*	*French*	*German*	*Spanish*
عقيقي	Agate	Agate	Achat	Agata
طابع بريد جوي	Air stamp	Timbre de la poste aérienne	Flugpostmarke	Sello de correo aéreo
أخضر تفاحي	Apple Green	Vert-pomme	Apfelgrün	Verde manzana
	Barred	Annulé par barres	Balkenentwertung	Anulado con barras
مقسوم الى شطرين	Bisected	Timbre coupé	Halbiert	Partido en dos
الذهبي المطفي - بيج	Bistre	Bistre	Bister	Bistre
بيج غامق	Bistre-brown	Brun-bistre	Bisterbraun	Castaño bistre
أسود	Black	Noir	Schwarz	Negro
بني مسود	Blackish Brown	Brun-noir	Schwärzlichbraun	Castaño negruzco
أخضر مسود	Blackish Green	Vert foncé	Schwärzlichgrün	Verde negruzco
زيتي مسود	Blackish Olive	Olive foncé	Schwärzlicholiv	Oliva negruzco
أربعة قطعة واحدة	Block of four	Bloc de quatre	Viererblock	Bloque de cuatro
أزرق	Blue	Bleu	Blau	Azul
أخضر مزرق	Blue-green	Vert-bleu	Blaugrün	Verde azul
بنفسجي مزرق	Bluish Violet	Violet bleuâtre	Bläulichviolett	Violeta azulado
دفتر طوابع	Booklet	Carnet	Heft	Cuadernillo
أزرق فاتح	Bright Blue	Bleu vif	Lebhaftblau	Azul vivo
أخضر فاتح	Bright Green	Vert vif	Lebhaftgrün	Verde vivo
بنفسجي فاتح	Bright Purple	Mauve vif	Lebhaftpurpur	Púrpura vivo
أخضر برونزي	Bronze Green	Vert-bronze	Bronzegrün	Verde bronce
بني	Brown	Brun	Braun	Castaño
بني قرميدي	Brown-lake	Carmin-brun	Braunlack	Laca castaño
البنفسجي الغامق	Brown-purple	Pourpre-brun	Braunpurpur	Púrpura castaño
أحمر غامق	Brown-red	Rouge-brun	Braunrot	Rojo castaño
أصفر داكن	Buff	Chamois	Sämisch	Anteado
الإلغاء	Cancellation	Oblitération	Entwertung	Cancelación
ملغى	Cancelled	Annulé	Gestempelt	Cancelado
قرمزي	Carmine	Carmin	Karmin	Carmín
أحمر قرمزي	Carmine-red	Rouge-carmin	Karminrot	Rojo carmín
متوسط	Centred	Centré	Zentriert	Centrado
أحمر فاتح	Cerise	Rouge-cerise	Kirschrot	Color de ceresa
ورق سطحه طباشيري	Chalk-surfaced paper	Papier couché	Kreidepapier	Papel estucado
أزرق طباشيري	Chalky Blue	Bleu terne	Kreideblau	Azul turbio
طابع خيري	Charity stamp	Timbre de bienfaisance	Wohltätigkeitsmarke	Sello de beneficenza
بني فاتح - كستناوي	Chestnut	Marron	Kastanienbraun	Castaño rojo
شوكولا	Chocolate	Chocolat	Schokolade	Chocolate
بني فاتح جدا - بيج	Cinnamon	Cannelle	Zimtbraun	Canela
أحمر داكن	Claret	Grenat	Weinrot	Rojo vinoso
أزرق سماوي	Cobalt	Cobalt	Kobalt	Cobalto
لون	Colour	Couleur	Farbe	Color
تخريم مشطي	Comb-perforation	Dentelure en peigne	Kammzähnung, Reihenzähnung	Dentado de peine
طابع تذكاري	Commemorative stamp	Timbre commémoratif	Gedenkmarke	Sello conmemorativo
أحمر داكن ـ قرزي	Crimson	Cramoisi	Karmesin	Carmesí
كحلي ـ أزرق غامق	Deep Blue	Blue foncé	Dunkelblau	Azul oscuro
أخضر غامق	Deep bluish Green	Vert-bleu foncé	Dunkelbläulichgrün	Verde azulado oscuro
التصميم	Design	Dessin	Markenbild	Diseño

Arabia	English	French	German	Spanish
قالب حديد يستخدم للصك	Die	Matrice	Urstempel. Type, Platte	Cuño
ضعف الكمية	Double	Double	Doppelt	Doble
لون كاكي	Drab	Olive terne	Trüboliv	Oliva turbio
أخضر باهت	Dull Green	Vert terne	Trübgrün	Verde turbio
بنفسجي باهت	Dull purple	Mauve terne	Trübpurpur	Púrpura turbio
نافر - بارز	Embossing	Impression en relief	Prägedruck	Impresión en relieve
الزمرد	Emerald	Vert-eméraude	Smaragdgrün	Esmeralda
منقوش - طباعة بالحفر	Engraved	Gravé	Graviert	Grabado
خطأ	Error	Erreur	Fehler, Fehldruck	Error
تجارب طباعية	Essay	Essai	Probedruck	Ensayo
طابع رسالة سريعه	Express letter stamp	Timbre pour lettres par exprès	Eilmarke	Sello de urgencia
طابع مالي	Fiscal stamp	Timbre fiscal	Stempelmarke	Sello fiscal
زهري غامق	Flesh	Chair	Fleischfarben	Carne
تزييف	Forgery	Faux, Falsification	Fälschung	Falsificación
إطار	Frame	Cadre	Rahmen	Marco
ورق الجرانيت	Granite paper	Papier avec fragments de fils de soie	Faserpapier	Papel con filamentos
أخضر	Green	Vert	Grün	Verde
أخضر مزرق	Greenish Blue	Bleu verdâtre	Grünlichblau	Azul verdoso
أخضر مصفر	Greenish Yellow	Jaune-vert	Grünlichgelb	Amarillo verdoso
رمادي	Grey	Gris	Grau	Gris
رمادي مزرق	Grey-blue	Bleu-gris	Graublau	Azul gris
رمادي مخضر	Grey-green	Vert gris	Graugrün	Verde gris
صمغ	Gum	Gomme	Gummi	Goma
فراغ أبيض يفصل بين طابعين	Gutter	Interpanneau	Zwischensteg	Espacio blanco entre dos grupos
غير مثقب - بدون تخريم	Imperforate	Non-dentelé	Geschnitten	Sin dentar
نيلي - أزرق غامق	Indigo	Indigo	Indigo	Azul indigo
النقش	Inscription	Inscription	Inschrift	Inscripción
معكوس - مقلوب	Inverted	Renversé	Kopfstehend	Invertido
اصدار	Issue	Émission	Ausgabe	Emisión
	Laid	Vergé	Gestreift	Listado
أحمر غامق جداً - أحمر دموي	Lake	Lie de vin	Lackfarbe	Laca
أحمر أجري	Lake-brown	Brun-carmin	Lackbraun	Castaño laca
لون الموف	Lavender	Bleu-lavande	Lavendel	Color de alhucema
ليموني	Lemon	Jaune-citron	Zitrongelb	Limón
أزرق فاتح	Light Blue	Bleu clair	Hellblau	Azul claro
لون نهدي	Lilac	Lilas	Lila	Lila
ثقب الخط	Line perforation	Dentelure en lignes	Linienzähnung	Dentado en linea
طباعة حجرية	Lithography	Lithographie	Steindruck	Litografía
محلي	Local	Timbre de poste locale	Lokalpostmarke	Emisión local
تخريم ناعم	Lozenge roulette	Percé en losanges	Rautenförmiger Durchstich	Picadura en rombos
قرمزي	Magenta	Magenta	Magentarot	Magenta
هامش	Margin	Marge	Rand	Borde
بنفسجي غامق	Maroon	Marron pourpré	Dunkelrotpurpur	Púrpura rojo oscuro
بنفسجي	Mauve	Mauve	Malvenfarbe	Malva
متعدد الألوان	Multicoloured	Polychrome	Mehrfarbig	Multicolores
أخضر غامق	Myrtle Green	Vert myrte	Myrtengrün	Verde mirto
أزرق جديد	New Blue	Bleu ciel vif	Neublau	Azul nuevo
طابع جريدة	Newspaper stamp	Timbre pour journaux	Zeitungsmarke	Sello para periódicos
طمس	Obliteration	Oblitération	Abstempelung	Matasello

Arabia	English	French	German	Spanish
لايستخدم	Obsolete	Hors (de) cours	Ausser Kurs	Fuera de curso
بيج	Ochre	Ocre	Ocker	Ocre
طابع حكومي	Official stamp	Timbre de service	Dienstmarke	Sello de servicio
بني زيتوني	Olive-brown	Brun-olive	Olivbraun	Castaño oliva
أخضر زيتوني	Olive-green	Vert-olive	Olivgrün	Verde oliva
رمادي زيتوني	Olive-grey	Gris-olive	Olivgrau	Gris oliva
أصفر زيتوني	Olive-yellow	Jaune-olive	Olivgelb	Amarillo oliva
برتقالي	Orange	Orange	Orange	Naranja
بني برتقالي	Orange-brown	Brun-orange	Orangebraun	Castaño naranja
أحمر برتقالي	Orange-red	Rouge-orange	Orangerot	Rojo naranja
أصفر برتقالي	Orange-yellow	Jaune-orange	Orangegelb	Amarillo naranja
توشيح	Overprint	Surcharge	Aufdruck	Sobrecarga
زوج	Pair	Paire	Paar	Pareja
شطب على القيمة أو	Pale	Pâle	Blass	Pálido
لوح	Pane	Panneau	Gruppe	Grupo
ورقة	Paper	Papier	Papier	Papel
رزمة طوابع البريد	Parcel post stamp	Timbre pour colis postaux	Paketmarke	Sello para paquete postal
ملغي بالقلم - مشطوب بالقلم	Pen-cancelled	Oblitéré à plume	Federzugentwertung	Cancelado a pluma
ثقب	Percé en arc	Percé en arc	Bogenförmiger Durchstich	Picadura en forma de arco
تخريم	Percé en scie	Percé en scie	Bogenförmiger Durchstich	Picado en sierra
صوة أبيض واسود	Perforated	Dentelé	Gezähnt	Dentado
ثقب دبوس	Perforation	Dentelure	Zähnung	Dentar
صفحة لتحديد مكان الطبع	Photogravure	Photogravure, Heliogravure	Rastertiefdruck	Fotograbado
لون خوخي	Pin perforation	Percé en points	In Punkten durchstochen	Horadado con alfileres
طابع أجرة بريد مستحق	Plate	Planche	Platte	Plancha
لون خوخي	Plum	Prune	Pflaumenfarbe	Color de ciruela
طابع مالي بريدي	Postage Due stamp	Timbre-taxe	Portomarke	Sello de tasa
طابع بريدي	Postage stamp	Timbre-poste	Briefmarke, Freimarke, Postmarke	Sello de correos
طابع مالي بريدي	Postal fiscal stamp	Timbre fiscal-postal	Stempelmarke als Postmarke verwendet	Sello fiscal-postal
ختم البريد	Postmark	Oblitération postale	Poststempel	Matasello
طباعة	Printing	Impression, Tirage	Druck	Impresión
بروفا	Proof	Épreuve	Druckprobe	Prueba de impresión
مؤقت - طابع محلي	Provisionals	Timbres provisoires	Provisorische Marken. Provisorien	Provisionales
أزرق مسود	Prussian Blue	Bleu de Prusse	Preussischblau	Azul de Prusia
أرجواني	Purple	Pourpre	Purpur	Púrpura
بني ارجواني	Purple-brown	Brun-pourpre	Purpurbraun	Castaño púrpura
طباعة زاحفة	Recess-printing	Impression en taille douce	Tiefdruck	Grabado
أحم	Red	Rouge	Rot	Rojo
بني محمر	Red-brown	Brun-rouge	Rotbraun	Castaño rojizo
أحمر زهري	Reddish Lilac	Lilas rougeâtre	Rötlichlila	Lila rojizo
أرجواني محمر	Reddish Purple	Poupre-rouge	Rötlichpurpur	Púrpura rojizo
بنفسجي محمر	Reddish Violet	Violet rougeâtre	Rötlichviolett	Violeta rojizo
برتقالي محمر	Red-orange	Orange rougeâtre	Rotorange	Naranja rojizo
طابع تسجيل - مسجل	Registration stamp	Timbre pour lettre chargée (recommandée)	Einschreibemarke	Sello de certificado lettere
إعادة طبع	Reprint	Réimpression	Neudruck	Reimpresión
معكوس - مقلوب	Reversed	Retourné	Umgekehrt	Invertido
وردي	Rose	Rose	Rosa	Rosa
أحمر وردي	Rose-red	Rouge rosé	Rosarot	Rojo rosado
وردي غامق	Rosine	Rose vif	Lebhaftrosa	Rosa vivo
تخريم ناعم	Roulette	Percage	Durchstich	Picadura

Arabia	English	French	German	Spanish
تخريم ناعم	Rouletted	Percé	Durchstochen	Picado
أزرق ملكي	Royal Blue	Bleu-roi	Königblau	Azul real
أخضر معتدل	Sage green	Vert-sauge	Salbeigrün	Verde salvia
برتقالي فاتح قريب للزهري	Salmon	Saumon	Lachs	Salmón
قرمزي	Scarlet	Écarlate	Scharlach	Escarlata
بني داكن	Sepia	Sépia	Sepia	Sepia
	Serpentine roulette	Percé en serpentin	Schlangenliniger Durchstich	Picado a serpentina
	Shade	Nuance	Tönung	Tono
صفحة	Sheet	Feuille	Bogen	Hoja
لون رصاصي	Slate	Ardoise	Schiefer	Pizarra
أزرق رمادي	Slate-blue	Bleu-ardoise	Schieferblau	Azul pizarra
أخضر مسود	Slate-green	Vert-ardoise	Schiefergrün	Verde pizarra
نهدي مزرق	Slate-lilac	Lilas-gris	Schierferlila	Lila pizarra
	Slate-purple	Mauve-gris	Schieferpurpur	Púrpura pizarra
	Slate-violet	Violet-gris	Schieferviolett	Violeta pizarra
خدمة البريد السريعة	Special delivery stamp	Timbre pour exprès	Eilmarke	Sello de urgencia
نموذج - عينة	Specimen	Spécimen	Muster	Muestra
أزرق فولاذي	Steel Blue	Bleu acier	Stahlblau	Azul acero
شريط	Strip	Bande	Streifen	Tira
الضريبة الاضافية	Surcharge	Surcharge	Aufdruck	Sobrecarga
	Tête-bêche	Tête-bêche	Kehrdruck	Tête-bêche
ورق لون خفيف	Tinted paper	Papier teinté	Getöntes Papier	Papel coloreado
طابع متأخر جداً	Too-late stamp	Timbre pour lettres en retard	Verspätungsmarke	Sello para cartas retardadas
أزرق تركوازي	Turquoise-blue	Bleu-turquoise	Türkisblau	Azul turquesa
أخضر تركوازي	Turquoise-green	Vert-turquoise	Türkisgrün	Verde turquesa
نوع من الطباعة	Typography	Typographie	Buchdruck	Tipografia
أزرق لازوردي	Ultramarine	Outremer	Ultramarin	Ultramar
غير مستخدم	Unused	Neuf	Ungebraucht	Nuevo
مستخدم	Used	Oblitéré, Usé	Gebraucht	Usado
لون بندقي - بني محمر	Venetian Red	Rouge-brun terne	Venezianischrot	Rojo veneciano
لون برتقالي محمر (قمرديني)	Vermilion	Vermillon	Zinnober	Cinabrio
بنفسج	Violet	Violet	Violett	Violeta
أزرق بنفسجي	Violet-blue	Bleu-violet	Violettblau	Azul violeta
علامة مائية	Watermark	Filigrane	Wasserzeichen	Filigrana
	Watermark sideways	Filigrane couché	Wasserzeichen liegend	Filigrana acostado
ورقة منسوجه	Wove paper	Papier ordinaire, Papier uni	Einfaches Papier	Papel avitelado
أصفر	Yellow	Jaune	Gelb	Amarillo
بني مصفر	Yellow-brown	Brun-jaune	Gelbbraun	Castaño amarillo
أخضر مصفر	Yellow-green	Vert-jaune	Gelbgrün	Verde amarillo
زيتوني مصفر	Yellow-olive	Olive-jaunâtre	Gelboliv	Oliva amarillo
برتقالي مصفر	Yellow-orange	Orange jaunâtre	Gelborange	Naranja amarillo
تخريم ناعم متعرج	Zig-zag roulette	Percé en zigzag	Sägezahnartiger Durchstich	Picado en zigzag

Guide to Entries

A **Country of Issue** – When a country changes its name, the catalogue listing changes to reflect the name change, for example Cambodia was formerly known as Kampuchea, the stamps in Part 21 South East Asia are all listed under Cambodia, but spilt into Kampuchea and then Cambodia. When a country spilts, for example Czechoslovakia split into Czech Republic and Slovakia, there will be a listing for Czechoslovakia and then separate sections for Czech Republic and Slovakia.

B **Currency** – Details of the currency, and dates of earliest use where applicable, on the face value of the stamps.

C **Country Information** – Brief geographical and historical details for the issuing country.

D **Illustration** – Generally, the first stamp in the set. Stamp illustrations are reduced to 75%, with overprints and surcharges shown actual size.

E **Illustration or Type Number** – These numbers are used to help identify stamps, either in the listing, type column, design line or footnote, usually the first value in a set. These type numbers are in a bold type face – **123**; when bracketed (**123**) an overprint or a surcharge is indicated. Some type numbers include a lower-case letter – **123a**, this indicates they have been added to an existing set. New cross references are also shown in bold.

F **Date of issue** – This is the date that the stamp/set of stamps was issued by the post office and was available for purchase. When a set of definitive stamps has been issued over several years the Year Date given is for the earliest issue. Commemorative sets are listed in chronological order. Stamps of the same design, or issue are usually grouped together, for example one of the French Marianne definitive series' was first issued in 2002 but includes stamps issued to the end of 2004.

G **Number Prefix** – Stamps other than definitives and commemoratives have a prefix letter before the catalogue number.
Their use is explained in the text: some examples are A for airmail, E for East Germany or Express Delivery stamps.

H **Footnote** – Further information on background or key facts on issues.

I **Stanley Gibbons Catalogue number** – This is a unique number for each stamp to help the collector identify stamps in the listing. The Stanley Gibbons numbering system is universally recognized as definitive.
Where insufficient numbers have been left to provide for additional stamps to a listing, some stamps will have a suffix letter after the catalogue number (for example 214a). If numbers have been left for additions to a set and not used they will be left vacant.
The separate type numbers (in bold) refer to illustrations (see **E**).

J **Colour** – If a stamp is printed in three or fewer colours then the colours are listed, working from the centre of the stamp outwards (see **R**).

K **Design line** – Further details on design variations

L **Key Type** – Indicates a design type on which the stamp is based. These are the bold figures found below each illustration, for example listed in Cameroun, in the Part 7 Germany catalogue is the Key type A and B showing the ex-Kaiser's yacht *Hohenzollern*. The type numbers are also given in bold in the second column of figures alongside the stamp description to indicate the design of each stamp. Where an issue comprises stamps of similar design, the corresponding type number should be taken as indicating the general design. Where there are blanks in the type number column it means that the type of the corresponding stamp is that shown by the number in the type column of the same issue. A dash (–) in the type column means that the stamp is not illustrated. Where type numbers refer to stamps of another country, e.g. where stamps of one country are overprinted for use in another, this is always made clear in the text.

M **Coloured Papers** – Stamps printed on coloured paper are shown – e.g. 'brown/*yellow*' indicates brown printed on yellow paper.

N **Surcharges and Overprints** – Usually described in the headings. Any actual wordings are shown in bold type. Descriptions clarify words and figures used in the overprint. Stamps with the same overprints in different colours are not listed separately. Numbers in brackets after the descriptions are the catalogue numbers of the non-overprinted stamps. The words 'inscribed' or 'inscription' refer to the wording incorporated in the design of a stamp and not surcharges or overprints.

O **Face value** – This refers to the value of each stamp and is the price it was sold for at the Post Office when issued. Some modern stamps do not have their values in figures but instead shown as a letter, shown as a letter, for example Great Britain use 1st or 2nd on their stamps as apposed to the actual value.

P **Catalogue Value** – Mint/Unused. Prices quoted for pre-1945 stamps are for lightly hinged examples.

Q **Catalogue Value** – Used. Prices generally refer to fine postally used examples. For certain issues they are for cancelled-to-order.

Prices
Prices are given in pence and pounds. Stamps worth £100 and over are shown in whole pounds:

Shown in Catalogue as	Explanation
10	10 pence
1·75	£1·75
15·00	£15
£150	£150
£2300	£2300

Prices assume stamps are in 'fine condition'; we may ask more for superb and less for those of lower quality. The minimum catalogue price quoted is 10p and is intended as a guide for catalogue users. The lowest price for individual stamps purchased from Stanley Gibbons is £1.
Prices quoted are for the cheapest variety of that particular stamp. Differences of watermark, perforation, or other details, often increase the value. Prices quoted for mint issues are for single examples. Those in *se-tenant* pairs, strips, blocks or sheets may be worth more. Where no prices are listed it is either because the stamps are not known to exist (usually shown by a †) in that particular condition, or, more usually, because there is no reliable information on which to base their value.
All prices are subject to change without prior notice and we cannot guarantee to supply all stamps as priced. Prices quoted in advertisements are also subject to change without prior notice.

R **Multicoloured** – Nearly all modern stamps are multicoloured (more than three colours); this is indicated in the heading, with a description of the stamp given in the listing.

S **Perforations** – Please see page x for a detailed explanation of perforations.

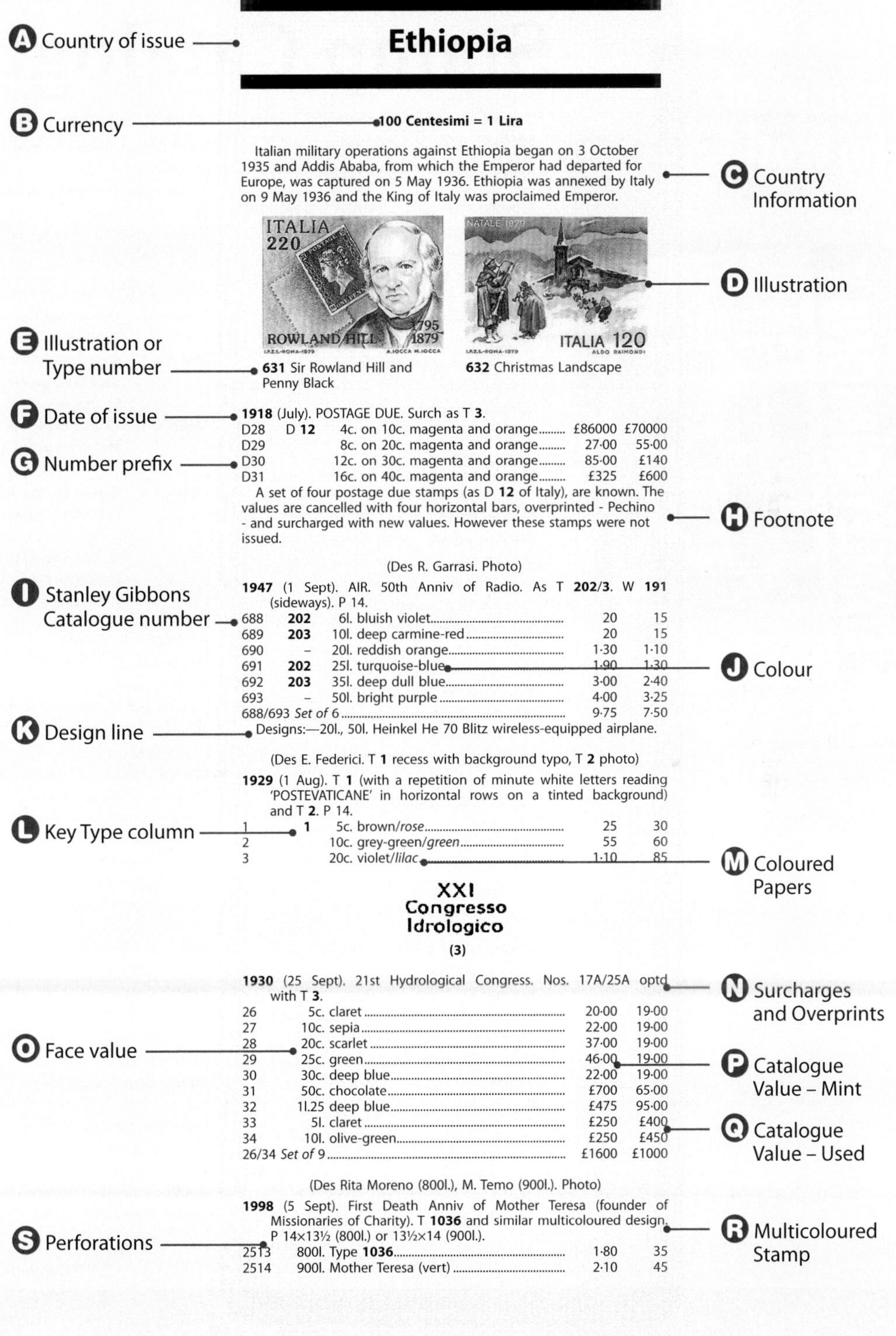

Ethiopia

100 Centesimi = 1 Lira

Italian military operations against Ethiopia began on 3 October 1935 and Addis Ababa, from which the Emperor had departed for Europe, was captured on 5 May 1936. Ethiopia was annexed by Italy on 9 May 1936 and the King of Italy was proclaimed Emperor.

631 Sir Rowland Hill and Penny Black

632 Christmas Landscape

1918 (July). POSTAGE DUE. Surch as T **3**.

D28	D **12**	4c. on 10c. magenta and orange	£86000	£70000
D29		8c. on 20c. magenta and orange	27·00	55·00
D30		12c. on 30c. magenta and orange	85·00	£140
D31		16c. on 40c. magenta and orange	£325	£600

A set of four postage due stamps (as D **12** of Italy), are known. The values are cancelled with four horizontal bars, overprinted - Pechino - and surcharged with new values. However these stamps were not issued.

(Des R. Garrasi. Photo)

1947 (1 Sept). AIR. 50th Anniv of Radio. As T **202/3**. W **191** (sideways). P 14.

688	**202**	6l. bluish violet	20	15
689	**203**	10l. deep carmine-red	20	15
690	–	20l. reddish orange	1·30	1·10
691	**202**	25l. turquoise-blue	1·90	1·30
692	**203**	35l. deep dull blue	3·00	2·40
693	–	50l. bright purple	4·00	3·25
688/693 *Set of 6*			9·75	7·50

Designs:—20l., 50l. Heinkel He 70 Blitz wireless-equipped airplane.

(Des E. Federici. T **1** recess with background typo, T **2** photo)

1929 (1 Aug). T **1** (with a repetition of minute white letters reading 'POSTEVATICANE' in horizontal rows on a tinted background) and T **2**. P 14.

1	**1**	5c. brown/*rose*	25	30
2		10c. grey-green/*green*	55	60
3		20c. violet/*lilac*	1·10	85

XXI Congresso Idrologico

(3)

1930 (25 Sept). 21st Hydrological Congress. Nos. 17A/25A optd with T **3**.

26	5c. claret	20·00	19·00
27	10c. sepia	22·00	19·00
28	20c. scarlet	37·00	19·00
29	25c. green	46·00	19·00
30	30c. deep blue	22·00	19·00
31	50c. chocolate	£700	65·00
32	1l.25 deep blue	£475	95·00
33	5l. claret	£250	£400
34	10l. olive-green	£250	£450
26/34 *Set of 9*		£1600	£1000

(Des Rita Moreno (800l.), M. Temo (900l.). Photo)

1998 (5 Sept). First Death Anniv of Mother Teresa (founder of Missionaries of Charity). T **1036** and similar multicoloured design. P 14×13½ (800l.) or 13½×14 (900l.).

2513	800l. Type **1036**	1·80	35
2514	900l. Mother Teresa (vert)	2·10	45

Gaza

EGYPTIAN OCCUPATION

1000 Milliemes = £1 (Egyptian)

On 15 May 1948, when the British mandate for Palestine ended, Egyptian troops seized the coastal town of Gaza. An Israeli offensive in October reduced the area in Egyptian occupation to a strip of territory along the coast from Gaza to the Egyptian frontier. On 22 September 1948 Arab states, except Jordan, recognised an Arab government for Palestine formed at Gaza. By the armistice terms of 24 February 1949 the Gaza Strip was to remain under Egyptian military control.

فلسطين

فلسطين

PALESTINE (1)

PALESTINE (2)

1948 (1 June). Various stamps of Egypt optd.

(a) POSTAGE. Optd with T **1** *(1 to 22m.) or as T* **2** *but with different spacing (30m. to 200m.)*

No.	Type	Description	Unused	Used
1	**91**	1m. orange-brown (G.)	60	60
		a. Opt inverted	£130	
2		2m. vermilion (G.)	60	60
		a. Opt inverted	£130	
		b. Opt double		
3	**78**	3m. sepia (G.)	70	70
		a. Opt inverted	£180	
4	**91**	4m. green (R.)	70	70
5		5m. red-brown	70	70
6	**78**	6m. yellow-green	85	85
		a. Opt double	£140	
7	**91**	10m. bright violet (R.)	85	85
8	**78**	13m. carmine (G.)	1·20	1·20
9	**91**	15m. deep purple (R.)	1·20	1·20
10		17m. olive-green (R.)	1·20	1·20
11		20m. slate-violet (R.)	1·50	1·50
12		22m. deep blue (R.)	1·70	1·70
13	–	30m. deep olive (No. 340) (R.)	2·10	2·10
14	**106**	40m. sepia (R.)	2·75	2·75
15	–	50m. greenish blue (No. 342) (R.)	3·75	3·75
16	–	100m. dull purple (No. 280) (R.)	7·50	7·50
17	–	200m. violet (No. 281) (R.)	19·00	19·00
18	**86**	50p. sepia and green (R.)	42·00	42·00
19	**87**	£E1 sepia and blue (R.)	70·00	70·00
1/19 *Set of 19*			£140	£140

(b) AIR. Optd with T **2**

No.	Type	Description	Unused	Used
20	**101**	2m. vermilion	85	85
		a. Opt inverted	£130	
21		3m. sepia (R.)	85	85
22		5m. brown-lake	85	85
23		7m. orange-brown	1·20	1·20
24		8m. green (R.)	1·20	1·20
25		10m. violet (R.)	1·40	1·40
26		20m. blue (R.)	2·20	2·20
27		30m. purple	4·25	4·25
28		40m. carmine	3·50	3·50
29		50m. greenish blue (R.)	4·75	4·75
30		100m. olive (R.)	7·50	7·50
31		200m. grey (R.)	37·00	37·00
20/31 *Set of 12*			60·00	60·00

(c) EXPRESS LETTER. Optd with T **2**

No.	Type	Description	Unused	Used
E32	E **52**	40m. black and brown (R.)	17·00	18·00
		a. Opt double	£150	

(d) POSTAGE DUE. Optd with T **1** *or* **2** *(30m.)*

No.	Type	Description	Unused	Used
D32	D **59**	2m. red-orange	2·75	3·00
D33	–	4m. yellow-green (R.)	2·10	2·40
D34	–	6m. grey-green	2·10	2·40
D35	–	8m. purple	2·10	2·40
D36	–	10m. rose-lake	2·10	2·40
D37	–	12m. lake	2·10	2·40
D38	–	30m. bright violet (R.)	6·25	12·00
D32/D38 *Set of 7*			18·00	24·00

(Optd at Survey Dept, Cairo; National Printing Press, Bulaq; and Railways Printing Press, Cairo)

1953. As above but with King Farouk's portrait obliterated with bars as T **134** of Egypt.

(a) POSTAGE. Nos. 1/19

No.	Type	Description	Unused	Used
32	**91**	1m. orange-brown	1·00	1·00
33		2m. vermilion	1·00	1·00
34	**78**	3m. sepia	1·00	1·00
35	**91**	4m. green	1·00	1·00
36		5m. red-brown	1·00	1·00
37	**78**	6m. yellow-green	1·00	1·00
38	**91**	10m. bright violet	1·10	1·10
39	**78**	13m. carmine	1·60	1·60
40	**91**	15m. deep purple	1·60	1·60
41		17m. olive-green	1·60	1·60
42		20m. slate-violet	1·60	1·60
43		22m. deep blue	2·50	2·50
44	–	30m. deep olive	3·25	3·25
45	**106**	40m. sepia	3·75	3·75
46	–	50m. greenish blue	7·50	7·50
47	–	100m. dull purple	20·00	20·00
48	–	200m. violet	40·00	40·00
49	**86**	50p. sepia and green	75·00	70·00
50	**87**	£E1 sepia and blue	£190	£180
32/50 *Set of 19*			£325	£300

(b) AIR. Nos. 20/31

No.	Type	Description	Unused	Used
51	**101**	2m. vermilion	2·40	2·40
52		3m. sepia	1·40	1·40
53		5m. brown-lake	20·00	20·00
54		7m. orange-brown	1·80	1·60
55		8m. green	3·75	3·50
56		10m. violet	3·75	3·50
57		20m. blue	3·75	3·50
58		30m. purple	3·75	3·50
59		40m. carmine	7·00	7·00
60		50m. greenish blue	28·00	28·00
61		100m. olive	£130	£130
62		200m. grey	19·00	19·00
51/62 *Set of 12*			£200	£200

1953. AIR. Various stamps of Egypt (Air stamps with Egypt–Sudan opt and with portrait obliterated) optd with T **2**.

No.	Type	Description	Unused	Used
63	**101**	2m. vermilion	1·10	1·10
64		3m. sepia	20·00	20·00
65		5m. brown-lake	3·50	3·50
66		10m. violet (R.)	31·00	31·00
67		50m. greenish blue (R.)	9·00	9·50
68		100m. olive (R.)	65·00	65·00
63/68 *Set of 6*			£120	£120

1955–56. Various stamps of Egypt optd as T **1** (1m. to 20m.) or T **2** (others).

No.	Type	Description	Unused	Used
69	**137**	1m. red-brown (B.)	75	75
70		2m. slate-purple (B.)	75	75
71		3m. blue (R.)	75	75
72		4m. deep bluish green (R.)	75	75
73		5m. carmine-red (B.)	75	75
74	**130**	10m. sepia (B.)	75	75
75		15m. grey (R.)	1·00	1·00
76		17m. deep turquoise-blue (R.)	1·00	1·00
77		20m. bright violet (R.)	1·00	1·00
78	**131**	30m. green (R.)	1·80	1·80
79		32m. blue (R.)	1·80	1·80
80		35m. bright violet (R.)	1·80	1·80
81		40m. red-brown (B.)	3·25	3·25
82		50m. dull purple (B.)	3·50	3·50
83	**132**	100m. brown-red (B.)	8·75	8·75
84		200m. deep turquoise-blue (R.)	20·00	20·00
85		500m. bright violet (R.)	75·00	75·00
86		£E1 red and bluish green (R.) (1956)	£130	£130
69/86 *Set of 18*			£225	£225

1955. AIR. T **133** of Egypt optd with T **2**.

No.	Type	Description	Unused	Used
86*a*	**133**	5m. red-brown	7·00	10·00
86*b*		15m. bronze-green (R.)	8·75	11·50

When war broke out between Egypt and Israel on 29 October 1956, Israeli troops occupied the Gaza Strip until 7 March 1957, when it was restored to Egyptian control. Israeli stamps were used in the Strip during the occupation.

فلسطين

PALESTINE

(**3**)

1957 (4 May). Re-occupation of Gaza Strip. As T **152** of Egypt but colour changed, optd with T **3**.

No.	Type	Description	Unused	Used
87	**152**	10m. blue-green	6·50	6·75

1957–58. Postage stamps of Egypt optd with T **3**, in red.

*(a) No. 539 (W **158**)*
87*a* 10m. bright violet (10.57) 3·75 3·75

*(b) Nos. 540/542 (W **161**)*
88 1m. deep turquoise-green (12.57) 65 65
89 5m. sepia (2.58) 1·10 1·10
90 10m. bright violet (12.57) 1·10 1·10
87*a*/90 *Set of* 4 6·00 6·00

1958 (15 Mar–30 Aug). Various stamps of Egypt optd with T **3**.
91 – 1m. carmine (G.) (2.6) 45 45
92 – 2m. blue (R.) (20.5) 45 45
93 **168** 3m. red-brown (15.3) 45 45
94 – 4m. green (R.) (16.4) 45 45
95 – 5m. sepia (R.) (20.8) 45 45
96 **160** 10m. bright violet (R.) (10.5) 60 45
96*a* – 35m. blue (R.) (30.8) 5·00 4·50
91/96*a* *Set of* 7 7·00 6·50

1958 (18 June). Fifth Anniversary of Republic. As T **172** of Egypt but colour changed, optd with T **3**.
97 **172** 10m. bistre-brown (R.) 2·75 3·25

1958 (10 Dec). Tenth Anniversary of Declaration of Human Rights. As T **178** of Egypt but colours changed, optd with T **3**.
98 **178** 10m. reddish purple (G.) 4·00 5·25
a. Opt double £275
b. Opt omitted £500
99 35m. red-brown (G.) 10·00 11·00
a. Brown opt £500
b. Opt omitted £500

1959 (20 Jan). T **132** of Egypt optd with T **3**, in green.
100 **132** 55m. on 100m. brown-red 6·00 9·00
a. Surch double £140
b. Opt double, one inverted £250
c. 'UAP' for 'UAR' (pos. 99) 35·00 45·00

NOTE. The following stamps are similar to those of Egypt (some with colours changed), but additionally inscr 'PALESTINE' in English and Arabic.

1960 (26 June–15 Dec). As Nos. 603 and 606/608. W **190**.
101 – 1m. brown-orange (15.12) 45 45
104 – 4m. olive-brown (21.11) 45 45
105 – 5m. deep reddish violet (15.10) 45 45
106 **160** 10m. bronze green (26.6) 45 45
101/106 *Set of* 4 1·60 1·60

1960 (29 Nov). World Refugee Year As T **205**.
109 **205** 10m. orange-brown 95 80
110 35m. black 2·50 2·20

1961 (6 Apr). World Health Day. As T **213**.
111 **213** 10m. blue 1·90 1·50

1961 (15 May). Palestine Day. As T **215**.
112 **215** 10m. deep reddish violet 90 90

1961 (24 Oct). UN Technical Co-operation Programme and 16th Anniversary of UN. As T **220**.
113 10m. blue and orange 85 65
114 35m. deep purple and red 1·30 1·00

1961 (18 Dec). Education Day. As T **223**.
115 **223** 10m. red-brown 85 70

1961 (23 Dec). Victory Day. As T **224**.
116 **224** 10m. brown and orange-brown 65 65

1962 (7 Mar). Fifth Anniversary of Egyptian Occupation of Gaza. As T **229**.
117 **229** 10m. red-brown 55 50

1962 (22 Mar). Arab League Week. As T **231**.
118 **231** 10m. deep maroon 55 55

1962 (20 June). Malaria Eradication. As T **235**.
119 10m. carmine and deep brown 55 55
120 35m. yellow and black 1·40 1·10

1962 (24 Oct). 17th Anniversary of UN and Hammarskjöld Commemoration. As T **245**.
121 **245** 5m. deep slate-blue and rose 45 45
122 10m. deep slate-blue and brown 55 55
123 35m. deep slate-blue and blue 1·10 1·10
121/123 *Set of* 3 1·90 1·90

1963 (20 Feb). As No. 91 for use on greeting cards.
124 4m. bright blue, orange and black 45 45

1963 (21 Mar). Freedom from Hunger. As T **252**.
125 5m. orange-brown and emerald 45 45
126 10m. yellow and olive 60 60
127 35m. yellow and slate-purple 90 90
125/127 *Set of* 3 1·80 1·80

1963 (8 May). Centenary of Red Cross. As T **253**.
128 10m. red, deep purple and ultramarine 60 50
129 35m. ultramarine, blue and red 1·10 1·00

1963 (1 Oct). UNESCO Campaign for Preservation of Nubian Monuments. As T **256**.
130 5m. greenish yellow and black-purple 50 50
131 10m. greenish yellow and black 55 55
132 35m. yellow and violet 1·90 1·50
130/132 *Set of* 3 2·75 2·30

1963 (24 Oct)–**64**. AIR. As T **191**.
133 50m. slate-purple and light blue (2.11.64) 1·40 1·60
134 80m. indigo and light blue 3·00 2·75
135 115m. greenish yellow and black 4·50 4·25
136 140m. orange-red and blue 5·25 5·00
133/136 *Set of* 4 12·50 12·00

1963 (10 Dec). 15th Anniversary of Declaration of Human Rights. As T **259a**.
137 5m. yellow and deep sepia 45 45
138 10m. black, grey and reddish purple 50 50
139 35m. black, pale green and turquoise-green. 1·20 1·20
137/139 *Set of* 3 1·90 1·90

1964 (1 Jan–July). As Nos. 769/783.
140 – 1m. violet and yellow-olive (1.6.64) 50 50
141 – 2m. slate-blue and red-orange (1.6.64) 50 50
142 – 3m. blue, chestnut and light blue (1.6.64) 50 50
143 – 4m. yellow-green, brown and pink (1.6.64) 50 50
144 – 5m. red, blue and pale pink (1.7.64) 50 50
145 – 10m. brown-red, brown and yellow-olive (1.6.64) 50 50
146 – 15m. yellow, violet and lilac (1.6.64) 55 55
147 **260** 20m. yellow-olive and black-violet 90 90
148 **261** 30m. slate-blue and orange 1·90 1·90
149 – 35m. orange-brown, emerald and pale orange (1.6.64) 1·50 1·50
150 – 40m. bright blue and emerald 2·00 2·00
151 – 60m. orange-brown and light blue 3·00 3·00
152 **263** 100m. yellow-brown and indigo 4·25 4·25
140/152 *Set of* 13 15·00 15·00

1964 (13 Jan). Arab League Heads of State Congress, Cairo. As T **266**.
153 **266** 10m. black and yellow-olive 45 45

1964 (10 Feb). Ramadan Festival. As T **267**.
154 **267** 4m. yellow-olive, red and brown-red 45 45

1964 (1 Apr). Tenth Anniversary of Arab Postal Union's Permanent Office. As T **271**.
155 **271** 10m. light blue and emerald-green 45 45

1964 (7 Apr). World Health Day. As T **272**.
156 **272** 10m. slate-purple and red 45 45

1965 (20 Jan). Ramadan Festival. As T **286a**.
157 **286a** 4m. brown and green 60 60

1965 (22 Mar). 20th Anniversary of Arab League. As T **289**.
158 10m. green and red 45 45
159 20m. bistre-brown and green 45 45

1965 (23 Mar). AIR. World Meteorological Day. As T **290**.
160 **290** 80m. orange and deep blue 3·75 3·75

1965 (7 Apr). World Health Day. As T **291**.
161 **291** 10m. red and emerald-green 55 55

1965 (9 Apr). Deir Vassin Massacre. As T **292**.
162 **292** 10m. rose-red and slate-blue 85 85

1965 (17 May). ITU Centenary. As T **293**.
163 **293** 5m. slate-blue, yellow and black-green 50 50
164 10m. rose-red, pale blue and carmine 55 55
165 35m. bright blue, yellow and deep ultramarine 1·80 1·20
163/165 *Set of* 3 2·50 2·00

1965 (1 July). AIR. Re-establishment of Egyptian Civil Airlines MISRAIR. As T **293**.
166 **295** 10m. deep green and light orange 2·30 2·30

1966 (24 Oct). UN Day. As T **321**.
167 5m. reddish violet and light red 45 45

168 10m. reddish violet and yellow-brown 50 50
169 35m. reddish violet and emerald .... 1·20 1·20
167/169 *Set of 3* .... 1·90 1·90

1966 (23 Dec). Victory Day. As T **324**.
170 **324** 10m. carmine and yellow-olive 50 50

1967 (22 Mar). Arab Publicity Week. As T **328**.
171 **328** 10m. yellow-brown and ultramarine........ 45 45

1967 (1 May). Labour Day. As T **331**.
172 **331** 10m. sepia and yellow-olive........................ 60 60

During the Six Day War, 5 to 10 June 1967, Israeli troops seized the Gaza Strip, which remained in occupation until 1994. The stamps of Israel were in use.

Under the Declaration of Principles between Israel and the Palestine Liberation Organisation, Israeli forces evacuated Gaza, together with Jericho on the West Bank, in May 1994 when they became autonomous under the Palestinian National Authority.

INDIAN UN FORCE IN GAZA

449 Jawaharlal Nehru (medallion)

UNEF
(G **1**)

1965 (15 Jan). No. 492 of India optd with T G **1**.
G1 **449** 15p. slate (C.) .... 3·50 10·00

Iraq

1917. 16 Annas = 1 Rupee
1931. 1000 Fils = 1 Dinar

Iraq, then known to the west as Mesopotamia, was part of the Turkish Empire from 1555 to 1612 and from 1638 to 1918. The Turkish postal system had a network of around 50 offices in this area.

Indian post offices were opened at Baghdad and Basra, then part of the Turkish Empire, on 1 January 1868. Unoverprinted stamps of India were used, Baghdad being allocated numeral cancellations '356', '18' and 'K-6', and Basra (also spelt Bussorah, Busreh, Busrah, Busra) '357', '19' and '1/K-6'.

Both offices closed on 30 September 1914, but Basra re-opened in December 1914 when Indian stamps overprinted 'I.E.F.' were used.

I. INDIAN POST OFFICES

Indian post offices were opened at Baghdad and Basra, then part of the Turkish Empire, on 1 January 1868. Unoverprinted stamps of India were used, cancels as detailed below.

Baghdad

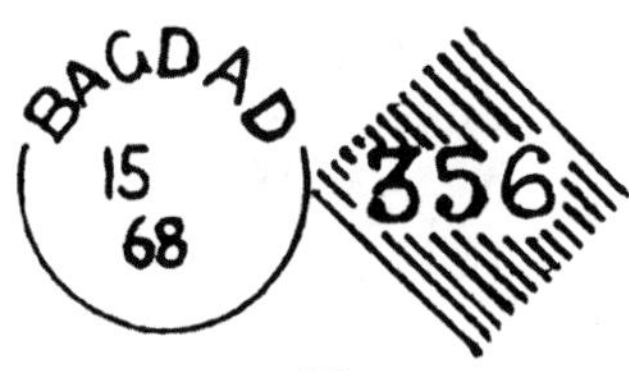

Z 1

Z 2

Z 3

Z 4

Z 5

Z 6

Z 7

Postmark Type	*Approx period of use*
Z **1**	1868–1869
Z **2**	1870–1875
Z **3**	1877–1880
Z **4**	1884–1885
Z **5**	1885–1886
Z **6**	1894–1914
Z **7**	1901–1914

Between 1881 and 1887 stamps were often cancelled with a 'B' in a square or circle of bars. Off cover, such stamps are indistinguishable from those used in other offices in the Bombay postal circle.

T Z **1** may be found with the numeral obliterator and datestamp applied separately.

T Z **4** exists with an acute accent over the first 'A' of 'BAGHDAD'.

Stamps of India cancelled at Baghdad between 1868 and 1914 with postmarks detailed above.

1856–64. P 14.

Z1	**11**	2a. yellow-buff	£110
Z2		4a. black	90·00

1865. W **13**. P 14.

Z3	**11**	½a. blue (Die I)	12·00
Z4		1a. pale brown	15·00
Z5		2a. orange	26·00
Z7		8a. carmine (Die I)	£250

1866–78. W **13**. P 14.

Z8	**17**	4a. green (Die I)	40·00
Z9		4a. blue-green (Die II)	42·00

1868. W **13**. P 14.

Z10	**11**	8a. rose (Die II)	45·00

1873. W **13**. P 14.

Z11	**11**	½a. blue (Die II)	9·00

1874. W **13**. P 14.

Z12	**19**	9p. mauve	75·00

1876. W **13**. P 14.

Z14	**21**	6a. olive-bistre	26·00
		a. Pale brown	26·00
Z15	**22**	12a. Venetian red	75·00

1882–90. W **34**. P 14.

Z16	**23**	½a. blue-green	5·50
Z18	**25**	1a. brown-purple	5·50
Z19	**26**	1a.6p. sepia	14·00
Z20	**27**	2a. blue	7·00
Z21	**28**	3a. orange	16·00
		a. Brown-orange	8·50
Z22	**29**	4a. olive-green	9·00
Z23	**30**	4a.6p. yellow-green	30·00
Z24	**31**	8a. dull mauve	20·00
Z25	**32**	12a. purple/*red*	30·00
Z26	**33**	1r. slate	26·00

1891. W **34**. P 14. Surch T **35**.

Z27	**30**	2½a. on 4a.6p. yellow-green	23·00

1892. W **34**. P 14.

Z28	**36**	2a.6p. yellow-green	11·00
Z29	**37**	1r. green and aniline carmine	60·00

1895. W **34**. P 14.

Z30	**38**	2r. carmine and yellow-brown	80·00

Z31		3r. brown and green	60·00
Z32		5r. ultramarine and violet	£100

1899. W **34**. P 14.

Z34	**40**	3p. aniline carmine	21·00

1900. W **34**. P 14.

Z36	**23**	½a. yellow-green	8·50
Z37	**25**	1a. carmine	10·00
Z38	**27**	2a. pale violet	13·00
Z39	**36**	2a.6p. ultramarine	13·00

1902–11. W **34**. P 14.

Z40	**41**	3p. grey	16·00
Z41	**42**	½a. yellow-green	8·00
Z42	**43**	1a. carmine	8·00
Z43	**44**	2a. violet	11·00
Z44		2a. mauve	7·50
Z45	**45**	2a.6p. ultramarine	5·50
Z46	**46**	3a. orange-brown	26·00
Z47	**47**	4a. olive	10·00
Z49	**49**	8a. purple	17·00
Z51	**51**	1r. green and carmine	35·00
Z52	**52**	2r. rose-red and yellow-brown	65·00
Z54		5r. ultramarine and violet	£120

1905. W **34**. P 14. Surch T **39**.

Z55	**42**	¼ on ½a. green	24·00

1906–07. W **34**. P 14.

Z56	**53**	½a. green	5·50
Z57	**54**	1a. carmine	5·50

1911–22. W **34**. P 14.

Z58	**55**	3p. grey	16·00
Z59	**56**	½a. light green	7·50
Z60	**57**	1a. carmine	7·50
Z61	**59**	2a. purple	9·50
Z62	**60**	2a.6p. ultramarine	13·00
Z63	**61**	2a.6p. ultramarine	11·00
Z64	**62**	3a. orange	20·00
Z67	**65**	8a. deep magenta	32·00
Z68	**66**	12a. carmine-lake	40·00

OFFICIAL STAMPS

1867–73. Optd with T O **7**.

Z76	**17**	4a. green (Die I)	50·00
Z77	**11**	8a. rose (Die II)	75·00

1874–82. Optd with T O **8** in black.

Z80	**11**	2a. orange	45·00

1883–99. Optd with T O **9**.

Z84	**23**	½a. blue-green	20·00
Z85	**25**	1a. brown-purple	22·00
Z86	**27**	2a. blue	25·00

1900. Optd with T O **9**.

Z90	**23**	½a. yellow-green	28·00
Z92	**27**	2a. pale violet	38·00

1902–09. Optd with T O **9**.

Z95	**43**	1a. carmine	19·00
Z96	**44**	2a. mauve	15·00
Z97	**47**	4a. olive	15·00
Z98	**48**	6a. olive-bistre	30·00
Z99	**49**	8a. purple	45·00

1906. Optd with T O **9**.

Z101	**53**	½a. green	15·00
Z102	**54**	1a. carmine	20·00

1912–13. Optd with T O **10**.

Z108	**56**	½a. light green	14·00
Z109	**57**	1a. carmine	16·00
Z112	**64**	6a. yellow-bistre	32·00

The post office at Baghdad closed on 30 September 1914.

Basra

Z **8**

Z **9**

Z **10**

Postmark Type	*Approx period of use*
Z **1** (inscr 'BUSSORAH/357')	1868–1873
Z **2** (inscr 'BUSREH/19')	1870–1873
Z **3** (inscr 'BUSREH/1/K-6')	1877–1879
Z **8**	1884
Z **4** (inscr 'BUSRAH')	1889–1892
Z **7**	1905–1918
Z **9**	1894–1916
Z **10**	1899–1903
Z **12** (inscr 'BUSRA')	1915–1918

Between 1881 and 1887 stamps were often cancelled with a 'B' in a square or circle of bars. As at Baghdad, such stamps are indistinguishable from those used at other offices in the Bombay postal circle.

Stamps of India cancelled at Basra between 1868 and 1918 with postmarks detailed above.

1865. W **13**. P 14.

Z121	**11**	½a. blue (Die I)	15·00
Z123		1a. pale brown	14·00
Z124		2a. orange	25·00
Z126		8a. carmine (Die I)	£250

1866–78. W **13**. P 14.

Z127	**17**	4a. green (Die I)	35·00
Z128		4a. blue-green (Die II)	42·00

1868. W **13**. P 14.

Z129	**11**	8a. rose (Die II)	75·00

1873. W **13**. P 14.

Z130	**11**	½a. blue (Die II)	9·00

1876. W **13**. P 14.

Z133	**21**	6a. pale brown	35·00
Z134		12a. Venetian red	90·00

1882–90. W **34**. P 14.

Z135	**23**	½a. blue-green	5·50
Z136	**24**	9p. rose	50·00
Z137	**25**	1a. brown-purple	5·50
Z138	**26**	1a.6p. sepia	12·00
Z139	**27**	2a. blue	7·00
Z140	**28**	3a. orange	16·00
		a. Brown-orange	8·50
Z141	**29**	4a. olive-green	10·00
Z142	**30**	4a.6p. yellow-green	17·00
Z143	**31**	8a. dull mauve	16·00
Z145	**33**	1r. slate	38·00

1891. W **34**. P 14. Surch T **35**.

Z146	**30**	2½a. on 4½a. yellow-green	13·00

1892–97. W **34**. P 14.

Z147	**36**	2a.6p. yellow-green	6·50
Z148	**37**	1r. green and aniline carmine	80·00

1898. W **34**. P 14. Surch T **39**.

Z152	**23**	¼ on ½a. blue-green	30·00

1899. W **34**. P 14.

Z153	**40**	3p. aniline carmine	11·00

1900. W **34**. P 14.

Z155	**23**	½a. yellow-green	8·50
Z156	**25**	1a. carmine	8·50

Z157	**27**	2a. pale violet	12·00
Z158	**36**	2a.6p. ultramarine	12·00

1902–11. W **34**. P 14.

Z159	**41**	3p. grey	18·00
Z160	**42**	½a. yellow-green	7·50
Z161	**43**	1a. carmine	9·50
Z162	**44**	2a. violet	10·00
		a. *Mauve*	9·50
Z163	**45**	2a.6p. ultramarine	5·50
Z165	**47**	4a. olive	14·00
Z167	**49**	8a. purple	20·00
Z169	**51**	1r. green and carmine	50·00

1905. W **34**. P 14. Surch T **39**.

Z172	**42**	¼ on ½a. green	20·00

1906–07. W **34**. P 14.

Z173	**53**	½a. green	7·50
Z174	**54**	1a. carmine	9·50

1911–22. W **34**. P 14.

Z175	**55**	3p. grey	19·00
Z176	**56**	½a. light green	5·50
Z177	**57**	1a. carmine	5·50
Z178	**59**	2a. purple	7·50
Z179	**60**	2a.6p. ultramarine	14·00
Z180	**61**	2a.6p. ultramarine	8·00
Z181	**62**	3a. orange	23·00
Z182	**63**	4a. deep olive	14·00
Z186	**67**	1r. brown and green	40·00

OFFICIAL STAMPS

1867–73. Optd with T O **7**.

Z196	**17**	4a. green (Die I)	80·00
Z197	**11**	8a. rose (Die II)	85·00

1874–82. Optd with T O **8** in black.

Z200	**11**	2a. orange	50·00

1883–99. Optd with T O **9**.

Z204	**23**	½a. blue-green	20·00
Z205	**25**	1a. brown-purple	20·00
Z206	**27**	2a. blue	27·00
Z207	**29**	4a. olive-green	32·00
Z208	**31**	8a. dull mauve	50·00

The post office at Basra closed on 30 September 1914. In November Basra was captured by the invading Indian Expeditionary Force and the post office was reopened the following month.

Basra City

Z **11** Z **12**

The office at Basra City opened in March 1915

Postmark Type	*Approx period of use*
Z **11**	1915
Z **12**	1915–1918

1911–22. W **34**. P 14.

Z222	**56**	½a. light green	20·00
Z223	**57**	1a. carmine	25·00
Z229	**65**	8a. deep mauve	50·00
Z230	**66**	12a. carmine-lake	60·00
Z231	**67**	1r. brown and green	50·00

The sale of Indian stamps by these offices was forbidden from 1 September 1918, being replaced by issues for Iraq, Nos. 1-14 (ex.4). The Indian post offices closed on 30 April 1919.

Other offices opened in Iraq after 1914 are believed to have been operated by the Indian Army, using stamps overprinted 'I.E.F.'. Unoverprinted Indian stamps are also known cancelled at these offices (Amara, Ezra's Tomb, Fao, Magil and Naseriyeh) but their status is unclear.

II. ISSUES FOR BAGHDAD

PRICES FOR STAMPS ON COVER TO 1945

Nos. 1/7	*from* × 8
No. 8	*from* × 4
Nos. 9/15	*from* × 8
No. 16	*from* × 3
Nos. 17/24	*from* × 8
No. 25	*from* × 5

BRITISH OCCUPATION

British and Indian troops occupied the port of Basra on 22 November 1914 to protect the oil pipeline. They then advanced up the rivers, and after a hard campaign, took Baghdad from the Turks on 11 March 1917.

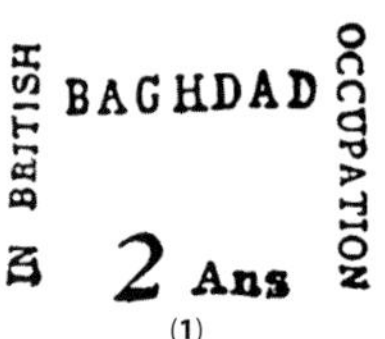

(**1**)

1917 (1 Sept). Stamps of Turkey, surch as T **1** in three operations.

		(a) Pictorial designs of 1914. T **32**, *etc., and* **31**. P12.		
1	**32**	¼a. on 2pa. claret (Obelisk)	£450	£500
		a. 'IN BRITISH' omitted	£16000	
2	**34**	¼a. on 5pa. dull purple (Leander's Tower)	£350	£375
		b. Value omitted	£2500	
3	**36**	½a. on 10pa. green (Lighthouse garden)	£1800	£2000
4	**31**	½a. on 10pa. green (Mosque of Selim)	£4000	£4250
		a. '½ An' double	£8000	
5	**37**	1a. on 20pa. red (Castle)	£1200	£1300
		a. 'BAGHDAD' double	£3000	
6	**38**	2a. on 1pi. bright blue (Mosque)	£500	£550
		(b) As (a), but overprinted with small five-pointed Star		
7	**37**	1a. on 20pa. red (B.)	£800	£850
		b. 'BAGHDAD' double	£3000	
8	**38**	2a. on 1pi. bright blue (R.)	£9000	£9500
		(c) Postal Jubilee stamps (Old GPO). P 12½		
9	**60**	½a. on 10pa. carmine	£1400	£1500
		a. Perf 13½	£5000	
10		1a. on 20pa. blue	£16000	
		a. Perf 13½	£3250	£3750
		ab. Value omitted	£20000	
11		2a. on 1pi. black and violet	£750	£800
		a. Value omitted	£18000	
		b. Perf 13½	£375	£400
		ba. 'IN BRITISH' twice	†	£17000
		(d) T **30** *(GPO, Constantinople) with opt T* **26**		
12	**30**	2a. on 1pi. ultramarine	£1400	£1600
		a. 'IN BRITISH' omitted	£18000	

No. 11ba shows 'BAGHDAD' superimposed on a second impression of 'IN BRITISH' at the top of the stamp. The only known example is *on cover*.

		(e) Stamps optd with six-pointed Star and Arabic date '1331' within Crescent. T **53** *(except No. 16, which has five-pointed Star and Arabic '1332', T* **57***)*		
13	**30**	½a. on 10pa. green (R.)	£350	£375
14		1a. on 20pa. rose	£1200	£1300
		a. Value omitted	£12000	£8000
		b. Optd with Type **26** (Arabic letter 'B') also	£12000	£12000
15	**23**	1a. on 20pa. rose (P 12×13½ comp)	£1300	£1400
		a. Value omitted	£20000	
16	**21**	1a. on 20pa. carmine	£11000	£14000
17	**30**	2a. on 1pi. ultramarine (R.)	£375	£400
		a. 'BAGHDAD' omitted	†	£18000
18	**21**	2a. on 1pi. dull blue (R.)	£500	£550
		a. 'OCCUPATION' omitted	£17000	
		(f) Stamps with similar opt, but date between Star and Crescent (Nos. 19 and 22, T **54***; others T* **55** *five-pointed Star)*		
19	**23**	½a. on 10pa. grey-green (P 13½) (R.)	£375	£425
		a. 'OCCUPATION' omitted	£16000	
		b. 'IN BRITISH' omitted	£18000	
20	**60**	½a. on 10pa. carmine (P 12½) (B.)	£500	£550
		a. Perf 13½	£1000	£1200
		ab. 'BAGHDAD' double	£6000	
		ac. Value double	£6000	
21	**30**	1a. on 20pa. rose	£375	£425
22	**28**	1a. on 20pa. rose (Plate II)	£1300	£1400

23 **15** 1a. on 10pa. on 20pa. claret £600 £650
a. 'OCCUPATION' omitted £17000
24 **30** 2a. on 1pi. ultramarine (R.) £500 £600
a. 'OCCUPATION' omitted £17000
b. 'BAGHDAD' omitted £15000
25 **28** 2a. on 1pi. ultramarine (Pl. II) £4250 £4500

The last group *(f)* have the Crescent obliterated by hand in violet-black ink, as this included the inscription, 'Tax for the relief of children of martyrs'.

III. ISSUES FOR MOSUL

PRICES FOR STAMPS ON COVER TO 1945	
Nos. 1/8	*from* × 50

BRITISH OCCUPATION

A British and Indian force occupied Mosul on 1 November 1918.

As the status of the vilayet was disputed stocks of 'IRAQ IN BRITISH OCCUPATION' surcharges were withdrawn in early 1919 and replaced by Nos. 1/8.

1

2

3

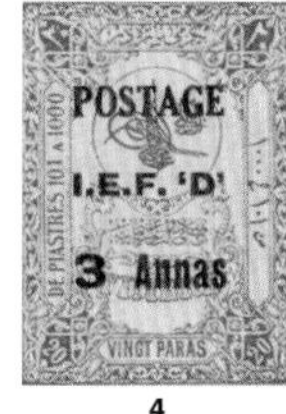

4

5

6

I

4

II

Two types of tougra in central design:
(a) Large 'tougra' or sign-manual of El Ghazi 7 mm high.
(b) Smaller 'tougra' of Sultan Rechad 5½ mm high.

Two types of 4a. surcharge:
I. Normal '4'. Apostrophes on D 3½ mm apart.
II. Small '4' Apostrophes on D 4½ mm apart.

1919 (1 Feb). Turkish Fiscal stamps surch as T **1** by Govt Press, Baghdad. P 11½ (½a.), 12 (1a.), or 12½ (others).

1 **1** ½a. on 1pi. green and red 2·25 1·90
2 **2** 1a. on 20pa. black/*red* (a) 1·40 1·75
a. Imperf between (horiz pair) £1000
b. Surch double £650
c. 'A' of 'Anna' omitted £275
3 1a. on 20pa. black/*red* (b) 4·00 3·00
b. Surch double £750
4 **3** 2½a. on 1pi. mauve and yellow (b) 1·50 1·50
a. No bar to fraction (R. 2/4) 85·00 £110
b. Surch double £1400
5 **4** 3a. on 20pa. green (a) 1·60 4·00
a. Surch double, one albino £550
6 3a. on 20pa. green and orange (b) £100 £140
7 **5** 4a. on 1pi. deep violet (a) (I) 3·00 3·50
a. '4' omitted £1900
c. Surch double £1200
7*d* 4a. on 1pi. deep violet (a) (II) 20·00 27·00
da. Surch double, one with '4' omitted £3250
8 **6** 8a. on 10pa. lake (a) 4·00 5·00
a. Surch inverted £900 £1000
b. Surch double £750 £850
c. No apostrophe after 'D' (R. 1/5) 65·00 85·00
d. Surch inverted. No apostrophe after 'D'
e. 'na' of 'Anna' omitted £325
f. Error. 8a. on 1pi. deep violet £3500

No. 4a occurs on some sheets only. No. 8c comes from the first setting only.

Nos. 1/8 were replaced by 'IRAQ IN BRITISH OCCUPATION' surcharges during 1921 and invalidated on1 September 1922.

In December 1925 the League of Nations awarded the vilayet of Mosul to Iraq.

IV. ISSUES FOR IRAQ

PRICES FOR STAMPS ON COVER	
Nos. 1/18	*from* × 6
Nos. 41/154	*from* × 2
Nos. O19/O171	*from* × 4

BRITISH OCCUPATION

1 Leander's Tower

1a Lighthouse Garden, Stamboul

1b Castle of Europe

1c Mosque of Sultan Ahmed

1d Martyrs of Liberty Monument

1e Fountains of Suleiman

1f Cruiser *Hamidiye*

1g Candilli, Bosphorus

1h Former Ministry of War

1i Sweet Waters of Europe

1j Suleiman Mosque

1k Bosphorus at Rumeli Hisar

1l Sultan Ahmed's Fountain

A

B

1918 (1 Sept)–**21**. Turkish pictorial issue of 1914, surch as T **1** by Bradbury Wilkinson. P 12.

(a) No wmk. Tougra as A (1 Sept 1918–1920)

1	**1**	¼a. on 5pa. dull purple	1·00	1·00
2	**1a**	½a. on 10pa. green	1·00	20
3	**1b**	1a. on 20pa. red	65	10
4	**1**	1½a. on 5pa. dull purple (1920)	20·00	50
5	**1c**	2½a. on 1pi. bright blue	1·75	1·40
		a. Surch inverted	£11000	
6	**1d**	3a. on 1½pi. grey and rose	1·75	25
		a. Surch double (Bk.+R.)	£4500	£5500
7	**1e**	4a. on 1¾pi. red-brown and grey	1·75	25
		a. Centre inverted	†	£32000
8	**1f**	6a. on 2pi. black and green (32 *mm* surch)	3·00	1·75
		a. Centre omitted	£22000	
		b. Surch 27 mm wide	£140	1·75
9	**1g**	8a. on 2½pi. green and orange (30 *mm* surch)	4·50	2·00
		a. Surch inverted	†	£20000
		b. Surch 27 mm wide	20·00	70
10	**1h**	12a. on 5pi. deep lilac	2·50	6·00
11	**1i**	1r. on 10pi. red-brown	2·75	1·40
12	**1j**	2r. on 25pi. yellow-green	13·00	3·25
13	**1k**	5r. on 50pi. rose (32 *mm* surch)	32·00	30·00
		a. Surch 27 mm wide	75·00	42·00
14	**1l**	10r. on 100pi. indigo	£110	17·00
1/14 *Set of* 14			£180	55·00
1s/14s (ex 1½a. on 5pa.) Perf 'Specimen' *Set of* 13			£850	

(b) No wmk. Tougra as B (one device instead of two) (1921)

15	**1i**	1r. on 10pi. red-brown	£350	27·00

(c) Wmk Mult Script CA (sideways on ½a., 1½a.) (1921)

16	**1a**	½a. on 10pa. green	7·50	2·75
17	**1**	1½a. on 5pa. dull purple	5·00	1·50
18	**1j**	2r. on 25pi. yellow-green	38·00	15·00
16/18 *Set of* 3			45·00	17·00
16s/18s Optd 'Specimen' *Set of* 3			£180	

The original settings of Nos. 1/18 showed the surcharge 27 mm wide, except for the 2½a. (24 *mm*), 4a. (26½ *mm*), 6a. (32 *mm*), 8a. (30½ *mm*), 12a. (33 *mm*), 1r. (31½ *mm*), 2r. (30 *mm*) and 5r. (32 *mm*). The 6a., 8a. and 5r. came from a subsequent setting with the surcharge was 27 mm wide. Minor variations in the width of the surcharge on other values exist but are not significant. On all surcharged values apart from the 2½a. and 12a. there is a stop after the 'An'. On those two values there is no stop.

Nos. 2, 3, 5, 6 and 7/9 are known bisected and used on philatelic covers. All such covers have Makinah or F.P.O. 339 cancellations.

During January 1923 an outbreak of cholera in Baghdad led to the temporary use for postal purposes of the above issue overprinted 'REVENUE'.

OFFICIAL STAMPS

ON STATE SERVICE

(O **2**)

1920 (16 May)–**23**. As Nos. 1/18, but surch includes additional wording 'ON STATE SERVICE' as T O **2** in black.

(a) No wmk. Tougra as A

O19	**1a**	½a. on 10pa. blue-green	29·00	2·00
O20	**1b**	1a. on 20pa. red	9·00	1·00
O21	**1**	1½a. on 5pa. purple-brown	70·00	3·00
O22	**1c**	2½a. on 1pi. blue	9·00	9·50
O23	**1d**	3a. on 1½pi. black and rose	28·00	1·25
O24	**1e**	4a. on 1¾pi. red-brown and grey-blue	60·00	5·50
O25	**1f**	6a. on 2pi. black and green	48·00	12·00
O26	**1g**	8a. on 2½pi. yellow-green and orange-brown	60·00	7·00
O27	**1h**	12a. on 5pi. purple	38·00	27·00
O28	**1i**	1r. on 10pi. red-brown	55·00	15·00
O29	**1j**	2r. on 25pi. olive-green	50·00	24·00
O30	**1k**	5r. on 50pi. rose-carmine	95·00	75·00
O31	**1l**	10r. on 100pi. slate-blue	£150	£180
O19/O31 *Set of* 13			£650	£325

(b) No wmk. Tougra as B (No. 15) (1922)

O32	**1i**	1r. on 10pi. red-brown	50·00	7·00

(c) Wmk Mult Script CA (sideways on ½a. to 8a.) (1921–1923)

O33	**1a**	½a. on 10pa. green	1·50	1·00
O34	**1b**	1a. on 20pa. red	13·00	1·00
O35	**1**	1½a. on 5pa. purple-brown	2·75	1·50
O36	**1e**	4a. on 1¾pi. red-brown and grey-blue	2·00	3·25
O37	**1f**	6a. on 2pi. black and green (10.3.23)	45·00	£190
O38	**1g**	8a. on 2½pi. yellow-green and orange-brown	3·50	2·25
O39	**1h**	12a. on 5pi. purple (10.3.23)	45·00	£110
O40	**1i**	2r. on 25pi. olive-green (10.3.23)	£130	£180
O33/O40 *Set of* 8			£200	£450
O33s/O40s Optd 'SPECIMEN' *Set of* 8			£500	

Nos. O25/O26, O30 and O37/O38 only exist from the setting with the surcharge 27½ mm wide.

On Nos. O19/O40 there is a stop after the 'An' on every value apart from the 2½a. (No. O22).

The 'SPECIMEN' opt on No. O34 is of a different type, without the full stop present on Nos. O33 and O35/O40.

LEAGUE OF NATIONS MANDATE

On 25 April 1920 the Supreme Council of the Allies assigned to the United Kingdom a mandate under the League of Nations to administer Iraq.

The Emir Faisal, King of Syria in 1920, was proclaimed King of Iraq on 23 August 1921.

King Faisal I

23 August 1921–1928 September 1933

2 Sunni Mosque, Muadhdham

3 Gufas on the Tigris

4 Winged Cherub

5 Bull from Babylonian wall-sculpture

6 Arch of Ctesiphon

7 Tribal Standard, Dulaim Camel Corps

8 Shiah Mosque, Kadhimain

9 Allegory of Date Palm

(Des Miss Edith Cheesman (½a., 1a., 4a., 6a., 8a., 2r., 5r., 10r.), Mrs. C. Garbett (Miss M. Maynard) (others). Typo (1r.) or recess (others) Bradbury Wilkinson)

1923 (1 June)–**25**. Types **2/4** and similar designs. Wmk Mult Script CA (sideways on 2a, 3a, 4a, 8a., 5r.). P 12.

41	**2**	½a. olive-green	3·50	10
42	**3**	1a. brown	7·50	10
43	**4**	1½a. lake	2·50	10
44	**5**	2a. orange-buff	3·00	15
45	**6**	3a. grey-blue (1923)	6·00	15
46	**7**	4a. violet	7·00	30
		w. Wmk crown to left of CA	£550	£250
47	**8**	6a. greenish blue	2·50	30
48	**7**	8a. olive-bistre	6·50	30
49	**9**	1r. brown and blue-green	35·00	1·50
50	**2**	2r. black	26·00	8·50
51		2r. olive-bistre (1925)	90·00	3·25
52	**7**	5r. orange	60·00	13·00
53	**8**	10r. lake	70·00	22·00
41/53 *Set of* 13			£300	45·00
41s/53s Optd 'SPECIMEN' *Set of* 13			£800	

The normal sideways watermark on Nos. 44, 45, 46, 48 and 52 shows the crown to right of CA, *as seen from the back of the stamp*.

With the exception of Nos. 49 and 50, later printings of these stamps and of No. 78 are on a thinner paper.

ON STATE SERVICE (O **6**)

ON STATE SERVICE (O **7**)

1923. Optd with T O **6** (horiz designs) or T O **7** (vert designs).

O54	**2**	½a. olive-green	1·50	1·75
O55	**3**	1a. brown	1·75	30
O56	**4**	1½a. lake	1·75	3·25
O57	**5**	2a. orange-buff	2·00	55
O58	**6**	3a. grey-blue	2·50	1·50
O59	**7**	4a. violet	4·25	3·25
O60	**8**	6a. greenish blue	4·00	1·25
O61	**7**	8a. olive-bistre	4·00	5·00
O62	**9**	1r. brown and blue-green	20·00	4·50
O63	**2**	2r. black (R.)	38·00	17·00
O64	**7**	5r. orange	90·00	65·00
O65	**8**	10r. lake	£200	85·00
O54/O65 *Set of* 12			£325	£160
O54s/O65s Optd 'SPECIMEN' *Set of* 12			£800	

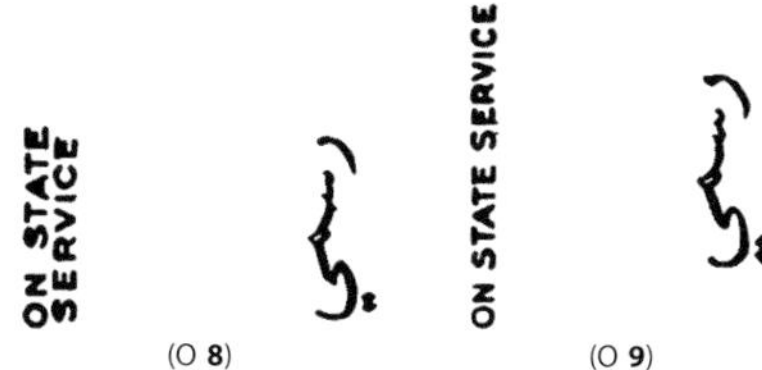

(O **8**) (O **9**)

1924–25. Optd with T O **8** (horiz designs) or T O **9** (vert designs).

O66	**2**	½a. olive-green	1·50	10
O67	**3**	1a. brown	1·25	10
O68	**4**	1½a. lake	1·25	30
O69	**5**	2a. orange-buff	1·50	10
O70	**6**	3a. grey-blue	2·00	10
O71	**7**	4a. violet	4·00	30
O72	**8**	6a. greenish blue	1·75	20
O73	**7**	8a. olive-bistre	3·75	35
O74	**9**	1r. brown and blue-green	22·00	4·25
O75	**2**	2r. olive-bistre (1925)	45·00	3·75
O76	**7**	5r. orange	95·00	65·00
O77	**8**	10r. lake	£180	42·00
O66/O77 *Set of* 12			£325	£100
O66s/O77s Optd 'SPECIMEN' *Set of* 12			£800	

10

11 King Faisal I

12

(Recess Bradbury Wilkinson)

1927 (1 Apr). Wmk Mult Script CA. P 12.

78	**10**	1r. red-brown	18·00	1·00
		s. Optd 'SPECIMEN'	£110	

See note below No. 53.

1927 (1 Apr). Optd with T O **9**.

O79	**10**	1r. red-brown	16·00	3·00
		s. Optd 'SPECIMEN'	£110	

(Recess Bradbury Wilkinson)

1931 (17 Feb). Wmk Mult Script CA (sideways on 1r. to 25r.). P 12.

80	**11**	½a. green	3·50	30
81		1a. red-brown	3·00	30
82		1½a. scarlet	3·50	50
83		2a. orange	3·00	10
84		3a. blue	3·00	20
85		4a. slate-purple	3·25	4·25
86		6a. greenish blue	3·25	80
87		8a. deep green	3·25	4·50
88	**12**	1r. chocolate	10·00	4·50
89		2r. yellow-brown	19·00	10·00
90		5r. orange	55·00	70·00
91		10r. scarlet	£170	£190
92	**10**	25r. violet	£1800	£2250
80/91 *Set of* 12			£250	£250
80s/92s Perf 'SPECIMEN' *Set of* 13			£1500	

ON STATE SERVICE

(O **12**) (O **13**)

1931. Optd.

(a) As T O **12**

O93	**11**	½a. green	65	2·75
O94		1a. red-brown	3·50	10
O95		1½a. scarlet	4·50	29·00
O96		2a. orange	80	10
O97		3a. blue	85	1·25
O98		4a. slate-purple	1·00	1·50
O99		6a. greenish blue	6·50	32·00
O100		8a. deep green	6·50	32·00

(b) As T O **13**, *horizontally*

O101	**12**	1r. chocolate	24·00	29·00
O102		2r. yellow-brown	40·00	90·00
O103		5r. orange	60·00	£180
O104		10r. scarlet	£225	£325

(c) As T O **13**, *vertically upwards*

O105	**10**	25r. violet	£1800	£2500
O93/O104 *Set of* 12			£325	£650
O93s/O105s Perf 'SPECIMEN' *Set of* 13			£1500	

(New Currency. 1000 Fils = 1 Dinar)

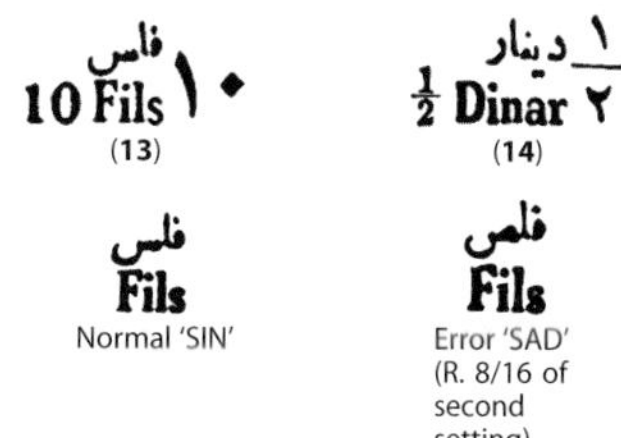

(**13**) (**14**)

Normal 'SIN' — Error 'SAD' (R. 8/16 of second setting)

(Surcharged at Govt Ptg Wks, Baghdad)

1932 (1–21 Apr). Nos. 80/92 and 46 surch in 'Fils' or 'Dinar' as T **13** or T **14**.

106	**11**	2f. on ½a. green (21.4.32) (R.)	50	10
		a. Wide space between '2' and 'Fils'	55·00	32·00
107		3f. on ½a. green	1·25	10
		a. Surch double	£350	
		b. Surch inverted	£300	
		c. Arabic letter 'SAD' instead of 'SIN'	70·00	38·00
		d. Wide space between '3' and 'Fils'	55·00	32·00
		e. Horiz pair one without surcharge	£1500	
108		4f. on 1a. red-brown (21.4.32) (G.)	3·25	25
		a. Wide space between '4' and 'Fils'	£120	50·00
109		5f. on 1a. red-brown	75	10
		a. Inverted Arabic '5' (R. 8/11)	85·00	60·00
		b. Surch inverted	£475	
110		8f. on 1½a. scarlet	1·00	50
		a. Surch inverted	£275	
111		10f. on 2a. orange	50	10
		a. Inverted Arabic '1' (R. 8/13)	65·00	38·00
		b. No space between '10' and 'Fils'	50	10
112		15f. on 3a. blue	1·50	1·00

No.	Type	Description	Unused	Used
113		20f. on 4a. slate-purple	3·50	3·50
		a. Surch inverted	£500	
114	7	25f. on 4a. violet (No. 46)	6·00	10·00
		a. 'Flis' for 'Fils' (R. 2/1, 10/8, 10/15)	£850	£1100
		b. Inverted Arabic '5' (R. 10/7, 10/14)	£1000	£1500
		c. Vars a and b in *se-tenant* pair	£2500	
		d. Error 20f. on 4a. violet (R. 10/1, 10/9)	£6500	
115	11	30f. on 6a. greenish blue	7·50	2·00
		a. Error 80f. on 6a. greenish blue	£6500	
116		40f. on 8a. deep green	4·50	8·50
117	12	75f. on 1r. chocolate	6·00	8·50
		a. Inverted Arabic '5'	£140	£160
118		100f. on 2r. yellow-brown	11·00	4·00
119		200f. on 5r. orange	60·00	55·00
120		½d. on 10r. scarlet	£140	£190
		a. No bar in English '½'	£1800	£2000
		b. Scarlet-vermilion	£160	£250
121	10	1d. on 25r. violet	£325	£450
106/121 *Set of* 16			£500	£650

Nos. 106/113 and 115/116 were in sheets of 160 (16×10) No. 114 sheets of 150 (15×10) and Nos. 117/121 sheets of 100 (10×10). There were three settings of the surcharge for the 3f. and two settings for the 5, 10, 25, 40, 100 and 200f. Nos. 109a and 111a come from the first setting and Nos. 107c, 111b and 114a/114b come from the second.

The 'wide space' varieties, Nos. 106a, 107a and 108a, show a 2 mm space between the numeral and 'Fils' instead of 1mm. On No. 106a it occurs R.8/5, and R. 8/13, on 107d on R.10/5 and R. 10/10 of the first setting and R. 6/6 of the second and on No. 108a on R. 7/1 and R. 7/9, although R 7/9 is also known with normal spacing.

No. 109a occurs in the first setting and can be easily identified as it shows the point of the Arabic numeral at the foot of the surcharge.

All 10f. stamps from the second setting are as No. 111b except for R. 4/7–8 and 15–16 where the spacing is the same as for the first setting (T **13**).

No. 114d shows '20' instead of '25'. Many examples of this error were removed from the sheets before issue. The Arabic value '25' was unaltered.

No. 115a shows the error in the English face value only.

No. 117a occurs on R. 1/2, 1/7 and a third position in the first vertical row not yet identified.

No. 120a occurs on R. 1/2, R. 2/3 and R. 10/11.

No. 120*b* was a special printing of No. 91 which does not exist unsurcharged.

1932 (1 Apr). Official issues of 1924–1925 and 1931 surch in 'FILS' or 'DINAR', as T **13** or T **14**.

No.	Type	Description	Unused	Used
O122	11	3f. on ½a. green	8·50	4·50
		a. Pair, one without surch	£1100	
O123		4f. on 1a. red-brown (G.)	2·50	10
O124		5f. on 1a. red-brown	2·50	10
		a. Inverted Arabic '5' (R. 8/11)	£120	50·00
O125	4	8f. on 1½a. lake (No. O68)	16·00	50
O126	11	10f. on 2a. orange	6·00	10
		a. Inverted Arabic '1' (R. 8/13)	£130	45·00
		b. '10' omitted	†	£3250
		c. No space between '10' and 'Fils'	6·00	10
O127		15f. on 3a. blue	4·25	8·50
O128		20f. on 4a. slate-purple	6·00	5·50
O129		25f. on 4a. slate-purple	4·75	2·00
O130	8	30f. on 6a. greenish blue (No. O72)	16·00	1·75
O131	11	40f. on 8a. deep green	4·75	3·50
		a. 'Flis' for 'Fils' (R. 7/5, 7/13)	£850	£950
O132	12	50f. on 1r. chocolate	22·00	5·00
		a. Inverted Arabic '5' (R. 1/2)	£325	£225
O133		75f. on 1r. chocolate	8·50	13·00
		a. Inverted Arabic '5'	£160	£180
O134	2	100f. on 2r. olive-bistre (surch at top)	48·00	3·50
		a. Surch at foot	48·00	15·00
O135	7	200f. on 5r. orange (No. O76)	28·00	26·00
O136	8	½d. on 10r. lake (No. O77)	£160	£180
		a. No bar in English '½' (R. 2/10)	£2000	£2500
O137	10	1d. on 25r. violet	£350	£500
O122/O137 *Set of* 16			£625	£700

Nos. O122/O124, O126/O129 and O131 were in sheets of 160 (16×10), Nos. O130, O134 and O136 150 (10×15), No. O135 150 (15×10) and Nos. O125, O132/O133 and O137 in sheets of 100 (10×10). There was a second setting of the surcharge for the 3f. (equivalent to the third postage setting), 10f. to 25f., 40f. to 100f. and 1d. Nos. O126c, O131a and O134a come from the second setting.

All 100f. stamps from the second setting are as No. O134a.

For notes on other varieties see below No. 121.

15

1932 (9 May–June). Types **10** to **12**, but with values altered to 'FILS' or 'DINAR' as in T **15**. Wmk Mult Script CA (sideways on 50f. to 1d.). P 12.

No.	Type	Description	Unused	Used
138	11	2f. ultramarine (6.32)	75	20
139		3f. green	50	10
140		4f. brown-purple (6.32)	2·00	10
141		5f. grey-green	1·25	10
142		8f. scarlet	3·00	10
143		10f. yellow	2·25	10
144		15f. blue	2·25	10
145		20f. orange	4·75	50
146		25f. mauve	5·00	50
147		30f. bronze-green	5·00	15
148		40f. violet	4·00	1·00
149	12	50f. brown	6·00	20
150		75f. dull ultramarine	14·00	5·50
151		100f. deep green	18·00	2·00
152		200f. scarlet	30·00	4·50
153	10	½d. deep blue	95·00	75·00
154		1d. claret	£225	£180
138/154 *Set of* 17			£375	£225
138s/154s Perf 'SPECIMEN' *Set of* 17			£800	

1932 (9 May). OFFICIAL. Optd.

No.	Type	Description	Unused	Used
		(a) As T O **12**		
O155	11	2f. ultramarine	1·75	10
O156		3f. green	1·50	10
O157		4f. brown-purple	1·50	10
O158		5f. grey-green	1·50	10
O159		8f. scarlet	1·50	10
O160		10f. yellow	2·25	10
O161		15f. blue	2·50	10
O162		20f. orange	2·50	15
O163		25f. mauve	2·50	15
O164		30f. bronze-green	3·50	20
O165		40f. violet	4·50	30
		(b) As T O **13***, horizontally*		
O166	12	50f. brown	3·25	20
O167		75f. dull ultramarine	2·50	1·00
O168		100f. deep green	11·00	4·00
O169		200f. scarlet	35·00	6·50
		(c) As T O **13***, vertically upwards*		
O170	10	½d. deep blue	27·00	48·00
O171		1d. claret	£150	£170
O155/O171 *Set of* 17			£2250	£200
O155s/O171s Perf 'SPECIMEN' *Set of* 17			£750	

INDEPENDENT KINGDOM

The British Mandate was given up on 3 October 1932 and Iraq became an independent Kingdom.

King Ghazi

8 September 1933–4 April 1939

16

17

18

King Ghazi

(Recess Bradbury Wilkinson)

1934 (11 June)–**38**. No wmk. P 12.

No.	Type	Description	Unused	Used
172	16	1f. violet (7.8.38)	85	50
173		2f. ultramarine	65	40
174		3f. green	65	40
175		4f. brown-purple	65	40
176		5f. grey-green	65	40
177		8f. scarlet	1·00	40
178		10f. yellow	1·20	40
179		15f. blue	1·20	40
180		20f. orange	1·20	40
181		25f. mauve	2·00	50
182		30f. bronze-green	1·60	40
183		40f. violet	2·20	40
184	17	50f. brown	4·50	40
185		75f. blue	4·00	55
186		100f. deep green	5·50	65
187		200f. scarlet	9·50	2·50
188	18	½d. deep blue	30·00	17·00

189		1d. claret	£110	31·00
172/189 *Set of* 18			£160	50·00
172s/189s Perf 'SPECIMEN' *Set of* 17			£400	

1934 (June)–**38**. OFFICIAL. Optd.

(a) As T O **12**

O190	**16**	1f. violet (7.8.38)	2·30	1·00
O191		2f. ultramarine	2·30	35
O192		3f. green	1·20	35
O193		4f. brown-purple	2·30	35
O194		5f. grey-green	1·90	35
O195		8f. scarlet	7·50	50
O196		10f. yellow	75	35
O197		15f. blue	16·00	2·50
O198		20f. orange	2·00	35
O199		25f. mauve	31·00	8·50
O200		30f. bronze-green	6·50	45
O201		40f. violet	8·00	70

(b) As T O **13**, *horizontally*

O202	**17**	50f. brown	1·90	1·10
O203		75f. blue	9·75	1·40
O204		100f. deep green	3·25	1·80
O205		200f. scarlet	8·00	4·00

(c) As T O **13**, *vertically upwards*

O206	**18**	½d. deep blue	22·00	29·00
O207		1d. claret	80·00	85·00
O190/O207 *Set of* 18			£190	£120
O191s/O207s Perf 'SPECIMEN' *Set of* 17			£400	

King Faisal II

4 April 1939–14 July 1958

(Abd-al-Ilah was Regent until 2 May 1953)

19 Mausoleum of Sitt Zubaidah

20 King Faisal's Mausoleum

21 Lion of Babylon

22 Spiral Tower of Samarra

23 Spiral Tower of Samarra

24 Oil Wells

25 Mosque of the Golden Dome, Samarra

Varieties

'Cloud'

Re-entry

Broken Arabic 'i' (Plate 1B R. 4/7)

(Recess De La Rue)

1941 (1 Apr)–**47**. Various perfs.

208	**19**	1f. purple (P 14) (20.4.42)	40	40
209		2f. chocolate (P 14) (20.4.42)	40	40
210	**20**	3f. emerald (P 14) (1.1.43)	40	40
		a. 'Cloud' flaw	80·00	
		b. 'Cloud' with punched hole	24·00	
		c. Re-entry in top inscription	11·00	8·75
211		4f. violet (P 14) (1.1.43)	40	40
		a. Re-entry in top inscription	11·00	8·75
		b. Broken Arabic 'i'	11·00	8·75
212		5f. lake (P 12×13½) (1.1.43)	40	40
		a. Re-entry in top inscription	13·50	8·75
		b. Perf 14	1·40	65
213	**21**	8f. carmine-rose (P 13½)	1·10	40
214		8f. yellow-buff (P 13½) (20.2.43)	40	40
		a. Perf 13×12½ (1947)	70	40
215		10f. yellow-buff (P 13½)	20·00	4·25
216		10f. carmine-rose (P 14) (1.6.42)	1·10	40
217		15f. blue (P 13½)	1·90	40
218		15f. black (P 13½) (20.2.43)	3·00	40
		a. Perf 13×12½ (1946)	1·90	65
219		20f. black (P 13½)	2·40	90
220		20f. blue (P 13½) (20.2.43)	95	40
		a. Perf 13×12½ (1946)	2·20	65
221	**22**	25f. purple (P 13½)	40	40
		a. Perf 12½×13 (1946)	2·40	65
222		30f. red-orange (P 13½)	40	40
		a. Perf 12½×13 (1946)	1·50	65
223		40f. Indian red (P 13½)	1·60	65
		a. Red-brown	1·10	65
		b. Dull chestnut	1·60	65
		ba. Perf 12½×13 (1946)	1·90	90
224	**23**	50f. ultramarine (P 14×13½)	11·00	2·30
		a. Perf 13½×12	5·50	1·10
		b. Perf 14×14½	3·75	90
225		75f. deep magenta (P 14×13½)	2·50	1·10
		a. Perf 14×14½	2·40	90
226	**24**	100f. grey-olive (P 14) (1.1.43)	2·50	1·50
		a. Perf 12½×13 (1947)	8·00	1·80
227		200f. red-orange (P 14) (1.1.43)	9·50	1·50
228	**25**	½d. blue (P 12×13½) (20.4.42)	27·00	7·50
		a. Perf 14½×14	30·00	7·50
229		1d. turquoise-green (P 12×13½) (20.4.42)	55·00	16·00
		a. Perf 14½×14	60·00	16·00
208/229 *Set of* 22 *(cheapest)*			£120	35·00
208s/213s, 215s, 217s, 219s, 221s/229s, Optd 'SPECIMEN' *Set of* 18			£450	

The earlier perforations of this issue were often irregular and stamps may be found differing slightly from the above gauges.

No. 210a exists with 'Cloud' partly erased officially by hand (*price £38 in block of four*). No. 210b is a further official endeavour to remove the flaw by punching a hole 9 mm diameter through the stamp; when the punching was not quite successful more portions of the flaw were removed by knife cuts. The flaw occurs on R. 9/2 of plate 1A.

The Re-entry on the 3f. occurs on R. 9/2 of plate 1A and on R. 6/6 of plate 1B; on the 4f. on R. 6/2 and 8/2 of plate 1A and on R. 4/8 and 5/8 of plate 1B (in both cases in only part of the printing); and on the 5f. on R. 3/2 and 4/7 of the 12×13½ perforation (plate 1B).

The prices quoted above for 'Cloud' flaws and Re-entries are for the variety in a block of four with three normals.

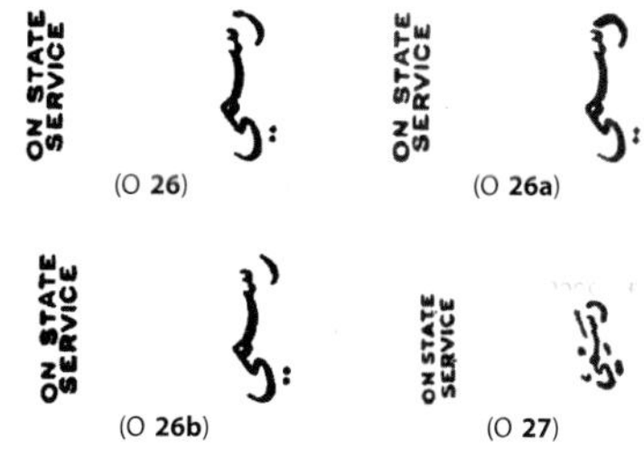

(O **26**) (O **26a**) (O **26b**) (O **27**)

In T O **26a** the top Arabic character is more sharply curved than in T O **26**. In T O **26b** it is flatter and shorter.

1941–**43**. OFFICIAL. Optd as T O **26**, or larger opt.

A. *Optd in small letters, 'ON STATE' 9½ mm long*

B. *Optd in larger letters, 'ON STATE' 11 mm long*

O230	**19**	1f. purple (P 14) (20.4.42)	55	40
		a. Optd with Type O **26a**	30·00	30·00
		b. Optd with Type O **26b**	30·00	30·00
O231		2f. chocolate (P 14) (20.4.42)	55	40
		a. Optd with Type O **26a**	30·00	30·00
		b. Optd with Type O **26b**	30·00	30·00
O232	**20**	3f. emerald (P 14) (1.1.43)	55	40
		a. Re-entry in top inscription	9·75	5·00
O233		4f. violet (P 14) (R.) (1.1.43)	55	40
		a. Re-entry in top inscription	9·75	5·00
		b. Broken Arabic 'i'	9·00	9·00

O234		5f. lake (P 12×13½) (1.1.43)	55	40
		a. Re-entry in top inscription	13·00	5·00
		b. Perf 14	55	40
		ba. Re-entry in top inscription	70·00	25·00
O235	**21**	8f. carmine-rose (P 13½)	1·80	40
O236		8f. yellow-buff (P 13½) (20.2.43)	55	40
		a. Optd with Type O **26b**	36·00	38·00
		b. Perf 12×13½	55	40
		ba. Optd with Type O **26b**	36·00	38·00
O237		10f. yellow-buff (P 13½)	12·00	75
O238		10f. carmine-rose (P 14) (1.6.42)	1·40	40
		a. Optd with Type O **26b**	36·00	38·00
O239		15f. blue (P 13½)	12·00	1·40
O240		15f. black (P 13½) (R.) (20.2.43)	2·20	75
		a. Optd with Type O **26b**	36·00	38·00
		b. Perf 13×12½	2·20	1·10
O241		20f. black (P 13½) (R.)	3·50	75
O242		20f. blue (P 13½) (20.2.43)	1·20	40
		a. Optd with Type O **26b**	36·00	38·00
O243	**22**	25f. purple (P 13½) (A.)	2·00	75
O244		25f. purple (P 13½) (B.)	2·00	75
O245		30f. red-orange (P 13½) (A.)	1·80	75
O246		30f. red-orange (P 13½) (B.)	1·80	75
		a. Perf 12½×13	80	75
O247		40f. Indian red (P 13½) (A.)	1·80	75
O248		40f. red-brown (P 13½) (B.)	1·10	50
		a. Dull chestnut (P 13½) (B.)	80	45
		ab. Perf 12½×13	1·80	50
O249	**23**	50f. ultramarine (P 14×13½)	3·50	75
		a. Optd with Type O **26a**	55·00	60·00
		b. Optd with Type O **26b**	55·00	60·00
		c. Perf 13½×12	2·20	1·30
		ca. Optd with Type O **26a**	55·00	60·00
		cb. Optd with Type O **26b**	55·00	60·00
		d. Perf 14×14½	3·50	1·00
		da. Optd with Type O **26a**	55·00	60·00
		db. Optd with Type O **26b**	55·00	60·00
O250		75f. deep magenta (P 14×13½)	2·20	75
		a. Optd with Type O **26a**	65·00	70·00
		b. Optd with Type O **26b**	65·00	70·00
		c. Perf 14×14½	2·00	75
		ca. Optd with Type O **26a**	55·00	60·00
		cb. Optd with Type O **26b**	55·00	60·00
O251	**24**	100f. grey-olive (P 14) (1.1.43)	4·25	65
O252		200f. red-orange (P 14) (1.1.43)	6·00	1·60
O253	**25**	½d. blue (P 12×13½) (20.4.42)	23·00	9·50
		a. Perf 14½×14	20·00	19·00
O254		1d. turquoise-green (P 12×13½) (20.4.42)	35·00	18·00
		a. Perf 14½×14	34·00	28·00
O230/O254 *Set of 25* (*cheapest*)			£100	38·00
O230s/O235s, O237s, O239s, O241s, O244s, O246s, O248s/O254s Optd 'SPECIMEN' *Set of 18*			£450	

The 'Cloud' flaw is not known with Service opt. The Re-entry on the 5f. perf 14 occurs on R. 7/7, 8/15, 8/7, 9/3, 9/4 and 9/5 of plate 1A and on R. 3/2 and 4/7 of plate 1B. The note on prices of Re-entries below No. 229 also applies here.

There were several settings of this overprint. Of those settings containing T O **26a** and T O **26b**, T O **26b** appears on R. 1/4 for the 8 and 10f. and on R. 9/10 for the other values; the position of T O **26b** varies but is known on R. 5/5, 5/7 and 5/8 lone position per setting).

26

27

28

King Faisal II

(Centre photo; frame litho Survey Dept, Cairo)

1942 (9 Feb–22 June). P 13½.

255	**26**	1f. sepia and violet (22.6)	45	40
256		2f. sepia and blue (22.6)	45	40
257		3f. sepia and yellow-green (22.6)	45	40
258		4f. sepia and brown (22.6)	45	40
259		5f. sepia and green (22.6)	45	40
260		6f. sepia and vermilion (22.6)	45	40
		a. Deep sepia and vermilion	4·75	4·50
261		10f. sepia and rose	45	40
262		12f. sepia and emerald-green (22.6)	45	40
255/262 *Set of 8*			3·25	3·25

1942 (9 Feb–22 June). OFFICIAL. Nos. 255/262 optd as T O **26**.

O263	**26**	1f. sepia and violet	55	50
O264		2f. sepia and blue	55	50
O265		3f. sepia and yellow-green	55	50
O266		4f. sepia and brown	55	50
O267		5f. sepia and green	70	65
O268		6f. sepia and vermilion	70	65
		a. Deep sepia and vermilion	5·00	3·00
O269		10f. sepia and rose	95	90
O270		12f. sepia and emerald-green	1·20	1·10
O263/O270 *Set of 8*			[illegible]	[illegible]

(Recess and litho (**MS**297) or recess (others) Bradbury Wilkinson)

1948 (15 Jan)–**51**. P 12 (T **27**) or 12×11½ (T **28**).

271	**27**	1f. indigo	70	25
272		2f. deep brown	40	25
273		3f. green	40	25
274		3f. brown-lake (15.5.51)	13·00	2·75
275		4f. deep lilac	40	25
276		5f. brown-lake	40	25
277		5f. emerald (15.5.51)	13·50	5·50
278		6f. deep magenta	2·50	25
279		8f. orange-brown	6·00	1·00
280		10f. rose-red	55	25
281		12f. brown-olive	55	25
282		14f. brown-olive (1.7.49)	3·75	40
283		15f. black	10·00	2·75
284		16f. rosine (15.5.51)	3·00	1·10
285		20f. blue	1·10	25
286		25f. purple	1·30	25
287		28f. blue (15.5.51)	3·25	75
288		30f. red-orange	1·30	25
289		40f. chestnut	3·25	1·00
290	**28**	50f. dull ultramarine (1.7.49)	10·00	1·90
291		60f. dull ultramarine	2·00	1·00
292		75f. magenta	2·00	1·00
293		100f. olive-green	8·75	1·90
294		200f. red-orange	7·00	1·90
295		½d. blue	18·00	6·25
296		1d. emerald	75·00	24·00
271/296 *Set of 26*			£170	50·00
271s/296s Optd 'SPECIMEN' *Set of 26*			£600	
MS297 161×179 mm. Nos. 273, 280, 285 and 292/294. Imperf or perf (21.5.49) *Each*			£190	£325
MS297s Optd 'SPECIMEN'. Imperf or perf *Each*			£250	

1948 (15 Jan)–**51**. OFFICIAL. T **27** optd with T O **27** and T **28** with a similar opt but more widely spaced.

O298	**27**	1f. indigo	35	50
O299		2f. deep brown	35	65
O300		3f. green	35	65
O301		3f. brown-lake (15.5.51)	4·75	1·50
		a. Optd both sides		
O302		4f. deep lilac	35	50
O303		5f. brown-lake	35	65
		a. Opt double		
O304		5f. emerald (15.5.51)	5·50	1·50
O305		6f. deep magenta	35	65
O306		8f. orange-brown	35	65
O307		10f. rose-red	35	50
O308		12f. brown-olive	45	50
O309		14f. brown-olive (1.10.49)	2·75	50
O310		15f. black	6·00	9·50
O311		16f. rosine (15.5.51)	4·75	50
O312		20f. blue	45	30
O313		25f. purple	45	30
O314		28f. blue (15.5.51)	1·50	50
O315		30f. red-orange	45	40
O316		40f. chestnut	85	65
O317	**28**	50f. dull ultramarine (1.7.49)	1·50	55
O318		60f. dull ultramarine	1·10	40
O319		75f. magenta	2·30	45
O320		100f. olive-green	2·30	1·50
O321		200f. red-orange	3·50	1·50
O322		½d. blue	30·00	23·00
O323		1d. emerald	42·00	48·00
O298/O323 *Set of 26*			£100	85·00
O298s/O323s Optd 'SPECIMEN' *Set of 26*			£600	

28a King Faisal II

28b King Faisal II

مالية

فلسان

انقاذ فلسطين

(**28c** 'Tax 2 Fils Save Palestine')

(**28d** 'Tax Save Palestine')

(**28e** 'Save Palestine') (12 *mm* wide)

(**28f** 'Save Palestine') (10 *mm* wide)

(**28g** 'Tax 10 Fils Save Palestine')

(**28h** 'Tax 5 Fils Save Palestine')

1948 (5 June)–**49** (17 Jan). OBLIGATORY TAX. Aid for Palestine.

(a) Nos. O300 and 278 surch as T **28c**

T324	**27**	2f. on 3f. green (R.) (17.1.49)	49·00	28·00
T325		2f. on 6f. deep magenta (17.1.49)	75·00	31·00
		a. Opt double	£250	

(b) Nos. O299 and O303 optd as T **28d** *but smaller*

T326	**27**	2f. deep-brown (R.) (17.1.49)	41·00	18·00
		a. Pair, one with opt omitted		
T327		5f. brown-lake (4.49)	80·00	40·00

(c) No. O234 optd with T **28d**

T328	**20**	5f. lake (P 12×13½) (17.1.49)	43·00	15·00
		a. Re-entry in top inscription	80·00	55·00
		b. Perf 14	43·00	10·00
		ba. Re-entry in top inscription	80·00	55·00

(d) Revenue stamp surch '2 Fils/Save Palestine' (as bottom two lines of T **28c***)*

T329	**28a**	2f. on 5f. deep blue (R.) (17.1.49)	30·00	15·00
		a. Opt double		
		b. Pair, one with opt omitted		

(e) Revenue stamps optd with T **28e**

T330	**28a**	5f. deep blue (R.) (5.49)	15·00	4·50
		a. Opt double		
T331		10f. red-orange (B.)	60·00	29·00
		a. Opt double (B.)		
		ab. Transposed opt		
		ac. 'SAVE' missing from opt		
		b. Opt in black	75·00	
		ba. Transposed opt		
		bb. 'SAVE' missing from opt		
T332	**28b**	10f. red-orange (B.) (3.8.48)	£200	70·00

(f) Revenue stamps optd with T **28f** *(T335) or similar opt 9 mm wide*

T333	**28a**	5f. deep blue (17.1.49)	55·00	
T334		10f. red-orange (17.1.49)	55·00	
T335		10f. red-orange (B.) (5.6.48)	32·00	14·00

The black overprint on Nos. T333/T334 is a similar size and reads the same as T **28f** but the lettering differs slightly in shape.

(g) Revenue stamps surch with T **28g** *(Arabic '1' 4 mm deep)*

T336	**28b**	10f. on 20f. slate-green (R.) (2.49)	95·00	40·00
		a. Small Arabic '10' ('1' 1¾ *mm* deep) (R.) (10.48)	£140	60·00

No. T336a came from a separate printing, the Arabic '1' is the second character from the right in the top line of the surcharge.

(h) No. 278 surch with T **28h**

T337	**27**	5f. on 6f. deep magenta (17.1.49)	80·00	28·00
		a. Opt double		60·00

Use of Nos. T324/T337 was obligatory from 17 January 1949 to 16 January 1951. Higher values than those listed were primarily for use on official documents, entertainment tickets etc, although occasional postal use is known.

29 Vickers Viking 1BYI-ABP *Al Mahfoutha* over Basra Aerodrome

30 Vickers Viking *Al Mahfoutha* over Dhiyala Railway Bridge

(Recess and litho (**MS**338) or recess (others) Bradbury Wilkinson)

1949 (1 Feb–25 Mar). AIR. T **30** and designs as T **29**. P 11½ or 11½×12 (T **30**).

330	**29**	3f. emerald	90	40
331	–	4f. bright purple	90	40
332	–	5f. lake-brown	95	40
333	**29**	10f. rosine	6·75	1·90
334	–	20f. blue	4·50	95
335	–	35f. red-orange	4·50	95
336	**30**	50f. yellow-olive	6·75	1·60
337		100f. reddish violet	13·50	3·50
330/337 *Set of 8*			35·00	9·00
330s/337s Optd 'SPECIMEN' *Set of 8*			£200	
MS338 235×165 mm. Nos. 330/337. Imperf or perf (25.3)			£120	£140
MS338s Optd 'SPECIMEN'. Imperf or perf *Each*			£200	

Designs: As T **29**—4, 20f. *Al Mahfoutha* over Kut Barrage; 5, 35f. *Al Mahfoutha* over Faisal II Bridge.

31 King Faisal I and Equestrian Statue

32 King Faisal II

(Recess Bradbury Wilkinson)

1949 (1 Nov). 75th Anniversary of Universal Postal Union. T **31** and similar horiz designs. P 13×13½.

339	–	20f. blue	3·75	2·50
340	**31**	40f. red-orange	5·75	2·50
341	–	50f. violet	13·50	9·50
339/341 *Set of 3*			21·00	13·00
339s/341s Optd 'SPECIMEN' *Set of 3*			£100	

Designs: 20f. King Ghazi and mounted postman; 50f. King Faisal II, globe and wreath.

(Recess Bradbury Wilkinson)

1953 (2 May). Coronation of King Faisal II. P 12.

342	**32**	3f. lake	1·90	1·80
343		14f. olive-brown	3·75	1·80
344		28f. greenish blue	11·00	2·50
342/344 *Set of 3*			15·00	5·50
342s/344s Optd 'SPECIMEN' *Set of 3*			£100	
MS345 134×138 mm. Nos. 342/344			£160	£375
MS345s Optd 'SPECIMEN'			£200	

33 King Faisal II

34 King Faisal II

(**35**)

(Recess Bradbury Wilkinson)

1954 (25 Oct)–**57**. P 12.

346	**33**	1f. grey-blue (15.1.56)	85	20
347		2f. deep brown	30	20
348		3f. lake	30	20
349		4f. blackish violet	30	20
350		5f. emerald	40	20
351		6f. deep magenta	40	20
352		8f. yellow-brown	40	20
353		10f. blue	40	20
354		15f. black	2·30	1·60
355		16f. carmine-red (20.10.57)	3·50	2·75
356		20f. olive-green	1·70	40
357		25f. reddish purple (12.2.55)	1·70	30
358		30f. red (12.2.55)	1·70	30
359		40f. chestnut (12.2.55)	2·00	65
360	**34**	50f. blue (12.2.55)	2·50	90
361		75f. magenta (12.2.55)	4·00	1·00
362		100f. olive-green (12.2.55)	7·75	1·00
363		200f. red-orange (12.2.55)	13·00	2·20
346/363 *Set of 18*			39·00	11·50
346s/363s Optd 'SPECIMEN' *Set of 18*			£350	

1955–58. OFFICIAL. Optd as T O **27**.

O364	**33**	1f. grey-blue (1958)	25	20
		a. Opt inverted	60·00	
O365		2f. deep brown	25	20
O366		3f. lake	25	20
O367		4f. blackish violet	40	20
O368		5f. emerald	40	20
O369		6f. deep magenta (1956)	40	20
O370		8f. yellow-brown	40	20

O371		10f. blue	40	20
O372		16f. carmine-red (1958)	35·00	35·00
		a. Optd on back only	£100	
		b. Vert pair, one without opt	£130	
O373		20f. olive-green	70	40
O374		25f. reddish purple	3·50	1·60
O375		30f. red	1·60	40
O376		40f. chestnut	70	40
O377	**34**	50f. blue	3·50	1·10
O378		60f. purple (1956)	23·00	8·25
O379		100f. olive-green (1956)	50·00	23·00
O364/O379 *Set of* 16			£110	65·00
O364s/O378s Optd 'SPECIMEN' *Set of* 15			£350	

Nos. O372a/O372b exist as a vertical strip of three with a normal at bottom.

1955 (6 Apr). Abrogation of Anglo-Iraqi Treaty. Nos. 348, 353 and 287 optd with T **35**.

380	**33**	3f. lake	1·60	65
		a. Opt double	80·00	
381		10f. blue	1·90	65
		a. Opt inverted	80·00	
		b. Opt double	80·00	
		c. Opt double, both inverted	£110	
382	**27**	28f. blue	3·00	1·40
380/382 *Set of* 3			5·75	2·40

36 King Faisal II

37 King Faisal and Globe

(Recess Bradbury Wilkinson)

1955 (26 Nov). Sixth Arab Engineers' Conference, Baghdad. P 13½.

383	**36**	3f. lake	1·40	65
384		10f. blue	2·40	90
385		28f. Prussian blue	3·25	2·30
383/385 *Set of* 3			6·25	3·50
383s/385s Optd 'SPECIMEN' *Set of* 3			£100	

(Recess Bradbury Wilkinson)

1956 (3 Mar). Third Arab Postal Union Conference, Baghdad. P 13×13½.

386	**37**	3f. lake	1·90	90
387		10f. blue	2·40	90
388		28f. Prussian blue	3·25	1·90
386/388 *Set of* 3			6·75	3·25
386s/388s Optd 'SPECIMEN' *Set of* 3			£100	

38 King Faisal II and Power Loom

39 King Faisal II and Exhibition Emblem

(Photo Courvoisier)

1957 (8 Apr–20 July). Development Week. T **38** and similar horiz designs. P 11½.

389		1f. steel-blue and yellow-buff	70	25
390		3f. multicoloured (20.7)	70	25
391		5f. multicoloured (20.7)	80	25
392		10f. multicoloured	1·20	25
393		40f. multicoloured	2·40	1·00
389/393 *Set of* 5			5·25	1·80

Designs: 1f. T **38**; 3f. Irrigation dam; 5f. Residential road, Baghdad; 10f. Cement kiln; 40f. Tigris Bridge.

(Photo Courvoisier)

1957 (1 June). Agricultural and Industrial Exhibition, Baghdad. P 11½.

394	**39**	10f. brown and cream	1·60	1·50

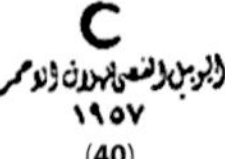

(**40**)

1957 (14 Nov). Silver Jubilee of Iraq Red Crescent Society. No. 388 optd with T **40**, in red.

395	**37**	28f. Prussian blue	6·75	3·25
		a. Opt double	£375	£425
		b. Vert pair, lower stamp without opt	£650	

No. 395a occurred on the top seven rows of one sheet.

41 King Faisal II

42 King Faisal II and Tanks

(Recess Bradbury Wilkinson)

1957 (18 Dec)–**58**. P 11½×12.

396	**41**	1f. slate-blue (6.58)	45	65
397		2f. brown (4.58)	45	65
398		3f. brown-lake (18.12.57)	45	65
399		4f. slate-violet (3.58)	45	65
400		5f. emerald (4.58)	1·30	1·10
401		6f. carmine-lake (5.58)	1·30	1·10
402		8f. orange-brown (6.58)	2·50	1·50
403		10f. blue (6.58)	2·50	1·50
396/403 *Set of* 8			8·50	7·00

15, 25, 30, 40, 50, 75, 100, 200f. values were also prepared but only issued overprinted (with Types **43**, **217**, O **218**/O **218a**). Small remainders of these unoverprinted were put on the market by the Post Office in October 1971. The 20f. value without overprint was already on the market in about 1959 and it is believed that this came from the unissued stock as it is not known with genuine used postmark. The 8, 30 and 50f. with official overprint were also prepared.

All values including the official overprints and the Army Day issue, Nos. 411/414 are know with 'SPECIMEN' overprints, but there is no evidence that they were distributed by the UPU.

1958. OFFICIAL. Optd as T O **27**.

O404	**41**	1f. slate-blue	7·25	2·75
O405		2f. brown	8·50	5·75
O406		3f. brown-lake	10·50	4·00
		a. Opt double	95·00	
O407		4f. slate-violet	12·50	2·75
		a. Opt double	80·00	
O408		5f. emerald	7·25	2·75
		a. Opt inverted	80·00	
O409		6f. carmine-lake	7·25	4·00
O410		10f. blue	7·25	2·10
O404/O410 *Set of* 7			55·00	22·00

(Recess Bradbury Wilkinson)

1958 (6 Jan). Army Day. T **42** and similar designs. P 12×11½ (30f.) or 13×13½ (others).

411	8f. deep grey-green and green	1·40	1·30
412	10f. black and brown	1·90	1·70
413	20f. brown and blue	1·90	1·70
414	30f. reddish violet and carmine	2·75	2·00
411/414 *Set of* 4		7·25	6·00

Designs: 8f. T **42**; As T **42**—King Faisal II and: 10f. Platoon marching; 20f. Mobile artillery unit and de Havilland DH.112 Venom FB.50 jet fighters. 22½×27½ mm—30f. King Faisal II (full-length portrait).

(Photo Courvoisier)

1958 (26 Apr). Development Week. Designs as T **38** inscr '1958'. P 11½.

415	3f. green, drab and slate-violet	75	40
416	5f. multicoloured	1·10	75
417	10f. multicoloured	2·40	1·50
415/417 *Set of* 3		3·75	2·40

Designs: Vert—3f. Sugar beet and refining plant. Horiz—5f. Building and pastoral scene; 10f. Irrigation dam.

REPUBLIC

14 July 1958

King Faisal II was killed on 14 July 1958 and a republic was proclaimed.

الجمهورية العراقية (**43**)

الجمهورية العراقية (**43a**)

1958–60. Various stamps optd with T **43** ('Iraqi Republic').

(i) POSTAGE

(a) 1934–1938 issue

418	**18**	1d. claret (13.12.58)	43·00	43·00

(b) 1948–1951 issue

418*a*	**27**	1f. indigo	49·00	19·00
419		12f. brown-olive (26.7.58)	1·10	40
420		14f. brown-olive (26.7.58)	1·50	40
421		16f. rosine	20·00	5·50
422		28f. blue (26.7.58)	1·90	1·00
423	**28**	60f. dull ultramarine (26.7.58)	5·50	1·00
424		½d. blue (26.7.58)	34·00	7·75
425		1d. emerald (26.7.58)	65·00	28·00

(c) 1954–1957 issue

426	**33**	1f. grey-blue (26.7.58)	95	40
		a. Lines of opt transposed (R. 7/1–4)	43·00	43·00
427		2f. deep brown (26.7.58)	95	40
		a. Lines of opt transposed (R. 1/5–10)	49·00	49·00
428		4f. blackish violet (11.59)	95	40
429		5f. emerald (17.11.59)	95	40
430		6f. deep magenta (26.7.58)	95	40
431		8f. yellow-brown (10.11.58)	95	40
432		10f. blue (26.7.58)	1·10	40
		a. Lines of opt transposed (R. 7/1–4)	49·00	49·00
433		15f. black (26.7.58)	1·40	40
434		16f. carmine-red (26.7.58)	3·50	75
435		20f. olive-green	1·60	90
436		25f. reddish purple (26.7.58)	1·10	50
437		30f. red (26.7.58)	1·60	50
438		40f. chestnut (26.7.58)	1·60	40
439	**34**	50f. blue (26.7.58)	7·50	4·25
440		75f. magenta (26.7.58)	5·75	1·30
441		100f. olive-green (26.7.58)	6·75	4·25
442		200f. red-orange (26.7.58)	20·00	8·25

*(d) On T **41** and similar portrait (22½×27½ mm) (Nos. 455/458)*

443	**41**	1f. slate-blue (26.7.58)	4·75	1·10
		a. Lines of opt transposed (R. 7/1–4)	55·00	55·00
444		2f. brown (26.7.58)	1·00	40
445		3f. brown-lake (26.7.58)	1·00	40
446		4f. slate-violet (26.7.58)	1·10	40
447		5f. emerald (26.7.58)	1·00	40
		a. Lines of opt transposed (R. 1/5–10)	49·00	49·00
448		6f. carmine-lake (26.7.58)	1·00	40
449		8f. orange-brown (26.7.58)	1·00	90
450		10f. blue (26.7.58)	1·00	40
451		20f. olive-green (26.7.58)	1·00	40
452		25f. purple (10.11.58)	2·20	1·10
453		30f. orange-red	2·40	40
454		40f. chestnut (1959)	6·00	2·20
455	–	50f. purple	4·75	1·10
456	–	75f. yellow-olive	4·75	2·10
457	–	100f. reddish orange	6·00	2·10
458	–	200f. blue	17·00	3·50

*(ii) OFFICIAL. Stamps already optd as Types O **26**/O **27***

(a) No. O252

O459	**24**	100f. grey-olive		
O459*a*		200f. red-orange (1960)	16·00	8·50

(b) 1948–1951 issue

O460	**27**	1f. indigo	55·00	50·00
		a. Lines of opt Type **43** transposed	70·00	80·00
		b. Optd with Type **43a**	55·00	50·00
O461		2f. deep brown	55·00	50·00
O462		3f. green	55·00	50·00
O463		3f. brown-lake	55·00	50·00
O464		4f. deep lilac	55·00	50·00
O465		5f. brown-lake	55·00	50·00
O466		5f. emerald	55·00	50·00
O467		6f. deep magenta	55·00	50·00
O468		8f. orange-brown	55·00	50·00
O470		12f. brown-olive	1·70	1·20
O471		14f. brown-olive	2·00	1·40
O472		15f. black	1·50	80
O473		16f. rosine	6·25	3·25
O474		25f. purple	5·50	3·25
O475		28f. blue	3·00	2·50
O476		40f. chestnut	2·10	1·50
O477	**28**	60f. dull ultramarine (1959)	7·75	3·75
O478		75f. magenta	3·75	2·75
O479		200f. red-orange	4·50	3·75
O480		½d. blue	28·00	9·25
O481		1d. emerald	43·00	18·00

(c) 1955–1958 issue

O482	**33**	1f. grey-blue	1·20	50
		a. Lines of opt Type **43** transposed	19·00	23·00
		b. Optd with Type **43a**	27·00	18·00
O483		2f. deep brown (1959)	1·20	50
		a. With Type O **27** on back instead of front	70·00	
O484		3f. lake	1·20	50
O485		4f. blackish violet	1·20	50
O486		5f. emerald (1959)	1·40	50
		a. Lines of opt Type **43** transposed	47·00	55·00
O487		6f. deep magenta	1·20	75
O488		8f. yellow-brown	1·10	50
		a. Optd with Type **43a**	27·00	18·00
O489		10f. blue (1959)	1·40	50
O490		16f. carmine-red	15·00	12·50
O491		20f. olive-green	1·20	50
		a. Optd with Type **43a**	27·00	18·00
O492		25f. reddish purple	1·20	50
O493		30f. red	1·40	75
O494		40f. chestnut	1·80	75
O495	**34**	50f. blue	1·80	1·00
O496		60f. purple	1·80	1·10
O497		100f. olive-green	4·00	1·10

(d) 1958 issue

O498	**41**	1f. slate-blue	40	40
		a. Lines of opt Type **43** transposed(R. 1/5–10)	19·00	23·00
		b. Optd with Type **43a**	39·00	25·00
O499		2f. brown	40	40
O500		3f. brown-lake	70	40
		a. Optd with Type **43a**	27·00	18·00
O501		4f. slate-violet	40	40
O502		5f. emerald	40	40
O503		6f. carmine-lake	40	40
		a. Optd with Type **43a**	27·00	18·00
O504		8f. orange-brown	95	25
		a. Optd with Type **43a**	27·00	18·00
O505		10f. blue	1·10	40

The 'lines transposed' setting error of T **43** occurs on only part of the printing.

The overprint T **43** is found double, inverted, misplaced and partially printed.

The overprint variety T **43a** has the two lines of the overprint slightly closer together and the second line is much shorter than the first. This was a separate printing and occurs in whole sheets.

(**44**)

1958 (26 Nov). Arab Lawyers Conference, Baghdad. No. 385 surch with T **44**, in red.

506	**36**	10f. on 28f. Prussian blue	2·50	1·50

45 Republican Soldier and Flag

45a Orange Tree

(Des and photo Courvoisier)

1959 (6 Jan). Army Day. P 11½.

507	**45**	3f. blue	65	40
508		10f. olive-green	1·10	65
509		40f. reddish violet	2·20	1·30
507/509 *Set of 3*			3·50	2·10

(Des and photo Courvoisier)

1959 (21 Mar). Afforestation Day. P 11½.

510	**45a**	10f. orange and deep bluish green	1·10	40

(**46**)

47 Worker and Buildings

1959 (1 June). International Children's Day. No. 388 surch with T **46**, in red.

511	**37**	10f. on 28f. Prussian blue	2·00	1·00
		a. Pair, one without surch	55·00	55·00

(Des and photo De La Rue)

1959 (14 July). First Anniversary of Revolution. T **47** and similar design inscr '14TH JULY 1958'. P 13.

512		10f. blue and yellow-ochre	85	80
513		30f. green and yellow-ochre	1·70	1·00

Designs: Vert—10f. T **47**. Horiz—30f. Revolutionaries brandishing weapons.

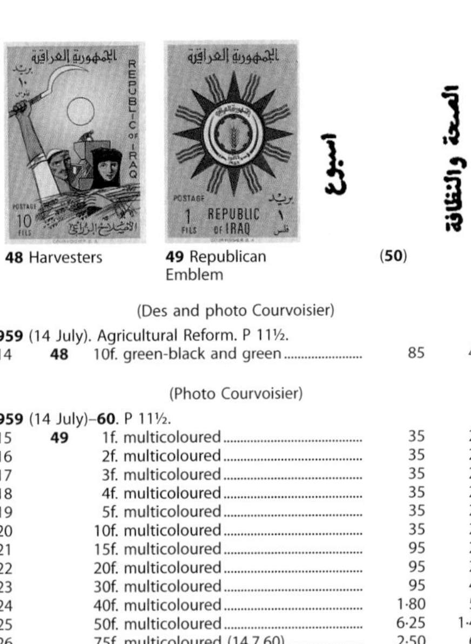

48 Harvesters **49** Republican Emblem (**50**)

(Des and photo Courvoisier)

1959 (14 July). Agricultural Reform. P 11½.

514	**48**	10f. green-black and green	85	40

(Photo Courvoisier)

1959 (14 July)–**60**. P 11½.

515	**49**	1f. multicoloured	35	20
516		2f. multicoloured	35	20
517		3f. multicoloured	35	20
518		4f. multicoloured	35	20
519		5f. multicoloured	35	20
520		10f. multicoloured	35	20
521		15f. multicoloured	95	25
522		20f. multicoloured	95	25
523		30f. multicoloured	95	45
524		40f. multicoloured	1·80	50
525		50f. multicoloured	6·25	1·40
526		75f. multicoloured (14.7.60)	2·50	65
527		100f. multicoloured (14.7.60)	4·00	1·30
528		200f. multicoloured (14.7.60)	7·00	1·30
529		500f. multicoloured (14.7.60)	11·50	4·50
530		1d. multicoloured (14.7.60)	25·00	11·50
515/530 *Set of* 16			55·00	21·00

1959 (23 Oct). 'Health and Hygiene'. No. 520 optd with T **50**.

531	**49**	10f. multicoloured	1·40	80
		a. Opt inverted	£120	£120

51 General Kassem and Military Parade

52 General Kassem

(Photo Courvoisier)

1960 (6 Jan). Army Day. T **51** and similar designs. P 11½.

532		10f. lake and blue-green	1·00	80
533		16f. red and blue	1·40	95
534		30f. olive-green, brown and buff	1·40	95
535		40f. violet and buff	2·30	1·30
536		60f. buff, chocolate and brown	3·00	1·60
532/536 *Set of* 5			8·25	5·00

Designs: Gen. Kassem and: Horiz—16f., Infantry on manoeuvres; 60f. Partisans. Vert—10f. T **51**; 30f. Anti-aircraft gun-crew; 40f. Oilfield guards on parade.

(Recess De La Rue)

1960 (1 Feb). General Kassem's Escape from Assassination. P 13.

537	**52**	10f. reddish violet	1·00	55
538		30f. emerald	1·90	85

53 Al Rasafi (poet)

54 General Kassem at Tomb of Unknown Soldier

(Photo Survey Dept, Cairo)

1960 (10 May). Al Rasafi Commemoration. Optd '1960' at top, in English and Arabic, in black. P 13½.

539	**53**	10f. lake	4·50	2·30
		a. Opt inverted	£250	£250
		b. Opt double	£400	

No. 539 was reissued without overprint in 1966, see No. 732.

(Photo Courvoisier)

1960 (14 July). Second Anniversary of Revolution. T **54** and similar design. P 11½.

540	–	6f. gold, bronze-green and orange	1·10	85
541	**54**	10f. orange, green and blue	1·10	85
542		16f. orange, violet and blue	1·40	1·30
543	–	18f. gold, bright blue and orange	1·40	1·30
544	–	30f. gold, brown and orange	1·80	1·50
545	**54**	60f. orange, sepia and blue	3·50	2·40
540/545 *Set of* 6			9·25	7·50

Designs: Vert—6f., 18f., 30f. Symbol of Republic.

55 Gen. Kassem, Flag and Troops

(O **56**)

(Photo Courvoisier)

1961 (6 Jan). Army Day. T **55** and similar vert design. P 11½.

546	**55**	3f. multicoloured	1·00	20
547		6f. multicoloured	1·00	20
548		10f. multicoloured	1·40	20
549	–	20f. black, yellow and emerald	1·40	40
550	–	30f. black, yellow and red-brown	1·70	55
551	–	40f. black, yellow and bright blue	2·20	1·00
546/551 *Set of* 6			7·75	2·30

Designs: 20f., 30f., 40f. Kassem and triumphal arch.

1961 (1 Apr). OFFICIAL. Optd as T O **56**.

O552	**49**	1f. multicoloured	55	55
O553		2f. multicoloured	55	55
O554		4f. multicoloured	55	55
O555		5f. multicoloured	70	55
O556		10f. multicoloured	1·30	1·00
O557		50f. multicoloured	25·00	16·00
O552/O557 *Set of* 6			21·00	17·00

56 General Kassem with Children

57 Gen. Kassem saluting

(Photo Courvoisier)

1961 (1 June). World Children's Day. P 11½.

558	**56**	3f. sepia and yellow	1·00	70
559		6f. sepia and light blue	1·40	70
560		10f. sepia and pink	2·00	70
561		30f. sepia and greenish yellow	2·00	70
562		50f. sepia and light green	3·50	1·10
558/562 *Set of* 5			9·00	3·50

(Photo Courvoisier)

1961 (14 July). Third Anniversary of Revolution. T **57** and similar vert design. P 11½.

No.	Type	Description	Mint	Used
563	–	1f. black, emerald, gold and reddish violet	40	20
564	–	3f. black, emerald, gold and violet	40	20
565	**57**	5f. multicoloured	40	20
566	–	6f. black, emerald, gold and ultramrine	40	20
567	–	10f. black, emerald, gold and carmine	55	40
568	**57**	30f. multicoloured	1·10	85
569		40f. multicoloured	1·40	85
570	–	50f. black, emerald, gold and greenish yellow	2·40	1·70
571	–	100f. black, emerald, gold and blue	7·75	4·25
563/571		*Set of* 9	13·50	8·00

Design: 1f., 3f., 6f., 10f., 50f., 100f. Gen. Kassem and Iraqi Flag.

58 Gen. Kassem and Army Emblem

مؤتمر
العالم الاسلامى
بغـــداد
١٣٨١هـ-١٩٦٢م

(**59**)

(Photo Courvoisier)

1962 (6 Jan). Army Day. T **58** and similar design. P 11½.

No.	Type	Description	Mint	Used
572	–	1f. yellow, carmine, green and sepia	1·00	40
573	–	3f. yellow, green, sepia and carmine	1·00	40
574	–	6f. yellow, carmine, sepia and green	1·00	40
575	**58**	10f. black, gold and lilac	1·40	40
576		30f. black, gold and orange	1·80	85
577		50f. black, gold and grey-green	3·00	1·70
572/577		*Set of* 6	8·25	3·75

Design: Vert—1f., 3f., 6f. Gen. Kassem saluting and part of speech.

1962 (29 May). Fifth Islamic Congress. Optd with T **59**.

No.	Type	Description	Mint	Used
578	**49**	3f. multicoloured	40	40
579		10f. multicoloured	40	40
580		30f. multicoloured	1·70	1·00
578/580		*Set of* 3	2·30	1·60

60 Gen. Kassem, Flag and Handclasp

ON STATE SERVICE

رسمي

(O **61**)

(Photo Courvoisier)

1962 (14 July). Fourth Anniversary of Revolution. P 11½.

No.	Type	Description	Mint	Used
581	**60**	1f. multicoloured	20	20
582		3f. multicoloured	20	20
583		6f. multicoloured	20	20
584		10f. multicoloured	70	70
585		30f. multicoloured	1·00	70
586		50f. multicoloured	2·00	1·30
581/586		*Set of* 6	4·00	3·00

1962. OFFICIAL. Optd as T O **61**.

No.	Type	Description	Mint	Used
O587	**49**	1f. multicoloured	70	70
O588		2f. multicoloured	70	70
O589		3f. multicoloured	70	70
O590		4f. multicoloured	70	70
O591		5f. multicoloured	70	70
O592		10f. multicoloured	70	70
O593		15f. multicoloured	70	70
O594		20f. multicoloured	70	70
O595		30f. multicoloured	85	70
O596		40f. multicoloured	85	70
O597		50f. multicoloured	1·00	70
O598		75f. multicoloured	1·80	85
O599		100f. multicoloured	1·80	1·40
O600		200f. multicoloured	6·75	2·75
O601		500f. multicoloured	20·00	9·75
O602		1d. multicoloured	39·00	20·00
O587/O602		*Set of* 16	70·00	38·00

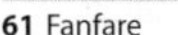
61 Fanfare

62 Republican Emblem

(Photo State Ptg Wks, Berlin)

1962 (1 Dec). Millenary of Baghdad. T **61** and similar vert designs. Multicoloured. P 14×13½.

No.	Type	Description	Mint	Used
603		3f. Type **61**	85	40
604		6f. Al Kindi (philosopher)	85	40
605		10f. Map of old 'Round City' of Baghdad	1·30	70
606		40f. General Kassem and Flag	3·50	1·70
603/606		*Set of* 4	5·75	3·00

(Litho Bradbury Wilkinson)

1962 (20 Dec). Aerogramme Stamps. P 13½×14.

No.	Type	Description	Mint	Used
607	**62**	14f. black and emerald	3·25	1·10
608		35f. black and vermilion	3·75	1·40

Nos. 607/608 were originally issued only attached to aerogramme forms, covering the old imprinted King Faisal II stamps, but later appeared in sheets.

63 Campaign Emblem

64 Gen. Kassem and Tank

65 Guffas, River Tigris

(Litho State Ptg Wks, Berlin)

1962 (31 Dec). Malaria Eradication. P 13½×14.

No.	Type	Description	Mint	Used
609	**63**	3f. multicoloured	40	40
610		10f. multicoloured	1·10	40
611		40f. multicoloured	2·00	1·00
609/611		*Set of* 3	3·25	1·60

(Photo Courvoisier)

1963 (6 Jan). Army Day. P 12×11½.

No.	Type	Description	Mint	Used
612	**64**	3f. black and greenish yellow	20	20
613		5f. sepia and purple	20	20
614		6f. black and pale green	20	20
615		10f. black and light blue	40	40
616		10f. black and pink	40	40
617		20f. black and bright blue	1·00	55
618		40f. black and mauve	1·70	1·00
619		50f. sepia and ultramarine	2·40	2·00
612/619		*Set of* 8	5·75	4·50

(Recess State Ptg Works, Prague)

1963 (16 Feb). Various vert designs as T **65**. P 12×11½.

No.	Type	Description	Mint	Used
620		1f. deep emerald-green	1·00	40
621		2f. reddish violet	1·00	40
622		3f. black	1·00	40
623		4f. black and greenish yellow	1·00	40
624		5f. purple and light green	1·10	40
625		10f. red	1·50	40
626		15f. red-brown and yellow	2·75	40
627		20f. bluish violet	2·75	40
628		30f. red-orange	2·00	55
629		40f. emerald	3·25	40
630		50f. deep chocolate	12·50	1·10
631		75f. black and light green	6·25	85
632		100f. purple	6·75	1·00
633		200f. brown	12·50	1·00
634		500f. blue	17·00	3·75
635		1d. brown-purple	22·00	6·25
620/635		*Set of* 16	85·00	16·00

Designs: 1f. T **65**; 2f., 500f. Spiral tower of Samarra; 3f. T **65**; 4f., 15f. Sumerian Harp; 5f., 75f. Republican emblem; 10f., 50f. Lion of Babylon; 20f., 40f. Koranic school of Abbasid period; 30f., 200f. Mosque and minarets; 100f., 1d. Winged Bull of Kharsabad.

66 Shepherd with Sheep

67 Centenary Emblem

(Litho State Ptg Wks, Berlin)

1963 (21 Mar). Freedom from Hunger. T **66** and similar horiz designs. P 13½×14.

636		3f. black and green	40	40
637		10f. magenta and chocolate (Harvester)	1·10	40
638		20f. red-brown and deep blue (Trees)	2·00	1·30
636/638 *Set of* 3			3·25	1·90
MS639 175×120 mm. Nos. 636/638 (*sold at* 50f.)			9·75	9·75

(Photo Postal Authority Press, Cairo)

1963 (30 Dec). Red Cross Centenary. T **67** and similar design but horiz. P 11½×11 (30f.) or 11×11½ (others).

640	**67**	3f. violet and red	40	40
641		10f. slate-blue and red	1·00	40
642	–	30f. light blue and red (Hospital)	1·70	1·10
640/642 *Set of* 3			2·75	1·70

68 Helmet, Rifle and Flag

69 Revolutionaries and Flag

(Photo Courvoisier)

1964 (6 Jan). Army Day. P 11½.

643	**68**	3f. sepia, green and light blue	40	40
644		10f. sepia, green and pink	85	40
645		30f. sepia, green and yellow	1·50	1·00
643/645 *Set of* 3			2·50	1·60

(Photo Courvoisier)

1964 (8 Feb). First Anniversary of Revolution of 14th Ramadan. P 11½.

646	**69**	10f. red, green, black and reddish violet	85	40
647		30f. red, green, black and brown	1·50	1·00
MS648 125×75 mm. Nos. 646/647 in new colours. Imperf (*sold at* 50f.)			11·00	8·50

See also No. **MS**746.

70 Shamash (Sun-God) and Hammurabi

71 Soldier raising Flag on Map of Iraq

(Des A. K. Refaat (10f.), A. Al-Jeboori (others). Litho Bradbury Wilkinson)

1964 (10 June). 15th Anniversary of Declaration of Human Rights. T **70** and similar horiz design. P 13½.

649	**70**	6f. pale grey-green and purple	1·00	85
650	–	10f. violet and yellow-orange	1·80	85
651	**70**	30f. light yellow-green and dull blue	2·75	1·30
649/651 *Set of* 3			5·00	2·75

Design: 10f. UN Emblem and Scales of Justice.

(Des Lt-Col. S. Salim. Photo Postal Authority Press, Cairo)

1964 (14 July). Sixth Anniversary of Revolution. T **71** and similar design. P 11×11½ (vert) or 11½×11 (horiz).

652		3f. yellow-orange, blue-grey and black	40	40
653		10f. red, black and green	40	40
654		20f. red, black and green	85	40
655		30f. yellow-orange, blue-grey and black	1·70	1·00
652/655 *Set of* 4			3·00	2·00

Designs: Horiz—3f., 30f. Soldier 'protecting' people and factories with outstretched arm. Vert—10f., 20f. T **71**.

72 Soldier, Civilians and Star Emblem

73 Musician

(Des Mohammed Kh. Al-Robaay. Photo Postal Authority Press, Cairo)

1964 (18 Nov). First Anniversary of Revolution of 18 November. P 11½.

656	**72**	5f. yellow-orange and sepia	70	40
657		10f. orange-yellow and blue	70	40
658		50f. red-orange and violet	2·00	85
656/658 *Set of* 3			3·00	1·50

(Litho State Ptg Wks, Berlin)

1964 (28 Nov). International Arab Music Conference, Baghdad. P 13×13½.

659	**73**	3f. multicoloured	1·70	40
660		10f. multicoloured	1·70	40
661		30f. multicoloured	2·50	1·70
659/661 *Set of* 3			5·25	2·30

74 Conference Emblem and Map

75 APU Emblem

(Des K. Hussain. Litho Pakistan Security Ptg Corp, Ltd)

1964 (13 Dec). Ninth Arab Engineers' Conference, Baghdad. P 12½×14.

662	**74**	10f. green and mauve	1·10	40

(Photo Postal Authority Press, Cairo)

1964 (21 Dec). Tenth Anniversary of Arab Postal Union's Permanent Office. P 11×11½.

663	**75**	3f. blue and red	40	30
664		10f. deep slate-purple and bright purple	1·00	30
665		30f. blue and yellow-orange	2·10	1·00
663/665 *Set of* 3			3·25	1·40

76 Soldier, Civilians and Flag

77 Cogwheel and Factory

(Des I. Alturki and I. el Tahtawi. Litho Pakistan Security Ptg Corp, Ltd)

1965 (6 Jan). Army Day. P 14×12½.

666	**76**	5f. multicoloured	40	30
667		15f. multicoloured	70	40
668		30f. multicoloured	2·10	1·10
666/668 *Set of 3*			3·00	1·60
MS669 110×83 mm. Stamp similar to No. 668 but without value shown together with stamp-size portrait of President Arif. Imperf (*sold at* 60f.)			14·00	14·00

(Des S. Rofeil. Litho Pakistan Security Ptg Corp, Ltd)

1965 (6 Jan). First Arab Ministers of Labour Conference, Baghdad. P 12½×14.

670	**77**	10f. multicoloured	85	40

78 Oil Tanker

(Litho State Ptg Wks, Berlin)

1965 (30 Jan). Inauguration of Deep Sea Terminal for Tankers. P 14.

671	**78**	10f. multicoloured	1·50	70

79 Armed Soldier with Flag

(Litho Pakistan Security Ptg Corp, Ltd)

1965 (8 Feb). Second Anniversary of Revolution of 14th Ramadan. P 13½.

672	**79**	10f. multicoloured	85	40
		a. Black printed double	£100	£110

80 Tree

(Litho Pakistan Security Ptg Corp, Ltd)

1965 (6 Mar). Tree Week. Multicoloured, colour of inscriptions given. P 13.

673	**80**	6f. magenta	45	45
674		20f. black	2·30	45
		a. Inscriptions in magenta	£275	

81 Federation Emblem

Short Arabic '3'

(Des I. Al-Shaikly. Litho; gold typo State Ptg Wks, Berlin)

1965 (24 Mar). Arab Insurance Federation. P 14.

675	**81**	3f. gold, ultramarine and light blue	45	45
		a. Short Arabic '3' (R. 9/4)	12·00	
676		10f. gold, black and silver-grey	45	45
677		30f. gold, carmine-red and pink	1·70	1·20
675/677 *Set of 3*			2·30	1·90

82 Dagger on Deir Yassin, Palestine

83 'Threat of Disease'

(Des A. Al-Jaboori. Litho Pakistan Security Ptg Corp, Ltd)

1965 (9 Apr). Deir Yassin Massacre. P 14×12½.

678	**82**	10f. drab and black	1·80	75
679		20f. light brown and deep blue	3·50	1·00

(Des M. Ali. Litho Pakistan Security Ptg Corp, Ltd)

1965 (30 Apr). World Health Day. P 14.

680	**83**	3f. multicoloured	90	45
681		10f. multicoloured	1·10	45
682		20f. multicoloured	2·50	1·30
680/682 *Set of 3*			4·00	2·00

Nos. 680/682 exist imperforate from a limited printing.

84 ITU Emblem and Symbols

85 Flag and Map

(Des A. Al-Jaboori. Litho Pakistan Security Ptg Corp, Ltd)

1965 (17 May). Centenary of International Telecommunications Union. P 14.

683	**84**	10f. multicoloured	1·20	30
684		20f. multicoloured	2·50	85
MS685 139×95 mm. Nos. 683/684. Imperf or perf (*sold at* 40f.)			30·00	25·00

(Des A. Al-Jaboori. Litho Pakistan Security Ptg Corp, Ltd)

1965 (26 May). First Anniversary of Iraq–UAR Pact. P 14×12½.

686	**85**	10f. multicoloured	75	30

85a Lamp and Burning Library

Large Flame

86 Revolutionary and Flames

(Photo Postal Authority Press, Cairo)

1965 (7 June). Reconstitution of Algiers University Library. P 11½×11.

687 **85a** 5f. red, emerald and black 60 45
688 10f. emerald, red and black .... 1·10 45
a. Large flame (R. 9/2) .... 7·50 7·50

(Des A. Al-Jaboori. Litho Pakistan Security Ptg Corp. Ltd)

1965 (30 June). 45th Anniversary of 1920 Rebellion. P 13×13½.

689 **86** 5f. multicoloured 45 30
690 10f. multicoloured 75 30

87 Mosque

(Des K. Hussain. Photo Courvoisier)

1965 (11 July). Mohammed's Birthday. P 12.

691 **87** 10f. multicoloured .... 1·20 1·20
MS692 110×75 mm. No. 691. Imperf (*sold at* 50f.) .... 13·00 12·50

88 Factory and Ear of Wheat

89 ICY Emblem

(Des A. Al-Jaboori. Litho Pakistan Security Ptg Corp, Ltd)

1965 (14 July). Seventh Anniversary of Revolution of 14 July. P 13×13½.

693 **88** 10f. multicoloured 75 75

Broken Arm

(Des A. Al-Jaboori. Litho Pakistan Security Ptg Corp, Ltd)

1965 (13 Aug). AIR. International Co-operation Year. P 13½×13.

694 **89** 5f. black and light orange-brown .... 1·40 45
a. Black and light olive-yellow £200
695 10f. bistre-brown and light yellow-olive .... 2·00 45
696 30f. black and light ultramarine .... 5·00 2·00
a. Broken arm (R. 7/5) .... 18·00
694/696 *Set of 3* .... 7·50 2·50

No. 696a occurs in part of the printing.

90 Fair Emblem

91 President Arif (photo by Studio Jean)

(Des H. Al-Sameraee. Litho Pakistan Security Ptg Corp, Ltd)

1965 (22 Oct). Baghdad Fair. P 13.

697 **90** 10f. multicoloured 75 45

(Photo Courvoisier)

1965 (18 Nov). Second Anniversary of Revolution of 18 November. P 11½.

698 **91** 5f. royal blue and orange 60 45
699 10f. sepia and light violet-blue 90 45
700 50f. indigo and mauve .... 3·75 1·50
698/700 *Set of 3* .... 4·75 2·20

92 Census Graph

(Des A. K. Refaat. Litho Pakistan Security Ptg Corp, Ltd)

1965 (29 Nov). National Census. P 13½×13.

701 **92** 3f. black and purple 75 30
702 5f. brown-red and bistre-brown 75 30
703 15f. bistre and blue .... 3·00 1·00
701/703 *Set of 3* .... 4·00 1·40

93 Hawker Siddeley Trident 1E Airliner

94 Date Palms

(Photo Courvoisier)

1965 (3 Dec). AIR. Inauguration of Trident Airliner by Iraqi Airways. P 11½×12.

704 **93** 5f. multicoloured 75 75
705 10f. multicoloured 75 75
706 40f. multicoloured .... 7·50 1·50
704/706 *Set of 3* .... 8·00 2·75

(Des A. Al-Jaboori. Litho Rosenbaum Brothers, Vienna)

1965 (27 Dec). Second Food and Agricultural Organisation Dates Conference, Baghdad. P 14.

707 **94** 3f. multicoloured 75 45
708 10f. multicoloured .... 1·80 45
709 15f. multicoloured .... 3·00 1·50
707/709 *Set of 3* .... 5·00 2·20

95 Army Memorial

96 'Eagle' and Flag

(Des M. El Khateeb. Litho State Ptg Wks, Vienna)

1966 (6 Jan). 45th Anniversary of Army Day. P 12.

710 **95** 2f. multicoloured 75 45
711 5f. multicoloured 75 45
712 40f. multicoloured .... 3·00 1·20
710/712 *Set of 3* .... 4·00 1·90

(Des M. Fahmi. Photo Delrieu)

1966 (8 Feb). Third Anniversary of Revolution of 14th Ramadan. P 12½.

713 **96** 5f. multicoloured 45 45
714 10f. multicoloured .... 1·10 45

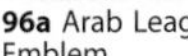

96a Arab League Emblem

97 Footballers

98 Footballer's Legs, and Iraq Football Union Emblem

(Photo Postal Authority Press, Cairo)

1966 (22 Mar). Arab Publicity Week. P 11.

715	**96a**	5f. emerald, brown and orange	75	30
716		15f. blue, reddish purple and yellow-olive	75	30

(Des A. Al-Jaboori. Photo State Ptg Wks, Vienna)

1966 (1 Apr). Arab Football Cup, Baghdad. T **97** and similar vert design and T **98**. Multicoloured. Imperf (50f.) or P 12 (others).

717	2f. Type **97**	75	45
718	5f. Goalkeeper with ball	90	45
719	15f. Type **97**	2·30	1·20
717/719 *Set of 3*		3·50	1·90
MS720 116×70 mm. 50f. Type **98**		13·00	16·00

99 Excavator

100 Queen Nefertari

(Des A. Al-Jaboori. Litho Rosenbaum Brothers, Vienna)

1966 (1 May). Labour Day. P 14.

721	**99**	15f. multicoloured	45	30
722		25f. black, silver and red	75	30

(Des A. Al-Jaboori. Litho German Bank Note Ptg Co, Leipzig)

1966 (20 May). Nubian Monuments Preservation. T **100** and similar design. P 13½×13 (40f.) or 12½×13 (others).

723	**100**	5f. greenish yellow, black and yellow-olive	60	45
724		15f. yellow, brown and light blue	60	45
725	–	40f. blackish brown, yellow-brown and red	3·25	2·50
723/725 *Set of 3*			4·00	3·00

Design: Horiz (41×32 *mm*)—40f. Rock temples, Abu Simbel.

101 President Arif

(Photo Courvoisier)

1966 (14 July). Eighth Anniversary of Revolution of 14 July. P 11½.

726	**101**	5f. brown, red, green and black	60	45
727		15f. blue, red, green and black	90	45
728		50f. violet, red, green and black	3·00	1·70
726/728 *Set of 3*			4·00	2·30

102

(Des K. Hussain. Litho De La Rue)

1966 (22 July). Mohammed's Birthday. P 12.

729	**102**	5f. multicoloured	30	15
730		15f. multicoloured	45	15
731		30f. multicoloured	2·40	2·00
729/731 *Set of 3*			2·75	2·10

1966. As No. 539 but without opt '1960'.

732	**53**	10f. lake	15·00	14·50

103 Iraqi Museum, Statue and Window

104 Revolutionaries

(Des J. Hamoudi. Litho De La Rue)

1966 (9 Nov). Inauguration of Iraqi Museum, Baghdad. T **103** and similar designs. Multicoloured. P 14.

733	15f. Type **103**	2·40	45
734	50f. Gold headdress	3·00	1·50
735	80f. Sumerian head (*vert*)	6·50	2·20
733/735 *Set of 3*		10·50	3·75

(Des Egyptian Artist Union. Litho De La Rue)

1966 (18 Nov). Third Anniversary of Revolution of 18 November. P 13½×13.

736	**104**	15f. multicoloured	1·10	85
		a. Imperf (pair)	41·00	
737		25f. multicoloured	1·70	1·60

105 'Magic Carpet'

106 UNESCO Emblem

(Des Y. Shaker. Litho State Ptg Wks, Vienna)

1966 (3 Dec). AIR. Meeting of Arab International Tourists Union, Baghdad. T **105** and similar multicoloured design. P 14×13½ (5f., 50f.) or 13½ (others).

738	2f. White Stork emblem (27½×39 *mm*)	60	45
739	5f. Type **105**	60	45
740	15f. As 2f.	75	75
741	50f. Type **105**	2·75	1·20
738/741 *Set of 4*		4·25	2·50

(Des S. Gabriel. Litho Rosenbaum Brothers, Vienna)

1966 (30 Dec). 20th Anniversary of United Nations Educational, Scientific and Cultural Organisation. P 13½.

742	**106**	5f. cinnamon, black and greenish blue	30	15
743		15f. bluish green, black and deep orange-red	90	45

107 Soldier and Rocket-launchers

108 Oil Refinery

(Des A. Al-Jaboori. Photo Courvoisier)

1967 (6 Jan). Army Day. P 11½.

744	**107**	15f. yellowow-ochre, blackish brown and light olive-yellow	75	30
745		20f. yellow-ochre, blackish brown and light lilac	1·10	45

1967 (8 Feb). Fourth Anniversary of Revolution of 14th Ramadan. No. **MS**648 with original inscriptions obliterated, '4th' in place of '1st', and sheet value amended to 70 fils.

MS746 125×75 mm. (Nos. 646/647). Imperf (*sold at* 70f.) ... 13·50 13·00

(Litho De La Rue)

1967 (6 Mar). Sixth Arab Petroleum Congress, Baghdad. T **108** and similar multicoloured design. P 14.

747	5f. Congress emblem (*vert*)	45	30
748	15f. Type **108**	60	30
749	40f. Congress emblem (*vert*)	1·40	1·20
750	50f. Type **108**	3·00	1·60
747/750 *Set of 4*		5·00	3·00

109 Spider's Web Emblem

110 Worker holding Cogwheel

(Des P. al-Bazirgan. Litho De La Rue)

1967 (11 Apr). Hajeer Year. P 13½.

751	**109**	5f. multicoloured	45	30
752		15f. multicoloured	75	45

(Litho De La Rue)

1967 (1 May). Labour Day. P 12½×13.

753	**110**	10f. multicoloured	45	15
754		15f. multicoloured	60	30

1967 FLOOD RELIEF SURCHARGES. A number of stamps bearing the face value of 5, 10, 15, 20 and 30f., were officially handstamped 'Aid for 1967 Flood Victims 5 fils' in Arabic, in black, red, violet or green, as a surcharge for compulsory use on all mail during the period 18 June to 18 December 1967. They exist with two sizes of handstamp. The stamps officially handstamped were Nos. 644, 650, 662, 671/672, 674, 678/679, 683, 686, 690, 693, 694/696, 697, 702/703 and 705. Other stamps are also known similarly handstamped but these are unofficial. Later No. T763 was used.

111

(Des A. al-Hadi. Litho De La Rue)

1967 (20 June). Mohammed's Birthday. P 14½.

755	**111**	5f. multicoloured	60	45
756		15f. multicoloured	75	45

112 Flag and Hands with Clubs

113 Um Qasr Port

(Litho De La Rue)

1967 (7 July). 47th Anniversary of 1920 Rebellion. P 13×13½.

757	**112**	5f. multicoloured	60	15
758		15f. multicoloured	90	15

(Litho De La Rue)

1967 (14 July). Ninth Anniversary of Revolution of 14 July and Inauguration of Um Qasr Port. T **113** and similar horiz design. Multicoloured. P 14×13½.

759	5f. Type **113**	60	30
760	10f. Freighter at quayside	1·20	60
761	15f. As 10f.	2·10	60
762	40f. Type **113**	3·50	2·00
759/762 *Set of 4*		6·75	3·25

113a

دفاع
وطني
(**113b**)

114 Costume

1967 (Aug). OBLIGATORY TAX. Flood Relief. Litho. P 13½.

T763	**113a**	5f. brown	90	60

1967 (Nov). OBLIGATORY TAX. Defence Fund. Optd locally with T **113b**.

T764	**113a**	5f. brown	90	85
		a. Lines of opt transposed	30·00	36·00
		b. Opt double	30·00	36·00
		c. Opt double, one albino	25·00	
		d. Opt inverted	30·00	

No. T764a is a setting error.

(Litho De La Rue)

1967 (10 Nov). Iraqi Costumes. T **114** and similar vert designs showing different costumes. P 13.

(a) POSTAGE

765	2f. multicoloured	60	45
766	5f. multicoloured	60	45
767	10f. multicoloured	1·40	45
768	15f. multicoloured	1·80	85
769	20f. multicoloured	2·30	85
770	25f. multicoloured	2·40	1·00
771	30f. multicoloured	2·75	1·00

(b) AIR

772	40f. multicoloured	3·00	1·20
773	50f. multicoloured	4·50	1·70
774	80f. multicoloured	6·00	2·20
765/774 *Set of 10*		23·00	9·25

115 President Arif and Map

(Photo Postal Authority Press, Cairo)

1967 (18 Nov). Fourth Anniversary of Revolution of 18 November. T **115** and similar design. Multicoloured. P 11×11½ (5f.) or 11½×11 (15f.).

775	5f. President Arif (*vert*)	60	45
776	15f. Type **115**	1·40	75

116 Ziggurat of Ur

117 Guide Emblem and Saluting Hand

(Litho De La Rue)

1967 (1 Dec). International Tourist Year. T **116** and similar multicoloured designs. P 13×13½ (horiz) or 13½×13 (vert).

(a) POSTAGE

777	2f. Type **116**	60	45
778	5f. Statues of Nimroud	60	45
779	10f. Babylon (arch)	90	45
780	15f. Minaret of Mosul (*vert*)	1·10	45
781	25f. Arch of Ctesiphon	1·20	45

(b) AIR

782	50f. Statue, Temple of Hatra (*vert*)	5·25	75
783	80f. Spiral Minaret of Samarra (*vert*)	5·75	1·00
784	100f. Adam's Tree (*vert*)	5·25	1·30
785	200f. Aladdin ('Aladdin's Cave') (*vert*)	12·00	5·25
786	500f. Golden Mosque of Kadhimain	55·00	32·00
777/786	*Set of* 10	80·00	38·00

(Litho De La Rue)

1967 (15 Dec). Iraqi Scouts and Guides. T **117** and similar horiz designs. Multicoloured. P 13.

787	2f. Type **117**	2·50	65
788	5f. Guides by camp-fire	3·00	75
789	10f. Scout emblem and saluting hand	3·00	1·20
790	15f. Scouts setting up camp	3·25	1·50
787/790	*Set of* 4	10·50	3·75
MS791	120×48 mm. Nos. 787/790. Imperf (*sold at* 50f.)	17·00	16·00

118 Soldiers Drilling

119 White-cheeked Bulbul (*Pyconotus leucotis*)

(Photo Postal Authority Press, Cairo)

1968 (6 Jan). Army Day. P 11½.

792	**118**	5f. deep brown, green and pale blue	60	30
793		15f. indigo, yellow-olive and pale blue	1·20	45

(Litho De La Rue)

1968 (19 Jan). Iraqi Birds. T **119** and similar multicoloured designs. P 14.

794	5f. Type **119**	1·20	45
795	10f. Hoopoe (*Upupa epops*)	1·50	45
796	15f. Jay (*Garrulus glandarius*)	2·30	45
797	25f. Peregrine Falcon (*Falco peregrinus*)	3·25	75
798	30f. White Stork (*Ciconia alba*)	4·50	75
799	40f. Black Partridge (*Francolinus francolinus*)	5·50	1·20
800	50f. Marbled Teal (*Arias angustirostris*)	7·50	1·90
794/800	*Set of* 7	23·00	5·25

120 Battle Scene

(Photo Postal Authority Press, Cairo)

1968 (14 Feb). Fifth Anniversary of Revolution of 14th Ramadan. P 11½.

801	**120**	15f. orange, black and blue	6·00	1·60

121 Symbols of Labour

122 Football

(Litho Pakistan Security Ptg Corp, Ltd)

1968 (1 May). Labour Day. P 13.

802	**121**	15f. multicoloured	60	45
803		25f. multicoloured	1·10	45

(Des and litho Rosenbaum Brothers, Vienna)

1968 (14 June). 23rd International Military Sports Council Football Championship. T **122** and similar multicoloured design. P 14.

804	2f. Type **122**	60	45
805	5f. Goalkeeper in mid air (*vert*)	60	45
806	15f. Type **122**	75	45
807	25f. As 5f. (*vert*)	4·25	1·30
804/807	*Set of* 4	5·50	2·40
MS808	59×61 mm. 70f. Championship shield. Imperf	17·00	17·00

123 Soldier with Iraqi Flag

124 Anniversary and WHO Emblems

(Photo State Ptg Wks, Vienna)

1968 (14 July). Tenth Anniversary of Revolution of 14 July. P 13½×14.

809	**123**	15f. multicoloured	75	30

(Litho De La Rue)

1968 (29 Nov). 20th Anniversary of World Health Organisation. T **124** and similar design. P 13½.

810	–	5f. multicoloured	45	30
811	–	10f. multicoloured	45	30
812	**124**	15f. red, greenish blue and black	90	30
813		25f. red, apple-green and black	1·20	60
810/813		*Set of* 4	2·75	1·40

Design: Vert—5, 10f. Combined anniversary and WHO emblems.

Nos. 810/813 exist imperforate from a limited printing.

125 Human Rights Emblem

126 Mother and Children

(Litho De La Rue)

1968 (22 Dec). Human Rights Year. P 14.

814	**125**	10f. bright scarlet, lemon and light new blue	60	45
815		25f. bright scarlet, lemon and bright green	60	45
MS816		55×75 mm. **125** 100f. bright scarlet, lemon and mauve. Imperf	9·75	9·50

(Litho De La Rue)

1968 (31 Dec). United Nations Children's Fund. P 14.

817	**126**	15f. multicoloured	75	45
818		25f. multicoloured	2·10	60
MS819		56×76 mm. **126** 100f. multicoloured. Imperf	15·00	9·50

127 Army Tanks

128 Agricultural Scene

(Photo Govt Ptg Wks, Tokyo)

1969 (6 Jan). Army Day. P 13½.

820 **127** 25f. multicoloured .... 6·75 3·75

(Photo Govt Ptg Wks, Tokyo)

1969 (14 Feb). Sixth Anniversary of Revolution of 14th Ramadan. P 13½.

821 **128** 15f. multicoloured 90 45

129 Mosque and Worshippers

130 Emblem of Iraqi Veterinary Medical Association

(Photo Govt Ptg Wks, Tokyo)

1969 (20 Mar). Hajeer Year. P 13½.

822 **129** 15f. multicoloured 90 85

(Litho State Ptg Wks, Damascus)

1969 (12 Apr). First Arab Veterinary Union Conference, Baghdad. P 12½×12.

823 **130** 10f. multicoloured .... 1·10 60

824 15f. multicoloured .... 1·70 60

131 Mahseer (*Barbus (tor) grypus*)

132 Kaaba, Mecca

(Des A. Mahrous. Litho De La Rue)

1969 (9 May–1 Sept). T **131** and similar horiz designs. Multicoloured. P 14.

(a) POSTAGE. Fish (9 May)

825 2f. Type **131** .... 2·75 75

826 3f. Sharpey's Barbel (*Barbus puntius sharpeyi*) .... 3·00 75

827 10f. Silver Pomfret (*Pampus argenteus*) .... 3·25 75

828 100f. Pike Barbel (*Barbus esocinus*) .... 11·50 5·75

825/828 *Set of 4* .... 18·50 7·25

(b) AIR. Fauna (1 Sept)

829 2f. Striped Hyena (*Hyena hyena*) .... 1·40 45

830 3f. Leopard (*Panthera pardus*) .... 1·40 45

831 5f. Mountain Gazelle (*Gazella gazella*) .... 1·40 45

832 10f. Head of Arab horse .... 1·80 60

833 200f. Arab horse .... 23·00 11·00

829/833 *Set of 5* .... 26·00 11·75

(Des J. Sherkham. Photo Govt Ptg Wks, Tokyo)

1969 (28 May). Mohammed's Birthday. P 12½.

834 **132** 15f. multicoloured .... 1·20 45

133 ILO Emblem

134 Weightlifting

(Des Kabeel and Badir. Litho De La Rue)

1969 (6 June). 50th Anniversary of International Labour Organisation. P 13×12½.

835 **133** 5f. yellow, ultramarine and black 30 15

836 15f. yellow, grey-green and black 30 15

837 50f. yellow, rose-red and black .... 2·40 1·60

835/837 *Set of 3* .... 2·75 1·70

MS838 75×55 mm. **133** 100f. multicoloured. Imperf .... 10·50 10·00

(Des A. Al-Jaboori. Litho De La Rue)

1969 (20 June). Olympic Games, Mexico (1968). T **134** and similar square design. Multicoloured. P 13½×13.

839 3f. Type **134** 90 45

840 5f. High jumping 90 45

841 10f. Type **134** .... 1·10 60

842 35f. As 5f. .... 2·00 1·50

839/842 *Set of 4* .... 4·50 2·75

MS843 91×116 mm. Nos. 839/842. Imperf (*sold at* 100f.) .... 20·00 19·00

135 Arms of Iraq and 'Industry'

136 Rebuilding Roads

(Photo Govt Ptg Wks, Tokyo)

1969 (14 July). 11th Anniversary of Revolution of 14 July. P 13½.

844 **135** 10f. multicoloured 60 45

845 15f. multicoloured 90 45

(Photo De La Rue)

1969 (17 July). Anniversary of 17 July Revolution, and Inauguration of Baghdad International Airport. T **136** and similar multicoloured designs. P 14×13½ (200f.) or 13½×14 (others).

846 10f. Type **136** 90 60

847 15f. Type **136** 90 60

848 20f. Airport building .... 2·75 75

849 200f. President Bakr (*vert*) .... 30·00 13·00

846/849 *Set of 4* .... 31·00 13·50

No. 849 exists imperforate from a limited printing.

137 Ear of Wheat and Fair Emblem

138 *Antara* (floating crane)

(Des I. Hanna. Photo Govt Ptg Wks, Tokyo)

1969 (1 Oct). Sixth International Baghdad Fair. P 13½.

850 **137** 10f. chestnut, gold and emerald .... 1·10 45

851 15f. red, gold and ultramarine .... 1·40 60

(Litho De La Rue)

1969 (8 Oct). 50th Anniversary of Port of Basra. T **138** and similar horiz designs. Multicoloured. P 12½.

852 15f. Type **138** 90 45

853 20f. *Al-Wald* (harbour tender) .... 1·20 75

854 30f. *Al-Rashid* (pilot boat) .... 1·80 85

855 35f. *Hillah* (dredger) .... 2·75 1·50

856 50f. *Al-Fao* (survey ship) .... 8·25 3·75

852/856 *Set of 5* .... 13·50 6·50

139 Radio Beacon and Outline of Palestine

140 Emblem, Book and Hands

(Des J. Sherkan. Litho De La Rue)

1969 (9 Nov). Tenth Anniversary of Iraqi News Agency. P 12½×13.

857	**139**	15f. multicoloured	2·00	75
858		50f. multicoloured	5·75	1·30

(Photo Govt Ptg Wks, Tokyo)

1969 (21 Nov). Campaign Against Illiteracy. P 13.

859	**140**	15f. multicoloured	45	30
860		20f. multicoloured	90	60

141 Ross and Keith Smith's Vickers Vimy G-EAOU Biplane

142 Newspaper Headline

(Litho De La Rue)

1969 (4 Dec). AIR. 50th Anniversary of First England–Australia Flight. P 14.

861	**141**	15f. multicoloured	4·50	2·20
862		35f. multicoloured	7·00	5·25
MS863		81×100 mm. Nos. 861/862. Imperf (*sold at* 100f.)	27·00	25·00

(Litho Govt Ptg Wks, Tokyo)

1969 (26 Dec). Centenary of Iraqi Press. P 13½.

864	**142**	15f. black, orange and light yellow	90	60

143 Soldier and Map

144 Iraqis supporting Wall

(Photo Pakistan Security Ptg Corp, Ltd)

1970 (6 Jan). Army Day. P 13.

865	**143**	15f. multicoloured	1·20	60
866		20f. multicoloured	2·40	1·20

(Des A. Al-Hadi. Litho Pakistan Security Ptg Corp, Ltd)

1970 (8 Feb). Seventh Anniversary of Revolution of 14th Ramadan. P 13.

867	**144**	10f. multicoloured	30	30
868		15f. multicoloured	75	30

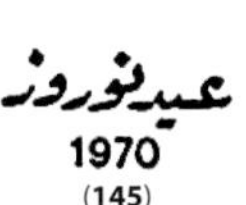

عيد نوروز
1970
(145)

146 Map of Arab Countries, and Slogans

1970 (21 Mar). New Year ('Nawrooz'). Nos. 891/896 optd with T **145**, in blue, by De La Rue.

869	2f. multicoloured	60	45
870	3f. multicoloured	60	45
871	5f. multicoloured	60	45
872	10f. multicoloured	1·20	45
873	15f. multicoloured	1·50	45
874	50f. multicoloured	4·00	2·20
869/874	*Set of 6*	7·75	4·00

(Litho De La Rue)

1970 (7 Apr). 23rd Anniversary of Al-Baath Party. T **146** and similar horiz design. Multicoloured. P 13½×13.

875	15f. Type **146**	75	45
876	35f. Type **146**	1·20	1·00
877	50f. Iraqis acclaiming Party	3·25	1·30
875/877	*Set of 3*	4·75	2·50
MS878	115×76 mm. 150f. As 50f. Imperf	20·00	19·00

مهرجان الربيع
الموصل
1970
(147)

148 Iraqis celebrating Labour Day

1970 (18 Apr). Mosul Spring Festival. Nos. 891/896 optd with T **147** by De La Rue.

879	2f. multicoloured	90	85
880	3f. multicoloured	90	85
881	5f. multicoloured	90	85
882	10f. multicoloured	90	85
883	15f. multicoloured	2·00	1·50
884	50f. multicoloured	4·25	1·70
879/884	*Set of 6*	8·75	6·00

(Litho De La Rue)

1970 (1 May). Labour Day. P 13½×13.

885	**148**	10f. multicoloured	60	45
886		15f. multicoloured	75	60
887		35f. multicoloured	2·40	1·20
885/887		*Set of 3*	3·50	2·00

149 Kaaba, Mecca, Broken Statues and Koran

150 Poppies

(Photo Pakistan Security Ptg Corp, Ltd)

1970 (17 May). Mohammed's Birthday. P 13.

888	**149**	15f. multicoloured	60	30
889		20f. multicoloured	60	45

(Litho De La Rue)

1970 (12 June). Flowers. Vert designs as T **150**. Multicoloured. P 13.

891	2f. Type **150**	75	45
892	3f. Narcissi	75	45
893	5f. Tulip	75	45
894	10f. Carnations	1·10	60
895	15f. Roses	1·80	85
896	50f. As 10f.	5·50	2·30
891/896	*Set of 6*	9·50	4·50

These stamps were first issued with overprints, see Nos. 869/874 and 879/884.

1970 ١٩٧٠
عيد الصحافة
(151)

152 Revolutionaries

1970 (15 June). Press Day. No. 864 optd locally with T **151**, in blue.

896*a*	**142**	15f. black, orange and light yellow	1·10	85
		b. Opt inverted	85·00	£160

(Photo Pakistan Security Ptg Corp, Ltd)

1970 (30 June). 50th Anniversary of the Revolution of 1920. T **152** and similar horiz design. P 13.

897	**152**	10f. black and light olive-green	30	30
898		15f. black and gold	[illegible]	[illegible]
899	–	35f. black and red-orange	1·50	75
897/899 *Set of 3*			2·20	1·20

MS900 119×71 mm. 100f. Designs as Nos. 897 and 899, but without face values. Imperf .... 9·00 8·75

Design: 35f. Revolutionary and rising sun.

153 Bomb-burst and Broken Chain

154 Hands and Map of Iraq

(Photo Pakistan Security Ptg Corp, Ltd)

1970 (14 July). 12th Anniversary of Revolution of 14 July. P 13½.

901	**153**	15f. multicoloured	45	30
902		20f. multicoloured	75	30

(Photo Pakistan Security Ptg Corp, Ltd)

1970 (17 July). Second Anniversary of Revolution of 17 July. P 13.

903	**154**	15f. multicoloured	45	30
904		25f. multicoloured	90	45

155 Pomegranates

156 Kaaba, Mecca

(Litho De La Rue)

1970 (21 Aug). Fruits. T **155** and similar multicoloured designs. P 13½.

905	3f. Type **155**	60	30
906	5f. Grapefruit	60	30
907	10f. Grapes	60	30
908	15f. Oranges	1·80	60
909	35f. Dates	5·50	3·00
905/909 *Set of 5*		8·25	4·00

The Latin inscriptions on Nos. 906/907 are transposed.

(Des K. Hussain. Photo Pakistan Security Ptg Corp, Ltd)

1970 (4 Sept). Hajeer Year. P 13.

910	**156**	15f. multicoloured	45	30
911		25f. multicoloured	90	45

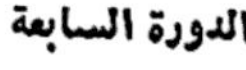

970 – ٩٧٠

(**157**)

158 Arab League Flag and Map

1970 (1 Oct). Seventh International Baghdad Fair. Nos. 850/851 optd locally with T **157**, in red.

912	**137**	10f. chestnut, gold and emerald	6·00	3·25
913		15f. red, gold and ultramarine	6·00	3·25

(Photo Postal Authority Press, Cairo)

1970 (1 Oct). 25th Anniversary of Arab League. P 11.

914	**158**	15f. deep plum, emerald and yellow-olive	45	15
915		35f. carmine, emerald and deep grey	90	75

159 Euphrates Bridge

(Litho De La Rue)

1970 (30 Oct). AIR. National Development. T **159** and similar horiz design. Multicoloured. P 13.

916	10f. Type **159**	3·00	85
917	15f. Type **159**	4·50	2·00
918	1d. President Bakr and banknotes (37×27 *mm*)	£100	44·00
916/918 *Set of 3*		95·00	42·00

160 IEY Emblem

(Photo Harrison & Sons)

1970 (13 Nov). International Education Year. P 13.

919	**160**	5f. multicoloured	45	30
920		15f. multicoloured	75	45

1970 (24 Nov). 25th Anniversary of United Nations. No. **MS**639 optd '1945 UNITED NATIONS 1970' together with other inscriptions and with the face values of the stamps in the miniature sheet obliterated.

MS921 175×120 mm. 50f. .... 13·00 12·50

161 Baghdad Hospital and Society Emblem

162 Union Emblem

(Litho State Ptg Wks, Budapest)

1970 (7 Dec). 50th Anniversary of Iraq Medical Society. P 12.

922	**161**	15f. multicoloured	45	30
923		40f. multicoloured	2·00	1·00

1970 (15 Dec). AIR. Tenth Arab Telecommunications Union Conference, Baghdad. Photo. P 14×13½.

924	**162**	15f. multicoloured	45	15
925		25f. multicoloured	90	75

163 Sugar Beet

164 OPEC Emblem

(Photo Pakistan Security Ptg Corp)

1970 (25 Dec). 12th Anniversary of Mosul Sugar Refinery. T **163** and similar multicoloured design. P 13½×13 (15f.) or 13×13½ (others).

926		5f. Type **163**	45	15
927		15f. Sugar refinery (*horiz*)	75	30
928		30f. Type **163**	2·50	1·20
926/928 *Set of 3*			3·50	1·50

(Litho De La Rue)

1970 (30 Dec). Tenth Anniversary of Organisation of Petroleum-Exporting Countries (OPEC). P 13½.

929	**164**	10f. cobalt, olive-bistre and deep claret	1·20	75
930		40f. cobalt, olive-bistre and bright green	5·50	2·30

(**164a**)

165 Soldiers, Tank and Aircraft

1970–71. OBLIGATORY TAX. Defence Fund.

(a) Nos. 620 and 625/629 surch locally with T **164a**

T931	**65**	5f. on 1f. deep emerald-green	9·00	10·00
T932	–	5f. on 10f. red	9·00	10·00
		a. Opt double	£170	£120
T933	–	5f. on 15f. red-brown and yellow	9·00	10·00
T934	–	5f. on 20f. bluish violet	9·00	10·00
T935	–	5f. on 30f. red-orange	9·00	10·00
T936	–	5f. on 40f. emerald	9·00	10·00
T931/T936 *Set of 6*			49·00	55·00

(b) No. 620 surch locally as T **164a***, but with crosses instead of dots obliterating original face value*

T937	**65**	5f. on 1f. deep emerald-green	38·00	44·00

(Litho De La Rue)

1971 (6 Jan). 50th Anniversary of Army Day. T **165** and similar design. P 13½×14 (15f.) or 11½×13 (40f.).

931		15f. black, bright magenta and gold	90	45
932		40f. multicoloured	5·00	1·70
MS933 124×91 mm. Nos. 931/932. Imperf (*sold at* 100f.)			17·00	16·00

Designs: 15f. T **165**. 42×35 mm—40f. Soldiers and map of Middle East.

166 'Revolutionary Army'

(Litho De La Rue)

1971 (8 Feb). Eighth Anniversary of Revolution of 14th Ramadan. P 11½×12½.

934	**166**	15f. multicoloured	85	50
935		40f. multicoloured	2·50	1·00

167 Pilgrims and Web

(Photo German Bank Note Ptg Co, Leipzig)

1971 (26 Feb). Hajeer Year. P 13.

936	**167**	10f. multicoloured	50	35
937		15f. multicoloured	85	50

168 President Bakr with Torch

169 Boatman in Marshland

(Litho De La Rue)

1971 (11 Mar). First Anniversary of Manifesto of 11 March. P 14.

938	**168**	15f. multicoloured	1·40	85
939		100f. multicoloured	5·75	2·75

(Litho De La Rue)

1971 (15 Mar). Tourism Week. T **169** and similar vert designs. Multicoloured. P 13½.

940		5f. Type **169**	85	50
941		10f. Stork over Baghdad	1·50	50
942		15f. Landscape ('Summer Resorts')	1·90	85
943		100f. Return of Sinbad	9·25	4·25
940/943 *Set of 4*			12·00	5·50

170 Blacksmith taming Serpent

يوم الأنواء
W.M. DAY
1971
(**171**)

(Litho De La Rue)

1971 (21 Mar). New Year ('Nawrooz'). P 11½×13.

944	**170**	15f. multicoloured	1·70	65
945		25f. multicoloured	3·25	1·30

1971 (23 Mar). World Meteorological Day. Nos. 780 and 783 optd locally with T **171**.

(a) POSTAGE

946		15f. multicoloured	6·75	2·50

(b) AIR

947		80f. multicoloured	13·50	10·00

172 Emblem and Workers

مهرجان الربيع
1971
(**173**)

1971 (7 Apr). 24th Anniversary of Al-Baath Party. T **172** and similar multicoloured design. Litho. P 14 (250f.) or 13½ (others).

948		15f. Type **172**	1·90	1·00
949		35f. Type **172**	3·25	2·00
950		250f. As Type **172**, but central portion of design only (42×42 *mm*)	24·00	23·00
948/950 *Set of 3*			26·00	23·00

On No. 950 the circular centre is also perforated.

1971 (14 Apr). Mosul Spring Festival. Nos. 765/766 and 770 optd locally with T **173**.

951	**114**	2f. multicoloured	85	50
952	–	5f. multicoloured	85	50
953	–	25f. multicoloured	3·75	1·80
951/953 *Set of 3*			5·00	2·50

174 Worker and Farm-girl

175 Muslim at Prayer

(Litho De La Rue)

1971 (1 May). Labour Day. P 13.

954	**174**	15f. multicoloured	70	50
955		40f. multicoloured	2·50	65

(Litho De La Rue)

1971 (7 May). Mohammed's Birthday. P 13.

956	**175**	15f. multicoloured	1·20	50
957		100f. multicoloured	4·25	2·75

176 Revolutionaries, and Hands with Broken Chains

177 Rising Sun and 'Prosperity'

(Photo German Bank Note Ptg Co, Leipzig)

1971 (14 July). 13th Anniversary of Revolution of 14 July. P 14.

958	**176**	25f. multicoloured	1·20	50
959		50f. multicoloured	3·75	1·30

(Photo German Bank Note Ptg Co, Leipzig)

1971 (17 July). Third Anniversary of Revolution of 17 July. P 13.

960	**177**	25f. multicoloured	1·20	65
961		70f. multicoloured	3·75	1·50

(O **178**) (O **179**) (O **179a**)
(O **180**) (O **181**)

1971–72. OFFICIAL. Various commemoratives optd or surch locally.

I. 1967 Costumes issue, Nos. 768 and 770/774, optd with T O **178** *(6.3.72).*

(a) POSTAGE

O962	15f. multicoloured	4·00	1·50
	a. Opt double	60·00	85·00
O963	25f. multicoloured	27·00	6·50
O964	30f. multicoloured	27·00	6·50

(b) AIR

O965	40f. multicoloured	11·00	3·25
O966	50f. multicoloured	14·50	3·25
O967	80f. multicoloured	13·50	3·25

II. 1967 Costumes issue, No. 768, optd with T O **179** *(1972).*

O968	15f. multicoloured	£130	14·00
	a. Optd with Type O **179a**	£250	85·00

III. 1967 International Tourist Year issue, Nos. 778 and 780/782, optd with T O **179** *(5, 25f.) or T O* **180** *(others) (28.8.71).*

(a) POSTAGE

O969	5f. multicoloured	14·50	85
O970	15f. multicoloured	14·50	1·50
O971	25f. multicoloured	20·00	4·00

(b) AIR

O972	50f. multicoloured	13·50	9·00

IV. 1968 20th Anniversary of WHO issue, Nos. 811/813, optd similar to T O **178** *but with wider spacing and Arabic inverted (1.7.71).*

O973	–	10f. multicoloured	16·00	10·00
		a. Opt inverted	50·00	60·00
O974	**124**	15f. red, greenish blue and black	16·00	10·00
		a. Opt inverted	50·00	60·00
O975	**124**	25f. red, apple-green and black	16·00	10·00

V. 1968 Human Rights Year issue, Nos. 814/815, optd with T O **178** *(11.5.72).*

O976	**125**	10f. red, yellow and light blue	12·00	1·20
O977		25f. red, yellow and light yellow-green	12·00	2·10
		a. Opt inverted	50·00	60·00

VI. 1968 UNICEF issue, Nos. 817/818, optd with T O **178** *(1972).*

O978	**126**	15f. multicoloured	12·00	1·00
O979		25f. multicoloured	12·00	2·75

VII. 1969 Army Day issue, No. 820, optd with T O **181** *(15.12.71).*

O980	**127**	25f. multicoloured	30·00	7·50

VIII. 1969 Fish and Fauna series, Nos. 825/827, 829/830 and 832, optd with T O **181**, *or surch in addition with bar over original value (29.9.71).*

(a) POSTAGE

O981	–	10f. multicoloured	15·00	10·00
O982	–	15f. on 3f. multicoloured	15·00	10·00
		a. Surch inverted	£150	£200
O983	**131**	25f. on 2f. multicoloured	15·00	10·00
		a. Surch inverted	£150	
		b. Surch double	£150	
		c. Surch double, one inverted	£150	

(b) AIR

O984	–	10f. multicoloured	15·00	10·00
O985	–	15f. on 3f. multicoloured	15·00	10·00
		a. Arabic word 'OFFICIAL' inverted (R. 4/10)	£190	£225
O986	–	25f. on 2f. multicoloured	15·00	10·00

IX. 1970 Fruits issue, Nos. 906/909, optd with T O **180**. *The 5f. and 10f. also have the incorrect Latin inscription blacked-out (29.4.72).*

O987	5f. multicoloured	12·00	9·00
O988	10f. multicoloured	12·00	9·00
O989	15f. multicoloured	12·00	9·00
O990	35f. multicoloured	12·00	9·00

X. 1966 Arab Football Cup issue, No. 717, optd as T O **179**, *but in sans-serif letters.*

O991	**97**	2f. multicoloured	13·50	10·00

XI. 1969 50th Anniversary of ILO issue, No. 836, optd with T O **179a**.

O992	**133**	15f. yellow, grey-green and black	13·50	10·00
		a. Opt inverted	£170	

182 Bank Emblem

التعداد الزراعى العام

١٩٧١/١٠/١٥

(**183**)

1971 (24 Sept). 30th Anniversary of Rafidain Bank. Photo.

(a) Size 34×34 mm. P 13½

989	**182**	10f. multicoloured	1·20	1·20
990		15f. multicoloured	1·90	1·80
991		25f. multicoloured	3·75	3·75

(b) Size 42×42 mm. P 14

992	**182**	65f. multicoloured	19·00	15·00
993		250f. multicoloured	48·00	43·00
989/993 *Set of 5*			65·00	60·00

Nos. 989/993 also have perforations around the circular centre of the design.

1971 (15 Oct). Agricultural Census. Nos. 905, 908/909 optd locally with T **183**.

994	**155**	3f. multicoloured	4·75	4·50
995	–	15f. multicoloured	4·75	4·50
996	–	35f. multicoloured	4·75	4·50
994/996 *Set of 3*			13·00	12·00

184 Football

(Litho De La Rue)

1971 (17 Nov). Fourth Pan-Arab Schoolboy Games, Baghdad. T **184** and similar horiz designs. Multicoloured. P 13.

997	15f. Type **184**	70	65
998	25f. Throwing the discus and running	1·50	85
999	35f. Table tennis	2·00	1·70
1000	70f. Gymnastics	8·25	3·00
1001	95f. Volleyball and basketball	13·50	5·00
997/1001	*Set of* 5	23·00	10·00
MS1002	195×146 mm. Nos. 997/1001. Imperf (*sold at* 200f.)	37·00	36·00

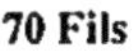

70 Fils

يوم الطالب
٢٣ تشرين الثاني
٩٦١ – ٩٧١
٧ فلسا

(**185**)

186 Society Emblem

1971 (23 Nov). Students' Day. Nos. 892/893 and 895 surch or optd only as T **185**, locally.

1003	15f. multicoloured	3·50	85
1004	25f. on 5f. multicoloured	5·00	2·50
1005	70f. on 3f. multicoloured	19·00	6·25
	a. Surch double	£100	
1003/1005	*Set of* 3	25·00	8·75

(Litho De La Rue)

1971 (30 Nov). AIR. 20th Anniversary of Iraqi Philatelic Society. P 13.

1006	**186**	25f. multicoloured	2·75	2·00
1007		70f. multicoloured	7·75	5·00

25th
Anniversary
971

(**187**)

188 Schoolchildren at Pedestrian Crossing

1971 (11 Dec). 25th Anniversary of United Nations Children's Fund. Nos. 817/818 optd locally with T **187**.

1008	**126**	15f. multicoloured	6·50	2·50
1009		25f. multicoloured	15·00	7·25

(Litho De La Rue)

1971 (17 Dec). Second Traffic Week. P 13.

1010	**188**	15f. multicoloured	3·00	1·50
1011		25f. multicoloured	5·75	2·75

189 APU Emblem

190 Racial Equality Year Symbol

(Photo Postal Authority Press, Cairo)

1971 (24 Dec). 25th Anniversary of Founding of Arab Postal Union at Sofar Conference. P 11½.

1012	**189**	25f. deep brown, lemon and emerald	85	50
1013		70f. vermilion, lemon and ultramarine	3·25	1·30

(Photo German Bank Note Ptg Co, Leipzig)

1971 (31 Dec). Racial Equality Year. P 13½×14.

1014	**190**	25f. multicoloured	50	35
1015		70f. multicoloured	2·00	1·80

191 Soldiers with Flag and Torch

192 Workers

(Photo German Bank Note Ptg Co, Leipzig)

1972 (6 Jan). Army Day. P 14×13½.

1016	**191**	25f. multicoloured	2·40	1·30
1017		70f. multicoloured	8·50	5·00

(Photo German Bank Note Ptg Co, Leipzig)

1972 (8 Feb). Ninth Anniversary of Revolution of 14th Ramadan. P 14×13½.

1018	**192**	25f. multicoloured	4·75	1·20
1019		95f. multicoloured	8·25	5·00

193 Mosque and Crescent

(Litho De La Rue)

1972 (16 Feb). Hajeer Year. P 13×13½.

1020	**193**	25f. multicoloured	70	35
1021		35f. multicoloured	1·40	85

المؤتمر التاسع للاتحاد الوطني
لطلبة العراق
٢٥ شباط – ٢ آذار / ١٩٧٢

(**194**)

1972 (25 Feb). AIR. Ninth Iraqi Students' Union Congress. Nos. 916/917 optd locally with T **194**.

1022	**159**	10f. multicoloured	4·75	4·50
		a. Opt inverted	£100	
1023		15f. multicoloured	4·75	4·50
		a. Opt inverted	£130	

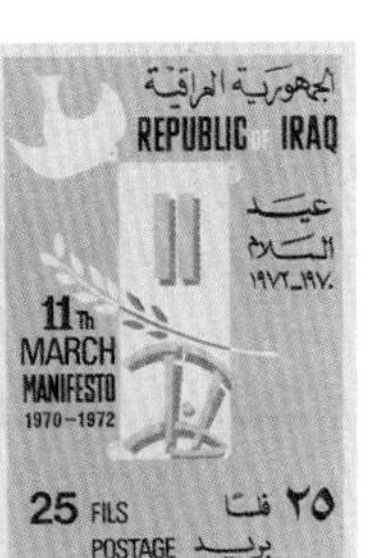

195 Dove, Olive Branch and Manifesto

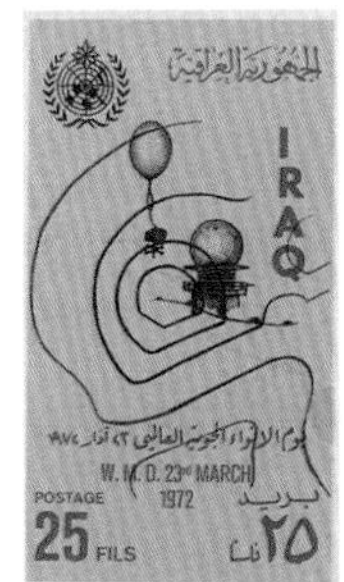

196 Observatory and Weather Balloon on Isobar Map

1972 (11 Mar). Second Anniversary of Manifesto of 11 March. Photo. P 11×12.

1024	**195**	25f. new blue, pale blue and black	3·00	65
1025		70f. reddish purple, mauve and black	8·25	3·25

(Photo German Bank Note Ptg Co, Leipzig)

1972 (23 Mar). World Meteorological Day. P 14×13½.

1026	**196**	25f. multicoloured	4·00	1·20
1027		35f. multicoloured	7·25	3·25

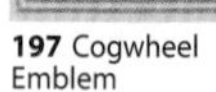

197 Cogwheel Emblem

198 Oil Rig and Flame

(Photo Postal Authority Press, Cairo)

1972 (25 Mar). Iraqi Chamber of Commerce. P 11×11½.

1028	**197**	25f. multicoloured	1·00	50
1029		35f. multicoloured	1·90	85

(Litho De La Rue)

1972 (7 Apr). Inauguration of North Rumaila Oilfield. P 13.

1030	**198**	25f. multicoloured	3·00	65
1031		35f. multicoloured	4·00	2·10

199 Party Emblem

(Litho De La Rue)

1972 (7 Apr). 25th Anniversary of Al-Baath Party. T **199** and similar multicoloured design. P 14 (10, 35f.) or 13½ (others).

1032	10f. Type **199**	70	35
1033	25f. Emblem and inscription (51×27 *mm*)	1·50	85
1034	35f. Type **199**	1·70	1·00
1035	70f. As 25f.	5·50	4·25
1032/1035	*Set of* 4	8·50	5·75

200 Mountain Scene

(Photo Postal Authority Press, Cairo)

1972 (14 Apr). New Year ('Nawrooz'). P 11½.

1036	**200**	25f. magenta, greenish yellow and blue	2·40	50
1037		70f. brown, greenish yellow and blue	7·75	2·75

201 Congress 'Quills' Emblem

202 Federation Emblem

(Photo Postal Authority Press, Cairo)

1972 (17 Apr). Third Arab Journalists Congress. P 11×11½.

1038	**201**	25f. orange, black and bright green	1·00	35
1039		35f. greenish blue, black and bright green	3·50	2·10

(Litho De La Rue)

1972 (22 Apr). Fourth Anniversary of Iraqi Women's Federation. P 13½.

1040	**202**	25f. multicoloured	1·00	65
1041		35f. multicoloured	3·50	2·50

رسمي

Official

(O **203**)

204 Hand holding Spanner

1972. OFFICIAL. Nos. 625/628 optd locally with T O **203**.

O1042	10f. red	15·00	15·00
	a. Opt inverted		50·00
O1043	15f. red-brown and yellow	15·00	15·00
O1044	20f. bluish violet	15·00	15·00
	a. Opt inverted		50·00
O1045	30f. red-orange	15·00	15·00
O1042/O1045	*Set of* 4	55·00	55·00

(Photo Postal Authority Press, Cairo)

1972 (1 May). Labour Day. P 11×11½.

1046	**204**	25f. multicoloured	85	35
1047		35f. multicoloured	1·50	85

205 Kaaba, Mecca

(Photo Postal Authority Press, Cairo)

1972 (26 May). Mohammed's Birthday. P 11½×11.

1048	**205**	25f. black, gold and emerald	1·00	35
1049		35f. black, gold and reddish violet	3·50	2·50

206 Shooting for Goal

(Litho De La Rue)

1972 (9 June). AIR. 25th International Military Sports Council Football Championship, Baghdad. T **206** and similar horiz designs. Multicoloured. P 13½.

1050	10f. Type **206**	1·00	50
1051	20f. Players in goalmouth	2·20	50
1052	25f. Type **206**	2·20	50
1053	35f. As 20f.	7·75	1·50
1050/1053	*Set of* 4	12·00	2·75
MS1054	77×64 mm. 100f. Olympic and CISM emblems. Imperf	34·00	33·00

207 Soldiers and Artillery

(Photo German Bank Note Ptg Co, Leipzig)

1972 (14 July). 14th Anniversary of the Revolution of 14 July. P 14.

1055	**207**	35f. multicoloured	2·00	85
1056		70f. multicoloured	6·50	2·50

208 'Spirit of Revolution'

(Photo German Bank Note Ptg Co, Leipzig)

1972 (17 July). Fourth Anniversary of Revolution of 17 July. P 13.

1057	**208**	25f. multicoloured	2·50	1·50
1058		95f. multicoloured	6·75	6·25

209 Scout Badge and Camp Scene

(Litho German Bank Note Ptg Co, Leipzig)

1972 (10 Aug). Tenth Jamboree and Conference of Arab Scouts, Mosul. P 14.

1059	**209**	20f. multicoloured	4·25	2·10
1060		25f. multicoloured	6·00	2·50

210 Guide Badge and Camp

(Litho German Bank Note Ptg Co, Leipzig)

1972 (24 Aug). Fourth Conference and Camp of Arab Guides, Mosul. P 14.

1061	**210**	10f. multicoloured	3·25	1·50
1062		45f. multicoloured	10·00	3·00

(**211**)

1972 (1 Oct). Third Traffic Week. Nos. 1010/1011 surch or optd only as T **211**, locally.

1063	**188**	25f. multicoloured	30·00	5·75
1064		70f. on 15f. multicoloured	30·00	14·00

(**212**)

213 Strong Man Statuette

1972 (13 Nov). Festival of Palm Trees and Feast of Dates. Nos. 707 and 709 surch locally as T **212**.

1065	**94**	25f. on 3f. multicoloured	8·25	5·00
1066		70f. on 15f. multicoloured	20·00	13·00

(Photo German Bank Note Ptg Co, Leipzig)

1972 (15 Nov). AIR. World Body-building Championships and Asian Congress, Baghdad. T **213** and similar vert designs. Multicoloured. P 14×13½.

1067	25f. Type **213**	2·50	1·30
1068	70f. Ancient warriors and modern Strong Man	6·75	4·25

214 Bank Building

(**215**)

(Photo German Bank Note Ptg Co, Leipzig)

1972 (16 Nov). 25th Anniversary of Central Bank of Iraq. P 13.

1069	**214**	25f. multicoloured	1·50	85
1070		70f. multicoloured	4·50	2·00

1972. OBLIGATORY TAX. Defence Fund. Nos. 607/608 surch locally with T **215**.

T1071	**62**	5f. on 14f. black and green	15·00	15·00
T1072		5f. on 35f. black and red	15·00	15·00

216 International Railway Union Emblem

(**217**)

(Photo German Bank Note Ptg Co, Leipzig)

1972 (29 Dec). 50th Anniversary of International Railway Union. P 13.

1073	**216**	25f. multicoloured	3·75	1·50
1074		45f. multicoloured	10·00	7·00

1973 (29 Jan). Various 'Faisal' definitives with portrait obliterated locally with T **217**.

(a) POSTAGE

(i) 1954–1957 issue

1075	**33**	10f. blue	6·75	2·50
1076		15f. black	6·75	2·50
1077		25f. reddish purple	6·75	2·50

(ii) 1957–1958 issue

1078	**41**	10f. blue	6·75	2·50
1079		15f. black	6·75	2·50
1080		25f. purple	6·75	2·50
1075/1080 *Set of 6*			36·00	13·50

*(b) OFFICIAL. Optd with T O **27** or similar opt*

(i) 1948–1951 issue

O1081	**27**	25f. purple	13·00	3·25
O1082	**28**	50f. dull ultramarine	13·00	11·50

(ii) 1955–1958 issue

O1083	**33**	25f. reddish purple	13·00	3·25
O1084	**34**	50f. blue	13·00	11·50

*(iii) Similar to T **41** but size 22½×27½ mm*

O1085	–	50f. purple	13·00	11·50
O1081/O1085 *Set of 5*			60·00	37·00

(O **218** Arabic word at right 7 *mm* long)

(O **218a** Arabic word at right 9 *mm* long)

1973. OFFICIAL. 'Faisal' postage stamps with portrait obliterated locally.

*(a) Optd with T O **218** over T **217***

O1086	**33**	10f. blue	9·25	9·00
		a. Opt on Type **41**	£120	£120
O1087	**41**	15f. black	9·25	9·00
		a. Opt on Type **33**	£160	£170

*(b) Optd with T O **218a** over T **217***

O1088	**41**	10f. blue	70·00	70·00
O1089	**33**	15f. black	70·00	70·00

*(c) Optd with T O **218** only*

O1090	**33**	15f. black	9·25	2·00
O1091	**41**	15f. black	9·25	2·00
O1092	**33**	25f. reddish purple	9·25	2·00
		a. Opt on Type **27**	29·00	13·00
O1093	**41**	25f. purple	9·25	2·00

*(d) Optd with T O **218a** only*

O1094	**33**	15f. black	11·00	10·50
O1095	**41**	15f. black	11·00	10·50
O1096	**27**	25f. purple	30·00	22·00
O1086/O1096 *Set of 11*			£225	£190

See also Nos. O1130*a*/O1147*a*.

المؤتمر الدولي
للتاريخ/١٩٧٣

(**219**)

220 Iraqi Oil Workers

1973 (25 Mar). International History Congress. Nos. 780, 783 and 786 optd locally as T **219**.

(a) POSTAGE

1094	15f. multicoloured	20·00	8·25

(b) AIR

1095	80f. multicoloured	44·00	15·00
1096	500f. multicoloured	£130	£130
1094/1096 *Set of 3*		£170	£140

(Photo German Bank Note Ptg Co, Leipzig)

1973 (1 June). First Anniversary of Nationalisation of Iraqi Oil Industry. P 13.

(a) POSTAGE

1097	**220**	25f. multicoloured	4·00	1·70
1098		70f. multicoloured	17·00	6·25

*(b) OFFICIAL. Optd as T O **179**, but in sans-serif letters*

O1099	**220**	25f. multicoloured	9·25	3·00

221 Harp

OFFICIAL

(O **222**)

(Litho German Bank Note Ptg Co, Leipzig)

1973 (June). T **221** and similar vert designs. P 13×12½.

1099	**221**	5f. black and orange	50	35
1100		10f. black and yellow-brown	50	35
1101		20f. black and cerise	70	35
1102	–	25f. black and violet-blue	1·00	50
1103	–	35f. black and turquoise-green	1·20	65
1104	–	45f. black and greenish blue	1·20	65
1105	–	50f. lemon and yellow-olive	1·70	65
1106	–	70f. lemon and bluish violet	2·40	1·20
1107	–	95f. lemon and brown	4·00	1·70
1099/1107 *Set of 9*			12·00	5·75

Designs: 25, 35, 45f. Minaret of Mosul; 50, 70, 95f. Statue of a Goddess.

1973 (June). OFFICIAL. Nos. 1099/1107 optd with T O **222**.

O1108	**221**	5f. black and orange	70	65
O1109		10f. black and yellow-brown	70	65
O1110		20f. black and cerise	1·20	65
O1111	–	25f. black and violet-blue	2·40	2·30
O1112	–	35f. black and turquoise-green	2·40	1·00
O1113	–	45f. black and greenish blue	2·40	1·20
O1114	–	50f. lemon and yellow-olive	3·25	1·30
O1115	–	70f. lemon and bluish violet	3·25	1·80
O1116	–	95f. lemon and brown	4·75	2·30
O1108/O1116 *Set of 9*			19·00	10·50

دفاع وطني
٥ فلوس

دفاع وطني
٥ فلوس

(**223**) (**224**) (**225**)

1973. OBLIGATORY TAX. Nos. 738, 765, 777, 787 and 891 surch locally with T **224** (No. T1119) or as T **223** (others).

T1117	–	5f. on 2f. multicoloured	17·00	17·00
T1118	**114**	5f. on 2f. multicoloured	17·00	17·00
		a. Old value obliterated with Type **225**	38·00	37·00
T1119	**116**	5f. on 2f. multicoloured	17·00	17·00
T1120	**117**	5f. on 2f. multicoloured	17·00	17·00
T1121	**150**	5f. on 2f. multicoloured	17·00	17·00
		a. Old English value obliterated with Type **225** (R. 3/6, 5/9)	£130	£120
T1117/T1121 *Set of 5*			75·00	75·00

On No. T1118 T **225** obliterates the left-hand (English) value on positions R. 1/4, 2/6, 3/3, 3/6, 3/10, 4/4 and 5/7, and the right-hand (Arabic) value on positions R. 1/10, 2/9, 4/1 and 5/8.

225a Iraqis and Flags

I.O.J.
SEPTEMBER
26-29, 1973

(**226**)

1973 (14 July). July Festivals. Litho. P 12.

1122	**225a**	25f. multicoloured	1·40	65
1123		35f. multicoloured	2·75	85

1973 (26 Sept). International Journalists' Conference. Nos. 857/858 optd locally with T **226**, in silver.

1124	**139**	15f. multicoloured	6·00	5·00
		a. Full point after '29'	6·75	5·75
1125		50f. multicoloured	8·50	7·50
		a. Full point after '29'	10·00	8·25

The full point variety occurs on all positions in vertical columns 3, 5 and 9.

227 Interpol Headquarters, Paris

228 Flags and Fair Emblems

1973 (30 Sept). 50th Anniversary of International Criminal Police Organisation (Interpol). Litho. P 12.

1126	**227**	25f. multicoloured	2·40	1·30
1127		70f. multicoloured	12·00	8·00

(Photo Postal Authority Press, Cairo)

1973 (8 Oct). Tenth Baghdad International Fair. P 11×11½.

1128	**228**	10f. multicoloured	85	50
1129		20f. multicoloured	1·50	65
1130		65f. multicoloured	3·50	1·80
1128/1130 *Set of 3*			5·25	2·75

1973. OFFICIAL. Various 'Faisal' Official stamps, optd locally with T O **27** or similar type, with portrait obliterated by 'leaf' motif similar to that used in T O **218a**.

(a) 1948–1951 issue

O1130*a*	**27**	12f. brown-olive	4·00	1·00
		b. Portrait obliterated with Type **225**	30·00	12·00
		c. Pair, one without leaf opt		
O1131		14f. brown-olive	4·00	1·30
O1132		15f. black	4·00	1·30
O1133		16f. carmine-rose	8·25	2·10

O1134		28f. blue	13·50	3·00
O1134*a*		30f. red-orange	13·00	3·00
O1134*b*		40f. chestnut	13·50	3·75
O1135	**28**	60f. ultramarine	13·50	12·50
O1136		100f. olive-green	50·00	20·00
O1137		½d. blue	£130	50·00
O1138		1d. emerald-green	£250	£225

(b) 1955–1958 issue

O1139	**33**	3f. lake	4·00	1·50
O1140		6f. deep magenta	4·00	1·50
O1141		8f. yellow-brown	4·00	1·50
O1142		16f. carmine-red	41·00	40·00
O1142*a*		20f. olive-green	4·00	1·50
O1142*b*		30f. red	4·00	2·50
O1142*c*		40f. chestnut	4·00	4·00
O1143	**34**	60f. purple	4·00	4·00
O1144		100f. olive-green	70·00	20·00

(c) 1958–1959 issue

O1145	**41**	3f. carmine-lake	12·00	3·00
O1146		6f. deep magenta	12·00	3·00
O1147		8f. light brown	12·00	3·00
O1147*a*		30f. orange-red	12·00	3·00
O1130*a*/O1147*a* *Set of 24*			£650	£400

The leaf motif points to the right or left, mixed in the same sheet.

T **225** (No. O1130*a*b) occurs with the diamond to the right on positions R. 1/10, 4/3, 7/2 and 8/4, and with the diamond to the left on positions R. 2/6, 3/10, 4/10, 5/4, 6/2, 8/6, 10/9 and 10/10.

229 WMO Emblem

230 Arab Flags and Map

1973 (20 Nov). Centenary of World Meteorological Organisation. Litho. P 12.

1148	**229**	25f. black, dull green and yellow-orange	1·40	35
1149		35f. black, dull green and reddish mauve	4·25	2·10

(Photo German Bank Note Ptg Co, Leipzig)

1973 (1 Dec). 11th Session of Arab States' Civil Aviation Council, Baghdad. P 14.

1150	**230**	20f. multicoloured	85	35
1151		35f. multicoloured	2·75	1·80

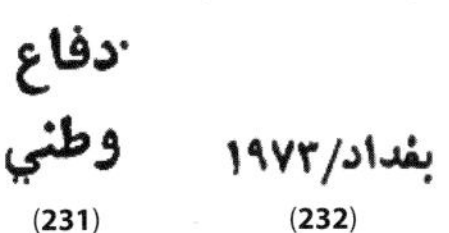

(**231**) (**232**)

233 Human Rights Emblem

1973. OBLIGATORY TAX. No. 1099 optd locally with T **231**.

T1152	**221**	5f. black and orange	12·00	8·25
		a. Opt double	£190	

1973 (12 Dec). Sixth Executive Council Meeting of Arab Postal Union, Baghdad. No. 665 optd locally with T **232**.

1153	**75**	30f. blue and yellow-orange	9·25	5·75

(Photo State Ptg Wks, Budapest)

1973 (25 Dec). 25th Anniversary of Declaration of Human Rights. P 11½×12.

1154	**233**	25f. multicoloured	50	50
1155		70f. multicoloured	1·70	1·00

234 Shield and Military Activities

235 Soldier

(Photo State Ptg Wks, Budapest)

1974 (6 Jan). 50th Anniversary of Military College. P 12×11½.

1156	**234**	25f. multicoloured	85	50
1157		35f. multicoloured	3·00	2·00

(Litho German Bank Note Ptg Co, Leipzig)

1974 (Feb). OBLIGATORY TAX. Defence Fund. P 13×12½.

T1158	**235**	5f. black, yellow and ochre	7·25	5·75

The use of Obligatory Tax stamps was discontinued as from 1 April 1974.

See also No. O1165.

236 UPU Emblem

(Photo State Ptg Wks, Budapest)

1974 (28 May). Centenary of Universal Postal Union. P 11½×12.

1159	**236**	25f. multicoloured	1·70	50
1160		35f. multicoloured	1·70	85
1161		70f. multicoloured	3·00	2·00
1159/1161 *Set of 3*			5·75	3·00

237 Allegory of Nationalisation

1974 (1 June). Second Anniversary of Nationalisation of Iraqi Oil Industry. Litho. P 12½.

1162	**237**	10f. multicoloured	85	35
1163		25f. multicoloured	1·70	50
1164		70f. multicoloured	5·00	4·25
1162/1164 *Set of 3*			6·75	4·50

بريد رسمي

(O **237a**)

238 Festival Time

1974. OFFICIAL. No. T1158 optd with T O **237a**.

O1165	**235**	5f. black, yellow and ochre	8·50	8·25
		a. Opt inverted	£200	
		b. Opt double, one inverted	£250	

This overprint was made in order to use up excess Obligatory Tax stamps.

(Litho State Ptg Wks, Budapest)

1974 (17 July). July Festivals. P 11½×12.

1165 **238** 20f. multicoloured 70 35
1166 35f. multicoloured .... 2·00 1·00

239 National Front Emblem and Heads

240 Cement Plant

(Litho State Ptg Wks, Budapest)

1974 (17 July). First Anniversary of Progressive National Front. P 12×11½.

1167 **239** 25f. multicoloured .... 1·20 50
1168 70f. multicoloured .... 3·00 1·50

(Litho State Ptg Wks, Budapest)

1974 (19 Oct). 25th Anniversary of Iraqi Cement Industry. P 11½×12.

1169 **240** 20f. multicoloured 85 50
1170 25f. multicoloured .... 1·20 65
1171 70f. multicoloured .... 2·75 2·10
1169/1171 *Set of 3* .... 4·25 3·00

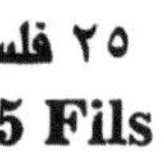

(**241**)

242 WPY Emblem

1975 (9 Jan). Nos. 905 and 892 surch as T **241**.

1172 **155** 10f. on 3f. multicoloured .... 7·50 5·00
1173 – 25f. on 3f. multicoloured .... 22·00 16·00
a. Surch inverted £125
b. Surch double £125

(Litho State Ptg Wks, Budapest)

1975 (30 Jan). World Population Year (1974). P 11½×12.

1174 **242** 25f. olive-green and cobalt .... 1·40 35
1175 35f. deep blue and magenta .... 2·40 1·30
1176 70f. violet and light yellow-olive .... 6·75 3·00
1174/1176 *Set of 3* .... 9·50 4·25

1975 (17 Apr). OFFICIAL. Nos. 780 and 798 optd as T O **179** but with different spacing between lines of opt (No. O1177, 4½ *mm;* O1178, 13½ *mm).*

O1177 15f. multicoloured .... 8·50 8·25
a. Surch inverted .... 60·00
O1178 30f. multicoloured .... 20·00 11·50
a. Surch inverted £100
b. Surch double, both inverted .... 60·00

243 Festival Emblems

(Litho State Ptg Wks, Budapest)

1975 (17 July). July Festivals. P 12×11½.

1177 **243** 5f. multicoloured 50 35
1178 10f. multicoloured 50 50
1179 35f. multicoloured .... 3·50 1·50
1177/1179 *Set of 3* .... 4·00 2·20

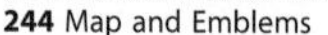

244 Map and Emblems

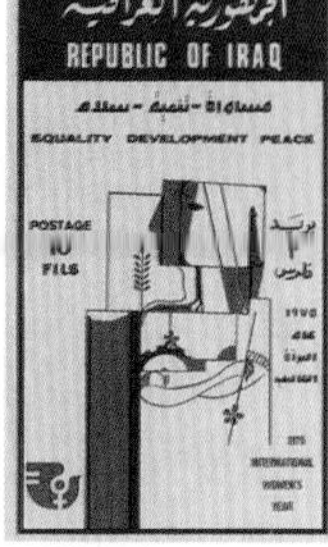

245 'Equality, Development, Peace'

1975 (5 Aug). Tenth Anniversary of Arab Labour Organisation. Photo. P 13.

1180 **244** 25f. multicoloured .... 1·00 35
1181 35f. multicoloured .... 1·70 1·20
1182 45f. multicoloured .... 1·90 1·30
1180/1182 *Set of 3* .... 4·25 2·50

1975 (15 Aug). International Women's Year. Photo. P 14×13½.

1183 **245** 10f. multicoloured .... 1·00 65
1184 35f. multicoloured .... 2·00 1·50
1185 70f. multicoloured .... 8·25 3·00
1183/1185 *Set of 3* .... 10·00 4·75
MS1186 100×83 mm. 100f. multicoloured. As T **245**, but face value outside design. Imperf .... 19·00 18·00

246 Diyala Barrage

247 Company Seal

(Litho State Ptg Wks, Budapest)

1975 (5 Sept). 25th Anniversary of International Commission on Irrigation and Drainage. P 12×11½.

1187 **246** 3f. multicoloured 35 15
1188 25f. multicoloured .... 1·40 50
1189 70f. multicoloured .... 5·50 2·75
1187/1189 *Set of 3* .... 6·50 3·00

1975 (11 Oct). 25th Anniversary of National Insurance Company of Baghdad. Photo. P 13.

1190 **247** 20f. multicoloured .... 1·50 50
1191 25f. multicoloured .... 1·90 85
MS1192 71×71 mm. **247** 100f. multicoloured. Imperf. 14·50 14·00

248 Court Musicians

O **249** Eagle Emblem

1975 (21 Nov). International Music Conference, Baghdad. Photo. P 14.

1193 **248** 25f. multicoloured .... 1·20 50
1194 45f. multicoloured .... 3·00 1·80

1975. OFFICIAL. Photo. P 14.

O1195 O **249** 5f. multicoloured .... 1·00 1·00
O1196 10f. multicoloured .... 1·00 1·00
O1197 15f. multicoloured .... 1·00 1·00
O1198 20f. multicoloured .... 1·50 1·50
O1199 25f. multicoloured .... 2·20 2·10
O1200 30f. multicoloured .... 2·50 2·50
O1201 50f. multicoloured .... 4·00 4·00
O1202 100f. multicoloured .... 7·75 7·50
O1195/O1202 *Set of 8* .... 19·00 19·00

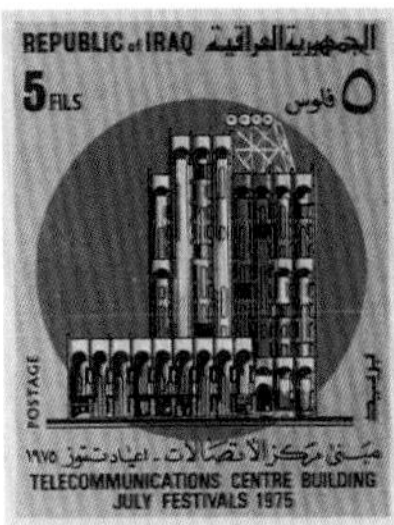

250 Telecommunications Centre

1975 (22 Dec). Opening of Telecommunications Centre. Litho. P 12½.

1203	**250**	5f. multicoloured	35	35
1204		10f. multicoloured	50	35
1205		60f. multicoloured	3·50	2·10
1203/1205 *Set of 3*			4·00	2·50

251 Diesel Train

252 Goddess (statue)

1975 (22 Dec). 15th Taurus Railway Conference, Baghdad. T **251** and similar horiz designs. Multicoloured. Photo. P 14.

1206	25f. Type **251**	11·00	2·00
1207	30f. Diesel locomotive	17·00	4·00
1208	35f. Tank locomotive and train	22·00	7·25
1209	50f. Steam locomotive	32·00	20·00
1206/1209 *Set of 4*		75·00	30·00

Nos. 1206/1209 are also known imperforate.

1976 (1 Jan). T **252** and similar vert designs. Litho. P 13×12½.

1210	**252**	5f. multicoloured	35	25
1211		10f. multicoloured	35	25
1212		15f. multicoloured	50	35
1213	–	20f. multicoloured	70	40
1214	–	25f. multicoloured	1·00	50
1215	–	30f. multicoloured	1·40	50
1216	–	35f. multicoloured	1·50	60
1217	–	50f. multicoloured	2·50	65
1218	–	75f. multicoloured	3·75	1·50
1210/1218 *Set of 9*			11·00	4·50

Designs: 20f., 25f., 30f. Two females forming column; 35f., 50f., 75f. Head of bearded man.

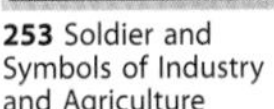

253 Soldier and Symbols of Industry and Agriculture

254 Crossed-out Thumbprint

1976 (6 Jan). Army Day. Photo. P 13.

1219	**253**	5f. multicoloured	35	15
1220		25f. multicoloured/*silver*	1·00	35
1221		50f. multicoloured/*gold*	3·00	1·20
1219/1221 *Set of 3*			4·00	1·50

1976 (8 Jan). Arab Illiteracy Day. Photo. P 13½×13.

1222	**254**	5f. multicoloured	50	50
1223		15f. multicoloured	85	50
1224		35f. multicoloured	3·00	2·00
1222/1224 *Set of 3*			4·00	2·75

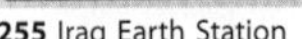

255 Iraq Earth Station

256 Early and Modern Telephones

1976 (8 Feb). 13th Anniversary of Revolution of 14th Ramadan. Photo. P 13×13½.

1225	**255**	10f. multicoloured	85	50
1226		25f. multicoloured/*silver*	2·20	85
1227		75f. multicoloured/*gold*	10·00	3·75
1225/1227 *Set of 3*			11·50	4·50

1976 (17 Mar). Telephone Centenary. Litho. P 12×12½.

1228	**256**	35f. multicoloured	2·50	85
1229		50f. multicoloured	5·00	1·30
1230		75f. multicoloured	7·75	2·10
1228/1230 *Set of 3*			13·50	3·75

257 Map and Emblem

258 Iraqi Family on Map

1976 (24 Mar). 20th International Arab Trade Unions Conference. Photo. P 13½.

(a) POSTAGE

1231	**257**	5f. multicoloured	70	35
1232		10f. multicoloured	70	35

(b) AIR

1233	**257**	75f. multicoloured	6·00	2·75
1231/1233 *Set of 3*			6·75	3·00

1976 (1 Apr). Police Day. Litho. P 12½.

1234	**258**	5f. multicoloured	35	15
1235		15f. multicoloured	85	35
1236		35f. multicoloured	4·25	2·00
1234/1236 *Set of 3*			5·00	2·30

259 'Strategy' Pipeline

260 Human Eye

(Des Y. M. Abdullah. Photo Heraclio Fournier)

1976 (1 June). Fourth Anniversary of Oil Nationalisation. T **259** and similar design. P 13½×13.

1237	**259**	25f. multicoloured	3·25	35
1238		75f. multicoloured	7·50	3·75
MS1239		80×90 mm. 150f. multicoloured. Imperf	60·00	60·00

Design: 35×33 mm—150f. President Bakr embracing Prime Minister.

No. **MS**1239 is known without control numbers.

(Des Y. M. Abdullah. Photo German Bank Note Ptg Co, Leipzig)

1976 (20 June). AIR. World Health Day. 'Foresight Prevents Blindness'. P 14.

1240	**260**	25f. cobalt and black	70	35
1241		35f. pale emerald and black	1·00	35
1242		50f. pale orange and reddish brown	2·00	1·20
1240/1242 *Set of 3*			3·25	1·70

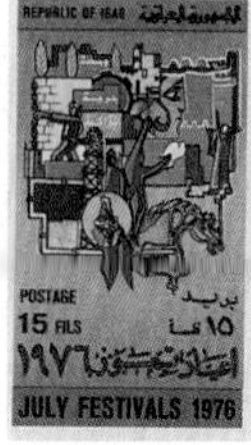

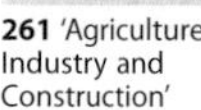

261 'Agriculture, Industry and Construction'

262 Basketball

(Des B. Aljoubori. Photo German Bank Note Ptg Co, Leipzig)

1976 (17 July). July Festivals. P 14.

1243	**261**	15f. multicoloured	70	50
1244		35f. multicoloured	2·00	1·30

(Des Y. M. Abdullah. Litho De La Rue)

1976 (30 July). AIR. Olympic Games, Montreal. T **262** and similar designs. Multicoloured. P 12×12½.

1245	25f. Type **262**	85	35
1246	35f. Volleyball	1·40	1·00
1247	50f. Wrestling	2·00	1·70
1248	75f. Boxing	3·75	2·75
1245/1248	*Set of* 4	7·25	5·25
MS1249	121×91 mm. 100f. Rifle-shooting. Imperf	13·50	13·00

263 Bishop Capucci, Wounded Dove and Map of Palestine

264 River Kingfisher (*Alcedo atthis*)

1976 (18 Aug). Second Anniversary of Arrest of Bishop Capucci. Litho. P 12.

1250	**263**	25f. multicoloured	1·40	50
1251		35f. multicoloured	1·50	85
1252		75f. multicoloured	5·00	2·75
1250/1252		*Set of* 3	7·00	3·75

1976 (15 Sept). Birds. T **264** and similar vert designs. Multicoloured. Litho. P 13½×14.

1253	5f. Type **264**	5·00	1·70
1254	10f. Turtle Dove (*Streptopelia turtur*)	5·00	1·70
1255	15f. Pin-tailed Sandgrouse (*Pterocles alchata*)	6·75	1·70
1256	25f. Blue Rock Thrush (*Monticola solitarius*)	13·50	2·00
1257	50f. Purple Heron (*Ardea purpurea*) and Grey Heron (*Ardea cinerea*)	20·00	3·00
1253/1257	*Set of* 5	45·00	9·00

1976 (15 Sept). OFFICIAL. Values and designs as Nos. 1253/1257 additionally inscr. 'OFFICIAL' in lined capitals and in Arabic across the centre of the stamp.

O1258	5f. multicoloured	3·25	1·80
O1259	10f. multicoloured	3·25	2·10
O1260	15f. multicoloured	3·25	2·10
O1261	25f. multicoloured	9·25	3·25
O1262	50f. multicoloured	14·50	5·25
O1258/O1262	*Set of* 5	30·00	13·00

265 Emblem within '15'

266 Children with Banner

1976 (23 Nov). 15th Anniversary of Iraqi Students' Union. Photo. P 13½.

1263	**265**	30f. multicoloured	1·20	50
1264		70f. multicoloured	4·25	1·80

1976 (25 Dec). 30th Anniversary of United Nations Educational, Scientific and Cultural Organisation. 'Children's Books'. T **266** and similar vert designs. Multicoloured. Litho. P 12×12½.

1265	10f. Type **266**	50	50
1266	25f. Children in garden	3·75	85
1267	75f. Children with Iraqi flag	6·75	2·50
1265/1267	*Set of* 3	10·00	3·50

267 *Rumaila* (tanker) and Emblem

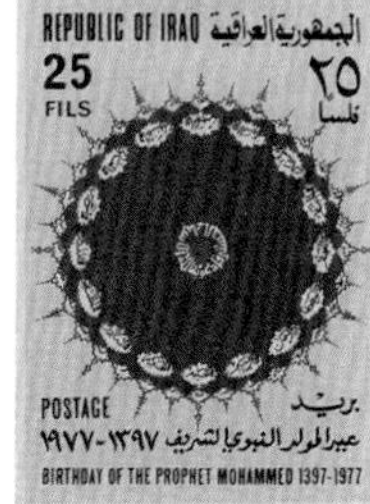

268 Islamic Design with Inscriptions

1976 (25 Dec). Fourth Anniversary of First Iraqi Oil Tanker and First Anniversary of Nationalisation of Basrah Petroleum Company. T **267** and similar horiz designs. Multicoloured. Litho. P 12½×12.

1268	10f. Type **267**	1·20	50
1269	15f. Type **267**	1·70	65
1270	25f. Oil jetty and installations	3·75	1·30
1271	50f. As 25f.	5·50	2·30
1268/1271	*Set of* 4	11·00	4·25

(Des M. R. al-Hashmi. Photo Heraclio Fournier)

1977 (2 Mar). Birthday of Prophet Mohammed. P 13½.

1272	**268**	25f. multicoloured	1·40	50
1273		35f. multicoloured	2·00	65

269 Dove Emblem

270 Dahlia

(Des Y. Hussain. Photo Heraclio Fournier)

1977 (11 Mar). Peace Day. P 14.

1274	**269**	25f. multicoloured	70	35
1275		30f. multicoloured	1·20	65

(Des S. Salman. Litho Harrison & Sons)

1977 (21 Mar). Flowers. T **270** and similar vert designs. Multicoloured. P 12½.

1276	5f. Type **270**	50	50
1277	10f. *Lathyrus odoratus*	85	50
1278	35f. *Chrysanthemum coronarium*	2·20	65
1279	50f. *Verbena hybrida*	4·25	1·30
1276/1279	*Set of* 4	7·00	2·75

271 'V' Emblem with Doves

1977 (7 Apr). 30th Anniversary of Al-Baath Party. T **271** and similar horiz designs. Multicoloured Photo. P 13.

No.		Description	Unused	Used
1280		25f. Type **271**	1·20	50
1281		75f. Human figures as a flame	4·00	2·30
MS1282		80×60 mm. 100f. Dove with olive-branch. Imperf	12·00	11·50

272 APU Emblem and Flags

273 1st May Emblem

1977 (12 Apr). 25th Anniversary of Arab Postal Union. Litho. P 14.

No.	Type	Description	Unused	Used
1283	**272**	25f. multicoloured	70	35
1284		35f. multicoloured	1·40	85

1977 (1 May). Labour Day. Litho. P 14½×14.

No.	Type	Description	Unused	Used
1285	**273**	10f. multicoloured	35	15
1286		30f. multicoloured	1·00	35
1287		35f. multicoloured	1·40	1·20
1285/1287 *Set of 3*			2·50	1·50

274 First Stage of Lift

275 Dome of the Rock

1977 (8 May). Eighth Asian Weightlifting Championship, Baghdad. T **274** and similar designs. Multicoloured. Photo. P 14.

No.		Description	Unused	Used
1288		25f. Type **274**	1·50	1·00
1289		75f. Press-up stage of lift	4·25	2·30
MS1290		60×80 mm. 100f. Championships emblem. Imperf	17·00	17·00

(Photo German Bank Note Ptg Co, Leipzig)

1977 (15 May). Palestinian Welfare. P 13½×14.

No.	Type	Description	Unused	Used
1291	**275**	5f. multicoloured	6·75	1·30

276 Arabian Garden

277 Dove and Ear of Wheat

(Des Y. M. Abdullah. Litho Kultura, Budapest)

1977 (15 June). Arab Tourism Year. T **276** and similar designs. Multicoloured. P 11½×12 (5f., 30f.) or 12×11½ (others).

No.		Description	Unused	Used
1292		5f. Type **276**	50	50
1293		10f. View of town with minarets (*horiz*)	50	50
1294		30f. Country stream	1·70	50
1295		50f. Oasis (*horiz*)	4·75	3·25
1292/1295 *Set of 4*			6·75	4·25

(Des Y. M. Abdullah, Photo German Bank Note Ptg Co, Leipzig)

1977 (17 July). July Festivals. P 13½×14.

No.	Type	Description	Unused	Used
1296	**277**	25f. multicoloured	1·00	35
1297		30f. multicoloured	1·40	65

278 Map of Middle East and North Africa

279 Emblem

(Des Y. M. Abdullah. Photo State Ptg Wks, Vienna)

1977 (9 Sept). UN Conference on Desertification. P 13½.

No.	Type	Description	Unused	Used
1298	**278**	30f. multicoloured	1·40	85
1299		70f. multicoloured	4·25	1·70

(Des J. H. Ali. Litho Harrison)

1977 (17 Oct). Census Day. P 14×14½.

No.	Type	Description	Unused	Used
1300	**279**	20f. multicoloured	70	50
1301		30f. multicoloured	1·50	50
1302		70f. multicoloured	3·00	1·70
1300/1302 *Set of 3*			4·75	2·40

280 Abstract Calligraphic Emblem

281 Kamal Jumblatt and Political Caricatures

(Photo German Bank Note Ptg Co, Leipzig)

1977 (1 Nov). Al-Mutanabby Festival. P 14.

No.	Type	Description	Unused	Used
1303	**280**	25f. multicoloured	50	15
1304		50f. multicoloured	1·20	85

(Des A. al-Mandalawi. Litho German Bank Note Ptg Co, Leipzig)

1977 (16 Nov). Kamal Jumblatt (Lebanese socialist) Commemoration. P 13½×14.

No.	Type	Description	Unused	Used
1305	**281**	20f. multicoloured	85	50
1306		30f. multicoloured	1·20	50
1307		70f. multicoloured	2·50	1·30
1305/1307 *Set of 3*			4·00	2·10

282 Hajeer Year Emblem

283 Girl, Boy and National Flag Ribbon

(Des M. Barsum. Photo German Bank Note Ptg Co, Leipzig)

1977 (12 Dec). Hajeer Year. P 13½×14.

No.	Type	Description	Unused	Used
1308	**282**	30f. multicoloured	70	35
1309		35f. multicoloured	1·00	50

(Des J. H. Ali. Photo State Security Ptg Wks, Warsaw)

1978 (7 Apr). Youth Day. P 11½×11.

No.	Type	Description	Unused	Used
1310	**283**	10f. multicoloured	35	15
1311		15f. multicoloured	35	35
1312		35f. multicoloured	1·00	65
1310/1312 *Set of 3*			1·50	1·00

284 Hand placing Coin in Box

285 Transmitting and Receiving Equipment

(Des M. R. al-Hasmi. Photo State Security Ptg Wks, Warsaw)

1978 (14 Apr). Sixth Anniversary of Postal Savings Bank. P 11×11½.

1313	**284**	15f. multicoloured	70	25
1314		25f. multicoloured	1·00	35
1315		35f. multicoloured	1·90	85
1313/1315 *Set of 3*			3·25	1·30

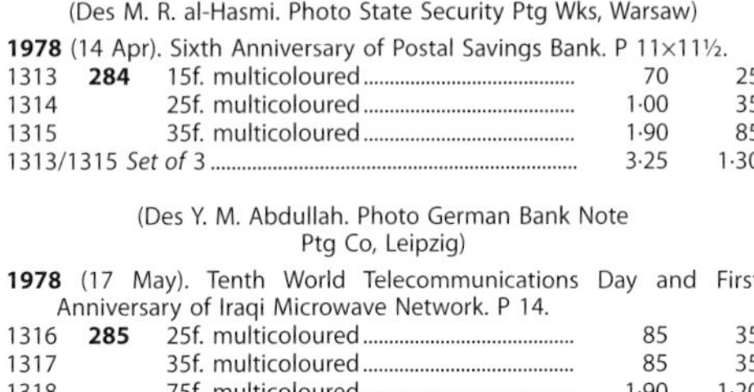

(Des Y. M. Abdullah. Photo German Bank Note Ptg Co, Leipzig)

1978 (17 May). Tenth World Telecommunications Day and First Anniversary of Iraqi Microwave Network. P 14.

1316	**285**	25f. multicoloured	85	35
1317		35f. multicoloured	85	35
1318		75f. multicoloured	1·90	1·20
1316/1318 *Set of 3*			3·25	1·70

286 Map and Flags

287 Silver Coins

(Des Y. M. Abdullah. Litho State Ptg Wks, Budapest)

1978 (19 June). First Conference of Arabian Gulf Postal Ministers. P 12×11½.

1319	**286**	25f. multicoloured	1·00	35
1320		35f. multicoloured	1·70	1·00

(Des Y. M. Abdullah. Photo State Ptg Wks, Budapest)

1978 (25 June). Ancient Iraqi Coins. T **287** and similar designs. P 12×11½ (75f.) or 11½×12 (others).

1321	**287**	1f. black, silver and olive-yellow	35	25
1322	–	2f. black, gold and blue	35	25
1323	–	3f. black, silver and salmon	35	25
1324	–	4f. black, gold and bright yellow-green	70	50
1325	–	75f. black, gold and turquoise-green	4·75	4·50
1321/1325 *Set of 5*			5·75	5·25

Designs: Horiz—2f. Two gold coins; 3f. Two silver coins; 4f. Two gold coins. Vert—75f. Gold coin.

288 Flower Emblem

289 Nurse, Hospital and Sick Child

(Des J. H. Ali and Y. M. Abdullah. Photo Heraclio Fournier)

1978 (17 July). July Festivals. P 13×13½ (100f.) or 13½×13 (others).

1326	**288**	25f. multicoloured	70	35
1327		35f. multicoloured	1·00	50
MS1328		80×60 mm. 100f. multicoloured (*horiz*)	13·00	12·50

Design: 100f. Flame and emblem.

(Des J. H. Ali. Photo German Bank Note Ptg Co, Leipzig)

1978 (18 Aug). Global Eradication of Smallpox. P 14.

1329	**289**	25f. multicoloured	50	15
1330		35f. multicoloured	1·20	50
1331		75f. multicoloured	3·50	1·80
1329/1331 *Set of 3*			4·75	2·20

290 Altharthar-Euphrates Canal

291 IMCO Emblem

1978. Photo. P 11½.

(a) POSTAGE

1332	**290**	5f. multicoloured	35	35
1333		10f. multicoloured	35	35
1334		15f. multicoloured	35	35
1335		25f. multicoloured	35	35
1336		35f. multicoloured	70	35
1337		50f. multicoloured	1·40	65
1332/1337 *Set of 6*			3·25	2·20

(b) OFFICIAL. As T **290** *but additionally inscr 'OFFICIAL' in English and Arabic*

O1338	**290**	5f. multicoloured	1·00	1·00
O1339		10f. multicoloured	1·00	1·00
O1340		15f. multicoloured	1·00	1·00
O1341		25f. multicoloured	2·20	1·00
O1338/O1341 *Set of 4*			4·75	3·50

(Des and photo State Ptg Wks, Budapest)

1978 (30 Aug). World Maritime Day. P 11×12.

1342	**291**	25f. multicoloured	1·20	65
1343		75f. multicoloured	3·00	1·20

292 Workers in the Countryside

293 Fair Emblem

(Des A. Albabaz. Photo German Bank Note Ptg Co, Leipzig)

1978 (12 Sept). Tenth Anniversary of People's Work Groups. P 14.

1344	**292**	10f. multicoloured	50	35
1345		25f. multicoloured	1·00	35
1346		35f. multicoloured	1·90	1·20
1344/1346 *Set of 3*			3·00	1·70

(Des Iraqi Exhibitions Administration. Photo German Bank Note Ptg Co, Leipzig)

1978 (1 Oct). Baghdad International Fair. P 14.

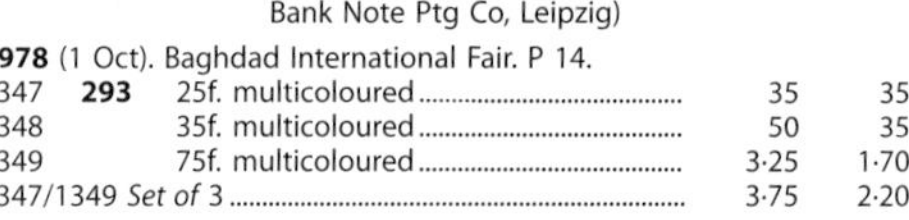

1347	**293**	25f. multicoloured	35	35
1348		35f. multicoloured	50	35
1349		75f. multicoloured	3·25	1·70
1347/1349 *Set of 3*			3·75	2·20

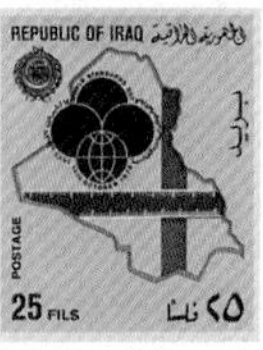
294 Map, Rule and Emblem

295 Conference Chamber

(Des and photo German Bank Note Ptg Co, Leipzig)

1978 (14 Oct). World Standards Day. P 14.

1350	**294**	25f. multicoloured	35	15
1351		35f. multicoloured	50	35
1352		75f. multicoloured	3·00	1·70
1350/1352 *Set of 3*			3·50	2·00

(Des and photo German Bank Note Ptg Co, Leipzig)

1978 (2 Nov). Ninth Arab Summit Conference, Baghdad. P 14.

1353	**295**	25f. multicoloured	50	35
1354		35f. multicoloured	70	35
1355		75f. multicoloured	2·20	1·70
1353/1355 *Set of 3*			3·00	2·20

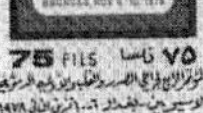

296 Congress Emblem

297 Pilgrims and Kaaba

1978 (8 Nov). Fourth Congress of Association of Thoracic and Cardiovascular Surgeons of Asia. Litho. P 12×11.

1356	**296**	25f. multicoloured	70	35
1357		75f. multicoloured	2·00	1·30

1978 (9 Nov). Pilgrimage to Mecca. Photo. P 14.

1358	**297**	25f. multicoloured	70	35
1359		35f. multicoloured	1·00	50

298 Map and Symbol

299 Hands holding Emblem

(Des Y. M. Abdullah. Photo State Ptg Wks, Vienna)

1978 (11 Nov). UN Conference for Technical Co-operation among Developing Countries. P 13½.

1360	**298**	25f. multicoloured	50	35
1361		50f. multicoloured	1·20	50
1362		75f. multicoloured	1·90	1·20
1360/1362 *Set of 3*			3·25	1·80

(Des Kh. Aziz. Litho Harrison)

1978 (30 Nov). International Year to Combat Racism. P 13.

1363	**299**	25f. multicoloured	85	50
1364		50f. multicoloured	1·50	65
		a. Face value omitted	£425	
1365		75f. multicoloured	4·50	1·30
1363/1365 *Set of 3*			6·25	2·20

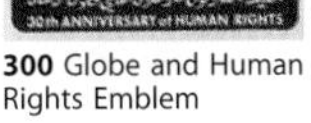

300 Globe and Human Rights Emblem

301 Candle and Emblem

(Des and photo Heraclio Fournier)

1978 (20 Dec). 30th Anniversary of Declaration of Human Rights. P 14.

1366	**300**	25f. multicoloured	85	35
1367		75f. multicoloured	3·00	2·10

(Des Y. M. Abdullah. Photo Heraclio Fournier)

1979 (9 Jan). Police Day. P 14.

1368	**301**	10f. multicoloured	70	50
1369		25f. multicoloured	70	50
1370		35f. multicoloured	1·20	50
1368/1370 *Set of 3*			2·30	1·40

302 Open Book, Pencil and Flame

303 School, Teacher and Assyrian Relief

(Des A. M. Asad. Photo Heraclio Fournier)

1979 (15 Feb). Anniversary of Application of Compulsory Education Law. P 14.

1371	**302**	15f. multicoloured	35	35
1372		25f. multicoloured	70	35
1373		35f. multicoloured	1·70	50
1371/1373 *Set of 3*			2·50	1·10

(Des Y. M. Abdullah. Photo Heraclio Fournier)

1979 (1 Mar). Teachers' Day. P 13.

1374	**303**	10f. multicoloured	35	35
1375		15f. multicoloured	35	35
1376		50f. multicoloured	1·70	1·00
1374/1376 *Set of 3*			2·20	1·50

304 Clenched Fist, Pencil and Book

305 World map, Koran and Symbols of Arab Achievements

(Des and photo Heraclio Fournier)

1979 (10 Mar). National Literacy Campaign. P 13.

1377	**304**	15f. multicoloured	50	50
1378		25f. multicoloured	85	50
1379		35f. multicoloured	1·40	50
1377/1379 *Set of 3*			2·50	1·40

(Photo Heraclio Fournier)

1979 (22 Mar). Arab Achievements. P 13.

1380	**305**	35f. multicoloured	1·00	35
1381		75f. multicoloured	3·00	1·30

306 Girl playing Flute

307 Iraqi Map and Flag with UPU Emblem

(Des and litho Enschedé)

1979 (15 Apr). Mosul Spring Festival. P 13½×13.

1382	**306**	15f. multicoloured	70	50
1383		25f. multicoloured	1·00	50
1384		35f. multicoloured	2·00	85
1382/1384 *Set of 3*			3·25	1·70

(Des and photo Heraclio Fournier)

1979 (22 Apr). 50th Anniversary of Admission to Universal Postal Union. P 13½×13.

1385	**307**	25f. multicoloured	1·20	50
1386		35f. multicoloured	1·20	50
1387		75f. multicoloured	3·00	1·30
1385/1387 *Set of 3*			4·75	2·10

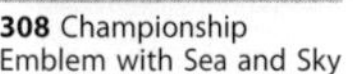

308 Championship Emblem with Sea and Sky

309 Child with Globe and Candle

(Des and photo Heraclio Fournier)

1979 (4 May). Fifth Arabian Gulf Football Championship. P 13.

1388	**308**	10f. multicoloured	35	35
1389		15f. multicoloured	70	35
1390		50f. multicoloured	1·70	1·00
1388/1390 *Set of 3*			2·50	1·50

(Des and photo Heraclio Fournier)

1979 (1 June). International Year of the Child. P 13.

1391	**309**	25f. multicoloured	1·40	65
1392		75f. multicoloured	3·50	2·10
MS1393		68×80 mm. 100f. multicoloured	48·00	46·00

Design: Vert—100f. Two children and UN emblem.

310 Flower and Branch

311 Children supporting Globe

(Des S. Ciba. Litho Cartor)

1979 (17 July). July Festivals. P 12½.

1394	**310**	15f. multicoloured	35	35
1395		25f. multicoloured	70	35
1396		35f. multicoloured	1·00	50
1394/1396 *Set of 3*			1·80	1·10

(Des Y. M. Abdullah. Litho Cartor)

1979 (25 July). 50th Anniversary of International Bureau of Education. P 12½.

1397	**311**	25f. multicoloured	1·00	50
1398		50f. multicoloured	1·90	1·00
1399		100f. multicoloured	3·00	2·00
1397/1399 *Set of 3*			5·25	3·25

312 Jawad Selim (sculptor)

313 The Kaaba, Mecca

(Des and litho Cartor)

1979 (15 Oct). Writers and Artists. T **312** and similar vert designs. Multicoloured. P 12½.

1400	25f. Type **312**	85	50
1401	25f. S. al-Hosari (philosopher)	85	50
1402	25f. Mustapha Jawad	85	50
1400/1402 *Set of 3*		2·30	1·40

(Litho Cartor)

1979 (25 Oct). Pilgrimage to Mecca. P 12½.

1403	**313**	25f. multicoloured	85	50
1404		50f. multicoloured	1·50	65

314 Figure '20' and Globe

315 Wave Pattern and Television Screen

(Des A. Hassan. Photo State Ptg Wks, Moscow)

1979 (9 Nov). 20th Anniversary of Iraqi News Agency. P 11½.

1405	**314**	25f. multicoloured	85	35
1406		50f. multicoloured	1·90	50
1407		75f. multicoloured	2·40	85
1405/1407 *Set of 3*			4·75	1·50

(Des Y. M. Abdullah. Litho State Ptg Wks, Budapest)

1979 (20 Nov). World Telecommunications Exhibition and Radio Conference, Geneva. P 12×11½.

1408	**315**	25f. multicoloured	85	35
1409		50f. multicoloured	1·40	65
1410		75f. multicoloured	2·40	1·20
1408/1410 *Set of 3*			4·25	2·00

316 Clenched Fists and Refugee

317 Ahmad Hassan al-Bakir

(Des Y. M. Abdullah. Photo State Ptg Wks, Moscow)

1979 (29 Nov). Palestinian Solidarity Day. P 11½×12.

1411	**316**	25f. multicoloured	1·50	50
1412		50f. multicoloured	3·00	85
1413		75f. multicoloured	4·00	1·50
1411/1413 *Set of 3*			7·75	2·50

(Des and photo Heraclio Fournier)

1979 (1 Dec). Inauguration of President Saddam Hussain. T **317** and similar vert design. Multicoloured. P 13.

1414	25f. Type **317**	70	50
1415	35f. President Hussain taking oath	1·00	50
1416	75f. Type **317**	1·90	85
1417	100f. As No. 1415	7·25	4·25
1414/1417 *Set of 4*		9·75	5·50

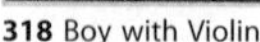

318 Boy with Violin

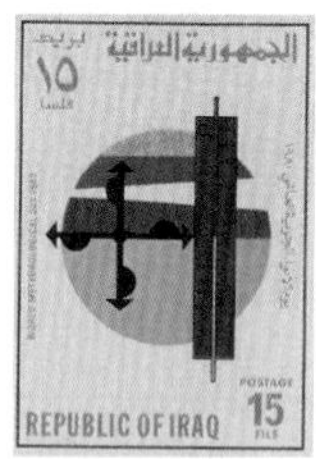

319 Wind speed Indicator and Thermometer

(Des Y. M. Abdullah. Photo Heraclio Fournier)

1979 (10 Dec). Activities of Vanguards (youth organisation). T **318** and similar vert designs. Multicoloured. P 14.

1418	10f. Type **318**	50	50
1419	15f. Boys on building site	50	50

1420		25f. Boys on assault course and in personal combat	70	50
1421		35f. Vanguards emblem	85	50
1418/1421		*Set of 4*	2·30	1·80

1980 (23 Mar). World Meteorological Day. Photo. P 14×13½.

1422	**319**	15f. multicoloured	35	35
1423		25f. multicoloured	50	35
1424		35f. multicoloured	1·20	50
1422/1424		*Set of 3*	1·80	1·10

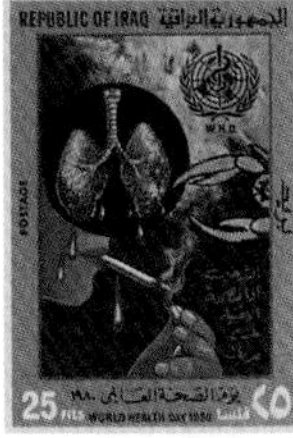

320 Lighting Cigarette and Cancerous Lungs

321 Festivals Emblem

(Des Y. M. Abdullah. Photo Heraclio Fournier)

1980 (7 Apr). World Health Day. Anti-smoking Campaign. P 14×13½.

1425	**320**	25f. multicoloured	70	50
1426		35f. multicoloured	85	50
1427		75f. multicoloured	3·50	1·00
1425/1427		*Set of 3*	4·50	1·80

1980 (17 July). July Festivals. T **321** and similar vert design. Multicoloured. Photo. P 13½×13.

1428		25f. Type **321**	85	65
1429		35f. Type **321**	1·00	65
MS1430		60×80 mm. 100f. President Hussain (27×44 *mm*). P 13×13½	13·50	13·00

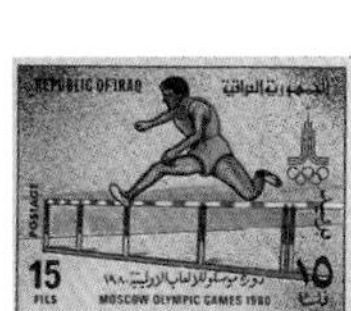

322 Hurdling

323 *Rubus sanctus*

(Photo Heraclio Fournier)

1980 (30 July). Olympic Games, Moscow. T **322** and similar multicoloured designs. P 14.

1431		15f. Type **322**	50	50
1432		20f. Weightlifting (*vert*)	85	65
1433		30f. Boxing	1·50	85
1434		35f. Football (*vert*)	3·00	1·50
1431/1434		*Set of 4*	5·25	3·25
MS1435		79×60 mm. 100f. Wrestling (37×29 *mm*). P 13×13½	20·00	19·00

1980 (15 Aug). Fruit. T **323** and similar vert designs. Multicoloured. Photo. P 14×13½.

1436		5f. Type **323**	50	35
1437		15f. Peaches (*Prunus persica*)	85	35
1438		20f. Pears (*Pyrus communis*)	1·20	35
1439		25f. Apples (*Pyrus malus*)	1·50	35
1440		35f. Plums (*Prunus domestica*)	2·00	65
1436/1440		*Set of 5*	5·50	1·80

324 Conference Emblem and Arabic Text

325 APU Emblem, Posthorn and Map

(Des R. Alnasri. Litho Cartor)

1980 (30 Aug). World Tourism Conference, Manila. P 12½.

1441	**324**	25f. multicoloured	70	35
1442		50f. multicoloured	1·50	50
1443		100f. multicoloured	3·00	1·70
1441/1443		*Set of 3*	4·75	2·30

1980 (8 Sept). 11th Congress of Arab Postal Union, Baghdad. Litho. P 12.

1444	**325**	10f. multicoloured	50	50
1445		30f. multicoloured	85	50
1446		35f. multicoloured	1·20	50
1444/1446		*Set of 3*	2·30	1·40

326 OPEC Emblem and Globe

327 *Danaus chrysippus*

(Litho Cartor)

1980 (30 Sept). 20th Anniversary of Organisation of Petroleum Exporting Countries. P 12½.

1447	**326**	30f. multicoloured	1·40	50
1448		75f. multicoloured	3·00	1·50

(Des S. Salman. Photo Heraclio Fournier)

1980 (20 Oct). Butterflies. T **327** and similar horiz designs. Multicoloured. P 13½×14.

1449		10f. *Papilio machaon*	3·75	65
1450		15f. Type **327**	4·25	1·20
1451		20f. *Vanessa atalanta*	5·75	1·50
1452		30f. *Colias croceus*	10·00	2·50
1449/1452		*Set of 4*	21·00	5·25

328 Mosque and Kaaba

329 Riflemen and Dome of the Rock on Map of Israel

(Des Y. M. Abdullah. Litho Oberthur, France)

1980 (9 Nov). 1400th Anniversary of Hegira. P 11½.

1453	**328**	15f. multicoloured	50	35
1454		25f. multicoloured	1·00	35
1455		35f. multicoloured	1·20	65
1453/1455		*Set of 3*	2·40	1·20

(Des Y. M. Abdullah. Litho State Ptg Wks, Moscow)

1980 (29 Nov). Palestinian Solidarity Day. P 12.

1456	**329**	25f. multicoloured	1·00	35
1457		35f. multicoloured	1·50	50
1458		75f. multicoloured	3·00	1·50
1456/1458		*Set of 3*	5·00	2·10

330 Soldier and Rocket

331 '8' and Flags forming Torch

(Photo Heraclio Fournier)

1981 (6 Jan). 60th Anniversary of Army Day. P 14×13½.

1459	**330**	5f. multicoloured	70	50
1460		30f. multicoloured	1·20	50
1461		75f. multicoloured	3·75	1·50
1459/1461		*Set of 3*	5·00	2·30

(Des Y. Hussain. Litho State Ptg Wks, Moscow)

1981 (8 Feb). 18th Anniversary of Revolution of 14th Ramadan (8 February). P 12.

1462	**331**	15f. multicoloured	50	35
1463		30f. multicoloured	85	35
1464		35f. multicoloured	1·20	50
1462/1464 *Set of 3*			2·30	1·10

332 Map of Arab States tied with Ribbon

333 President Saddam, Hussain and Modern Military Equipment

(Des Y. M. Abdullah. Litho Cartor)

1981 (22 Mar). Arab Achievements. P 12½.

1465	**332**	5f. multicoloured	35	35
1466		25f. multicoloured	85	35
1467		35f. multicoloured	1·20	50
1465/1467 *Set of 3*			2·20	1·10

(Des Sh. Kh. Shalash. Photo Heraclio Fournier)

1981 (7 Apr). Saddam's Battle of Qadisiya. T **333** and similar multicoloured design. P 13½×13.

1468	**333**	30f. multicoloured	1·20	65
1469		35f. multicoloured	1·70	85
1470		75f. multicoloured	3·00	1·50
1468/1470 *Set of 3*			5·25	2·75
MS1471 80×59 mm. 100f. President Hussain, military equipment and flag (37×29 *mm*). P 13			11·00	10·50

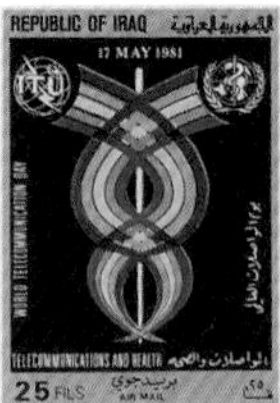

334 ITU and WHO Emblems and Ribbons forming Caduceus

335 Mil Mi-24 Helicopters attacking Ground Forces

(Litho Cartor)

1981 (17 May). AIR. World Telecommunications Day. P 12½.

1472	**334**	25f. multicoloured	1·20	65
1473		50f. multicoloured	2·40	1·00
1474		75f. multicoloured	4·00	2·00
1472/1474 *Set of 3*			6·75	3·25

(Des Sh. Kh. Shalash and Y. M. Abdullah. Photo Heraclio Fournier)

1981 (1 June). 50th Anniversary of Air Force. T **335** and similar multicoloured designs. P 14×13½ (120f.) or 13½×14 (others).

(a) POSTAGE

1475	5f. Type **335**	35	35
1476	10f. Antonov An-2 biplane trainer	70	35
1477	15f. 'SAM-15' missile	85	35

(b) AIR. Inscr 'AIR MAIL'

1478	120f. Mikoyan Gurevich MiG-21 jet fighters and de Havilland DH.89 Dragon Rapide biplane (*vert*)	7·25	4·25
1475/1478 *Set of 4*		8·25	4·75

336 Map and Flower enclosing Ballot Box

337 Festivals Emblem

(Des Y. M. Abdullah. Litho Cartor)

1981 (20 June). First Anniversary of National Assembly Election. P 12½.

1479	**336**	30f. multicoloured	1·00	50
1480		35f. multicoloured	1·20	50
1481		45f. multicoloured	2·00	85
1479/1481 *Set of 3*			3·75	1·70

(Litho Cartor)

1981 (17 July). July Festivals. P 12½.

1482	**337**	15f. multicoloured	50	15
1483		25f. multicoloured	70	35
1484		35f. multicoloured	1·20	35
1482/1484 *Set of 3*			2·20	75

338 Basket Weaver

339 Saddam Hussain Gymnasium

(Des and photo Heraclio Fournier)

1981 (15 Aug). Popular Industries. T **338** and similar multicoloured designs. P 14.

1485	5f. Type **338**	35	35
1486	30f. Copper worker	1·00	35
1487	35f. Potter	1·40	50
1488	50f. Weaver (*horiz*)	1·70	65
1485/1488 *Set of 4*		4·00	1·70

(Litho Enschedé)

1981 (26 Sept). Modern Buildings. T **339** and similar horiz design. Multicoloured. P 12×12½.

1489	45f. Type **339**	1·40	50
1490	50f. Palace of Conferences	1·40	50
1491	120f. As No. 1490	3·75	2·75
1492	150f. Type **339**	5·00	3·00
1489/1492 *Set of 4*		10·50	6·00

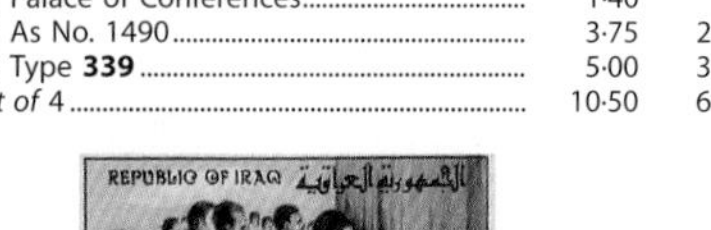

340 Pilgrims

(Photo State Ptg Wks, Budapest)

1981 (7 Oct). Pilgrimage to Mecca. P 12×11½.

1493	**340**	25f. multicoloured	1·20	35
1494		45f. multicoloured	2·20	85
1495		50f. multicoloured	2·20	85
1493/1495 *Set of 3*			5·00	1·80

341 Harvesting

O **342** Entrance to Baghdad University

(Photo Heraclio Fournier)

1981 (16 Oct). World Food Day. P 13½×14.

1496	**341**	30f. multicoloured	1·00	35
1497		45f. multicoloured	1·90	85
1498		75f. multicoloured	2·75	1·50
1496/1498 *Set of 3*			5·00	2·40

(Litho Enschedé)

1981 (21 Oct). OFFICIAL. P 12×12½.

O1499	O **342**	45f. multicoloured	1·70	1·30
O1500		50f. multicoloured	2·00	1·50

343 Teacher and Deaf Child

344 Medal and Map

(Photo Heraclio Fournier)

1981 (15 Nov). International Year of Disabled Persons. P 14×13½.

1501	**343**	30f. multicoloured	85	50
1502		45f. multicoloured	1·40	65
1503		75f. multicoloured	1·90	1·20
1501/1503 *Set of 3*			3·75	2·10

(Des M. al-Habeeb. Photo Heraclio Fournier)

1981 (1 Dec). Martyr's Day. P 14×13½.

(a) POSTAGE

1504	**344**	45f. multicoloured	1·00	85
1505		50f. multicoloured	1·50	1·50
1506		120f. multicoloured	3·00	2·30
1504/1506 *Set of 3*			5·00	4·25

(b) OFFICIAL

O1507	**344**	45f. multicoloured	3·50	1·70
O1508		50f. multicoloured	3·50	1·70
O1509		120f. multicoloured	8·50	3·25
O1507/O1509 *Set of 3*			14·00	6·00

345 *Ibn Khaldoon* (freighter)

346 Woman and Symbols of Technology

(Photo Heraclio Fournier)

1981 (2 Dec). Fifth Anniversary of United Arab Shipping Company. P 13.

1507	**345**	50f. multicoloured	2·50	1·20
1508		120f. multicoloured	6·75	3·25

(Des Y. M. Abdullah. Litho Cartor)

1982 (4 Mar). Iraqi Women's Day. P 12½.

1509	**346**	25f. multicoloured	1·20	50
1510		45f. multicoloured	2·00	1·00
1511		50f. multicoloured	2·00	1·20
1509/1511 *Set of 3*			4·75	2·40

347 President Hussain, '7' and Flowers

348 APU Emblem and Globe

(Des Ministry of Culture. Photo Heraclio Fournier)

1982 (7 Apr). 35th Anniversary of Al-Baath Party. T **347** and similar vert designs. Multicoloured. P 13½×13.

1512	25f. Type **347**	85	35
1513	30f. Rainbow in National Colours and '7 7 7'	85	35
1514	45f. Type **347**	1·40	85
1515	50f. As No. 1513	1·40	85
1512/1515 *Set of 4*		4·00	2·20

MS1516 99×53 mm. 150f. President Hussain, globe and Arabic '7' (27×39 *mm*). Imperf ... 10·00 10·00

(Des M. al-Habeeb. Litho Cartor)

1982 (12 Apr). 30th Anniversary of Arab Postal Union. P 12½.

1517	**348**	25f. multicoloured	1·20	50
1518		45f. multicoloured	2·00	85
1519		50f. multicoloured	2·00	85
1517/1519 *Set of 3*			4·75	2·00

349 White Storks

350 World Map, Factories and '1'

(Litho State Ptg Wks, Budapest)

1982 (15 Apr). Mosul Spring Festival. T **349** and similar vert design. Multicoloured. P 11½×12.

1520	25f. Type **349**	2·00	35
1521	30f. Doll	1·20	35
1522	45f. Type **349**	2·00	1·00
1523	50f. As No. 1521	1·90	85
1520/1523 *Set of 4*		6·50	2·30

(Des Y. M. Abdullah. Litho Cartor)

1982 (1 May). Labour Day. P 12½.

1524	**350**	25f. multicoloured	85	15
1525		45f. multicoloured	1·20	65
1526		50f. multicoloured	1·40	85
1524/1526 *Set of 3*			3·00	1·50

351 Geometric Figure and ITU Emblem

352 Oil Gusher

(Des Y. M. Abdullah. Photo Heraclio Fournier)

1982 (17 May). World Telecommunications Day. P 13×13½.

1527	**351**	5f. multicoloured	35	25
1528		45f. multicoloured	1·50	85
1529		100f. multicoloured	3·50	2·10
1527/1529 *Set of 3*			4·75	3·00

(Litho Cartor)

1982 (1 June). Tenth Anniversary of Oil Nationalisation. T **352** and similar vert design. Multicoloured. P 12½.

1530	5f. Type **352**	50	25
1531	25f. Type **352**	1·00	35
1532	45f. Bronze statue of bull and horse flanking couple holding model of oil rig	2·00	85
1533	50f. As No. 1532	2·40	85
1530/1533 *Set of 4*		5·25	2·10

353 Nuclear Power Emblem and Lion

354 Footballers

(Photo Heraclio Fournier)

1982 (7 June). First Anniversary of Attack on Iraqi Nuclear Reactor. T **353** and similar vert design. P 14.
1534 30f. Type **353** .... 1·20 65
1535 45f. Bomb aimed at egg .... 2·00 65
1536 50f. Type **353** .... 2·20 1·00
1537 120f. As No. 1535 .... 4·00 3·00
1534/1537 *Set of 4* .... 8·50 4·75

1982 (1 July). World Cup Football Championship, Spain. T **354** and similar multicoloured designs. Litho. P 11½×12.
1538 5f. Type **354** .... 1·20 50
1539 45f. Three footballers .... 1·70 85
1540 50f. Type **354** .... 1·90 1·00
1541 100f. As No. 1539 .... 3·50 2·10
1538/1541 *Set of 4* .... 7·50 4·00
MS1542 85×60 mm. 150f. Two footballers (*horiz*). P 12½ .... 7·25 7·00

355 President Hussain and Fireworks

356 European Green Lizard (*Lacerta viridis*)

(Des M. al-Habeeb. Litho Harrison)

1982 (17 July). July Festivals. P 14½×14.
1543 **355** 25f. multicoloured 70 50
1544 45f. multicoloured .... 1·40 65
1545 50f. multicoloured .... 1·40 85
1543/1545 *Set of 3* .... 3·25 1·80

(Des S. Salman. Litho Cartor)

1982 (20 Aug). Reptiles. T **356** and similar horiz designs. Multicoloured. P 12½.
1546 25f. Type **356** .... 4·00 1·50
1547 30f. Asp (*Vipera aspis*) .... 4·00 1·50
1548 45f. Two European Green Lizards (*Lacerta viridis*) .... 5·50 2·10
1549 50f. *Natrix tessellata* .... 6·50 3·00
1546/1549 *Set of 4* .... 18·00 7·25

357 Pandit Nehru (India)

358 Microscope and Bacilli

(Photo Heraclio Fournier)

1982 (6 Sept). Seventh Non-Aligned Countries Conference, Baghdad. T **357** and similar vert designs. Multicoloured. P 13×13½.
1550 50f. Type **357** .... 1·50 65
1551 50f. Josef Tito (Yugoslavia) .... 1·50 65
1552 50f. Abdul Nasser (Egypt) .... 1·50 65
1553 50f. Kwame Nkrumah (Ghana) .... 1·50 65
1554 100f. President Hussain (Iraq) .... 3·50 1·80
1550/1554 *Set of 5* .... 8·50 4·00

(Des Y. M. Abdullah. Litho Harrison)

1982 (1 Oct). Centenary of Discovery of Tubercule Bacillus. P 14×14½.
1555 **358** 20f. multicoloured .... 1·20 35
1556 50f. multicoloured .... 2·20 65
1557 100f. multicoloured .... 3·75 1·70
1555/1557 *Set of 3* .... 6·50 2·40

Nos. 1558/1560 are vacant.

359 UPU Building, Berne

360 Drums

(Litho State Ptg Wks, Budapest)

1982 (9 Oct). Universal Postal Union Day. P 12×11½.
1561 **359** 5f. multicoloured 50 35
1562 45f. multicoloured .... 1·40 85
1563 100f. multicoloured .... 3·50 2·00
1561/1563 *Set of 3* .... 4·75 3·00

(Litho Cartor)

1982 (15 Nov). Musical Instruments. T **360** and similar vert designs. Multicoloured. P 12½×13.
1564 5f. Type **360** 50 25
1565 10f. Stringed board instrument 50 35
1566 35f. Bowed instruments .... 1·50 50
1567 100f. Mandolin .... 5·00 1·80
1564/1567 *Set of 4* .... 6·75 2·50

361 Mosque and Minaret, Mecca

362 Flowers

(Litho State Ptg Wks, Budapest)

1982 (27 Dec). Birth Anniversary of Prophet Mohammed. T **361** and similar horiz designs. Multicoloured. P 12×11½.
1568 25f. Type **361** 50 35
1569 30f. Mosque courtyard 70 35
1570 45f. Type **361** .... 1·00 65
1571 50f. As No. 1569 .... 1·20 65
1568/1571 *Set of 4* .... 3·00 1·80

1982. Flowers. Booklet stamps. T **362** and similar vert designs. Multicoloured. Photo. P 15×14.
1572 10f. Type **362** 50 35
a. Booklet pane. Nos. 1572/1577 .... 10·50
1573 20f. Flowers (*different*) 85 35
1574 30f. Type **362** .... 1·00 50
1575 40f. As No. 1573 .... 1·70 85
1576 50f. Type **362** .... 2·00 1·00
1577 100f. As No. 1573 .... 4·00 2·00
1572/1577 *Set of 6* .... 9·00 4·50

The booklet pane has its outer edges guillotined; stamps are therefore found with one or more edges imperforate.

60
فلسا

(**363**)

364 President Hussain

1983 (15 May). Various stamps surch as T **363**.

(a) POSTAGE. Nos. 1489/1491
1578 60f. on 50f. Palace of Conferences .... 2·75 1·00
1579 70f. on 45f. Type **339** .... 3·50 1·20
1580 160f. on 120f. Palace of Conferences .... 8·00 4·00
1578/1580 *Set of 3* .... 13·00 5·50

(b) OFFICIAL. Nos. O1499/O1500
O1581 **O 342** 60f. on 45f. multicoloured .... 6·00 1·70
O1582 70f. on 50f. multicoloured .... 6·75 2·00

(Litho Harrison)

1983 (17 July). July Festivals. P 15×14.
1583 **364** 30f. multicoloured 85 50
1584 60f. multicoloured .... 1·90 85
1585 70f. multicoloured .... 2·40 1·20
1583/1585 *Set of 3* .... 4·75 2·30

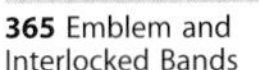

365 Emblem and Interlocked Bands

366 Horseman and Map

(Des H. M. A. Ahmad. Litho State Ptg Wks, Budapest)

1983 (20 Oct). World Communications Year. T **365** and similar vert designs. Multicoloured. P 11½×12.

1586	5f. Type **365**	25	15
1587	25f. Hexagons of primary colours	50	35
1588	60f. Type **365**	1·90	1·00
1589	70f. As No. 1587	2·00	1·20
1586/1589 *Set of 4*		4·25	2·40
MS1590	80×60 mm. 200f. Emblem. Imperf	8·50	8·25

(Des H. M. A. Ahmad. Litho Cartor)

1983 (30 Oct). Battle of Thiqar. T **366** and similar vert designs. Multicoloured. P 12½×13.

1591	20f. Type **366**	50	35
1592	50f. Eagle and pyre	1·40	65
1593	60f. Type **366**	1·70	85
1594	70f. As No. 1592	1·90	1·00
1591/1594 *Set of 4*		5·00	2·50

367 Fair Emblem and Silhouette of Baghdad

368 President Hussain within Figure '9'

(Litho Cartor)

1983 (1 Nov). Baghdad International Fair. P 12½×13.

1595	**367**	60f. multicoloured	1·40	85
1596		70f. multicoloured	1·70	1·00
1597		160f. multicoloured	3·75	2·75
1595/1597 *Set of 3*			6·25	4·25

(Photo Heraclio Fournier)

1983 (10 Nov). Ninth Al-Baath Party Congress. T **368** and similar vert designs. Multicoloured. P 14.

1598	30f. Type **368**	70	50
1599	60f. Eagle, torch, map and book	1·40	85
1600	70f. Type **368**	1·70	1·00
1601	100f. As No. 1599	2·50	1·30
1598/1601 *Set of 4*		5·75	3·25

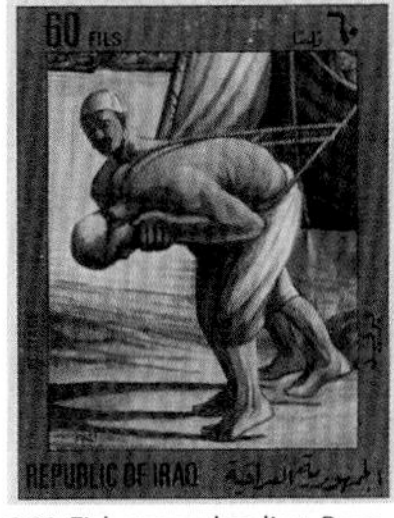

369 Fishermen hauling Boat

370 Dove and Victim

1983 (20 Nov). Paintings. T **369** and similar horiz designs. Multicoloured. Litho. P 12½.

1602	60f. Type **369**	3·00	1·20
1603	60f. Festive crowd	3·00	1·20
1604	60f. Hanging decorations	3·00	1·20
1605	70f. Crowd	3·75	1·70
1606	70f. Bazaar	3·75	1·70
1602/1606 *Set of 5*		15·00	6·25

1983 (29 Nov). Massacre of Palestinians in Sabra and Shatila Refugee Camps, Lebanon. T **370** and similar vert designs. Multicoloured. Litho. P 11½×12.

1607	10f. Type **370**	50	35
1608	60f. Type **370**	1·90	85
1609	70f. Dove and fist shedding blood and victims	2·20	1·00
1610	160f. As No. 1609	4·75	2·75
1607/1610 *Set of 4*		8·50	4·50

371 Apartment Building

372 President Hussain

1983 (31 Dec). Buildings. T **371** and similar horiz designs. Litho. P 14.

(a) POSTAGE

1611	60f. bright yellow-green, black and sage-green	1·40	85
1612	70f. bright purple, black and bluish grey	1·70	1·00
1613	160f. bright purple, black and lavender-grey	4·25	2·10
1614	200f. bright yellow-green, black and pale yellow-olive	5·00	2·75
1611/1614 *Set of 4*		11·00	6·00

(b) OFFICIAL

O1615	60f. greenish yellow, black and brown-rose	2·20	1·70
O1616	70f. greenish yellow, black and flesh	3·00	2·00

Designs: Nos. 1611, 1614, T **371**; 1612/1613, Apartment building (*different*); O1615/O1616, Aerial view of building.

1983. Fourth Anniversary of President Hussain as Party and State Leader. Photo. P 13½×13.

1617	**372**	60f. multicoloured	1·50	85
1618		70f. multicoloured	2·20	1·20
1619		250f. multicoloured	7·25	4·25
1617/1619 *Set of 3*			9·75	5·75

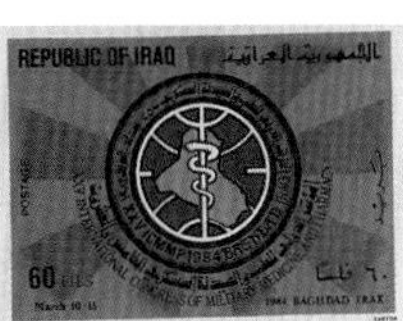

373 Congress Emblem

374 President Hussain and Flowers

(Litho Cartor)

1984 (10 Mar). 25th International Military Medicine and Pharmacy Congress. P 13×12½.

1620	**373**	60f. multicoloured	1·50	85
1621		70f. multicoloured	1·90	1·00
1622		200f. multicoloured	5·00	2·75
1620/1622 *Set of 3*			7·50	4·25

(Litho and thermography Cartor)

1984 (27 Apr). 47th Birthday of President Saddam Hussain. T **374** and similar vert designs. Multicoloured. P 12½×13.

1623	60f. Type **374**	1·40	85
1624	70f. President Hussain in army uniform	1·50	1·00
1625	160f. As No. 1623	4·25	3·00
1626	200f. Type **374**	5·00	3·75
1623/1626 *Set of 4*		11·00	7·75
MS1627	81×61 mm. 250f. President Hussain and rose (*horiz*). P 12½	9·25	9·00

375 Boxing

376 President Hussain and Horses' Heads

1984 (12 Aug). Olympic Games, Los Angeles. T **375** and similar horiz designs. Multicoloured. Litho. P 12×11½.

1628	50f. Type **375**	1·40	1·00
1629	60f. Hurdling, weightlifting and wrestling	1·70	1·00
1630	70f. Type **375**	2·00	1·20
1631	100f. As No. 1629	3·00	1·80
1628/1631 *Set of 4*		7·25	4·50
MS1632 80×60 mm. 200f. Footballers (30×40 *mm*). P 12½		9·25	9·00

1984 (22 Sept). Battle of Qadisiya. T **376** and similar vert designs. Multicoloured. Litho. P 11½×12.

1633	50f. Type **376**	1·00	65
1634	60f. President Hussain and symbolic representation of battle	1·40	85
1635	70f. Type **376**	1·50	1·00
1636	100f. As No. 1634	2·40	1·30
1633/1636 *Set of 4*		5·75	3·50
MS1637 80×60 mm. 200f. Shield and eagle (30×40 *mm*). P 12½		9·25	9·00

377 Flag as Ribbon and Two Domes

378 Text

(Litho Cartor)

1984 (1 Dec). Martyr's Day. T **377** and similar vert design. Multicoloured. P 13½.

(a) POSTAGE

1638	50f. Type **377**	85	65
1639	60f. Woman holding rifle and medal	1·20	65
1640	70f. Type **377**	1·40	85
1641	100f. As No. 1639	1·90	1·30
1638/1641 *Set of 4*		4·75	3·00

(b) OFFICIAL

O1642	20f. Type **377**	1·00	85
O1643	30f. Type **377**	1·00	85
O1644	50f. As No. 1639	1·40	1·00
O1645	60f. As No. 1639	1·70	1·00
O1642/O1645 *Set of 4*		4·50	3·25

(Photo Delrieu)

1985 (2 Apr). Fifth Anniversary of President Hussain's Visit to Al-Mustansiriyah University. P 12×11½.

1646	**378**	60f. deep bright rose and deep violet-blue	1·20	85
1647		70f. deep bright rose and bronze green	1·50	1·00
1648		250f. deep bright rose and black	5·00	3·25
1646/1648 *Set of 3*			7·00	4·50

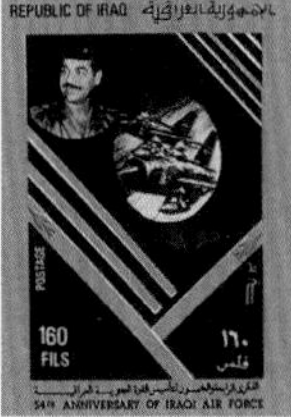

379 President Hussain and Jet Fighters

380 President Hussain within Flower

1985 (22 Apr). 54th Anniversary of Iraqi Air Force. T **379** and similar multicoloured designs. Photo. P 13½.

1649	10f. Type **379**	70	35
1650	60f. Fighter aeroplanes trailing flag and '54' (*horiz*)	3·00	1·50
1651	70f. As No. 1650	3·00	1·50
1652	160f. Type **379**	7·75	4·00
1649/1652 *Set of 4*		13·00	6·50
MS1653 80×60 mm. 200f. As No. 1650. P 12½		11·00	10·50

1985 (28 Apr). 48th Birthday of President Saddam Hussain. T **380** and similar vert designs. Multicoloured. Photo. P 13½.

1654	30f. Type **380**	85	65
1655	60f. President Hussain, candle and flowers	1·50	85
1656	70f. Type **380**	1·70	1·00
1657	100f. As No. 1655	2·40	1·30
1654/1657 *Set of 4*		5·75	3·50
MS1658 87×60 mm. 200f. '28', flowers and text. P 13×12½		7·25	7·00

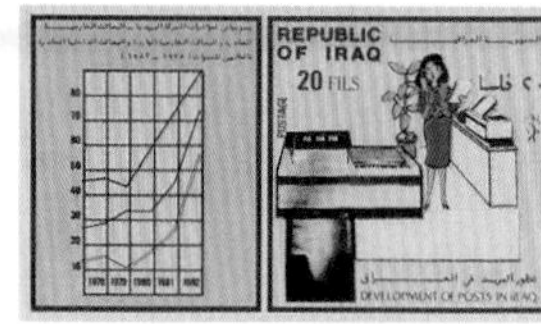

381 Graph and Modern Office

1985 (11 Aug). Posts and Telecommunications Development. T **381** and similar horiz design. Multicoloured. Litho. P 12½.

1659	20f. Type **381**	70	35
1660	50f. Dish aerial and graph	1·40	65
1661	60f. Type **381**	1·40	65
1662	70f. As No. 1660	1·70	1·00
1659/1662 *Set of 4*		4·75	2·40

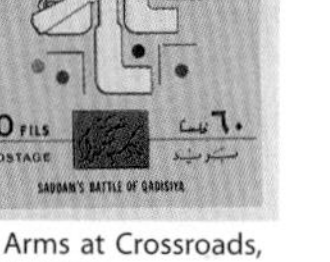

382 Arms at Crossroads, and Building

383 Solar Energy Research Centre

(Litho State Ptg Wks, Budapest)

1985 (4 Sept). Saddam's Battle of Qadisiya. T **382** and similar vert designs. Multicoloured. P 11½×12.

1663	10f. Type **382**	35	35
1664	20f. President Hussain and emblem of Al-Baath Party	50	35
1665	60f. Type **382**	1·70	85
1666	70f. As No. 1664	1·90	1·30
1663/1666 *Set of 4*		4·00	2·50
MS1667 80×60 mm. 200f. Peace Dove and soldiers (27×43 *mm*). P 12×12½		5·75	5·50

(Litho Cartor)

1985 (19 Sept). P 13½.

1668	**383**	10f. multicoloured	35	15
1669		50f. multicoloured	1·70	85
1670		100f. multicoloured	3·50	1·80
1668/1670 *Set of 3*			5·00	2·50

384 Disabled Children

385 Hand holding Quill

(Litho Cartor)

1985 (10 Oct). UNICEF Child Survival Campaign. T **384** and similar vert design. Multicoloured. P 13½.

1671	10f. Type **384**	25	15
1672	15f. Toddler and baby	35	35
1673	50f. Type **384**	1·40	65
1674	100f. As No. 1672	2·75	1·70
1671/1674 *Set of 4*		4·25	2·50

(Litho Cartor)

1985 (20 Oct). Death Millenary of Al-Sharif Al-Radhi (poet). P 13½.

1675	**385**	10f. multicoloured	70	35
1676		50f. multicoloured	1·20	85
1677		100f. multicoloured	2·75	1·70
1675/1677 *Set of 3*			4·25	2·50

386 UN Emblem

387 World Map

(Litho Cartor)

1985 (24 Oct). 40th Anniversary of United Nations Organisation. P 13½.

1678 **386** 10f. multicoloured 35 25
1679 40f. new blue, black and bistre-yellow .... 1·20 50
1680 100f. multicoloured .... 3·00 1·70
1678/1680 *Set of 3* .... 4·00 2·20

(Litho Cartor)

1985 (29 Nov). Palestinian Solidarity Day. P 13½.

1681 **387** 10f. multicoloured 50 25
1682 50f. multicoloured .... 1·70 85
1683 100f. multicoloured .... 3·75 1·80
1681/1683 *Set of 3* .... 5·25 2·50

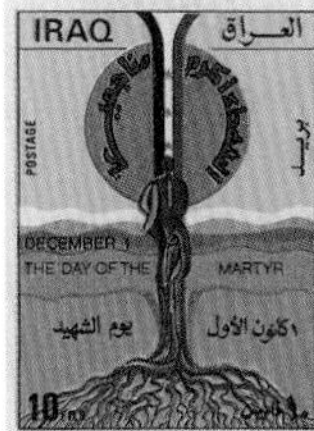

388 Flag, Man and Blood Vessels as Roots

389 IYY Emblem and Soldier with Flag

(Litho State Ptg Wks, Budapest)

1985 (1 Dec). Martyr's Day. P 11½×12.

1684 **388** 10f. multicoloured 50 35
1685 40f. multicoloured .... 1·00 50
1686 100f. multicoloured .... 3·00 1·70
1684/1686 *Set of 3* .... 4·00 2·30

(Des F. Y. Taha. Litho State Ptg Wks, Budapest)

1985 (10 Dec). International Youth Year. T **389** and similar vert design. Multicoloured. P 11½×12.

1687 40f. Type **389** 85 50
1688 50f. Young couple, flag and IYY emblem .... 1·20 65
1689 100f. Type **389** .... 2·50 1·50
1690 200f. As No. 1688 .... 4·75 4·00
1687/1690 *Set of 4* .... 8·25 6·00
MS1691 80×60 mm. 250f. Cogwheel, flag, rifle and symbols of agriculture, industry and science (29×44 *mm*). P 12×12½ or imperf .... 9·25 9·00

390 President Hussain, Soldier and '6'

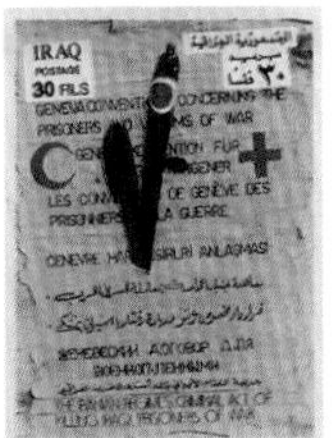

391 Pen as Knife in Sheet of Text

(Des Y. M. Abdullah. Litho State Ptg Wks, Budapest)

1986 (6 Jan). Army Day. T **390** and similar horiz designs. Multicoloured. P 11½×12 (vert) or 12×11½ (horiz).

1692 10f. Type **390** 35 35
1693 40f. President Hussain, cogwheel, '6' and missiles (*horiz*) .... 1·20 50
1694 50f. Type **390** .... 1·50 65
1695 100f. As No. 1693 .... 3·25 1·80
1692/1695 *Set of 4* .... 5·75 3·00
MS1696 80×60 mm. 200f. President Hussain, '6' in star and rifle (51×36 *mm*). P 12½×11½ .... 9·25 9·00

(Des Y. M. Abdullah. Litho State Ptg Wks, Budapest)

1986 (1 Feb). Iraqi Prisoners of War Commemoration. T **391** and similar vert design. Multicoloured. P 14.

1697 30f. Type **391** 70 50
1698 70f. Dove, cherub holding flag and three prisoners .... 1·40 85
1699 100f. Type **391** .... 2·00 1·30
1700 200f. As No. 1698 .... 4·50 2·75
1697/1700 *Set of 4* .... 7·75 4·75
MS1701 110×80 mm. 250f. As Nos. 1699/1700 .... 9·25 9·00

392 President Hussain with Children

393 Worker, Globe and Cogwheel

(Des F. Y. Taha and Y. M. Abdullah. Litho State Ptg Wks, Budapest)

1986 (28 Apr). 49th Birthday of President Saddam Hussain. T **392** and similar multicoloured designs. P 11½×12.

1702 30f. Type **392** 85 50
1703 50f. President Hussain and Doves holding flag .... 1·40 65
1704 100f. Type **392** .... 2·75 1·30
1705 150f. As. Nos. 1703 .... 3·75 1·80
1702/1705 *Set of 4* .... 8·00 3·75
MS1706 80×60 mm. 250f. President Hussain, flag and flowers. Imperf .... 9·25 9·00

(Litho State Ptg Wks, Budapest)

1986 (1 July). Labour Day. T **393** and similar vert design. Multicoloured. P 11½×12.

1707 10f. Type **393** 50 50
1708 40f. Candle in cogwheel .... 1·40 50
1709 100f. Type **393** .... 2·50 1·30
1710 150f. As No. 1708 .... 3·75 1·80
1707/1710 *Set of 4* .... 7·25 3·75

394 President Hussain and '30 July 17'

395 President Hussain and Jet Fighter

(Litho State Ptg Wks, Budapest)

1986 (17 July). July Festivals and Seventh Anniversary of President Hussain's State Leadership. T **394** and similar multicoloured designs. P 11½×12.

1711 20f. Type **394** 70 35
1712 30f. President Hussain and '17 1986' 85 35
1713 100f. Type **394** .... 3·00 1·50
1714 150f. As No. 1712 .... 4·00 2·50
1711/1714 *Set of 4* .... 7·75 4·25
MS1715 80×60 mm. 250f. President Hussain within laurel wreath and text. Imperf .... 7·25 7·00

(Litho State Ptg Wks, Budapest)

1986 (6 Aug). 55th Anniversary of Iraqi Airforce. T **395** and similar horiz designs. Multicoloured. P 12×11½.

1716 30f. Type **395** .... 1·40 50
1717 50f. President Hussain and jet fighters .... 2·50 65
1718 100f. Type **395** .... 5·00 2·75
1719 150f. As No. 1717 .... 7·75 3·75
1716/1719 *Set of 4* .... 15·00 7·00
MS1720 80×60 mm. 250f. Air Force Medal. P 12½ or imperf .... 9·25 9·00

396 Refinery **397** Arab Warrior

(Litho State Ptg Wks, Budapest)

1986 (6 Aug). Oil Nationalisation Day. T **396** and similar multicoloured design. P 12×11½ (horiz) or 11½×12 (vert).

1721	10f. Type **396**	20	15
1722	40f. Derrick and pipeline within flags (*vert*)	1·00	35
1723	100f. Type **396**	2·75	1·50
1724	150f. As No. 1722	3·75	2·75
1721/1724	*Set of 4*	7·00	4·25

1986 (15 Aug). First Battle of Qadisiya. T **397** and similar multicoloured design. P 13×13½ (vert) or 13½×13 (horiz).

1725	20f. Type **397**	70	15
1726	60f. President Hussain and battle scene (*horiz*)	1·50	85
1727	70f. Type **397**	1·70	1·00
1728	100f. As No. 1726	3·00	1·30
1725/1728	*Set of 4*	6·25	3·00

398 President Hussain, Battlefield and Cheering Soldiers **399** President Hussain

(Litho State Ptg Wks, Budapest)

1986 (4 Sept). Saddam's Battle of Qadisiya. T **398** and similar multicoloured designs. P 11½×12½ (vert) or 12½×11½ (horiz).

1729	30f. Type **398**	1·70	50
1730	40f. President Hussain within flag 'swords' and symbols of ancient and modern warfare (*horiz*)	2·20	85
1731	100f. Type **398**	4·50	2·30
1732	150f. As No. 1730	7·75	3·25
1729/1732	*Set of 4*	14·50	6·25
MS1733	80×60 mm. 250f. President Hussain, soldiers and flag 'swords'. Imperf	8·50	8·25

1986 (1 Oct). Litho. P 12½×12.

1734	**399**	30f. multicoloured	1·20	35
1735		50f. multicoloured	1·70	50
1736		100f. multicoloured	3·50	1·30
1737		150f. multicoloured	4·50	1·70
1738		250f. multicoloured	8·50	2·75
1739		350f. multicoloured	12·00	3·75
1734/1739		*Set of 6*	28·00	9·25

O **400** President Hussain **401** Women

1986 (1 Oct). OFFICIAL. Litho. P 12½×12.

O1740	O **400**	30f. multicoloured	1·20	35
O1741		50f. multicoloured	1·70	50
O1742		100f. multicoloured	3·50	1·30
O1743		150f. multicoloured	4·75	2·50
O1740/O1743		*Set of 4*	20·00	4·25

Nos. O1740/O1743 are inscribed 'POSTAGE'.

(Litho State Ptg Wks, Budapest)

1986 (1 Nov). Iraqi Women's Day. T **401** and similar multicoloured design. P 11½×12 (vert) or 12×11½ (horiz).

1744	30f. Type **401**	85	50
1745	50f. Woman and battle scenes (*horiz*)	1·20	65
1746	100f. Type **401**	2·50	1·50
1747	150f. As No. 1745	4·00	2·10
1744/1747	*Set of 4*	7·75	4·25

402 Flag and Treble Clef forming Dove **403** *Al Alwah* (freighter) and Map

(Litho State Ptg Wks. Budapest)

1986 (24 Nov). International Peace Year. T **402** and similar multicoloured designs. P 11½×12.

1748	50f. Type **402**	1·20	50
1749	100f. Globe, Dove with flag and hand holding rifle and olive branch	2·20	1·20
1750	150f. Type **402**	3·25	2·10
1751	250f. As No. 1749	4·50	2·75
1748/1751	*Set of 4*	10·00	6·00
MS1752	80×60 mm. 200f. IPY emblem, flag and Dove and fist on map. Imperf	5·50	5·25

1987 (1 Apr). Tenth Anniversary of United Arab Shipping Company. T **403** and similar horiz designs. Multicoloured. Litho. P 12½×12.

1753	50f. Type **403**	1·00	50
1754	100f. *Khaled Ibn Al Waleed* (container ship)	2·00	1·20
1755	150f. Type **403**	3·25	1·70
1756	250f. As No. 1754	5·00	2·75
1753/1756	*Set of 4*	10·00	5·50
MS1757	100×90 mm. 200f. *Khaled Ibn Al Waleed* at wharf. Imperf	7·25	7·00

404 Activities on Tree **405** President Hussain in '6'

1987 (25 Aug). 40th Anniversary (1986) of United Nations Children's Fund. T **404** and similar multicoloured design. Litho. P 12×12½ (vert) or 12½×12 (horiz).

1758	20f. Type **404**	50	50
1759	40f. Doves and '40' containing children and UNICEF emblem (*horiz*)	70	65
1760	90f. Type **404**	1·70	1·70
1761	100f. As No. 1759	1·90	1·80
1758/1761	*Set of 4*	4·25	4·25

1987 (1 Nov). Army Day. T **405** and similar vert design. Multicoloured. Litho. P 12×12½.

1762	20f. Type **405**	50	50
1763	40f. President Hussain and military scenes	70	65
1764	90f. Type **405**	1·70	1·70
1765	100f. As No. 1763	1·90	1·80
1762/1765	*Set of 4*	4·25	4·25

406 Torch, Cogwheel, Wheat and Map

407 President Hussain

1987 (1 Nov). 40th Anniversary of Al-Baath Party. T **406** and similar vert design. Multicoloured. Litho. P 12×12½.

1766	20f. Type **406**	50	50
1767	40f. President Hussain, map and flag as '7'	70	65
1768	90f. Type **406**	1·70	1·70
1769	100f. As No. 1767	1·90	1·80
1766/1769	*Set of 4*	4·25	4·25

1987 (1 Nov). 50th Birthday of President Saddam Hussain. T **407** and similar horiz design. Multicoloured. Litho. P 12½×12.

1770	20f. Type **407**	70	65
1771	40f. Anniversary dates, flowers and President Hussain	85	85
1772	90f. Type **407**	2·00	2·00
1773	100f. As No. 1771	2·20	2·10
1770/1773	*Set of 4*	5·25	5·00

408 Civilians, Soldiers and Buried Soldier

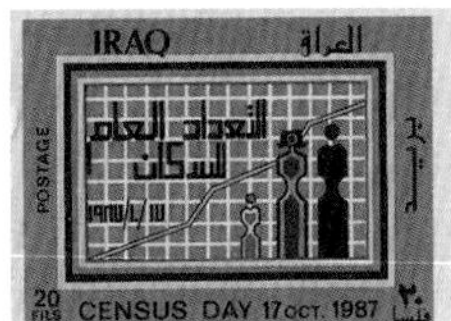

409 Symbolic Family on Graph

1987 (1 Nov). July Festivals and Eighth Anniversary of President Hussain's State Leadership. T **408** and similar multicoloured design. Litho. P 12½×12 (horiz) or 12×12½ (vert).

1774	20f. President Hussain and flag (*horiz*)	70	65
1775	40f. Type **408**	85	85
1776	90f. As No. 1774	2·00	2·00
1777	100f. Type **408**	2·20	2·10
1774/1777	*Set of 4*	5·25	5·00

(Des M. Abdullah. Litho)

1987 (1 Dec). Census. T **409** and similar horiz design. Multicoloured. P 12×11½.

1778	20f. Type **409**	50	35
1779	30f. People on graph	70	50
1780	50f. As No. 1779	1·00	50
1781	500f. Type **409**	9·25	7·00
1778/1781	*Set of 4*	10·50	7·50

410 President Hussain in '6' and Troops

411 '8' and President Hussain

1988 (6 Jan). Army Day. T **410** and similar multicoloured design. Litho. P 11½×12 (vert) or 12×11½ (horiz).

1782	20f. Type **410**	50	50
1783	30f. Soldier and medal (*horiz*)	50	50
1784	50f. Type **410**	1·00	50
1785	150f. As No. 1783	3·00	1·20
1782/1785	*Set of 4*	4·50	2·40

1988 (8 Feb). 18th Anniversary of People's Army (1786, 1788) and 25th Anniversary of 8th February Revolution (others). T **411** and similar multicoloured design. Litho. P 12×11½ (horiz) or 11½×12 (vert).

1786	20f. Type **411**	70	50
1787	30f. President Hussain and Eagle in '8' (*vert*)	85	50
1788	50f. Type **411**	1·20	65
1789	150f. As No. 1787	3·75	1·30
1786/1789	*Set of 4*	5·75	2·75

412 Flag as 'V', and Lyre

413 Rally and Ears of Wheat

1988 (1 Mar). Art Day. T **412** and similar vert designs. Multicoloured. Litho. P 11½×12.

1790	20f. Type **412**	70	50
1791	30f. President Hussain, rifle as torch, clef and Dove on film strip	85	65
1792	50f. Type **412**	1·20	65
1793	100f. As No. 1791	2·40	85
1790/1793	*Set of 4*	4·75	2·40
MS1794	60×80 mm. 150f. Musical notes, lute and keyboard. Imperf	5·00	5·00

1988 (7 Apr). 41st Anniversary of Al-Baath Party. T **413** and similar multicoloured design. Litho. P 12½×12 (horiz) or 12×12½ (vert).

1795	20f. Type **413**	70	50
1796	30f. Flowers and '7 April 1947–1988' (*vert*)	85	65
1797	50f. Type **413**	1·20	65
1798	150f. As No. 1796	3·75	1·20
1795/1798	*Set of 4*	5·75	2·75

414 Emblem

415 President Hussain

1988 (24 Apr). Regional Marine Environment Day. T **414** and similar multicoloured design. Litho. P 12×12½ (vert) or 12½×12 (horiz).

1799	20f. Type **414**	85	50
1800	40f. Fish (*horiz*)	85	65
1801	90f. Type **414**	2·20	85
1802	100f. As No. 1800	2·40	85
1799/1802	*Set of 4*	5·75	2·50

1988 (28 Apr). 51st Birthday of President Saddam Hussain. T **415** and similar vert design. Multicoloured. Litho. P 12×12½.

1803	20f. Type **415**	85	65
1804	30f. President Hussain and hands holding flowers	1·00	85
1805	50f. Type **415**	1·50	85
1806	100f. As No. 1804	3·00	1·20
1803/1806	*Set of 4*	5·75	3·25
MS1807	90×100 mm. 150f. President Hussain and flowers within flag as heart. Imperf	6·00	5·75

416 Emblem

417 Bomb and Open Book showing School, Child and Wreath

1988 (1 June). 40th Anniversary of World Health Organisation. T **416** and similar multicoloured design. Litho. P 12½×12 (horiz) or 12×12½ (vert).

1808	20f. Type **416**	70	50
1809	40f. Red crescent protecting line of people (*vert*)	85	65
1810	90f. Type **416**	2·20	85
1811	100f. As No. 1809	2·40	85
1808/1811 *Set of 4*		5·50	2·50

1988 (1 June). Bilat Al-Shuhada School Bomb Victims. T **417** and similar multicoloured designs. Litho. P 11½×12 (vert) or 12×11½ (horiz).

1812	20f. Type **417**	70	50
1813	40f. Explosion and girl (*horiz*)	85	65
1814	90f. Type **417**	2·40	85
1815	100f. As No. 1813	2·40	85
1812/1815 *Set of 4*		5·75	2·50
MS1816	80×60 mm. 150f. Child's severed head in clawed hand (49×39 *mm*). P 12½	4·00	4·00

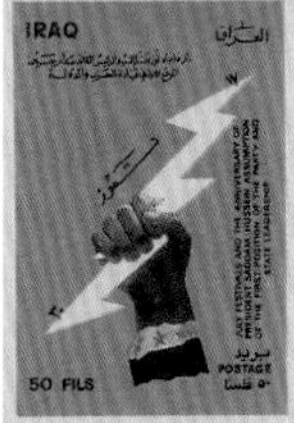

418 Hand holding Flash of Lightning

419 President Hussain and al-Sail al-Kabir Miqat

1988 (17 July). July Festivals and Ninth Anniversary of President Hussain's State Leadership. T **418** and similar multicoloured designs. Litho. P 12×12½.

1817	50f. Type **418**	1·50	85
1818	90f. Sun, map and President Hussain	2·75	1·00
1819	100f. Type **418**	3·00	1·00
1820	150f. As No. 1818	4·25	1·20
1817/1820 *Set of 4*		10·50	3·75
MS1821	90×70 mm. 250f. President Hussain and flag. Imperf	8·25	8·00

1988 (24 July). President Hussain's Pilgrimage to Mecca. Litho. P 13½.

1822 **419**	90f. multicoloured	2·75	1·00
1823	100f. multicoloured	3·00	1·50
1824	150f. multicoloured	4·50	1·50
1822/1824 *Set of 3*		9·25	3·50

420 Mosul

421 President Hussain and Soldiers

1988 (31 July). Tourism. T **420** and similar multicoloured designs. Litho. P 11½×12 (150f.) or 12×11½ (others).

1825	50f. Type **420**	2·00	65
1826	100f. Basrah	3·00	1·50
1827	150f. Baghdad (*vert*)	6·25	2·30
1825/1827 *Set of 3*		10·00	4·00

1988 (8 Aug). 'Victorious Iraq'. Litho. P 12×11½.

1828 **421**	50f. multicoloured	10·00	10·00
1829	100f. multicoloured	18·00	17·00
1830	150f. multicoloured	26·00	25·00
1828/1830 *Set of 3*		45·00	42·00

422 Emblem

423 Map and Hands holding Flag

1988 (12 Aug). Navy Day. T **422** and similar multicoloured designs. Litho. P 12×12½.

1831	50f. Type **422**	2·20	85
1832	90f. Missile boats	4·25	1·20
1833	100f. Type **422**	4·50	1·50
1834	150f. As No. 1832	6·75	2·10
1831/1834 *Set of 4*		16·00	5·00
MS1835	90×70 mm. 250f. Emblem and President Hussain decorating officers. Imperf	13·50	13·00

1988 (1 Sept). Liberation of Fao City. Litho. P 12×11½.

1836 **423**	100f. multicoloured	3·75	1·20
1837	150f. multicoloured	5·50	1·80
MS1838	60×80 mm. 500f. multicoloured. Imperf	27·00	26·00

Design: 500f. President Hussain and document.

424 Missile Launch from Winged Map

425 Boxer and Hodori (mascot)

1988 (10 Sept). Iraq Missile Research. T **424** and similar horiz design. Litho. P 11½×12.

1839 **424**	100f. multicoloured	3·00	1·00
1840	150f. multicoloured	4·50	1·50
MS1841	80×60 mm. 500f. multicoloured. Imperf	15·00	15·00

Design: 500f. President Hussain, map and missiles.

1988 (19 Sept). Olympic Games, Seoul. T **425** and similar multicoloured designs. Litho. P 12×12½.

1842	100f. Type **425**	4·50	1·50
1843	150f. Games emblem	6·75	2·10
MS1844	100×90 mm. 500f. President Hussain presenting football trophy. Imperf	27·00	26·00

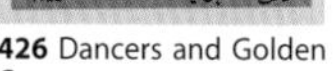

426 Dancers and Golden Cow

427 Crescent and Camel Train

1988 (30 Sept). Second Babylon International Festival. Litho. P 11½×12.

1845 **426**	100f. multicoloured	3·00	1·00
1846	150f. multicoloured	4·00	1·50
MS1847	60×80 mm. 500f. multicoloured. Imperf	15·00	15·00

Design: 500f. Medallion and laurel wreath.

1988 (Oct). Mohammed's Birth Anniversary. Litho. P 11½×12.

1848 **427**	100f. multicoloured	3·00	1·20
1849	150f. multicoloured	4·25	1·80
1850	1d. multicoloured	27·00	11·50
1848/1850 *Set of 3*		31·00	13·00

428 Hand holding Candle

انتصار العراق
١٩٨٨/٨/٨

(**429** 'Victory')

1988 (1 Dec). Martyr's Day. Litho. P 13½.

1851 **428**	100f. multicoloured	1·90	85
1852	150f. multicoloured	3·50	1·50
1853	500f. multicoloured	12·00	4·25
1851/1853 *Set of 3*		16·00	6·00

1988 (Dec). Nos. 1738/1739 optd with T **429**.

1854 **399** 250f. multicoloured .... 10·00 3·75
1855 350f. multicoloured .... 15·00 5·75
a. Opt inverted £170 £250

430 Family on Pedestrian Crossing

431 Children and Money

1989 (9 Jan). Police Day. Litho. P 12×11½.

1856 **430** 50f. multicoloured .... 1·50 85
1857 100f. multicoloured .... 3·00 1·00
1858 150f. multicoloured .... 4·00 1·80
1856/1858 *Set of 3* .... 7·75 3·25

1989 (28 Jan). Postal Savings Bank. T **431** and similar square design. Litho.

(a) Size 32×32 mm. P 12

1859 **431** 50f. multicoloured .... 3·50 1·70

(b) Size 24×25 mm. With Arabic overprint. P 13½×13

1860 – 100f. multicoloured .... 10·00 5·00
1861 – 150f. multicoloured .... 12·00 6·25
1859/1861 *Set of 3* .... 23·00 11·50

Design: 100, 150f. Motif as T **431** but with inscriptions differently arranged and inscribed 'REPUBLIC OF IRAQ'.

For Nos. 1860/1861 without overprint, see Nos. 1928/1929.

432 Members' Flags and Leaders

433 Dates

1989 (16 Feb). Formation of Arab Co-operation Council (Egypt, Iraq, Jordan and Yemen Arab Republic). T **432** and similar horiz design. Multicoloured. Litho. P 12×11½.

1862 100f. Type **432** .... 3·00 1·00
1863 150f. Leaders in formal pose .... 4·00 1·50

1989 (17 Apr). First Anniversary of Liberation of Fao City. T **433** and similar vert design. Litho. P 12×11½.

1864 **433** 100f. multicoloured .... 2·75 1·00
1865 150f. multicoloured .... 3·75 1·00
MS1866 60×80 mm. 250f. multicoloured. Imperf .... 5·50 5·25

Design: 250f. Calendar.

434 President Hussain

435 Khairalla

1989 (28 Apr). 52nd Birthday of President Saddam Hussain. T **434** and similar vert design. Litho. P 12×11½.

1867 **434** 100f. multicoloured .... 2·75 1·00
1868 150f. multicoloured .... 3·75 1·00
MS1869 60×80 mm. 250f. multicoloured. Imperf .... 8·50 8·25

Design: 250f. Hussain and laurel branches.

1989 (6 May). General Adnan Khairalla Commemoration. Litho. P 13½.

1870 **435** 50f. multicoloured .... 1·90 85
1871 100f. multicoloured .... 3·50 1·00
1872 150f. multicoloured .... 5·00 1·80
1870/1872 *Set of 3* .... 9·25 3·25

436 Hussain laying Mortar

437 Crane and Buildings

1989 (14 June). Completion of Basrah Re-construction Project. Litho. P 13½.

1873 **436** 100f. multicoloured .... 3·00 85
1874 150f. multicoloured .... 4·25 1·50

1989 (25 June). Start of Re-construction of Fao City. Litho. P 13½.

1875 **437** 100f. multicoloured .... 3·00 85
1876 150f. multicoloured .... 4·25 1·50

438 Women

439 President Hussain

1989 (25 June). Litho. P 11½×12.

1877 **438** 100f. multicoloured .... 1·70 65
1878 150f. multicoloured .... 2·50 1·00
1879 1d. multicoloured .... 17·00 6·50
1880 5d. multicoloured .... 85·00 28·00
1877/1880 *Set of 4* .... 95·00 33·00

1989 (17 July). July Festivals and Tenth Anniversary of President Hussain's State Leadership. Litho. P 12×12½.

1881 **439** 50f. multicoloured .... 1·50 1·00
1882 100f. multicoloured .... 3·00 1·00
1883 150f. multicoloured .... 4·50 1·50
1881/1883 *Set of 3* .... 8·00 3·25

440 Flag and Victory Signs

1989 (8 Aug). Victory Day. T **440** and similar vert design. Litho. P 12×12½.

1884 **440** 100f. multicoloured .... 2·40 85
1885 150f. multicoloured .... 3·75 1·30
MS1886 70×90 mm. 250f. multicoloured. Imperf .... 7·25 7·00

Design: 250f. President Hussain, palm, Boeing 737 airliner and *Khawla* (container ship).

441 Children, Heart and Bride

1989 (1 Sept). Iraqi Family. Litho. P 13½.

1887 **441** 50f. multicoloured .... 2·20 1·00
1888 100f. multicoloured .... 4·00 1·80
1889 150f. multicoloured .... 12·00 5·00
1887/1889 *Set of 3* .... 16·00 7·00

442 Najaf

443 Map and Means of Transport

1989 (15 Oct). Tourism. T **442** and similar vert designs. Multicoloured. Litho. P 11½×12½.

1890		100f. Type **442**	3·75	1·20
1891		100f. Arbil	3·75	1·20
1892		100f. Marsh Arab punter and Ziggurat of Ur	3·75	1·20
1890/1892		*Set of 3*	10·00	3·25

1989 (21 Oct). Fifth Session of Arab Ministers of Transport Council, Baghdad. T **443** and similar multicoloured designs. Litho. P 11½×12 (150f.) or 12×11½ (others).

1893		50f. Type **443**	2·50	1·20
1894		100f. Sun, means of transport and map	5·00	1·50
1895		150f. Means of transport and members' flags (*vert*)	7·25	2·30
1893/1895		*Set of 3*	13·50	4·50

444 City and President Hussain placing Final Stone

445 Anniversary Emblem

1989 (25 Oct). Completion of Fao City Reconstruction. Litho. P 13½.

1896	**444**	100f. multicoloured	3·25	1·00
1897		150f. multicoloured	4·50	1·50

1989 (9 Nov). 30th Anniversary of Iraqi News Agency. Litho. P 13½.

1898	**445**	50f. multicoloured	1·00	65
1899		100f. multicoloured	2·00	85
1900		150f. multicoloured	3·00	1·30
1898/1900		*Set of 3*	5·50	2·50

446 Emblem

447 Pansies

1989 (15 Nov). First Anniversary of Declaration of Palestinian State. T **446** and similar vert design. Multicoloured. Litho. P 12×12½.

1901		25f. Type **446**	50	50
1902		50f. Crowd of children	1·20	65
1903		100f. Type **446**	2·40	85
1904		150f. As No. 1902	3·75	1·20
1901/1904		*Set of 4*	7·00	2·40

1989 (20 Nov). Flowers. T **447** and similar vert designs. Multicoloured. Litho. P 13½×13.

1905		25f. Type **447**	70	65
1906		50f. Antirrhinums	1·40	65
1907		100f. *Hibiscus trionum*	2·50	85
1908		150f. Mesembryanthemums	4·00	1·30
1905/1908		*Set of 4*	7·75	3·00
MS1909		90×110 mm. As Nos. 1905/1908 but larger (*26½×36 mm*). P 12½×11½ (*sold at 500f.*)	18·00	17·00

448 Map and Emblem

449 Sun, Flag, Doves and Mosque Domes

1989 (25 Nov). Centenary of Interparliamentary Union. Litho. P 12½×12.

1910	**448**	25f. multicoloured	70	50
1911		100f. multicoloured	2·40	85
1912		150f. multicoloured	3·75	1·30
1910/1912		*Set of 3*	6·25	2·40

1989 (1 Dec). Martyr's Day. Litho. P 13½.

1913	**449**	50f. multicoloured	1·50	85
1914		100f. multicoloured	2·75	1·00
		a. Opt double, one albino		
1915		150f. multicoloured	3·75	1·50
1913/1915		*Set of 3*	7·25	3·00

450 Dove, Red Crescent and President Hussain

451 Members' Flags on Map

1989 (10 Dec). Iraqi Red Crescent Society. Litho. P 13½.

1916	**450**	100f. multicoloured	1·50	85
1917		150f. multicoloured	4·00	1·70
1918		500f. Multicoloured	13·00	5·00
1916/1918		*Set of 3*	17·00	6·75

1990 (16 Feb). First Anniversary of Arab Co-operation Council. Litho. P 13×13½.

1919	**451**	50f. multicoloured	2·20	1·20
1920		100f. multicoloured	5·50	2·10
MS1921		80×60 mm. **451** 250f. multicoloured. Imperf.	14·50	14·00

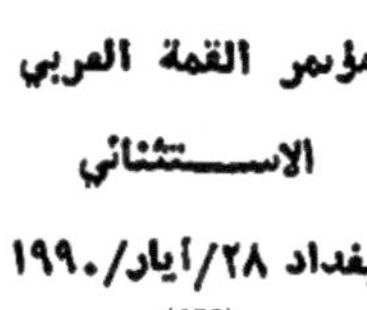

(**452**)

453 Doves and Flag as Flame

1990 (28 May). Arab League Summit Conference, Baghdad. Nos. 1906 and 1908 optd with T **452**.

1922		50f. multicoloured	2·50	2·00
1923		150f. Multicoloured	7·75	4·50

A miniature sheet was prepared for the 1990 World Cup Football Championship. This miniature sheet was not put on sale at the time but a number are believed to have been sold during March 1997.

1990 (30 Aug). Second Anniversary of Liberation of Fao City. P 13½×13.

1924	**453**	50f. multicoloured	1·40	1·30
1925		100f. multicoloured	2·75	2·75

First day covers are dated 17 April 1990.

No. 1926 is vacant.

(454)

455 Children and Currency

FORGERIES. From 1992 to 1996 numerous forged overprints are known.

1992 (23 Nov). No. 1291 surch with T **454**.

1927	100f. on 5f. multicoloured	7·75	7·50
	a. Opt inverted	60·00	
	b. Opt double	60·00	

1993 (1 Apr). Postal Savings. T **455** and similar square designs. P 13½×13.

1928	**455**	100f. multicoloured	70	65
1929		150f. multicoloured	85	85
1930		250f. multicoloured	1·50	1·50
1928/1930 *Set of 3*			2·75	2·75

(456) (457)

1993 (1 July). No. O1742 surch with T **456**.

1931	1d. on 100f. multicoloured	17·00	17·00
	a. Opt inverted	£170	

1993 (1 Aug). No. 1901 surch with T **457**.

1932	10d. on 25f. multicoloured	50·00	50·00

458 Satellite and Receiver

459 *Ibn Khaldoon* (trading vessel)

1993 (22 Sept). Re-building. T **458** and similar vert designs. Multicoloured. Litho. P 14.

1933	250f. Type **458**	1·40	1·30
1934	500f. Bridge over Tigris River	2·50	2·50
1935	750f. Power transformers	3·75	3·75
1936	1d. Damaged and restored buildings	5·00	5·00
1933/1936 *Set of 4*		11·50	11·25

1993 (26 Dec). Litho. P 14.

1937	**459**	2d. multicoloured	4·25	4·25
1938		5d. multicoloured	11·00	10·50

(460) (461) (461a)

(461b) (461c) (461d)

(462) (462a) (463)

(463a) (464) (464a)

(464b) (464c) (465)

(466) (466a) (467)

1994 (5 Feb). No. 1291 surch with Types **460/467**.

1939	500f. on 5f. multicoloured (Type **460**) (opt 14 *mm*)	5·00	5·00
1940	500f. on 5f. multicoloured (Type **460**) (opt 17 *mm*)	34·00	33·00
1941	1d. on 5f. multicoloured (Type **461**)	3·50	3·25
1942	1d. on 5f. multicoloured (Type **461a**)	5·00	5·00
1943	1d. on 5f. multicoloured (Type **461b**)	11·00	10·50
1944	1d. on 5f. multicoloured (Type **461c**)	5·00	5·00
1945	1d. on 5f. multicoloured (Type **461d**)	5·00	5·00
1946	2d. on 5f. multicoloured (Type **462**)	6·00	6·25
1947	2d. on 5f. multicoloured (Type **462a**)	8·50	8·25
1948	3d. on 5f. multicoloured (Type **463**)	3·50	3·25
1949	3d. on 5f. multicoloured (Type **463a**)	3·50	3·25
1950	5d. on 5f. multicoloured (Type **464**)	3·50	3·25
1951	5d. on 5f. multicoloured (Type **464a**)	5·00	5·00
1952	5d. on 5f. multicoloured (Type **464b**)	10·00	10·00
1953	5d. on 5f. multicoloured (Type **464c**)	13·50	13·00
1954	10d. on 5f. multicoloured (Type **465**)	7·25	7·00
1955	25d. on 5f. multicoloured (Type **466**)	14·50	14·00
1956	25d. on 5f. multicoloured (Type **466a**)	24·00	23·00
1957	50d. on 5f. multicoloured (Type **467**)	48·00	46·00

Types **468/471** and Nos. 1958/1966 are vacant.

(472) (473)

1994 (28 Apr). 57th Birth Anniversary of President Hussain. No. 1739 surch with Types **472/473**.

1967	**399**	5d. on 350f. multicoloured (Type **472**)	10·00	10·00
1968	**399**	5d. on 350f. multicoloured (Type **473**)	10·00	10·00

474 Al Qaid Bridge

(475)

1994 (17 July). Litho. P 14.

1969	**474**	1d. multicoloured	2·40	2·30
		a. Pair. Nos. 1969/1970	8·75	8·50
		b. Face value and inscription missing	43·00	
1970		3d. multicoloured	6·00	6·00
		b. Inscription missing	43·00	

1994 (8 Aug). Victory Day. No. 1739 surch with T **475**.

1971	**399**	5d. on 350f. multicoloured	9·25	9·00

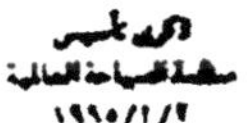

(476)

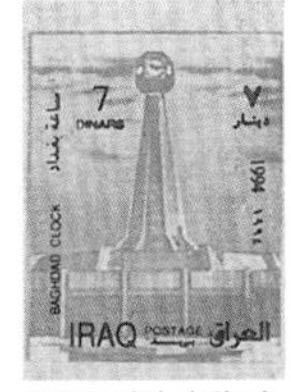

477 Baghdad Clock

1995 (2 Jan). 20th Anniversary of World Tourism Organisation. No. 1878 surch with T **476**.

1972	**438**	5d. on 150f. multicoloured (Arabic inscription)	7·75	7·50
1973	**438**	5d. on 150f. multicoloured (English inscription)	7·75	7·50

1995 (28 Feb). T **477** and similar vert design. Litho. P 11.

1974	**477**	7d. blue and black	4·25	4·25
		a. Size 25×31 mm	4·25	4·25
MS1975		86×110 mm. 25d. As No. 1974 but with design enlarged (multicoloured). Imperf	26·00	25·00
		a. Missing date inscription	£170	

478 Saddam Tower (television transmitter)

479 President Hussain

1995 (12 Mar). Litho. P 14.

1976	**478**	2d. multicoloured	2·00	2·00
1977		5d. multicoloured	4·25	4·25

1995 (28 Apr). 58th Birth Anniversary of President Hussain. Two sheets. Litho. Imperf.

MS1978 (a) 60×78 mm. 25d. Type **479**; (b) 78×60 mm. 25d. President and child (*horiz*)	60·00	60·00

480 Woman and River Basin

481 Barbed Wire, Tower, Woman and Child

1995 (17 July). Completion of 'Saddam River' (canal between Iraq and Persian Gulf). Litho. P 14.

1979	**480**	4d. red and new blue	6·50	6·25
		a. Imperf between (pair)	70·00	
1980		4d. ochre and new blue	6·50	6·25
MS1981		106×86 mm. **480** 25d. multicoloured	26·00	25·00

1995 (6 Aug). Litho. P 11.

1982	**481**	10d. new blue and red	5·00	5·00
		a. Imperf between (vert pair)	95·00	
		b. Imperf between (horiz pair)	£120	
MS1983		85×110 mm. **481** 25d. multicoloured	26·00	25·00

✻ ٢٥ دينار ✻

(**482**)

1995 (1 Oct–12 Dec). No. 1739 surch with T **482** in either blue (No. 1985) or black (others).

1984	**399**	25d. on 350f. multicoloured	2·40	2·30
		a. Opt double	70·00	
		b. Opt double, top and bottom	£100	
1985		250d. on 350f. multicoloured (B.)	14·50	14·00
		a. Opt inverted	55·00	
1986		350d. on 350f. multicoloured (12.12)	34·00	33·00
		a. Opt inverted	60·00	
		b. Pair, one with opt omitted	£140	
1987		1000d. on 350f. multicoloured (12.12)	70·00	65·00
		a. Opt inverted	£200	

(**483**)

(**484**)

(**485**)

(**486**)

1995 (1 Oct–12 Dec). Nos. 1930 surch as Types **483**/**486**.

1988	**455**	50d. on 250f. multicoloured (Type **483**)	6·00	5·75
		a. Opt inverted	£160	
1989		500d. on 250f. multicoloured (12.12) (Type **484**)	48·00	46·00
		a. Opt inverted	£160	
1990		2500d. on 250f. multicoloured (12.12) (Type **485**)	£170	£170
1991		5000d. on 250f. multicoloured (12.12) (Type **486**)	£375	£375

يوم الاستفتاء
١٩٩٥/١٠/١٥
✻ ٢٥ دينار ✻

(**487**)

Referendum
15/10/1995
✻25 Dinars✻

(**488**)

1995 (15 Oct). Referendum Day. No. 1739 surch with Types **487**/**488**.

1992	**399**	25d. on 350f. multicoloured (Type **487**)	6·00	5·75
		a. Arabic opt inverted	95·00	
1993		25d. on 350f. multicoloured (Type **488**)	6·00	5·75
		a. English opt inverted	95·00	

✻ ٢٥ دينار

(**489**)

1996 (Feb). No. 1927 surch with T **489** (overprint on overprint).

1994	**275**	25d. on 100f. on 5f. multicoloured	9·25	9·00
		a. Opt inverted	70·00	

٢٥ دينار

(**490**)

(**490a**)

(**490b**)

مائة دينار

(**491**)

1996 (Feb). Nos. 1859/1861 surch with Types **490**/**490a**/**490b**.

1995	25d. on 100f. multicoloured (Type **490**)	3·00	2·75
	a. Opt inverted	70·00	
	b. Opt double	75·00	

1996 25d. on 150f. multicoloured (Type **490a**) 3·00 2·75
a. Opt inverted 70·00
b. Opt double 70·00
1997 50d. on 50f. multicoloured (32×32 *mm.*) (Type **490b**) 5·50 5·25
a. Opt inverted 70·00
b. Pair, one with opt, one without 85·00

1996 (Feb). No. O1616 surch with T **491**.
1998 100d. on 70f. greenish yellow, black and flesh 12·00 11·50

492 Flag, Doves and Flames

1996 (13 Feb). Sheet 86×62 mm. Litho. Imperf.
MS1999 **492** 100d. multicoloured 26·00 25·00

(**493**)

1996 (15 Feb). No. 1878 surch with T **493**.
2000 **438** 100d. on 150f. multicoloured 8·50 8·25
a. Opt inverted £130

(**494**) (**495**)

1996 (15 Feb). Nos. 1989/1991 surch with Types **494/495** (overprint on overprint).
2001 25d. on 500d. on 250f. multicoloured (Type **494**) 10·00 10·00
2002 25d. on 5000d. on 250f. multicoloured (Type **494**) 10·00 10·00
2003 50d. on 2500d. on 250f. multicoloured (Type **495**) 20·00 20·00
a. Opt double 70·00

(**496**) (**497**)

1996 (Feb–Mar). Un-issued stamps surch with Types **496/497**. P 13.
2004 25d. on 10f. multicoloured (3.96) (Type **496**) 65·00 65·00
2005 25d. on 25f. multicoloured (Type **496**) 5·00 5·00
2006 50d. on 10f. multicoloured (3.96) (Type **497**) £100 £100
2007 50d. on 50f. multicoloured (Type **497**) 6·75 6·50
Designs: Nos. 2004/2007 School children in classroom.

(**498**) (**499**)

1996 (15 Apr). No. 1906 surch with T **498**.
2008 100d. on 50f. Antirrhinums 50·00 50·00

1996 (Apr). No. 1930 surch with T **499**.
2009 25d. on 250f. multicoloured 3·50 3·25
a. Opt inverted 70·00

(**500**)

1996 (1 Dec). No. O1645 surch with T **500**.
2010 100d. on 60f. multicoloured 10·00 10·00

(**501/501a**)

1996 (16 Dec). Nos. 1572/1577 surch as Types **501/501a**.
2011 25d. on 10f. multicoloured (Type **501**) 3·25 3·25
a. Booklet pane. Nos. 2011/2016
b. Opt inverted £150
2012 25d. on 30f. multicoloured (Type **501**) 3·25 3·25
b. Opt inverted £150
2013 25d. on 50f. multicoloured (Type **501**) 3·25 3·25
b. Opt inverted £150
2014 100d. on 20f. multicoloured (Type **501a**) 13·50 13·00
b. Opt inverted £150
2015 100d. on 40f. multicoloured (Type **501a**) 13·50 13·00
b. Opt inverted £150
2016 100d. on 100f. multicoloured (Type **501a**) 13·50 13·00
b. Opt inverted £150

(**502**) (**503**)

1996 (Dec). No. 1924 surch with T **502**.
2017 100d. on 50f. multicoloured 8·50 8·25

1997 (17 Jan). No. 1933 surch as T **503**.
2018 25d. on 250f. multicoloured 2·40 2·30
a. Opt inverted 70·00

504 Geometric Design (**505**)

1997 (13 Feb). Litho. P 10 (25d.) or 11 (others).
2019 **504** 25d. emerald, black and rosine 2·00 2·00
a. Imperf (between pair) 70·00
2020 100d. emerald, new blue and orange vermilion 10·00 10·00
a. Arabic inscription to right of design reversed (upside down) 29·00 28·00

1997 (7 Apr). 50th Anniversary of Baath Party. No. 1920 surch with T **505**.
2021 25d. on 100f. multicoloured 3·00 3·00

(**506**) **507** President Hussain

1997 (22 Apr). 45th Anniversary of Arab Post Union. No. 1878 surch with T **506**.
2022 25d. on 150f. multicoloured 7·25 7·00

1997 (15 June–20 Aug). Second Anniversary of Referendum. Litho. P 14.
2023 **507** 25d. multicoloured 3·00 3·00
2024 100d. multicoloured (20.8) 12·00 11·50
a. Blue omitted 70·00
MS2025 96×81 mm. 250d. President Hussain and map. Imperf (17.7) 20·00 20·00

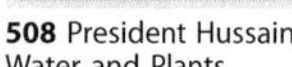

508 President Hussain, Water and Plants

509 Saladin and President Hussain

1997 (15 Nov). Completion of Al Qaid Water Project. T **508** and similar vert designs. Multicoloured. Litho. P 14.

(a) Sheet stamps

(i) Ordinary gum

2026 25d. Type **508** .... 1·20 1·20

(ii) Self-adhesive gum

2027 100d. As No. 2026 .... 4·75 4·50

(b) Miniature Sheets. Ordinary gum

MS2028 Two sheets. (a) 79×91 mm. 250d. As No. 2026; (b) 75×92 mm. 250d. President Hussain and pipeline .... 27·00 26·00

1998 (28 Feb–3 Mar). Jerusalem Day. Litho. Self-adhesive. Die-cut perf 14.

2029 **509** 25d. multicoloured .... 1·40 1·30
a. Imperf .... 2·50 2·50
2030 100d. multicoloured (3.3) .... 5·00 5·00
a. Imperf (3.3) .... 11·00 10·50
MS2031 88×75 mm. **509** 250d. multicoloured. Imperf .... 13·50 13·00

510 Zinnias

1998 (21 Mar). Kurdish New Year. Two sheets containing T **510** and similar vert design. Litho. Imperf.

MS2032 (a) 71×93 mm. 250d. Type **510**; (b) 68×93 mm. 250d. Iris .... 43·00 41·00

511 Goalkeeper and Players (½-size illustration)

1998 (9 June). World Cup Football Championship, France (1st issue). Two sheets containing T **511** and similar multicoloured design. Litho. Imperf.

MS2033 (a) 72×85 mm. 250d. Type **511**; (b) 84×62 mm. 250d. Two players (*vert*) .... 29·00 28·00

See also Nos. 2061/2062.

512 Emblem (⅔ *size illustration*)

1998 (12 July). 25th Anniversary of Arab Police Security Chiefs' Conference. Sheet 93×67 mm. Litho. P 14.

MS2034 **512** 250d. multicoloured .... 13·50 13·00

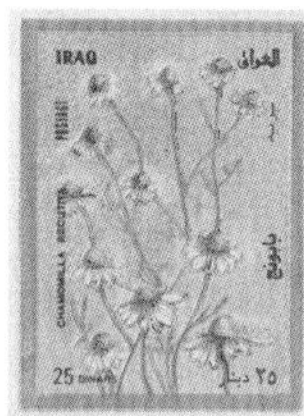

513 *Chamomile recutita*

514 President Hussain and Map

1998 (10–30 Sept). Flora. T **513** and similar vert designs. Multicoloured. Litho.

(a) Ordinary gum. P 14

2035 25d. Type **513** 70 65
2036 50d. *Helianthus annuus* .... 1·00 1·00
2037 1000d. *Carduus nutans* .... 17·00 17·00
2035/2037 *Set of 3* .... 17·00 17·00

(b) Self-adhesive gum. Die-cut perf 14

2038 25d. Type **513** (30.9) .... 3·25 3·25

1998 (25 Oct). Arab Languages Day. T **514** and similar vert design. Multicoloured. Litho. P 14.

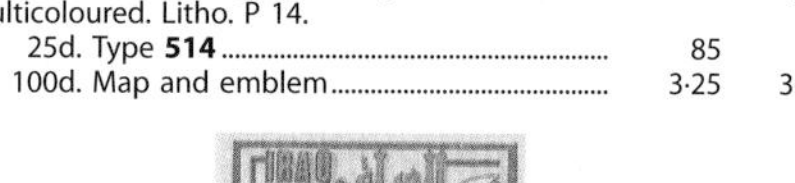

2039 25d. Type **514** 85 85
2040 100d. Map and emblem .... 3·25 3·25

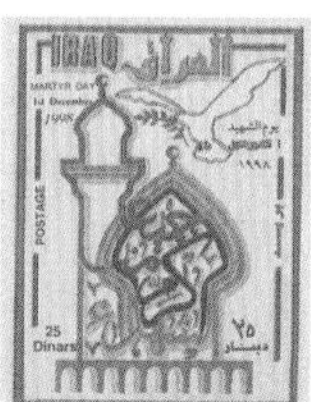

515 Mosque Outline, Calligraphy and Dove

1998 (1 Dec). Martyrs Day. T **515** and similar multicoloured designs. Litho. P 14.

2041 25d. Type **515** 85 85
a. Imperf .... 2·50 2·50
2042 100d. Calligraphy and banner .... 3·25 3·25
a. Imperf .... 10·00 10·00
MS2043 94×74 mm. 250d. Emblem. Imperf .... 8·50 8·25

516 *Precis orithya*

1998 (20 Dec). Butterflies. T **516** and similar horiz designs. Multicoloured. Litho. P 14.

2044 100d. Type **516** .... 6·00 6·00
a. Imperf .... 13·00 12·50
2045 150d. *Anthocharis euphome* .... 8·50 8·25
a. Imperf .... 19·00 18·00

517 Ishtar Gate, Babylon

518 Tower and Dam

1999 (Feb). Tower of Babylon and Borsippa Ziggurat Conference. T **517** and similar vert designs. Multicoloured. Litho. P 14.

2046 25d. Type **517** ... 70 65
2047 50d. Ishtar Gate (*different*) ... 1·40 1·30
MS2048 71×90 mm. 250d. Ziggurat, Borsippa ... 13·00 12·50

1999 (28 Apr). Dams on the Tigris River. T **518** and similar vert design. Multicoloured. Litho. P 14.

2049 25d. Type **518** ... 85 85
2050 100d. Dam, flowers, fruit and pylon ... 3·25 3·25
MS2051 71×93 mm. 250d. As No. 2050. Imperf ... 13·00 12·50

519 President Hussain

520 Emblem and President Hussain

1999 (28 Apr). 62nd Birthday of President Hussain. T **519** and similar multicoloured designs. Litho. P 14.

2052 25d. Type **519** ... 50 50
2053 50d. With flag in background ... 1·00 1·00
2054 150d. With tree in background ... 2·75 2·75
2055 500d. Wearing uniform facing right ... 7·25 7·00
2056 1000d. Wearing uniform facing left ... 17·00 17·00
2057 5000d. Seated with clasped hands (*horiz*) ... 70·00 65·00
2052/2057 *Set of* 6 ... 90·00 85·00

1999 (28 Apr). Saddamiya al Therthar. T **520** and similar horiz design. Multicoloured. Litho. P 14.

2058 25d. Type **520** ... 1·70 1·70
2059 100d. Flowers, tower and gateway ... 3·50 3·25
MS2060 93×71 mm. 250d. Emblem, tower and President Hussain. Imperf ... 13·50 13·00

521 Two Players

522 Bees (*Apis mellifica*)

1999 (14 July). World Cup Football Championship, France (2nd issue). T **521** and similar multicoloured design. Litho. P 14.

2061 25d. Type **521** ... 2·50 2·50
2062 100d. Goalkeeper and players (*horiz*) ... 6·00 5·75

(Litho)

1999 (17 July). Apiculture. T **522** and similar vert design. P 14.

2063 **522** 25d. multicoloured ... 2·50 2·50
2064 50d. As Type **522** ... 6·00 5·75

523 Dome of the Rock

524 Flags and President Hussain

1999 (1 Oct). Jerusalem Day. T **523** and similar multicoloured designs. Litho. P 14.

2065 25d. Type **523** ... 85 85
2066 50d. Dome and map (*horiz*) ... 1·70 1·70
2067 100d. Dome, flag and shield ... 3·50 3·25
2068 150d. Dome and President Hussain (*horiz*) ... 4·25 4·25
2065/2068 *Set of* 4 ... 9·25 9·00
MS2069 93×71 mm. 250d. As No. 2068. Imperf ... 12·00 11·50

1999 (17 Dec). Victory Day. T **524** and similar horiz design. Multicoloured. Litho. P 14.

2070 25d. Type **524** ... 85 85
2071 50d. President Hussain and crowd ... 1·50 1·50
MS2072 93×71 mm. 250d. Eagle's head and President Hussain. Imperf ... 12·00 11·50

525 President Hussain and Flowers

526 Men and Women holding Tools (detail)

2000 (28 Apr). 63rd Birthday of President Hussain. T **525** and similar multicoloured design. Litho. P 14.

2073 25d. Type **525** ... 70 65
2074 50d. President Hussain and '28' (*horiz*) ... 1·40 1·30
MS2075 93×71 mm. 500d. President Hussain wearing coat with fur collar. Imperf ... 17·00 17·00

2000 (17 July). *Nasb al-Hurriyah* (sculpture by Jawad Salim). T **526** and similar horiz designs. Multicoloured. P 14.

2076 25d. Type **526** ... 70 65
a. Strip of 5. Nos. 2076/2080 ... 3·75
b. Imperf ... 1·40 1·30
ba. Strip of 5. Nos. 2076b/2080b ... 7·25
2077 25d. Women and child carrying corn ... 70 65
b. Imperf ... 1·40 1·30
2078 25d. Men and broken fence ... 70 65
b. Imperf ... 1·40 1·30
2079 25d. Grieving women ... 70 65
b. Imperf ... 1·40 1·30
2080 25d. Men with raised arms ... 70 65
b. Imperf ... 1·40 1·30
2076/2080 *Set of* 5 ... 3·25 3·00
2076b/2080b *Set of* 5 ... 6·25 5·75

Nos. 2076/2080 and 2076b/2080b, respectively, were issued in horizontal *se-tenant* strips of five stamps within the sheets.

527 President Hussain

528 Mallards (*Anas platyrhynchos*)

2000 (8 Aug). Victory Day. T **527** and similar vert designs. Multicoloured. Litho. P 14.

2081 25d. Type **527** ... 1·40 1·30
2082 50d. Flag and guns ... 2·75 2·75
MS2083 72×92 mm. 255d. As No. 2081. Imperf ... 10·00 10·00

2000 (21 Aug). Birds. T **528** and similar horiz designs. Multicoloured. Litho. P 14.

2084 25d. Type **528** 85 85
2085 50d. House Sparrow (*Passer domesticus*) 1·90 1·80
2086 100d. Purple Swamphen (*Porphyrio porphyrio*) 5·50 5·25
2084/2086 *Set of 3* 7·50 7·00
MS2087 92×71 mm. 500d. Goldfinch (*Carduelis carduelis*). Imperf 19·00 18·00

529 Emblem

530 Flag, President Hussain and Voting Cards

2000 (30 Sept). 430th Birth Anniversary of Mohammed. T **529** and similar vert design. Multicoloured. Litho. P 14.

2088 25d. Type **529** 1·50 1·50
2089 50d. Emblem (*different*) 3·00 2·75

2000 (15 Oct). Fifth Anniversary of Referendum. T **530** and similar multicoloured designs. Litho. P 14.

2090 25d. Type **530** 70 65
2091 50d. President Hussain wearing uniform (*horiz*) 1·50 1·50
MS2092 93×72 mm. 250d. President Hussain wearing traditional clothes. Imperf 10·00 10·00

531 Emblem

532 Woman carrying Child

2000 (23 Nov). 1200th Anniversary of Bayt al-Hikmah. T **531** and similar vert design. Litho. P 14.

2093 **531** 50d. multicoloured 1·00 1·00
2094 100d. multicoloured 2·00 2·00

2001 (13 Feb). Tenth Anniversary of Al-Amiriyah. T **532** and similar vert designs. Multicoloured. Litho. P 14.

2095 25d. Type **532** 85 85
2096 50d. National Colours and Doves 1·70 1·70
MS2097 93×71 mm. 250d. As No. 2095. Imperf 7·25 7·00

533 Inscribed Tablet and Statuette

534 Arabic Script as Torch Flame and Crowd

2001 (20 Mar). 5000th Anniversary of Writing in Mesopotamia. T **533** and similar vert designs. Multicoloured. Litho. P 14.

2098 25d. Type **533** 50 50
2099 50d. Sumerian script and figures 1·00 1·00
2100 75d. As No. 2098 1·50 1·50
2101 100d. As No. 2099 1·90 1·80
2102 150d. Figure wearing skirt (statue) 3·00 3·00
2103 250d. As No. 2102 4·75 4·50
2098/2103 *Set of 6* 11·50 11·00

2001 (7 Apr). 54th Anniversary of Al Baath Party. T **534** and similar horiz designs. Multicoloured. Litho. P 14.

2104 25d. Type **534** 70 65
2105 50d. Michael Aflaq (founder) and President Hussain 1·00 1·00
2106 100d. Map of Arab states 2·00 2·00
2104/2106 *Set of 3* 3·25 3·25

535 President Hussain

536 President Hussain

2001 (17 Apr). 13th Anniversary of Cessation of Hostilities. T **535** and similar multicoloured design. Litho. P 14.

2107 25d. Type **535** 70 65
2108 100d. President Hussain, soldier and map (*horiz*) 2·00 2·00

(Litho)

2001 (28 Apr). 64th Birthday of President Hussain. T **536** and similar multicoloured designs. P 14.

2109 25d. Type **536** 35 35
2110 50d. Wearing dark suit (*horiz*) 70 65
2111 100d. Seated with children (*horiz*) 1·40 1·30
2109/2111 *Set of 3* 2·20 2·10
MS2112 90×69 mm. 250d. With children carrying flowers. Imperf 8·50 8·25

537 *Barbus sharpeyi*

538 Gazelle (*Gazella subgutturosa*)

2001 (3 Aug). Fish. T **537** and similar horiz designs. Multicoloured. Litho. P 14.

2113 25d. Type **537** 55 50
2114 50d. *Barbus esocinus* 1·10 1·00
2115 100d. *Barbus xanthopterus* 2·20 2·00
2116 150d. *Pampus argenteus* 3·50 3·25
2113/2116 *Set of 4* 6·50 6·00

2001 (3 Aug). Fauna. T **538** and similar multicoloured designs. Litho. P 14.

2117 100d. Type **538** 1·40 1·30
2118 250d. Hare (*Lepus europaeus*) (*vert*) 3·50 3·25
2119 500d. Dromedary (*Camelus dromedaries*) 7·25 6·50
2117/2119 *Set of 3* 11·00 10·00
MS2120 92×70 mm. 1000d. Horse, Gazelle, Sheep and Camel. Imperf 15·00 14·00

539 Hawk and Flags

540 National Colours joining Maps of Palestine and Iraq

2001 (4 Aug). Tenth Anniversary of Um Al Marik. T **539** and similar vert design. Litho. P 14.

2121 **539** 25d. multicoloured 35 35
2122 100d. multicoloured 2·00 1·80

2001 (3 Sept). Al Asqa Intifada. T **540** and similar multicoloured designs. Litho. P 14.

2123 25d. Type **540** 70 65
2124 25d. Dome of the Rock, flag and man carrying gun (*vert*) 70 65

2125 50d. Dome of the Rock, leaves and man with raised arms (*vert*) 1·30 1·20
2123/2125 *Set of 3* 2·40 2·30
MS2126 Two sheets, each 89×67 mm. (a) 250d. Mohammed Dorra and father; (b) 250d. Tank and protester. Imperf 11·00 10·00

541 Drilling Rig and Workers

542 World Map and Footballers

2001 (16 Sept). 29th Anniversary of Nationalisation of Oil Industry. T **541** and similar vert design. Multicoloured. Litho. P 14.
2127 25d. Type **541** 70 65
2128 50d. Flaming tower, processing plant and oil 1·30 1·20

2001 (7 Oct). Under 20 Junior World Cup Football Championship, Argentina. T **542** and similar multicoloured design. Litho. P 14.
2129 25d. Type **542** 70 65
2130 50d. Player and trophy (*vert*) 1·30 1·20

543 Sick Child

544 Soldiers and Flag

2001 (26 Nov). Tenth Anniversary of Gulf War. T **543** and similar multicoloured designs. Litho. P 14.
2131 25d. Type **543** 1·80 1·70
2132 25d. Woman and children 1·80 1·70
2133 50d. Flag and family (*horiz*) 3·50 3·25
2131/2133 *Set of 3* 6·50 6·00
MS2134 70×92 mm. 250d. As No. 2131. Imperf 12·50 11·50

2002 (6 Jan). Army Day. T **544** and similar multicoloured designs. Litho. P 14.
2135 25d. Type **544** 1·10 1·00
2136 50d. Statue of soldiers (*vert*) 2·20 2·00
2137 100d. Soldier (*vert*) 4·25 4·00
2135/2137 *Set of 3* 6·75 6·25
MS2138 70×90 mm. 250d. As No. 2115 Imperf 7·50 7·00

545 Aircraft, Flames and Girl

546 President Hussain

2002 (16 Jan). 11th Anniversary of Gulf War. Litho. P 14.
2139 **545** 100d. multicoloured 3·50 3·25

2002 (20 Jan). Jerusalem Day. T **546** and similar vert designs. Litho. P 14.
2140 **546** 25d. multicoloured 70 65
2141 50d. multicoloured 1·10 1·00
2142 100d. multicoloured 2·20 2·00
2140/2142 *Set of 3* 3·50 3·25

547 Flags and Fist

548 Aircraft Sights

2002 (8 Feb). 39th Anniversary of 8 February 1963. T **547** and similar multicoloured designs. Litho. P 14.
2143 50d. Type **547** 1·10 1·00
2144 100d. Sumerians, Saladin and modern crowd (*horiz*) 2·20 2·00

2002 (13 Feb). 11th Anniversary of Al-Amiriyah. Litho. P 14.
2145 **548** 25d. multicoloured 70 65
2146 50d. multicoloured 1·10 1·00

549 Orange Roses

550 Web and Mosques

2002 (21 Mar). Flowers. T **549** and similar vert designs. Litho. P 14.
2147 25d. Type **549** 70 65
2148 50d. Pink and red Roses 1·10 1·00
2149 150d. Carnations, Anemone and Narcissi 3·50 3·25
2147/2149 *Set of 3* 4·75 4·50
MS2150 73×91 mm. 250d. Bouquet. Imperf 8·00 7·50

2002 (11 Apr). Hajeer New Year. T **550** and similar multicoloured designs. Litho. P 14.
2151 25d. Type **550** 70 65
2152 50d. Crescent moon and mosque (*vert*) 1·10 1·00
2153 75d. Web and Doves 1·60 1·50
2151/2153 *Set of 3* 3·00 2·75

551 Envelope

552 President Hussain as Boy

2002 (22 Apr). Post Day. T **551** and similar horiz design. Multicoloured. Litho. P 14.
2154 50d. Type **551** 1·30 1·20
2155 100d. Aircraft, ship and train 2·50 2·30
MS2156 70×91 mm. 250d. Envelope and globe. Imperf 11·00 10·00

2002 (28 Apr). 65th Birth Anniversary of President Hussain. T **552** and similar vert designs. Multicoloured. Litho. P 14.
2157 25d. Type **552** 55 50
2158 50d. As young man 90 85
2159 75d. With flag at left 1·40 1·30
2160 100d. With flag at right 1·80 1·70
2157/2160 *Set of 4* 4·25 4·00
MS2161 Two sheets, each 74×91 mm. (a) 250d. Wearing traditional clothes; (b) 250d. Surrounded by flowers. Imperf 13·00 12·00

553 Trophy and Player

554 Soldier, Child and Woman

2002 (30 May). World Cup Football Championship, Japan and South Korea. T **553** and similar vert designs. Multicoloured. Litho. P 14.

2162 50d. Type **553** ... 1·10 1·00
2163 100d. Player chasing ball ... 2·20 2·00
2164 150d. Player kicking ball ... 3·50 3·25
2162/2164 *Set of* 3 ... 6·00 5·75
MS2165 69×91 mm. 250d. Championship emblem and trophy enclosing players. Imperf ... 8·25 7·50

2002 (5 June). Second Anniversary of Al Asqa Intifada. Litho. P 14.

2166 **554** 5000d. multicoloured ... 55·00 50·00

555 Sheikh Maruf Mosque

556 Stylised Eagle, Flag and President Hussain

2002 (10 June). Mosques. T **555** and similar vert designs. Multicoloured. Litho. P 14.

2167 25d. Type **555** ... 70 65
2168 50d. Al- Mouiz ... 1·30 1·20
2169 75d. Um Al Marik ... 2·00 1·80
2167/2169 *Set of* 3 ... 3·50 3·25

2002 (8 Aug). Victory Day. Litho. P 14.

2170 **556** 25d. multicoloured ... 70 65
2171 50d. multicoloured ... 1·10 1·00
MS2172 70×91 mm. 150d. Eagle's head. Imperf ... 7·25 6·50

557 Reed Boats and Guffa

558 Jameel Sidqi Al-Zahawi

2002 (10 Sept). Traditional Watercraft. T **557** and similar horiz designs. Multicoloured. Litho. P 14.

2173 150d. Type **557** ... 3·50 3·25
2174 250d. Galley ... 5·75 5·25
2175 500d. Sail boat ... 11·50 10·50
2173/2175 *Set of* 3 ... 19·00 17·00

2002 (15 Oct). Writers. T **558** and similar vert designs. Multicoloured. Litho. P 14.

2176 25d. Type **558** ... 55 50
2177 50d. Abdul Musin Al-Qadumi ... 90 85
2178 75d. Badr Shaker Al-Sayab ... 1·40 1·30
2179 100d. Ma'rouf Al-Rasafi ... 1·80 1·70
2176/2179 *Set of* 4 ... 4·25 4·00
MS2180 71×91 mm. 150d. Badr Shaker Al-Sayab and rose. Imperf ... 7·25 6·50

559 Hands holding Flowers and President Hussain

560 Woman Spinning

2002 (15 Oct). Referendum. T **559** and similar vert designs. Multicoloured. Litho. P 14.

2181 100d. Type **559** ... 2·20 2·00
2182 150d. Fist and ballot box ... 3·50 3·25
MS2183 70×92 mm. 250d. As No. 2181. Imperf ... 5·75 5·25

2002 (15 Nov). Baghdad Day. T **560** and similar multicoloured designs. Litho. P 14.

2184 25d. Type **560** ... 70 65
2185 50d. Street performer and children ... 1·10 1·00
2186 75d. Two women talking (*horiz*) ... 1·60 1·50
2184/2186 *Set of* 3 ... 3·00 2·75
MS2187 91×71 mm. 250d. Musicians. Imperf ... 11·00 10·00

561 *Oryx leucoryx*

2003 (10 Jan). Fauna. T **561** and similar multicoloured designs. Litho. P 14.

2188 25d. Type **561** ... 1·10 1·00
2189 50d. *Acinonyx jubatus* (*vert*) ... 1·40 1·30
2190 75d. *Panthera leo* (*vert*) ... 2·75 2·50
2191 100d. *Castor fiber* ... 3·25 3·00
2192 150d. *Equus hemionus* ... 5·00 4·50
2188/2192 *Set of* 5 ... 12·00 11·00
MS2193 69×93 mm. 250d. As No. 2188. Imperf ... 12·50 11·50

562 Emblem

2003 (5 Feb). Tenth Anniversary of Saddam University. T **562** and similar horiz design. Litho. P 14.

2194 **562** 50d. multicoloured ... 1·10 1·00
2195 100d. multicoloured ... 2·20 2·00

NOTE. 13 stamps issued by the Saddam Hussein regime with overprints and surcharges reading **Iraq/In Coalition/Occupation** were declared illegal by the Iraqi Coalition Provisional Authority.

563 Guffa

2004 (15 Jan). Transportation. T **563** and similar horiz designs. Multicoloured. P 14.

2196 50d. Type **563** ... 90 85
2197 100d. Horse-drawn cab ... 1·20 1·10
2198 250d. Tram ... 1·80 1·70
2199 500d. Skiff carrying reeds ... 3·25 3·00
2200 5000d. Camel train ... 27·00 25·00
a. Imperf ... 27·00 25·00
2196/2200 *Set of* 5 ... 31·00 28·00

564 Woman and Flowers

565 Women and Map

(Des Saadgh)

2006 (16 Mar). New Year. P 13½.

2201	**564** 250d. multicoloured	3·00	2·75

(Des Atheer (100d.) or Farooq Hassan (250d.))

2006 (7 Sept). Installation of Interim Government–30 June 2004. T **565** and similar vert design. Multicoloured. Phosphor markings. P 14½.

2202	100d. Type **565**	1·20	1·10
2203	250d. Map and hands enclosing sun	3·00	2·75

566 Bust wearing Headdress

567 Football

(Des Farooq Hassan (**MS**2207) or Atheer (others))

2006 (11 Sept). Iraqi Civilisation. T **566** and similar multicoloured designs. Phosphor markings. P 14.

2204	100d. Type **566**	1·20	1·10
2205	150d. Golden bull	1·80	1·70
2206	200d. Carved bull with human head	2·40	2·20
2204/2206	*Set of* 3	4·75	4·50
MS2207	80×61 mm. 250d. Tiled mosaic animals Imperf	6·00	5·50

(Des Farooq Hassan (**MS**2210) or Dhargham Al Jasim (others))

2006 (24 Sept). Olympic Games, Athens (2004). T **567** and similar designs. Multicoloured. Phosphor markings. P 14.

2208	100d. Type **567**	1·20	1·10
2209	150d. Athletics	1·80	1·70
MS2210	100×70 mm. 500d. Sportsmen Imperf	6·25	6·00

568 *Two Women* (Akram Shukri)

569 *Anemone* sp.

(Des Atheer (**MS**2214) or Dhargham Al Jasim (others))

2006 (9 Oct). Paintings. T **568** and similar horiz designs. Multicoloured. Phosphor markings. P 14½.

2211	100d. Type **568**	1·20	1·10
2212	150d. *Abstract* (Hafidh Al Duroubi)	1·80	1·70
2213	200d. *Horseman* (Faiq Hassan)	2·40	2·20
2211/2213	*Set of* 3	4·75	4·50
MS2214	88×70 mm. 250d. *Abstract* (*different*) Imperf	3·25	3·00

2007. Flowers. T **569** and similar vert designs. Multicoloured. Self-adhesive. Die-cut.

2215	250d. Type **569**	3·00	2·75
2216	750d. *Viola mamola*	9·00	8·50
2217	1000d. *Atropa belladonna*	13·00	12·00
2215/2217	*Set of* 3	23·00	21·00
MS2218	88×70 mm. Nos. 2215/2217	26·00	24·00

570 *Papilio demodocus*

572 Rug Maker

2007 (23 Apr). Butterflies. T **570** and similar horiz designs. Multicoloured. P 14½×14.

2219	100d. Type **570**	1·20	1·10
2220	250d. Inscr 'Precis orithua'	3·00	2·75
2221	500d. Inscr 'Ciotas croceus'	6·00	5·50
2219/2221	*Set of* 3	9·25	8·50
MS2222	81×60 mm. 1000d. *Papilio demodocus* (*different*)	13·50	12·50

2007 (23 Apr). Folklore. Vert designs showing folklore traditions. Litho. P 13.

2223	500d. Singers wearing traditional dress	36·00	28·00

T **571** is unavailable.

2007 (22 May). Artisans. T **572** and similar vert designs. Multicoloured. Self-adhesive. Die-cut.

2224	250d. Type **572**	3·00	2·75
2225	350d. Blanket maker	4·25	4·00
2226	500d. Basket maker	6·00	5·50
2224/2226	*Set of* 3	12·00	11·00
MS2227	106×60 mm. Nos. 2224/2226	14·50	13·50

573 Women and Children (*Illustration reduced. Actual size* 111×80 *mm*)

2007 (7 June). Folklore. Sheet 111×80 mm. Imperf.

MS2228	**573** 1000d. multicoloured	13·50	12·50

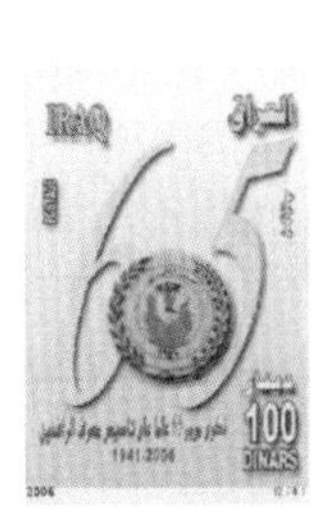
574 Anniversary Emblem

575 Ducks

2007 (10 July). 65th Anniversary (2006) of Rafidain Bank. P 14.

2229	**574** 100d. multicoloured	1·20	1·10
2230	150d. multicoloured	1·80	1·70
2231	250d. multicoloured	3·00	2·75
2232	500d. multicoloured	6·00	5·50
2229/2232	*Set of* 4	11·00	10·00

2007 (Sept). Birds. T **575** and similar horiz designs. Multicoloured. P 14.

2233	150d. *Anser anser* (Greylag Goose)	1·80	1·70
2234	250d. *Merops superciliosus* (Olive Bee-eater)	3·00	2·75
2235	500d. *Pterocles alchata* (Pin-tailed Sandgrouse)	6·00	5·50
2233/2235	*Set of 3*	9·75	9·00
MS2236	80×83 mm. 1500d. Type **575**. Imperf	20·00	18·00

576 Mohammad Al-Qubanchi (singer)

2007 (1 Oct). Theatre Personalities. T **576** and similar multicoloured designs. Self-adhesive. Die-cut.

(a) Size 30×40 mm

2237	250d. Type **576**	3·00	2·75
2238	500d. Haqi Al Shibly (theatre manager) (*horiz*)	6·00	5·50
2239	750d. Nadhum Al Ghazali (singer) (*horiz*)	9·00	8·50
2240	1000d. Munir Bashir (musician) (*horiz*)	13·00	12·00
2237/2240	*Set of 4*	28·00	26·00

(b) Size 30×42 mm

2241	250d. Type **576**	3·00	2·75
	a. Vert strip of 4. Nos. 2237/2240		
	b. With vertical black border		
	ba. Vert strip of 4. Nos. 2241b/2244b		
	bb. Sheetlet of 12. Nos. 2241b/2244b, each×3		
2242	500d. As No. 2238 (*horiz*)	6·00	5·50
	b. With vertical black border		
2243	700d. As No. 2239 (*horiz*)	9·00	8·50
	b. With vertical black border		
2244	1000d. As No. 2240 (*horiz*)	13·00	12·00
	b. With vertical black border		
2241/2244	*Set of 4*	28·00	26·00

Nos. 2241/2244 and Nos. 2241b/2244b were printed, *se-tenant*, in vertical strips of four stamps.

Nos. 2241 and 2241b are laid at right angles giving the appearance of a strip of four horiz stamps.

577 Clasped Hands, Girl holding Map and Ship

2008 (27 Oct). National Reconciliation. T **577** and similar horiz designs. Multicoloured. P 14.

2245	250d. Type **577**	3·00	2·75
2246	500d. Symbols of conflict (40×40 *mm*)	6·00	5·50
2247	750d. Child holding rifle (40×40 *mm*)	9·00	8·50
2245/2247	*Set of 3*	16·00	15·00

578 Flags Intertwined

2008 (28 Oct). 50th Anniversary of Iraq–China Diplomatic Relations. P 12.

2248	**578** 500d. multicoloured	6·00	5·50

No. 2249 is vacant.

579 Buraq and Statue

2008 (24 Nov). Wasit Poetry Competition. P 13½.

2250	**579** 5000d. multicoloured	33·00	31·00

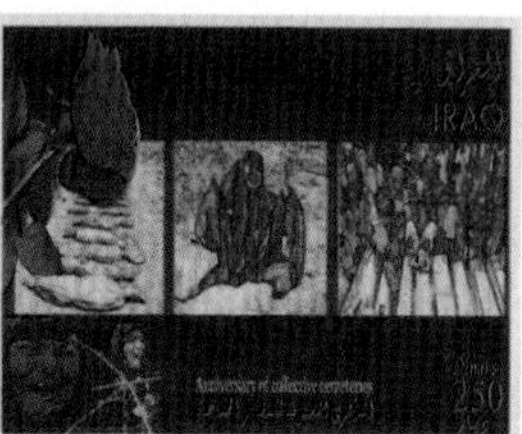

580 Graves and grieving Woman

2008 (14 Dec). Collective Cemeteries. T **580** and similar horiz design. Multicoloured. P 13½.

2251	250d. Type **580**	3·00	2·75
2252	500d. Bones	6·00	5·50

581 Gateway, Female and Animal Statues

582 Cooling Towers, Crayfish, Geese and Trees

2009 (17 Mar). Campaign to Regain Iraqi Antiques. T **581** and similar horiz designs. Multicoloured. P 13½.

2253	250d. Type **581**	3·00	2·75
2254	500d. Gateway, two statues and head	6·00	5·50
2255	750d. Gateway, head and plaque	9·00	8·50
2253/2255	*Set of 3*	16·00	15·00

It is reported that an imperforate miniature sheet, value 1000d. (Baghdad at Night), two perforated stamps value 250d., 1000d. (Calligraphy) and an imperforated miniature sheet, value 1500d. (Calligraphy), were printed but not issued due to poor printing quality.

2009 (29 Mar). Environmental Protection. P 13×13½.

2256	**582** 1000d. multicoloured	13·00	12·00

583 Boats and Wildfowl

584 Couple

2009 (22 Apr). International Campaign to Reclaim Marshes. P 13½.

2257	**583** 10000d. multicoloured	£100	95·00

2009 (1 June). International Children's Day. Children's Paintings. T **584** and similar multicoloured designs. P 13½.

2258	50d. Type **584**	60	55
2259	50d. Two girls	60	55
2260	50d. Family	60	55
2261	50d. Mother and daughter	60	55
2262	50d. Three girls	60	55
2258/2262	*Set of 5*	2·75	2·50
MS2263	80×60 mm. 500d. Mother cradling baby. Imperf	6·25	6·00

585 Emblem and Goalkeeper

2009 (13 June). FIFA Confederations Cup, South Africa. T **585** and similar multicoloured designs. P 13½.

2264	100d. Type **585**	1·20	1·10
2265	250d. Emblem and player	3·00	2·75
2266	500d. Emblem and player with leg extended	6·00	5·50
2264/2266	*Set of* 3	9·25	8·50
MS2267	80×80 mm. 750d. Emblem	9·75	9·00

586 Musicians and Seated Men

2009 (14 July). Tourism Week. T **586** and similar horiz designs. Multicoloured. P 13½.

2268	250d. Type **586**	3·00	2·75
	a. Horiz pair. Nos. 2268/2269	6·25	5·75
2269	250d. Market, draughtsman and apothecary	3·00	2·75
2270	250d. Women	3·00	2·75
	a. Horiz pair. Nos. 2270/2271	6·25	5·75
2271	250d. Men working	3·00	2·75
2268/2271	*Set of* 4	11·00	10·00
MS2272	90×60 mm. 500d. Horsemen. Imperf	6·25	6·00

Nos. 2268/2269 and 2270/2271, respectively, were printed, *se-tenant*, in horizontal pairs within the sheet, each pair forming a composite design.

587 Emblem

588 Ammo Baba

2009 (14 July). al-Quds–2009 Capital of Arab Culture. T **587** and similar vert design. Multicoloured. P 13½.

2273	250d. Type **587**	3·00	2·75
MS2274	60×80 mm. 750d. As Type **587**. Imperf	9·75	9·00

2009 (30 Dec). Emmanuel Baba Dawud (Ammo Baba) (football coach) Commemoration. T **588** and similar horiz design. Multicoloured. P 13.

2275	250d. Type **588**	3·00	2·75
2276	500d. As older man	6·00	5·50

589 Steam Locomotive

589a Stylised Figures and Palm Tree

2010 (25 Jan). National Railways. T **589** and similar multicoloured designs. P 14.

2277	250d. Type **589**	3·00	2·75
2278	500d. Diesel locomotive	6·00	5·50
2279	750d. Green steam locomotive	9·00	8·50
2277/2279	*Set of* 3	16·00	15·00
MS2280	80×80 mm. 1000d. Locomotive Baghdad Train Station. Imperf	13·50	12·50

2010 (7 Mar). Elections. P 13½.

2280*a*	**589a** 250d. multicoloured	3·00	2·75
2280*b*	500d. multicoloured	6·00	5·50
2280*c*	1000d. multicoloured	13·00	12·00
2280*a*/2280*c*	*Set of* 3	20·00	18·00

590 Girl Scouts

591 Envelope and Letterbox

2010 (23 Mar). Arabian Brotherhood Scout Day. T **590** and similar horiz designs. Multicoloured. P 13½.

2281	250d. Type **590**	3·00	2·75
2282	250d. Boy bugler	3·00	2·75
2283	250d. Girls on parade	3·00	2·75
2284	250d. Boys saluting flag	3·00	2·75
2281/2284	*Set of* 4	11·00	10·00
MS2285	80×60 mm. 1000d. Parading scouts enclosed in knot. Imperf	13·50	12·50

2010 (27 Apr). Post Day. T **591** and similar vert design. Multicoloured. P 13½.

2286	250d. Type **591**	3·00	2·75
2287	500d. Envelope and Dove	6·00	5·50

592 Pterodactyls

2010 (28 June). Pre-Historic Animals. T **592** and similar horiz designs. Multicoloured. P 13½.

2288	250d. Type **592**	3·00	2·75
	a. Block of 8. Nos. 2288/2295	25·00	
2289	250d. Pterodactyls and trees	3·00	2·75
2290	250d. Archaeopteryx, flight-less Birds and Brachiosaurus	3·00	2·75
2291	250d. Tyranosaurus Rex, Iguanadon and Archaeopteryx in flight	3·00	2·75
2292	250d. Albertosaurus and Stegosaurus	3·00	2·75
2293	250d. Stegosaurus, Brontosaurus and Ankylosaurus	3·00	2·75
2294	250d. Ankylosaurus and early Crocodiles	3·00	2·75
2295	250d. Spinosaurus	3·00	2·75
2288/2295	*Set of* 8	22·00	20·00
MS2296	Two sheets, each 104×78 mm. 500d. Deinonychus; 500d. Dinosaur. Imperf	13·50	12·50

Nos. 2288/2295 were printed, *se-tenant*, in blocks of eight stamps within the sheet, each block forming a composite design.

593 Throwing Ball

2010 (13 July). World Cup Football Championships, South Africa. T **593** and similar horiz designs. Multicoloured. P 13½.

2297	250d. Type **593**	3·00	2·75

2298 500d. Player celebrating 6·00 5·50
2299 750d. Player wearing green shorts and ball 9·00 8·50
2300 1000d. Player wearing red shorts and ball 13·00 12·00
2297/2300 *Set of 4* 28·00 26·00
MS2301 125×70 mm. 1000d. Emblem and players. Imperf 13·50 12·50

594 Koran

2010 (11 Aug). National Campaign for the Koran. T **594** and similar horiz design. Multicoloured. P 13½.
2302 250d. Type **594** 3·00 2·75
MS2303 90×70 mm. 500d. Koran (*different*). Imperf 6·25 6·00

595 Young Couple

596 Anniversary Emblem and Symbols of Iraq

2010 (8 Sept). United Nations International Year of Youth. T **595** and similar vert design. Multicoloured. P 13½.
2304 250d. Type **595** 3·00 2·75
2305 250d. Two faces in profile and hand holding candle 3·00 2·75

2010 (14 Sept). 50th Anniversary of Organisation of Petroleum Exporting Countries (OPEC). T **596** and similar vert design. Multicoloured. P 13½.
2306 250d. Type **596** 3·00 2·75
2307 500d. Ishtar Gate, Samorra Mosque, Al-Najaf and Shedu (human-headed winged Bull) 6·00 5·50

597 Kirkuk Citadel

2010 (4 Oct). Kirkuk–Iraqi City of Culture. P 13½.
2308 **597** 1000d. multicoloured 13·00 12·00

598 Child holding Adult's Hand

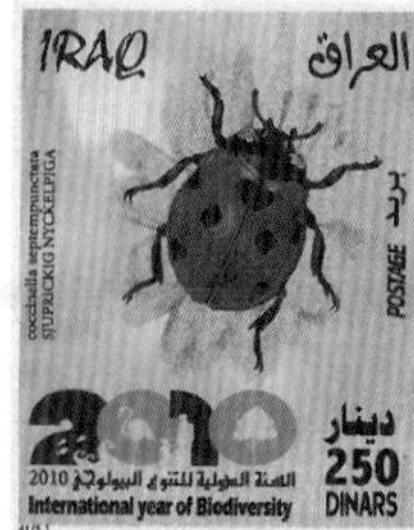

599 *Coccinella septempunctata* (Ladybird)

2010 (20 Oct). United Nations Convention on the Rights of the Child. T **598** and similar vert designs. Multicoloured. P 13½.
2309 500d. Type **598** 6·00 5·50
2310 750d. Boy writing on blackboard 9·00 8·50
2311 1000d. Children on carousel 13·00 12·00
2309/2311 *Set of 3* 25·00 23·00

2011 (11 Jan). International Year of Biodiversity. T **599** and similar multicoloured designs. P 13½.
2312 250d. Type **599** 3·00 2·75
2313 500d. *Egretta alba* (Great Egret) (inscr 'Great White Heron') 6·00 5·50
2314 750d. Persian Gazelle (*horiz*) 9·00 8·50
2315 1000d. *Ophisops elegans* (Snake-eyed Lizard) (*horiz*) 13·00 12·00
2312/2315 *Set of 4* 28·00 26·00
MS2316 151×75 mm. 1000d. Ducks (108×25 *mm*). Imperf 13·50 12·50

No. 2317 is vacant.

600 Goalkeeper and Ball

2011 (27 Jan). Asia Cup Football Championships, Qatar. T **600** and similar multicoloured designs. P 13.
2318 250d. Type **600** 3·00 2·75
2319 500d. Player and ball facing left 6·00 5·50
2320 750d. Player and ball facing right 9·00 8·50
2321 1000d. Player with right knee raised and ball 13·00 12·00
2318/2321 *Set of 4* 28·00 26·00
MS2322 60×60 mm. 1000d. Two players and central emblem. Imperf 13·50 12·50

601 *Metapenaeus affinis*

2011 (13 Feb). Biodiversity of Shatt al Arab and Northern Gulf. T **601** and similar horiz designs. Multicoloured. P 13½.
2323 250d. Type **601** 3·00 2·75
2324 500d. *Torpedo panthera* 6·00 5·50
2325 750d. *Eupagurus prideaux* (inscr 'Eupagurus prideauxl') 9·00 8·50
2326 1000d. Carp 13·00 12·00
2323/2326 *Set of 4* 28·00 26·00
MS2327 80×60 mm. 1000d. Lionfish. Imperf 13·50 12·50

602 Child, Seedling and Desert

603 Lungs, Diseased and Healthy Tissue

2011 (19 Apr). National Day to Control Desertification. T **602** and similar horiz design. Multicoloured. P 13½.

2328 750d. Type **602** .... 9·00 8·50
2329 1000d. Hands holding seedling and desert .... 13·00 12·00

2011 (21 June). International Day of TB Awareness. P 13½.

2330 **603** 250d. multicoloured .... 3·00 2·75
2331 500d. multicoloured .... 6·00 5·50

604 Babylon

605 Abd al-Wahhab Al-Bayati

2011 (29 June). Archaeology. T **604** and similar multicoloured designs. P 13½.

2332 250d. Type **604** .... 3·00 2·75
2333 500d. Hatra .... 6·00 5·50
2334 750d. Ziggurat of Ur .... 9·00 8·50
2335 1000d. Nineveh .... 13·00 12·00
2332/2335 *Set of 4* .... 28·00 26·00
MS2336 60×80 mm. 1000d. Spiral Minaret. Imperf .... 13·50 12·50

2011 (7 July). Personalities. Poets. T **605** and similar vert designs. Multicoloured. P 13½.

2337 250d. Type **605** .... 3·00 2·75
2338 500d. Muhammad Mahdi Al-Jawahiri .... 6·00 5·50
2339 750d. Nazik Al-Malaika .... 9·00 8·50
2337/2339 *Set of 3* .... 16·00 15·00

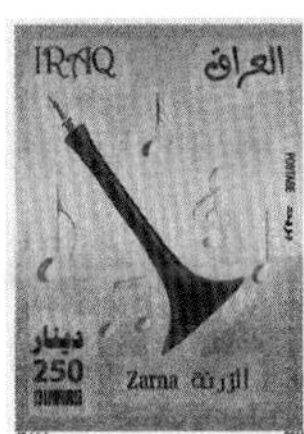

606 Zarna

607 Black Horse

(Litho)

2011 (30 July). Musical Instruments. T **606** and similar vert designs. Multicoloured. P 13½×13.

2340 250d. Type **606** .... 1·80 1·40
2341 500d. Rababa .... 3·50 2·75
2342 750d. Ud .... 5·50 4·25
2343 1000d. Qanun .... 7·25 5·50
2340/2343 *Set of 4* .... 16·00 12·50

(Litho)

2011 (2 Oct). Arab Horses. T **607** and similar horiz designs showing horses. Multicoloured. P 13×13½.

2344 250d. Type **607** .... 1·80 1·50
2345 500d. Grey .... 3·50 3·00
2346 750d. Grey, cantering and head of Chestnut .. 5·25 4·50
2347 1000d. Grey leaping .... 7·00 6·00
2344/2347 *Set of 4* .... 16·00 13·50
MS2348 105×85 mm. 1000d. Five horses. Imperf .... 7·25 6·25

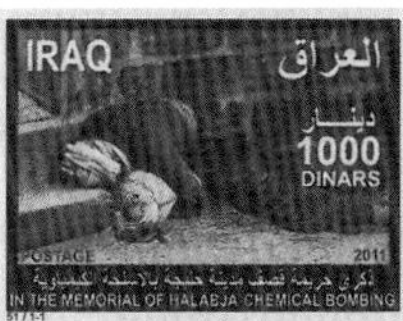

608 Mother and Child

609 Couple wearing Traditional Dress

(Litho)

2011 (1 Nov). Victims of Chemical Attack at Halabja Commemoration. P 13×13½.

2349 **608** 1000d. multicoloured .... 7·00 6·00

(Litho)

2011 (8 Nov). Traditional Iraqi Costumes. T **609** and similar multicoloured designs showing couples wearing traditional dress, womans clothing given. P 13½×13.

2350 500d. Type **609** .... 3·50 3·00
2351 500d. Woman wearing dark patterned dress and black cloak .... 3·50 3·00
2352 500d. Woman wearing purple patterned dress .... 3·50 3·00
2353 500d. Woman wearing outfit including orange tabard .... 3·50 3·00
2354 500d. Woman wearing patterned skirt, black top and green coat .... 3·50 3·00
2350/2354 *Set of 5* .... 16·00 13·50
MS2355 80×80 mm. 500d. Headdresses. Imperf .... 3·75 3·25

610 Emblem

611 Eurasian Reed Warbler (*Acrocephalus scirpaceus*)

(Litho)

2011 (25 Nov). Stamp Day. 60th Anniversary of Iraq Philatelic Society. T **610** and similar multicoloured design. P 13½.

2356 250d. Type **610** .... 1·80 1·50
2357 500d. Coins and stamps (*horiz*) .... 3·50 3·00

(Litho)

2011 (12 Dec). 40th Anniversary of Ramsar Convention. Birds. T **611** and similar multicoloured designs. P 13½.

2358 500d. Type **611** .... 3·50 3·00
2359 750d. *Acrocephalus scirpaceus* (*different*) .... 5·25 4·50
2360 1000d. *Acrocephalus griseldis* (Basra Reed Warbler) (*vert*) .... 7·00 6·00
2358/2360 *Set of 3* .... 14·00 12·00

612 Couple and Symbols of AIDS Campaign

(Litho)

2012 (2 Jan). 30th Anniversary of Fight against AIDS. P 13½.
2361 **612** 10000d. multicoloured .... 70·00 60·00

613 Camels leading Prisoners in Chains

(Litho and gold foil)

2012 (14 Jan). Revolution of Imam Hussain. T **613** and similar horiz designs. Multicoloured. P 13½.
2362 250d. Type **613** .... 1·80 1·50
a. Horiz strip of 4. Nos. 2362/2365 .... 19·00
2363 500d. Imam Hussain's Horse (Murtajiz/Zuljana) .... 3·50 3·00
2364 750d. Trampling Imam Hussain's body .... 5·25 4·50
2365 1000d. Vision of Imam Hussain riding Murtajiz .... 7·00 6·00
2362/2365 *Set of* 4 .... 16·00 13·50
MS2366 103×85 mm. 1000d. Dome of Imam Hussain, Karbala. Imperf .... 7·25 6·25

Nos. 2362/2365 were printed, *se-tenant*, in horizontal strips of four stamps within the sheet, each strips forming a composite design.

614 Protesters, Coffins and Women

615 Emblem

(Litho)

2012 (4 Mar). Martyrs' Day. T **614** and similar vert design. Multicoloured. P 13×13½.
2367 750d. Type **614** .... 5·25 4·50
2368 1000d. Coffins, screaming face and emblem .... 7·00 6·00

(Litho)

2012 (3 May). Arab Summit Conference, Baghdad. P 13½×13.
2369 **615** 250d. multicoloured .... 1·80 1·50
2370 500d. multicoloured .... 3·50 3·00
2371 750d. multicoloured .... 5·25 4·50
2369/2371 *Set of* 3 .... 9·50 8·00

616 Sunflowers

617 Mosque

(Litho)

2012 (6 May). Flowers. T **616** and similar multicoloured designs.

(a) Ordinary gum. P 13.

2372 250d. Type **616** .... 1·80 1·50
2373 500d. Gardenias .... 3·50 3·00
2374 750d. Snap Dragons .... 5·25 4·50
2375 1000d. Carnations .... 7·00 6·00
2372/2375 *Set of* 4 .... 16·00 13·50

(b) Self-adhesive. Die-cut.

2376 250d. Zinnias .... 1·80 1·50
2377 500d. Anemones .... 3·50 3·00
2378 750d. Roses .... 5·25 4·50
2379 1000d. Chrysanthemums .... 7·00 6·00
2376/2379 *Set of* 4 .... 16·00 13·50

(c) Miniature sheet. 80×80 mm. Imperf.

MS2380 1000d. Mixed bouquet .... 7·25 6·25

(Litho)

2012 (16 June). Al-Kadhimiya Mosque. T **617** and similar horiz designs. Multicoloured. P 13½×13.
2381 250d. Type **617** .... 1·80 1·50
2382 250d. Tomb of Musa ibn Ja'far al-Kazim .... 1·80 1·50
2383 250d. As Type **617** but with arch and blue and gold background .... 1·80 1·50
2381/2383 *Set of* 3 .... 4·75 4·00
MS2384 100×70 mm. 500d. 'Al-Kadimiya the Holy Threshold'. Imperf .... 3·75 3·25

618 Refugees

(Litho)

2012 (21 June). Genocide of the Kurdish Faylee. T **618** and similar horiz design. Multicoloured. P 13½×13.
2385 750d. Type **618** .... 5·25 4·50
2386 1000d. Woman, children and tent .... 7·00 6·00

619 Symbols of Education and Culture

(Litho)

2012 (27 July). National Board of Education, Culture and Science. P 13½×13.
2387 **619** 5000d. multicoloured .... 35·00 30·00

620 Archer

(Litho)

2012 (12 Aug). Olympic Games, London. T **620** and similar horiz designs. Multicoloured. P 13×13½.
2388 250d. Type **620** .... 1·80 1·50
2389 500d. Gymnasts .... 3·50 3·00
2390 750d. Fencer .... 5·25 4·50
2391 1000d. Hurdlers .... 7·00 6·00
2388/2391 *Set of* 4 .... 16·00 13·50
MS2392 120×70 mm. 1000d. Stadium, mascots and female athlete throwing javelin. Imperf .... 7·25 6·25
MS2393 120×70 mm. 1000d. Athletes. Imperf .... 7·25 6·25

621 King Faisal II

(Litho)

2012 (1 Oct). Iraqi Kings. T **621** and similar horiz designs. Multicoloured. P 14½.

2394	500d. Type **621**	3·50	3·00
2395	750d. King Ghazi (1933–1939)	5·25	4·50
2396	1000d. King Faisal I (1921–1933)	7·00	6·00
2394/2396	*Set of* 3	14·00	12·00
MS2397	90×70 mm. 1000d. Iraqi Kings. Imperf	7·25	6·25

622 Kirkuk Castle

(Litho)

2012 (22 Nov). Kirkuk Castle. P 13½×13.

2398	**622**	500d. multicoloured	3·50	3·00

623 Dove and Map

624 Waterwheel

(Litho)

2012 (27 Nov). Arab Post Day. P 13×13½.

2399	**623**	250d. multicoloured	1·80	1·50

(Litho)

2012 (3 Dec). Noria Waterwheel. P 13×13½.

2400	**624**	10000d. multicoloured	70·00	60·00

625 Gyr Falcon

(Litho)

2012 (19 Dec). Falcons. T **625** and similar horiz designs. Multicoloured. P 13×13½.

2401	250d. Type **625**	1·80	1·50
2402	500d. Lanner Falcon (inscr 'Lamer')	3·50	3·00
2403	750d. Saker Falcon (inscr 'Cherrug')	5·25	4·50
2404	1000d. Peregrine Falcon (inscr 'Peregine')	7·00	6·00
2401/2404	*Set of* 4	16·00	13·50
MS2405	90×70 mm. 1000d. Falcon on wrist. Imperf	7·25	6·25

626 Striding Forward

(Litho)

2013 (6 Jan). First Anniversary of Evacuation of Coalition Forces. P 13½×13.

2406	**626**	250d. multicoloured	1·80	1·50
2407		1000d. multicoloured	7·00	6·00

627 Map and Ruins

(Des Ghaith Al-Makhzoomi. Litho)

2013 (28 Jan). Iraqi Landmarks. T **627** and similar multicoloured designs. P 13½.

2408	250d. Type **627**	1·80	1·50
2409	250d. As Type **627** but with Great Minaret, Samara Mosque and other sites	1·80	1·50
2410	250d. As Type **627** but with Blue Gateway, Babylon and other sites	1·80	1·50
2411	250d. As Type **627** but with other sites	1·80	1·50
2412	500d. Map and landmarks (*horiz*)	3·50	3·00
2413	750d. Kirkuk Castle, other landmarks and map (*horiz*)	5·25	4·50
2414	1000d. Central map surrounded by landmarks (*horiz*)	7·00	6·00
2408/2414	*Set of* 7	21·00	18·00
MS2415	100×80 mm. 1000d. Map and landmarks. Imperf	7·25	6·25

628 Mohammed Ghani Hikmat

629 Symbols of Modern Telecommunications

(Des Ali Al-Shekerchi. Litho)

2013 (23 Mar). Baghdad–Arab Capital of Culture. T **628** and similar multicoloured designs. P 13½×13.

2416	250d. Type **628** (sculptor)	1·80	1·50
2417	500d. Baheeja Al-Hakeem (artist)	3·50	3·00
2418	750d. Hashem Al-Khattat (calligrapher)	5·25	4·50
2419	1000d. Ali Alwardi (social scientist)	7·00	6·00
2416/2419	*Set of* 4	16·00	13·50
MS2420	60×60 mm. 1000d. 10th-century Bagdad. Imperf	7·25	6·25

(Des Ghaith Al-Makhzoomi. Litho)

2013 (17 May). World Telecommunication Day. T **629** and similar multicoloured design. P 13½.

2421	250d. Type **629**	1·80	1·50
2422	1000d. Globe of flags, satellites and receiver (*horiz*)	7·00	6·00

630 *Anthocharis cardamines*

631 Camels

(Des Ghaith Al-Makhzoomi. Litho)

2013 (4 Sept). Butterflies. T **630** and similar vert designs. Multicoloured. P 13½.

2423 200d. Type **630** ... 1·40 1·20
2424 250d. *Precis orithya* ... 1·80 1·50
2425 500d. *Ascia buneae sublineata* (inscr 'White Glider') ... 3·50 3·00
2426 750d. *Colias croceus* ... 5·25 4·50
2427 1000d. *Papilio machaon* ... 7·00 6·00
2428 5000d. *Vanessa atlanta* ... 35·00 30·00
2429 10000d. *Danaus chrysippus* ... 70·00 60·00
2423/2429 *Set of 7* ... £110 95·00

(Des Wathiq Mohammed and Ali Al-Shekerchi. Litho)

2013 (9 Sept). Camels. T **631** and similar multicoloured designs. P 13½.

2430 250d. Type **631** ... 1·80 1·50
2431 500d. Camel, facing right ... 3·50 3·00
2432 750d. Two Camels ... 5·25 4·50
2433 1000d. Four young Camels ... 7·00 6·00
2430/2433 *Set of 4* ... 16·00 13·50
MS2434 110×75 mm. 1000d. Two Camels with cloth covered saddles. Imperf ... 7·25 6·25
MS2435 110×75 mm. 1000d. Four Camels with saddles. Imperf ... 7·25 6·25

632 Clock Tower, 1930

633 Emblem

(Des Ali Al-Shekerchi. Litho)

2013 (13 Sept). Clock Towers. T **632** and similar vert designs. Multicoloured. P 13½×13.

2436 250d. Type **632** ... 1·80 1·50
2437 500d. Clock Tower, 1869 ... 3·50 3·00
2438 750d. Clock Tower, Railway Station, 1952 ... 5·25 4·50
2439 1000d. Clock Tower, Mūsá Al-Kāzim Shrine, 1882 ... 7·00 6·00
2436/2439 *Set of 4* ... 16·00 13·50

(Des Ali Al-Shekerchi. Litho)

2014 (9 Jan). Arabic Language Day. P 13×13½.

2440 **633** 500d. multicoloured ... 3·50 3·00
2441 1000d. multicoloured ... 7·00 6·00

634 Woman's Profile

635 Apricots

(Des Wathiq Mohammed. Litho)

2014 (9 Jan). Iraqi Women's Day. P 13×13½.

2442 **634** 1500d. multicoloured ... 10·50 9·00

(Des Ghaith Al-Makhzoomi. Litho)

2014 (26 Jan). Fruit. T **635** and similar vert designs. Multicoloured. P 13½×13.

2443 250d. Type **635** ... 1·80 1·50
2444 500d. Pomegranates ... 3·50 3·00
2445 750d. Figs ... 5·25 4·50
2446 1000d. Apples ... 7·00 6·00
2447 1000d. Grapes ... 7·00 6·00
2443/2447 *Set of 5* ... 22·00 19·00

636 Rolls-Royce Phantom VI

(Des Sa'ad Ghazi. Litho)

2014 (26 Jan). Classic Cars–'Royal Chariots'. T **636** and similar horiz designs. Multicoloured. P 13½.

2448 250d. Type **636** ... 1·80 1·50
2449 500d. Bentley, 1950's ... 3·50 3·00
2450 750d. Mercedes, 1932 ... 5·25 4·50
2451 1000d. Cadillac, 1950's ... 7·00 6·00
2448/2451 *Set of 4* ... 16·00 13·50

637 Aircraft and Control Tower

(Des Wathiq Mohammed and Dhurgham Al-Jasim. Litho)

2014 (28 Jan). 70th Anniversary (2013) of ICAO (International Civil Aviation Organisation). T **637** and similar horiz designs. Multicoloured. P 13×13½.

2452 500d. Type **637** ... 3·50 3·00
2453 1000d. Aircraft and airport buildings ... 7·00 6·00
2454 1500d. Aircraft and world map ... 10·50 9·00
2452/2454 *Set of 3* ... 19·00 16·00

638 Symbols of Iraq

639 Emblem

(Des Ghaith Al-Makhzoomi. Litho)

2014 (30 Apr). 'Iraq Votes'–Elections. T **638** and similar multicoloured designs. P 13½×13.

2455 500d. Type **638** ... 3·50 3·00
2456 1000d. Dove, map, ballot box and emblem ... 7·00 6·00
2457 1500d. Emblem and map (*horiz*) ... 10·50 9·00
2455/2457 *Set of 3* ... 19·00 16·00

(Des Sa'ad Ghazi. Litho)

2014 (15 May). Environmental Year in Iraq. P 13½×13.

2458 **639** 250d. multicoloured ... 1·80 1·50
2459 500d. multicoloured ... 3·50 3·00
2460 750d. multicoloured ... 5·25 4·50
2458/2460 *Set of 3* ... 9·50 8·00

640 Trophy and Pitch

641 Symbols of Japan and Iraq

(Des Ghaith Al-Makhzoomi)

2014 (12 June). World Cup Football Championships, Brazil. T **640** and similar square designs. Multicoloured. P 13½.

2461	250d. Type **640**	1·80	1·50
2462	500d. Player, trophy and flags	3·50	3·00
2463	750d. Mascot, pitch and flags	5·25	4·50
2464	1000d. Football, trophy and player	7·00	6·00
2461/2464	*Set of* 4	16·00	13·50
MS2465	70×70 mm. 1000d. Flags and trophy. Imperf.	7·25	6·25

Nos. 2461/2464 were perforated in a circle contained in an outer perforated square.

(Des Husain Muhsin Hejair and Omar Sa'ad Fa'iq. Litho)

2014 (1 Nov). 75th Anniversary of Iraq–Japan Diplomatic Relations. P 13½×13.

2466	**641** 250d. multicoloured	1·80	1·50
2467	500d. multicoloured	3·50	3·00
2468	1000d. multicoloured	7·00	6·00
2466/2468	*Set of* 3	11·00	9·50
MS2469	90×62 mm. 1000d. As Nos. 2456/2458. Imperf	7·25	6·25

642 Destroyer

643 Sparrow

(Des Sa'ad Ghazi. Litho)

2015 (6 Jan). Army Day. T **642** and similar square designs. Multicoloured. P 13×13½.

2470	250d. Type **642**	1·80	1·50
2471	500d. Tank	3·50	3·00
2472	750d. Soldiers	5·25	4·50
2473	1000d. Military aircraft	7·00	6·00
2470/2473	*Set of* 4	16·00	13·50

(Des Sa'ad Ghazi. Litho)

2015 (21 Jan). Birds. T **643** and similar multicoloured designs. P 13×13½.

2474	250d. Type **643**	1·80	1·50
2475	500d. Blue-cheeked Flycatcher	3·50	3·00
2476	750d. Robin	5·25	4·50
2477	1000d. Goldfinch	7·00	6·00
2478	1000d. Kingfisher	7·00	6·00
2474/2478	*Set of* 5	22·00	19·00
MS2479	125×102 mm. 1000d. Design showing all five birds (with perforations around Robin, Goldfinch and Kingfisher). Imperf	11·50	9·75

644 Potter

645 Lake

(Des Sa'ad Ghazi. Litho)

2015 (25 Jan). Trades. T **644** and similar vert designs. Multicoloured. P 14½×14.

2480	250d. Type **644**	1·80	1·50
2481	500d. Leather worker	3·50	3·00
2482	750d. Cloth salesman	5·25	4·50
2483	1000d. Knife sharpener	7·00	6·00
2480/2483	*Set of* 4	16·00	13·50

(Des Sa'ad Ghazi. Litho)

2015 (8 Feb). Southern Iraqi Marshes. T **645** and similar horiz design. Multicoloured. P 13×13½.

2484	250d. Type **645**	1·80	1·50
2485	500d. Cattle and reed hut	3·50	3·00

646 Mosque of the Prophet Jonah

(Des Dhurgham Al-Jasim. Litho)

2015 (9 Feb). Land of the Prophets. T **646** and similar horiz designs. Multicoloured. P 13½.

2486	250d. Type **646**	1·80	1·50
2487	500d. Tomb of Ezekiel	3·50	3·00
2488	750d. Shrine of Seth, Mosul	5·25	4·50
2489	1000d. Shrine of Job	7·00	6·00
2486/2489	*Set of* 4	16·00	13·50

647 Disability Support Signs

(Des Wathiq Mohammed. Litho)

2015 (17 Sept). National Day for the Disabled. T **647** and similar horiz designs. Multicoloured. P 14.

2490	250d. Type **647**	1·80	1·50
2491	500d. Stylised couple and wheelchair user	3·50	3·00
2492	1000d. Umbrella shielding symbols for various disabilities	7·00	6·00
2490/2492	*Set of* 3	11·00	9·50

648 Fist, Flags and Tank ('Amerli Victorious')

(Des Ghaith Al-Makhzoomi. Litho)

2015 (26 Oct). Fight Against ISIS in Iraq. T **648** and similar horiz designs. Multicoloured. P 14.

2493	500d. Type **648**	3·50	3·00
2494	750d. Oil field, helicopter, tank and armoured vehicles	5·25	4·50
2495	1000d. Soldiers and tank (Liberation of Jurf Al-Nasr)	7·00	6·00
2493/2495	*Set of* 3	14·00	12·00

649 Head of Fallen Babylonian Statue

(Des Sa'ad Ghazi. Litho)

2015 (23 Nov). Destruction of Iraqi Antiquities. T **649** and similar multicoloured designs. P 13½.

2496	500d. Type **649**	3·50	3·00
2497	1000d. Two cracked Babylonian statues (*vert*)	7·00	6·00
MS2498	65×85 mm. 1500d. As Type **649**. Imperf	11·50	9·75

650 Rabbits

(Litho)

2016 (22 Mar). Farm Animals. T **650** and similar multicoloured designs inscribed 'Farm Pets'. P 14.

2499	250d. Type **650**	1·80	1·50
2500	500d. Two Pigeons	3·50	3·00
2501	750d. Cat and Dog (*vert*)	5·25	4·50
2502	1000d. Cockerel, Hen and Chicks	7·00	6·00
2499/2502	*Set of 4*	16·00	13·50
MS2503	103×84 mm. 15000d. Composite design including all four stamps (with perforations around images). Imperf	11·50	9·75

651 Alhazen and Anniversary Emblem

652 Hopscotch

(Litho)

2016 (3 Apr). 70th Anniversary of UNESCO. International Year of Light and Abu 'Ali al-Hasan ibn al-Hasan ibn al-Haytham (Alhazen) (scientist, mathematician, astronomer) Commemoration. P 14.

2504	**651** 10000d. multicoloured	70·00	60·00

(Litho)

2016 (14 Apr). Childrens' Games. T **652** and similar multicoloured designs. P 14.

2505	250d. Type **652**	1·80	1·50
2506	500d. Marbles (*horiz*)	3·50	3·00
2507	750d. Nine Men's Morris (Merels or Mill) (*horiz*)	5·25	4·50
2508	1000d. Skipping	7·00	6·00
2505/2508	*Set of 4*	16·00	13·50

653 Zaha Hadid, 1950–2016

654 Bouquet

(Litho)

2016 (26 June). Iraqi Architects. T **653** and similar horiz design. Multicoloured. P 14.

2509	750d. Type **653**	5·25	4·50
2510	1000d. Mohammed Makiya, 1914–2014	7·00	6·00

(Litho)

2016 (6 May). Flowers. Bouquets. T **654** and similar multicoloured designs. P 14.

2511	250d. Type **654**	1·80	1·50
2512	500d. Tall mixed boquet with pink roses in centre	3·50	3·00
2513	750d. Bouquet of blue, cream and pink lilac (*horiz*)	5·25	4·50
2514	1000d. Pink, white and red bouquet	7·00	6·00
2515	1500d. Tall mixed bouquet of roses, delphiniums and white chrysanthemums	10·50	9·00
2511/2515	*Set of 5*	25·00	22·00

655 Emblem, Globe and Envelopes

2016 (5 Sept). Arab Post Day. T **655** and similar horiz design. Multicoloured. P 14.

2516	500d. Type **655**	3·50	3·00
	a. Pair. Nos. 2516/2517	11·00	9·25
2517	1000d. As Type **655** but with design reversed	7·00	6·00

656 Syndicate of Iraqi Pharmacists

(Litho)

2016 (21 Sept). Medical Associations in Iraq. T **656** and similar horiz designs. Multicoloured. P 14.

2518	250d. Type **656**	1·80	1·50
	a. Block of 4. Nos. 2518/2521	11·00	
2519	250d. Iraqi Medical Association	1·80	1·50
2520	500d. Iraqi Red Crescent Society	3·50	3·00
2521	500d. Anti Tuberculosis and Chest Deseases Society	3·50	3·00
2518/2521	*Set of 4*	9·50	8·00

Nos. 2518/2521 were printed, *se-tenant*, in blocks of four stamps within the sheet.

657 Civilians and Soldiers celebrating

(Litho)

2016 (5 Oct). Liberation of Anbar. P 14.

2522	**657** 1000d. multicoloured	7·00	6·00

(Litho)

2016 (23 Oct). Rio 2016–Olympic Games, Brazil. Horiz designs showing athletes. Multicoloured. P 14.

2523	250d. Hurdling	1·80	1·50
	a. Sheet of 8. Nos. 2523/2530	36·00	
2524	250d. Football	1·80	1·50
2525	500d. High Jump	3·50	3·00
2526	500d. Handball	3·50	3·00
2527	750d. Show jumping	3·50	3·00
2528	750d. Javelin	5·25	4·50
2529	1000d. Boxing	5·25	4·50
2530	1000d. Fencing	7·00	6·00
2523/2530	*Set of 8*	32·00	27·00
MS2531	140×70 mm. 1000d. Pole vault, gymnastics, basketball and long jump. Imperf	7·25	6·25

Nos. 2523/2530 were printed both in sheets, and together, *se-tenant*, in sheets of eight stamps.

T **658** is unavailable.

No. 2532 is vacant.

659 Ahmed Al-Wáili

660 Babylonian Statue

(Litho)

2016 (13 Nov). Ahmed Al-Wáili Al-Laithi Al-Kinani (writer and cleric) Commemoration. P 14.

2533 **659** 1000d. multicoloured .... 7·00 6·00

(Litho)

2016 (1 Dec). UNESCO World Heritage–South Iraq Marshes and Antiques. T **660** and similar multicoloured designs. P 14.

2534 250d. Type **660** .... 1·80 1·50
2535 500d. Early Lion-shaped statuette .... 3·50 3·00
2536 750d. Ziggurat of Ur (*horiz*) .... 5·25 4·50
2537 1000d. Marshland lake and boat (*horiz*) .... 7·00 6·00
2534/2537 *Set of* 4 .... 16·00 13·50
MS2538 95×90 mm. 1000d. Composite design including all four stamp images. Imperf .... 7·25 6·25

661 Cathedral of Santiago de Compostela (Spain) and Ishtar Gate (Iraq)

(Litho)

2017 (5 Feb). 70th Anniversary of Iraq–Spain Diplomatic Relations. Iraq–Spain Cultural Week. Multicoloured. P 14.

2539 **661** 1000d. multicoloured .... 7·00 6·00

662 Oud (musical instrument), Books, Textiles and Metalwork

(Litho)

2017 (1 Mar). Hobbies and Crafts Festival. T **662** and similar multicoloured design. P 14.

2540 500d. Type **662** .... 3·50 3·00
MS2541 95×90 mm. 1000d. Bull-headed harp (lyre), textiles and painter's palette. Imperf .... 7·25 6·25

663 Al Rasheed Street, Past and Present

(Litho)

2017 (30 Mar). Centenary of Al Rasheed Street. Multicoloured. P 14.

2542 **663** 1000d. multicoloured .... 7·00 6·00

664 Gypsy Moth, 1931

665 Liberation of Mosul

2017 (5 July). Transportation in Iraq. T **664** and similar horiz designs. Multicoloured. P 14.

2543 250d. Type **664** .... 1·80 1·50
2544 250d. DHL 136 Locomotive, 2004 .... 1·80 1·50
2545 250d. Ikarus Bus, 1971 ....
2546 500d. de Havilland Dragon, 1933 .... 1·80 1·50
2547 500d. DEM 2745 Locomotive, 2001 .... 3·50 3·00
2548 500d. Leyland Double Decker Bus, 1976 .... 3·50 3·00
2549 750d. Gloster Gladiator, 1937 .... 3·50 3·00
2550 750d. DEM 2006 Locomotive, 1964 .... 5·25 4·50
2551 750d. AC Bus, 1956 .... 5·25 4·50
2552 1000d. de Havilland Dove, 1948 .... 5·25 4·50
2553 1000d. DMU Locomotive, 2014 .... 7·00 6·00
2554 1000d. Alba Bus, 2013 .... 7·00 6·00
2543/2554 *Set of* 12 .... 47·00 41·00
MS2555 125×70 mm. 1000d. Steam Locomotive, Aircraft and Double Decker Bus. Imperf .... 7·25 6·25

No. 2556 is vacant.

(Des Ahmed Sahib Majeed. Litho)

2017 (18 July). Liberation of Mosul. T **665** and similar multicoloured design. P 14.

2557 500d. Type **665** .... 3·50 3·00
MS2558 100×68 mm. 1000d. Woman and soldiers. Imperf .... 7·25 6·25

666 1917 ½a. on 2pa. (Obelisk) (As No. 1 of Baghdad)

667 Al-Abbas Shrine

(Des Sa'ad Ghazi)

2017 (21 Oct). Centenary (2018) of First Iraqi Stamps. T **666** and similar multicoloured designs showing stamps of Turkey overprinted 'BAGHDAD'. P 13½.

2559 250d. Type **666** .... 1·80 1·50
2560 500d. 2a.on 1pi (Mosque) (No. 11) (*horiz*) .... 3·50 3·00
2561 1000d. ½a. on 10pa. (Mosque of Selim) (No. 4) (*horiz*) .... 7·00 6·00
2559/2561 *Set of* 3 .... 11·00 9·50
MS2562 95×70 mm. 1000d. First day covers. Imperf .... 7·25 6·25

(Des Sa'ad Ghazi)

2017 (3 Dec). Al-Abbas Shrine. T **667** and similar horiz designs. Multicoloured. P 13½.

2563 250d. Type **667** .... 1·80 1·50
2564 1000d. Worshiper at gate .... 7·00 6·00
MS2565 95×70 mm. 1000d. Dome and minarets Imperf .... 7·25 6·25

STAMP BOOKLETS

Price is for complete booklet

Booklet No.	*Date*	*Contents and Cover Price*	*Price*
SB1	1982	Flowers 1 pane, No. 1572a (250f.)	11·00

Israel

1948. 1000 Prutot (Mils) = 1 Israeli Pound
1960. 100 Agorot = 1 Israeli Pound
1980. 100 Agorot = 1 Shekel

Following disturbances the United Kingdom requested the termination of its mandate to administer Palestine (q.v.) and this came to an end on 14 May 1948. On the same day the State of Israel was proclaimed.

On 15 May 1948 forces of Egypt, Iraq, Jordan, Lebanon and Syria invaded Israel in an attempt to destroy the new state. They were driven back, and Israeli forces occupied considerable areas in Galilee and the Negev. Armistice agreements in 1949 ended the war.

It had been expected that the United Nations would accept responsibility for the continuance of the postal services until a new state postal organisation could be set up after the termination of the British Mandate. This did not happen but in the meanwhile the Postmaster-General at Jerusalem issued a direction on 13 April 1948 notifying the suspension of the postal services and all the post offices were closed down on various dates during the period 15 April to 5 May. To prevent complete disruption of the services the Jewish Agency and National Council instructed all employees in the Jewish sectors of the country to remain at their posts and provisional postmarks were supplied. Many interim commemorative and local stamps made their appearance. These are outside the scope of this catalogue.

'TABS'. Almost all Israeli stamps (except the Postage Dues) exist with descriptive sheet margin attached. These so-called 'Tabs' are popular and in some cases scarce. Individual prices for issues in sets of two or more are for stamps without tab; set prices are quoted for stamps both without and with tab. For single stamps, the first price quoted is for stamp without tab and the price on the following line is for stamp with tab.

Some tabs are separated from the edge of the sheet by a line of perforation, giving an area of plain selvedge. In such cases our prices are for 'full tabs', i.e. with selvedge attached.

1

2

Ancient Jewish Coins

(Des O. Wallish. Typo Haaretz Ptg Press, Sarona)

1948 (16 May). Ancient Jewish Coins (1st issue). P 11. As T **1**.

1	3m. orange	1·20	60
	a. Rouletted	9·00	2·30
	b. Perf 10	£140	60·00
	c. Perf 10×11	2·10	1·50
2	5m. emerald-green	1·20	60
	a. Rouletted	12·00	2·30
	b. Perf 10	£160	£150
3	10m. magenta	1·20	60
	a. Grey paper	9·00	4·50
	b. Rouletted	30·00	2·75
	c. Perf 10×11	18·00	15·00
4	15m. scarlet	2·30	60
	a. Perf 10	£200	£200
5	20m. blue	4·50	90
	c. Perf 10×11	45·00	38·00
6	50m. brown	27·00	3·25
	a. Grey paper	42·00	12·00
	b. Perf 10	£225	£180
	c. Perf 10×11	45·00	38·00
	T **2**. *(a) Size 34½×21½ mm*		
7	250m. deep green	60·00	30·00
	a. Perf 10	£450	£425
	b. Perf 10×11	£350	£350
8	500m. brown-red/*buff*	£300	£140
	a. Perf 10	£700	£650
	b. Perf 10×11	£550	£550
	(b) Size 36×24 mm		
9	1000m. indigo/*blue*	£550	£275
	a. Perf 10	£1700	£1600
	b. Perf 10×11	£1100	£1100
1/9	*Set of 9* (*cheapest*)	£850	£400
1/9	*Set of 9 with tabs*	£1800	£5500

Designs shown on coins: As T **1**—3m. Palm tree and baskets with dates; 5m. Vine leaf; 10m. Ritual jar; 15m. Bunch of grapes; 20m. Ritual cup; 50m. Tied palm branches and lemon. T **2**—Silver shekel and pomegranates.

These stamps were printed on various papers, thin yellowish, medium white etc.

All values exist imperforate and there are many imperf between varieties in combination with the various gauges of perforation.

See also Nos. 21/26, 40/51 and 90/93.

דמי דאר

(D **3**)

3 Flying Scroll Emblem

1948 (28 May). POSTAGE DUE. T **1** and similar designs showing ancient coins, optd with T D **3**. P 11.

D10	3m. orange/*yellow*	4·50	3·00
D11	5m. emerald-green/*yellow*	6·00	4·50
D12	10m. magenta/*yellow*	15·00	10·50
D13	20m. blue/*yellow*	45·00	38·00
D14	50m. brown/*yellow*	£180	£140
D10/D14	*Set of 5*	£225	£180
D10/D14	*Set of 5 with 'tab' margins*	£4500	£2250

(Des O. Wallish. Litho)

1948 (26 Sept). Jewish New Year. P 11½.

10	**3**	3m. red-brown and light blue	1·20	75
11		5m. blue-green and light blue	1·20	75
12		10m. claret and light blue	1·50	1·20
13		20m. blue and light blue	6·00	2·75
14		65m. yellow-brown and scarlet	30·00	13·50
10/14		*Set of 5*	36·00	17·00
10/14		*Set of 5 with tabs*	£550	£300

PRINTERS. The following stamps of Israel in litho were printed by Lewin-Epstein Ltd at Bat Yam and those in photo by the Government Printer at Hakirya, Tel Aviv, later at Jerusalem, *unless otherwise stated.*

4 Road to Jerusalem

5 National Flag

(Des M. and G. Shamir. Litho)

1949 (16 Feb). Inauguration of Constituent Assembly. P 11½.

15	**4**	250pr. red-brown and grey	3·75	3·00
		With tab	90·00	60·00

This stamp continued in use as a regular issue.

(Des F. Krausz. Litho)

1949 (31 Mar). Adoption of new National Flag. P 11½.

16	**5**	20pr. blue	1·80	90
		With tab	£120	60·00

(Des O. Wallish. Litho)

1949 (1 May). First Anniversary of Israeli Postage Stamps. Sheet containing stamp similar to T **8**, in block of four. Imperf.

MS16*a*	75×95 mm. 10pr. claret	£225	£110

The above sheet was sold at TABUL the First National Stamp Exhibition in Tel Aviv, 1st–6th May 1949, for 100pr. which covered the entrance fee and one sheet.

6 Petah Tiqwa Well

7 Air Force Badge

(Des O. Wallish. Litho)

1949 (10 Aug). 70th Anniversary of Founding of Petah Tiqwa. P 11.

17	**6**	40pr. sepia and green	23·00	3·75
		With tab	£200	£110

(Des M. and G. Shamir. Litho)

1949 (20 Sept). Jewish New Year. As T **7** (badges). P 11½.

18		5pr. dark blue (Type **7**)	1·50	75
19		10pr. blue-green (Navy)	1·50	75
20		35pr. chocolate (Army)	12·00	7·50
18/20		*Set of 3*	13·50	8·00
18/20		*Set of 3 with tabs*	£1400	£550

8 Ancient Jewish Coin

D **9**

(Des O. Wallish. Litho)

1949 (18 Dec)–**50**. Jewish Coins (2nd issue). As T **8**. Design 20×24½ mm. Inscr at left 9 mm. P 11½.

21	**8**	3pr. olive-grey	30	30
22		5pr. violet	30	30
		a. *Tête-bêche* (pair) (5.4.50)	12·00	11·50
23		10pr. green	30	30
		a. *Tête-bêche* (pair) (5.4.50)	18·00	18·00
24		15pr. carmine	60	30
		a. *Tête-bêche* (pair) (5.4.50)	30·00	30·00
25		30pr. blue	1·10	60
		a. *Tête-bêche* (pair) (5.4.50)	38·00	38·00
26		50pr. brown	3·50	90
21/26		*Set of 6*	5·50	2·40
21/26		*Set of 6 with tabs*	£200	£110

Design: subjects—Similar to Nos. 1/6 (30pr. Ritual vessel).

Tête-bêche pairs come from uncut sheets printed for booklets. They do not exist with tabs.

(Des O. Wallish. Litho)

1949 (18 Dec). POSTAGE DUE. P 11½.

D27	D **9**	2pr. yellow-orange	45	30
D28		5pr. violet	75	45
D29		10pr. green	75	30
D30		20pr. vermilion	90	30
D31		30pr. blue	1·20	60
D32		50pr. brown	2·10	1·80
D27/D32		*Set of 6*	5·50	3·50
D27/D32		*Set of 6 with blank tab margins*	£225	£150

10 Stag and Globe

11 Landing of Immigrants

(Des O. Wallish. Litho)

1950 (26 Mar). Israel's Membership and 75th Anniversary of Universal Postal Union. P 11½.

27	**10**	40pr. bright violet	2·30	1·20
28		80pr. rose-carmine	2·75	1·50
		a. Nos. 27/28 *tête-bêche*	55·00	49·00
27/28		*Set of 2*	4·50	2·40
27/28		*Set of 2 with tabs*	£150	90·00

Tête-bêche pairs come from uncut sheets printed for booklets. They do not exist with tabs.

(Des M. Kara (20pr.), Wind-Struski (40pr.). Litho)

1950 (23 Apr). Second Anniversary of Independence. T **11** and similar design. P 11½.

29		20pr. chocolate (Type **11**)	6·00	3·00
30		40pr. green (Line of immigrant ships)	24·00	13·50
29/30		*Set of 2*	27·00	15·00
29/30		*Set of 2 with tabs*	£1000	£400

12 Library and Book

13 Eagle

(Des F. Krausz. Litho)

1950 (9 May). 25th Anniversary of Founding of Hebrew University, Jerusalem. P 11½.

31	**12**	100pr. blue-green	90	90
		With tab	55·00	38·00

This stamp continued in use as a regular issue.

(Des O. Wallish. Litho)

1950 (25 June). AIR. As T **13** (ornamental bird types). P 11½.

32		5pr. light-blue	1·20	75
33		30pr. blue-grey	75	75
34		40pr. blue-green	75	75
35		50pr. brown-red	75	75
36		100pr. carmine	38·00	24·00
37		250pr. grey-blue	4·50	3·00
32/37		*Set of 6*	41·00	27·00
32/37		*Set of 6 with tabs*	£400	£250

Designs: Vert—5pr. Doves pecking grapes; 30pr. Eagle; 40pr. Ostrich; 50pr. Dove. Horiz—100pr. T **13**; 250pr. Dove with olive branch.

14 Star of David and Fruit

15 Ancient Jewish Coin

(Des A. Szyk. Litho)

1950 (31 Aug). Jewish New Year. P 14.

38	**14**	5pr. violet and orange	30	30
39		15pr. brown and green	1·50	1·50
38/39		*Set of 2*	1·60	1·60
38/39		*Set of 2 with tabs*	75·00	60·00

(Des O. Wallish. Litho)

1950 (19 Sept)–**54**. Jewish Coins (3rd issue). T **15** and similar vert designs. Design 19¾×25½ mm. Inscr at left 11 mm. P 14.

40		3pr. olive-grey (24.10.50)	30	30
41		5pr. violet (4.10.50)	30	30
		a. *Tête-bêche* (pair) (26.2.53)	6·00	4·50
42		10pr. green (19.9.50)	30	30
		a. *Tête-bêche* (pair) (26.2.53)	4·50	3·00
43		15pr. carmine (22.9.50)	30	30
		a. *Tête-bêche* (pair) (26.2.53)	4·50	3·00
44		20pr. orange (30.3.52)	30	30
		a. *Tête-bêche* (pair) (26.2.53)	6·00	4·50
45		30pr. deep blue (31.12.50)	30	30
		a. *Tête-bêche* (pair) (26.2.53)	7·50	6·00
46		35pr. olive-green (30.3.52)	1·10	60
47		40pr. orange-brown (30.3.52)	40	40
48		45pr. deep mauve (30.3.52)	40	40
		a. *Tête-bêche* (pair) (15.6.54)	23·00	15·00
49		50pr. brown (13.12.50)	45	40
50		60pr. rose-red (30.3.52)	40	40
51		85pr. turquoise-blue (30.3.52)	1·10	60
40/51		*Set of 12*	5·00	4·25
40/51		*Set of 12 with tabs*	42·00	30·00

Designs shown on coins:—3pr., 20pr. Palm tree and baskets with dates; 5pr., 35pr. Vine leaf; 10pr., 40pr. Ritual jar; 15pr., 45pr. Bunch of grapes; 30pr., 60pr. Ritual vessel; 50pr., 85pr. Tied palm branches and lemon.

16 Runner and Track

17 The Negev (after R. Rubin)

(Des A. Games. Litho)

1950 (1 Oct). Third Maccabiah. P 14.

52	**16**	80pr. blackish green and olive-green	7·50	3·75
		With tab	£130	75·00

(Des R. Rubin. Litho)

1950 (26 Dec). Opening of Post Office at Elat. P 14.

53	**17**	500pr. brown and orange-brown	23·00	18·00
		With tab	£450	£375

This stamp continued in use as a regular issue.

בול שרות

(O **18**)

19 Memorial Tablet

1951 (1 Feb). OFFICIAL. As Nos. 41 etc, but colours changed. Optd with T O **18**.

O54	5pr. magenta	30	25
O55	15pr. vermilion	30	25
O56	30pr. light blue	55	45
O57	40pr. red-brown	70	45
O54/O57	*Set of 4*	1·70	1·30
O54/O57	*Set of 4 with tabs*	27·00	23·00

(Des M. and G. Shamir. Litho)

1951 (22 Mar). 40th Anniversary of Founding of Tel Aviv. P 14.

54	**19** 40pr. purple-brown	1·40	90
	With tab	45·00	38·00

20 Supporting Israel

21 Metsudat Yesha

(Des A. Games. Litho)

1951 (30 Apr). Independence Bonds Campaign. P 14.

55	**20** 80pr. brown-lake	90	90
	With tab	6·75	5·25

(Des O. Wallish. Litho)

1951 (9 May). Third Anniversary of State of Israel. T **21** and similar design. P 14.

56	15pr. brown-lake (Type **21**)	45	45
57	40pr. deep blue (Hakastel)	1·40	1·40
56/57	*Set of 2*	1·70	1·70
56/57	*Set of 2 with tabs*	90·00	65·00

22 Tractor

23 Ploughing and Savings Stamp

(Des O. Wallish (15pr. and 25pr.), Wind-Struski (80pr.). Litho)

1951 (24 June). 50th Anniversary of Jewish National Fund T **22** and similar design and T **23**. P 14.

58	**22** 15pr. brown	30	30
59	– 25pr. blue-green (Stylised tree)	30	30
60	**23** 80pr. blue	3·00	2·10
58/60	*Set of 3*	3·25	2·40
58/60	*Set of 3 with tabs*	£225	£130

24 Dr. T. Herzl

25 Carrier Pigeons

(Des M. and G. Shamir. Litho)

1951 (14 Aug). 23rd Zionist Congress. P 14.

61	**24** 80pr. grey-green	90	75
	With tab	7·50	6·00

(Des M. Kara (15pr.), Wind-Struski (others). Litho)

1951 (16 Sept). Jewish New Year. T **25** and similar vert designs. P 14.

62	5pr. blue (Type **25**)	30	15
63	15pr. rose (Woman and Dove)	30	15
64	40pr. reddish violet (Scroll of the Law)	45	45
62/64	*Set of 3*	95	70
62/64	*Set of 3 with tabs*	7·50	6·00

26 Menorah and Emblems

26a Haifa Bay, Mt. Carmel and City Seal

(Des O. Wallish. Litho)

1952 (27 Feb). P 14.

64*a*	**26** 1000pr. black and blue	36·00	23·00
	With tab	£600	£375

(Des O. Wallish. Litho)

1952 (13 Apr). AIR. National Stamp Exhibition (TABA). T **26a** and similar design. P 14.

64*b*	100pr. cobalt and black	1·50	1·10
64*c*	120pr. purple and black	2·10	1·50
64*b*/64*c*	*Set of 2*	3·25	2·30
64*b*/64*c*	*Set of 2 with tabs*	45·00	26·00

Designs: 100pr. Haifa Bay and City Seal; 120pr. T **26a**.

The above were only sold at the Exhibition, at 340pr. including entrance fee.

27 Thistle and Yad Mordechai

28 New York Skyline and ZOA Building

(Des O. Wallish. Litho)

1952 (29 Apr). Fourth Anniversary of Independence. T **27** and similar designs. P 14.

65	30pr. red-brown and magenta	45	30
66	60pr. slate-black and ultramarine	75	45
67	110pr. grey-brown and red	1·50	1·10
65/67	*Set of 3*	2·40	1·70
65/67	*Set of 3 with tabs*	55·00	38·00

Designs: 30pr. T **27**; 60pr. Cornflowers and Deganya; 100pr. Anemone and Safed.

(Des Wind-Struski. Litho)

1952 (13 May). Opening of American Zionist Building. Tel Aviv. P 14.

68	**28** 220pr. grey and deep blue	1·80	90
	With tab	38·00	30·00

29 Figs

D **30**

(Des O. Wallish. Litho)

1952 (3 Sept). Jewish New Year. T **29** and similar vert designs. P 14.

69	15pr. greenish yellow and blue-green	60	30
70	40pr. yellow, pale blue and reddish violet	90	60
71	110pr. grey and carmine	1·40	1·20
72	220pr. pale yellow-green, brown and yellow-orange	2·00	1·50
69/72	*Set of 4*	4·50	3·25
69/72	*Set of 4 with tabs*	75·00	45·00

Designs: 15pr. T **29**; 40pr. Lily ('Rose of Sharon'); 110pr. Dove; 220pr. Nuts.

(Des O. Wallish. Litho)

1952 (30 Nov). POSTAGE DUE. P 14.

D73	D **30**	5pr. orange-brown	25	15
D74		10pr. greenish blue	25	15
D75		20pr. reddish purple	40	30
D76		30pr. black	25	15
D77		40pr. emerald	25	15
D78		50pr. sepia	25	15
D79		60pr. reddish violet	25	15
D80		100pr. scarlet	40	30
D81		250pr. blue	60	30
D73/D81		*Set of 9*	2·50	1·60
D73/D81		*Set of 9 with blank tab margins*	30·00	30·00

30 Dr. C. Weizmann (from sketch by R. Errell)

31

(Des Wind-Struski. Litho)

1952 (9 Dec). Death of First President. P 14.

73	**30**	30pr. indigo	45	30
74		110pr. grey-black	1·40	1·10
73/74		*Set of 2*	1·70	1·30
73/74		*Set of 2 with tabs*	33·00	23·00

(Des G. Hamori. Litho)

1952 (31 Dec). 70th Anniversary of Bet Yaakov Lechu Venelcha Immigration Organisation. P 14.

75	**31**	110pr. buff, green and brown	1·40	90
		With tab	33·00	23·00

32 Douglas DC-4 Airliner over Tel Aviv-Yafo

33 Anemones and Arms

(Des G. Hamori. Litho)

1953 (16 Mar)–**56**. AIR. T **32** (inscr 'POSTE AERIENNE'). P 14.

76	10pr. bronze-green and sage-green (2.3.54)	60	40
77	70pr. violet and lilac (6.4.54)	60	40
78	100pr. deep green and pale green (2.3.54)	60	40
79	150pr. brown and brown-orange (6.4.54)	60	40
80	350pr. carmine-red and pink (6.4.54)	90	90
81	500pr. deep blue and pale blue (2.3.54)	2·00	1·50
81*a*	750pr. sepia and yellow-brown (21.8.56)	30	30
82	1000pr. deep bluish green and turquoise-green	7·50	6·00
82*a*	3000pr. dull purple (13.11.56)	75	75
76/82*a*	*Set of 9*	12·50	10·00
76/82*a*	*Set of 9 with tabs*	£200	90·00

Designs: Horiz—10pr. Olive tree; 70pr. Sea of Galilee; 100pr. Shaar Hogay on road to Jerusalem; 150pr. Lion Rock, Negev; 350pr. Bay of Elat. Vert—500pr. Tanour Falls, near Metoulla; 750pr. Lake Hula; 1000pr. T **32**; 3000pr. Tomb of Meir Baal Haness.

(Des Wind-Struski. Litho)

1953 (19 Apr). Fifth Anniversary of Independence. P 14.

83	**33**	110pr. red, deep blue-green and turquoise-blue	75	45
		With tab	7·50	5·00

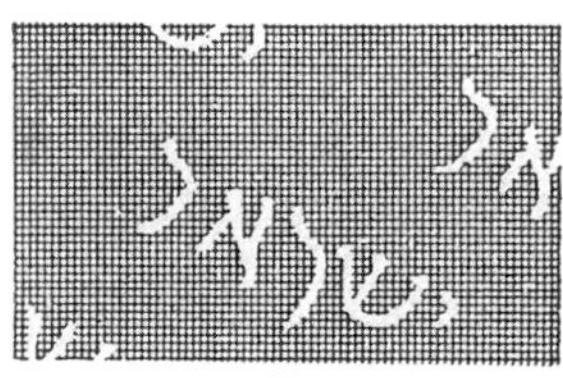

34

35 Maimonides (philosopher)

(Des Wind-Struski. Photo)

1953 (3 Aug). Seventh International Congress of History of Science. W **34**. P 14×13.

84	**35**	110pr. brown	2·50	1·10
		With tab	17·00	9·75

36 Holy Ark, Petah Tiqwa

37 Hand holding Globe/Football

38 Exhibition Emblem

(Des G. Hamori. Photo)

1953 (11 Aug). Jewish New Year. T **36** and similar vert designs showing Holy Arks. W **34**. P 14×13.

85	20pr. blue (at Jerusalem)	15	15
86	45pr. deep rose-red (Type **36**)	30	30
87	200pr. reddish violet (at Zefat)	1·40	90
85/87	*Set of 3*	1·70	1·20
85/87	*Set of 3 with tabs*	23·00	13·50

(Des Wind-Struski. Litho)

1953 (20 Sept). Fourth Maccabiah. P 14.

88	**37**	110pr. red-brown and pale blue	90	45
		With tab	7·50	5·75

(Des A. Games. Litho)

1953 (22 Sept). Conquest of the Desert Exhibition. P 14.

89	**38**	200pr. multicoloured	90	45
		With tab	10·50	6·00

39 Ancient Jewish Coin

40 Gesher and Narcissus

(Des O. Wallish. Litho)

1954 (5 Jan). Jewish Coins (4th issue). As T **39**. P 14.

90	80pr. bistre	15	15
91	95pr. bright bluish green	30	15
92	100pr. light red-brown	30	15
93	125pr. ultramarine	45	30
90/93	*Set of 4*	1·10	70
90/93	*Set of 4 with tabs*	7·00	3·00

Designs: shown on coins—80pr. T **39**; 95pr. Leaf; 100pr. Building facade; 125pr. Musical instrument.

(Des O. Wallish. Litho)

1954 (5 May). Sixth Anniversary of Independence. T **40** and similar vert design. P 14.

94	60pr. deep blue, greenish grey and magenta	15	15
95	350pr. brown, green and yellow	90	60
94/95	*Set of 2*	95	70
94/95	*Set of 2 with tabs*	4·75	3·25

Designs: 60pr. Yehiam and helichrysum; 350pr. T **40**.

41 Dr. T. Z. Herzl

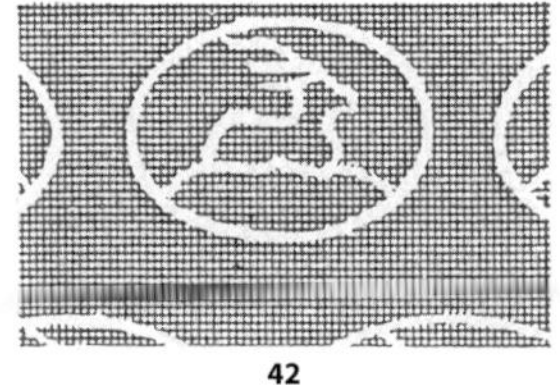

42

(Des R. Errell. Litho)

1954 (21 July). 50th Death Anniversary of Herzl (founder of World Zionist Movement). W **42** P 14.

96	**41** 160pr. brown-black, buff and deep blue..	75	45
	With tab	1·80	1·20

43

44 19th-century Mail Coach and Post Office

(Des G. Hamori. Photo)

1954 (8 Sept). Jewish New Year. W **34**. P 13×14.

97	**43** 25pr. sepia	25	25
	With tab	75	60

(Des O. Wallish. Litho)

1954 (13 Oct). National Stamp Exhibition. T **44** and similar horiz design. W **42**. P 14.

98	60pr. black, yellow and blue	15	15
99	200pr. grey-black, red and deep dull green	75	75
98/99	*Set of 2*	80	80
98/99	*Set of 2 with tabs*	4·50	2·75

Designs: 60pr. T **44**; 200pr. Post van and GPO, 1954.

45 Baron Edmond de Rothschild

46 Lamp of Knowledge

(Des G Hamori. Photo)

1954 (23 Nov). 20th Anniversary of Death of De Rothschild (financier). W **42**. P 13×14.

100	**45** 300pr. deep turquoise-green	75	45
	With tab	1·80	1·50

(Des G. Hamori. Photo)

1955 (13 Jan). 50th Anniversary of Teachers Association. W **42**. P 13×14.

101	**46** 250pr. blue	60	45
	With tab	1·50	1·50

47 Parachutist and Barbed Wire

48 Menorah and Olive Branches

(Des M. and G. Shamir. Litho)

1955 (31 Mar). Jewish Mobilisation During Second World War. W **42** (sideways). P 14.

102	**47** 120pr. greenish black and turquoise-green	45	30
	With tab	90	90

(Des G. Hamori. Litho)

1955 (26 Apr). Seventh Anniversary of Independence. W **42**. P 14.

103	**48** 150pr. orange, black and green	75	45
	With tab	75	75

49 Immigrants and Ship

50 Musicians playing Timbrel and Cymbals

(Des Miriam Karoly. Litho)

1955 (10 May). 20th Anniversary of Youth Immigration Scheme. T **49** and similar horiz designs. No wmk. P 14.

104	5pr. black and bright blue	15	15
105	10pr. black and rose-red	15	15
106	25pr. black and green	15	15
107	30pr. black and orange	15	15
108	60pr. black and bright reddish violet	15	15
109	750pr. black and pale bistre-brown	1·80	1·10
104/109	*Set of 6*	2·30	1·70
104/109	*Set of 6 with tabs*	5·25	3.75

Designs: 5pr. T **49**; 10pr. Immigrants and Douglas DC-3 aeroplane; 25pr. Boy and calf; 30pr. Girl watering flowers; 60pr. Boy making pottery; 750pr. Boy using theodolite.

(Des Miriam Karoly. Photo (25pr.). Litho (others))

1955 (25 Aug). Jewish New Year. T **50** and similar vert designs. W **42** (25pr.), no wmk (others). P 14×13 (25pr.) or 14 (others).

110	25pr. deep myrtle-green and orange	15	15
111	60pr. grey and red-orange	15	15
112	120pr. pale blue and yellow	15	15
113	250pr. chocolate and red-orange	60	45
110/113	*Set of 4*	95	80
110/113	*Set of 4 with tabs*	1·80	1·40

Designs: 25pr. T **50**. Musicians playing—60pr. Ram's horn; 120pr. Tuba; 250pr. Harp.

51 Ambulance

52 'Reuben'

(Des G. Hamori. Litho)

1955 (1 Nov). 25th Anniversary of Magen David Adom (Jewish Red Cross). W **34**. P 14.

114	**51** 160pr. emerald, black and red	30	30
	With tab	75	60

(Des G. Hamori. Photo)

1955 (8 Nov)–**59**. 12 Tribes of Israel. T **52** and similar vert designs. P 13×14.

A. W **42**

115A	10pr. emerald	15	15
116A	20pr. deep mauve	15	15
117A	30pr. ultramarine	15	15
118A	40pr. brown	15	15
119A	50pr. light blue	15	15
120A	60pr. bistre	15	15
121A	80pr. bluish violet	15	15
122A	100pr. red	15	15
123A	120pr. deep yellow-olive	30	15
124A	180pr. magenta	90	45
125A	200pr. myrtle-green	45	30
126A	250pr. grey	60	30
115A/126A	*Set of 12*	3·00	2·20
115A/126A	*Set of 12 with tabs*	10·50	7·50

B. No wmk

115B	10pr. emerald	20	20
116B	20pr. deep mauve	30	20
117B	30pr. ultramarine	†	
118B	40pr. brown	7·50	3·25
119B	50pr. light blue	75	30
120B	60pr. bistre	1·10	45
121B	80pr. bluish violet	†	
122B	100pr. red	75	60
123B	120pr. deep yellow-olive	2·30	1·10

124B	180pr. magenta	†	
125B	200pr. myrtle-green	†	
126B	250pr. grey	†	
115B/123B	*Set of 7*	11·50	5·50
115B/123B	*Set of 7 with tabs*	£130	£100

Emblems: 10pr. T **52**; 20pr. 'Simeon' (castle); 30pr. 'Levi' (High Priest's breastplate); 40pr. 'Judah' (Lion), 50pr. 'Dan' (scales); 60pr, 'Naphtali' (Gazelle); 80pr. 'Gad' (tents); 100pr. 'Asher' (tree); 120pr. 'Issachar' (sun and stars); 180pr. 'Zebulun' (ship); 200pr. 'Joseph' (sheaf of wheat); 250pr. 'Benjamin' (Wolf).

Date of issue: W **42**—8.11.55, 10, 30, 60, 100pr. 10.1.56, 20, 40, 80, 180pr.; 5.6.56, 50, 120, 200, 250pr. No wmk—7.57, 50pr.; 9.57, 60, 100pr.; 10.57, 20pr.; 11.57, 10pr.; 1.1.59, 120pr.; 1959, 40pr.

53 Professor Einstein

54 Technion

(Des G. Hamori. Photo)

1956 (3 Jan). Einstein Commemoration. W **42**. P 13×14.

127	**53** 530pr. brown	60	45
	With tab	1·50	1·20

(Des G. Hamori. Photo)

1956 (3 Jan). 30th Anniversary of Israel Institute of Technology, Haifa. W **42**. P 13×14.

128	**54** 350pr. yellow-olive and black	45	45
	With tab	75	60

55 Eight Years of Independence

56 Oranges

57 Musician playing Lyre

(Des M. and G. Shamir. Litho)

1956 (12 Apr). Eighth Anniversary of Independence. W **42**. P 14.

129	**55** 150pr. multicoloured	30	20
	With tab	75	60

(Des M. and G. Shamir. Litho)

1956 (20 May). Fourth International Congress of Mediterranean Citrus Fruit Growers. W **42** (sideways). P 14.

130	**56** 300pr. multicoloured	45	45
	With tab	75	60

(Des Miriam Karoly. Photo (30pr.), litho (others))

1956 (14 Aug). Jewish New Year. T **57** and similar designs. W **42** (sideways on vert designs). P 14×13 (30pr.) or 14 (others).

131	30pr. bistre-brown and blue	15	15
132	50pr. reddish violet and yellow-orange	15	15
133	150pr. deep turquoise-green and orange	30	30
131/133	*Set of 3*	55	55
131/133	*Set of 3 with tabs*	90	90

Designs: Vert—30pr. T **57**; 50pr. Musician playing sistrum. Horiz—150pr. Musician playing double oboe.

58 Insignia of 'Haganah'

59 Aeroplane sky-writing Figure '9'

(Des O. Wallish. Photo)

1957 (1 Jan). Defence Fund. W **42**. P 13×14.

134	**58** 80pr. +20 emerald	15	15
135	150pr. +50 bright carmine	15	15
136	350pr. +50 bright blue	25	20
134/136	*Set of 3*	50	45
134/136	*Set of 3 with tabs*	75	70

(Des O. Wallish. Litho)

1957 (29 Apr). Ninth Anniversary of Independence. W **42** (sideways). P 14.

137	**59** 250pr. black, blue and pale blue	45	30
	With tab	75	45

60 Bezalel Museum and Candelabrum

61 Seal of Tamach and Horse

(Des M. and G. Shamir. Litho)

1957 (29 Apr). 50th Anniversary of the Bezalel Museum, Jerusalem. W **42** (sideways). P 14.

138	**60** 400pr. multicoloured	30	30
	With tab	75	45

(Des Miriam Karoly. Litho (50pr.), photo (others))

1957 (4 Sept). Jewish New Year. Ancient Hebrew Seals. T **61** and similar vert designs. W **42** (sideways) (50pr.), no wmk (others). P 14 (50pr.) or 14×13 (others).

139	50pr. black and yellow-brown/*blue*	15	15
140	160pr. black and green/*buff*	15	15
141	300pr. black and carmine/*pink*	30	15
139/141	*Set of 3*	55	40
139/141	*Set of 3 with tabs*	1·40	1·10

Designs: 50pr. T **61**; 160pr. Seal of Shema and Lion; 300pr. Seal of Netanyahuv Ne'avadyahu and Gazelle.

TAB SHEETS. Nos. 137, 138 and 139 were officially re-printed in small sheets of five stamps and five tabs to prevent speculation in the tabbed stamps. Most of the sheets were broken up and sold through the Israeli Post Office's mail order service, but some have survived intact.

61a Part of Ancient 'Bet Alpha' Synagogue Floor Mosaic

(Des R. Errell. Litho)

1957 (17 Sept). First Israeli International Stamp Exhibition. Sheet containing four triangular stamps, which together form the complete centre-piece of floor mosaic. Multicoloured. Roul 13.

MS141*a*	103×105 mm. 100pr. (Type **61a**); 200pr., 300pr., 400pr. (*similar*)	90	90

62 Throwing the Hammer

63 Ancient Hebrew Ship

(Des A. Games. Photo)

1958 (20 Jan). 25th Anniversary of Maccabiah Games. No wmk. P 14×13.

142	**62** 500pr. carmine and bistre	45	30
	With tab	90	60

(Des Miriam Karoly. Litho (10pr.), photo (others))

1958 (27 Jan). Israel Merchant Marine Commemoration. T **63** and similar horiz designs. W **42**. P 14 (10pr.) or 13×14 (others).

143	10pr. red, indigo and yellow-ochre	15	15
144	20pr. brown and bluish green	15	15
145	30pr. blue-grey and carmine	30	15
146	1000pr. deep green and greenish blue	60	60
143/146	*Set of 4*	1·10	95
143/146	*Set of 4 with tabs*	2·10	2·00

Designs: 10pr. T **63**; 20pr. *Nirit* (immigrant ship); 30pr. *Shomron* (freighter); 1000pr. (57×22½ *mm*) *Zion* (liner).

64 Menorah and Olive Branch

65 Dancing Children forming '10'

(Des O. Wallish. Litho)

1958 (21 Apr). Tenth Anniversary of Independence. No wmk. P 14.

147	**64** 400pr. green, black and gold	45	45
	With tab	60	60

(Des G. Rothschild and Z. Lippmann. Photo)

1958 (2 July). First World Conference of Jewish Youth, Jerusalem. No wmk. P 13×14.

148	**65** 200pr. blackish green and brown-orange	45	30
	With tab	75	45

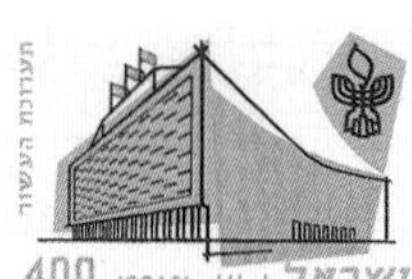

66 Convention Centre, Jerusalem and Exhibition Emblem

(Des M. and G. Shamir. Litho)

1958 (2 July). Tenth Anniversary (of Israel) Exhibition, Jerusalem. No wmk. P 14.

149	**66** 400pr. orange and lilac/*cream*	45	45
	With tab	75	60

67 Wheat

68 Ancient Stone

(Des Z. Narkiss. Photo)

1958 (27 Aug). Jewish New Year. Vert designs as T **67**. No wmk. P 14×13.

150	50pr. brown and yellow-ochre (Type **67**)	15	15
151	60pr. black and olive-yellow (Barley)	15	15
152	160pr. bright purple and violet (Grapes)	15	15
153	300pr. green and apple-green (Figs)	45	45
150/153	*Set of 4*	80	80
150/153	*Set of 4 with tabs*	1·50	1·40

See also Nos. 166/168.

(Des I. Blaushild. Litho)

1958 (10 Dec). Tenth Anniversary of Declaration of Human Rights. No wmk. P 14.

154	**68** 750pr. black, yellow and turquoise-blue	60	45
	With tab	1·40	1·40

69 Post Office Emblem

70 Sholem Aleichem

(Des G. Rothschild and Z. Lippmann. Litho)

1959 (25 Feb). Tenth Anniversary of Israeli Postal Services. Designs as T **69**. W **42** (reversed; sideways on 250pr. and 500pr.). P 14.

155	60pr. black, red and olive	15	15
156	120pr. black, red and olive	30	25
157	250pr. black, red and olive	40	30
158	500pr. black, red and olive	50	45
155/158	*Set of 4*	1·20	1·00
155/158	*Set of 4 with tabs*	2·00	1·90

Designs: Horiz—60pr. T **69**; 120pr. Post van. Vert—250pr. Radio-telephone equipment; 500pr. Telex dial and keyboard.

(Des M. and G. Shamir. Photo)

1959 (30 Mar). Birth Centenary of Sholem Aleichem (writer). No wmk. P 14×13.

159	**70** 250pr. red-brown and yellow-green	40	30
	With tab	80	45

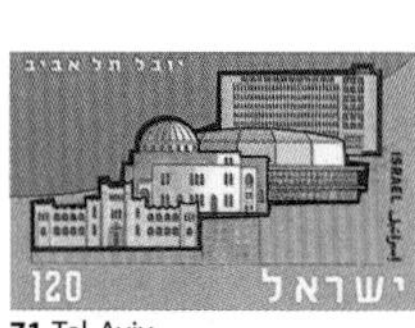

71 Tel Aviv

72 Anemone

(Des M. and G. Shamir. Litho)

1959 (4 May). 50th Anniversary of Tel Aviv. W **42**. P 14.

160	**71** 120pr. multicoloured	50	30
	With tab	95	60

(Des Z. Narkiss. Litho)

1959 (11 May). 11th Anniversary of Independence. Vert designs as T **72**. W **42** (sideways). P 14.

161	60pr. red, black, yellow-green and bluish green	15	15
162	120pr. carmine, brown, green and purple	15	15
163	300pr. yellow, green, drab and turquoise-blue	15	15
161/163	*Set of 3*	40	40
161/163	*Set of 3 with tabs*	80	55

Flowers: 60pr. T **72**; 120pr. Cyclamen; 300pr. Narcissus.

See also Nos. 188/189, 211/213, 257/259.

73 C. N. Bialik

74 Bristol 175 Britannia 313 Airliner and Wind-sock

(Des M. and G. Shamir. Photo)

1959 (22 July). 25th Death Anniversary of Chaim Bialik (poet). No wmk. P 14×13.

164	**73** 250pr. deep olive and yellow-orange	50	30
	With tab	80	45

(Des P. Kor. Litho)

1959 (22 July). Tenth Anniversary of Civil Aviation in Israel. W **42**. P 14.

165	**74** 500pr. multicoloured	65	45
	With tab	80	60

(Des Z. Narkiss. Photo)

1959 (9 Sept). Jewish New Year. Vert designs as T **67**. No wmk. P 14×13.

166		60pr. rose-red and chocolate	30	25
167		200pr. yellow-olive and deep olive	50	30
168		350pr. orange and sepia	65	45
166/168 *Set of* 3			1·30	90
166/168 *Set of* 3 *with tabs*			2·10	1·70

Designs: 60pr. Pomegranates; 200pr. Olives; 350pr. Dates.

76 E. Ben-Yehuda

77 Merhavya Settlement

(Des Z. Narkiss. Litho)

1959 (25 Nov). Birth Centenary of Eliezer Ben-Yehuda (pioneer of Hebrew language). No wmk. P 14.

169	**76**	250pr. deep blue and blue	50	45
		With tab	80	75

(Des M. and G. Shamir. Photo)

1959 (25 Nov). 50th Anniversary of Merhavya and Deganya Settlements, and 75th Anniversary of Yesud Ha-Maala Settlement. Horiz designs as T **77**. P 13×14.

170		60pr. deep green and olive-yellow	15	15
171		120pr. red-brown and yellow-brown	50	30
172		180pr. deep green and turquoise-blue	80	60
170/172 *Set of* 3			1·30	95
170/172 *Set of* 3 *with tabs*			3·25	2·50

Designs: Views of—60pr. T **77**; 120pr. Yesud Ha-Maala; 180pr. Deganya.

New Currency

78 Ancient Jewish Coin

79 Tiberias

(Des O. Wallish. Photo)

1960 (6 Jan–6 July). Values in black. No wmk. P 13×14.

173	**78**	1a. deep bistre/*pink*	15	10
		a. White-backed paper	2·00	1·70
174		3a. red/*pink*	15	10
175		5a. slate/*pink*	15	10
176		6a. emerald-green/*azure*	15	10
176*a*		7a. grey/*azure* (6.7.60)	15	10
177		8a. magenta/*azure*	20	10
178		12a. greenish blue/*azure*	20	10
179		18a. orange	25	10
180		25a. blue	30	20
181		30a. carmine-red	35	20
182		50a. reddish lilac	45	25
173/182 *Set of* 11			2·30	1·30
173/182 *Set of* 11 *with tabs*			4·75	2·75

(Des F. Stern. Photo)

1960 (24 Feb)–**61**. AIR. T **79** and similar designs. No wmk. P 13×14 (horiz) or 14×13 (vert).

183		15a. black and reddish lilac	40	25
184		20a. black and light green	50	40
184*a*		25a. black and orange (14.6.61)	80	65
184*b*		30a. black and turquoise-blue (14.6.61)	1·30	1·30
184*c*		35a. black and green (14.6.61)	1·70	1·30
184*d*		40a. black and lilac (26.10.61)	3·25	2·50
184*e*		50a. black and yellow-olive (26.10.61)	1·30	1·30
185		65a. black and cobalt	3·25	3·25
185*a*		I£1 black and pink (26.10.61)	7·25	7·00
183/185*a* *Set of* 9			18·00	16·00
183/185*a* *Set of* 9 *with tabs*			39·00	35·00

Designs: Vert—15a. Old Town, Zefat; 20a. Tower, Ashqelon; 25a. Akko Tower and boats; 30a. View of Haifa from Mt. Carmel. Horiz—35a. Ancient synagogue, Capernaum; 40a. Kefar Hittim—Tomb of Jethro; 50a. City walls, Jerusalem; 65a. T **79**; I£1, Old city, Yafo (Jaffa).

ERRORS. Various errors exist from issues made between 1960 and 1987. It is believed that the majority of these are printer's waste which escaped from the official destruction process. Only those examples which are known to have been sold for postal purposes are listed.

80 Operation Magic Carpet

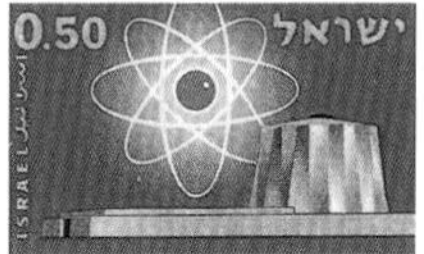

81 Atomic Symbol and Reactor Building

(Des O. Wallish. Photo)

1960 (7 Apr). World Refugee Year. T **80** and similar horiz design. No wmk. P 13×14.

186		25a. chestnut (Type **79**)	40	40
187		50a. green (Resettled family)	40	40
186/187 *Set of* 2			70	70
186/187 *Set of* 2 *with tabs*			1·60	1·50

(Des Z. Narkiss. Litho)

1960 (27 Apr). 12th Anniversary of Independence. Vert floral designs as T **72**. No wmk. P 14.

188		12a. yellow, grey, green and blue	50	40
189		32a. yellow, green and brown	80	40
188/189 *Set of* 2			1·20	70
188/189 *Set of* 2 *with tabs*			2·50	1·50

Flowers: 12a. *Pancratium maritimum*; 32a. *Oenothera drummondi*.

(Des P. Kor. Litho)

1960 (6 July). Inauguration of Atomic Reactor. W **42**. P 14.

190	**81**	50a. red, black and blue	1·30	75
		With tab	2·50	1·50

83 King Saul

84 Dr. Theodor Herzl

(Des A. Kalderon. Litho)

1960 (31 Aug). Jewish New Year. Various vert designs as T **83**. Centres multicoloured; background colours below. W **42** sideways (7a.), no wmk (others). P 14.

191	**83**	7a. green	50	25
192	–	25a. brown (King David)	1·00	50
193	–	40a. bright blue (King Solomon)	1·30	75
191/193 *Set of* 3			2·50	1·40
191/193 *Set of* 3 *with tabs*			3·75	3·00

(Des M. and G. Shamir. Litho)

1960 (31 Aug). Birth Centenary of Dr. Theodor Herzl (founder of World Zionist Movement). W **42**. P 14.

194	**84**	25a. black-brown and cream	80	75
		With tab	1·60	1·50

85 Postal Courier, Prague, 1741

86 Henrietta Szold

(Des P. Kor, from old engraving. Photo)

1960 (9 Oct). TAVIV National Stamp Exhibition, Tel Aviv. No wmk. P 13×14.

195	**85**	25a. black and pale olive-grey	2·30	1·40
		With tab	4·75	2.75

MS195*a* 192×135 mm. No. 195 but in olive-brown and light sage-green (*sold at* 50a.) .... 50·00 50·00

No. **MS**195*a* was only sold at the stamp exhibition.

(Des O. Adler. Photo)

1960 (14 Dec). Birth Centenary of Henrietta Szold (founder of Youth Immigration Scheme). No wmk. P 13×14.

196	**86**	25a. slate-violet and greenish blue	65	40
		With tab	1·30	75

87 Badges of First Zionist Congress, and Jerusalem

(Des O. Wallish. Litho)

1960 (14 Dec). 25th Zionist Congress, Jerusalem. No wmk. P 14.

197	**87**	50a. light blue and deep ultramarine	2·00	90
		With tab	4·00	1·80

88 Ram (Aries)

89 The Twelve Signs

(Des J. Blaushild. Litho (**89**) or photo (others))

1961 (27 Feb)–**65**. Signs of the Zodiac. As Types **88/89**. P 14 (No. 210) or 13×14 (others).

198	1a. emerald	25	15
199	2a. scarlet	25	15
200	6a. ultramarine	25	15
201	7a. brown	25	15
202	8a. deep green	25	15
	a. *Tête-bêche* (horiz pair) (4.1.65)	1·60	1·50
203	10a. red-orange	25	15
204	12a. violet	40	25
	a. *Tête-bêche* (horiz pair) (4.1.65)	1·60	1·50
205	18a. magenta	80	50
206	20a. yellow-olive	40	30
207	25a. purple	65	40
208	32a. black	1·00	75
209	50a. turquoise-blue	1·20	90
210	I£1 blue, gold and deep blue	2·75	2·30
198/210	*Set of* 13	7·75	5·75
198/210	*Set of* 13 *with tabs*	17·00	12·00

Designs: (As T **88**)—1a. T **88**; 2a. Bull (Taurus); 6a. Twins (Gemini); 7a. Crab (Cancer); 8a. Lion (Leo); 10a. Virgin (Virgo); 12a. Scales (Libra); 18a. Scorpion (Scorpio); 20a. Archer (Sagittarius); 25a. Goat (Capricorn); 32a. Waterman (Aquarius); 50a. Fish (Pisces); I£1 T **89**.

The *tête-bêche* pairs come from sheets printed for making up into booklets. These sheets also give horizontal *tête-bêche* pairs and vertical pairs of the 8a. and 12a. separated by a stamp-size label with ornamental pattern.

The 1a. and 10a. were also issued in coils.

(Des Z. Narkiss. Litho)

1961 (18 Apr). 13th Anniversary of Independence. Vert floral designs as T **72**. P 14.

211	7a. yellow, brown and deep green	35	25
212	12a. yellow-green, purple and magenta	60	45
213	32a. red, yellow-green and greenish blue	80	60
211/213	*Set of* 3	1·60	1·20
211/213	*Set of* 3 *with tabs*	3·50	2·50

Flowers: 7a. Myrtle; 12a. Squill; 32a. Oleander.

91 Throwing the Javelin

92 A Decade of Israel Bonds

(Des O. Adler. Litho)

1961 (18 Apr). Seventh Hapoel Sports Association International Congress, Ramat Gan. P 14.

214	**91**	25a. multicoloured	80	70
		With tab	1·60	1·40

(Des M. and G. Shamir. Photo)

1961 (14 June). Tenth Anniversary of Israel Bond Issue. P 14×13.

215	**92**	50a. slate-blue	80	70
		With tab	1·60	1·40

93 Samson

94 Bet Hamidrash (synagogue), Medzibozh (Russia)

(Des A. Kalderon. Litho)

1961 (21 Aug). Jewish New Year. Heroes of Israel. Vert designs as T **93**. Centres multicoloured; background colours below. P 14.

216	**93**	7a. orange-red	70	45
217	–	25a. lilac-grey (Yehuda Maccabi)	80	60
218	–	40a. bright reddish lilac (Bar Kochba)	80	70
216/218		*Set of* 3	2·10	1·60
216/218		*Set of* 3 *with tabs*	4·50	3·50

(Des E. Vardimon. Photo)

1961 (21 Aug). Bicentenary of Death of Rabbi Baal Shem Tov (founder of Hassidism movement). P 13×14.

219	**94**	25a. sepia and pale yellow	70	45
		With tab	1·40	90

95 Fir Cone

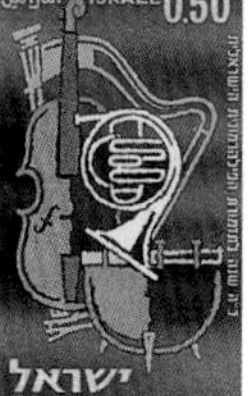

96 Musical Instruments

(Des Z. Narkiss (25a.), P. Kor (30a.). Photo)

1961 (26 Dec). Afforestation Achievements. T **95** and similar horiz design. P 13×14.

220	25a. yellow, black and green	1·40	1·20
221	30a. multicoloured	1·50	1·30
220/221	*Set of* 2	2·50	2·30
220/221	*Set of* 2 *with tabs*	5·75	4·75

Designs: 25a. T **95**; 30a. Symbol of afforestation.

(Des M. and G. Shamir. Litho)

1961 (26 Dec). 25th Anniversary of Israel Philharmonic Orchestra. P 14.

222	**96**	50a. multicoloured	3·00	2·75
		With tab	6·00	5·50

97 Bay of Elat

0.03
(**98**)

(Des F. Stern. Litho)

1962 (21 Feb). AIR. W **42** (sideways). P 14.

223	**97**	I£3 multicoloured	20·00	15·00
		With tab	39·00	30·00

1962 (18 Mar). As Nos. 198, 201 and 208 (colours changed), surch as T **98**.

224	3a. on 1a. mauve	35	25
225	5a. on 7a. grey	35	25

226 30a. on 32a. emerald 35 25
a. Surch omitted £170 £170
224/226 *Set of 3* 95 70
224/226 *Set of 3 with tabs* .... 2·10 1·40

The 5a. was also issued in coils.

99 Symbolic Flame

100 Sud Aviation SO 4050 Vatour IIA Jet-fighters

(Des Mrs. C. Menusy, Mrs. C. Ornan: Photo (12a.). Des J. Zim. Litho (55a.))

1962 (30 Apr). Heroes' and Martyrs' Day. T **99** and similar vert design. P 14×13 (12a.) or 14 (55a.).
227 12a. yellow, red and black 45 35
228 55a. yellow, red, blue and black .... 1·40 1·20
227/228 *Set of 2* .... 1·70 1·40
227/228 *Set of 2 with tabs* .... 3·75 3·00

Designs: 12a. T **99**; 55a. Nazi 'Yellow Star' and candles.

(Des M. and G. Shamir. Photo)

1962 (30 Apr). 14th Anniversary of Independence. T **100** and similar horiz design. P 13×14.
229 12a. blue 90 90
230 30a. bronze-green .... 1·60 1·40
229/230 *Set of 2* .... 2·30 2·10
229/230 *Set of 2 with tabs* .... 5·00 4·50

Designs: 12a. T **100**; 30a. Flight of Vatour IIA jet-fighters.

101 Mosquito and Malaria Graph

102 Rosh Pinna

(Des G. Rothschild and Z. Lippmann. Photo)

1962 (30 Apr). Malaria Eradication. P 14×13.
231 **101** 25a. yellow-bistre, red and black 70 60
With tab 1·40 1·20

(Des M. and G. Shamir. Photo)

1962 (30 Apr). 80th Anniversary of Rosh Pinna. P 14×13.
232 **102** 20a. deep bluish green and pale yellow 70 60
With tab 1·40 1·20

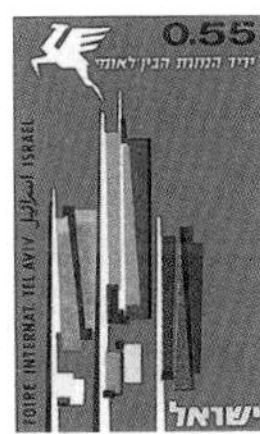

103 Fair Flags

104 'The wolf also shall dwell with the lamb'

(Des D. Reisinger. Litho)

1962 (5 June). Near East International Fair, Tel Aviv. P 14.
233 **103** 55a. multicoloured .... 1·20 1·00
With tab 2·30 2·10

(Des Mrs. C. Menusy and Mrs. C. Ornan. Photo)

1962 (5 Sept). Jewish New Year. T **104** and similar vert designs illustrating quotations from *Book of Isaiah*. P 14×13.
234 8a. black, red and olive 60 45
235 28a. black, bright purple and olive .... 1·20 70
236 43a. black, orange and olive .... 1·70 1·40
234/236 *Set of 3* .... 3·25 2·30
234/236 *Set of 3 with tabs* .... 7·00 5·00

Designs: 8a. T **104**; 28a. 'And the leopard shall lie down with the kid...'; 43a. 'And the sucking child shall play on the hole of the asp...'

105 Boeing 707 Jetliner

106 Pennant Coralfish

(Des M. and G. Shamir. Photo)

1962 (7 Nov). El Al Airline Commemoration. P 13×14.
237 **105** 55a. indigo, lilac and light blue .... 1·50 1·40
With tab 3·00 2·75

MS237*a* 195×136 mm. **105** 55a. indigo, lilac and turquoise-blue (*sold at* I£1) .... 9·25 9·25

(Des M. and G. Shamir. Litho)

1962 (26 Dec). Red Sea Fish (1st series). T **106** and similar horiz designs. Multicoloured. P 14.
238 3a. Type **106** 25 25
239 6a. Racoon Butterflyfish 25 25
240 8a. Indian Ocean Lionfish 45 35
241 12a. Regal Angelfish (*Holacanthus imperator*) 45 35
238/241 *Set of 4* .... 1·30 1·10
238/241 *Set of 4 with tabs* .... 2·75 2·30

See also Nos. 265/268.

107 Symbolic Cogwheels

108 J. Korczak (child educator)

(Des I. Blaushild. Photo)

1962 (26 Dec). 25th Anniversary of United Jewish Appeal. P 13×14.
242 **107** 20a. blue, silver and red 80 70
With tab 1·60 1·40

(Des O. Adler. Photo)

1962 (26 Dec). Janusz Korczak Commemoration. P 13×14.
243 **108** 30a. sepia and olive-grey 80 70
With tab 1·60 1·40

109 Houbara Bustard (*Chlamydotis undulata*)

110 Bird in the Hand

(Des Miriam Karoly. Photo)

1963 (13 Feb–23 Oct). AIR. T **109** and similar designs. P 14×13 (vert) or 13×14 (horiz).
244 5a. rose, brown and violet (25.4) 35 25
245 20a. turquoise, sepia and red (25.4) 60 35
246 28a. black, brown and green (25.4) 60 35
247 30a. multicoloured (19.6) 60 35
248 40a. multicoloured (19.6) 80 35
249 45a. multicoloured (19.6) .... 1·20 80
250 55a. orange, black and turquoise .... 1·20 80
251 70a. bistre, brown and black .... 1·40 1·00
252 I£1 orange, black and carmine-red .... 1·60 1·00
253 I£3 multicoloured (23.10) .... 4·50 4·00
244/253 *Set of 10* .... 11·50 8·25
244/253 *Set of 10 with tabs* .... 25·00 18·00

Birds: Horiz—5a. Sinai Rosefinch (*Erythrina sinoica*); 20a. White-breasted Kingfisher (*Halcyon smyrnensis*); 28a. Mourning Wheatear (*Oenanthe lugens*). Vert—30a. Madagascar Bee-eater (*Merops superciliosus*); 40a. Graceful Prinia (*Prinia gracilis*); 45a. Palestine Sunbird (*Cinnyris osea*); 55a. T **109**; 70a. Eurasian Scops Owl (*Otus scops*); I£1, Purple Heron (*Ardea purpurea*); I£3, White-tailed Sea Eagle (*Haliaetus albicilla*).

(Des A. Kalderon. Photo)

1963 (21 Mar). Freedom from Hunger. P 13×14.

254 **110** 55a. olive-grey and black .... 1·40 1·40
With tab 2·75 2·75
a. Deep grey and black .... 11·50 10·50
ab. *Tête-bêche* (pair) .... 31·00 31·00

No. 254*a* comes from booklets and does not exist with tabs. The *tête-bêche* pair comes from sheets of 16 printed for making up into booklets.

111 Construction at Daybreak **112** Compositor

(Des P. Kor. Litho)

1963 (21 Mar). 25th Anniversary of Stockade and Tower Settlements. T **111** and similar horiz design. P 14.

255 12a. yellow-brown, black and yellow 45 45
256 30a. reddish purple, black and light blue 90 90
255/256 *Set of 2* .... 1·20 1·20
255/256 *Set of 2 with tabs* .... 2·75 2·75

Designs: 12a. T **111**; 30a. Settlement at night.

(Des Z. Narkiss. Litho)

1963 (25 Apr). 15th Anniversary of Independence. Vert floral designs as T **72**. Flowers multicoloured; background colours below. P 14.

257 8a. slate (White Lily) 60 45
258 30a. yellow-green (Bristly Hollyhock) .... 1·50 1·40
259 37a. dull purple (Sharon Tulip) .... 2·50 1·20
257/259 *Set of 3* .... 4·25 2·75
257/259 *Set of 3 with tabs* .... 9·25 8·00

(Des O. Wallish. Photo)

1963 (19 June). Centenary of Hebrew Press. P 14×13.

260 **112** 12a. brown-purple and buff .... 1·40 1·20
With tab 2·75 2·30
a. Sheet of 16 .... £140 £140

No. 260 was issued in sheets of 16 (4×4) with an overall background consisting of a replica of the first page of the first issue of the Hebrew newspaper *Halbanon*, published in Jerusalem in 1863.

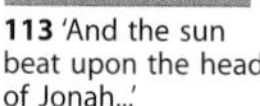

113 'And the sun beat upon the head of Jonah...' **114** Hoe clearing Thistles

(Des J. David. Photo)

1963 (21 Aug). Jewish New Year. T **113** and similar designs illustrating quotations from the *Book of Jonah*. Multicoloured. P 14×13 (8a.) or 13×14 (others).

261 8a. Type **113** 60 60
262 30a. 'And there was a mighty tempest in the sea' (*horiz*) .... 1·50 1·50
263 55a. 'And Jonah was in the belly of the fish' (*horiz*) .... 3·00 3·00
261/263 *Set of 3* .... 4·50 4·50
261/263 *Set of 3 with tabs* .... 9·75 9·75

(Des E. Weishoff. Litho)

1963 (21 Aug). 80th Anniversary of Israeli Agricultural Settlements. P 14.

264 **114** 37a. multicoloured .... 1·40 1·00
With tab 2·75 2·10

(Des M. and G. Shamir. Litho)

1963 (16 Dec). Red Sea Fish (2nd series). Horiz designs as T **106**. Multicoloured. P 14.

265 2a. Undulate Triggerfish 25 25
266 6a. Radial Lionfish 35 35
267 8a. Catalufa 45 45
268 12a. Emperor Angelfish (*Pomacanthus imperator*) 70 60
265/268 *Set of 4* .... 1·60 1·50
265/268 *Set of 4 with tabs* .... 3·50 3·25

115 *Shalom*

(Des Mrs. C. Menusy and Mrs. C. Ornan. Photo)

1963 (16 Dec). Maiden Voyage of Liner *Shalom*. P 13×14.

269 **115** I£1 ultramarine, turquoise and purple 11·50 8·75
With tab 23·00 17·00

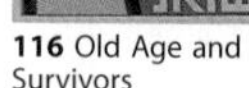

116 Old Age and Survivors **117** President Ben-Zvi

(Des E. Weishoff. Litho)

1964 (24 Feb). Tenth Anniversary of National Insurance. T **116** and similar vert designs. Multicoloured. P 14.

270 12a. Type **116** .... 1·70 80
271 25a. Nurse and child within hands (Maternity) .... 3·00 1·50
272 37a. Family within hand (Large families) .... 3·50 1·70
273 50a. Hand with arm and crutch (Employment injuries) .... 5·75 3·00
270/273 *Set of 4* .... 12·50 6·25
270/273 *Set of 4 with tabs* .... 28·00 14·00

(Des M. Krup. Photo)

1964 (13 Apr). First Anniversary of Death of President Izhak Ben-Zvi. P 14×13.

274 **117** 12a. brown 35 35
With tab 70 70

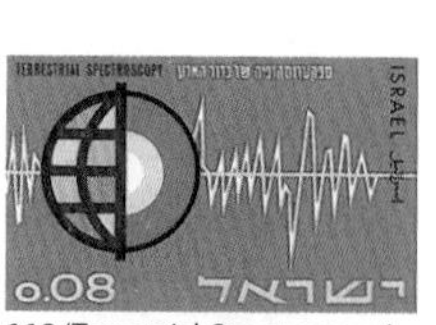

118 'Terrestrial Spectroscopy' **119** Running

(Des A. Kalderon. Litho)

1964 (13 Apr). 16th Anniversary of Independence. Israel's Contribution to Science. Horiz scientific designs as T **118**. Multicoloured. P 14.

275 8a. Type **118** 45 45
276 35a. Macromolecules of living cell .... 1·40 1·20
277 70a. Electronic computer .... 3·00 2·50
275/277 *Set of 3* .... 4·25 3·75
275/277 *Set of 3 with tabs* .... 9·75 8·75

(Des D. Reisinger. Photo)

1964 (24 June). Olympic Games, Tokyo. T **119** and similar vert designs. P 14×13.

278	8a. black and red	35	25
279	12a. black and mauve	45	30
280	30a. carmine, black and light blue	60	35
281	50a. red, deep maroon and yellow-green	70	60
278/281	*Set of 4*	1·90	1·40
278/281	*Set of 4 with tabs*	4·25	2·75

Designs: 8a. T **119**; 12a. Throwing the discus; 30a. Basketball; 50a. Football.

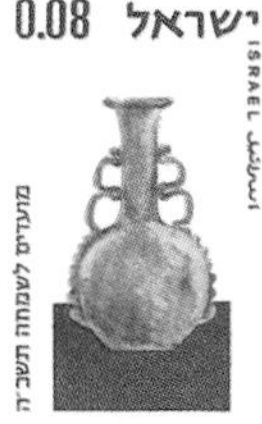

120 3rd-century Glass Vessel

121 Congress Emblem

(Des Mrs. C. Menusy and Mrs. C. Ornan. Photo (8a.) or litho (others))

1964 (5 Aug). Jewish New Year. T **120** and similar vert designs showing ancient glass vessels in Haaretz Museum, Tel Aviv. Multicoloured. P 14×14 (8a.) or 14 (others).

282	8a. Type **120**	25	25
283	35a. 1st/2nd-century vessel	60	45
284	70a. 1st-century vessel	80	60
282/284	*Set of 3*	1·50	1·20
282/284	*Set of 3 with tabs*	3·25	2·50

(Des M. and G. Shamir. Photo)

1964 (5 Aug). Sixth Israel Medical Associations World Congress. P 14×13.

285	**121**	I£1 multicoloured	1·40	1·20
		With tab	2·75	2·30

122 *Exodus* (immigrant ship)

123 Eleanor Roosevelt

(Des M. and G. Shamir. Litho)

1964 (2 Nov). Year of the Blockade-runners. P 14.

286	**122**	25a. black, slate-blue and turquoise	70	60
		With tab	1·40	1·20

(Des M. Krup. Photo)

1964 (2 Nov). 80th Birth Anniversary of Eleanor Roosevelt. P 14×13.

287	**123**	70a. plum	80	70
		With tab	1·60	1·40

124 Olympics Symbols and Knight

(Des M. and G. Shamir. Photo)

1964 (2 Nov). 16th Chess Olympiad, Tel Aviv. T **124** and similar horiz design. P 13×14.

288	12a. deep brown	60	35
289	70a. deep green	2·50	1·70
288/289	*Set of 2*	2·75	1·80
288/289	*Set of 2 with tabs*	6·25	4.25

Designs: 12a. T **124**; 70a. Olympics symbol and rook.

125 African–Israeli Friendship

126 Masada

(Des A. Kalderon. Photo)

1964 (30 Nov). TABAI National Stamp Exhibition. Haifa. P 14×13.

290	**125**	57a. multicoloured	2·50	1·40
		With tab	5·00	2·75
MS290*a*		125×81 mm. No. 290. Imperf (*sold at* I£1)	4·00	3·50

No. **MS**290*a* was only sold at the stamp exhibition.

(Des G. Rothschild and Z. Lippmann. Photo)

1965 (3 Feb). Masada. T **126** and similar designs. P 14×13 (I£1) or 13×14 (others).

291	25a. deep green	60	35
292	36a. blue	80	60
293	I£1 brown	1·20	90
291/293	*Set of 3*	2·30	1·70
291/293	*Set of 3 with tabs*	5.00	3·75

Designs: Horiz—25a. T **126**; 36a. Northern Palace, lower section. Vert—I£1. Northern Palace aerial view.

127 Ashdod

128 Fair Emblem

(Des M. and G. Shamir. Photo)

1965 (24 Mar)–**75**. Civic Arms (1st series). T **127** and similar vert designs showing Arms. P 13×14 or 14×13 (70a., I£1, I£3).

294	1a. brown (2.2.66)	25	25
295	2a. magenta (2.2.66)	25	25
296	5a. blackish brown (2.2.66)	25	25
297	6a. violet (2.2.66)	25	25
298	8a. red-orange (2.2.66)	25	25
	a. *Tête-bêche* (horiz pair) (14.3.66)	1·20	1·20
299	10a. emerald (2.2.66)	25	25
	a. Booklet pane. Nos. 299 and 417×5 (12.12.72)	4·75	
300	12a. maroon (2.2.66)	25	25
	a. *Tête-bêche* (horiz pair) (14.3.66)	1·20	1·20
301	15a. green	25	25
302	20a. red	25	25
303	25a. ultramarine	45	25
304	35a. reddish purple	45	25
305	37a. yellow-olive (2.2.66)	1·60	1·40
305*a*	40a. olive-brown (8.2.67)	70	45
306	50a. turquoise-blue (2.2.66)	70	45
306*a*	55a. crimson (8.2.67)	70	45
307	70a. deep brown (2.2.66)	1·20	90
307*a*	80a. Venetian red (8.2.67)	1·60	1·40
308	I£1 blackish green (15.12.65)	1·40	1·20
	p. Two phosphor bands (30.1.75)	3·00	3·00
309	I£3 magenta (14.3.66)	1·80	1·60
294/309	*Set of 19* (*cheapest*)	11·50	9·50
294/309	*Set of 19 with tabs* (*cheapest*)	25·00	21·00

Arms: As T **127**—1a. Lod; 2a. Qiryat Shmona; 5a. Petah Tiqwa; 6a. Nazareth; 8a. Beer Sheva; 10a. Bet Shean; 12a. Tiberias; 15a. T **127**; 20a. Elat; 25a. Akko; 35a. Dimona; 37a. Zefat; 40a. Mizpe Ramon; 50a. Rishon Le Zion; 55a. Ashqelon; 80a. Rosh Pinna. 22½×27 mm—70a. Jerusalem; I£1, Tel Aviv-Yafo; I£3, Haifa.

The 1, 5 and 10a. were issued in coils on 10 January 1967.

Nos. 298a and 300a come from uncut sheets printed for making booklets. From the same sheets come horizontal *tête-bêche* gutter pairs and vertical gutter pairs of the 8a, or 12a., and also horizontal *tête-bêche* gutter pairs of Nos. 299 and 417 together.

See also Nos. 413/424.

(Des N. Wolfensohn. Photo)

1965 (24 Mar). Second International Book Fair, Jerusalem. P 13×14.

310	**128**	70a. black, blue and light grey-green	60	60
		With tab	1·20	1·20

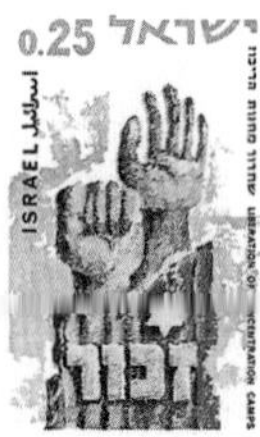

129 Hands reaching for Barbed Wire

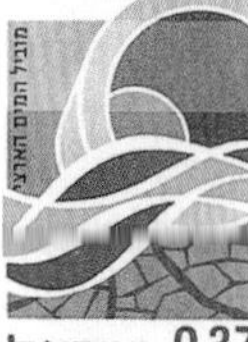

130 National Water Supply

(Des J. Zim. Photo)

1965 (27 Apr). 20th Anniversary of Concentration Camps Liberation. P 14×13.

311	**129**	25a. black, yellow and olive-grey	70	45
		With tab	1·40	90

(Des Z. Narkiss. Photo)

1965 (27 Apr). 17th Anniversary of Independence. P 14×13.

312	**130**	37a. olive-brown, deep new blue and new blue	45	45
		With tab	90	90

131 Potash Works, Sedom

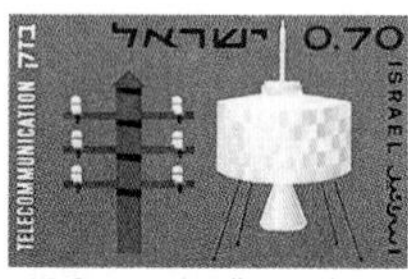

132 *Syncom* Satellite and Telegraph Pole

(Des Z. Narkiss. Litho)

1965 (21 July). Dead Sea Industrial Development. T **131** and similar vert design. Multicoloured. P 14.

313	12a. Potash Works, Sedom (*different*)	35	10
314	50a. Type **131**	90	45
313/314	*Set of 2*	1·10	50
313/314	*Set of 2 with tabs*	2·50	1·20

The two stamps form one composite design when placed side by side.

(Des Mrs. C. Menusy. Photo)

1965 (21 July). Centenary of International Telecommunications Union. P 13×14.

315	**132**	70a. bluish violet, black and greenish blue	80	60
		With tab	1·60	1·20

133 'Co-operation'

134 'Light'

(Des M. and G. Shamir. Litho)

1965 (21 July). International Co-operation Year. P 14.

316	**133**	36a. multicoloured	60	45
		With tab	1·20	90

(Des A. Kalderon. Photo)

1965 (7 Sept). Jewish New Year. 'The Creation'. T **134** and similar vert designs. Multicoloured. P 13×14.

317	6a. Type **134**	25	25
318	8a. 'Heaven'	25	25
319	12a. 'Earth'	25	25
320	25a. 'Stars'	45	45
321	35a. 'Birds and Beasts'	70	70
322	70a. 'Man'	1·20	1·20
317/322	*Set of 6*	2·75	2·75
317/322	*Set of 6 with tabs*	5·75	5·75

135 *Charaxes jasius*

136 War of Independence Memorial

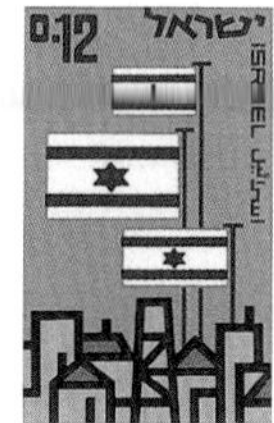

137 Flags

(Des M. and G. Shamir. Litho)

1965 (15 Dec). Butterflies and Moths. T **135** and similar vert designs. Multicoloured. P 14.

323	2a. Type **135**	25	25
324	6a. *Papilio alexanor*	35	35
325	8a. *Deilephila nerii* (*Daphnis nerii*)	35	35
326	12a. *Zegris eupheme*	45	45
323/326	*Set of 4*	1·30	1·30
323/326	*Set of 4 with tabs*	2·50	2·50

(Des O. Adler. Photo)

1966 (20 Apr). Memorial Day. P 14×13.

327	**136**	40a. olive-brown and black	45	45
		With tab	90	90

(Des E. Weishoff. Litho)

1966 (20 Apr). 18th Anniversary of Independence. T **137** and similar vert designs. Multicoloured. P 14.

328	12a. Type **137**	25	25
329	20a. Fireworks	30	25
330	80a. Dassault Mirage IIICJ jet fighters and warships	35	35
328/330	*Set of 3*	80	75
328/330	*Set of 3 with tabs*	1·60	1·60

138 Knesset Building

139 Scooter Rider

(Des G. Rothschild and Z. Lippmann. Photo)

1966 (22 June). Inauguration of Knesset Building, Jerusalem. P 13×14.

331	**138**	I£1 blue	1·00	90
		With tab	2·60	1·80

(Des E. Weishoff. Photo)

1966 (22 June). Road Safety. T **139** and similar designs. Multicoloured. P 14.

332	2a. Type **139**	10	10
333	5a. Cyclist	10	10
334	10a. Pedestrian on crossing	10	10
335	12a. Child with ball	10	10
336	15a. Motorist in car	25	25
332/336	*Set of 5*	60	60
332/336	*Set of 5 with tabs*	1·20	1·20

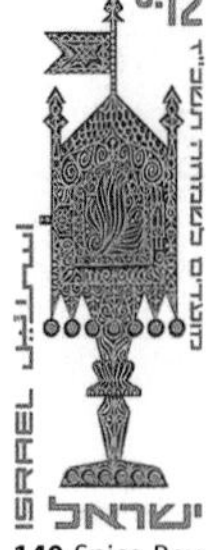

140 Spice Box

141 Panther (bronze)

(Des E. Weishoff. Photo)

1966 (24 Aug). Jewish New Year. Religious Ceremonial Objects. T **140** and similar vert designs. Multicoloured. P 13×14.

337	12a. Type **140**	15	15
338	15a. Candlesticks	25	25
339	35a. Kiddush cup	25	25
340	40a. Torah pointer	25	25
341	80a. Hanging lamp	60	60
337/341	*Set of 5*	1·40	1·40
337/341	*Set of 5 with tabs*	2·75	2·75

(Des O. Adler. Litho)

1966 (25 Oct). Israel Museum Exhibits. T **141** and similar designs. Multicoloured. P 14.

342	15a. Type **141**	1·70	1·70
343	30a. Synagogue menora (stone)	2·30	2·30
344	40a. Phoenician sphinx (ivory)	3·00	3·00
345	55a. Earring (gold)	3·50	3·50
346	80a. Miniature capital (gold)	4·50	4·50
347	I£1.15 Drinking horn (gold) (*vert*)	8·00	8·00
342/347	*Set of 6*	21·00	21·00
342/347	*Set of 6 with tabs*	46·00	46·00

142 Levant Postman and Mail Coach

143 'Fight Cancer and Save Life'

(Des M. and G. Shamir. Photo)

1966 (14 Dec). Stamp Day. T **142** and similar designs. P 14.

348	12a. green and yellow-brown	10	10
349	15a. cerise, brown and yellow-green	25	25
350	40a. slate-blue and magenta	35	35
351	I£1 bistre-brown and turquoise-blue	70	60
348/351	*Set of 4*	1·30	1·20
348/351	*Set of 4 with tabs*	2·75	2·50

Designs: 12a. T **142**; 15a. Turkish postman and camels; 40a. Palestine postman and steam locomotive; I£1, Israeli postman and Boeing 707.

(Des H. Frank. Photo)

1966 (14 Dec). Cancer Research. P 14×13.

352	**143**	15a. slate-green and red	60	35
		With tab	1·20	70

144 Akko (Acre)

145 Book and Crowns

(Des O. Adler. Photo)

1967 (15 Mar). Ancient Israeli Ports. T **144** and similar horiz designs. P 13×14.

353	15a. dull purple (Type **144**)	35	25
354	40a. deep bluish green (Caesarea)	60	45
355	80a. deep blue (Yafo or Jaffa)	80	70
353/355	*Set of 3*	1·60	1·30
353/355	*Set of 3 with tabs*	3·50	2·75

(Des E. Weishoff. Photo)

1967 (15 Mar). *Shulhan Arukh* (Book of Wisdom). P 14×13.

356	**145**	40a. multicoloured	60	60
		With tab	1·20	1·20

146 War of Independence Memorial

147 Taylorcraft Auster AOP.5 Reconnaissance Aeroplane

(Des O. Adler. Photo)

1967 (10 May). Memorial Day. P 13×14.

357	**146**	55a. silver, deep blue and greenish blue	70	60
		With tab	1·40	1·20

(Des M. and G. Shamir. Photo)

1967 (10 May). Independence Day. Military Aircraft. T **147** and similar horiz designs. P 13×14.

358	15a. deep greenish blue and olive-green	25	25
359	30a. brown and yellow-orange	45	45
360	80a. violet-blue and turquoise	70	70
358/360	*Set of 3*	1·30	1·30
358/360	*Set of 3 with tabs*	2·75	2·75

Designs: 15a. T **147**; 30a. Dassault Mystère IVA jet fighter; 80a. Dassault Mirage IIICJ jet fighters.

> During the Six-day War, 5 to 10 June 1967, Israeli troops occupied the Gaza Strip, the Sinai Peninsula, Jordanian territory west of the River Jordan and the Golan Heights in Syria. Israeli stamps were brought into use in these areas.

148 *Dolphin* (freighter) in Straits of Tiran

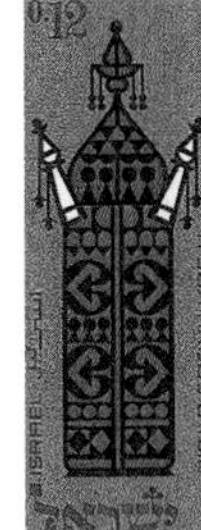

149 Law Scroll

(Des 'Roli' team (G. Rothschild and Z. Lippmann). Photo)

1967 (16 Aug). Victory in Arab–Israeli War. T **148** and similar designs. P 14×13 (15a.) or 13×14 (others).

361	15a. black, yellow and red	10	10
362	40a. deep bluish green	25	25
363	80a. bluish violet	25	25
361/363	*Set of 3*	55	55
361/363	*Set of 3 with tabs*	1·20	1·20

Designs: Vert—15a. Sword emblem of Zahal (Israeli Defence Forces). Horiz—40a. T **148**; 80a. Wailing Wall, Jerusalem.

(Des E. Weishoff. Photo)

1967 (13 Sept). Jewish New Year. *Scrolls of the Torah* (Mosaic Law). T **149** and similar designs. P 13×14.

364	12a. multicoloured	25	25
365	15a. multicoloured	25	25
366	35a. multicoloured	35	35
367	40a. multicoloured	35	35
368	80a. multicoloured	35	35
364/368	*Set of 5*	1·40	1·40
364/368	*Set of 5 with tabs*	3·00	2·75

150 'Welcome to Israel'

151 Lord Balfour

(Des A. Kalderon. Litho)

1967 (2 Nov). International Tourist Year. T **150** and similar vert designs each with 'Sun' emblem. Multicoloured. P 14.

369	30a. Type **150**	25	25
370	40a. 'Air hostess'	35	35
371	80a. 'Orange' child	35	35
369/371	*Set of 3*	85	85
369/371	*Set of 3 with tabs*	1·90	1·80

(Des O. Adler. Photo)

1967 (2 Nov). 50th Anniversary of Balfour Declaration. T **151** and similar horiz design. P 13×14.

372	15a. blackish green (Dr. C. Weizmann)	25	25
373	40a. brown (Type **151**)	35	35
372/373	*Set of 2*	55	55
372/373	*Set of 2 with tabs*	1·20	1·20

152 Ibex

153 Diamond

(Des M. and G. Shamir. Litho)

1967 (27 Dec). Israeli Nature Reserves. T **152** and similar square designs. Multicoloured. P 13.

374	12a. Type **152**	25	25
375	18a. Caracal (*Felis caracal*)	50	45
376	60a. Dorcas Gazelle (*Gazella dorcas*)	60	60
374/376	*Set of 3*	1·20	1·20
374/376	*Set of 3 with tabs*	2·75	2·50

(Des O. Adler. Photo)

1968 (7 Feb–23 Dec). AIR. Israeli Exports. T **153** and similar horiz designs. P 13×14.

377	10a. multicoloured (11.3)	25	25
378	30a. multicoloured (11.3)	25	25
379	40a. multicoloured (11.3)	35	25
380	50a. multicoloured (11.3)	60	45
381	55a. multicoloured (6.11)	60	45
382	60a. multicoloured (6.11)	70	45
383	80a. multicoloured (23.12)	70	45
384	I£1 multicoloured (6.11)	95	70
385	I£1.50 multicoloured (23.12)	95	70
386	I£3 reddish violet and pale turquoise-green	1·70	1·30
377/386	*Set of 10*	6·25	4·75
377/386	*Set of 10 with tabs*	13·00	10·50

Designs: 10a. Draped curtains ('Textiles'); 30a. 'Stamps'; 40a. Jar and necklace ('Arts and Crafts'); 50a. Chick and egg ('Chicks'); 55a. Melon, avocado and strawberries ('Fruits'); 60a. Gladioli ('Flowers'); 80a. Telecommunications equipment ('Electronics'); I£1, Atomic equipment ('Isotopes'); I£1.50, Models ('Fashion'); I£3, T **153**.

154 Beflagged Football

155 Immigration

(Des E. Weishoff. Litho)

1968 (11 Mar). Pre-Olympic Football Tournament. P 13.

387	**154**	80a. multicoloured	60	45
		With tab	1·20	90

(Des M. and G. Shamir. Litho)

1968 (24 Apr). Independence Day. T **155** and similar vert design. P 14.

388	15a. Type **155**	25	25
389	80a. Settlement	35	35
388/389	*Set of 2*	55	55
388/389	*Set of 2 with tabs*	1·40	1·40

156 Rifles and Helmet

157 Zahal Emblem

(Des E. Weishoff. Litho)

1968 (24 Apr). Memorial Day. P 14.

390	**156**	55a. multicoloured	60	35
		With tab	1·20	70

(Des E. Weishoff. Litho)

1968 (24 Apr). Independence Day (Zahal–Israel Defence Forces). P 14.

391	**157**	40a. multicoloured	60	35
		With tab	1·20	70

158 Resistance Fighter (detail from Warsaw monument)

159 Moshe Sharett

(Des M. and G. Shamir. Photo)

1968 (24 Apr). 25th Anniversary of Warsaw Ghetto Uprising. P 14×13.

392	**158**	60a. bistre	60	45
		With tab	1·20	90

(Des O. Adler. Photo)

1968 (5 June). 27th Zionist Congress, Jerusalem. P 14×13.

393	**159**	I£1 sepia	50	45
		With tab	95	90

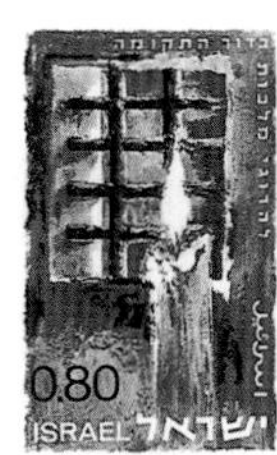
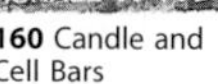

160 Candle and Cell Bars

161 Jerusalem

(Des J. Zim. Photo)

1968 (5 June). Fallen Freedom Fighters. P 13×13.

394	**160**	80a. black, grey and brown	50	45
		With tab	95	90

(Des D. Ben Dov. Photo)

1968 (21 Aug). Jewish New Year. T **161** and similar vert designs. P 14×13.

395	12a. multicoloured	25	25
396	15a. multicoloured	50	45
397	35a. multicoloured	60	60
398	40a. multicoloured	70	70
399	60a. multicoloured	95	90
395/399	*Set of 5*	2·75	2·50
395/399	*Set of 5 with tabs*	6·00	5·75

Designs: Jerusalem—views of the Old City (12, 15, 35a.) and of the New City (40, 60a.).

162 Scout Badge and Knot

163 Lions' Gate, Jerusalem (*detail*)

(Des E. Weishoff. Litho)

1968 (21 Aug). 50th Anniversary of Jewish Scout Movement. P 13.

400 **162** 30a. multicoloured ... 60 35
With tab 1·20 70

(Des O. Adler. Photo)

1968 (8 Oct). Tabira Stamp Exhibition, Jerusalem. P 13×14.

401 **163** I£1 chestnut ... 60 35
With tab 1·20 70

MS402 122×75 mm. No. 401. Imperf (*sold at* I£1.50)... 7·25 7·00

164 A. Mapu

165 Disabled playing Basketball

(Des O. Adler. Photo)

1968 (8 Oct). Death Centenary of Abraham Mapu (writer). P 14×13.

403 **164** 30a. deep olive ... 60 35
With tab 1·20 70

(Des Z. Narkiss. Photo)

1968 (6 Nov). International Games for the Disabled. P 14×13.

404 **165** 40a. deep green and light yellow-green ... 60 35
With tab 1·20 70

166 Elat

(Des O. Adler. Photo)

1969 (19 Feb). Israeli Ports. T **166** and similar horiz designs. P 13×14.

405 30a. deep magenta (Type **166**) ... 95 90
406 60a. brown (Ashdod) ... 1·20 1·20
407 I£1 deep green (Haifa) ... 1·40 1·40
405/407 *Set of 3* ... 3·25 3·25
405/407 *Set of 3 with tabs* ... 7·25 7·00

167 'Worker' and ILO Emblem

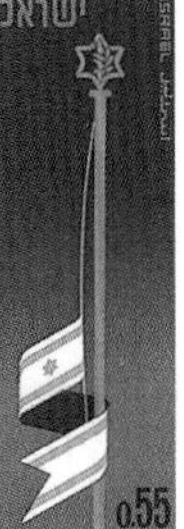

168 Israeli Flag at Half-mast

(Des O. Adler. Photo)

1969 (16 Apr). 50th Anniversary of International Labour Organisation. P 13×14.

408 **167** 80a. deep bluish green and pale lilac... 60 45
With tab 1·20 90

(Des A. Kalderon. Photo)

1969 (16 Apr). Memorial Day. P 13×14.

409 **168** 55a. gold, light blue and violet ... 60 45
With tab 1·20 90

169 Army Tank

170 Flaming Torch

(Des Y. Yoresh. Photo)

1969 (16 Apr). Independence Day. T **169** and similar horiz design. Multicoloured. P 13×14.

410 15a. Type **169** ... 35 35
411 80a. *Elat* (destroyer) ... 50 45
410/411 *Set of 2* ... 75 70
410/411 *Set of 2 with tabs* ... 1·70 1·60

(Des E. Weishoff. Photo)

1969 (9 July). Eighth Maccabiah. P 14×13.

412 **170** 60a. multicoloured ... 85 80
With tab 1·70 1·60

171 Arms of Hadera

172 Building the Ark

(Des M. and G. Shamir. Photo)

1969 (9 July)–**73**. Civic Arms (2nd series). T **171** and similar vert designs. P 13×14.

413 2a. green ... 35 35
414 3a. bright purple (3.11.69) ... 50 45
415 5a. red-orange ... 60 60
416 15a. bright carmine ... 70 70
a. Booklet pane. Nos. 416×2 and 417×4 (25.5.71) ... 5·00
b. *Tête-bêche* pair with 18a. (No. 417) (25.5.71) ... 4·75 4·50
417 18a. ultramarine (18.10.70) ... 85 80
a. *Tête-bêche* (pair) (25.5.71) ... 4·75 4·50
418 20a. yellow-brown (18.10.70) ... 85 80
a. Reddish brown (1973) ... 50 45
ab. Booklet pane. No. 418*a*×5 plus label (1.10.73) ... 2·75
419 25a. deep blue ... 1·10 1·00
420 30a. bright magenta (6.5.70) ... 60 45
421 40a. reddish violet ... 1·30 1·30
422 50a. turquoise-blue (3.11.69) ... 1·90 1·80
423 60a. yellow-olive (18.10.70) ... 1·20 1·20
424 80a. deep green ... 2·75 2·50
413/424 *Set of 12* ... 11·00 10·50
413/424 *Set of 12 with tabs* ... 25·00 24.00

Arms: 2a. T **177**; 3a. Herzliyya; 5a. Holon; 15a. Bat Yam; 18a. Ramla; 20a. Kefar Sava; 25a. Giv'atayim; 30a. Rehovot; 40a. Netanya; 50a. Bene Beraq; 60a. Nahariyya; 80a. Ramat Gan.

Nos. 416b and 417a come from uncut sheets printed for making booklets. From the same sheets come *tête-bêche* or *se-tenant* gutter pairs of Nos. 416/417 together, and also horizontal *tête-bêche* or vertical gutter pairs of No. 417.

25a. with phosphor bands was an experimental printing used for trial runs of cancelling machines. Used copies dated 13 January 1974 were included in kiloware later sold by the Post Office.

For booklet pane containing 18a. *se-tenant* with 10a., see No. 299a.

(Des D. Grebu and I. Schwadron. Photo)

1969 (13 Aug). Jewish New Year. T **172** and similar horiz designs, showing scenes from *The Flood*. Multicoloured. P 14½.

425 12a. Type **172** ... 10 10
426 15a. Animals boarding the Ark ... 15 15
427 35a. Ark afloat ... 30 30
428 40a. Dove with olive branch ... 35 35
429 60a. Ark on Mount Ararat ... 35 35
425/429 *Set of 5* ... 1·10 1·10
425/429 *Set of 5 with tabs* ... 2·75 2·50

173 *King David* (Chagall) **174** Atomic 'Plant'

1969 (24 Sept). Litho. P 14.

430	**173**	I£3 multicoloured	2·40	2·30
		With tab	4·75	4·50

(Des E. Weishoff. Photo)

1969 (3 Nov). 25th Anniversary of Weizmann Institute of Science. P 14×13.

431	**174**	I£1.15 multicoloured	1·90	1·80
		With tab	3·75	3·75

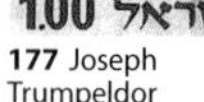

175 Dum Palms, Emeq He-Arava **176** Immigrant 'Aircraft'

(Des G. Rothschild and Z. Lippmann. Photo)

1970 (21 Jan). Nature Reserves. T **175** and similar vert designs. P 14×13.

432	2a. yellow-olive	10	10
433	3a. blue	10	10
434	5a. red	10	10
435	6a. deep myrtle-green	10	10
436	30a. reddish violet	25	25
432/436	*Set of 5*	60	60
432/436	*Set of 5 with tabs*	1·40	1·40

Designs: 2a. T **175**; 3a. Tahana Waterfall, Nahal Iyon; 5a. Nahal Baraq Canyon, Negev; 6a. Ha-Masreq, Judean Hills; 30a. Soreq Cave, Judean Hills.

(Des A. Prath. Litho)

1970 (21 Jan). 20th Anniversary of Operation Magic Carpet (immigration of Yemenite Jews). P 13.

437	**176**	30a. multicoloured	60	35
		With tab	1·20	70

177 Joseph Trumpeldor **178** Prime Minister Levi Eshkol

1970 (21 Jan). 50th Anniversary of Defence of Tel Hay. Photo. P 14×13.

438	**177**	I£1 deep slate-violet	1·20	1·20
		With tab	2·40	2·30

1970 (11 Mar). Levi Eshkol Commemoration. Litho. P 14.

439	**178**	15a. multicoloured	60	35
		With tab	1·20	70

179 Ze'ev Jabotinsky (commander) **180** Camel and Diesel Train

(Des F. Horn. Photo)

1970 (11 Mar). 50th Anniversary of Defence of Jerusalem. P 14×13.

440	**179**	80a. myrtle-green and pale cream	70	60
		With tab	1·40	1·20

(Des O. and E. Schwarz. Litho)

1970 (11 Mar). Opening of Dimona–Oron Railway. P 13.

441	**180**	80a. multicoloured	1·30	1·30
		With tab	2·75	2·50

181 Mania Shochat (author) **182** Scene from *The Dybbuk*

(Des F. Horn. Photo)

1970 (11 Mar). 60th Anniversary of Ha-Shomer. P 14×13.

442	**181**	40a. maroon and pale cream	70	60
		With tab	1·40	1·20

(Des E. Weishoff. Photo)

1970 (11 Mar). 50th Anniversary of Habimah National Theatre. P 14×13.

443	**182**	I£1 multicoloured	95	90
		With tab	1·90	1·80

183 Memorial Flame **184** *Orchis laxiflorus*

(Des R. Vero. Photo)

1970 (6 May). Memorial Day. P 13×14.

444	**183**	55a. black, rose and light violet	60	45
		With tab	1·20	90

(Des Heather Wood. Litho)

1970 (6 May). Independence Day. Israeli Wild Flowers. T **184** and similar vert designs. Multicoloured. P 13×14.

445	12a. Type **184**	35	35
446	15a. *Iris mariae*	60	45
447	80a. *Lupinus pilosus*	95	80
445/447	*Set of 3*	1·70	1·40
445/447	*Set of 3 with tabs*	3·75	3·25

185 C. Netter (founder)

186 Israeli Aircraft Industry IAI-201 Arava

(Des E. Weishoff. Photo)

1970 (6 May). Centenary of Miqwe Yisrael Agricultural College. T **185** and similar vert design. Multicoloured. P 14×13.

448 40a. Type **185** ... 85 60
449 80a. College building and gate ... 1·40 90
448/449 *Set of 2* ... 2·00 1·40
448/449 *Set of 2 with tabs* ... 4·50 3·00

(Des D. Pessach and S. Ketter. Photo)

1970 (8 July). Israel Aircraft Industries. P 13×14.

450 **186** I£1 silver, bluish violet and new blue.. 70 60
With tab 1·40 1·20

187 Dinghies

188 Keren Hayesod

(Des A. Berg. Photo)

1970 (8 July). World 420 Class Sailing Championships. T **187** and similar vert designs. Multicoloured. P 14×13.

451 15a. Type **187** ... 50 45
452 30a. Dinghy with spinnaker ... 60 45
453 80a. Dinghies racing ... 85 70
451/453 *Set of 3* ... 1·80 1·40
451/453 *Set of 3 with tabs* ... 3·75 3·25

(Des G. Rothschild and Z. Lippmann. Photo)

1970 (8 July). 50th Anniversary of Keren Hayesod. P 13×14.

454 **188** 40a. multicoloured ... 60 45
With tab 1·20 90

189 Old Synagogue, Cracow

190 Jewish 'Bird' heading for Sun

(Des E. Weishoff. Photo)

1970 (7 Sept). Jewish New Year. Synagogues. T **189** and similar square designs. Multicoloured. P 13 (15a.) or 14×14½ (others).

455 12a. Type **189** ... 10 10
456 15a. Great Synagogue, Tunis ... 10 10
a. Perf 14×14½ ... 95·00 60·00
457 35a. Portuguese Synagogue, Amsterdam ... 15 15
458 40a. Great Synagogue, Moscow ... 25 25
459 60a. Shearith Israel Synagogue, New York ... 35 35
455/459 *Set of 5* ... 85 85
455/459 *Set of 5 with tabs* ... 1·90 1·80

(Des M. and G. Shamir. Litho)

1970 (7 Sept). Operation Ezra and Nehemiah (Exodus of Iraqi Jews to Israel). P 14.

460 **190** 80a. multicoloured ... 60 45
With tab 1·20 90

191 Mother and Child

192 Tel Aviv Post Office, 1920

(Des M. Amar and G. Elmaliah. Photo)

1970 (18 Oct). 50th Anniversary of Women's International Zionist Organisation (WIZO). P 13×14.

461 **191** 80a. greenish yellow, deep blue-green and silver ... 85 70
With tab 1·70 1·40

(Des A. Prat. Photo)

1970 (18 Oct). Tabit Stamp Exhibition and 50th Anniversary of Tel Aviv Post Office. P 14.

462 **192** I£1 multicoloured ... 60 60
With tab 1·20 1·20
MS463 115×70 mm. No. 462. Imperf (*sold at* I£1.50).... 7·25 7·00

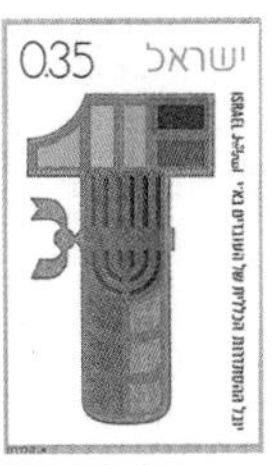

193 Histadrut Emblem

194 *Landscape with Bridge* (C. Pissarro)

(Des A. Kalderon. Litho)

1970 (22 Dec). 50th Anniversary of Histadrut. (General Federation of Labour). P 14.

464 **193** 35a. multicoloured ... 60 35
With tab 1·20 70

1970 (22 Dec). Paintings in Tel Aviv Museum. T **194** and similar horiz designs. Multicoloured. Litho. P 14.

465 85a. *Jewish Wedding* (J. Israels) ... 35 35
466 I£1 Type **194** ... 60 60
467 I£2 *Flowers in a Vase* (F. Léger) ... 95 90
465/467 *Set of 3* ... 1·70 1·70
465/467 *Set of 3 with tabs* ... 3·75 3·75

195 *Inn of the Ghosts* (Cameri Theatre)

(Des E. Weishoff. Photo)

1971 (16 Feb). Israeli Theatre. T **195** and similar horiz designs. Multicoloured. P 14×13.

468 50a. Type **195** ... 50 45
469 50a. *Samson and Delilah* (National Opera Company) ... 50 45
470 50a. *A Psalm of David* (INBAL Dance Theatre). 50 45
468/470 *Set of 3* ... 1·40 1·20
468/470 *Set of 3 with tabs* ... 3·00 2·75

196 Fallow Deer (*Dama mesopotamica*)

197 Haganah Emblem

(Des M. and G. Shamir. Litho)

1971 (16 Feb). Nature Reserves. Animals of Biblical Times. T **196** and similar square designs. Multicoloured. P 13.

471	2a. Type **196**	25	25
472	3a. Asiatic Wild Ass (*Equus hemionus*)	35	35
473	5a. Arabian Oryx (*Oryx leucoryx*)	35	35
474	78a. Cheetah (*Acinonyx jubatus*)	60	60
471/474	*Set of 4*	1·40	1·40
471/474	*Set of 4 with tabs*	3·00	2·75

(Des D. Tel Vardi. Photo)

1971 (13 Apr). Memorial Day. P 14×13.

475	**197** 78a. multicoloured	60	60
	With tab	1·20	1·20

198 Jaffa Gate

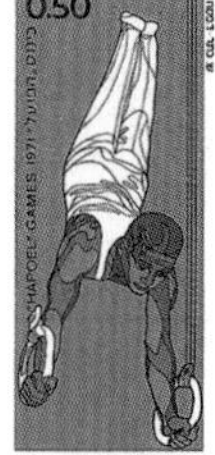

199 Gymnastics

(Des E. Weishoff. Photo)

1971 (13 Apr). Independence Day. Gates of Jerusalem (1st series). T **198** and similar square designs. Multicoloured. P 14.

476	15a. Type **198**	60	60
477	18a. New Gate	70	70
478	35a. Damascus Gate	95	90
479	85a. Herod's Gate	1·60	1·50
476/479	*Set of 4*	3·50	3·25
476/479	*Set of 4 with tabs*	7·75	7·25
MS480	93×93 mm. As Nos. 476/479, but each in 28×28 mm format. P 13×14 (*sold at* I£2)	12·00	11·50

No. **MS**480 was issued in connection with the Gates of Jerusalem Exhibition.

See also Nos. 527/**MS**531.

(Des D. Pessach and S. Ketter. Litho)

1971 (13 Apr). Ninth Hapoel Games. T **199** and similar vert designs. Multicoloured. P 14.

481	50a. Type **199**	35	35
482	50a. Basketball	35	35
483	50a. Running	35	35
481/483	*Set of 3*	95	95
481/483	*Set of 3 with tabs*	2·20	2·10

200 '... and he wrote upon the tables...'

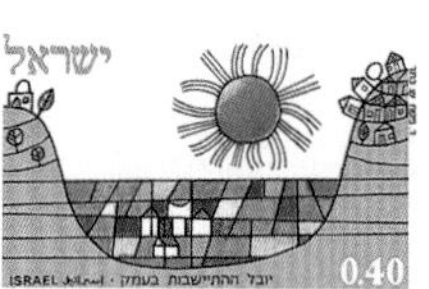

201 Sun over the Emeq

(Des A. Kalderon. Photo)

1971 (25 May). Feast of Weeks (*Shavuot*). T **200** and similar vert designs, showing illuminated verses from the Bible. Multicoloured. P 14×13.

484	50a. Type **200**	60	60
485	85a. 'The first of the first fruits...'	85	70
486	I£1.50 '...and ye shall observe the feast...'	1·20	1·00
484/486	*Set of 3*	2·40	2·10
484/486	*Set of 3 with tabs*	5·25	4·50

See also Nos. 488/492.

(Des D. Pessach and S. Ketter. Litho)

1971 (24 Aug). 50th Anniversary of Settlements in the Emeq (Yezreel Valley). P 14.

487	**201** 40a. multicoloured	60	35
	With tab	1·20	70

(Des A. Kalderon. Photo)

1971 (24 Aug). Jewish New Year. Feast of Tabernacles (*Sukkot*). Vert designs as T **200**, showing illuminated verses, but without *Shavuot* inscr. Multicoloured. P 14×13.

488	15a. 'You shall rejoice in your feast'	25	25
489	18a. 'You shall dwell in booths...'	25	25
490	20a. 'That I made the people...'	35	35
491	40a. '... gathered in the produce'	35	35
492	65a. '...I will give you your rains...'	35	35
488/492	*Set of 5*	1·40	1·40
488/492	*Set of 5 with tabs*	3·00	2·75

202 Kinneret

203 'Agricultural Research'

(Des G. Rothschild and Z. Lippmann. Photo)

1971 (25 Oct)–**79**. Landscapes. T **202** and similar horiz designs. P 14 (I£10) or 13×14 (others).

493	3a. ultramarine (7.11.72)	60	60
494	5a. bluish green (7.11.72)	35	35
495	15a. salmon	35	35
496	18a. bright purple	2·20	2·10
497	20a. slate-green (23.10.73)	1·20	1·20
	p. One phosphor band (17.3.75)	3·00	3·00
498	22a. new blue (4.1.72)	2·75	2·50
498*a*	25a. orange-red (5.11.74)	60	60
	ap. One phosphor band (30.1.75)	3·25	3·00
499	30a. bright magenta (7.11.72)	50	45
	p. One phosphor band (2.10.75)	3·50	3·50
500	35a. purple (20.12.73)	1·20	1·20
	p. One phosphor band (23.4.75)	5·50	5·25
501	45a. grey-blue (16.1.73)	50	45
	p. One phosphor band (9.5.76)	3·00	3·00
502	50a. green	70	70
	pa. Two phosphor bands (24.8.75)	5·50	5·25
	pb. One phosphor band (1976)	6·00	5·75
503	55a. yellow-olive (4.1.72)	70	70
504	65a. blackish brown (23.10.73)	1·40	1·40
	p. One phosphor band (21.8.77)	6·50	6·25
505	70a. rose-red (4.1.72)	70	70
505*a*	80a. ultramarine (5.11.74)	2·40	2·30
	ap. One phosphor band (21.8.77)	6·00	5·75
	apa. Two phosphor bands (27.11.77)	6·00	5·75
506	88a. greenish blue	2·75	2·75
507	95a. brown-red (16.1.73)	2·75	2·75
508	I£1.10 olive-brown (20.12.73)	2·20	2·10
	p. One phosphor band (10.4.78)	6·50	6·25
508*a*	I£1.30 blue (5.11.74)	1·20	1·20
	ap. Two phosphor bands (16.3.76)	7·75	7·50
	apa. One phosphor band (27.2.78)	7·75	7·50
508*b*	I£1.70 sepia (*two phosphor bands*) (17.6.75)	70	60
509	I£2 brown (16.1.73)	2·40	2·30
	p. Two phosphor bands (23.4.75)	9·00	8·75
	pa. One phosphor band (7.10.79)	3·50	3·50
510	I£3 bluish violet (7.11.72)	2·40	2·30
	p. Two phosphor bands (21.12.75)	9·00	8·75
	pa. One phosphor band (26.11.79)	12·00	11·50
510*a*	I£10 deep greenish blue (17.8.76)	3·00	3·00
	ap. Two phosphor bands (23.1.78)	12·00	11·50
493/510*a*	*Set of 23* (*cheapest*)	30·00	29·00
493/510*a*	*Set of 23 with tabs* (*cheapest*)	65·00	65·00

Designs: 3a. Judean desert; 5a. Gan Ha-Shelosha; 15a. Negev desert; 18a. T **202**; 20a. Tel Dan; 22a. Yafo; 25a. Arava; 30a. En Avedat; 35a. Brekhat Ram: 45a. Mount Hermon; 50a. Rosh Pinna; 55a. Netanya; 65a. Plain of Zebulun; 70a. Engedi; 80a. Beach, Elat; 88a. Akko (Acre); 95a. Hamifratz Hane'Elam; I£1.10, Aqueduct near Akko; I£1.30, Zefat; I£1.70, Nazerat Illit; I£2, Coral Island; I£3, Haifa. 28×27 mm—I£10, Elat.

The 5, 15, 18, 20, 30, 35, 45, 50, 55, 65, 70a, I£1.10, I£2 and I£3 were all available issued on two different types of paper; thin paper with shiny gum and thick paper with matte gum.

Nos. 497 and 499 were re-issued in 1976, No. 498*a* in 1977, No. 502 in 1978 and No. 509 in 1979.

3 and 18a. values with phosphor bands and 35a. with two bands were not issued but were experimental printings used for trial runs of cancelling machines. Used copies were included in kiloware subsequently sold by the Post Office, all being postmarked 13 January 1974. An early printing of No. 499p is similarly found.

Nos. 500p, 501p and 504p are found on covers with special commemorative cachets, dated earlier than the dates of issue. Covers of this type are made up by the Philatelic Service in batches and backdated; stamps with phosphor bands were used in error.

For similar views but with inscriptions arranged differently and different tabs see Nos. 682/684*a*.

(Des M. and G. Shamir. Litho)

1971 (25 Oct). 50th Anniversary of Volcani Institute of Agricultural Research. P 14.

511	**203**	I£1 multicoloured	60	60
		With tab	1·20	1·20

204 Hebrew Text

205 *The Scribe* (sculpture, B. Schatz)

(Des M. Faraj and E. Rivkind. Litho)

1972 (4 Jan). Educational Development. T **204** and similar vert designs. Multicoloured. P 14.

512	15a. Type **204**	15	15
513	18a. Mathematical formulae	15	15
514	20a. Engineering symbols	15	15
515	40a. University degree abbreviations	25	25
512/515	*Set of 4*	65	65
512/515	*Set of 4 with tabs*	1·40	1·40

1972 (7 Mar). Jewish Art. T **205** and similar designs. Litho (40, 85a.) or photo (others). P 13×14 (40, 85a.) or 14 (others).

516	40a. blackish brown, copper and black	35	35
517	55a. multicoloured	35	35
518	70a. multicoloured	60	60
519	85a. black and pale yellow	70	70
520	I£1 multicoloured	70	70
516/520	*Set of 5*	2·40	2·40
516/520	*Set of 5 with tabs*	5·25	5·00

Designs: Vert—40a. T **205**; 55a. *Sarah* (A. Pann); 85a. *Old Jerusalem* (woodcut, J. Steinhardt); I£1, *Resurrection* (A. Kahana). Horiz—70a. *Zefat* (M. Shemi).

206 The Flight from Egypt

207 'Let My People Go'

(Des D. Ben Dov. Litho)

1972 (7 Mar). Feast of the Passover (*Pesah*). T **206** and similar square designs. Multicoloured. P 13.

521	18a. Type **106**	50	45
522	45a. Baking unleavened bread	60	60
523	95a. *Seder* table	85	80
521/523	*Set of 3*	1·80	1·70
521/523	*Set of 3 with tabs*	3·75	3·75

(Des M. Faraj. Litho)

1972 (7 Mar). Campaign for Jewish Immigration. P 14.

524	**207**	55a. multicoloured	3·00	3·00
		With tab	6·00	5·75

208 Bouquet

209 Jethro's Tomb

(Des E. Weishoff. Litho)

1972 (17 Apr). Memorial Day. P 14.

525	**208**	55a. multicoloured	60	45
		With tab	1·20	90

(Des M. Amar. Litho)

1972 (17 Apr). 'Nebi Shuaib' (Jethro's Tomb) (Druse shrine). P 13.

526	**209**	55a. multicoloured	60	45
		With tab	1·20	90

(Des E. Weishoff. Photo)

1972 (17 Apr). Independence Day. Gates of Jerusalem (2nd series). Square designs similar to T **198**. Multicoloured. P 14.

527	15a. Lions' Gate	95	70
528	18a. Golden Gate	1·20	80
529	45a. Dung Gate	1·20	90
530	55a. Zion Gate	1·40	1·00
527/530	*Set of 4*	4·25	3·00
527/530	*Set of 4 with tabs*	9·50	7·00
MS531	93×93 mm. As Nos. 527/530, but each in format 28×28 mm (*sold at* I£2)	12·00	11·50

210 Ghetto Entrance

211 Book Year Texts

(Des J. Zim. Litho)

1972 (6 June). 400th Death Anniversary of Rabbi Yizhaq Luria ('Ari'). P 13.

532	**210**	70a. multicoloured	3·50	3·50
		With tab	7·25	7·00

(Des M. Faraj. Photo)

1972 (6 June). International Book Year. P 14×13.

533	**211**	95a. black, red and light blue	70	70
		With tab	1·40	1·40

212 Dish Aerial

213 Ancona Ark

(Des A. Kalderon. Litho)

1972 (6 June). Opening of Satellite Earth Station. P 13.

534	**212**	I£1 multicoloured	60	45
		With tab	1·20	90

(Des O. Adler. Photo)

1972 (8 Aug). Jewish New Year. Holy Arks from Italy. T **213** and similar vert designs. P 14×13.

535	15a. red-brown and pale yellow	25	25
536	45a. myrtle-green, gold and bright green	35	35
537	70a. carmine-red, cobalt and yellow	60	60
538	95a. bright purple and gold	85	80
535/538	*Set of 4*	1·80	1·80
535/538	*Set of 4 with tabs*	4·00	4·00

Designs: 15a. T **213**; 45a. Soragna Ark; 70a. Padua Ark; 95a. Reggio Emilia Ark.

214 Menorah Emblem

215 Hanukkah Lamp (Morocco 18th/19th-century)

(Des M. Faraj. Photo)

1972 (8 Aug). 25th Anniversary of State of Israel. P 14×13.

539	**214**	I£1 light blue, purple and silver	60	35
		With tab	1·20	70

(Des Z. Narkiss. Litho)

1972 (7 Nov). Festival of Lights (*Hanukkah*). T **215** and similar horiz designs, showing ceremonial lamps. Multicoloured. P 14×13.

540	12a. Type **215**	25	25
541	25a. 18th-century Polish lamp	25	25
542	70a. 17th-century German silver lamp	50	45
540/542	*Set of 3*	90	85
540/542	*Set of 3 with tabs*	1·90	1·80

216 Pendant

217 *Horse and Rider*

(Des D. Ben Dov and A. Kalderon. Photo)

1973 (16 Jan). Immigration of Jews from North Africa. P 14×13.

543	**216**	18a. multicoloured	60	35
		With tab	1·20	70

1973 (16 Jan). Children's Drawings. T **217** and similar vert designs. Multicoloured. Litho. P 14.

544	2a. Type **217**	25	25
545	3a. *Balloon Ride* (17×48 *mm*)	25	25
546	55a. *Party-time*	50	35
544/546	*Set of 3*	90	75
544/546	*Set of 3 with tabs*	1·90	1·60

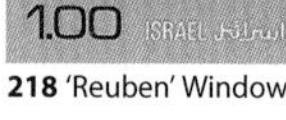

218 'Reuben' Window

219 Flame of Remembrance

1973 (26 Mar–21 Aug). Tribes of Israel Stained-glass Windows by Chagall, Hadassah Synagogue, Jerusalem. T **218** and similar vert designs. Multicoloured centres, background colours given. Litho. P 14.

547	I£1 ochre ('Levi')	1·20	1·20
548	I£1 grey-green ('Simeon')	1·20	1·20
549	I£1 yellow-olive (Type **218**)	1·20	1·20
550	I£1 grey-blue ('Issachar')	1·20	1·20
551	I£1 olive-yellow ('Zebulun')	1·20	1·20
552	I£1 drab ('Judah')	1·20	1·20
553	I£1 dull yellow-green ('Asher') (21.8)	1·80	1·70
554	I£1 greenish grey ('Gad') (21.8)	1·80	1·70
555	I£1 turquoise-green ('Dan') (21.8)	1·80	1·70
556	I£1 pale olive-brown ('Benjamin') (21.8)	1·80	1·70
557	I£1 light bronze-green ('Joseph') (21.8)	1·80	1·70
558	I£1 brownish grey ('Naphtali') (21.8)	1·80	1·70
547/558	*Set of 12*	16·00	16·00
547/558	*Set of 12 with tabs*	36·00	35·00

(Des M. Faraj. Litho)

1973 (3 May). Memorial Day. P 14.

559	**219**	65a. multicoloured	60	45
		With tab	1·20	90

220 Skeletal Hand

221 Signatures of Declaration of Independence

(Des A. Games. Photo)

1973 (3 May). Holocaust (Persecution of European Jews 1933–1945) Memorial. P 14.

560	**220**	55a. blackish blue	60	35
		With tab	1·20	70

(Des M. Amar. Photo)

1973 (3 May). Independence Day. P 14.

561	**221**	I£1 multicoloured	60	45
		With tab	1·20	90
MS562		65×147 mm. No. 561 (*sold at* I£1.50)	3·50	3·50
		a. Error. Imperf	£1000	

222 Star of David and Runners

223 Isaiah

(Des D. Reisinger. Litho)

1973 (3 May). Ninth Maccabiah. P 14.

563	**222**	I£1.10 multicoloured	60	35
		With tab	1·20	70

(Des P. Grebu. Photo)

1973 (21 Aug). Jewish New Year. Prophets of Israel. T **223** and similar vert designs. Multicoloured. P 13×14.

564	18a. Type **223**	10	10
565	65a. Jeremiah	15	15
566	I£1.10 Ezekiel	25	25
564/566	*Set of 3*	45	45
564/566	*Set of 3 with tabs*	1·10	1·00

224 Jews in Boat, and Danish Flag

225 Institute Emblem and Cogwheel

(Des A. Berg. Photo)

1973 (23 Oct). 30th Anniversary of Rescue of Danish Jews. P 13×14.

567 **224** I£5 black, scarlet and yellow-brown ..... 1·40 1·30
With tab 3·00 2·50

(Des D. Pessach and S. Ketter. Photo)

1973 (23 Oct). 50th Anniversary of Technion Israel Institute of Technology. P 14×13.

568 **225** I£1.25 multicoloured 60 35
With tab 1·20 70

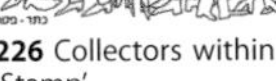

226 Collectors within 'Stamp'

227 Soldier with Prayer Shawl

(Des D. Pessach and S. Ketter. Litho)

1973 (20 Dec)–**74**. Jerusalem 73 International Stamp Exhibition. T **226** and similar square design. Multicoloured. P 13.

569 20a. Type **226** 25 25
570 I£1 Collectors within 'stamp' (*different*) 35 35
569/570 *Set of 2* 55 55
569/570 *Set of 2 with tabs* ..... 1·40 1·40
MS571 Three sheets, each 121×75 mm (a) I£1 250m. stamp of 1948; (b) I£2 500m. stamp of 1948; (c) I£3 1000m. stamp of 1948 (19.2.74) ..... 11·00 10·50

(Des M. Pereg. Photo)

1974 (23 Apr). Memorial Day. P 13×14.

572 **227** I£1 black and new blue 60 35
With tab 1·20 70

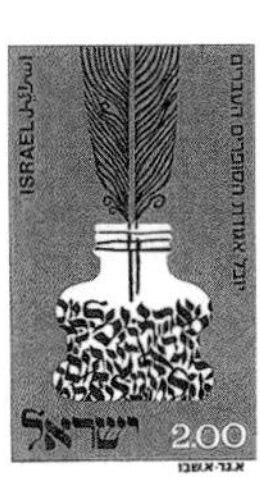

228 Quill and Bottle of Ink

229 *Woman in Blue* (M. Kisling)

(Des A. Gad and A. Shevo. Photo)

1974 (23 Apr). 50th Anniversary of Hebrew Writers' Association. P 14×13.

573 **228** I£2 black and gold 60 45
With tab 1·20 90

1974 (11 June). Jewish Art. T **229** and similar vert designs. Multicoloured. Litho. P 14.

574 I£1.25 Type **229** 35 35
575 I£2 *Mother and Child* (bronze, C. Orloff) 50 35
576 I£3 *Girl in Blue* (C. Soutine) 50 45
574/576 *Set of 3* ..... 1·20 1·00
574/576 *Set of 3* with *tabs* ..... 2·75 2·50

See also Nos. 604/606.

230 Spanner

(Des M. Pereg. Litho)

1974 (11 June). 50th Anniversary of Young Workers Movement. P 14.

577 **230** 25a. multicoloured 35 35
With tab 1·20 70

231 Lady Davis Technical Centre, Tel Aviv

(Des O. Adler. Photo)

1974 (6 Aug). 'Architecture in Israel' (1st series). T **231** and similar horiz designs. P 13×14.

578 25a. agate 25 25
579 60a. steel-blue 25 25
580 I£1.45 red-brown 25 25
578/580 *Set of 3* 70 70
578/580 *Set of 3 with tabs* ..... 1·40 1·40

Designs: 25a. T **231**; 60a. Elias Sourasky Library, Tel Aviv University; I£1.45, Mivtahim Rest Home, Zikhron Yaaqov.

See also Nos. 596/598.

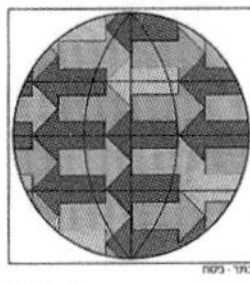

232 Istanbuli Synagogue

233 Arrows on Globe

(Des M. Amar. Photo)

1974 (6 Aug). Jewish New Year. Rebuilt Synagogues in Jerusalem's Old City. T **232** and similar vert designs. Multicoloured. P 13×14.

581 25a. Type **232** 25 25
582 70a. Emtzai Synagogue 25 25
583 I£1 Raban Yohanan Ben Zakkai Synagogue 25 25
581/583 *Set of 3* 70 70
581/583 *Set of 3 with tabs* ..... 1·40 1·40

(Des A. Glaser, D. Pessach and S. Ketter. Litho (25a.); photo (I£1.30))

1974 (5 Nov). Centenary of Universal Postal Union. T **233** and similar multicoloured design. P 14.

584 25a. Type **233** 25 25
585 I£1.30 Dove 'postman' (27×27 *mm*) 35 35
584/585 *Set of 2* 55 55
584/585 *Set of 2 with tabs* ..... 1·40 1·40

234 David Ben Gurion (statesman)

236 Child with Plant, and Rainbow

(Des O. Adler. Photo)

1974 (5 Nov). Ben Gurion Memorial. P 14.

586 **234** 25a. reddish brown 25 25
587 I£1.30 myrtle-green 35 35
586/587 *Set of 2* 55 55
586/587 *Set of 2 with tabs* ..... 1·20 1·20

(Des A. Kalderon. Litho)

1975 (14 Jan). Arbour Day. T **236** and similar vert designs. Multicoloured. P 14.

588	1a. Type **236**	25	25
589	35a. Bird in tree	25	25
590	I£2 Child with plant, and sun	50	35
588/590	*Set of 3*	90	75
588/590	*Set of 3 with tabs*	1·90	1·60

237 Hebrew University, Jerusalem

(Des A. Kalderon. Litho)

1975 (14 Jan). 50th Anniversary of Hebrew University. Jerusalem. P 13.

591	**237** I£2.50 multicoloured	60	45
	With tab	1·20	90

238 Welding

239 Harry S. Truman

(Des A. Berg. Photo)

1975 (14 Jan). Occupational Safety. T **238** and similar vert designs. Multicoloured. P 14×13.

592	30a. Type **238**	25	25
593	80a. Tractor-driving	30	30
594	I£1.20 Telephone line maintenance	35	35
592/594	*Set of 3*	80	80
592/594	*Set of 3 with tabs*	1·40	1·40

1975 (4 Mar). Truman Commemoration. Recess. P 14.

595	**239** I£5 sepia	85	70
	With tab	1·80	1·40

(Des O. Adler. Photo)

1975 (4 Mar). 'Architecture in Israel' (2nd series). Horiz designs as T **231**. P 14.

596	80a. sepia	15	15
597	I£1.30 grey-brown	30	30
598	I£1.70 olive-brown	35	35
596/598	*Set of 3*	70	70
596/598	*Set of 3 with tabs*	1·70	1·60

Designs: 80a. Hebrew University Synagogue, Jerusalem; I£1.30, Yad Mordechai Museum; I£1.70, City Hotel, Bat Yam.

240 Memorial

241 Text and Poppy

(Des A. Berg. Photo)

1975 (10 Apr). Memorial Day. Two phosphor bands. P 14×13.

599	**240** I£1.45 black, red and magenta	40	40
	With tab	85	80

(Des E. Greenman. Photo)

1975 (10 Apr). Fallen Soldiers Memorial. Two phosphor bands. P 13×14.

600	**241** I£1.45 black, red and grey	40	40
	With tab	85	80

242 Hurdling

243 Old People

(Des M. Pereg. Photo)

1975 (10 Apr). Tenth Hapoel Games. T **242** and similar horiz designs. Multicoloured. P 13×14.

601	25a. Type **242**	15	15
602	I£1.70 Cycling	30	30
603	I£3 Volleyball	35	35
601/603	*Set of 3*	70	70
601/603	*Set of 3 with tabs*	1·70	1·60

1975 (17 June). Jewish Art. Multicoloured designs as T **229**. Two phosphor bands. Litho. P 14.

604	I£1 *Hanukkah* (M. Oppenheim)	35	35
605	I£1.40 *The Purim Players* (J. Adler) (*horiz*)	50	45
606	I£4 *Yom Kippur* (M. Gottlieb)	60	60
604/606	*Set of 3*	1·30	1·30
604/606	*Set of 3 with tabs*	3·00	2·75

(Des Z. Narkiss. Photo)

1975 (17 June). Gerontology. Two phosphor bands. P 13×14.

607	**243** I£1.85 multicoloured	60	35
	With tab	1·20	70

244 Gideon

245 Zalman Shazar

(Des D. Ben Dov. Photo)

1975 (5 Aug). Jewish New Year. Judges of Israel. T **244** and similar vert designs. Multicoloured. One phosphor band (35a.), or two phosphor bands (others). P 13×14.

608	35a. Type **244**	25	25
609	I£1 Deborah	30	30
610	I£1.40 Jephthah	35	35
608/610	*Set of 3*	80	80
608/610	*Set of 3 with tabs*	1·70	1·60

(Des A. Berg. Photo)

1975 (5 Aug). First Death Anniversary of Zalman Shazar (President, 1963–1973). One phosphor band. P 14×13.

611	**245** 35a. black and silver	60	35
	With tab	1·20	70

246 Emblem of Pioneer Women

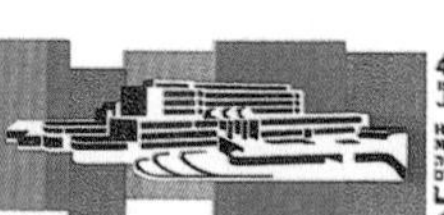

247 New Hospital Buildings

(Des A. Kalderon. Photo)

1975 (5 Aug). 50th Anniversary of Pioneer Women's Organisation. Two phosphor bands. P 14.

612	**246** I£5 multicoloured	60	60
	With tab	1·20	1·20

(Des E. Greenman. Photo)

1975 (14 Oct). Return of Handassah Hospital to Mt. Scopus. Two phosphor bands. P 14×13.

613	**247** I£4 multicoloured	60	45
	With tab	1·20	90

248 Pratincole (*Glareola pratincola*)

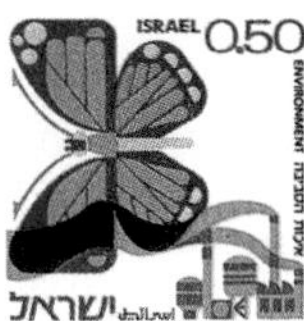

249 Air Pollution

(Des W. Ferguson. Litho)

1975 (14 Oct). Protected Wild Birds. T **248** and similar square designs. Multicoloured. Two phosphor bands. P 13.

614	I£1.10 Type **248**	35	35
615	I£1.70 Spur-winged Plover (*Hoplopterus spinosus*)	50	45
616	I£2 Black-winged Stilt (*Himantopus himantopus*)	60	60
614/616	*Set of 3*	1·30	1·30
614/616	*Set of 3 with tabs*	3·00	2·75

(Des E. Weishoff. Photo)

1975 (9 Dec). Environmental Quality. T **249** and similar square designs. Multicoloured. Two phosphor bands. P 14.

617	50a. Type **249**	25	25
618	80a. Water pollution	30	30
619	I£1.70 Noise pollution	35	35
	a. Perf 13	70·00	70·00
617/619	*Set of 3*	80	80
617/619	*Set of 3 with tabs*	1·70	1·60

250 Star of David

251 Symbolic Key

(Des N. Felheim. Photo)

1975 (9 Dec)–**80**. One phosphor band (75a., I£1.80, I£2.70, I£4.30) or two phosphor bands (others). P 13×14.

620	**250**	75a. ultramarine and rose-carmine (5.12.77)	50	45
621		I£1.80 ultramarine and slate (*band on right*) (22.5.79)	60	60
		a. Phosphor band on left (20.8.79)	35	45
622		I£1.85 ultramarine and orange-brown	60	45
623		I£2.45 ultramarine and emerald (22.6.76)	50	45
623*a*		I£2.70 ultramarine and bright mauve (*band on left*) (25.12.79)	70	70
		ab. Phosphor band on right (1979)	25	10
623*b*		I£4.30 ultramarine and scarlet-vermilion (26.5.80)	50	35
624		I£5.40 ultramarine and bistre (23.5.78)	1·40	1·40
625		I£8 ultramarine and greenish blue (22.5.79)	1·10	1·00
620/625		*Set of 8* (*cheapest*)	5·25	4·75
620/625		*Set of 8 with tabs* (*cheapest*)	10·00	9·75

The 75a. is found on philatelic covers bearing a special cancellation for WIZO and dated 1 December 1977. Such covers were made up in batches and backdated; No. 620 was used on the covers in error.

(Des A. Hecht. Litho)

1976 (17 Feb). 70th Anniversary of Bezalel Academy of Arts and Design, Jerusalem. Two phosphor bands. P 14.

626	**251**	I£1.85 multicoloured	60	45
		With tab	1·20	90

252 Border Settlements

253 'In the days of Ahasuerus...'

(Des M. Pereg. Litho)

1976 (17 Feb). Jewish Border Settlements. P 14.

627	**252**	I£1.50 multicoloured	60	45
		With tab	1·20	90

(Des O. and E. Schwarz. Litho)

1976 (17 Feb). Purim Festival. T **253** and similar vert designs. Multicoloured. One phosphor band (40a.) two phosphor bands (80a., I£1.60) or no bands (**MS**631). P 14.

628	40a. Type **253**	25	25
629	80a. 'He set the royal crown ...'	30	30
630	I£1.60 'Thus shall it be done ...'	35	35
628/630	*Set of 3*	80	80
628/630	*Set of 3 with tabs*	1·70	1·60
MS631	127×86 mm. Nos. 628/630 (*sold at* I£4)	1·90	1·80

254 Monument to the Fallen

255 *Dancers of Meron* (R. Rubin)

(Des D. Cohen. Photo)

1976 (25 Apr). Memorial Day. Two phosphor bands. P 14×13.

632	**254**	I£1.85 multicoloured	60	45
		With tab	1·20	90

1976 (25 Apr). Lag Ba-Omer Festival Two phosphor bands. P 14.

633	**255**	I£1.30 multicoloured	70	60
		With tab	1·40	1·20

256 '200' Flag

257 Diamond (Industry)

(Des A. Lucaci. Photo)

1976 (25 Apr). Bicentenary of American Revolution. Two phosphor bands. P 13×14.

634	**256**	I£4 multicoloured	70	70
		With tab	1·40	1·40

(Des E. Weishoff. Photo)

1976 (25 Apr). Netanya 76 National Stamp Exhibition. Sheet 112×75 mm, containing T **257** and similar vert designs. Multicoloured. P 14×13.

MS635 I£1 Type **257**; I£2 Sailing (sport); I£4 Beach umbrella (tourism) (*sold at* I£10) 3·50 3·50

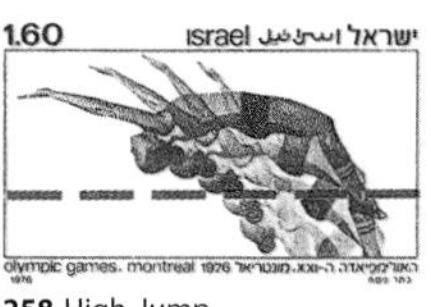

258 High Jump

259 Multiple Tent Emblems

(Des D. Pessah and S. Ketter. Photo)

1976 (22 June). Olympic Games, Montreal. T **258** and similar horiz designs. Two phosphor bands. P 13×14.

636	I£1.60 black and vermilion	50	45
637	I£2.40 black and ultramarine	50	45
638	I£4.40 black and bright magenta	60	60

636/638	*Set of 3*	1·40	1·40
636/638	*Set of 3 with tabs*	3·00	3·00

Designs: I£1.60, T **258**; I£2.40, Swimming; I£4.40, Gymnastics.

(Des M. Felheim. Photo)

1976 (22 June). Camping. Two phosphor bands. P 14.

639	**259** I£1.50 multicoloured	60	35
	With tab	1·20	70

260 'Truth'

261 Excavated Byzantine House

(Des A. Kalderon. Photo)

1976 (17 Aug). Jewish New Year. T **260** and similar vert designs. Multicoloured. One phosphor band (45a.) or two phosphor bands (others). P 14×13.

640	45a. Type **260**	60	60
641	I£1.50 'Judgement'	60	60
642	I£1.90 'Peace'	60	60
640/642	*Set of 3*	1·60	1·60
640/642	*Set of 3 with tabs*	3·50	3·50

(Des M. Pereg. Litho)

1976 (19 Oct). Archaeology in Jerusalem (1st series). T **261** and similar vert designs. Multicoloured. Two phosphor bands. P 14.

643	I£1.30 Type **261**	35	35
644	I£2.40 Arch of Second Temple	60	60
645	I£2.80 Staircase to Second Temple	70	70
643/645	*Set of 3*	1·50	1·50
643/645	*Set of 3 with tabs*	3·25	3·25

See Nos. 648/649.

262 Pawn

263 Clearing Ground

(Des D. Ben Dov and E. Weishoff. Litho)

1976 (19 Oct). 22nd Chess Olympiad, Haifa. T **262** and similar vert design. Multicoloured. Two phosphor bands. P 14.

646	I£1.30 Type **262**	70	70
647	I£1.60 Rook	70	70
646/647	*Set of 2*	1·30	1·30
646/647	*Set of 2 with tabs*	3·00	2·75

(Des M. Pereg. Litho)

1976 (14 Dec). Archaeology in Jerusalem (2nd series). Vert designs as T **261**. Multicoloured. Two phosphor bands. P 14.

648	70a. City wall, First Temple period	25	25
649	I£5 Omayyad palace	1·20	1·20
648/649	*Set of 2*	1·30	1·30
648/649	*Set of 2 with tabs*	3·00	2·75

(Des Z. Narkiss. Photo)

1976 (14 Dec). Pioneers. T **263** and similar designs. One phosphor band (60a.), two phosphor bands (I£1.40, I£1.80). P 14×13 (60a.) or 13×14 (others).

650	5a. deep brown and gold	25	25
651	10a. deep rose lilac and gold	25	25
652	60a. deep carmine and gold	25	25
653	I£1.40 indigo and gold	35	35
654	I£1.80 blackish olive and gold	35	35
650/654	*Set of 5*	1·30	1·30
650/654	*Set of 5 with tabs*	3·00	2·75

Designs: Vert—60a. Road construction. Horiz—5a. T **263**; 10a. Building breakwater; I£1.40, Ploughing; I£1.80, Ditch-clearing.

264 Grandfather's Carrot

(Des L. Halabin. Litho)

1977 (15 Feb). Voluntary Service. Two phosphor bands. P 14.

655	**264** I£2.60 multicoloured	60	60
	With tab	1·20	1·20

265 *By the Rivers of Babylon*

1977 (15 Feb). Drawings of E. M. Lilien. T **265** and similar designs. Two phosphor bands. Photo. P 13×14 (I£1.80) or 14×13 (others).

656	I£1.70 brown, grey and black	35	35
657	I£1.80 blue-black, yellow-ochre and reddish brown	50	45
658	I£2.10 blackish green, sage green and blue-black	60	60
656/658	*Set of 3*	1·30	1·30
656/658	*Set of 3 with tabs*	3·00	2·75

Designs: Vert—I£1.80, *Abraham*. Horiz—I£1.70, T **265**; I£2.10, *May Our Eyes Behold.*

266 Jew and Arab Shaking Hands

267 Parachute Troops Memorial

1977 (15 Feb). Children's Drawings on Peace. T **266** and similar horiz designs. Multicoloured. Two phosphor bands Photo. P 14.

659	50a. Type **266**	25	25
660	I£1.40 Arab and Jew holding hands	35	35
661	I£2.70 Peace Dove, Jew and Arab	70	70
659/661	*Set of 3*	1·20	1·20
659/661	*Set of 3 with tabs*	3·00	2·75

(Des Z. Narkiss. Photo)

1977 (19 Apr). Memorial Day. Two phosphor bands. P 13×14.

662	**267** I£3.30 multicoloured	85	80
	With tab	1·70	1·60

268 Embroidery showing Sabbath Loaves

269 Trumpet

(Des G. Almaliah. Litho)

1977 (19 Apr). Sabbath. Two phosphor bands. P 13×14.

663	**268** I£3 multicoloured	60	60
	With tab	1·20	1·20

(Des A. Glaser. Litho)

1977 (19 Apr). Ancient Musical instruments, T **269** and similar vert designs. Multicoloured. Two phosphor bands. P 14.

664	I£1.50 Type **269**	35	35
665	I£2 Lyre	35	35
666	I£5 Jingle	50	45
664/666	*Set of 3*	1·10	1·00
664/666	*Set of 3 with tabs*	2·40	2·30

270 Fencing

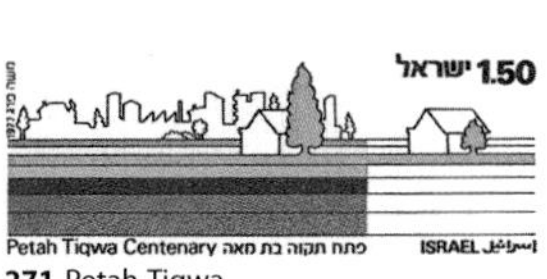

271 Petah Tiqwa

(Des A. Berg. Photo)

1977 (23 June). Tenth Maccabiah Games. T **270** and similar vert designs. Two phosphor bands. P 14×13.

667	I£1 grey, greenish blue and black	35	35
668	I£2.50 lilac-grey, orange-vermilion and black	50	45
669	I£3.50 greenish grey, yellowish green and black	60	60
667/669	*Set of 3*	1·30	1·30
667/669	*Set of 3 with tabs*	3·00	2·75

Designs: I£1, T **270**; I£2.50, Putting the shot; I£3.50, Judo.

(Des M. Pereg. Photo)

1977 (23 June). Petah Tiqwa Centenary. Two phosphor bands. P 14×13.

670	**271** I£1.50 multicoloured	50	45
	With tab	95	90

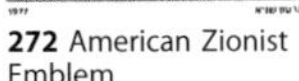

272 American Zionist Emblem

273 Page of 16th-century Book *Kohelet Yaakov*

(Des G. Sagi. Photo)

1977 (23 June). Zionist Organisation of America Convention, Two phosphor bands. P 14.

671	**272** I£4 multicoloured	85	80
	With tab	1·70	16·00

(Des Z. Narkiss. Photo)

1977 (16 Aug). 400th Anniversary of Hebrew Printing at Zefat. Two phosphor bands. P 14×13.

672	**273** I£4 black, gold and carmine-vermilion	95	60
	With tab	1·90	1·20

274 Sarah

275 Police

(Des A. Kalderon and M. Pereg. Photo)

1977 (16 Aug). Jewish New Year. Matriarchs of Israel. T **274** and similar square designs. Multicoloured. One phosphor band (70a.) or two phosphor bands (others). P 14.

673	70a. Type **274**	25	25
674	I£1.50 Rebekah	30	30
675	I£2 Rachel	35	35
676	I£3 Leah	60	60
673/676	*Set of 4*	1·40	1·40
673/676	*Set of 4 with tabs*	3·00	2·75

See also Nos. 728/730.

(Des O. and E. Schwarz. Litho)

1977 (16 Aug). National Police Force. T **275** and similar vert designs. Multicoloured. Two phosphor bands. P 14.

677	I£1 Type **275**	35	35
678	I£1 Civil Guard	35	35
679	I£1 Frontier Guard	35	35
677/679	*Set of 3*	95	95
677/679	*Set of 3 with tabs*	2·20	2·10

276 Helmet and Model Settlement

277 Accelerator Building, Weizmann Institute

(Des G. Sagi. Litho)

1977 (18 Oct). Nahal Pioneering Fighting Youth. Two phosphor bands. P 14.

680	**276** I£3.50 multicoloured	60	60
	With tab	1·20	1·20

(Des Z. Narkiss. Photo)

1977 (18 Oct). Inauguration of Koffler Accelerator. P 14×13.

681	**277** I£8 grey-blue and black	1·10	1·00
	With tab	2·20	2·10

278 Caesarea

279 American-built Mogul Steam Locomotive, 1892

(Des I. Amit and A. Glaser; litho (I£50).
Des A. Glaser; photo (others))

1977 (18 Oct)–**80**. Landscapes. T **278** and similar designs. P 14 (I£20), 13×14 (I£50) or 13½×14 (others).

682	10a. deep ultramarine	1·20	1·20
683	I£1 bistre (*two phosphor bands*)	1·40	1·40
	a. One phosphor band (13.7.78)	1·80	1·70
	b. No phosphor bands (13.12.79)	1·80	1·70
684	I£20 deep dull green and red-orange (4.7.78)	3·00	3·00
	p. Two phosphor bands (13.11.78)	12·00	11·50
684*a*	I£50 multicoloured (15.1.80)	3·50	3·50
682/684*a*	*Set of 4 (cheapest)*	8·25	8·25
682/684*a*	*Set of 4 with tabs (cheapest)*	16·00	15·00

Designs: 10a. T **278**. As T **278**—I£1, Arava. 29×27 mm—I£20, Rosh Pinna. 27½×36½ mm—I£50, Soreq Cave.

(Des A. Kalderon. Photo)

1977 (13 Dec). Railways in the Holy Land. T **279** and similar horiz designs. Multicoloured. One phosphor band (65a.) or two phosphor bands (others). P 13×14.

685	65a. Type **279**	35	35
686	I£1.50 Steam locomotive, Jezreel Valley	50	45
687	I£2 4-6-0 P class steam locomotive, Lydda station	50	45
688	I£2.50 Diesel locomotive	60	60
685/688	*Set of 4*	1·80	1·70
685/688	*Set of 4 with tabs*	3·75	3·75
MS689	112×75 mm. Nos. 685/688	5·25	5·00

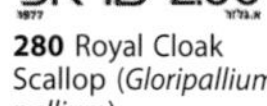

280 Royal Cloak Scallop (*Gloripallium pallium*)

281 The Marriage Parties (Dutch Ketubah)

(Des A. Glaser. Photo)

1977 (13 Dec). Red Sea Shells. T **280** and similar vert designs. Multicoloured. Two phosphor bands. P 14.

690	I£2 Type **280**	35	35
691	I£2 Pacific Grinning Tun (*Malea pomum*)	35	35
692	I£2 Isabelle Cowrie (*Cypraea isabella*)	35	35
693	I£2 Camp Pitar Venus (*Lioconcha castrensis*)	35	35
690/693	*Set of 4*	1·30	1·30
690/693	*Set of 4 with tabs*	3·00	2·75

1978 (14 Feb). Illuminated Jewish Marriage Contracts (Ketubah). T **281** and similar horiz designs. Multicoloured. One phosphor band (75a.), two phosphor bands (I£3.90) or no bands (I£6). Litho. P 14.

694	75a. Type **281**	25	25
695	I£3.90 Moroccan Ketubah	50	45
696	I£6 Jerusalem Ketubah	60	60
694/696	*Set of 3*	1·20	1·20
694/696	*Set of 3 with tabs*	2·75	2·50

282 *A Street in Jerusalem* (H. Gliksberg)

283 Eliyahu Golomb (leader of Hagana)

1978 (14 Feb). Jewish Art. T **282** and similar vert designs. One phosphor band (I£3.80) or two phosphor bands (others). Photo (I£3.80) or litho (others). P 13×14 (I£3.80) or 14 (others).

697	I£3 multicoloured	35	35
698	I£3.80 black, pale yellow and grey	50	45
699	I£4.40 multicoloured	60	60
697/699	*Set of 3*	1·30	1·30
697/699	*Set of 3 with tabs*	3·00	2·75

Designs: I£3, T **282**; I£3.80, *Thistles* (L. Krakauer); I£4.40, *An Alley in Zefat* (M. Levanon).

(Des Z. Narkiss. Photo)

1978 (23 Apr). Historical Personalities (1st series). T **283** and similar vert designs. P 14×13.

700	I£2 blackish green and pale greenish yellow	40	40
701	I£2 indigo and pale bluish grey	40	40
702	I£2 blackish purple and pale stone	40	40
703	I£2 blackish brown and stone	40	40
704	I£2 brownish black and pale brownish grey	40	40
700/704	*Set of 5*	1·80	1·80
700/704	*Set of 5 with tabs*	4·00	4·00

Designs: No. 700, T **283**; No. 701, David Raziel (Irgun commander); No. 702, Yitzhak Sadeh (nationalist and military commander); No. 703, Dr. Moshe Sneh (Zionist politician); No. 704, Abraham Stern (underground fighter).

See also Nos. 721/722, 725/726, 732/733, 738/740, 763/765, 809/811 and 831/833.

284 Children's Flower Paintings (from mural, Petah Tiqwa Museum)

285 Jerusalem (detail from Madaba mosaic map)

1978 (23 Apr). Memorial Day. T **284** and similar horiz designs. Litho. P 14.

705	I£1.50 multicoloured	15	15
706	I£1.50 multicoloured	15	15
707	I£1.50 multicoloured	15	15
708	I£1.50 multicoloured	15	15
709	I£1.50 multicoloured	15	15
710	I£1.50 multicoloured	15	15
711	I£1.50 multicoloured	15	15
712	I£1.50 multicoloured	15	15
713	I£1.50 multicoloured	15	15
714	I£1.50 multicoloured	15	15
715	I£1.50 multicoloured	70	70
716	I£1.50 multicoloured	70	70
717	I£1.50 multicoloured	70	70
718	I£1.50 multicoloured	70	70
719	I£1.50 multicoloured	70	70
705/719	*Set of 15*	4·50	4·50
705/719	*Sheet of 15 with tabs*	11·00	10·50

Nos. 705/719 were issued together *se-tenant*. Each stamp depicts a part of the Memorial Wall, together making a composite design.

1978 (23 Apr). Tabir 78 National Stamp Exhibition. Sheet 111×77 mm, containing T **285** and similar horiz designs. Multicoloured. Litho. P 14.

MS720	I£1 Type **285**; I£2 N.W. corner of map; I£3 S.E. corner of map; I£4 S.W. corner of map (*sold at* I£15)	6·00	5·75

(Des Z. Narkiss. Photo)

1978 (4 July). Historical Personalities (2nd series). Vert designs as T **283**. Two phosphor bands (No. 721) or one phosphor band (No. 722). P 14×13.

721	I£2 indigo and stone	90	85
722	I£2 deep olive-brown and pale grey	90	85
721/722	*Set of 2*	1·60	1·50
721/722	*Set of 2 with tabs*	3·50	3·50

Designs: No. 721, Dr. Chaim Weizmann (first President of Israel); No. 722, Dr. Theodor Herzl (founder of Zionism).

286 YMCA Building, Jerusalem

287 Verse of National Anthem

(Des A. Kalderon. Litho)

1978 (4 July). Centenary of Jerusalem Young Men's Christian Association. P 13.

723	**286** I£5.40 multicoloured	70	70
	With tab	1·40	1·40

(Des D. Cohen. Photo)

1978 (4 July). Centenary of Publication of *Hatiqwa* (Jewish National Anthem). Two phosphor bands. P 13×14.

724	**287** I£8.40 silver, deep blue and new blue	95	90
	With tab	1·90	1·80

(Des Z. Narkiss. Photo)

1978 (22 Aug). Historical Personalities (3rd series). Vert designs as T **283**. P 14×13.

725	I£2 blackish purple and cream	50	35
726	I£2 blackish green and cream	50	35
725/726	*Set of 2*	90	65
725/726	*Set of 2 with tabs*	1·90	1·40

Designs: No. 725, Rabbi Ouziel; No. 726, Rabbi Kook.

288 Family Groups

289 Star of David, Young Tree and Globe showing USA

(Des G. Sagi and D. Ben Dov. Photo)

1978 (22 Aug). Social Welfare. Two phosphor bands. P 13×14.

727	**288** I£5.10 multicoloured	70	70
	With tab	1·40	1·40

(Des A. Kalderon and M. Pereg. Photo)

1978 (22 Aug). Jewish New Year. Patriarchs of Israel. Square designs as T **274**. Multicoloured. One phosphor band (I£1.10) or two phosphor bands (others). P 14.

728	I£1.10 Abraham	35	35
729	I£5.20 Isaac	50	45
730	I£6.60 Jacob	60	60
728/730	*Set of 3*	1·30	1·30
728/730	*Set of 3 with tabs*	3·00	2·75

(Des D. Pessah and S. Ketter. Litho)

1978 (31 Oct). United Jewish Appeal. Two phosphor bands. P 14.

731	**298** I£8.40 multicoloured	95	90
	With tab	1·90	1·80

(Des Z. Narkiss. Photo)

1978 (31 Oct). Historical Personalities (4th series). Vert designs as T **283**. One phosphor band. P 14×13.

732	I£2 blackish purple and pale stone	50	45
733	I£2 indigo and pale grey	50	45
732/733	*Set of 2*	90	80
732/733	*Set of 2 with tabs*	1·90	1·80

Designs: No. 732, David Ben-Gurion (first Prime Minister of Israel); No. 733, Ze'ev Jabotinsky (Zionist leader).

290 Shaare Zedek Medical Centre, New and Old Buildings

291 Indian Silver and Enamelled Vase

(Des D. Pessah and S. Ketter. Litho)

1978 (31 Oct). Opening of New Shaare Zedek Medical Centre, Jerusalem. P 14.

734	**290** I£5.40 multicoloured	60	60
	With tab	1·20	1·20

(Des M. Pereg. Litho)

1978 (31 Oct). Institute for Islamic Art, Jerusalem. T **291** and similar vert designs. Multicoloured. Two phosphor bands. P 14.

735	I£2.40 Type **291**	25	25
736	I£3 13th-century Persian pottery chess rook (elephant with howdah)	35	35
737	I£4 Syrian mosque lamp	50	45
735/737	*Set of 3*	1·00	95
735/737	*Set of 3 with tabs*	2·20	2·10

(Des Z. Narkiss. Photo)

1978 (26 Dec). Historical Personalities (5th series). Vert designs as T **283**. One phosphor band. P 14×13.

738	I£2 olive-black and pale stone	35	35
739	I£2 deep blue and pale bluish grey	35	35
740	I£2 brownish black and pale stone	35	35
738/740	*Set of 3*	95	95
738/740	*Set of 3 with tabs*	2·20	2·10

Designs: No. 738, Menahem Ussishkin (President of Jewish National Fund); No. 739, Berl Katzenelson (pioneer of Zionist socialism); No. 740, Dr. Max Nordau (journalist).

292 *Iris lortetii*

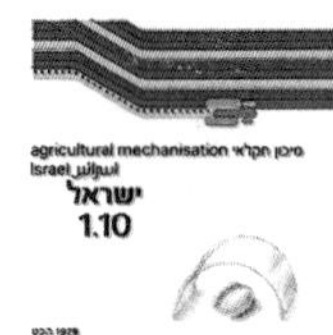

293 Agricultural Mechanisation

(Des A. Glaser. Litho)

1978 (26 Dec). Wild Irises. T **292** and similar vert designs. Multicoloured. One phosphor band (I£1.10), two phosphor bands (I£8.40) or no bands (I£5.40). P 14.

741	I£1.10 Type **292**	35	35
742	I£5.40 *Iris haynei*	60	60
743	I£8.40 *Iris nazarena*	70	70
741/743	*Set of 3*	1·50	1·50
741/743	*Set of 3 with tabs*	3·25	3·25

(Des A. Hecht. Litho)

1979 (13 Feb). Technological Achievements. T **293** and similar square designs. Multicoloured. One phosphor band (I£1.10, I£2.40) or two phosphor bands (others). P 13.

744	I£1.10 Type **293**	10	10
745	I£2.40 Sea water desalination	25	25
746	I£4.30 Electronics	25	25
747	I£5 Chemical fertilisers	25	25
744/747	*Set of 4*	75	75
744/747	*Set of 4 with tabs*	1·70	1·60

294 Jewish Brigade Flag

295 Good from Evil

(Des A. Oron. Photo)

1979 (13 Feb). Yishuv Volunteers Serving in Second World War. Two phosphor bands. P 14.

748	**294** I£5.10 lemon, pale greenish blue and deep grey-blue	70	70
	With tab	1·40	1·40

(Des N. Rosner. Litho)

1979 (13 Feb). 'Salute to the Righteous among Nations'. P 13.

749	**295** I£5.40 multicoloured	70	70
	With tab	1·40	1·40

296 Prayer for Peace in Western Wall

297 Naval Memorial, Ashdod

(Des R. and A. Hecht. Photo)

1979 (26 Mar). Signing of Egyptian–Israeli Peace Treaty. P 14×13.

750	**296** I£10 multicoloured	85	80
	With tab	1·70	1·60
MS751	119×78 mm. I£10 No. 750. Imperf.	1·90	1·80

(Des Z. Narkiss. Photo)

1979 (23 Apr). Memorial Day. Two phosphor bands. P 13×14.

752	**297** I£5.10 multicoloured	60	60
	With tab	1·20	1·20

298 Weightlifting

299 '50' and Rotary Emblem

(Des A. Hecht. Litho)

1979 (23 Apr). 11th Hapoel Games. T **298** and similar square designs. Multicoloured. One phosphor band (I£1.50) or two phosphor bands (others). P 13.

753	I£1.50 Type **298**	35	35
754	I£6 Tennis	60	60
755	I£11 Gymnastics	95	90
753/755	*Set of 3*	1·70	1·70
753/755	*Set of 3 with tabs*	3·75	3·75

(Des A. Ron. Photo)

1979 (23 Apr). 50th Anniversary of Rotary in Israel. P 14×13.

756	**299** I£7 multicoloured	85	80
	With tab	1·70	1·60

300 Rabbi Joshua Ben Hananiah (blacksmith)

301 Tiberias Hot Springs

(Des A. Glaser. Photo)

1979 (4 Sept). Jewish New Year. The Hazal (sages and craftsmen). T **300** and similar vert designs. Multicoloured. One phosphor band (I£1.80) or two phosphor bands (others). P 14×13.

757	I£1.80 Type **300**	25	25
758	I£8.50 Rabbi Meir Ba'al Ha-Nes (scribe)	35	35
759	I£13 Rabbi Johanan the Sandal-maker	60	60
757/759	*Set of 3*	1·10	1·10
757/759	*Set of 3 with tabs*	2·40	2·30

(Des A. Kalderon. Litho)

1979 (4 Sept). Health Resorts. T **301** and similar vert design. Multicoloured. Two phosphor bands. P 14.

760	I£8 Type **301**	35	35
761	I£12 Dead Sea Hot Springs	70	70
760/761	*Set of 2*	95	95
760/761	*Set of 2 with tabs*	2·20	2·10

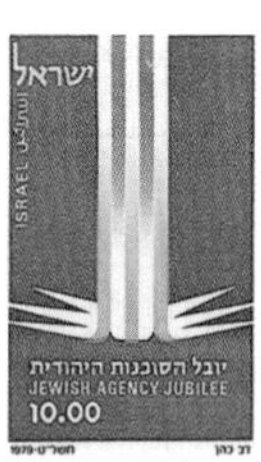
302 Searchlight Beam

303 Arab and Jew before Jerusalem

(Des D. Cohen. Photo)

1979 (4 Sept). 50th Anniversary of Jewish Agency. Two phosphor bands. P 14×13.

762	**302** I£10 new blue, grey and deep turquoise-blue	60	60
	With tab	1·20	1·20

(Des Z. Narkiss. Photo)

1979 (6 Nov). Historical Personalities (6th series). Vert designs as T **283**. Two phosphor bands. P 14×13.

763	I£7 deep claret and pale grey	35	35
764	I£9 deep turquoise-blue	35	35
765	I£13 olive-black and pale stone	60	60
763/765	*Set of 3*	1·20	1·20
763/765	*Set of 3 with tabs*	2·75	2·50

Designs: I£7, Dr. Arthur Ruppin (father of Zionist settlement); I£9, Joseph Trumpeldor (founder of Zion Mule Corps and Jewish Legion); I£13, Aaron Aaronsohn (botanist).

(Des E. Weishoff. Litho)

1979 (6 Nov). Children Paint Jerusalem. T **303** and similar horiz designs. Multicoloured. One phosphor band. P 14.

766	I£1.80 Type **303**	10	10
767	I£4 Jewish, Christian and Muslim citizens of Jerusalem	25	25
768	I£5 Worshippers at the Western Wall	25	25
766/768	*Set of 3*	55	55
766/768	*Set of 3 with tabs*	1·40	1·40

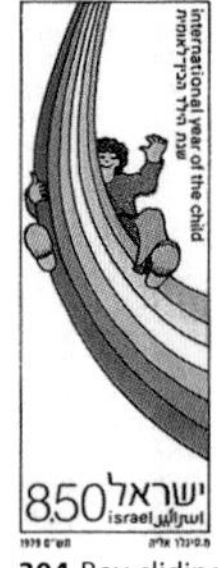
304 Boy sliding down Rainbow

305 Cog with Star of David

(Des M. Siegler Eliya. Photo)

1979 (6 Nov). International Year of the Child. Two phosphor bands. P 13×14.

769	**304** I£8.50 multicoloured	60	60
	With tab	1·20	1·20

(Des M. Pereg. Photo)

1980 (15 Jan). Centenary of Organisation for Rehabilitation through Training. Two phosphor bands. P 14.

770	**305** I£13 multicoloured	95	90
	With tab	1·90	1·80

306 *Scolymus maculatus*

307 Road of Courage Monument

(Des A. Glaser. Photo)

1980 (15 Jan). Thistles. T **306** and similar vert designs. Multicoloured. P 14.

771	50a. Type **306**	25	25
772	I£5.50 *Echinops viscosus*	35	35
773	I£8.50 *Cynara syriaca*	50	45
771/773	*Set of 3*	1·00	95
771/773	*Set of 3 with tabs*	2·20	2·10

1980 (15 Apr). Memorial Day. Two phosphor bands. Photo. P 14.

774	**307** I£12 multicoloured	60	60
	With tab	1·20	1·20

308 Symbolical Human Figure with Blood-drop

309 Sabbath Lamp, Netherlands, 18th-century

(Des A. Vanooijen. Photo)

1980 (15 Apr). 50th Anniversary of Magen David Adom (voluntary medical corps). T **308** and similar vert design. One phosphor band (I£2.70), two phosphor bands (I£13) or no bands (No. **MS**777). P 14×13.

775	I£2.70 red, brownish grey and grey-black	35	35
776	I£13 multicoloured	70	70
775/776	*Set of 2*	95	95
775/776	*Set of 2 with tabs*	2·20	2·10
MS777	124×64 mm. Nos. 775/776×2	7·25	7·00

Designs: I£2.70, T **308**; I£13, Mobile intensive care unit and graph.

(Des A. Vanooijen. Photo)

1980 (12 Aug). Jewish New Year. Sabbath Lamps. T **309** and similar vert designs. Multicoloured. One phosphor band (I£4.30) or two phosphor bands (others). P 13×14.

778	I£4.30 Type **309**	25	25
779	I£20 Sabbath lamp, Germany, 18th-century	70	70
780	I£30 Sabbath lamp, Morocco, 19th-century	95	90
778/780	*Set of 3*	1·70	1·70
778/780	*Set of 3 with tabs*	3·75	3·75

310 Yizhak Gruenbaum

311 Tree and Flowers

(Des M. Krup. Photo)

1980 (12 Aug). Tenth Death Anniversary of Yizhak Gruenbaum (Zionist and politician). Two phosphor bands. P 14×13.

781	**310**	I£32 sepia	1·40	1·40
		With tab	3·00	2·75

(Des D. Ben-Hador. Photo)

1980 (12 Aug). Renewal of Jewish Settlement in Gush Etzion. P 14×13.

782	**311**	I£19 multicoloured	85	80
		With tab	1·70	1·60

New Currency

(1 (new) Shekel = 10 (old) Israeli Pounds).

312 Haifa

313 Shekel

1980 (28 Sept). Haifa 80 National Stamp Exhibition. Sheet 100×84 mm containing T **312** and similar vert design showing details of 17th-century engraving of Haifa. Multicoloured. Litho. P 14×13.

MS783	2s. Type **312** Haifa (*different*) (*sold at* 7s.50)	6·00	5·75

(Des G. Sagi. Photo)

1980 (16 Dec)–**84**. No phosphor bands (5 to 50a. and 10s.) or with phosphor bands (others). P 13×14.

784	**313**	5a. bright green and emerald	50	45
785		10a. orange-vermilion and bright magenta	50	45
786		20a. greenish blue and Prussian blue	50	45
787		30a. reddish violet and violet	50	45
788		50a. red-orange and brown-red	60	45
789		60a. yellow-green and maroon (*1 band on right*)	1·40	1·40
		a. No phosphor bands (21.1.82)	60	45
790		70a. greenish blue and grey-black (*1 band on right*) (5.5.81)	1·40	1·40
		a. No phosphor bands (1983)	6·00	5·75
791		90a. violet and orange-brown (*1 band on right*) (25.8.81)	1·80	1·70
		a. One band on left	3·50	3·50
792		1s. bright magenta and deep green (*2 bands*)	70	70
		a. One band on right (21.1.82)	3·00	3·00
		b. No phosphor bands (25.4.82)	85	80
793		1s.10 brown-olive and orange-vermilion (*1 band on right*) (11.2.82)	85	80
794		1s.20 blue and vermilion (*1 band on right*) (16.3.82)	85	80
795		2s. bluish green and brown-purple (*2 bands*)	2·20	2·10
		a. One band on right (30.5.82)	6·00	5·75
		b. No phosphor bands (1983)	1·10	90
796		2s.80 olive-sepia and emerald (*2 bands*)	1·10	1·00
797		3s. deep rose-red and deep violet-blue (*2 bands*) (25.8.81)	3·00	3·00
		a. No phosphor bands (1984)	4·75	4·50
798		3s.20 deep grey and bright carmine (*2 bands*)	1·20	1·00
799		4s. deep reddish purple and bright magenta (*2 bands*) (25.8.81)	2·20	2·10
		a. One band on right (1983)	7·25	7·00
		b. No phosphor bands (1984)	6·00	5·75
800		4s.20 ultramarine and violet (*2 bands*)	1·20	1·00
801		5s. emerald and grey-black (*2 bands*)	2·20	1·30
		a. No phosphor bands (1984)	1·20	1·00
802		10s. orange-brown and deep brown	3·50	3·00
		p. Two phosphor bands (21.1.82)	6·00	5·25
		pa. One band on right (1984)	17·00	16·00
784/802		*Set of 19* (*cheapest*)	21·00	19·00
784/802		*Set of 19 with tabs* (*cheapest*)	38·00	37·00

314 Golda Meir

315 *Landscape* (Anna Ticho)

(Des M. Krup. Photo)

1981 (10 Feb). Golda Meir (former Prime Minister) Commemoration. P 14×13.

803	**314**	2s.60 plum	85	80
		With tab	1·70	1·60

1981 (10 Feb). Paintings of Jerusalem. T **315** and similar multicoloured designs. One phosphor band (50a.) or two phosphor bands (others). Litho. P 14.

804	50a. Type **315**	25	25
805	1s.50 *View of City* (Joseph Zaritsky) (*vert*)	50	45
806	2s.50 *Landscape* (Mordechai Ardon)	60	60
804/806	*Set of 3*	1·20	1·20
804/806	*Set of 3 with tabs*	2·75	2·50

316 Hand putting Coin into Light Bulb

317 A. H. Silver (Zionist)

(Des D. Ben-Hador. Photo)

1981 (17 Mar). Energy Conservation. T **316** and similar square design. Multicoloured. Two phosphor bands. P 14.

807 2s.60 Type **316** ... 60 60
808 4s.20 Hand squeezing energy from sun ... 85 80
807/808 *Set of 2* ... 1·30 1·30
807/808 *Set of 2 with tabs* ... 3·00 2·75

(Des R. Beckman; photo (2s., 2s.80). Des A. Vanooijen; litho (3s.20))

1981 (17 Mar). Historical Personalities (7th series). T **317** and vert designs as T **283**. Two phosphor bands. P 14 (3s.20) or 14×13 (others).

809 2s. deep dull blue ... 70 70
810 2s.80 bottle green ... 70 70
811 3s.20 yellow-ochre and black ... 70 70
809/811 *Set of 3* ... 1·90 1·90
809/811 *Set of 3 with tabs* ... 4·25 4·25

Designs: 2s. Shmuel Yosef Agnon (writer); 2s.80, Moses Montefiore (Zionist); 3s.20, T **317**.

318 Biq'at Ha-yarden Memorial

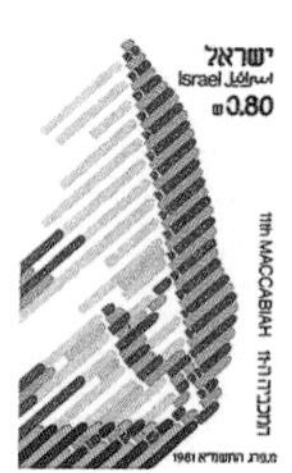

319 Board Sailing

(Des D. Cohen. Photo)

1981 (5 May). Memorial Day. Two phosphor bands. P 13×14.

812 **318** 1s. multicoloured ... 60 45
With tab 1·20 90

(Des M. Pereg. Photo)

1981 (5 May). 11th Maccabiah Games. T **319** and similar vert designs. Multicoloured. One phosphor band (80a.) or two phosphor bands (others). P 14×13.

813 80a. Type **319** ... 50 45
814 4s. Basketball ... 70 70
815 6s. High jump ... 95 90
813/815 *Set of 3* ... 1·90 1·80
813/815 *Set of 3 with tabs* ... 4·25 4·25

320 'Family Tree'

321 Moses and the Burning Bush

(Des A. Hecht. Litho)

1981 (5 May). Jewish Family Heritage. Two phosphor bands. P 14.

816 **320** 3s. multicoloured ... 85 80
With tab 1·70 1·60

(Des A. Glaser. Photo)

1981 (25 Aug). Jewish New Year. Moses. T **321** and similar vert designs. Multicoloured. One phosphor band (70a., 1s.) or two phosphor bands (others). P 13×14.

817 70a. Type **321** ... 25 25
818 1s. Moses and Aaron petitioning Pharaoh for freedom of Israelites ... 35 35
819 3s. Israelites crossing Red Sea ... 70 70
820 4s. Moses with Tablets ... 85 80
817/820 *Set of 4* ... 1·90 1·90
817/820 *Set of 4 with tabs* ... 4·25 4·25

322 *Rosa damascena*

323 Ha-Shiv'a Interchange

(Des A. Glaser. Litho)

1981 (22 Oct). Roses. T **322** and similar vert designs. Multicoloured. One phosphor band (90a.) or two phosphor bands (others). P 14.

821 90a. Type **322** ... 35 35
822 3s.50 *Rosa phoenicia* ... 85 80
823 4s.50 *Rosa hybrida* ... 95 90
821/823 *Set of 3* ... 1·90 1·80
821/823 *Set of 3 with tabs* ... 4·25 4·25

(Des D. Cohen. Photo)

1981 (22 Oct). Ha-Shiv'a Motorway Interchange. P 14×13.

824 **323** 8s. multicoloured ... 1·40 1·40
With tab 3·00 2·75

324 Balonea Oak(*Quercus ithaburensis*)

325 Elat Stone

(Des I. Granot. Litho)

1981 (29 Dec). Trees. T **324** and similar vert designs. Multicoloured. Two phosphor bands. P 14.

825 3s. Type **324** ... 60 60
a. Strip of 3. Nos. 825/827 ... 1·90
826 3s. Wild Strawberry (*Arbutus andrachne*) ... 60 60
827 3s. Judas Tree (*Cercis siliquastrum*) ... 60 60
825/827 *Set of 3* ... 1·60 1·60
825/827 *Set of 3 with tabs* ... 3·50 3·50

Nos. 825/827 were printed together in *se-tenant* vertical and horizontal strips of three within sheets of nine stamps.

(Des D. Pessah and S. Ketter. Litho)

1981 (29 Dec). Precious Stones. T **325** and similar vert designs. Multicoloured. Two phosphor bands. P 14.

828 2s.50 Type **325** ... 60 60
829 5s.50 Star sapphire ... 95 90
830 7s. Emerald ... 1·30 1·30
828/830 *Set of 3* ... 2·50 2·50
828/830 *Set of 3 with tabs* ... 5·75 5·50

326 Perez Bernstein (politician)

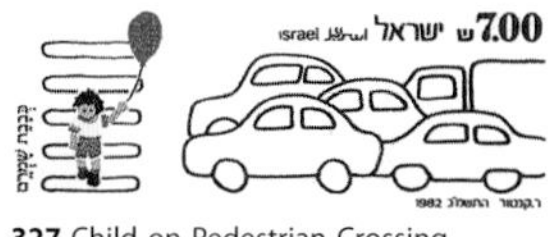

327 Child on Pedestrian Crossing

(Des M. Pereg (7s.), R. Beckman (others). Litho (8s.) or photo (others))

1982 (2 Mar). Historical Personalities (8th series). T **326** and vert designs as T **283**. Two phosphor bands. P 14 (8s.) or 14×13 (others).

831 7s. multicoloured 95 90
832 8s. sepia, stone and black 95 90
833 9s. deep slate-blue and pale grey 95 90
831/833 *Set of 3* 2·50 2·40
831/833 *Set of 3 with tabs* 5·75 5·50

Designs: 7s. T **326**; 8s. Rabbi Arye Levin; 9s. Joseph Gedaliah Klausner (writer, editor and President of Hebrew Language Academy).

(Des R. Kantor. Photo)

1982 (2 Mar). Road Safety. Two phosphor bands (No. 834) or no phosphor bands (**MS**835). P 14×13.

834 **327** 7s. multicoloured 1·10 1·00
With tab 2·20 2·10
MS835 127×79 mm. 7s. No. 834 (*sold at* 10s.) 6·00 5·75

328 Armoured Brigade Memorial, Ein Zetim

329 *Landscape* (Aryeh Lubin)

(Des D. Cohen. Litho)

1982 (22 Apr). Memorial Day. One phosphor band. P 14.

836 **328** 1s.50 multicoloured 60 45
With tab 1·20 90

(Des A. Vanooijen. Litho)

1982 (22 Apr). Israeli Art. T **329** and similar multicoloured designs depicting landscapes of Eastern Israel by artists named. No phosphor bands (15s.) or two phosphor bands (others). P 14.

837 7s. Type **329** 95 90
838 8s. Sionah Tagger (*vert*) 1·20 1·20
839 15s. Israel Paldi 2·00 2·00
837/839 *Set of 3* 3·75 3·75
837/839 *Set of 3 with tabs* 8·50 8·00

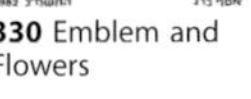

330 Emblem and Flowers

331 Agricultural Products

332 Joshua and Israelites setting out for Canaan

(Des A. Berg. Photo)

1982 (22 Apr). 40th Anniversary of Gadna (Youth Corps). Two phosphor bands. P 14×13.

840 **330** 5s. multicoloured 95 90
With tab 1·90 1·80

(Des E. Wieshoff. Photo)

1982 (22 June)–**85**. No phosphor bands (40, 80a., 100, 500s.) or with phosphor bands (others). P 13×14.

841 **331** 40a. bright turquoise-blue and green (11.1.83) 1·20 1·20
842 80a. blue and deep mauve (11.1.83) 1·20 1·20
843 1s.40 dull yellow-green and deep carmine-red (*1 band*) 85 80
844 6s. deep magenta and orange-red (*2 bands*) (11.1.83) 1·40 1·40
a. One band on right (1984) 9·00 8·75
845 7s. Indian red and deep olive (*2 bands*) (11.10.83) 60 60
a. Value omitted
846 8s. light green and Indian red (*2 bands*) (11.10.83) 60 60
847 9s. yellow-olive and deep brown (*2 bands*) (11.10.83) 2·40 2·30
848 15s. rosine and light green (*2 bands*) (11.10.83) 12·00 11·50
a. One band (1984) 30·00 29·00
b. No phosphor bands 9·50 9·25
849 30s. maroon and scarlet-vermilion (*2 bands*) (26.4.84) 5·50 5·25
a. No phosphor bands (1985) 19·00 18·00
850 50s. deep olive-bistre and brown-lake (*2 bands*) (26.4.84) 3·50 3·50
a. One band (1984) 13·00 12·50
b. No phosphor bands (1985) 32·00 31·00
851 100s. grey-black and bluish green (26.4.84) 7·25 7·00
a. Two bands (1984) 20·00 20·00
b. One band on right 12·00 11·50
852 500s. orange-red and blue-black (20.11.84) 9·00 8·75
a. Two phosphor bands (1985) 42·00 40·00
841/852 *Set of 12* (*cheapest*) 39·00 38·00
841/852 *Set of 12 with tabs* (*cheapest*) 70·00 70·00

No. 845a occurred on the entire middle horizontal row of at least one sheet (10×5).

Nos. 853/859 are vacant.

(Des M. Pereg. Photo)

1982 (17 Aug). Jewish New Year. Joshua. T **332** and similar square designs. Multicoloured. One phosphor band (1s.50) or two phosphor bands (others). P 14.

860 1s.50 Type **332** 35 35
861 5s.50 Priests carrying Ark of the Covenant over River Jordan 50 45
862 7s.50 The fall of the walls of Jericho 60 60
863 9s.50 The suspension of twilight during the battle against the five kings of the Amorites 70 70
860/863 *Set of 4* 1·90 1·90
860/863 *Set of 4 with tabs* 4·25 4·25

333 Rosh Pinna

334 Symbolic Figures on Star of David

(Des Z. Rosenberg. Photo)

1982 (17 Aug). Centenaries of Rosh Pinna and Rishon LeZion Settlements. T **333** and similar horiz design. Multicoloured. Two phosphor bands. P 13×13½.

864 2s.50 Type **333** 60 60
865 3s.50 Rishon LeZion 60 60
864/865 *Set of 2* 1·10 1·10
864/865 *Set of 2 with tabs* 2·40 2·30

See also Nos. 868/869, 905/906 and 967.

(Des G. Sagi. Litho)

1982 (17 Aug). 70th Anniversary of Hadassah (Women's Zionist Organisation of America). Two phosphor bands. P 14.

866 **334** 12s. multicoloured 1·40 1·40
With tab 3·00 2·75

335 Branch

336 Flower

(Des D. Cohen. Photo)

1982 (12 Sept)–**88**. No value expressed. One phosphor band. P 13×14.

867 **335** (–) reddish brown and orange ... 70 70
With tab 1·40 1·40
a. Booklet pane. No. 867×8 (4.9.84)... 11·50
b. Reddish brown and bright yellow-orange (1988) ... 4·25 4·00
ba. Booklet pane. No. 867*b*×8 (1988).. 35·00

No. 867 was sold at the current inland letter rate, initially 1s.70. Subsequently this value was increased several times.

Nos. 867a and 867ba have a selvedge round the outer edges of the pane.

(Des Z. Rosenberg. Photo)

1982 (5 Oct). Centenaries of Zikhron Yaaqov and Mazkeret Batya. Horiz designs as T **333**. Multicoloured. Two phosphor bands. P 13×14.

868 6s. Zikhron Yaaqov ... 95 90
869 9s. Mazkeret Batya ... 1·20 1·20
868/869 *Set of 2* ... 1·90 1·90
868/869 *Set of 2 with tabs* ... 4·25 4·25

(Des R. Hamburg. Litho)

1982 (5 Oct). Council for a Beautiful Israel. P 14.

870 **336** 17s. multicoloured ... 1·80 1·70
With tab 3·50 3·50

(Des R. Hamburg. Litho)

1982 (5 Oct). Beer Sheva 82 National Stamp Exhibition. Sheet 130×78 mm. Imperf.

MS871 17s. No. 870 (*sold at* 25s.) ... 6·00 5·75

337 Eliahu Bet Tzuri

338 Honey Bee, Honeycomb and Flowers

(Des R. Beckman. Photo)

1982 (22 Dec). Martyrs of Struggle for Israel's Independence. T **337** and similar vert designs. P 14×13½.

872 3s. grey, black and reddish brown ... 35 35
873 3s. grey, black and brown-olive ... 35 35
874 3s. grey, black and greenish blue ... 35 35
875 3s. grey, black and brown-olive ... 35 35
876 3s. grey, black and reddish brown ... 35 35
877 3s. grey, black and greenish blue ... 35 35
878 3s. grey, black and reddish brown ... 35 35
879 3s. grey, black and brown-olive ... 35 35
880 3s. grey, black and greenish blue ... 35 35
881 3s. grey, black and brown-olive ... 35 35
882 3s. grey, black and reddish brown ... 35 35
883 3s. grey, black and brown-olive ... 35 35
884 3s. grey, black and greenish blue ... 35 35
885 3s. grey, black and reddish brown ... 35 35
886 3s. grey, black and greenish blue ... 35 35
887 3s. grey, black and brown-olive ... 35 35
888 3s. grey, black and greenish blue ... 35 35
889 3s. grey, black and reddish brown ... 35 35
890 3s. grey, black and brown-olive ... 35 35
891 3s. grey, black and reddish brown ... 35 35
872/891 *Set of 20* ... 6·25 6·25
872/891 *Sheetlet of 20 with tabs* ... 17·00 16·00

Designs: No. 872, T **337**; No. 873, Hannah Szenes; No. 874, Shlomo Ben Yosef; No. 875, Yosef Lishanski; No. 876, Naaman Belkind; No. 877, Eliezer Kashani; No. 878, Yechiel Dresner; No. 879, Dov Gruner; No. 880, Mordechai Alkachi; No. 881, Eliahu Hakim; No. 882, Meir Nakar; No. 883, Avshalom Haviv; No. 884, Yaakov Weiss; No. 885, Meir Feinstein, No. 886, Moshe Barazani; No. 887, Eli Cohen; No. 888, Samuel Azaar; No. 889, Dr. Moshe Marzouk; No. 890, Shalom Salih; No. 891, Yosef Basri.

Nos. 872/891 were printed together in sheetlets of 20 stamps.

(Des D. Ben-Hador. Photo)

1983 (15 Feb). Bee-keeping. P 13×14.

892 **338** 30s. multicoloured ... 3·00 3·00
With tab 6·00 5·75

339 Sweets in Ashtray

340 Golan Settlement

(Des Naomi and M. Eshel. Litho)

1983 (15 Feb). Anti-smoking Campaign. Two phosphor bands. P 13.

893 **339** 7s. multicoloured ... 85 80
With tab 1·70 1·60

(Des D. Ben Dov. Litho)

1983 (15 Feb). Settlements. T **340** and similar horiz designs. Multicoloured. Two phosphor bands. P 14.

894 8s. Type **340** ... 95 90
895 15s. Galil settlement ... 1·20 1·20
896 20s. Yehuda and Shomeron settlements ... 1·40 1·40
894/896 *Set of 3* ... 3·25 3·25
894/896 *Set of 3 with tabs* ... 7·25 7·00

341 84th Division of Steel Memorial, Besor (Israel Godowitz)

342 Star of David

(Des D. Pessah and S. Ketter. Litho)

1983 (12 Apr). Memorial Day. One phosphor band. P 13.

897 **341** 3s. multicoloured ... 60 60
With tab 1·20 1·20

(Des Y. Agam. Litho)

1983 (12 Apr). 35th Anniversary of Independence. P 14.

898 **342** 25s. multicoloured ... 2·75 2·50
With tab 5·25 5·00

MS899 120×84 mm. 25s. No. 898. Imperf (*sold at* 35s.). 7·75 7·25

343 Running

344 Missile and Blueprint

(Des A. Prath. Photo)

1983 (12 Apr). 12th Hapoel Games. Two phosphor bands. P 14×13.

900 **343** 6s. multicoloured ... 70 70
With tab 1·40 1·40

(Des E. Weishoff. Photo)

1983 (12 Apr). 50th Anniversary of Israel Military Industries. Two phosphor bands. P 14×13.

901 **344** 12s. multicoloured ... 1·10 1·00
With tab 2·20 2·10

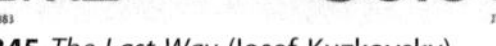

345 *The Last Way* (Iosef Kuzkovsky) **346** Yosef Glazman

(Des Y. Zim. Litho)

1983 (7 June). Babi Yar Massacre, 1941. P 14.

902	**345**	35s. multicoloured	2·40	2·30
		With tab	4·75	4·50

(Des A. Glaser. Litho)

1983 (7 June). 40th Anniversary of Warsaw and Vilna Ghettos Uprising. Sheet 120×86 mm containing T **346** and similar square designs. Multicoloured. P 14½.

MS903 10s. Type **346**, 10s. Commemorative text, 10s. Mordechai Anielewicz (*sold at* 45s.) 9·50 9·25

347 Raoul Wallenberg **348** Ohel Moed Synagogue,Tel Aviv

(Des R. Beckman. Photo)

1983 (7 June). Raoul Wallenberg (Swedish diplomat) Commemoration. Two phosphor bands. P 14×13.

904	**347**	14s. stone and blackish brown	1·80	1·70
		With tab	3·50	3·50

(Des Z. Rosenberg. Litho)

1983 (23 Aug). Centenaries of Yesud Ha-Maala and Nes Ziyyona. Horiz designs as T **333**. Multicoloured. Two phosphor bands. P 14.

905	11s. Yesud Ha-Maala	95	90
906	13s. Nes Ziyyona	95	90
905/906	*Set of 2*	1·70	1·70
905/906	*Set of 2 with tabs*	3·75	3·75

(Des A. Berg. Litho)

1983 (23 Aug). Jewish New Year. Synagogues. T **348** and similar horiz designs. Multicoloured. One phosphor band (*3s.*) or two bands (others). P 14.

907	3s. Type **348**	35	35
908	12s. Yeshurun Synagogue, Jerusalem	60	60
909	16s. Ohel Aharon Synagogue, Haifa	1·10	1·00
910	20s. Khalaschi Synagogue, Beer Sheva	1·20	1·20
907/910	*Set of 4*	3·00	2·75
907/910	*Set of 4 with tabs*	6·50	6·25

349 Afula Landscape **350** Promenade, Tel Aviv

(Des M. Pereg. Litho)

1983 (23 Aug). Afula Urban Centre, Jezreel Valley. Two phosphor bands. P 14.

911	**349**	15s. multicoloured	1·30	1·30
		With tab	2·75	2·50

(Des M. Pereg Litho)

1983 (25 Sept). Tel Aviv 83 Stamp Exhibition. Sheet 142×88 mm containing T **350** and similar vert design. Multicoloured. P 14×13.

MS912 30s. Type **350**, 50s. Promenade (*different*) (*sold at* 120s.) 22·00 21·00

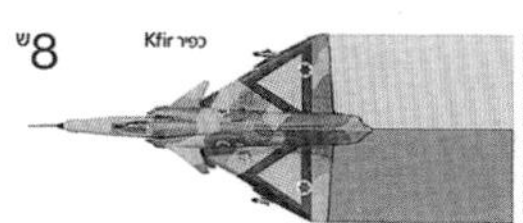

351 Israeli Aircraft Industry Kfir-C2 Jet Fighter **352** Rabbi Meir Bar-Ilan

(Des A. Kalderon. Litho)

1983 (13 Dec). Military Equipment. T **351** and similar horiz designs. Multicoloured. Two phosphor bands. P 14.

913	8s. Type **351**	35	35
914	18s. *Reshef* (missile vessel)	60	60
915	30s. Merkava battle tank	95	90
913/915	*Set of 3*	1·70	1·70
913/915	*Set of 3 with tabs*	3·75	3·75

(Des A. Glaser. Photo)

1983 (13 Dec). 34th Death Anniversary of Rabbi Meir Bar-Ilan (Zionist leader). Two phosphor bands. P 14×13.

916	**352**	9s. deep blue and olive-green	60	60
		With tab	1·20	1·20

353 'Aliya' (immigration) **354** Michael Halperin

(Des Z. Rosenberg. Photo)

1983 (13 Dec). 50th Anniversary of Jewish Immigration from Germany. Two phosphor bands. P 13×14.

917	**353**	14s. scarlet-vermilion, gold and deep new blue	70	70
		With tab	1·40	1·40

(Des R. Beckman. Photo)

1984 (15 Mar). 65th Death Anniversary of Michael Halperin (nationalist). One phosphor band. P 14×13½.

918	**354**	7s. reddish brown, pale yellow-ochre and blackish brown	50	45
		With tab	95	90

355 Yigal Allon **356** Uri Zvi Grinberg

(Des A. Glaser. Litho)

1984 (15 Mar). Fourth Death Anniversary of Yigal Allon (politician). Two phosphor bands. P 14.

919 **355** 15s. cobalt, yellow-olive and black......... 50 45
With tab 95 90

(Des Z. Narkiss. Litho)

1984 (15 Mar). Third Death Anniversary of Uri Zvi Grinberg (poet). Two phosphor bands. P 13.

920 **356** 16s. deep brown and dull scarlet........... 50 45
With tab 95 90

357 Hevel Ha-besor

(Des Naomi and M. Eshel. Litho)

1984 (15 Mar). Settlements. T **357** and similar vert designs. Multicoloured. Two phosphor bands. P 14.

921 12s. Type **357**........ 50 45
922 17s. Arava........ 60 60
923 40s. Hevel Azza........ 1·20 1·20
921/923 *Set of 3*........ 2·10 2·00
921/923 *Set of 3 with tabs*........ 4·50 4·25

The right hand phosphor band on Nos. 921/923 is shorter than that on the left.

358 Alexander Zaid Monument (David Polus)

(Des A. Berg. Photo)

1984 (15 Mar). Sculptures. T **358** and similar vert designs. P 13×14.

924 15s. pale stone, black and azure........ 60 60
925 15s. pale stone, black and pale brown........ 60 60
926 15s. pale blue-green, black and pale drab.... 60 60
924/926 *Set of 3*........ 1·60 1·60
924/926 *Set of 3 with tabs*........ 3·50 3·50

Designs: No. 924, T **358**; No. 925, Tel Hay memorial (Abraham Melnikov); No. 926, Dov Gruner monument (Chana Orloff).

359 Oliphant House, Dalyat Al Karmil (memorial to Druse Community)

360 Worker with Flag

(Des R. Dayagi. Photo)

1984 (26 Apr). Memorial Day. One phosphor band. P 14×13.

927 **359** 10s. multicoloured........ 60 35
With tab 1·20 70

(Des Naomi and M. Eshel. Photo)

1984 (26 Apr). 50th Anniversary of National Labour Federation. Two phosphor bands. P 14×13.

928 **360** 35s. multicoloured........ 85 80
With tab 1·70 1·60

361 Leon Pinsker

362 Stars and Hearts

(Des R. Beckman. Photo)

1984 (19 June). 93rd Death Anniversary of Leon Pinsker (Zionist leader). Two phosphor bands. P 14×13.

929 **361** 20s. grey-lilac and maroon........ 50 45
With tab 95 90

(Des A. Hecht. Photo)

1984 (19 June). 70th Anniversary of American Jewish Joint Distribution Committee. Two phosphor bands. P 14×13.

930 **362** 30s. vermilion, new blue and black....... 70 70
With tab 1·40 1·40

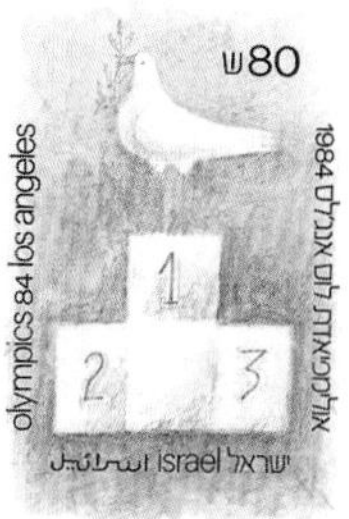

363 Dove on Olympic Podium

364 General Charles Orde Wingate

(Des D. Pessah. Litho)

1984 (3 July). Olympic Games, Los Angeles. Two phosphor bands. P 14.

931 **363** 80s. multicoloured........ 1·30 1·30
With tab 2·75 2·50

MS932 119×80 mm. Type **363** 240s. multicoloured (23×37 *mm*) (no phosphor bands). P 14×13 (*sold at* 350s.)........ 19·00 18·00

(Des A. Vanooijen. Photo)

1984 (3 July). 40th Death Anniversary of General Charles Orde Wingate (military strategist). Two phosphor bands. P 14×13.

933 **364** 20s. greenish slate, black and emerald. 50 45
With tab 95 90

365 Hannah

366 Nahalal (first Moshav)

(Des A. Kalderon. Photo)

1984 (4 Sept). Jewish New Year. Women in the Bible. T **365** and similar vert designs. Multicoloured. One phosphor band (15s.) or two bands (others). P 13×14.

934 15s. Type **365**........ 50 45
935 70s. Ruth........ 95 90

936 100s. Huldah the prophetess........ 1·20 1·20
934/936 *Set of 3*........ 2·40 2·30
934/936 *Set of 3 with tabs*........ 5·25 5·00

(Des Naomi and M. Eshel. Litho)

1984 (4 Sept). Moshavim (Co-operative Workers' Settlements). Two phosphor bands. P 14.
937 **366** 80s. multicoloured........ 1·10 1·00
With tab 2·20 2·10

367 David Wolffsohn

368 *Apartment to Let* (Leah Goldberg, illus Shemuel Katz)

(Des Z. Narkiss. Photo)

1984 (4 Sept). 70th Death Anniversary of David Wolffsohn (president of Zionist Organisation). P 14½.
938 **367** 150s. olive-sepia, grey-blue and black.... 2·20 2·10
With tab 4·25 4·25

(Des D. Ben Dov. Litho)

1984 (20 Nov). Children's Books. T **368** and similar multicoloured designs showing scenes from children's books. One phosphor band (20s.) or two bands (others). P 13 (30s.) or 14 (others).
939 20s. Type **368**........ 35 35
940 30s. *Why is the Zebra wearing Pyjamas?* (O. Hillel, illus Alona Frankel) (28×28 *mm*)........ 50 45
941 50s. *Across the Sea* (Haim Nahman Bialik, illus Nahum Gutman)........ 60 60
939/941 *Set of 3*........ 1·30 1·30
939/941 *Set of 3 with tabs*........ 3·00 2·75

369 Bread and Wheat

370 Isaac Herzog

(Des D. Pessah. Litho)

1984 (20 Nov). World Food Day. P 14.
942 **369** 200s. multicoloured........ 1·80 1·70
With tab 3·50 3·50

(Des Z. Narkiss. Photo)

1984 (20 Nov). 25th Death Anniversary of Isaac Herzog (Israel's first Chief Rabbi). P 14½.
943 **370** 400s. muulticoloured........ 3·25 3·00
With tab 6·50 6·25

371 Lappet-faced Vulture (*Trogos tracheliotus negevensis*)

(Des A. Glaser. Litho)

1985 (5 Feb). Biblical Birds of Prey (1st series). T **371** and similar horiz designs. Multicoloured. Two phosphor bands (100, 200s.). P 14.
944 100s. Type **371**........ 1·20 1·20
945 200s. Bonelli's Eagle (*Hieraetus fasciatus*)........ 1·80 1·70
946 300s. Sooty Falcon (*Falco concolor*)........ 3·00 3·00
947 500s. Griffon Vulture (*Gyps fulvus*)........ 4·75 4·50
944/947 *Set of 4*........ 9·75 9·25
944/947 *Set of 4 with tabs*........ 22·00 21·00
MS948 120×82 mm. As Nos. 944/947 but smaller (33×23 *mm*) and without phosphor bands (*sold at* 1650s.)........ 29·00 28·00
See also Nos. 1015/**MS**1019.

372 Golani Brigade Monument and Museum

(Des D. Cohen. Photo)

1985 (2 Apr). Memorial Day. One phosphor band. P 14×13.
949 **372** 50s. multicoloured........ 70 70
With tab 1·40 1·40

373 Blériot XI

374 Zivia and Yitzhak Zuckerman

(Des D. Cohen. Litho)

1985 (2 Apr). Aviation in the Holy Land. T **373** and similar horiz designs. Multicoloured. One phosphor band (50s.), two bands (150s.). P 14.
950 50s. Type **373** (landing by Jules Vedrines, 1913)........ 50 45
951 150s. Short S.17 Kent flying boat *Scipio* (Imperial Airways regular flights via Palestine, 1931–1942)........ 95 90
952 250s. de Havilland DH.82A Tiger Moth (foundation of Palestine Flying Club, 1934)........ 1·60 1·50
953 300s. Short S.16 Scion II (international flights by Palestine Airways, 1937–1940)........ 1·80 1·70
950/953 *Set of 4*........ 4·25 4·00
950/953 *Set of 4 with tabs*........ 9·50 9·25

(Des A. Glaser. Photo)

1985 (2 Apr). Zivia and Yitzhak Zuckerman (Polish Jewish freedom fighters) Commemoration. Two phosphor bands. P 13×14.
954 **374** 200s. deep yellow-brown, lavender-grey and black........ 1·40 1·40
With tab 3·00 2·75

375 Nurses tending Patients

(Des M. Pereg. Litho)

1985 (2 Apr). 18th International Congress of Nurses. P 14.
955 **375** 400s. multicoloured........ 2·20 2·10
With tab 4·25 4·25

376 Dome of the Rock

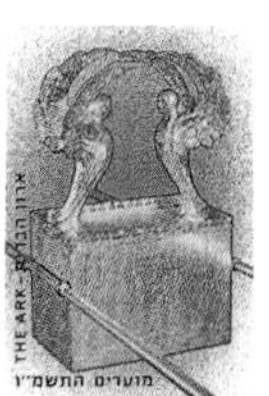

377 Ark of the Covenant

(Des M. Pereg. Litho)

1985 (14 May). Israphil 85 International Stamp Exhibition, Tel Aviv. Three sheets containing various designs.

MS956 Three sheets (a) 120×80 mm. 200s. Type **376**; 200s. Western wall; 200s. Church of the Holy Sepulchre. P 13×14 (*sold at* 900s.); (b) 120×80 mm. 350s. 16th-century relief; 350s. 18th-century relief; 350s. 12/13th-century relief (each 25×39 *mm*). P 14×13 (*sold at* 1500s.); (c) 79×120 mm. 800s. Adam and Eve with serpent (30×30 *mm*). P 14½ (*sold at* 1200s.) .... 50·00 48·00

The three sheets with additional private overprints 'Under the patronage of Fédération International de Philatelie' were sold at the FIP stand at the exhibition for US$10 per set.

(Des A. Berg. Litho)

1985 (16 July). Jewish New Year. Tabernacle Furnishings. T **377** and similar vert designs. Multicoloured. One phosphor band (100, 150s.) or two bands (others). P 14.

957	100s. Type **377**	60	60
958	150s. The table	60	60
959	200s. Candlestick	70	70
960	300s. Incense altar	1·10	1·00
957/960	*Set of 4*	2·75	2·50
957/960	*Set of 4 with tabs*	6·00	5·75

378 'Medals'

379 Basketball

(Des Naomi and M. Eshel. Litho)

1985 (16 July). International Youth Year. One phosphor band. P 14.

961	**378** 150s. multicoloured	70	70
	With tab	1·40	1·40

(Des Z. Rosenberg. Litho)

1985 (16 July). 12th Maccabiah Games. T **379** and similar vert designs. Multicoloured. P 14.

962	400s. Type **379**	1·20	1·20
963	500s. Tennis	1·80	1·70
964	600s. Windsurfing	2·40	2·30
962/964	*Set of 3*	4·75	4·75
962/964	*Set of 3 with tabs*	11·00	10·50

380 Recanati

381 Dizengoff (after J. Steinhardt and M. Sima)

(Des E. Weishoff. Litho)

1985 (5 Nov). 40th Death Anniversary of Leon Yehuda Recanati (founder of Palestine Discount Bank). One phosphor band. P 14.

965	**380** 200s. sepia, pale greenish grey and deep blue	85	80
	With tab	1·70	1·60

(Des Y. Granot. Litho)

1985 (5 Nov). 49th Death Anniversary of Meir Dizengoff (founder and Mayor of Tel Aviv). Two phosphor bands. P 14.

966	**381** 500s. black, pale grey-brown and silver	2·20	2·10
	With tab	4·25	4·25

(Des Z. Rosenberg. Photo)

1985 (5 Nov). Centenary of Gedera. Horiz design as T **333**. Multicoloured. P 13×14.

967	600s. Gedera	1·80	1·70
	With tab	3·50	3·50

382 Kibbutz Members

383 Dr. Theodor Herzl

(Des D. Ben Dov. Litho)

1985 (5 Nov). The Kibbutz. P 14.

968	**382** 900s. multicoloured	3·00	2·75
	With tab	5·75	5·50

Currency Reform. 1000 (old) Shekalim = 1 (new) Shekel.

(Des Z. Narkiss. Photo)

1986 (1 Jan)–**96**. One phosphor band (20, 30a.), two bands (50a.), no bands (others). P 13×14.

969	**383** 1a. dull royal blue and vermilion	85	80
970	2a. dull royal blue and yellowish green	95	90
971	3a. dull royal blue and bistre	1·20	1·20
972	5a. dull royal blue and greenish blue.	1·40	1·40
	a. Deep violet-blue and greenish blue (1996)		
973	10a. dull royal blue and bright orange.	2·20	2·10
	a. Deep violet-blue and bright orange		
974	20a. dull royal blue and bright purple..	9·00	8·75
	a. No phosphor bands (1989)	30·00	29·00
	b. Deep violet-blue and bright purple..		
975	30a. dull royal blue and olive-yellow	9·00	8·75
	a. No phosphor bands (1988)	30·00	29·00
	b. Two phosphor bands (1986)		
976	50a. dull royal blue and bluish violet	4·75	4·50
	a. One phosphor band (1989)	7·25	7·00
	b. Deep violet-blue and bluish violet		
969/976	*Set of 8 (cheapest)*	26·00	26·00
969/976	*Set of 8 with tabs (cheapest)*	60·00	55·00

384 Corinthian Capital, 1st-century BC

385 *Balanophyllia coccinea*

(Des Martha Ritmeyer and E. Weishoff. Litho (70, 80, 90a., 2, 10s.), photo (others))

1986 (1 Jan)–**94**. Jerusalem Archaeology. T **384** and similar horiz designs. One phosphor band (40a.), two bands (60 to 90a.), no bands (others). P 14 (70, 80, 90a., 2, 10s.) or 13½×14 (others).

977	40a. blue-green, yellow-orange and black (22.12.88)	4·25	4·00
	a. No phosphor bands (1992)	22·00	21·00
978	60a. drab, bluish violet and black (22.12.88)	9·00	8·75
	a. One phosphor band (1991)	36·00	35·00
	b. No phosphor bands		
979	70a. yellowish green, olive-sepia and black (11.6.89)	4·25	3·50
980	80a. reddish purple, olive-bistre and black (11.6.89)	4·75	4·00
981	90a. olive-yellow, reddish lilac and black (17.10.89)	3·75	3·00
982	1s. brown-ochre, bright yellow-green and black	4·75	4·50
	a. One phosphor band (1994)	14·50	14·00
	b. Two phosphor bands (1989)	£475	£475
983	2s. violet-blue, dull green and black (12.6.90)	4·25	4·25
	a. Two phosphor bands (1994)	13·00	12·50
984	3s. deep mauve, new blue and black	7·25	7·00
985	10s. turquoise-green, violet-blue and black (30.4.89)	13·00	12·50
977/985	*Set of 9*	50·00	46·00
977/985	*Set of 9 with tabs*	£110	£100

Designs: As T **384**—40a. Relief, 1st-century BC (Second Temple); 60a. Byzantine capital, 6th-century AD; 1s. T **384**; 3s. Archaic Ionic capital, 1st-century BC (Second Temple). 32×23 mm—70a. Relief from palace of Umayyad Caliphs, 8th-century AD; 80a. Crusader capital from Church of Ascension, Mount of Olives, 12/13th-centuries; 90a. Relief from Suleiman's Wall, 16th-century AD; 2s. Insignia of Sayif addin Attaz from Mameluke academy, 14th-century AD; 10s. Frieze from burial cave entrance, end of Second Temple period.

Designs as T **384** and No. 978 but with face values of 1000 and 1500s. were prepared before the currency reform but not issued.

Nos. 986/990 are vacant.

(Des A. Glaser. Litho)

1986 (4 Mar). Red Sea Corals. T **385** and similar horiz designs. Multicoloured. One phosphor band (30a.) or two bands (others). P 14.

991	30a. Type **385**	1·40	1·40
992	40a. *Goniopora*	1·60	1·50
993	50a. *Dendronephthya*	1·80	1·70
991/993	*Set of 3*	4·25	4·25
991/993	*Set of 3 with tabs*	9·50	9·25

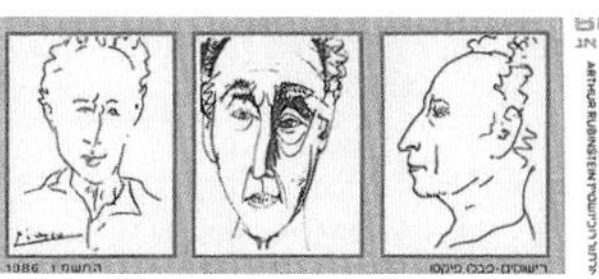

386 Sketches of Rubinstein (Pablo Picasso)

(Des Y. Granot. Photo)

1986 (4 Mar). Birth Centenary (1987) of Arthur Rubinstein and Fifth International Rubenstein Piano Competition. P 13×14.

994	**386**	60a. multicoloured	2·40	2·30
		With tab	4·75	4·50

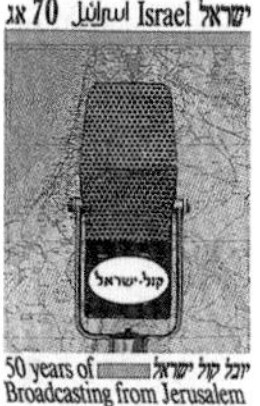

387 Microphone and Map

388 Negev Brigade Monument, Beer Sheva

(Des D. Pessah. Litho)

1986 (4 Mar). 50th Anniversary of Broadcasting from Jerusalem. P 14.

995	**387**	70a. multicoloured	1·80	1·70
		With tab	3·50	3·50

(Des R. Dayagi. Litho)

1986 (4 May). Memorial Day. One phosphor band. P 13.

996	**388**	20a. multicoloured	95	90
		With tab	1·90	1·80

389 El-Jazzar Mosque, Akko

390 Hebrew Union College, Cincinnati

(Des A. Berg. Photo)

1986 (4 May). Eid-al-Fitr (end of Ramadan). Two phosphor bands. P 14×13.

997	**389**	30a. bright emerald, blackish olive and yellow-olive	95	90
		With tab	1·90	1·80

(Des E. Weisshof. Litho)

1986 (4 May). Ameripex '86 International Stamp Exhibition, Chicago. Jewish Institutes of Higher Learning. T **390** and similar horiz designs. Multicoloured. Two phosphor bands. P 14.

998	50a. Type **390**	1·70	1·60
999	50a. Yeshiva University, New York	1·70	1·60
1000	50a. Jewish Theological Seminary, New York	1·70	1·60
998/1000	*Set of 3*	4·50	4·25
998/1000	*Set of 3 with tabs*	10·00	9·75
MS1001	100×70 mm. 75a.×3, As Nos. 998/1000 but smaller (35×22 *mm*) and without phosphor bands (*sold at* 3s.)	19·00	18·00

391 Nabi Sabalan's Tomb, Hurfeish

(Des A. Berg. Litho)

1986 (22 July). Feast of Nabi Sabalan (Druse Festival). Two phosphor bands. P 14.

1002	**391**	40a. multicoloured	1·20	1·20
		With tab	2·40	2·30

392 Graffiti on Wall

(Des R. Dayagi. Litho)

1986 (22 July). Anti-racism Campaign. Two phosphor bands. P 14.

1003	**392**	60a. multicoloured	2·20	2·10
		With tab	4·25	4·25

393 Sprinzak

394 Airport through Cabin Windows

(Des Z. Narkiss. Litho)

1986 (22 July). Birth Centenary (1985) of Joseph Sprinzak (first Speaker of Knesset). P 13.

1004	**393**	80a. indigo, grey-green and black	2·20	2·10
		With tab	4·25	4·25

(Des M. Pereg. Litho)

1986 (22 July). 50th Anniversary of Ben Gurion Airport. P 14×13.

1005	**394**	90a. multicoloured	2·40	2·30
		With tab	4·75	4·50

395 Gates of Heaven with Jerusalem above, opening to Power of Prayer

396 David Ben Gurion

(Des D. Ben-Hador. Litho)

1986 (23 Sept). Jewish New Year. Pages from *Worms Mahzor* (prayer book). T **395** and similar vert designs. Multicoloured. One phosphor band (20a.). two bands (40a.), no bands (90a.). P 13×14.

1006	20a. Type **395** (prayers for Yom Kippur)	1·40	1·40

1007 40a. Man weighing shekel for Temple (prayer for Sheqalim, first special Sabbath) .... 1·60 1·50
1008 90a. Roses (illustration of liturgical poem) .... 2·00 2·00
1006/1008 *Set of 3* .... 4·50 4·50
1006/1008 *Set of 3 with tabs* .... 10·00 9·75

(Des Z. Narkiss. Litho)

1986 (19 Oct). Birth Centenary of David Ben Gurion (Prime Minister, 1948–1953 and 1955–1963). P 14×13.
1009 **396** 1s. olive-bistre, purple-brown and black .... 2·75 2·50
With tab 5·25 5·00

397 Map of Holy Land by Gerard de Jode, 1578

398 Satellite and Isobars over Map

(Des Naomi and M. Eshel. Litho)

1986 (19 Oct). Netanya 86 National Stamp Exhibition. Sheet 126×80 mm. P 14½.
MS1010 **397** 2s. multicoloured (*sold at* 3s.) .... 22·00 21·00

(Des Naomi and M. Eshel. Litho)

1986 (18 Dec). 50th Anniversary of Meteorological Service. P 13.
1011 **398** 50a. multicoloured .... 1·80 1·70
With tab 3·50 3·50

399 Basilica of the Annunciation, Nazareth

400 Bronislaw Huberman (violinist and founder)

(Des A. Berg. Litho)

1986 (18 Dec). Christmas. P 14.
1012 **399** 70a. multicoloured .... 3·00 2·75
With tab 5·75 5·50

(Des A. Vanooijen. Litho)

1986 (18 Dec). 50th Anniversary of Israel Philharmonic Orchestra. T **400** and similar horiz design. P 14.
1013 1s.50 dull chocolate, black and lemon .... 5·50 5·25
a. Pair. Nos. 1013/1014 .... 11·50 11·00
1014 1s.50 slate, black and lemon .... 5·50 5·25
1013/1014 *Set of 2* .... 10·00 9·50
1013/1014 *Set of 2 with tabs* .... 22·00 21·00

Design: No. 1013, T **400**; No. 1014, Arturo Toscanini (conductor of Orchestra's first concert, 1936).

Nos. 1013/1014 were issued together in *se-tenant* pairs within the sheet.

401 Hume's Owl (*Strix butleri*)

402 Six Day War Memorial, Ammunition Hill, Jerusalem

(Des A. Glaser. Litho)

1987 (24 Feb). Biblical Birds of Prey (2nd series). Owls. T **401** and similar horiz designs. Multicoloured. One phosphor band (30a.), two bands (40, 50a.) or no bands (80a.). P 14×13.
1015 30a. Desert Eagle Owl (*Bubo bubo*) .... 1·20 1·20
1016 40a. Pallid Scops Owl (*Otus brucei*) .... 1·80 1·70
1017 50a. Barn Owl (*Tyto alba*) .... 2·40 2·30
1018 80a. Type **401** .... 4·25 4·00
1015/1018 *Set of 4* .... 8·75 8·25
1015/1018 *Set of 4 with tabs* .... 19·00 18·00
MS1019 102×82 mm. As Nos. 1015/1018 but smaller (31×23 *mm*) and without phosphor bands. P 14 (*sold at* 3s.) .... 22·00 21·00

(Des D. Cohen. Litho)

1987 (16 Apr). Memorial Day. One phosphor band. P 14.
1020 **402** 30a. multicoloured .... 2·40 1·70
With tab 4·75 3·50

403 Emblem

404 1952 120pr. 'TABA' Stamp

(Des G. Almaliah. Litho)

1987 (16 Apr). 13th Hapoel Games. P 14.
1021 **403** 90a. multicoloured .... 3·00 2·75
With tab 5·75 5·50

(Des Y. Granot. Litho)

1987 (16 Apr). Haifa 87 National Stamp Exhibition. Sheet 111×77 mm. P 14×13.
MS1022 **404** 2s.70 multicoloured (*sold at* 4s.) .... 24·00 23·00

405 Street Cleaner

406 Saluki

(Des A. Berg. Litho)

1987 (14 June). 'A Clean Environment'. Two phosphor bands. P 13.
1023 **405** 40a. multicoloured .... 1·40 1·40
With tab 3·00 2·75

(Des A. Vanooijen. Litho)

1987 (14 June). World Dog Show. Dogs of Israeli Origin. T **406** and similar vert designs. Multicoloured. No phosphor bands (2s.) or two bands (others). P 14.
1024 40a. Type **406** .... 2·40 2·30
1025 50a. Sloughi .... 2·40 2·30
1026 2s. Canaan Dog .... 5·50 5·25
1024/1026 *Set of 3* .... 9·25 8·75
1024/1026 *Set of 3 with tabs* .... 20·00 20·00

407 Radio Operators and Globe

408 Altneuschul Synagogue, Prague

(Des M. Pereg. Litho)

1987 (14 June). Israel Radio Amateurs. P 14.
1027 **407** 2s.50 multicoloured .... 7·75 7·50
With tab 16·00 15·00

(Des D. Ben Dov. Litho)

1987 (10 Sept). Jewish New Year Synagogue Models in Museum of the Diaspora, Tel Aviv (1st series). T **408** and similar vert designs. Multicoloured. One phosphor band (30a.) or two bands (others). P 13×14.
1028 30a. Type **408** 95 90

1029 50a. Main Synagogue, Aleppo, Syria .... 1·70 1·60
1030 60a. Israelite Temple, Florence .... 2·20 2·10
1028/1030 *Set of 3* .... 4·25 4·25
1028/1030 *Set of 3 with tabs* .... 9·50 9·25

See also Nos. 1054/1056.

409 Rabbi Amiel

410 Family

(Des D. Beckham. Litho)

1987 (10 Sept). 104th Birth Anniversary of Rabbi Moshe Avigdor Amiel (Chief Rabbi of Tel Aviv). P 14.

1031 **409** 1s.40 multicoloured .... 4·25 4·25
With tab 8·75 8·25

(Des R. Dayagi. Litho)

1987 (10 Sept). 75th Anniversary of Kupat Holim Health Insurance Institution. P 14.

1032 **410** 1s.50 multicoloured .... 4·25 4·25
With tab 8·75 8·25

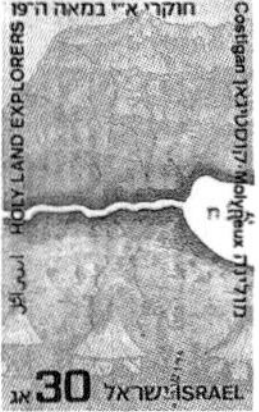

411 Camp

412 Rosen

(Des A. Glaser. Litho)

1987 (24 Nov). 19th-century Holy Land Explorers. T **411** and similar vert designs. Multicoloured. One phosphor band (30a.) or two bands (others). P 14.

1033 30a. Type **411** (Christopher Costigan, 1835, and Thomas Howard Molyneux, 1847).. 1·40 1·40
1034 50a. Map of River Jordan (William Francis Lynch, 1848) .... 1·80 1·70
1035 60a. Men in canoe (John MacGregor, 1868–1869) .... 2·20 2·10
1033/1035 *Set of 3* .... 4·75 4·75
1033/1035 *Set of 3 with tabs* .... 11·00 10·50

MS1036 106×75 mm. 40a. Type **411**; 50a. As No. 1034; 80a. As No. 1035; but each smaller (22×35 *mm*) and without phosphor bands (*sold at* 2s.50) .... 14·50 14·00

(Des R. Beckman. Litho)

1987 (24 Nov). Birth Centenary of Pinhas Rosen (lawyer and politician). Two phosphor bands. P 13.

1037 **412** 80a. multicoloured .... 2·20 2·10
With tab 4·25 4·25

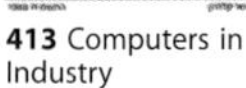

413 Computers in Industry

414 Corked Tap

(Des A. Kalderon. Litho)

1988 (26 Jan). Centenary of Israeli Industry. T **413** and similar vert designs. Multicoloured. P 14.

1038 10a. Type **413** 85 80
1039 80a. Genetic engineering .... 3·00 3·00
1040 1s.40 Medical engineering .... 3·50 3·50
1038/1040 *Set of 3* .... 6·50 6·50
1038/1040 *Set of 3 with tabs* .... 15·00 14·50

(Des Z. Rosenberg. Litho)

1988 (26 Jan). 'Save Water'. Two phosphor bands. P 14.

1041 **414** 40a. multicoloured .... 1·40 1·40
With tab 3·00 2·75

415 Kangaroos holding Birthday Cake

416 Sunflower

(Des G. Sagi. Litho)

1988 (26 Jan). Bicentenary of Australian Settlement. P 14.

1042 **415** 1s. multicoloured .... 3·50 3·50
With tab 7·25 7·00

(Des R. Beckman. Photo)

1988 (9 Mar). No value expressed. One phosphor band. P 13×14.

1043 **416** (30a.) bronze green and greenish yellow 1·40 1·40
With tab 3·00 2·75

417 Hebrew Year 5748

418 Anne Frank and House, Amsterdam

(Des M. Pereg. Litho)

1988 (19 Apr). Memorial Day (No. 1044) and 40th Anniversary of Independence (**MS**1045). P 14×13.

1044 **417** 40a. multicoloured .... 1·40 1·40
With tab 3·00 2·75

MS1045 86×70 mm. As No. 1044 but smaller (33×25 *mm*). P 14 (*sold at* 60a.) .... 9·50 9·25

(Des A. Vanooijen. Litho)

1988 (19 Apr). 43rd Death Anniversary of Anne Frank (concentration camp victim). Two phosphor bands. P 13×14.

1046 **418** 60a. multicoloured .... 2·40 2·30
With tab 4·75 4·50

419 Jerusalem

420 1963 37a. Kibbutzim Stamp (Settling)

(Des A. Berg. Litho)

1988 (19 Apr). Independence 40 National Stamp Exhibition, Jerusalem. T **419** and similar horiz design. P 13×14.

1047 **419** 1s. pale cinnamon and yellow-brown 3·00 3·00
With tab 6·00 5·75

MS1048 68×85 mm. 2s. cinnamon and deep reddish brown. P 14 (*sold at* 3s.) .... 24·00 23·00

Designs: 1s. T **419**. 34×25 mm. 2s. Jerusalem (detail of No. 1047).

(Des A. Glaser. Litho)

1988 (9 June). 40th Anniversary of Independence Exhibition, Tel Aviv. Sheet 118×88 mm containing T **420** and similar horiz designs showing stamps. Multicoloured. P 14.

MS1049 20a.×9: Type **420**; 1965 50a. Potash Works (Industry); 1956 300pr. Oranges (Agriculture); 1955 25pr. Youth Immigration (Immigrant absorption); 1981 8s. Ha-Shiv'a motorway interchange (Construction); 1964 25a. National Insurance (Welfare); 1966 15a. Cancer Research (Health); 1972 40a. Educational Development (Education) (*sold at* 2s.40) .... 24·00 23·00

Booklets containing the above sheet were privately produced by the Israel Philatelic Federation.

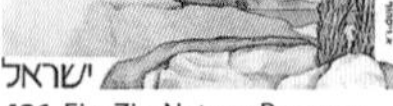

421 Ein Zin Nature Reserve

422 Jerusalem Lodge

(Des E. Weishoff. Litho)

1988 (27 June). Nature Reserves in the Negev. T **421** and similar horiz designs. Multicoloured. Two phosphor bands. P 14.

1050	40a. Type **421**	1·40	1·40
1051	60a. She'zaf	1·80	1·70
1052	70a. Ramon	2·00	2·00
1050/1052	*Set of 3*	4·75	4·50
1050/1052	*Set of 3 with tabs*	11·00	10·50

(Des Naomi and M. Eshel. Litho)

1988 (27 June). Centenary of B'nai B'rith in Jerusalem. Two phosphor bands. P 14.

1053	**422**	70a. multicoloured	2·00	2·00
		With tab	4·00	4·00

(Des D. Ben Dov. Litho)

1988 (1 Sept). Jewish New Year. Synagogue Models in Museum of the Diaspora, Tel Aviv (2nd series). Vert designs as T **408**. Multicoloured. One phosphor band (35a.) or two bands (others). P 13×14.

1054	35a. Kai-Feng Fu Synagogue, China	1·30	1·30
1055	60a. Zabludow Synagogue, Poland	1·40	1·40
1056	70a. Touro Synagogue, Newport. Rhode Island	1·60	1·50
1054/1056	*Set of 3*	3·75	3·75
1054/1056	*Set of 3 with tabs*	8·75	8·25

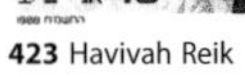

423 Havivah Reik

424 Dayan

(Des R. Beckman (40a.). Z. Narkiss (1s.65). Litho)

1988 (1 Sept). Jewish World War II Underground Fighters. T **423** and similar horiz design. One phosphor band (40a.). no bands (1s.65). P 14.

1057	40a. multicoloured	1·20	1·20
1058	1s.65 indigo, deep blue and black	4·75	4·50
1057/1058	*Set of 2*	5·25	5·25
1057/1058	*Set of 2 with tabs*	12·00	11·50

Designs: 40a. T **423**; 1s.65, Enzo Hayyim Sereni.

(Des R. Beckman. Litho)

1988 (9 Nov). Seventh Death Anniversary of Moshe Dayan (soldier and politician). Two phosphor bands. P 13.

1059	**424**	40a. multicoloured	5·50	5·25
		With tab	11·00	10·50

425 Burning Illustration of German Synagogue

426 Menorah and Soldiers

(Des D. Pessah. Litho)

1988 (9 Nov). 50th Anniversary of 'Kristallnacht' (Nazi pogrom). Two phosphor bands. P 14.

1060	**425**	80a. multicoloured	3·75	3·50
		With tab	7·75	7·00

(Des Z. Narkiss. Litho)

1988 (9 Nov). 74th Anniversary of Formation of Jewish Legion. P 14.

1061	**426**	2s. deep brown, yellow-brown and olive-bistre	6·00	5·75
		With tab	12·00	11·50

427 Avocado (fruit-growing)

428 Red Sea

(Des G. Sagi. Litho)

1988 (22 Dec). Agricultural Achievements in Israel. T **427** and similar horiz designs. Multicoloured. Two phosphor bands. P 14.

1062	50a. Type **427**	1·40	1·40
1063	60a. Easter Lily (*Lilium longiflorum*) (plant breeding)	1·80	1·70
1064	90a. Plants and drip-pipe (irrigation systems)	2·20	2·10
1062/1064	*Set of 3*	4·75	4·75
1062/1064	*Set of 3 with tabs*	11·00	10·50

(Des O. and E. Schwarz. Litho)

1989 (12 Mar). Tourism. T **428** and similar square designs. Multicoloured. No bands (1s.70) or two bands (others). P 13.

1065	40a. Type **428**	95	90
1066	60a. Dead Sea	1·20	1·20
1067	70a. Mediterranean	1·40	1·40
1068	1s.70 Sea of Galilee	3·00	3·00
1065/1068	*Set of 4*	6·00	5·75
1065/1068	*Set of 4 with tabs*	13·00	12·50

429 Rabbi Maimon

430 'Rashi' in Rashi Script

(Des R. Beckman. Litho)

1989 (12 Mar). 114th Birth Anniversary of Rabbi Judah Leib Maimon (writer). P 14.

1069	**429**	1s.70 multicoloured	4·25	4·25
		With tab	8·75	8·25

(Des E. Rapoport and O. Paz. Litho)

1989 (12 Mar). 950th Birth Anniversary of Rashi (Rabbi Solomon Ben Isaac of Troyes) (scholar). P 14.

1070	**430**	4s. cream and agate	9·00	8·75
		With tab	18·00	17·00

431 Airforce Memorial, Har Tayassim

432 Child

(Des D. Pessah. Litho)

1989 (30 Apr). Memorial Day. Two phosphor bands. P 14.
1071 **431** 50a. multicoloured .... 1·30 1·30
With tab 2·75 2·50

(Des A. Vanooijen. Litho)

1989 (30 Apr). 20th Anniversary of Israel United Nations Children's Fund National Committee. Two phosphor bands. P 14.
1072 **432** 90a. multicoloured .... 2·40 2·30
With tab 4·75 4·50

433 Games Emblem

434 Smoira

(Des R. Dayagi, M. Gallitziano and D. Reisinger. Photo)

1989 (11 June). 13th Maccabiah Games. Two phosphor bands. P 13×14.
1073 **433** 80a. multicoloured .... 1·80 1·70
With tab 3·50 3·50

(Des Z. Narkiss. Litho)

1989 (11 June). Birth Centenary (1988) of Moshe Smoira (first President of Israel's Supreme Court). Two phosphor bands. P 13.
1074 **434** 90a. indigo .... 2·75 2·75
With tab 5·50 5·25

435 Tree of Liberty

(Des A. Vanooijen. Litho)

1989 (7 July). Bicentenary of French Revolution. Sheet 120×80 mm. P 14.
MS1075 **435** 3s.50, multicoloured (*sold at* 5s.) .... 36·00 35·00

436 Garganey

437 Printed Circuit and Pencil

(Des A. Vanooijen. Litho)

1989 (18 July). Ducks. T **436** and similar horiz designs. Multicoloured. Two phosphor bands. P 14.
1076 80a. Type **436** .... 2·40 2·30
a. Horiz strip of 4. Nos. 1076/1079 .... 9·75
1077 80a. Mallard .... 2·40 2·30
1078 80a. Green-winged Teal .... 2·40 2·30
1079 80a. Common Shelduck .... 2·40 2·30
1076/1079 *Set of 4* .... 8·75 8·25
1076/1079 *Set of 4 with tabs* .... 19·00 18·00

Nos. 1077/1079 were printed together in *se-tenant* horizontal strips of four within sheets of 12 stamps.

See also No. **MS**1091.

(Des G. Almaliah. Litho)

1989 (18 July). 13th International Council of Graphic Design Associations Congress. P 14.
1080 **437** 1s. multicoloured .... 2·75 2·50
With tab 5·25 5·00

438 Lion Design (Ukraine, 1921)

439 Founders of Safa Brurah

(Des Naomi and M. Eshel. Litho)

1989 (3 Sept). Jewish New Year. Paper-cuts. T **438** and similar horiz designs. Multicoloured. One phosphor band (50a.) or two bands (others). P 14×13.
1081 50a. Type **438** 95 90
1082 70a. Hand design (Morocco, 1800s) .... 1·20 1·20
1083 80a. Stag design (Germany, 1818) .... 1·80 1·70
1081/1083 *Set of 3* .... 3·50 3·50
1081/1083 *Set of 3 with tabs* .... 8·50 8·00

(Des D. Pessah. Litho)

1989 (3 Sept). Centenaries of Safa Brurah (Clear Language) and Hebrew Language Committee (precursors of Hebrew Language Council). P 13×14.
1084 **439** 1s. multicoloured .... 2·40 2·30
With tab 4·75 4·50

440 Rabbi Alkalai

441 'Stag'

(Des R. Beckman. Litho)

1989 (3 Sept). 111th Death Anniversary of Rabbi Hai Alkalai (Zionist). P 14.
1085 **440** 2s.50 multicoloured .... 5·00 4·75
With tab 10·00 9·75

(Des D. Gottlib. Photo)

1989 (12 Oct). Tevel 89 Youth Stamp Exhibition. P 13×14.
1086 **441** 50a. multicoloured .... 2·40 2·30
With tab 4·75 4·50

No. 1086 was issued in sheetlets of eight stamps and eight tabs.

442 Postal Authority Emblem

443 'See You Again'

(Des Orna Cohen. Litho)

1989 (17 Oct). First Stamp Day. P 14.

1087	**442**	1s. multicoloured	1·40	1·40
		With tab	3·00	2·75

(Des Zmira Rosenman. Photo)

1989 (17 Nov)–**93**. Greetings Stamps. No value expressed. T **443** and similar horiz designs. Multicoloured. One phosphor band. P 13½×14.

1088	(–) Type **443** (*band at right*)	4·75	4·50
	a. Phosphor band at left. Booklets (29.6.93)	4·75	4·50
	ab. Booklet pane. No. 1088a×10	49·00	
1089	(–) Patched heart ('With Love')	4·75	4·50
	a. Booklet pane. No. 1089×10 (7.8.90)	49·00	
1090	(–) Flower ('Good Luck')	4·75	4·50
1088/1090	*Set of 3*	13·00	12·00
1088/1090	*Set of 3 with tabs*	29·00	28·00

The stamps in the booklet panes are arranged in two horizontal *tête-bêche* rows.

Nos. 1088/1090 were sold at the current inland letter rate, initially 50a. Subsequently this value was increased.

For same designs but with face values, see Nos. 1111/1113, and for new designs with no value see Nos. 1128/1130.

(Des A. Vanooijen. Litho)

1989 (17 Nov). World Stamp Expo '89 International Stamp Exhibition, Washington DC. Sheet 99×64 mm containing designs as Nos. 1076/1079 but smaller, size 27×22 mm, and without phosphor bands. P 14.

MS1091	80a.×4 multicoloured (*sold at* 5s.)	24·00	23·00

444 Rebab and Carpet

445 Traditional Dancing

(Des Y. Granot. Litho)

1990 (13 Feb). The Bedouin in Israel. P 13.

1092	**444**	1s.50 multicoloured	2·75	2·75
		With tab	5·50	5·25

(Des A. Berg. Photo)

1990 (13 Feb). Circassians in Israel. P 14×13.

1093	**445**	1s.50 multicoloured	3·50	3·50
		With tab	7·25	7·00

446 Photograph Album and Orange

447 Artillery Corps Monument, Zikhron Yaaqov

(Des D. Pessah. Litho)

1990 (13 Feb). Centenary of Rehovot Settlement. P 14.

1094	**446**	2s. multicoloured	4·25	4·00
		With tab	8·50	8·00

(Des A. Berg. Photo)

1990 (17 Apr). Memorial Day. One phosphor band. P 13×14.

1095	**447**	60a. multicoloured	1·30	1·30
		With tab	2·75	2·50

448 Ruins of Gamla, Yehudiyya

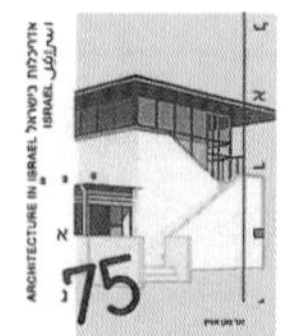

449 School, Deganya Kibbutz (Richard Kauffmann)

(Des E. Weishoff. Litho)

1990 (17 Apr). Nature Reserves (1st series). T **448** and similar horiz designs. Multicoloured. Two phosphor bands. P 14.

1096	60a. Type **448**	1·20	1·20
1097	80a. Huleh	1·70	1·60
1098	90a. Mt. Meron	1·90	1·80
1096/1098	*Set of 3*	4·25	4·25
1096/1098	*Set of 3 with tabs*	9·50	9·25

See also Nos. 1200/1202.

(Des A. Vanooijen. Photo)

1990 (17 Apr)–**99**. Architecture. T **449** and similar vert designs. Two phosphor bands. P 14×13½.

1099	75a. Type **449**	48·00	46·00
	a. One phosphor band (3.8.92)	2·40	90
	b. No phosphor bands (1994)	19·00	18·00
1100	1s.10 Dining hall, Tel Yosef Kibbutz (Leopold Krahauer) (12.12.90)	1·80	1·70
	a. One phosphor band	3·00	3·00
1101	1s.20 Engel House, Tel Aviv (Ze'ev Rechter) (12.12.90)	1·80	1·70
	a. One phosphor band (20.4.99)	3·00	3·00
1102	1s.40 Weizmann House, Rehovot (Erich Mendelsohn) (9.4.91)	2·40	2·30
	a. One phosphor band (2.2.97)	7·25	7·00
1103	1s.60 National Institutions Building, Jerusalem (Yohanan Ratner) (26.4.92)	2·20	2·10
1099/1103	*Set of 5* (*cheapest*)	9·50	7·75
1099/1103	*Set of 5 with tabs* (*cheapest*)	21·00	17·00

Nos. 1104/1109 are vacant.

450 Roads to Jerusalem

(Des Y. Granot. Litho)

1990 (17 Apr). Stamp World London 90 International Stamp Exhibition. Stained Glass Windows by Mordecai Ardon in National and University Library illustrating Book of Isaiah. Sheet 151×67 mm containing T **450** and similar vert design. Multicoloured. P 14.

MS1110	1s.50, Type **450**; 1s.50, Weapons beaten into ploughshares (*sold at* 4s.50)	36·00	35·00

Imperforate sheets were presented to subscribers of the Philatelic Service. They are inscribed on the back.

(Des Zmira Rosenman. Photo)

1990 (12 June)–**92**. Greetings Stamps. As Nos. 1088/1090 but with value. One phosphor band (55a.) or two bands (others). P 13½×14.

1111	55a. As No. 1090	6·00	5·75
1112	80a. Type **443**	6·00	5·75
	a. One band on right (1993)	22·00	21·00
1113	1s. As No. 1089	6·00	5·75
	a. One band on right (1992)	36·00	35·00
	b. No phosphor bands		
1111/1113	*Set of 3* (*cheapest*)	16·00	16·00
1111/1113	*Set of 3 with tabs* (*cheapest*)	36·00	35·00

451 Badges

(Des R. Dayagi and M. Gallitziano. Litho)

1990 (12 June). 70th Anniversary of Formation of Hagana (underground military organisation). P 14.

1114	**451**	1s.50 multicoloured	3·50	3·50
		With tab	7·25	7·00

452 Dancers

453 19th-century Austro-Hungarian Spice Box

(Des O. and E. Schwarz. Litho)

1990 (12 June). Eighth International Folklore Festival, Haifa. T **452** and similar vert design. Multicoloured. P 14.

1115	1s.90 Type **452**	6·00	5·75
	a. Horiz pair. Nos. 1115/1116	12·50	11·50
1116	1s.90 Dancers and accordion player	6·00	5·75
1115/1116	*Set of 2*	11·00	10·50
1115/1116	*Set of 2 with tabs*	24·00	23·00

Nos. 1115/1116 were issued together in *se-tenant* pairs within the sheet, each pair forming a composite design.

(Des A. Vanooijen. Litho)

1990 (4 Sept). Jewish New Year. Silver Spice Boxes. T **453** and similar vert designs. Multicoloured. One phosphor band (55a.) or two bands (others). P 13×14.

1117	55a. Type **453**	1·40	1·40
	a. Booklet pane. Nos. 1117×3, 1118×2 and 1119	17·00	
1118	80a. 19th-century Italian box	1·60	1·50
1119	1s. German painted and gilt box by Matheus Wolf, 1700	1·80	1·70
1117/1119	*Set of 3*	4·25	4·25
1117/1119	*Set of 3 with tabs*	9·50	9·25

454 People forming Star of David

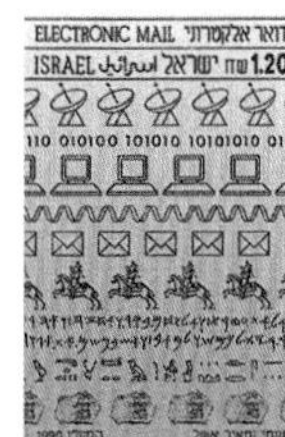

455 Ancient and Modern Means of Communication

(Des Anna Popescu and Maya Gross. Litho)

1990 (4 Sept). Absorption of Immigrants. Two phosphor bands. P 13.

1120	**454** 1s.10 multicoloured	2·20	2·10
	With tab	4·25	4·25

(Des Naomi and M. Eshel. Photo)

1990 (4 Sept). Electronic Mail. P 14×13.

1121	**455** 1s.20 emerald, black and greenish yellowish	2·20	2·10
	With tab	4·25	4·25

456 Abraham's Well (after 17th-century engraving)

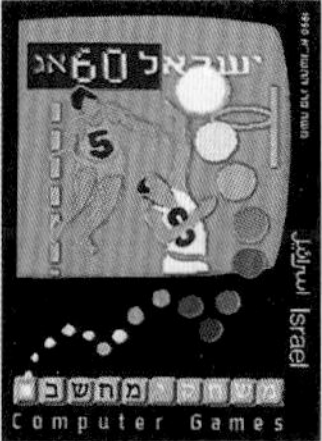

457 Basketball

(Des A. Berg. Litho)

1990 (5 Oct). Beer Sheva 90 National Stamp Exhibition. Sheet 90×86 mm. P 13×14.

MS1122	**456** 3s. multicoloured (*sold at* 4s.)	18·00	17·00

(Des M. Pereg. Litho)

1990 (12 Dec). Computer Games. T **457** and similar vert designs. Multicoloured. One phosphor band (1124) or no bands (others). P 13×14.

1123	60a. Type **457**	1·20	1·20
1124	60a. Chess	1·20	1·20
1125	60a. Racing cars	1·20	1·20
1123/1125	*Set of 3*	3·25	3·25
1123/1125	*Set of 3 with tabs*	7·25	7·00

458 Tel Aviv-Yafo Post Office and 1948 20m. Stamp

459 Jabotinsky

(Des M. and Momi Alon. Litho)

1990 (12 Dec). Stamp Day. Two phosphor bands. P 14.

1126	**458** 1s.20 multicoloured	3·75	3·75
	With tab	7·75	7·25

(Des R. Beckman. Litho)

1990 (12 Dec). 50th Death Anniversary of Ze'ev Jabotinsky (Zionist leader). P 13×14.

1127	**459** 1s.90 multicoloured	2·75	2·75
	With tab	5·50	5·25

(Des Zmira Rosenman. Photo)

1991 (19 Feb)–**94**. Greetings Stamps. No value expressed. Horiz designs as T **443**. Multicoloured. One phosphor band. P 13½×14.

1128	(–) Birthday cake ('Happy Birthday')	6·00	5·75
1129	(–) Champagne bottle ('Greetings')	6·00	5·75
	a. Phosphor band at right (1992)	12·00	11·50
1130	(–) Envelopes ('Keep in Touch')	6·00	5·75
	a. Booklet pane. No. 1130×10 plus two blank labels (18.4.94)	65·00	
1128/1130	*Set of 3*	16·00	16·00
1128/1130	*Set of 3 with tabs*	36·00	35·00

The stamps in the booklet pane are arranged in two horizontal *tête-bêche* rows.

Nos. 1128/1130 were sold at the current inland letter rate.

460 Sarah Aaronsohn (intelligence agent)

(Des R. Beckman. Litho)

1991 (19 Feb). Anniversary. T **460** and similar horiz designs. Multicoloured. P 14.

1131	1s.30 Type **460** (birth centenary (1990))	1·40	1·40
1132	1s.30 Rahel Bluwstein (poet, 60th death anniversary)	1·40	1·40
1133	1s.30 Lea Goldberg (writer and translator, 80th birth anniversary)	1·40	1·40
1131/1133	*Set of 3*	3·75	3·75
1131/1133	*Set of 3 with tabs*	8·75	8·25

461 Eucalyptus Tree and Hadera

(Des Ruth (Beckman) Malka. Litho)

1991 (19 Feb). Centenary of Hadera. P 13.

1134	**461** 2s.50 multicoloured	3·50	3·50
	With tab	7·25	7·00

462 Karate

463 Intelligence Services Memorial, Centre for Special Studies, Tel Aviv

(Des M. Gallitziano and R. Dayagi. Litho)

1991 (9 Apr). 14th Hapoel Games. T **462** and similar horiz designs. Multicoloured. One phosphor band (60a.) or two bands (others). P 14.

1135	60a. Type **462**	2·20	2·10
1136	90a. Table tennis	1·20	1·20
1137	1s.10 Football	1·40	1·40
1135/1137	*Set of 3*	4·25	4·25
1135/1137	*Set of 3 with tabs*	7·25	7·00

The left hand phosphor band on No. 1137 is interrupted by a short break.

(Des A. Vanooijen. Litho)

1991 (9 Apr). Memorial Day. P 14.

1138	**463** 65a. multicoloured	1·30	1·30
	With tab	2·75	2·50

464 First (Diesel) Power Station, Tel Aviv

465 Rabbi Shimon Hakham (co-founder) and Armon Building

(Des Ruth Malka. Litho)

1991 (11 June). Inauguration of Rutenberg Power Station. T **464** and similar square designs. Multicoloured. P 13.

1139	70a. Type **464**	1·20	1·20
1140	90a. Yarden hydro-electric station, Naharayim	1·60	1·50
1141	1s.20 Rutenberg coal-fired power station, Ashqelon	2·00	2·00
1139/1141	*Set of 3*	4·25	4·25
1139/1141	*Set of 3 with tabs*	9·50	9·25

(Des Ruth Malka. Litho)

1991 (11 June). Centenary (1990) of Bukharim Quarter of Jerusalem. P 13.

1142	**465** 2a.10 multicoloured	3·00	3·00
	With tab	6·00	5·75

466 Cover bearing Israeli, Palestine and Turkish Stamps

467 Ram's Head and Man blowing Shofar

(Des E. Weishoff. Litho)

1991 (11 June). Tel Aviv Postal and Philatelic Museum Project. Sheet 120×89 mm. P 14×13.

MS1143	**466** 3s.40, multicoloured (*sold at* 5s.)	19·00	18·00

(Des O. and E. Schwarz. Litho)

1991 (27 Aug). Festivals. T **467** and similar vert designs. Multicoloured. P 14.

1144	65a. Type **467** (Jewish New Year)	95	90
1145	1s. 'Penitence Cock', father blessing children and men blowing shofars (Day of Atonement)	1·60	1·50
1146	1s.20 Family in booth (Festival of Tabernacles)	1·70	1·60
1144/1146	*Set of 3*	3·75	3·50
1144/1146	*Set of 3 with tabs*	8·50	8·00

468 Front Page of First Edition

469 Colonists and Baron Maurice de Hirsch (founder)

(Des A. Berg. Photo)

1991 (27 Aug). 150th Anniversary of *Jewish Chronicle* (weekly newspaper). P 14½.

1147	**468** 1s.50 black, deep ultramarine and rosine	2·40	2·30
	With tab	4·75	4·50

(Des A. Kalderon. Litho)

1991 (27 Aug). Centenary of Jewish Colonisation Association. P 14.

1148	**469** 1s.60 multicoloured	2·75	2·50
	With tab	5·25	5·00

470 *Haifa, 1898* (Gustav Bauernfeind)

471 Cancelled 1948 5m. Stamp

(Des Y. Granot. Litho)

1991 (27 Aug). Haifa 91 Israel–Poland Stamp Exhibition. Sheet 104×62 mm. P 14×13.

MS1149	**470** 3s. multicoloured (*sold at* 4s.)	19·00	18·00

Imperforate sheets come from a limited issue sold in a commemorative folder.

(Des Naomi and M. Eshel. Litho)

1991 (2 Dec). Stamp Day. P 13.

1150	**471** 70a. multicoloured	1·20	1·20
	With tab	2·40	2·30

472 Rahel Yanait Ben-Zvi

473 Runner

(Des Ruth Malka. Litho)

1991 (2 Dec). T **472** and similar horiz design. Multicoloured. P 14.

1151	1s. Type **472** (Zionist)	2·00	2·00
1152	1s.10 Dona Gracia Nasi (supporter of 16th-century Jewish settlement in Tiberias)	2·30	2·20
1151/1152	*Set of 2*	3·75	3·75
1151/1152	*Set of 2 with tabs*	8·75	8·25

(Des Ruth Kantor. Litho)

1991 (2 Dec). Olympic Games, Barcelona. P 14.

1153	**473** 1s.10 multicoloured	2·20	2·10
	With tab	4·25	4·25

474 Flame and Hebrew Script

475 Southern Wing of Acre Prison

(Des G. Almaliah. Litho)

1991 (2 Dec). 51st Anniversary of Lehi (resistance organisation). P 14.
1154 **474** 1s.50 multicoloured .... 2·40 2·30
With tab 4·75 4·50

(Des A. Berg. Photo)

1991 (2 Dec). 60th Anniversary of Etzel (resistance organisation). P 14.
1155 **475** 1s.50 black, bright scarlet and brownish grey .... 2·40 2·30
With tab 4·75 4·50

476 Mozart and Score of *Don Giovanni*

477 Anemone

(Des Naomi and M. Eshel. Litho)

1991 (2 Dec). Death Bicentenary of Wolfgang Amadeus Mozart (composer). P 13.
1156 **476** 2s. multicoloured .... 5·50 5·25
With tab 11·00 10·50
a. Booklet pane. No. 1156×4 (including *tête-bêche* pair) .... 45·00
The booklet pane has a decorated margin around the outer edge.

(Des Ruth Malka. Photo)

1992 (18 Feb). No value expressed. One phosphor band at left. P 13×14.
1157 **477** (–) bright scarlet and bottle green ...... 3·00 3·00
With tab 6·00 5·75
a. Phosphor band at right .... 3·00 3·00
With tab 6·00 5·75
ab. Booklet pane. No. 1157a×20 .... 65·00
In the booklet pane the left-hand block of ten stamps is inverted, giving two horizontal *tête-bêche* pairs.
No. 1157 was sold at the current inland letter rate, initially 75a.

478 Hanna Rovina (actress)

479 Trees

(Des Ruth Malka. Litho)

1992 (18 Feb). T **478** and similar horiz design. Multicoloured. P 14.
1158 80a. Type **478** .... 1·40 1·40
1159 1s.30 Rivka Guber (teacher and writer) .... 1·80 1·70
1158/1159 *Set of 2* .... 3·00 2·75
1158/1159 *Set of 2 with tabs* .... 6·50 6·25

(Des R. Salomon. Litho)

1992 (18 Feb). Sea of Galilee. T **479** and similar vert designs. Multicoloured. One phosphor band. P 14.
1160 85a. Type **479** .... 3·00 2·30
a. Strip of 3. Nos. 1160/1162 .... 9·25
1161 85a. Sailboard .... 3·00 2·30
1162 85a. Fish .... 3·00 2·30
1160/1162 *Set of 3* .... 8·00 6·25
1160/1162 *Set of 3 with tabs* .... 18·00 14·00
Nos. 1160/1162 were issued together in *se-tenant* strips of three stamps within the sheet.

480 Palmah Emblem

481 Samaritans praying on Mount Gerizim

(Des G. Sagi. Litho)

1992 (18 Feb). 51st Anniversary of Palmah (resistance organisation). P 14.
1163 **480** 1s.50 gold, deep bright blue and deep bright mauve .... 2·75 2·50
With tab 5·25 5·50

(Des D. Pessah. Litho)

1992 (18 Feb). The Samaritans. P 14.
1164 **481** 2s.60 multicoloured .... 4·25 4·00
With tab 8·50 8·00

482 Border Guard Memorial, Eiron Junction (Yechiel Arad)

483 Azulai

(Des I. Gabay. Litho)

1992 (26 Apr). Memorial Day. P 13.
1165 **482** 85a. multicoloured .... 1·40 1·40
With tab 3·00 2·75

(Des M. Yozefpolsky. Litho)

1992 (26 Apr). 186th Death Anniversary of Rabbi Hayyim Joseph David Azulai (scholar). P 13.
1166 **483** 85a. multicoloured .... 2·40 2·30
With tab 4·75 4·50

484 Hayyim

485 *Almanach Perpetuum* and Models of Columbus's Ships

(Des J. Rac. Litho)

1992 (26 Apr). 83rd Death Anniversary of Rabbi Joseph Hayyim Ben Elijah. P 14.
1167 **484** 1s.20 multicoloured .... 2·40 2·30
With tab 4·75 4·50

(Des O. Meirav. Litho)

1992 (26 Apr). 500th Anniversary of Discovery of America by Columbus. Two phosphor bands. P 14.
1168 **485** 1s.60 multicoloured .... 2·75 2·50
With tab 5·25 5·00

486 Bedridden Patient and Map

(Des A. Vanooijen. Litho)

1992 (26 Apr). 500th Anniversary of Expulsion of Jews from Spain. Sheet 140×71 mm containing T **486** and similar horiz designs showing details of map by Abraham Cresques. Multicoloured. P 14.

MS1169	80a. Type **486**; 1s.10, Doctor and map; 1s.40, Writer-philosopher and map	17·00	16·00

487 Diesel Trains, Greasing of Wheels and Blueprint of Baldwin Engine

(Des A. Vanooijen. Litho)

1992 (16 June–Sept). Centenary of Jaffa–Jerusalem Railway. T **487** and similar horiz designs. Multicoloured. P 14.

1170	85a. Type **487**	1·20	1·20
	a. Booklet pane. Nos. 1170/1173 (including two *tête-bêche* pairs)	7·25	
1171	1s. Scottish steam locomotive, track plan at Lod, electric signalling board at Tel Aviv, semaphore arms and points at Lod	1·60	1·50
1172	1s.30 Diesel locomotive, interior and exterior of passenger carriages, Palestine Railways ticket and 1926 timetable	1·90	1·80
1173	1s.60 Diesel train, drawing of façade of Jerusalem station, platform at Lod, Jaffa station in 1900 and points at Bar-Giora station	2·20	2·10
1170/1173	*Set of 4*	6·25	6·00
1170/1173	*Set of 4 with tabs*	13·50	13·00
MS1174	140×71 mm. 4×50a. As Nos. 1170/1173 (17.9)	17·00	16·00

488 Cover of *Or-HaHayyim* (*Light of Life*) (Rabbi Hayyim Benatar)

489 Leopard (*Panthera pardus*)

(Des Y. Granot. Litho)

1992 (16 June). Death Anniversaries. T **488** and similar vert design. P 13.

1175	1s.30 pale lilac, bottle green and gold	1·80	1·70
1176	3s. deep rose-lilac, pale green and gold	4·75	4·50
1175/1176	*Set of 2*	6·00	5·50
1175/1176	*Set of 2 with tabs*	13·00	12·50

Designs: 1s.30, T **488** (250th (1993) anniversary); 3s. 19th-century drawing of Bet-El Yeshiva, Jerusalem (Rabbi Shalom Sharabi, (215th anniversary)).

(Des D. Bochman. Litho)

1992 (17 Sept). Zoo Animals. T **489** and similar horiz designs. Multicoloured. P 14.

1177	50a. Type **489**	70	70
	a. Horiz strip of 4. Nos. 1177/1180	3·00	
1178	50a. Indian Elephant (*Elephas maximus*)	70	70
1179	50a. Chimpanzee (*Pan troglodytes*)	70	70
1180	50a. Lion (*Panthera leo*)	70	70
1177/1180	*Set of 4*	2·50	2·50
1177/1180	*Set of 4 with tabs*	5·75	5·50

Nos. 1177/1180 were issued together in horizontal *se-tenant* strips of four stamps within the sheet.

490 *Parables* (Yitzhak ben Shlomo ibn Sahula) (1st edition, Brescia, 1491)

491 Court Building

(Des D. Ben Dov. Litho)

1992 (17 Sept). Jewish New Year. Centenary of Jewish National and University Library, Jerusalem. T **490** and similar vert designs. Multicoloured. P 13×14.

1181	85a. Type **490**	1·20	1·20
1182	1s. *Mahzor* (prayer book) (15th-century manuscript by Leon ben Yehoshua de Rossi)	1·30	1·30
1183	1s.20 Draft of translation by Martin Buber of Leviticus 25: 10-13	1·40	1·40
1181/1183	*Set of 3*	3·50	3·50
1181/1183	*Set of 3 with tabs*	8·00	7·50

(Des D. Ben-Hador. Litho)

1992 (17 Sept). Inauguration of New Supreme Court Building. P 14.

1184	**491** 3s.60 multicoloured	4·75	4·50
	With tab	9·50	9·25

492 Wallcreeper

493 *Judah Released*

(Des J. Smith. Photo)

1992 (8 Dec)–**98**. Songbirds. T **492** and similar vert designs. Multicoloured. No phosphor bands (10 to 50a.), one band (85a. to 1s.) or two bands (others). P 13×14.

1185	10a. Type **492**	35	35
1186	20a. Tristram's Grackle	35	35
1187	30a. Pied (White) Wagtail	50	45
1188	50a. Palestine Sunbird (16.2.93)	2·20	1·70
1189	85a. Sinai Rosefinch (8.2.94)	1·90	1·80
1190	90a. Barn Swallows	1·40	1·40
1191	1s. Trumpeter Finches (7.6.95)	2·40	2·30
	a. No phosphor bands (1997)	4·25	4·00
1192	1s.30 Graceful Prinia (warbler) (9.12.93)	2·40	2·30
	a. One phosphor band (1997)	3·50	3·50
1193	1s.50 Black-eared Wheatear (16.2.93)	3·00	2·75
	a. One phosphor band (4.12.98)	3·50	3·50
1194	1s.70 White-eyed (Common) Bulbuls (9.12.93)	3·00	2·75
1185/1194	*Set of 10*	16·00	14·50
1185/1194	*Set of 10 with tabs*	25·00	23·00

No. 1192 (1s.30) was re-issued during 1998 with two phosphor bands.

(Des H. Khoury. Litho)

1992 (8 Dec). 75th Anniversary of First All-Hebrew Film. T **493** and similar square designs showing scenes from films. Multicoloured. P 13.

1195	80a. Type **493** (first Hebrew film)	1·80	1·70
1196	2s.70 *Oded the Wanderer* (first Hebrew feature film)	3·50	3·50
1197	3s.50 *This is the Land* (first Hebrew talking film)	4·75	4·50
1195/1197	*Set of 3*	9·00	8·75
1195/1197	*Set of 3 with tabs*	20·00	20·00

494 European Community Emblem on Graph

495 Begin

(Des R. Hefer. Litho)

1992 (8 Dec). Stamp Day. European Single Market. Two phosphor bands. P 13.

1198	**494**	1s.50 multicoloured	3·50	3·25
		With tab	3·75	3·50

(Des A. Vanooijen. Litho)

1993 (16 Feb). First Death Anniversary of Menachem Begin (Prime Minister, 1977–1983). One phosphor band. P 13.

1199	**495**	80a. multicoloured	1·90	1·70
		With tab	2·00	1·90

(Des E. Weishoff. Litho)

1993 (16 Feb). Nature Reserves (2nd series). Horiz designs as T **448**. Multicoloured. Two phosphor bands. P 14.

1200	1s.20 Hof Dor	2·75	2·50
1201	1s.50 Nahal Ammud	3·25	3·00
1202	1s.70 Nahal Ayun	4·00	3·75
1200/1202	*Set of 3*	9·00	8·25
1200/1202	*Set of 3 with tabs*	10·00	9·25

496 Seat of the Universal House of Justice

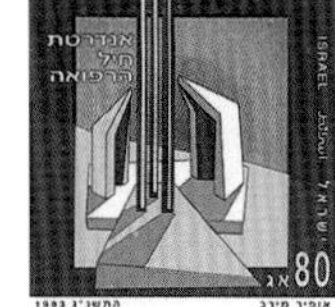

497 Medical Corps Memorial, Carmel, Haifa (Akiva Lomnitz)

(Des R. Salomon. Litho)

1993 (16 Feb). Baha'i World Centre, Haifa. P 13.

1203	**496**	3s.50 multicoloured	6·00	5·50
		With tab	6·50	6·00

(Des O. Meirav. Litho)

1993 (18 Apr). Memorial Day. One phosphor band. P 13.

1204	**497**	80a. multicoloured	1·70	1·50
		With tab	1·90	1·70

498 'The Eye's Memory'

499 Prisoner

(Des Naomi and M. Eshel. Litho)

1993 (18 Apr). Illustration of Scientific Concepts. T **498** and similar vert designs showing exhibits from the Israel National Museum of Science, Haifa (Nos. 1205/1206) or the Bernard M. Bloomfield Science Museum, Jerusalem (others). Multicoloured. One phosphor band. P 14.

1205	80a. Type **498**	1·90	1·70
	a. Horiz strip of 4. Nos. 1205/1208	7·75	
1206	80a. Colour mixing	1·90	1·70
1207	80a. Waves	1·90	1·70
1208	80a. Floating balls (principle of lift)	1·90	1·70
1205/1208	*Set of 4*	6·75	6·00
1205/1208	*Set of 4 with tabs*	7·50	6·75

Nos. 1205/1208 were issued together in horizontal *se-tenant* strips of four within sheetlets of eight stamps.

(Des Ruth Avrahami. Litho)

1993 (18 Apr). 50th Anniversary of Uprisings in the Ghettos and Concentration Camps. P 14.

1209	**499**	1s.20 black, lemon and azure	2·20	2·00
		With tab	2·40	2·20

A stamp of a similar design was issued by Poland.

500 Hurbat Rabbi Yehuda Hasid Synagogue, Jerusalem

(Des Y. Granot. Litho)

1993 (18 Apr). 45th Anniversary of Independence. P 14.

1210	**500**	3s.60 multicoloured	7·75	7·25
		With tab	8·25	7·75

501 Giulio Racah

502 Family using Crossing (Lior Abohovsky)

(Des S. Dozorets. Photo)

1993 (29 June). Physicists. T **501** and similar horiz design. Each gold, deep reddish purple and royal blue. One phosphor band (80a.) or two bands (1s.20). P 13×14.

1211	80a. Type **501**	1·70	1·50
1212	1s.20 Aharon Katchalsky-Katzir	2·40	2·20
1211/1212	*Set of 2*	3·75	3·25
1211/1212	*Set of 2 with tabs*	4·50	4·00

(Des M. and Momi Alon. Litho)

1993 (29 June). Road Safety. T **502** and similar vert designs showing children's paintings. Multicoloured. One phosphor band (80a.) or two bands (others). P 14.

1213	80a. Type **502**	1·90	1·70
1214	1s.20 Vehicles and road signs (Elinor Paz)	2·75	2·50
1215	1s.50 Road signals on 'man' (Moran Dadush)	3·25	3·00
1213/1215	*Set of 3*	7·00	6·50
1213/1215	*Set of 3 with tabs*	8·25	7·75

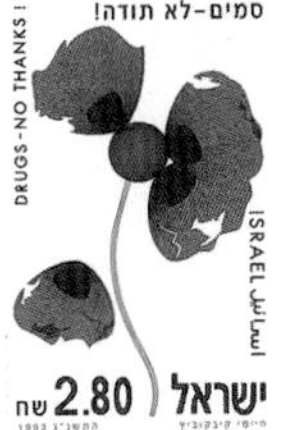

503 Poppy

504 Passing Baton

(Des H. Kivkovich. Litho)

1993 (29 June). Anti-drugs Campaign. P 14.

1216	**503**	2s.80 multicoloured	6·00	5·50
		With tab	6·75	6·00

(Des D. Zilberman. Litho)

1993 (29 June). 14th Maccabiah Games. P 14.

1217	**504**	3s.60 multicoloured	7·75	7·25
		With tab	8·25	7·50

505 Tree

506 Ear of Wheat

(Des Yael Gavish. Litho)

1993 (22 Aug). International Day of the Elderly. Two phosphor bands. P 14.

1218	**505**	80a. multicoloured	1·60	1·40
		With tab	1·70	1·50

(Des Marion Codner. Litho)

1993 (22 Aug). Jewish New Year. T **506** and similar vert designs. Multicoloured. One phosphor band (80a.) or two bands (others). P 14.

1219	80a. Type **506**	1·40	1·30
1220	1s.20 Grapes	2·20	2·00
1221	1s.50 Olives	2·75	2·50
1219/1221	*Set of 3*	5·75	5·25
1219/1221	*Set of 3 with tabs*	6·75	6·00

The left-hand phosphor band on No. 1220 is cut to fit the design.

507 Environmental Concerns

508 Emblems

(Des D. Ben-Hador. Litho)

1993 (22 Aug). Environment Year. Two phosphor bands. P 14.

1222	**507** 1s.20 multicoloured	1·90	1·70
	With tab	2·00	1·90

(Des G. Almaliah and A. Shevo. Litho)

1993 (22 Aug). 150th Anniversary of B'nai B'rith (cultural and social organisation). Two phosphor bands. P 13.

1223	**508** 1s.50 multicoloured	3·00	2·75
	With tab	3·25	3·00

509 *Immigrant Ship* (Marcel Janco)

(Des Zmira Rosenman. Litho)

1993 (22 Aug). Telafila 93 Israel–Rumania Stamp Exhibition, Tel Aviv. Sheet 60×90 mm. P 14×13.

MS1224	**509** 3s.60 multicoloured	11·00	10·00

510 Talmudic Oil Lamp

(Des I. Gabay. Litho)

1993 (9 Dec). Festival of Hanukkah. T **510** and similar horiz designs. Multicoloured. One phosphor band (90a.) or two bands (others). P 14.

1225	90a. Type **510**	1·40	1·30
1226	1s.30 Hanukkah lamp in shape of building	2·75	2·50
1227	2s. *Lighting the Hanukkah Lamp* (illustration from the *Rothschild Miscellany*)	3·50	3·25
1225/1227	*Set of 3*	7·00	6·25
1225/1227	*Set of 3 with tabs*	8·25	7·50

511 Cover of First Issue

(Des A. Vanooijen. Litho)

1993 (9 Dec). Stamp Day. Centenary (1992) of *Miniature World* (children's magazine). Two phosphor bands. P 14.

1228	**511** 1s.50 multicoloured	3·00	2·75
	With tab	3·25	3·00

512 Yellow-banded Borer (*Chlorophorus varius*)

513 Man carrying Car ('Exercise Regularly')

(Des A. Vanooijen. Litho)

1994 (8 Feb). Beetles. T **512** and similar horiz designs. Multicoloured. One phosphor band. P 14.

1229	85a. Type **512**	2·20	2·00
	a. Booklet pane. Nos. 1229/1232, each×2.	19·00	
1230	85a. Copper Beetle (*Potosia cuprea*)	2·20	2·00
1231	85a. Pied Ground Beetle (*Graphopterus serrator*)	2·20	2·00
1232	85a. Seven-spotted Ladybird (*Coccinella septempunctata*)	2·20	2·00
1229/1232	*Set of 4*	8·00	7·25
1229/1232	*Set of 4 with tabs*	9·50	8·75

The stamps in the booklet pane are arranged in two horizontal *tête-bêche* rows.

(Des Ruth Avrahami. Litho)

1994 (8 Feb). Health and Well-being. T **513** and similar horiz designs. Multicoloured. One phosphor band (85a.) or two bands (others). P 13.

1233	85a. Type **513**	1·40	1·30
1234	1s.30 Blowing soap bubbles ('Don't Smoke')	1·90	1·70
1235	1s.60 Inspecting food through magnifying glass ('Eat Sensibly')	2·40	2·20
1233/1235	*Set of 3*	5·25	4·75
1233/1235	*Set of 3 with tabs*	6·00	5·50

514 Haffkine

515 Communications, Electronics and Computer Corps Memorial, Yehud (Claude Grundman)

(Des A. Vanooijen. Litho Govt Printers)

1994 (8 Feb). 64th Death Anniversary of Dr. Mordecai Haffkine (bacteriologist). P 14.

1236	**514** 3s.85 multicoloured	6·00	5·50
	With tab	6·25	5·75

(Des D. Ben-Hador. Litho Govt Printers)

1994 (5 Apr). Memorial Day. One phosphor band. P 14.

1237	**515** 85a. multicoloured	1·60	1·40
	With tab	1·70	1·50

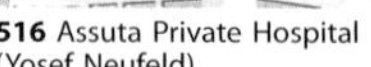

516 Assuta Private Hospital (Yosef Neufeld)

517 Battered Child

(Des I. Gabay. Litho)

1994 (5 Apr). International Style Architecture in Tel Aviv. T **516** and similar horiz designs. Each grey, greenish blue and turquoise-green. One phosphor band. P 14.

1238	85a. Type **516**	1·80	1·60
	a. Strip of 3. Nos. 1238/1240	5·75	
1239	85a. Co-operative workers' housing (flats with separate balconies) (Arieh Sharon)	1·80	1·60

1240 85a. Citrus House (Karl Rubin) ... 1·80 1·60
1238/1240 *Set of 3* ... 4·75 4·25
1238/1240 *Set of 3 with tabs* ... 5·50 5·00

Nos. 1238/1240 were issued together in *se-tenant* strips of three stamps within the sheet.

(Des Yael Arad. Litho Govt Printers)

1994 (5 Apr). 'No to Violence' Campaign. P 13.
1241 **517** 3s.85 black and bright scarlet ... 4·75 4·25
With tab 5·00 4·75

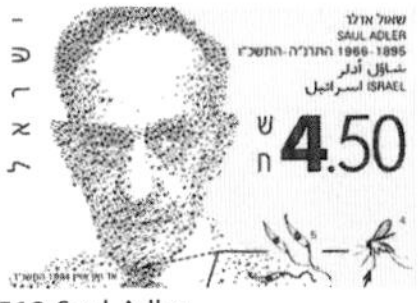

518 Saul Adler

519 Inflating Balloon

(Des A. Vanooijen. Litho Govt Printers)

1994 (5 Apr). Birth Centenary (1995) of Saul Adler (scientist). P 14.
1242 **518** 4s.50 multicoloured ... 5·00 4·75
With tab 5·50 5·00

(Des D. Ben-Hador. Litho)

1994 (21 June). Ayalon Valley International Hot-Air Balloon Race. T **519** and similar horiz designs. Multicoloured. One phosphor band. P 14.
1243 85a. Type **519** ... 1·60 1·40
1244 85a. Balloons in air ... 1·60 1·40
1245 85a. Balloon hovering over target (cross on ground) ... 1·60 1·40
1243/1245 *Set of 3* ... 4·25 3·75
1243/1245 *Set of 3 with tabs* ... 5·00 4·50

520 Chemistry Class at Bialystok and Physical Education at Wolyn

521 Israeli Team at Munich Games, 1972, and National Committee Emblem

(Des M. Pereg. Litho Govt Printers)

1994 (21 June). 75th Anniversary of Tarbut Schools (Hebrew schools in Eastern Europe). Two phosphor bands. P 14.
1246 **520** 1s.30 multicoloured ... 1·80 1·60
With tab 1·90 1·70

(Des Ruth Kantor and R. Meller. Litho)

1994 (21 June). Centenary of International Olympic Committee. P 14.
1247 **521** 2s.25 multicoloured ... 3·00 2·75
With tab 3·25 3·00

522 The Little Prince (book character) and Saint-Exupéry

523 *Adam and Eve* (Itai Cohen)

(Des Y. Granot. Litho)

1994 (21 June). 50th Death Anniversary of Antoine de Saint-Exupéry (writer and pilot). P 14.
1248 **522** 5s. multicoloured ... 6·00 5·50
With tab 6·50 6·00

(Des D. Gotlib. Litho)

1994 (23 Aug). Jewish New Year. T **523** and similar multicoloured designs showing entries in the Children and Young People draw the Bible exhibition. No phosphor bands (4s.), one band (85a.) or two bands (others). P 14.
1249 85a. Type **523** ... 1·20 1·10
a. Booklet pane. Nos. 1249, 1250×2 and 1251×3 ... 13·00
1250 1s.30 *Jacob's Dream* (Moran Sheinberg) ... 1·80 1·60
1251 1s.60 *Moses in the Bulrushes* (Carmit Crspi) ... 2·20 2·00
1249/1251 *Set of 3* ... 4·75 4·25
1249/1251 *Set of 3 with tabs* ... 5·50 5·00
MS1252 65×90 mm. 4s. *Parting of the Red Sea* (Avital Kaisar) (39×50 *mm*). P 13×14 ... 7·50 6·75

524 Jewish and Arab Houses merging

525 Silicat Brick Factory, Tel Aviv (Fourth Aliya, 1924–1928)

(Des Ruth Kantor. Litho)

1994 (23 Aug). Israeli–Palestinian Peace Process. One phosphor band. P 14.
1253 **524** 90a. multicoloured ... 3·00 2·75
With tab 3·25 3·00

(Des D. Ben-Hador. Litho Govt Printers)

1994 (23 Aug). Aliyot (immigration of Jews to Israel). T **525** and similar square design. Multicoloured. Two phosphor bands. P 13.
1254 1s.40 Settlers and booklet distributed in Poland to encourage Jews to settle the Valley of Jezreel (Third Aliya, 1919–1923) ... 1·40 1·30
1255 1s.70 Type **525** ... 1·90 1·70
1254/1255 *Set of 2* ... 3·00 2·75
1254/1255 *Set of 2 with tabs* ... 3·50 3·25

526 Road to Peace

527 Ford Model T Bus (1920s)

(Des R. Goldberg. Litho)

1994 (26 Oct). Signing of Israel–Jordan Peace Treaty. P 14.
1256 **526** 3s.50 multicoloured ... 5·50 5·00
With tab 6·00 5·50

(Des Naomi & M. Eshel. Litho)

1994 (27 Nov). Public Transport. T **527** and similar horiz designs. Multicoloured. One phosphor band (90a.) or two bands (others). P 14.
1257 90a. Type **527** ... 1·40 1·30
1258 1s.40 White Super bus (1940s) ... 2·00 1·90
1259 1s.70 Leyland Royal Tiger bus (1960s) ... 2·20 2·00
1257/1259 *Set of 3* ... 5·00 4·75
1257/1259 *Set of 3 with tabs* ... 6·00 5·50

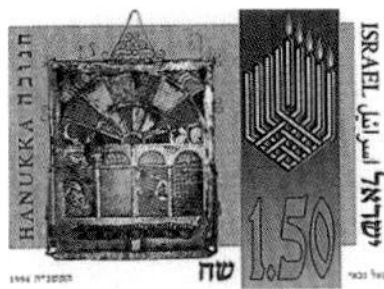

528 Hanukkah Lamp from Mazagan, Morocco

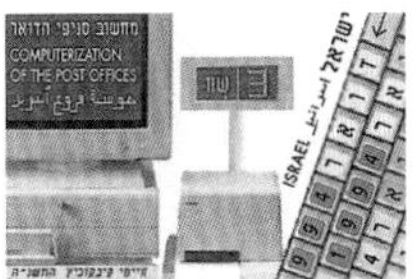

529 Computerised Post Office Counter

(Des I. Gabay. Litho)

1994 (27 Nov). Festival of Hanukkah. Two phosphor bands. P 14.
1260 **528** 1s.50 multicoloured .... 2·20 2·00
With tab 2·40 2·00

(Des H. Kivkovich. Litho Govt Printers)

1994 (27 Nov). Stamp Day. Computerisation of the Post Office. P 14.
1261 **529** 3s. multicoloured .... 3·00 2·75
With tab 3·25 3·00

530 Breaking Dreyfus's Sword

531 *Serpentine* (Itzhak Danziger), Yarkon Park, Tel Aviv

(Des R. Dayagi. Litho Govt Printers)

1994 (27 Nov). Centenary of 'The Dreyfus Affair' (conviction for treason of French Army Captain Alfred Dreyfus). P 14.
1262 **530** 4s.10 multicoloured .... 5·50 5·00
With tab 6·00 5·50

(Des A. Vanooijen. Litho Govt Printers)

1995 (7 Feb). Outdoor Sculptures. T **531** and similar horiz designs. Multicoloured. One phosphor band (90a.) or two bands (others). P 14×13.
1263 90a. Type **531** .... 1·60 1·40
1264 1s.40 *Stabile* (Alexander Calder), Mount Herzl, Jerusalem .... 2·40 2·20
1265 1s.70 Hall of Remembrance Gate (David Palombo), Yad Vashem, Jerusalem .... 3·00 2·75
1263/1265 *Set of 3* .... 6·25 5·75
1263/1265 *Set of 3 with tabs* .... 7·50 6·75

532 Score from *Schelomo*, Solomon (after Doré) and Ernest Bloch

533 Ordnance Corps Memorial, Netanya

(Des Naomi and M. Eshel. Litho)

1995 (7 Feb). Composers (1st series). T **532** and similar horiz design. Multicoloured. P 14.
1266 4s.10 Type **532** .... 6·00 5·50
1267 4s.10 Score from *Jeremiah*, Jeremiah (after Gustave Doré) and Leonard Bernstein .... 6·00 5·50
1266/1267 *Set of 2* .... 11·00 10·00
1266/1267 *Set of 2 with tabs* .... 12·00 11·00
See also Nos. 1272/1273, 1330 and 1338.

(Des O. Meirav. Litho)

1995 (25 Apr). Memorial Day. One phosphor band. P 13.
1268 **533** 1s. multicoloured .... 1·60 1·40
With tab 1·70 1·50

534 Liberation of Dachau Concentration Camp

535 UN Projects

(Des A. Vanooijen. Litho)

1995 (25 Apr). 50th Anniversary of End of Second World War. One phosphor band. P 14×13.
1269 **534** 1s. multicoloured .... 2·75 2·50
With tab 3·00 2·75
MS1270 140×70 mm. 2s.50, As No. 1269 but larger (50×39 *mm*) and without phosphor band .... 7·50 6·75

(Des G. Sagi. Litho Govt Printers)

1995 (25 Apr). 50th Anniversary of United Nations Organisation. Two phosphor bands. P 14.
1271 **535** 1s.50 multicoloured .... 2·50 2·40
With tab 2·75 2·50

(Des Naomi & M. Eshel. Litho)

1995 (25 Apr). Composers (2nd series). Horiz designs as T **532**. Multicoloured. P 14.
1272 2s.40 Arnold Schoenberg and scene from *Moses and Aaron* .... 3·50 3·25
1273 2s.40 Darius Milhaud and score and scene from opera *David* .... 3·50 3·25
1272/1273 *Set of 2* .... 6·25 5·75
1272/1273 *Set of 2 with tabs* .... 7·50 6·75

536 Soldier teaching Children Hebrew

(Des G. Sagi. Litho Govt Printers)

1995 (25 Apr). Jewish Brigades of Second World War. Sheet 95×65 mm. P 14.
MS1274 **536** 2s.50 multicoloured .... 8·25 7·75

537 Canoeist

538 Box kite and Cody War kite

(Des H. Kivkovich. Litho Govt Printers)

1995 (7 June). 15th Hapoel Games. One phosphor band. P 14.
1275 **537** 1s. multicoloured .... 3·50 3·25
With tab 3·75 3·50

(Des Naomi and M. Eshel. Litho Govt Printers)

1995 (7 June). Kites. T **538** and similar vert designs. Multicoloured. One phosphor band. P 14.
1276 1s. Type **538** .... 1·20 1·10
a. Strip of 3. Nos. 1276/1278 .... 3·75
1277 1s. Bird-shaped, hexagonal Tiara and rhombic Eddy kites .... 1·20 1·10
1278 1s. Multiple rhombic and triangular Deltic aerobatic kites .... 1·20 1·10
1276/1278 *Set of 3* .... 3·25 3·00
1276/1278 *Set of 3 with tabs* .... 4·00 3·50
Nos. 1276/1278 were issued together in horizontal or vertical *se-tenant* strips of three, each horiz strip forming a composite design.

539 *Stars in a Bucket* (Anda Amir-Pinkerfeld, illus. Hava Nathan)

540 *Zim Israel* (container ship)

(Des R. Goldenberg. Litho)

1995 (7 June). Children's Books. T **539** and similar horiz designs illustrating poems. Multicoloured. One phosphor band (1s.) or two bands (others). P 14.
1279 1s. Type **539** .... 1·90 1·70
1280 1s.50 *Hurry, Run, Dwarfs* (Miriam Yallan-Stekelis, illus. Tirzah Tanny) .... 3·25 3·00

1281 1s.80 *Daddy's Big Umbrella* (Levin Kipnis, illus. Pazit Meller-Dushi) 3·75 3·50
1279/1281 *Set of 3* 8·00 7·50
1279/1281 *Set of 3 with tabs* 9·25 8·50

(Des Ruth Avrahami. Litho Govt Printers)

1995 (7 June). 50th Anniversary of Zim Navigation Company. P 14.
1282 **540** 4s.40 multicoloured 8·25 7·75
With tab 9·00 8·25

541 Elijah's Chair (German, 1768)

542 King David playing Harp (mosaic pavement, Gaza Synagogue)

(Des Y. Granot. Litho Govt Printers)

1995 (4 Sept). Jewish New Year. T **541** and similar horiz designs. Multicoloured. One phosphor band (1s.) or two bands (others). P 14.
1283 1s. Type **541** (circumcision) 1·90 1·70
1284 1s.50 Velvet bag for prayer shawl (Moroccan, 1906) (Bar-Mitzvah) 2·75 2·50
1285 1s.80 Marriage stone (from Bingen Synagogue, Germany, 1700) 3·75 3·50
1283/1285 *Set of 3* 7·50 7·00
1283/1285 *Set of 3 with tabs* 8·25 7·75

(Des Ruth Kantor and A. Friedman. Litho)

1995 (4 Sept). 3000th Anniversary of City of David (Jerusalem) (1st issue). T **542** and similar horiz designs. Multicoloured. One phosphor band (1s.) or two bands (others). P 14.
1286 1s. Type **542** 2·00 1·90
1287 1s.50 Illustration of Jerusalem from 19th-century map by Rabbi Pinie 3·50 3·25
1288 1s.80 Aerial view of Knesset (parliament) 4·25 4·00
1286/1288 *Set of 3* 8·75 8·25
1286/1288 *Set of 3 with tabs* 10·00 9·25
See also Nos. **MS**1296 and **MS**1310.

543 *Sheep* (Menashe Kadishman)

544 Rabin

(Des M. Pereg. Litho Govt Printers)

1995 (4 Sept). 75th Anniversary of Veterinary Services. P 14.
1289 **543** 4s.40 multicoloured 7·75 7·25
With tab 8·25 7·50

(Des Y. Granot. Litho)

1995 (5 Dec). Yitzhak Rabin (Prime Minister) Commemoration. P 14.
1290 **544** 5s. multicoloured 8·75 8·00
With tab 9·25 8·50

545 Putting out Fire

546 Miniature Silver Menorah (Zusia Ejbuszyc)

(Des G. Paran. Litho Govt Printers)

1995 (14 Dec). 70th Anniversary of Fire and Rescue Service. T **545** and similar horiz design. Multicoloured. One phosphor band. P 14.
1291 1s. Type **545** 1·80 1·60
1292 1s. Cutting crash victim out of car 1·80 1·60
1291/1292 *Set of 2* 3·25 3·00
1291/1292 *Set of 2 with tabs* 3·75 3·50

(Des I. Gabay. Litho)

1995 (14 Dec). Festival of Hanukkah. Two phosphor bands. P 14.
1293 **546** 1s.50 multicoloured 2·50 2·40
With tab 2·75 2·50

547 Flying Model Aeroplane

548 Film Stars

(Des I. Gabay. Litho Govt Printers)

1995 (14 Dec). Stamp Day. Two phosphor bands. P 14.
1294 **547** 1s.80 multicoloured 3·25 3·00
With tab 3·25 3·00

(Des M. Pereg. Litho)

1995 (14 Dec). Centenary of Motion Pictures. P 14×13.
1295 **548** 4s.40 multicoloured 5·00 4·75
With tab 5·50 5·00
The stars depicted are the Marx Brothers, Simone Signoret, Peter Sellers, Danny Kaye and Al Jolson.

549 Illustration of Jerusalem from 19th-century Map by Rabbi Pinie

550 Cycling

(Des R. Kantor and A. Friedman. Litho)

1995 (16 Dec). 3000th Anniversary of City of David (Jerusalem) (2nd issue) and Jerusalem 3000 Israeli-European Stamp Exhibition. Sheet 140×70 mm containing T **549** and similar horiz designs. Multicoloured. P 14.
MS1296 1s. King David playing Harp (mosaic pavement, Gaza Synagogue); 1s.50, Type **549**; 1s.80, Aerial view of Knesset (Parliament) (*sold at* 6s.) 12·00 11·00
The stamps in No. **MS**1296 depict the same motifs as Nos. 1286/1288 but with differences in inscriptions.

(Des A. Berg. Litho Govt Printers (1s.80, 2s.20) or photo (others))

1996 (20 Feb)–**98**. Sport. T **550** and similar vert designs. Multicoloured. One phosphor band (1s.05, 1s.10), no bands (3s., 5s., 10s.) or two bands (others). P 14 (1s.80, 2s.20) or 13×14 (others).
1301 1s.05 Type **550** 2·20 2·00
1302 1s.10 Show jumping (*band at right*) (13.2.97). 2·00 1·90
a. Phosphor band at left. Booklets (13.2.97) 3·75 3·50
ab. Booklet pane. No. 1302a×20 (13.2.97) 80·00
1303 1s.80 Water skiing (17.2.98) 2·75 2·50
1304 1s.90 Paragliding 4·00 3·50
1305 2s. Volleyball 4·50 4·00
1306 2s.20 Whitewater rafting (17.2.98) 3·75 3·50
a. Photo. Perf 13½×14 (23.8.98) 5·00 4·75
1307 3s. Bat and ball (23.9.97) 3·75 3·50
1308 5s. Archery (13.2.97) 5·50 5·00
1309 10s. Abseiling (8.7.97) 11·00 10·00
1301/1309 *Set of 9* 36·00 32·00
1301/1309 *Set of 9 with tabs* 39·00 36·00
The stamps in the booklet pane (No. 1302ab) are arranged in two *tête-bêche* blocks of ten stamps.
Numbers have been left for additions to this series.

551 'Temple and Walls of Jerusalem'

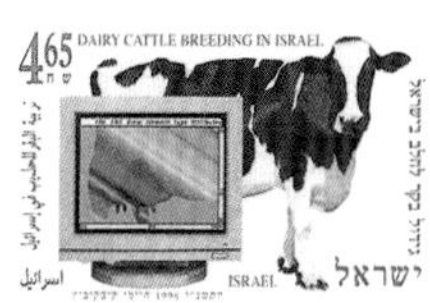

552 Cow and Computer

(Des A. Vanooijen. Litho)

1996 (20 Feb). 3000th Anniversary of City of David (Jerusalem) (3rd issue). 3rd-century Murals from Dura-Europos Synagogue, Syria. Sheet 141×71 mm containing T **551** and similar vert designs. Multicoloured. P 14×13.

MS1310 1s.05, Type **551**; 1s.60, Torah Ark niche; 1s.90, 'Prophet Samuel anointing David as King' (*sold at* 5s.) .... 15·00 13·50

(Des H. Kivkovich. Litho Govt Printers)

1996 (20 Feb). 70th Anniversary of Israel Dairy Cattle Breeders' Association. P 14.

1311	**552** 4s.65 multicoloured	7·50	6·75
	With tab	7·75	7·25

(Des J. Smith. Litho Govt Printers)

1996 (17 Apr). China '96 International Stamp Exhibition, Peking. Birds. Sheet 128×89 mm containing designs as Nos. 1185/1194 but face values and colours changed. P 14.

MS1312 30a.×10, multicoloured .... 22·00 20·00

553 Abraham Shlonsky (poet)

554 Fallen Policemen Monument, National Police Academy, Kiryat Ata (Yosef Assa)

(Des A. Vanooijen, M. Yozefpolsky, Galia Lerech and R. Beckman. Litho)

1996 (17 Apr). Modern Hebrew Writers, T **553** and similar vert designs. Multicoloured. P 14.

1313	40a. Type **553**	65	60
	a. Sheetlet of 14. Nos. 1313/1326	9·25	
1314	40a. Joseph Brenner (novelist and essayist)	65	60
1315	40a. Judah Gordon (poet)	65	60
1316	40a. Haim Hazaz (novelist)	65	60
1317	40a. Devorah Baron (novelist)	65	60
1318	40a. Yehuda Burla (novelist)	65	60
1319	40a. Micha Berdyczewski (novelist and historian)	65	60
1320	40a. Yaakov Shabtai (novelist)	65	60
1321	40a. Isaac Peretz (novelist)	65	60
1322	40a. Nathan Alterman (poet)	65	60
1323	40a. Saul Tchernichowsky (poet)	65	60
1324	40a. Amir Gilboa (poet)	65	60
1325	40a. Yokheved Bat-Miriam (poet)	65	60
1326	40a. Mendele Sefarim (novelist)	65	60
1313/1326	*Set of* 14	8·25	7·50
1313/1326	*Set of* 14 *with tabs*	10·50	9·50

Nos. 1313/1326 were issued together in *se-tenant* sheetlets of 14 stamps, the two rows of seven arranged *tête-bêche*.

(Des R. Beckman. Litho Govt Printers)

1996 (17 Apr). Memorial Day. One phosphor band. P 14.

1327	**554** 1s.05 multicoloured	7·50	6·75
	With tab	8·25	7·75

555 Circuit Boards

556 Emblem and Old Photographs

(Des G. Sagi. Litho)

1996 (17 Apr). 75th Anniversary of Manufacturers' Association. One phosphor band. P 14.

1328	**555** 1s.05 multicoloured	4·00	3·50
	With tab	4·00	3·75

(Des D. Harel. Litho Govt Printers)

1996 (17 Apr). Centenary of Metulla. Two phosphor bands. P 13.

1329	**556** 1s.90 multicoloured	7·00	6·50
	With tab	7·50	6·75

(Des Naomi and M. Eshel. Litho)

1996 (17 Apr). Composers (3rd series). Horiz design as T **532**. P 14.

1330	4s.65 multicoloured	13·00	12·00
	With tab	13·50	12·50

Design: 4s.65, Gustav Mahler, score from *Resurrection Symphony* and creation of light.

557 Plant growing in Cracked Earth

558 Fencing

(Des I. Gabai. Litho)

1996 (25 June). 50th Anniversary of the 11 Negev Settlements. One phosphor band. P 14.

1331	**557** 1s.05 multicoloured	2·50	2·40
	With tab	2·75	2·50

(Des R. Sadeh. Litho Govt Printers)

1996 (25 June). Olympic Games, Atlanta. T **558** and similar vert designs. Multicoloured. One phosphor band (1s.05) or two bands (others). P 14.

1332	1s.05 Type **558**	2·20	2·00
	a. Booklet pane. Nos. 1332, 1333×2 and 1334×3	20·00	
1333	1s.60 Pole vaulting	3·00	2·75
1334	1s.90 Wrestling	3·50	3·25
1332/1334	*Set of* 4	7·75	7·25
1332/1334	*Set of* 4 *with tabs*	11·00	10·00

559 Jaffa Orange Tree and Citrus Fruit

560 Road Systems

(Des A. Vanooijen. Litho)

1996 (25 June). Israeli Fruit Production. T **559** and similar horiz designs. Multicoloured. One phosphor band (1s.05.) or two bands (others). P 14.

1335	1s.05 Type **559**	2·20	2·00
1336	1s.60 Grape vine, avocado, date, sharon fruit and mango	3·00	2·75
1337	1s.90 Star fruit plant and exotic fruit	3·50	3·25
1335/1337	*Set of* 3	7·75	7·25
1335/1337	*Set of* 3 *with tabs*	11·00	10·00

(Des Naomi and M. Eshel. Litho)

1996 (25 June). Composers (4th series). Horiz design as T **532.** P 14.

1338	4s.65 multicoloured	8·25	7·75
	With tab	8·50	8·00

Design: 4s.65, Felix Mendelssohn, Prophet Elijah (after Albrecht Dürer) and score from oratorio *Elijah*.

(Des Molcholand Studio. Litho Govt Printers)

1996 (3 Sept). 75th Anniversary of Public Works Department. One phosphor band. P 14.

1339	**560** 1s.05 multicoloured	3·25	3·00
	With tab	3·75	3·50

561 New Year

562 Herzl looking out at David's Tower (wall hanging)

(Des H. Kivkovich. Litho)

1996 (3 Sept). Jewish Festivals. Paintings by Sahar Pick. T **561** and similar horiz designs. Multicoloured. One phosphor band (1s.05) or two bands (others). P 14.

1340 1s.05 Type **561** .... 2·20 2·00
1341 1s.60 Booth decoration (Festival of Tabernacles) .... 3·00 2·75
1342 1s.90 Pulpit (Simchat Torah Festival) .... 3·50 3·25
1340/1342 *Set of 3* .... 7·75 7·25
1340/1342 *Set of 3 with tabs* .... 11·00 10·00

(Des O. Meirav; litho Govt Printers (No. 1343). Des H. Kivkovich; litho Lewin-Epstein (No. **MS**1344))

1996 (3 Sept). Centenary of First Zionist Congress, Basel, Switzerland. T **562** and similar vert design. P 14.

1343 4s.65 Type **562** .... 12·00 11·00
With tab 13·00 12·00
MS1344 70×97 mm. 5s. Casino, Basel (venue) (39×50 *mm*) .... 15·00 13·50

563 Lighted Candles

564 Bird and Fighter Aircraft

(Des Hannah Smotrich. Photo Avery Dennison, Clinton, South Carolina, USA)

1996 (22 Oct). Festival of Hanukkah. Phosphorescent paper. Self-adhesive. Die-cut perf 11.

1345 **563** 2s.50 multicoloured .... 4·00 3·50
With tab 4·00 3·75

A stamp of a similar design was issued by USA.

(Des Kati Messing. Litho)

1996 (5 Dec). Coexistence between Man and Animals. T **564** and similar horiz designs. Multicoloured. One phosphor band (1s.10) or two bands (others). P 14.

1346 1s.10 Type **564** .... 2·00 1·90
1347 1s.75 Dog, people and cat .... 3·25 3·00
1348 2s. Dolphins and diver .... 3·75 3·50
1346/1348 *Set of 3* .... 8·00 7·50
1346/1348 *Set of 3 with tabs* .... 9·00 8·25

565 Ahad Ha'am

(Des D. Goldberg. Litho Govt Printers)

1996 (5 Dec). Centenary of First Edition of *Ha-Shilo ah* (periodical) and 140th Birth Anniversary of Ahad Ha'am (editor and Zionist). One phosphor band. P 14.

1349 **565** 1s.15 multicoloured .... 2·20 2·00
With tab 2·40 2·20

566 Shavit Rocket, Earth and *Ofeq-3* (satellite)

567 Equal Opportunities Emblem

(Des G. Sagi. Litho)

1996 (5 Dec). Stamp Day. Space Research. Two phosphor bands. P 14.

1350 **566** 2s.05 multicoloured .... 4·50 4·00
With tab 4·75 4·25

(Des D. Reisinger. Litho Govt Printers)

1996 (5 Dec). Equal Opportunities for Disabled People. P 14.

1351 **567** 5s. multicoloured .... 8·75 8·00
With tab 9·25 8·50

568 Woman, Ethiopia

569 Alexander Graham Bell demonstrating Telephone

(Des A. Vanooijen. Litho)

1997 (13 Feb). Traditional Costumes of Jewish Communities Abroad. T **568** and similar horiz designs. Multicoloured. One phosphor band (1s.10) or two bands (others). P 14.

1352 1s.10 Type **568** .... 2·00 1·70
1353 1s.70 Man, Kurdistan .... 3·25 3·00
1354 2s. Woman, Salonica .... 4·00 3·75
1352/1354 *Set of 3* .... 8·25 7·50
1352/1354 *Set of 3 with tabs* .... 9·25 8·50

(Des M. Pereg. Litho Govt Printers)

1997 (13 Feb). Hong Kong '97 International Stamp Exhibition. Inventors' 150th Birth Anniversaries. Sheet 90×56 mm containing T **561** and similar vert design. P 13.

MS1355 1s.50, Type **569**; 2s. Thomas Edison and light bulb .... 10·00 9·25

570 Windmills, Don Quixote and Sancho Panza (Ya'acov Farkas (Ze'ev))

571 Logistics Corps Memorial, Hadir

(Des Y. Granot. Litho)

1997 (13 Feb). 450th Birth Anniversary of Miguel de Cervantes (writer). P 14.

1356 **570** 3s. multicoloured .... 5·00 4·75
With tab 5·50 5·00

(Des H. Kivkovich. Litho Govt Printers)

1997 (30 Apr). Memorial Day. One phosphor band. P 14.

1357 **571** 1s.10 multicoloured .... 2·00 1·90
With tab 2·20 2·00

572 Ark of the Torah, Old-New Synagogue (east side)

573 Rabbi Elijah (Mario Sermoneta)

(Des J. Janicek. Litho Govt Printers)

1997 (30 Apr). Jewish Monuments in Prague. T **572** and similar vert design. Multicoloured. Two phosphor bands. P 14.

1358 1s.70 Type **572** .... 3·50 3·25
1359 1s.70 Grave of Rabbi Loew (chief Rabbi of Prague), Old Jewish Cemetery .... 3·50 3·25
1358/1359 *Set of 2* .... 6·25 5·75
1358/1359 *Set of 2 with tabs* .... 7·50 6·75

Nos. 1358/1359 were issued both in separate sheets of 15 stamps and five tabs and also together in sheetlets containing each design in a block of four, the blocks separated by an inscribed gutter.

Stamps of a similar design were issued by Czech Republic.

(Des Y. Granot. Litho)

1997 (30 Apr). Death Bicentenary of Vilna Gaon (Rabbi Elijah ben Solomon). Two phosphor bands. P 14.

1360	**573**	2s. multicoloured	4·00	3·50
		With tab	4·00	3·75

574 *Exodus* (immigrant ship), 1947 in Haifa Port

575 Ben Ezra Synagogue, Cairo

(Des D. Ben-Hador. Litho)

1997 (30 Apr)–**98**. Clandestine Immigration, 1934–1948. P 14.

1361	**574**	5s. multicoloured	8·25	7·75
		With tab	9·25	8·50
		a. Perf 14×13 Booklets (13.5.98)		
		ab. Booklet pane. No. 1361a		

No. 1361ab has a large illustrated pane.

(Des A. Vanooijen. Litho)

1997 (29 May). Pacific 97 International Stamp Exhibition, San Francisco. Sheet 90×60 mm containing T **575** and similar square design. Multicoloured. P 13.

MS1362 2s. Type **575** (centenary of discovery of Cairo Hebrew archives); 3s. Qumran and the Dead Sea, Prof. E. Sukenik and Shrine of the Book (50th anniversary of discovery of Dead Sea Scrolls) ... 10·00 9·25

576 Classroom (Navit Mangashsa)

577 Drunk Driver

(Des Y. Barnea-Givoni. Litho)

1997 (8 July). Winning Entry in 'Hello First Grade!' Stamp Drawing Competition. One phosphor band. P 14.

1363	**576**	1s.10 multicoloured	2·20	2·00
		With tab	2·40	2·20

(Des G. Harlap. Litho Govt Printers)

1997 (8 July). Road Safety. T **577** and similar square designs. Multicoloured. One phosphor band. P 13.

1364	1s.10 Type **577** ('Don't Drink and Drive')	2·40	2·20
1365	1s.10 Car sinking in water ('Keep in Lane')	2·40	2·20
1366	1s.10 Car hitting bird ('Keep your Distance')	2·40	2·20
1364/1366	*Set of 3*	6·50	6·00
1364/1366	*Set of 3 with tabs*	7·50	6·75

578 Ice Skating

579 Abraham and Tamarisk Tree

(Des I. Gabay. Litho)

1997 (8 July). 15th Maccabiah Games. P 14.

1367	**578**	5s. multicoloured	8·75	8·00
		With tab	9·25	8·50

(Des E. Lorentsov. Litho Govt Printers)

1997 (23 Sept). Festival of Sukkot. The Visiting Patriarchs (1st series). T **579** and similar vert designs showing paintings from the Sukkah of Rabbi Loew Immanuel of Szeged, Hungary. Multicoloured. One phosphor band (1s.10) or two bands (others). P 14.

1368	1s.10 Type **579**	2·00	1·90
	a. Booklet pane. Nos. 1368, 1369×2 and 1370×3	22·00	
1369	1s.70 Abraham preparing to sacrifice Isaac	3·50	3·25
1370	2s. Jacob dreaming of Angels on ladder to heaven	4·00	3·75
1368/1370	*Set of 3*	8·50	8·00
1368/1370	*Set of 3 with tabs*	10·00	9·25

See also Nos. 1453/1456.

580 Mt. Scopus (Jerusalem) and Choirs

581 *The Night of 29th November* (Ya'acov Eisenscher)

(Des D. Grebu. Litho Govt Printers)

1997 (23 Sept). Music and Dance Festivals. T **580** and similar square designs. Multicoloured. One phosphor band (1s.10), two bands (2s.) or no bands (3s.). P 13.

1371	1s.10 Type **580** (Zimriya World Assembly of Choirs, Hebrew University)	1·90	1·70
1372	2s. Fireworks over Karmiel and dancers (Dance Festival)	3·50	3·25
1373	3s. Zefat and klezmers (Hassidic musicians) (Klezmer Festival)	5·00	4·75
1371/1373	*Set of 3*	9·25	8·75
1371/1373	*Set of 3 with tabs*	11·00	10·00

(Des H. Kivkovich. Litho)

1997 (23 Sept)–**98**. 50th Anniversary of United Nations Resolution of Establishment of State of Israel. One phosphor band. P 13×14.

1374	**581**	5s. multicoloured	8·75	8·00
		a. Booklet pane. No. 1374 (13.5.98)		
		With tab		

No. 1374a has a large illustrated pane.

582 Sketch by Pushkin of Himself and Onegin

583 National Flag and Srulik with Flower

(Des Marina Pekarskaya. Litho)

1997 (19 Nov). Translation into Hebrew by Abraham Shlonsky of *Eugene Onegin* (poem) by Aleksandr Pushkin. Sheet 75×60 mm. P 14×13.

MS1375 **582** 5s. multicoloured ... 9·25 8·50

The miniature sheet also bears the emblem of Israel 98 Stamp Exhibition in the margin.

(Des Dosh (K. Gardosh). Printed Govt Printers)

1997 (23 Dec)–**98**. 50th Anniversary (1998) of State of Israel (1st issue). No value expressed. One phosphor band.

(a) Size 18×23½ mm Litho. P 14

1376	**583**	(–) multicoloured	3·75	3·50
		a. One band at left	4·75	4·25
		b. Perf 13×14. Booklets (13.5.98)		
		ba. Booklet pane. No. 1376b		
		c. Size 17×22 mm (17.2.98)	2·00	1·90
		ca. Booklet pane. No. 1376c×20 (17.2.98)	41·00	
		cb. Booklet pane. No. 1376c×20 plus 10 labels (13.5.98)		

(b) Size 17½×21½ mm. One phosphor band. Photo. P 13×14

1377 **583** (–) multicoloured (3.5.98) .... 5·50 5·00
1376/1377 *Set of 2* .... 6·75 6·25
1376/1377 *Set of 2 with tabs* .... 7·75 7·25

No. 1376ba has a large illustrated margin.

In No. 1376ca, the stamps are arranged in a block (10×2), with the ten stamps at the left inverted. No. 1376cb has two horizontal strips of ten, the strips separated by a row of ten labels showing a flower; the five stamps at the left of each strip are inverted. Two horizontal *tête-bêche* pairs are therefore available from each booklet.

See also Nos. 1395.

584 Norseman Aircraft, Soldier, Battleship *Achi Hagana* K 20 and Cannon *Napoleon-Chick*

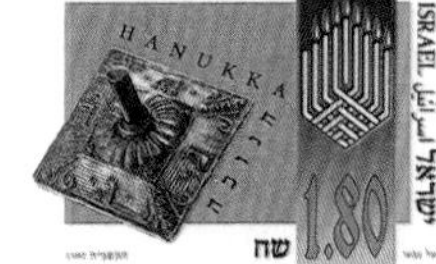

585 Bezalel (spinning-top)

(Des R. Kantor. Litho)

1997 (23 Dec)-**98**. 50th Anniversary of Arrival in Israel of Machal (overseas volunteers) (No. 1378) and Gachal (overseas recruits) (No. 1379). T **584** and similar horiz design. Multicoloured. One phosphor band (No. 1378) or two bands (No. 1379). P 14.

1378 1s.15 Type **584** .... 1·60 1·40
a. Perf 13×14. Booklets (13.5.98) ....
ab. Booklet pane. Nos. 1378a and 1379a ....
1379 1s.80 Infantry soldier and Holocaust survivors 1·90 1·70
a. Perf 13×14. Booklets (13.5.98) ....
1378/1379 *Set of 2* .... 3·25 2·75
1378/1379 *Set of 2 with tabs* .... 3·75 3·50

No. 1378ab has a large illustrated margin.

(Des I. Gabay. Litho Govt Printers)

1997 (23 Dec). Festival of Hanukkah. Museum Exhibits. T **585** and similar horiz design. Multicoloured. Two phosphor bands. P 14.

1380 1s.80 Type **585** (Eretz Israel Museum, Tel Aviv) .... 2·50 2·40
1381 2s.10 Coin of Bar-Kokhba during war against the Romans (Israel Museum, Jerusalem) .... 3·25 3·00
1380/1381 *Set of 2* .... 5·25 4·75
1380/1381 *Set of 2 with tabs* .... 6·25 5·75

586 Children leaving Airliner

587 Julia Set Fractal

(Des E. Carmli. Litho)

1997 (23 Dec). Chabad Children of Chernobyl Organisation (for evacuation of Jewish children from radiated areas of Europe to Israel). Two phosphor bands. P 14.

1382 **586** 2s.10 multicoloured .... 2·50 2·40
With tab 2·75 2·50

(Des Y. Granot. Litho Govt Printers)

1997 (23 Dec). Stamp Day. P 14.

1383 **587** 2s.50 multicoloured .... 3·75 3·50
With tab 4·00 3·75

588 Photograph of Soldiers of Palmach Battalion and Civilians (Zefat)

589 Herzog

(Des M. Pereg. Litho)

1998 (17 Feb–13 May). 50th Anniversary of War of Independence. Battle Fronts. T **588** and similar vert designs. Multicoloured. No phosphor bands (**MS**1386) or one band (others). P 14.

1384 1s.15 Type **588** .... 2·00 1·90
a. Booklet pane. Nos. 1384/1386 (13.5.98)
1385 1s.15 *Castel Conquered* (Arieh Navon) superimposed on military vehicles (Jerusalem) .... 2·00 1·90
1386 1s.15 Soldiers raising flag (Elat) .... 2·00 1·90
1384/1386 *Set of 3* .... 5·50 5·25
1384/1386 *Set of 3 with tabs* .... 6·75 6·00
MS1387 140×70 mm. 1s.50, 2s.50, 3s. showing enlarged details of Nos. 1384/1386. P 14×13 .... 13·50 12·00

The miniature sheet also bears the emblem of Israel 98 Stamp Exhibition in the margin.

No. 1384a has a large illustrated margin.

(Des R. Beckman. Litho Govt Printers)

1998 (17 Feb). 80th Birth Anniversary of Chain Herzog (President 1983–1993). P 14.

1388 **589** 5s.35 multicoloured .... 6·00 5·50
With tab 6·50 6·00

590 Franz Kafka (writer)

591 Declaration Ceremony, 1948

(Des H. Rashelbach, A. Vanooijen, Ruth Beckman, D. Goldberg, M. Yozefpolsky and M. Sermoneta. Litho Govt Printers)

1998 (27 Apr). Jewish Contribution to World Culture (1st series). T **590** and similar horiz designs. Multicoloured. P 14.

1389 90a. Type **590** .... 1·20 1·10
a. Sheetlet of 6. Nos. 1389/1394 .... 7·50
1390 90a. George Gershwin (composer) .... 1·20 1·10
1391 90a. Lev Davidovich Landau (physicist) .... 1·20 1·10
1392 90a. Albert Einstein (physicist and mathematician) .... 1·20 1·10
1393 90a. Leon Blum (writer) .... 1·20 1·10
1394 90a. Elizabeth Rachel Felix (actress) .... 1·20 1·10
1389/1394 *Set of 6* .... 6·50 6·00
1389/1394 *Set of 6 with tabs* .... 7·75 7·25

Nos. 1389/1389 were issued together in *se-tenant* sheetlets of six stamps.

See also Nos. 1436/1441.

(Des Batia Ton. Litho)

1998 (27 Apr–May). 50th Anniversary of State of Israel (2nd issue). One phosphor band. P 14.

1395 **591** 1s.15 multicoloured .... 1·60 1·40
With tab 1·70 1·50
a. Perf 14×13. Booklets (13.5.98) ....
ab. Booklet pane. No. 1395a ....

No. 1395ab has a large illustrated margin.

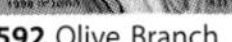

592 Olive Branch

593 Swearing In Ceremony in 1948 and Badge entwined with Medal Ribbons

(Des I. Gabay. Litho)

1998 (27 Apr). Memorial Day. One phosphor band. P 14.

1396 **592** 1s.15 multicoloured .... 1·60 1·40
With tab 1·70 1·50

(Des O. Meirav. Litho Govt Printers)

1998 (27 Apr–May). 50th Anniversary of Defence Forces. P 14.
1397 **593** 5s.35 multicoloured .... 5·50 5·00
With tab 7·00 6·50
a. Perf 14×13. Booklets (13.5.98) ....
ab. Booklet pane. No. 1397a ....
No. 1397ab has a large illustrated margin.

594 Giorgio Perlasca, Aristides de Sousa Mendes, Charles Lutz, Sempo Sugihara and Selahattin Ulkumen (diplomats) (*⅓ size illustration*)

(Des A. Vanooijen. Litho)

1998 (27 Apr). Holocaust Memorial Day. Righteous Among the Nation (non-Jews who risked their lives to save Jews during the Holocaust). P 13.
1398 **594** 6s. multicoloured .... 8·25 7·75
With tab 9·00 8·25

595 Kitten **596** Srulik at Post Office Counter

(Des M. Sermoneta. Litho Govt Printers)

1998 (13 May). Children's Pets. T **595** and similar pentagonal designs. Multicoloured. P 13.
1399 60a. Type **595** 85 75
a. Sheetlet of 6. Nos. 1399/1404 plus 6 labels .... 5·25
1400 60a. Puppy 85 75
1401 60a. Parrot 85 75
1402 60a. Common Rosella 85 75
1403 60a. Hamster 85 75
1404 60a. Rabbit 85 75
1399/1404 *Set of 6* .... 4·50 4·00
1399/1404 *Set of 6 with tabs* .... 5·50 5·00
Nos. 1399/1404 were issued together in *se-tenant* sheetlets of six stamps and six triangular labels bearing the emblem of Israel 98 International Stamp Exhibition, each label with an adjacent stamp completing a square. The complete sheetlet forms a composite design.

(Des Batia Ton. Litho)

1998 (13 May). Inauguration of Postal and Philatelic Museum, Tel Aviv. Sheet 142×72 mm containing T **596** and similar horiz designs showing illustrations by K. Gardosh. Multicoloured. P 14.
MS1405 1s.50, Type **596**; 2s.50, Srulik viewing stamp through magnifying glass; 3s. Srulik posting letter (*sold at* 8s.) .... 11·00 10·00

597 Drawing of Temple Entrance **598** de Havilland DH.89 Dragon Rapide

(Des A. Shevo. Litho Govt Printers)

1998 (13 May). Israel 98 International Stamp Exhibition, Tel Aviv (1st issue). King Solomon's Temple. Sheet 92×66 mm containing T **597** and similar square design. Multicoloured. P 13.
MS1406 2s. Type **597**; 3s. Inscribed ivory pomegranate (*sold at* 7s.) .... 8·25 7·75
See also No. **MS**1410.

(Des T. Kurz. Litho)

1998 (13 May). Aircraft of War of Independence. T **598** and similar horiz designs. Multicoloured. Two phosphor bands. P 14.
1407 2s.20 Type **598** .... 1·90 1·70
a. Horiz strip of 3. Nos. 1407/1409 .... 6·00
b. Perf 13×14. Booklets ....
ba. Booklet pane. Nos. 1407b, 1408a and 1409a ....
1408 2s.20 Supermarine Spitfire .... 1·90 1·70
a. Perf 13×14. Booklets ....
1409 2s.20 Boeing B-17 Flying Fortress .... 1·90 1·70
a. Perf 13×14. Booklets ....
1407/1409 *Set of 3* .... 5·25 4·50
1407/1409 *Set of 3 with tabs* .... 6·00 5·50
Nos. 1407/1409 were issued together in horizontal *se-tenant* strips of three stamps within sheetlets containing two such strips separated by a row of three labels bearing the emblem of Israel 98 International Stamp Exhibition. One of the horizontal strips was inverted.
No. 1407ba has a large illustrated margin.

599 Woman's Head (mosaic from Zippori) **600** *Amos* Satellite, Immigration, Grapes, Dove and Lion's Gate, Jerusalem

(Des G. Sagi. Litho)

1998 (13 May). Israel 98 International Stamp Exhibition, Tel Aviv (2nd issue). Sheet 90×60 mm. P 14.
MS1410 **599** 5s. multicoloured (*sold at* 6s.) .... 8·25 7·75

(Des H. Kivkovich. Litho)

1998 (3 Aug). Israel Jubilee Exhibition, Tel Aviv. P 14×13.
1411 **600** 5s.35 multicoloured .... 5·50 5·00
With tab 6·00 5·50

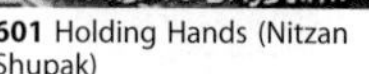

601 Holding Hands (Nitzan Shupak) **602** Birds (Hechal Yitshak Synagogue, Moshav Yonatan)

(Des E. Carmeli. Litho)

1998 (8 Sept). Living in a World of Mutual Respect Elementary Education Programme. One phosphor band. P 14.
1412 **601** 1s.15 multicoloured .... 1·40 1·30
With tab 1·50 1·40

(Des K. Soip. Litho)

1998 (8 Sept). Jewish New Year. Synagogue Curtains. T **602** and similar horiz designs. Multicoloured. One phosphor band (1s.15) or two bands (others). P 14.
1413 1s.15 Type **602** .... 1·20 1·10
1414 1s.80 Lions (Ohal Chanah Synagogue, Neve Tsuf) .... 2·00 1·90
1415 2s.20 Leaves (Hatzvi Israel Synagogue, Jerusalem) .... 2·50 2·40
1413/1415 *Set of 3* .... 5·25 4·75
1413/1415 *Set of 3 with tabs* .... 6·25 5·75

603 Hebron **604** State Flag

(Des Naomi and M. Eshel. Litho Govt Printers)

1998 (8 Sept). Jewish Life in Eretz Israel (1st series). T **603** and similar horiz design showing section from Holy Cities Wall Plaque. Multicoloured. Two phosphor bands. P 14.
1416 1s.80 Type **603** .... 1·80 1·60
1417 2s.20 Jerusalem .... 2·40 2·20
1416/1417 *Set of 2* .... 3·75 3·50
1416/1417 *Set of 2 with tabs* .... 4·50 4·00
See also Nos. 1430/1431.

(Des I. Gabay. Litho Glilon Industries Ltd.)

1998 (24 Nov). Phosphorescent security markings (Nos. 1419/1421). Self-adhesive. Die-cut.

1418	**604**	1s.15 bright blue and new blue	1·90	1·70
1419		2s.15 bright blue and yellowish green	3·50	3·25
1420		3s.25 bright blue and magenta	5·00	4·75
1421		5s.35 bright blue and orange-yellow	8·75	8·00
1418/1421		*Set of 4*	17·00	16·00
1418/1421		*Set of 4 with tabs*	20·00	19·00

Nos. 1422/1425 are vacant.

605 Hanukkah Lamp showing Mattathias (Boris Schatz)

606 *Hyacinthus orientalis*

(Des I. Gabay. Litho)

1999 (5 Jan). Festival of Hanukkah. Two phosphor bands. P 14.

1426	**605**	2s.15 multicoloured	2·00	1·90
		With tab	2·20	2·00

(Des Ruth Malka. Photo De La Rue)

1999 (1 Feb). Wild Hyacinths. No value expressed. Phosphorescent paper. P 15.

1427	**606**	(1s.15) bright green and bright lilac	1·20	1·10
		With tab	1·30	1·20

See also No. 1671.

607 The Knesset, Menorah and Knesset Stone Wall (des. Danny Karavan)

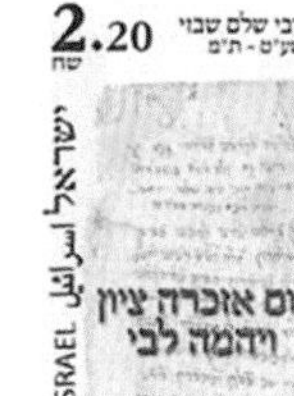

608 Manuscript

(Des D. Goldberg. Litho Govt Printers)

1999 (1 Feb). 50th Anniversary of the Knesset (Parliament). Two phosphor bands. P 14.

1428	**607**	1s.80 multicoloured	1·50	1·40
		With tab	1·70	1·50

(Des Y. Granot. Litho Govt Printers)

1999 (1 Feb). 380th Birth Anniversary of Rabbi Shalem Shabazi (Yemeni poet). Two phosphor bands. P 14.

1429	**608**	2s.20 multicoloured	1·90	1·70
		With tab	2·20	2·00

(Des Naomi & M. Eshel. Litho Govt Printers)

1999 (16 Feb). Jewish Life in Eretz Israel (2nd series). Horiz designs as T **603** showing sections from Holy Cities Wall Plaque. Multicoloured. One phosphor band (1s.15) or no bands (5s.35). P 14.

1430	1s.15 Zefat	1·10	1·00
1431	5s.35 Tiberias	4·75	4·25
1430/1431	*Set of 2*	5·25	4·75
1430/1431	*Set of 2 with tabs*	6·50	6·00

609 Part of £1 Share Certificate

610 Yemeni Woman

(Des D. Ben-Hador. Litho Govt Printers)

1999 (16 Feb). Centenary of Jewish Colonial Trust. Two phosphor bands. P 14.

1432	**609**	1s.80 multicoloured	1·70	1·50
		With tab	1·90	1·70

(Des A. Vanooijen. Litho Govt Printers)

1999 (16 Feb). Traditional Costumes of Jewish Communities (1st series). T **610** and similar horiz design. Multicoloured. Two phosphor bands (2s.15) or no bands (3s.25). P 14.

1433	2s.15 Type **610**	1·90	1·70
1434	3s.25 Woman wearing sari, India	2·75	2·50
1433/1434	*Set of 2*	4·25	3·75
1433/1434	*Set of 2 with tabs*	5·00	4·50

See also Nos. 1457/1458.

611 Reconstruction of Ship

612 Memorial to Bedouin Soldiers, Rish Lakish

(Des Y. Granot. Litho Govt Printers)

1999 (19 Mar). Australia 99 International Stamp Exhibition, Melbourne. Excavation of Ancient Ship, *Sea of Galilee*. Sheet 100×63 mm containing T **611** and similar square design. Multicoloured. P 13.

MS1435 3s. Type **611**; 5s. Remains of ship	7·75	7·25

(Des H. Rashelbach, A. Vanooijen, Ruth Beckman, D. Goldberg, Masha Yozefpolsky and M. Sermoneta. Litho Govt Printers)

1999 (18 Apr). Jewish Contribution to World Culture (2nd series). Horiz designs as T **590**. Multicoloured. P 14.

1436	90a. Emile Durkheim (sociologist)	1·10	1·00
	a. Sheetlet of 6. Nos. 1436/1441	6·75	
1437	90a. Paul Ehrlich (medical researcher)	1·10	1·00
1438	90a. Rosa Luxemburg (revolutionary)	1·10	1·00
1439	90a. Norbert Wiener (mathematician)	1·10	1·00
1440	90a. Sigmund Freud (psychologist)	1·10	1·00
1441	90a. Martin Buber (philosopher)	1·10	1·00
1436/1441	*Set of 6*	6·00	5·50
1436/1441	*Set of 6 with tabs*	7·75	7·25

Nos. 1436/1441 were issued together in *se-tenant* sheetlets of six stamps.

1999 (18 Apr). Memorial Day. One phosphor band. P 14.

1442	**612**	1s.20 multicoloured	1·10	1·00
		With tab	1·30	1·20

613 Flags of UN, Israel and Other States

614 Holtzberg

(Des A. Kalderon. Litho Govt Printers)

1999 (18 Apr). 50th Anniversary of Israel's Admission to United Nations. Two phosphor bands. P 14.

1443	**613**	2s.30 multicoloured	1·90	1·70
		With tab	2·20	2·00

1999 (18 Apr). 75th Birth Anniversary of Simcha Holtzberg. P 14.

1444	**614**	2s.50 multicoloured	2·00	1·90
		With tab	2·40	2·20

615 *My Favourite Room* (detail)

(Des Myriam Voz and T. Martin. Photo Belgian Stamp Ptg Wks, Malines)

1999 (16 May). 50th Death Anniversary of James Ensor (artist). P 11½.

1445	**615**	2s.30 multicoloured	2·40	2·20
		With tab	2·75	2·50

A stamp of a similar design was issued by Belgium.

616 Ouza the Goose

(Des T. Kurtz. Litho Govt Printers)

1999 (22 June). *Lovely Butterfly* (children's television programme). T **616** and similar horiz designs. One phosphor band. Multicoloured. P 14.

1446	1s.20 Type **616**	95	85
	a. Strip of 3. Nos. 1446/1448	3·00	
1447	1s.20 Nooly the chick and Shabi the snail	95	85
1448	1s.20 Batz the tortoise and Pingi the penguin	95	85
1446/1448	*Set of 3*	2·50	2·30
1446/1448	*Set of 3 with tabs*	3·25	3·00

Nos. 1446/1448 were issued together in *se-tenant* strips of three stamps within the sheet.

617 *Church of the Holy Sepulchre, Jerusalem* (F. Geyer)

(Des H. Khoury. Litho Govt Printers)

1999 (22 June). Paintings of Christian Pilgrimage Sites (1st series). T **617** and similar horiz design. Multicoloured. P 14×13.

1449	3s. Type **617**	3·25	3·00
1450	3s. *Mary's Well, Nazareth* (W. H. Bartlett)	3·25	3·00
1451	3s. *The River Jordan* (E. Finden after A. W. Callcott)	3·25	3·00
1449/1451	*Set of 3*	8·75	8·00
1449/1451	*Set of 3 with tabs*	10·00	9·25

See also Nos. 1476/1478.

618 Illustration from Nehemia Emshel's Manuscript of *Musa-Nameh* by Shahin (poet)

(Des E. Carmeli. Litho Govt Printers)

1999 (22 June). 205th Death Anniversary of Rabbi Or Sharga (Persian Jew). P 14.

1452	**618**	5s.60 multicoloured	5·00	4·75
		With tab	5·25	5·00

(Des E. Lorentsov. Litho Govt Printers)

1999 (1 Sept). Festival of Sukkot. The Visiting Patriarchs (2nd series). Vert designs as T **579** showing paintings from the Sukkah of Rabbi Loew Immanuel of Szeged, Hungary. Multicoloured. One phosphor band (1s.20), two phosphor bands (1s.90, 2s.30) or no bands (5s.60). P 14.

1453	1s.20 Joseph interpreting Pharaoh's dreams	1·50	1·40
	a. Booklet pane. Nos. 1453×3 and 1454/1456	15·00	
1454	1s.90 Moses and the burning bush	2·00	1·90
1455	2s.30 Aaron and Holy Ark	2·20	2·00
1456	5s.60 David playing harp	6·00	5·50
1453/1456	*Set of 4*	10·50	9·75
1453/1456	*Set of 4 with tabs*	13·00	12·00

(Des A. Vanooijen. Litho Govt Printers)

1999 (1 Sept). Traditional Costumes of Jewish Communities (2nd series). Horiz designs as T **610**. Multicoloured. Two phosphor bands (2s.30) or no bands (3s.40). P 14.

1457	2s.30 Woman from Seus region, Morocco	2·20	2·00
1458	3s.40 Man from Bukhara	3·25	3·00
1457/1458	*Set of 2*	5·00	4·50
1457/1458	*Set of 2 with tabs*	6·00	5·50

619 Family and Part of 1948 250m. Stamp

620 18th-century Ceramic Urn showing Funeral Procession

(Des M. Kichka. Litho Govt Printers)

1999 (1 Sept). Stamp Day. P 14.

1459	**619**	5s.35 multicoloured	4·75	4·50
		With tab	5·25	4·75

(Des H. Khoury. Litho)

1999 (23 Nov). Jewish Culture in Slovakia. T **620** and similar vert design. Multicoloured. Two phosphor bands. P 14.

1460	1s.90 Type **620**	2·00	1·90
1461	1s.90 18th-century urn showing visit to a sick man	2·00	1·90
1460/1461	*Set of 2*	3·50	3·50
1460/1461	*Set of 2 with tabs*	4·75	4·50

Stamps of a similar design were issued by Slovakia.

621 View over Town from Arch of Columns

622 *The Street of the Jews in Old Jersusalem* (Ludwig Blum)

(Des Zina and Z. Roitman. Litho Govt Printers)

1999 (7 Dec). 50th Anniversary of Kiryat Shemona. One phosphor band. P 14.

1462	**621**	1s.20 multicoloured	1·10	1·00
		With tab	1·30	1·20

(Des A. Kalderon. Litho Govt Printers)

1999 (7 Dec). 50th Anniversary of Proclamation of Jerusalem as Capital. P 13×14.

1463	**622**	3s.40 multicoloured	4·25	4·00
		With tab	4·75	4·25

623 Sali

624 Children and Aliens holding Hands (Renana Barak)

(Des D. Goldberg. Litho Govt Printers)

1999 (7 Dec). 15th Death Anniversary of Admor (Rabbi) Israel Abihssira Sidna 'Baba Sali'. P 13.

1464	**623**	4s.40 multicoloured	4·75	4·25
		With tab	5·25	4·75

(Des M. Sofer. Litho Enschedé)

2000 (1 Jan). Stampin' the Future Children's Painting Competition. T **624** and similar horiz designs. Multicoloured. One phosphor band (1s.20) or two bands (others). P 13.

1465	1s.20 Type **624**	1·20	1·00
1466	1s.90 Man and robot (Tal Engelsten)	1·70	1·60
1467	2s.30 Futuristic street scene (Asia Aizenshteyn)	2·20	2·00

1468	3s.40 Alien and child's heads (Ortal Hasid)	3·25	3·00
1465/1468	*Set of 4*	7·50	6·75
1465/1468	*Set of 4 with tabs*	9·50	8·50

625 Globe, Joggers and Skiers

626 *The Little Mermaid*

(Des M. Pereg. Photo)

2000 (1 Jan). Year 2000. T **625** and similar square designs. Multicoloured. One phosphor band (1s.40), two bands (1s.90, 2s.30) or no bands (2s.80). P 13.

1469	1s.40 Type **625** (quality of life)	1·50	1·30
1470	1s.90 Da Vinci's *Proportion of Man*, ear of corn and scientist (biotechnology)	1·60	1·40
1471	2s.30 Computer, satellite dish and website address (information technology)	1·90	1·70
1472	2s.80 Moon's surface, astronaut and globe (space research)	2·75	2·50
1469/1472	*Set of 4*	7·00	6·25
1469/1472	*Set of 4 with tabs*	8·25	7·50

(Des S. Katz. Litho Govt Printers)

2000 (15 Feb). 125th Death Anniversary of Hans Christian Andersen (writer). T **626** and similar vert designs depicting illustrations by Samuel Katz. Multicoloured. One phosphor band (1s.20) or two bands (others). P 13×14.

1473	1s.20 Type **626**	85	80
1474	1s.90 *The Emperor's New Clothes*	1·70	1·60
1475	2s.30 *The Ugly Duckling*	2·20	2·00
1473/1475	*Set of 3*	4·25	4·00
1473/1475	*Set of 3 with tabs*	5·25	4·75

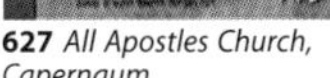

627 *All Apostles Church, Capernaum*

628 Fort Shuni (Zina Roitman)

(Des Zvika Roitman. Litho)

2000 (15 Feb). Paintings of Christian Pilgrimage Sites (2nd series). T **627** and similar horiz designs depicting paintings by Zina Roitman. Multicoloured. Two phosphor bands. P 14×13.

1476	1s.40 Type **627**	1·30	1·20
1477	1s.90 *St Andrew's Church, Jerusalem*	2·00	1·80
1478	2s.30 *The Church of the Visitation, Ein Kerem*	2·30	2·10
1476/1478	*Set of 3*	5·00	4·50
1476/1478	*Set of 3 with tabs*	6·00	5·50

(Des Y. Granot. Photo Questa)

2000 (15 Feb). Buildings and Historical Sites. Two phosphor bands. P 14 (with one elliptical hole on each vert side).

1479	**628** 2s.30 multicoloured	2·00	1·80
	With tab	2·20	2·00

629 King Hussein

630 Monument to Jewish Volunteers in British Army, Jerusalem

(Des D. Goldberg. Litho)

2000 (15 Feb). King Hussein of Jordan Commemoration. P 14.

1480	**629** 4s.40 multicoloured	4·00	3·50
	With tab	4·25	4·00

(Des D. Goldberg. Litho Govt Printers)

2000 (3 May). Memorial Day. One phosphor band. P 14.

1481	**630** 1s.20 multicoloured	1·50	1·30
	With tab	1·60	1·40

631 Fox yawning

632 Mobile Telephone

(Des A. Balaban and A. Vanooijen. Litho)

2000 (3 May). Endangered Species. Blanford's Fox (*Vulpes cana*). T **631** and similar vert designs. Multicoloured. One phosphor band. P 14.

1482	1s.20 Type **631**	1·00	90
	a. Block of 4. Nos. 1482/1485	4·25	
	b. Strip of 4. Nos. 1482/1485, plus central label	4·25	
1483	1s.20 Fox watching bird	1·00	90
1484	1s.20 Fox	1·00	90
1485	1s.20 Three Foxes	1·00	90
1482/1485	*Set of 4*	3·50	3·25
1482/1485	*Set of 4 with tabs*	5·25	4·75

Nos. 1482/1485 were issued together in either *se-tenant* blocks or strips of four stamps within sheetlets of eight.

(Des I. Gabai. Litho Govt Printers)

2000 (3 May). International Communications Day. Two phosphor bands. P 13.

1486	**632** 2s.30 multicoloured	2·20	2·00
	With tab	2·50	2·20

633 Cross, Crescent and Menorah

634 Bach (bust) and Manuscript of *Chaconne for Violin Solo*

(Des Z. Roitman. Litho Govt printers)

2000 (3 May). The Holy Land. P 13.

1487	**633** 3s.40 multicoloured	4·25	4·00
	With tab	5·00	4·50

(Des D. Goldberg. Litho Govt Printers)

2000 (3 May). 250th Death Anniversary of Johann Sebastian Bach (composer). P 13.

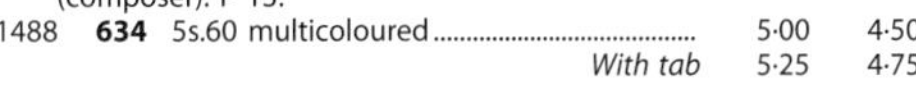

1488	**634** 5s.60 multicoloured	5·00	4·50
	With tab	5·25	4·75

635 Fortified Stone Building, Juara (Zina Roitman)

636 Couscous

(Des Y. Granot. Photo Enschedé)

2000 (25 July). Buildings and Historical Sites. Phosphorescent paper. P 14 (with one elliptical hole on each vert side).

1489 **635** 1s.20 multicoloured .... 1·50 1·30
With tab 1·60 1·40

(Des O. Meiray. Litho Enschedé)

2000 (25 July). Traditional Foods. T **636** and similar vert designs. Multicoloured. One phosphor band (1s.40) or two bands (others). P 13½×13.

1490 1s.40 Type **636** .... 1·30 1·20
a. Booklet pane. No. 1490, 1491×2 and 1492×3 .... 12·00
1491 1s.90 Stuffed Carp .... 1·60 1·40
1492 2s.30 Falafel .... 2·30 2·10
1490/1492 *Set of 3* .... 4·75 4·25
1490/1492 *Set of 3 with tabs* .... 5·75 5·00

637 Olympic Rings and Koala

638 King Hassan II

(Des A. Vanooijen. Litho Govt Printers)

2000 (25 July). Olympic Games, Sydney. P 13.

1493 **637** 2s.80 multicoloured .... 3·00 2·75
With tab 3·25 2·75

(Des D. Goldberg. Litho Govt Printers)

2000 (25 July). First Death Anniversary of King Hassan II of Morocco. P 14.

1494 **638** 4s.40 multicoloured .... 4·00 3·50
With tab 4·25 4·00

639 Young Boy and Girl

640 Adam and Eve

(Des H. Shtayer. Litho)

2000 (19 Sept). Festivals. New Year Cards. T **639** and similar vert designs. Multicoloured. One phosphor band (1s.20) or two bands (others).

1495 1s.20 Type **639** .... 1·20 1·00
1496 1s.90 Young woman holding Zionist flag .... 1·60 1·40
1497 2s.30 Man presenting flowers to woman .... 2·00 1·80
1495/1497 *Set of 3* .... 4·25 3·75
1495/1497 *Set of 3 with tabs* .... 5·25 4·75

(Des Ela Whitten. Litho Govt Printers)

2000 (19 Sept). Dental Health Campaign. Two phosphor bands. P 14.

1498 **640** 2s.20 multicoloured .... 2·50 2·20
With tab 2·50 2·30

641 Menorah and Interior of Synagogue

642 Revivim Observatory, Negev (Zina Roitman)

(Des Zina and Z. Roitman. Litho Govt Printers)

2000 (19 Sept). Dohany Synagogue, Budapest. P 13×14.

1499 **641** 5s.60 multicoloured .... 4·75 4·25
With tab 5·25 4·75

A stamp of a similar design was issued by Hungary.

(Des Y. Granot. Photo Enschedé)

2000 (5 Dec). Buildings and Historical Sites. Two phosphor bands. P 14 (with one elliptical hole on each vert side).

1500 **642** 2s.20 multicoloured .... 2·20 2·00
With tab 2·30 2·10

643 Struthiomimus running

644 Robot (*I, Robot*, Isaac Asimov)

(Des T. Kurz. Litho Govt Printers)

2000 (5 Dec). Dinosaurs. T **643** and similar square designs. Multicoloured. Two phosphor bands. P 13.

1501 2s.20 Type **643** .... 1·70 1·60
a. Strip of 3. Nos. 1501/1503 .... 5·25
1502 2s.20 Head of Struthiomimus .... 1·70 1·60
1503 2s.30 Struthiomimus standing by tree .... 1·70 1·60
1501/1503 *Set of 3* .... 4·50 4·25
1501/1503 *Set of 3 with tabs* .... 5·75 5·00

Nos. 1501/1503 were issued together in horizontal or vertical *se-tenant* strips of three stamps within sheetlets of nine.

(Des A. Katz. Litho)

2000 (5 Dec). Science Fiction Novels. T **644** and similar horiz designs. Multicoloured. P 14.

1504 2s.80 Type **644** .... 2·75 2·50
1505 3s.40 Time travel machine (*The Time Machine*, H. G. Wells) .... 3·25 3·00
1506 5s.60 Space rocket (*Journey to the Moon*, Jules Verne) .... 5·00 4·50
1504/1506 *Set of 3* .... 10·00 9·00
1504/1506 *Set of 3 with tabs* .... 11·00 10·50

645 Open Book

646 Tof

(Des A. Shevo. Litho Govt Printers)

2000 (5 Dec). *Aleppo Codex* (earliest known manuscript of the Bible). P 13.

1507 **645** 4s.40 multicoloured .... 4·00 3·50
With tab 4·25 4·00

(Des E. Lorentsov. Litho De La Rue (1508/1529) or Govt Printers (others))

2001 (13 Feb). Hebrew Alphabet. T **646** and similar multicoloured designs each showing a different Hebrew letter. P 15 (No. 1508/1529) or 14 (others).

1508 10a. Type **646** 15 15
a. Sheetlet of 22. Nos. 1508/1529 .... 3·50
1509 10a. Shin 15 15
1510 10a. Reish 15 15
1511 10a. Kuf 15 15
1512 10a. Tzadi Kekufa 15 15
1513 10a. Pay Kekufah 15 15
1514 10a. Ayin 15 15
1515 10a. Samech 15 15
1516 10a. Nun 15 15
1517 10a. Mem 15 15
1518 10a. Lamed 15 15
1519 10a. Chof Kefufa 15 15
1520 10a. Yud 15 15
1521 10a. Tes 15 15
1522 10a. Ches 15 15
1523 10a. Zayin 15 15
1524 10a. Vov 15 15

1525	10a. Heh	15	15
1526	10a. Daled	15	15
1527	10a. Gimel	15	15
1528	10a. Beis	15	15
1529	10a. Aleph	15	15
1530	10a. Tzade Peshuta	15	15
	a. Horiz strip of 5. Nos. 1530/1534	80	
1531	10a. Pay Peshuta	15	15
1532	10a. Chof Peshuta	15	15
1533	10a. Mem Stumah	15	15
1534	10a. Vov	15	15
1535	1s. Aleph and Beis	75	65
1508/1535	*Set of 28*	4·25	4·25
1508/1535	*Set of 28 with tabs*	4·75	4·25

Nos. 1508/1529 were issued together in sheetlets of 22, the stamps arranged in two horizontal *tête-bêche* rows.

Nos. 1530/1534 were issued together in sheetlets of ten stamps comprising of two horizontal strips *tête-bêche*.

647 Pupils in front of School (Yavne'el)

648 Segera Spring, Ilaniyya

(Des M. Eshel. Litho Govt Printers)

2001 (13 Feb). Village Centenaries. T **647** and similar horiz designs. Multicoloured. Two phosphor bands (2s.50) or no bands (others). P 14.

1536	2s.50 Type **647**	2·75	2·50
1537	4s.70 Farmers, horses and cart (Kefar Tavor)	4·25	4·00
1538	5s.90 Cart full of flowers (Menahamia)	5·00	4·50
1536/1538	*Set of 3*	11·00	10·00
1536/1538	*Set of 3 with tabs*	13·00	11·50

(Des Y. Granot. Photo Questa)

2001 (13 Feb). Buildings and Historical Sites. P 14 (with one elliptical hole on each vert side).

1539	**648** 3s.40 multicoloured	3·25	3·00
	With tab	3·50	3·00

649 Prairie Gentian

650 Lesser Kestrel

(Des A. Vanooijen. Litho Govt Printers)

2001 (18 Mar). Flowers. T **649** and similar vert designs. Multicoloured. One phosphor band. P 14.

1540	1s.20 Type **649**	1·20	1·00
	a. Horiz strip of 4. Nos. 1540/1543 plus 4 labels	5·00	
1541	1s.20 Barberton Daisy	1·20	1·00
1542	1s.20 Star of Bethlehem	1·20	1·00
1543	1s.20 Florists Calla	1·20	1·00
1540/1543	*Set of 4*	4·25	3·50
1540/1543	*Set of 4 with tabs*	5·25	4·75

Nos. 1540/1543 were issued together in sheets of 16, each stamp having a *se-tenant* label attached at the left. Visitors to the Jerusalem 2001 International Stamp Exhibition could, for an extra charge, personalise the sheets by having a photograph taken at the show and printed on the labels.

(Des A. Vanooijen. Litho)

2001 (18 Mar). Endangered Species. T **650** and similar vert designs. Multicoloured. One phosphor band (1s.20) or two bands (others). P 14.

1544	1s.20 Type **650**	1·20	1·00
	a. Booklet pane. Nos. 1544/1547, each×2, with margins all round	16·00	
1545	1s.70 Kuhl's Pipistrelle	1·60	1·40
1546	2s.10 Roe Deer	2·20	2·00
1547	2s.50 Greek Tortoise	2·50	2·20
1544/1547	*Set of 4*	6·75	6·00
1544/1547	*Set of 4 with tabs*	8·00	7·25

651 Jerusalem (detail of ceramic tile, Ze'ev Rabin)

(Des Y. Gabay. Litho Govt Printers)

2001 (18 Mar). Jerusalem 2001 International Stamp Exhibition. Sheet 131×67 mm. P 14.

MS1548	**651** 10s. multicoloured	11·50	10·50

652 Monument for the Fallen Nahal Soldiers, Pardes Hanna

653 Marquise Diamond

(Des M. Pereg. Litho Govt Printers)

2001 (18 Apr). Memorial Day. One phosphor band. P 13.

1549	**652** 1s.20 multicoloured	1·60	1·40
	With tab	1·70	1·60

(Des M. Pereg. Litho Questa)

2001 (23 May). Belgica 2001 International Stamp Exhibition, Brussels. Diamonds. Sheet 117×70 mm containing T **653** and similar vert designs. Multicoloured. P 15×14½.

MS1550	1s.40 Type **653**; 1s.70 Round diamond; 4s.70 Square diamond	11·00	9·75

654 Sha'ar HaGay Inn

655 Shrine of the Bahá'í and Terraces

(Des Y. Granot. Photo Enschedé)

2001 (23 May). Buildings and Historical Sites. Two phosphor bands. P 14 (with one elliptical hole on each vert side).

1551	**654** 2s. multicoloured	2·00	1·80
	With tab	2·20	2·00

(Des M. Pereg. Photo Questa)

2001 (23 May). Shrine of the Báb, Haifa. P 13×13½.

1552	**655** 3s. multicoloured	3·00	2·50
	With tab	3·25	2·75

656 Prayer Shawl and Tassel

657 Hebron

(Des E. Carmeli. Litho)

2001 (23 May). Karaite Jews. P 14.

1553	**656** 5s.60 multicoloured	5·00	4·50
	With tab	5·50	5·00

(Des A. Kalderon. Litho)

2001 (17 July). Ceramic Tiles. T **657** and similar vert designs showing tiles from façade of Ahad Ha'am Municipal Boys School, Tel Aviv. Multicoloured. One phosphor band (1s.20) or two bands (others). P 13×14.

1554	1s.20 Type **657**	1·00	90
1555	1s.40 Jaffa	1·30	1·20
1556	1s.90 Haifa	1·90	1·70
1557	2s.30 Tiberias	2·50	2·20
1554/1557	*Set of 4*	6·00	5·50
1554/1557	*Set of 4 with tabs*	7·25	6·50

658 *and me? I want to ride in a hot air balloon* (Eyar Shteiman)

659 Clasped Hands and Hikers

(Des Sharon Murro. Litho Questa)

2001 (17 July). PHILA NIPPON '01 International Stamp Exhibition, Tokyo. Winning Entries in Children's Painting Competition. Sheet 120×75 mm containing T **658** and similar vert designs. Multicoloured. P 15×14½.

MS1558	1s.20 Type **658**; 1s.40 *I wish I had a kitten* (Rony Schechter-Malve); 2s.50 *My dream is to be a vet* (Dana Srebrnik); 4s.70 *to swim with dolphins* (Hila Malka)	11·00	9·75

(Des R. Radzeli. Litho Govt Printers)

2001 (17 July). Israeli Council of Youth Movements. P 14.

1559	**659** 5s.60 multicoloured	5·00	4·50
	With tab	5·50	5·00

660 Soldier and Peace Dove

661 Rustaveli

(Des H. Shtayer. Litho)

2001 (3 Sept). Festivals. New Year Cards. T **660** and similar vert designs. Multicoloured. One phosphor band (1s.20) or two bands (others). P 14.

1560	1s.20 Type **660**	1·00	90
1561	1s.90 Two women	1·70	1·60
1562	2s.30 Boy carrying flowers	2·30	2·10
1560/1562	*Set of 3*	4·50	4·25
1560/1562	*Set of 3 with tabs*	5·50	5·00

(Des Y. Granot. Litho)

2001 (3 Sept). 32nd Anniversary of the Translation into Hebrew of *The Knight in a Tiger's Skin* (poem by Shota Rustaveli). P 13×14.

1563	**661** 3s.40 multicoloured	3·00	2·75
	With tab	3·25	2·75

A stamp of a similar design was issued by Georgia.

662 Field, Leaves and Sky

(Des M. Sofer. Litho)

2001 (3 Sept). Centenary of Jewish National Fund. P 14.

1564	**662** 5s.60 multicoloured	4·75	4·25
	With tab	5·00	4·50

663 Amichai

(Des R. Hartman. Litho Govt Printers)

2001 (3 Sept). First Death Anniversary of Yehuda Amichai (poet). P 13×14.

1565	**663** 5s.60 multicoloured	4·75	4·25
	With tab	5·25	4·75

664 Sunshade on Beach

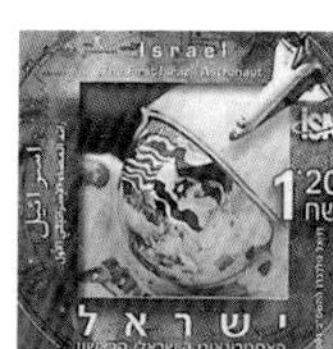

665 Flags reflected in Helmet Visor

(Des Yael Minian. Photo Enschedé)

2001 (11 Dec). Coastal Conservation. P 13.

1566	**664** 10s. multicoloured	9·00	8·25
	With tab	9·50	8·50

(Des D. Goldberg. Litho)

2001 (11 Dec). First Israeli Astronaut. One phosphor band. P 13.

1567	**665** 1s.20 multicoloured	1·30	1·20
	With tab	1·50	1·30

666 Child Painting (Yaffa Dahan)

667 *Heinrich Heine* (painting, Moritz Daniel Oppenheim)

(Des Y. Granot. Litho)

2001 (11 Dec). 50th Anniversary of Association for Rehabilitation of the Disabled (AKIM). Two phosphor bands. P 13×14.

1568	**666** 2s.20 multicoloured	2·00	1·80
	With tab	2·20	2·00

(Des H. Khoury. Litho)

2001 (11 Dec). 145th Death Anniversary of Heinrich Heine (poet and satirist). P 13×14.

1569	**667** 4s.40 multicoloured	4·00	3·50
	With tab	4·25	4·00

668 *Israel* in Braille

669 Lily

(Des I. Gabay. Litho and embossed Questa)

2001 (11 Dec). Centenary of Institute for the Blind, Jerusalem. P 14½.

1570 **668** 5s.60 multicoloured .... 5·50 5·00
With tab 5·75 5·25

(Des A. Vanooijen. Litho)

2002 (24 Feb). One phosphor band. P 14.

1571 **669** 1s.20 multicoloured .... 1·20 1·00
With tab 1·30 1·20

670 Hat and Rattle (Adar)

671 Field Mushroom

(Des Miri Sofer. Photo Enschedé)

2002 (24 Feb). Months of the Year. T **670** and similar vert designs. Multicoloured. Phosphorised paper.

(a) Sheet stamps. Ordinary gum. P 14

1572 1s.20 Type **670** .... 1·20 1·10
a. Sheetlet of 12. Nos, 1572/1583 .... 15·00
1573 1s.20 Almond twig, flowers and fruit (Shevat) 1·20 1·10
1574 1s.20 Grapefruit and Anemones (Tevet) .... 1·20 1·10
1575 1s.20 Spinning top and candles (Kislev) .... 1·20 1·10
1576 1s.20 Autumn leaves (Heshvan) .... 1·20 1·10
1577 1s.20 Ram's horn and Pomegranates (Tishrei) 1·20 1·10
1578 1s.20 Cup, unleavened bread and flowers (Nisan) .... 1·20 1·10
1579 1s.20 Bow, arrows and Oleanders (Iyyar) .... 1·20 1·10
1580 1s.20 Sickle and grains (Sivian) .... 1·20 1·10
1581 1s.20 Sunflower and shells (Tammuz) .... 1·20 1·10
1582 1s.20 Couple wearing wedding dress and Grapes (Av) .... 1·20 1·10
1583 1s.20 Torah, cotton and Figs (Elul) .... 1·20 1·10
1572/1583 *Set of 12* .... 13·00 12·00
1572/1583 *Set of 12 with tabs* .... 16·00 14·50

(b) Booklet stamps. Self-adhesive gum. Die-cut perf 16

1584 1s.20 As Type **670** .... 1·30 1·20
1585 1s.20 Almond twig, flowers and fruit (Shevat) 1·30 1·20
1586 1s.20 Grapefruit and Anemones (Tevet) .... 1·30 1·20
1587 1s.20 Spinning top and candles (Kislev) .... 1·30 1·20
1588 1s.20 Autumn leaves (Heshvan) .... 1·30 1·20
1589 1s.20 Ram's horn and Pomegranates (Tishrei) 1·30 1·20
1590 1s.20 Cup, unleavened bread and flowers (Nisan) .... 1·30 1·20
1591 1s.20 Bow, arrows and Oleanders (Iyyar) .... 1·30 1·20
1592 1s.20 Sickle and grains (Sivian) .... 1·30 1·20
1593 1s.20 Sunflower and shells (Tammuz) .... 1·30 1·20
1594 1s.20 Couple wearing wedding dress and Grapes (Av) .... 1·30 1·20
1595 1s.20 Torah, cotton and Figs (Elul) .... 1·30 1·20
1584/1595 *Set of 12* .... 14·00 13·00

Nos. 1572/1583 were issued in sheetlets of 12, the stamps arranged in two horizontal *tête-bêche* rows. The booklet stamps, Nos. 1584/1595 were arranged similarly.

(Des A. Vanooijen. Litho)

2002 (24 Feb). Fungi. T **671** and similar vert designs. Multicoloured. Two phosphor bands. P 13×14.

1596 1s.90 Type **671** (*Agaricus campestri*) (inscr 'campester') .... 1·70 1·60
1597 2s.20 Fly Agaric (*Amanita muscaria*) .... 1·90 1·70
1598 2s.80 Granulated Boletus (*Suillus granulatus*). 2·50 2·20
1596/1598 *Set of 3* .... 5·50 5·00
1596/1598 *Set of 3 with tabs* .... 6·50 5·75

672 'Ladino' in Rashi Script

673 Military Police Memorial and Eternal Flame, Bet Lid

(Des B-T Nahmias and Z. Roitman. Litho)

2002 (24 Feb). Judaic Languages. T **672** and similar vert design. Multicoloured. Two phosphor bands. P 13×14.

1599 2s.10 Type **672** (Judeo-Spanish) .... 1·90 1·70
1600 2s.10 Peacock (Yiddish) .... 1·90 1·70
1599/1600 *Set of 2* .... 3·50 3·00
1599/1600 *Set of 2 with tabs* .... 4·00 3·75

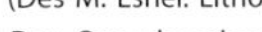

(Des M. Eshel. Litho)

2002 (10 Apr). Memorial Day. One phosphor band. P 14.

1601 **673** 1s.20 multicoloured .... 1·30 1·20
With tab 1·50 1·30

674 Heinrich Graetz

675 King and Torah

(Des A. Vanooijen. Litho)

2002 (10 Apr). Historians (1st series). T **674** and similar vert design. Multicoloured. Two phosphor bands. P 14.

1602 2s.20 Type **674** .... 1·90 1·70
1603 2s.20 Simon Dubnow .... 1·90 1·70
1604 2s.20 Benzion Dinur .... 1·90 1·70
1605 2s.20 Yitzhak Baer .... 1·90 1·70
1602/1605 *Set of 4* .... 6·75 6·00
1602/1605 *Set of 4 with tabs* .... 8·00 7·25

See also Nos. 1686/1688.

(Des A. Shevo. Litho)

2002 (10 Apr). Hakel Ceremony. P 13×14.

1606 **675** 4s.70 multicoloured .... 4·25 4·00
With tab 4·75 4·25

676 '50' and Wheels

677 Cable Cars, Menara

(Des Y. Lemel. Litho)

2002 (10 Apr). 50th Anniversary of ILAN (Israel Foundation for Disabled Children). P 13×14.

1607 **676** 5s.90 multicoloured .... 4·75 4·25
With tab 5·00 4·50

(Des M. Eshel. Litho)

2002 (18 June). Tourism. Cable Cars. T **677** and similar vert designs. Two phosphor bands. Multicoloured. P 14.

1608 2s.20 Type **677** .... 1·90 1·70
1609 2s.20 Rosh Haniqra .... 1·90 1·70
1610 2s.20 Haifa .... 1·90 1·70
1611 2s.20 Massada .... 1·90 1·70
1608/1611 *Set of 4* .... 6·75 6·00
1608/1611 *Set of 4 with tabs* .... 8·00 7·25

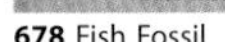

678 Fish Fossil

679 Hatsar Kinneret

(Des M. Pereg. Litho)

2002 (18 June). Geology. Sheet 115×70 mm containing T **678** and similar vert designs. Multicoloured. P 14.

MS1612 2s.20 Type **678**; 3s.40 Copper mineral; 4s.40 Ammonite	10·00	9·00

(Des Zina Roitman and Y. Granot. Photo Questa)

2002 (10 June). Buildings and Historical Sites. P 14 (with one elliptical hole on each vert side).

1613	**679**	3s.30 multicoloured	3·25	3·00
		With tab	3·50	3·00

680 Rechavam Ze'evy

681 Grape Scissors and Grapes

(Des Tuvia Kurtz and D. Goldberg. Litho)

2002 (27 Aug). First Death Anniversary of Rechavam Ze'evy (Minister for tourism). One phosphor band. P 14.

1614	**680**	1s.20 multicoloured	1·20	1·00
		With tab	1·30	1·20

(Des Y. Gabay. Litho)

2002 (27 Aug). Festivals. Wine. T **681** and similar vert designs. Multicoloured. One phosphor band (1s.20) or two phosphor bands (others). P 14.

1615	1s.20 Type **681**	1·00	90
1616	1s.90 Cork screw and cork	1·70	1·60
1617	2s.30 Wine glass and bottle	2·20	2·00
1615/1617	*Set of 3*	4·50	4·00
1615/1617	*Set of 3 with tabs*	5·25	4·75

682 Golden Eagle

(Des Tuvia Kurtz and Y. Granot. Litho Questa)

2002 (27 Aug). Birds of Jordan Valley. T **682** and similar horiz designs. Multicoloured. Two phosphor bands. P 14½×14.

1618	2s.20 Type **682**	1·90	1·70
1619	2s.20 Black Stork	1·90	1·70
1620	2s.20 Crane	1·90	1·70
1618/1620	*Set of 3*	5·25	4·50
1618/1620	*Set of 3 with tabs*	6·00	5·50

683 Kadoorie School

684 Baruch Spinoza

(Des Zina Roitman and Y. Granot. Photo Questa)

2002 (27 Aug). Buildings and Historical Sites. P 14 (with one elliptical hole on each vert side).

1621	**683**	4s.60 multicoloured	4·00	3·50
		With tab	4·25	4·00

(Des Ruth Bekman-Malka and H. Khoury. Litho)

2002 (27 Aug). 370th Birth Anniversary of Baruch (Benedictus) Spinoza. P 13×14.

1622	**684**	5s.90 multicoloured	4·75	4·25
		With tab	5·25	4·75

685 Menorah Candlestick

686 Abba Ahimeir

(Des I. Gabay. Litho Enschedé)

2002 (26 Nov)–**03**. P 15.

1623	**685**	20a. scarlet-vermilion	30	20
1624		30a. olive brown	30	20
1625		40a. slate-green (11.2.03)	30	20
1626		50a. brown olive (11.2.03)	30	25
1627		1s. deep reddish violet	75	65
1628		1s.30 steel blue (11.2.03)	85	80
1623/1628		*Set of 6*	2·50	2·10
1623/1628		*Set of 6 with tabs*	3·25	2·75

See also Nos. 1918*a*/1918*c* and 1979*a*.

No. 1629 is vacant.

(Des I. Gaby. Litho)

2002 (26 Nov). Political Journalists. T **686** and similar horiz designs. Multicoloured. One phosphor band (1s.20). P 14.

1630	1s.20 Type **686**	1·00	90
1631	3s.30 Israel Eldad	2·50	2·30
1632	4s.70 Moshe Beilinson	3·75	3·25
1633	5s.90 Rabbi Binyamin (Yehoshua Radler-Feldman)	4·75	4·25
1630/1633	*Set of 4*	11·00	9·75
1630/1633	*Set of 4 with tabs*	13·00	11·50

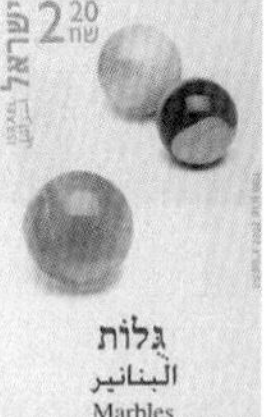

687 Marbles

688 Students

(Des S. Murro. Litho)

2002 (26 Nov). Stamp Day. Children's Toys. T **687** and similar vert designs. Multicoloured. Two phosphor bands. P 14.

1634	2s.20 Type **687**	1·90	1·70
1635	2s.20 Spinning-top	1·90	1·70
1636	2s.20 Five stones	1·90	1·70
1637	2s.20 Yo-yo	1·90	1·70
1634/1637	*Set of 4*	6·75	6·00
1634/1637	*Set of 4 with tabs*	8·00	7·25

(Des Ruth Bekman-Malka. Litho)

2003 (11 Feb). Yeshivot Hahesder (college). One phosphor band. P 14.

1638	**688**	1s.20 multicoloured	1·20	1·00
		With tab	1·30	1·20

689 *11 September 2001* (Michael Gross)

690 Wright Glider (1902)

2003 (11 Feb). Two phosphor bands. Litho. P 13×14.

1639	**689**	2s.30 multicoloured	2·00	1·80
		With tab	2·20	2·00

(Des A. Vanooijen. Litho)

2003 (11 Feb). Centenary of Powered Flight. T **690** and similar horiz designs. Multicoloured. Two phosphor bands. P 14.

1640	2s.30 Type **690**	1·60	1·40
1641	3s.30 Engine and Wright brothers	2·50	2·20

1642 5s.90 Orville Wright flying *Wright Flyer* .... 4·00 3·50
1640/1642 *Set of 3* .... 7·25 6·50
1640/1642 *Set of 3 with tabs* .... 8·75 7·75

691 Memorial Monument, Mount Herzl

(Des Y. Granot. Litho)

2003 (11 Feb). P 14×13.
1643 **691** 4s.70 multicoloured .... 3·50 3·00
With tab 3·75 3·25

692 Burnt-out Vehicle

693 Opened Box

(Des Eva Cohen Saban. Litho)

2003 (27 Apr). Memorial Day. One phosphor band. P 14.
1644 **692** 1s.20 multicoloured .... 1·00 90
With tab 1·20 1·00

(Des E. Carmeli, A. Shevo and M. Kichka. Litho)

2003 (27 Apr). Greetings Stamps (1st issue). T **693** and similar vert designs. Multicoloured. One phosphor band. P 14.
1645 (1s.20) Type **693** .... 1·00 90
1646 (1s.20) Boy and growing heart .... 1·00 90
1647 (1s.20) Married couple .... 1·00 90
1645/1647 *Set of 3* .... 2·75 2·40
1645/1647 *Set of 3 with tabs* .... 3·50 3·00
See also Nos. 1655/1657.

694 Ya'akov Meridor

695 Star of David

(Des Ruth Beckman-Malka. Litho)

2003 (27 Apr). 90th Birth Anniversary of Ya'akov Meridor (politician). Two phosphor bands. P 13.
1648 **694** 1s.90 multicoloured .... 1·60 1·40
With tab 1·70 1·60

(Des G. Sagi. Litho)

2003 (27 Apr). Holocaust Memorial Day. Two phosphor bands. P 13.
1649 **695** 2s.20 multicoloured .... 2·20 2·00
With tab 2·30 2·10

696 Ya'akov Dori

697 Sheikh Ameen Tarif

(Des Ruth Beckman-Malka. Litho)

2003 (27 Apr). 30th Death Anniversary of Ya'akov Dori (Chief of Staff 1948–1950). Two phosphor bands. P 13.
1650 **696** 2s.20 multicoloured .... 2·20 2·00
With tab 2·30 2·10

(Des Ruth Beckman-Malka. Litho)

2003 (27 Apr). Tenth Death Anniversary of Sheikh Ameen Tarif (Druze (religious sect) leader). Two phosphor bands. P 13.
1651 **697** 2s.80 multicoloured .... 2·30 2·10
With tab 2·50 2·20

698 Soldier

(Des D. Goldberg. Litho)

2003 (27 Apr). Jewish Immigration from Yemen, 1881. P 14.
1652 **698** 3s.30 multicoloured .... 2·75 2·50
With tabs 3·00 2·50

699 Paper Aeroplane and Computer Circuit Board

700 '55'

(Des G. Almaliah and A. Shevo. Litho)

2003 (27 Apr). 50th Anniversary of Israel Aircraft Industries. P 14.
1653 **699** 3s.30 multicoloured .... 2·75 2·50
With tab 3·00 2·50

(Des E. Hendel. Litho)

2003 (27 Apr). 55th Anniversary of Israel. P 14.
1654 **700** 5s.90 multicoloured .... 4·00 3·50
With tab 4·25 4·00

(Des Zina Roitman, B. Maori and W. Bulba. Litho)

2003 (24 June). Greetings Stamps (2nd issue). Vert designs as T **693**. Multicoloured. One phosphor band. P 14.
1655 (1s.20) Flowers .... 1·00 90
1656 (1s.20) Air balloon .... 1·00 90
1657 (1s.20) Boy holding teddy bear .... 1·00 90
1655/1657 *Set of 4* .... 2·75 2·40
1655/1657 *Set of 4 with tabs* .... 3·50 3·00

701 Prague Jewish Community Flag (15th-century)

702 Coast, Ruined Castle and Houses (Atlit)

(Des A. Vanooijen. Litho)

2003 (24 June). Development of Israel State Flag. T **701** and similar horiz designs. Multicoloured. Two phosphor bands (No. 1658/1659). P 14.
1658 1s.90 Type **701** .... 1·40 1·20
1659 2s.30 Ness Ziona (Jewish settlement) (1891) .... 1·60 1·40
1660 4s.70 Draft design from *Der Judenstaat* (Theodor Herzl) (1896) .... 3·25 3·00
1661 5s.90 State flag (1948) .... 4·00 3·50
1658/1661 *Set of 4* .... 9·25 8·25
1658/1661 *Set of 4 with tabs* .... 11·00 9·75

(Des Zina and Zvika Roitman. Litho)

2003 (24 June). Village Centenaries. T **702** and similar horiz designs. Multicoloured. P 14.
1662 3s.30 Type **702** .... 2·50 2·20
1663 3s.30 Tractor, crops and houses (Givat-Ada) .... 2·50 2·20
1664 3s.30 Houses and bungalow amongst trees (Kfar-Saba) .... 2·50 2·20
1662/1664 *Set of 3* .... 6·75 6·00
1662/1664 *Set of 3 with tabs* .... 7·75 7·00

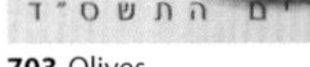

703 Olives

704 Teddy Bear and Page of Testimony

(Des Zvika Roitman. Litho)

2003 (9 Sept). Olive Oil Production. T **703** and similar horiz designs. Multicoloured. One phosphor band (1s.30) or two phosphor bands (others). P 14.

1665	1s.30 Type **703**	1·30	1·20
	a. Booklet pane. Nos. 1665, 1666×2, 1667×3	11·00	
1666	1s.90 Mill stone and wheel	1·70	1·60
1667	2s.30 Oil	2·00	1·80
1665/1667	*Set of 3*	4·50	4·25
1665/1667	*Set of 3 with tabs*	5·50	5·00

(Des M. Eshel and Y. Gabay. Litho)

2003 (9 Sept). 50th Anniversary of Vad Yashem (Holocaust remembrance organisation). T **704** and similar vert design. Multicoloured. Two phosphor bands. P 14.

1668	2s.20 Type **704**	2·00	1·80
	a. Pair. Nos. 1668/1669	4·25	3·75
1669	2s.20 Rail tracks and list of forced labourers	2·00	1·80
1668/1669	*Set of 2*	3·50	3·25
1668/1669	*Set of 2 with tabs*	4·25	4·00

Nos. 1668/1669 were issued in horizontal and vertical *se-tenant* pairs within sheets of 15 stamps.

705 Deer and Flowers (Karakashian-Balian studio, *c.*1940)

(Des H. Khoury. Litho D.L.R.)

2003 (9 Sept). Armenian Ceramics in Jerusalem. Sheet 120×65 mm containing T **705** and similar circular designs showing ceramic patterns. Multicoloured. P 10.

MS1670	2s.30 Type **705**; 3s.30 Bird (Stepan Karakashian, *c.*1980); 4s.70 Tree of life (Marie Balian, *c.* 1990)	11·00	9·75

(Ruth Beckman-Malka. Photo Enschedé)

2003 (3 Nov). Booklet Stamp. No value expressed. Vert design as T **606**. Self-adhesive. Die-cut perf 14.

1671	**606** (1s.30) bright green and bright lilac	1·20	1·10
	With tabs	1·30	1·20

706 Yehoshua Hankin

707 Boy riding Bicycle

(Des Ruth Beckman-Malka. Litho)

2003 (4 Nov). 58th Death Anniversary of Yehoshua Hankin (Zionist pioneer). P 14.

1672	**706** 6s.20 multicoloured	6·25	5·50
	With tab	6·50	5·75

(Des Tamar Moshkovitz. Litho D.L.R.)

2003 (9 Dec). Philately Day. Children and Wheels. T **707** and similar square designs. Multicoloured. P 14.

1673	1s.30 Type **707**	1·10	1·00
	a. Strip of 4. Nos. 1673/1676	4·75	
1674	1s.30 Girl on roller skates	1·10	1·00
1675	1s.30 Girl pushing scooter	1·10	1·00
1676	1s.30 Boy on skateboard	1·10	1·00
1673/1676	*Set of 4*	4·00	3·50
1673/1676	*Set of 4 with tabs*	4·75	4·25

Nos. 1673/1676 were issued in horizontal *se-tenant* strips of four within sheets of 12 stamps.

708 Leibowitch Family and Administrative Building, Zikhron Ya'akov

709 Aharon David Gordon

(Des Y. Gabay. Litho)

2003 (9 Dec). First and Second Aliya (immigration to Eretz Yisrael). T **708** and similar square design. Multicoloured. Two phosphor bands (2s.10). P 13.

1677	2s.10 Type **708** (1st Aliya)	2·20	2·00
1678	6s.20 Young men (2nd Aliya)	6·25	5·50
1677/1678	*Set of 2*	7·50	6·75
1677/1678	*Set of 2 with tabs*	8·75	7·75

(Des Ruth Beckman-Malka. Litho)

2003 (9 Dec). Personalities. T **709** and similar vert design. Multicoloured. P 14.

1679	3s.30 Type **709** (land purchase pioneer) (81st death anniversary)	3·50	3·00
1680	4s.90 Emile Habiby (writer) (82nd death anniversary)	4·75	4·25
1679/1680	*Set of 2*	7·50	6·50
1679/1680	*Set of 2 with tabs*	8·75	8·00

710 Two-banded Anemonefish (*Amphirion bicinctus*)

711 Menachem Begin and Building

(Des Tuvia Kurz and H. Khoury. Litho)

2004 (30 Jan). Fish. T **710** and similar horiz designs. Multicoloured. One phosphor band. P 14.

1681	1s.30 Type **710**	1·20	1·10
1682	1s.30 Butterfly Perch (*Pseudanthias squamipinnis*)	1·20	1·10
1683	1s.30 *Pseudochromis fridmani*	1·20	1·10
1684	1s.30 Crown Butterflyfish (*Chaetodon paucifasciatus*)	1·20	1·10
1681/1684	*Set of 4*	4·25	4·00
1681/1684	*Set of 4 with tabs*	5·00	4·50
MS1685	118×77 mm. Nos. 1681/1684	5·00	4·50

(Des A. Vanooijen. Litho)

2004 (24 Feb). Historians (2nd series). Vert designs as T **674**. Multicoloured. Two phosphor bands (2s.40). P 14.

1686	2s.40 Emanuel Ringelblum	1·70	1·60
1687	3s.70 Jacob Talmon	2·30	2·10
1688	6s.20 Jacob Herzog	4·75	4·25
1686/1688	*Set of 3*	8·00	7·25
1686/1688	*Set of 3 with tabs*	9·50	8·50

(Des R. Goldberg. Litho)

2004 (24 Feb). Menachem Begin Heritage Centre, Jerusalem. Two phosphor bands. P 13.

1689	**711** 2s.50 multicoloured	2·50	2·20
	With tab	2·50	2·30

712 Ilan Ramon

713 Memorial Garden, Mount Herzl

(Des D. Goldberg. Litho)

2004 (24 Feb). First Death Anniversary of Ilan Ramon (astronaut on *Columbia* Space Shuttle). Two phosphor bands. P 13.

1690	**712**	2s.60 multicoloured	2·50	2·20
		With tab	2·50	2·30

(Des H. Kivkovich. Litho)

2004 (20 Apr). Memorial Day. One phosphor bar. P 14.

1691	**713**	1s.30 multicoloured	1·20	1·10
		With tab	1·30	1·20

714 Saraya Clock Tower, Safed

715 Football and Israel–USA Match, 1948

(Des Zina and Zvika Roitman. Litho)

2004 (3 May). Ottoman Clock Towers. T **714** and similar vert designs. One phosphor bar (1s.30). P 13.

1692	1s.30 Type **714**	1·20	1·10
1693	1s.30 Khan El-Umdan, Acre	1·20	1·10
1694	1s.30 El-Jarina Mosque, Haifa	1·20	1·10
1695	1s.30 Jaffa Gate, Jerusalem	1·20	1·10
1696	1s.30 Clock Square, Jaffa	1·20	1·10
1697	3s.10 No. 1692	1·70	1·60
	a. Booklet pane. No. 1697×5	1·80	
	b. Booklet pane. Nos. 1697/1701	16·00	
1698	3s.70 No. 1693	2·30	2·10
	a. Booklet pane. No. 1698×5	2·40	
1699	5s.20 No. 1694	3·00	2·75
	a. Booklet pane. No. 1699×5	3·25	
1700	5s.50 No. 1695	3·50	3·00
	a. Booklet pane. No. 1700×5	3·75	
1701	7s. No. 1696	4·25	4·00
	a. Booklet pane. No. 1701×5	4·50	
1692/1701	*Set of 10*	19·00	17·00
1692/1696	*Set of 5 with tabs*	21·00	19·00

Nos. 1697/1701 were issued in booklets containing six panes, five panes containing a single example of each stamp and one pane containing examples of all five stamps.

(Des A. Shevo and G. Almaliah. Litho)

2004 (3 May). Centenary of FIFA (Fédération Internationale de Football Association). Two phosphor bars. P 13.

1702	**715**	2s.10 multicoloured	1·90	1·70
		With tab	2·00	1·80

No. 1702 was issued in sheets of 12 stamps surrounding four stamp size labels forming a composite design of a football.

716 Football

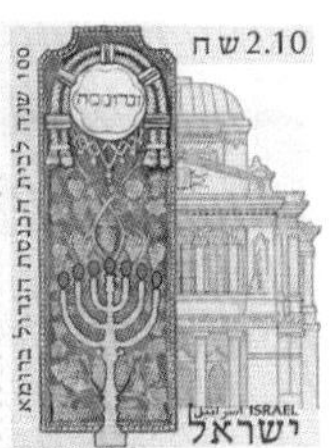

717 Candlestick, Ornamental Panel and Synagogue Façade

(Des M. Pereg. Litho)

2004 (3 May). 50th Anniversary of UEFA (Union of European Football Associations). P 14.

1703	**716**	6s.20 multicoloured	4·25	4·00
		With tab	4·75	4·25

(Des Anna Maresca (1704) and A. Merenda (1705). Litho)

2004 (20 May). Centenary of the Great Synagogue, Rome. T **717** and similar vert design. Multicoloured. Two phosphor bars. P 13.

1704	2s.10 Type **717**	1·90	1·70
1705	2s.10 Synagogue (*different*)	1·90	1·70
1704/1705	*Set of 2*	3·50	3·00
1704/1705	*Set of 2 with tabs*	4·00	3·75

Stamps of the same design were issued by Italy.

718 Judo and Israeli Silver Medal (Barcelona, 1992)

719 Theodor Herzl

(Des D. Goldberg. Litho)

2004 (6 July). Olympic Games, Athens. T **718** and similar horiz designs. Multicoloured. One phosphor bar (1s.50), two phosphor bars (2s.40), or no phosphor (6s.90). P 14.

1706	1s.50 Type **718**	1·00	90
1707	2s.40 Windsurfing and Israeli bronze medal (Atlanta, 1996)	2·00	1·80
1708	6s.90 Kayaking and Israeli bronze medal (Sydney, 2000)	5·00	4·50
1706/1708	*Set of 3*	7·25	6·50
1706/1708	*Set of 3 with tabs*	8·75	7·75

(Des A. Vanooijen. Litho)

2004 (6 July). Death Centenary of Theodor Herzl (writer and Zionist pioneer). Two phosphor bars. P 13.

1709	**719**	2s.50 multicoloured	2·20	2·00
		With tab	2·30	2·10

A stamp of a similar design was issued by Austria and Hungary.

720 Anniversary Emblem

721 Ear of Corn

(Des Sharon Muro. Litho)

2004 (6 July). 50th Anniversary of National Insurance Institute. P 13.

1710	**720**	7s. multicoloured	5·50	5·00
		With tab	5·75	5·25

(Des Hayyimi Kivkovich. Litho)

2004 (31 Aug). Bread. T **721** and similar horiz design. Multicoloured. One phosphor bar (No. 1711) or two phosphor bars (others). P 14×13.

1711	1s.50 Type **721**	1·50	1·30
1712	2s.40 Grinding stones	2·20	2·00
1713	2s.70 Bread in oven	2·50	2·20
1711/1713	*Set of 3*	5·50	5·00
1711/1713	*Set of 3 with tabs*	6·50	5·75

722 Building Façade and Test Tubes

723 Parachutist

(Des Hayyimi Kivkovich. Litho)

2004 (31 Aug). Centenary (2005) of Herzliya Hebrew High School. Two phosphor bands. P 13×14.

1714 **722** 2s.20 multicoloured .... 1·90 1·70
With tab 2·00 1·80

(Des Miri Nistor. Litho)

2004 (31 Aug). Children's Adventure Stories. T **723** and similar vert designs showing illustrations from book covers. Multicoloured. Two phosphor bars. P 13.

1715 2s.20 Type **723** (*Eight on the Trail of One* by Yemima Avidar-Tchernovitz) .... 1·60 1·40
1716 2s.50 Children and donkey (*Hasamba* by Igal Mossinsohn) .... 2·00 1·80
1717 2s.60 Faces (*Our Gang* by Pucho) .... 2·20 2·00
1715/1717 *Set of 3* .... 5·25 4·75
1715/1717 *Set of 3 with tabs* .... 6·25 5·50

724 Building and David Ben-Gurion

725 Airport Buildings

(Des Hayyimi Kivkovich. Litho)

2004 (31 Aug). Ben-Gurion Heritage Institute. Two phosphor bands. P 13.

1718 **724** 2s.50 multicoloured .... 2·75 2·50
With tab 3·00 2·50

(Des R. Goldberg. Litho)

2004 (31 Aug). Ben Gurion Airport. Two phosphor bands. P 14×13.

1719 **725** 2s.70 multicoloured .... 2·30 2·10
With tab 2·50 2·50

726 Post Woman and Envelope

727 Ottoman Period Austrian Mail box

2004 (14 Dec). Telabul 2004 International Stamp Exhibition, Tel Aviv. Design a Stamp Competition Winner. One phosphor band. Litho. P 14×13.

1720 **726** 1s.30 multicoloured .... 1·20 1·00
With tab 1·50 1·30

(Des G. Sagi. Litho)

2004 (14 Dec). Stamp Day. Mail boxes. T **727** and similar horiz designs. Multicoloured. Two phosphor bands (No. 1721/1722) or no phosphor bands (1723). P 14×13.

1721 2s.10 Type **727** .... 1·20 1·10
1722 2s.20 British Mandate period .... 1·50 1·30
1723 3s.30 Modern .... 2·75 2·50
1721/1723 *Set of 3* .... 5·00 4·50
1721/1723 *Set of 3 with tabs* .... 5·75 5·25

728 '20, 50, 100, 200'

729 Brown Bear

(Des E. Lida. Litho)

2004 (14 Dec). 50th Anniversary of Bank of Israel. P 14×13.

1724 **728** 6s.20 multicoloured .... 4·75 4·25
With tab 5·00 4·50

(Des T. Kurz. Litho)

2005 (22 Feb). Biblical Animals. T **729** and similar horiz designs. Multicoloured. One phosphor bar (No. 1725/1726) or two phosphor bars (1727/1728). P 14×13.

1725 1s.30 Type **729** .... 1·40 1·20
1726 1s.30 Ostrich .... 1·40 1·20
1727 2s.20 Nile Crocodile .... 1·70 1·60
1728 2s.20 Wolf .... 1·70 1·60
1725/1728 *Set of 4* .... 5·50 5·00
1725/1728 *Set of 4 with tabs* .... 6·50 5·75
MS1729 110×72 mm. 1s.30 No. 1726 (40×26 *mm*); 2s.10 Type **729** (40×26 *mm*); 2s.30 No. 1728 (40×26 *mm*); 2s.80 No. 1727 (40×26 *mm*) (*sold at 12s.*) .... 8·00 7·25

730 Tunnel and Spoon

731 Last of Kin Monument (Micha Ullman)

(Des E. Weishoff. Litho)

2005 (22 Feb). Ancient Water Systems. T **730** and similar horiz designs. Multicoloured. Two phosphor bars (No.1730/1731). P 14×13.

1730 2s.10 Type **730** (Hazor) (9th/8th-century BC). 1·40 1·20
1731 2s.20 Top of shaft (Megiddo) (10th-century).. 1·70 1·60
1732 3s.30 Aqueduct (Caesarea) (BC) .... 2·30 2·10
1733 6s.20 Tunnel and pool (Hezekiah's Tunnel) (8th-century) .... 4·00 3·50
1730/1733 *Set of 4* .... 8·50 7·50
1730/1733 *Set of 4 with tabs* .... 10·00 9·00

(Des H. Kivkovich. Litho)

2005 (3 May). Memorial Day. One phosphor bar. P 14.

1734 **731** 1s.50 multicoloured .... 1·40 1·20
With tab 1·50 1·30

732 Hebrew Kindergarten, Rishon Le-Zion

733 University Buildings

(Des H. Kivkovich. Litho)

2005 (3 May). Educational Institutions. T **732** and similar vert design. Two phosphor bands (6s.20). Multicoloured. P 14.

1735 2s.10 Type **732** .... 1·70 1·60
1736 6s.20 Lemel Elementary School, Jerusalem ..... 4·25 4·00
1735/1736 *Set of 2* .... 5·25 5·00
1735/1736 *Set of 2 with tabs* .... 6·50 5·75

(Des M. Lasky. Litho)

2005 (3 May). 50th Anniversary of Bar-Ilan University. Two phosphor bars. P 14.

1737 **733** 2s.20 multicoloured .... 1·70 1·60
With tab 1·90 1·70

734 Family and Soldiers

735 Jewish Partisans

(Des E. Landsberg. Litho)

2005 (3 May). National Reserve Force. Two phosphor bars. P 14.

1738 **734** 2s.20 multicoloured .... 1·70 1·60
With tab 1·90 1·70

(Des R. Goldberg. Litho)

2005 (3 May). 60th Anniversary of End of World War II. T **735** and similar horiz design. Multicoloured. P 14.

1739	3s.30 Type **735**	2·75	2·50
	a. Pair. Nos. 1739/1740	5·75	5·25
1740	3s.30 Jewish soldiers with Allied Forces	2·75	2·50
1739/1740	*Set of 2*	5·00	4·50
1739/1740	*Set of 2 with tabs*	5·75	5·25

Nos. 1739/1740 were issued in horizontal *se-tenant* pairs within the sheet.

736 Pope John Paul II

737 Emblem

2005 (18 May). Pope John Paul II Commemoration. Litho. P 14.

1741	**736**	3s.30 multicoloured	2·75	2·50
		With tab	3·00	2·50

(Des G. Brickman. Litho)

2005 (11 July). Maccabiah 2005 Sports Festival. Litho. P 14.

1742	**737**	3s.30 multicoloured	2·75	2·50
		With tab	3·00	2·50

738 *Gagea Commutata*

(Des Ruth Malka. Photo Enschedé)

2005 (26 July)–**06**. No value expressed.

(a) Ordinary gum. Phosphorescent paper (No. 1743) or short phosphor bar (No. 1743aa). P 14×14½ (with one elliptical hole on each horiz side) (No. 1743) or P ? (No. 1743aa). Photo (No. 1743) or litho (No. 1743aa)

1743	**738**	(1s.30) multicoloured	1·10	1·00
1743*aa*		(1s.50) multicoloured (20.9.06)	1·10	1·00

(b) Self-adhesive booklets. One phosphor band. Die-cut perf 14 (Nos. 1743ba/1743bb) or P 11 (Nos. 1743bc/1743bd). Photo (Nos. 1743ba and 1743bc) or litho (Nos. 1743bb and 1743bd)

1743*ba*	(1s.30) multicoloured (30.11.05)	1·10	1·00
1743*bb*	(1s.30) multicoloured (30.11.05)	1·10	1·00
1743*bc*	(1s.50) multicoloured (30.9.06)	1·40	1·20
1743*bd*	(1s.50) multicoloured (30.9.06)	1·40	1·20
1743/1743*bd*	*Set of 6*	6·50	5·75
1743/1743*bd*	*Set of 6 with tabs*	7·25	6·50

Nos. 1743*ba* and 1743*bc* are drawn with heavier lines and are on thicker board, Nos. 1743*bb* and 1743*bd* are on thinner ATM paper.

739 *Agrippas Street* (Arie Aroch)

(Des A. Vanooijen. Litho)

2005 (26 July). Art. T **739** and similar vert designs. Two phosphor bars (No. 1744). P 14×14½.

1744	2s.20 Type **739**	1·40	1·20
1745	4s.90 *Tablets of the Covenant* (Moshe Castel)	3·50	3·00
1746	6s.20 *The Rift in Time* (Moshe Kupferman)	4·00	3·50
1744/1746	*Set of 3*	8·00	7·00
1744/1746	*Set of 3 with tabs*	9·50	8·50

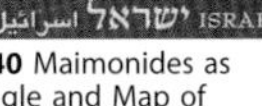

740 Maimonides as Eagle and Map of Mediterranean

741 Sack of Grain (Order of Zeraim)

(Des A. Shevo. Litho)

2005 (26 July). 800th Death Anniversary of Maimonides (Rabbi Moses Ben Maimon) (Jewish scholar). P 14.

1747	**740**	8s.20 multicoloured	6·25	5·50
		With tab	6·50	5·75

(Des D. Zada. Litho)

2005 (27 Sept). Mishnah (laws). T **741** and similar horiz designs. Multicoloured. One phosphor bar (No. 1748) or two phosphor bars (others). P 14.

1748	1s.30 Type **741**	95	85
1749	2s.10 Zodiac and wine goblet (Order of Moed)	1·40	1·20
1750	2s.30 Two rings (Order of Nashim)	1·70	1·60
1748/1750	*Set of 3*	3·75	3·25
1748/1750	*Set of 3 with tabs*	4·25	4·00

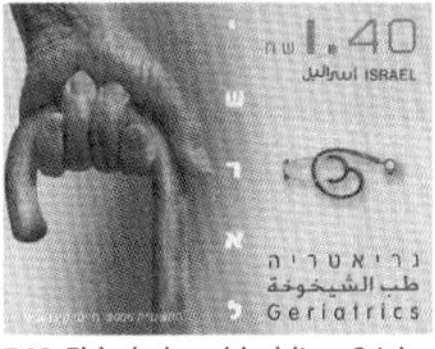

742 Elderly hand holding Stick and Stethoscope (geriatrics)

743 Yitzhak Rabin

(Des H. Kivkovich. Litho)

2005 (27 Sept). Medicine. T **742** and similar horiz designs. Multicoloured. One phosphor bar (No. 1751), two bars (No.s 1752/1753) or none (No. 1754). P 14.

1751	1s.40 Type **742**	95	85
1752	2s.20 Wheelchair user and dumb-bell (rehabilitation)	1·40	1·20
1753	2s.20 Child holding teddy bear and thermometer (paediatrics)	1·40	1·20
1754	6s.20 Bi-coloured face and tablet (mental health)	3·75	3·25
1751/1754	*Set of 4*	6·75	5·75
1751/1754	*Set of 4 with tabs*	8·00	7·25

(Des Z. Roitman. Litho)

2005 (27 Sept). Yitzhak Rabin Centre. Two phosphor bars. P 13.

1755	**743**	2s.20 multicoloured	1·70	1·40
		With tab	1·70	1·60

744 Albert Einstein

745 Wall

(Des A. Shevo and G. Almaliah. Litho)

2005 (27 Sept). International Year of Physics. Centenary of Publication of *Special Theory of Relativity* by Albert Einstein. P 13×13½.

1756	**744**	3s.30 multicoloured	2·50	2·20
		With tab	2·50	2·30

(Des A. Shevo and G. Almaliah. Litho)

2005 (27 Sept). Priestly Blessing. P 14.

1757	**745**	6s.20 multicoloured	3·50	3·00
		With tab	3·75	3·25

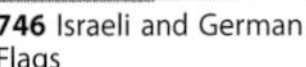

746 Israeli and German Flags

747 *Childhood is Happiness* (Lya Kasif)

(Des S. Klein and O. Neumann. Litho)

2005 (3 Nov). 40th Anniversary of Diplomatic Relations with Germany. Two phosphor bars. P 14.

1758 **746** 2s.20 multicoloured .... 1·40 1·20
With tab 1·50 1·30

A stamp of the same design was issued by Germany.

(Des D. B. Hador. Litho)

2005 (27 Dec). International Convention on the Rights of the Child. Winning Designs in Children's Painting Competition. T **747** and similar vert designs. Multicoloured. One phosphor bar. P 14.

1759 1s.30 Type **747** 95 85
1760 1s.30 *A Warm Home* (Menahem Mendel Albo) 95 85
1761 1s.30 *Indifference Hurts* (Irina Rogozinsky) 95 85
1759/1761 *Set of 3* .... 2·50 2·30
1759/1761 *Set of 3 with tabs* .... 3·00 2·75

748 Moshe Halevy (director)

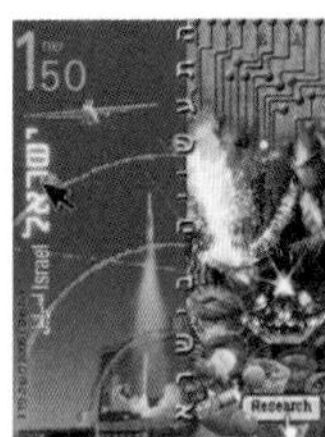

749 Symbols of Industry

(Des M. Pereg. Litho)

2005 (27 Dec). Theatre Personalities. T **748** and similar vert designs. Multicoloured. Two phosphor bars (Nos. 1762/1763). P 14.

1762 2s.20 Type **748** .... 1·20 1·10
1763 2s.20 Joeseph Millo (actor and director) .... 1·20 1·10
1764 6s.20 Shai K. Ophir (Isaiah Goldstein) (actor and director) .... 3·50 3·00
1765 6s.20 Nissim Aloni (playwright and director) . 3·50 3·00
1762/1765 *Set of 4* .... 8·50 7·50
1762/1765 *Set of 4 with tabs* .... 10·00 9·00

(Des A. Shevo and G. Almaliah. Litho)

2005 (27 Dec). Stamp Day. International Year of Physics. Sheet 84×59 mm. P 13×13½.

MS1766 **744** 8s.20 multicoloured (*sold at* 12s.) .... 8·00 7·25

(Des M. Pereg. Litho)

2005 (29 Dec). 85th Anniversary of Manufacturers' Association. P 14.

1767 **749** 1s.50 multicoloured .... 1·10 1·00
With tab 1·20 1·00

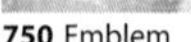

750 Emblem

751 *Desert Bloom* (Yael Blldner)

(Des E. Carmli. Litho)

2006 (28 Feb). Inauguration of Israel Post Ltd (1 March 2006). One phosphor bar. P 14.

1768 **750** 1s.50 multicoloured .... 1·20 1·10
With tab 1·30 1·20

(Des G. Sagi. Litho)

2006 (28 Feb). Winning Designs in Jewish-American Children's Design-a-Stamp Competition. T **751** and similar horiz designs. Multicoloured. One phosphor bar (1s.50), two phosphor bars (2s.40) or no bars (others). P 14.

1769 1s.50 Type **751** .... 1·10 1·00
1770 2s.40 *Harmony* (Michela Janower) .... 1·70 1·60
1771 3s.60 *Together in Israel* (Jessica Deautsch) .... 2·30 2·10
1772 7s.40 *Colours in Israel* (Marissa Galli) .... 5·00 4·50
1769/1772 *Set of 4* .... 9·00 8·25
1769/1772 *Set of 4 with tabs* .... 11·00 9·75
MS1772*a* 110×75mm. 2s.20, As Type **751**; 2s.40 As No. 1772; 3s.60 As No. 1770; 5s.10 As No. 1771 (*sold at* 15s.) .... 10·00 9·00

752 Rebbe

753 Ezer Weizman

(Des D. Zada. Litho)

2006 (28 Feb). Chabad-Lubavitch Chassism (religious movement). Two phosphor bars. P 14.

1773 **752** 2s.50 multicoloured .... 1·70 1·60
With tab 1·90 1·70

(Des D. Goldberg. Litho)

2006 (28 Feb). First Death Anniversary of Ezer Weizman (president 1993–2000). P 14.

1774 **753** 7s.40 multicoloured .... 4·75 4·25
With tab 5·25 4·75

754 Latrun Memorial

755 Aquilegia

(Des R. Goldberg. Litho)

2006 (8 May). Memorial Day. One phosphor bar. P 14.

1775 **754** 1s.50 multicoloured .... 1·10 1·00
With tab 1·20 1·00

(Des A. Vanoojen. Litho)

2006 (8 May). Flowers. T **755** and similar vert design. Multicoloured. One phosphor bar. P 14.

1776 1s.50 Type **755** .... 1·10 1·00
1777 1s.50 Tulip .... 1·10 1·00
1776/1777 *Set of 2* .... 2·00 1·80
1776/1777 *Set of 2 with tabs* .... 2·30 2·10

756 Uranus

757 Symbols of Art and Science

(Des D. Ben Hader. Litho)

2006 (8 May). Solar System. Jerusalem 2006 National Stamp Exhibition. T **756** and similar square designs. Multicoloured.

(a) Sheet stamps. Ordinary gum. P 13

1778 2s.50 Type **756** .... 1·50 1·30
a. Sheetlet of 6. Nos. 1778/1783 .... 9·25
1779 2s.50 Saturn .... 1·50 1·30
1780 2s.50 Jupiter .... 1·50 1·30
1781 2s.50 Neptune and Pluto .... 1·50 1·30
1782 2s.50 Earth and Mars .... 1·50 1·30
1783 2s.50 Mercury and Venus .... 1·50 1·30

1778/1783	*Set of 6*	8·00	7·00
1778/1783	*Set of 6 with tabs*	9·25	8·25

(b) Booklet stamps. Self-adhesive gum. Die-cut perf 11½

1784	2s.50 As Type **756**	1·50	1·30
1785	2s.50 As No. 1779	1·50	1·30
1786	2s.50 As No. 1780	1·50	1·30
1787	2s.50 As No. 1781	1·50	1·30
1788	2s.50 As No. 1782	1·50	1·30
1789	2s.50 As No. 1783	1·50	1·30
1784/1789	*Set of 6*	8·00	7·00
1784/1789	*Set of 6 with tabs*	9·25	8·25

Nos. 1778/1783 were issued in sheetlets of six, the stamps arranged in two horizontal *tête-bêche* rows. The booklet stamps, Nos. 1784/1789 were arranged similarly.

(Des Hayyimi Kivkovich. Litho)

2006 (8 May). 50th Anniversary of Tel Aviv University. P 14.

1790	**757**	3s.60 multicoloured	2·20	2·00
		With tab	2·30	2·10

758 Postal Emblem

(Des E. Carneli. Litho)

2006 (8 May). Israeli Post. Sheet 92×67 mm. Imperf.

MS1791	**758**	5s.90 multicoloured (*sold at* 7s.50)	6·50	5·75

759 Mosaic

(Des Y. Granot. Litho)

2006 (8 May). 3rd-century Mosaic, Megiddo. Jerusalem 2006 National Stamp Exhibition. Sheet 62×74 mm. P 14.

MS1792	**759**	10s. multicoloured (*sold at* 15s.)	11·00	9·75

760 Jacob Saul Eliachar

761 Moroccan Khamsa

(Des A. Shevo. Litho)

2006 (25 July). Rabbis. T **760** and similar vert designs. One phosphor bar (No. 1793) or two phosphor bars (others). Multicoloured. P 14.

1793	1s.50 Type **760**	95	85
1794	2s.20 Samuel Salant	1·50	1·30
1795	2s.40 Jacob Meir	1·60	1·40
1793/1795	*Set of 3*	3·75	3·25
1793/1795	*Set of 3 with tabs*	4·25	4·00

(Des M. Eshel. Litho)

2006 (25 July). Khamsa (protective amulets). T **761** and similar vert designs. Multicoloured. One phosphor bar (No. 1796), two phosphor bars (No. 1797) or none (No. 1798). P 14.

1796	1s.50 Type **761**	95	85
1797	2s.50 Tunisian	1·50	1·30
1798	7s.40 Iranian	4·75	4·25
1796/1798	*Set of 3*	6·50	5·75
1796/1798	*Set of 3 with tabs*	7·25	6·50

762 Rabbis, Children and Star of David

763 Man on Wheel

(Des H. Shechter. Litho)

2006 (25 July). Centenary of Religious Zionist Education. P 14.

1799	**762**	3s.60 multicoloured	2·50	2·30
		With tab	2·75	2·50

(Des D. Zada. Litho)

2006 (12 Sept). Mishnah (laws). Horiz designs as T **741**. Multicoloured. One phosphor bar (No. 1800) or two phosphor bars (others). P 14.

1800	1s.50 Bull (Order of Nezikin)	95	85
1801	2s.20 Pigeon (Order of Kodashim)	1·50	1·30
1802	2s.40 Hand washing vessel (Order of Tohorot)	1·60	1·40
1800/1802	*Set of 3*	3·75	3·25
1800/1802	*Set of 3 with tabs*	4·25	4·00

(Des Talya Stein. Litho)

2006 (12 Sept). Centenary of Bezalel Academy of Arts and Design. Two phosphor bands. P 14.

1803	**763**	2s.50 bright emerald	1·50	1·30
		a. Strip of 3. Nos. 1803/1805	4·75	
1804		2s.50 bright ultramarine	1·50	1·30
1805		2s.50 bright orange	1·50	1·30
1803/1805		*Set of 3*	4·00	3·50
1803/1805		*Set of 3 with tabs*	4·75	4·25

764 Abba Eban

765 *Coriandrum sativum*

(Des A. David. Litho)

2006 (12 Sept). Abba Eban (politician and diplomat) Commemoration. P 14.

1806	**764**	7s.30 multicoloured	4·75	4·25
		With tab	5·00	4·50

(Des Y. Garbay. Litho)

2006 (17 Dec). Medicinal Plants. T **765** and similar horiz designs. Multicoloured. One phosphor bar (No. 1807), two phosphor bars (No. 1808) or none (No. 1809). P 14.

1807	1s.50 Type **765**	95	85
1808	2s.50 *Micromeria fructicosa*	1·70	1·60
1809	3s.30 *Mentha piperita*	2·00	1·80
1807/1809	*Set of 3*	4·25	3·75
1807/1809	*Set of 3 with tabs*	5·00	4·50

766 Oriental Style Fabric, 1882–1948

767 Atlit

(Des O. Shemer. Litho)

2006 (17 Dec). Fashion in Israel. T **766** and similar square designs showing fabric. Multicoloured. One phosphor bar (No. 1810), two phosphor bars (No. 1811) or none (others). P 14.

1810	1s.50 Type **766**	95	85
1811	2s.50 Ethnic style, 1948–1973	1·70	1·60
1812	3s.30 International style, 1973–1990	2·00	1·80
1813	7s.30 Technological style, 1990–2006	4·75	4·25
1810/1813	*Set of 4*	8·50	7·75
1810/1813	*Set of 4 with tabs*	10·00	9·00

(Des E. Weishoff. Litho)

2006 (17 Dec). Crusader Sites in Israel. T **767** and similar horiz designs. Multicoloured. Two phosphor bars. P 14.

1814 2s.50 Type **767** ... 1·60 1·40
1815 2s.50 Caesarea ... 1·60 1·40
1816 2s.50 Montfort ... 1·60 1·40
1817 2s.50 Belvoir ... 1·60 1·40
1814/1817 *Set of 4* ... 5·75 5·00
1814/1817 *Set of 4 with tabs* ... 7·00 6·25

The phosphor bars on No. 1816 are placed to the left of the stamp, whilst on the other stamps they are placed at either side.

768 Lazarus Ludwig Zamenhof (creator)

769 Ma Pit'om

(Des M. Pereg. Litho)

2006 (17 Dec). 120th Anniversary of Esperanto (international constructed language). P 14.

1818 **768** 3s.30 multicoloured ... 2·30 2·10
With tab 2·50 2·20

(Des Miri Nestor. Litho)

2007 (20 Feb). 40th Anniversary of Educational Television. T **769** and similar vert designs. Multicoloured. Two phosphor bands.

(a) Ordinary gum. P 11½

1819 2s.50 Type **769** ... 1·50 1·30
a. Horiz strip of 3. Nos. 1819/1821 ... 4·75
1820 2s.50 Krovim ... 1·50 1·30
1821 2s.50 No Secrets ... 1·50 1·30
1819/1821 *Set of 3* ... 4·00 3·50
1819/1821 *Set of 3 with tabs* ... 4·75 4·25

(b) Self-adhesive booklet stamps. Die-cut perf

1822 2s.50 As Type **769** ... 1·40 1·20
1823 2s.50 As No. 1820 ... 1·40 1·20
1824 2s.50 As No. 1821 ... 1·40 1·20
1822/1824 *Set of 3* ... 3·75 3·25
1822/1824 *Set of 3 with tabs* ... 4·25 4·00

Nos. 1819/1821 were issued in horizontal *se-tenant* strips on three stamps within the sheet.

770 Negev

(Des Marion Codner and M. Pereg. Litho)

2007 (20 Feb). Development of Negev and Galilee. T **770** and similar horiz design. Multicoloured. Two phosphor bands (2s.50). P 11½.

1825 2s.50 Type **770** ... 1·60 1·40
1826 3s.30 Galilee ... 2·50 2·20
1825/1826 *Set of 2* ... 3·75 3·25
1825/1826 *Set of 2 with tabs* ... 4·25 4·00

771 Physical Education in Schools

(Des Marion Codner and M. Pereg. Litho)

2007 (20 Feb). Physical Education and Sport in Israel. T **771** and similar horiz designs. Multicoloured. P 14.

1827 2s.90 Type **771** ... 1·60 1·40
1828 3s.00 Wingate Institute for Sport ... 1·70 1·60
1829 7s.30 Sport for All ... 4·00 3·50
1827/1829 *Set of 3* ... 6·50 5·75
1827/1829 *Set of 3 with tabs* ... 8·00 7·25

772 Givati Brigade Memorial

773 Founding Members

(Des Miri Nestor. Litho)

2007 (17 Apr). Memorial Day. One phosphor band. P 14.

1830 **772** 1s.50 multicoloured ... 1·10 1·00
With tab 1·20 1·00

(Des David Tartakover. Litho)

2007 (17 Apr). 120th Anniversary of Neve-Tzedek. Sheet 125×72 mm containing T **773** and similar vert designs. Multicoloured. P 14.

MS1831 2s.20 Type **773**: 3s.30 Neve-Tzedek; 5s.80 Intellectuals (*sold at* 15s.) ... 9·50 8·50

774 Scouts

(Des Hadar Shechter. Litho)

2007 (17 Apr). Centenary of Scouting. Two phosphor bands. P 14.

1832 **774** 2s.50 multicoloured ... 1·90 1·70
With tab 2·00 1·80

775 Sederot (southern Israel)

776 Circle of Stylised Figures

(Des Gideon Sagi. Litho)

2007 (17 Apr). Urban Development in Israel. T **775** and similar horiz designs. Multicoloured. Two phosphor bands (2s.50). P 14.

1833 2s.50 Type **775** ... 1·40 1·20
1834 3s.30 Aqiva (central Israel) ... 1·90 1·70
1835 7s.30 Migdal Ha'emeq (northern Israel) ... 4·00 3·50
1833/1835 *Set of 3* ... 6·50 5·75
1833/1835 *Set of 3 with tabs* ... 7·75 7·00

(Des Aharon Shevo. Litho)

2007 (16 May). 40th Anniversary of Reunification of Jerusalem. P 14.

1836 **776** 1s.50 multicoloured ... 1·10 1·00
With tab 1·20 1·00

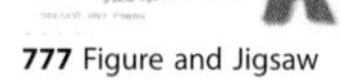

777 Figure and Jigsaw

778 Ballet Dancers

(Des Levona Caspi. Litho)

2007 (20 June). Volunteer Organisations. One phosphor bar. P 14.

1837 **777** 1s.50 multicoloured ... 1·10 1·00
With tab 1·20 1·00

(Des Moshe Pereg. Litho)

2007 (20 June). Dance. T **778** and similar vert designs. Multicoloured. Two phosphor bars. P 14.

1838 2s.20 Type **778** ... 1·60 1·40
a. Horiz strip of 4. Nos. 1838/1841 ... 6·75
1839 2s.20 Ethnic ... 1·60 1·40
1840 2s.20 Folk ... 1·60 1·40
1841 2s.20 Modern ... 1·60 1·40
1838/1841 *Set of 4* ... 5·75 5·00
1838/1841 *Set of 4 with tabs* ... 7·00 6·25

Nos. 1838/1841 were issued in horizontal *se-tenant* strips of four stamps within the sheet.

779 Prison Officers

2007 (20 June). National Prison Service. Two phosphor bars. P 14.

1842 **779** 2s.50 multicoloured ... 1·60 1·40
With tab 1·70 1·60

780 Dining Hall, Knights Hospitaller's Compound, Acre

(Des Ronen Goldberg. Litho)

2007 (20 June). UNESCO World Heritage Sites. T **780** and similar horiz designs. Multicoloured. P 14.

1843 3s.30 Type **780** ... 2·00 1·80
1844 5s. Zina Dizengoff Circle, Tel Aviv ... 3·00 2·75
1845 5s.80 Mosaic floor, Western Palace, Masada ... 4·00 3·50
1843/1845 *Set of 3* ... 8·00 7·25
1843/1845 *Set of 3 with tabs* ... 9·50 8·50

781 Beach and 'Israel' (in Hebrew)

782 Jael (killed Sisera to deliver Israel from the troops of King Jabin)

(Des Meir Eshel. Litho)

2007 (27 Aug). Personalised Stamp. No value expressed. One phosphor bar. P 14.

1846 **781** (1s.50) multicoloured ... 1·40 1·20
With tab 1·50 1·30

No. 1846 could be personalised by the addition of a photograph or logo.

(Des Ora and Eliahu Schwarts. Litho)

2007 (27 Aug). Women from the Bible. T **782** and similar vert designs. Multicoloured. One phosphor bar (1s.50) or two phosphor bars (others). P 14.

1847 1s.50 Type **782** ... 95 85
1848 2s.20 Esther (risked her life to save her adoptive father and the Jewish people) ... 1·40 1·20
1849 2s.40 Miriam (sister of Moses) ... 1·60 1·40
1847/1849 *Set of 3* ... 3·50 3·00
1847/1849 *Set of 3 with tabs* ... 4·25 3·75

783 Horsemen

784 Soldiers and Reservists

(Des Mali and Momi Alon. Litho)

2007 (27 Aug). Centenary of Hashomer (The Watchmen) (early Jewish defence organisation). P 14.

1850 **783** 3s.30 multicoloured ... 2·00 1·80
With tab 2·20 2·00

(Des Gal Najari and Yigal Gabay. Litho)

2007 (27 Aug). National Reserve Force. P 14.

1851 **784** 7s.30 multicoloured ... 4·25 4·00
With tab 4·75 4·25

785 Rabbi Chalom Messas

786 Zina Dizengff Circle (As No. 1844)

(Des Gal Najari and Yigal Gabay. Litho)

2007 (27 Aug). Rabbi Chalom Messas (Moroccan Jewish Halachic scholar) Commemoration. P 14.

1852 **785** 7s.30 multicoloured ... 4·25 4·00
With tab 4·75 4·25

(Des Ronen Goldberg. Litho)

2007 (27 Aug). Centenary (2009) of Tel Aviv. Sheet 96×70. P 14.

MS1853 **786** 10s. multicoloured (*sold at* 15s.) ... 9·50 8·50

787 Bay Leaves

788 Mother and Child

(Des Yigal Gabay and Tuvia Kurtz. Litho)

2007 (5 Nov). Herbs. T **787** and similar horiz design. Multicoloured. P 14.

1854 1s.55 Type **787** ... 95 85
1855 2s.25 Wild Thyme ... 1·60 1·40
1854/1855 *Set of 2* ... 2·30 2·00
1854/1855 *Set of 2 with tabs* ... 2·75 2·50

See also Nos. 1903/1905.

(Des Galia Armland. Litho)

2007 (5 Dec). Family Love. T **788** and similar vert designs. Multicoloured. One phosphor bar (No. 1856), two phosphor bars (No. 1857) or no phosphor (No. 1858). P 14.

1856 1s.55 Type **788** ... 95 85
1857 2s.25 Brother and sister ... 1·40 1·20
1858 3s.55 Father and child ... 2·00 1·80
1856/1858 *Set of 3* ... 4·00 3·50
1856/1858 *Set of 3 with tabs* ... 4·75 4·25

789 Otter, Catfish and Cranes **790** Dove

(Des Galia Armland. Litho)

2007 (5 Dec). Hula Nature Reserve. T **789** and similar horiz designs. Multicoloured. Two phosphor bars.

(a) Ordinary gum. P 14

1859 2s.25 Type **789** .... 1·50 1·30
a. Horiz strip of 3. Nos. 1859/1861 .... 4·75
1860 2s.25 Terrapins, Iris and Pelicans .... 1·50 1·30
1861 2s.25 Water Buffalo, Duck, Warbler and Jungle Cat .... 1·50 1·30
1859/1861 *Set of 3* .... 4·00 3·50
1859/1861 *Set of 3 with tabs* .... 4·75 4·25

(b) Self-adhesive booklet stamps. Die-cut perf 11

1862 2s.25 As Type **789** .... 1·50 1·30
1863 2s.25 As No. 1860 .... 1·50 1·30
1864 2s.25 As No. 1861 .... 1·50 1·30
1862/1864 *Set of 3* .... 4·00 3·50
1862/1864 *Set of 3 with tabs* .... 4·75 4·25

Nos. 1859/1861 were issued in horizontal *se-tenant* strips of three stamps within the sheet, each strip forming a composite design.

Nos. 1862/1864, each×2 were issued in booklets of six stamps.

(Des Aaron Shevo. Litho)

2007 (5 Dec). Noah's Ark. Sheet 159×93 mm containing T **790** and similar horiz designs. Multicoloured. P 14.

MS1865 2s.25×6, Type **790**; Noah, family, Ark and animals; Elephants; Peacocks, Bears and Tiger; Lions and Wolves; Wolf, Leopards and Kangaroos (*sold at* 16s.) .... 10·50 9·25

The stamps and margins of No. **MS**1865 form a composite design of the Ark and animals on dry land.

791 1927 Western Electric Projector, Pianist and Screen showing *The Jazz Singer* **792** Rabbi Itzhak Kaduri

(Des David Ben-Hador. Litho)

2007 (5 Dec). Stamp Day. Israeli Cinema. T **791** and similar horiz design. Multicoloured. P 14.

1866 4s.50 Type **791** .... 3·00 2·75
1867 4s.60 1937 BTH projector and wide-screen showing *The Robe* .... 3·00 2·75
1866/1867 *Set of 2* .... 5·50 5·00
1866/1867 *Set of 2 with tabs* .... 6·50 5·75

(Des Itzhak Yamin and Meir Eshel. Litho)

2007 (5 Dec). Rabbi Itzhak Kaduri Commemoration. P 14.

1868 **792** 8s.15 multicoloured .... 5·25 4·75
With tab 5·50 5·00

793 Israel Rokach **794** 'Shema Servant of Jeroboam' Seal and Tel Hazor ('The Biblical Tels')

(Des Ruthie El Hanan. Litho)

2008 (27 Jan). Israel Rokach (mayor of Tel Aviv 1936–1953) Commemoration. Two phosphor bars. P 14.

1869 **793** 2s.25 multicoloured .... 1·80 1·60
With tab 1·90 1·70

(Des Ronen Goldberg. Litho)

2008 (27 Jan). World Heritage Sites. T **794** and similar horiz design. Multicoloured. Two phosphor bars. P 14.

1870 2s.25 Type **794** .... 1·80 1·60
1871 3s.40 Camel figurine and Nabatean temple ('The Incense Route') .... 2·40 2·20
1870/1871 *Set of 2* .... 3·75 3·50
1870/1871 *Set of 2 with tabs* .... 4·50 4·00

795 Members of Ahuzat-Bayit Association

(Des David Ben-Hador. Litho)

2008 (27 Jan). Ahuzat-Bayit Land Lottery (the founding of Tel Aviv). P 14.

1872 **795** 4s.50 multicoloured .... 3·25 3·00
With tab 3·50 3·25

796 Barbed Wire becoming Flowers

(Des Matias Delfino)

2008 (27 Jan). International Holocaust Remembrance Day. P 14.

1873 **796** 4s.60 multicoloured .... 3·00 2·75
With tab 3·25 3·00

Stamps of a similar design were issued by United Nations Geneva, New York and Vienna.

797 Symbols of Water **798** Akiva Weiss

(Des Ronen Goldberg. Litho)

2008 (27 Jan). 70th Anniversary of Mekorot–National Water System. P 14.

1874 **797** 5s.80 multicoloured .... 3·75 3·50
With tab 4·25 3·75

(Des Daniel Goldberg. Litho)

2008 (27 Jan). 140th Birth Anniversary of Akiva Aryeh Weiss (chairman of Ahuzat-Bayit association). P 14.

1875 **798** 8s.15 multicoloured .... 5·25 4·75
With tabs 5·75 5·25

799 Fireworks and Emblem **800** Srulik (created by Dosh (cartoonist))

(Des Miri Nestor. Litho)

2008 (28 Apr). 60th Anniversary of Independence. One phosphor bar. P 14.

1876 **799** 1s.55 multicoloured .... 1·20 1·10
With tab 1·30 1·20

(Des Eli Karmeli. Litho)

2008 (28 Apr). The Israeli. One phosphor bar. T **800** and similar vert design. No value expressed. Multicoloured.

(a) Sheet Stamp. Ordinary gum. P 14

1877 (1s.55) Type **800** .... 1·20 1·10

(b) Self-adhesive Booklet stamp. Die-cut wavy edge

1878 (1s.55) As Type **800** .... 1·20 1·10
1877/1878 *Set of 2* .... 2·20 2·00
1877/1878 *Set of 2 with tabs* .... 2·50 2·30

No. 1878 was issued in booklets of 20 stamps (5×2, 5×2).

801 *Hemerocallis* Flower

802 Women and Corn (Paul Kor) (1952)

(Des Ronen Goldberg. Litho)

2008 (28 Apr). Memorial Day. One phosphor bar. P 14.

1879 **801** 1s.55 multicoloured .... 1·20 1·10
With tab 1·30 1·20

(Des Haimi Kivkovich. Litho)

2008 (28 Apr). Independence Day Posters. T **802** and similar vert designs. Multicoloured. Two phosphor bars. P 14.

1880 2s.55 Type **802** .... 1·50 1·40
a. *Tête-bêche* pair. Nos. 1880/1881 .... 3·25 3·00
b. Sheetlet of 6. Nos. 1880/1885 .... 9·25
1881 2s.55 Heart as Landscape (Hila Biran) (2006). 1·50 1·40
1882 2s.55 Boy watering flowers (Amram Prat) (1965) .... 1·50 1·40
a. *Tête-bêche* pair. Nos. 1882/1883 .... 3·25 3·00
1883 2s.55 Star of David as ship containing immigrants (Assaf Berg) (1989) (inscr '1991' on tab) .... 1·50 1·40
1884 2s.55 Lions supporting tulips as menorah (Kopel Gurwin) (1968) (inscr '1971' on tab) .... 1·50 1·40
a. *Tête-bêche* pair. Nos. 1884/1885 .... 3·25 3·00
1885 2s.55 Landscape with steeples, mosques, synagogues and water towers (Assaf Berg) (1979) (inscr '1981' on tab) .... 1·50 1·40
1880/1885 *Set of 6* .... 8·00 7·50
1880/1885 *Set of 6 with tabs* .... 9·50 8·75

Nos. 1880/1881, 1882/1883 and 1884/1885, respectively were issued in *tête-bêche* pairs within sheetlets of six stamps.

803 Israeli Flag and World Map as Clasped Hands

804 Rose

(Des David Ben-Hador. Litho)

2008 (28 Apr). 50th Anniversary of Export Institute. P 14.

1886 **803** 2s.80 multicoloured .... 2·10 1·90
With tab 2·20 2·00

(Des Tuvia Kurtz and Yigal Gabay. Litho)

2008 (28 Apr). Flowers. T **804** and similar vert design. Multicoloured. No value expressed. One phosphor bar. P 14.

1887 (1s.55) Type **804** .... 1·00 95
1888 (1s.55) *Cyclamen persicum* .... 1·00 95
1887/1888 *Set of 2* .... 1·80 1·70
1887/1888 *Set of 2 with tabs* .... 2·20 2·00

Nos. 1887/1888 were impregnated with floral scent.

805 Emblem

(Des Baruch Naeh. Litho Cartor)

2008 (28 Apr). 120th Anniversary of *Hatikvah* (hope) (song now National Anthem). Sheet 140×85 mm. P 14.

MS1889 **805** 10s. multicoloured (*sold at* 15s.) .... 10·50 9·50

806 Girl with Telescope (*Israel's 60th*) (Daniel Hazan)

807 First Concert

2008 (14 May). 60th Anniversary of Independence. Children's Drawings. T **806** and similar vert designs. Multicoloured. P 14.

1890 2s.25 Type **806** .... 1·80 1·60
1891 2s.25 Script (*Israel is my Home*) (Yuval Sulema and Eden Vilker) .... 1·80 1·60
1892 2s.25 House and script (*I Love Israel*) (Etai Epstein) .... 1·80 1·60
1890/1892 *Set of 3* .... 4·75 4·25
1890/1892 *Set of 3 with tabs* .... 5·75 5·25

(Des Galia Armland)

2008 (14 May). Hula Nature Reserve. Children's self-adhesive booklet stamps. Horiz designs as T **789**. Multicoloured. Die-cut wavy edge.

1892*a* 2s.25 As No. 1861 (Water Buffalo) .... 2·40 2·20
a. Booklet pane. Nos. 1892*a*/1892*c*, each×2 .... 15·00
1892*b* 2s.25 As No. 1859 (Otter) .... 2·40 2·20
1892*c* 2s.25 As No. 1860 (Terrapins) .... 2·40 2·20
1892*a*/1892*c* *Set of 3* .... 6·50 6·00
1892*a*/1892*c* *Set of 3 with tabs* .... 9·50 8·75

Nos. 1892*a*/1892*c*, each×2, were printed, *se-tenant* in a block of six stamps, within a single pane of stamps, in booklets with nine pages of text, containing games and puzzles for children.

2008 (14 May). Noah's Ark. Children's self-adhesive booklet stamps. Horiz designs as T **790**. Multicoloured. Die-cut wavy edge.

1892*d* 2s.25 As Type **790** .... 2·40 2·20
a. Booklet pane. Nos. 1892*d*/1892*i* .... 15·00
1892*e* 2s.25 Noah, family, Ark and animals .... 2·40 2·20
1892*f* 2s.25 Elephants .... 2·40 2·20
1892*g* 2s.25 Peacocks, Bears and Tiger .... 2·40 2·20
1892*h* 2s.25 Lions and Wolves .... 2·40 2·20
1892*i* 2s.25 Wolf, Leopards and Kangaroos .... 2·40 2·20
1892*d*/1892*i* *Set of 6* .... 13·00 12·00

Nos. 1892*d*/1892*i*, were printed, *se-tenant* in a block of six stamps, the block forming a composite design, within a single pane of stamps, in booklets with nine pages of text, containing games and puzzles for children.

A prestige booklet containing eight panes of text and four panes of stamps, as Nos. **MS**1853; 1866/1867; 1869×2 (with no phosphor bars); 1872 and 1875×2, was on sale for 68s.

(Des Yigal Gabay)

2008 (14 May). Centenary of Tel-Aviv (2009). Sheet 150×85 mm containing T **807** and similar horiz designs showing drawings of Ahuzat Bayit (Tel-Aviv) by Nahum Gutman. P 14.

MS1893 3s.50 Type **807**; 4s.50 First Lamp Post; 5s.50 Dr Hisin (physician) riding his Donkey (*sold at* 15s.) .. 12·00 11·00

808 Circle of Stylised Figures (As T **776**)

809 Seashore, Neve Dekalim, Greenhouses, Tomatoes and Children

(Des Aaron Shevo. Litho and gold foil embossed)

2008 (14 May). *Jerusalem of Gold* (song by Naomi Shemer). Sheet 110×70 mm. P 14.

MS1894 **808** 18s. multicoloured (*sold at* 22s.50) .... 16·00 14·50

(Des Aaron Shevo. Litho)

2008 (14 July). Gush Katif. One phosphor bar. P 14.

1895 **809** 1s.55 multicoloured .... 1·20 1·10
With tab 1·30 1·20

810 Swimming

811 Capernaum-Tabgha Promenade, Sea of Galilee

(Des Ruti El Hanan. Litho)

2008 (14 July). Olympic Games, Beijing. T **810** and similar horiz designs. Multicoloured. One phosphor bar (1s.55) or two phosphor bars (others). P 14.

1896 1s.55 Type **810** .... 1·00 95
1897 1s.55 Rhythmic gymnastics .... 1·00 95
1898 2s.25 Tennis .... 1·60 1·50
1899 2s.25 Sailing, Laser Radial .... 1·60 1·50
1896/1899 *Set of 4* .... 4·75 4·50
1896/1899 *Set of 4 with tabs* .... 5·75 5·25

(Des Zina and Zvika Roitman. Litho)

2008 (14 July). Promenades. T **811** and similar horiz designs. Multicoloured. P 14.

1900 4s.50 Type **811** .... 3·00 2·75
1901 4s.60 Armon Hanatziv Promenade, Jerusalem .... 3·00 2·75
1902 8s.15 Rishom Promenade, Netanya .... 4·75 4·25
1900/1902 *Set of 3* .... 9·75 8·75
1900/1902 *Set of 3 with tabs* .... 11·50 10·50

812 *Artemisia arborescens*

813 Aden

(Des Yigal Gabay and Tuvia Kurz.)

2008 (17 Sept). Herbs. T **812** and similar horiz design. Multicoloured. One phosphor band (No. 1903).

(a) Ordinary gum.

1903 1s.60 Type **812** .... 1·20 1·10
1904 (2s.90) *Salvia fruticosa* .... 2·10 1·90

(b) Size 24×18 mm. Self-adhesive. Die-cut perf 11.

1905 (2s.90) As No. 1904 .... 2·20 2·00

No. 1905 was also available in sheets of 12 stamps and 12 labels which could be personalised by the addition of a photograph or logo.

(Des Meir Eshel)

2008 (17 Sept). Torah Crowns. T **813** and similar horiz designs showing crowns. Multicoloured. One phosphor band (No. 1906) or two phosphor bands (others). P 14.

1906 1s.60 Type **813** .... 1·20 1·10
1907 3s.80 Turkey .... 2·75 2·50
1908 3s.80 Poland .... 2·75 2·50
1906/1908 *Set of 3* .... 6·00 5·50
1906/1908 *Set of 3 with tabs* .... 7·00 6·50

814 Rabbi Samuel Mohilewer

(Des Aharon Shevo)

2008 (17 Sept). Pioneers of Zionism. T **814** and similar horiz design. Multicoloured. P 14.

1909 2s.30 Type **814** .... 1·90 1·80
1910 8s.50 Rabbi Zevi Hirsch Kalischer .... 6·25 5·50
1909/1910 *Set of 2* .... 7·25 6·50
1909/1910 *Set of 2 with tabs* .... 8·75 8·00

815 Air France DC3, Envelope and Haifa

(Des Meir Eshel and Pierre-André Cousin. Photo)

2008 (6 Nov). 60th Anniversary of France–Israel Relations. 60th Anniversary of First Flight from Israel to France. T **815** and similar horiz design. One phosphor bar (1s.60) or two phosphor bars (3s.80). P 13½×13.

1911 1s.60 Type **815** .... 1·50 1·40
1912 3s.80 Paris, envelope and aircraft .... 3·25 3·00
1911/1912 *Set of 2* .... 4·25 4·00
1911/1912 *Set of 3 with tabs* .... 5·00 4·75

Stamps of a similar design were issued by France.

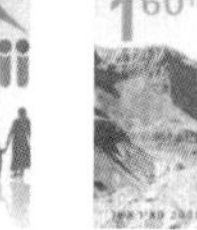

816 Families and Calculations

817 Bar Kokhba Letter

(Des Huri Haviv. Litho)

2008 (17 Dec). 2008-Census. One phosphor bar. P 14×13.

1913 **816** 1s.60 multicoloured .... 1·50 1·40
With tab 1·60 1·40

(Des Meir Eishel. Litho)

2008 (17 Dec). Stamp Day. Ancient Letters. T **817** and similar horiz designs. Multicoloured. One phosphor bar (1s.60). P 14×13.

1914 1s.60 Type **817** .... 1·30 1·20
1915 2s.30 Lachish letter .... 1·90 1·80
1916 8s.50 Letter from Ugarit .... 6·50 6·00
1914/1916 *Set of 3* .... 8·75 8·00
1914/1916 *Set of 3 with tabs* .... 10·50 9·50

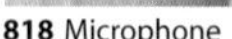

818 Microphone

819 Young People enclosed in Frame

(Des Osnat Eshel. Litho)

2008 (17 Dec). 50th (2010) Anniversary of Galei Zahal (IDF Broadcasting Service). P 14×13.

1917 **818** 2s.30 multicoloured .... 1·90 1·80
With tab 2·10 1·90

(Des David Harel. Litho)

2008 (17 Dec). Taglit–Birthright Israel (young adults educational tour of Israel). P 14×13.

1918	**819**	5s.60 multicoloured	4·25	3·75
		With tab	4·50	4·25

819a Menorah

820 Grapes

2009 (1 Jan). Menorah. Self-adhesive. Die-cut wavy edge.

1918*a*	**819a**	30a. olive-brown	50	50
1918*b*		50a. brown-olive	70	65
1918*c*		1s. deep reddish violet	90	80
1918*a*/1918*c* *Set of 3*			1·90	1·80

(Des Meir Eshel. Litho)

2009 (17 Feb). Fruit. T **820** and similar vert designs. No Value Expressed. Multicoloured. One phosphor bar. P 14.

1919	(1s.60) Type **820**	1·30	1·20
	a. Strip of 5. Nos. 1919/1923	6·75	
1920	(1s.60) Lemon	1·30	1·20
1921	(1s.60) Avocado	1·30	1·20
1922	(1s.60) Orange	1·30	1·20
1923	(1s.60) Pomegranate	1·30	1·20
1919/1923 *Set of 5*		5·75	5·50
1919/1923 *Set of 5 with tabs*		7·00	6·50

Nos. 1919/1923 were printed, *se-tenant*, in horizontal strips of five stamps within sheets of 25 stamps.

See also Nos. 1975/1979.

821 Coastal Scenes

(Des Moshe Pereg. Litho)

2009 (17 Feb). Centenary of Tel Aviv. T **821** and similar horiz designs. Multicoloured. One phosphor bar (1s.60), two phosphor bars (3s.80) or none (2s.30). P 14×13½.

1924	1s.60 Type **821**	1·30	1·20
1925	2s.30 White City (World Heritage Site of Bauhaus style buildings)	1·90	1·80
1926	3s.80 Parks and gardens	3·25	3·00
1924/1926 *Set of 3*		5·75	5·50
1924/1926 *Set of 3 with tabs*		7·00	6·50

822 Mountain Biking

(Des Igal Gabai. Litho)

2009 (17 Feb). Extreme Sports. T **822** and similar horiz designs. Multicoloured. Two phosphor bars. P 14×13½.

1927	4s.40 Type **822**	3·75	3·25
1928	5s.40 Sky diving	4·25	3·75
1929	5s.60 Surfing	4·75	4·25
1927/1929 *Set of 3*		11·50	10·00
1927/1929 *Set of 3 with tabs*		13·00	12·00

2009 (Feb). Children's Sheets. Eight sheets, each 148×200 mm containing various vert designs. Die-cut rouletted.

MS1929*a* (1s.20) As No. 1645 (open box)	8·75	8·00
MS1929*b* (1s.20) As No. 1646 (boy growing heart)	8·75	8·00
MS1929*c* (1s.20) As No. 1655 (flowers)	8·75	8·00
MS1929*d* (1s.20) As No. 1656 (air balloon)	8·75	8·00
MS1929*e* (1s.20) As No. 1657 (boy and teddy)	8·75	8·00
MS1929*f* (1s.50) As No. 1846 (Israel written in sand)	8·75	8·00
MS1929*g* (1s.50) As No. 1887 (rose)	8·75	8·00
MS1929*h* (1s.55) As No. 1888 (cyclamen)	8·75	8·00

Nos. **MS**1929*a*/**MS**1929*h* contained one example of the stamp named, a stamp-size label and three stickers, each 54×77 mm.

823 Yossi Banai

824 Jacob's Staff (tool for mapping stars invented by Gersonides)

(Des Miri Nestor. Litho)

2009 (22 Apr). Israeli Music. T **823** and similar square designs. Multicoloured. P 13.

1930	1s.60 Type **823**	1·10	1·00
	a. Strip of 4. Nos. 1930/1933	13·50	
	b. Sheetlet of 12. Nos. 1930/1941		
1931	1s.60 Meir Ariel	1·10	1·00
1932	1s.60 Sasha Argov	1·10	1·00
1933	1s.60 Zohar Argov	1·10	1·00
1934	1s.60 Naomi Shemer	1·10	1·00
	a. Pair. Nos 1934/1935		
1935	1s.60 Yair Rosenblum	1·10	1·00
1936	1s.60 Ehud Manor	1·10	1·00
	a. Strip of 4. Nos. 1936/1939		
1937	1s.60 Arik Lavie	1·10	1·00
1938	1s.60 Uzi Hitman	1·10	1·00
1939	1s.60 Ofra Hazi	1·10	1·00
1940	1s.60 Moshe Wilensky	1·10	1·00
	a. Pair. Nos. 1940/1941		
1941	1s.60 Shoshana Damari	1·10	1·00
1930/1941 *Set of 12*		12·00	11·00
1930/1941 *Set of 12 with tabs*		15·00	14·00

Nos. 1930/1933 and 1936/1939 were printed *se-tenant*, in horizontal strips of four, Nos. 1934/1935 and 1940/1941 in horizontal pairs, each strip or pair sharing a composite background design, surrounding a block of four stamp-size labels, each showing part of a disc.

The stamps were arranged so that each have *se-tenant* tab at foot, the tabs forming the margin of the sheet.

(Des David Ben-Hador. Litho)

2009 (22 Apr). Astronomy. T **824** and similar horiz designs. Multicoloured. P 14½×14.

1942	2s.30 Type **824**	1·90	1·80
1943	3s.80 Gravitational Lensing	3·00	2·75
1944	8s.50 Laser Interferometer Space Antenna	6·50	6·00
1942/1944 *Set of 3*		10·50	9·50
1942/1944 *Set of 3 with tabs*		12·50	11·00

825 Memorial Day Badge

826 *Berek Joselewicz* (Juliusz Kossak)

(Des Hayyimi Kivkovitch. Litho)

2009 (22 Apr). Memorial Day. P 14½×14.

1945	**825**	1s.60 multicoloured	1·30	1·20
		With tab	1·40	1·30

(Des Marzanna Dabrowska and Zvika Roitman. Litho Enschedé)

2009 (22 Apr). Polish Year in Israel. Sheet 70×90 mm. P 14.

MS1946 **826**	6s.10 multicoloured	6·00	5·50

A stamp of a similar design was issued by Poland.

827 Heart

828 Floating Tourist and Ibex

(Des Miri Nestor. Litho)

2009 (30 June). Love. No value expressed. One phosphor bar. P 14.

1947 **827** (1s.60) multicoloured 1·60 1·50

With tab 1·70 1·60

No. 1947 was originally on sale for 1s.60.

(Des Meir Eshel. Litho)

2009 (30 June). Dead Sea–Lowest Place on Earth. P 14.

1948 **828** 2s.30 multicoloured 2·10 1·90

With tab 2·30 2·10

829 Globe as Kettle

830 Athletes

(Des Igal Gabai. Litho)

2009 (30 June). Global Warming. T **829** and similar multicoloured designs. P 14.

1949 2s.30 Type **829** 1·90 1·80

a. Strip of 3. Nos. 1949/1951 6·00

1950 2s.30 Globe melting in frypan (61×31 *mm*) 1·90 1·80

1951 2s.30 Solar powered house 1·90 1·80

1949/1951 *Set of 3* 5·25 4·75

1949/1951 *Set of 3 with tabs* 6·25 5·75

Nos. 1949/1951 were printed, *se-tenant*, in horizontal strips of three stamps within the sheet.

(Des Ronen Goldberg. Litho)

2009 (30 June). 18th Maccabiah (games). Two phosphor bars. P 14.

1952 **830** 5s.60 multicoloured 5·00 4·50

With tab 5·25 4·75

831 Harpist

832 Honeybee and Flower

(Des David Ben-Hader. Litho)

2009 (30 June). 50th Anniversary of International Harp Contest, Israel. P 14.

1953 **831** 8s.50 multicoloured 7·25 6·50

With tab 7·50 7·00

(Des Igal Gabai. Litho)

2009 (8 Sept). Honey. T **832** and similar horiz designs. Multicoloured. One phosphor bar (1s.60) or two phosphor bars (others). P 14.

1954 1s.60 Type **832** 1·40 1·30

1955 4s.60 Honeycomb 4·00 3·75

1956 6s.70 Pouring honey 5·25 4·75

1954/1956 *Set of 3* 9·50 8·75

1954/1956 *Set of 3 with tabs* 11·50 10·50

833 Woman with Dog

834 Instant Messaging Software

(Des Meir Eshel and Tuvia Kurtz. Litho)

2009 (8 Sept). Animal Assisted Therapy. T **833** and similar horiz designs. Multicoloured.

(a) Sheet stamps. Ordinary gum. P 14.

1957 2s.40 Type **833** 1·90 1·80

1958 2s.40 Girl with Dolphin 1·90 1·80

1959 2s.40 Girl with Horse 1·90 1·80

1957/1959 *Set of 3* 5·25 4·75

1957/1959 *Set of 3 with tabs* 6·25 5·75

(b) Booklet stamps. Self-adhesive. Die-cut perf 14.

1960 2s.40 As Type **833** 1·90 1·80

1961 2s.40 As No 1958 1·90 1·80

1962 2s.40 As No. 1959 1·90 1·80

1960/1962 *Set of 3* 5·25 4·75

1960/1962 *Set of 3 with tabs* 6·25 5·75

(Des Hayyimi Kivovitch. Litho)

2009 (8 Sept). Virtual Communication. T **834** and similar horiz designs. Multicoloured. No phosphor bar (2s.40) or two phosphor bars (others). P 14.

1963 2s.40 Type **834** 1·60 1·50

1964 5s.30 USB flash drive 4·25 4·00

1965 6s.50 Voice over internet protocol 5·75 5·25

1963/1965 *Set of 3* 10·50 9·75

1963/1965 *Set of 3 with tabs* 12·50 11·50

835 Child playing Doctor

836 Stage

(Des Yael Arad-Arami and Tuvia Kurtz. Litho)

2009 (8 Sept). 75th Anniversary of Leumit Health Fund. P 14.

1966 **835** 8s.80 multicoloured 7·25 6·50

With tab 7·50 7·00

(Des David Ben-Hador)

2009 (26 Nov). Death Centenary of Avram Goldfaden (founder of first Yiddish theatre (No. 1876), Iasi, Romania). Two phosphor bars. P 14.

1967 **836** 4s.60 multicoloured 4·00 3·75

With tab 4·25 3·75

A stamp of a similar design was issued by Romania.

837 Jaffa

838 Amphora

(Des Osnat Eshel. Litho)

2009 (26 Nov). Stamp Day. Lighthouses. T **837** and similar horiz designs. Multicoloured. Two phosphor bars (No. 1968/1969). P 14.

1968 4s.60 Type **837** 3·50 3·25

1969 6s.70 Tel Aviv 5·25 4·75

1970 8s.80 Ashdod 7·25 6·50

1968/1970 *Set of 3* 14·50 13·00

1968/1970 *Set of 3 with tabs* 17·00 16·00

(Des Eliezer Weishoff. Litho)

2009 (26 Nov). Marine Archaeology. T **838** and similar horiz designs. Multicoloured. Two phosphor bars (3s.60). P 14.

1971 2s.40 Type **838** 1·90 1·80

1972 2s.40 Figurines 1·90 1·80

1973 3s.60 Weaponry 2·75 2·75

1974 5s. Anchors 4·25 4·00

1971/1974 *Set of 4* 9·75 9·25

1971/1974 *Set of 4 with tabs* 12·00 11·00

(Des Meir Eshel. Litho)

2009 (26 Nov). Fruit. Vert designs as T **820**. No Value Expressed. Multicoloured. Self-adhesive. One phosphor bar. Die-cut perf 14.

1975 (1s.60) As Type **820** 1·20 1·10

1976 (1s.60) Lemon (As No. 1920) ... 1·20 1·10
1977 (1s.60) Avocado (As No. 1921) ... 1·20 1·10
1978 (1s.60) Orange (As No. 1922) ... 1·20 1·10
1979 (1s.60) Pomegranate (As No. 1923) ... 1·20 1·10
1975/1979 *Set of 5* ... 5·50 5·00
1975/1979 *Set of 5 with tabs* ... 6·75 6·25

Nos. 1975/1979, each×4 were printed in booklets of 20 stamps, the stamps peeled directly from the booklet cover.

2010 (10 Jan). Menorah. Self-adhesive. Die-cut wavy edge.
1979*a* **819a** 40a slate-green ... 65 60
With tab 75 70

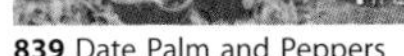

839 Date Palm and Peppers

840 *Carduelis carduelis* (Gold Finch)

(Des Eli Carmeli)

2010 (27 Jan). 50th Anniversary of Settling the Arava. One phosphor bar. P 14.
1980 **839** 1s.60 multicoloured ... 1·40 1·30
With tab 1·50 1·40

(Des Tuvia Kurtz and Ronen Goldberg)

2010 (27 Jan). Birds. T **840** and similar vert designs. Multicoloured. P 14.
1981 2s.40 Type **840** ... 1·90 1·80
a. Strip of 3. Nos. 1981/1983 ... 6·00
1982 2s.40 *Upupa epops* (Hoopoe) (National Bird) .. 1·90 1·80
1983 2s.40 *Prinia gracilis* (Graceful Prinia) ... 1·90 1·80
1981/1983 *Set of 3* ... 5·25 4·75
1981/1983 *Set of 3 with tabs* ... 6·25 5·75

Nos. 1981/1983 were printed, *se-tenant*, in horizontal strips of three stamps within the sheet, each strip forming a composite design.

841 Child and Dove

(Des Igal Gabai)

2010 (27 Jan). 50th Anniversary of Lions, Israel. Two phosphor bands. P 14.
1984 **841** 4s.60 multicoloured ... 4·50 4·25
With tab 4·75 4·50

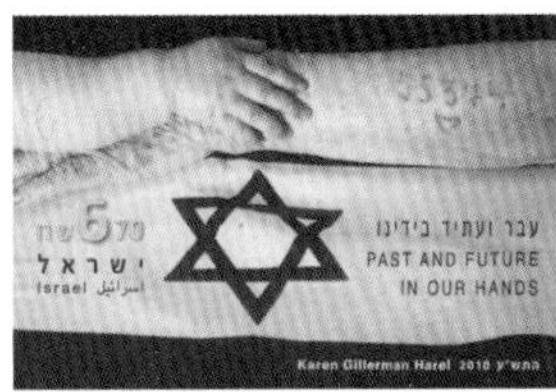

842 Child's and Camp Inmate's Arms

(Des Osnat Eshel)

2010 (27 Jan). Holocaust Remembrance Day. Two phosphor bars. P 14.
1985 **842** 6s.70 multicoloured ... 6·00 5·50
With tab 6·50 6·00

843 Gymnasts and Students, Alliance School, Tehran, May 1936

844 Flower and Rocks

(Des Zvika Roitman)

2010 (27 Jan). 150th Anniversary of Alliance Israelite Universelle. P 14.
1986 **843** 8s.80 multicoloured ... 8·25 7·50
With tab 8·75 8·00

(Des Osnat Ethel)

2010 (14 Apr). Memorial Day. One phosphor bar. P 14.
1987 **844** 1s.60 multicoloured ... 1·70 1·50
With tab 1·80 1·60

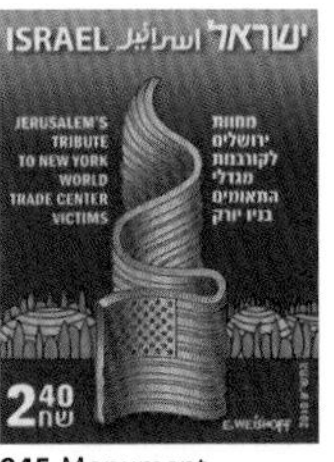

845 Monument, Jerusalem

846 Drip Irrigation (agriculture)

2010 (14 Apr). Living Memorial Plaza (designed by Eliezer Weishoff) (tribute to World Trade Centre victims). P 14.
1988 **845** 2s.40 multicoloured ... 2·40 2·20
With tab 2·75 2·40

(Des Meir Eshel)

2010 (14 Apr). Expo 2010, Shanghai. Israeli Innovations. T **846** and similar horiz designs. Multicoloured. P 14.
1989 2s.40 Type **846** ... 2·20 2·00
1990 2s.40 Intel chips and processors (information technology) ... 2·20 2·00
1991 2s.40 Pill camera (medicine) ... 2·20 2·00
1989/1991 *Set of 3* ... 6·00 5·50
1989/1991 *Set of 3 with tabs* ... 7·25 6·50

847 Theodor Herzl

848 Figures forming Maple Leaf and Star of David

(Des Moshe Pereg)

2010 (14 Apr). 150th Birth Anniversary of Theodor Binyamin Ze'ev Herzl (Zionist pioneer). Sheet 140×76 mm containing T **847** and similar horiz designs. Multicoloured. P 14.
MS1992 3s.70 Type **847**; 4s Builders, houses and tents; 6s.70 Modern Israelis ... 18·00 16·00

(Des Karen Henricks, Yarek Waszul and Miri Nestor)

2010 (14 Apr). 60th Anniversary of Israel–Canada Diplomatic Relations. Two phosphor bars. P 14.
1993 **848** 4s.60 bright rose-red, blue and dull yellow-green ... 5·50 5·00
With tab 5·50 5·00

A similar design was issued Canada.

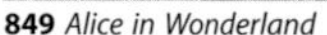

849 *Alice in Wonderland*

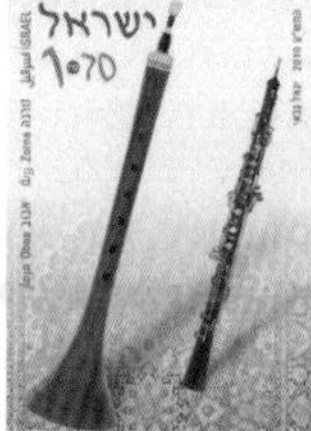

850 Oboe and Zorna

(Des Danny Kerman and Igal Gabai)

2010 (14 Apr). Europa. Children's Books. Sheet 142×75 mm containing T **849** and similar horiz designs. Multicoloured. P 14.

MS1994 4s.60×3, Type **849**; *Peter Pan*; *Gulliver's Travels* .... 16·00 15·00

(Des Igal Gabai. Litho Enschedé)

2010 (14 June). Musical Instruments of the Middle East. T **850** and similar vert designs showing instruments and oriental rugs. Multicoloured. P 13½×14.

1995	1s.70 Type **850**	2·10	2·00
	a. Horiz strip of 5. Nos. 1995/1999	11·00	
1996	1s.70 Rebab and violin	2·10	2·00
1997	1s.70 Darbuka (inscr 'Darbouka') and drum	2·10	2·00
1998	1s.70 Qanun and piano	2·10	2·00
1999	1s.70 Oud and guitar	2·10	2·00
1995/1999	*Set of 5*	9·50	9·00
1995/1999	*Set of 5 with tabs*	11·50	10·50

Nos. 1995/1999 were printed, *se-tenant*, in horizontal strips of five stamps within the sheet.

851 Water Tower (security), Orange (agriculture) and Mill Wheel (industry)

852 *Shmulikipod* (Shmuel the Hedgehog) (Noga Yudkowitz)

(Des Ronen Goldberg. Litho Enschedé)

2010 (14 June). Centenary of Kibbutz. P 14×13½.

2000	**851**	2s.50 multicooured	2·75	2·50
		With tab	3·00	2·75

(Des David Ben-Hador. Litho Enschedé)

2010 (14 June). Story Gardens, Holon. T **852** and similar horiz designs showing sculptures from the gardens, artists' names given. Multicoloured.

2001	2s.50 Type **852**	2·75	2·50
2002	2s.50 *Where is Pluto* (Dorit Levinstein)	2·75	2·50
2003	2s.50 *Soul Bird* (David Gerstein)	2·75	2·50
2001/2003	*Set of 3*	7·50	6·75
2001/2003	*Set of 3 with tabs*	9·00	8·25

853 Tikun Clali Assembly at Rabi Nachman's Gravesite, Uman, Ukraine

(Des Rabbi Israel Yitzchak Bezanson and David Ben-Hador. Litho Enschedé)

2010 (14 June). Death Bicentenary of Rabbi Nachman of Breslev (Hasidic philosopher). P 13½×14.

2004	**853**	3s.70 multicoloured	4·25	4·00
		With tab	4·50	4·25

854 Simon Wiesenthal in Star of David

(Des Michael Rosenfeld. British Thai Security Ptg (litho) Outer Aspect (laser printing))

2010 (14 June). Simon Wiesenthal (holocaust survivor and pursuer of war criminals) Commemoration. P 14.

2005	**854**	5s. multicoloured	6·00	5·50
		With tab	6·25	5·75

A stamp of a similar design was issued by Austria.

855 Dinghies

(Des Mali and Momi Alon. Litho Enschedé)

2010 (14 June). International 420 Sailing World Championship, 2010, Haifa. P 14.

2006	**855**	9s. multicoloured	10·50	9·75
		With tab	11·50	10·50

On 26 July 2010 a personalised sheet entitled 'A year of Fun. My First Hebrew Calendar' containing 12 examples of No. 1888 and 12 labels was on sale for 38s. The face value of the stamps was 20s.40

856 Wine Glass ('Happy Holidays')

857 Two Chicks

(Des Miri Nestor. Litho Enschedé)

2010 (25 Aug). Greetings Stamps. T **856** and similar vert designs. Multicoloured. One phosphor bar.

(a) Ordinary gum. P 14.

2007	(1s.70) As Type **856**	1·90	1·70
2008	(1s.70) Script and pen ('With compliments')	1·90	1·70
2007/2008	*Set of 2*	3·50	3·00
2007/2008	*Set of 2 with tabs*	4·00	3·75

(b) Booklet stamps. Self-adhesive. Die-cut perf 13.

2009	(1s.70) As Type **856**	1·90	1·70
2010	(1s.70) As No. 2008	1·90	1·70
2009/2010	*Set of 2*	3·50	3·00
2009/2010	*Set of 2 with tabs*	4·00	3·75

Nos. 2007/2008 were printed in sheets of 12 stamps each with a *se-tenant* label which could be personalised by the addition of a photograph.

Nos. 2009/2010, each×6, were printed in booklets of 12 stamps with 12 small square labels for attaching to correspondence.

(Des Hila Havkin and Miri Nestor. Litho Cartor)

2010 (25 Aug). Domestic Animals and their Young. T **857** and similar horiz designs. Multicoloured. One phosphor bar. P 13×13½.

2011	1s.70 Type **857**	1·90	1·70
	a. Horiz strip of 2. Nos. 2011/2012 plus central label	4·00	
	b. Vert strip of 3. Nos. 2011, 2013 and 2015	6·00	
	c. Sheetlet. Nos. 2011/2016, plus 3 labels	12·00	

2012 1s.70 Hen .... 1·90 1·70
a. Vert strip of 3. Nos. 2012, 2014 and 2016........ 6·00
2013 1s.70 Kitten and ball of wool .... 1·90 1·70
a. Horiz strip of 2. Nos. 2013/2014 plus central label .... 4·00
2014 1s.70 Cat........ 1·90 1·70
2015 1s.70 Rabbit kitten........ 1·90 1·70
a. Horiz strip of 2. Nos. 2015/2016 plus label........ 4·00
2016 1s.70 Rabbit........ 1·90 1·70
2011/2016 *Set of 6*........ 10·50 9·25
2011/2016 *Set of 6 with tabs*........ 12·00 11·00

Nos. 2011/2012, 2013/2014 and 2015/2016 were each printed, *se-tenant*, in horizontal strips of two stamps surrounding a central stamp size label, each strip forming a composite design, and also forming (Nos. 2011, 2013 and 2016, and 2012, 2014 and 2016), *se-tenant*, vertical strips of three stamps within the sheet.

858 Ram's Horn Shofar

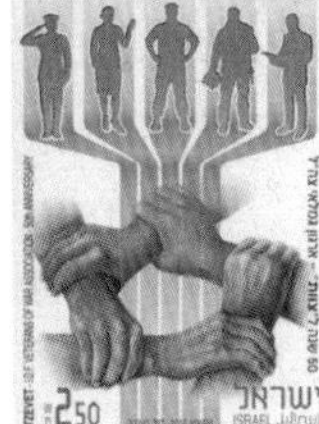

859 Clasped Hands

(Des Aharon Shevo. Litho Cartor)

2010 (25 Aug). Festivals. Shofars. T **858** and similar vert designs showing shofars (horns used for religious purposes, incorporated in synagogue services on Rosh Hashanah and Yom Kippur). Multicoloured. One phosphor bar (1s.70) or two phosphor bars (others). P 13½×13.

2017 1s.70 Type **858**........ 1·90 1·70
2018 4s.20 Yemeni shofar made from Kudu horn... 4·50 4·25
2019 6s.10 Ram's horn shofar (*different*)........ 6·75 6·25
2017/2019 *Set of 3*........ 12·00 11·00
2017/2019 *Set of 3 with tabs*........ 14·00 12·50

(Des David Ben-Hador. Litho Cartor)

2010 (25 Aug). 50th Anniversary of Tzevet (Israel Defence Forces Veterans' Association). P 13½×13.

2020 **859** 2s.50 multicoloured........ 3·00 2·75
With tab 3·25 3·00

860 Early Apartments and Windmill

2010 (25 Aug). 150th Anniversary of First Habitations outside Jerusalem Old City Walls. P 13½.

2021 **860** 3s.70 multicoloured........ 4·25 4·00
With tab 4·50 4·25

861 Woman with Dog and City Street Scene

(Des Igal Gabai. Litho Cartor)

2010 (25 Aug). Urban Renaissance. P 13½.

2022 **861** 8s.90 multicoloured........ 9·50 8·75
With tab 10·00 9·25

862 Church of All Nations and Garden of Gethsemane, Jerusalem

863 Star of David

(Des Meir Eshel. Litho Cartor)

2010 (15 Nov). Visit of Pope Benedict XVI to Israel, May 2009. P 13½.

2023 **862** 4s.20 multicoloured........ 4·75 4·25
With tab 5·00 4·50

A stamp of a similar design was issued by Vatican City.

(Des Osnat Eshel. Litho Enschedé)

2010 (21 Nov). National Flag. No value expressed. One phosphor bar. P 14.

2024 **863** (1s.70) pale dull ultramarine and black..... 1·90 1·70
With tab 2·00 1·80

A sheet of 12 examples of No. 2024 and 12 stamp size labels, issued for the Bicentenary of Latin America, was on sale, above face value, for 38s.

No. 2024 was also printed in sheets of 12 stamps each with a *se-tenant* label which could be personalised by the addition of a photograph.

864 Jonah and the Whale (inscr 'Fish')

(Des Diana Shimon and Meir Eshel. Litho Cartor)

2010 (21 Nov). Bible Stories. T **864** and similar multicoloured designs. One phosphor bar (1s.70). P 14½.

2025 1s.70 Type **864**........ 2·10 2·00
2026 1s.70 Samson and the Lion........ 2·10 2·00
2027 1s.70 Adam and Eve........ 2·10 2·00
2025/2027 *Set of 3*........ 5·75 5·50
2025/2027 *Set of 3 with tabs*........ 6·75 6·25
MS2028 100×70 mm. 6s. Parting of the Red Sea (30×40 *mm*)........ 11·50 10·50

865 Farmer picking Sabra Fruit

866 Armon Cinema, Haifa

(Des Mysh. Litho Cartor)

2010 (21 Nov). 50th Anniversary of ASIFA (Association Internationale du Film d' Animation), France and 25th Anniversary of ASIFA, Israel. T **865** and similar horiz designs showing animation sequence. Multicoloured. One phosphor bar.

(a) Sheet stamps. Ordinary gum. P 13½.

2029 1s.70 Type **865**........ 1·90 1·70
a. Sheet of 15. Nos. 2029/2043........ 30·00
2030 1s.70 Farmer smiling, grasping fruit, girl with clasped hands........ 1·90 1·70
2031 1s.70 Farmer squashing fruit, girl reaching forward........ 1·90 1·70
2032 1s.70 Farmer squashing fruit, girl reaching forward (*different*)........ 1·90 1·70
2033 1s.70 Farmer facing forward........ 1·90 1·70
2034 1s.70 Farmer facing left, opening hands, girl with hands between gloves........ 1·90 1·70

2035	1s.70 Girl taking fruit, farmer with open hands	1·90	1·70
2036	1s.70 Girl eating fruit	1·90	1·70
2037	1s.70 Girl with both hands to mouth	1·90	1·70
2038	1s.70 Girl with both hands to mouth, farmer looking worried	1·90	1·70
2039	1s.70 Girl with eyes closed, farmer looking worried	1·90	1·70
2040	1s.70 Girl smiling, farmer looking worried	1·90	1·70
2041	1s.70 Farmer laughing	1·90	1·70
2042	1s.70 Farmer looking over left shoulder at sabra cactus	1·90	1·70
2043	1s.70 Girl with hands behind back, farmer turning towards cactus	1·90	1·70
2029/2043	*Set of* 15	26·00	23·00
2029/2043	*Set of* 15 *with tabs*	30·00	28·00

(b) Booklet stamps. Self-adhesive. Die-cut wavy edge.

2044	1.70 Type **865**	1·90	1·70
2045	1.70 As No. 2030	1·90	1·70
2046	1.70 As No. 2031	1·90	1·70
2047	1.70 As No. 2032	1·90	1·70
2048	1.70 As No. 2033	1·90	1·70
2049	1.70 As No. 2034	1·90	1·70
2050	1.70 As No. 2035	1·90	1·70
2051	1.70 As No. 2036	1·90	1·70
2052	1.70 As No. 2037	1·90	1·70
2053	1.70 As No. 2038	1·90	1·70
2054	1.70 As No. 2039	1·90	1·70
2055	1.70 As No. 2040	1·90	1·70
2056	1.70 As No. 2041	1·90	1·70
2057	1.70 As No. 2042	1·90	1·70
2058	1.70 As No. 2043	1·90	1·70
2044/2058	*Set of* 15	26·00	23·00
2044/2058	*Set of* 15 *with tabs*	30·00	28·00

Nos. 2029/2043 were printed, *se-tenant*, in sheets of 15 stamps.

Nos. 2044/2058 were printed in booklets of 15 stamps, which, when the pages were flicked, give the appearance of animation.

(Des David Ben-Hador. Litho Cartor)

2010 (21 Nov). Stamp Day. Cinemas. T **866** and similar horiz design. Multicoloured. Two phosphor bars (9s.). P 13×13½.

2059	4s.20 Type **866**	4·75	4·25
2060	9s. Zion Cinema, Jerusalem	9·50	8·75
2059/2060	*Set of* 2	13·00	11·50
2059/2060	*Set of* 2 *with tabs*	15·00	14·00

867 Ubiquitin (protein destructor) (Aaron Ciechanover, Avram Hershko and Irwin Rose's Nobel Prize in Chemistry, 2004)

868 Leopard

(Des Hayyimi Kivkovitch)

2011 (4 Jan). International Year of Chemistry. T **867** and similar horiz design. Multicoloured. Two phosphor bars. P 14.

2061	4s.20 Type **867**	4·50	4·25
2062	6s.10 Ribosome (protein constructor) (Venkatraman Ramakrishnan, Thomas A. Steitz and Ada E. Yonath's Nobel Prize in Chemistry, 2009)	6·75	6·25
2061/2062	*Set of* 2	10·00	9·50
2061/2062	*Set of* 2 *with tabs*	12·00	11·00

(Des Tuvia Kurtz and Ronen Goldberg)

2011 (7 Feb). Endangered Species. Persian Leopard (*Panthera pardus saxicolor*). T **868** and similar vert designs showing Leopards. Multicoloured. One phosphor bar. P 14.

2063	1s.70 Type **868**	2·10	2·00
	a. Pair. Nos. 2063/2064	4·50	4·25
	b. Block fo 4. Nos. 2063/2066	8·75	
2064	1s.70 Leaping	2·10	2·00
2065	1s.70 Drinking	2·10	2·00
	a. Pair. Nos. 2065/2066	4·50	4·25
2066	1s.70 Mother and cub	2·10	2·00
2063/2066	*Set of* 4	7·50	7·25
2063/2066	*Set of* 4 *with tabs*	9·00	8·25

Nos. 2063/2064 and 2065/2066, respectively, were printed, *se-tenant*, in horizontal pairs within the sheet.

869 Ceasarea

870 Plant with Hebrew Language as Roots and Soil

(Des Meir Eshel and Tuvia Kurtz)

2011 (7 Feb). Herod`s Building Projects. T **869** and similar vert designs. Multicoloured. One phosphor band (1s.70). P 14.

2067	1s.70 Type **869**	2·10	2·00
2068	1s.70 Masada	2·10	2·00
2069	2s.50 Jerusalem	2·75	2·50
2070	2s.50 Herodian	2·75	2·50
2067/2070	*Set of* 4	8·75	8·00
2067/2070	*Set of* 4 *with tabs*	10·50	9·75

(Des David Beb-Hador)

2011 (7 Feb). Hebrew Language. P 14.

2071	**870** 3s.70 multicoloured	4·25	4·00
	With tab	4·50	4·25

871 Baby and Laptop showing Health Care Providers

(Des Zvika Roitman)

2011 (7 Feb). Centenary of Clalit Health Services. P 14.

2072	**871** 9s. multicoloured	10·50	9·75
	With tab	11·50	10·50

872 *Papilio machaon syriacus*

(Des Tuvia Kurtz and Miri Nestor. Litho Cartor (sheet stamps))

2011 (12 Apr). Butterflies. T **872** and similar vert designs. Multicoloured. One phosphor bar.

(a) Ordinary gum. P 14.

2073	(1s.70) Type **872**	1·90	1·70
	a. Strip of 3. Nos. 2073/2075	6·00	
	b. Sheetlet. Nos. 2073/2078	12·00	
2074	(1s.70) *Vanessa atalanta*	1·90	1·70
2075	(1s.70) *Anaphaeis aurota*	1·90	1·70
2076	(1s.70) *Apharitis acamas*	1·90	1·70
	a. Strip of 3. Nos. 2076/2078	6·00	
2077	(1s.70) *Danaus chrysippus*	1·90	1·70
2078	(1s.70) *Polyommatus icarus zelleri*	1·90	1·70
2073/2078	*Set of* 6	10·50	9·25
2073/2078	*Set of* 6 *with tabs*	12·00	11·00

(b) Self-adhesive. Die-cut perf 13½×14.

2078*a*	(1s.70) As Type **872**	1·90	1·70
2078*b*	(1s.70) *Vanessa atalanta*	1·90	1·70
2078*c*	(1s.70) *Anaphaeis aurota*	1·90	1·70
2078*d*	(1s.70) *Apharitis acamas*	1·90	1·70
2078*e*	(1s.70) *Danaus chrysippus*	1·90	1·70
2078*f*	(1s.70) *Polyommatus icarus zelleri*	1·90	1·70
2078*a*/2078*f*	*Set of* 6	10·50	9·25
2078*a*/2078*f*	*Set of* 6 *with tabs*	12·00	11·00

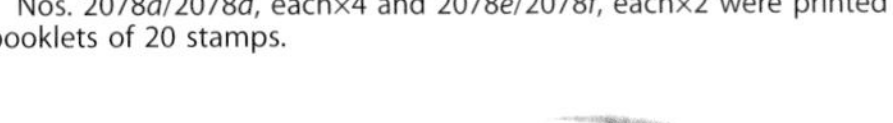

Nos. 2073/2075 and 2076/2078, respectively were printed, *se-tenant*, in horizontal strips of three stamps within sheetlets of six stamps.

Nos. 2076/2078 are laid reversed to Nos. 2073/2075, separated by an illustrated gutter.

Nos. 2078*a*/2078*d*, each×4 and 2078*e*/2078*f*, each×2 were printed in booklets of 20 stamps.

873 Crowd

(Des Igal Gabai)

2011 (12 Apr). Aliyah of Ethiopian Jewry. P 14½.

2079	**873**	2s.50 multicoloured	3·25	3·00
		With tab	3·50	3·25

874 Country Road

875 Sea of Galilee

(Des Osnat Eshel)

2011 (12 Apr). Memorial Day. One phosphor bar. P 13½×13.

2080	**874**	1s.70 multicoloured	2·10	2·00
		With tab	2·30	2·10

(Des Meir Eshel)

2011 (12 Apr). Tourism. Visit Israel. T **875** and similar horiz designs. Multicoloured. Two phosphor bars (4s.20 and 6s.10). P 14×13½.

2081	4s.20 Type **875**	4·75	4·25
2082	6s. Tower and fort, Jerusalem	7·00	6·25
2083	6s.10 Fish (Red Sea)	7·00	6·25
2081/2083	*Set of 3*	17·00	15·00
2081/2083	*Set of 3 with tabs*	20·00	18·00

876 Stylised Figures circling Globe

(Des Igal Gabai)

2011 (12 Apr). 50th Anniversary of Mount Carmel Training Centre, Haifa. P 13×13½.

2084	**876**	5s. multicoloured	6·00	5·50
		With tab	6·25	5·75

877 Ephraim Katzir

(Des Daniel Goldberg)

2011 (12 Apr). Ephraim Katzir (Ephraim Katchalski) (President 1973–1978, biophysicist and politician) Commemoration. P 13×13½.

2085	**877**	9s. multicoloured	10·00	9·25
		With tab	10·50	9·75

878 Rabbi Goren

879 Sea of Galilee Beach

(Des Moshe Pereg)

2011 (26 June). Rabbi Shlomo Goren (scholar and soldier) Commemoration. One phosphor bar. P 14.

2086	**878**	1s.70 multicoloured	1·90	1·70
		With tab	2·00	1·80

(Des Osnat Eshel)

2011 (27 June). Tourism. Beaches. T **879** and similar horiz designs. Multicoloured. One phosphor bar. P 14.

2087	1s.70 Type **879**	1·90	1·70
	a. Pair. Nos. 2087/2088	4·00	3·75
	b. Sheetlet of 10. Nos. 2087/2096	20·00	
2088	1s.70 Sea of Galilee beach, right	1·90	1·70
2089	1s.70 Caesarea beach, left	1·90	1·70
	a. Pair. Nos. 2089/2090	4·00	3·75
2090	1s.70 Caesarea beach, right	1·90	1·70
2091	1s.70 Tel-Aviv beach, left	1·90	1·70
	a. Pair. Nos. 2091/2092	4·00	3·75
2092	1s.70 Tel-Aviv beach, right	1·90	1·70
2093	1s.70 Dead Sea beach, left	1·90	1·70
	a. Pair. Nos. 2093/2094	4·00	3·75
2094	1s.70 Dead Sea beach, right	1·90	1·70
2095	1s.70 Eilat beach, left	1·90	1·70
	a. Pair. Nos. 2095/2096	4·00	3·75
2096	1s.70 Eilat beach, right	1·90	1·70
2087/2096	*Set of 10*	17·00	15·00
2087/2096	*Set of 10 with tabs*	20·00	18·00

Nos. 2087/2096, respectively, were printed, *se-tenant*, in horizontal pairs within sheets of ten stamps, each pair, with the tabs, forming a composite design of the beach mentioned.

880 Irrigating with Reclaimed Water

(Des Meir Eshel)

2011 (27 June). Israeli Achievements–Agriculture. T **880** and similar horiz designs. Multicoloured. P 14.

2097	2s.50 Type **880**	2·75	2·50
2098	2s.50 Improving Tomatoes through Breeding	2·75	2·50
2099	2s.50 Growing Crops with Saline Water	2·75	2·50
2097/2099	*Set of 3*	7·50	6·75
2097/2099	*Set of 3 with tabs*	9·00	8·25

881 Clown Doctor and Child

(Des Dudi Shmay and Igal Gabay)

2011 (27 June). Clown Care (programme in hospitals and medical centres involving visits from specially trained clowns). P 14.

2100	**881**	9s. multicoloured	10·00	9·25
		With tab	10·50	9·75

882 Arik Einstein and Shalom Hanoch in Concert

883 Player and Album Covers (*image reduced by 68% of original size*)

(Des David Ben-Hador. Litho Enschedé)

2011 (13 Sept). Israeli Music-Albums. T **882** and similar square designs showing album covers and forming the overall design T **883**. Multicoloured. P 14.

2101	1s.70 Type **882**	1·90	1·70
	a. Sheetlet. Nos. 2101/2112	24·00	
2102	1s.70 Shlomo Artzi–*Ways*	1·90	1·70
2103	1s.70 The Israel Andalusian Orchestra Hosts Jo Amar	1·90	1·70
2104	1s.70 Kaveret–*Poogy Tales*	1·90	1·70
2105	1s.70 Lehakat Tsliley Ha'ud	1·90	1·70
2106	1s.70 Corinne Allal–*Antarctica*	1·90	1·70
2107	1s.70 Lamb on green field and tree (HaKeves HaShisha Asar)	1·90	1·70
2108	1s.70 Boy seated on crossing bar watching train pass (Yehuda Poliker–*Ashes and Dust*)	1·90	1·70
2109	1s.70 Stylised face (Ehud Banai and the Refugees)	1·90	1·70
2110	1s.70 Yehoram Gaon–*The Middle of the Road*	1·90	1·70
2111	1s.70 The Doodaim	1·90	1·70
2112	1s.70 Woman seated outside radio shack (The Idan Raichel Project–*Out of the Depths*)	1·90	1·70
2101/2112	*Set of* 12	21·00	18·00
2101/2112	*Set of* 12 *with tabs*	24·00	22·00

Nos. 2101/2104 and 2109/2112 were printed *se-tenant*, in horizontal strips of four, Nos. 2105/2106 and 2107/2108 in vertical pairs, each strip or pair sharing a composite background design, surrounding a block of four stamp-size labels, each showing part of a disc.

The stamps were arranged so that each have a *se-tenant* tab, illustrating a song from the album, at foot, the tabs forming the margin of the sheet.

884 Apple and Honey

885 Tag

(Des Aharon Shevo. Litho Enschedé)

2011 (13 Sept). Festivals. Rosh Hashanah Feast. T **884** and similar horiz design. Multicoloured. One phosphor bar (1s.70) or two phosphor bars (others). P 14.

2113	1s.70 Type **884**	1·90	1·70
2114	4s. Fish head	4·25	4·00
2115	5s.90 Pomegranate	6·25	5·75
2113/2115	*Set of* 3	11·00	10·50
2113/2115	*Set of* 3 *with tabs*	13·00	12·00

(Des Eitan Kedmy and Miri Nestor. Litho Enschedé)

2011 (13 Sept). Children's Games. T **885** and similar horiz designs. Multicoloured.

(a) Ordinary gum. P 14.

2116	2s.60 Type **885**	2·75	2·50
2117	2s.60 Hopscotch	2·75	2·50
2118	2s.60 Hide and seek	2·75	2·50
2116/2118	*Set of* 3	7·50	6·75
2116/2118	*Set of* 3 *with tabs*	9·00	8·25

(b) Self-adhesive. Die-cut perf 13½×14.

2119	2s.60 As Type **885**	2·75	2·50
2120	2s.60 As No 2117	2·75	2·50
2121	2s.60 As No. 2118	2·75	2·50
2119/2121	*Set of* 3	7·50	6·75
2119/2121	*Set of* 3 *with tabs*	9·00	8·25

Nos. 2119/2121, each×2 were printed in booklets of six stamps.

886 Emblem

887 Avi Cohen

(Des Tali (Kahalon) Ovadia. Litho Enschedé)

2011 (13 Sept). Israel–Organisation for Economic Co-operation and Development (OECD) Member. P 14.

2122	**886** 9s.30 multicoloured	10·00	9·25
	With tab	10·50	9·75

(Des Ofir Begun and Meir Eshel. Litho Enschedé)

2011 (6 Dec). Israeli Football Legends. T **887** and similar horiz designs. Multicoloured. One phosphor bar. P 14.

2123	1s.70 Type **887** (Maccabi Tel Aviv, Liverpool and National Team player)	1·90	1·70
	a. Vert strip of 5. Nos. 2123/2127	9·75	
	b. Sheet of 10. Nos. 2123/2132	20·00	
2124	1s.70 Nahum Stelmach (Hapoel Petach Tikva player and National Team player and captain)	1·90	1·70
2125	1s.70 Eli Fuchs (Maccabi Tel Aviv player and National Team player and captain)	1·90	1·70
2126	1s.70 Natan Panz (Maccabi Tel Aviv, Beitar and National Team player)	1·90	1·70
2127	1s.70 Avi Ran (Maccabi Haifa and National Team goalkeeper)	1·90	1·70
2128	1s.70 Menachem Ashkenazi (international referee)	1·90	1·70
	a. Vert strip of 5. Nos. 2128/2132	9·75	
2129	1s.70 Jerry Beit Halevi (Maccabi Tel Aviv player and manager)	1·90	1·70
2130	1s.70 Shmuel Ben-Dror (Maccabi Avshalom Petach Tikva player and captain of National Team)	1·90	1·70
2131	1s.70 Ya'akov Grundman (Bnei Yehuda Tel Aviv player and National Team player and manager)	1·90	1·70
2132	1s.70 Ya'akov Hodorov (Hapoel Tel Aviv and National Team goalkeeper)	1·90	1·70
2123/2132	*Set of* 10	17·00	15·00
2123/2132	*Set of* 10 *with tabs*	20·00	18·00

Nos. 2123/2127 and 2128/2132, respectively were printed, *se-tenant*, in vertical strips of five within sheets of ten stamps (No. 2123b), with an enlarged illustrated central gutter.

The stamps were arranged so that each have a *se-tenant* tab, illustrating player's signature at left (Nos. 2123/2127), or right (Nos. 2128/2132) the tabs forming the vertical margins of the sheet.

888 Hartmann 2-8-2 Steam Engine and Train in Jezreel Valley

889 Love Message on Stylised Tree

(Des Ronen Goldberg and Tuvia Kurz. Litho Enschedé)

2011 (6 Dec). The Valley Railway (Rakevet HaEmek) (Hebrew nickname for Haifa branch line of Hijaz Railway). P 14.

2133	**888** 2s.60 multicoloured	2·75	2·50
	With tab	3·00	2·75

(Des Achva Kahana. Litho Enschedé)

2011 (6 Dec). Rescue Forces. P 14.

2134	**889** 3s.80 scarlet and apple-green	3·75	3·50
	With tab	4·00	3·75

890 Script

891 Script

(Des Meir Eshel. Litho Enschedé)

2011 (6 Dec). 75th Anniversary of Israel Philharmonic Orchestra. Two phosphor bars. P 14.

2135	**890**	4s. multicoloured	4·25	4·00
		With tab	4·50	4·25

(Des Aharon Shevo. Litho Cartor)

2012 (7 Jan). Death Bicentenary of Rabbi Shneur Zalman of Liadi (founder of Chabad Hasidism and a leader of Czarist Russia's Jewish community). One phosphor bar. P 13×13½.

2136	**891**	1s.70 multicoloured	1·90	1·70
		With tab	2·00	1·80

892 Candle

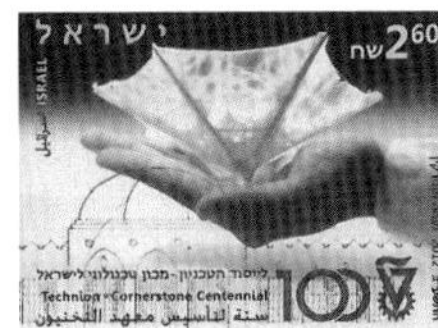

893 'Nano-parachute' (detector of airborne toxins) and Schematic of Building Façade

(Des Zvika Roitman. Litho Cartor)

2012 (7 Feb). In Memory. No Value Expressed. One phosphor bar. P 14.

2137	**892**	(1s.70) multicoloured	1·90	1·70
		With tab	2·00	1·80

No. 2137 was also available in sheets of 12 stamps and 12 stamp-size labels which could be personalised by the additon of photograph or logo.

(Des Naama Tumarkin. Litho Cartor)

2012 (7 Feb). Centenary of Technion–Israel Institute of Technology. P 13½.

2138	**893**	2s.60 multicoloured	2·75	2·50
		With tab	3·00	2·75

894 Reuven–Carnelian

(Des David Ben-Hador. Litho Cartor)

2012 (7 Feb). Jewels of the Choshen–The High Priest's Breastplate (1st issue). T **894** and similar horiz designs. Multicoloured. P 13×13½.

2139	2s.60 Type **894**	2·75	2·50
2140	2s.60 Shimon–Topaz	2·75	2·50
2141	2s.60 Levi–Emerald	2·75	2·50
2142	2s.60 Yehuda–Turquoise	2·75	2·50
2139/2142	*Set of 4*	10·00	9·00
2139/2142	*Set of 4 with tabs*	12·00	11·00

Nos. 2139/2142 show jewels inscribed with one of the 12 tribes of Israel.

See also Nos. 2160/2163, 2168/2171 and **MS**2192.

895 Bracha Zefira (singer)

(Des Rutie El Hanan. Litho Cartor)

2012 (7 Feb). Pioneering Women. T **895** and similar horiz design. Multicoloured. Two phosphor bars. P 13×13½.

2143	4s. Type **895**	4·25	4·00
2144	5s.90 Batia Makov (pioneer of the First Aliyah)	6·50	6·00
2143/2144	*Set of 2*	9·75	9·00
2143/2144	*Set of 2 with tabs*	11·50	10·50

896 Accusing Finger of Gideon Hausner (Attorney General and trial prosecutor) (Miron Sima)

897 Waxwing

(Des Liat Dessau. Litho Cartor)

2012 (7 Feb). 50th Anniversary of Execution of Adolf Eichman (war criminal). P 13½×13.

2145	**896**	9s.30 multicoloured	9·50	8·75
		With tab	10·00	9·25

(Des Chen Shaohua. Litho Enschedé)

2012 (20 Mar). Peace Birds. 20th Anniversary of Israel–China Diplomatic Relations. T **897** and similar vert design. Multicoloured. One phosphor band (2s.). P 13½×14.

2146	2s. Type **897**	2·10	2·00
2147	3s. White Dove	3·25	3·00
2146/2147	*Set of 2*	4·75	4·50
2146/2147	*Set of 2 with tabs*	5·75	5·25

Stamps of a similar design were issued by China.

898 Child and Balloon (image from song *Mi Shechalam* (He Who Dreamt) (by Didi Menusiand Yochanan Zarai)

899 Girl with Balloon (*A Tale of Five Balloons* (Miriam Roth and Ora Eyal))

(Des Igal Gabay. Litho Enschedé)

2012 (17 Apr). Memorial Day. One phosphor band. P 14×13½.

2148	**898**	1s.70 multicoloured	1·90	1·70
		With tab	2·00	1·80

(Des Miri Nestor. Litho Enschedé)

2012 (17 Apr). Children's Books. T **899** and similar horiz designs. Multicoloured. P 14×13½.

2149	2s. Type **899**	2·10	2·00
	a. Strip of 4. Nos. 2149/2152	8·75	
2150	2s. Whale and script (*Caspion the Little Fish* (Paul Kor))	2·10	2·00
2151	2s. *Itamar Walks on Walls* (David Grossman and Ora Eyal)	2·10	2·00
2152	2s. *The Lion that Loved Strawberries* (Tirtza Atar and Danny Kerman)	2·10	2·00
2153	2s. Lion and Giraffe (*Raspberry Juice* (Haya Shenhav and Tamara Rikman))	2·10	2·00
	a. Strip of 4. Nos. 2153/2156	8·75	
2154	2s. *The Absent-Minded Guy from Kefar Azar* (Leah Goldberg)	2·10	2·00
2155	2s. Children eating sweetcorn (*Hot Sweet Corn* (Miriam Roth and Ora Eyal))	2·10	2·00
2156	2s. *Come to Me, Nice Butterfly* (Fania Bergstein and Ilse Kantor)	2·10	2·00
2149/2156	*Set of 8*	15·00	14·50
2149/2156	*Set of 8 with tabs*	18·00	16·00

Nos. 2149/2152 and 2153/2156, respectively, were each printed *se-tenant*, in vertical strips of four, within sheets of eight stamps with an enlarged illustrated central gutter.

The stamps were arranged so that each have a *se-tenant* tab, illustrating a scene from the book, at left (Nos. 2149/2152) or right (Nos. 2153/2156), the tabs forming the margin of the sheet.

900 *Hehalutz*, 1919, Jaffa

901 The Western Wall

(Des Ronen Goldberg and Tuvia Kurtz. Litho Enschedé)

2012 (17 Apr). Renaissance of Jewish Seamanship. Multicoloured. P 14×13½.

2157	3s. Type **900**	3·00	2·75
2158	3s. *Sarah A*, 1936, Haifa	3·00	2·75
2159	3s. *Har Zion*, 1936, Tel-Aviv	3·00	2·75
2157/2159	*Set of 3*	8·00	7·50
2157/2159	*Set of 3 with tabs*	9·75	9·00

(Des David Ben-Hador. Litho Enschedé)

2012 (17 Apr). Jewels of the Choshen–The High Priest's Breastplate (2nd issue). Horiz designs as T **894**. Multicoloured. P 14×13½.

2160	3s. Issachar–Lazurite	3·00	2·75
2161	3s. Zevulun–Quartz	3·00	2·75
2162	3s. Dan–Zircon	3·00	2·75
2163	3s. Naftali–Amethyst	3·00	2·75
2160/2163	*Set of 4*	11·00	10·00
2160/2163	*Set of 4 with tabs*	13·00	12·00

Nos. 2160/2163 show jewels inscribed with one of the 12 tribes of Israel.

(Des Meir Eshel. Litho Enschedé)

2012 (17 Apr). Chain of Generations Visitor Centre, Western Wall. P 13½×14.

2164	**901**	9s.30 multicoloured	9·50	8·75
		With tab	9·75	9·00

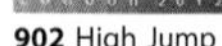

902 High Jump

903 Teddy Kollek

(Des Moshe Pereg. Litho Cartor)

2012 (26 June). Olympic Games, London. T **902** and similar horiz designs. Multicoloured. P 13×13½.

2165	2s. Type **902**	2·10	2·00
2166	2s. Gymnastics	2·10	2·00
2167	4s.50 Taekwondo	5·25	4·75
2165/2167	*Set of 3*	8·50	8·00
2165/2167	*Set of 3 with tabs*	10·00	9·25

(Des David Harel (after David Gerstein). Litho Cartor)

2012 (26 June). Teddy Kollek (Mayor of Jerusalem (1965–1993)) Commemoration. P 13½×13.

2172	**903**	9s.40 multicoloured	10·50	9·75
		With tab	11·50	10·50

A premium booklet entitled Birds of Israel – Tel Aviv 2013, containing six stamps with the face value 2s.20, six stamps with the face value 2s.40 and five pages of text was on sale for 49s.

(Des David Ben-Hador. Litho Cartor)

2012 (26 June). Jewels of the Choshen–The High Priest's Breastplate (3rd issue). Horiz designs as T **894**. Multicoloured. P 13×13½.

2168	3s. Gad–Agate	3·00	2·75
2168	3s. Asher–Aquamarine	3·00	2·75
2168	3s. Yosef–Onyx	3·00	2·75
2168	3s. Binyamin–Jasper	3·00	2·75
2168/2171	*Set of 4*	11·00	10·00
2168/2171	*Set of 4 with tabs*	13·00	12·00

Nos. 2160/2163 show jewels inscribed with one of the 12 tribes of Israel.

904 Tashlikh, Rosh Hashanah

905 Rosh Hanika

(Des Aharon Shevo. Litho Cartor)

2012 (4 July). Festivals. The Month of Tishrei. T **904** and similar horiz design. Multicoloured. P 13×13½.

2173	2s. Type **904**	1·90	1·70
2174	4s.20 Kol Nidrei Prayer, Yom Kippur	4·25	4·00
2175	6s.20 Bearing the Lulav, Sukkot	6·25	5·75
2173/2175	*Set of 3*	11·00	10·50
2173/2175	*Set of 3 with tabs*	13·00	12·00

(Des Pini Hamou. Litho Cartor)

2012 (4 Sept). Tourism. Visit Israel. T **905** and similar horiz designs. Multicoloured.

(a) Sheet stamps. Ordinary gum. P 14.

2176	3s. Type **905**	3·25	3·00
2177	3s. Old Jaffa, port and Tel Aviv	3·25	3·00
2178	3s. Solomon's Pillars, Timna	3·25	3·00
2176/2178	*Set of 3*	8·75	8·00
2176/2178	*Set of 3 with tabs*	10·50	9·75

(b) Booklet stamps. Self-adhesive. Die-cut perf 14.

2179	3s. As Type **905**	3·25	3·00
2180	3s. As No. 2177	3·25	3·00
2181	3s. As No. 2178	3·25	3·00
2179/2181	*Set of 3*	8·75	8·00

906 Mount Everest and Dead Sea

907 Anniversary Emblem

(Des Osnat Eshel. Litho Cartor)

2012 (4 Sept). Highest and Lowest Places on Earth. Israel–Nepal Diplomatic Relations. P 14.

2182	**906**	5s. multicoloured	5·50	5·00
		With tab	5·50	5·00

A stamp of a similar design was issued by Nepal.

(Des Ronen Goldberg. Litho Cartor)

2012 (4 Sept). 50th Anniversary of International Police Association, Israel. P 14.

2183	**907**	4s.20 multicoloured	4·25	4·00
		With tab	4·50	4·25

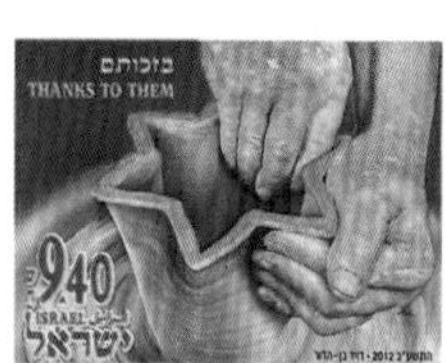

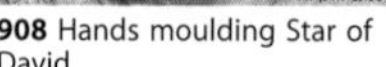

908 Hands moulding Star of David

909 Symbols of Organisation

(Des David Ben-Hador. Litho Cartor)

2012 (4 Sept). Senior Citizens' Contribution to Israel. P 14.

2184	**908**	9s.40 multicoloured	10·00	9·25
		With tab	10·50	9·75

(Des Zvika Roitman. Litho Cartor)

2012 (4 Sept). Centenary of Hadassah–Women's Zionist Organisation of America. P 14.

2185	**909**	6s.20 multicoloured	6·25	5·75
		With tab	6·50	6·00

910 Hanukkah

911 Mediterranean Spur-thighed Tortoise (*Testudo graeca*)

(Des Ronen Goldberg and Elka Sharma. Litho Cartor)

2012 (5 Nov). Festivals of Lights. 20th Anniversary of Israel–India Diplomatic Relations. T **910** and similar horiz design. Multicoloured. P 14.

2186	2s. Type **910**	1·90	1·70
2187	2s. Deepavali	1·90	1·70
2186/2187	*Set of 2*	3·50	3·00
2186/2187	*Set of 2 with tabs*	4·00	3·75

Stamps of a similar design were issued by India.

(Des Igal Gabai and Tuvia Kurtz. Litho Cartor)

2012 (12 Dec). Wildlife Conservation. Israeli Wildlife Hospital. T **911** and similar horiz designs. Multicoloured. P 14.

2188	3s. Type **911**	2·75	2·50
	a. Strip of 3. Nos. 2188/2190	8·50	
2189	3s. Mountain Gazelle fawn (*Gazella gazella*)	2·75	2·50
2190	3s. Imperial Eagle (*Aquila heliaca*)	2·75	2·50
2188/2190	*Set of 3*	7·50	6·75
2188/2190	*Set of 3 with tabs*	9·00	8·25

Nos. 2188/2190 were printed, *se-tenant*, in two strips of three stamps in sheets of six, surrounding a central illustrated gutter.

912 Off-shore Drilling Platform

(Des Ronen Goldberg and Tuvia Kurtz. Litho Cartor)

2012 (12 Dec). Energy Resources in Israel. P 14.

2191	**912** 4s.20 multicoloured		4·00	3·75
		With tab	4·25	4·00

913 High Priest wearing Breastplate

(Des Tuvia Kurtz and David Ben-Hador. Litho Cartor)

2012 (12 Dec). Jewels of the Choshen–The High Priest's Breastplate (4th issue). Sheet 85×150 mm. P 13×13½.

MS2192	**913** 5s. multicoloured (*sold at 7s.*)	7·50	7·00

914 Bible and National Flag

915 Light Pink Duplex Bloom

(Des Ronen Goldberg)

2012 (12 Dec). 50th Anniversary of Koren Jerusalem Bible. P 13½×13.

2193	**914** 9s.50 multicoloured		9·50	8·75
		With tab	10·00	9·25

(Des Tuvia Kurtz and Miri Nestor. Litho Cartor)

2013 (5 Feb). Gerberas. T **915** and similar vert designs. Multicoloured.

(a) Ordinary gum. P 14.

2194	20a. Type **915**	25	25
2195	30a. Orange crested bloom	40	35
2196	40a. White single (flower structure) bloom	50	45
2197	50a. Yellow single (flower structure) bloom	65	60
2198	1s. Dark pink duplex bloom	1·30	1·20
2194/2198	*Set of 5*	2·75	2·50
2194/2198	*Set of 5 with tabs*	3·25	3·00

(b) Self-adhesive. Die-cut perf 13½×14.

2199	20a. As Type **915**	25	25
2200	50a. As No. 2197	65	60
2201	1s. As No. 2198	1·30	1·20
2199/2201	*Set of 3*	2·00	1·80
2199/2201	*Set of 3 with tabs*	2·30	2·10

Nos. 2194/2198, each×2 were printed, *se-tenant*, in two horizontal strips of five stamps within sheets of ten, the strips laid *tête-bêche* to one another.

See also No. 2260.

916 Symbols of Arad

917 Man-made Lake

(Des Zvika and Zina Roitman. Litho Cartor)

2013 (5 Feb). 50th Anniversary of Arad. P 14.

2202	**916** 2s. multicoloured		2·50	2·30
		With tab	2·75	2·50

(Des Shlomit Ben-Zur and Gustavo Viselner. Litho Cartor)

2013 (5 Feb). Water–The Source of Life. P 14½.

2203	**917** 3s. multicoloured		3·75	3·50
		With tab	4·00	3·75

918 School Buildings

919 Symbols of International Movement

(Des Mali and Momi Alon. Litho Cartor)

2013 (5 Feb). Centenary of Hebrew Reali School. P 13×13½.

2204	**918** 4s.20 multicoloured		5·25	4·75
		With tab	5·50	5·00

(Des Igal Gabay. Litho Cartor)

2013 (5 Feb). Israel Customs Directorate. P 13×13½.

2205	**919** 9s.50 multicoloured		12·00	11·00
		With tab	12·50	11·50

920 *Torgos tracheliotos* (Lappet-faced Vulture) and *Neophron percnopterus* (Egyptian Vulture)

921 Service Personnel (illustrating *The Silver Platter* (poem by Natan Alterman))

(Des Zvika Roitman and Tuvia Kurtz. Litho Cartor)

2013 (13 Mar). Taking Vultures under our Wing (1st issue). P 13×13½.

2206 **920** 3s. multicoloured ... 3·75 3·50
With tab 4·00 3·75

See also Nos. 2208/2209.

(Des Moshe Pereg. Litho Cartor)

2013 (2 Apr). Memorial Day–*The Silver Platter*. P 13½×13.

2207 **921** 2s. multicoloured ... 2·50 2·30
With tab 2·75 2·50

(Des Zvika Roitman and Tuvia Kurtz. Litho Cartor)

2013 (2 Apr). Taking Vultures under our Wing (2nd issue). Horiz designs as T **920**. Multicoloured. P 13×13½.

2208 3s. *Gyps fulvus* (Griffon Vulture) ... 3·75 3·50
2209 3s. *Gypaetus barbatus* (Bearded Vulture) ... 3·75 3·50
2208/2209 *Set of 2* ... 6·75 6·25
2208/2209 *Set of 2 with tabs* ... 8·25 7·50

922 Percutaneous Heart Valve (transcatheter aortic valve replacement (TAVR))

923 Pawel Frenkel

(Des Meir Eshel. Litho Cartor)

2013 (2 Apr). Israeli Achievements–Cardiology. T **922** and similar horiz designs. Multicoloured. P 13×13½.

2210 3s. Type **922** ... 3·75 3·50
2211 4s.20 Stent ... 5·25 4·75
2212 5s. Implantable defibrillator ... 6·25 5·75
2210/2212 *Set of 3* ... 13·50 12·50
2210/2212 *Set of 3 with tabs* ... 16·00 14·50

(Des Pini Hamo and Tuvia Kurtz. Litho Cartor)

2013 (2 Apr). Flags Over the Ghetto–70th Anniversary of Warsaw Uprising. P 13.

2213 **923** 9s.50 multicoloured ... 12·00 11·00
With tab 12·50 11·50

924 Horseman (statue, Australian Soldier Park)

(Des Simon Sakinofsky (Australia) and Shlomit Ben-Zur (Israel). Litho Cartor)

2013 (10 May). Australian Light Horse Brigade and Battle of Beersheba, 1917. 95th Anniversary of Israel–Australia Relations. T **924** and similar horiz design. Multicoloured. P 13×13½.

2214 2s. Type **924** ... 2·50 2·30
2215 6s.10 Bridge and horsemen (re-enactment of battle) ... 7·50 7·00
2214/2215 *Set of 2* ... 9·00 8·25
2214/2215 *Set of 2 with tabs* ... 10·50 9·75

Stamps of a similar design were issued by Australia.

925 Hang-glider

(Des David Ben-Hador and Ishai Oron)

2013 (26 May). Israel National Trail. Sheet 160×190 mm containing T **925** and similar horiz designs showing part of trail. Multicoloured. P 14×13½.

MS2216 2s.x10, Type **925**; Deer sniffing girl's nose; Windsurfer and Scoutmaster; Picnic, father and son hiking and cable car; Woman leaning against ruin and quad bike; Abseiling, reading, cliffs and jumping; Cyclist and pedalo; Ostrich, ladder, girl in tree and Antelope; Dolphin and tower; Off-road vehicle, dog and sitting under palm trees ... 26·00 24·00

The stamps and margins of **MS**2216 form a composite design.

926 Austrian Post Carriage and Jaffa Gate, Jerusalem

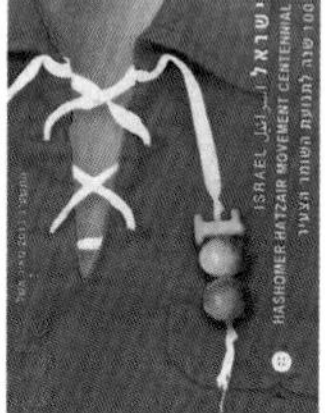

927 Blue Shirt with White String (Hashomer Hatzair uniform) and '100'

(Des Tuvia Kurtz and Ronen Goldberg. Litho Enschedé)

2013 (26 May). Postal Vehicles in Eretz Israel. Sheet 140×75 mm containing T **926** and similar horiz designs. Multicoloured. P 14×13½.

MS2217 2s. Type **926**; 3s. Mail sorting train car, operated by Mandatory Railway; 5s. 'The Red Van' (early post van) (*sold at* 15s.) ... 13·00 12·00

(Des Meir Eshel. Litho Enschedé)

2013 (26 May). Centenary of Hashomer Hatzair Movement. P 13½×14.

2218 **927** 3s. multicoloured ... 3·75 3·50
With tab 4·00 3·75

928 Athletes

929 Yitzhak Shamir

(Des Tal Hoover. Litho Enschedé)

2013 (26 May). 19th Maccabiah (games). P 14×13½.

2219 **928** 3s. multicoloured ... 3·75 3·50
With tab 4·00 3·75

(Des Ilan Hagari. Litho Enachedé)

2013 (26 May). Yitzhak Shamir (Icchak Jeziernicky) (prime minister 1983–1984 and 1986–1992) Commemoration. P 13½×14.

2220 **929** 9s.50 multicoloured ... 12·00 11·00
With tab 12·50 11·50

930 Dorcas Gazelle (*Gazella dorcas*)

931 *Buba Zehava* (Doll)

(Des Zina and Zvika Roitman. Litho Enschedé)

2013 (11 June). Endangered Species. Animals from Arctic to Desert. Sheet 90×70 mm. P 14×13½.

MS2221 **930** multicoloured ... 9·50 8·75

A stamp of a similar theme was issued by Greenland.

(Des Renat Abudraham Dadon. Litho Enschedé)

2013 (26 Aug). Israeli Music–Children's Songs. Multicoloured. P 13½×14.

2222	2s. Type **931**	2·50	2·30
2223	2s. *I Wanted You To Know*	2·50	2·30
2224	2s. *What Do the Does Do?*	2·50	2·30
2225	2s. *A Brave Clock*	2·50	2·30
2226	2s. *I Am Always Me*	2·50	2·30
2227	2s. *Merry Choir*	2·50	2·30
2228	2s. *Brave Danny*	2·50	2·30
2229	2s. *Horse Rider*	2·50	2·30
2230	2s. *My Dad*	2·50	2·30
2231	2s. *The Post Van*	2·50	2·30
2232	2s. *The Prettiest Girl in Kindergarten*	2·50	2·30
2233	2s. *Why Does the Zebra Wear Pajamas?*	2·50	2·30
2222/2233	*Set of 12*	27·00	25·00
2222/2233	*Set of 12 with tabs*	31·00	29·00

Nos. 2222/2225 and 2228/2231 were printed *se-tenant*, in horizontal strips of four and Nos. 2226/2227 and 2232/2233 in horizontal pairs, each strip or pair sharing a composite background design, surrounding a block of four stamp size labels, each showing part of a disc.

The stamps were arranged so that each have a *se-tenant*, inscribed tab, at foot, the tabs forming part of the design and the margin of the sheet.

932 Etrog Box, Bezalel, Jerusalem

933 Young People

(Des Osnat Eshel. Litho Enschede)

2013 (26 Aug). Festivals–Etrog (citrus fruit) Boxes. T **932** and similar horiz designs. Multicoloured. P 14×13½.

2234	2s. Type **932**	2·50	2·30
2235	3s.90 Shallow oval Etrog box, Austria	5·00	4·50
2236	5s.70 Bird-shaped Etrog box, Iraq	7·00	6·25
2234/2236	*Set of 3*	13·00	11·50
2234/2236	*Set of 3 with tabs*	15·00	14·00

(Des Osnat Eshel. Litho Enschedé)

2013 (26 Aug). 80th Anniversary of Betar–World Zionist Youth Movement. P 14×13½.

2237	**933**	3s.10 multicoloured	4·00	3·75
		With tab	4·25	4·00

934 Missiles

935 *The Annunciation of Sarah* (José Gurvich)

(Des Meir Eshel. Litho Enschedé)

2013 (26 Aug). Israel Military Industries. P 14×13½.

2238	**934**	9s.60 multicoloured	12·00	11·00
		With tab	12·50	11·50

(Des Rinat Gilboa. Litho Cartor)

2013 (28 Oct). 65th Anniversary of Friendship with Uruguay. P 13×13½.

2239	**935**	2s. multicoloured	2·50	2·30
		With tab	2·75	2·50

936 Rachel weeping for her Children and Tomb

937 Menorah

(Des Osnat Eshel. Litho Cartor)

2013 (28 Oct). Rachel's Tomb. P 13.

2240	**936**	5s. multicoloured	6·25	5·75
		With tab	7·00	6·25

(Des Limor Peretz. Litho Cartor)

2013 (3 Dec). Holiday of Holidays–Haifa. P 13.

2241	**937**	3s.10 multicoloured	4·00	3·75
		With tab	4·25	4·00

938 Fouga Magister IDF Air Force Training Aeroplane, 1960

939 Verdi and Scene from *Nabucco* at Israeli Opera's Opera Festival, Masada

(Des Igal Gabay. Litho Cartor)

2013 (3 Dec). Centenary of Aviation in Israel. T **938** and similar horiz designs. Multicoloured.

(a) Ordinary gum. P 13×13½.

2242	3s.10 Type **938**	4·00	3·75
2243	3s.10 Blériot XI	4·00	3·75
2244	3s.10 Heron I (unmanned aerial vehicle), 1994	4·00	3·75
2242/2244	*Set of 3*	11·00	10·50
2242/2244	*Set of 3 with tabs*	12·50	11·50

(b) Self-adhesive. Die-cut perf 12½.

2245	3s.10 As Type **938**	4·00	3·75
2246	3s.10 As No. 2243	4·00	3·75
2247	3s.10 AS No. 2244	4·00	3·75
2245/2247	*Set of 3*	11·00	10·50

(Des Shlomit Ben-Zur. Litho Cartor)

2013 (3 Dec). Birth Bicentenary of Giuseppe Verdi. P 13.

2248	**939**	3s.90 multicoloured	5·00	4·50
		With tab	5·25	4·75

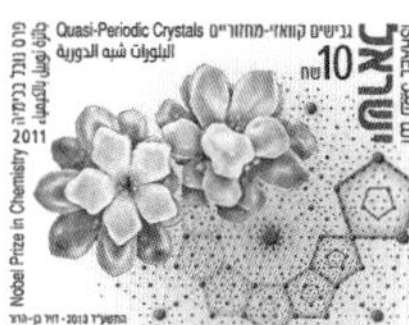

940 Quasicrystal of Aluminium-Manganese Alloy

941 Halls of the Knights Hospitallers, Valletta, Malta and Acre, Israel

(Des David Ben-Hador. Litho Cartor)

2013 (3 Dec). International Year of Crystallography. Stamp Day. P 13×13½.

2249	**940**	10s. multicoloured	12·50	11·50
		With tab	13·00	12·00

(Des Ronen Goldberg. Litho Cartor)

2014 (28 Jan). The Halls of the Knights Hospitallers. P 13×13½.

2250	**941**	3s.90 multicoloured	5·00	4·50
		With tab	5·25	4·75

A stamp of a similar design was issued by Malta.

942 Independence Hall, Tel Aviv

943 Abseiling, Makhtesh Ramon

(Des Ronen Goldberg. Litho Cartor)

2014 (11 Feb). National Heritage. Landmarks. T **942** and similar horiz designs. Multicoloured. P 13×13½.

2251	2s. Type **942**	2·50	2·30
	a. Horiz strip of 5. Nos 2251/2255	13·00	

2252 2s. Dention Camp, Atlit ..... 2·50 2·30
2253 2s. Synagogue, Peki'in ..... 2·50 2·30
2254 2s. Ein Keshatot, Golan ..... 2·50 2·30
2255 2s. City of David, Jerusalem ..... 2·50 2·30
2251/2255 *Set of 5* ..... 11·50 10·50
2251/2255 *Set of 5 with tabs* ..... 13·00 12·00

Nos. 2251/2255 were printed, *se-tenant*, in horizontal strips of five stamps within the sheet.

(Des Tuvia Kurtz and Meir Eshel. Litho Cartor)

2014 (11 Feb). Ancient Erosion Craters in Israel. T **943** and similar horiz designs. Multicoloured. P 13×13½.

2256 3s.10 Type **943** ..... 4·00 3·75
2257 3s.10 Three off-road vehicles, Makhtesh Gadol ..... 4·00 3·75
2258 3s.10 Cyclists, Makhtesh Katan ..... 4·00 3·75
2256/2258 *Set of 3* ..... 11·00 10·50
2256/2258 *Set of 3 with tabs* ..... 12·50 11·50

944 Broadcasting

945 Soldiers

(Des Osnat Eshel. Litho Cartor)

2014 (11 Feb). Resistance Radio (1939–1948). P 13.

2259 **944** 9s.60 multicoloured ..... 12·00 11·00
With tab 12·50 11·50

(Des Tuvia Kurtz and Miri Nestor. Litho Cartor)

2014 (11 Feb). Gerberas. Vert design as T **915**. Multicoloured. P 14.

2260 10a. Dark red bloom 15 10
With tab 25 25

(Des Rinat Gilboa. Litho Enschedé)

2014 (8 Apr). Memorial Day. P 13×13½.

2261 **945** 2s. multicoloured ..... 2·50 2·30
With tab 2·75 2·50

946 Rings and Hearts

947 Thanks

(Des Renat Abudraham Dadon. Litho Enschedé)

2014 (8 Apr). Mazal Tov. Marriage. P 14.

2262 **946** (2s.) multicoloured ..... 2·50 2·30
With tab 2·75 2·50

(Des Miri Nestor. Litho Enschedé)

2014 (8 Apr). Israeli Sign Language. T **947** and similar vert designs. Multicoloured.

(a) Ordinary gum. P 14.

2263 (2s.) Type **947** ..... 2·50 2·30
2264 (2s.) Kiss ..... 2·50 2·30
2265 (2s.) Friendship ..... 2·50 2·30
2266 (2s.) Love ..... 2·50 2·30
2267 (2s.) Goodbye ..... 2·50 2·30
2263/2267 *Set of 5* ..... 11·50 10·50
2263/2267 *Set of 5 with tabs* ..... 13·00 12·00

(b) Self-adhesive. Die-cut perf 14.

2268 (2s.) As Type **947** ..... 2·50 2·30
2269 (2s.) As No. 2264 ..... 2·50 2·30
2270 (2s.) As No. 2265 ..... 2·50 2·30
2271 (2s.) As No. 2266 ..... 2·50 2·30
2272 (2s.) As No. 2267 ..... 2·50 2·30
2268/2272 *Set of 5* ..... 11·50 10·50

948 Symbols of Area

949 Cable Water Skiing

(Des Osnat Eshel. Litho Enschedé)

2014 (8 Apr). 50th Anniversary of Mateh Yehuda Regional Council. P 14.

2273 **948** 3s.10 multicoloured ..... 4·00 3·75
With tab 4·25 4·00

(Des Tal Hoover. Litho Enschedé)

2014 (8 Apr). Non-Olympic Sports. T **949** and similar vert designs. Multicoloured. P 14.

2274 3s.90 Type **949** ..... 5·00 4·50
2275 5s. Wushu ..... 6·25 5·75
2276 5s.70 Paragliding ..... 7·00 6·25
2274/2276 *Set of 3* ..... 16·00 15·00
2274/2276 *Set of 3 with tabs* ..... 19·00 17·00

950 Violin

951 Pomegranate (Israel) and Mangosteen (Thailand)

(Des David Ben-Hador. Litho Enschedé)

2014 (8 Apr). Violins that Survived the Holocaust. P 14.

2277 **950** 9s.60 multicoloured ..... 12·00 11·00
With tab 12·50 11·50

(Des Rinat Gilboa. Litho Enschedé)

2014 (5 June). 60th Anniversary of Israel–Thailand Friendship. Fruit. P 14.

2278 **951** 3s.10 multicoloured ..... 4·00 3·75
With tab 4·25 4·00

A stramp of a similar design was issued by Thailand.

952 *Pelobates syriacus* (Eastern Spadefoot Toad)

953 Sara Levi-Tanai (writer and dancer)

(Des Pini Hamo. Litho Enschedé)

2014 (23 June). Amphibians in Israel. T **952** and similar horiz designs. Multicoloured. P 14.

2279 2s. Type **952** ..... 2·50 2·30
a. Pair. Nos. 2279/2280 ..... 5·25 4·75
b. Block of 4. Nos. 2279/2282 ..... 10·50
2280 2s. *Salamandra infraimmaculata* (Near Eastern Fire Salamander) ..... 2·50 2·30
2281 2s. *Ommatotriton vittatus* (Southern Banded Newt) ..... 2·50 2·30
a. Pair. Nos. 2281/2282 ..... 5·25 4·75
2282 2s. *Lantonia nigriventer* (Hula Painted Frog) ..... 2·50 2·30
2279/2282 *Set of 4* ..... 9·00 8·25
2279/2282 *Set of 4 with tabs* ..... 10·50 9·75

Nos. 2279/2280 and 2281/2282, respectively, were printed, *se-tenant*, in horizontal pairs and in blocks of four stamps within sheets of eight, the blocks separated by an illustrated gutter.

(Des Mario Sermoneta and Meir Eshel. Litho Enschedé)

2014 (23 June). Pioneering Women. T **953** and similar horiz design. Multicoloured. P 14.

2283	6s. Type **953**	7·50	7·00
2284	10s. Esther Raab (writer)	12·50	11·50
2283/2284	*Set of 2*	18·00	17·00
2283/2284	*Set of 2 with tabs*	21·00	19·00

954 Palmer Gate Street, Port, and City Fish (statue (Zvika Cantor))

955 1930's Flag

(Des Aharon Shevo. Litho Enschedé)

2014 (23 June). Palmer Gate, Haifa. P 14.

2285	**954**	9s.60 multicoloured	12·00	11·00
		With tab	12·50	11·50

(Des Limor Perez-Samia, Zvi Livni and Arie Moskovitz. Litho Cartor)

2014 (9 Sept). Festivals–Simchat Tora Flags. T **955** and similar horiz designs. Multicoloured. P 13×13½.

2286	2s. Type **955**	2·50	2·30
2287	3s.80 1950's flag	4·75	4·25
2288	5s.60 1960's flag	7·00	6·25
2286/2288	*Set of 3*	13·00	11·50
2286/2288	*Set of 3 with tabs*	15·00	14·00

956 Fiddler on the Roof

957 Symbols of Tel Aviv

(Des Miri Nestor and Chaim Topol Stamps. Litho Cartor)

2014 (9 Sept). 50th Anniversary of *Fiddler on the Roof*. T **956** and similar horiz designs. Multicoloured.

(a) Ordinary gum. P 13×13½.

2289	3s.10 Type **956**	4·00	3·75
2290	3s.10 Teva the Dairyman	4·00	3·75
2291	3s.10 'Do you love me?'	4·00	3·75
2289/2291	*Set of 3*	11·00	10·50
2289/2291	*Set of 3 with tabs*	12·50	11·50

(b) Self-adhesive. Die-cut perf 12½.

2292	3s.10 As Type **956**	4·00	3·75
2293	3s.10 As No. 2290	4·00	3·75
2294	3s.10 As No. 2291	4·00	3·75
2292/2294	*Set of 3*	11·00	10·50

(Des Barufh Nae. Litho Cartor)

2014 (9 Sept). Tel Aviv–Global City. P 13×13½.

2295	**957**	4s.50 multicoloured	5·75	5·25
		With tab	6·00	5·50

958 Wolfgang von Weisl

959 Rabbi Yosef

(Des Osnat Eshel. Litho Cartor)

2014 (9 Sept). 40th Death Anniversary of Benjamin Zeev (Wolfgang Johannes) von Weisl (physician, writer, orientalist and Zionist pioneer). P 13×13½.

2296	**958**	9s.70 multicoloured	12·00	11·00
		With tab	12·50	11·50

(Des Meir Eshel. Litho Cartor)

2014 (28 Sept). First Death Anniversary of Rabbi Ovadia Yosef. P 13.

2297	**959**	2s. multicoloured	2·50	2·30
		With tab	2·75	2·30

960 Arik Einstein

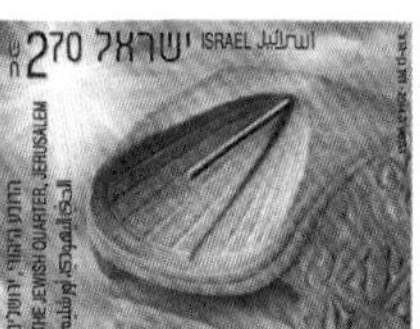

961 Jewish Quarter, Jerusalem

(Des Miri Nestor. Litho Cartor)

2014 (16 Dec). First Death Anniversary of Arik Einstein (singer). P 13.

2298	**960**	1s.80 multicoloured	2·30	2·10
		With tab	2·40	2·20

(Des David Ben-Hador. Litho Cartor)

2014 (16 Dec). Sundials in Israel. T **961** and similar horiz designs showing sundials. Multicoloured. P 13×13½.

2299	2s.70 Type **961**	3·50	3·25
2300	3s.80 Al Jezzar Mosque, Acre	4·75	4·25
2301	5s.60 Zoharei Chama Synagogue, Jerusalem	7·00	6·25
2299/2301	*Set of 3*	13·50	12·50
2299/2301	*Set of 3 with tabs*	16·00	14·50

962 Standard Carmel, 1936

963 Bee Orchid and Monkey Orchid

(Des Pini Hamou. Litho Cartor)

2014 (16 Dec). Israel's Automotive Industry. T **962** and similar horiz designs. Multicoloured. P 13×13½.

2302	3s.80 Type **962**	4·75	4·25
2303	4s. Sabra Sport, 1961	5·00	4·50
2304	4s.10 Kaiser Manhattan, 1951	5·25	4·75
2305	8s.30 Sufa Jeep, 1992	10·50	9·50
2302/2305	*Set of 4*	23·00	21·00
2302/2305	*Set of 4 with tabs*	26·00	24·00

(Des Zina and Zvika Roitman. Litho Cartor)

2014 (16 Dec). Orchids. P 13.

2306	**963**	5s. multicoloured	6·25	5·75
		With tab	7·00	6·25

A stamp of a similar design was issued by Ecuador.

964 Menorah and Children

965 Ariel Sharon

(Des Rinat Gilboa. Litho Cartor)

2014 (16 Dec). Hanukkah. P 13×13½.

2307	**964**	9s.70 multicoloured	12·00	11·00
		With tab	12·50	11·50

(Des Zvika Roitman. Litho Cartor)

2015 (27 Jan). First Death Anniversary of Ariel Sharon (prime minister 2001–2006). P 13.

2308	**965**	2s.10 multicoloured	2·50	2·30
		With tab	2·75	2·50

966 Open Doors Monument

967 *Anthemis leucanthemifolia*

(Des Ronen Goldberg. Litho Cartor)

2015 (27 Jan). Philippine Rescue of Jews. Open Doors Monument. P 13.

2309	**966**	4s.50 multicoloured	5·75	5·25
		With tab	6·00	5·50

A stamp of a similar design was issued by Philippines.

(Des Tuvia Kurtz and Ronen Goldberg. Litho Cartor)

2015 (10 Feb). Winter Flowers. T **967** and similar vert designs. Multicoloured. P 13.

2310	1s.80 Type **967**	2·30	2·10
2311	2s.10 *Alkanna tinctoria*	2·50	2·30
2312	2s.70 *Anemone coronaria*	3·50	3·25
2310/2312	*Set of 3*	7·50	7·00
2310/2312	*Set of 3 with tabs*	8·75	8·00

968 Chess Pieces on Star of David

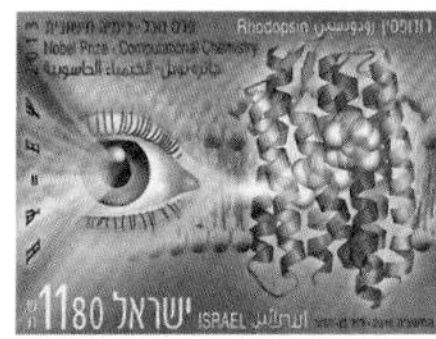

969 Rhodopsin, Schrödinger Equation and Eye

(Des David Ben-Hador. Litho Cartor)

2015 (10 Feb). Chess. European Individual Chess Championship 2015, Jerusalem. P 13×13½.

2313	**968**	4s.10 multicoloured	5·25	4·75
		With tab	5·50	5·00

(Des David Ben-Hador. Litho Cartor)

2015 (10 Feb). International Year of Light 2015. P 13×13.

2314	**969**	11s.80 multicoloured	15·00	13·50
		With tab	16·00	14·50

970 *The Wheat grows Again* (poem by Dorit Tzameret)

971 Shrine of the Book

(Des Rinat Gilboa. Litho Cartor)

2015 (14 Apr). Memorial Day. P 13×13½.

2315	**970**	2s.20 multicoloured	2·75	2·50
		With tab	3·00	2·75

(Des Osnat Eshel. Litho Cartor)

2015 (14 Apr). 50th Anniversary of Israel Museum, Jerusalem. T **971** and similar horiz designs. Multicoloured. P 13×13½.

2316	4s.10 Type **971**	5·25	4·75
2317	4s.10 Synagogue Hanukkah Lamp, Eastern Europe, 18th-century	5·25	4·75
2318	4s.10 *Turning the World Upside Down, Jerusalem*, (sculpture) Anish Kapoor, 2010	5·25	4·75
2316/2318	*Set of 3*	14·00	13·00
2316/2318	*Set of 3 with tabs*	16·00	15·00

972 Container Ship

973 Fruit and Vegetables emerging from Field

(Des Pini Hemo. Litho Cartor)

2015 (14 Apr). 50th Anniversary of Ashdod Port. P 13×13½.

2319	**972**	4s.30 multicoloured	5·50	5·00
		With tab	5·75	5·25

(Des Zvika Roitman. Litho Cartor)

2015 (14 Apr). Expo Milano 2015–Fields of Tomorrow. P 13½×13.

2320	**973**	6s.50 multicoloured	8·25	7·50
		With tab	8·75	8·00

974 Inscribed Clay Cylinder (cylinder of Cyrus)

975 Mule Corps

(Des Renat Abudraham Dadon. Litho Cartor)

2015 (14 Apr). The Cyrus Declaration. P 13×13.

2321	**974**	8s.30 multicoloured	10·50	9·50
		With tab	11·00	10·00

(Des Osnat Eshel and Tuvia Kurtz. Litho Cartor)

2015 (14 Apr). Centenary of Zion Mule Corps. P 13×13½.

2322	**975**	11s.80 multicoloured	15·00	14·00
		With tab	16·00	14·50

976 Biet Bruno Building (Bauhaus designed), White City Tel Aviv

977 Bell AH-1 Cobra

(Des Zvika Roitman. Litho Cartor)

2015 (7 May). 50th Anniversary of Israel–Germany Diplomatic Relations. P 13×13½.

2323	**976**	7s.40 multicoloured	9·50	8·75
		With tab	10·00	9·25

A stamp of similar design was issued by Germany.

(Des Igal Gabai. Litho Cartor)

2015 (16 June). Bell AH-1 Cobra–First Attack Helicopter in Israeli Air Force. P 13×13½.

2324	**977**	2s.20 multicoloured	2·75	2·50
		With tab	3·00	2·75

978 Carrots

979 Bridal Jewellery, Yemen, 1930s

(Des Tal Huber. Litho Cartor (Nos. 2326/2329))

2015 (16 June). Vegetables. T **978** and similar vert designs. Multicoloured.

(a) Ordinary gum. P 14.

2325	(2s.20) Type **978**	2·75	2·50
2326	(2s.20) Red cabbage	2·75	2·50
2327	(2s.20) Lettuce	2·75	2·50
2328	(2s.20) Onion	2·75	2·50
2329	(2s.20) Tomato	2·75	2·50
2325/2329	*Set of 5*	12·50	11·50
2325/2329	*Set of 5 with tabs*	14·50	13·00

(b) Self-adhesive. One phosphor bar. Die-cut perf 13½×14.

2330	(2s.20) Type **978**	2·75	2·50
2331	(2s.20) As No. 2326	2·75	2·50
2332	(2s.20) As No. 2327	2·75	2·50
2333	(2s.20) As No. 2328	2·75	2·50
2334	(2s.20) As No. 2329	2·75	2·50
2330/2334	*Set of 5*	12·50	11·50

Nos. 2330/2334 each×4 were printed in booklets of 20 stamps.

(Des Limor Peretz-Samia. Litho Cartor)

2015 (16 June). Jewellery from Jewish Communities. T **979** and similar vert designs. Multicoloured. P 13½×13.

2335	4s.10 Type **979**	5·25	4·75
2336	4s.10 Bridal head ornament, Bukhara, late 19th-century	5·25	4·75
2337	4s.10 Wedding ring, Italy, 17th-century	5·25	4·75
2335/2337	*Set of 3*	14·00	13·00
2335/2337	*Set of 3 with tabs*	16·00	15·00

980 Turkish Train at Beer Sheva Station and Moshe Shertok (later Prime Minister) in Turkish Military Uniform

980a Rosh Hashana

(Des Ronen Goldberg. Litho Cartor)

2015 (16 June). Centenary of World War I in Israel. Military Railway, 1915. P 13×13½.

2338	**980** 11s.80 multicoloured	15·00	14·00
	With tab	16·00	14·50

(Des Rinat Gilboa. Enschede Litho)

2015 (2 Sept). Festivals. Childhood Memories. T **980a** and similar horiz designs. Multicoloured. P 14.

2338*a*	2s.20 Type **980a**	2·75	2·50
2339	7s.40 Yom Kippur	9·50	8·75
2340	8s.30 Sukkot	10·50	9·75
2338*a*/2340	*Set of 3*	20·00	19·00
2338*a*/2340	*Set of 3 with tabs*	23·00	21·00

981 Kziv River

(Des Miri Nestor. Litho Enschedé)

2015 (2 Sept). Rivers. Booklet Stamps. T **981** and similar horiz designs. Multicoloured.

(a) Ordinary gum. P 13×13½.

2341	4s.10 Type **981**	5·25	4·75
2342	4s.10 Taninim River	5·25	4·75
2343	4s.10 Zin River	5·25	4·75
2341/2343	*Set of 3*	14·00	13·00
2341/2343	*Set of 3 with tabs*	16·00	14·50

(b) Self-adhesive. Die-cut perf 12½

2344	4s.10 As Type **981**	5·25	4·75
2345	4s.10 Taninim River	5·25	4·75
2346	4s.10 Zin River	5·25	4·75
2344/2346	*Set of 3*	14·00	13·00

Nos. 2344/2346, each×2, were printed in booklets of six stamps.

982 Church of the Holy Sepulchre

(Des Renat Abudraham Dadon. Litho Enschedé)

2015 (2 Sept). Pope Francis's Visit to the Holy Land, 24–26 May 2014. Church of the Holy Sepulchre. P 14.

MS2347	**982** 7s. multicoloured	9·25	8·50

983 Ginat Ha'Machtarot Monument (Menashe Kadishman), Ramat Gan

984 Soda Siphon

(Des Zvika Roitman. Litho Enschedé)

2015 (2 Sept). 70th Anniversary of Jewish Resistance Movement. P 14.

2348	**983** 11s.80 multicoloured	15·00	14·00
	With tab	16·00	14·50

(Des Baruch Nae and Sharon Targal. Litho Cartor)

2015 (8 Dec). Israeli Nostalgia. T **984** and similar horiz designs. Multicoloured. P 13×13½.

2349	2s.30 Type **984**	3·00	2·75
	a. Strip of 3. Nos. 2349/2351	9·25	
2350	2s.30 Tembel hat	3·00	2·75
2351	2s.30 Sussita car	3·00	2·75
2349/2351	*Set of 3*	8·00	7·50
2349/2351	*Set of 3 with tabs*	9·00	8·25

Nos. 2349/2351 were printed, *se-tenant*, in horizontal strips of three stamps within the sheet.

985 Sefi Rivlin

986 House from where Group Signalled and Ship

(Des Zvika Roitman. Litho Cartor)

2015 (8 Dec). Personalities. Theatre and Entertainment. T **985** and similar vert design. Multicoloured. P 13½×13.

2352	2s.30 Type **985** (comedian)	3·00	2·75
2353	4s.10 Channa Marron (actress)	5·25	4·75
2352/2353	*Set of 2*	7·50	6·75
2352/2353	*Set of 2 with tabs*	8·25	7·50

(Des Pini Hamou and Rotem Palma. Litho Cartor)

2015 (8 Dec). Centenary of Nili (Netzach Israel Lo Yishaker) (undercover group working to assist the British effort to conquer Eretz Israel by gathering information). P 13×13½.

2354	**986** 5s. multicoloured	6·50	6·00
	With tab	6·75	6·25

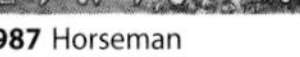

987 Horseman

988 Piles of Coins

(Des David Ben-Hador. Litho Cartor)

2015 (8 Dec). Stamp Day. Mamluk Postal Road. P 13×13½.

2355	**987**	10s. multicoloured	13·00	12·00
		With tab	13·50	12·50

(Des Meir Eshel. Litho Cartor)

2015 (8 Dec). Pension Savings. P 13×13½.

2356	**988**	11s.70 multicoloured	15·00	14·00
		With tab	16·00	14·50

989 *Eretmochelys imbricata* (Hawksbill Turtle)

990 Nehama Pohatchevsky

(Des Tuvia Kurttz and Ronen Goldberg. Litho Enschedé)

2016 (9 Feb). Marine Life. T **989** and similar horiz designs. Multicoloured. P 14.

2357	2s.30 Type **989**	3·00	2·75
	a. Block of 4. Nos. 2357/2360	12·50	
2358	2s.30 *Dermochelys coriacea* (Leatherback Turtle)	3·00	2·75
2359	2s.30 *Chelonia mydas* (Green Turtle)	3·00	2·75
2360	2s.30 *Caretta caretta* (Loggerhead Turtle)	3·00	2·75
2357/2360	*Set of 4*	11·00	10·00
2357/2360	*Set of 4 with tabs*	11·50	10·50

Nos. 2357/2360 were printed, *se-tenant*, as blocks of four stamps within sheets of eight, the blocks separated by stamp-width gutter.

(Des Osnat Eshel. Litho Enschedé)

2016 (9 Feb). Pioneering Women. T **990** and similar horiz design. Multicoloured. P 14.

2361	2s.30 Type **990** (writer)	3·00	2·75
2362	5s. Zelda Schneersohn Mishkovsky (poet)	6·50	6·00
2361/2362	*Set of 2*	8·50	8·00
2361/2362	*Set of 2 with tabs*	9·50	8·75

991 Haifa and Thessaloniki Ports

992 Children and Snowman

(Des Ronen Goldberg. Litho Enschedé)

2016 (9 Feb). 25th Anniversary of Israel–Greece Diplomatic Relations. P 14.

2363	**991**	4s.10 multicoloured	5·25	4·75
		With tab	5·50	5·00

(Des Miri Nestor and Tamar Nahir-Yanai. Litho Enschedé)

2016 (9 Feb). Seasons in Israel–Winter. P 14.

2364	**992**	4s.10 multicoloured	5·25	4·75
		With tab	5·50	5·00

993 Ephraim Kishon

994 Beach

(Des Pini Hamou and Renana Kishon. Litho Enschedé)

2016 (9 Feb). Ephraim Kishon (writer) Commemoration. P 14.

2365	**993**	11s.70 multicoloured	15·00	14·00
		With tab	16·00	14·50

(Des Meir Eshel. Litho Cartor)

2016 (19 Apr). Memorial Day. 'The Sand will Remember'. P 13×13½.

2366	**994**	2s.30 multicoloured	3·00	2·75
		With tab	3·25	3·00

995 Stylised Building

996 Digital Prepress

(Des Rinat Gilboa. Litho Cartor)

2016 (19 Apr). 50th Anniversary of Knesset Building, Jerusalem. P 13×13½.

2367	**995**	2s.30 multicoloured	3·00	2·75
		With tab	3·25	3·00

(Des Meir Eshel. Litho Cartor)

2016 (19 Apr). Israeli Achievements. Printing. T **996** and similar horiz design. Multicoloured. P 13×13½.

2368	2s.30 Type **996**	3·00	2·75
2369	8s.30 Digital printing	10·50	9·75
2368/2369	*Set of 2*	12·00	11·50
2368/2369	*Set of 2 with tabs*	13·50	12·50

997 Children in Poppy Field

998 Flea Market, Jaffa

(Des Miri Nestor and Tamar Nahir-Yanai. Litho Cartor)

2016 (19 Apr). Seasons in Israel–Spring. P 13×13½.

2370	**997**	4s.10 multicoloured	5·25	4·75
		With tab	5·50	5·00

(Des David Ben-Hador. Litho Cartor)

2016 (19 Apr). Markets. T **998** and similar horiz designs. Multicoloured. P 13×13½.

2371	4s.10 Type **998**	5·25	4·75
2372	4s.10 Machane Yehuda Market, Jerusalem	5·25	4·75
2373	4s.10 Old Acre Market	5·25	4·75
2371/2373	*Set of 3*	14·00	13·00
2371/2373	*Set of 3 with tabs*	16·00	14·50

999 Bridge of Strings, Jerusalem (Santiago Calatrava (Spanish architect))

1000 Guide Dogs

(Des Meir Eshel. Litho Cartor)

2016 (19 Apr). 30th Anniversary of Israel–Spain Diplomatic Relations. P 13×13½.

2374	**999**	7s.40 multicoloured	9·50	8·75
		With tab	9·75	9·00

A stamp of a similar design was issued by Spain.

(Des Meir Eshel. Litho Cartor)

2016 (21 June). Service Dogs. T **1000** and similar horiz design. Multicoloured. P 13×13½.

2375	2s.30 Type **1000**	3·00	2·75
2376	10s. Search and Rescue Dogs	13·00	12·00
2375/2376	*Set of 2*	14·50	13·50
2375/2376	*Set of 2 with tabs*	16·00	14·50

1001 Boy and Dog on Beach

1002 Windsurfing

(Des Tamar Nahir-Yanai. Litho Cartor)

2016 (21 June). Seasons in Israel–Summer. P 13×13½.

2377 **1001** 4s.10 multicoloured .... 5·25 4·75
With tab 5·50 5·00

(Des Osnat Eshel. Litho Cartor)

2016 (21 June). Rio 2016–Olympic Games, Brazil. T **1002** and similar vert designs. Multicoloured. P 13½×13.

2378 4s.10 Type **1002** .... 5·25 4·75
2379 4s.10 Judo .... 5·25 4·75
2380 4s.10 Triple jump .... 5·25 4·75
2378/2380 *Set of 3* .... 14·00 13·00
2378/2380 *Set of 3 with tabs* .... 16·00 14·50

1003 German Pilot and Aircraft, Merhavia Co-operative Landing Strip

1004 Hands reaching

(Des Ronen Goldberg. Litho Cartor)

2016 (21 June). Centenary of World War I in Israel. Aerial Warfare, 1916. P 13×13½.

2381 **1003** 11s.70 multicoloured .... 15·00 14·00
With tab 16·00 14·50

(Des Zvika Roitman. Litho Enschedé)

2016 (13 Sept). Casualties of War and Terror Appreciation Day. P 14.

2382 **1004** 2s.30 multicoloured .... 3·00 2·75
With tab 3·25 3·00

1005 'The Potter'

1006 *The Fox in the Vineyard*

(Des David Ben-Hador. Litho Enschedé)

2016 (13 Sept). Festivals. Yom Kippur Poem. T **1005** and similar horiz designs. Multicoloured. P 14.

2383 2s.30 Type **1005** .... 3·00 2·75
2384 7s.40 'The Silversmith' .... 9·50 8·75
2385 8s.30 'The Glazier' .... 10·50 9·75
2383/2385 *Set of 3* .... 21·00 19·00
2383/2385 *Set of 3 with tabs* .... 23·00 21·00

(Des Rinat Gilboa. Litho Enschedé)

2016 (13 Sept). Parables of the Sages. T **1006** and similar horiz designs. Multicoloured.

(a) Ordinary gum. P 14.

2386 4s.10 Type **1006** .... 5·25 4·75
2387 4s.10 *The Lion and the Heron* .... 5·25 4·75
2388 4s.10 *The Reed and the Cedar* .... 5·25 4·75
2386/2388 *Set of 3* .... 14·00 13·00
2386/2388 *Set of 3 with tabs* .... 16·00 14·50

(b) Self-adhesive. Booklet stamps. Die-cut perf 12½.

2389 4s.10 As Type **1006** .... 5·25 4·75
2390 4s.10 As No. 2387 .... 5·25 4·75
2391 4s.10 As No. 2388 .... 5·25 4·75
2389/2391 *Set of 3* .... 14·00 13·00

Nos. 2389/2391, each×2, were printed in booklets of six stamps.

1007 Children flying Kite

1008 Stork migrating, Israeli and Bulgarian Flags

(Des Miri Nestor. Litho Enschedé)

2016 (13 Sept). Seasons–Autumn. P 14.

2392 **1007** 4s.10 multicoloured .... 5·25 4·75
With tab 5·50 5·00

MS2392*a* 4s.10×4, As Nos. 2367, 2370, 2377, 2392 .... 22·00 20·00

(Des Tuvia Kurtz and Miri Nistor. Enschede Litho)

2016 (13 Sept). Fauna. Bird Migration–White Stork. P 14.

2393 **1008** 5s. multicoloured .... 6·50 6·00
With tab 6·75 6·25

A stamp of a similar design was issued by Bulgaria.

1009 Animals from Biblical Zoo

1010 Synagogue, Gaza, 6th-century

(Des Osnat Eshel. Litho Cartor)

2016 (13 Nov). Tourism in Jerusalem. T **1009** and similar horiz designs. Multicoloured. P 13×13½.

2394 2s.40 Type **1009** .... 3·00 2·75
a. Booklet pane. Nos. 2394/2398, each×2. 32·00
b. Strip of 5. Nos. 2394/2398 .... 16·00
2395 2s.40 First Railway Station .... 3·00 2·75
2396 2s.40 Via Dolorosa .... 3·00 2·75
2397 2s.40 Jaffa Street .... 3·00 2·75
2398 2s.40 City Ramparts .... 3·00 2·75
2394/2398 *Set of 5* .... 13·50 12·50
2394/2398 *Set of 5 with tabs* .... 15·00 14·00

Nos. 2394/2398 were printed, *se-tenant*, both in horizontal strips of five stamps within the sheet, and, each×2, in booklets of ten stamps.

(Des Meir Eshel. Litho Cartor)

2016 (13 Nov). Mosaics in Israel. T **1010** and similar horiz designs. Multicoloured. P 13×13½.

2399 4s.10 Type **1010** .... 5·25 4·75
a. Strip of 3. Nos. 2399/2401 .... 16·00
2400 4s.10 Dolphins, Villa, Lod, 3rd-century .... 5·25 4·75
2401 4s.10 Peacock, Synagogue, Maon (Negev), 6th-century .... 5·25 4·75
2399/2401 *Set of 3* .... 14·00 13·00
2399/2401 *Set of 3 with tabs* .... 16·00 14·50

Nos. 2399/2401 were printed, *se-tenant*, in horizontal strips of three stamps within the sheet.

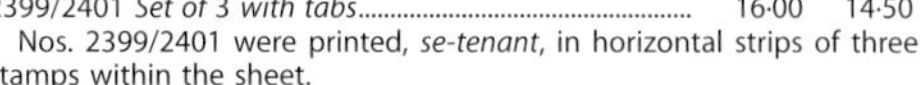

1011 Ship

(Des Tuvia Kurtz and Meir Eshel. Litho Cartor)

2016 (13 Nov). JERUSALEM 2016 International Stamp Exhibition. King Solomon's Ships. Sheet 138×83 mm. P 13×13½.

MS2402 **1011** 5s. multicoloured .... 6·75 6·25

1012 Yitzhak Navon

1013 Members

(Des David Ben-Hador. Litho Cartor)

2016 (13 Nov). First Death Anniversary of Yitzhak Navon (president 1978–1983). P 13×13½.

2403 **1012** 11s.70 multicoloured .... 15·00 14·00
With tab 16·00 14·50

(Des Ronen Goldberg. Litho Cartor)

2017 (7 Feb). Brit Hayyale Ha'Etsel Organisation. P 13½×13.

2404 **1013** 2s.40 multicoloured .... 3·00 2·75
With tab 3·25 3·00

1014 Nahal Me'arot Caves

1015 Frankincense

(Des Ronen Goldberg. Litho Cartor)

2017 (7 Feb). UNESCO World Heritage Sites in Israel. T **1014** and similar horiz designs. Multicoloured. P 13×13½.

2405 2s.40 Type **1014** .... 3·00 2·75
2406 5s. Bet She'arim Necropolis .... 6·50 6·00
2407 10s. Maresha and Bet-Guvrin Caves .... 13·00 12·00
2405/2407 *Set of 3* .... 20·00 19·00
2405/2407 *Set of 3 with tabs* .... 23·00 21·00

(Des Tuvia Kurtz and Osnat Eshel. Litho Cartor)

2017 (7 Feb). Flora–Aromatic Plants. T **1015** and similar horiz designs. Multicoloured.

(a) Ordinary gum. P 13×13½.

2408 4s.10 Type **1015** .... 5·25 4·75
2409 4s.10 Myrrh .... 5·25 4·75
2410 4s.10 Balsam .... 5·25 4·75
2408/2410 *Set of 3* .... 14·00 13·00
2408/2410 *Set of 3 with tabs* .... 16·00 14·50

(b) Self-adhesive. Booklet stamps. Die-cut perf 12½.

2410*a* 4s.10 As Type **1015** .... 5·25 4·75
2410*b* 4s.10 Myrrh (As No. 2409) .... 5·25 4·75
2410*c* 4s.10 Balsam (As No. 2410) .... 5·25 4·75
2410*a*/2410*c* *Set of 3* .... 14·00 13·00

Nos. 2410*a*/2410*c*, each×2, were printed in booklets of six stamps.

1016 Statue of Liberty

1017 Fighters

(Des Osnat Eshel. Litho Cartor)

2017 (7 Feb). 120th Anniversary of Zionist Organisation of America. P 13½×13.

2411 **1016** 8s.30 multicoloured .... 10·50 9·75
With tab 11·00 10·00

(Des Pini Hamou. Litho Cartor)

2017 (7 Feb). Krav Maga Self-defence System. P 13×13½.

2412 **1017** 11s.70 multicoloured .... 15·00 14·00
With tab 16·00 14·50

1018 National Memorial Hall

1019 Waterfall, Golan Heights

(Des Miri Nestor. Litho Cartor)

2017 (4 Apr). Memorial Day. National Memorial Hall at Mount Herzel, Jerusalem. P 13×13½.

2413 **1018** 2s.40 multicoloured .... 3·00 2·75
With tab 3·25 3·00

(Des Ronen Goldberg. Litho Cartor)

2017 (4 Apr). 50th Anniversary of Settlements in Golan, Jordan Valley, Judea and Samaria. T **1019** and similar vert designs. P 13½×13.

2414 2s.40 Type **1019** .... 3·00 2·75
2415 2s.40 Jordan Valley .... 3·00 2·75
2416 2s.40 Judea and Samaria .... 3·00 2·75
2414/2416 *Set of 3* .... 8·00 7·50
2414/2416 *Set of 3 with tabs* .... 9·00 8·25

1020 Kibbutz Ein Gev, 1944

1021 Hebrew University of Jerusalem

(Des Zina and Zvika Roitman. Litho Cartor)

2017 (4 Apr). Passover Haggadah. T **1020** and similar horiz designs. Multicoloured. P 13×13½.

2417 4s. Type **1020** .... 5·25 4·75
2418 4s. Kibbutz Artzi Federation, 1944 .... 5·25 4·75
2419 4s. Pirkei Pesach Haganah, 1948 .... 5·25 4·75
2417/2419 *Set of 3* .... 14·00 13·00
2417/2419 *Set of 3 with tabs* .... 16·00 14·50

(Des Meir Eshel. Litho Cartor)

2017 (4 Apr). 50th Anniversary of Re-unification of Jerusalem. Sheet 138×83 mm containing T **1021** and similar vert designs. Multicoloured. P 13½×13.

MS2420 4s.10×2, Type **1021**; Western Wall .... 11·00 10·00

1022 Bottlenose Dolphin

1023 Athletes

(Des Ronen Goldberg. Litho Cartor)

2017 (4 Apr). Dolphin Research–40th Anniversary of Israel–Portugal Friendship. P 13×13½.

2421 **1022** 7s.40 multicoloured .... 9·50 8·75
With tab 9·75 9·00

A stamp of a similar design was issued by Portugal.

(Des Itay Balaish. Litho Cartor)

2017 (13 June). 20th Maccabiah (games). P 13½×13.

2422 **1023** 2s.40 multicoloured .... 3·00 2·75
With tab 3·25 3·00

1024 *Atur Mitzchech Zahav Shachor* (Your Forehead is Decorated in Gold and Black)

1025 Love Songs (*image reduced by 69% of original size*)

(Des Baruch Nae and Anat Warshavsky. Litho Cartor)

2017 (13 June). Israeli Music–Love Songs. T **1024** and similar square designs forming the overall design T **1025**. Multicoloured. P 13.

2423	2s.40 Type **1024**	3·00	2·75
	a. Sheet of 12. Nos. 2423/2434	37·00	
2424	2s.40 *Take Me Under Your Wings*	3·00	2·75
2425	2s.40 *A Meeting to Eternity*	3·00	2·75
2426	2s.40 *Rosa Rosa*	3·00	2·75
2427	2s.40 *Apples and Dates*	3·00	2·75
2428	2s.40 *When the Light is on in your Window*	3·00	2·75
2429	2s.40 *The Flower in my Garden*	3·00	2·75
2430	2s.40 *Forgiveness*	3·00	2·75
2431	2s.40 *There were Nights*	3·00	2·75
2432	2s.40 *Melancholy Song*	3·00	2·75
2433	2s.40 *Everyone Has*	3·00	2·75
2434	2s.40 *Universal Convenant*	3·00	2·75
2423/2434	*Set of 12*	32·00	30·00
2423/2434	*Set of 12 with tabs*	36·00	33·00

Nos. 2423/2426 and 2429/2432 were printed *se-tenant*, in horizontal strips of four and Nos. 2427/2428 and 2433/2434 in horizontal pairs, each strip or pair sharing a composite background design, surrounding a block of four stamp size labels, within the sheet No. 2423a.

The stamps were arranged so that each have a *se-tenant*, inscribed tab, at foot, the tabs forming part of the design and the margin of the sheet.

1026 Soldier

1027 Crown Anemone and Croatian Iris

(Des Ronen Goldberg. Litho Cartor)

2017 (4 Sept). Centenary of World War I in Israel. General Allenby Entering Jerusalem, 1917. P 13×13½.

2435	**1026** 11s.60 multicoloured	15·00	14·00
	With tab	16·00	14·50

(Des Sabina Rešié. Litho Cartor)

2017 (4 Sept). Israel–Croatia Friendship. P 14.

2436	**1027** 6s.50 multicoloured	8·50	7·75
	With tab	8·75	8·00

1028 Composite Scene from Production of Play

1029 Shimom Peres

(Des Rinat Gilboa. Litho Cartor)

2017 (12 Sept). Centenary of Habimah National Theatre. P 13½.

2437	**1028** 2s.40 multicoloured	3·00	2·75
	With tab	3·25	3·00

(Des Limor Peretz-Samia. Litho Cartor)

2017 (12 Sept). First Death Anniversary of Shimom Peres (president 2007–2014). P 13½.

2438	**1029** 2s.40 multicoloured	3·00	2·75
	With tab	3·25	3·00

1030 Selichot Prayers

(Des Diana Shimon. Litho Cartor)

2017 (12 Sept). Festivals–Month of Tishrei. T **1030** and similar horiz designs. Multicoloured. P 13×13½.

2439	2s.40 Type **1030**	3·00	2·75
2440	7s.40 Building a Sukkah	9·50	8·75
2441	8s.30 Second Hakafot	10·50	9·75
2439/2441	*Set of 3*	21·00	19·00
2439/2441	*Set of 3 with tabs*	23·00	21·00

1031 'His Majesty's Government Views with Favour the Establishment in Palestine of a National Home for the Jewish People'

(Des David Ben-Hador. Litho Cartor)

2017 (12 Sept). Centenary of the Balfour Declaration. P 13½.

2442	**1031** 5s. multicoloured	6·50	6·00
	With tab	6·75	6·25

1032 Gorny Convent

1033 Gal Class Submarine

(Des Ivan Ulyanovskiy. Litho Enschedé)

2017 (14 Nov). Architecture–Gorny Convent, Ein Karem. P 13½.

2443	**1032** 6s.50 multicoloured	8·50	7·75
	With tab	8·75	8·00

A stamp of a similar design was issued by Russia.

(Des Meir Eshel and Tuvia Kurtz. Littho Enschedé)

2017 (19 Dec). Stamp Day. Submarines. T **1033** and similar horiz designs showing submarines. Multicoloured. P 13½.

2444	2s.50 Type **1033**	3·25	3·00
2445	2s.50 S Class	3·25	3·00
2446	2s.50 T Class from below	3·25	3·00
2444/2446	*Set of 3*	8·75	8·00
2444/2446	*Set of 3 with tabs*	[illegible]	[illegible]

1034 Theatre, Beit She'an

1035 *Dolichophis jugularis* (Large Whip Snake)

(Des David Ben-Hador. Litho Enschede)

2017 (19 Dec). Ancient Roman Arenas. T **1034** and similar horiz designs. Multicoloured. P 13½.

2447	4s.10 Type **1034**	5·25	4·75
2448	4s.10 Amphitheatre, Beit Guvrin	5·25	4·75
2449	4s.10 Hippodrome, Caesarea	5·25	4·75
2447/2449	*Set of 3*	14·00	13·00
2447/2449	*Set of 3 with tabs*	16·00	14·50

(Des Tuvia Kurtz and Ronen Goldberg. Litho Enschedé)

2017 (19 Dec). Snakes in Israel. T **1035** and similar vert designs. Multicoloured. P 14.

2450	4s.10 Type **1035**	5·25	4·75
	a. Strip. Nos. 2450/2452	17·00	
2451	4s.10 *Psammophis schokari* (Schokari Sand Racer)	5·25	4·75
2452	4s.10 *Daboia palaestinae* (Palestine Viper)	5·25	4·75
2450/2452	*Set of 3*	14·00	13·00
2450/2452	*Set of 3 with tabs*	16·00	14·50

Nos. 2450/2452 were printed, *se-tenant*, in horizontal strips of three stamps within sheets of nine.

1036 Wheelchair Users and Able-bodied

(Des Meir Eshel. Litho Enschedé)

2017 (19 Dec). Integration of the Disabled into Society. P 13½.

2453	**1036** 11s.60 multicoloured	15·00	14·00
	With tab	16·00	14·50

MACHINE LABELS

A. FRAMA

From 17 November 1988 gummed labels were available from three Frama automatic machines, two machines were installed in post offices in Tel Aviv-Yafo and one in Ramat Gan. Further machines were later installed.

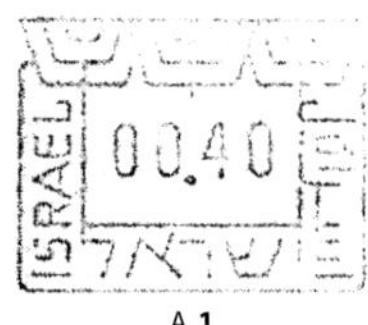

A **1**

1988 (17 Nov). Design as T A **1** in red. Face values 5a. to 15s. in steps of 5a.

Fixed values:

17.11.88	40, 60, 70a.
25.5.89	45, 70, 80a.
1.9.89	50, 70, 80a.
1.5.90	55, 80a., 1s.
2.12.90	60, 90a., 1s.10
12.7.91	70a., 1s., 1s.30
25.11.91	75a., 1s.10, 1s.40
23.12.92	80a., 1s.20, 1s.50
10.11.93	85a., 1s.30, 1s.60
1.9.94	90a., 1s.05, 1s.40, 1s.70
19.3.95	1s., 1s.10, 1s.50, 1s.80
24.1.96	1s.05, 1s.20, 1s.60, 1s.90
[illegible]	[illegible]
23.12.97	1s.15, 1s.40, 1s.80, 2s.20

A **2** Exhibition Emblem

1998 (13 May). Israel '98 World Stamp Exhibition. Multicoloured design as T A **2**. Face values 5a. to 15s. in 5a. steps.
Fixed values: 13.5.98 1s.15, 1s.80, 2s.20

B. KLUSSENDORF

On 9 July 1990 Klussendorf machines started operating, with further machines added later. At first these labels were manufactured in Germany with shiny gum and one phosphor band about a third from the left; later labels were produced in Israel with matt gum and the phosphor band at the extreme left of the design. A number specific to the issuing machine appears on the front (some 40 numbers have appeared); labels produced by the Philatelic Service are unnumbered.

B **1** Running Stag and Star of David

(Des D. Ben-Hador)

1990 (9 July). Design as T B **1**. Scarlet, ultramarine and black. Face values 5a. to 5s. in 5a. steps.
Fixed values: 9.7.90 9.7.90 9.7.90

Withdrawn from sale 8 January 1999.

Every fifth stamp has a control number on the back.

(Des Y. Granot)

1992 (2 Nov). Christmas. Multicoloured design inscr 'Season's Greetings from the Holy Land'. Face values 5a. to 5s. in 5a. steps.
Fixed values: 2.11.92 75a., 1s.10, 1s.40 (Candle, bell and holly)

Withdrawn from sale 8 January 1993.

Christmas labels were dispensed by the Philatelic Service (unnumbered) and the machines at Bethlehem and Tel Aviv (both numbered 023).

(Des Y. Granot)

1993 (16 Nov). Christmas. Multicoloured design showing a view of Bethlehem and inscr 'Season's Greetings from the Holy Land'. Face values 5a. to 5s. in 5a. steps.
Fixed values: 16.11.93 85a., 1s.30, 1s.60 (View of Bethlehem)

Withdrawn from sale 10 January 1994.

Christmas labels were dispensed by the Philatelic Service (unnumbered) and the machines at Bethlehem and Tel Aviv (both numbered 023).

B **2** Nazareth

(Des Marion Codner)

1994 (21 June). Tourist Sites (1st series). Designs as T B **2** showing tourist sites of Israel. Black. Face values 5a. to 15s. in 5a. steps.

Fixed values:

21.7.94	85a., 1s.30, 1s.60 (Type B **2**)
	85a., 1s.30, 1s.60 (Akko)
	85a., 1s.30, 1s.60 (Tiberias)
	85a., 1s.30, 1s.60 (Yafo)

85a., 1s.30, 1s.60 (Bethlehem)
85a., 1s.30, 1s.60 (David's Tower, Jerusalem)

Withdrawn from sale 8 January 1999.

(Des Marion Codner)

1994 (23 Aug). Tourist Sites (2nd series). Designs as T B **2** showing tourist sites of Israel. Black. Face values 5a. to 15s. in 5a. steps.
Fixed values: 23.8.94 85a., 1s.30, 1s.60 (Massada)
85a., 1s.30, 1s.60 (Church of Holy Sepulchre, Jerusalem)
85a., 1s.30, 1s.60 (Capernaum)

(Des Y. Granot)

1994 (27 Nov). Christmas. Multicoloured design showing an Angel and inscr 'Season's Greetings from the Holy Land'. Face values 5a. to 5s. in 5a. steps.
Fixed values: 27.11.94 90a., 1s.40, 1s.70 (Angel)

Withdrawn from sale 10 January 1995.

Christmas labels were dispensed by the Philatelic Service (unnumbered), the machines at Bethlehem and Tel Aviv (both numbered 023), and Nazareth (numbered 018).

(Des Y. Granot)

1995 (16 Nov). Christmas. Multicoloured design showing the Nativity Scene and inscr 'Season's Greetings from the Holy Land'. Face values 5a. to 5s. in 5a. steps.
Fixed values: 16.11.95 1s., 1s.50, 1s.80 (Nativity scene)

Withdrawn from sale 12 January 1996.

Christmas labels were dispensed by the Philatelic Service (unnumbered) and the machines at Tel Aviv and Nazareth (both numbered 023).

(Des Y. Granot)

1995 (16 Dec). Jerusalem 3000 European Stamp Exhibition. Multicoloured design showing exhibition emblem. Face values 5a. to 15s. in 5a. steps.
Fixed values: 16.12.95 1s., 1s.50, 1s.80 (Exhibition emblem)

Withdrawn from sale 21 December 1995.

B **3** Fish and Loaves of Bread

(Des Y. Granot)

1996 (19 Nov). Christmas. Multicoloured design as T B **3** inscr 'Season's Greetings from the Holy Land'. Face values 5a. to 5s. in 5a. steps.
Fixed values: 19.11.96 1s.05, 1s.60, 1s.90 (Type B **3**)

Withdrawn from sale 10 January 1997.

Christmas labels were dispensed by the Philatelic Service (unnumbered) and the machines at Tel Aviv and Nazareth (both numbered 023).

(Des Ruth Beckman)

1996 (5 Dec). Tourist Sites (3rd series). Design as T B **2** showing tourist sites of Israel. Black. Face values 5a. to 15s. in 5a. steps.
Fixed values: 5.12.96 1s.05, 1s.60, 1s.90 (Haifa)
17.12.96 1s.10, 1s.70, 2s. (Haifa)
23.12.97 1s.15, 1s.80, 2s.20 (Haifa)

Withdrawn from sale 8 January 1999.

B **4** Jerusalem

(Des A. Berg)

1997 (19 Nov). Christmas. Design as T B **4** inscr 'Season's Greetings from the Holy Land'. Face values 5a. to 15s. in 5a. steps.
Fixed values: 19.11.97 1s.10, 1s.70, 2s.

Withdrawn from sale 9 January 1998.

Christmas labels were dispensed by the Philatelic Service (unnumbered) and the machines at Tel Aviv and Nazareth (both numbered 023).

1997 (23 Dec). Tourist Sites (4th series). Design as T B **2** showing tourist sites of Israel. Black. Face values 5a. to 15s. in 5a. steps.
Fixed values: 23.12.97 1s.15, 1s.80, 2s.20 (Be'er Sheva)

Withdrawn from sale 8 January 1999.

1997 (28 Dec). Tourist Sites (5th series). Design as T B **2** showing tourist sites of Israel. Black. Face values 5a. to 15s. in 5a. steps.
Fixed values: 28.12.97 1s.15, 1s.80, 2s.20 (The Knesset, Jerusalem)

Withdrawn from sale 8 January 1999.

B **5** Exhibition Emblem

(Des I. Gabay)

1998 (13 May). Israphil '98 World Stamp Exhibition, Tel Aviv. Multicoloured design as T B **5**. Face values 5a. to 15s. in 5a. steps.
Fixed values: 13.5.98 1s.15, 1s.80, 2s.20, 2s.70

Withdrawn from sale 21 May 1998.

B **6** Birds

(Des I. Gabay)

1998 (16 Nov). Christmas. Design as T B **6** inscr 'Season's Greetings from the Holy Land'. Face values 5a. to 15s. in 5a. steps.
Fixed values: 16.11.98 1s.15, 1s.80, 2s.20, 2s.70

Withdrawn from sale 8 January 1999.

Christmas labels were dispensed by the Philatelic Service (unnumbered) and the machines at Tel Aviv and Nazareth (both numbered 023).

B **7** Methods of Communication

2004 (19 Feb). Methods of Communications. Multicoloured design as T B **7**.
Fixed values: 19.2.04 1s.30, 1s.40, 2s.10, 2s.20, 2s.30, 2s.80, 2s.90, 4s.10

Nos. 001, 002, 003, 004, 005, 006, 007, 008, 009, 010, 011, 012, 013, 015.

2004 (3 May). TELABUL 2004 National Stamp Exhibition, Tel Aviv. Multicoloured design showing clock tower and clock face.
Fixed values: 3.5.04 1s.30, 1s.40, 2s.10, 2s.20, 2s.30, 2s.80, 2s.90, 4s.10

Nos. 001, 002, 003, 004, 005, 006, 007, 008, 009, 010, 011, 012, 013, 014.

B **8** Christmas Tree and Decorations

2004 (14 Dec). Christmas. Multicoloured designs as T B **8** inscr 'Season's Greetings from the Holy Land'.
Fixed values: 14.12.04 1s.30, 1s.40, 2s.10, 2s.20, 2s.30, 2s.80, 2s.90, 4s.10

Nos. 001, 002, 003, 004, 005, 006, 007, 008, 009, 010, 011, 012, 013, 014, 015.

B **9** Emblem

2005 (22 Feb). 800th Death Anniversary (2004) of Moses Maimonides (philosopher). Multicoloured design as T B **9**.
Fixed values: 22.2.05 1s.30, 1s.40, 2s.10, 2s.20, 2s.30, 2s.80, 2s.90, 4s.10

Nos. 001, 002, 003, 004, 005.

B **10** Soldier raising Flag

2005 (9 May). 60th Anniversary of End of Second World War. Multicoloured design as T B **10**.
Fixed values: 9.5.05 1s.30, 1s.40, 2s.10, 2s.20, 2s.30, 2s.80, 2s.90, 4s.10

Nos. 001, 004, 006, 008, 010, 012.
Withdrawn from sale 15 August 2005.

B **11** Christmas Decorations and View over Nazareth

2005 (12 Dec). Christmas. Multicoloured design as T B **11** inscr 'Seasons Greetings from the Holy Land'.
Fixed values: 12.12.05 1s.30, 1s.40, 2s.10, 2s.20, 2s.30, 2s.80, 2s.90, 4s.10

Nos. 001, 002, 003, 004, 005, 006, 007, 008, 009, 010, 011, 012, 013, 014, 015.
Withdrawn from sale 19 January 2006.

B **12** Emblem

2006 (1 Mar). New Postal Emblem. Multicoloured design as T B **12**.
Fixed values: 1.3.06 1s.50, 2s.20, 2s.40, 2s.50, 2s.90, 3s., 4s.30, 4s.90

Nos. 001, 002, 004, 005, 006, 008, 009, 010, 011, 012, 013, 015, 016.
Withdrawn from sale 20 February 2007.

B **13** Jerusalem

2006 (8 May). JERUSALEM 2006 National Philatelic Exhibition. Multicoloured designs as T B **13**. Face values in violet.
Fixed values: 8.5.06 1s.50, 2s.20, 2s.40, 2s.50, 2s.90, 3s., 4s.30, 4s.90

Nos. 001, 002, 003, 004, 005, 006, 007, 008, 009, 010, 011, 012, 013, 014, 015, 016, 017.

B **14** Building Façade

2006 (12 Sept). Rehovot. Multicoloured design as T B **14**. Face values available in black or violet.
Fixed values: 12.9.06 1s.50, 2s.20, 2s.40, 2s.50, 2s.90, 3s., 4s.30, 4s.90

Nos. 001, 002, 003, 004, 005, 006, 007, 008, 009, 010, 011.

2006 (5 Dec). Christmas. Multicoloured design showing Angel and trumpet inscr 'Season's Greetings from the Holy Land'. Face values in violet.
Fixed values: 5.12.06 1s.50, 2s.20, 2s.40, 2s.50, 2s.90, 3s., 4s.30, 4s.90

Nos. 001, 010, 015.

2007 (20 Feb). New Postal Emblem. Multicoloured design as T B **12** but with change of background. Face values available in black and violet.
Fixed values: 20.2.07 1s.50, 2s.20, 2s.40, 2s.50, 2s.90, 3s., 4s.30, 4s.90

Nos. 001, 004, 006, 008, 013, 015.

B **15** Ashdod Museum of Art

2007 (20 June). Tourism (1st issue). Ashdod. Multicoloured design as T B **15**. Face values available in black and violet.
Fixed values: 20.6.07 1s.50, 2s.20, 2s.40, 2s.50, 2s.90, 3s., 4s.30, 4s.90

Nos. 001, 002, 003, 004, 005, 006, 007, 008, 009, 010, 011, 012, 013, 014, 015, 016, 017, 018.

B **16** Coral World Underwater Observatory, Eilat

2007 (27 Aug). Tourism (2nd issue). Eilat. Multicoloured design as T B **16**. Face values available in black and violet.
Fixed values: 27.8.07 1s.55, 2s.25, 2s.80, 3s.30, 3s.40, 4s.50, 4s.60, 5s.80

Nos. 001, 002, 003, 004, 005, 006, 007, 008, 009, 010, 011, 012, 013.

B **17** Nazareth

2007 (5 Dec). Christmas. Multicoloured design as T B **17** inscr 'Season's Greetings from the Holy Land'. Face values in violet.
Fixed values: 5.12.07 1s.55, 2s.25, 2s.80, 3s.30, 3s.40, 4s.50, 4s.60, 5s.80

Nos. 001, 010, 015.

B **18**

2008 (14 May). World Stamp Championship Exhibition 2008, Tel Aviv. Multicoloured designs as T B **18**. Face values in black.
Fixed values: 14.5.08 1s.55, 2s.25, 2s.80, 3s.30, 3s.40, 4s.50, 4s.60, 5s.80

Nos. 001 to 060.

B **19** Dove

2008 (8 Dec). Christmas. Multicoloured design as T B **19** inscr 'Season's Greetings from the Holy Land'. Face values in black.
Fixed values: 8.12.08 1s.60, 2s.30, 2s.90, 3s.40
Nos. 001, 010, 015.

B **20** Birds flying

2009 (1 Jan). Birds. Multicoloured design as T B **20**.
Fixed values: 1.1.09 1s.60, 2s.30, 3s.20, 3s.50, 3s.80, 4s.40, 5s.40, 5s.60
Nos. 001, 006, 008, 010.

B **21** Griffin Vulture *Gypus fluvus*

2009 (17 Feb–8 Sept). Birds of Prey. Multicoloured design as T B **21**.
Fixed values: 17.2.09 1s.60, 2s.30, 3s.20, 3s.50, 3s.80, 4s.40, 5s.40, 5s.60 (Type B **21**)
Nos. 001, 006.
22.4.09 1s.60, 2s.30, 3s.20, 3s.50, 3s.80, 4s.40, 5s.40, 5s.60 (Lesser Kestrel (*Falco naumanni*))
Nos. 001, 010.
30.6.09 1s.60, 2s.30, 3s.20, 3s.80, 4s.40, 5s.40, 5s.60 (Short-toed Snake Eagle (*Circaetus gallicus*))
Nos. 001, 012.
8.9.09 1s.60, 2s.30, 3s.20, 3s.50, 3s.80, 4s.40, 5s.40, 5s.60 (Bonelli's Eagle (*Hieraaetus fasciatus*))
Nos. 001, 004.

B **22**

2009 (4 May). Visit of Pope Benedict XVI. Multicoloured design T B **22**.
Fixed values: 4.5.09 1s.60, 2s.30, 3s.20, 3s.50, 3s.80, 4s.40, 5s.40, 5s.60
Nos. 001, 010, 015.

B **23**

2009 (26 Nov). Christmas. Multicoloured design as T B **23** inscr 'Season's Greetings from the Holy Land'.
Fixed values: 26.11.09 1s.60, 2s.40, 3s.60, 3s.80, 4s.60, 5s.30, 6s.50, 6s.70
Nos. 010, 015.

B **24** Birds

2010 (3 Jan). Birds. Multicoloured design as T B **24**.
Fixed values: 3.1.10 1s.60, 1s.70, 3s.50, 3s.80, 4s.20, 4s.60, 6s.10, 6s.70
Nos. 001, 006, 008, 010, 012, 013, 015, 018.

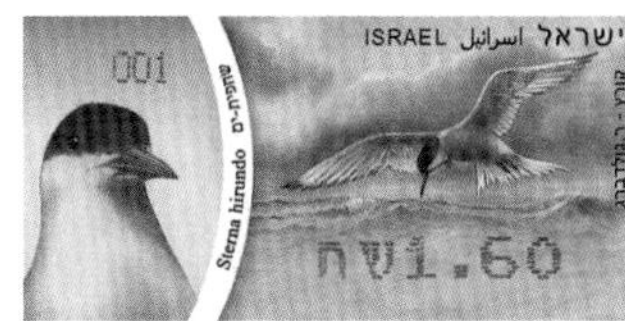

B **25** Common Tern (*Sterna hirundo*)

2010 (27 Jan). Birds. Multicoloured design as T B **25**.
Fixed values: 27.1.10 1s.60, 1s.70, 3s.50, 3s.80, 4s.20, 4s.60, 6s.10, 6s.70 (Type B **25**)
Nos. 001, 008.
14.3.10 1s.60, 1s.70, 3s.50, 3s.80, 4s.20, 4s.60, 6s.10, 6s.70 (Flamingo (*Phoenicopterus ruber*))
Nos. 001, 013.
14.6.10 1s.60, 1s.70, 3s.50, 3s.80, 4s.20, 4s.60, 6s.10, 6s.70 (Pallas's Gull (*Larus ichthyaetus*))
Nos. 001, 018.
25.8.10 1s.60, 1s.70, 3s.50, 3s.80, 4s.20, 4s.60, 6s.10, 6s.70 (Kingfisher (*Alcedo atthis*))
Nos. 001, 011.

B **26** Emblem

2010 (2 June). Multicoloured design as T B **26**.
Fixed values: 2.6.10 1s.60, 1s.70, 3s., 3s.10, 3s.20, 3s.30, 3s.50, 3s.80, 4s., 4s.20

B **27** Wrapped Present

2010 (19 Nov). Christmas. Multicoloured design as T B **27** inscr 'Season's Greetings from the Holy Land'.
Fixed values: 19.11.10 1s.70, 2s.50, 3s.50, 3s.70, 4s.20, 4s.90, 6s., 6s.10
Nos. 001, 010, 015, 062.

B **28** Menorah and Knesset

2010 (21 Nov). Jerusalem 2010 International Philatelic Exhibition. Multicoloured design as T B **28**.
Fixed values: 21.11.10 1s.70, 2s.50, 3s.50, 3s.70, 4s.20, 4s.90, 6s., 6s.10
Nos. 001, 061.

B **29** Deer

2011 (2 Jan–13 Sept). Animals. Multicoloured designs as T B **29**.
Fixed values: 2.1.11 1s.70, 3s.30, 3s.50, 4s., 4s.20, 5s.90, 6s.10 (Type B **29**)
Nos. 001, 006, 008, 010, 012, 013, 015, 018.
7.2.11 1s.70, 3s.30, 3s.50, 4s., 4s.20, 5s.90, 6s.10 (Roe Deer (*Capreolus capreolus*))
Nos. 001, 006.
12.4.11 1s.70, 3s.30, 3s.50, 4s., 4s.20, 5s.90, 6s.10 (Persian Fallow Deer (*Dama mesopotamica*))
Nos. 001, 004.
27.6.11 1s.70, 3s.30, 3s.50, 4s., 4s.20, 5s.90, 6s.10 (Arabian Oryx (*Oryx leucoryx*))
Nos. 001, 013.
13.9.11 1s.70, 2s.60, 3s.30, 3s.80, 4s., 4s.70, 5s.80, 5s.90 (Mountain Gazelle (*Gazella gazelle acacia*)
Nos. 001, 012.

B **30** Emblem

2011 (2 Aug). Wikimania 2011. Multicoloured design as T B **30**.
Fixed values: 2.8.11 1s.70, 2s.60, 3s.30, 3s.80, 4s., 4s.70, 5s.80, 5s.90
Nos. 001, 006.

B **31** Christmas Tree

2011 (22 Nov). Christmas. Multicoloured designs as T B **31** inscr 'Season's Greetings from the Holy Land'.
Fixed values: 22.11.11 1s.70, 2s.60, 3s.30, 3s.80, 4s., 4s.70, 5s.80, 5s.90
Nos. 001, 010, 015.

B **32** Fish, Turtle and Dolphin

2012 (1 Jan–4 Sept). Marine Life. Multicoloured designs as T B **32**.
Fixed values: 1.1.12 1s.70, 2s., 2s.60, 3s. 3s.30, 3s.80, 4s., 4s.20, 4s.50, 4s.70, 5s.80, 5s.90 (Type B **32**)
Nos. 001, 004, 006, 008, 010, 011, 012, 013, 015, 018.
7.2.12 1s.70, 2s., 2s.60, 3s. 3s.30, 3s.80, 4s., 4s.20, 4s.50, 4s.70, 5s.80, 5s.90 (Diver and coral)
Nos. 001, 013.
17.4.12 2s., 3s., 3s.30, 3s.50, 4s., 4s.20, 4s.50, 4s.70, 5s., 5s.80, 5s.90, 6s.10, 6s.20 (Bottlenose Dolphin (*Tursiops truncates*))
Nos. 001, 006.
26.6.12 2s., 3s., 3s.30, 3s.50, 4s., 4s.20, 4s.50, 4s.70, 5s., 5s.80, 5s.90, 6s.10, 6s.20 (Green Sea Turtle (*Chelonia mydas*))
Nos. 001, 008.
4.9.12 2s., 3s., 3s.50, 4s.20, 4s.50, 5s., 6s.10, 6s.20 (Grouper (*Epinephelus marginatus*))
Nos. 001, 006.

B **33** Presents and Decorations

2012 (22 Dec). Christmas. Multicoloured design as T B **33** inscr 'Season's Greetings from the Holy Land'.
Fixed values: 22.12.12 2s., 3s., 3s.50, 4s.20, 4s.50, 5s., 6s.10, 6s.20
Nos. 001, 010, 015.

B **34** Flowers

2013 (1 Jan–26 Aug). Flowers. Multicoloured designs as T B **34**.
Fixed values: 1.1.13 2s., 3s.20, 3s.50, 4s.20, 4s.90, 5s.70, 6s.20 (Type B **34**)
Nos. 001, 004, 006, 008, 010, 011, 012, 013, 015, 018.
5.2.13 2s., 3s.20, 3s.50, 4s.20, 4s.90, 5s.70, 6s.20 (Iris (*Iris mariae*))
Nos. 001, 012.
2.4.13 2s., 3s.20, 3s.50, 4s.20, 4s.90, 5s.70, 6s.20 (Peony (*Paeonia mascula*)
Nos. 001, 004.
25.5.13 2s., 3s.20, 3s.50, 4s.20, 4s.90, 5s.70, 6s.20 (Spotted Rock Rose (*Tuberaria guttata*))
Nos. 001, 011.
26.8.13 2s., 3s.10, 3s.20, 3s.90, 4s.60, 5s.20, 5s.60, 5s.70 (Lotus (*Nymphaea caerulea*))
Nos. 001, 006.

B **35** Flag and Beach

2013 (26 May). Tel Aviv 2013. Multicoloured design as T B **35**.
Fixed values: 26.5.13 2s., 3s., 3s.50, 4s.20, 4s.50, 5s. 6s.10, 6s.20
Nos. 001, 065.

B **36** Angel

2013 (25 Nov). Christmas. Multicoloured design as T B **36** inscr 'Season's Greetings from the Holy Land'.
Fixed values: 25.11.13 2s., 3s.10, 3s.20, 3s.90, 4s.60, 5s.20, 5s.60, 5s.70
Nos. 001, 010, 015.

B **37** Badgers and Weasels

2014 (1 Jan–9 Sept). Fauna. Multicoloured designs as T B **37**.
Fixed values: 1.1.14 2s., 3s.10, 3s.20, 3s.90, 4s.60, 5s.20, 5s.60, 5s.70 (Type B **37**)
Nos. 001, 004.

11.2.14 2s., 3s.10, 3s.20, 3s.90, 4s.60, 5s.20, 5s.60, 5s.70 (Polecat (*Vormela peregusna*))
Nos. 001, 008, 010, 020.
8.4.14 2s., 3s.10, 3s.20, 3s.90, 4s.60, 5s.20, 5s.60, 5s.70 (Beech Martin (*Martes foina*))
Nos. 001, 004.
23.6.14 2s., 3s.10, 3s.20, 3s.90, 4s.60, 5s.20, 5s.60, 5s.70 (Honey Badger (*Mellivora capensis*))
Nos. 001, 011.
9.9.14 1s.80, 2s.70, 3s.20, 3s.80, 4s., 5s.10, 5s.50, 5s.60 (Badger (*Meles meles*))
Nos. 001, 015.

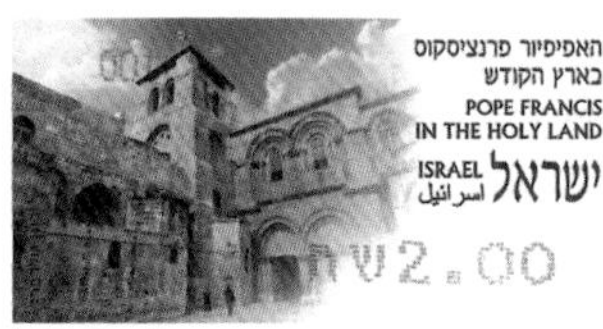

B **38** Façade

2014 (26 May). Pope Francis in the Holy Land. Multicoloured design as T B **38**.
Fixed values: 26.5.14 2s., 3s.10, 3s.20, 3s.90, 4s.60, 5s.20, 5s.60, 5s.70
Nos. 001, 020.

B **39** Mary and Jesus

2014 (25 Nov). Christmas. Multicoloured design as T B **39** inscr 'Season's Greetings from the Holy Land'.
Fixed values: 25.11.14 1s.80, 2s.70, 3s.20, 3s.80, 4s., 5s.10, 5s.50, 5s.60
Nos. 001, 015, 020.

B **40** Partridge (*Phasianidae*)

2015 (11 Feb–8 Dec). Birds. Multicoloured designs as T B **40**.
Fixed values: 11.2.15 2s.20, 4s.10, 6s.50, 7s.40, 8s.30, 9s. (Type B **40**)
Nos. 001, 004, 008, 011, 015, 020.
14.4.15 2s.20, 4s.10, 6s.50, 7s.40, 8s.30, 9s. (Partridge (*Alectoris chukar*))
Nos. 001, 004.
16.6.15 2s.20, 4s.10, 6s.50, 7s.40, 8s.30, 9s. (Sand Partridge (*Ammordix heyi*))
Nos. 001, 003.
2.9.15 2s.20, 4s.10, 6s.50, 7s.40, 8s.30, 9s. (Black Francolin (*Francolinus francolinus*))
Nos. 001, 011.
8.12.15 2s.20, 4s.10, 6s.50, 7s.40, 8s.30, 9s. (Common Quail (*Coturnix coturnix*))
Nos. 001, 022.

B **41** Postal Vehicles

2015 (1 June). Postal Vehicles. Multicoloured design as T B **41**.
Fixed values: 1.6.15 2s.20, 4s.10, 6s.50, 7s.40, 8s.30, 9s.
Nos. 001, 101, 220, 300, 326, 450, 636, 714, 900.

B **42**

2015 (24 Nov). Christmas. Multicoloured design as T B **42** inscr 'Season's Greetings from the Holy Land'.
Fixed values: 24.11.15 2s.20, 4s.10, 6s.50, 7s.40, 8s.30, 9s.
Nos. 001, 101, 987.

B **43** Silhouette of Dog and Owner

2016 (1 Jan–13 Nov). Dog Adoption. Multicoloured designs as T B **43**.
Fixed values: 1.1.16 2s.30, 4s.10, 6s.50, 7s.40, 8s.30, 9s. (Type B **43**)
Nos. 001, 101, 220, 300, 326, 450, 636, 714.
9.2.16 2s.30, 4s.10, 6s.50, 7s.40, 8s.30, 9s. (Willy)
Nos. 001, 220, 450.
21.6.16 2s.30, 4s.10, 6s.50, 7s.40, 8s.30, 9s. (Viki and Riki)
Nos. 001, 101.
13.9.16 2s.30, 4s.10, 6s.50, 7s.40, 8s.30, 9s. (Teddy)
Nos. 001, 714.
13.11.16 2s.30, 4s.10, 6s.50, 7s.40, 8s.30, 9s. (Bob)
Nos. 001.

B **44** Wailing Wall, Jerusalem

2016 (13 Nov). Jerusalem 2016 Stamp Exhibition. Multicoloured design as T B **44**.
Fixed values: 13.11.16 2s.30, 4s.10, 6s.50, 7s.40, 8s.30, 9s.
Nos. 001, 1601.

B **45** Nativity Scene

2016 (13 Nov). Christmas. Multicoloured design as T B **45** inscr 'Season's Greetings from the Holy Land'.
Fixed values: 13.11.16 2s.30, 4s.10, 6s.50, 7s.40, 8s.30, 9s.
Nos. 001, 101, 987, 1602.

STAMP BOOKLETS

The following checklist covers, in simplified form, booklets issued by Israel. It is intended that it should be used in conjunction with the main listings and details of stamps and panes listed there are not repeated.

Some booklets exist in more than one version, differing, for example, in the advertisements on the cover. Such differences are not covered by this list, prices quoted being for the cheapest version.

Prices are for complete booklets

Booklet No.	*Date*	*Contents and Cover Price*	*Price*
SB1	9.9.49	First Coins issue 2 panes, No. 2×6; 1 pane, No. 3×6 (120m.)	£350
SB2	9.9.49	First Coins issue 1 pane, No. 2×6; 1 pane, No. 3×6;1 pane, No. 4×6 (180m.)	
		a. Green cover	£750
		b. Front cover green, back cover white	£350
		c. White cover	£800
SB3	9.9.49	First Coins issue 1 pane, No. 2×6; 1 pane, No. 3×6;1 pane, No. 4×6; 1 pane, No. 5×6 (300m.)	
		a. Orange cover	£450
		b. White cover	£500
SB4	1.6.50	Second Coins issue 2 panes, No. 22×6; 1 pane, No. 23×6 (120pr.)	£100
SB5	1.6.50	Second Coins issue 1 pane, No. 22×6; 1 pane, No. 23×6;1 pane, No. 24×6 (180pr.)	£140
SB6	1.6.50	Second Coins issue 1 pane, No. 22×6; 1 pane, No. 23×6;1 pane, No. 24×6; 1 pane, No. 25×6 (360pr.)	
		a. White cover	£220
		b. Blue cover	£250
SB7	7.1.51	UPU 1 pane, No. 27×4; 1 pane, No. 28×4 (480pr.)	55·00
SB8	4.1.53	Third Coins issue 1 pane, No. 41×6; 1 pane, No. 42×6; 2 panes, No. 45×6 (450pr.)	11·00
SB9	15.3.56	12 Tribes 3 panes, No. 121A×6 (1440pr.)	16·00
SB10	16.6.57	12 Tribes 3 panes, No. 122A×6 (1800pr.)	17·00
SB11	3.6.58	12 Tribes 1 pane, No. 119B×6; 2 panes, No. 122B×6 (1500pr.)	16·00
SB12	21.3.63	Freedom from Hunger 1 pane, No. 254*a*×4 (I£2·20)	47·00
SB13	20.1.65	Signs of the Zodiac 1 pane, No. 202×6; 2 panes, No. 204×6 (I£1·92)	16·00
SB14	14.3.66	Civic Arms (1st series) 1 pane, No. 298×6; 2 panes, No. 300×6 (I£1.92)	9·00
SB15	25.5.71	Civic Arms (2nd series) 2 panes, No. 416a (I£2.04)	10·50
SB16	25.5.71	Civic Arms (2nd series) 2 panes, No. 417×6 (I£2.16)	10·50
SB17	12.12.72	Civic Arms (1st and 2nd series) 1 pane, No. 299a (I£1)	5·00
SB18	1.10.73	Civic Arms (2nd series) 1 pane, No. 418ab (I£1)	3·00
SB19	4.9.84-91	Undenominated Stamp. Branch (T **335**) 2 panes *tête-bêche* (separated by gutter). Cover rose-vermilion, greenish yellow and one other colour as indicated	
		a. No. 867a. Cover dull ultramarine	24·00
		b. No. 867ba. Cover deep bright ultramarine (1988)	75·00
		c. No. 867ba. Cover deep grey (25.11.91)	75·00
SB20	7.8.90	Undenominated Greetings Stamp. 'With Love' 1 pane, No. 1089a	50·00
SB21	4.9.90	Silver Spice Boxes 1 pane, No. 1117a (4s.25)	37·00
SB22	2.12.91	Mozart (T **476**) 1 pane, No. 1156a (8s.)	46·00
SB23	18.2.92	Undenominated Stamp. Anemone (T **477**) 1 pane, No. 1157ab	70·00
SB24	17.9.92	Jaffa–Jerusalem Railway 1 pane, No. 1170a (4s.75)	7·50
SB25	29.6.93	Undenominated Greetings Stamp. 'See You Again' (T **443**) 1 pane, No. 1088ab	50·00
SB26	8.2.94	Beetles 1 pane, No. 1229a (6s.80)	20·00
SB27	18.4.94	Undenominated Greetings Stamp. 'Keep in Touch' 1 pane, No. 1130a	70·00
SB28	23.8.94	Jewish New Year. Children Draw the Bible 1 pane, No. 1249a (8s.25)	15·50
SB29	25.6.96	Olympic Games, Atlanta 1 pane, No. 1332a (9s.95)	21·00
SB30	13.2.97	Show Jumping 1 pane, No. 1302ab (22s.)	85·00
SB31	23.9.97	Festival of Sukkot 1 pane, No. 1368a (10s.50)	23·00
SB32	17.2.98	50th Anniversary of State of Israel (T **583**) 1 pane, No. 1376ab	42·00
SB33	13.5.98	50th Anniversary of State of Israel 9 panes, Nos. 1361ab, 1374a, 1376ba, 1376cb, 1378ab, 1384a, 1395ab, 1397ab, 1407ba	£180
SB34	1.9.99	Festival of Sukkot 1 pane, No. 1453a (13s.40)	16·00
SB35	25.7.00	Traditional Foods 1 pane, No. 1490a (12s.10)	12·50
SB36	18.3.01	Animals 1 pane, No. 1544a (15s.)	17·00
SB36*a*	24.2.02	Months of the Year Nos. 1584/1595 (14s.40)	17·00
SB37	9.9.03	Olive Oil Production (T **703**) 1 pane, No. 1665a (11s.)	11·50
SB38	3.11.03	Wild Hyacinth No. 1671×20 (26s.)	25·00
SB39	3.5.04	Ottoman Clock Towers 6 panes, Nos. 1697a/1701a and 1697b (147s.)	33·00
SB39*a*	26.7.05	Gagea commutata Nos. 1743*ba*/1743*bd* (5s.60)	
SB40	8.5.06	Solar System Nos. 1784/1789 (15s.)	9·25
SB41	5.12.07	Hula Nature Reserve Nos. 1862/1864, each×2 (13s.50)	9·25
SB42	28.4.08	The Israeli No. 1878×20 (31s.)	24·00
SB42a	14.5.08	Hula Nature Reserve 1 pane, No. 1892*a*/1892*c* (31s.50)	17·00
SB42b	14.5.08	Noah's Ark 1 pane, No. 1892*d*/1892*i* (31s.50)	17·00
SB43	17.9.08	Herbs/24 hour post No. 1905×12 (34s.80)	26·00
SB44	8.9.09	Animal Assisted Therapy 1 pane. Nos. 1960/1962, each×2 (14s.40)	12·00
SB45	26.11.09	Fruit 1 pane, Nos. 1975/1979, each×4 (32s.)	2·00
SB45*a*	25.8.10	Greeting Stamps 1 pane, Nos. 2009/2010, each×6 (20s.40)	24·00
SB46	21.11.10	50th Anniversary of ASIFA 1 pane, Nos. 2044/2058 (25s.50)	30·00
SB47	7.2.11	Butterflies 1 pane, Nos. 2078*a*/2078*d*, each×4 and 2078*e*/2078*f*, each×2 (34s.)	39·00
SB48	13.9.11	Children's Games 1 pane, Nos. 2119/2121, each×3 (15s.60)	26·00
SB49	4.9.12	Visit Israel 1 pane, Nos. 2176/2178, each×2 (18s.)	21·00
SB50	3.12.13	Centenary of Aviation in Israel 1 pane, Nos. 2245/2247, each×2 (18s.60)	25·00
SB51	8.4.14	Israeli Sign Language 1 pane, Nos. 2268/2272, each×2 (20s.)	26·00
SB52	9.9.14	50th Anniversary of *Fiddler on the Roof* 1 pane, Nos. 2292/2294 each×2 (18s.60)	25·00
SB53	16.6.15	Vegetables 1 pane, Nos. 2330/2334 each×4 (44s.)	60·00
SB54	2.9.15	Rivers. Self-adhesive 1 pane, Nos. 2341/2346, each×2 (24s.60)	33·00
SB55	13.9.16	Parables of the Sages. Self-adhesive 1 pane, Nos. 2389/2391, each×2 (24s.60)	33·00
SB56	13.11.16	Tourism in Jerusalem 1 pane, Nos. 2394/2398, each×2 (24s.)	31·00
SB57	7.2.17	Flora 1 pane, Nos. 2410*a*/2410*c*, each×2 (24s.60)	33·00

DESIGN INDEX

This index provides in a condensed form a key to designs and subjects of portraits and pictorial stamps of Israel. In order to save space, portrait stamps are listed under surname only, views under the name of the town or area and works of art under the name of the artist. In order to save space people are listed under surname only, except for Rabbis, who are all listed under the title of Rabbi followed by their full name. In cases of difficulty part of the inscription has been used to identify the stamp.

A. SUBSIDIARY GROUPS

B. AIR STAMPS

C. POSTAGE STAMPS

B

C

D

E

F

G

Jordan

TRANSJORDAN

1920. 1000 Milliemes = 100 Piastres = £1 Egyptian
1927. 1000 Milliemes = £1 Palestinian
1950. 1000 Fils = 1 Jordanian Dinar
2004. 1 Dinar = 100 Qirsh/piastre = 100 Fils

PRICES FOR STAMPS ON COVER TO 1945	
Nos. 1/88*a*	*from* × 10
Nos. 89/142	*from* × 5
Nos. 143/243	*from* × 3
Nos. D112/24	*from* × 6
Nos. D159/248	*from* × 4
No. O117	—

Transjordan was part of the Turkish Empire from 1516 to 1918.

Turkish post offices are known to have existed at Ajlun ('Adjiloun'), Amman ('Omman'), Amman Station, Kerak ('Kerek'), Ma'an ('Mohan' or 'Maan'), Qatrana, Salt and Tafila ('Tafile'). Stamps cancelled 'Ibin' may have been used at Ibbin.

The area was overrun by British and Arab forces, organised by Colonel T. E. Lawrence, in September 1918, and as Occupied Enemy Territory (East), became part of the Syrian state under the Emir Faisal, who was king of Syria from 11 March to 24 July 1920. During 1920 the stamps of the Arab Kingdom of Syria were in use. On 25 April 1920 the Supreme Council of the Allies assigned to the United Kingdom a mandate to administer both Palestine and Transjordan, as the area to the east of the Jordan was called. The mandate came into operation on 29 September 1923.

E.E.F. post offices, using the stamps of Palestine, operated in the area from September 1918.

FORGERIES. Collectors are warned that the early provisional overprints and surcharges on T **3** or Palestine have been extensively forged. This particularly concerns Nos. 1/8, 20/88a and 98A/109. Nos. 9/19 and 106A/106B and 107A/107B must, however, always be genuine, as the underlying stamps of Palestine T **3** were never issued perf 14 without opt.

BRITISH MANDATED TERRITORY

'EAST'. Where the word 'East' appears in Arabic overprints it is not used in its widest sense but as implying the land or government 'East of Jordan'.

شرقي الاردن — (**1**) ('East of Jordan')

شرقي الاردن — (**1a**)

(Optd at Greek Orthodox Convent, Jerusalem)

1920 (Nov). T **3** of Palestine optd with T **1**.

No.	Type	Description	Unused	Used
		(a) P 15×14		
1	**1**	1m. sepia	3·75	6·00
		a. Opt inverted	£140	£275
2		2m. blue-green	23·00	26·00
		a. Silver opt		
3		3m. yellow-brown	4·00	4·75
		a. Opt Type **1a**	£1100	
4		4m. scarlet	4·25	4·50
		a. Arabic '40'	75·00	
5		5m. yellow-orange	11·00	3·75
5*a*		1p. deep indigo (Silver)	£2000	
6		2p. olive	15·00	17·00
		a. Opt Type **1a**	£850	
7		5p. deep purple	50·00	80·00
		a. Opt Type **1a**	£1400	
8		9p. ochre	£850	£1400
1/7 (*ex 5a*) *Set of 7*			95·00	£120
		(b) P 14		
9	**1**	1m. sepia	1·40	6·00
		a. Opt inverted	£170	
10		2m. blue-green	3·50	5·50
		a. Silver opt	£550	£600
11		3m. yellow-brown	23·00	32·00
12		4m. scarlet	17·00	48·00
		a. Arabic '40'	£150	
13		5m. orange	2·75	3·75
14		1p. deep indigo (Silver)	3·75	4·75
15		2p. deep olive	15·00	15·00
16		5p. purple	7·50	17·00
17		9p. ochre	7·50	55·00
18		10p. ultramarine	18·00	55·00
19		20p. pale grey	20·00	90·00
9/19 *Set of* 11			£100	£300

Nos. 1/19 were surcharged from five different settings of 120 (12×10) which produced eight sub-types of T **1**. T **1a** occurred on R. 8/12 from one setting. The 9p. also exists with this overprint, but no example appears to have survived without further overprint or surcharge.

Nos. 9/19 (P 14) were never issued without opt, and the T **1** opt on this perforation must always be genuine.

The T **1** opt ('Sharqi Al-urdun') comprises seven Arabic characters, reading (from right to left) Sh-R-Qi-Al-R-D-N. The key features of the rare T **1a** are a) the absence of the dots above 'Qi' and b) the short left stroke of the 'Al'. Other variants exist with the missing dots, but only T **1a** also has the short left stroke. T **1a** is often misidentified, and forgeries exist.

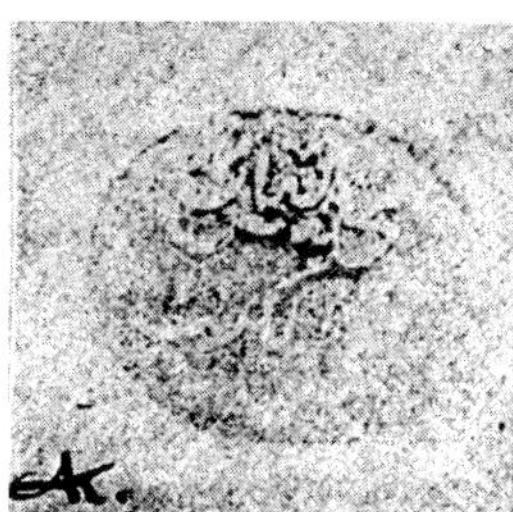

1b Moab District Seal (*full size*)

1920 (Nov). Issued at Kerak. Handstamped. Manuscript initials 'AK' in violet. Imperf.

No.	Type	Description	Unused	Used
19*a*	**1b**	(1p.) pale blue	£3500	£4000

No. 19*a* was issued in November 1920 by the political officer for Moab District, Captain (later Sir) Alex Kirkbride, and was used until supplies of Nos. 1/19 reached the area in March 1921. The local Turkish canceller was used as a postmark.

Emir Abdullah

1 April 1921–22 May 1946

Abdullah, a son of the King of the Hejaz, was made Emir of Transjordan in 1921. On 26 May 1923 Transjordan was recognised as an autonomous state and on 20 February 1928 it was accorded a degree of independence.

(**2**) ('Tenth of a piastre') (**3**) ('Piastre')

1922 (Nov). Nos. 1/19 additionally handstamped with steel dies at Amman as T **2** or **3**.

No.	Type	Description	Unused	Used
		(a) P 15×14		
20	**2**	1/10p. on 1m. sepia	29·00	50·00
		a. Red surch	70·00	70·00
		b. Violet surch	70·00	70·00
21		2/10p. on 2m. blue-green	35·00	35·00
		a. Error. Surch '3/10' for '2/10'	£120	£110
		b. Red surch	80·00	80·00
		c. Violet surch	£100	£100
		ca. Error. '3/10' for '2/10'		
22		3/10p. on 3m. yellow-brown	15·00	15·00
		a. Pair, one without surch	£800	
		b. Opt Type **1a**	£1200	£1200
		c. Error. '2/10' for '3/10'		
		d. Violet surch	£150	£150
		da. Opt Type **1a**	£2750	
23		4/10p. on 4m. scarlet	60·00	65·00
		a. Violet surch		
24		5/10p. on 5m. yellow-orange	£180	£100
		a. Pair, one without surch		
		b. Violet surch	£250	£225
25	**3**	2p. on 2p. olive	£250	75·00
		a. Opt Type **1a**	£1300	
		b. Red surch	£325	80·00
		ba. Opt Type **1a**		
		c. Violet surch	£300	90·00
26		5p. on 5p. deep purple	65·00	80·00
		a. Opt Type **1a**	£1600	
		b. Violet surch		
27		9p. on 9p. ochre	£300	£350
		a. Red surch	£130	£140
		b. Violet surch		

(b) P 14

28	2	1/10p. on 1m. sepia	25·00	30·00
		a. Pair, one without surch	£1500	
		b. Red surch	60·00	60·00
		c. Violet surch	£250	£300
29		2/10p. on 2m. blue-green	29·00	29·00
		a. Pair, one without surch	£1500	
		b. Error. Surch '3/10' for '2/10'	£110	£110
		c. Red surch	80·00	80·00
		ca. Error. Surch '3/10' for '2/10'		
		d. Violet surch	80·00	80·00
30		5/10p. on 5m. orange	£225	£100
		a. Pair, one without surch	†	£2000
		b. Violet surch	£275	
31	3	1p. on 1p. deep indigo (R.)	£200	60·00
		a. Pair, one without surch	£1800	
		b. Violet surch	£400	
32		9p. on 9p. ochre (R.)	£550	£550
		a. Violet surch		
33		10p. on 10p. ultramarine	£850	£1000
		a. Violet surch inverted		
34		20p. on 20p. pale grey	£650	£850
		a. Violet surch	£900	£950

*T **3** of Palestine (perf 15×14) similarly surch*

35	3	10p. on 10p. ultramarine	£1800	£2500
36		20p. on 20p. pale grey	£2500	£3000
		a. Violet surch		

T **2** reads 'tenths of a piastre' and T **3** 'the piastre', both with Arabic figures below. These surcharges were applied in order to translate the Egyptian face values of the stamps into the currency of the Arab Kingdom of Syria, but the actual face value of the stamps remained unchanged.

Being handstamped the surcharge may be found either at the top or bottom of the stamp, and exists double on most values.

The Types **2/3** handstamped surcharges have been extensively forged. Forged examples of Nos. 20/27 also often have a forged T **1** opt.

(**4**) ('Arab Government of the East, April 1921')

حكومة الشرق
العربية
نيسان سنة ١٩٢١

(**5**) ('Arab Government of the East, April 1921')

1922 (Dec). Stamps of 1920 handstamped with a steel die as T **4** in red-purple, violet or black.*

(a) P 15×14

37	4	1m. sepia (R.P.)	29·00	30·00
		a. Violet opt	30·00	35·00
		b. Black opt	26·00	26·00
38		2m. blue-green (R.P.)	27·00	27·00
		a. Violet opt	24·00	24·00
		b. Black opt	23·00	23·00
39		3m. yellow-brown (R.P.)	48·00	48·00
		a. Opt Type **1a**	£1600	
		b. Violet opt	9·00	9·00
		ba. Pair, one without opt	£1300	
		bb. Opt Type **1a**	£1500	£2000
		c. Black opt	10·00	10·00
		ca. Opt Type **1a**		
40		4m. scarlet (R.P.)	60·00	65·00
		b. Violet opt	60·00	65·00
		c. Black opt	60·00	65·00
41		5m. yellow-orange (R.P.)	45·00	12·00
		a. Violet opt	19·00	12·00
42		2p. olive (R.P.)	60·00	45·00
		a. Opt Type **1a**	£1500	
		b. Violet opt	26·00	18·00
		ba. Opt Type **1a**	£1500	£1300
		c. Black opt	17·00	12·00
43		5p. deep purple (R.P.)	£100	£120
		a. Pair, one without opt	£1600	
		b. Violet opt	65·00	85·00
		c. Black opt		
44		9p. ochre (R.P.)	£400	£450
		a. Violet opt	£200	£250
		ab. Opt Type **1a**	£2250	
		b. Black opt	70·00	85·00

(b) P 14

45	4	1m. sepia (R.P.)	16·00	20·00
		a. Pair, one without opt	£1300	
		b. Violet opt	27·00	24·00
		c. Black opt	23·00	23·00
46		2m. blue-green (R.P.)	32·00	32·00
		a. Violet opt	10·00	10·00
		b. Black opt	15·00	15·00
46c		3m. yellow-brown (V.)	£800	£350
47		5m. orange (R.P.)	£300	75·00
		a. Violet opt	32·00	22·00
48		1p. deep indigo (R.P.)	38·00	17·00
		a. Violet opt	22·00	11·00
49		2p. deep olive (V.)	80·00	85·00
50		5p. purple (R.P.)	£100	£110
		a. Violet opt	£110	£120
		b. Black opt		
51		9p. ochre (V.)	£900	£1000
52		10p. ultramarine (R.P.)	£1800	£1900
		a. Violet opt	£1100	£1600
		b. Black opt		
53		20p. pale grey (R.P.)	£1600	£2000
		a. Violet opt	£1100	£1800
		b. Black opt		

* The ink of the 'black' overprint is not a true black, but is caused by a mixture of inks from different ink-pads. The colour is, however, very distinct from either of the others.

Most values are known with inverted and/or double overprints.

The T **4** handstamp has been extensively forged, often in conjunction with a forged T **1** opt on stamps perf 15×14.

1923 (1 Mar). Stamps of 1920, with typographed overprint, T **5** applied by Govt Printing Press, Amman.

(a) P 15×14

54	5	1m. sepia (Gold)	£1500	£1800
55		2m. blue-green (Gold)	24·00	26·00
56		3m. yellow-brown (Gold)	18·00	19·00
		a. Opt double	£500	
		b. Opt inverted	£550	
		c. Black opt	75·00	85·00
57		4m. scarlet	20·00	19·00
58		5m. yellow-orange	60·00	50·00
		a. Opt Type **1** albino	£1200	£1400
59		2p. olive (Gold)	23·00	21·00
		a. Opt Type **1a**	£1200	£1000
		b. Black opt	£250	£250
		ba. Opt Type **1a**		
60		5p. deep purple (Gold)	75·00	£100
		a. Opt inverted	£225	
		b. Opt Type **1a**	£2000	
		ba. Opt inverted	£2500	
		c. Black opt inverted	£1500	

(b) P 14

62	5	1m. sepia (Gold)	19·00	32·00
		a. Opt inverted	£750	
63		2m. blue-green (Gold)	18·00	21·00
		a. Opt inverted	£350	£350
		b. Opt double	£300	
		c. Black opt	£300	
		ca. Opt double	£1500	
64		5m. orange	14·00	14·00
65		1p. deep indigo (Gold)	14·00	18·00
		a. Opt double	£500	£550
		b. Black opt	£800	£850
66		9p. ochre	90·00	£130
		a. Gold opt	£3000	
67		10p. ultramarine (Gold)	85·00	£130
		a. Black opt		
68		20p. pale grey (Gold)	85·00	£130
		a. Opt inverted	£375	
		b. Opt double	£450	
		c. Opt double, one inverted	£450	
		e. Opt double, one gold, one black, latter inverted	£750	
		f. Opt treble, one inverted	£1100	
		g. Black opt	£850	
		ga. Opt inverted	£1100	
		gb. Opt double, one inverted	£1300	

The gold overprints were created by sprinkling gold dust on wet black ink.

There are numerous constant minor varieties in this overprint in all values.

The 9p. perforated 15×14 was also prepared with this overprint, but the entire stock was used for No. 85.

The 20p. exists with top line of overprint only or with the lines transposed, both due to misplacement.

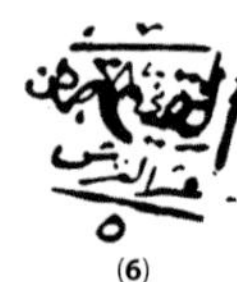

(**6**)

(7)

(8) (9)

1923 (Apr–Oct). Stamps of the preceding issues and of Palestine further surch by means of handstamps.

No.	Type	Description	Unused	Used
		(a) Issue of Nov 1920		
70	–	2½/10thsp. on 5m. (No. 13) (B.–Blk.)	£170	£170
		a. Black surch	£170	£170
		b. Violet surch	£170	£170
70*c*	6	5/10p. on 3m. (No. 3)	†	£5000
70*d*		5/10p. on 5m. (No. 13)	£2500	
70*e*	9	2p. on 20p. (No. 19)		
		(b) Stamp of Palestine		
71	6	5/10p. on 3m. (P 15×14)	£3000	
		(c) Issue of Nov 1922		
72	6	5/10p. on 3m. (No. 22)	£7000	
		a. Pair, one without surch	£7500	
73		5/10p. on 5p. (No. 26) (V.)	75·00	85·00
		a. Black surch		
		ab. Opt Type **3** omitted	£1200	
73*b*		5/10p. on 9p. (No. 27a)	£1300	
74	7	½p. on 5p. (No. 26)	75·00	85·00
		a. Pair, one without surch	£750	
75		½p. on 9p. (No. 27)	£3500	
		a. On No. 27a	£350	£400
		ab. Opt Type **1a**	£3500	
76		½p. on 9p. (No. 32)	—	£8000
77	8	1p. on 5p. (No. 26)	85·00	£110
		(d) Issue of Dec 1922		
78	6	5/10p. on 3m. (No. 39) (V.)	85·00	£100
		a. Black surch	£750	
		ab. Opt Type **1a**		
		b. On No. 39v	50·00	60·00
		ba. Pair, one without surch	£1400	
		bb. Without numeral of value		
		bc. Black surch	£750	
79		5/10p. on 5p. (No. 43b) (Blk.)	10·00	19·00
		a. Opt Type **1a**	£2000	
		b. Pair, one without surch	£500	
		c. Violet surch		
79*d*		5/10p. on 9p. (No. 44b)	—	£1200
		da. On No. 44a. Violet surch	—	£1300
80	7	½p. on 2p. (No. 42)	£100	£120
		a. Opt Type **1a**	£2000	
		b. On No. 42b	80·00	£110
		c. On No. 42c	60·00	£110
		ca. Pair, one without surch	£1000	
		w. Wmk inverted		
81		½p. on 5p. (No. 43)	£3000	
		a. On No. 43b	£1000	
82		½p. on 5p. (No. 50)	£2000	
		a. On No. 50a	£2500	
83	8	1p. on 5p. (No. 43)	£3750	
		b. On No. 43b	£2000	£2250
83*c*		1p. on 5p. (No. 50)	£2500	
		(e) Issue of 1 March 1923		
84	6	5/10p. on 3m. (No. 56)	29·00	45·00
		a. On No. 56c	£750	
85	7	½p. on 9p. (P 15×14)	95·00	£160
		a. Pair, one without surch	£5000	
86		½p. on 9p. (No. 66)	£170	
87	9	1p. on 10p. (No. 67)	£2250	£2500
		a. Violet surch	£2750	
88		2p. on 20p. (No. 68)	65·00	85·00
88*a*		2p. on 20p. (No. 68g)	£2000	

The handstamp on Nos. 70*c*, 88 and 88*a* has an Arabic '2' in place of the '1' shown in the illustration of T **9**.

Being handstamped many of the above exist inverted or double.

The Types **6/9** provisional surcharges have been extensively forged and should only be acquired from reliable sources.

TYPES OF SAUDI ARABIA. The following illustrations are repeated here for convenience from Saudi Arabia.

11 20 21 22 47 49

(**10**) ('Arab Government of the East, 9 Sha'ban 1341')

(**11**) ('Arab Government of the East. Commemoration of Independence, 25 May 1923')

It should be noted that as Arabic is read from right to left, the overprint described as reading downwards appears to the English reader as though reading upwards. Our illustration of T **11** shows the overprint reading downwards.

1923 (Apr). Stamps of Saudi Arabia. T **11**, with typographed opt, T **10**.

No.	Type	Description	Unused	Used
89	10	⅛p. chestnut	5·50	4·25
		a. Opt double	£200	
		b. Opt inverted	£110	
90		½p. scarlet	5·50	4·25
		a. Opt inverted		
91		1p. blue	4·25	1·25
		a. Opt inverted	£120	£140
92		1½p. lilac	4·50	2·50
		a. Opt double	£150	
		b. Top line omitted	—	£250
		c. Pair, one without opt	£250	
		d. Imperf between (horiz pair)	£170	
93		2p. orange	5·50	8·00
94		3p. brown	14·00	20·00
		a. Opt inverted	£225	
		b. Opt double	£225	£250
		c. Pair, one without opt	£375	
95		5p. olive	32·00	45·00
89/95 *Set of 7*			65·00	75·00
		On same stamps, surcharged with new values (Saudi Arabia, Nos. 47 and 49)		
96	10	¼p. on ⅛p. chestnut	16·00	8·00
		a. Opt and surch inverted	£150	
		b. Ditto but 2nd and 3rd lines of opt omitted	£200	
		c. Opt double	†	£200
97		10p. on 5p. olive	35·00	40·00
		a. Top line omitted	£350	

In this setting the third line of the overprint measures 19–21 mm. On 35 stamps out of the setting of 36 the Arabic '9' (right-hand character in bottom line) is widely spaced from the rest of the inscription. Minor varieties of this setting exist on all values.

For later setting, varying from the above, see Nos. 121/124.

Normal. '923'   Error. '933'

An error reading '933' instead of '923' occurs as No. 3 in the setting of 24 on all values. Only 24 stamps are believed to have been overprinted for each of Nos. 103A, 108A, 105B and 107B so that for these stamps only one example of the error can exist. No example has yet been confirmed for Nos. 103A or 105B.

1923 (25 May). T **3** of Palestine optd with T **11**, reading up or down, in black or gold by Govt Press, Amman, in a setting of 24 (12×2). P 14 (9p., 10p.) or 15×14 (other values).

A. Reading downwards

No.	Description	Unused	Used
98A	1m. (Blk)	23·00	23·00
	a. Opt double, one inverted (Blk.)	£650	£650
	b. Arabic '933'	£100	
	c. Gold opt	£150	£160
	ca. Opt double, one inverted (Gold)	£900	
	cb. Opt double (Blk.+Gold)	£900	£900
	cc. Arabic '933'	£550	
99A	2m. (Blk)	42·00	50·00
	a. Arabic '933'	£180	
100A	3m. (Blk.)	14·00	18·00
	a. Arabic '933'	80·00	
101A	4m. (Blk.)	15·00	18·00
	a. Arabic '933'	85·00	
102A	5m. (Blk.)	70·00	80·00
	a. Arabic '933'	£375	
103A	1p. (Gold)	£750	£850
	a. Opt double	£800	£900
104A	2p. (Blk.)	70·00	90·00
	a. Arabic '933'	£375	
105A	5p. (Gold)	80·00	90·00
	a. Opt double (Gold)	£650	
	b. Arabic '933'	£400	
	c. Opt double (Blk.)	£1500	
106A	9p. (Blk.)	90·00	£130
	a. Arabic '933'	£425	
107A	10p. (Blk)	80·00	£100
	a. Arabic '933'	£400	
108A	20p. (Blk.)	£800	£800
	a. Arabic '933'	£3000	

B. Reading upwards

No.	Description	Unused	Used
98B	1m. (Blk.)	95·00	£120
	b. Arabic '933'	£400	
	c. Gold opt	£150	£160
	cc. Arabic '933'	£550	
99B	2m. (Blk.)	60·00	70·00
	a. Arabic '933'	£300	
100B	3m. (Blk.)	£100	£130
	a. Arabic '933'	£400	
101B	4m. (Blk.)	32·00	45·00
	a. Arabic '933'	£150	
103B	1p. (Gold)	70·00	85·00
	a. Opt double	£600	
	b. Black opt		
	c. Arabic '933'	£375	
105B	5p. (Gold)	£800	£650
	a. Opt double		
106B	9p. (Blk.)	70·00	85·00
	a. Arabic '933'	£375	
107B	10p. (Blk.)	£700	
	a. Arabic '933'	£3000	
108B	20p. (Blk.)	85·00	£110
	a. Arabic '933'	£425	

The T **11** opt has been extensively forged on all values, but note that the 9p. and 10p. (Nos. 106A/106B and 107A/107B) will always be genuine, if correctly perf 14. The genuine T **11** opt shows numerous breaks in the Arabic lettering, which tend to be absent from the more heavily printed forged opts.

No. 107A surch with T **9**

No.	Description	Unused	Used
109	1p. on 10p. ultramarine	£6000	

نصف قرش

(12)

1923 (Sept). No. 92 surch with T **12**.

(a) Handstamped

No.	Type	Description	Unused	Used
110	**12**	½p. on 1½p. lilac	12·00	14·00
		a. Surch and opt inverted	55·00	
		b. Opt double	75·00	
		c. Opt double, one inverted	90·00	£100
		d. Pair, one without opt	£150	

This handstamp is known inverted, double and double, one inverted.

(b) Typographed

No.	Type	Description	Unused	Used
111	**12**	½p. on 1½p. lilac	55·00	55·00
		a. Surch inverted	£150	
		b. Surch double	£180	
		c. Pair, one without surch	£500	

مستحق

(D **12** 'Due')

مستحق
الشرق العربية
٩ شعبان ١٣٤١

(D **13**)

1923 (Sept). Issue of April, 1923, with opt T **10** with further typographed opt T D **12** (the 3p. with handstamped surch as T **12** at top).

No.	Description	Unused	Used
D112	½p. on 3p. brown	40·00	42·00
	a. 'Due' inverted	50·00	55·00
	b. 'Due' double	50·00	60·00
	ba. 'Due' double, one inverted	£150	
	c. Arabic 't' & 'h' transposed (R. 1/2)	£110	
	ca. As c, inverted	£350	
	d. Surch at foot of stamp	48·00	
	da. Ditto, but with var. c	£130	
	e. Surch omitted	£200	
D113	1p. blue	24·00	26·00
	a. Type **10** inverted	80·00	
	b. 'Due' inverted	48·00	42·00
	c. 'Due' double	50·00	
	d. 'Due' double, one inverted	£150	
	e. Arabic 't' & 'h' transposed (R. 1/2)	75·00	
	f. 'Due' omitted (in vertical pair with normal)	£200	
D114	1½p. lilac	35·00	38·00
	a. 'Due' inverted	48·00	48·00
	b. 'Due' double	50·00	
	ba. 'Due' double, one diagonal	75·00	
	c. Arabic 't' & 'h' transposed (R. 1/2)	75·00	
	ca. As c, inverted	£275	
	d. 'Due' omitted (in pair with normal)	£200	
D115	2p. orange	38·00	40·00
	a. 'Due' inverted	60·00	60·00
	b. 'Due' double	65·00	
	ba. 'Due' double, one diagonal	£100	
	c. 'Due' treble	£150	
	d. Arabic 't' & 'h' transposed (R. 1/2)	80·00	
	e. Arabic 'h' omitted	£100	

The variety, Arabic 't' and 'h' transposed, occurred on R. 1/2 of all values in the first batch of sheets printed. The variety, Arabic 'h' omitted, occurred on every stamp in the first three rows of at least three sheets of the 2p.

Genuine examples of Nos. D113/D115 are known with additional forged T D **12** opts, in imitation of the 'double' and 'double, one inverted' errors. Most such forged opts show the left-hand Arabic character dropped out of alignment with the other characters.

Handstamped in four lines as T D **13** *and surch as on No. D112*

No.	Description	Unused	Used
D116	½p. on 3p. brown	55·00	60·00
	a. Opt and surch inverted	£200	
	b. Opt double	£200	
	c. Surch omitted	£225	
	d. Opt inverted. Surch normal, but at foot of stamp	£150	
	e. Opt omitted and opt inverted (pair)	£300	
	f. 'Due' double, one inverted	£160	
	h. Surch double	£250	

الشرق العربية
مستحق
٩ شعبان ١٣٤١

(D **14**)

مستحق
شرق الاردن

(D **20**) ('Due. East of the Jordan')

1923 (Oct). T **11** of Saudi Arabia handstamped with T D **14**.

D117	½p. scarlet	4·25	9·00
D118	1p. blue	8·50	8·50
	a. Pair, one without handstamp		
D119	1½p. lilac	6·00	9·50
D120	2p. orange	8·50	10·00
D121	3p. brown	20·00	26·00
	a. Pair, one without handstamp	£600	
D122	5p. olive	22·00	42·00
D117/D122	*Set of 6*	60·00	95·00

There are three types of this handstamp, differing in some of the Arabic characters. They occur inverted, double etc.

(**13a**) (**13b**)

('Arab Government of the East, 9 Sha'ban, 1341')

These two types differ in the spacing of the characters and in the position of the bottom line which is to the left of the middle line in T **13a** and centrally placed in T **13b**.

1923 (Oct). T **11** of Saudi Arabia handstamped as T **13a** or **13b**.

112	**13a**	½p. scarlet	15·00	16·00
113	**13b**	½p. scarlet	15·00	16·00

No. 112 exists with handstamp inverted.

1923 (Nov). T **11** of Saudi Arabia with opt similar to T D **14** but first three lines typo and fourth handstruck.

D123	1p. blue	80·00	
D124	5p. olive	28·00	
	a. Imperf between (vert pair)	£750	

15 ('Arab Government of the East')

(**16**) ('Commemorating the coming of His Majesty the King of the Arabs' and date)

1924 (Jan). T **11** of Saudi Arabia with typographed opt T **15**.

114	**15**	½p. scarlet	22·00	16·00
		a. Opt inverted	£180	
115		1p. blue	£300	£200
116		1½p. lilac	£350	
		a. Pair, one without opt	£1500	

The ½p. exists with thick, brown gum, which tints the paper, and with white gum and paper.

The 2p. in the same design was also overprinted, but was not issued without the subsequent T **16** overprint.

(O **16**) ('Arab Government of the East, 1342' = 1924)

1924. OFFICIAL. T **11** of Saudi Arabia with typographed opt, T O **16**.

O117	½p. scarlet	32·00	£110
	a. Arabic '1242' (R. 2/2, 3/6, 4/5, 4/6)	£160	
	b. Imperf between (vert pair)		

1924 (18 Jan). Visit of King Hussein of Hejaz. Nos. 114/116 and unissued 2p. with further typographed opt T **16** in black.

117	**16**	½p. scarlet	3·25	3·25
		a. Type **15** omitted	£150	
		b. Type **16** inverted	£150	
		c. Imperf between (pair)	£110	
		d. Type **16** in gold	3·25	3·25
		dc. Imperf between (pair)	£250	
118		1p. blue	4·00	3·50
		a. Type **15** omitted	£150	
		b. Both opts inverted	£200	
		c. Imperf between (pair)		
		d. Type **16** in gold	4·00	3·50
		db. Both opts inverted	£300	
		dc. Imperf between (pair)	£225	
119		1½p. lilac	4·25	4·50
		a. Type **15** omitted		
		b. Type **15** inverted	£130	
		d. Type **16** in gold	4·25	4·50
		da. Type **15** inverted	£150	
120		2p. orange	13·00	13·00
		d. Type **16** in gold	12·00	12·00

The spacing of the lines of the overprint varies considerably, and a variety dated '432' for '342' occurs on the 12th stamp in each sheet (*Price £75 un*).

(**16a**)

'Shaban' (normal) 'Shabal' (R. 4/6) 'Shabn' (R. 5/3)

1924 (Mar–May). T **11** of Saudi Arabia optd with T **16a** (new setting of Type **10**).

121	⅛p. chestnut	45·00	22·00
	a. Opt inverted	£100	
122	½p. scarlet	14·00	4·50
	a. 'Shabal'	55·00	
	b. 'Shabn'	55·00	
	c. Opt inverted	£120	
123	1p. blue	24·00	2·25
	a. 'Shabal'	80·00	
	b. 'Shabn'	80·00	
	c. Opt double	£120	
	d. Imperf between (horiz pair) with opt double	£500	
124	1½p. lilac	28·00	28·00
	a. 'Shabal'	95·00	
	b. 'Shabn'	95·00	

This setting is from fresh type with the third line measuring 18¼ mm.

On all stamps in this setting (except Nos. 1, 9, 32 and 33) the Arabic '9' is close to the rest of the inscription.

The dots on the character 'Y' (the second character from the left in the second line) are on many stamps vertical (:) instead of horizontal (..).

On some sheets of the ⅛p. and ½p. the right-hand character, 'H', in the first line, was omitted from the second stamp in the first row of the sheet.

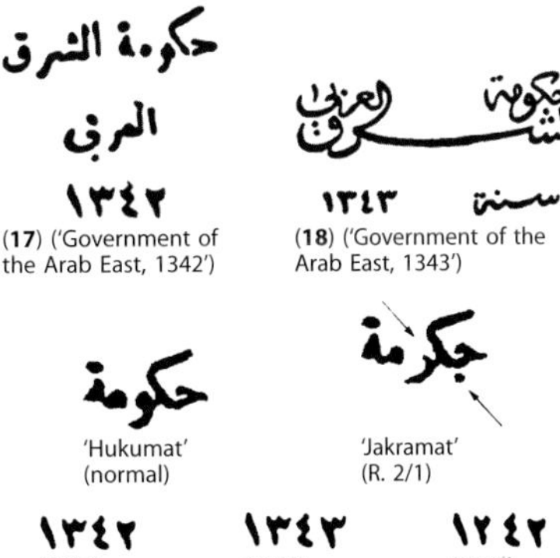

(**17**) ('Government of the Arab East, 1342') (**18**) ('Government of the Arab East, 1343')

'Hukumat' (normal) 'Jakramat' (R. 2/1)

'1342' (normal) '1343' (R. 4/2) '1242' (R. 6/1)

1924 (Sept–Nov). T **11** of Saudi Arabia with type-set opt as T **17** by Govt Press, Amman.

No.	Type	Description	Unused	Used
125	**17**	1/8p. chestnut	1·50	1·25
		a. Opt inverted	£130	
		b. 'Jakramat'	30·00	
		c. '1242'	30·00	
126		¼p. green	1·50	70
		a. *Tête-bêche* (pair, both opts normal)	9·00	12·00
		b. Opt inverted	85·00	
		c. *Tête-bêche* (pair, one with opt inverted)	£300	
		d. 'Jakramat'	30·00	
		e. '1242'	30·00	
127		½p. bright scarlet	1·50	70
		a. Deep rose-red		
		b. '1343'	30·00	
129		1p. blue	10·00	1·50
		a. Imperf between (horiz pair)	£130	
		b. Opt inverted		
		c. 'Jakramat'	50·00	
		d. '1242'	50·00	
130		1½p. lilac	6·50	6·50
		a. '1343'	55·00	
131		2p. orange	4·75	3·50
		a. Opt double		
		b. '1343'	55·00	
132		3p. brown-red	4·75	4·75
		a. Opt inverted	£100	
		b. Opt double	£100	
		c. '1343'	75·00	
133		5p. olive	6·50	6·50
		a. 'Jakramat'	60·00	
		b. '1242'	60·00	
134		10p. brown-purple and mauve (R.)	15·00	16·00
		a. Centre inverted	£2500	
		b. Black opt	£250	
		c. 'Jakramat'	£100	
		d. '1242'	£100	
125/134 *Set of 9*			45·00	38·00

T **11** of Saudi Arabia was printed in sheets of 36 (6×6). The ¼p. value had the bottom three rows inverted, giving six vertical *tête-bêche* pairs. A few sheets were overprinted with the normal setting of T **17**, with the result that the overprints on the bottom rows were inverted in relation to the stamp, including on one of the stamps in the *tête-bêche* pair (No. 126c). A corrected setting with the overprint inverted on the lower rows was used for the majority of the printing giving *tête-bêche* pairs with the overprints both normal in relation to the stamps (No. 126a).

1925 (2 Aug). Types **20/22** of Saudi Arabia with lithographed opt T **18** applied in Cairo.

No.	Type	Description	Unused	Used
135	**18**	⅛p. chocolate	1·00	1·50
		a. Imperf between (horiz pair)	£130	£150
		b. Opt inverted	70·00	
136		¼p. ultramarine	2·00	3·00
		a. Opt inverted	70·00	
137		½p. carmine	1·50	60
		a. Opt inverted	70·00	
138		1p. green	1·50	1·50
139		1½p. orange	3·50	4·00
		a. Opt inverted	70·00	
140		2p. blue	4·50	6·00
		a. Opt treble	£160	£225
141		3p. sage-green (R.)	5·00	8·00
		a. Imperf between (horiz pair)	£130	£170
		b. Opt inverted	90·00	
		c. Black opt	£130	£160
142		5p. chestnut	7·50	15·00
		a. Opt inverted	85·00	
135/142 *Set of 8*			24·00	35·00

All values exist imperforate.

No. 141 imperforate with gold overprint comes from a presentation sheet for the Emir.

(**19**) ('East of the Jordan')

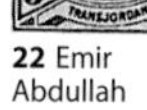
22 Emir Abdullah

23 Emir Abdullah

(Opt typo by Waterlow)

1925 (1 Nov)–**26**. Stamps of Palestine, 1922 (without the three-line Palestine opt), optd with T **19**. Wmk Mult Script CA. P 14.

No.	Type	Description	Unused	Used
143	**19**	1m. deep brown	55	3·50
144		2m. yellow	1·00	75
145		3m. greenish blue	2·75	1·75
146		4m. carmine-pink	2·75	4·00
147		5m. orange	3·25	50
		a. Yellow-orange	42·00	22·00
148		6m. blue-green	2·75	2·50
149		7m. yellow-brown	2·75	2·50
150		8m. scarlet	2·75	1·25
151		1p. grey	2·75	70
152		13m. ultramarine	3·25	3·00
153		2p. olive	4·25	4·75
		a. Olive-green	£120	35·00
154		5p. deep purple	9·50	10·00
155		9p. ochre	14·00	27·00
		a. Perf 15×14 (1926)	£900	£1400
156		10p. light blue	29·00	40·00
		a. Error. 'EFF' in bottom panel (R.10/3)	£800	£1000
		b. Perf 15×14 (1926)	80·00	£100
157		20p. light violet	48·00	85·00
		a. Perf 15×14 (1926)	£850	£1000
143/157 *Set of 15*			£110	£160
143s/157s Optd 'SPECIMEN' *Set of 15*			£350	

(Opt typo by Waterlow)

1925 (Nov). Stamps of Palestine 1922 (without the three-line Palestine opt), optd with T D **20**. P 14.

No.	Description	Unused	Used
D159	1m. deep brown	2·50	15·00
D160	2m. yellow	4·75	9·50
D161	4m. carmine-pink	4·75	22·00
D162	8m. scarlet	7·00	23·00
D163	13m. ultramarine	11·00	24·00
D164	5p. deep purple	13·00	40·00
	a. Perf 15×14	65·00	£100
D159/D164 *Set of 6*		38·00	£120
D159s/D164s Optd 'SPECIMEN' *Set of 6*		£140	

Stamps as No. D164, but with a different top line to overprint T D **20**, were for revenue purposes.

مستحق

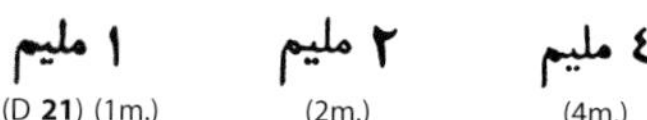
(D **21**) (1m.) (2m.) (4m.)

٨ مليم (8m.) ١٣ مليم (13m.) ٥ قروش (5p.)

(Surch typo at Jerusalem)

1926 (Feb–May). Postage stamps of 1 November 1925, surch 'Due' and new value as T D **21** by Greek Orthodox Printing Press, Jerusalem. Bottom line of surcharge differs for each value as illustrated.

No.	Description	Unused	Used
D165	1m. on 1m. deep brown	14·00	38·00
	a. Red opt	£160	
D166	2m. on 1m. deep brown	13·00	38·00
D167	4m. on 3m. greenish blue	14·00	40·00
D168	8m. on 3m. greenish blue	14·00	40·00
D169	13m. on 13m. ultramarine	19·00	45·00
D170	5p. on 13m. ultramarine	23·00	65·00
D165/D170 *Set of 6*		85·00	£225

(New Currency. 1000 milliemes = £1 Palestinian)

(Recess Perkins Bacon & Co)

1927 (1 Nov)–**29**. New Currency. Wmk Mult Script CA. P 14.

No.	Type	Description	Unused	Used
159	**22**	2m. greenish blue	3·50	1·75
160		3m. carmine-pink	4·75	4·00
161		4m. green	6·50	8·00
162		5m. orange	3·25	30
163		10m. scarlet	5·50	8·00
164		15m. ultramarine	4·50	65
165		20m. olive-green	4·50	4·75
166	**23**	50m. purple	4·50	14·00
167		90m. bistre	7·50	35·00
168		100m. blue	8·50	25·00
169		200m. violet	17·00	50·00
170		500m. brown (5.29)	60·00	85·00
171		1000m. slate-grey (5.29)	£100	£150
159/171 *Set of 13*			£200	£350
159s/171s Optd or Perf (500, 1000m.) 'SPECIMEN' *Set of 13*			£375	

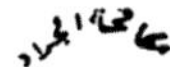

(24) ('Constitution') (27)

1928 (1 Sept). New Constitution of 20 February 1928. Optd with T **24** by Atwood, Morris & Co, Cairo.

No.	Type	Description	Unused	Used
172	**22**	2m. greenish blue	7·00	7·00
173		3m. carmine-pink	8·00	12·00
174		4m. green	8·00	15·00
175		5m. orange	8·00	4·25
176		10m. scarlet	8·00	16·00
177		15m. ultramarine	8·00	4·75
178		20m. olive-green	16·00	26·00
179	**23**	50m. purple	21·00	29·00
180		90m. bistre	25·00	£100
181		100m. blue	25·00	£100
182		200m. violet	90·00	£180
172/182 *Set of* 11			£200	£450

(D **25** 'Due') Extra Arabic character in opt (R. 4/10)

1929 (1 Jan). Nos. 159 etc. optd only or surch in addition as T D **25** by Whitehead, Morris & Co, Alexandria.

No.	Type	Description	Unused	Used
D183	**22**	1m. on 3m. carmine-pink	1·75	8·00
		a. Extra Arabic character	40·00	
D184		2m. greenish blue	4·00	7·50
		a. Pair, one without opt	£475	
D185		4m. on 15m. ultramarine	4·75	18·00
		a. Surch inverted	£190	£325
D186		10m. scarlet	9·00	9·50
D187	**23**	20m. on 100m. blue	7·50	29·00
		a. Horiz pair, one without surch	£800	
D188		50m. purple	6·00	27·00
		a. Horiz pair, one without opt	£800	
D183/D188 *Set of* 6			30·00	90·00

D **26**

28

29

(Recess Perkins, Bacon)

1929 (1 Apr)–**39**. Wmk Mult Script CA. P 14.

No.	Type	Description	Unused	Used
D189	D **26**	1m. red-brown	2·50	15·00
		a. Perf 13½×13 (1939)	£160	£130
D190		2m. orange-yellow	5·00	8·00
D191		4m. green	6·50	18·00
D192		10m. scarlet	12·00	14·00
D193		20m. olive-green	16·00	27·00
D194		50m. blue	20·00	35·00
D189/D194 *Set of* 6			55·00	£100
D189s/D194s Perf 'SPECIMEN' *Set of* 6			£150	

1930 (1 Apr). Locust Campaign. Optd as T **27** by Whitehead, Morris & Co, Alexandria.

No.	Type	Description	Unused	Used
183	**22**	2m. greenish blue	3·25	7·50
		a. Opt inverted	£300	£600
184		3m. carmine-pink	2·50	6·50
185		4m. green	3·75	19·00
186		5m. orange	23·00	14·00
		a. Opt double	£425	£700
		b. Vert pair, top stamp opt double. Lower stamp without bottom line of opt	£1800	
187		10m. scarlet	2·25	4·25
188		15m. ultramarine	2·25	4·00
		a. Opt inverted	£225	£450
189		20m. olive-green	4·00	4·00
190	**23**	50m. purple	5·00	11·00
191		90m. bistre	10·00	48·00
192		100m. blue	12·00	50·00
193		200m. violet	32·00	85·00
194		500m. brown	75·00	£200
		a. 'C' of 'LOCUST' omitted (R. 5/3)	£800	£1200
183/194 *Set of* 12			£500	£400

No. 186a was sold at Kerak.

(Re-engraved with figures of value at left only. Recess Perkins Bacon)

1930 (1 June)–**39**. Wmk Mult Script CA. P 14.

No.	Type	Description	Unused	Used
194*b*	**28**	1m. red-brown (6.2.34)	9·00	1·00
		c. Perf 13½×13 (1939)	18·00	7·00
195		2m. greenish blue	2·00	50
		a. Perf 13½×13. *Bluish green* (1939)	24·00	4·50
196		3m. carmine-pink	5·50	70
196*a*		3m. green (6.2.34)	10·00	85
		b. Perf 13½×13 (1939)	35·00	8·00
197		4m. green	5·50	8·00
197*a*		4m. carmine-pink (6.2.34)	10·00	1·00
		b. Perf 13½×13 (1939)	£140	45·00
198		5m. orange	3·50	40
		a. Coil stamp. Perf 13½×14 (29.2.36)	32·00	23·00
		b. Perf 13½×13 (1939)	70·00	3·00
199		10m. scarlet	4·50	15
		a. Perf 13½×13 (1939)	£190	4·25
200		15m. ultramarine	4·50	20
		a. Coil stamp. Perf 13½×14 (29.2.36)	29·00	22·00
		b. Perf 13½×13 (1939)	42·00	5·50
201		20m. olive-green	4·75	35
		a. Perf 13½×13 (1939)	65·00	12·00
202	**29**	50m. purple	6·00	1·25
203		90m. bistre	3·50	4·25
204		100m. blue	4·50	4·25
205		200m. violet	22·00	14·00
206		500m. brown	32·00	55·00
207		£P1 slate-grey	70·00	£110
194*b*/207 *Set of* 16			£170	£180
194*b*s/207s Perf 'SPECIMEN' *Set of* 16			£375	

For stamps perf 12 see Nos. 230/243, and for T **28** lithographed, perf 13½, see Nos. 222/229.

30 Mushetta

30a Nymphaeum, Jerash

30b Kasr Kharana

30c Kerak Castles

30d Temple of Artemis, Jerash

31 Ajlun Castle

31a The Khazneh at Petra

31b Allenby Bridge over the Jordan

31c Threshing scene

31d Kasr Kharana

32 Temple of Artemis, Jerash

32a Ajlun Castle

32b The Khazneh at Petra

33 Emir Abdullah

(Vignettes from photographs; frames des Yacoub Sukker. Recess Bradbury Wilkinson)

1933 (1 Feb). As Types **31/33**. Wmk Mult Script CA. P 12.

208	**30**	1m. black and maroon	1·75	1·60
209	**30a**	2m. black and claret	6·00	1·40
210	**30b**	3m. blue-green	6·00	1·75
211	**30c**	4m. black and brown	12·00	7·00
212	**30d**	5m. black and orange	7·00	1·40
213	**31**	10m. carmine	15·00	4·75
214	**31a**	15m. blue	8·50	1·40
215	**31b**	20m. black and sage-green	8·50	5·50
216	**31c**	50m. black and purple	35·00	21·00
217	**31d**	90m. black and yellow	35·00	60·00
218	**32**	100m. black and blue	35·00	60·00
219	**32a**	200m. black and violet	65·00	£150
220	**32b**	500m. scarlet and red-brown	£250	£500
221	**33**	£P1 black and yellow-green	£550	£1300
208/221 *Set of* 14			£900	£1900
208s/221s Perf 'SPECIMEN' *Set of* 14			£900	

34

D 35

(Litho Survey Dept, Cairo)

1942 (18 May). T **28**, but with Arabic characters above portrait and in top left circle modified as in T **34**. No wmk. P 13½.

222	**34**	1m. red-brown	1·25	8·50
223		2m. green	3·50	3·25
224		3m. yellow-green	4·00	7·50
225		4m. carmine-pink	4·00	7·50
226		5m. yellow-orange	7·50	1·75
227		10m. scarlet	14·00	3·75
228		15m. blue	27·00	8·50
229		20m. olive-green	48·00	50·00
222/229 *Set of* 8			95·00	80·00

Forgeries of the above exist on whiter paper with rough perforations.

(Litho Survey Dept, Cairo)

1942 (22 Dec). Redrawn. Top line of Arabic in taller lettering. No wmk. P 13½.

D230	D **35**	1m. red-brown	4·50	25·00
D231		2m. orange-yellow	12·00	13·00
D232		10m. scarlet	19·00	7·00
D230/D232 *Set of* 3			32·00	40·00

Forgeries of the above exist on whiter paper with rough perforations.

(Recess Bradbury Wilkinson)

1943 (1 Jan)–**46**. Wmk Mult Script CA. P 12.

230	**28**	1m. red-brown	30	75
231		2m. bluish green	4·25	2·75
232		3m. green	2·00	3·50
233		4m. carmine-pink	1·75	3·50
234		5m. orange	1·75	20
235		10m. red	3·00	1·25
236		15m. blue	3·00	2·75
237		20m. olive-green (26.8.46)	3·00	1·00
238	**29**	50m. purple (26.8.46)	3·00	1·00
239		90m. bistre (26.8.46)	5·50	9·00
240		100m. blue (26.8.46)	5·50	1·75
241		200m. violet (26.8.46)	12·00	16·00
242		500m. brown (26.8.46)	14·00	12·00
243		£P1 slate-grey (26.8.46)	26·00	22·00
230/243 *Set of* 14			75·00	70·00

Nos. 237/243 were released in London by the Crown Agents in May 1944, but were not put on sale in Transjordan until 26 August 1946.

Printings of the 3, 4, 10, 15 and 20m. in changed colours, together with a new 12m. value, were released on 12 May 1947.

(Recess Bradbury Wilkinson)

1944–49. Wmk Mult Script CA. P 12.

D244	D **26**	1m. red-brown	1·50	8·50
D245		2m. orange-yellow	2·50	8·50
D246		4m. green	2·50	13·00
D247		10m. carmine	7·50	16·00
D248		20m. olive-green (1949)	80·00	£100
D244/D248 *Set of* 5			85·00	£130

KINGDOM OF TRANSJORDAN

By treaty of 22 March 1946 with the United Kingdom, Transjordan was proclaimed an independent kingdom on 25 May 1946.

King Abdullah

25 May 1946–20 July 1951

35 Map of Jordan

(Litho Catholic Press, Beirut)

1946 (25 May). Installation of King Abdullah and National Independence. P 11½.

249	**35**	1m. brown-purple	30	30
250		2m. orange	30	30
251		3m. grey-green	30	30
252		4m. violet	30	30
253		10m. chestnut	30	30
254		12m. carmine	30	30
255		20m. deep blue	45	40
256		50m. ultramarine	1·10	1·00
257		200m. bright green	4·50	4·25
249/257 *Set of* 9			7·00	6·75

Imperforate sets were distributed as souvenirs.

1947 (12 May). As 1943–1944. Colours changed and new value.

258	**28**	3m. carmine-pink	45	40
259		4m. green	45	40
260		10m. bright violet	45	40
261		12m. scarlet	1·10	1·00
262		15m. olive-green	1·40	1·30
263		20m. blue	1·50	1·40
258/263 Set of 6			4·75	4·50
258s/263s Perf 'SPECIMEN' *Set of* 6			£250	

OBLIGATORY TAX STAMPS. In 1946 a law was passed decreeing that special stamps should be issued for compulsory use on all letters and parcels to half the amount of the postage, the proceeds to be transferred by the Post Office to a special fund to aid Arabs suffering hardship in Palestine.

After the Arab-Jewish war of 1948 when the Jordanian forces had occupied parts of Palestine adjoining their border, these stamps were overprinted 'PALESTINE' for use there (see under Occupation of Palestine). Later, due to a general shortage of ordinary stamps they were overprinted 'POSTAGE' for use throughout Jordan and from time to time they did duty without overprint as ordinary stamps in local areas where stamps were lacking.

T **36** Mosque in Hebron

T **37** Dome of the Rock

T **38** Acre

(Des Es Sayed Yacoub Sukker. Recess De La Rue)

1947 (31 May). OBLIGATORY TAX. Values in MILS. No wmk. P 11½×12½.

T264	T **36**	1m. ultramarine	90	50
T265		2m. carmine	1·10	65
T266		3m. emerald	1·20	85
T267		5m. claret	1·50	1·00
T268	T **37**	10m. carmine	1·70	1·40
T269		15m. grey-black	2·40	1·50
T270		20m. purple-brown	3·50	2·00
T271		50m. reddish violet	6·00	4·00
T272	T **38**	100m. orange-red	18·00	12·00
T273		200m. blue	55·00	28·00
T274		500m. green	£110	85·00
T275		£P1 brown	£225	£180
T264/T275 *Set of 12*			£375	£275

39 Parliament Building

(Recess De La Rue)

1947 (1 Nov). Inauguration of First National Parliament. P 12.

276	**39**	1m. violet	30	30
277		3m. orange-red	30	30
278		4m. yellow-green	30	30
279		10m. brown-purple	30	30
280		12m. carmine	30	30
281		20m. blue	30	30
282		50m. claret	45	40
283		100m. pink	90	85
284		200m. blue-green	2·00	1·80
276/284 *Set of 9*			4·75	4·25

Imperforate sets were distributed as souvenirs.

HASHEMITE KINGDOM OF THE JORDAN

The kingdom was renamed on 2 June 1949, after the acquisition of territory to the west of Jordan.

40 Globe and Forms of Transport

41 King Abdullah

(Recess De La Rue)

1949 (1 Aug). 75th Anniversary of Universal Postal Union. Wmk Mult Script CA. P 13×12½.

285	**40**	1m. brown	60	55
286		4m. green	1·10	1·00
287		10m. carmine	1·40	1·30
288		20m. blue	2·30	2·10
289	**41**	50m. dull green	3·75	3·50
285/289 *Set of 5*			8·25	7·50

اعانة
Aid
(T **42**) (Small 'Aid')

اعانة
Aid
(T **42a**) (Large 'Aid' with broad 'd')

1950. OBLIGATORY TAX.

(a) Optd with Type T **42**

T290	**28**	5m. orange (No. 234)	29·00	27·00
		a. Opt double		
T291		10m. bright violet (No. 260)	38·00	35·00
		a. Opt double	90·00	
		b. Opt double (Bk.+R.)	90·00	
T292		15m. olive-green (No. 262)	45·00	42·00
		a. Opt double	£110	

*(b) Optd with Type T***42a**

T293	**28**	5m. orange (No. 234)	19·00	
T294		10m. bright violet (No. 260)	30·00	
T295		15m. olive-green (No. 262)	1·50	1·10
		a. Opt double	£110	

T **43** Ruins at Palmyra, Syria

اعانة
Aid
(T **43a**)

اعانة
Aid
(T **43b**)

اعانة
Aid
(T **43c**)

اعانة
Aid
(T **43d**)

44 Lockheed Constellation Airliner and Globe

Type T **43a**. Top line 5 mm wide; lines 7½ mm apart; 'A' normally with serifs.
Type T **43b**. Top line 5 mm wide; lines 6 mm apart; 'Aid' with serifs.
Type T **43c**. Top line 5 mm wide; lines 9 mm apart; 'Aid' with serifs.
Type T **43d**. Top line 8 mm wide; lines 9 mm apart; 'Aid' without serifs.

1950–51. OBLIGATORY TAX. Revenue stamps optd. Wmk Mult Script CA. Recess. P 13½×13.

(a) Optd with Type T **43a**

T296	T **43**	5m. orange	33·00	24·00
		a. Dot below top of Arabic letter	24·00	15·00
		b. 'A' without serifs	60·00	49·00
		c. Vars. a and b together	£200	£200
T297		10m. violet (C.)	33·00	28·00
		a. Dot below top of Arabic letter	26·00	15·00
		b. 'A' without serifs	55·00	38·00
		c. Vars. a and b together	£200	£200
		d. Opt double		
		e. Opt double (Blk.+R.)		

In a setting of 50 (5×10), repeated on each vertical half of the sheet, there are 35 normals, 11 of variety a (positions 2, 4, 8, 9, 13, 18, 33, 34, 43, 48, 50), three with variety b (positions 5, 10, 20) and one with variety c (position 15).

(b) Optd with T **43b**

T298	T **43**	5m. orange	1·50	1·30
		a. 'A' omitted	£200	
		b. 'd' inverted	£200	
		c. Two dots in place of single dot on Arabic letter	£200	
		d. Opt double	£200	

(c) Optd with Type T **43c**

T299	T **43**	5m. orange	2·50	1·30

(d) Optd with Type T **43d** *(1951)*

T300	T **43**	5m. orange	4·25	2·75
		a. Lines of opt 7 mm apart	18·00	14·00

After the area of Palestine occupied by Jordanian forces was united with Jordan on 24 April 1950, the objects of the Palestine Aid Fund became redundant. In May 1951 an ordinance was issued earmarking the money raised by the tax for reconstruction and development.

New Currency

(Recess De La Rue)

1950 (16 Sept). AIR. Wmk Mult Script CA. P 13½×13.

295	**44**	5f. reddish purple and orange-yellow	1·50	1·00
296		10f. chocolate and violet	1·50	1·00
297		15f. carmine and sage-green	1·50	1·00
298		20f. black and deep blue	2·10	1·70
299		50f. green and magenta	3·50	1·70
300		100f. sepia and light blue	6·00	4·00
301		150f. red-orange and black	9·00	5·50
295/301 *Set of 7*			23·00	14·50

1951. OBLIGATORY TAX. Values in FILS. Wmk Mult Script CA. P 11½×12½.

T302	T **36**	5f. claret	1·10	1·00
T303	T **37**	10f. carmine-red	1·10	1·00
T304		15f. black	1·20	1·10
T305		20f. chocolate	1·50	1·40
T306	T **38**	100f. orange	7·50	7·00
T302/T306 *Set of 5*			11·00	10·50

King Talal

20 July 1951–11 August 1952

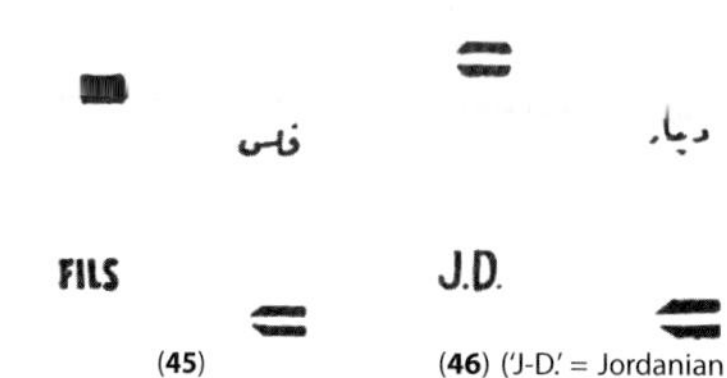

(**45**) (**46**) ('J-D.' = Jordanian Dinar)

(Optd by Catholic Press, St Joseph's University, Beirut)

1952 (26 Feb). Optd with T **45** (1f. to 20f.) or larger (50f. to 500f.) or with T **46** (1d.).

(a) On 1942 issue. No wmk. P 13½

307	**34**	1f. on 1m. red-brown	13·50	5·50
308		2f. on 2m. green (R.)	13·50	5·50
		a. Black opt	70·00	
309		3f. on 3m. yellow-green (R.)	13·50	5·50
310		4f. on 4m. carmine-pink (R.)	11·00	5·25
311		5f. on 5m. yellow-orange (G.)	13·50	5·50
		a. Opt inverted	65·00	
312		15f. on 15m. blue (R.)	48·00	24·00

(b) On 1943–1947 issues. Wmk Mult Script CA. P 12

313	**28**	1f. on 1m. red-brown	75	70
		a. Opt inverted	23·00	21·00
314		2f. on 2m. bluish green (R.)	75	70
		a. Opt double	30·00	
		b. Opt inverted	30·00	
		c. Black opt	65·00	
		d. On Palestine P2, P 12 (R.)	£150	£140
		e. On Palestine P2c, P 13½×13 (R.)	£150	£140
		f. On Palestine P2d, P 13½ (R.)	£150	£140
315		3f. on 3m. green (R.)	45·00	
		a. Opt double	85·00	
		b. On Palestine P3 (R.)	£150	£140
316		3f. on 3m. carmine-pink	75	70
		a. Opt double	48·00	
317		4f. on 4m. carmine-pink	48·00	
318		4f. on 4m. green (R.)	75	70
		a. Opt inverted	30·00	
		b. Opt double	48·00	
		c. Black opt	48·00	
319		5f. on 5m. orange (G.)	1·10	1·00
		a. Black opt	60·00	
320		10f. on 10m. red	45·00	
321		10f. on 10m. bright violet (R.)	1·40	1·30
		a. Black opt	60·00	
322		12f. on 12m. scarlet	1·40	1·30
323		15f. on 15m. ultramarine. P 13½×13 (No. 200b) (R.)	70·00	
324		15f. on 15m. blue (R.)	44·00	
325		15f. on 15m. olive-green (R.)	1·80	1·00
		a. Opt double	70·00	
		b. Black opt	75·00	
326		20f. on 20m. olive-green (R.)	47·00	
327		20f. on 20m. blue (R.)	3·25	1·40
		a. Opt inverted	70·00	
		b. Black opt	85·00	
328	**29**	50f. on 50m. purple (G.)	3·25	2·20
		a. Black opt	£110	
329		90f. on 90m. bistre (G.)	24·00	15·00
330		100f. on 100m. blue (R.)	15·00	5·00
331		200f. on 200m. violet (R.)	21·00	6·25
332		500f. on 500m. brown (R.)	48·00	20·00
333		1d. on £P1 slate-grey (R.)	£110	25·00

The first printings of Nos. 319, 321 and 325/329 were in dark colours and are worth considerably more.

1952. OBLIGATORY TAX. Nos. T264/T275 optd as T **45** or T **46** (1d.).

T334	T **36**	1f. on 1m. ultramarine (R.)	60	55
		a. Black opt	60·00	
T335		2f. on 2m. carmine	£140	
T336		3f. on 3m. emerald (R.)	90	55
		a. Opt double, one inverted	£110	
T337	T **37**	10f. on 10m. carmine	1·10	55
T338		15f. on 15m. grey-black (R.)	2·10	1·40
T339		20f. on 20m. purple-brown (R.)	2·40	2·20
T340		50f. on 50m. reddish violet (R.)	4·50	4·25
T341	T **38**	100f. on 100m. orange-red (R.)	26·00	13·50
T342		200f. on 200m. blue (R.)	65·00	36·00
T343		500f. on 500m. green (R.)	£140	£100
T344		1d. on £P1 brown (R.)	£250	£200

FILS FILS

(D **47**)

48 Dome of the Rock and Khazneh at Petra

49 King Abdullah

1952 (31 Mar). POSTAGE DUE. Optd with T D **47**.

(a) Wmk Mult Script CA. P 14

D345	D **26**	20f. on 20m. olive-green (R.)	10·50	11·00
D346		50f. on 50m. blue (R.)	13·00	12·00
		a. Opt inverted	45·00	
		b. Black opt	60·00	

(b) Redrawn. No wmk. P 13½

D347	D **35**	1f. on 1m. red-brown	55·00	
D348		2f. on 2m. orange-yellow (G.)	55·00	
		a. Black opt	70·00	
D349		10f. on 10m. scarlet	75·00	

(c) Wmk Mult Script CA. P 12

D350	D **26**	1f. on 1m. red-brown	1·50	1·80
		a. Opt double	60·00	
		b. Optd with T **45**	£375	
D351		2f. on 2m. orange-yellow (G.)	1·50	1·80
		a. Black opt	55·00	
D352		4f. on 4m. green (R.)	2·30	2·75
		a. Black opt	70·00	
D353		10f. on 10m. carmine	6·00	6·75
D354		20f. on 20m. olive-green (R.)	12·50	11·50
		a. Black opt	70·00	

(Recess De La Rue)

1952 (1 Apr). Unification of Jordan and Arab Palestine. Wmk Mult Script CA. P 13.

355	**48**	1f. yellow-green and red-brown	60	55
356		2f. scarlet and deep blue-green	60	55
357		3f. black and carmine	60	55
358		4f. orange and green	60	55
359		5f. purple and chocolate	75	70
360		10f. brown and violet	75	70
361		20f. black and deep blue	1·80	1·00
362		100f. sepia and blue	6·50	4·50
363		200f. orange and deep violet	17·00	8·50
355/363 *Set of 9*			26·00	16·00

1952 (14 June). Recess. Wmk Mult Script CA.

(a) Size 18×21½ mm. P 11½

364	**49**	5f. yellow-orange	60	55
365		10f. lilac	60	55
366		12f. carmine	2·40	1·70
367		15f. olive	1·50	55
368		20f. deep blue	1·50	70

(b) Size 20×24½ mm. P 12×13

369	**49**	50f. plum	3·75	1·40
370		90f. brown-orange	10·50	5·00
371		100f. deep blue	11·50	3·25
364/371 *Set of 8*			29·00	12·50

King Hussein

11 August 1952–7 February 1999

D **50**

(**51**)

(Recess Bradbury Wilkinson)

1952 (13 Aug). POSTAGE DUE. Wmk Mult Script CA. P 11½.

D372	D **50**	1f. red-brown	90	1·10
D373		2f. orange-yellow	90	1·10
D374		4f. green	90	1·10
D375		10f. carmine-red	1·80	2·00
D376		20f. bistre-brown	1·80	2·20
D377		50f. blue	5·00	5·25
D372/D377 *Set of 6*			10·00	11·50

See also Nos. D465/D469.

PAID HANDSTAMPS. Between May and July 1953, during a shortage of stamps, a double-circle handstamp inscribed with the date, name of town and 'PAID' was applied directly to covers at Amman and Jerusalem. *Price on cover from*: £120.

1953 (18 May). Nos. 355/363 with two horiz bars across central commemorative inscription.

A. Bars 1¼ mm apart

No.	Type	Description	Unused	Used
378A	**48**	1f. yellow-green and red-brown	60	55
		c. Traces of third bar	12·00	11·00
		d. Bars 2 mm apart	12·00	11·00
		e. Pair, one without bars	£425	—
379A		2f. scarlet and deep blue-green	60	55
		c. Traces of third bar	12·00	11·00
		d. Bars 2 mm apart	12·00	11·00
380A		3f. black and carmine	60	55
		c. Traces of third bar	12·00	11·00
		d. Bars 2 mm apart	12·00	11·00
381A		4f. orange and green	60	55
		c. Traces of third bar	12·00	11·00
		d. Bars 2 mm apart	12·00	11·00
382A		5f. purple and chocolate	60	55
		c. Traces of third bar	12·00	11·00
		d. Bars 2 mm apart	12·00	11·00
383A		10f. brown and violet	1·80	1·00
		c. Traces of third bar	18·00	17·00
		d. Bars 2 mm apart	18·00	17·00
384A		20f. black and deep blue	1·80	1·30
		c. Traces of third bar	18·00	17·00
		d. Bars 2 mm apart	18·00	17·00
385A		100f. sepia and blue	10·50	2·75
		c. Traces of third bar	23·00	21·00
		d. Bars 2 mm apart	23·00	21·00
386A		200f. orange and deep violet	14·50	8·50
		c. Traces of third bar	23·00	21·00
		d. Bars 2 mm apart	23·00	21·00
378A/386A *Set of 9*			28·00	14·50

B. Bars ½ mm apart

No.	Type	Description	Unused	Used
378B	**48**	1f. yellow-green and red-brown	3·50	3·25
379B		2f. scarlet and deep blue-green	3·50	3·25
380B		3f. black and carmine	3·50	3·25
381B		4f. orange and green	3·50	3·25
382B		5f. purple and chocolate	85·00	75·00
383B		10f. brown and violet	85·00	70·00
384B		20f. black and deep blue	65·00	55·00
385B		100f. sepia and blue	29·00	21·00
386B		200f. orange and deep violet	36·00	27·00
378B/386B *Set of 9*			£275	£225

On the 'Traces of third bar' variety the upper and lower bars are 1½ mm apart and there are traces at left and right of a third bar between them; this variety occurs on R. 3/9 of the 1¼ mm setting. The same setting contains the 'Bars 2 mm apart' on R 4/5: on R. 4/7 there is a further variety with the bars 1½ mm apart which is difficult to distinguish as a single but is noticeable in pair with a normal. The bars ½ mm apart are a separate setting.

Varieties of bars inverted or double occur in this issue.

1953 (June)–**56**. Obligatory Tax stamps optd as T **51** for ordinary postal use. P 11½×12½.

No.	Type	Description	Unused	Used
		(a) Inscr 'MILS'. No wmk (Nos. T264/T272)		
387	T **36**	1m. ultramarine (R.) (5.1.56)	60	55
		a. Opt inverted	24·00	22·00
		b. Opt double	24·00	22·00
		c. Black opt	90·00	65·00
388		3m. emerald (R.) (5.1.56)	60	55
		a. Opt inverted	24·00	22·00
		b. Opt double	24·00	22·00
		c. Black opt	£100	65·00
389		5m. claret	£200	£200
390	T **37**	10m. carmine	85·00	65·00
		a. Opt double	90·00	85·00
391		15m. grey-black (R.)	5·25	2·75
		a. Opt double		
392		20m. purple-brown (R.)	£180	£130
		a. Opt inverted		
		b. Opt double		
393		50m. reddish violet (R.) (5.1.56)	1·50	1·30
		a. Opt inverted	75·00	55·00
		b. Opt double		
394	T **38**	100m. orange-red (5.1.56)	17·00	12·50
		a. Opt inverted		
		b. Opt double		
		*(b) Inscr 'MILS', with Palestine opt Type P T **4** (Nos. PT35 etc)*		
395	T **36**	1m. ultramarine (R.)	£110	65·00
		a. Type **51** in black		
396		3m. emerald (R.)	£110	65·00
		a. Type **51** inverted		
		b. Type **51** double		
397		5m. claret	£110	65·00
398	T **37**	10m. carmine	£110	65·00
		a. Opt Type P T **4** double	£170	
399		15m. grey-black (R.)	£110	65·00
400		20m. purple-brown (R.)	£110	65·00
400*a*		50m. reddish violet (R.)		
401	T **38**	100m. orange-red	£110	65·00
		(c) Inscr 'MILS', optd 'FILS' (Nos. T334, etc) (1955)		
402	T **36**	1f. on 1m. ultramarine (R.)	£100	75·00
403		3f. on 3m. emerald (R.)	£100	75·00
		a. Type **51** inverted	£130	
404	T **37**	10f. on 10m. carmine	£100	75·00
405		15f. on 15m. grey-black (R.)	£100	75·00
406		20f. on 20m. purple-brown (R.)	£100	75·00
		a. 'FILS' opt in black	£225	£200
407	T **38**	100f. on 100m. orange-red	£110	£100
		(d) Inscr 'FILS'. Wmk Mult Script CA (Nos. T302/T306).		
408	T **36**	5f. claret	60	30
		a. Optd both sides	£150	
		b. Opt inverted	23·00	21·00
		c. Opt double	£130	
409	T **37**	10f. carmine-red (9.6.53)	75	30
		a. Optd both sides	£150	
		b. Opt inverted	23·00	21·00
		c. Opt double	£130	
410		15f. black (R.) (9.6.53)	1·80	1·40
		a. Opt inverted	23·00	21·00
		b. Opt double	75·00	
411		20f. chocolate (R.)	3·50	2·20
		a. Opt inverted	26·00	24·00
		b. Opt double	75·00	
		c. Opt double, one inverted	£130	
412	T **38**	100f. orange (5.1.56)	9·00	4·50

51a King Hussein

(Recess De La Rue)

1953 (1 Oct). Enthronement of King Hussein. P 12.

No.	Type	Description	Unused	Used
413	**51a**	1f. black and green	30	30
414		4f. black and deep claret	45	40
415		15f. black and deep bright blue	2·75	55
416		20f. black and deep slate-lilac	4·75	55
417		50f. black and bluish green	10·50	4·50
418		100f. black and deep blue	21·00	13·50
413/418 *Set of 6*			36·00	18·00

52 El-Deir Temple, Petra

53 King Hussein

54 El Aqsa Mosque

54a Temple of Artemis, Jerash

55

(Recess Bradbury Wilkinson)

1954 (9 Feb–19 Oct). No wmk.

No.	Type	Description	Unused	Used
		*(a) POSTAGE. Types **52/54** and similar designs. P 13*		
419	**52**	1f. red-brown and deep blue-green	75	70
420	**53**	2f. black and scarlet	75	70
421	**52**	3f. bluish violet and reddish purple	75	70
422	**53**	4f. myrtle-green and orange-brown	75	70
423	**52**	5f. deep blue-green and deep violet	75	70
424	–	10f. bluish green and deep purple (10.5)	1·10	70
425	**54**	12f. sepia and carmine (10.5)	2·40	1·40

426	–	20f. deep grey-green and blue (2.54)	2·40	70
427	**54**	50f. scarlet and deep blue (19.10)	7·50	7·00
428		100f. greenish blue and myrtle-green (19.10)	5·50	1·70
429		200f. deep turquoise-blue and brown-lake (19.10)	23·00	2·75
430	–	500f. purple and red-brown (19.10)	55·00	17·00
431	–	1d. brown-lake and deep olive (19.10)	85·00	35·00
419/431 *Set of* 13			£170	65·00

Designs: Vert—500f., 1d. As T **53** but arched frame, tablet below portrait. Horiz—10f., 20f. Dome of the Rock, Jerusalem.

(b) AIR. P 12

432	**54a**	5f. orange and indigo	1·10	1·00
433		10f. vermilion and chocolate	1·10	1·00
434		25f. pale blue and emerald (19.10)	1·50	1·00
435		35f. turquoise-blue and deep mauve (19.10)	1·80	1·00
436		40f. slate and carmine (19.10)	2·30	1·00
437		50f. brown-orange and deep bright blue (19.10)	3·00	1·40
438		100f. chocolate and deep blue (19.10)	3·50	2·50
439		150f. brown-lake and deep turquoise-green (19.10)	6·00	3·25
432/439 *Set of* 8			18·00	11·00

See also Nos. 445/458 and 470/475.

(Photo Survey Dept, Cairo)

1955 (1 Jan). Arab Postal Union. W **48** of Egypt. P 13½×13.

440	**55**	15f. green	1·10	55
441		20f. violet	1·10	55
442		25f. yellow-brown	1·40	1·00
440/442 *Set of* 3			3·25	1·90

56 King Hussein and Queen Dina

(Photo Survey Dept, Cairo)

1955 (19 Apr). Royal Wedding. W **48** of Egypt. P 11×11½.

443	**56**	15f. blue	3·25	1·30
		a. Imperf (pair)	£3000	
444		100f. brown-lake	12·00	5·00
		a. Imperf (pair)	£3000	

57

1955 (July)–**65**. As Nos. 419/431 and new value (15f.), but W **57**. P 13.

445	**52**	1f. red-brown and deep blue-green (18.7.57)	30	20
446	**53**	2f. black and scarlet (18.7.57)	30	20
447	**52**	3f. bluish violet and reddish purple (1956)	30	20
448	**53**	4f. myrtle-green and orange-brown (1956)	30	20
449	**52**	5f. deep blue-green and deep violet (1956)	60	30
450	–	10f. bluish green and deep purple (18.7.57)	5·50	3·50
451	**54**	12f. sepia and carmine	2·30	30
452	–	15f. vermilion and brown	1·40	30
453	–	20f. deep grey-green and blue (18.7.57)	1·10	30
454	**54**	50f. scarlet and deep blue	2·30	30
455		100f. greenish blue and myrtle-green (1962)	4·75	1·70
456		200f. deep turquoise-blue and brown-lake (1965)	13·50	3·50
457	–	500f. purple and red-brown (1965)	48·00	18·00
458	–	1d. brown-lake and deep olive (1965)	85·00	27·00
445/458 *Set of* 14			£150	50·00

Design: Horiz—15f. Dome of the Rock, Jerusalem.

58 Envelope with Postmarks in English and Arabic

59 'Flame of Freedom'

(Des R. T. Ledger. Recess)

1956 (15 Jan). First Arab Postal Congress, Amman. W **57**. P 14.

459	**58**	1f. brown and black	45	40
460		4f. carmine and black	45	40
461		15f. blue and black	45	40
462		20f. olive-bistre and black	45	40
463		50f. indigo and black	1·10	40
464		100f. orange-red and black	1·70	1·00
459/464 *Set of* 6			4·25	2·75

1957 (Jan). POSTAGE DUE. Redrawn. As T D **50** but inscr 'THE HASHEMITE KINGDOM OF JORDAN'. W **57**. P 11½.

D465	1f. red-brown	1·50	1·80
D466	2f. orange-yellow	1·50	1·80
D467	4f. green	1·50	2·50
D468	10f. carmine-red	2·30	2·50
D469	20f. yellow-brown	4·00	5·00
D465/D469 *Set of* 5		9·75	12·00

1958–59. AIR. As Nos. 432/437 but W **57**.

470	**54a**	5f. orange and indigo	40	30
471		10f. vermilion and chocolate	60	30
472		25f. pale blue and emerald	1·10	55
473		35f. turquoise-blue and deep mauve	1·50	85
474		40f. slate and carmine	2·10	1·00
475		50f. orange-brown and deep blue (1959)	4·50	1·50
470/475 *Set of* 6			9·25	4·00

(Recess Waterlow)

1958 (Dec). Tenth Anniversary of Declaration of Human Rights. W **57**. P 12½.

476	**59**	5f. brown-red and ultramarine	15	15
477		15f. black and yellow-brown	45	40
478		35f. purple and grey-green	90	85
479		45f. grey-black and carmine (10.12)	1·20	1·10
476/479 *Set of* 4			2·40	2·30

60 King Hussein

61 Arab League Centre, Cairo

(Recess De La Rue)

1959 (3 June). Centres in black. W **57**. P 12×11½.

480	**60**	1f. deep green	25	15
481		2f. violet	30	15
482		3f. carmine-red	60	15
483		4f. black-purple	75	15
484		7f. bluish green	90	20
485		12f. carmine-red	1·10	20
486		15f. vermilion	1·20	30
487		21f. emerald-green	1·50	30
488		25f. yellow-brown	1·80	30
489		35f. deep blue	2·75	30
490		40f. bronze-green	3·75	30
491		50f. orange-red	4·50	30
492		100f. blue-green	6·00	1·00
493		200f. brown-purple	17·00	4·25
494		500f. slate-blue	38·00	17·00
495		1d. deep purple	70·00	42·00
480/495 *Set of* 16			£140	60·00

(Photo Survey Dept, Cairo)

1960 (22 Mar). Inauguration of Arab League Centre, Cairo. W **190** of Egypt. P 13×13½.

496	**61**	15f. black and green	55	30

62 'Care of Refugees'

(Litho Enschedé)

1960 (7 Apr). World Refugee Year. W **57** (sideways). P 14×13½.

No.	Type	Description	Unused	Used
497	**62**	15f. red and grey blue	45	30
498		35f. blue and bistre	90	70

63 Shah of Iran and King Hussein

(Litho Enschedé)

1960 (15 May). Visit of Shah of Iran. W **57** (sideways). P 13½×14.

No.	Type	Description	Unused	Used
499	**63**	15f. multicoloured	75	70
500		35f. multicoloured	1·10	1·00
501		50f. multicoloured	1·50	1·40
499/501 *Set of 3*			3·00	2·75

64 Petroleum Refinery, Zarka

65 Jordanian Families and Graph

(Recess Enschedé)

1961 (1 May). Inauguration of Jordanian Petroleum Refinery. W **57**. P 14×13.

No.	Type	Description	Unused	Used
502	**64**	15f. blue and slate-violet	45	30
503		35f. chestnut and slate-violet	75	55

1961 (15 Oct). First Jordanian Census Commemoration. Litho. P 13×13½.

No.	Type	Description	Unused	Used
504	**65**	15f. orange-brown	45	30

(**66**)

67 Campaign Emblem

1961 (28 Nov). Dag Hammarskjöld Memorial Issue. Optd with T **66**.

No.	Type	Description	Unused	Used
505	**62**	15f. red and grey-blue	8·25	7·75
		a. Opt inverted	60·00	
506		35f. blue and bistre	8·25	7·75
		a. Opt inverted	60·00	

IMPERFORATE STAMPS. Many of the following issues (including miniature sheets) exist imperforate from limited printings.

(Litho Bradbury Wilkinson)

1962 (15 Apr). Malaria Eradication. P 11×11½.

No.	Type	Description	Unused	Used
507	**67**	15f. magenta	45	40
508		35f. blue	90	55
MS509 75×76 mm. Nos. 507/508			11·50	11·00

68 Telephone Exchange, Amman

69 *Rida* (freighter), Aqaba Port and King Hussein

(Recess and litho (dial) Bradbury Wilkinson)

1962 (11 Dec). Inauguration of Amman's Automatic Telephone Exchange. W **57**. P 11×11½.

No.	Type	Description	Unused	Used
510	**68**	15f. greenish blue and purple	30	35
511		35f. purple and emerald	90	85

(Recess Bradbury Wilkinson)

1962 (11 Dec). Opening of Aqaba Port. W **57**. P 11×11½.

No.	Type	Description	Unused	Used
512	**69**	15f. black and purple	1·10	30
513		35f. black and ultramarine	2·00	70
MS514 80×93 mm. Nos. 512/513			7·50	7·25

70 Dag Hammarskjöld and UN Headquarters

71 Church of Holy Virgin's Tomb, Jerusalem

(Photo Harrison)

1963 (24 Jan). 17th Anniversary of United Nations Organisation. P 14×14½.

No.	Type	Description	Unused	Used
515	**70**	15f. brown-red, olive and blue	75	30
516		35f. blue, brown-red and olive	1·80	85
517		50f. olive, blue and brown-red	3·00	1·70
515/517 *Set of 3*			5·00	2·50
MS518 135×95 mm. Nos. 515/517. Imperf			20·00	19·00

(Photo Harrison)

1963 (5 Feb). Holy Places. T **71** and similar vert designs. Multicoloured. P 14½×14.

No.	Description	Unused	Used
519	50f. Type **71**	2·30	2·10
	a. Vert strip of 4. Nos. 519/522	9·50	
520	50f. Basilica of the Agony, Gethsemane	2·30	2·10
521	50f. Holy Sepulchre, Jerusalem	2·30	2·10
522	50f. Nativity Church, Bethlehem	2·30	2·10
523	50f. Haram of Ibrahim, Hebron	2·30	2·10
	a. Vert strip of 4. Nos. 523/526	9·50	
	b. Yellow omitted		
524	50f. Dome of the Rock, Jerusalem	2·30	2·10
	a. Yellow omitted		
525	50f. Omar el-Khetab Mosque, Jerusalem	2·30	2·10
	a. Yellow omitted		
526	50f. El-Aqsa Mosque, Jerusalem	2·30	2·10
	a. Yellow omitted		
519/526 *Set of 8*		17·00	15·00

The above stamps were issued in two groups, four designs in a sheet of 16 (4×4) arranged vertically *se-tenant*, i.e. each design in a horiz row of four stamps.

72 League Centre, Cairo, and Emblem

73 Wheat and FAO Emblem

(Photo Postal Authority Press, Cairo)

1963 (16 July). Arab League. P 13½×13.

527	**72**	15f. deep greenish blue	45	30
528		35f. orange-red	1·50	55

1963 (15 Sept). Freedom from Hunger. Litho. W **57**. P 11½×13.

529	**73**	15f. deep green, black and light blue	60	30
530		35f. deep green, black and light yellow-green	90	55
MS531		98×85 mm. Nos. 529/530	3·00	2·40

74 Canal and Symbols

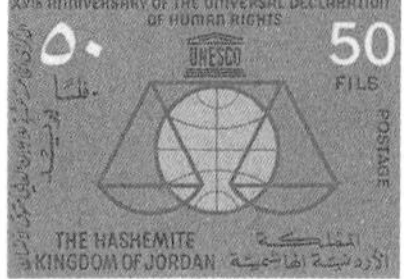

75 Scales of Justice and Globe

1963 (20 Sept). East Ghor Canal Project. Litho. W **57**. P 14.

532	**74**	1f. black and yellow-bistre	30	15
533		4f. black and light blue	30	15
534		5f. black and light purple	30	15
535		10f. black and yellow-green	60	15
536		35f. black and orange	3·25	2·20
532/536 *Set of 5*			4·25	2·50

(Litho De La Rue)

1963 (10 Dec). 15th Anniversary of Declaration of Human Rights. P 13½×13.

537	**75**	50f. red and grey-blue	1·50	1·40
538		50f. grey-blue and red	1·50	1·40

1 Fils ١ فلس

(**76**)

77 King Hussein and Red Crescent

1963 (Dec). Surch as T **76**.

539	**60**	1f. on 21f. black and emerald-green	45	40
540		2f. on 21f. black and emerald-green	45	40
541		4f. on 12f. black and carmine-red	27·00	42·00
542	**54**	4f. on 12f. sepia and carmine (No. 451)	60	55
543	**60**	5f. on 21f. black and emerald-green	1·20	85
544		25f. on 35f. black and deep blue	4·50	1·80
539/544 *Set of 6*			31·00	41·00

No. 541 with '4 Fils' omitted or with the English and Arabic transposed result from the surcharge being misplaced.

Similar surcharges in other denominations or the same denominations surcharged on other stamps exist but were unauthorised.

(Photo Harrison)

1963 (24 Dec). Red Crescent Commemoration. P 14×14½.

545	**77**	1f. purple and red	30	30
546		2f. turquoise and red	30	30
547		3f. deep blue and red	30	30
548		4f. deep bluish green and red	30	30
549		5f. sepia and red	30	30
550		85f. deep green and red	4·00	3·00
545/550 *Set of 6*			5·00	4·00
MS551		90×65 mm. 100f. purple and red (larger). Imperf	48·00	46·00

78 Red Cross Emblem

(Photo Harrison)

1963 (24 Dec). Centenary of Red Cross. P 14×14½.

552	**78**	1f. purple and red	45	40
553		2f. turquoise and red	45	40
554		3f. deep blue and red	45	40
555		4f. deep bluish green and red	45	40
556		5f. sepia and red	45	40
557		85f. deep green and red	6·25	4·25
552/557 *Set of 6*			7·75	5·75
MS558		90×65 mm. 100f. purple and red (larger). Imperf	45·00	43·00

79 Kings Hussein of Hejaz and Hussein of Jordan

1963 (25 Dec). Arab Renaissance Day. Litho. W **57**. P 11×11½.

559	**79**	15f. multicoloured	1·20	55
560		25f. multicoloured	1·70	85
561		35f. multicoloured	3·00	1·80
562		50f. multicoloured	6·25	5·00
559/562 *Set of 4*			11·00	7·50
MS563		112×93 mm. Nos. 559/562	13·50	13·00

80 El Aqsa Mosque, Pope Paul and King Hussein

(Des P. Koroleff, Litho Yacoub Slim Press, Beirut)

1964 (4 Jan). Pope Paul's Visit to the Holy Land. T **80** and similar horiz designs. P 13×13½.

564	15f. emerald and black	60	40
565	35f. cerise and black	90	55
	a. Black (portraits etc) omitted	£300	
566	50f. brown and black	1·80	1·30
	a. Imperf (pair)	£375	
567	80f. violet-blue and black	3·25	2·20
564/567 *Set of 4*		6·00	4·00
MS567*a*	138×108 mm. Nos. 564/567. Imperf	39·00	37·00

Designs: 15f. T **80**; 35f. Dome of the Rock (Mosque of Omar), Jerusalem; 50f. Church of the Holy Sepulchre, Jerusalem; 80f. Church of the Nativity, Bethlehem.

81 Prince standing by wall

82 Basketball

(Photo Harrison)

1964 (1 Mar). Second Birthday of Prince Abdullah (30 January). T **81** and similar multicoloured designs. P 14.

568	5f. Type **81**	75	30
569	10f. Head of Prince and roses (*diamond, 63×63 mm*)	90	70
	a. Gold omitted	£550	
570	35f. Prince Abdullah (*horiz*)	2·00	1·40
	a. Gold omitted	£550	
568/570 *Set of 3*		3·25	2·20

A set of ten triangular 20f. stamps and two 100f. miniature sheets showing astronauts and rockets was issued but very few were put on sale at the Post Office and we are not satisfied as to their status.

(Photo Harrison)

1964 (1 June). Olympic Games, Tokyo (1st issue). T **82** and similar designs. P 14½×14.

571	1f. carmine (Type **82**)	30	30
572	2f. blue (Volleyball)	30	30
573	3f. turquoise-green (Football)	30	30

574		4f. cinnamon (Table tennis) (*horiz*)	30	30
575		5f. violet (Running)	30	30
576		35f. vermilion (Cycling) (*horiz*)	3·25	1·40
577		50f. bright green (Fencing) (*horiz*)	6·00	2·75
578		100f. chocolate (Pole-vaulting) (*horiz*)	9·00	5·00
571/578 *Set of 8*			18·00	9·50
MS579 88×64 mm. 200f. light blue (as 100f. but larger). Imperf			70·00	65·00

See also Nos. 610/**MS**618 and 641/**MS**647.

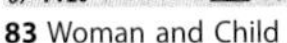

83 Woman and Child

84 King Hussein Sports Stadium, Amman

(Litho De La Rue)

1964 (12 June). Fourth Session of Social Studies Seminar, Amman. W **57** (sideways). P 14.

580	**83**	5f. multicoloured	75	70
581		10f. multicoloured	75	70
582		25f. multicoloured	75	70
580/582 *Set of 3*			2·00	1·90

(Litho Bradbury Wilkinson)

1964 (12 July). AIR. Inauguration of Hussein Sports City. W **57**. P 11×11½.

583	**84**	1f. multicoloured	45	40
584		4f. multicoloured	45	40
585		10f. multicoloured	45	40
586		35f. multicoloured	90	85
583/586 *Set of 4*			2·00	1·80
MS587 120×94 mm. Nos. 583/586			4·50	4·25

85 President Kennedy

(Litho Harrison)

1964 (15 July). President Kennedy Memorial Issue. P 14.

588	**85**	1f. violet	60	55
589		2f. carmine	60	55
590		3f. ultramarine	60	55
591		4f. yellow-brown	60	55
592		5f. blue-green	60	55
593		85f. vermilion	30·00	17·00
588/593 *Set of 6*			30·00	18·00
MS594 110×77 mm. **85** 100f. sepia (larger). Imperf			33·00	32·00

86 Statues at Abu Simbel

87 King Hussein and Map of Palestine in 1920

1964 (1 Aug). Nubian Monuments Preservation. Litho. W **57**. P 14½×14.

595	**86**	4f. black and light blue	75	70
596		15f. violet and yellow	75	70
597		25f. carmine-red and light yellow-green	75	70
595/597 *Set of 3*			2·00	1·90

1964 (5 Sept). Arab Summit Conference. Litho. P 12.

598	**87**	10f. multicoloured	30	15
599		15f. multicoloured	45	20
600		25f. multicoloured	60	30
601		50f. multicoloured	1·40	40
602		80f. multicoloured	2·50	2·00
598/602 *Set of 5*			4·75	2·75
MS603 110×90 mm. Nos. 598/602. Imperf. No gum			8·25	8·00

88 Pope Paul VI, King Hussein and Ecumenical Patriarch

1964 (18 Sept). Meeting of Pope, King and Patriarch, Jerusalem. Multicoloured; background colour given. Litho. P 12.

604	**88**	10f. deep bluish green (*shades*)	30	30
605		15f. purple	45	40
606		25f. chocolate	60	55
607		50f. light blue	1·40	1·30
608		80f. emerald	2·50	2·40
604/608 *Set of 5*			4·75	4·50
MS609 130×100 mm. Nos. 604/608. Imperf. No gum			13·50	13·00

No. 604 became available in 1967 in a pale dull green.

89 Olympic Flame

1964 (21 Nov). Olympic Games, Tokyo (2nd issue). Litho. P 14.

610	**89**	1f. brown-red	15	15
611		2f. violet	25	20
612		3f. turquoise-green	30	30
613		4f. brown	40	35
614		5f. Venetian red	45	40
615		35f. indigo	1·50	1·40
616		50f. yellow-olive	2·30	2·10
617		100f. deep ultramarine	5·25	5·00
610/617 *Set of 8*			9·50	9·00
MS618 108×76 mm. **89** 100f. carmine-rose (larger). Imperf			33·00	32·00

90 Scouts crossing River

(Des V. Whiteley and D. Slater. Litho Harrison)

1964 (7 Dec). Jordanian Scouts. T **90** and similar designs. P 14.

619	1f. brown (Type **90**)	25	20
620	2f. violet (First Aid)	25	20
621	3f. yellow-brown (Exercising)	30	30
622	4f. brown-lake (Practising knots)	30	30
623	5f. yellow-green (Cooking meal)	30	30
624	35f. blue (Sailing)	8·25	3·00
625	50f. deep grey-green (Around campfire)	9·00	4·75
619/625 *Set of 7*		17·00	8·25
MS626 108×76 mm. 100f. deep violet-blue (as 50f. but larger). Imperf		39·00	19·00

91 Four-coloured Bush Shrike

(Photo Harrison)

1964 (18 Dec). AIR. Birds. T **91** and similar multicoloured designs. P 14×14½ (150f.) or 14½×14 (others).

627	150f. Type **91**	45·00	21·00
628	500f. Ornate Hawk Eagle (*vert*)	£120	55·00
629	1000f. Grey-headed Kingfisher (*vert*)	£200	£100
627/629 *Set of 3*		£325	£160

92 Bykovsky

1965 (20 Jan). Russian Cosmonauts. T **92** and similar designs. Litho. P 14.

630	40f. red-brown and sage-green (Type **92**)	2·10	1·40
631	40f. slate-violet and brown (Gagarin)	2·10	1·40
632	40f. maroon and cobalt (Nikolayev)	2·10	1·40
633	40f. deep lilac and pale bistre (Popovich)	2·10	1·40
634	40f. olive-brown and violet-blue (Tereshkova)	2·10	1·40
635	40f. bronze-green and pink (Titov)	2·10	1·40
630/635 *Set of 6*		11·50	7·50
MS636 115×83 mm. 100f. blue and black (space ship and the six cosmonauts). Imperf		38·00	36·00
MS637 As above opt 'VOSKHOD 12/10/64/ VLADIMIR KOMAROV/KONSTANTIN FEOK-TISTOV/BORIS YEGEROV'		38·00	36·00

93 UN Headquarters and Emblem

(Des V. Whiteley. Litho Harrison)

1965 (15 Feb). 19th Anniversary (1964) of United Nations. P 14×15.

638	**93**	30f. reddish violet, turquoise-blue and light brown	90	70
639		70f. light brown, turquoise-blue and reddish violet	1·80	1·00
MS640 76×102 mm. Nos. 638/639. Imperf			30·00	29·00

94 Olympic Flame

(Litho Harrison)

1965 (6 Mar). AIR. Olympic Games, Tokyo (3rd issue). P 14.

641	**94**	10f. rose	60	55
642		15f. violet	60	55
643		20f. greenish blue	60	55
644		30f. bluish green	60	55
645		40f. greyish brown	90	85
646		60f. magenta	1·20	1·10
641/646 *Set of 6*			4·00	3·75
MS647 102×102 mm. **94** 100f. violet-blue (larger). Imperf			29·00	27·00

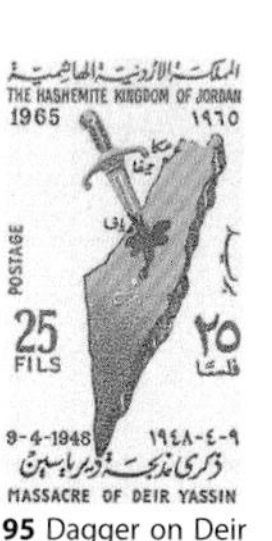

95 Dagger on Deir Yassin, Palestine

96 Horse-jumping

97 Volleyball Player and Cup

(Photo Postal Authority Press, Cairo)

1965 (9 Apr). Deir Yassin Massacre. P 11×11½.

648	**95**	25f. red and yellow-olive	6·50	3·50

(Des V. Whiteley and D. Slater. Litho Harrison)

1965 (24 May). Army Day. T **96** and similar vert designs. P 14½×14.

649	5f. deep bluish green	30	15
650	10f. ultramarine	60	30
651	35f. purple-brown	2·00	70
649/651 *Set of 3*		2·50	1·00

Designs: 5f. T **96**; 10f. Tank; 35f. King Hussein making inspection in army car.

(Des V. Whiteley. Litho Harrison)

1965 (June). Arab Volleyball Championships. P 14½×14.

652	**97**	15f. light yellow-olive	1·70	55
653		35f. lake	3·25	1·40
654		50f. turquoise-blue	5·25	3·00
652/654 *Set of 3*			9·25	4·50
MS655 63×89 mm. **97** 100f. orange-brown (larger). Imperf			42·00	40·00

98 President J. F. Kennedy

(Des V. Whiteley and D. Slater. Litho)

1965 (June). First Death Anniversary of President Kennedy. W **57**. P 14.

656	**98**	10f. black and blue-green	75	70
657		15f. violet and yellow-orange	1·10	70
658		25f. brown and light blue	1·70	1·00
659		50f. brown-purple and bright green	3·25	1·80
656/659 *Set of 4*			6·00	3·75
MS660 114×90 mm. **98** 50f. salmon and blue. Imperf			30·00	29·00

99 Pope Paul, King Hussein and Dome of the Rock

100 Cathedral Steps

1965 (22 June). First Anniversary of Pope Paul's Visit to the Holy Land. Litho. W **57**. P 13½×14½.

No.	Type	Description	Unused	Used
661	**99**	5f. brown and mauve	75	15
662		10f. brown-lake and pale yellow-green	1·50	55
663		15f. blue and flesh	2·10	70
664		50f. olive-grey and pink	5·50	2·40
661/664 *Set of 4*			8·75	3·50
MS665		102×76 mm. **99** 50f. blue and reddish violet. Imperf	42·00	40·00

(Photo Harrison)

1965 (22 June). AIR. Jerash Antiquities. T **100** and similar multicoloured designs. P 14½×14.

No.	Type	Description	Unused	Used
666		55f. Type **100**	2·50	2·40
		a. Horiz strip of 4. Nos. 666/669	10·50	
667		55f. Artemis Temple Gate	2·50	2·40
668		55f. Street of Columns	2·50	2·40
669		55f. Columns of South Theatre	2·50	2·40
670		55f. Forum (*horiz*)	2·50	2·40
		a. Horiz strip of 4. Nos. 670/673	10·50	
		b. Pink (frame) omitted		
671		55f. South Theatre (*horiz*)	2·50	2·40
		a. Pink omitted		
672		55f. Triumphal Arch (*horiz*)	2·50	2·40
673		55f. Temple of Artemis (*horiz*)	2·50	2·40
		a. Pink omitted		
666/673 *Set of 8*			18·00	17·00

Nos. 666/669 and 670/673 were arranged together *se-tenant* in horizontal rows within the sheets of 16.

101 Jordanian Pavilion at Fair

(Des V. Whiteley. Photo Harrison)

1965 (July). New York World's Fair. P 14×13½.

No.	Type	Description	Unused	Used
674	**101**	15f. multicoloured	30	30
675		25f. multicoloured	75	40
676		50f. multicoloured	1·70	1·00
674/676 *Set of 3*			2·50	1·50
MS677		113×75 mm. **101** 100f. multicoloured. Imperf	5·75	5·50

102 Lamp and Burning Library

103 ITU Emblem and Symbols

(Photo Postal Authority Press, Cairo)

1965 (14 July). Reconstruction of Algiers University Library. P 11½×11.

No.	Type	Description	Unused	Used
678	**102**	25f. green, red and black	75	40

(Litho Bradbury Wilkinson)

1965 (15 Aug). Centenary of International Telecommunications Union. W **57**. P 14×13½.

No.	Type	Description	Unused	Used
679	**103**	25f. blue and light blue	75	30
680		45f. black and sage-green	1·20	70
MS681		40×32 mm. **103** 100f. lake and orange-red (larger). Imperf	4·50	4·25

104 *Syncom* Satellite and Pagoda

(Des V. Whiteley and D. Slater. Litho Harrison)

1965 (5 Sept). Space Achievements. T **104** and similar designs. Multicoloured. W **57**. P 14.

No.	Type	Description	Unused	Used
682		5f. Type **104**	60	55
683		10f. North American X-15 being launched from Boeing B-52H Stratofortress	60	55
684		15f. Astronauts	90	70
685		20f. As 10f.	1·20	85
686		50f. Type **104**	2·75	2·00
682/686 *Set of 5*			5·50	4·25
MS687		101×76 mm. 50f. *Syncom* Satellite and Earth's sphere. Imperf	29·00	27·00

105 Dead Sea

(Photo Harrison)

1965 (23 Sept). Dead Sea T **105** and similar horiz designs. Multicoloured. P 14.

No.	Type	Description	Unused	Used
688		35f. Type **105**	1·40	85
		a. Vert strip of 4. Nos. 688/691	5·75	
689		35f. Boats and palms	1·40	85
690		35f. Qumran Caves	1·40	85
691		35f. Dead Sea Scrolls	1·40	85
688/691 *Set of 4*			5·00	3·00

Nos. 688/691 were printed together in *se-tenant* vertical strips of four within sheets of 16 stamps.

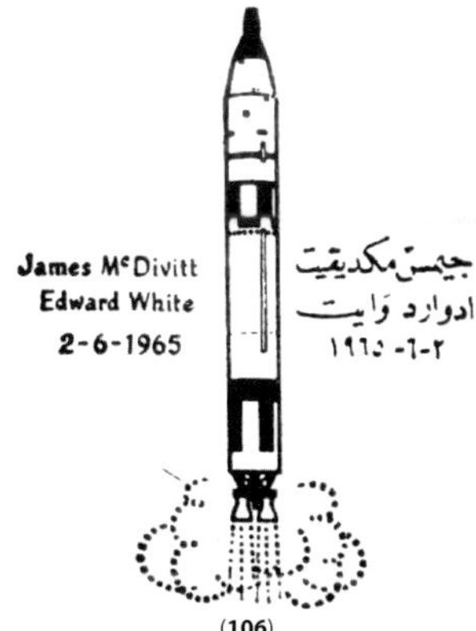

(106)

1965 (25 Sept). AIR. Space Flight of McDivitt and White. Nos. 641/**MS**647 optd with T **106**.

No.	Type	Description	Unused	Used
692	**94**	10f. rose	2·30	2·10
693		15f. violet	3·00	2·75
694		20f. greenish blue	4·25	4·00
695		30f. bluish green	6·25	6·00
696		40f. greyish brown	8·25	7·75
697		60f. magenta	12·00	11·00
692/697 *Set of 6*			32·00	30·00
MS698		102×102 mm. **94** 100f. violet-blue (larger). Imperf	45·00	43·00

107 King Hussein, UN Emblem and Headquarters

108 ICY Emblem

(Litho Harrison)

1965 (5 Oct). King Hussein's Visit to France and the USA. T **107** and similar designs. W **57**. P 14.

699 **107** 5f. sepia, light greenish blue and pale pink ... 60 55
700 – 10f. sepia, green and pale grey ... 60 55
701 – 20f. agate, red-brown and light blue ... 1·10 1·00
702 **107** 50f. slate-lilac, red-brown and light blue ... 2·50 2·40
699/702 *Set of 4* ... 4·25 4·00
MS703 102×102 mm. **107** 50f. slate-lilac, red-brown and light blue. Imperf. ... 18·00 17·00

Designs: 5f. T **107**; 10f. King Hussein, President de Gaulle and Eiffel Tower; 20f. King Hussein, President Johnson and Statue of Liberty.

(Litho Bradbury Wilkinson)

1965 (24 Oct). International Co-operation Year. W **57**. P 14×13.

704 **108** 5f. red and orange ... 45 30
705 10f. violet and new blue ... 1·10 40
706 45f. purple and bluish green ... 4·00 2·75
704/706 *Set of 3* ... 5·00 3·00

109 APU Emblem

110 Dome of the Rock

(Litho Harrison)

1965 (5 Nov). Tenth Anniversary (1964) of Arab Postal Union's Permanent Office at Cairo. W **57**. P 14½×14.

707 **109** 15f. black and violet-blue ... 30 30
708 25f. black and yellow-green ... 1·10 40

(Litho Harrison)

1965 (20 Nov). Dome of the Rock Inauguration (1964). P 14×14½.

709 **110** 15f. multicoloured ... 1·70 55
710 25f. multicoloured ... 2·75 1·70

111 King Hussein

(Photo Harrison)

1966 (15 Jan). P 14½×14.

(a) POSTAGE. Portraits in slate-blue (1f. to 15f.) or brown-purple (21f. to 150f.); background colours given

711 **111** 1f. orange ... 15 15
712 2f. ultramarine ... 15 15
713 3f. reddish violet ... 15 15
714 4f. reddish purple ... 15 15
715 7f. chestnut ... 45 15
716 12f. magenta ... 45 15
717 15f. bistre-brown ... 60 15
718 21f. emerald-green ... 90 20
719 25f. greenish blue ... 1·10 20
720 35f. yellow-ochre ... 1·40 30
721 40f. orange-yellow ... 1·50 40
722 50f. olive-green ... 1·70 70
723 100f. bright-green ... 2·75 1·50
724 150f. bluish violet ... 6·25 2·40

(b) AIR. Portraits in bistre-brown; background colours given

725 **111** 200f. turquoise ... 9·75 2·75
726 500f. light green ... 17·00 10·50
727 1d. blue ... 29·00 17·00
711/727 *Set of 17* ... 65·00 33·00

Alexei Leonov
Pavel Belyaev
18 3-1965

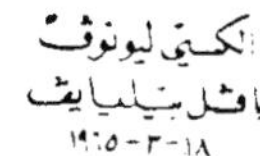

(**112**)

1966 (15 Jan). Space Flights of Belyaev and Leonov. Nos. 630/**MS**637 optd with T **112**.

728 40f. red-brown and sage-green ... 9·00 8·50
a. Opt sideways (reading down) ... £100
729 40f. slate-violet and brown ... 9·00 8·50
a. Opt sideways (reading down) ... £100
730 40f. maroon and cobalt ... 9·00 8·50
a. Opt sideways (reading down) ... £100
b. Opt sideways (reading up) ... £150
731 40f. deep lilac and pale bistre ... 9·00 8·50
a. Opt sideways (reading down) ... £100
732 40f. olive-brown and violet-blue ... 9·00 8·50
a. Opt sideways (reading down) ... £100
733 40f. bronze-green and pink ... 9·00 8·50
a. Opt sideways (reading down) ... £100
728/733 *Set of 6* ... 49·00 46·00
MS734 115×83 mm. 100f. blue and black (No. **MS**636) ... 90·00 85·00
a. Opt inverted ... £250
MS735 115×83 mm. 100f. blue and black (No. **MS**637) ... 90·00 85·00
a. Opt inverted ... £250

PAPA PAULUS VI WORLD PEACE VISIT . TO UNITED NATIONS 1965

(**113**)

1966 (27 Apr). Pope Paul's Visit to UN (1965). Nos. 604/**MS**609 optd with T **113**. Background colours given.

736 **88** 10f. deep bluish green ... 45 15
737 15f. purple ... 1·10 40
738 25f. chocolate ... 1·10 55
739 50f. light blue ... 2·00 1·00
740 80f. emerald ... 3·25 1·50
736/740 *Set of 5* ... 7·00 3·25
MS740*a* 130×100 mm. Nos. 736/740. Imperf. No gum ... 20·00 19·00

114 Agricultural Symbols

115 First Station of the Cross

(Photo Harrison)

1966 (17 May). Anti-tuberculosis Campaign. Unissued 'Freedom from Hunger' stamps optd with UN emblem and 'ANTI-TUBERCULOSIS CAMPAIGN' in English and Arabic. P 14×14½.

(a) T **114**

741	15f. multicoloured	75	55
742	35f. multicoloured	2·00	1·30
743	50f. multicoloured	3·00	2·75
741/743 *Set of 3*		5·25	4·25
MS744 108×76 mm. Nos. 741/743. Gold background. Simulated perfs		23·00	22·00
MS744*a* 108×76 mm. Nos. 741/743 White background. Imperf		23·00	22·00

(b) As T **114** *but with additional premium in red obliterated by bars*

745	15f. +15f. multicoloured	75	55
746	35f. +35f. multicoloured	2·00	1·30
747	50f. +50f. multicoloured	3·00	2·75
745/747 *Set of 3*		5·25	4·25

(Des V. Whiteley. Photo Harrison)

1966 (14 Sept). Christ's Passion. The Stations of the Cross. T **115** and similar vert designs. P 14½×14.

749	1f. multicoloured (Type **115**)	30	15
750	2f. multicoloured	30	15
751	3f. multicoloured	45	30
752	4f. multicoloured	45	30
753	5f. multicoloured	75	40
754	6f. multicoloured	1·10	55
755	7f. multicoloured	1·50	85
756	8f. multicoloured	1·70	90
757	9f. multicoloured	2·00	1·00
758	10f. multicoloured	2·10	1·30
759	11f. multicoloured	2·50	1·50
760	12f. multicoloured	2·50	1·50
761	13f. multicoloured	2·75	1·70
762	14f. multicoloured	2·75	1·80
749/762 *Set of 14*		19·00	11·00
MS763 101×76 mm. **115** 100f. multicoloured. Imperf		55·00	50·00

Designs: The 14 Stations. The denominations, expressed in Roman numerals, correspond to the numbers of the Stations.

116 Schirra and *Gemini 6*

117 The Three Kings

(Photo Harrison)

1966 (15 Nov). Space Achievements. T **116** and similar vert designs. P 14½×14.

764	1f. Prussian blue, violet and deep bluish green	30	30
765	2f. deep bluish green, violet and Prussian blue	30	30
766	3f. violet, Prussian blue and deep bluish green	30	30
767	4f. violet, deep bluish green and ochre	45	30
768	30f. turquoise-blue, yellow-brown and violet	3·00	2·00
769	60f. yellow-brown, turquoise-blue and violet	4·00	2·75
764/769 *Set of 6*		7·50	5·25
MS770 114×88 mm. 100f. multicoloured (The six astronauts etc). Imperf		36·00	34·00

Designs: 1f. T **116**; 2f. Stafford and *Gemini 6*; 3f. Borman and *Gemini 7*; 4f. Lovell and *Gemini 7*; 30f. Armstrong and *Gemini 8*; 60f. Scott and *Gemini 8*.

(Photo Harrison)

1966 (26 Dec). Christmas. T **117** and similar multicoloured designs. P 14½×14 (35f.) or 14×14½ (others).

771	5f. Type **117**	45	15
772	10f. The Magi presenting gifts to the infant Christ	60	30
773	35f. The Flight to Egypt (*vert*)	5·75	1·80
771/773 *Set of 3*		6·00	2·00
MS774 115×90 mm. 50f. As 10f. Imperf		42·00	40·00

Although not issued at post offices until 26 December, copies were available from commercial sources before Christmas at extortionate prices.

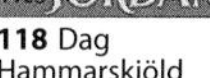

118 Dag Hammarskjöld

119 King Hussein

(Photo Harrison)

1967 (5 Jan). 'Builders of World Peace'. T **118** and similar vert portrait designs. Multicoloured. P 14½×14.

(a) First issue

775	5f. Type **118**	30	30
776	10f. Pandit Nehru	45	30
	a. 'FILS' omitted	48·00	45·00
777	35f. President Kennedy	1·70	85
778	50f. Pope John XXIII	4·00	1·10
779	100f. King Abdullah (of Jordan)	4·50	3·25
775/779 *Set of 5*		9·75	5·25
MS780 99×64 mm. 100f. The above five portraits. Imperf		36·00	34·00

(b) Second issue

781	5f. U Thant	30	30
782	10f. President De Gaulle	45	30
783	35f. President Johnson	1·70	85
	a. Gold (portrait frame) omitted	£350	
784	50f. Pope Paul VI	4·00	1·10
785	100f. King Hussein	4·50	3·25
781/785 *Set of 5*		9·75	5·25
MS786 99×64 mm. 100f. The above five portraits. Imperf		36·00	34·00

No. 776a occurs in every fourth sheet as four sheets were printed at a time.

(Die-stamped and photo Harrison)

1967 (7 Feb). Gold Coins. Circular designs, centre and rim embossed on gold foil. Imperf.

(a) As T **119**

(i) Diameter 41 mm

787	5f. light salmon and ultramarine	1·10	1·00
788	10f. light salmon and bluish violet	1·10	1·00

(ii) Diameter 47 mm

789	50f. lavender and blackish brown	5·75	5·25
790	100f. light pink and grey-green	7·25	6·75

(iii) Diameter 54 mm

791	200f. light blue and deep blue	17·00	15·00
787/791 *Set of 5*		29·00	26·00

(b) Crown Prince Hassan of Jordan

(i) Diameter 41 mm

792	5f. black and bright green	1·10	1·00
793	10f. black and lilac	1·10	1·00

(ii) Diameter 47 mm

794	50f. black and light blue	5·75	5·25
795	100f. black and orange-brown	7·25	6·75

(iii) Diameter 54 mm

796	200f. gold, black and magenta	17·00	15·00
792/796 *Set of 5*		29·00	26·00

(c) John F. Kennedy (President of USA, 1961–1963)

(i) Diameter 41 mm

796*a*	5f. new blue and bright yellow green	1·10	1·00
796*b*	10f. emerald and rose-pink	1·10	1·00

(ii) Diameter 47 mm

796*c*	50f. rose carmine and yellow	5·75	5·25
796*d*	100f. olive brown and olive yellow	7·25	6·75

(iii) Diameter 54 mm

796*e*	200f. purple and bright yellow green	17·00	15·00
796*a*/796*e* *Set of 5*		29·00	26·00

120 University City Statue and Olympic Torch

(Des V. Whiteley. Photo Harrison)

1967 (Mar). Preparation for Olympic Games in Mexico (1968). T **120** and similar horiz designs. P 14×14½.

797	1f. crimson, black and bluish violet	45	40
798	2f. black, bluish violet and crimson	45	40
799	3f. bluish violet, crimson and black	45	40
800	4f. ultramarine, brown and green	45	40
801	30f. green, ultramarine and brown	1·10	1·00
802	60f. brown, green and ultramarine	2·10	2·00
797/802 *Set of 6*		4·50	4·25
MS803 115×90 mm. 100f. brown, green and ultramarine (as 60f.). Imperf		36·00	34·00

Designs: (each with Olympic torch)—1f. T **120**; 2f. Fishermen on Lake Patzcuaro; 3f. University City and skyscraper, Mexico City; 4f. Avenida de la Reforma, Mexico City; 30f. Guadalajara Cathedral; 60f, 100f. Fine Arts Theatre, Mexico City.

121 Decade Emblem

(Des V. Whiteley. Litho Harrison)

1967 (1 Mar). International Hydrological Decade. W **57**. P 14½×14.

804	**121**	10f. black and light brown-red	45	15
805		15f. black and turquoise	90	40
806		25f. black and bright purple	1·70	1·00
804/806 *Set of 3*			2·75	1·40

122 UNESCO Emblem

(Des V. Whiteley. Litho Harrison)

1967 (16 Mar). 20th Anniversary of United Nations Educational, Scientific and Cultural Organisation. W **57**. P 14½×14.

807	**122**	100f. multicoloured	2·30	2·10

123 Dromedary

(Photo Harrison)

1967 (Apr). Animals. T **123** and similar horiz designs. Multicoloured. P 14×15.

(a) POSTAGE

808	1f. Type **123**	3·50	55
809	2f. Karakul Sheep	3·50	55
810	3f. Angora Goat	3·50	55

(b) AIR

811	4f. Striped Hyena	3·50	55
812	30f. Arab Horses	4·75	1·10
813	60f. Arabian Oryx	8·25	2·10
808/813 *Set of 6*		24·00	4·75
MS814 115×89 mm. 100f. (as 30f.). Imperf		50·00	48·00

124 WHO Building

125 Arab League Emblem, Open Book and Reaching Hands

1967 (7 Apr). Inauguration of World Health Organisation Headquarters, Geneva. Litho. P 14½×14.

815	**124**	5f. black and light emerald	30	30
816		45f. black and light yellow-orange	1·20	55

(Photo De La Rue)

1968 (5 May). Literacy Campaign. P 11.

817	**125**	20f. bronze green and red orange	1·20	[illegible]
818		20f. blue and magenta	90	40

126 WHO Emblem and '20'

(Litho Harrison)

1968 (10 Aug). 20th Anniversary of World Health Organisation. W **57**. P 14½×14.

819	**126**	30f. multicoloured	1·20	40
820		100f. multicoloured	3·50	1·80

127 Eurasian Goldfinch

128 Human Rights Emblem

(Des V. Whiteley. Photo State Ptg Wks, Vienna)

1968 (5 Oct). Game Protection. T **127** and similar multicoloured designs. P 13½.

(a) POSTAGE

821	5f. Type **127**	5·00	2·10
822	10f. Chukar Partridge (*vert*)	9·00	2·10
823	15f. Ostrich (*vert*)	13·00	2·75
824	20f. Sand Partridge	13·00	3·00
825	30f. Mountain Gazelle	8·25	2·40
826	40f. Arabian Oryx	11·50	2·75
827	50f. Houbara Bustard	18·00	6·00

(b) AIR

828	60f. Ibex (*vert*)	14·50	7·00
829	100f. Flock of Mallard	23·00	13·50
821/829 *Set of 9*		£100	37·00

(Litho Pakistan Security Ptg Corp Ltd)

1968 (10 Dec). Human Rights Year. P 13.

830	**128**	20f. black, buff and orange-brown	45	30
831		60f. black, pale blue and blue-green	1·80	1·40

129 ILO Emblem

130 Horses in Pasture

1969 (10 June). 50th Anniversary of International Labour Organisation. Photo. P 13½×14.

832	**129**	10f. black and light greenish blue	45	15
833		20f. black and orange-brown	45	30
834		25f. black and apple-green	60	40
835		45f. black and magenta	1·10	70
836		60f. black and yellow-orange	1·50	1·00
832/836 *Set of 5*			3·75	2·30

1969 (6 July). Arab Horses. T **130** and similar horiz designs. Multicoloured. Photo. P 14.

837	10f. Type **130**	2·30	40
838	20f. White horse	6·25	1·50
839	45f. Black mare and foal	11·50	4·75
837/839	*Set of* 3	18·00	6·00

131 Kaaba, Mecca, and Dome of the Rock, Jerusalem

1969 (9 Oct). Dome of the Rock. T **131** and similar horiz design. Multicoloured. Photo. P 12.

840	5f. Type **131**	60	15
841	10f. Dome of the Rock (30×36 *mm*)	1·10	70
842	20f. As 10f.	2·00	1·00
843	45f. Type **131**	4·75	1·10
840/843	*Set of* 4	7·50	2·75

132 Oranges

133 Prince Hassan and Bride

1969 (22 Nov). Fruits. T **132** and similar vert designs. Multicoloured. Photo. P 12.

844	10f. Type **132**	45	15
845	20f. Gooseberry	75	40
846	30f. Lemons	1·70	50
847	40f. Grapes	2·40	55
848	50f. Olives	3·25	1·50
849	100f. Apples	5·25	2·75
844/849	*Set of* 6	12·50	5·25

(Photo Harrison)

1969 (2 Dec). Wedding of Prince Hassan (1968). T **133** and similar designs, showing Prince and bride. P 12½.

850	20f. multicoloured	90	85
	a. Strip of 3. Nos. 850/852	6·75	
851	60f. multicoloured	2·10	1·70
852	100f. multicoloured	3·50	3·25
850/852	*Set of* 3	5·75	5·25

Nos. 850/852 were issued in *se-tenant* strips of each design within the sheet.

134 Wrecked Houses

135 Bombed Mosque

1969 (10 Dec). 'Tragedy of the Refugees'. Vert designs as T **134** with similar inscr. Multicoloured. Photo. P 14×13.

853/882	1f. to 30f. inclusive *Set of* 30	55·00	55·00

1969 (10 Dec). 'Tragedy in the Holy Lands'. Vert designs as T **135** with similar inscr. Multicoloured. Photo. P 14×13.

883/912	1f. to 30f. inclusive *Set of* 30	55·00	55·00

Nos. 853/882 and 883/912 were issued in sheets of ten, each sheet containing five different values in *se-tenant* horizontal strips.

136 Pomegranate

137 Football

1970 (21 Mar). Flowers. T **136** and similar vert designs. Multicoloured. Photo. P 14×13½.

913	5f. Type **136**	75	30
914	15f. Wattle	1·20	30
915	25f. Caper	2·00	30
916	35f. Convolvulus	2·75	40
917	45f. Desert Scabious	3·75	1·30
918	75f. Black Iris	6·00	4·75
913/918	*Set of* 6	15·00	6·50

Nos. 913/915 and 917 are wrongly inscribed.

1970 (6 June). Sports. T **137** and similar multicoloured designs. Photo. P 13½×14 (horiz) or 14×13½ (vert).

919	5f. Type **137**	30	15
920	10f. Diving	45	30
921	15f. Boxing	75	30
922	50f. Running	2·30	1·00
923	100f. Cycling (*vert*)	5·50	1·80
924	150f. Basketball (*vert*)	8·25	4·25
919/924	*Set of* 6	16·00	7·00

138 Arab Children

139 Black Scrub Robin

1970 (15 July). Children's Day. T **138** and similar multicoloured designs. Photo. P 13½×14 (5f.) or 14×13½ (others).

925	5f. Type **138**	45	15
926	10f. Refugee boy with kettle (*vert*)	45	20
927	15f. Refugee girl in camp (*vert*)	1·10	30
928	20f. Refugee child in tent (*vert*)	1·50	40
925/928	*Set of* 4	3·25	95

1970 (1 Sept). Birds. T **139** and similar vert designs. Photo. P 13½.

929	120f. black and salmon	21·00	4·25
930	180f. multicoloured	26·00	9·00
931	200f. multicoloured	33·00	12·50
929/931	*Set of* 3	70·00	23·00

Designs: 120f. T **139**; 180f. Masked Shrike; 200f. Palestine Sunbird.

140 Grotto of the Nativity, Bethlehem

(Photo State Ptg Wks, Vienna)

1970 (25 Dec). Christmas. Church of the Nativity, Bethlehem. T **140** and similar horiz designs. Multicoloured. P 13½.

932	5f. Type **140**	60	30
933	10f. Christmas crib	1·10	35
934	20f. Crypt altar	1·40	55
935	25f. Nave, Church of the Nativity	1·80	70
932/935	*Set of* 4	4·50	1·70

141 Arab League Flag, Emblem and Map

142 Heads of Four Races and Emblem

(Photo Postal Authority Press, Cairo)

1971 (22 Mar). 25th Anniversary (1970) of Arab League. P 11½×11.

936	**141**	10f. green, violet and red-orange	30	20
937		20f. green, brown and light blue	75	30
938		30f. green, blue and yellow-olive	1·10	40
936/938 *Set of 3*			1·90	80

1971 (15 June). Racial Equality Year. T **142** and similar multicoloured designs. Photo. P 11.

939	5f. Type **142**	45	40
940	10f. 'Plant' and emblem	45	40
941	15f. 'Doves' and emblem (*horiz*)	60	40
939/941 *Set of 3*		1·40	1·10

No. 939 is inscribed 'KINIGDOM' in error.

143 Shore of the Dead Sea

144 Ibn Sina (Avicenna)

1971 (7 Aug). Tourism. T **143** and similar multicoloured designs. Photo. P 13½.

942	5f. Type **143**	60	40
943	30f. Ed Deir Temple, Petra	2·10	85
944	45f. Via Dolorosa, Jerusalem (*vert*)	3·00	1·10
945	60f. River Jordan	5·00	2·40
946	100f. Christmas Bell, Bethlehem (*vert*)	7·25	4·75
942/946 *Set of 5*		16·00	8·50

1971 (7 Sept). Famous Arab Scholars. T **144** and similar vert portraits. Multicoloured. Photo. P 12.

947	5f. Type **144**	45	15
948	10f. Ibn Rushd	60	15
949	20f. Ibn Khaldun	90	30
950	26f. Ibn Tufail	1·50	30
951	30f. Ibn El Haytham	2·30	1·00
947/951 *Set of 5*		5·25	1·70

145 New Headquarters Building

146 Young Pupil

1971 (9 Oct). Inauguration of New Universal Postal Union Headquarters Building, Berne. Photo. P 11½×11.

952	**145**	10f. chocolate, pale turquoise-green and yellow	1·10	40
953		20f. slate-purple, turquoise-green and yellow	1·40	40

1972 (9 Feb). International Education Year. Photo. P 11.

954	**146**	5f. multicoloured	15	15
955		15f. multicoloured	45	15
956		20f. multicoloured	75	30
957		30f. multicoloured	1·70	85
954/957 *Set of 4*			2·75	1·30

147 Mothers and Children

148 Pope Paul VI leaving Church of the Holy Sepulchre, Jerusalem

1972 (22 Feb). Mothers' Day. T **147** and similar multicoloured designs. Photo. P 13½×14 (10f.) or 14×13½ (others).

958	10f. Type **147**	90	40
959	20f. Mother and child (*vert*)	90	40
960	30f. Bedouin mother and child (*vert*)	1·10	40
958/960 *Set of 3*		2·50	1·10

1972 (2 Apr). Easter. T **148** and similar vert designs. Photo. P 14×13½.

(a) POSTAGE

961	30f. Type **148**	1·10	30

(b) AIR

962	60f. The Calvary, Church of the Holy Sepulchre	2·10	70
963	100f. *The Washing of Feet*, Jerusalem	3·75	1·40
961/963 *Set of 3*		6·25	2·20

149 Children and UNICEF Emblem

150 Dove of Peace

1972 (27 May). 25th Anniversary of United Nations Children's Fund. T **149** and similar designs. P 11×11½ (20f.) or 11½×11 (others).

964	10f. greenish blue, deep blue and blackish brown	90	40
965	20f. brown, myrtle-green and bright purple	1·10	40
966	30f. brown, reddish mauve and greenish blue	1·40	40
964/966 *Set of 3*		3·00	1·10

Designs: Vert—20f. Child with toy bricks. Horiz—10f. T **149**; 30f. Nurse holding baby.

1972 (26 June). 25th Anniversary of United Nations (1970). Photo. P 11×11½.

967	**150**	5f. bluish violet, blue-green and yellow	30	30
968		10f. carmine-lake, emerald and yellow	45	30
969		15f. multicoloured	1·10	35
970		20f. multicoloured	1·40	40
971		30f. orange-brown, emerald and yellow	2·50	1·10
967/971 *Set of 15*			5·25	2·20

151 Al Aqsa Mosque and Pilgrims

152 Arab with Kestrel

1972 (21 Aug). Burning of Al Aqsa Mosque (1970). T **151** and similar horiz designs. Multicoloured. Litho. P 14½.

972	30f. Type **151**	3·25	40
973	60f. Mosque in flames	8·25	2·10
974	100f. Mosque interior	11·50	4·25
972/974 *Set of 3*		21·00	6·00

1972 (21 Oct). Jordanian Desert Life. T **152** and similar multicoloured designs. Photo. P 14×13½ (5f.) or 13½×14 (others).

975	5f. Type **152**	90	40
976	10f. Desert bungalow (*horiz*)	90	40
977	15f. Camel trooper, Arab Legion (*horiz*)	90	40
978	20f. Boring operations (*horiz*)	1·40	50
979	25f. Shepherd (*horiz*)	1·40	50
980	30f. Dromedaries at water-trough (*horiz*)	2·40	70
981	35f. Chicken farm (*horiz*)	2·50	1·30
982	45f. Irrigation scheme (*horiz*)	4·00	2·20
975/982	*Set of* 8	13·00	5·75

153 Wasfi el Tell and Dome of the Rock, Jerusalem

154 Clay-pigeon Shooting

1972 (28 Nov). Wasfi el Tell (assassinated statesman) Memorial Issue. T **153** and similar multicoloured design. P 13½.

983	5f. Type **153**	45	15
984	10f. Wasfi el Tell, map and flag (*vert*)	60	30
985	20f. Type **153**	1·40	30
986	30f. As 10f.	1·50	1·10
983/986	*Set of* 4	3·50	1·70

1972 (25 Dec). World Clay-pigeon Shooting Championship. T **154** and similar multicoloured designs. Photo. P 13½.

987	25f. Type **154**	1·10	40
988	75f. Marksman on range (*horiz*)	2·10	1·70
989	120f. Taking aim (*horiz*)	4·00	2·50
987/989	*Set of* 3	6·50	4·25

155 Aero Club Emblem

156 Dove and Flag

1973 (24 Jan). Royal Jordanian Aero Club. T **155** and similar horiz designs. Multicoloured. Photo. P 13½×14.

(a) POSTAGE

990	5f. Type **155**	1·10	40
991	10f. Type **155**	1·10	40

(b) AIR

992	15f. Two Piper PA-28 Cherokee 140 aircraft.	1·10	40
993	20f. Beech B55 Baron aeroplane	1·20	50
994	40f. Winged horse emblem	2·40	1·00
990/994	*Set of* 5	6·25	2·40

1973 (Mar). 50th Anniversary of Hashemite Kingdom of Jordan. T **156** and similar square designs. Multicoloured. Photo. P 11½.

995	5f. Type **156**	15	15
996	10f. Anniversary emblem	45	20
997	15f. King Hussein	1·10	30
998	30f. Map and emblems	2·30	1·80
995/998	*Set of* 4	3·50	2·20

157 Map and Jordanian Advance

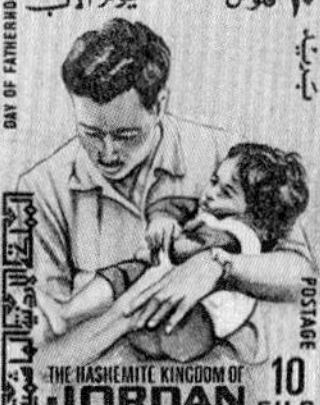

158 Father and Son

1973 (10 Apr). Fifth Anniversary of Battle of Karama. T **157** and similar horiz designs. Multicoloured. Photo. P 11½×11.

999	5f. Type **157**	45	30
1000	10f. Jordanian attack, and map	90	40
1001	15f. Map, and King Hussein on tank	2·30	1·40
999/1001	*Set of* 3	3·25	1·90

1973 (20 Apr). Fathers' Day. T **158** and similar vert designs. Multicoloured. Photo. P 13½.

1002	10f. Type **158**	30	30
1003	20f. Father and daughter	1·10	30
1004	30f. Family group	1·70	70
1002/1004	*Set of* 3	2·75	1·20

159 Phosphate Mines

160 Racing Camel

1973 (25 June). Development Projects. T **159** and similar horiz designs. Multicoloured. Photo. P 13½×14.

1005	5f. Type **159**	60	15
1006	10f. Cement factories	1·10	30
1007	15f. Sharhabil Dam	1·50	30
1008	20f. Kafrein Dam	2·00	70
1005/1008	*Set of* 4	4·75	1·30

1973 (21 July). Camel Racing. T **160** and similar horiz designs. Multicoloured. Photo. P 13½×14.

1009	5f. Type **160**	1·40	40
1010	10f. Camels in paddock	1·40	40
1011	15f. Start of race	1·40	40
1012	20f. Camel racing	1·40	55
1009/1012	*Set of* 4	5·00	1·60

161 Book Year Emblem

1973 (25 Aug). International Book Year (1972). Photo. P 13×13½.

1013	**161**	30f. multicoloured	90	40
1014		60f. multicoloured	2·10	55

162 Family Group

(Photo Rosenbaum Brothers, Vienna)

1973 (18 Sept). Family Day. T **162** and similar horiz designs. Multicoloured. P 13½.

1015	20f. Type **162**	90	40
1016	30f. Family group (*different*)	90	40
1017	60f. Family group (*different*)	1·70	55
1015/1017	*Set of* 3	3·25	1·20

163 Shah of Iran, King Hussein, Cyrus's Tomb and Mosque of Omar

1973 (12 Oct). 2,500th Anniversary of Iranian Monarchy. Litho. P 13.

1018	**163**	5f. multicoloured	90	30
1019		10f. multicoloured	1·20	35
1020		15f. multicoloured	1·40	40
1021		30f. multicoloured	3·25	1·00
1018/1021		*Set of* 4	6·00	1·80

164 Emblem of Palestine Week

(Photo Postal Authority Press, Cairo)

1973 (15 Nov). Palestine Week. T **164** and similar multicoloured designs. P 11 (15f.) or 11½×11 (others).

1022	5f. Type **164**	75	40
1023	10f. Torch and emblem	1·10	50
1024	15f. Refugees (26×47 *mm*)	1·20	55
1025	30f. Children and map on Globe	2·75	85
1022/1025	*Set of* 4	5·25	2·10

165 Traditional Harvesting **166** Long-nosed Butterflyfish

(Photo Rosenbaum Brothers, Vienna)

1973 (25 Dec). Ancient and Modern Agriculture. T **165** and similar horiz designs. Multicoloured. P 13½.

(a) POSTAGE

1026	5f. Type **165**	30	30
1027	10f. Modern harvesting	45	30
1028	15f. Traditional seeding	90	35
1029	20f. Modern seeding	1·40	35
1030	30f. Traditional ploughing	1·50	40
1031	35f. Modern ploughing	1·80	40
1032	45f. Pest control	2·30	50
1033	60f. Horticulture	4·00	1·80

(b) AIR

1034	100f. Agricultural landscape	4·50	2·10
1026/1034	*Set of* 9	15·00	5·75

(Photo Rosenbaum Brothers, Vienna)

1974 (15 Feb). Red Sea Fish. T **166** and similar horiz designs. Multicoloured. P 14.

1035	5f. Type **166**	75	30
1036	10f. Monacle Bream	90	30
1037	15f. As No. 1036	1·10	30
1038	20f. Slender-spined Mojarra	1·40	40
1039	25f. As No. 1038	1·90	75
1040	30f. Russell's Snapper	3·00	85
1041	35f. As No. 1040	3·50	1·40
1042	40f. Blue-barred Orange Parrotfish	4·25	1·50
1043	45f. As No. 1042	4·50	1·70
1044	50f. As No. 1035	7·50	1·80
1045	60f. Yellow-edged Lyretail	9·50	2·40
1035/1045	*Set of* 11	34·00	10·50

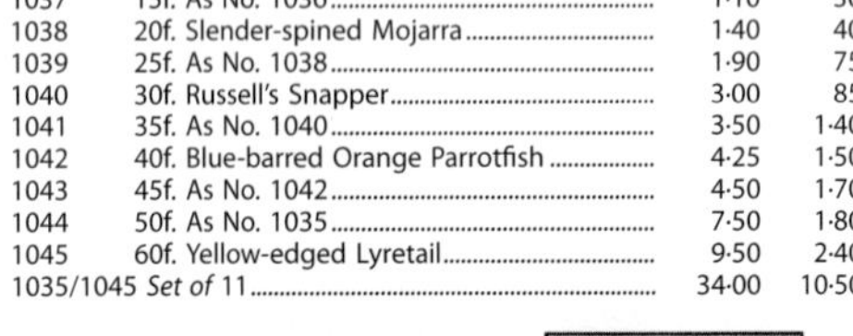

167 Battle of Muta **168** *The Club-footed Boy* (Murillo)

(Photo Rosenbaum Brothers, Vienna)

1974 (15 Mar). Islamic Battles against the Crusaders. T **167** and similar horiz designs. Multicoloured. P 13½.

1046	10f. Type **167**	90	30
1047	20f. Battle of Yarmouk	2·30	55
1048	30f. Battle of Hattin	3·75	1·50
1046/1048	*Set of* 3	6·25	2·10

(Photo Rosenbaum Brothers, Vienna)

1974 (15 Apr). Paintings. T **168** and similar multicoloured designs. P 13½×14 (40f., 60f.) or 14×13½ (others).

1049	5f. Type **168**	2·00	55
1050	10f. *Praying Hands* (Dürer)	2·00	55
1051	15f. *St. George and the Dragon* (Uccello)	2·00	55
1052	20f. *The Mona Lisa* (Da Vinci)	2·00	55
1053	30f. *Hope* (Watts)	2·00	55
1054	40f. *The Angelus* (Millet) (*horiz*)	2·40	65
1055	50f. *The Artist and her Daughter* (Angelica Kaufhnann)	3·00	70
1056	60f. *Whistler's Mother* (J. Whistler) (*horiz*)	4·50	1·50
1057	100f. *Master Hare* (Reynolds)	6·25	2·50
1049/1057	*Set of* 9	24·00	7·25

المؤتمر الدولي لتاريخ بلاد الشام
٢٠ – ١٩٧٤/٤/٢٥
الجامعة الاردنية

(**169**)

170 UPU Emblem

1974 (20 Apr). International Conference for Damascus History. Nos. 1013/1014 optd with T **169**.

1058	**161**	30f. multicoloured	90	55
1059		60f. multicoloured	2·10	1·30

(Photo Enschedé)

1974 (15 May). Centenary of Universal Postal Union. P 13×12½.

1060	**170**	10f. gold, yellow-green, yellowish green and reddish brown	60	55
1061		30f. gold, new blue, blue and violet	90	65
1062		60f. gold, magenta, bright carmine and black	1·70	70
		a. Bright carmine (face value) omitted	£300	
1060/1062		*Set of* 3	3·00	1·70

171 Camel Caravan **172** WPY Emblem

(Photo Rosenbaum Brothers, Vienna)

1974 (25 June). The Dead Sea. T **171** and similar multicoloured designs. P 14.

1063	2f. Type **171**	30	15
1064	3f. Palm and shore	45	15
1065	4f. Hotel on coast	60	15
1066	5f. Jars from Qumran Caves	1·10	55
1067	6f. Copper scrolls (*vert*)	1·20	55
1068	10f. Cistern steps, Qumran (*vert*)	1·40	55
1069	20f. Type **171**	1·50	30
1070	30f. As 3f.	2·10	40
1071	40f. As 4f.	2·30	85
1072	50f. As 5f.	3·00	70
1073	60f. As 6f.	3·75	85
1074	100f. As 10f.	6·00	1·30
1063/1074	*Set of* 12	21·00	5·75

1974 (20 Aug). World Population Year. Photo. P 11.

1075	**172**	5f. plum, emerald and black	30	15
1076		10f. carmine-red, emerald and black	45	30
1077		20f. yellow-orange, emerald and black	1·10	40
1075/1077		*Set of* 3	1·70	75

173 Water-skier **174** Kaaba, Mecca, and Pilgrims

(Photo Rosenbaum Brothers, Vienna)

1974 (20 Sept). Water-skiing. T **173** and similar multicoloured designs. P 14×13½ (5f., 50f.) or 13½×14 (others).

1078	5f. Type **173**	60	55
1079	10f. Water-skier, side view (*horiz*)	60	55
1080	20f. Skier turning (*horiz*)	60	55
1081	50f. Type **173**	1·20	70
1082	100f. As 10f.	2·10	1·00
1083	200f. As 20f.	4·50	2·00
1078/1083	*Set of* 6	8·75	4·75

(Photo Postal Authority Press, Cairo)

1974 (Nov). Pilgrimage Season. P 11.

1084	**174**	10f. multicoloured	45	30
1085		20f. multicoloured	1·40	85

175 Amrah Palace

176 King Hussein at Wheel of Car

1974 (25 Nov). Desert Ruins. T **175** and similar horiz designs. Multicoloured. Photo. P 13×13½.

1086	10f. Type **175**	45	30
1087	20f. Hisham Palace	1·10	85
1088	30f. Kharana Castle	2·75	1·30
1086/1088	*Set of* 3	3·75	2·20

1974 (20 Dec). AIR. Royal Jordanian Automobile Club. Photo. P 12.

1089	**176**	30f. multicoloured	90	30
1090		60f. multicoloured	2·75	1·40

177 Woman in Costume

178 Treasury, Petra

179 King Hussein

1975 (1 Feb). Jordanian Women's Costumes. T **177** and similar vert designs. Photo. P 12.

1091	5f. multicoloured (Type **177**)	30	15
1092	10f. multicoloured	45	20
1093	15f. multicoloured	90	30
1094	20f. multicoloured	1·40	40
1095	25f. multicoloured	1·80	1·00
1091/1095	*Set of* 5	4·25	1·80

(Photo Rosenbaum Brothers, Vienna)

1975 (1 Mar). Tourism. T **178** and similar multicoloured designs. P 14×13½ (15f., 50f.) or 13½×14 (others).

(a) POSTAGE

1096	15f. Type **178**	1·50	55
1097	20f. Omayyad Palace, Amman (*horiz*)	1·50	55
1098	30f. Dome of the Rock, Jerusalem (*horiz*)	2·10	65
1099	40f. Forum columns, Jerash (*horiz*)	2·75	70

(b) AIR. Inscr 'AIRMAIL'

1100	50f. Palms, Aqaba	2·10	70
1101	60f. Obelisk Tomb, Petra (*horiz*)	3·25	85
1102	80f. Fort of Wadi Rum (*horiz*)	3·50	90
1096/1102	*Set of* 7	15·00	4·50

1975 (8 Apr). Photo.

(a) Size 19×24 mm

1103	**179**	5f. indigo and green	45	15
1104		10f. indigo and violet	45	15
1105		15f. indigo and rose	15	15
1106		20f. indigo and bistre-brown	90	30
1107		25f. indigo and ultramarine	90	30
1108		30f. indigo and red-brown	30	30
1109		35f. indigo and reddish violet	45	30
1110		40f. indigo and rose-red	1·10	40
1111		45f. indigo and deep mauve	60	40
1112		50f. indigo and blue-green	60	40

(b) Size 22×27 mm

1113	**179**	60f. brown and myrtle-green	2·00	70
1114		100f. brown and orange-brown	3·25	85
1115		120f. brown and blue	1·70	1·30
1116		180f. brown and magenta	2·75	1·80
1117		200f. brown and turquoise-blue	3·25	2·50
1118		400f. brown and purple	5·50	4·25
1119		500f. brown and orange-red	7·00	6·25
1103/1119		*Set of* 17	28·00	18·00

180 Globe and 'Desert'

182 Emblem of Chamber

181 Satellite and Earth Station

(Photo Postal Authority Press, Cairo)

1975 (15 June). Tenth Anniversary of ALIA (Royal Jordanian Airlines). T **180** and similar multicoloured designs. P 11×11½ (30f.) or 11½×11 (others).

1120	10f. Type **180**	45	15
1121	30f. Boeing 707 airliner linking globe and map of Jordan (*horiz*)	1·50	55
1122	60f. Globe and ALIA logo	3·00	1·30
1120/1122	*Set of* 3	4·50	1·80

1975 (1 Aug). Opening of Satellite Earth Station. Photo. P 11.

1123	**181**	20f. multicoloured	1·20	30
1124		30f. multicoloured	2·10	1·00

1975 (15 Oct). 50th Anniversary of Amman Chamber of Commerce. Photo. P 11.

1125	**182**	10f. multicoloured	30	30
1126		15f. multicoloured	60	30
1127		20f. multicoloured	90	55
1125/1127		*Set of* 3	1·40	1·00

183 Emblem and Hand with Spanner

1975 (Nov). Completion of Three Year Development Plan. Photo. P 11½.

1128	**183**	5f. black, red and green	30	30
1129		10f. black, red and green	45	40
1130		20f. black, red and green	1·10	55
1128/1130		*Set of* 3	1·70	1·10

184 Jordanian Family

185 ALO Emblem and Salt Mine

(Des M. el Zoghbi and R. Lahham. Litho)

1976 (27 Apr). International Women's Year (1975). T **184** and similar horiz designs. Multicoloured. P 14.

1131	5f. Type **184**	15	15
1132	25f. Woman scientist	90	40
1133	60f. Woman graduate	2·40	1·30
1131/1133 *Set of 3*		3·00	1·70

(Des M. el Zoghbi. Litho)

1976 (1 June). Arab Labour Organisation. T **185** and similar vert designs. Multicoloured. P 14.

1134	10f. Type **185**	75	55
1135	30f. Welding	75	55
1136	60f. Quayside, Aqaba	1·50	70
1134/1136 *Set of 3*		2·75	1·60

25 Fils ٢٥ فلسا

(**186**)

1976 (18 July). Nos. 853/882 ('Tragedy of the Refugees') surch in English and Arabic as T **186**.

1137/1146	25f. on 1f. to 10f.		
1147/1149	40f. on 11f. to 13f.		
1150	40f. on 14f.		
	a. Arabic numeral in place of '40'	£110	
1151	40f. on 15f.		
1152/1156	50f. on 16f. to 20f.		
1157/1161	75f. on 21f. to 25f.		
1162/1166	125f. on 26f. to 30f.		
1137/1166 *Set of 30*		£250	£250

The overprint on Nos. 1137/1141 (25f. on 1f. to 5f.) differs from T **186** in the figure '25', and in the size of 'Fils' which is smaller.

No. 1150a occurs on Row 1, stamp 2 of the sheet of ten.

1976 (18 July). Nos. 883/912 ('Tragedy in the Holy Lands') surch in English and Arabic as T **186**.

1167/1176	25f. on 1f. to 10f.		
1177/1179	40f. on 11f. to 13f.		
1180	40f. on 14f.		
	a. Arabic numeral in place of '40'	£110	
1181	40f. on 15f.		
1182/1186	50f. on 16f. to 20f.		
1187/1191	75f. on 21f. to 25f.		
1192/1196	125f. on 26f. to 30f.		
1167/1196 Set of 30		£250	£250

No. 1180a occurs on Row 1, stamp 2 of the sheet of ten.

187 Tennis

188 Shu'aib Dam

1976 (1 Nov). Sports and Youth. T **187** and similar horiz designs. Multicoloured. Litho. P 14×13½.

1197	5f. Type **187**	30	15
1198	10f. Body-building	45	20
1199	15f. Football	60	30
1200	20f. Show jumping	90	35
1201	30f. Weightlifting	1·50	55
1202	100f. Sports Stadium, Amman	6·00	3·00
1197/1202 *Set of 6*		8·75	4·00

1976 (7 Dec). Dams. T **188** and similar horiz designs. Multicoloured. Photo. P 14×13½.

1203	30f. Type **188**	1·20	55
1204	60f. Al-Kafrein Dam	2·40	70
1205	100f. Ziqlab Dam	4·00	1·30
1203/1205 *Set of 3*		6·75	2·30

189 Early and Modern Telephones

190 Road Crossing and Traffic Lights

1977 (17 Feb). Telephone Centenary (1976). T **189** and similar vert designs. Multicoloured. Litho. P 11½×12.

1206	75f. Type **189**	2·30	1·30
1207	125f. Early telephone and modern receiver	3·75	2·10

(Des M. el Zoghbi. Photo State Ptg Wks, Budapest)

1977 (4 May). International Traffic Day. T **190** and similar horiz designs. Multicoloured. P 11×12.

1208	5f. Type **190**	1·10	40
1209	75f. Traffic lights and roundabout	3·25	1·50
1210	125f. Traffic lights, road signs and motorcycle policeman	5·00	2·10
1208/1210 *Set of 3*		8·50	3·50

191 Airliner over Liner

192 Child, Toys and Money-box

(Des M. el Zoghbi. Litho State Ptg Wks, Budapest)

1977 (11 Aug). Silver Jubilee of King Hussein. T **191** and similar horiz designs. Multicoloured. P 11½×12.

1211	10f. Type **191**	30	15
1212	25f. Pylons and factories	60	30
1213	40f. Fertiliser plant	90	35
1214	50f. Ground-to-air missile	1·20	55
1215	75f. Mosque	2·10	1·00
1216	125f. Ground satellite receiving aerial	3·25	2·00
1211/1216 *Set of 6*		7·50	4·00
MS1217 100×70 mm. 100f. Silver Jubilee emblem. Imperf		15·00	14·50

(Des M. el Zoghbi. Litho State Ptg Wks, Budapest)

1977 (1 Sept). Postal Savings Bank. T **192** and similar vert designs. Multicoloured. P 11½×12.

1218	10f. Type **192**	15	15
1219	25f. Child with piggy-bank	60	30
1220	50f. Savings Bank emblem	1·40	55
1221	75f. Boy and bank teller	2·75	1·30
1218/1221 *Set of 4*		4·50	2·10

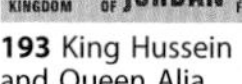

193 King Hussein and Queen Alia

194 Queen Alia

(Des M. el Zoghbi. Litho State Ptg Wks, Budapest)

1977 (1 Nov). P 11½×12.

1222	**193**	10f. multicoloured	30	30
1223		25f. multicoloured	60	30
1224		40f. multicoloured	1·10	40
1225		50f. multicoloured	1·40	85
1222/1225 *Set of 4*			3·00	1·70

(Des M. el Zoghbi. Litho State Ptg Wks, Budapest)

1977 (1 Dec). Queen Alia Commemoration. P 11½×12.

1226	**194**	10f. multicoloured	30	30
1227		25f. multicoloured	60	30
1228		40f. multicoloured	1·10	40
1229		50f. multicoloured	1·40	85
1226/1229 *Set of 4*			3·00	1·70

195 Mohammed Ali Jinnah

196 APU Emblem and Flags

(Des M. el Zoghbi. Litho State Ptg Wks, Budapest)

1977 (20 Dec). Birth Centenary of Mohammed Ali Jinnah (first Governor-General of Pakistan). P 11½.

1230 **195** 25f. multicoloured ... 1·10 40
1231 75f. multicoloured ... 3·00 1·10

(Des M. el Zoghbi. Litho State Ptg Wks, Budapest)

1978 (12 Apr). 25th Anniversary of Arab Postal Union (1977). P 12×11.

1232 **196** 25f. multicoloured ... 1·20 70
1233 40f. multicoloured ... 2·00 1·30

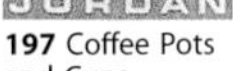

197 Coffee Pots and Cups

198 Roman Amphitheatre, Jerash

(Des M. el Zoghbi. Photo State Ptg Wks, Budapest)

1978 (30 May). Handicrafts. T **197** and similar vert designs. Multicoloured. P 11½×12.

1234 25f. Type **197** ... 60 30
1235 40f. Porcelain plate and ashtray ... 90 35
1236 75f. Vase, necklace and chains ... 2·10 85
1237 125f. Containers holding pipes ... 3·25 2·10
1234/1237 *Set of 4* ... 6·25 3·25

(Des M. el Zoghbi. Litho State Ptg Wks, Budapest)

1978 (30 July). Tourism. T **198** and similar horiz designs. Multicoloured. P 12.

1238 5f. Type **198** ... 90 40
1239 20f. Roman columns, Jerash ... 90 40
1240 40f. Roman mosaic, Madaba ... 1·20 55
1241 75f. Rock formations, Rum ... 2·75 1·10
1238/1241 *Set of 4* ... 5·25 2·20

199 King Hussein and President Sadat

200 Cement Works

(Des M. el Zoghbi. Litho State Ptg Wks, Budapest)

1978 (20 Aug). Visits of Arab Leaders to Jordan. T **199** and similar horiz designs. Multicoloured. P 11½×12 (No. 1242) or 12×11½. (others).

1242 40f. Type **199** ... 90 30
1243 40f. King Hussein and President Assad ... 90 30
1244 40f. King Hussein and King Khalid ... 90 30
1242/1244 *Set of 3* ... 2·40 80

(Des M. el Zoghbi. Litho State Ptg Wks, Budapest)

1978 (25 Sept). Industrial Development. T **200** and similar horiz designs. Multicoloured. P 12.

1245 5f. Type **200** ... 15 15
1246 10f. Science laboratory ... 60 30
1247 25f. Printing press ... 1·50 40
1248 75f. Fertiliser plant ... 3·75 1·40
1245/1248 *Set of 4* ... 5·50 2·00

201 UNESCO Emblem

202 King Hussein

(Des M. el Zoghbi. Litho State Ptg Wks, Budapest)

1978 (5 Dec). 30th Anniversary of United Nations Educational, Scientific and Cultural Organisation. P 12×11½.

1249 **201** 40f. multicoloured ... 1·20 85
1250 75f. multicoloured ... 2·75 1·80

1979 (9 July). Dated 1979. Litho. P 13½×13.

1251 **202** 25f. bistre-brown, flesh and blue ... 90 30
1252 40f. bistre-brown, flesh and bright purple ... 1·50 35

See Nos. 1265/1272 and 1309/1313.

203 Emblems within Cogwheels

204 IYC Emblem and Flag of Jordan

(Des M. el Zoghbi. Litho De La Rue)

1979 (25 Oct). Five Year Development Plan. P 12½×12.

1253 **203** 25f. multicoloured ... 75 30
1254 40f. multicoloured ... 1·10 35
1255 50f. multicoloured ... 1·20 70
1253/1255 *Set of 3* ... 2·75 1·20

(Des B. Abu Bakr. Litho De La Rue)

1979 (15 Nov). International Year of the Child. P 12×12½.

1256 **204** 25f. multicoloured ... 90 40
1257 40f. multicoloured ... 1·40 50
1258 50f. multicoloured ... 2·10 55
1256/1258 *Set of 3* ... 4·00 1·30

205 Census Emblem

206 Nurse holding Baby

(Des K. el Dairy. Litho De La Rue)

1979 (25 Dec). Population and Housing Census. P 12½×12.

1259 **205** 25f. multicoloured ... 60 30
1260 40f. multicoloured ... 1·10 35
1261 50f. multicoloured ... 1·50 70
1259/1261 *Set of 3* ... 3·00 1·20

(Litho De La Rue)

1980 (12 May). International Nursing Day. P 12×12½.

1262 **206** 25f. multicoloured ... 90 30
1263 40f. multicoloured ... 1·50 55
1264 50f. multicoloured ... 1·80 1·00
1262/1264 *Set of 3* ... 3·75 1·70

(Litho Harrison)

1980 (3 Sept–Dec). T **202** redrawn. Dated 1980. P 13.

1265 **202** 5f. bistre-brown, flesh and emerald ... 30 30
1266 10f. bistre-brown, flesh and reddish violet ... 30 30
1267 20f. bistre-brown and flesh ... 30 30
1268 25f. bistre-brown, flesh and bright blue (16.12) ... 45 40
1269 40f. bistre-brown, flesh and magenta (16.12) ... 1·10 50
1270 50f. bistre-brown, flesh and turquoise-green (16.12) ... 1·20 1·00

1271	75f. bistre-brown, flesh and slate	1·20	70
1272	125f. bistre-brown, flesh and rosine	3·75	1·10
1265/1272 *Set of 8*		7·75	4·25

In addition to the date, the redrawn design differs from Nos. 1251/1252 in the word 'FILS', which is larger, in the shading and in minor details of the design. On Nos. 1268/1269 the figures of value have also been redrawn.

Nos. 1268/1270 were issued only in booklets.

207 El-Deir Temple, Petra

208 Mosque and Kaaba, Mecca

(Des R. Lahham. Litho Harrison)

1980 (27 Sept). World Tourism Conference, Manila. P 14½×14.

1273	**207**	25f. black, drab and blue-green	90	40
1274		40f. black, drab and pale blue	1·70	55
1275		50f. black, drab and claret	2·10	70
1273/1275 *Set of 3*			4·25	1·50

(Litho Harrison)

1980 (11 Nov). 1400th Anniversary of Hegira. P 14×14½.

1276	**208**	25f. multicoloured	45	40
1277		40f. multicoloured	1·10	55
1278		50f. multicoloured	1·40	70
1279		75f. multicoloured	2·40	1·10
1280		100f. multicoloured	2·40	1·50
1276/1280 *Set of 5*			7·00	3·75
MS1281 127×89 mm. Nos. 1276/1280. Imperf			11·50	11·00

209 Conference Emblem

210 Picking Crops, examining Patients and Flag-raising Ceremony

(Litho Harrison)

1980 (25 Nov). 11th Arab Summit Conference, Amman. P 14½×14.

1282	**209**	25f. multicoloured	45	40
1283		40f. multicoloured	90	55
1284		50f. multicoloured	1·20	70
1285		75f. multicoloured	2·00	1·10
1286		100f. multicoloured	2·40	1·50
1282/1286 *Set of 5*			6·25	3·75
MS1287 100×100 mm. Nos. 1282/1286. Imperf			11·50	11·00

(Litho Harrison)

1981 (8 May). Red Crescent. P 14×14½.

1288	**210**	25f. multicoloured	1·10	40
1289		40f. multicoloured	1·40	70
1290		50f. multicoloured	1·50	85
1288/1290 *Set of 3*			3·50	1·80

211 ITU and WHO Emblems and Ribbons forming Caduceus

212 Jordan Stamps of 1934 and 1975

(Des M. el Zoghbi. Litho Bradbury Wilkinson)

1981 (17 June). World Telecommunications Day. P 14×14½.

1291	**211**	25f. multicoloured	1·10	40
1292		40f. multicoloured	1·80	70
1293		50f. multicoloured	2·40	1·30
1291/1293 *Set of 3*			4·75	2·20

(Litho Harrison)

1981 (1 July). Opening of Postal Museum. T **212** and similar multicoloured designs. P 14½×13½ (40f.) or 13½×14½ (others).

1294	25f. Type **212**	1·10	30
1295	40f. Jordan stamps of 1933 and 1954 (*vert*)	1·50	55
1296	50f. Jordan stamps of 1946 and 1952	2·10	1·00
1294/1296 *Set of 3*		4·25	1·70

213 Khawla Bint el-Azwar

214 FAO Emblem and Olive Branches

(Des M. Muraish. Litho Harrison)

1981 (25 Aug). Arab Women in History. T **213** and similar vert designs. Multicoloured. P 14½×13½.

1297	25f. Type **213**	1·50	40
1298	40f. El-Khansa (writer)	2·50	70
1299	50f. Rabia el-Adawiyeh (Sufi religious leader)	4·25	2·00
1297/1299 *Set of 3*		7·50	2·75

(Des M. el Zoghbi. Litho Bradbury Wilkinson)

1981 (16 Oct). World Food Day. P 14×14½.

1300	**214**	25f. multicoloured	75	40
1301		40f. multicoloured	1·40	70
1302		50f. multicoloured	1·70	70
1300/1302 *Set of 3*			3·50	1·60

215 IYDP Emblem

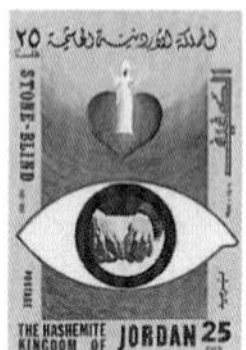

216 Hands reading Braille

(Des M. el Zoghbi. Litho Bradbury Wilkinson)

1981 (14 Nov). International Year of Disabled Persons. P 14½×14.

1303	**215**	25f. multicoloured	75	40
1304		40f. multicoloured	1·70	55
1305		50f. multicoloured	2·10	70
1303/1305 *Set of 3*			4·00	1·50

(Des M. el Zoghbi. Litho Bradbury Wilkinson)

1981 (14 Nov). The Blind. P 14×14½.

1306	**216**	25f. multicoloured	75	40
1307		40f. multicoloured	1·70	55
1308		50f. multicoloured	2·10	70
1306/1308 *Set of 3*			4·00	1·50

(Litho State Ptg Wks, Moscow)

1982 (18 Jan). T **202** redrawn again. Dated 1981. P 12½.

1309	**202**	5f. olive-sepia, flesh and light green	40	30
1310		10f. olive-sepia, flesh and bright reddish violet	45	30
1311		20f. olive-sepia and flesh	55	30
1312		25f. olive-sepia, flesh and ultramarine	60	30
1313		40f. olive-sepia, flesh and bright purple	90	40
1309/1313 *Set of 5*			2·50	1·40

217 Hand holding Jug and Stone Tablet

218 APU Emblem

(Des M. el Zoghbi. Litho Bradbury Wilkinson)

1982 (10 Mar). Jordan Monuments. P 14×14½.

1314	**217**	25f. multicoloured	1·10	30
1315		40f. multicoloured	1·70	40
1316		50f. multicoloured	2·10	1·00
1314/1316 *Set of* 3			4·50	1·50

(Des M. el Zoghbi. Litho Bradbury Wilkinson)

1982 (12 Apr). 30th Anniversary of Arab Postal Union. P 14×14½.

1317	**218**	10f. multicoloured	90	40
1318		25f. multicoloured	1·20	50
1319		40f. multicoloured	1·70	55
1320		50f. multicoloured	2·10	70
1321		100f. multicoloured	4·25	1·40
1317/1321 *Set of* 5			9·25	3·25

219 King Hussein and Jet Fighter

220 Salt Secondary School

(Des M. el Zoghbi. Litho Bradbury Wilkinson)

1982 (25 May). Independence, Army Day and 30th Anniversary of King Hussein's Accession to Throne. T **219** and similar horiz designs. Multicoloured. P 14½×14.

1322	10f. King Hussein and rockets	45	30
1323	25f. King Hussein and tanks	90	35
1324	40f. Type **219**	1·70	55
1325	50f. King Hussein and tanks (*different*)	2·10	1·00
1326	100f. King Hussein and flag being hoisted by armed forces	4·25	2·75
1322/1326 *Set of* 5		8·50	4·50

Nos. 1322/1323 and 1325/1326 show King Hussein in army uniform.

(Des M. el Zoghbi. Litho Bradbury Wilkinson)

1982 (12 Sept). Salt Secondary School. P 14½×14.

1327	**220**	10f. multicoloured	75	40
1328		25f. multicoloured	1·10	50
1329		40f. multicoloured	1·70	55
1330		50f. multicoloured	1·80	85
1331		100f. multicoloured	3·50	1·40
1327/1331 *Set of* 5			8·00	3·25

221 City Gate, Jerusalem

222 Soldiers, Flags and Badge

(Des M. el Zoghbi. Litho Bradbury Wilkinson)

1982 (14 Nov). Jerusalem. T **221** and similar vert designs. Multicoloured. P 14×14½.

1332	10f. Type **221**	45	40
1333	25f. Minaret	1·50	70
1334	40f. Mosque	2·40	1·30
1335	50f. Mosque (*different*)	2·75	1·40
1336	100f. Dome of the Rock	6·00	3·00
1332/1336 *Set of* 5		12·00	6·00

(Des M. el Zoghbi. Litho Bradbury Wilkinson)

1982 (14 Nov). Yarmouk Forces. P 14½×14.

1337	**222**	10f. multicoloured	45	15
1338		25f. multicoloured	90	30
1339		40f. multicoloured	1·50	55
1340		50f. multicoloured	1·80	1·00
1341		100f. multicoloured	3·25	2·20
1337/1341 *Set of* 5			7·00	3·75
MS1342 71×51 mm. 100f. multicoloured (Forces badge). Imperf			26·00	25·00

223 Dish Aerial, Earth and UN Emblem

224 King Abdullah and Dome of the Rock

(Des M. el Zoghbi. Litho Bradbury Wilkinson)

1982 (1 Dec). Second United Nations Conference on the Exploration and Peaceful Uses of Outer Space, Vienna. P 14½×14.

1343	**223**	10f. multicoloured	45	15
1344		25f. multicoloured	90	30
1345		40f. multicoloured	1·50	55
1346		50f. multicoloured	1·80	1·00
1347		100f. multicoloured	3·25	2·50
1343/1347 *Set of* 5			7·00	4·00

(Des and litho Bradbury Wilkinson)

1982 (13 Dec). Birth Centenary of King Abdullah. P 14½.

1348	**224**	10f. multicoloured	45	15
1349		25f. multicoloured	90	30
1350		40f. multicoloured	1·50	55
1351		50f. multicoloured	1·80	1·00
1352		100f. multicoloured	3·25	2·50
1348/1352 *Set of* 5			7·00	4·00

225 King Hussein and Temple Colonnade

226 King Hussein

(Des M. el Zoghbi. Litho Bradbury Wilkinson)

1982 (29 Dec). Roman Ruins at Jerash. T **225** and similar horiz designs. Multicoloured. P 15.

1353	10f. Type **225**	1·20	55
1354	25f. Archway	1·50	55
1355	40f. Temple of Artemis	2·10	70
1356	50f. Amphitheatre	2·75	70
1357	100f. Hippodrome	5·50	1·50
1353/1357 *Set of* 5		12·00	3·50

(Des M. el Zoghbi. Litho Harrison)

1983 (1 Feb–Mar). P 14½×14.

1358	**226**	10f. multicoloured	45	40
1359		25f. multicoloured (3.3)	45	40
1360		40f. multicoloured (8.2)	75	55
1361		60f. multicoloured	1·20	70
1362		100f. multicoloured (3.3)	1·80	1·10
1363		125f. multicoloured (3.3)	2·40	1·30
1358/1363 *Set of* 6			6·25	4·00

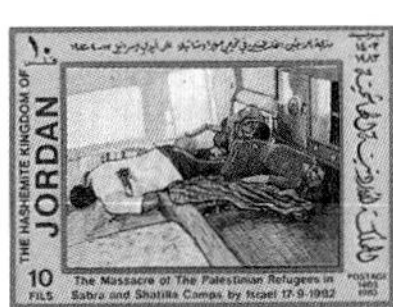

227 Massacre Victims

228 Control Tower and Airport Buildings

(Des M. el Zoghbi. Litho Bradbury Wilkinson)

1983 (9 Apr). Massacre of Palestinian Refugees in Sabra and Shatila Camps, Lebanon. T **227** and similar horiz designs. Multicoloured. P 14½.

1364	10f. Type **227**	45	30
1365	25f. Covered bodies	1·40	35
1366	40f. Orphans	2·00	55
1367	50f. Massacre victims in street	2·75	1·10
1368	100f. Massacre victims (*different*)	4·50	2·75
1364/1368 *Set of* 5		10·00	4·50
MS1369 80×59 mm. 100f. Wounded child in hospital. Imperf (*sold at* 1500f.)		30·00	29·00

(Des B. Ammari. Litho State Ptg Wks, Budapest)

1983 (25 May). Opening of Queen Alia International Airport. T **228** and similar horiz designs. Multicoloured. P 12.

1370	10f. Type **228**	45	15
1371	25f. Tower and terminal building	1·20	30
1372	40f. Tower and hangar	2·00	55
1373	50f. Tower and aerial view of airport	2·40	1·10
1374	100f. Tower and embarkation bridge	4·50	2·75
1370/1374	*Set of 5*	9·50	4·25

229 King Hussein and Radio Equipment

230 Academy Building, Amman

(Des B. Ammari. Litho State Ptg Wks, Budapest)

1983 (11 Aug). Royal Jordanian Radio Amateurs Society. P 12.

1375 **229**	10f. multicoloured	45	15
1376	25f. multicoloured	1·20	30
1377	40f. multicoloured	1·80	55
1378	50f. multicoloured	2·00	1·10
1379	100f. multicoloured	4·00	2·75
1375/1379	*Set of 5*	8·50	4·25

(Des B. Ammari, F. el Afghani and M. el Qaddoumi. Litho State Ptg Wks, Budapest)

1983 (16 Sept). Establishment of Royal Academy for Islamic Civilisation Research. T **230** and similar horiz designs. Multicoloured. P 12.

1380	10f. Type **230**	60	55
1381	25f. Silk rug	1·20	70
1382	40f. View of Amman	1·80	1·10
1383	50f. Panorama of Jerusalem	2·10	1·40
1384	100f. Holy sites of Islam	4·75	2·75
1380/1384	*Set of 5*	9·50	5·75
MS1385	80×60 mm. 100f. Letter from Mohammed to Heraclius. Imperf	26·00	25·00

231 Irrigation Canal

232 Switchboard and Emblem

(Des M. el Qaddoumi. Litho State Ptg Wks, Budapest)

1983 (16 Oct). Food Security. T **231** and similar horiz designs. Multicoloured. P 12.

1386	10f. Type **231**	45	30
1387	25f. Growing crops under glass	1·20	30
1388	40f. Battery hens	2·00	55
1389	50f. Harvesting	2·30	1·00
1390	100f. Flock of sheep	4·00	2·75
1386/1390	*Set of 5*	9·00	4·50

(Des M. el Qaddoumi, B. Ammari and M. el Zoghbi. Litho State Ptg Wks, Budapest)

1983 (14 Nov). World Communications Year. T **232** and similar horiz designs. Multicoloured. P 12.

1391	10f. Type **232**	90	50
1392	25f. Aerial view of satellite receiving station	1·40	55
1393	40f. Antenna and communication emblems	2·00	65
1394	50f. WCY emblems	2·50	70
1395	100f. Airmail letter	5·25	1·70
1391/1395	*Set of 5*	11·00	3·75

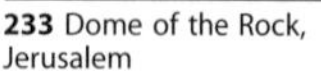

233 Dome of the Rock, Jerusalem

234 Human Rights Emblems

(Des M. el Qaddoumi. Litho State Ptg Wks, Budapest)

1983 (29 Nov). Palestinian Welfare. P 12.

1396 **233**	5f. multicoloured	90	55
1397	10f. multicoloured	1·80	70

(Des M. el Qaddoumi. Litho State Ptg Wks, Budapest)

1983 (10 Dec). 35th Anniversary of Human Rights Declaration. P 12.

1398 **234**	10f. multicoloured	45	15
1399	25f. multicoloured	1·20	30
1400	40f. multicoloured	1·80	55
1401	50f. multicoloured	2·00	1·10
1402	100f. multicoloured	3·75	2·75
1398/1402	*Set of 5*	8·25	4·25

235 Campaign Emblem

236 Bomb and Cogwheel

(Des M. el Qaddoumi. Litho State Ptg Wks, Budapest)

1984 (7 Apr). Anti-Poliomyelitis Campaign. P 13½×11½.

1403 **235**	40f. orange, black and ultramarine	1·70	40
1404	60f. silver, black and carmine	2·75	1·10
1405	100f. myrtle green, black and bright lemon	4·50	2·40
1403/1405	*Set of 3*	8·00	3·50

(Des M. el Zoghbi. Litho State Ptg Wks, Budapest)

1984 (7 June). Israel's Attack on Iraqi Nuclear Reactor. T **236** and similar horiz designs. Multicoloured. P 13½×11½.

1406	40f. Type **236**	2·30	70
1407	60f. Hand with dagger attacking nuclear symbol	3·00	85
1408	100f. Aircraft bombing nuclear symbol	4·50	1·50
1406/1408	*Set of 3*	8·75	2·75

237 King Hussein and Tanks

238 Sports Pictograms

(Des M. el Qaddoumi and M. el Zoghbi. Litho State Ptg Wks,Budapest)

1984 (10 June). Independence and Army Day. T **237** and similar horiz designs. Multicoloured. P 13½×11½.

1409	10f. Type **237**	45	30
1410	25f. King and Naval patrol boat	1·20	35
1411	40f. King and Camel Corps	2·00	55
1412	60f. King and soldiers at Independence Monument	3·00	1·10
1413	100f. Parading soldiers	4·00	2·75
1409/1413	*Set of 5*	9·50	4·50

(Des B. Ammari and M. el Zoghbi. Litho State Ptg Wks, Budapest)

1984 (28 July). Olympic Games, Los Angeles. T **238** and similar horiz designs. Multicoloured. P 13½×11½.

1414	25f. Type **238**	1·20	55
1415	40f. Swimming	2·00	70
1416	60f. Shooting and archery pictograms	3·00	1·40
1417	100f. Gymnastics (floor exercises)	5·50	2·20
1414/1417	*Set of 4*	10·50	4·25
MS1418	90×70 mm. 100f. Pole vaulting. Imperf	23·00	22·00

239 Amman Power Station

240 Omayyad Coins

(Des M. el Zoghbi and M. el Qaddoumi. Litho State Ptg Wks,Budapest)

1984 (11 Aug). Water and Electricity Year. T **239** and similar horiz designs. Multicoloured. P 13½×11½.

1419	25f. Power lines and factories	75	30
1420	40f. Type **239**	1·40	40
1421	60f. Reservoirs and water pipe	2·00	1·10
1422	100f. Telephone lines, street light, water tap and pipeline	3·00	1·80
1419/1422	*Set of 4*	6·50	3·25

(Des M. el Zoghbi. Litho State Ptg Wks, Budapest)

1984 (26 Sept). Coins. T **240** and similar horiz designs. Multicoloured. P 13.

1423	40f. Type **240**	1·70	70
1424	60f. Abbasid coins	2·40	1·00
1425	125f. Hashemite coins	5·00	2·40
1423/1425	*Set of 3*	8·25	3·75

241 Shield and Antelope

242 Mu'tah Military University, Karak City

(Des M. el Zoghbi, M. el Qaddoumi and B. Ammari. Photo State Ptg Wks, Budapest)

1984 (18 Oct). Release of Antelope in Jordan. T **241** and similar vert designs. Multicoloured. P 13.

1426	25f. Type **241**	1·10	30
1427	40f. Four antelope	1·80	55
1428	60f. Three antelope	2·75	1·30
1429	100f. Duke of Edinburgh, King Hussein and Queen Alia	4·75	2·00
1426/1429	*Set of 4*	9·25	3·75

(Des M. el Zoghbi and B. Ammari. Photo State Ptg Wks, Budapest)

1984 (14 Nov). Jordanian Universities. T **242** and similar horiz designs. Multicoloured. P 13.

1430	40f. Type **242**	1·20	40
1431	60f. Yarmouk University, Irbid City	1·80	85
1432	125f. Jordan University, Amman	3·00	1·80
1430/1432	*Set of 3*	5·50	2·75

243 Tombs of El-Hareth bin Omier el-Azdi and Derar bin el-Azwar

244 Soldier descending Mountain and King Hussein

(Des M. el Zoghbi. Litho State Ptg Wks, Budapest)

1984 (5 Dec). Al Sahaba Tombs. T **243** and similar horiz designs. Multicoloured. P 13½×11½.

1433	10f. Type **243**	45	15
1434	25f. Tombs of Sharhabil bin Hasna and Abu Obaidah Amer bin el-Jarrah	1·10	30
1435	40f. Muath bin Jabal's tomb	1·50	40
1436	50f. Tombs of Zaid bin Haretha and Abdullah bin Rawaha	1·70	70
1437	60f. Tomb of Amer bin Abi Waqqas	2·00	1·10
1438	100f. Jafar bin Abi Taleb's tomb	3·25	1·80
1433/1438	*Set of 6*	9·00	4·00

(Des M. el Zoghbi, R. Lahham and M. el Qaddoumi. Litho State Ptg Wks, Budapest)

1985 (10 June). Independence and Army Day. T **244** and similar horiz designs. Multicoloured. P 13.

1439	25f. Type **244**	90	30
1440	40f. Flags on map, King Abdullah and King Hussein	1·50	40
1441	60f. Flag, monument and Arms	2·30	1·10
1442	100f. King Hussein, flag, King Abdullah and Arms	4·00	2·75
1439/1442	*Set of 4*	7·75	4·00

245 Sir Rowland Hill (instigator of first stamps)

246 Emblem and Delegates round Table

(Des M. el Zoghbi. Litho State Ptg Wks, Budapest)

1985 (1 July). Postal Celebrities. T **245** and similar horiz designs. Multicoloured. P 13×13½.

1443	40f. Type **245**	1·40	40
1444	60f. Heinrich von Stephan (founder of Universal Postal Union)	2·00	1·10
1445	125f. Yacoub Sukker (first Jordanian stamp designer)	4·00	2·75
1443/1445	*Set of 3*	6·75	3·75

(Des A. Haddadeen and M. el Qaddoumi. Litho State Ptg Wks,Budapest)

1985 (20 July). First Jordanians Abroad Conference. T **246** and similar horiz designs. Multicoloured. P 13×13½.

1446	40f. Type **246**	1·40	40
1447	60f. Conference emblem and globe and hand over torch	2·00	1·10
1448	125f. Globe encircled by Jordanian flags	4·00	2·75
1446/1448	*Set of 3*	6·75	3·75

247 IYY Emblem

248 El-Deir Temple, Petra

(Des R. Lahham and M. el Zoghbi. Litho State Ptg Wks, Budapest)

1985 (11 Aug). International Youth Year. T **247** and similar vert designs. Multicoloured. P 13×13½.

1449	10f. Type **247**	45	30
1450	25f. Arab couple on map, flag and emblem	1·10	40
1451	40f. Stylised figures flanking globe, flag and emblem	1·50	50
1452	60f. Part of cogwheel, laurel branch and ribbons in jug decorated with emblem	2·30	1·10
1453	125f. Stylised figures and emblem	4·00	2·75
1449/1453	*Set of 5*	8·50	4·50

(Des R. Lahham and M. el Zoghbi. Litho State Ptg Wks, Budapest)

1985 (13 Sept). Tenth Anniversary of World Tourist Organisation. T **248** and similar horiz designs. Multicoloured. P 13½×13.

1454	10f. Type **248**	45	30
1455	25f. Temple of Artemis (ruins), Jerash	1·10	40
1456	40f. Amrah Palace	1·50	50
1457	50f. Hill town, Jordan valley	1·80	70
1458	60f. Sailing in Aqaba bay	2·30	1·40
1459	125f. Roman amphitheatre, Amman, and city Arms	4·00	3·00
1454/1459	*Set of 6*	10·00	5·75
MS1460	90×70 mm. 100f. Flower with emblem as vase, and flag. Imperf	11·50	11·00

249 Mother with Baby and Hospital

250 Dancers

(Des M. el Zoghbi and R. Lahham. Litho State Ptg Wks, Budapest)

1985 (7 Oct). UNICEF Child Survival Campaign. T **249** and similar multicoloured designs. P 13.

1461	25f. Type **249**	1·10	40
1462	40f. Weighing child	1·50	55
1463	60f. Childrens' heads as balloons	2·30	1·40
1464	125f. Mother feeding baby	4·00	3·00
1461/1464	*Set of 4*	8·00	4·75
MS1465	90×70 mm. 100f. Hands cradling children's heads. Imperf	20·00	19·00

(Litho State Ptg Wks, Budapest)

1985 (21 Oct). Fifth Anniversary of Jerash Festival. T **250** and similar horiz designs. Multicoloured. P 13½×13.

1466	10f. Opening ceremony, 1980	45	30
1467	25f. Type **250**	1·10	40
1468	40f. Dancers (*different*)	1·50	55
1469	60f. Men's choir at Roman theatre	2·30	1·40
1470	100f. King Hussein and his wife	4·00	2·75
1466/1470	*Set of 5*	8·50	4·50

251 Flag and Emblem forming '40'

(Des M. el Zoghbi. Photo State Ptg Wks, Budapest)

1985 (25 Oct). 40th Anniversary of United Nations Organisation. P 13×13½.

1471	**251**	60f. multicoloured	2·50	1·50
1472		125f. multicoloured	4·00	2·75

252 Hussein comforting Boy

(Des M. el Zoghbi. Litho Harrison)

1985 (14 Nov). 50th Birthday of King Hussein. T **252** and similar horiz designs. Multicoloured. P 14½.

1473	10f. Type **252**	45	15
1474	25f. Hussein in Arab robes	1·10	55
1475	40f. Hussein piloting aircraft	1·50	85
1476	60f. Hussein in army uniform	2·30	1·40
1477	100f. Hussein in Arab headdress	4·00	2·75
1473/1477	*Set of 5*	8·50	5·25
MS1478	90×70 mm. 200f. Hussein in uniform, flags and Dome of the Rock, Jerusalem. Imperf	26·00	25·00

253 El Aqsa Mosque

254 Policeman beside Car

(Litho State Ptg Wks, Budapest)

1985 (25 Nov). COMPULSORY TAX. Restoration of El Aqsa Mosque, Jerusalem. P 13×13½.

1479	**253**	5f. multicoloured	1·80	1·70
1480		10f. multicoloured	4·00	2·75

(Litho State Ptg Wks, Budapest)

1985 (18 Dec). The Police. T **254** and similar horiz designs. Multicoloured. P 13×13½.

1481	40f. Type **254**	1·70	55
1482	60f. Traffic policeman and crowd of children	2·30	85
1483	125f. Policeman taking oath	5·00	1·50
1481/1483	*Set of 3*	8·00	2·50

255 Satellite over Map of Arab Countries

256 King presenting Colours

(Litho State Ptg Wks, Budapest)

1986 (8 Feb). First Anniversary of Launch of *Arabsat 1* Communications Satellite. T **255** and similar horiz design. Multicoloured. P 13½×13.

1484	60f. Satellite	1·40	55
1485	100f. Type **255**	2·50	85

(Litho State Ptg Wks, Budapest)

1986 (1 Mar). 30th Anniversary of Arabisation of Jordanian Army. T **256** and similar multicoloured designs. P 11½×12½.

1486	40f. Type **256**	1·20	30
1487	60f. King Hussein shaking hands with soldier	1·70	55
1488	100f. King Hussein addressing Army	2·75	1·50
1486/1488	*Set of 3*	5·00	2·10
MS1489	90×70 mm. 100f. Text and Hussein addressing Army. Imperf	18·00	17·00

257 King Abdullah decorating Soldier

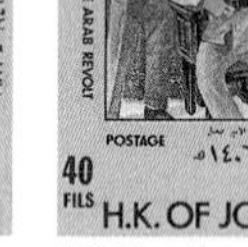

258 King Hussein of Hejaz and Sons

(Litho State Ptg Wks, Budapest)

1986 (25 May). 40th Anniversary of Independence. P 12½×11½.

1490	**257**	160f. multicoloured	4·50	2·40

(Litho State Ptg Wks, Budapest)

1986 (10 June). 70th Anniversary of Arab Revolt. T **258** and similar horiz designs. Multicoloured. P 11½×12½ (40f.) or 12½×11½ (others).

1491	40f. Type **258**	1·20	30
1492	60f. King Abdullah with armed men	2·10	70
1493	160f. King leading soldiers on horseback	4·00	2·75
1491/1493	*Set of 3*	6·50	3·50
MS1494	90×70 mm. King Abdullah and Independence declaration. Imperf	15·00	14·50

259 Emblem

260 Cardiac Centre Building

(Litho State Ptg Wks, Budapest)

1986 (1 July). International Peace Year. P 13½×13.

1495	**259**	160f. multicoloured	4·00	2·40
1496		240f. black, yellow-orange and emerald	5·25	3·25

(Litho State Ptg Wks, Budapest)

1986 (11 Aug). King Hussein Medical City. T **260** and similar horiz designs. Multicoloured. P 13½×13.

1497	40f. Type **260**	1·20	40

1498 60f. Patient undergoing operation 2·10 1·00
1499 100f. View of operating theatre during operation 3·00 1·70
1497/1499 *Set of 3* 5·75 2·75

261 Extract of Speech in Arabic

(Litho State Ptg Wks, Budapest)

1986 (27 Sept). King Hussein's Speech on 40th Anniversary of United Nations Organisation. T **261** and similar horiz designs. Multicoloured. P 12½×11½.
1500 40f. Type **261** 1·20 30
1501 80f. Extract of speech in Arabic (*different*) 2·00 1·10
1502 100f. Extract of speech in English 2·75 1·50
1500/1502 *Set of 3* 5·25 2·50
MS1503 90×70 mm. 200f. Extracts of speech in Arabic and English and King Hussein making speech. Imperf 14·50 14·00

262 Head Post Office, Amman

263 Jaber ibn Hayyan al-Azdi

(Litho State Ptg Wks, Budapest)

1987 (12 Apr). 35th Anniversary of Arab Postal Union. T **262** and similar horiz designs. Multicoloured. P 13½×13.
1504 80f. Type **262** 1·70 85
1505 160f. Ministry of Communications, Amman 3·00 2·10

(Litho State Ptg Wks, Budapest)

1987 (24 Apr). Arab and Muslim Pharmacists. T **263** and similar horiz designs. Multicoloured. P 13½×13.
1506 60f. Type **263** 1·40 55
1507 80f. Abu-al-Qasem al-Majreeti 1·70 85
1508 240f. Abu-Bakr al-Razi 4·50 3·75
1506/1508 *Set of 3* 6·75 4·75

264 Village

(Litho State Ptg Wks, Budapest)

1987 (7 May). SOS Children's Village, Amman. T **264** and similar horiz design. Multicoloured. P 13½×13.
1509 80f. Type **264** 2·75 1·30
1510 240f. Child and mural 4·75 3·75

265 Soldiers on Wall

(Litho State Ptg Wks, Budapest)

1987 (10 June). 40th Anniversary of Fourth Army Brigade. T **265** and similar multicoloured designs. P 13½×13.
1511 60f. Type **265** 2·10 1·00
1512 80f. Mortar crew 3·00 1·30
MS1513 70×90 mm. 160f. Soldiers on parade 13·50 13·00

266 Black-headed bunting (*Emberiza melanocephala*)

267 King Hussein

(Litho State Ptg Wks, Budapest)

1987 (24 June). Birds. T **266** and similar horiz designs. Multicoloured. P 13½×13.
1514 10f. Hoopoe (*Upupa epops*) 1·70 70
1515 40f. Palestine Sunbird (*Nectarinia osea*) 2·75 1·10
1516 50f. Type **266** 3·25 1·40
1517 60f. Spur-winged Plover (*Vanellus spinosus*) 4·25 1·50
1518 80f. Western Greenfinch (*Carduelis chloris*) 5·50 2·75
1519 100f. Black-winged Stilt (*Himantopus himantopus*) 6·50 3·00
1514/1519 *Set of 6* 22·00 9·50

(Litho State Ptg Wks, Budapest)

1987 (24 June). P 13×13½.
1520 **267** 60f. multicoloured 90 70
1521 80f. multicoloured 1·40 1·00
1522 160f. multicoloured 3·00 2·10
1523 240f. multicoloured 4·25 2·75
1520/1523 *Set of 4* 8·50 6·00

268 Horsemen charging

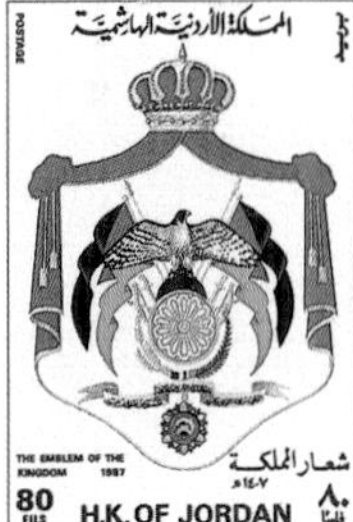
269 Arms

(Des M. el Qaddoumi and F. Yanouh. Litho State Ptg Wks,Budapest)

1987 (4 July). 800th Anniversary of Battle of Hattin. T **268** and similar multicoloured designs. P 13½×13.
1524 60f. Type **268** 2·00 85
1525 80f. Horseman and Dome of the Rock 2·50 1·40
1526 100f. Saladin, horsemen and Dome of the Rock 3·00 2·00
1524/1526 *Set of 3* 6·75 3·75
MS1527 90×70 mm. 100f. Saladin (29×44 *mm*). P 12×12½ or imperf 13·50 13·00

1987 (11 Aug). Litho. P 11½×12½.
1528 **269** 80f. multicoloured 1·70 1·10
1529 160f. multicoloured 3·50 2·10

270 Amman Industrial Estate, Sahab

271 University Crest

(Litho State Ptg Wks, Budapest)

1987 (11 Aug). P 13½×13.
1530 **270** 80f. multicoloured 1·70 40

(Des University Technical Section (60f.). Litho State Ptg Wks,Budapest)

1987 (2 Sept). 25th Anniversary of Jordan University. T **271** and similar horiz design. Multicoloured. P 11 (60f.) or 12½×11½ (80f.).
1531 60f. Type **271** 1·70 40
1532 80f. Entrance to campus (47×32 *mm*) 2·00 85

272 Child's Head in Droplet

273 Parliament in Session, 1987

(Des F. Bannouh. Litho State Ptg Wks, Budapest)

1987 (5 Oct). UNICEF Child Survival Campaign. T **272** and similar vert design. Multicoloured. P 13×13½.

1533		60f. Type **272**	1·40	70
1534		80f. Hands reaching towards child and flag as 'J'	2·50	1·50
1535		160f. Baby on scales and children reading	3·50	2·40
1533/1535 *Set of 3*			6·75	4·25

1987 (20 Oct). 40th Anniversary of Jordanian Parliament. T **273** and similar horiz design. P 13½×13.

1536		60f. deep mauve and gold	1·70	1·10
1537		80f. multicoloured	3·00	2·40

Design: 60f. 1947 opening ceremony; 80f. T **273**.

274 Emblem

275 King Hussein receiving Cape

(Lithe State Ptg Wks, Budapest)

1987 (8 Nov). Extraordinary Arab Summit Conference, Amman. T **274** and similar horiz design. Multicoloured. P 13½×13.

1538	**274**	60f. multicoloured	1·40	40
1539		80f. multicoloured	1·80	70
1540		160f. multicoloured	3·00	1·80
1541		240f. multicoloured	4·50	2·75
1538/1541 *Set of 4*			9·75	5·00
MS1542 90×66 mm. 100f. Emblem, King Hussein and map. Imperf			13·00	12·50

(Litho State Ptg Wks, Budapest)

1988 (6 Feb). Award of 1987 Dag Hammarskjöld Peace Prize to King Hussein. T **275** and similar horiz design. Multicoloured. P 12½.

1543		80f. Type **275**	1·80	70
1544		160f. King Hussein receiving Prize	3·00	1·80

276 Golden Sword

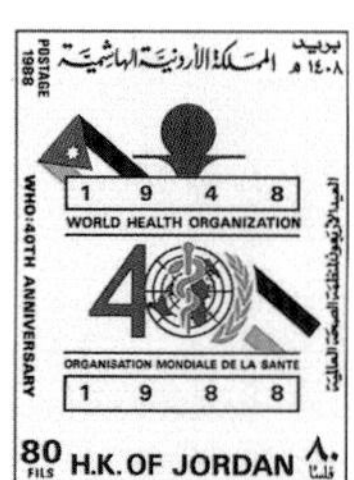

277 Anniversary Emblem and National Flag

(Litho State Ptg Wks, Budapest)

1988 (1 Mar). Jordanian Victory in 1987 Arab Military Basketball Championship. T **276** and similar horiz designs. Multicoloured. P 13½×13.

1545		60f. Type **276**	1·40	40
1546		80f. King Hussein congratulating winners	1·80	1·00
1547		160f. Match scene	3·75	2·75
1545/1547 *Set of 3*			6·25	3·75

(Des M. el Qaddoumi. Litho State Ptg Wks, Budapest)

1988 (7 Apr). 40th Anniversary of World Health Organisation. P 13×13½.

1548	**277**	60f. multicoloured	1·70	55
1549		80f. multicoloured	2·10	1·00

278 Emblems and Globe

279 Crested Lark (*Galerida cristata*)

(Des F. Bannouh. Litho State Ptg Wks, Budapest)

1988 (2 July). 75th Anniversary of Arab Scout Movement. P 13×13½.

1550	**278**	60f. multicoloured	1·70	55
1551		80f. multicoloured	2·10	1·00

(Des N. el Zagha. Litho State Ptg Wks, Moscow)

1988 (21 July). Birds. T **279** and similar horiz designs. Multicoloured. P 11½×12.

1552		10f. Type **279**	3·50	55
1553		20f. Stone Curlew (*Burhinus oedicnemus saharae*)	3·50	55
1554		30f. Common Redstart (*Phoenicurus phoenicurus*)	3·50	55
1555		40f. Blackbird (*Turdus merula*)	5·25	70
1556		50f. Feral Rock Pigeon (*Columba livia*)	6·25	85
1557		160f. White-throated Kingfisher (*Halcyon smymensis*)	20·00	2·75
1552/1557 *Set of 6*			38·00	5·25
MS1558 70×90 mm. 310f. Birds as in Nos. 1552/1557. Imperf			26·00	25·00

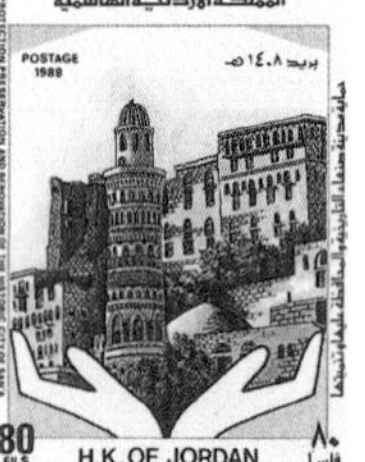

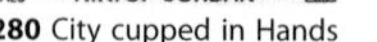

280 City cupped in Hands

281 Umm al-Rasas

(Des F. Bannouh. Litho State Ptg Wks, Moscow)

1988 (11 Aug). Restoration of Sana'a, Yemen Arab Republic. P 12×11½.

1559	**280**	80f. multicoloured	1·50	1·10
1560		160f. multicoloured	3·25	2·20

(Des M. el Qaddoumi and A. Ramadan. Litho State Ptg Wks,Budapest)

1988 (11 Aug). Historic Sites. T **281** and similar horiz designs. Multicoloured. P 13½×13.

1561		60f. Type **281**	1·20	85
1562		80f. Umm Qais	1·70	1·10
1563		160f. Iraq al-Amir	3·25	2·20
1561/1563 *Set of 3*			5·50	3·75
MS1564 100×70 mm. Nos. 1561/1563. Imperf			9·00	8·75

282 Tennis

283 Flame and Figures

(Des M. el Zoghbi, M. el Qaddoumi, F. Bannouh and F. Hejazeen. Litho State Ptg Wks, Budapest)

1988 (17 Sept). Olympic Games, Seoul. T **282** and similar vert designs. Multicoloured. P 13×13½.

1565		10f. Type **282**	60	40
1566		60f. Games mascot	1·50	85
1567		80f. Running and swimming	2·00	1·10
1568		120f. Basketball	3·00	1·70
1569		160f. Football	4·25	2·20
1565/1569 *Set of 5*			10·00	5·75
MS1570 70×90 mm. 100f. Games emblem. Imperf			26·00	25·00

Nos. 1565/1569 were also issued imperforate in restricted numbers.

(Litho State Ptg Wks, Moscow)

1988 (10 Dec). 40th Anniversary of Declaration of Human Rights. P 11½×12.

1571	**283**	80f. multicoloured	1·70	85
1572		160f. multicoloured	2·50	1·40

284 El-Deir Temple, Petra

(Litho State Ptg Wks, Moscow)

1988 (15 Dec). 25th Anniversary of Royal Jordanian Airline. T **284** and similar horiz design. Multicoloured. P 11½×12.

1573		60f. Type **284**	1·70	1·10
1574		80f. Boeing 737 airliner and map of world	2·40	1·30

285 Dome of the Rock, Jerusalem

1989 (5 June). Palestinian Welfare. Litho. P 14½.

1575	**285**	5f. multicoloured	45	30
1576		10f. multicoloured	45	30

286 Treasury, Petra, Flags and King Hussein

1989 (10 June). Formation of Arab Co-operation Council (economic grouping of four states). T **286** and similar horiz designs. Multicoloured. Litho. P 13½×13.

1577		10f. Type **286**	15	15
1578		30f. Sana'a, Yemen	60	30
1579		40f. Spiral Tower of Samarra, Iraq	75	40
1580		60f. Pyramids, Egypt	1·20	55
1577/1580 *Set of 4*			2·40	1·30

287 Jordanian Parliament Building

1989 (20 Sept). Centenary of Interparliamentary Union. Litho. P 12.

1581	**287**	40f. multicoloured	45	30
1582		60f. multicoloured	1·10	55

288 Modern Flats and Emblems

1989 (2 Oct). Arab Housing Day and World Refugee Day. T **288** and similar multicoloured designs. Litho. P 12.

1583		5f. Type **288**	90	30
1584		40f. Hand supporting refugee family (*horiz*)	1·70	40
1585		60f. Modern blocks of flats (*horiz*)	3·00	55
1583/1585 *Set of 3*			5·00	1·10

289 King Abdullah, Mosque and King Hussein

1989 (12 Oct). Inauguration of King Abdullah Ibn al-Hussein Mosque, Amman. Litho. P 12.

1586	**289**	40f. multicoloured	75	30
1587		60f. multicoloured	1·20	40
MS1588 90×70 mm. **289** 100f. multicoloured. Imperf			11·50	11·00

290 Horse's Head

291 Trees

1989 (1 Nov). Arabian Horse Festival. T **290** and similar multicoloured designs. P 12.

1589		5f. Horse in paddock and emblem of Royal Stables (*horiz*)	1·10	30
1590		40f. Horse rearing and Treasury, Petra (*horiz*)	1·80	35
1591		60f. Type **290**	3·50	40
1589/1591 *Set of 3*			5·75	95
MS1592 90×70 mm. 100f. Mare and foal. Imperf			45·00	43·00

1989 (14 Nov). 50th Anniversary of Ministry of Agriculture. T **291** and similar vert designs. Multicoloured. P 12.

1593		5f. Type **291**	1·40	40
1594		40f. Tree and '50'	1·50	50
1595		60f. Orange trees and hives	1·80	55
1593/1595 *Set of 3*			4·25	1·30

292 Open Book, Globe and Flags

1989 (3 Dec). Jordan Library Association. P 12.

1596	**292**	40f. multicoloured	90	30
1597		60f. multicoloured	1·20	40

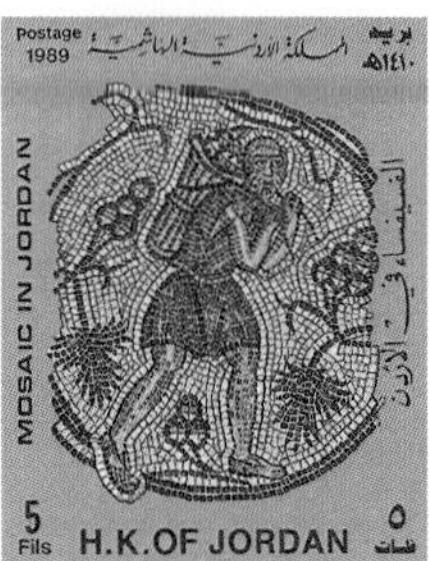

293 Man carrying Basket

1989 (23 Dec). Mosaics. T **293** and similar multicoloured designs. P 12.

1598	5f. Type **293**	1·10	40
1599	10f. Philadelphia (modern Amman)	1·20	50
1600	40f. Deer	2·30	70
1601	60f. Man with stick	3·25	1·00
1602	80f. Jerusalem (*horiz*)	4·50	1·40
1598/1602	*Set of* 5	11·00	3·50
MS1603	90×70 mm. 100f. As No. 1602. Imperf	26·00	25·00

294 Flags and Map

1990 (16 Feb). First Anniversary of Arab Co-operation Council. P 13.

1604	**294**	5f. multicoloured	45	40
1605		20f. multicoloured	55	50
1606		60f. multicoloured	1·20	70
1607		80f. multicoloured	1·50	1·00
1604/1607		*Set of* 4	3·25	2·30

295 Wild Asses at Oasis

1990 (22 Apr). Nature Conservation. T **295** and similar horiz designs. Multicoloured. Litho. P 13×13½.

1608	40f. Type **295**	90	40
1609	60f. Rock formation, Rum	1·40	50
1610	80f. Desert palm trees	1·80	55
1608/1610	*Set of* 3	3·75	1·30

296 Horsemen and Building

1990 (21 Nov). 70th Anniversary of Arrival of Prince Abdullah in Ma'an. T **296** and similar horiz design. Litho. P 13×13½.

1611	**296**	40f. multicoloured	45	40
1612		60f. multicoloured	60	50
MS1613		90×73 mm. 200f. multicoloured. Imperf	10·50	10·00

Design: 200f. King Abdullah, flags and horsemen.

297 Emblem

298 King Hussein

1990 (1 Dec). 40th Anniversary of United Nations Development Programme. Litho. P 13.

1614	**297**	60f. multicoloured	60	40
1615		80f. multicoloured	75	50

1990–91. Multicoloured, frame colour given. Litho. P 12×13½.

(a) Small head. Dated 1990

1616	**298**	5f. orange-yellow	45	40
1617		60f. blue	75	40
1618		80f. mauve	1·20	40

(b) Large head. Dated 1991

1619	**298**	5f. orange-yellow	45	40
1620		20f. emerald	45	40
1621		40f. orange-red	45	40
1622		80f. rose-lilac	1·20	40
1623		240f. orange-brown	2·30	85
1624		320f. bright purple	3·00	1·10
1625		1d. bright yellow-green	4·50	3·25
1616/1625		*Set of* 10	13·50	7·25

Nos. 1626/1630 are vacant.

299 Nubian Ibex

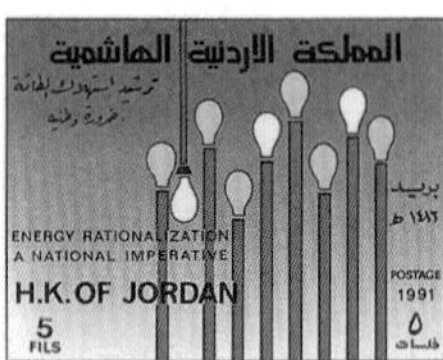

300 Electric Light Bulbs

1991 (1 Sept). Endangered Animals. T **299** and similar vert designs. Multicoloured. Litho. P 13×13½.

1631	5f. Type **299**	30	30
1632	40f. Onager	90	40
1633	80f. Arabian gazelles	1·80	70
1634	160f. Arabian oryx	3·75	1·50
1631/1634	*Set of* 4	6·00	2·50

1991 (3 Oct). Energy Rationalisation. T **300** and similar multicoloured designs. Litho. P 13½×13 (5f.) or 13×13½ (others).

1635	5f. Type **300**	45	40
1636	40f. Solar energy (*vert*)	55	40
1637	80f. Angle-poise lamp by window (*vert*)	90	40
1635/1637	*Set of* 3	1·70	1·10

301 Grain

302 Drops of Blood on Hand

1991 (16 Oct). Grain Production. T **301** and similar horiz designs. Multicoloured. Litho. P 13½×13.

1638	5f. Type **301**	45	40
1639	40f. Ear of wheat and leaves	55	40
1640	80f. Ear of wheat and field	90	40
1638/1640	*Set of* 4	1·70	1·10

1991 (14 Nov). National Blood Donation Campaign. Litho. P 13½×13.

1641	**302**	80f. multicoloured	1·40	70
1642		160f. multicoloured	2·40	1·00

303 Jerusalem and Map

304 Emblem

1991 (29 Nov). Palestinian 'Intifida' Movement. Litho. P 11–11½.

1643	**303**	20f. multicoloured	1·80	85

(Litho State Ptg Wks, Budapest)

1992 (20 Feb). Expo '92 World's Fair, Seville. P 13½×13.

1644	**304**	80f. multicoloured	75	40
1645		320f. multicoloured	3·00	1·80

305 Man and Woman balancing Scales

306 Children

(Litho State Ptg Wks, Budapest)

1992 (7 Apr). World Health Day. 'Heartbeat–the Rhythm of Health'. T **305** and similar multicoloured design. P 13×13½ (80f.) or 13½×13 (125f.).

1646	80f. Type **305**	1·10	40
1647	125f. Man and heart in balance and cardiograph (*horiz*)	1·50	70

(Litho State Ptg Wks, Budapest)

1992 (30 Apr). SOS Children's Village, Aqaba. T **306** and similar horiz design. Multicoloured. P 13½×13.

1648	80f. Type **306**	1·10	40
1649	125f. Village	1·50	70

307 Judo and Olympic Flame

(Litho State Ptg Wks, Budapest)

1992 (25 July). Olympic Games, Barcelona. T **307** and similar multicoloured designs. P 13½×13 (horiz) or 13×13½ (vert).

1650	5f. Type **307**	45	40
1651	40f. Runners and track (*vert*)	55	40
1652	80f. Gymnast	90	40
1653	125f. Mascot (*vert*)	1·70	70
1654	160f. Table tennis	2·00	85
1650/1654 *Set of 5*		5·00	2·50
MS1655 70×90 mm. 100f. Motifs as Nos. 1650/1654. Imperf		26·00	25·00

308 King Hussein

309 African Monarch (*Danaus chrysippus*)

(Litho State Ptg Wks, Budapest)

1992 (11 Aug). 40th Anniversary of King Hussein's Accession. T **308** and similar multicoloured designs. P 13×13½ (40f.) or 13½×13 (others).

1656	40f. Type **308**	45	40
1657	80f. National Colours, crown and King (*horiz*)	75	55
1658	125f. King and flags (*horiz*)	1·40	65
1659	160f. King, crown and anniversary emblem (*horiz*)	1·70	85
1656/1659 *Set of 4*		3·75	2·20
MS1660 90×70 mm. 200f. King Hussein and flame. Imperf		12·00	11·50

(Litho State Ptg Wks, Budapest)

1992 (20 Dec). Butterflies. T **309** and similar horiz designs. Multicoloured. P 13½×13.

1661	5f. Type **309** (inscr 'Danus chrysippus')	45	30
1662	40f. Black-veined White (*Aporia crataegi*)	90	40
1663	80f. Swallowtail (*Papilio machaon*)	2·30	70
1664	160f. Turanian Grayling *Pseudochazara telephassa*	4·25	1·50
1661/1664 *Set of 4*		7·00	2·50
MS1665 90×70 mm. 200f. Butterflies as in Nos. 1661/1664. Imperf		24·00	23·00

The Latin inscriptions on Nos. 1661/1662 contain errors of spelling.

310 Hadrian's Triumphal Arch, Jerash

311 Customs Co-operation Council Emblem, Flag and Laurel

BORDER TYPES

I II III

(Litho State Ptg Wks, Budapest)

1993 (13 Jan)–**2003**. Border Type I. P 12×13.

1666	**310**	5f. light brown, cobalt and black (dated 1992)	15	15
1667		50f. chestnut, lemon and black (perf 12½×13, dated 2003)	45	30
1668		80f. light brown, apple green and black (dated 1992)	60	30
1669		100f. light brown, rose-red and black (dated 1992)	75	30
1670		125f. light brown, flesh and black (dated 1992)	90	30
1671		160f. light brown, greenish yellow and black (dated 1992)	1·20	40
1672		240f. light brown, bright mauve and black (dated 1992)	1·70	40
1673		320f. light brown, chestnut and black (dated 1992)	2·30	55
1674		400f. brown, light new blue and black (perf 12½×13) (dated 1997)	4·50	4·25
1675		500f. light brown, ochre and black (dated 1992)	3·50	1·40
		a. Perf 12½×13. Dated 1997	4·50	4·25
1676		1d. light brown, olive-yellow and black (dated 1992)	7·00	2·10
1666/1676 *Set of 12*			21·00	9·50

See also Nos. 1718/1724, 1788/1793, 1798/1805, 2036*a*/2036*b*, 2311*a* and 2613/2622.

Nos. 1677/1679 are vacant.

(Litho State Ptg Wks, Budapest)

1993 (26 Jan). International Customs Day. P 13½×13.

1680	**311**	80f. multicoloured	1·10	40
1681		125f. multicoloured	1·50	70

312 King Hussein and Military Equipment

(Litho Security Printers (M), Malaysia)

1993 (10 June). Army Day and 77th Anniversary of Arab Revolt. T **312** and similar horiz designs. Multicoloured. P 12.

1682 5f. Type **312** 30 30
1683 40f. King Hussein, soldier, surgeons and tank 45 35
1684 80f. King Abdullah and Dome of the Rock .. 90 40
1685 125f. King Hussein of Hejaz, Dome of the Rock and horsemen .... 1·40 50
1682/1685 *Set of 4* .... 2·75 1·40
MS1686 90×70 mm. 100f. King Hussein, flags of Jordan and Palestine and army emblem. Imperf .... 9·75 9·50

313 Society Emblem and Natural Energy Resources

(Litho Security Printers (M), Malaysia)

1993 (10 June). 23rd Anniversary of Royal Scientific Society. P 12½.

1687 **313** 80f. multicoloured 90 55

314 Courtyard

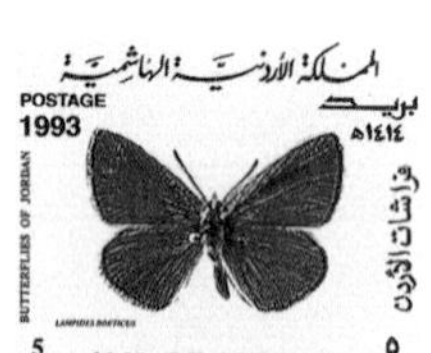

315 Long-tailed Blue (*Lampides boeticus*)

(Des M. el Qaddoumi. Litho Security Printers (M), Malaysia)

1993 (1 Sept). Centenary of Salt Municipality. P 12.

1688 **314** 80f. multicoloured .... 1·10 40
1689 125f. multicoloured .... 1·50 70
MS1690 90×71 mm. Nos 1688/1689. Imperf (*sold at* 200f.) .... 10·50 10·00

(Litho Security Printers (M), Malaysia)

1993 (10 Oct). Butterflies. T **315** and similar horiz designs. Multicoloured. P 12.

1691 5f. Type **315** 75 30
1692 40f. *Melanargria titea* .... 1·20 55
1693 80f. *Allancastria deyrollei* .... 1·70 70
1694 160f. *Gonepteryx cleopatra* .... 4·00 1·70
1691/1694 *Set of 4* .... 7·00 3·00
MS1695 91×72 mm. 100f. Butterflies as in Nos. 1691/1694. Imperf .... 38·00 36·00

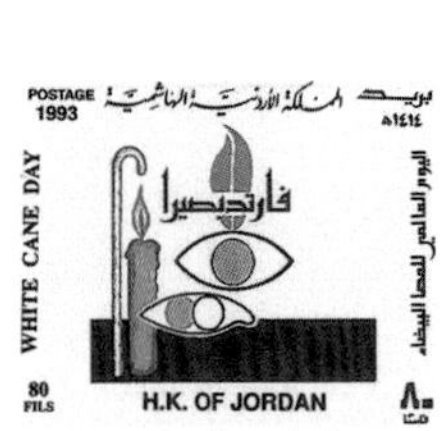

316 Eyes, Candle and White Cane

317 King Hussein in Army Uniform

(Des R. Lahham (80f.), M. el Qaddoumi (125f.). Litho Security Printers (M), Malaysia)

1993 (23 Oct). White Cane Day. T **316** and similar multicoloured design. P 12.

1696 80f. Type **316** .... 1·10 40
1697 125f. Globe, white cane and eye (*vert*) .... 1·50 70

(Litho Security Printers (M), Malaysia)

1993 (14 Nov). 40th Anniversary of King Hussein's Enthronement. T **317** and similar multicoloured designs. P 12.

1698 40f. Type **317** 45 40
1699 80f. King wearing Bedouin costume 90 55
1700 125f. King wearing suit .... 1·40 65
1701 160f. King with Queen Noor (*horiz*) .... 1·80 85
1698/1701 *Set of 4* .... 4·00 2·20
MS1702 90×71 mm. 100f. As No. 1701. Imperf .... 13·50 13·00

318 Saladin and Dome of the Rock, Jerusalem

(Des M. el Qaddoumi. Litho Security Printers (M), Malaysia)

1993 (25 Nov). 800th Death Anniversary of Saladin. P 12.

1703 **318** 40f. multicoloured 45 40
1704 80f. multicoloured 75 50
1705 125f. multicoloured .... 1·40 70
1703/1705 *Set of 3* .... 2·30 1·40

319 King Hussein and Crowd

320 Virus, Emblem and Silhouettes

(Litho Security Printers (M), Malaysia)

1993 (25 Nov). King Hussein's Return from Surgery in USA (1992). T **319** and similar horiz designs. Multicoloured. P 12.

1706 80f. Type **319** 90 40
1707 125f. King waving at crowd .... 1·40 70
1708 160f. King embracing his mother .... 1·80 85
1706/1708 *Set of 3* .... 3·75 1·80
MS1709 90×70 mm. 100f. King Hussein at top of steps. Imperf .... 9·00 8·75

(Des M. el Qaddoumi. Litho Security Printers (M), Malaysia)

1993 (1 Dec). World AIDS Day. P 12.

1710 **320** 80f. multicoloured 90 55
1711 125f. multicoloured .... 1·40 85
MS1712 91×71 mm. Nos. 1710/1711. Imperf (*sold at* 200f.) .... 10·50 10·00

321 Emblems and Flag

(Des R. Lahham. Litho Security Printers (M), Malaysia)

1993 (10 Dec). 45th Anniversary of United Nations Declaration of Human Rights. P 12.

1713 **321** 40f. multicoloured 45 40
1714 160f. multicoloured .... 1·80 85

322 Loading Aeroplane

(Des M. Jarrar. Litho Security Printers (M), Malaysia)

1994 (20 Mar). Jordan Hashemite Charity Organisation. T **322** and similar horiz design. Multicoloured. P 12.

1715	80f. Type **322**	90	55
1716	125f. Transport plane	1·40	85

No. 1717 is vacant.

(Litho Security Printers (M), Malaysia)

1994 (23 Mar)–**95**. T **310** redrawn. Border Type II or III. P 12.

1718	**310**	40f. light brown, light green and black (II) (dated 1993)	30	30
1720		100f. light brown, rose-red and black (25.1.95) (III) (dated 1993)	75	30
1721		125f. light brown, cobalt and black (20.5.95) (III) (dated 1994)	1·10	1·00
1722		160f. light brown, greenish yellow and black (20.10.94) (III) (dated 1993)	1·20	55
		a. Dated 1994 (20.5.95) (III)	1·40	55
1723		240f. light brown, mauve and black (9.4.94) (III) (dated 1993)	1·80	85
		a. Dated 1994 (20.5.95) (III)	2·10	85
1724		320f. light brown, orange-brown and black (22.12.94) (III) (dated 1993)	3·00	2·75
1718/1724 *Set of* 6			7·25	5·25

For details of border types see Nos. 1666/1674.

Apart from imprint dates and perforations, Nos. 1718/1723 most noticeably differ from Nos. 1666/1674 in the design of the outer frame.

Nos. 1719 and 1725 are vacant.

323 Mosque and King Hussein

(Des R. Lahham. Litho Press Directory and Official Newspaper,Damascus, Syria)

1994 (18 Apr). Refurbishment of El Aqsa Mosque and Dome of the Rock. T **323** and similar horiz designs. P 12½.

1726	80f. Type **323**	90	40
1727	125f. Dome of the Rock and King Hussein	1·20	70
1728	240f. Dome of the Rock and King Hussein (*different*)	2·50	1·10
1726/1728 *Set of* 3		4·25	2·00
MS1729 90×70 mm. 100f. King Hussein and interior and exterior view of dome. Imperf		13·50	13·00

324 Emblems on Doves

(Des S. Tamimi (80f.), M. el Qaddoumi (160f.). Litho Security Printers (M), Malaysia)

1994 (8 May). 75th Anniversary of International Federation of Red Cross and Red Crescent Societies. T **324** and similar multicoloured design. P 12.

1730	80f. Child and emblems (*horiz*)	1·50	40
1731	160f. Type **324**	2·30	85
MS1732 70×90 mm. As Nos. 1721/1722 but smaller (*sold at* 200f.)		21·00	20·00

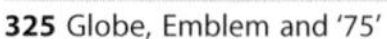

325 Globe, Emblem and '75'

326 Sports Pictograms and Olympic Rings

(Des S. Tamimi. Litho Security Printers (M), Malaysia)

1994 (13 June). 75th Anniversary of International Labour Organisation. P 12.

1733	**325**	80f. multicoloured	75	40
1734		125f. multicoloured	1·20	55

(Des B. Osman (80f.), M. el Qaddoumi (125, 160f.), R. Lahham (others). Litho Security Printers (M), Malaysia)

1994 (23 June). Centenary of International Olympic Committee. T **326** and similar multicoloured designs. P 12.

1735	80f. Type **326**	75	40
1736	125f. Sports pictograms, flame and '100'	1·40	65
1737	160f. Olympic rings, track and athlete (*horiz*)	1·70	70
1738	240f. Olympic rings and hand holding torch (*horiz*)	2·50	1·50
1735/1738 *Set of* 4		5·75	3·00
MS1739 90×70 mm. 100f. Olympic rings and Jordanian flag forming 'J'. Imperf		14·50	14·00

327 King Hussein greeting Soldiers

(Des M. Jarrar. Litho Security Printers (M), Malaysia)

1994 (11 Aug). Jordanian Participation in United Nations Peace-keeping Forces. T **327** and similar horiz designs. Multicoloured. P 12.

1740	80f. Type **327**	75	40
1741	125f. King Hussein inspecting troops	1·20	65
1742	160f. United Nations road checkpoint	1·40	70
1740/1742 *Set of* 3		3·00	1·60

328 Flag, Emblem, Globe, Wheat and Family

(Des S. Tamimi. Litho Security Printers (M), Malaysia)

1994 (11 Aug). International Year of the Family. P 12.

1743	**328**	80f. multicoloured	75	40
1744		125f. multicoloured	1·40	65
1745		160f. multicoloured	1·70	70
1743/1745 *Set of* 3			3·50	1·60

329 Aircraft and Emblem

(Litho Security Printers (M), Malaysia)

1994 (25 Oct). 50th Anniversary of International Civil Aviation Organisation. P 12.

1746	**329**	80f. multicoloured	90	70
1747		125f. multicoloured	1·20	1·00
1748		160f. multicoloured	1·70	1·40
1746/1748 *Set of 3*			3·50	2·75

330 Hands around Water Droplet

(Litho Security Printers (M), Malaysia)

1994 (14 Nov). Water Conservation Campaign. T **330** and similar vert designs. Multicoloured. P 14.

1749	80f. Type **330**	1·20	50
1750	125f. Glass beneath running tap, foodstuffs and industry	1·80	70
1751	160f. Water droplets and boy on lush hillside	2·30	70
1749/1751 *Set of 3*		4·75	1·70

331 Crown Prince Hassan **332** University Emblem

(Litho Security Printers (M), Malaysia)

1994 (11 Dec). Tenth Anniversary of Crown Prince's Award. T **331** and similar horiz designs. P 12.

1752	**331**	80f. multicoloured	1·20	55
1753		125f. multicoloured	1·80	65
1754		160f. multicoloured	2·30	70
1752/1754 *Set of 3*			4·75	1·70

(Litho Security Printers (M), Malaysia)

1995 (6 Feb). Inauguration of Al al-Bayt University. P 12.

1755	**332**	80f. gold, bright greenish blue and black	75	55
1756		125f. gold, yellow-green and black	1·50	65
MS1757 89×70 mm. Nos. 1743/1744. Imperf (*sold at* 200f.)			6·25	6·00

333 UN Emblem and '50'

(Des M. el Qaddoumi. Litho Alexandros Matsoukis, Athens, Greece)

1995 (1 Apr). 50th Anniversary of United Nations Organisation. P 14.

1758	**333**	80f. multicoloured	1·10	55
1759		125f. multicoloured	1·70	70

334 Labour Emblem and Crowd with Flag

(Litho Alexandros Matsoukis, Athens)

1995 (1 May). Labour Day. T **334** and similar horiz designs. Multicoloured. P 14.

1760	80f. Type **334**	75	70
1761	125f. Emblem, world map and miner's head	1·10	1·00
1762	160f. Hands holding spanner and torch	1·50	1·40
1760/1762 *Set of 3*		3·00	2·75

335 Flags and Globe

(Des R. Lahham. Litho Alexandros Matsoukis, Athens)

1995 (22 May). Jordan Week in Japan. T **335** and similar horiz designs. Multicoloured. P 14.

1763	80f. Type **335**	1·10	70
1764	125f. Hemispheres and flags	1·70	85
1765	160f. Flags, brick wall and globe	2·00	1·00
1763/1765 *Set of 3*		4·25	2·30

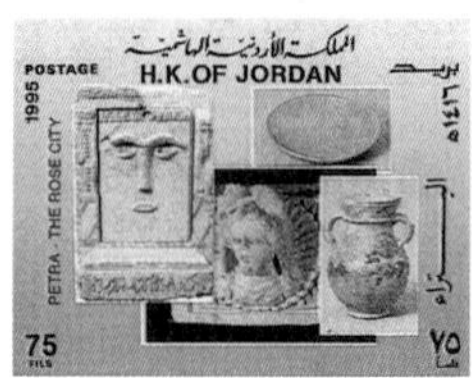

336 Artefacts

(Litho Alexandros Matsoukis, Athens)

1995 (11 Aug). Petra, 'The Rose City'. T **336** and similar multicoloured designs. P 14.

1766	50f. Amphitheatre	1·20	50
1767	75f. Type **336**	1·50	55
1768	80f. Treasury seen through cleft in rocks (*vert*)	1·80	65
1769	160f. Treasury (*vert*)	3·00	70
1766/1769 *Set of 4*		6·75	2·20
MS1770 90×70 mm. 200f. El-Deir Temple. Imperf		30·00	29·00

337 Emblem

(Litho Alexandros Matsoukis, Athens)

1995 (20 Sept). 50th Anniversary of Arab League. P 14.

1771	**337**	80f. multicoloured	75	70
1772		125f. multicoloured	1·10	1·00
1773		160f. multicoloured	1·50	1·40
1771/1773 *Set of 3*			3·00	2·75

338 Leaves and Emblems

1995 (16 Oct). 50th Anniversary of Food and Agriculture Organisation. T **338** and similar horiz designs. Multicoloured. Litho. P 14.

1774 80f. Type **338** 75 55
1775 125f. Ears of wheat and '50' incorporating FAO emblem .... 1·40 65
1776 160f. United Nations emblem and '50' incorporating FAO emblem .... 1·80 70
1774/1776 *Set of 3* .... 3·50 1·70

339 Knotted Ropes, Summit Emblem and National Flags

1995 (29 Oct). Middle Eastern and North African Economic Summit, Amman. Litho. P 12.

1777 **339** 80f. multicoloured 75 55
1778 125f. multicoloured .... 1·40 65

340 King Hussein

(Litho Alexandros Matsoukis, Athens, Greece)

1995 (14 Nov). 60th Birthday of King Hussein. T **340** and similar horiz designs. Multicoloured. P 14.

1779 25f. Type **340** 60 55
1780 40f. Hussein within shield 60 55
1781 80f. Dove incorporating '60', El-Deir Temple (Petra) and Hussein 75 55
1782 100f. Hussein in military uniform and anniversary emblem .... 1·10 65
1783 125f. King Hussein .... 1·40 70
1784 160f. Hussein, National Flag and '60 60 60' .... 1·80 70
1779/1784 *Set of 6* .... 5·75 3·25
MS1785 90×70 mm. 200f. Dome of the Rock and King Hussein within '60'. Imperf .... 10·50 10·00

341 Hands and Hard of Hearing Emblem

1995 (30 Nov). The Deaf. T **341** and similar horiz design. Multicoloured. Litho. P 14.

1786 80f. Type **341** 75 55
1787 125f. Emblems, sign language and hard of hearing emblem .... 1·40 65

1995. T **310** redrawn. Border Type II or III. Litho. P 12.

1788 **310** 25f. chestnut, pale reddish purple and black (III) (dated 1995) 30 30
1789 50f. chestnut, lemon and black (III) (dated 1995) 45 40
a. Dated 1996 (III) 45 40
1790 100f. chestnut, bright yellow-green and black (III) (dated 1995) 90 85
a. Dated 1996 (III) 90 85
1791 200f. chestnut, bluish grey and black (III) (dated 1995) .... 2·00 1·80
1792 300f. chestnut, rose-pink and black (III) (dated 1995) .... 3·25 3·00
1793 500f. chestnut, ochre and black (II) (dated 1995) .... 3·75 1·40
1788/1793 *Set of 6* .... 9·50 7·00

For details of border types see Nos. 1666/1674.

342 Anniversary Emblem and Map of Jordan

1996 (25 May). 50th Anniversary of Independence. T **342** and similar horiz designs. Multicoloured. Litho. P 12.

1794 100f. Type **342** .... 1·10 55
1795 200f. King Hussein, map of Jordan and King Abdullah .... 2·00 1·00
1796 300f. King Hussein .... 2·75 1·50
1794/1796 *Set of 3* .... 5·25 2·75
MS1797 85×66 mm. 200f. King Hussein in military uniform. Imperf .... 11·50 11·00

1996 (15 May). T **310** redrawn. Border Type II. Dated 1996. P 13½×14.

1798 **310** 50f. brown, lemon and black 45 40
1799 75f. brown, cinnamon and black 75 70
1800 100f. brown, bright yellow-green and black 90 85
1801 120f. brown, blue-green and black .... 1·20 1·10
1802 150f. brown, salmon-pink and black .... 1·70 1·50
1803 200f. brown, bluish grey and black .... 2·00 1·80
1804 300f. brown, rose-red and black .... 3·25 3·00
1805 400f. brown, light new blue and black .... 4·50 4·25
1798/1805 *Set of 8* .... 13·50 12·00

For details of border types see Nos. 1666/1674.

343 Games Emblem, Olympic Rings and Pictograms

344 Hand protecting Animals and Plants

1996 (19 July). Olympic Games, Atlanta. T **343** and similar horiz designs. Multicoloured. Litho. P 12.

1806 50f. Type **343** 90 55
1807 100f. Games emblem and pictograms .... 1·50 65
1808 200f. Games emblem forming torch and figure .... 2·75 85
1809 300f. Games emblem, torch and National Flag .... 3·75 1·30
1806/1809 *Set of 4* .... 8·00 3·00

1996 (16 Sept). Protection of the Ozone Layer. Litho. P 12.

1810 **344** 100f. multicoloured .... 3·00 1·00

345 Anniversary Emblem

1996 (11 Dec). 50th Anniversary of United Nations Children's Fund. Litho. P 12.

1811	**345**	100f. multicoloured	1·40	70
1812		200f. multicoloured	2·40	1·00

346 Playing Polo

347 Karak

1997 (20 Mar). 50th Birthday of Crown Prince Hassan. T **346** and similar multicoloured designs. Litho. P 12.

1813	50f. Type **346**	75	70
1814	100f. Wearing western dress (*vert*)	1·10	75
1815	200f. Wearing Arab headdress and uniform	2·30	1·00
1813/1815	*Set of 3*	3·75	2·20
MS1816	90×69 mm. 200f. Wearing graduation robes. Imperf	13·00	12·50

1997 (7 Apr). Centenary of Discovery of Madaba Mosaic Map. T **347** and similar multicoloured designs. Litho. P 12.

1817	100f. Type **347**	1·40	70
1818	200f. River Jordan (*horiz*)	2·75	1·00
1819	300f. Jerusalem	4·25	1·70
1817/1819	*Set of 3*	7·50	3·00
MS1820	90×70 mm. 100f. Remains of map. Imperf	23·00	22·00

348 Von Stephan

349 Rosefinch

1997 (8 Apr). Death Centenary of Heinrich von Stephan (founder of Universal Postal Union). P 12.

1821	**348**	100f. multicoloured	2·10	70
1822		200f. multicoloured	4·00	1·00

1997 (25 May). The Jordanian Rosefinch. Litho. P 12.

1823	**349**	50f. multicoloured	75	40
1824		100f. multicoloured	1·50	1·00
1825		150f. multicoloured	2·30	1·50
1826		200f. multicoloured	3·00	2·10
1823/1826		*Set of 4*	6·75	4·50

350 Performers and Hadrian's Triumphal Arch

(Litho Security Printers (M), Malaysia)

1997 (23 July). 15th Anniversary of Jerash Festival. T **350** and similar horiz designs. Multicoloured. P 12.

1827	50f. Type **350**	45	40
1828	100f. Orchestra, Festival emblem and Jerash ruins	1·10	1·00
1829	150f. Temple of Artemis and marching band	1·70	1·50
1830	200f. Women dancers and audience at performance	2·30	2·10
1827/1830	*Set of 4*	5·00	4·50
MS1831	90×70 mm. 200f. Torch-lighting ceremony. Imperf	14·50	14·00

351 Current and Previous Parliament Buildings

(Litho Security Printers (M), Malaysia)

1997 (1 Nov). 50th Anniversary of First National Parliament. T **351** and similar horiz design. Multicoloured. P 12 (200f.) or 12½ (100f.).

1832	100f. Type **351**	1·10	1·00
1833	200f. King Hussein addressing, and view of, Chamber of Deputies	2·10	2·00

352 Meeting Emblem

353 King Hussein and Queen Noor

1997 (3 Nov). 53rd International Air Transport Association Annual General Meeting, Amman. Litho. P 13×13½.

1834	**352**	100f. multicoloured	1·10	1·00
1835		200f. multicoloured	2·10	2·00
1836		300f. multicoloured	3·25	3·00
1834/1836		*Set of 3*	5·75	5·50

(Litho Cartor)

1997 (14 Nov). 62nd Birthday of King Hussein. P 13×13½.

1837	**353**	100f. multicoloured	1·10	1·00
1838		200f. multicoloured	2·10	2·00
1839		300f. multicoloured	3·25	3·00
1837/1839		*Set of 3*	5·75	5·50
MS1840		70×90 mm. 200f. As No. 1838 but 44×61 mm.	13·00	12·50

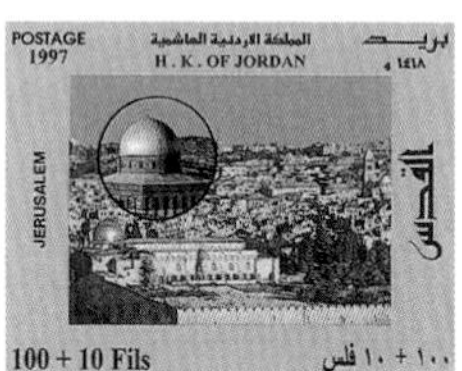

354 Jerusalem and Dome of the Rock

1997 (29 Nov). Jerusalem. Litho. P 13½×13.

1841	**354**	100f. +10f. multicoloured	1·10	1·00
1842		200f. +20f. multicoloured	2·40	2·20
1843		300f. +30f. multicoloured	3·50	3·25
1841/1843		*Set of 3*	6·25	5·75

355 Opening Ceremony

356 Women

1997 (14 Dec). Jordan, Arab Football Champions, 1997. T **355** and similar horiz designs. Multicoloured. Litho. P 12.

1844	50f. Type **355**	60	55
1845	75f. Team saluting National Anthem	75	70

1846 100f. Posing for team photograph and police officers patrolling crowd .... 1·10 1·00
1844/1846 *Set of 3* .... 2·20 2·00
MS1847 91×71 mm. 200f. King Hussein and Queen Noor among dignitaries and motorcade. Imperf .... 18·00 17·00

1997 (20 Dec). National Women's Forum. T **356** and similar multicoloured designs. Litho. P 12.
1848 50f. Type **356** 60 55
1849 100f. National Flag, women's profiles and emblems (*horiz*) .... 1·10 1·00
1850 150f. Forum meeting and emblem (*horiz*) .... 1·80 1·70
1848/1850 *Set of 3* .... 3·25 3·00

357 Air Pollution by Factories and Cars

1998 (29 Apr). Earth Day. Children's Paintings. T **357** and similar multicoloured designs. Litho. P 13½.
1851 50f. Polluted air, land and water 90 55
1852 100f. Type **357** .... 1·50 1·00
1853 150f. 'Earth' being strangled by pollution (*vert*) .... 2·30 1·70
1851/1853 *Set of 3* .... 4·25 3·00

Nos. 1854/1863 have been left for stamps not yet received.

358 King Abdullah and Camel in Desert

359 Thistle

1998 (25 May). 75th Anniversary of Recognition of Transjordan as Autonomous State. T **358** and similar horiz designs. Multicoloured. Litho. P 12.
1864 100f. Type **358** .... 1·20 1·00
1865 200f. King Hussein and camel in desert .... 2·40 2·10
1866 300f. King Abdullah, King Hussein and May 1923 9p. stamp .... 4·00 3·25
1864/1866 *Set of 3* .... 6·75 5·75
MS1867 89×74 mm. 300f. As No. 1866 but 78×70 mm. Imperf .... 13·00 12·50

1998 (7 July). Flowers. T **359** and similar vert designs. Multicoloured. Litho. P 14.
1868 50f. Type **359** .... 1·10 70
1869 100f. Poppy .... 1·50 1·30
1870 150f. Carnation .... 2·50 2·00
1868/1870 *Set of 3* .... 4·50 3·50
MS1871 70×90 mm. 200f. Iris. Imperf .... 13·00 12·50

360 Animals and Trees

361 Honey Bee and Honeycomb

1998 (22 July). Mosaics from Um ar-Rasas. T **360** and similar vert designs. Multicoloured. Litho. P 14.
1872 100f. Type **360** .... 1·20 1·00
1873 200f. City buildings .... 2·40 2·10
1874 300f. Mosaic panel .... 4·00 3·25
1872/1874 *Set of 3* .... 6·75 5·75

1998 (3 Aug). Second Arab Bee-keeping Conference. T **361** and similar multicoloured designs. Litho. P 13½.
1875 50f. Type **361** 75 70
1876 100f. Bee on flower (*vert*) .... 1·40 1·30
1877 150f. Bee, flower and honeycomb .... 2·10 2·00
1875/1877 *Set of 3* .... 3·75 3·50
MS1878 90×70 mm. 200f. Bees on flowers. Imperf .... 13·00 12·50

362 Dove with Stamp

1998 (9 Oct). International Stamp Day. T **362** and similar horiz designs. Multicoloured. Litho. P 14.
1879 50f. Type **362** .... 1·10 65
1880 100f. World map and Universal Postal Union emblem .... 1·80 1·10
1881 150f. Stamps encircling globe .... 3·00 1·80
1879/1881 *Set of 3* .... 5·25 3·25

363 King Hussein and Map of Jordan

1998 (14 Nov). 63rd Birthday of King Hussein. Litho. P 14.
1882 **363** 100f. multicoloured .... 1·10 1·00
1883 200f. multicoloured .... 2·30 2·10
1884 300f. multicoloured .... 3·50 3·25
1882/1884 *Set of 3* .... 6·25 5·75
MS1885 90×70 mm. 300f. King Hussein and map of Jordan (*different*). Imperf .... 13·00 12·50

364 King Hussein and Emblem

1998 (18 Nov). 25th Anniversary of Arab Police and Security Chiefs' Meeting. T **364** and similar multicoloured designs. Litho. P 13½.
1886 100f. Type **364** .... 1·10 1·00
1887 200f. Flags of member countries of Arab League (*vert*) .... 2·30 2·10
1888 300f. Police beret and map of Jordan .... 3·50 3·25
1886/1888 *Set of 3* .... 6·25 5·75

365 Family and Anniversary Emblem

366 Wahbi al Tal

1998 (10 Dec). 50th Anniversary of Universal Declaration of Human Rights. T **365** and similar horiz design. Multicoloured. Litho. P 14½.
1889 100f. Type **365** .... 1·10 1·00

1890 200f. Silhouettes of people and United Nations emblem .... 2·30 2·10

King Abdullah II

7 February 1999

1999 (25 May). Birth Centenary and 50th Death Anniversary of Mustafa Wahbi al Tal (poet). Litho. P 14½.

1891 **366** 100f. multicoloured .... 2·10 1·30

367 Mascot and Sports Pictograms

1999 (15 Aug). Ninth Arab Sports Tournament. T **367** and similar multicoloured designs. Litho. P 14×13½ (200f.) or 13½×14 (others).

1892 50f. Type **367** 75 40
1893 100f. Emblem, mascot and torch .... 1·10 70
1894 200f. Sportsmen, emblem and '9' (*vert*) .... 2·40 1·40
1895 300f. Jordanian flag, mascot and emblem .... 3·25 2·10
1892/1895 *Set of 4* .... 6·75 4·25
MS1896 90×70 mm. 200f. Mascot and sports pictograms. Imperf .... 5·25 5·00

368 Railway Map, Station and Train

1999 (7 Sept). Hijazi Railway Museum. T **368** and similar horiz design. Multicoloured. Litho. P 13½×14.

1897 100f. Type **368** .... 1·50 1·40
1898 200f. Type **368** .... 3·00 2·75
1899 300f. Train and station building .... 4·50 4·25
1897/1899 *Set of 3* .... 8·00 7·50

369 *Pachyseris speciosa*

(Litho Enschedé)

1999 (2 Oct). Marine Life in the Gulf of Aqaba. Corals. T **369** and similar horiz designs. Multicoloured. P 13½×14.

1900 50f. Type **369** 75 55
1901 100f. *Acropora digitfera* .... 1·50 1·30
1902 200f. *Oxypora lacera* .... 2·50 2·20
1903 300f. *Fungia echinata* .... 4·00 3·25
1900/1903 *Set of 4* .... 8·00 6·50
MS1904 90×70 mm. 200f. *Gorgonia*. Imperf .... 12·00 11·50

370 '125' and Emblem on Envelope

(Des A. Haddadin (1905), R. Taha (1906), A. Omer (**MS**1907). Litho Enschedé)

1999 (9 Oct). 125th Anniversary of Universal Postal Union. T **370** and similar horiz designs. Multicoloured. P 13½×14.

1905 100f. Type **370** .... 1·10 1·00
1906 200f. UPU emblem on envelope, target and post emblem .... 2·40 2·20
MS1907 90×70 mm. 200f. As No. 1906. Imperf .... 2·40 2·30

371 Children helping Sick Globe

(Des M. el Qaddoumi. Litho Enschedé)

1999 (14 Oct). Environmental Protection. T **371** and similar horiz design. Multicoloured. P 13½×14.

1908 100f. Type **371** .... 1·10 1·00
1909 200f. Hands holding globe as apple .... 1·90 1·70

372 Aerial View of Temple

(Des A. Mahredijian. Litho Enschedé)

1999 (24 Oct)–**2000**. Cradle of Civilisation. T **372** and similar horiz designs. Multicoloured. P 13½×14.

(a) Petra

1910 100f. Type **372** .... 1·10 1·00
a. Sheet of 30. Nos. 1910/1939 (3.12.00) ... 70·00
1911 200f. Front view of temple .... 2·10 1·80
1912 300f. Building in cliffs .... 3·25 2·75

(b) Jerash

1913 100f. Path between columns .... 1·10 1·00
1914 200f. Columns .... 2·10 1·80
1915 300f. Columns and ruined building .... 3·25 2·75

(c) Amman

1916 100f. Auditorium (30.10.99) .... 1·10 1·00
1917 200f. Columns (30.10.99) .... 2·10 1·80
1918 300f. Statues (30.10.99) .... 3·25 2·75

(d) Aqaba

1919 100f. Camels, Wadi Rum (30.10.99) .... 1·10 1·00
1920 200f. Building with wooden door (30.10.99) .. 2·10 1·80
1921 300f. Fort (30.10.99) .... 3·25 2·75

(e) Baptism Site

1922 100f. Rushes at water's edge (22.11.99) .... 1·10 1·00
1923 200f. Aerial view of site (22.11.99) .... 2·10 1·80
1924 300f. Archaeological site (22.11.99) .... 3·25 2·75

(f) Madaba

1925 100f. Mosaic of man (22.11.99) .... 1·10 1·00
1926 200f. Temple (22.11.99) .... 2·10 1·80
1927 300f. Mosaic of town (22.11.99) .... 3·25 2·75

(g) Pella

1928 100f. Columns and steps (7.3.00) .... 1·10 1·00
1929 200f. Columns and wall (7.3.00) .... 2·10 1·80
1930 300f. Columns and sheep (7.3.00) .... 3·25 2·75

(h) Ajloun

1931 100f. Castle (7.3.00) .... 1·10 1·00
1932 200f. Castle from below (7.3.00) .... 2·10 1·80
1933 300f. Hill top castle (7.3.00) .... 3·25 2·75

(i) Um Quais

1934 100f. Arches and columns (7.4.00) .... 1·10 1·00
1935 200f. Amphitheatre (7.4.00) .... 2·10 1·80
1936 300f. Columns and rubble (7.4.00) .... 3·25 2·75

(j) Desert Palaces

1937 100f. Mushatta (7.4.00) .... 1·10 1·00
1938 200f. Kharaneh (7.4.00) .... 2·10 1·80
1939 300f. Amra (7.4.00) .... 3·25 2·75
1910/1939 *Set of 30* .... 60·00 50·00

Nos. 1910/1939 were issued together in *se-tenant* sheets of 30 stamps.

373 Jordanian Stamps

(Des Philatelic Club. Litho)

1999 (14 Nov). 20th Anniversary of Jordan Philatelic Club. T **373** and similar horiz design. Multicoloured. P 14½.

1940 100f. Type **373** .... 1·10 1·00
1941 200f. Jordanian stamps (*different*) .... 2·10 1·80

374 Assembly Room

375 Jordanian Flag and Emblems

1999 (14 Nov). Museum of Political History. T **374** and similar horiz designs. Multicoloured. Litho. P 13½×14.

1942 100f. Type **374** .... 1·10 1·00
1943 200f. Courtyard .... 2·10 1·80
1944 300f. Entrance .... 3·25 2·75
1942/1944 *Set of 3* .... 5·75 5·00

1999 (23 Nov). 50th Anniversary of SOS Children's Villages. T **375** and similar vert design. Multicoloured. Litho. P 14½.

1945 100f. Type **375** .... 1·10 1·00
1946 200f. Woman and children .... 2·10 1·80

376 King Abdullah II

(Photo Courvoisier)

1999 (27 Dec). Coronation of King Abdullah II Bin Al-Hussein. T **376** and similar vert designs. P 11½.

1947 **376** 100f. multicoloured .... 1·10 1·00
1948 200f. multicoloured .... 2·10 1·80
1949 300f. multicoloured .... 3·25 2·75
1947/1949 *Set of 3* .... 5·75 5·00
MS1950 70×89 mm. 200f. No. 1948 but with gold border .... 3·25 3·00

377 King Abdullah II and Queen Rania

(Photo Courvoisier)

1999 (27 Dec). Coronation of King Abdullah II Bin Al-Hussein and Queen Rania al-Abdullah. T **377** and similar vert designs. P 11½.

1951 **377** 100f. multicoloured .... 1·10 1·00
1952 200f. multicoloured .... 2·10 1·80
1953 300f. multicoloured .... 3·25 2·75
1951/1953 *Set of 3* .... 5·75 5·00
MS1954 70×89 mm. 200f. No. 1952 but with gold border .... 3·25 3·00

378 Crowned Portrait

379 Red Cross Emblem and Jordanian Flag

2000 (30 Jan). 38th Birth Anniversary of King Abdullah II. T **378** and similar multicoloured designs. Litho. P 12.

1955 100f. Type **378** .... 1·10 1·00
1956 200f. King Abdullah II (*horiz*) .... 2·10 1·80
1957 300f. King Abdullah II and flag (*horiz*) .... 3·25 2·75
1955/1957 *Set of 3* .... 5·75 5·00
MS1958 90×74 mm. 200f. As No. 1956. Imperf .... 3·25 3·00

2000 (15 Feb). 50th Anniversary of Geneva Red Cross Conventions. T **379** and similar horiz designs. Multicoloured. Litho. P 13½×14.

1959 **379** 100f. multicoloured .... 1·10 1·00
a. Strip of 3. Nos. 1959/1961 .... 7·00
1960 200f. multicoloured .... 2·20 2·00
1961 300f. multicoloured .... 3·50 3·00
1959/1961 *Set of 3* .... 6·00 5·50

Nos. 1959/1961 were issued in *se-tenant* strips of three stamps within the sheet.

380 Flag and '2000 AD'

381 King Abdullah II, Rooves and Pope John Paul II

2000 (22 Feb). New Millennium. T **380** and similar vert designs. Multicoloured. Litho. P 13½.

1962 100f. Type **380** .... 1·10 1·00
a. Strip of 3. Nos. 1962/1964 .... 7·00
1963 200f. Palms, sand and fish swimming .... 2·20 2·00
1964 300f. As No. 1962 but inscription in Arabic .... 3·50 3·00
1962/1964 *Set of 3* .... 6·00 5·50

Nos. 1962/1964 were issued in *se-tenant* strips of three stamps within the sheet.

2000 (20 Mar). 36th Anniversary of Pope Paul VI's Visit to Jordan. T **381** and similar horiz designs. P 12.

1965 **381** 100f. multicoloured .... 1·10 1·00
1966 200f. multicoloured .... 2·20 2·00
1967 300f. multicoloured .... 3·50 3·00
1965/1967 *Set of 3* .... 6·00 5·50

382 Pope John Paul II and King Abdullah II

2000 (20 Mar). Pope John Paul II's Visit to Jordan. T **382** and similar horiz designs. Litho. P 12.

No.	Description	Unused	Used
1968	100f. Type **382**	1·10	1·00
1969	200f. Pope John Paul II, river and King Abdullah II	2·20	2·00
1970	300f. Pope John Paul II, flags and King Abdullah II	3·50	3·00
1968/1970	*Set of* 3	6·00	5·50
MS1971	70×90 mm. 200f. Pope John Paul II. Imperf.	8·00	7·25

383 Globe and Emblem

2000 (28 Mar). 50th Anniversary of World Meteorological Organisation. T **383** and similar horiz design. Multicoloured. Litho. P 12.

No.	Description	Unused	Used
1972	100f. Type **383**	1·60	1·40
1973	200f. Globe and emblem (*different*)	3·25	2·75

384 Emblem, Flag and '90'

385 Clinic Building and Emblem

2000 (11 May). 90th Anniversary of Jordan Boy Scouts. T **384** and similar horiz designs. Multicoloured. Litho. P 12.

No.	Description	Unused	Used
1974	100f. Type **384**	1·80	1·50
1975	200f. Pyramids	3·50	3·00
1976	300f. '90', flag and pyramids	5·00	4·50
1974/1976	*Set of* 3	9·25	8·00
MS1977	90×70 mm. 200f. As No. 1974 but with design enlarged. Imperf.	6·50	6·00

2000 (17 June). Al-Amal Cancer Centre. T **385** and similar vert designs. Multicoloured. Granite paper. Photo. P 11½.

No.	Description	Unused	Used
1978	200f. Type **385**	2·75	2·40
1979	300f. Emblem and family	4·25	3·75

386

387 Scales enclosing Palace of Justice

2000 (26 June). Palace of Justice, Amman. T **387** and similar horiz design. Multicoloured. W **386** (200f.). Litho. P 12.

No.	Description	Unused	Used
1980	100f. Type **387**	1·40	1·30
1981	200f. Building façade	2·75	2·40

388 Dove

389 Iris

2000 (28 Sept). Booklet Stamps. Endangered Species. T **388** and similar vert designs. Multicoloured. Litho. P 14.

No.	Description	Unused	Used
1982	50f. Type **388**	65	55
	a. Booklet pane. Nos. 1982/1983, each×2.	4·25	
1983	100f. Oryx	1·40	1·30
1984	150f. Caracal	2·20	2·00
	a. Booklet pane. Nos. 1984/1985, each×2.	11·00	
1985	200f. Red fox	3·00	2·50
1986	300f. Iris	4·50	4·00
	a. Booklet pane. Nos. 1986/1987, each×2.	22·00	
1987	400f. White broom	5·75	5·00
1982/1987	*Set of* 6	16·00	14·00

2000 (4 Oct). World Conservation Union Conference, Amman. T **389** and similar vert design. Granite paper. Photo. P 11½.

No.	Description	Unused	Used
1988	**389** 200f. multicoloured	3·00	2·50
1989	300f. multicoloured	4·50	4·00

390 Petra

391 Column Capital

2000 (9 Oct). Booklet Stamps. Tourism. T **390** and similar horiz designs. Multicoloured. Litho. P 14.

No.	Description	Unused	Used
1990	50f. Type **390**	65	40
	a. Booklet pane. Nos. 1990/1991, each×2.	4·25	
1991	100f. Jerash	1·30	1·00
1992	150f. Mount Nebo	1·90	1·50
	a. Booklet pane. Nos. 1992/1993, each×2.	9·00	
1993	200f. Dead Sea	2·50	2·00
1994	300f. Aqaba	3·75	3·00
	a. Booklet pane. Nos. 1994/1995, each×2.	18·00	
1995	400f. Wadi Rum	4·75	4·00
1990/1995	*Set of* 6	13·00	10·50

2000 (9 Oct). Expo 2000, Hanover. T **391** and similar multicoloured designs. Granite paper. Photo. P 11½.

No.	Description	Unused	Used
1996	200f. Type **391**	3·00	2·50
1997	300f. Statuette	4·50	4·00
MS1998	90×70 mm. 200f. King Abdullah, Queen Rania Al-Abdullah and Expo 2000 buildings	6·50	6·00

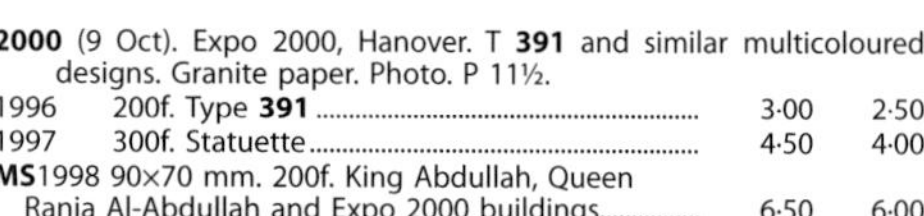

392 King Hussein

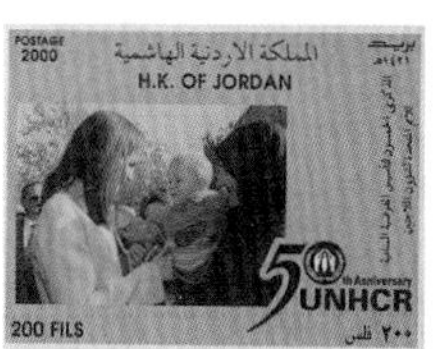
393 Women and Child

2000 (14 Nov). First Death Anniversary of King Hussein. T **392** and similar multicoloured designs. Granite paper. P 11½.

No.	Description	Unused	Used
1999	50f. Type **392**	65	55
2000	150f. King Hussein enclosed in wreath (*horiz*)	2·20	2·00
2001	200f. Symbols of industry and King Hussein (*horiz*)	3·00	2·50
1999/2001	*Set of* 3	5·25	4·50
MS2002	90×70 mm. 200f. As No. 2000 but with design enlarged	4·00	3·75

2000 (14 Dec). 50th Anniversary of United Nations High Commissioner for Refugees (2001). T **393** and similar horiz design. Granite paper. Photo. P 11½.

2003 200f. multicoloured .... 3·00 2·50
2004 300f. light turquoise green, deep ultramarine and black .... 4·50 4·00

Designs: 200f. Type **393**; 300f. UNHCR emblem.

394 Conference Emblem and Jordanian Flag

2001 (1 Aug). 13th Arab Summit Conference, Amman. T **394** and similar horiz designs. Multicoloured. Litho. P 14.

2005 50f. Type **394** 65 55
2006 200f. Flags, emblem and map of Arab countries .... 2·40 2·10
2007 250f. King Abdullah II and emblem .... 3·25 2·75
2005/2007 *Set of 3* .... 5·75 4·75

395 Muhammed al Durrah, his Father and Dome

2001 (5 Aug). First Death Anniversary of Muhammed al Durrah. T **395** and similar horiz design. Multicoloured. P 14.

2008 200f. Type **395** .... 2·40 2·10
2009 300f. Muhammed al Durrah and father .... 3·75 3·25

396 Dome of the Rock with Arms

397 Wheelchair User

2001 (5 Aug). Al Aqsa Intifada. T **396** and similar horiz design. Multicoloured. Litho. P 14.

2010 200f. Type **396** .... 2·40 2·10
2011 300f. Dome of the Rock and protesters .... 3·75 3·25

2001 (31 Oct). Sports for Special Needs. T **397** and similar vert design. Multicoloured. Litho. P 14.

2012 200f. Type **397** .... 2·40 2·10
2013 300f. Woman holding medal .... 3·75 3·25

No. 2013 is inscribed 'JORDON' instead of 'JORDAN'.

398 School Children and No-Smoking Sign

399 Olive Branches and Map of Jordan

2001 (31 Oct). Anti-Smoking Campaign. T **398** and similar multicoloured design. Litho. P 14.

2014 200f. Type **398** .... 2·40 2·10
2015 300f. Stylised student holding no-smoking sign (*vert*) .... 3·75 3·25

2001 (15 Nov). Olive Cultivation. T **399** and similar multicoloured design. Litho. P 14.

2016 200f. Type **399** .... 2·40 2·10
2017 300f. Girl holding olives (*vert*) .... 3·75 3·25

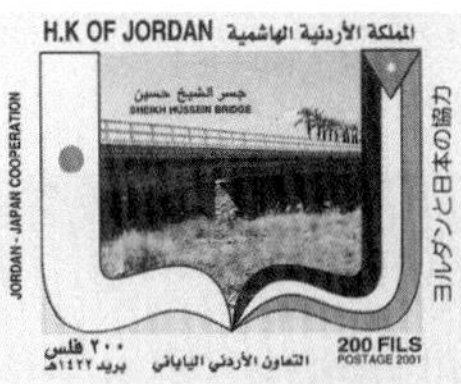

400 Family and World Map

401 Sheik Hussein Bridge and Japanese and Jordanian Flags

2001 (15 Nov). United Nations Year of Dialogue among Civilisations. T **400** and similar horiz design. Multicoloured. P 14.

2018 200f. Type **400** .... 2·40 2·10
2019 300f. Emblem, clasped hands and olive tree .... 3·75 3·25

No. 2019 is inscribed 'JORDON' instead of 'JORDAN'.

2001 (6 Dec). Japan–Jordan Co-operation. T **401** and similar horiz design. Multicoloured. P 14½.

2020 200f. Type **401** .... 2·40 2·10
2021 300f. King Hussein bridge and clasped hands .... 3·75 3·25

402 Emblem, Star and National Colours

403 Buildings

2002 (1 Jan). Amman, Arab Cultural Capital, 2002. T **402** and similar horiz designs. Multicoloured. Litho. P 14½.

2022 100f. Type **402** .... 1·10 1·00
2023 200f. Flame and pen .... 1·90 1·70
2024 300f. Emblem and amphitheatre .... 3·00 2·75
2022/2024 *Set of 3* .... 5·50 5·00

2002 (2 July). Jordanian Artists. T **403** and similar multicoloured designs. Litho. P 13.

2025 100f. Type **403** .... 1·10 1·00
2026 150f. *Abstract* (Mahmoud Taha) (*horiz*) .... 1·40 1·30
2027 200f. *Woman* (Mohanna Durra) .... 1·90 1·70
2028 300f. *Hilltop castle* (Wijdan) (*horiz*) .... 3·00 2·75
2025/2028 *Set of 4* .... 6·75 6·00

404 Bird carrying Envelope

405 Goldfinch

2002 (2 July). 25th Anniversary of Jordan–China Diplomatic Relations. T **404** and similar horiz design. Multicoloured. Litho. P 12.

2029 200f. Type **404** .... 1·90 1·70
2030 300f. King Abdullah II and President Jiang Zemin .... 3·00 2·75

2002 (18 July). Birds. T **405** and similar multicoloured designs. Litho. P 13.

2031 100f. Type **405** .... 1·40 1·30
2032 200f. Rufous Scrub Robin (inscr 'Rufous Bush Robin') .... 2·50 2·20
2033 300f. Stork .... 4·00 3·50
2031/2033 *Set of 3* .... 7·00 6·25
MS2034 70×90 mm. 200f. Golden Oriole, Goshawk, Bunting and Hoopoe .... 18·00 17·00

406 Symbols of Industry **407** Building Façade

2002 (15 Aug). Jordan Vision 2002 (campaign for economic development). T **406** and similar vert design. Multicoloured. Litho. P 13.

2035 200f. Type **406** ... 1·90 1·70
2036 300f. Hand and computer circuit board ... 3·00 2·75

2003 (Jan). Hadrian's Triumphal Arch, Jerash. Dated 2003. As T **310**. Multicoloured. P 12×13½.

2036*a* 25f. As Type **310** ... 30 30
2036*b* 25f. As Type **310** ... 65 55

2003 (2 July). Archaeological Museum. T **407** and similar horiz design. Multicoloured. Litho. P 14.

2037 150f. Type **407** ... 1·40 1·30
2038 250f. Building from below ... 2·50 2·20

408 Sherif Hussein bin Ali **409** *Cistanche tubulosa*

2003 (2 July). Hashemite Dynasty. Sheet 230×90 mm containing T **408** and similar vert designs. Multicoloured. Litho. P 14.

MS2039 200f.×5 Type **408**; King Abdullah; King Talal bin Abdullah; King Hussein bin Talal; King Abdullah II ... 9·50 9·00

2003 (7 Aug). Flora. T **409** and similar multicoloured designs. Litho. P 14.

2040 50f. Type **409** ... 65 55
2041 100f. *Ophioglossum polyphyllum (vert)* ... 1·40 1·30
2042 150f. *Narcissus tazetta* ... 1·90 1·70
2043 200f. *Gynandriris sisyrinchium (vert)* ... 2·50 2·20
2040/2043 *Set of* 4 ... 5·75 5·25

410 Italian Cypress (*Cupressus sempervirens*) **411** Short-toed Eagle (*Ciraetus gallicus*)

2003 (7 Aug). Trees. T **410** and similar horiz designs. Multicoloured. Litho. P 14.

2044 50f. Type **410** ... 1·10 1·00
2045 100f. *Pistacia atlantica* ... 1·40 1·30
2046 200f. *Quercus aegilops* ... 1·90 1·70
2044/2046 *Set of* 3 ... 4·00 3·50

2003 (9 Dec). Birds of Prey. T **411** and similar vert designs. Litho. P 14.

2047 100f. Type **411** ... 1·40 1·30
2048 200f. Peregrine Falcon (*Falco peregrinus*) ... 2·50 2·20
2049 300f. Northern Sparrow Hawk (*Accipter nisus*) ... 4·00 3·50
2047/2049 *Set of* 3 ... 7·00 6·25

MS2050 70×90 mm. 200f. *Ciraetus gallicus (different)*. Imperf ... 13·00 12·50

412 Company Emblem, Colours and Arch **413** Ferrari F40 (1989)

2003 (23 Dec). Jordan Post Company. T **412** and similar multicoloured design. P 14.

2051 50f. Type **412** ... 65 55
2052 100f. Columns, stamp outline and emblem ... 1·40 1·30

2003 (23 Dec). Royal Car Museum, Amman. T **413** and similar horiz designs. Multicoloured. Litho. P 14.

2053 100f. Type **413** ... 1·40 1·30
2054 150f. Rolls Royce Phantom V (1968) ... 1·90 1·70
2055 300f. Mercedes Benz Cabriolet D (1961) ... 3·75 3·25
2053/2055 *Set of* 3 ... 6·25 5·75

MS2056 90×70 mm. 200f. Panther J72 convertible (1972), Mercedes Benz 300 sc roadster (1956) and Cadillac 53 (1916). Imperf ... 12·00 11·00

CURRENCY

1 dinar = 100 qirsh/piastre = 1000 fils

414 Grey **415** Camels

2004 (27 Dec). Arabian Horses. T **414** and similar multicoloured designs. Litho. P 14.

2057 5pt. Type **414** ... 50 40
2058 7pt.50 Light bay, red bridle ... 80 70
2059 12pt.50 Dark bay ... 1·30 1·10
2060 15pt. Grey, long mane ... 1·60 1·40
2061 25pt. Chestnut ... 2·50 2·20
2057/2061 *Set of* 5 ... 6·00 5·25

MS2062 90×70 mm. 10pt. Two horses. Imperf ... 13·50 12·50

2004 (27 Dec). Children's Paintings. T **415** and similar horiz designs. Multicoloured. P 14.

2063 5pt. Type **415** ... 50 40
2064 7pt.50 Valley ... 65 55
2065 12pt.50 Sun ... 1·10 1·00
2066 15pt. Sea and buildings ... 1·30 1·10
2067 25pt. Buildings and tree ... 2·20 2·00
2063/2067 *Set of* 5 ... 5·25 4·50

MS2068 90×70 mm. 10pt. Collage of Nos. 2063/2067 (detail). Imperf ... 12·00 11·00

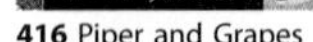

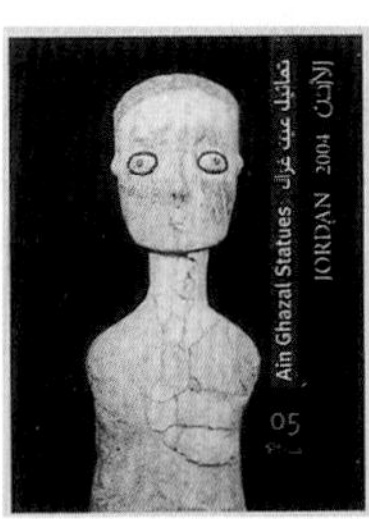

416 Piper and Grapes **417** Statue

2004 (27 Dec). Mosaics, Church of the Holy Martyrs, Mount Nebo. Sheet 205×110 mm containing T **416** and similar vert designs. Multicoloured. Litho. P 14.

MS2069 10pt. Type **416**; 10pt. Man using sickle (68×90 *mm*); 15pt. House; 25pt. Man carrying basket ... 13·00 12·00

2004 (29 Dec). Statues from Ain Ghazal (Neolithic site). T **417** and similar vert designs. Multicoloured. Litho. P 14.

2070	5pt. Type **417**	50	40
2071	7pt.50 Female statue	65	55
2072	12pt.50 Armless statue	1·10	1·00
2073	15pt. Statue with arms	1·30	1·10
2074	25pt. Two-headed statue	2·20	2·00
2070/2074	*Set of 5*	5·25	4·50
MS2075	70×90 mm. 10pt. Two statues. Imperf	12·00	11·00

418 **418** Nazareth Iris

419 Salt Deposit

2004 (29 Dec). Nazareth Iris (*Iris bismarkiana*). Sheet 224×167 mm containing T **418** and similar vert designs. Multicoloured. P 14.

MS2076 5pt. Type **418**; 7pt.50 Speckled petals; 10pt. Iris and bud (70×90 *mm*); 12pt.50 Lined petals; 15pt. Speckled petals below, striped petal above; 25pt. Throat of Iris flower ... 13·00 12·00

2005 (7 July). EXPO 2005, Aichi, Japan. Sheet 321×111 mm containing T **419** and similar vert designs. Multicoloured. P 14.

MS2077 5pt. Type **419**; 7pt.50 Encrusted salt deposit; 12pt.50 Layered salt deposit; 20pt. Cliffs and Dead Sea (70×90 *mm*) ... 8·00 7·75

420 Twoband Anemonefish

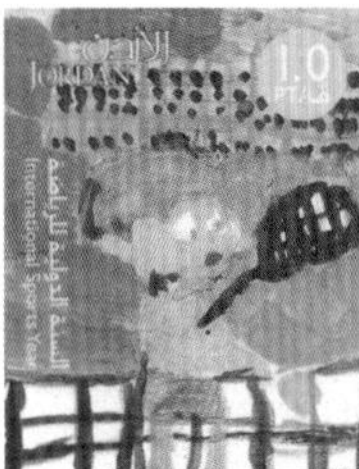
421 Tennis

2005 (27 Dec). Red Sea Fish. T **420** and similar vert designs. Multicoloured. Litho. P 14.

2078	0.5pt. Type **420**	30	30
2079	5pt. Emperor Angelfish	80	70
2080	7pt.50 Blue-masked Butterflyfish	1·30	1·10
2081	12pt.50 Pufferfish	2·20	2·00
2078/2081	*Set of 4*	4·25	3·75
MS2082	90×70 mm. 20pt. Ragged-finned Firefish	9·50	9·00

2005 (27 Dec). Children's Drawings. International Year of Sports and Sports Education. T **421** and similar multicoloured designs. Litho. P 14.

2083	1pt. Type **421**	30	30
2084	10pt. Medal winner	1·10	1·00
2085	15pt. Football (*horiz*)	1·80	1·50
2086	20pt. Swimmer (*horiz*)	2·40	2·10
2083/2086	*Set of 4*	5·00	4·50
MS2087	70×90 mm. 20pt. Boy. Imperf	8·75	8·50

422 Oryx

2005 (27 Dec). Arabian Oryx (*Oryx leucoryx*). T **422** and similar horiz designs. Multicoloured. Litho. P 14.

2088	1pt.50 Type **422**	50	40
2089	5pt. Mother and calf	1·30	1·10
2090	7pt.50 Calf and adults (*horiz*)	1·80	1·50
2091	12pt.50 Two adults (*horiz*)	3·00	2·50
2088/2091	*Set of 4*	6·00	5·00
MS2092	90×70 mm. 20pt. Head and shoulders	19·00	18·00

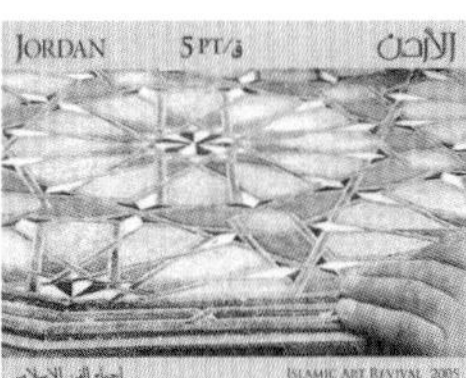
423 Mosaic

2005 (27 Dec). Islamic Art Revival. T **423** and similar horiz designs. Multicoloured. Litho. P 14.

2093	5pt. Type **423**	80	70
2094	7pt.50 Metalwork	1·10	1·00
2095	10pt. Calligraphy	1·40	1·30
2096	15pt. Wood carving	2·10	1·80
2093/2096	*Set of 4*	4·75	4·25
MS2097	90×70 mm. 20pt. Circular calligraphy. Imperf	9·50	9·00

424 Adult Hand holding Child's Hand

2005 (27 Dec). Child Protection. T **424** and similar horiz designs. Litho. P 14.

2098	7pt.50 silver and new blue	1·10	1·00
2099	10pt. silver and bright orange	1·60	1·40
2100	12pt.50 silver and bright carmine	2·10	1·80
2098/2100	*Set of 3*	4·25	3·75
MS2101	70×90 mm. 20pt. silver and gold. Imperf	9·50	9·00

Designs: 7pt.50 T **424**; 10pt. Child enclosed in adult arms; 12pt.50 Adult arms holding toddler; 20pt. Boy with head on hand.

425 Japanese Calligraphy

2005 (27 Dec). Jordan–Japan Friendship. T **425** and similar multicoloured designs. Litho. P 14.

2102	7pt.50 Type **425**	95	85
2103	12pt.50 Floodlit buildings	1·60	1·40
2104	15pt. Museum by day	1·90	1·70
2102/2104	*Set of 3*	4·00	3·50
MS2105	70×90 mm. 20pt. Museum exhibits. Imperf	10·50	9·75

426 Omayyad Coin

427 '2006 FIFA World Cup, Germany'

2006 (1 Jan). Coins. T **426** and similar multicoloured designs showing early coins. Litho. P 14.

2106 5pt. Type **426** ... 80 70
2107 7pt.50 Hisham (obverse) ... 1·10 1·00
2108 10pt. Abbasid ... 1·60 1·40
2109 12pt.50 Omayyad ... 2·10 1·80
2110 15pt. Hisham (reverse) ... 2·40 2·10
2106/2110 *Set of* 5 ... 7·25 6·25
MS2111 90×70 mm. 30pt. Omayyad. Imperf ... 9·50 9·00

2006 (1 Jan). World Cup Football Championship, Germany. T **427** and similar multicoloured designs. Litho. P 14.

2112 5pt. Type **427** ... 80 70
2113 7pt.50 As Type **427** ... 1·10 1·00
2114 10pt. Championship emblem ... 1·60 1·40
2115 12pt.50 As No. 2112 ... 2·10 1·80
2116 15pt. As No. 2112 ... 2·40 2·10
2112/2116 *Set of* 5 ... 7·25 6·25
MS2117 90×70 mm. 30pt. Championship emblem. Imperf ... 9·50 9·00

428 Waterfront Development

429 Police Vehicle

2006 (1 Jan). Contemporary Architecture. T **428** and similar multicoloured designs. Litho. P 14.

2118 7pt.50 Type **428** ... 1·10 1·00
2119 10pt. Interior (*horiz*) ... 1·60 1·40
2120 12pt.50 Garden (*horiz*) ... 2·10 1·80
2118/2120 *Set of* 3 ... 4·25 3·75
MS2121 90×70 mm. 20pt. Curved façade. Imperf ... 8·00 7·75

2006 (1 Jan). Public Service Vehicles. T **429** and similar horiz designs. Multicoloured. Litho. P 14.

2122 10pt. Type **429** ... 1·10 1·00
2123 12pt.50 Fire engine ... 1·60 1·40
2124 17pt.50 Waste disposal truck ... 2·10 1·80
2125 20pt. Support vans ... 2·50 2·20
2122/2125 *Set of* 4 ... 6·50 5·75
MS2126 90×70 mm. 20pt. Ambulance. Imperf ... 7·75 7·25

430 Blue Lizard

431 Hearts

2006 (21 Oct). Desert Reptiles. T **430** and similar multicoloured designs. Litho. P 14.

2127 5pt. Type **430** ... 70 65
2128 7pt.50 Snake ... 1·10 95
2129 10pt. Two Lizards ... 1·40 1·30
2130 12pt.50 Lizard ... 1·80 1·60
2131 15pt. Small Lizard (*horiz*) ... 2·20 1·90
2132 20pt. Viper ... 3·00 2·50
2127/2132 *Set of* 6 ... 9·25 8·00
MS2133 90×70 mm. 20pt. Monitor Lizard. Imperf ... 9·00 8·75

2006 (21 Oct). Art. T **431** and similar multicoloured designs. Litho. P 14.

2134 5pt. Type **431** ... 70 65
2135 10pt. Dancers ... 1·40 1·30
2136 15pt. Buildings ... 2·20 1·90
2137 20pt. Abstract ... 3·00 2·50
2134/2137 *Set of* 4 ... 6·50 5·75
MS2138 90×70 mm. 20pt. Four paintings. Imperf ... 9·00 8·75

432 King Abdullah II

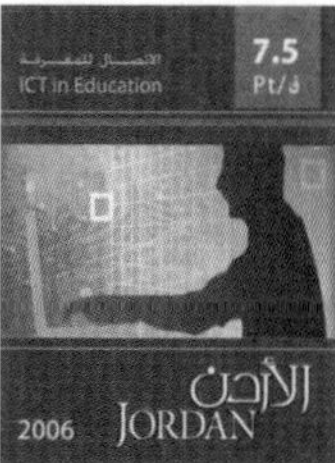

433 Laptop User

2006 (11 Nov). National Celebration. T **432** and similar multicoloured designs. Litho. P 14.

2139 5pt. Type **432** ... 70 65
2140 7pt.50 King Abdullah II wearing suit ... 1·10 95
2141 10pt. Armed forces (*horiz*) ... 1·40 1·30
2142 12pt.50 King Abdullah II wearing army uniform ... 1·80 1·60
2143 15pt. National Flag (*horiz*) ... 2·20 1·90
2144 20pt. Sharif Hussein bin Ali during a visit to Amman, 1924 (*horiz*) ... 3·00 2·50
2145 25pt. Army tanks in parade (*horiz*) ... 3·50 3·25
2146 30pt. Rose on flag (*horiz*) ... 4·25 3·75
2139/2146 *Set of* 8 ... 16·00 14·50

2006 (11 Nov). ICT in Education. T **433** and similar vert designs. Multicoloured. Litho. P 14.

2147 7pt.50 Type **433** ... 1·10 95
2148 12pt.50 Woman using touch screen ... 1·80 1·60
2149 15pt. Man using touch screen ... 2·20 1·90
2150 20pt. Woman using mobile telephone ... 3·00 2·50
2147/2150 *Set of* 4 ... 7·25 6·25
MS2151 70×90 mm. 20pt. Hand and key pad. Imperf ... 9·00 8·75

Nos. 2152 and 2153 are vacant.

434 Orange

435 Mafraq

2007 (16 July). Fruit. T **434** and similar vert designs. Multicoloured. Paper with fluorescent fibres. P 14.

2154 10p. Type **434** ... 1·40 1·30
2155 15p. Cherries ... 2·10 1·90
2156 20p. Figs ... 2·75 2·50
2157 25p. Pomegranate ... 3·50 3·25
2158 30p. Grapes ... 4·25 3·75
2154/2158 *Set of* 5 ... 12·50 11·50

2007 (16 July). Traditional Women's Clothes. T **435** and similar vert designs. Multicoloured. Paper with fluorescent fibres. P 14.

2159 10p. Type **435** ... 1·40 1·30
2160 15p. Ma'an ... 2·10 1·90
2161 20p. Amman ... 2·75 2·50
2162 25p. Jerash ... 3·50 3·25
2163 30p. Salt ... 4·25 3·75
2159/2163 *Set of* 5 ... 12·50 11·50

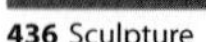

436 Sculpture

437 Doorway

2007 (16 July). Petra. T **436** and similar vert designs. Multicoloured. Paper with fluorescent fibres. P 14.

2164	10p. Type **436**	1·40	1·30
2165	15p. Ceramic plate	2·10	1·90
2166	20p. Carved leaves	2·75	2·50
2167	25p. Siq al Barid	3·50	3·25
2168	30p. Rock formation	4·25	3·75
2164/2168	*Set of* 5	12·50	11·50
MS2168*a*	87×105 mm 40p. Treasury. P 13½.	11·50	11·00
MS2168*b*	71×91 mm. As **MS**2168*a*. Imperf	12·50	12·00

2007 (16 July). Aqaba. T **437** and similar vert designs. Multicoloured. Paper with fluorescent fibres. P 14.

2169	10p. Type **437**	1·40	1·30
2170	15p. Scuba diver	2·10	1·90
2171	20p. Marina	2·75	2·50
2172	30p. Yacht	4·25	3·75
2169/2172	*Set of* 4	9·50	8·50

438 Butterfly

439 Metal Jug

2007 (31 Dec). Butterflies. T **438** and similar multicoloured designs. P 14.

2173	10p. Type **438**	1·40	1·30
2174	15p. Brimstone	2·10	1·90
2175	20p. Large White	2·75	2·50
2176	25p. White Admiral (*horiz*)	3·50	3·25
2177	30p. Orange Tip (*horiz*)	4·25	3·75
2173/2177	*Set of* 5	12·50	11·50
MS2178	90×70 mm. 40p. Clouded Yellow. Imperf	9·25	9·00

2007 (31 Dec). Islamic Art. T **439** and similar multicoloured designs. P 14.

2179	10p. Type **439**	1·40	1·30
2180	20p. Iron jug with legs and animal head spout	2·75	2·50
2181	30p. Octagonal incised jug	4·25	3·75
2179/2181	*Set of* 3	7·50	6·75
MS2182	90×70 mm. 25p. Jug with tall spout. Imperf	8·00	7·50

440 Pile of Books

441 Suspension Bridge

2007 (31 Dec). Culture and Identity. T **440** and similar vert designs. Multicoloured. P 14.

2183	10p. Type **440**	1·40	1·30
2184	20p. Lute	2·75	2·50
2185	25p. Desert scene enclosed in bottle	3·50	3·25
2186	30p. Script	4·25	3·75
2183/2186	*Set of* 4	10·50	9·75
MS2186*a*	70×90 mm. 20p. Details of designs from Nos. 2183/2186 and paint brushes. Imperf	7·00	6·50

2008 (22 Sept). 50th Anniversary of Engineers' Association. T **441** and similar multicoloured designs. Granite paper. P 14.

2187	15p. Type **441**	2·10	1·90
2188	20p. '50' (*vert*)	2·75	2·50
2189	25p. Pylons	3·50	3·25
2187/2189	*Set of* 3	7·50	7·00

442 Taekwondo

443 Oud

2008 (22 Sept). Olympic Games, Beijing. T **442** and similar vert designs. Multicoloured. Granite paper. P 14.

2190	20p. Type **442**	2·75	2·50
2191	30p. Equestrian	4·25	3·75
2192	40p. Table Tennis	5·50	5·00
2193	50p. Athletics	7·00	6·25
2190/2193	*Set of* 4	18·00	16·00

2008 (22 Sept). Musical Instruments. T **443** and similar multicoloured designs. P 14.

2194	20p. Type **443**	1·80	1·70
2195	40p. Rababah	3·75	3·25
2196	60p. Kanoun	5·50	5·00
2197	80p. Flute	7·25	6·75
2198	100p. Drum	9·25	8·50
2194/2198	*Set of* 5	25·00	23·00
MS2199	90×70 mm. 50p. Instruments	7·00	6·50

444 *Silene aegyptiaca* (inscr 'Egyptian Catchfly')

445 Fresco

2008 (15 Nov). Flowers. T **444** and similar multicoloured designs. P 14.

2200	5p. Type **444**	45	40
2201	10p. Inscr 'Lupin'	90	85
2202	15p. Judean Viper's Bugloss (*Echium judaeum*)	1·40	1·30
2203	20p. Blue Pimpernel	1·80	1·70
2204	30p. Inscr 'Asiatic Crowfoot'	2·75	2·50
2205	40p. Grape Hyacinth	3·75	3·25
2206	50p. Large Flowered Sage	4·50	4·25
2207	60p. Star of Bethlehem	5·50	5·00
2208	80p. Orchid Pyramidalis	7·25	6·75
2209	100p. Calotropis (inscr 'calotrpis')	9·25	8·50
2200/2209	*Set of* 10	34·00	31·00
MS2210	90×70 mm. 50p. Cyclamen. Imperf	7·00	6·50

2008 (15 Nov). World Heritage Site. Quseir Amra (early 8th-century castle, one of the most important examples of early Islamic art). T **445** and similar horiz designs showing frescoes. Multicoloured. P 14.

2211	40pt. Type **445**	3·75	3·25
2212	60pt. Grapes and vine	5·50	5·00
2213	80pt. Games	7·25	6·75
2214	100pt. Face	9·25	8·50
2211/2214	*Set of* 4	23·00	21·00
MS2215	90×70 mm. 50pt. Quseir Amra	7·00	6·50

2009 (2 Feb). Centenary of Hejaz Railway. Horiz designs showing railway. Multicoloured. P 14.

2216	20pt. Steam train crossing bridge	2·30	1·70
2217	30pt. Steam locomotive	3·50	2·50
2218	50pt. Railway station	5·75	4·25
2216/2218	*Set of* 3	10·50	7·50

T **446** is unavailable.

2009 (2 Feb). Birds. Horiz designs as T **405**. Multicoloured. P 14.

2219	10pt. *Anas platyrhynchos* (Mallard)	90	85
2220	15pt. *Falco cherrug* (Saker Falcon)	1·40	1·30

2221	20pt. *Cursorius cursor* (Cream-coloured Courser)	1·80	1·70
2222	30pt. Palestine Sunbird (*Nectarinia osea*)	2·75	2·50
2223	40pt. *Upupa epops* (Hoopoe)	3·75	3·25
2224	50pt. *Francolinus francolinus* (Black Francolin)	4·50	4·25
2225	60pt. *Merops orientalis* (Green Bee-eater)	5·50	5·00
2226	80pt. *Carpodacus synoicus* (Sinai Rosefinch)	7·25	6·75
2219/2226	*Set of* 8	25·00	23·00

T **447**, No. 2227 is vacant.

448 Coffee Grinder

449 Woman wearing Dress with Embroidered Bodice

2009 (1 Mar). Coffee Drinking. T **448** and similar vert designs. Multicoloured. P 14.

2228	40p. Type **448**	3·75	3·25
2229	60p. Coffee pots and coffee roasting over embers	5·50	5·00
2230	80p. Coffee pot and cups	7·25	6·75
2231	100p. Coffee and coffee roasting implements	9·25	8·50
2228/2231	*Set of* 4	23·00	21·00
MS2232	70×90 mm. 50p. Coffee making equipment. Imperf	7·00	6·50

2009 (1 Mar). Traditional Clothes. T **449** and similar vert designs. Multicoloured. P 14.

2233	40p. Type **449**	3·75	3·25
2234	60p. Woman wearing brown dress and white veil	5·50	5·00
2235	80p. Woman wearing red headdress and coin jewellery	7·25	6·75
2236	100p. Couple	9·25	8·50
2233/2236	*Set of* 4	23·00	21·00
MS2237	70×90 mm. 50p. As Type **449** (enlarged detail). Imperf	7·00	6·50

450 Pope Benedict XVI and King Abdullah II

451 King Abdullah II

2009 (8 May). Visit of Pope Benedict XVI. T **450** and similar horiz designs. Multicoloured. P 14.

2238	20p. Type **450**	1·80	1·70
2239	30p. Pope Benedict XVI	2·75	2·50
2240	40p. Pope Benedict XVI and King Abdullah II (*different*)	3·75	3·25
2238/2240	*Set of* 3	7·50	6·75
MS2241	90×70 mm. 50p. As No. 2240 (enlarged detail). Imperf	8·00	7·50

2009 (June). Tenth Anniversary of Accession of King Abdullah II. P 14.

2242	**451**	10p. multicoloured	90	85
2243		15p. multicoloured	1·40	1·30
2244		20p. multicoloured	1·80	1·70
2245		25p. multicoloured	2·30	2·10
2246		30p. multicoloured	2·75	2·50
2247		35p. multicoloured	3·25	3·00
2248		40p. multicoloured	3·75	3·25
2249		45p. multicoloured	4·25	3·75
2250		50p. multicoloured	4·50	4·25
2251		1d. multi-coloured	9·25	8·50
2242/2251		*Set of* 10	31·00	28·00

452 Diana, the Huntress (As T **2342** of USA)

453 Horse

2009 (25 Aug). Breast Cancer Awareness Campaign. P 14.

2252	**452**	30pt. +50pt. multicoloured	7·25	6·75

2009 (26 Aug). Fauna. T **453** and similar horiz designs. Multicoloured. P 14.

2253	10pt. Type **453**	90	85
2254	20pt. Rabbits	1·80	1·70
2255	30pt. Fox	2·75	2·50
2256	40pt. Oryx (inscr 'Maha Gazelle')	3·75	3·25
2257	50pt. Gazelle	4·50	4·25
2253/2257	*Set of* 5	12·50	11·50
MS2258	90×70 mm. 60pt. Camel. Imperf	7·00	6·50

No. 2259 is vacant.

454 Cables

455 Spring-fed Waterfalls

2009 (26 Aug). e-Government Programme. T **454** and similar vert designs. Multicoloured. P 14.

2260	20pt. Type **454**	1·80	1·70
2261	30pt. Emblem	2·75	2·50
2262	40pt. 'www.jordan.gov.jo'	3·75	3·25
2263	50pt. Symbols of communication	4·50	4·25
2260/2263	*Set of* 4	11·50	10·50

2009 (7 Oct). Hammamat Ma'een Hot Springs. T **455** and similar vert designs. Multicoloured. P 14.

2264	10pt. Type **455**	90	85
2265	20pt. Resort	1·80	1·70
2266	30pt. Waterfall and pool	2·75	2·50
2267	40pt. Waterfalls (*different*)	3·75	3·25
2268	50pt. Springs and dam	4·50	4·25
2264/2268	*Set of* 5	12·50	11·50
MS2269	70×90 mm. 60pt. Single waterfall	7·00	6·50

456

457

458

459

460

461

462

463

464

465

466 Sweetcorn

2009 (7 Oct). Jordanian Universities. P 14.

2270 **456** 20pt. multicoloured ..... 1·80 1·70
2271 **457** 20pt. multicoloured ..... 1·80 1·70
2272 **458** 20pt. multicoloured ..... 1·80 1·70
2273 **459** 20pt. multicoloured ..... 1·80 1·70
2274 **460** 20pt. multicoloured ..... 1·80 1·70
2275 **461** 20pt. multicoloured ..... 1·80 1·70
2276 **462** 20pt. multicoloured ..... 1·80 1·70
2277 **463** 20pt. multicoloured ..... 1·80 1·70
2278 **464** 20pt. multicoloured ..... 1·80 1·70
2279 **465** 20pt. multicoloured ..... 1·80 1·70
2270/2279 *Set of* 10 ..... 16·00 15·00

2009 (7 Oct). Vegetables. T **466** and similar horiz designs. Multicoloured. P 14.

2280 20pt. Type **466** ..... 1·80 1·70
a. Sheetlet of 10. Nos. 2280/2289 ..... 19·00
2281 20pt. Garlic and Onions ..... 1·80 1·70
2282 20pt. Peas, Beans and Okra ..... 1·80 1·70
2283 20pt. Cabbages ..... 1·80 1·70
2284 20pt. Aubergines ..... 1·80 1·70
2285 20pt. Pumpkin ..... 1·80 1·70
2286 20pt. Sweet Peppers ..... 1·80 1·70
2287 20pt. Chilli Peppers ..... 1·80 1·70
2288 20pt. Turnips, Swedes and Radishes ..... 1·80 1·70
2289 20pt. Tomatoes and Courgettes ..... 1·80 1·70
2280/2289 *Set of* 10 ..... 16·00 15·00

Nos. 2280/2289 were printed, *se-tenant*, in sheetlets of ten stamps.

467 Distressed Tree and Litter

2009 (13 Dec). Environmental Protection. T **467** and similar vert design. Multicoloured. P 14.

2290 20pt. Type **467** ..... 1·80 1·70
2291 30pt. Litter on fire and children running ..... 2·75 2·50
2292 40pt. Farm animals eating litter ..... 3·75 3·25
2293 50pt. Litter in stream and recycling bins ..... 4·50 4·25
2290/2293 *Set of* 4 ..... 11·50 10·50

No. 2294 is vacant.

468 Emblem

469 Stag Beetle

2009 (13 Dec). al-Quds–2009 Arab Capital of Culture. P 14.

2295 **468** 20pt. +25pt. multicoloured ..... 4·25 3·75
2296 30pt. +25pt. multicoloured ..... 5·00 4·50
2297 40pt. +25pt. multicoloured ..... 6·00 5·50
2298 50pt. +25pt. multicoloured ..... 7·00 6·25
2295/2298 *Set of* 4 ..... 20·00 18·00

2009 (13 Dec). Insects. T **469** and similar vert designs. Multicoloured. Granite paper. P 13½.

2299 10pt. Type **469** 90 85
2300 15pt. Butterfly ..... 1·40 1·30
2301 20pt. Ladybird ..... 1·80 1·70
2302 25pt. Honey Bee ..... 2·30 2·10
2303 30pt. Mantis ..... 2·75 2·50
2304 40pt. Moth ..... 3·75 3·25
2305 50pt. Dragon Fly ..... 4·50 4·25
2306 60pt. Fly ..... 5·50 5·00
2307 80pt. Grasshopper ..... 7·25 6·75
2308 100pt. Dragon Fly and Damsel Fly ..... 9·25 8·50
2299/2308 *Set of* 10 ..... 35·00 33·00

(**470**)

2009 (20 Dec). Nos. 929/931 surch as T **470**. P 13½.

2309 80pt. on 120f. black and salmon (Type **139**) ..... 7·25 6·75
2310 80pt. on 180f. black, deep brown and lilac (No. 930) ..... 7·25 6·75
2311 80pt. on 200f. multicoloured (No. 931) ..... 7·25 6·75
2309/2311 *Set of* 3 ..... 20·00 18·00

80 pt

(**470a**)

471 Ajlun

2009 (20 Dec). Un-listed Stamp 25f. of 2003 (as No. 1788) surch T **470a**. Granite paper. P 13×13½.

2311*a* 80pt. on 25f. chestnut, pale reddish purple and black (Type **310**) ..... 7·25 6·75

2010 (3 Oct). Tourism. T **471** and similar horiz designs. Multicoloured. P 14.

2312 10pt. Type **471** 90 85
2313 20pt. Column and capital, Amman ..... 1·80 1·70
2314 30pt. Stone corridor, Karak ..... 2·75 2·50
2315 40pt. Stone staircase, Showbak ..... 3·75 3·25
2312/2315 *Set of* 4 ..... 8·25 7·50
MS2316 90×70 mm. 50pt. Partial façade, Jerash. Imperf ..... 4·50 4·25

472 *Cortinarius balteatus*

473 Jordan University Mosque

2010 (3 Oct). Fungi. T **472** and similar horiz designs. Multicoloured. P 12.

2317 20pt. Type **472** ..... 1·80 1·70
a. Sheetlet of 8. Nos. 2317/2324 ..... 15·00
2318 20pt. *Russula bicolor* ..... 1·80 1·70
2319 20pt. Fly agaric (inscr 'Red Fly Agaric') ..... 1·80 1·70
2320 20pt. Inscr 'Amanita muscaria' ..... 1·80 1·70
2321 20pt. *Boletus edulis* ..... 1·80 1·70
2322 20pt. *Amanita ocreata* (inscr 'Amanita albocreata') ..... 1·80 1·70

2323 20pt. Inscr 'Agaricus Anderwij' 1·80 1·70
2324 20pt. *Agaricus bisporus* 1·80 1·70
2317/2324 *Set of* 8 13·00 12·00

Nos. 2317/2324 were printed, *se-tenant*, in sheetlets of eight stamps.

2010 (30 Nov). Mosques. T **473** and similar horiz designs showing mosques. Multicoloured. P 14.

2325 10pt. Type **473** 90 85
2326 20pt. Abu-Darwiesh 1·80 1·70
2327 30pt. Al-Hussainy 2·75 2·50
2328 40pt. King Abdullah Mosque 3·75 3·25
2329 50pt. King Hussain Bin Talal Mosque 4·50 4·25
2325/2329 *Set of* 5 12·50 11·50

474 Skydiving

475 Ma'an Development Area

2010 (30 Nov). Sports. T **474** and similar vert designs. Multicoloured. P 14.

2330 10pt. Type **474** 90 85
2331 20pt. Swimming 1·80 1·70
2332 30pt. Air ballooning 2·75 2·50
2333 40pt. Yacht racing 3·75 3·25
2330/2333 *Set of* 4 8·25 7·50
MS2334 70×90 mm. 50pt. Rallying. Imperf 4·50 4·25

2011 (27 Feb). Developmental Zones. T **475** and similar vert designs. Multicoloured. P 14.

2335 20pt. Type **475** 1·80 1·70
2336 20pt. King Hussain Bin Talal Development Area 1·80 1·70
2337 20pt. Dead Sea Development Zone 1·80 1·70
2338 20pt. Jabal Ajloun Development Area 1·80 1·70
2339 20pt. Irbid Development Area 1·80 1·70
2335/2339 *Set of* 5 8·00 7·75

476 *Ocimum basilicum*

477 Millstone

2011 (27 Feb). Wild Herbs. T **476** and similar vert designs. Multicoloured. P 14.

2340 20pt. Type **472** 1·80 1·70
2341 20pt. *Matricaria chamomilia* 1·80 1·70
2342 20pt. *Salvia officinalis* 1·80 1·70
2343 20pt. *Thymus serpyllum* (inscr 'Thymus seryvllum') 1·80 1·70
2344 20pt. *Lavender* (inscr 'Lavandulaivera') 1·80 1·70
2345 20pt. *Artemisia herba alba* 1·80 1·70
2346 20pt. *Capparis spinsa* (inscr 'Capparis spinsa') 1·80 1·70
2347 20pt. *Trignella foenum-graecum* 1·80 1·70
2340/2347 *Set of* 8 13·00 12·00

2011 (27 Feb). Antique Tools. T **477** and similar horiz designs. P 14.

2348 20pt. Type **477** 1·80 1·70
2349 20pt. Horse drawn flail 2·75 2·50
2350 20pt. Pitchfork 3·75 3·25
2351 20pt. Donkey powered olive crusher 4·50 4·25
2348/2351 *Set of* 4 11·50 10·50

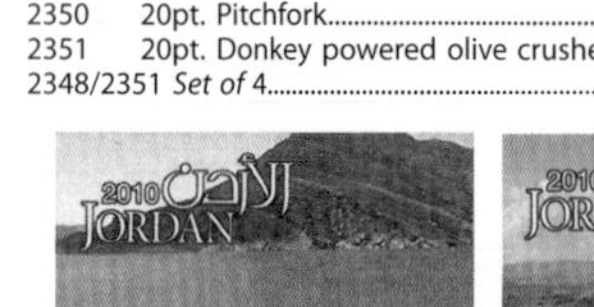

478 Dam

479 Dam

480 Dam

481 Dam

482 Dam

483 Dam

484 Dam

485 Dam

486 Dam

487 Dam

2011 (10 May). Dams. P 14.

2352 **478** 20pt. multicoloured 1·80 1·70
2353 **479** 20pt. multicoloured 1·80 1·70
2354 **480** 20pt. multicoloured 1·80 1·70
2355 **481** 20pt. multicoloured 1·80 1·70
2356 **482** 20pt. multicoloured 1·80 1·70
2357 **483** 20pt. multicoloured 1·80 1·70
2358 **484** 20pt. multicoloured 1·80 1·70
2359 **485** 20pt. multicoloured 1·80 1·70
2360 **486** 20pt. multicoloured 1·80 1·70
2361 **487** 20pt. multicoloured 1·80 1·70
2352/2361 *Set of* 10 16·00 15·00
MS2362 90×70 mm. 30pt. As Type **480**. Imperf 5·75 5·25

488 Necklace

489 Fencers

2011 (10 May). Traditional Jewellery. T **488** and similar vert designs. P 14.

2363 20pt. Type **488** 1·80 1·70
2364 30pt. Turquoise and gold 'doughnut', Hand of Fatima pendant and gold chain with decorative inserts 2·75 2·50
2365 40pt. Large decorated gold ring 3·75 3·25
2366 50pt. Necklace with several pendants 4·50 4·25
2363/2366 *Set of* 4 11·50 10·50
MS2367 77×76 mm. 30pt. Pierced work bangle. Imperf 5·75 5·50

2011 (6 Apr). Fencing Championship. T **489** and similar multicoloured designs showing fencers, background colour given. P 14.

2368 10pt. Type **489** 90 85
2369 20pt. Hit (purple) 1·80 1·70
2370 30pt. Attack (green) 2·75 2·50
2371 40pt. Lunge (bistre) 3·75 3·25

2372 50pt. Lunge and parry (grey) 4·50 4·25
2368/2372 *Set of* 5 12·50 11·50
MS2373 75×94 mm. 50pt. Lunge and leap. Imperf 7·00 6·50

490 Red Bull Citroën Rally Car

2011 (14 Apr). FIA World Rally Championship (WRC), Jordan. T **490** and similar horiz designs showing rally cars. Multicoloured. P 14.

2374 10pt. Type **490** 90 85
2375 20pt. Sports Academy Racing Team Mitsubishi race car 1·80 1·70
2376 30pt. BP Ford Abu Dhabi race car 2·75 2·50
2377 40pt. Rally Jordan P-WRC winner Patrik Flodin (No. 48) 3·75 3·25
2378 50pt. Red Mitsubishi race car 4·50 4·25
2374/2378 *Set of* 5 12·50 11·50
MS2379 93×74 mm. 50pt. Subaru race car (No. 3). Imperf 7·00 6·50

491 *Diploria strigosa*

492 Tall Jug and Head

2011 (28 Sept). Marine Life. Red Sea Coral Reefs. T **491** and similar horiz designs. Multicoloured. P 14.

2380 20pt. Type **491** 1·80 1·70
2381 30pt. Coral and fish 2·75 2·50
2382 40pt. *Diploastrea heliopora* 3·75 3·25
2383 50pt. *Acropora hyacinthus* 4·50 4·25
2384 60pt. *Pectinia lactuca* 5·50 5·00
2380/2384 *Set of* 5 16·00 15·00
MS2385 90×70 mm. 40pt. Coral bed and fish. Imperf 5·75 5·50

2011 (28 Sept). Ceramics. T **492** and similar vert designs. Multicoloured. P 14.

2386 10pt. Type **492** 90 85
2387 20pt. Complex plaque with raised fortified decoration 1·80 1·70
2388 30pt. Circular jug with script decoration 2·75 2·50
2389 40pt. Flat circular tile with lower left extrusion 3·75 3·25
2390 50pt. Flat circular tile with lower right eroded 4·50 4·25
2391 60pt. Circular vessel on stand 5·50 5·00
2386/2391 *Set of* 6 17·00 16·00
MS2392 70×90 mm. 30pt. Tiles. Imperf 3·50 3·25

493 King Abdullah II

494 Astrolabe

2011 (28 Sept). Historical Path. T **493** and similar multicoloured designs. P 14.

2393 20pt. Type **493** 1·80 1·70
2394 20pt. Harpist, carving 1·80 1·70
2395 20pt. White buildings on hillside (*horiz*) 1·80 1·70
2396 20pt. Assyrian bas-relief with figures and tree (*horiz*) 1·80 1·70
2397 20pt. Antelopes and figues, carving (*horiz*) 1·80 1·70
2398 20pt. Damaged fresco showing ships (*horiz*) 1·80 1·70
2399 20pt. Stylised multicoloured decorative buildings (*horiz*) 1·80 1·70
2400 20pt. Building (*horiz*) 1·80 1·70
2401 20pt. Circular plaque with woman's head (*horiz*) 1·80 1·70
2402 20pt. Ceres, bas-relief (*horiz*) 1·80 1·70
2393/2402 *Set of* 10 16·00 15·00

2012 (23 Jan). Old Astronomical Instruments. T **494** and similar vert designs. Multicoloured. Granite paper. P 14.

2403 10pt. Type **494** 90 85
2404 20pt. Telescope 1·80 1·70
2405 30pt. Sextant 2·75 2·50
2406 40pt. Sundial 3·75 3·25
2403/2406 *Set of* 4 8·25 7·50

495 Crown Prince Hussein

2012 (23 Jan). Crown Prince Hussein bin Abdullah. Granite paper. P 14.

2407 **495** 20pt. multicoloured 1·80 1·70
2408 30pt. multicoloured 2·75 2·50
2409 50pt. multicoloured 4·50 4·25
2407/2409 *Set of* 3 8·25 8·50

496 Penguins

2012 (23 Jan). Preserve the Polar Regions and Glaciers. Sheet 120×80 mm containing T **496** and similar horiz design. Multicoloured. Granite paper. P 14.

MS2410 80pt. Type **496**; 1d. Stranded Polar Bear 17·00 16·00

497 Royal Jordanian Falcons

498 Raised Fists

2012 (27 Feb). Royal Jordanian Falcons. T **497** and similar horiz designs. Multicoloured. Granite paper. P 14.

2411 10pt. Type **497** 90 85
2412 20pt. Lead pilot 1·80 1·70
2413 30pt. Flying over wadi 2·75 2·50
2414 40pt. Flying over river 3·75 3·25
2411/2414 *Set of* 4 8·25 7·50
MS2415 90×70 mm. 50pt. Falcons and flag. Imperf 4·75 4·50

2012 (1 May). International Labour Day. Granite paper. P 14.

2416 **498** 20pt. orange-yellow and black 1·80 1·70
2417 30pt. Indian red 2·75 2·50
2418 40pt. agate 3·75 3·25
2419 50pt. multicoloured 4·50 4·25
2416/2419 *Set of* 4 11·50 10·50

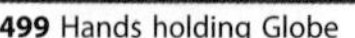

499 Hands holding Globe

500 King Abdullah II and Khazne al-Firaun, Petra

2012 (17 May). World Telecommunication Day. T **499** and similar vert designs. Multicoloured. Granite paper. P 14.

2420	30pt. Type **499**	2·75	2·50
2421	40pt. Satellite dish	3·75	3·25
2422	50pt. Laptop computer	4·50	4·25
2420/2422	*Set of 3*	10·00	9·00

2012 (30 June). 50th Birthday of King Abdullah II ibn al-Hussein. T **500** and similar multicoloured designs showing King Abdullah II in front of landmarks. Granite paper. P 14.

2423	20pt. Type **500**	1·80	1·70
2424	20pt. Mosque, Amman	1·80	1·70
2425	20pt. Palace of Justice, Amman	1·80	1·70
2426	20pt. Oil refinery	1·80	1·70
2427	20pt. *Zhen Hua 16* freighter with containers	1·80	1·70
2428	20pt. Abdoun suspension bridge	1·80	1·70
2423/2428	*Set of 6*	9·75	9·25
MS2429	90×70 mm. 50pt. King Abdullah. Imperf	4·75	4·50

501 Dressage

502 King and Queen

2012 (27 July). Olympic Games, London. T **501** and similar vert designs. Multicoloured. Granite paper. P 14.

2430	20pt. Type **501**	1·80	1·70
2431	30pt. Football	2·75	2·50
2432	40pt. Tennis	3·75	3·25
2433	50pt. Canoeing	4·50	4·25
2430/2433	*Set of 4*	11·50	10·50

2013 (18 Sept). Chess. T **502** and similar horiz designs. Multicoloured. P 14.

2434	20pt. Type **502**	1·80	1·70
2435	20pt. Chess board	1·80	1·70
2436	20pt. Rook and pawn	1·80	1·70
2434/2436	*Set of 3*	4·75	4·50

Nos. 2434/2436 have '2012' imprint date.

503 Kumquats

504 Tyrannosaurus Rex

2013 (18 Oct). Fruit. T **503** and similar vert designs. Multicoloured. P 14.

2437	10pt. Type **503**	90	85
2438	20pt. Mandarines	1·80	1·70
2439	30pt. Lemons	2·75	2·50
2440	40pt. Oranges	3·75	3·25
2441	50pt. Pomelos	4·50	4·25
2437/2441	*Set of 5*	12·50	11·50

Nos. 2437/2441 have '2012' imprint date.

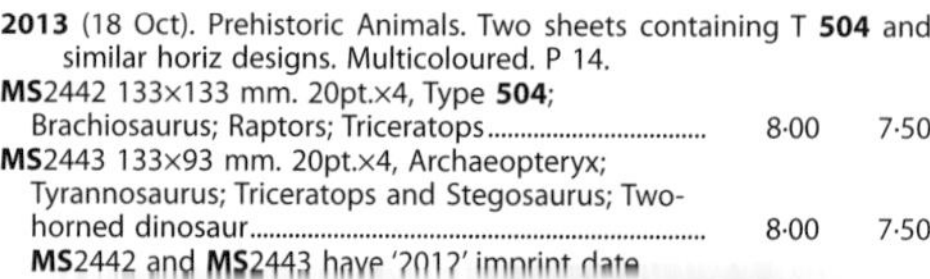

2013 (18 Oct). Prehistoric Animals. Two sheets containing T **504** and similar horiz designs. Multicoloured. P 14.

MS2442	133×133 mm. 20pt.×4, Type **504**; Brachiosaurus; Raptors; Triceratops	8·00	7·50
MS2443	133×93 mm. 20pt.×4, Archaeopteryx; Tyrannosaurus; Triceratops and Stegosaurus; Two-horned dinosaur	8·00	7·50

MS2442 and **MS**2443 have '2012' imprint date.

505 Book surmounting Globe

506 Mare and Foal

2013 (23 Oct). 50th Anniversary of Jordan Library and Information Association. T **505** and similar vert design. Multicoloured. P 14.

2444	40pt. Type **505**	3·75	3·25
2445	50pt. Anniversary emblem	4·50	4·25

2013 (2 Dec). Horses. T **506** and similar multicoloured designs showing horses. P 14.

2446	10pt. Type **506**	90	85
2447	20pt. Chestnut with white blaze galloping (*horiz*)	1·80	1·70
2448	30pt. Chestnut Mare and foal (*horiz*)	2·75	2·50
2449	40pt. Head of Bright Bay with black mane (*horiz*)	3·75	3·50
2450	50pt. Bay galloping through sea (*horiz*)	4·50	4·25
2446/2450	*Set of 5*	12·50	11·50
MS2451	90×70 mm. 50pt. Herd. Imperf	4·75	4·50

Nos. 2446/**MS**2451 have '2012' imprint date.

507 Tawfiq Nimri

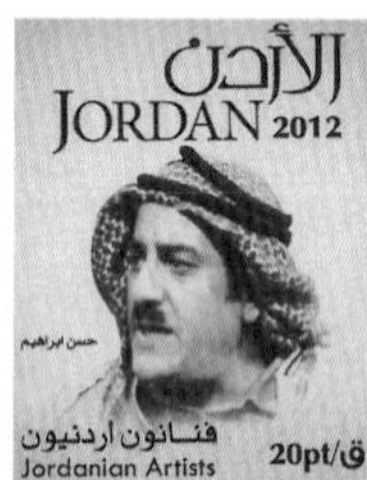

508 Hassan Ibrahim

509 Moses

510 Mahmoud Saymeh

511 Jordanian Artist

512 Jordanian Artist

513 Jordanian Artist

514 Jordanian Artist

2013 (2 Dec). Jordanian Artists. P 14.

2452 **507** 20pt. multicoloured .... 1·80 1·70
2453 **508** 20pt. multicoloured .... 1·80 1·70
2454 **509** 20pt. multicoloured .... 1·80 1·70
2455 **510** 20pt. multicoloured .... 1·80 1·70
2456 **511** 20pt. multicoloured .... 1·80 1·70
2457 **512** 20pt. multicoloured .... 1·80 1·70
2458 **513** 20pt. multicoloured .... 1·80 1·70
2459 **514** 20pt. multicoloured .... 1·80 1·70
2452/2459 *Set of 8* .... 13·00 12·50

Nos. 2452/2459 have '2012' imprint date.

515 Full Sail

2013 (2 Dec). Sailing Ships. T **515** and similar horiz designs showing sailing ships. Multicoloured. P 14.

2460 20pt. Type **515** .... 1·80 1·70
2461 30pt. In harbour .... 2·75 2·50
2462 40pt. On stormy sea .... 3·75 3·50
2463 50pt. Partially rigged .... 4·50 4·25
2460/2463 *Set of 4* .... 11·50 11·00
MS2464 90×70 mm. 50pt. Armada of ships. Imperf .... 4·75 4·50

Nos. 2460/**MS**2464 have '2012' imprint date.

516 *Landscape with Rainbow* (Peter Paul Rubens)

517 Amethyst

2013 (25 Dec). Paintings. Masterpieces of Art. T **516** and similar multicoloured designs showing paintings. P 11½×12 (horiz) or 12×11½ (vert).

2465 20pt. Type **516** .... 1·80 1·70
2466 20pt. *The Milkmaid* (Johannes Vermeer) (*vert*) .... 1·80 1·70
2467 20pt. *Slavers throwing overboard the Dead and Dying–Typhoon coming on* (JMW. Turner) .... 1·80 1·70
2468 20pt. *Women in the Garden* (Claude Monet) (*vert*) .... 1·80 1·70
2469 20pt. *Impression. Soleil Levant* (Claude Monet) .... 1·80 1·70
2470 20pt. *Les Meules à Giverny* (Claude Monet) .... 1·80 1·70
2471 20pt. *The Red Vineyard* (Vincent van Gogh) .... 1·80 1·70
2472 20pt. *Strolling along the Seashore* (Joaquin Sorolla y Bastida) .... 1·80 1·70
2465/2472 *Set of 8* .... 13·00 12·00

(Litho Henan Post Printing)

2013 (25 Dec). Precious Stones. T **517** and similar vert designs. P 12×11½.

2473 20pt. Type **517** .... 1·80 1·70
a. Sheet of 6. Nos. 2473/2478 .... 11·50
2474 20pt. Red Diamond .... 1·80 1·70
2475 20pt. Emerald .... 1·80 1·70
2476 20pt. Black Opal .... 1·80 1·70
2477 20pt. Pearl .... 1·80 1·70
2478 20pt. Ruby .... 1·80 1·70
2473/2478 *Set of 6* .... 9·75 9·25

Nos. 2473/2478 were printed, *se-tenant*, in sheets of six stamps.

518 Mountain Pass

519 Grey-crowned Crane

2014 (9 Feb). Nature Reserves in Jordan. Dana Nature Reserve. T **518** and similar multicoloured designs. P 14.

2479 10pt. Type **518** 90 85
2480 20pt. Succulent flower (*horiz*) .... 1·80 1·70
2481 30pt. Lake (*horiz*) .... 2·75 2·50
2482 40pt. Hillside (*horiz*) .... 3·75 3·50
2483 50pt. Oryx (*horiz*) .... 4·50 4·25
2479/2483 *Set of 5* .... 12·50 11·50
MS2484 90×70 mm. 50pt. Cliffs and valley. Imperf .... 4·75 4·50

Nos. 2479/**MS**2454 have '2013' imprint date.

2014 (9 Feb). Migratory Birds. T **519** and similar multicoloured designs. P 14.

2485 20pt. Type **519** .... 1·80 1·70
2486 20pt. Great White Pelican .... 1·80 1·70
2487 20pt. Mallard (Duck) .... 1·80 1·70
2488 20pt. Collared Flycatcher .... 1·80 1·70
2489 20pt. Common Buzzard .... 1·80 1·70
2490 20pt. Female Eurasian Blackcap .... 1·80 1·70
2491 20pt. European Bee-eater (*vert*) .... 1·80 1·70
2492 20pt. Glossy Ibis (*vert*) .... 1·80 1·70
2485/2492 *Set of 8* .... 13·00 12·00

Nos. 2485/2492 have '2013' imprint date.

520 1933 500m. Stamp (As No. 220), Map and Ruins of Petra (*image reduced by 54% of original size*)

2014 (9 Feb). 80th Anniversary of Petra Stamps. Two sheets each 115×70 mm, horiz designs as T **520**. Multicoloured. Imperf.

MS2493 Type **520** .... 7·50 7·25
MS2494 80pt. 1933 15m. Stamp (As No. 214), map and ruins of Petra .... 7·50 7·25

MS2493/**MS**2494 have '2013' imprint date.

521 Pope Francis

2014 (24 May). 50th Anniversary of First Papal Visit to Jordan. T **521** and similar multicoloured designs. P 14.

2495 20pt. Type **521** .... 1·80 1·70
2496 30pt. Pope Francis and HM King Abdulla II .... 2·75 2·50
2497 40pt. Pope Francis releasing Dove (*vert*) .... 3·75 3·50
2495/2497 *Set of 3* .... 7·50 7·00
MS2498 90×70 mm. 50pt. Images of Papal visits, 1964, 2000, 2009 and 2014. Imperf .... 4·00 3·75

522 Cartoon by Osama Hajjaj

523 Cartoon by Osama Hajjaj

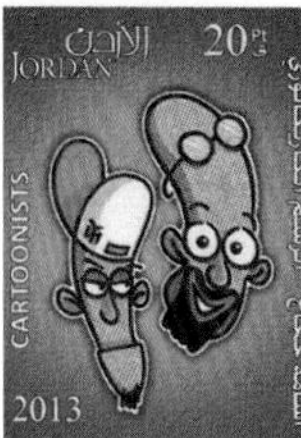

524 Cartoon by Osama Hajjaj

525 Abu Mohammad (cartoon by Emad Hajjaj)

526 Abu Mohammad and Abu Mahjoob (cartoon by Emad Hajjaj)

527 Abu Mahjoob (cartoon by Emad Hajjaj)

2014 (1 June). Cartoonists. P 14.

2499	**522**	20pt. multicoloured	1·80	1·70
2500	**523**	20pt. multicoloured	1·80	1·70
2501	**524**	20pt. multicoloured	1·80	1·70
2502	**525**	20pt. multicoloured	1·80	1·70
2503	**526**	20pt. multicoloured	1·80	1·70
2504	**527**	20pt. multicoloured	1·80	1·70
2499/2504 *Set of 6*			9·75	9·25

Nos. 2499/2504 have '2013' imprint date.

528 Doorway, Justice Palace

529 Mediterranean

2014 (1 July). Architecture. Doors and Windows. T **528** and similar multicoloured designs. P 14.

2505	20pt. Type **528**	1·80	1·70
2506	20pt. Circular window, Al-Salt	1·80	1·70
2507	20pt. Glazed door, Alt-Salt School	1·80	1·70
2508	20pt. Arched window, Raghadan Palace	1·80	1·70
2509	20pt. Doorway, Royal Hashemite Court	1·80	1·70
2510	20pt. Doorway, King Hussein's Mosque (*horiz*)	1·80	1·70
2511	20pt. Doorway, Umayyad Palace (*horiz*)	1·80	1·70
2505/2511 *Set of 7*		11·50	10·50

Nos. 2505/2511 have '2013' imprint date.

No. 2512 is vacant.

(Des Helen Aposttolou)

2014 (9 July). EUROMED. Euromed 2014 Postal Conference. P 14.

2513	**529**	80pt. multicoloured	7·25	7·00

530 Emblem

531 Statue of Soldier and Emblem

2015 (9 Mar). 90th Anniversary of Amman Chamber of Commerce. P 14.

2514	**530**	40pt. multicoloured	3·75	3·50

No. 2514 has '2014' imprint date.

2015 (9 Mar). Economic and Social Foundation for Military Retirees and Veterans. P 14.

2515	**531**	40pt. multicoloured	3·75	3·50

No. 2515 has '2014' imprint date.

532 Scales

2015 (9 Mar). Arab Lawyers' Union. P 14.

2516	**532**	40pt. multicoloured	3·75	3·50

No. 2516 has '2014' imprint date.

533 Signing

2015 (9 Mar). Jordanian Deaf Women's Association. P 14.

2517	**533**	40pt. multicoloured	3·75	3·50

534 1 dinar Banknote

2015 (13 Dec). Jordanian Currency. T **534** and similar horiz designs. Multicoloured. P 14 (with one star-shaped hole on each vert side).

2518	10pt. Type **534**	90	85
2519	20pt. 5d. banknote	1·80	1·70
2520	40pt. 10d. banknote	3·75	3·50
2521	60pt. 15d. banknote	5·50	5·25
2522	80pt. 50d. banknote	7·25	7·00
2518/2522 *Set of 5*		17·00	16·00

535 Order of Independence

2015 (13 Dec). Royal Medals. T **535** and similar multicoloured designs. P 14 (with one star-shaped hole on each vert side (horiz designs) or each horiz side (vert designs)).

2523 50pt. Type **535** ... 4·50 4·25
2524 50pt. Order of Renaissance (green 'leaves', red circle, crossed flags) ... 4·50 4·25
2525 50pt. Al-Hussein Order of Military Merit–Second Class (white star, red centre, crown and wreath) ... 4·50 4·25
2526 50pt. Order of Renaissance (green 'leaves', red circle, crossed flags) (*different*) ... 4·50 4·25
2527 50pt. Al-Hussein Decoration for Distinguished Service–First Class (gold circle and central profile) ... 4·50 4·25
2528 50pt. The Order of Hussein ibn Ali (gold, oval, surmounted by crown) (*vert*) ... 4·50 4·25
2529 50pt. Order of Military Gallantry (head of King Abdullah ibn Hussein facing left) (*vert*) ... 4·50 4·25
2530 50pt. Medal of Honour (gold medal and bar) (*vert*) ... 4·50 4·25
2531 50pt. Order of the Star of Jordan (seven gold stars, green circle) ... 4·50 4·25
2532 50pt. Order of the Hashemite Star (white star, central profile, surmounted by crown) (*vert*) ... 4·50 4·25
2523/2532 *Set of* 10 ... 41·00 38·00

2015 (13 Dec). 70th Anniversary of United Nations. Horiz design showing anniversary emblem. Multicoloured. P 14 (with one star-shaped hole on each vert side).

2533 80pt. '70' and 'Strong UN Better World' ... 7·25 7·00

T **536** is unavailable.

2015 (28 Dec). Traditional Costumes. Vert designs showing women wearing traditional dress, area name given. Multicoloured. P 14 (with one star-shaped hole each horiz side).

2534 20pt. Salt ... 1·80 1·70
2535 20pt. Um Qais ... 1·80 1·70
2536 20pt. Jerash ... 1·80 1·70
2537 20pt. Karak ... 1·80 1·70
2538 20pt. Tafilah ... 1·80 1·70
2539 20pt. Wadi Rum ... 1·80 1·70
2540 20pt. Amman ... 1·80 1·70
2541 20pt. Ma'an ... 1·80 1·70
2542 20pt. Badawi ... 1·80 1·70
2543 20pt. Ajloun ... 1·80 1·70
2544 20pt. Mafraq ... 1·80 1·70
2545 20pt. Madaba ... 1·80 1·70
2534/2545 *Set of* 12 ... 19·00 18·00

T **537** is unavailable.

2015 (28 Dec). The Four Seasons. Sheet 150×100 mm containing four vert stamps showing a tree during all four seasons at once. Multicoloured. P 14 (with one star-shaped hole on each horiz side).

MS2546 30pt.×4, Tips of bough in Spring time; Boughs and trunk in Summer; Upper and lower bough in Autumn; Tips of boughs in winter ... 11·00 10·50

T **538** is unavailable.

2015 (28 Dec). Jordanian Mosaics. Five horiz designs showing mosaics. Multicoloured. P 14 (with one star-shaped hole on each vert side).

2547 30pt. Male figure ... 2·75 2·50
2548 30pt. Horse ... 2·75 2·50
2549 30pt. City ... 2·75 2·50
2550 30pt. Ox in a roundel ... 2·75 2·50
2547/2550 *Set of* 4 ... 10·00 9·00
MS2551 90×70 mm. 60pt. Woman and fish. Imperf ... 5·75 5·50

T **539** is unavailable.

540 Decorated Bottles

2015 (28 Dec). Jordanian Handicrafts. T **540** and similar horiz designs. Multicoloured. P 14 (with one star-shaped hole on each vert side).

2552 30pt. Type **540** ... 2·75 2·50
2553 30pt. Mosaic box ... 2·75 2·50
2554 30pt. Coloured sand in bottles ... 2·75 2·50
2555 30pt. Decorated pot ... 2·75 2·50
2556 30pt. Jewellery ... 2·75 2·50
2552/2556 *Set of* 5 ... 12·50 11·00
MS2557 90×70 mm. 60pt. Coloured sand in bottles (*different*). Imperf ... 5·75 5·50

541 Umm Aljemal

2015 (28 Dec). Decapolis. T **541** and similar horiz designs. Multicoloured. P 14 (with one star-shaped hole on each vert side).

2558 50pt. Type **541** ... 4·50 4·25
2559 50pt. Um Qais ... 4·50 4·25
2560 50pt. Beit Ras ... 4·50 4·25
2561 50pt. Quwayliba ... 4·50 4·25
2562 50pt. Gerasa ... 4·50 4·25
2558/2562 *Set of* 5 ... 20·00 19·00

542 Camel Riders

2016 (10 June). Centenary of Great Arab Revolt. T **542** and similar multicoloured designs. P 14½ (with one star-shaped hole on each vert side).

2563 10pt. Type **542** ... 90 85
2564 20pt. Horseman ... 1·80 1·70
2565 30pt. Leaders ... 2·75 2·50
2566 50pt. King Abdullah II ... 4·50 4·25
2567 100pt. Sherif Hussein bin Ali and emblem ... 9·00 8·75
2563/2567 *Set of* 5 ... 17·00 16·00
MS2568 70×90 mm. 60pt. Emblem (*different*). Imperf ... 5·75 5·50

543 Scorpion Fish

2016 (30 June). Fish of the Mediterranean Sea. T **543** and similar horiz designs. Multicoloured. P 14½ (with one star-shaped hole on each vert side).

2569 40pt. Type **543** ... 3·75 3·50
2570 40pt. Axillary Wrasse ... 3·75 3·50
2571 40pt. Lionfish ... 3·75 3·50
2572 40pt. Black Back Butterflyfish ... 3·75 3·50
2573 40pt. Butterfly Blenny ... 3·75 3·50
2569/2573 *Set of* 5 ... 17·00 16·00

544 Emblem

2016 (28 July). First Amman International Numismatic and Philatelic Fair. Multicoloured. P 14½ (with one star-shaped hole on each vert side).

2574 **544** 30pt. multicoloured ... 2·75 2·50
2575 50pt. multicoloured ... 4·50 4·25

545 Wadi Rum

2016 (28 July). Tourism. Hiking Destinations in Jordan. T **545** and similar multicoloured designs. P 14 (with one star-shaped hole on each vert side (horiz designs) or each horiz side (vert designs)).

2576	40pt. Type **545**	3·75	3·50
2577	40pt. Madaba	3·75	3·50
2578	40pt. Karak	3·75	3·50
2579	40pt. Ajlun (*vert*)	3·75	3·50
2580	40pt. Wadi Al Dab (*vert*)	3·75	3·50
2581	40pt. Ma'in (*vert*)	3·75	3·50
2582	40pt. Madaba (*different*)	3·75	3·50
2576/2582	*Set of 7*	24·00	22·00

546 Emblem

2016 (3 Aug). Arab Post Day. T **546** and similar horiz design. Multicoloured. P 14½ (with one star-shaped hole on each vert side).

2583	40pt. Type **546**	3·75	3·50
2584	40pt. As Type **546** but with design reversed	3·75	3·50

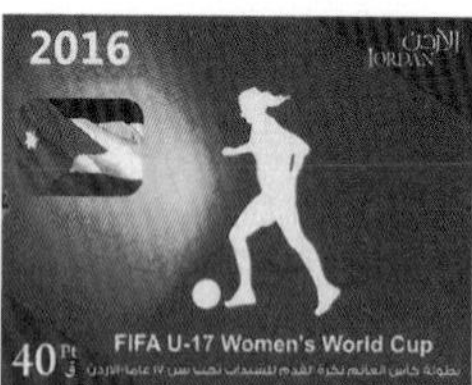

547 Player

2016 (25 Sept). Football. FIFA U-17 Women's World Cup. T **547** and similar horiz designs. Multicoloured. P 14½ (with one star-shaped hole on each vert side).

2585	40pt. Type **547**	3·75	3·50
2586	50pt. Two players	4·50	4·25
2587	60pt. Player (*different*)	5·50	5·25
2588	70pt. Player kicking ball	6·25	6·00
2585/2588	*Set of 4*	18·00	17·00

548 Ajlun Castle

2016 (20 Oct). Ancient Castles in Jordan. T **548** and similar horiz designs. Multicoloured. P 14½ (with one star-shaped hole on each vert side).

2589	30pt. Type **548**	2·75	2·50
2590	30pt. Al-Azraq	2·75	2·50
2591	30pt. Omayyad Palace	2·75	2·50
2592	40pt. Shobak Castle	3·75	3·50
2593	40pt. Karak Castle	3·75	3·50
2594	40pt. Aqaba Castle	3·75	3·50
2589/2594	*Set of 6*	18·00	16·00

549 Emblem

2016 (7 Nov). Museum of Parliamentary Life. T **549** and similar horiz designs. Multicoloured. P 14½ (with one star-shaped hole on each vert side).

2595	20pt. Type **549**	1·80	1·70
2596	30pt. Gateway	2·75	2·50
2597	40pt. Meeting room	3·75	3·50
2598	50pt. Dias and chamber	4·50	4·25
2599	60pt. King Abdullah II	5·50	5·25
2595/2599	*Set of 5*	16·00	15·00

550 Map and Flags of Participants

(Litho)

2017 (29 Mar). 28th Arab League Summit, Amman, Jordan. T **550** and similar horiz designs. Multicoloured. Granite paper. Fluorescent markings. P 10.

2600	10pt. Type **550**	90	85
2601	20pt. Amman	1·80	1·70
2602	30pt. Mosque	2·75	2·50
2603	40pt. '28'	3·75	3·50
2600/2603	*Set of 4*	8·25	7·75
MS2604	95×80 mm. 50pt. King Abdullah II bin Al-Hussein. Imperf	4·75	4·50

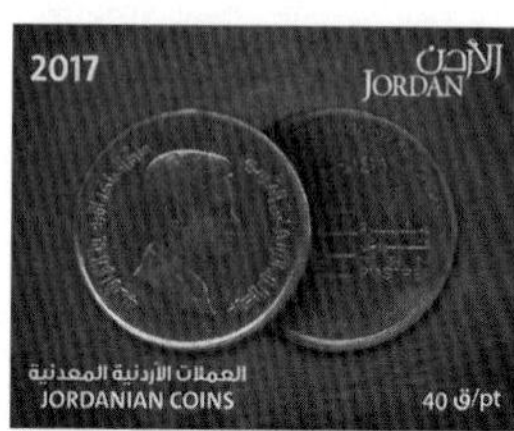

551 Coins

552 Coins

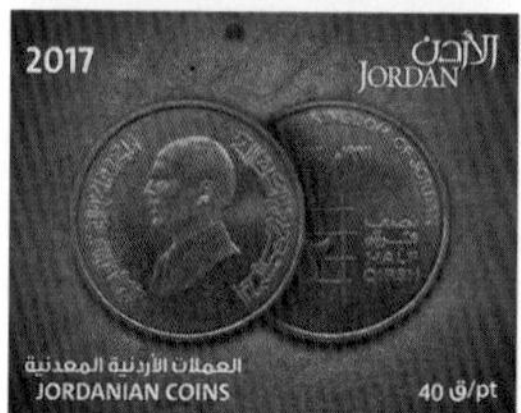

553 Coins

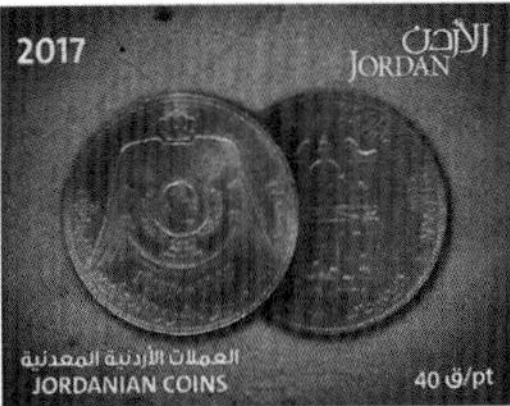

554 Coins

555 Coins

556 Coins

(Litho)

2017 (4 May). Coins. Multicoloured. Granite paper. Fluorescent markings. P 10.

2605	**551**	40pt. multicoloured	3·75	3·50
2606	**552**	40pt. multicoloured	3·75	3·50
2607	**553**	40pt. multicoloured	3·75	3·50
2608	**554**	40pt. multicoloured	3·75	3·50
2609	**555**	40pt. multicoloured	3·75	3·50
2610	**556**	40pt. multicoloured	3·75	3·50
2605/2610		*Set of* 6	20·00	19·00

557 Spanish Fir

10pt ١٠ قروش

(**558**)

(Litho)

2017 (10 July). EUROMED. Mediterranean Trees. T **557** and similar vert design. Multicoloured. P 14½ (with a star-shaped hole on each horiz side).

2611	30pt. Type **557**	2·75	2·50
2612	50pt. Turkey Oak	4·50	4·25

2017 (20 July). No. 2036*b* (Hadrian's Triumphal Arch, Jerash–2003) (T **310**) surch as T **558**. Granite paper. P 12×13½.

2613	10pt. on 50f. multicoloured	90	85
2614	15pt. on 50f. multicoloured	1·40	1·30
2615	20pt. on 50f. multicoloured	1·80	1·70
2616	25pt. on 50f. multicoloured	2·30	2·20
2617	30pt. on 50f. multicoloured	2·75	2·50
2618	35pt. on 50f. multicoloured	3·25	3·00
2619	40pt. on 50f. multicoloured	3·75	3·50
2620	45pt. on 50f. multicoloured	4·25	3·75
2621	50pt. on 50f. multicoloured	4·50	4·25
2622	60pt. on 50f. multicoloured	5·50	5·25
2613/2622	*Set of* 10	27·00	25·00

559 Strawberries

(Litho)

2017 (12 Oct). Fruit. T **559** and similar horiz designs. Multicoloured. Fluorescent markings. P 14½ (with one star-shaped hole on each vert side).

2623	20pt. Type **559**	1·80	1·70
2624	20pt. Pomegranates	1·80	1·70
2625	20pt. Figs	1·80	1·70
2626	20pt. Mulberries	1·80	1·70
2627	20pt. Grapes	1·80	1·70
2628	20pt. Prickly Pears	1·80	1·70
2629	20pt. Peaches	1·80	1·70
2630	20pt. Cantaloupe Melon	1·80	1·70
2631	20pt. Plums	1·80	1·70
2632	20pt. Watermelon	1·80	1·70
2623/2632	*Set of* 10	16·00	15·00

20 pt ٢٠ قرش

(**560**)

2017 (12 Oct). Various stamps (Cradle of Civilisation) surch as T **560**. P 13½×14.

2633	20pt. on 100f. multicoloured (No. 1910) (Temple, Petra)	1·80	1·70
2634	20pt. on 100f. multicoloured (No. 1913) (Path between columns, Jerash)	1·80	1·70
2635	20pt. on 100f. multicoloured (No. 1919) (Camels, Wadi Rum)	1·80	1·70
2636	20pt. on 100f. multicoloured (No. 1928) (Columns and steps, Pella)	1·80	1·70
2637	20pt. on 100f. multicoloured (No. 1931) (Castle, Ajloun)	1·80	1·70
2638	20pt. on 100f. multicoloured (No. 1934) (Arches and columns, um Quais)	1·80	1·70
2639	20pt. on 100f. multicoloured (No. 1937) (Mushatta Palace)	1·80	1·70
2633/2639	*Set of* 7	11·50	10·50

30pt ٣٠قرش

(**561**)

2017 (12 Oct). No. 1918 (Statues (Cradle of Civilisation)) surch as T **561**. P 13½×14.

2640	30pt. on 300f. multicoloured	2·75	2·50
2641	50pt. on 300f. multicoloured	4·50	4·25

562 Rock Dove (inscr 'Carrier Pigeon')

(Litho)

2017 (12 Oct). Birds. Sheet 166×160 mm containing T **562** and similar horiz designs. Multicoloured. P 14½ (with one star-shaped hole on each vert side).

MS2642 30pt.×6, Type **562**; Goldfinch; Long-legged Buzzard (Inscr 'Buteo rufinus'); Blackbird; Chukar Partridge (Inscr 'Shunnarbird'); Rose Finch 17·00 16·00

563 Badge and Soldier

564 Badge and Soldier

565 Badge and Soldier

566 Badge and Soldier

567 Badge and Soldier

568 Badge and Soldier

569 Badge and Soldier

(Litho)

2017 (Nov). Jordanian Armed Forces. P 14½ (with one star-shaped hole on each vert side).

2643	**563**	30pt. multicoloured	2·75	2·50
2644	**564**	30pt. multicoloured	2·75	2·50
2645	**565**	30pt. multicoloured	2·75	2·50
2646	**566**	30pt. multicoloured	2·75	2·50
2647	**567**	30pt. multicoloured	2·75	2·50
2648	**568**	30pt. multicoloured	2·75	2·50
2649	**569**	30pt. multicoloured	2·75	2·50
2643/2649		*Set of 7*	17·00	16·00

570 Afra Baths

(Litho)

2017 (Dec). Medical Tourism in Jordan. T **570** and similar horiz designs. Multicoloured. Granite paper. P 14½ (with one star-shaped hole on each vert side).

2650	40pt. Type **570**	3·75	3·50
2651	40pt. Maeen Baths	3·75	3·50
2652	40pt. Dead Sea	3·75	3·50
2653	40pt. Jordan's natural springs	3·75	3·50
2650/2653	*Set of 4*	13·50	12·50

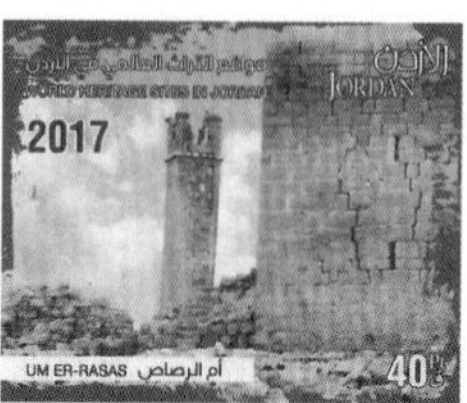

571 Um Er-Rasas

(Litho)

2017 (Dec). World Heritage Sites in Jordan. T **571** and similar horiz designs. Multicoloured. P 14½ (with one star-shaped hole on each vert side).

2654	40pt. Type **571**	3·75	3·50
2655	40pt. Wadi Rum	3·75	3·50
2656	40pt. Petra	3·75	3·50
2657	40pt. Qusayr Amra	3·75	3·50
2658	40pt. Inscr 'Baptism'	3·75	3·50
2654/2658	*Set of 5*	17·00	16·00

STAMP BOOKLETS

Prices are for complete booklets

Booklet No.	*Date*	*Contents and Cover Price*	*Price*
SB1	16.12.80	King Hussein (T **202**) 1 pane, No. 1268×4; 1 pane, No. 1269×4; 1 pane, No. 1270×4; 1 pane, No. 1271×4; 1 pane, No. 1272×4 (1260f.)	32·00
SB2	28.9.00	Endangered Species (T **388**) 3 panes. Nos. 1982/1983, each×2; 1984/1985, each×2; 1986/1987, each×2	38·00
SB3	9.10.00	Tourism (T **390**) 3 panes. Nos. 1990/1991, each×2; 1992/1993, each×2; 1994/1995, each×2	32·00

OCCUPATION OF PALESTINE

On the day after the proclamation of the state of Israel on 14 May 1948, Transjordanian troops (the Arab Legion) crossed the Jordan into Palestine and, before the armistice of 3 April 1949, were able to take and hold the Old City of Jerusalem; an area to the north including Jenin, Tulkarm, Qalqiliya and Latrun; and an area to the south round Bethlehem and Hebron.

PALESTINE (P 1) PALESTINE (PD 2)

1948 (2 Dec). T **28/29** of Jordan optd with T P **1**. P 12.

No.	Type	Description		
P1	**28**	1m. red-brown	1·10	95
		a. Opt inverted	80·00	
		b. Opt double	80·00	
P2		2m. bluish green (R.)	1·10	95
		a. Opt inverted	50·00	50·00
		b. Opt double	50·00	50·00
		c. Perf 13½×13 (No. 195*a*)	3·25	3·00
		ca. Opt inverted	70·00	70·00
		d. Perf 13½ (No. 223)	10·00	10·00
		da. Opt inverted	70·00	70·00
P3		3m. green (R.)	1·10	1·10
		a. Opt inverted	90·00	90·00
		b. Opt double	90·00	90·00
P4		3m. carmine-pink	65	65
		a. Opt double	50·00	50·00
		b. Opt inverted	50·00	50·00
P5		4m. green (R.)	65	65
		a. Opt double	50·00	50·00
		b. Opt inverted		
P6		5m. orange (G.)	65	65
		a. Opt inverted	50·00	50·00
		b. Opt double	50·00	50·00
		c. Optd in black	£130	£130
P7		10m. bright violet (R.)	1·90	1·80
		a. Opt inverted	50·00	
		b. Opt double	50·00	
P8		12m. scarlet	1·80	1·10
		a. Opt inverted	80·00	
		b. Opt double	50·00	
		c. Optd in green	£120	
P9		15m. olive-green (R.)	2·50	2·50
		a. Opt inverted	70·00	
		b. Opt double	70·00	
P10		20m. blue (R.)	3·50	1·90
		a. Opt inverted	70·00	
		b. Opt double	70·00	
		c. Opt both sides	65·00	
P11	**29**	50m. purple (G.)	3·75	3·75
		a. Opt double	£100	£100
		b. Opt inverted	£100	
		c. Opt double, one inverted	£250	
P12		90m. bistre (G.)	19·00	4·00
P13		100m. blue (R.)	22·00	12·00
P14		200m. violet (R.)	10·00	18·00
		a. Perf 14 (No. 205)	95·00	65·00
P15		500m. brown (R.)	75·00	33·00
P16		£P1 slate-grey (R.)	£150	80·00
P1/P16 *Set of 16*			£275	£150

A second overprinting was made of some Postage and Postage Due values which produced variations in shade, notably in Nos. P11 and P12, which may be found either with a deep blue-green or pale green overprint.

Nos. P2. P2c, P2d and P3 exist overprinted 'FILS' as T **45** of Jordan and are listed under Jordan Nos. 314d/314f and 315b.

1948 (2 Dec). POSTAGE DUE. Postage Due stamps of Jordan optd with T PD **2**.

(a) Wmk Mult Script CA. P 14

No.	Type	Description		
PD17	**D 26**	1m. red-brown (P 13½×13)	95·00	65·00
PD18		4m. green (R.)	5·00	7·00
PD19		10m. scarlet	£375	
PD20		20m. olive-green (R.)	4·50	5·50
PD21		50m. blue (R.)	5·25	7·00
		a. Opt inverted		

(b) Redrawn. No wmk. P 13½

No.	Type	Description		
PD22	**D 35**	1m. red-brown	£225	£225
PD23		2m. orange-yellow	24·00	28·00
		a. Opt inverted	£250	
PD24		10m. scarlet	22·00	28·00
		a. Opt inverted	80·00	90·00
		b. Opt double	£110	£110

(c) Wmk Mult Script CA. P 12

No.	Type	Description		
PD25	**D 26**	1m. red-brown	4·50	6·00
		a. Opt inverted	65·00	
		b. Opt double		
		c. Horiz pair, one without opt	£425	
PD26		2m. orange-yellow	5·00	7·00
		a. Opt inverted	£110	
		b. Opt double	£110	
		c. Optd closer (5 *mm*) (G.)	90·00	55·00
PD27		4m. green (R.)	19·00	23·00
		a. Opt inverted	£100	£100
		b. Opt double	£100	
		c. Opt closer (5 *mm*)	44·00	44·00
PD28		10m. scarlet	5·00	6·25
		a. Opt inverted	£110	
		b. Opt double	£110	
PD29		20m. olive-green (R.)	£120	£120
		a. Opt inverted	£140	
		b. Opt double	£140	

Nos. PD23/PD24 exist with either line of overprint omitted or with the lines transposed due to misplaced overprints.

PALESTINE (P 3) PALESTINE (PT 4)

1949 (Aug). 75th Anniversary of Universal Postal Union. Nos. 285/289 of Jordan optd with T P **3** or arranged in one line (50m.).

No.	Type	Description		
P30	**40**	1m. brown	90	90
		a. Opt inverted	£130	
		b. Opt double	£120	
		c. Optd in vermilion	55·00	
		d. Opt double, one inverted	41·00	
		e. Opt double, both inverted	41·00	
P31		4m. green (Vm.)	90	90
		a. Error. 'PLAESTINE' (R. 7/5)	95·00	
		b. Opt inverted	90·00	
		c. Opt double	£130	
		d. Opt double, both inverted	£180	
		e. Opt in one line (as 50m.)	£160	
		ea. Opt double		
P32		10m. carmine	1·40	1·40
		a. Opt inverted	£100	
		b. Opt double	£150	
		c. Opt double, both inverted	£180	
P33		20m. blue (Vm.)	1·40	1·40
		a. Arabic omitted	£200	
		b. Opt inverted	95·00	
		c. Opt double	£120	
		d. Opt treble	£150	
P34	**41**	50m. dull green (Vm.)	3·50	3·50
		a. Error. 'PLAESTINE' (R. 1/4)	90·00	
		b. Opt inverted	95·00	
P30/P34 *Set of 5*			7·25	7·25

No. P33a is a setting error which was later corrected.

1949 (Sept–Oct). OBLIGATORY TAX. Nos. T264/T275 optd with T PT **4**.

No.	Type	Description		
PT35	T **36**	1m. ultramarine (R.)	40	90
		a. Opt inverted		
		b. Opt double		
PT36		2m. carmine	40	90
		a. Opt inverted		
		b. Opt double		
PT37		3m. emerald (R.)	90	1·00
		a. Opt inverted		
		b. Opt double		
PT38		5m. claret	1·10	90
		a. Opt inverted		
		b. Opt double		
PT39	T **37**	10m. carmine	1·30	90
		a. Opt inverted		
		b. Opt double		
PT40		15m. grey-black (R.)	3·50	1·10
		a. Opt inverted		
		b. Opt double		
PT41		20m. purple-brown (R.) (9.49)	5·50	1·90
		a. Opt inverted		
		b. Opt double		
PT42		50m. reddish violet (R.)	8·25	3·75
		a. Opt inverted		
PT43	T **38**	100m. orange-red	14·00	6·00
		a. Opt inverted		
		b. Opt double		
PT44		200m. blue (R.)	35·00	18·00
		a. Opt inverted		
PT45		500m. green (R.)	£100	55·00
PT46		£P1 brown (R.)	£190	£100
PT35/PT46 *Set of 12*			£325	£170

The occupied areas were incorporated into the Kingdom of Jordan on 24 April 1950, after which the stamps of Jordan came into use in them. In the Six Day War, 5 to 10 June 1967, all this territory was lost by Jordan and it has since been administered by Israel.

DESIGN INDEX

Where the same design, or subject, appears more than once in a set only the first number is given. Scenes and buildings are listed under the town or geographical area in which they are situated. Portraits are listed under surnames only. In cases of difficulty part of the inscription has been used to identify the stamp.

Lebanon

100 Centiemes = 1 Piastre

100 Piastres = 1 Lebanese Pound

The Lebanon area, inhabited mainly by Maronite Christians and Moslem Druses, came under Turkish rule in 1516 and was allowed a degree of self-government. From 1697 to 1842 it had Emirs of the Shihab family of Sunni Moslems. After a civil war, won by the Druses in 1860, the Powers intervened, and, by the Organic Law of 1861, The Lebanon received autonomy under a Christian governor appointed by the Sultan.

The Turkish postal system had a large network of offices in this area; it is thought that there were over 200 although used examples from a little less than that number have been identified. In addition several foreign powers operated offices at Beirut and/or Tripoli: Austria, Great Britain, Egypt, France, Germany, Italy and Russia. Details of the Egyptian offices are given at the end of that country; for details of the others see Stanley Gibbons *Central Asia* catalogue.

FRENCH MANDATED TERRITORY OF GREATER LEBANON

After the defeat of Turkey in 1918, The Lebanon came under French military administration, and on 25 April 1920 France was given a mandate by the League of Nations to administer Syria, including The Lebanon which was given a separate status on 1 September. To The Lebanon as defined in 1861 were added Beirut and other coastal towns and the inland Bekaa area, and the whole was renamed Greater Lebanon (Grand Liban). The mandate came into effect on 29 September 1923.

Until September 1923 the French military occupation stamps of Syria were used in The Lebanon, and then, until the end of 1923, the joint issues for Syria and Greater Lebanon (Syria Nos. 97 etc). From 21 October 1918 to September 1920 stamps issued by the British Military Administration for Palestine were available from EEF offices in Lebanon.

Types of France

D **11**

11

13

14

15

18

30

31

35

GRAND
LIBAN
10
CENTIEMES
(**1**)

GRAND LIBAN
2 PIASTRES
(**2**)

1924 (1 Jan–June). Stamps of France surch.

(a) Definitive stamps

(i) Surch as T **1**

No.	Type	Description	Unused	Used
1	**11**	10c. on 2c. claret	1·90	2·50
		a. 'CE' omitted	95·00	
		b. Surch inverted	70·00	70·00
		c. Surch double	70·00	70·00
2	**18**	25c. on 5c. orange	2·10	2·40
3		50c. on 10c. green	2·30	2·40
		a. 'R' omitted	£110	85·00
		b. Surch double	70·00	70·00
4	**15**	75c. on 15c. olive-green	3·75	5·75
5	**18**	1p. on 20c. chocolate	3·00	2·10
		a. Surch inverted	70·00	70·00
		b. Surch double	70·00	70·00
6		1.25p. on 25c. blue	7·00	4·50
7		1.50p. on 30c. orange	4·50	8·25
8		1.50p. on 30c. scarlet (4.24)	3·75	8·50
9	**15**	2.50p. on 50c. blue	3·25	3·00
		a. Figure '0' omitted	60·00	55·00
		b. Surch inverted	70·00	70·00
1/9 *Set of 9*			28·00	35·00

(ii) Surch as T **2**

No.	Type	Description	Unused	Used
10	**13**	2p. on 40c. red and pale blue	5·00	3·75
		a. '2' omitted	£160	£150
		b. Surch inverted	65·00	65·00
11		3p. on 60c. violet and blue	11·00	13·50
12		5p. on 1f. lake and yellow	12·00	12·00
13		10p. on 2f. orange and blue-green	20·00	20·00
		a. Surch inverted	£110	£110
14		25p. on 5f. deep blue and buff	36·00	60·00
		a. Error. 'LIABN'	£600	
		b. Surch inverted	£180	£180
10/14 *Set of 5*			75·00	£100

(b) Pasteur type surch as T **1** *(June)*

No.	Type	Description	Unused	Used
15	**30**	50c. on 10c. green	3·25	4·00
		a. Surch inverted	60·00	60·00
16		1.50p. on 30c. red	4·25	9·50
17		2.50p. on 50c. blue	2·75	4·25
		a. Error. '250.' (pos. 40)	£110	£110
		b. Surch inverted	70·00	70·00
		c. Surch double	55·00	55·00
15/17 *Set of 3*			9·25	16·00

(c) Olympic Games stamps surch as Types **1** *or* **2** *(June)*

No.	Type	Description	Unused	Used
18	**31**	50c. on 10c. green and yellow-green	41·00	70·00
		a. Surch inverted	£450	
19	–	1.25p. on 25c. deep and dull carmine	41·00	70·00
		a. Figure '1' omitted	£275	
		b. Surch inverted	£450	
20	–	1.50p. on 30c. red and black	41·00	70·00
		a. Surch inverted	£450	
21	–	2.50p. on 50c. ultramarine	41·00	70·00
		a. Surch inverted	£450	
18/21 *Set of 4*			£150	£250

Designs: Horiz—25c. Notre Dame and Pont Neuf. Vert—30c. *Milan de Crotone* (statue), 50c. The Victor.

All values exist with thin 'G' in 'GRAND' and there are many other minor varieties of type and spacing.

Poste par Avion
GRAND LIBAN
2 PIASTRES
(**2a**)

(Surch by Capuchin Fathers, Beirut)

1924 (1 Jan). AIR. Stamps of France surch as T **2a**.

No.	Type	Description	Unused	Used
22	**13**	2p. on 40c. red and pale blue	16·00	38·00
23		3p. on 60c. violet and blue	16·00	38·00
24		5p. on 1f. lake and yellow	16·00	23·00
		a. Figure '5' omitted	£375	
25		10p. on 2f. orange and blue-green	18·00	35·00
		a. Surch and opt inverted	£160	
22/25 *Set of 4*			60·00	£120

1924 (1 Jan). POSTAGE DUE. Postage Due stamps of France surch as T **1**.

No.	Type	Description	Unused	Used
D26	D **11**	50c. on 10c. pale brown	6·25	8·75
D27		1p. on 20c. olive-green	6·25	11·00
D28		2p. on 30c. carmine	6·25	8·75
D29		3p. on 50p. dull claret	6·25	8·75
D30		5p. on 1f. claret/*straw*	6·25	8·75
D26/D30 *Set of 5*			28·00	41·00

The note after No. 21 also applies here.

G^d Liban
1 Piastre
لبنان الكبير
غرش ١
(**3**)

Grand Liban
2 Piastres
لبنان الكبير
غروش ٢٠
(**4**)

غرش ٢
(a) (singular)

غروش ٢
(b) (plural)

1924 (1 July)–**25**. Stamps of France surch as T **4** (on T **13**) or as T **3** (others).

(a) Definitive stamps

No.	Type	Description	Unused	Used
26	**11**	0p.10 on 2c. claret	1·30	1·50
		a. Figure '1' inverted	60·00	60·00
		b. Surch inverted	60·00	60·00
		c. Surch double	60·00	60·00
27	**18**	0p.25 on 5c. orange	1·60	1·50
		a. Surch inverted	60·00	60·00
		b. Surch double	60·00	60·00
28		0p.50 on 10c. green	3·25	3·50
		a. Surch inverted	60·00	60·00
		b. Surch double	60·00	60·00
29	**15**	0p.75 on 15c. sage-green	2·00	4·25
		a. Surch inverted	60·00	60·00
		b. Surch double	60·00	60·00
30	**18**	1p. on 20c. lake-brown	1·90	1·40
		a. Surch inverted	60·00	60·00
		b. Surch double	60·00	60·00
31		1p.25 on 25c. blue	3·50	5·00
		a. Surch inverted	70·00	70·00
		b. Surch double	70·00	70·00
32		1p.50 on 30c. scarlet	2·75	2·75
		a. Surch inverted	70·00	70·00
		b. Surch double	70·00	70·00
33		1p.50 on 30c. orange (1.25)	85·00	85·00
		a. Surch inverted	£250	£250
34		2p. on 35c. violet (26.2.25)	3·00	8·50
		a. Surch inverted	60·00	60·00
35	**13**	2p. on 40c. red and pale blue	4·25	2·40
		a. Surch inverted	60·00	60·00
		b. Surch double	70·00	70·00
		c. 4th line of Type **4** as (a) instead of (b) (11.24)	4·75	2·75
		ca. Surch inverted	70·00	70·00
36		2p. on 45c. deep green and blue (26.2.25)	29·00	40·00
		a. Surch inverted	£110	£110
37		3p. on 60c. violet and blue	3·50	3·75
		a. Surch inverted	60·00	60·00
38	**15**	3p. on 60c. violet (26.2.25)	3·75	10·00
39		4p. on 85c. vermilion (2.2.25)	3·25	4·00
40	**13**	5p. on 1f. lake and yellow	5·25	5·00
		a. Surch inverted	70·00	70·00
		b. Surch double	80·00	80·00
41		10p. on 2f. orange and blue-green	11·50	18·00
42		25p. on 5f. deep blue and buff	19·00	34·00
26/42 *Set of 17*			£170	£200

(b) Pasteur type

No.	Type	Description	Unused	Used
43	**30**	0p.50 on 10c. green	1·40	1·30
		a. Surch inverted	65·00	65·00
		b. Surch double	60·00	60·00
44		0p.75 on 15c. green (26.2.25)	3·25	8·75
45		1p.50 on 30c. red	3·00	1·50
		a. Figure '1' omitted	80·00	80·00
		b. Line under 'd'	60·00	55·00
		c. 'C' for 'G'	55·00	55·00
		d. Surch inverted	65·00	60·00
46		2p. on 45c. scarlet (26.2.25)	6·25	8·75
		a. Surch inverted	65·00	60·00
47		2p.50 on 50c. blue	2·50	1·40
		a. Comma omitted after '2' (12.24)	3·00	3·00
		b. Surch inverted	60·00	60·00
		c. Surch double	60·00	60·00
48		4p. on 75c. blue (1.25)	4·00	4·75
43/48 *Set of 6*			18·00	24·00

(c) Olympic Games stamps (25.9.24)

No.	Type	Description	Unused	Used
49	**31**	0p.50 on 10c. green and yellow-green	41·00	65·00
		a. Surch inverted	£350	
50	–	1p.25 on 25c. deep and dull carmine	41·00	65·00
		a. Surch inverted	£350	
51	–	1p.50 on 30c. red and black	41·00	65·00
		a. Surch inverted	£350	
52	–	2p.50 on 50c. ultramarine and blue	41·00	65·00
		a. Surch inverted	£350	
49/52 *Set of 4*			£150	£225

(d) Ronsard stamp (12.24)

No.	Type	Description	Unused	Used
53	**35**	4p. on 75c. blue/*bluish*	3·75	10·50
		a. Surch inverted	£110	£110

G^d Liban
2 Piastres
لبنان الكبير
غروش ٢
طيارة
Avion
(**4a**)

1924 (1 July). AIR. Olivier Merson type of France surch as T **4a**.

No.	Type	Description	Unused	Used
54	**13**	2p. on 40c. red and pale blue	12·00	35·00
55		3p. on 60c. violet and blue	12·00	35·00
56		5p. on 1f. lake and yellow	12·00	35·00
		a. Surch inverted	70·00	
57		10p. on 2f. orange and blue-green	15·00	38·00
		a. Surch inverted	70·00	
		b. Surch double	70·00	
54/57 *Set of 4*			46·00	£130

1924 (1 July). POSTAGE DUE. T D **11** of France surch as T **3**.

No.	Type	Description	Unused	Used
D58	D **11**	0p.50 on 10c. pale brown	7·25	8·00
D59		1p. on 20c. olive-green	7·25	8·00
D60		2p. on 30c. carmine	7·25	8·00
		a. 4th line of Type **3** as (a) instead of (b)	18·00	21·00
D61		3p. on 50c. dull claret	7·25	9·75
		a. 4th line of Type **3** as (a) instead of (b)	18·00	21·00
D62		5p. on 1f. claret/*straw*	7·25	9·75
D58/D62 *Set of 5*			33·00	39·00

5 Cedar of Lebanon

6 Beirut

6a Beit ed-Din

6b Baalbek Ruins

6c Mouktara

7 Tripoli

(Des J. de la Nézière. 0p.10, litho; others photo Vaugirard, Paris)

1925 (1 Mar). T **5** and various views as Types **6** to **7**. P 12½ (No. 58) or 13½ (remainder).

No.	Type	Description	Unused	Used
58	**5**	0p.10 violet	90	1·60
59	**6**	0p.25 olive-black	1·20	2·30
60	–	0p.50 yellow-green	1·60	1·40
61	**6a**	0p.75 brown-red	2·00	4·00
62	**6b**	1p. bright claret	2·75	1·20
63	**6c**	1p.25 green	3·75	4·00
64	–	1p.50 bright rose	2·50	70
65	–	2p. sepia	3·25	1·30
66	–	2p.50 light blue	2·75	1·70
67	–	3p. brown	3·50	1·70
68	–	5p. bright violet	7·00	7·25
69	**7**	10p. plum	9·25	6·50
70	–	25p. bright blue	16·00	28·00
58/70 *Set of 13*			50·00	55·00

Designs: Horiz—0p.50, Tripoli; 1p.50, Tyre; 2p. Zahle; 2p.50, Baalbek; 3p. Deir el-Kamar; 5p. Sidon; 25p. Beirut (*different*).

AVION

طيارة

(7a)

D 7 Nahr el-Kalb

1925 (1 Mar). AIR. Nos. 65 and 67/69 optd with T **7a**, in green.

71	–	2p. sepia	5·75	11·50
72	–	3p. brown	5·75	11·50
73	–	5p. bright violet	5·75	11·50
		a. Opt inverted		
74	**7**	10p. plum	5·75	11·50
71/74 *Set of 4*			21·00	41·00

(Des J. de la Nézière. Photo Vaugirard, Paris)

1925 (1 Mar). POSTAGE DUE. As T D **7** (views). P 13½.

D75	0p.50 brown/*yellow*	1·30	3·50
D76	1p. brown-lake/*rose*	1·40	5·50
D77	2p. black/*blue*	2·40	4·00
D78	3p. deep brown/*salmon*	3·75	11·50
D79	5p. black/*green*	4·25	10·50
D75/D79 *Set of 5*		12·00	32·00

Designs: 0p.50, T D **7**; 1p. Pine forest, Beirut; 2p. Pigeon Grotto, Beirut; 3p. Beaufort Castle; 5p. Baalbek.

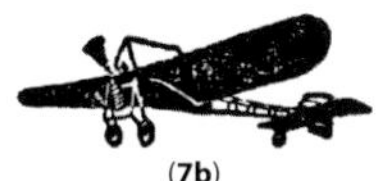

(**7b**)

1926 (1 May). AIR. Nos. 65 and 67/69 optd with T **7b**, in red (sideways (facing downwards) on 10p.).

75	–	2p. sepia	5·75	14·50
		a. Opt inverted	55·00	
76	–	3p. brown	5·75	14·50
		a. Opt inverted	55·00	
77	–	5p. bright violet	5·75	14·50
		a. Opt inverted	55·00	
78	**7**	10p. plum	5·75	14·50
		a. Opt inverted	55·00	
75/78 *Set of 4*			21·00	50·00

Secours aux Réfugiés

اعانات للاجئين

Afft الاجرة

0P·50 ١/٢ غ

(**7c**)

Secours aux Réfugiés

اعانات للاجئين

Afft الاجرة

0P·50 ١/٢ غ

(**7d**)

1926 (1 May). War Refugee Charity stamps.

(a) POSTAGE. Nos. 59/70 surch as T **7c** *or T* **7d** *(No. 89)*

79	0p.25 +0p.25 olive-black (R.)	3·25	7·00
80	0p.50 +0p.25 yellow-green	3·75	14·00
81	0p.75 +0p.25 brown-red	3·00	11·00
82	1p. +0p.50 bright claret	4·25	13·50
83	1p.25 +0p.50 green (R.)	4·50	17·00
	a. Black surch	£160	£160
84	1p.50 +0p.50 bright rose	5·75	14·00
	a. Surch double	70·00	70·00
85	2p. +0p.75 sepia (R.)	5·50	13·00
86	2p.50 +0p.75 light blue (R.)	4·75	20·00
87	3p. +1p. brown (R.)	5·25	19·00
	a. Black surch	£150	£150
88	5p. +1p. bright violet	7·50	22·00
89	10p. +2p. plum	7·50	28·00
90	25p. +5p. bright blue (R.)	7·25	34·00
79/90 *Set of 12*		55·00	£190

All values exist with surcharge inverted (*Price £65 each unused*).

(b) AIR. Nos. 75/78 surch as T **7c***, in black (new value in red on Nos. 91/93)*

91	2p. +1p. sepia	10·00	17·00
	a. Type **7c** inverted		
92	3p. +2p. brown	10·00	17·00
	a. Figure '2' omitted	£1000	£1000
93	5p. +3p. bright violet	10·00	17·00
94	10p. +5p. plum (Type **7c** vert up)	10·00	17·00
	a. 'au' for 'aux' in opt	48·00	48·00
91/94 *Set of 4*		36·00	60·00

These stamps were sold at face value plus the value indicated by the surcharge, but were only available for postage to the first amount, the difference going to the Refugee Fund.

REPUBLIC UNDER FRENCH MANDATE

The Lebanese Republic was proclaimed by the French on 23 May 1926.

3P·50 غرش ١/٢

(**7e**)

4P. غ٢

(**7f**)

4P. غ٤

(**7g**)

1926 (Sept–Dec). Nos. 59, 61, 63, 66 and 70 surch as Types **7e**/**7g**.

95	**7e**	3p.50 on 0p.75 brown-red	3·25	3·75
96	**7f**	4p. on 0p.25 olive-black (8.10)	3·75	4·50
		a. Surch double	70·00	70·00
97	**7g**	4p. on 0p.25 olive-black (12.11)	4·50	2·30
		a. Surch inverted	75·00	75·00
		b. Left-hand Arab character omitted.	50·00	50·00
		c. Comma after 'P'		
98		4p.50 on 0p.75 brown-red (12.26)	4·50	3·75
		a. Left-hand Arab character omitted.	41·00	37·00
		b. Surch inverted	70·00	70·00
99	**7e**	6p. on 2p.50 light blue	4·00	4·00
		a. Surch inverted	70·00	70·00
100	**7g**	7p.50 on 2p.50 light blue (12.26)	3·75	4·00
		a. Surch inverted	70·00	70·00
		b. Surch double	80·00	80·00
101	**7e**	12p. on 1p.25 green	3·00	4·25
		a. Surch inverted	70·00	70·00
		b. Surch back and front	47·00	
102	**7g**	15p. on 25p. bright blue (12.26)	5·00	4·50
		a. Left-hand Arab character omitted.	30·00	30·00
		b. Comma after 'P'		
103	**7e**	20p. on 1p.25 green (8.10)	10·00	19·00
		a. Surch back and front	47·00	
95/103 *Set of 9*			38·00	45·00

On Nos. 99/101 and 103 the new figures of value are below the bars.

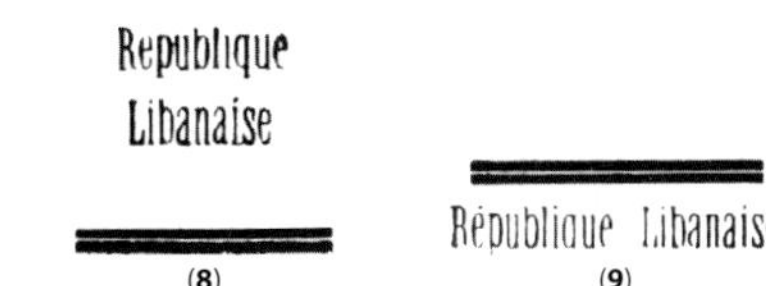

(**8**) (**9**)

Two types of 15p. on 25p.
(a) Surcharge at top. 'République Libanaise' at foot.
(b) Surcharge at foot. 'République Libanaise' at top.

1927 (1 July–Oct). Stamps of 1925 and provisionals as for 1926 optd as T **8** (vert designs) or **9** (horiz designs).

104	0p.10 violet (R.)	70	1·80
	a. Opt in black	70·00	
	b. Surch double	60·00	
105	0p.50 yellow-green	1·20	65
	a. Opt inverted	60·00	60·00
	b. Surch double	55·00	55·00
106	1p. bright claret	65	45
	a. Opt inverted	60·00	60·00
107	1p.50 bright rose	2·00	1·70
	a. Opt inverted	65·00	65·00
	b. Opt double	60·00	60·00
108	2p. sepia	3·75	2·00
109	3p. brown	1·80	65
110	4p. on 0p.25 olive-black (Type **7g**)	1·90	65
111	4p.50 on 0p.75 brown-red	1·60	90
	a. Opt inverted	55·00	
112	5p. bright violet	3·75	4·25
113	7p.50 on 2p.50 light blue	2·30	80
114	10p. plum	4·50	4·50
115	15p. on 25p. bright blue (a)	11·00	7·50
116	15p. on 25p. bright blue (b) (10.27)	16·00	16·00
117	25p. bright blue	14·00	42·00
	a. Opt inverted	65·00	65·00
104/117 *Set of 14*		60·00	75·00

The figures of the surcharges on Nos. 110 and 111 are below the cancelling bars, instead of above them as in Nos. 97 and 98.

On 5p. and 7p.50 'République Libanaise' is above the bars.

1927 (1 July). AIR. Nos. 75/78 optd as T **8** (10p.) or T **9** (others).

118 2p. sepia 7·00 14·50
  a. Aeroplane inverted £120 £120
119 3p. brown 7·00 14·50
120 5p. bright violet 7·00 14·50
121 10p. plum 7·00 14·50
118/121 *Set of 4* 25·00 50·00

On the 5p. 'République Libanaise' is above the bars.

1927 (1 July). POSTAGE DUE. Nos. D75/D79 optd as T **9**.

D122 0p.50 brown/*yellow* 1·50 4·25
  a. Opt inverted
D123 1p. brown-lake/*rose* 1·80 7·25
D124 2p. black/*blue* 3·50 9·00
D125 3p. deep brown/*salmon* 5·25 6·50
D126 5p. black/*green* 7·00 16·00
D122/D126 *Set of 5* 17·00 39·00

الجمهورية اللبنانية

(**10**)

1928. Nos. 113 and 116 additionally optd above the surch with T **10**.

122 7p.50 on 2p.50 light blue (R.)* 7·50 6·00
123 15p. on 25p. bright blue (R.)* 14·00 38·00
  a. Arabic opt inverted £130 £130

Red cancelling bars (as for No. 135), cover the Arabic inscription at foot of No. 123.

* See footnote below No. 136*a*.

1928 (May–Dec). Stamps of 1927, further optd as T **10** and with additional bars (except No. 131), above or below, obliterating former Arabic inscription.

124 0p.10 violet (R.) 80 90
  a. French opt omitted £130 £130
  b. Arabic opt vert 45·00 45·00
  c. Pair, one with entire opt omitted £160
125 0p.50 yellow-green 2·75 2·30
  a. Arabic opt inverted 70·00 70·00
  b. Entire opt inverted 55·00 55·00
126 1p. bright claret 1·60 1·10
  a. Entire opt inverted 60·00 60·00
127 1p.50 bright rose 3·50 3·50
  a. Entire opt inverted £140 £140
128 2p. sepia (R.)† 5·75 13·00
  a. Error. 'épublique Libana' 30·00 30·00
128*b* 2p. sepia (a Bk., b R.)‡ £150 £150
129 3p. brown 3·25 1·80
130 4p. on 0p.25 olive-black (a Bk., b R.)‡ 4·25 2·75
131 4p.50 on 0p.75 brown-red 3·00 3·00
132 5p. bright violet (a Bk., b R.)‡ 4·75 5·25
132*a* 5p. bright violet (R.)† (14.12) 3·50 9·00
132*b* 5p. bright violet (R.)† (12.28) 48·00 65·00
133 7p.50 on 2p.50 light blue (R.)* 10·00 8·00
134 10p. plum 11·00 10·50
  a. Entire opt inverted £160 £160
  b. Entire opt double £170 £170
135 15p. on 25p. bright blue (R.)* 16·00 44·00
136 25p. bright blue (a Bk., b R.)‡ 14·50 19·00
136*a* 25p. bright blue (R.)† 16·00 36·00
124/136*a* *Set of 17* £275 £350

* There were three issues of the 7p.50 on 2p.50 and 15p. on 25p. In the first only the Arabic overprint is in red and is applied above the surcharge (Nos. 122/123), whereas in the second printing (Nos. 133 and 135) both the French and Arabic overprints are in red below it. For the third, see Nos. 149/150.

† The French and Arabic overprints on Nos. 128, 132*a* and 136*a* are both red. On No. 132*a* 'République Libanaise' is above the Arabic overprint, but on No. 132*b* it is below it and closer. These overprints were applied, in each case, at one operation.

‡ On Nos. 128*b*, 130, 132 and 136 the overprints are bicoloured, a and b denote French and Arabic overprints respectively.

1928 (May). AIR. Nos. 118/121 further optd with T **10** and with additional bars (except on No. 139) obliterating former Arabic inscription.

137 2p. sepia 16·00 21·00
138 3p. brown 16·00 21·00
139 5p. bright violet 16·00 21·00
140 10p. plum 16·00 21·00
137/140 *Set of 4* 60·00 75·00

(**11**)

1928 (May). AIR. Nos. 65 and 67/69 optd as T **11**.

141 2p. sepia (R.) 5·25 8·00
  a. Error. On 2p. No. 71
  b. Opt double £140
142 3p. brown (R.) 3·50 4·50
  a. Error. On 3p. No. 72
  b. Opt double
143 5p. bright violet (R.) 5·25 6·50
  a. Error. On 5p. No. 73
144 10p. plum (R.) 5·25 6·25
  a. Error. On 10p., No. 74 £950
  b. Opt reading down
  c. 'Républiqne' for 'République' 25·00
141/144 *Set of 4* 17·00 23·00

The overprint on No. 144 is vertical (reading upwards) with the exception of the bars.

1928 (May). POSTAGE DUE. Nos. D122/D126 additionally optd as T **10** but with bars in upper corners obliterating the old Arabic inscriptions (except on 2p.).

D145 0p.50 brown/*yellow* (R.) 2·75 7·00
D146 1p. brown-lake/*rose* 2·75 8·25
D147 2p. black/*blue* (R.) 3·75 8·25
D148 3p. deep brown/*salmon* 7·50 14·00
D149 5p. black/*green* (R.) 8·50 21·00
D145/D149 *Set of 5* 23·00 55·00

See also Nos. D151/D153.

05 ٠٥
République
Libanaise
الجمهورية اللبنانية

(**12**)

République Libanaise
7P.50 ٧ ١/٢ غ
الجمهورية اللبنانية

(**13**)

1928 (June)–**29**. Nos. 58/59, 61, 63, 66 and 70 surch with T **12** or as T **13**.

145 05 on 0p.10 violet (2.11.28) 50 1·20
  a. Surch double 55·00 55·00
  b. Thick '5'
146 0p.50 on 0p.75 brown-red (7.29) 1·90 1·70
147 2p. on 1p.25 green (R.) 2·00 1·50
  a. Surch double 60·00 60·00
148 4p. on 0p.25 olive-black (R.) 3·50 1·10
  a. '4' inverted £650
  b. Surch inverted 80·00 80·00
  c. Surch double 65·00 65·00
149 7p.50 on 2p.50 light blue (R.) 3·00 1·80
  a. Opt inverted £170
  b. Opt double 70·00 70·00
  c. Opt on back
  d. Surch '5p.70' instead of '7p.50' £1300
  e. 'Républiqne' for 'République' 18·00 18·00
150 15p. on 25p. bright blue (R.) 14·00 15·00
  a. Surch double 55·00 55·00
145/150 *Set of 6* 22·00 20·00

No. 145b occurs on positions 2 and 52 of the sheet of 100.

1928 (July–Oct). POSTAGE DUE. Nos. D75, D77 and D79 optd with T **9** and **10** at one operation.

D151 1p.50 brown/*yellow* (R.) 3·25 5·00
D152 2p. black/*blue* (R.) (10.28) 12·00 18·00
D153 5p. black/*green* (R.) (10.28) 14·50 34·00
D151/D153 *Set of 3* 27·00 50·00

In Nos. D145/D149, bars obliterating the old Arabic inscriptions are found on all values except the 2p., whereas in this set the only exception is the 5p. The overprints are entirely in red on Nos. D151/D153, whereas T **9** on Nos. D145/D157 is in black.

15 (I) **15** (II)

1929–30. Stamps of 1925–1928 optd with an aeroplane only (No. 152) or as T **11**. Nos. 154/155 have surcharges and bars in addition.

151 0p.50 yellow-green (R.) (10.6.29) 1·30 5·00
  a. 'Républiqne' for 'République' 7·50
  b. Opt inverted 70·00
152 0p.50 on 0p.75 brown-red (B.) (No. 146) (9.29) 1·70 2·75
  a. 'Républiqne' for 'République' 8·75
  b. Surch normal, aeroplane inverted £170
  c. Aeroplane normal, surch inverted £170
  d. Surch double £170

No.	Description	Unused	Used
153	1p. bright claret (7.29)	2·50	3·75
	a. 'Républiqne' for 'République'	12·50	
	b. Opt inverted	70·00	
154	2p. on 1p.25 green (R.) (1.30)	2·50	3·25
	a. 'Républiqne' for 'République'	15·00	
	b. Surch inverted	70·00	
	c. Surch double	70·00	
155	15p. on 25p. bright blue (I) (R.) (7.29)	£275	£275
	a. 'Républiqne' for 'République'		
	b. Type II	£1300	£1300
156	25p. bright blue (R.) (7.29)	£225	£225
	a. 'Républiqne' for 'République'		
	b. Opt inverted	£650	£650
151/156	*Set of* 6	£450	£475

Beware of forgeries of No. 155.

14 Silkworm Larva, Cocoon and Moth

(Typo Imp Gédéon, Beirut)

1930 (11 Feb). Silk Congress. P 11.

No.	Type	Description	Unused	Used
157	**14**	4p. sepia	19·00	23·00
158		4½p. vermilion	19·00	23·00
159		7½p. deep blue	19·00	23·00
160		10p. violet	19·00	23·00
161		15p. deep green	19·00	23·00
162		25p. pale claret	19·00	23·00
157/162		*Set of* 6	£100	£120

The above exist imperforate from a limited supply used only for presentation purposes.

IMPERFORATE STAMPS. Most of the following issues up to 1945 exist imperforate from very limited printings.

FORGERIES. Forgeries exist of stamps as Types **15** and **20** and of most issues between 1944 and 1955. The details of the designs and lettering are less sharp and the colours generally paler than in the originals.

15 Cedars of Lebanon

16 Nahr el-Kalb

16a Baalbek

A

B

C

D

E

F

G

H

I

J. 'HASBAYA' 5 mm long.
K. 'HASBAYA' 6½ mm long.
L. 'CHUTES D'AFKA' 8 mm long.
M. 'CHUTES D'AFKA' 9½ mm long.

(Des J. de la Nézière. Ptd Vaugirard, Paris)

1930–36. Various views and frames.

(a) As T **15**, *lithographed. P 12½*

No.	Description	Unused	Used
163	0p.10 brown-orange (A) (12.30)	80	4·50
163*a*	0p.10 brown-orange (B) (1932)	8·25	5·00
163*b*	0p.10 yellow-orange (C) (1936)	2·30	1·70
164	0p.20 yellow-brown (10.30)	1·20	2·30
165	0p.25 blue (D) (6.31)	75	2·10
165*a*	0p.25 blue (E) (1932)	2·75	90
163/165*a*	*Set of* 6	14·50	15·00

(b) As Types **16** *and* **16a** *in photogravure. P 13½*

No.	Description	Unused	Used
166	0p.50 red-brown (F) (7.30)	2·50	1·50
166*a*	0p.50 red-brown (G)	16·00	10·50
166*b*	0p.75 brown (8.32)	3·75	3·00
167	1p. green (10.30)	5·50	1·10
167*a*	1p. deep plum (1.10.35)	8·25	70
168	1p.50 deep plum (7.30)	4·50	2·40
168*a*	1p.50 green (11.32)	10·50	1·10
169	2p. greenish blue (4.31)	6·50	1·70
170	3p. sepia (5.31)	7·75	1·70
171	4p. red-brown (9.30)	7·75	1·70
172	4p.50 carmine (10.30)	6·50	1·70
173	5p. blackish green (7.30)	3·50	1·50
174	6p. purple (10.30)	9·25	2·75
175	7p.50 deep blue (H) (5.30)	6·75	1·70
175*a*	7p.50 deep blue (I)	10·00	3·50
176	10p. deep green (J) (6.30)	11·00	1·90
176*a*	10p. deep green (K)	11·00	2·40
177	15p. blackish purple (L) (10.30)	13·00	3·75
177*a*	15p. blackish purple (M)	15·00	4·75
178	25p. blue-green (9.30)	16·00	6·00
179	50p. yellow-green (10.30)	60·00	20·00
180	100p. slate-black (10.30)	60·00	26·00
166/180	*Set of* 22	£275	90·00

Designs: As T **15**—0p10, Beirut; 0p.25, Baalbek. 0p.20. T **15**. 4p. T **16**. 7p.50, T **16a**. As Types **16** and **16a**—0p.50, Bickfaya; 1p. Saida (Sidon); 1p.50, 5p. Beit ed-Din (*different*); 2p. Tripoli; 0p.75, 3p., 100p. Baalbek (*different*); 4p.50, Beaufort, 6p. Tyre; 10p. Hasbaya; 15p. Afka Falls; 25p. Beirut; 50p. Deir el-Kamar.

See also Nos. 248/251.

17 Jebeil (Byblos)

(Photo Vaugirard, Paris)

1930–31. AIR. As T **17** (views). P 13½.

No.	Description	Unused	Used
181	0p.50 deep purple (1.31)	1·80	2·00
182	1p. yellow-green (4.31)	1·10	1·60
183	2p. orange (4.31)	2·50	2·50
184	3p. carmine (4.31)	2·50	2·75
185	5p. blackish green (6.30)	2·50	2·75
186	10p. orange-vermilion ('KADICHA' 4 *mm*) (10.30)	3·75	3·25
	a. 'KADICHA' 5 mm long	5·50	6·00
187	15p. red-brown (10.30)	3·75	3·25
188	25p. deep-violet (1.31)	5·75	5·25
189	50p. lake (10.30)	10·00	8·25
190	100p. brown (10.30)	15·00	15·00
181/190	*Set of* 10	44·00	42·00

Designs: Potez 29-4 biplane over—0p.50, Rachaya; 1p. Broumana; 2p. Baalbek; 3p. Hasroun; 5p. T **17**; 10p. Kadisha; 15p. Beirut; 25p. Tripoli; 50p. Kabelais; 100p. Zahle.

D **18**

D **19** Bas-relief from Sarcophagus of King Ahiram at Byblos

(Des J. de la Nézière. Photo Vaugirard, Paris)

1931 (Apr). POSTAGE DUE. As T D **18** and T D **19** (various designs). P 13½.

No.	Description	Unused	Used
D191	0p.50 black/*rose*	1·30	2·50
D192	1p. black/*blue*	2·30	2·75
D193	2p. black/*yellow*	2·50	2·50

D194		3p. black/*green*	3·75	3·00
D195		5p. black/*red*	12·00	13·00
D196		8p. black/*rose*	7·00	11·50
D197		15p. black/*white*	7·75	7·00
D191/D197 *Set of 7*			33·00	38·00

Designs with Arabic and French inscriptions: 0p.50, T D **18**; 1p. Bas-relief of Phoenician galley; 2p. Arabesque; 3p. Garland; 5p. As T D **32**; 8p. T D **19**; 15p. Statuettes.

For 10p. see No. D252.

18 Skiing

19 Jounieh Bay

(Des M. Farrouk and P. Mourani. Photo Vaugirard, Paris)

1936 (12 Oct). AIR. Tourist Propaganda. P 13½.

191	**18**	0p.50 deep green	3·50	3·75
192	**19**	1p. orange-vermilion	4·50	5·25
193	**18**	2p. blackish violet	4·50	5·25
194	**19**	3p. yellow-green	4·50	5·25
195	**18**	5p. lake	6·00	5·75
196	**19**	10p. chestnut	6·50	7·25
197		15p. carmine-lake	55·00	55·00
198	**18**	25p. green	£160	£160
191/198 *Set of 8*			£225	£225

20 Cedar of Lebanon

21 President Eddé

22 Lebanese Landscape

23 Exhibition Pavilion, Paris

(Des P. Mourani. T **20**; Die eng G. Hourriez. Typo. Types **21**/**22**; Eng H. Cheffér and J. Piel. Recess French Govt Ptg Wks, Paris)

1937–40. P 14×13½ (T **20**) or 13 (Types **21**/**22**).

199	**20**	0p.10 carmine (11.37)	55	35
200		0p.20 greenish blue (1940)	1·00	5·50
201		0p.25 rose-lilac (1940)	75	5·25
202		0p.50 cerise (1.9.37)	65	35
203		0p.75 brown (1940)	80	1·70
204	**21**	3p. bright violet (4.11.37)	5·00	1·90
205		4p. purple-brown (1.11.37)	3·00	60
206		4p.50 carmine (26.6.37)	2·75	85
207	**22**	10p. brown-lake (1.9.37)	3·75	95
208		12½p. ultramarine (1940)	2·10	55
209		15p. bluish green (1938)	5·00	1·10
210		20p. chestnut (1940)	2·50	95
211		25p. rose-carmine (1940)	7·50	90
212		50p. violet (1940)	12·50	3·25
213		100p. sepia (1940)	17·00	5·50
199/213 *Set of 15*			60·00	27·00

Nos. 214/217 are vacant.

(Des P. Mourani. Photo Vaugirard, Paris)

1937 (1 July). AIR. Paris International Exhibition. P 13½.

218	**23**	0p.50 greenish black	2·20	3·25
219		1p. yellow-green	2·20	3·25
220		2p. chestnut	2·20	3·25
221		3p. blackish green	2·20	3·25
222		5p. green	2·20	3·25
223		10p. rose-red	11·50	23·00
224		15p. claret	10·50	27·00
225		25p. red-brown	18·00	42·00
218/225 *Set of 8*			46·00	95·00

24 Beit ed-Din

25 Ruins of Baalbek

(Des P Mourani. Eng A. Delzers and Feltesse (10p.). Recess French Govt Ptg Wks, Paris)

1937–40. AIR. P 13.

226	**24**	0p.50 bright blue (1.3.38)	40	40
227		1p. brown-red (1940)	2·00	2·30
228		2p. sepia (1940)	2·40	2·75
229		3p. rose-carmine (1940)	6·00	5·00
230		5p. light green (1940)	2·75	2·30
231	**25**	10p. dull violet (1.12.37)	2·30	85
232		15p. turquoise-blue (1940)	2·75	3·50
233		25p. violet (1940)	7·25	6·50
234		50p. yellow-green (1940)	14·00	7·25
235		100p. brown (1940)	7·50	7·25
226/235 *Set of 10*			43·00	34·00

(**26**)

27 Medical College, Beirut

1938–41. Nos. 204/205 surch as T **26**.

236	**21**	2p. on 3p. bright violet	2·00	1·10
237		2½p. on 4p. purple-brown	3·00	75
		a. Surch in red (1941)	5·25	2·30

(Des P. Mourani. Photo Vaugirard, Paris)

1938 (9 May). AIR. Medical Congress. P 13½.

238	**27**	2p. green	3·75	7·75
239		3p. orange-vermilion	4·25	5·00
240		5p. deep violet	6·50	11·00
241		10p. carmine	13·00	23·00
238/241 *Set of 4*			25·00	42·00

28 Maurice Noguès and Liore et Olivier LeO H.24-3 Flying Boat over Beirut

(Des P. Mourani. Photo Vaugirard, Paris)

1938 (15 July). AIR. Tenth Anniversary of First Air Service between France and Lebanon. P 11.

242	**28**	10p. maroon	7·50	14·50
MS242*a* 161×120 mm. No. 242 in block of four. P 13½			70·00	75·00

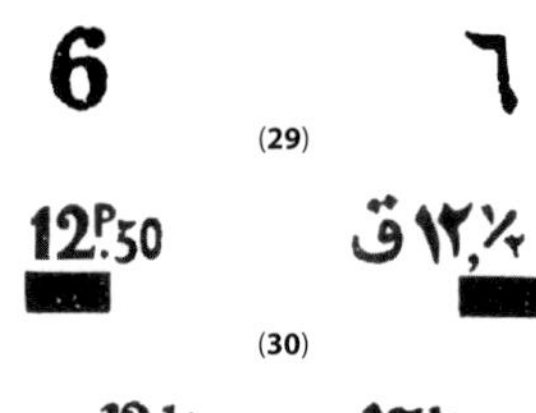
6 ٦

(**29**)

12P.50 ق١٢,٥٠

(**30**)

12½ ١٢½

(**31**)

1938–39. Surch with Types **29**/**31**.

243	**29**	6p. on 7p.50 (No. 175) (R.)	3·75	3·00
243*a*		6p. on 7p.50 (No. 175*a*) (R.)		
244	**30**	7p.50 on 50p. (No. 179)	3·75	4·00
245		7p.50 on 100p. (No. 180) (R.)	3·25	3·75
246		12p.50 on 7p.50 blue (Type **22**) (R.)	6·50	4·50

247	**31**	12½p. on 7p.50 blue (Type **22**) (R.) (1939)	3·25	1·10
243/247 *Set of 5*			18·00	15·00

(Litho Imprimerie Catholique, Beirut)

1939. As T **16a**, but view of Beit ed-Din. P 11½.

248	1p. slate-green	1·80	85
249	1p.50 slate-purple	2·40	1·50
250	7p.50 rose-carmine	2·75	1·60
248/250 *Set of 3*		6·25	3·50

In Nos. 248/250, the figures and Arabic inscriptions, in the side panels, differ from those of T **16a** and the imprint 'HELIO VAUGIRARD' is replaced by 'IMP. CATHOLIQUE-BEY-ROUTH-LIBAN'.

(Des J. de la Nézière. Eng Degorce. Recess Govt Ptg Wks, Paris)

1940. Nahr el-Kalb design but with 'DEGORCE' (engraver) at bottom instead of printer's imprint. P 13.

251	**16**	5p. greenish blue	3·50	1·00

D **32**

(Des J. de la Nézière. Eng Feltesse. Recess Govt Ptg Wks, Paris)

1940. POSTAGE DUE. P 13.

D252	D **32**	10p. deep green	14·50	18·00

British and Free French forces took control of Syria and Lebanon from the Vichy-controlled French régime in June 1941 and on 26 November 1941 Lebanon was proclaimed independent. The powers exercised by France were transferred to the republic on 1 January 1944.

INDEPENDENT REPUBLIC

British and Free French forces took control of Syria and Lebanon from the Vichy-controlled French régime in June 1941 and on 26 November 1941 Lebanon was proclaimed independent. The powers exercised by France were transferred to the republic on 1 January 1944.

The issues for the Free French Forces made in 1942–1943 are listed at the end of Syria.

PRINTERS, PROCESS AND DESIGNER. Nos. 252/D469 were all lithographed by the Imprimerie Catholique, Beirut and were also designed by P. Koroleff, *except where otherwise stated.*

32 Emir Bechir Chehab

33 Aeroplane over Mountains

1942 (18 Sept). First Anniversary of Proclamation of Independence. P 11½.

(a) POSTAGE

252	**32**	0p.50 emerald green	4·25	3·75
253		1p.50 brown-purple	4·25	3·75
254		6p. rose-carmine	4·25	3·75
255		15p. blue	4·25	3·75

(b) AIR

256	**33**	10p. purple	7·25	6·50
257		50p. blue-green	7·75	7·25
252/257 *Set of 6*			29·00	26·00

Nos. 252/255 and 256/257 exist imperforate in miniature sheets of which only 200 of each were printed.

(**34**) (**35**)

(**36**)

1943–45. Various surcharges as Types **34/36**.

(a) No. 208 (President Eddé) surch with T **34**

258	**21**	2p. on 4p. purple-brown (B.)	8·50	7·75

(b) Nos. 250 (Beit ed-Din) and 212 (Landscape) surch as T **35**

259	–	6p. on 7p.50 rose-carmine (G.)	3·00	1·70
260	**22**	10p. on 12½p. ultramarine	2·75	1·30

(c) Nos. 251 (Nahr el-Kalb) and 212 surch as T **36** *(1945)*

261	**16**	2p. on 5p. greenish blue (V.)	1·70	95
262		3p. on 5p. greenish blue	1·70	95
263	**22**	6p. on 12½p. ultramarine	2·50	1·70
264		7½p. on 12½p. ultramarine (R.)	2·75	2·30
258/264 *Set of 7*			21·00	15·00

37 Parliament House

38 Bechamoun

(Des P. Koroleff (Nos. 269/272); S. Kalaajy (others))

1944 (1 May). Second Anniversary of Proclamation of Independence. P 11½.

(a) POSTAGE. As T **37** *(buildings)*

265	25p. carmine	13·00	12·00
266	50p. greenish blue	13·00	12·00
267	150p. blue	13·00	12·00
268	200p. dull purple	13·00	12·00

(b) AIR. As T **38** *(aeroplane and views)*

269	25p. emerald-green	5·25	3·00
270	50p. red-orange	5·25	3·00
271	100p. cinnamon	5·25	4·25
272	200p. violet	6·50	4·25
273	300p. grey-green	22·00	20·00
274	500p. purple-brown	60·00	38·00
265/274 *Set of 10*		£140	£110

Designs: Postage—25p, 150p. T **37**; 50p., 200p. Government House. Air—25p., 50p. T **38**; 100p., 200p. Rachaya Citadel; 300p., 500p. Beirut.

38a Beirut Isolation Hospital

(**39**)

1944 (8 July). Sixth Arabic Medical Congress. T **38a** and similar horiz design, optd with T **39**. P 11½.

(a) POSTAGE

275	**38a**	10p. carmine	8·50	7·75
276		20p. bright blue	9·75	9·00

(b) AIR. Inscr 'POSTE AERIENNE'

277	–	20p. red-orange	4·25	3·75
278	–	50p. greenish blue	5·50	5·00
279	–	100p. purple	7·25	6·50
275/279 *Set of 5*			32·00	29·00

Design: 20p. (air) to 100p. Bhannes Sanatorium.

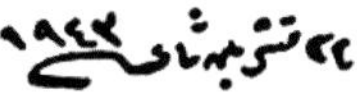
(**40** Trans 'Nov, 23, 1943')

1944 (23 Nov). First Anniversary of President's Return to Office. Nos. 265/274 optd with T **40**.

(a) POSTAGE. As T **37** *(buildings)*

280	25p. carmine (B.)	22·00	20·00
281	50p. greenish blue (V.)	22·00	20·00
282	150p. blue (R.)	22·00	20·00
283	200p. dull purple (Bk.)	22·00	20·00

(b) AIR. As T **38** *(aerpolane and views)*

284	25p. emerald-green (R.)	11·00	10·00
285	50p. red-orange (B.)	18·00	17·00
286	100p. cinnamon (V.)	23·00	22·00
287	200p. violet (R.)	36·00	34·00

288		300p. grey-green (R.)	49·00	46·00
289		500p. purple-brown (B.)	85·00	80·00
280/289		*Set of* 10	£275	£250

POSTAL TAX STAMPS. These were issued between 1945 and 1962 for compulsory use on inland mail (and sometimes also on mail to Arab countries) to provide funds for various purposes. All were printed on watermarked paper. The majority being multiple 'AT 30' (sideways).

T **41**

(T **42**)

1945 (Apr). POSTAL TAX. Lebanese Army. Fiscal stamp as Type T **41** surch with Type T **42**. P 13½.

T289	T **41**	5p. on 30c. red-brown (V.)	£800	4·25

Earliest date of use reported was May 1945.

41 Crusader Castle, Byblos

42 Falls of R. Litani

1945. As Types **41/42** (views). P 11½.

(a) POSTAGE

290	**41**	15p. purple-brown	6·50	5·75
291		20p. green	7·75	5·75
292	–	25p. blue	7·75	5·75
293	–	50p. carmine	9·00	5·75

Design: Horiz—25p., 50p. Crusader Castle, Tripoli.

(b) AIR. Inscr 'POSTE AERIENNE'

294	**42**	25p. sepia	4·25	2·75
295		50p. bright purple	7·25	4·50
296	–	200p. violet	21·00	7·25
297	–	300p. black	36·00	14·50
290/297		*Set of* 8	90·00	47·00

Design: Horiz—200p., 300p. Cedar of Lebanon and skier.

For other values and colour changes in T **41**, see Nos. 397/401.

D **43** National Museum

1945. POSTAGE DUE. P 11½.

D298	D **43**	2p. black/*lemon*	6·25	5·75
D299		5p. blue/*rose*	7·75	7·25
D300		25p. blue/*green*	10·50	9·50
D301		50p. purple/*blue*	11·50	11·00
D298/D301		*Set of* 4	32·00	30·00

43 V(ictory) and National Flag

44 V(ictory) and Lebanese Soldiers at Bir-Hakeim

1946 (8 May). Victory issue. 'V' in design. P 11½.

(a) POSTAGE

298	**43**	7p.50 red and chocolate	1·00	10
299		10p. red and purple	1·60	10
300		12p.50 claret, blue and red	2·30	20
301		15p. green, yellow-green and red	4·00	25
302		20p. blue-green, yellow-green and red	3·50	25
303		25p. blue, grey-blue and red	5·25	50
304		50p. ultramarine, violet and red	8·50	2·75
305		100p. black, grey-blue and red	14·50	5·00

(b) AIR

306	**44**	15p. blue, yellow and red	90	25
307		20p. vermilion, blue and red	1·00	60
308		25p. blue, yellow and red	1·30	60
309		50p. black, violet and red	2·50	60
310		100p. violet, rose and red	6·50	1·80
311		150p. brown, rose and red	7·75	3·00
298/311		*Set of* 14	55·00	14·50

MS311*a* 142×230 mm. Nos. 298/311. Colours changed. Text in brown (with gum) or blue (without gum) £160 £140

The above sheet also exists on thick buff paper with blue inscriptions, of which 300 were printed (*Price* £600 *un*.).

1946. As T **43**, but without V(ictory) sign. P 11½.

312		7p.50 lake, mauve and red	2·50	25
313		10p. violet, mauve and red	4·00	25
314		12p.50 brown, yellow-green and red	5·25	30
315		15p. chocolate, rose and red	6·50	35
316		20p. blue, rose and red	7·75	35
317		25p. green, yellow-green and red	10·50	50
318		50p. blue, grey-blue and red	16·00	2·20
319		100p. black, grey-blue and red	26·00	5·25
312/319		*Set of* 8	70·00	8·50

45 Grey Herons

1946 (11 Sept). P 11½.

(a) POSTAGE. Inscr 'POSTES'

320	**45**	12p.50 carmine	46·00	4·75

(b) AIR

321	**45**	10p. orange	10·50	1·40
322		25p. blue	13·00	70
323		50p. green	29·00	2·00
324		100p. slate-purple	50·00	9·00
320/324		*Set of* 5	£130	16·00

46 Cedar of Lebanon

47

1946–47. P 11.

325	**46**	0p.50 red-brown (1947)	90	25
326		1p. brown-purple (1947)	1·70	25
327		2p.50 bright violet	5·25	25
328		5p. carmine	5·75	25
329		6p. grey (1947)	5·75	25
325/329		*Set of* 5	17·00	1·10

1946 (22 Nov). AIR. Arab Postal Congress. P 11½.

330	**47**	25p. blue	2·00	85
331		50p. green	2·50	1·30
332		75p. orange-red	4·50	2·20
333		150p. blackish violet	9·00	3·75
330/333		*Set of* 4	16·00	7·25

Nos. 330/333 exist imperforate in a miniature sheet of which 500 were printed (*Price* £550 *un*.).

48 Cedar of Lebanon

49 President, Bridge and Tablet

1947. P 14×13½.

333*a*	**48**	0p.50 deep brown	2·10	25
333*b*		2p.50 green	2·75	25
333*c*		5p. rose-carmine	5·25	50
333*a*/333*c*		*Set of* 3	9·00	90

1947 (11 Feb). AIR. Evacuation of Foreign Troops from Lebanon. P 11½.

334	**49**	25p. blue	2·50	1·20
335		50p. brown-lake	4·50	1·80
336		75p. black	7·75	3·50
337		150p. green	13·00	6·00
334/337		*Set of 4*	25·00	11·50

Nos. 334/337 exist imperforate in a miniature sheet of which 500 were printed (*Price* £500 *un.*).

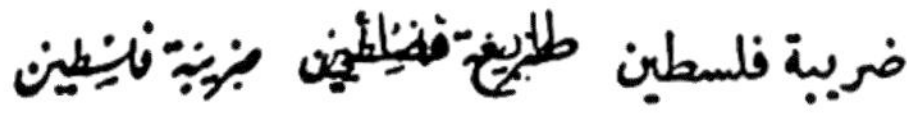

(T **50**) (T **51**) (T **52**)

1947 (Feb)–**49**. POSTAL TAX. Aid to War in Palestine. Surch as Type T **42**.

(a) With top line Type T **50**

T338	T **41**	5p. on 25c. deep bluish green (R.) (12.48)	36·00	3·00
T339		5p. on 30c. red-brown (B.) (4.49)	47·00	6·00
T340		5p. on 60c. pale grey-blue (Br.) (7.48)	80·00	4·25
T341		5p. on 3p. pale salmon-rose (B.)	36·00	5·50
T342		5p. on 15p. Prussian blue (R.) (8.49)	36·00	2·20
		a. Brown surch (10.48)	85·00	6·50

(b) With top line Type T **51**

T343	T **41**	5p. on 10p. red (7.48)	£160	9·50

(c) With top line Type T **52**

T344	T **41**	5p. on 3p. pale salmon-rose (Bk.+V.) (5.49)	33·00	3·00
		a. Type T **42** omitted	£650	60·00
		b. On 3p. rose-red (1949)	33·00	5·00

(d) As No. T344 but with figure '5' at left instead of 'O' and without inscr between figures

T345	T **41**	5p. on 3p. pale salmon-rose (Bk.+V.)	£600	38·00

Dates given are those of earliest recorded use.

In addition to 'AT 39' No. T338 is also known with watermark 'AT 37' and 'AT 38'. For general note regarding watermarks see above No. T289.

50 Crusader Castle, Tripoli

51 Jounieh Bay

52 Grand Serail Palace

D **53**

(Des P. Koroleff (Types **50**/**51**), M. Farrouk (T **52**))

1947 (17 May–June). P 11½.

(a) POSTAGE

338	**50**	12p.50 carmine	13·00	65
339		25p. ultramarine	16·00	65
340		50p. green	50·00	1·40
341		100p. violet	65·00	10·50

(b) AIR

342	**51**	5p. green (27.6)	80	25
343		10p. mauve (27.6)	90	25
344		15p. vermilion	1·60	25
344*a*		15p. deep green	26·00	4·00
345		20p. orange	2·50	25
345*a*		20p. vermilion	2·75	50
346		25p. blue	3·25	25
347		50p. brown-red	7·25	65
348		100p. brown-purple	16·00	1·00
349	**52**	150p. brown-purple (27.6)	30·00	2·20
350		200p. blue-slate (27.6)	31·00	10·50
351		300p. black (27.6)	60·00	23·00
338/351		*Set of 16*	£300	50·00

For other stamps in T **51** but redrawn with larger boat, see Nos. 402/406.

1947. POSTAGE DUE. P 11½.

D352	D **53**	5p. black/*green*	8·50	2·20
D353		25p. black/*lemon*	85·00	5·75
D354		50p. black/*blue*	44·00	14·50
D352/D354		*Set of 3*	£120	20·00

53 Posthorn

54 Phoenician Galley

1947 (17 June). AIR. Participation in 12th Congress of Universal Postal Union, Paris. P 11½.

352	**53**	10p. ultramarine	2·00	90
353		15p. carmine	2·50	1·60
354		25p. blue	4·25	1·80
355	**54**	50p. grey-green	9·00	2·50
356		75p. violet	9·75	4·00
357		100p. grey-brown	13·00	6·75
352/357		*Set of 6*	36·00	16·00

55 Faraya Bridge and Statue

(T **56** 'Palestine Stamp')

1947 (27 June). AIR. Red Cross. T **55** and similar horiz design. Cross in red. P 11½.

358	**55**	12p.50 +25p. blue-green	12·50	9·00
359		25p. +50p. blue	16·00	10·50
360	–	50p. +100p. red-brown	21·00	13·00
361	–	75p. +150p. violet	43·00	26·00
362	–	100p. +200p. slate	80·00	46·00
358/362		*Set of 5*	£160	95·00

Design: Nos. 360/362, Djounié Bay and statue.

1948 (June). POSTAL TAX. Palestine Aid. No. T289 optd with Type T **56**. P 13½.

T363	T **41**	5p. on 30c. red-brown	33·00	4·25

For general note regarding watermarks see above No. T289.

56 Cedar of Lebanon

57 Zebaide Aqueduct

58 Lebanese Landscape

D **59** Monument at Hermel

1948 (1 Sept). P 14×13 (T **56**) or 11½ (Types **57**/**58**).

(a) POSTAGE

363	**56**	0p.50 light blue	40	15
364		1p. light brown	90	20
365		2p.50 dull mauve	1·30	20
366		3p. emerald-green	3·00	25
367		5p. rose-red	4·00	25
368	**57**	7p.50 scarlet	9·75	40
369		10p. slate-purple	7·00	50
370		12p.50 blue	16·00	50
371		25p. ultramarine	23·00	1·30
372		50p. green	49·00	9·00

(b) AIR

373	**58**	5p. orange-vermilion	1·30	25
374		10p. magenta	2·00	25
375		15p. red-brown	5·00	25
376		20p. slate	7·50	35
377		25p. greenish blue	13·00	1·80
378		50p. black	26·00	2·50
363/378		*Set of 16*	£150	16·00

For similar values at T **56** but in redrawn designs and different colours, see Nos. 394/396 and 407/410.

1948. POSTAGE DUE. P 11½.

D379	D **59**	2p. black/*lemon*	5·50	1·40
D380		3p. black/*rose*	11·50	5·25
D381		10p. black/*azure*	31·00	9·75
D379/D381 *Set of 3*			43·00	15·00

59 Europa on Bull

60 Avicenna (philosopher and scientist)

61 Apollo on Sun Chariot

62 Symbolical Figure

(Des M. Farrouk (T **60**), P. Koroleff (others))

1948 (23 Nov). Third Meeting of United Nations Educational, Scientific and Cultural Organisation, Beirut. P 11½.

(a) POSTAGE

379	**59**	10p. orange and carmine	4·00	2·30
380		12p.50 mauve and violet	5·25	3·50
381		25p. green and olive-green	5·75	3·50
382	**60**	30p. buff and orange-brown	7·75	4·25
383		40p. grey-green and bluish green	11·50	4·25

(b) AIR

384	**61**	7p.50 blue and pale blue	3·25	2·30
385		15p. black and grey	4·00	2·30
386		20p. lake-brown and pink	6·50	3·50
387	**62**	35p. carmine and pink	11·00	4·50
388		75p. emerald and yellow-green	23·00	10·50
379/388 *Set of 10*			75·00	37·00
MS388*a* 142×205 mm. Nos. 379/388. Imperf. No gum			£425	£425

63 Camel

64 Sikorsky S-51 Helicopter

1949 (16 Aug). 75th Anniversary of Universal Postal Union. P 11½.

(a) POSTAGE

389	**63**	5p. violet	2·20	1·40
390		7p.50 red	3·00	2·50
391		12p.50 bright blue	5·25	3·00

(b) AIR

392	**64**	25p. blue	11·00	5·00
393		50p. grey-green	17·00	7·75
389/393 *Set of 5*			35·00	18·00
MS393*a* 135×190 mm. Nos. 389/393. Sheet inscr in green. Imperf (*sold at* 150p.)			£110	£110

The above sheet exists with the sheet inscriptions in brown, without price (150p.) and without gum. Of this 500 were printed (*Price* £500 *un.*).

No. 363

No. 364

No. 365

No. 394

No. 395

No. 396

Small boat. Nos. 343/347

Large boat. Nos. 402/406

(Des Koroleff (Types **41** and **56**); M. Farrouk (T **51**))

1949.

*(a) POSTAGE. As T **56**, but redrawn. P 14×13. T **41**, new values and colour changes. P 11½*

394	**56**	0p.50 blue	1·20	15
395		1p. red-orange	2·00	15
396		2p.50 bright mauve	14·50	1·30
397	**41**	7p.50 scarlet	4·50	25
398		10p. brown-purple	6·50	40
399		12p.50 blue	16·00	40
400		25p. violet	30·00	90
401		50p. green	65·00	7·25

*(b) AIR. As T **51**, but redrawn. P 11½*

402	**51**	10p. bright mauve	9·75	1·60
403		15p. green	14·50	2·00
404		20p. orange	33·00	3·50
405		25p. deep blue	£120	4·75
406		50p. brown-red	£350	50·00
394/406 *Set of 13*			£600	65·00

T **51**. Nos. 344*a* and 402/406. White paper, yellow gum. Others grey paper, white gum. Nos. 402, 404 and 406 have a broader opening to the '0' of the value than the earlier versions.

65 Cedar of Lebanon

66 Nahr el-Kalb Bridge

1950.

*(a) As T **56**, but redrawn. P 14×13*

407	**65**	0p.50 rose-red	65	25
408		1p. orange-red	1·60	25
409		2p.50 violet	2·20	25
410		5p. reddish purple	4·25	25

*(b) T **66**. P 11½*

411	**66**	7p.50 rose-red	5·25	25
412		10p. reddish lilac	6·50	25
413		12p.50 pale blue	9·75	40
414		25p. deep blue	18·00	1·70
415		50p. emerald-green	49·00	9·00
407/415 *Set of 9*			90·00	11·50

D **67**

1950. POSTAGE DUE. P 11½.

D416	D **67**	1p. carmine	1·30	25
D417		5p. ultramarine	6·50	1·30
D418		10p. blue-green	9·00	2·50
D416/D418 *Set of 3*			15·00	3·75

67 Congressional Flags

68 House Martins

69 President Bechara el-Khoury

70 Crusader Castle, Sidon

1950 (8 Aug). Lebanese Emigrants' Congress. P 11½.

		(a) POSTAGE		
416	**67**	7p.50 grey-green	1·60	40
417		12p.50 magenta	2·00	40
		(b) AIR		
418	**68**	5p. violet-blue	4·25	90
419		15p. violet	5·50	1·30
420	**69**	25p. purple-brown	3·25	1·30
421		35p. blue-green	5·50	2·30
416/421 *Set of 6*			20·00	6·00
MS421*a* 134×184 mm. Nos. 416/421. Imperf. No gum			£130	£130

1950 (8 Sept). AIR. P 11½.

422	**70**	10p. brown	1·30	25
423		15p. green	2·00	25
424		20p. rose-carmine	5·25	65
425		25p. blue	9·00	1·60
426		50p. olive-grey	16·00	4·00
422/426 *Set of 5*			30·00	6·00

(**71**) (**72**)

1950 (Nov). Surch with Types **71**/**72**.

427	**56**	1p. on 3p. emerald-green (R.)	90	40
428	**46**	2p.50 on 6p. grey (R.)	1·30	40

73 Cedar of Lebanon

74 Nahr el-Kalb Bridge

75 Crusader Castle, Sidon

1951 (9 June). P 14×13 (T **73**) or 11½ (others).

		(a) POSTAGE		
429	**73**	0p.50 rose-red	65	15
430		1p. brown	1·20	15
431		2p.50 greenish grey	5·25	15
432		5p. claret	5·75	15
433	**74**	7p.50 vermilion	6·75	50
434		10p. purple	9·00	40
435		12p.50 turquoise-blue	16·00	65
436		25p. blue	23·00	2·30
437		50p. green	49·00	12·50
		(b) AIR		
438	**75**	10p. blue-green	1·80	25
439		15p. deep brown	4·00	25
440		20p. scarlet	4·00	40
441		25p. blue	4·25	40
442		35p. magenta	9·75	4·50
443		50p. violet-blue	18·00	3·50
429/443 *Set of 15*			£140	24·00

For redrawn stamps as T **74** but inscribed 'LIBAN', see Nos. 561/563.

76 Cedar of Lebanon

77 Baalbek

1952. T **76** and designs as T **77**. P 14×13 (T **76**) or 11½ (others).

		(a) POSTAGE		
444	**76**	0p.50 green	1·30	15
445		1p. chestnut	1·30	15
446		2p.50 light blue	2·00	40
447		5p. rose-red	3·25	40
448	**77**	7p.50 scarlet	4·50	80
449		10p. bright violet	9·00	90
450		12p.50 blue	9·00	90
451		25p. ultramarine	11·00	2·30
452	–	50p. blue-green	33·00	4·25
453	–	100p. brown	70·00	13·00
		(b) AIR		
454	–	5p. scarlet	50	15
455	–	10p. grey	80	25
456	–	15p. magenta	1·40	25
457	–	20p. orange	2·30	50
458	–	25p. light blue	2·30	65
459	–	35p. ultramarine	4·00	80
460	–	50p. emerald-green	13·00	90
461	–	100p. blue	90·00	4·00
462	–	200p. blue-green	50·00	7·25
463	–	300p. blackish brown	70·00	16·00
444/463 *Set of 20*			£350	49·00

Designs: Horiz—5p. to 35p. Beirut Airport; 50p., 100p. (Nos. 452/453), Beaufort Castle; 50p., 100p. (Nos. 460/461), 200p., 300p. Amphitheatre, Byblos.

D **78**

1952. POSTAGE DUE. P 11½.

D464	D **78**	1p. magenta	40	15
D465		2p. bright-violet	65	40
D466		3p. blue-green	80	40
D467		5p. blue	1·20	50
D468		10p. brown	2·20	90
D469		25p. black	17·00	2·20
D464/D469 *Set of 6*			20·00	4·00

PROCESS. Nos. 464/860 were all lithographed by various printers.

78 Cedar of Lebanon

79 General Post Office

80 Douglas DC-4

(Des V. Pliss. Imp J. Saikali)

1953 (Sept–Oct). P 14×13½ (T **78**) or 11½ (others).

		(a) POSTAGE		
464	**78**	0p.50 pale blue	1·70	15
465		1p. crimson	1·70	15
466		2p.50 dull violet	2·10	40
467		5p. emerald	3·25	40
468	**79**	7p.50 carmine	5·25	65
469		10p. deep yellow-green	6·00	90
470		12p.50 turquoise-green	8·50	1·00
471		25p. ultramarine	12·50	2·10
472		50p. purple-brown	22·00	4·75
		(b) AIR (1 Oct)		
473	**80**	5p. bright green	65	15
474		10p. crimson	1·30	15
475		15p. vermilion	1·80	15
476		20p. turquoise-green	2·50	15

477		25p. blue	6·50	25
478		35p. chestnut	9·50	40
479		50p. deep violet-blue	12·50	80
480		100p. blackish sepia	23·00	7·75
464/480 *Set of* 17			£110	18·00

On Nos. 464 and 466 the '50' of the face value aligns at the foot with 'P.'. For redrawn design with the '50' projecting below 'P.' see Nos. 559/560.

For 20p. as T **79** see No. 636.

D **81**

(Des V. Pliss. Imp J. Saikali)

1953 (Sept). POSTAGE DUE. P 11½.

D481	D **81**	1p. carmine	25	15
D482		2p. blue-green	40	25
D483		3p. yellow-orange	50	25
D484		5p. bright purple	65	40
D485		10p. brown	1·30	50
D486		15p. deep blue	2·50	1·20
D481/D486 *Set of* 6			5·00	2·50

81 Cedar of Lebanon

82 Beit ed-Din Palace

83 Baalbek

(Des V. Pliss. Imp J. Saikali)

1954 (Mar). P 14×13½ (T **81**), 11½ (others).

(a) POSTAGE

481	**81**	0p.50 blue	40	25
482		1p. red-orange	65	25
483		2p.50 violet	1·00	40
484		5p. bluish green	2·10	40
485	**82**	7p.50 carmine-red	3·50	80
486		10p. green	5·25	80
487		12p.50 blue	8·50	1·00
488		25p. deep ultramarine	11·50	4·25
489		50p. turquoise-green	21·00	7·25
490		100p. purple-brown	50·00	14·50

(b) AIR. T **83** *and another horiz design*

491	**83**	5p. green	65	15
492		10p. deep lilac	1·30	15
493		15p. carmine	1·40	15
494		20p. bistre-brown	2·10	15
495		25p. deep blue	2·30	40
496		35p. blackish brown	3·25	40
497	–	50p. bronze-green	10·50	65
498	–	100p. lake	17·00	1·00
499	–	200p. sepia	34·00	3·50
500	–	300p. deep state-blue	60·00	7·25
481/500 *Set of* 20			£200	39·00

Design: 50p. to 300p. (Nos. 497/500) Litani irrigation canal.

For redrawn stamps as Nos. 497/500, see Nos. 564/567.

84 Khalde Airport, Beirut

84a

(Des P. Koroleff. Imp Catholique)

1954 (23 Apr). AIR. Inauguration of Beirut International Airport. P 11½.

501	**84**	10p. rosine and carmine	1·30	40
502		25p. deep blue and blue	2·50	65
503		35p. yellow-brown and brown	4·00	1·20
504		65p. yellowish green and pale green	9·00	4·50
501/504 *Set of* 4			15·00	6·00

(Photo Survey Dept, Cairo)

1955 (1 Jan). Arab Postal Union. W **48** of Egypt. P 13½×13.

(a) POSTAGE

505	**84a**	12p.50 emerald	1·30	65
506		25p. bright violet	2·00	65

(b) AIR. Inscr 'POSTE AERIENNE'

507	**84a**	2p.50 yellow-brown	1·30	50
505/507 *Set of* 3			4·25	1·60

85 Rotary Emblem

(Des P. Koroleff. Imp J. Saikali)

1955 (24 Feb). AIR. 50th Anniversary of Rotary International. P 11½.

508	**85**	35p. dull green	2·00	1·30
509		65p. dull deep blue	3·25	2·00

86 Cedar of Lebanon

87 Jeita Grotto

88 Skiers

(Des V. Pliss (T **86**), P. Koroleff (others). Imp J. Saikali)

1955 (Mar). P 14×13½ (T **86**) or 11½ (others).

(a) POSTAGE

510	**86**	0p.50 deep bright blue	50	25
511		1p. red	65	25
512		2p.50 reddish violet	1·00	25
513		5p. emerald	1·70	25
514	**87**	7p.50 red-orange	2·30	25
515		10p. bright green	3·25	25
516		12p.50 blue	3·75	25
517		25p. deep violet-blue	8·50	50
518		50p. deep grey-green	13·00	1·30

(b) AIR

519	**88**	5p. bluish green	90	65
520		15p. rose-red	1·60	40
521		20p. bright violet	2·50	40
522		25p. pale blue	5·25	50
523		35p. olive-brown	7·75	90
524		50p. deep brown	14·50	1·30
525		65p. chalky blue	26·00	4·25
510/525 *Set of* 16			85·00	11·00

On No. 510 the face value reads '0.50 PIASTRE' and on No. 512 the '2' and '50' are different sizes. For redrawn stamps with the 0p.50 reading 'P', the 2p.50 with figures same size and the 1 and 5p. with short dash under 'P', see Nos. 582/585*b*. For 2p.50 stamp with imprint 'I. C. Beyrouth', see No. 552.

89 Visitor from Abroad

90 Cedar of Lebanon

91 Globe and Columns

92 Oranges

D **93**

(Des M. Farrouk. Imp Catholique)

1955 (10 Sept). AIR. Tourist Propaganda. P 13½×13.

526	**89**	2p.50 maroon and pale blue	25	15
527		12p.50 ultramarine and pale blue	65	40
528		25p. indigo and pale blue	1·60	65
529		35p. yellow-green and pale blue	2·10	90
526/529 *Set of 4*			4·25	1·90
MS529*a* 159×110 mm. Nos. 526/529. Imperf			36·00	34·00

(Des F. Ott. Imp Catholique)

1955 (Sept–Oct).

(a) POSTAGE. P 13×13½ (T **90***) or 13½×13 (T* **91***)*

530	**90**	0.50p. blue	25	15
531		1p. orange	50	15
532		2p.50 violet	90	15
533		5p. bluish green	1·30	15
534	**91**	7p.50 brown-red and yellow-orange	2·00	15
535		10p. emerald and orange-brown	2·20	20
536		12p.50 ultramarine and turquoise-green	2·50	20
537		25p. deep blue and pale magenta	4·00	35
538		50p. deep green and pale blue	5·75	65
539		100p. deep brown and salmon	8·50	1·60

(b) AIR. T **92** *and similar designs. P 13×13½ (horiz) or 13½×13 (vert) (15 Oct)*

540	**92**	5p. lemon and green	65	20
541		10p. orange and myrtle-green	1·30	20
542		15p. red-orange and green	1·60	20
543		20p. yellow-orange and deep olive-brown	2·00	20
544	–	25p. deep violet-blue and blue	2·75	25
545	–	35p. brown-purple and green	4·75	40
546	–	50p. yellow and olive-black	5·25	45
547	–	65p. lemon and bluish green	9·75	50
548	–	100p. orange and bright yellow-green	13·00	1·40
549	–	200p. brown-red and bluish green	26·00	7·25
530/549 *Set of 20*			85·00	13·50

Designs: Vert—25p., 35p., 50p. Grapes. Horiz—65p., 100p., 200p. Quinces.

(Des F. Ott. Imp Catholique)

1955. POSTAGE DUE. P 13×13½.

D550	D **93**	1p. yellow-brown	25	25
D551		2p. yellow-green	40	25
D552		3p. turquoise-green	50	25
D553		5p. claret	65	25
D554		10p. bronze-green	90	40
D555		15p. ultramarine	1·00	45
D556		25p. purple	2·20	1·30
D550/D556 *Set of 7*			5·25	2·75

93 United Nations Emblem

94 Masks, Columns and Gargoyle

(Des P. Koroleff. Imp J. Saikali)

1956 (23 Jan). AIR. Tenth Anniversary of United Nations. P 11½.

550	**93**	35p. deep ultramarine	7·25	5·75
551		65p. deep green	9·75	7·25
MS551*a* 90×70 mm. Nos. 550/551. Imperf			£130	£130

(Imp Catholique)

1956 (Feb). As No. 512 but without designer's name and with new imprint 'I. C. Beyrouth' below design. Colour changed. P 14×13½.

552	**86**	2p.50 violet-blue	11·00	25

(Des P. Koroleff. Imp J. Saikali)

1956 (10 Dec). AIR. Baalbek International Drama Festival. T **94** and similar design inscr 'FESTIVAL INTERNATIONAL DE BAALBECK'. P 13×13½ (12p.50, 25p.) or 13½×13 (others).

553	**94**	2p.50 blackish brown	65	25
554		10p. deep dull green	90	40
555	–	12p.50 light blue	1·00	65
556	–	25p. deep violet-blue	1·60	80
557	–	35p. deep bright purple	3·50	1·30
558	–	65p. blackish slate	5·50	2·75
553/558 *Set of 6*			11·50	5·50

Designs: Horiz—12p.50, 25p. Temple ruins at Baalbek. Vert—35p., 65p. Double bass, masks and columns.

T **95** Family and Ruined House

95 President Chamoun and King Faisal II of Iraq

96 Arab Leaders

(Des P. Koroleff. Imp J. Saikali)

1956. POSTAL TAX. Earthquake Victims. P 13½.

T559	T **95**	2p.50 brown	5·75	40

1957. As earlier designs but redrawn.

(a) POSTAGE

(i) As T **78** *but numerals of value redrawn*

559	0p.50 bright blue	50	20
560	2p.50 claret	1·20	20

(ii) As T **74** *but inscr 'LIBAN' and Arabic inscription changed*

561	7p.50 red	2·20	20
562	10p. chestnut	3·00	20
563	12p.50 deep grey-blue	3·75	20

(b) AIR

(i) As Nos. 497/500 but Arabic inscription changed

564	10p. bright violet	65	20
565	15p. orange	90	20
566	20p. green	1·30	25
567	25p. slate-blue	1·70	25

(ii) As T **88** *but Arabic inscription changed*

568	35p. bronze-green	4·00	40
569	65p. reddish purple	7·25	1·00
570	100p. bistre-brown	11·00	2·20
559/570 *Set of 12*		34·00	5·00

(Des E. Ognyanov. Imp J. Saikali)

1957 (15 July). AIR. Arab Leaders' Conference, Beirut, 1956. T **95** and similar designs and T **96**. P 13 (100p.) or 13×13½ (others).

571	15p. red-orange	1·30	65
572	15p. deep blue	1·30	65
573	15p. maroon	1·30	65
574	15p. bright purple	1·30	65
575	15p. deep green	1·30	65
576	25p. greenish blue	2·00	70
577	100p. red-brown	9·00	4·25
571/577 *Set of 7*		16·00	7·50
MS577*a* 106×151 mm. Nos. 571/576. Imperf		£120	£100

Designs: No. 571, T **95**. Horiz as T **95**—President Chamoun and: No. 572, King Hussein of Jordan; No. 573, Abdallah Khalil of Sudan; No. 574, President Shukri Bey al-Quwatli of Syria; No. 575, King Saud of Saudi Arabia; No. 576, Lebanon map. Diamond—No. 577, T **96**.

97 Runners

(Des V. Pliss (2p.50), Wembe (others). Imp J. Saikali)

1957 (12 Sept). Second Pan-Arabian Games, Beirut. Various designs as T **97** inscr '2 èmes JEUX SPORTIFS PAN-ARABES BEYROUTH 1957'. P 13½×13.

	(a) POSTAGE		
578	2p.50 deep chocolate	1·20	65
579	12p.50 indigo	1·70	90
	(b) AIR. P 13×13½		
580	35p. maroon	4·50	1·80
581	50p. green	5·50	2·50
578/581 *Set of 4*		11·50	5·25
MS581*a* 132×185 mm. Nos. 578/581. Imperf. No gum		£170	£160

Designs: Vert—2p.50, T **97**; 12p.50, Footballers. Horiz—35p. Fencers; 50p. Stadium.

98 Miners

1957–60. As T **86** but figures redrawn and colours changed, and various designs as T **98**. P 13×13½ (Nos. 582/585*b*, 592/593, 596, 598, 600) 11½ (Nos. 586/588, 594/595, 597, 599) or 13½×13 (Nos. 589/591).

		(a) POSTAGE		
582	**86**	0p.50 blue (16½×20½ *mm*)	50	20
582*a*		0p.50 violet (17×21½ *mm*) (1960)	40	20
583		1p. light brown (16½×20½ *mm*)	65	20
583*a*		1p. brown-purple (17×21½ *mm*) (1960)	50	20
584		2p.50 bright violet (16½×20½ *mm*)	90	20
584*a*		2p.50 ultramarine (17×21¼ *mm*) (1960)	80	20
584*b*		2p.50 blue (17×21¼ *mm*) (1960)	80	20
585		5p. green (16½×20½ *mm*)	1·30	20
585*a*		5p. emerald (17×21¼ *mm*) (1960)	1·00	20
585*b*		5p. yellow-green (17×21¼ *mm*) (1960)	1·00	20
586	**98**	7½p. rose-pink	1·60	20
587		10p. purple-brown	2·10	25
588		12½p. blue	2·75	25
589	–	25p. grey-blue	3·25	35
590	–	50p. yellow-green	5·25	50
591	–	100p. sepia	9·00	1·60
		(b) AIR. Inscr 'POSTE AERIENNE'		
592	–	5p. emerald	40	15
593	–	10p. yellow-orange	45	15
594	–	15p. brown	60	15
595	–	20p. brown-purple	90	20
596	–	25p. deep violet-blue	1·20	25
597	–	35p. dull purple	1·80	50
598	–	50p. deep green	3·00	80
599	–	65p. sepia	5·00	85
600	–	100p. deep grey	6·50	2·20
582/600 *Set of 25*			46·00	9·25

Designs: Nos. 582/582*a*, 584/584*b*. As T **86** but figures of value uniform in size; Nos. 583/583*a*, 585/585*b*. As T **86** but short dash under 'P'. Vert—Nos. 589/591, Potter. Horiz—Nos. 592/596, Cedar of Lebanon within signs of the Zodiac, with bird and ship; Nos. 597/600, Chamoun Electric Power Station.

T **99** Rebuilding

T **100** Rebuilding

(Des D. Akiskalian. Imp J. Saikali)

1957–59. POSTAL TAX. Earthquake Victims. P 13½.

T601	T **99**	2p.50 sepia	5·75	40
T602		2p.50 grey-green (1958)	3·25	40
T603	T **100**	2p.50 brown (1959)	4·00	25
T601/T603 *Set of 3*			11·50	95

99 Cedar of Lebanon

100 Soldier and flag

101 Douglas DC-6B at Khalde Airport

(Des D. Akiskalian (Types **99**/**101**). Imp J. Saikali)

1958–59. P 13½×13 (T **100**), 13×13½ (others).

		(a) POSTAGE		
601	**99**	0p.50 blue	40	20
602		1p. yellow-orange	65	20
603		2p.50 bright violet	90	20
604		5p. deep yellow-green	1·20	20
605	**100**	12p.50 blue	2·10	25
606		25p. indigo	2·30	25
607		50p. brown	4·00	40
608		100p. sepia	7·25	80
		*(b) AIR. T **101** and similar horiz design*		
609	**101**	5p. green	1·30	15
610		10p. claret	1·60	15
611		15p. deep violet	1·80	20
612		20p. orange-red	2·30	25
613		25p. deep violet-blue	2·75	40
614	–	35p. bronze-green	2·30	40
615	–	50p. turquoise-blue	3·00	45
616	–	65p. sepia	5·75	80
617	–	100p. ultramarine	6·50	1·30
601/617 *Set of 17*			41·00	6·00

Design: Nos. 614/617, Factory, cogwheel and telegraph pylons.

(**102**)

(**103**)

1959 (Sept). Lawyers' Conference. Nos. 538 and 546 surch as T **102**.

	(a) POSTAGE		
618	30p. on 50p. deep green and pale blue	2·20	1·00
	(b) AIR		
619	40p. on 50p. yellow and olive-black	2·50	1·20

1959 (Sept). AIR. Engineers' Conference. Nos. 614 and 616 surch as T **103**.

620	30p. on 35p. bronze-green	1·30	90
621	40p. on 65p. sepia (B.)	2·20	1·30

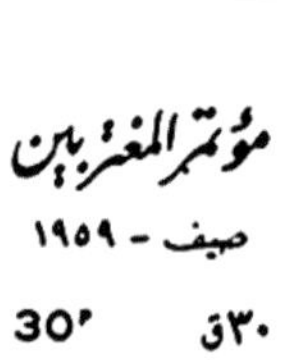
(**104**)

105 *The Discus Thrower*

1959 (Oct). Emigrants' Conference. No. 590 surch as T **104**.

622	30p. on 50p. yellow-green	1·80	40
623	40p. on 50p. yellow-green	2·50	90

(Imp Catholique)

1959 (11 Oct). AIR. Third Mediterranean Games, Beirut. T **105** and similar designs inscr 'IIIe JEUX MEDITERRANEENS—1959'. P 11½.

624		15p. grey-green	90	40
625		30p. chocolate	1·30	65
626		40p. ultramarine	3·00	1·20
624/626		*Set of* 3	4·75	2·00

MS626*a* 106×130 mm. Nos. 624/626. Without sheet values in margins. Imperf (*sold at* 100p.) £325 £325
MS626*b* As last but with sheet values in margins £100 £100

Designs: Vert—15p. T **105**; 30p. Weightlifting. Horiz—40p. Games emblem.

106 Soldiers with Standard

(**107**)

1959 (25 Nov). AIR. 16th Anniversary of independence. P 13½×13.

627	**106**	40p. orange-red and slate-black	1·70	85
628		60p. orange-red and green	2·20	1·10

Nos. 627/628 exist imperforate in a miniature sheet of which 500 were printed (*Price* £160 *un and used*.).

1959 (Dec). Various issues surch as T **107**.

(a) POSTAGE

629	**100**	7p.50 on 12p.50 blue	1·00	15
630		10p. on 12p.50 blue	1·20	15
631		15p. on 25p. indigo	1·40	20
632	–	40p. on 50p. yellow-green (No. 590)	4·00	65

(b) AIR

633	–	40p. on 65p. reddish purple (No. 569)	4·75	80
629/633		*Set of* 5	11·00	1·80

108 Planting Tree

109 President Chehab

1960 (18 Jan). AIR. 25th Anniversary of Friends of the Tree Society. P 11½.

634	**108**	20p. reddish purple and green	1·30	90
635		40p. sepia and green	2·10	1·30

1960 (Feb). AIR. Design similar to T **79**. P 13½×13.

636	**79**	20p. green	1·30	80

(Photo State Ptg Works, Vienna)

1960 (12 Mar). AIR. P 14.

637	**109**	5p. green	20	15
638		10p. Prussian blue	20	15
639		15p. orange-brown	25	20
640		20p. sepia	25	20
641		30p. yellow-olive	50	25
642		40p. brown-red	60	40
643		50p. blue	1·00	45
644		70p. purple	2·00	50
645		100p. deep emerald-green	4·25	1·00
637/645		*Set of* 9	8·25	3·00

110 Arab League Centre

111 Uprooted Tree

(Imp Catholique)

1960 (23 May). Inauguration of Arab League Centre, Cairo. P 13×13½.

646	**110**	15p. blue-green	1·00	65

(Imp Catholique)

1960 (7 Apr). AIR. World Refugee Year. P 13½×13.

(a) Size 20½×36½ mm

647	**111**	25p. light brown	1·30	90
648		40p. deep green	2·10	1·30

MS648*a* 90×110 mm. Nos. 647/648. Imperf (*sold at* 150p.) 65·00 65·00

(b) 2nd printing. Size 19½×35½ mm

648*b*	**111**	25p. light brown	1·80	1·80
648*c*		40p. deep green	2·20	2·20

112 Martyrs' Monument

(Imp Catholique)

1960 (6 May). AIR. Martyrs' Commemoration. T **112** and similar design. P 13½×13 (70p.) or 13×13½ (others).

649	**112**	20p. purple and deep green	90	50
650		40p. greenish blue and deep green	1·30	90
651	–	70p. deep olive-green and black	3·00	1·30
649/651		*Set of* 3	4·75	2·40

Design: Vert—70p. Detail of statues on monument.

Nos. 649/651 exist in a miniature sheet imperforate and without gum of which 1000 were printed (*Price* £130 *un*, £100 *used*).

113 President Chehab and King Mohammed V

114 President Chehab

(Imp Catholique)

1960 (1 June). AIR. Visit of King Mohammed V of Morocco. P 13×13½.

652	**113**	30p. chocolate and brown	1·40	65
653		70p. orange-brown and black	2·75	1·00

Nos. 652/653 exist in a miniature sheet imperforate and without gum of which 1000 were printed (*Price* £170 *un*, £130 *used*).

(Photo State Ptg Wks, Vienna)

1960. P 14.

654	**114**	0p.50 deep green	25	20
655		2p.50 yellow-olive	35	20
656		5p. green	50	20
657		7p.50 brown-red	80	25
658		15p. blue	1·20	40
659		50p. purple	2·50	50
660		100p. brown	5·00	90
654/660		*Set of* 7	9·50	2·40

115 Child

116 Dove, Map and Flags

(Des P. Koroleff. Imp Catholique)

1960 (Aug). AIR. Mother and Child Days. T **115** and similar vert design. P 13½×13.

661	**115**	20p. brown-red and orange-yellow	90	25
662		20p. +10p. brown-red and orange-yellow	1·00	40
663	–	60p. blue and pale blue	2·50	1·60
664	–	60p. +15p. blue and pale blue	3·75	1·70
661/664		*Set of* 4	7·25	3·50

Design: 60p., 60p.+15p. Mother and child.

(Des P. Koroleff. Imp Catholique)

1960 (20 Sept). AIR. World Lebanese Union Meeting, Beirut. T **116** and similar designs inscr 'UNION DES LIBANAIS DANS LE MONDE'. P 13×13½ (70p.) or 13½×13 (others).

665	20p. red, ultramarine, yellow and blue	40	40
666	40p. green, black, violet and blue	1·30	65
667	70p. orange-brown, green, blue and indigo	1·60	90
665/667 *Set of 3*		3·00	1·80
MS667*a* 110×139 mm. Nos. 665/667. Imperf (*sold at* 150p.)		36·00	33·00

Designs: Vert—20p. T **116**; 40p. Cedar of Lebanon and homing pigeons. Horiz—70p. Globes and Cedar.

(**117**)

٢٠ق+١٠ق

20 P. + 10 P.

(**118**)

1960 (Nov). Arabian Oil Congress, Beirut. Nos. 585*a* and 646 optd with T **117**, in red.

668	**86**	5p. emerald	90	15
669	**110**	15p. blue-green	1·80	65

1960 (7 Nov). AIR. World Refugee Year. Nos. 648*b*/648*c* surch as T **118**, in red.

669*a*	**111**	20p. +10p. on 40p. deep green	13·00	13·00
669*b*		30p. +15p. on 25p. light brown	18·00	18·00

119 Boxing

(Imp Catholique)

1961 (12 Jan). Olympic Games. T **119** and similar designs inscr 'XVIIe OLYMPIADE'. P 13.

(a) POSTAGE

670	2p.50 +2p.50 red-brown and blue	25	25
671	5p. +5p. red-brown and yellow-orange	50	40
672	7p.50 +7p.50 red-brown and bright violet	80	65

(b) AIR. Inscr 'POSTE AERIENNE'

673	15p. +15p. red-brown and scarlet	4·25	4·00
674	25p. +25p. red-brown and blue-green	4·25	4·00
675	35p. +35p. red-brown and ultramarine	4·50	4·00
670/675 *Set of 6*		13·00	12·00
MS675*a* 137×118 mm. Nos. 673/675. Imperf (*sold at* 150p.)		47·00	47·00

Designs: 2p.50, T **119**; 5p. Wrestling; 7p.50, Putting the shot; 15p. Fencing; 25p. Cycling; 35p. Swimming.

120 President Chehab

121 President Chehab and Map of Lebanon

122 UN Emblem and Map

(Des J. A. Kufédjian. Imp Catholique)

1961 (Feb). T **120/121** and similar design. P 13×13½ (200p.) or 13½×13 (others).

(a) POSTAGE

676	**120**	2p.50 bright blue and light blue	40	20
677		7p.50 blackish violet and mauve	80	20
678		10p. brown-lake and yellow	1·30	20

(b) AIR

679	**121**	5p. blue-green and pale green	25	25
680		10p. brown and yellow-ochre	65	25
681		70p. violet and mauve	3·25	80
682	–	200p. blue and bistre-brown	7·75	3·25
676/682 *Set of 7*			13·00	4·75

Design: Horiz—200p. Casino, Maameltein.

(Des P. Koroleff. Imp Catholique)

1961 (5 May). AIR. 15th Anniversary of United Nations Organisation. T **122** and similar designs. P 13×13½ (50p.) or 13½×13 (others).

683	20p. maroon and light blue	80	40
684	30p. green and brown	1·30	65
685	50p. light blue and ultramarine	2·20	1·00
683/685 *Set of 3*		3·75	1·80
MS685*a* 100×132 mm. Nos. 683/685. Imperf (*sold at* 125p.)		13·00	13·00

Designs: Vert—20p. T **122**; 30p. UN emblem and Baalbek ruins. Horiz—50p. View of UN Headquarters and Manhattan.

123 Cedar of Lebanon

124 Bay of Maameltein

(Des V. Pliss. Imp Catholique)

1961. P 13×13½.

686	**123**	2p.50 deep myrtle-green	80	15

See also Nos. 695/957.

(Des J. A. Kufédjian. Imp J. Saikali)

1961 (10 May). AIR. P 13×13½.

687	**124**	15p. lake	80	25
688		30p. greenish blue	1·20	50
689		40p. sepia	2·00	80
687/689 *Set of 3*			3·50	1·40

125 Weaving

126 Water-skiers

(Des P. Koroleff. Imp J. Saikali)

1961 (11 July). AIR. Labour Day. T **125** and similar horiz design. P 13×13½.

690	30p. claret (Pottery)	2·20	1·00
691	70p. ultramarine (Type **125**)	4·25	2·20

(Des P. Koroleff. Imp J. Saikali)

1961 (30 Aug). AIR. Tourist Month. T **126** and similar designs inscr 'LE MOIS TOURISTIQUE'. P 13½×13 (15p.) or 13×13½ (others).

692	15p. bright violet and deep blue	1·00	50
693	40p. blue and flesh	2·20	80
694	70p. olive-green and flesh	3·25	1·70
692/694 *Set of 3*		5·75	2·75

Designs: Vert—15p. Firework display. Horiz—40p. T **126**; 70p. Tourists in punt.

(Des V. Pliss. Imp J. Saikali)

1961 (Aug). As T **123** but with plain background. P 13×13½.

695	2p.50 orange-yellow	1·00	20
696	5p. lake	1·30	20
697	10p. black	1·60	25
695/697 *Set of 3*		3·50	60

127 GPO, Beirut

127a Motor Highway, Dora

(Des P. Koroleff. Imp Cortbawi, Aley)

1961 (1 Aug–Oct). P 11½.

(a) POSTAGE

698	**127**	2p.50 deep magenta (8.61)	1·00	25
699		5p. emerald (10.61)	1·30	35
700		15p. blue (8.61)	1·80	50

(b) AIR. Inscr 'POSTE AERIENNE'

701	**127a**	35p. olive-green (1.8)	1·00	50
702		50p. brown (9.61)	1·80	65
703		100p. grey-black (9.61)	2·50	1·00
698/703 *Set of 6*			8·50	3·00

128 Cedars of Lebanon

129 Tyre Waterfront

(Des P. Koroleff. Imp J. Saikali)

1961 (Oct). Small figures of values as in Types **128/129**. P 13½.

(a) POSTAGE

704	**128**	0p.50 green	20	20
705		1p. bistre-brown	25	20
706		2p.50 ultramarine	40	25
707		5p. carmine	65	25
708		7p.50 violet	90	35
709	–	10p. deep purple	2·00	35
710	–	15p. deep grey-blue	2·50	50
711	–	50p. deep green	3·00	1·70
712	–	100p. black	7·25	2·50

(b) AIR. Inscr 'POSTE AERIENNE'

713	**129**	5p. carmine	50	20
714		10p. bright violet	65	20
715		15p. greenish blue	1·00	20
716		20p. yellow-orange	1·20	25
717		30p. emerald-green	1·30	35
718	–	40p. brown-purple	1·60	50
719	–	50p. ultramarine	2·10	80
720	–	70p. green	2·50	1·30
721	–	100p. sepia	4·75	2·10
704/721 *Set of 18*			29·00	11·00

Designs: Horiz—Nos. 709/712, Zahle. Vert—Nos. 718/721, Afka Falls.

See also Nos. 729/734.

130 UNESCO Building, Beirut

131 Tomb of Unknown Soldier

(Des Shammout. Imp Cortbawi, Aley)

1961 (20 Nov). AIR. 15th Anniversary of United Nations Educational, Scientific and Cultural Organisation. T **130** and similar designs. P 12.

722	20p. multicoloured	80	35
723	30p. multicoloured	1·00	65
724	50p. multicoloured	2·10	1·00
722/724 *Set of 3*		3·50	1·80

Designs: Vert—30p. UNESCO emblem and cedar. Horiz—20p. T **130**; 50p. UNESCO Building, Paris.

(Des Shammout. Imp Cortbawi, Aley)

1961 (31 Dec). Independence, and Evacuation of Foreign Troops Commemoration. T **131** and similar designs. P12.

(a) POSTAGE

725	10p. multicoloured	1·00	20
726	15p. multicoloured	1·40	40

(b) AIR. Inscr 'POSTE AERIENNE'

727	25p. multicoloured	1·00	80
728	50p. multicoloured	1·40	1·00
725/728 *Set of 4*		4·25	2·20

Designs: Vert—10p. T **131**; 15p. Soldier and flag. Horiz—25p. Cedar emblem; 50p. Emirs Bashir and Fakhreddine.

T **132** Rebuilding

T **133** Rebuilding

(Des J. A. Kufédjian. Imp Catholique)

1961–62. POSTAL TAX. Earthquake Victims. P 13½×13 or 13 (No. T730).

T729	T **132**	2p.50 red-brown	3·50	25
T730	T **133**	2p.50 turquoise (1962)	3·50	25

131a

1962. As Nos. 704, etc., but tablet redrawn with larger figures of value, as T **131a.**

(a) POSTAGE

729	**128**	0p.50 green	50	25
730		1p. bistre-brown	65	35
731		2p.50 ultramarine	80	40
732	–	15p. deep grey-blue	5·25	65

(b) AIR. Inscr 'POSTE AERIENNE' (March)

733	**129**	5p. carmine	50	20
734	–	40p. brown-purple	11·00	1·30
729/734 *Set of 6*			17·00	2·75

132 Scout Bugler

133 Arab League Centre, Cairo, and Emblem

(Des Shammout. Imp Cortbawi, Aley)

1962 (1 Mar). Lebanese Scout Movement. Designs as T **132**. P 12.

(a) POSTAGE

735	½p. black, yellow and green	20	15
736	1p. green, yellow-green, red and black	25	15
737	2½p. green, black and red	45	15
738	6p. multicoloured	1·00	15
739	10p. yellow, black and blue	1·40	20

(b) AIR. Inscr 'POSTE AERIENNE'

740	15p. red, green, yellow and black	1·80	25
	a. Black (value, inscr and trunk) omitted		
741	20p. yellow, black and violet	2·20	40
742	25p. green, ochre, red and black	2·75	1·30
735/742 *Set of 8*		9·00	2·50

Designs: Horiz—1p. Scout with flag, cedar and badge; 2½p. Stretcher-party, badge and laurel; 10p. Scouts at campfire; 15p. Cedar and Guide badge; 25p. Cedar and Scout badge. Vert—½p. T **132**; 6p. Lord Baden-Powell; 20p. Saluting hand.

(Des P. Koroleff. Imp Catholique)

1962 (20 Mar). AIR. Arab League Week. P 13½×13.

743	**133**	20p. ultramarine and pale blue	80	40
744		30p. brown-red and pink	1·00	65
745		50p. deep green and turquoise	1·80	1·00
743/745 *Set of 3*			3·25	1·80

See also Nos. 792/795.

134 Blacksmith

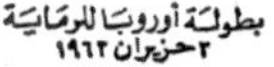

CHAMPIONNAT D'EUROPE DE TIR
2 JUIN 1962

(**135**)

(Des P. Koroleff. Imp J. Saikali)

1962 (1 May). AIR. Labour Day. T **134** and similar design. P 13½×13 (vert) or 13×13½ (horiz).

746	**134**	5p. green and pale blue	35	15
747		10p. blue and pink	50	20
748	–	25p. violet and pink	90	40
749	–	35p. magenta and pale blue	1·80	65
746/749 *Set of 4*			3·25	1·30

Design: Horiz—25p., 35p. Tractor.

1962 (5 June). European Shooting Championships. Nos. 670/675 optd with T **135**.

(a) POSTAGE

750	2p.50 +2p.50 red-brown and blue	40	40
751	5p. +5p. red-brown and yellow-orange (G.)	90	90
752	7p.50 +7p.50 red-brown and bright violet (B.)	1·00	1·00

(b) AIR. Inscr 'POSTE AERIENNE'

753	15p. +15p. red-brown and scarlet (Ol.)	1·60	1·60
754	25p. +25p. red-brown and blue-green (Lake)	3·50	3·50
755	35p. +35p. red-brown and ultramarine (R.)	4·25	4·25
750/755 *Set of 6*		10·50	10·50

136 Hand grasping Emblem

137 Rock Temples of Abu Simbel

(Des P. Koroleff. Imp J. Saikali)

1962 (2 July). AIR. Malaria Eradication. T **136** and similar vert design. P 13½×13.

756	30p. deep brown and pale chocolate	1·60	80
757	70p. bluish violet and lilac	2·30	1·40

Designs: 30p. T **136**; 70p. Campaign emblem.

(Des P. Koroleff. Imp J. Saikali)

1962 (1 Aug). Nubian Monuments. T **137** and similar vert design. P 13½×13.

(a) POSTAGE

758	**137**	5p. blue and ultramarine	90	25
759		15p. lake-brown and red-brown	1·30	40

(b) AIR. Inscr 'POSTE AERIENNE'

760	–	30p. yellow-green and green	3·00	90
761	–	50p. olive-grey and grey	5·25	2·00
758/761 *Set of 4*			9·50	3·25

Design: 30p., 50p. Bas-relief.

138 Playing-card Symbols

139 Schoolboy

(Des P. Koroleff. Imp J. Saikali)

1962 (1 Sept). AIR. European Bridge Championships, Beirut. P 13½×13.

762	**138**	25p. black, red, magenta and pink	5·75	3·75
763		40p. black, red, yellow-brown and yellow	6·00	3·75

(Des Shammout. Imp Cortbawi, Aley)

1962 (1 Oct). Schoolchildren's Day. T **139** and similar vert design. P 12.

(a) POSTAGE

764	**139**	30p. multicoloured	1·00	40

(b) AIR. Inscr 'POSTE AERIENNE'

765	–	45p. multicoloured (Teacher)	1·60	90

140

141 Cherries

(Des P. Koroleff. Imp Saikali)

1962 (22 Nov). AIR. 19th Anniversary of Independence. P 13½×13.

766	**140**	25p. emerald, red and pale blue	1·40	80
767		25p. violet, red and pale blue	1·40	80
768		25p. blue, red and pale blue	1·40	80
766/768 *Set of 3*			3·75	2·20

(Des P. Koroleff. Imp J. Saikali)

1962 (Dec)–**63**. Fruits. T **141** and similar vert designs. Multicoloured. P 13½×13.

(a) POSTAGE

769	0p.50 Type **141**	40	15
770	1p. Figs	65	15
771	2p.50 As Type **141** (*different*)	80	15
772	5p. As Figs (*different*)	90	15
773	7p.50 As Type **141** (*different*)	40	15
774	10p. Grapes	65	20
775	17p.50 As Grapes (*different*)	1·30	25
776	30p. As Grapes (*different*)	2·30	40
777	50p. Oranges	4·25	90
778	100p. Pomegranates	8·50	2·30

(b) AIR. Inscr 'POSTE AERIENNE'

779	5p. Apricots	25	15
780	10p. Plums	50	20
781	20p. Apples	90	25
782	30p. As Plums (1.63) (*different*)	1·30	50
783	40p. As Apples (*different*)	1·40	60
784	50p. Pears (1.63)	1·70	65
785	70p. Medlars	2·50	80
786	100p. Lemons (1.63)	4·75	1·60
769/786 *Set of 18*		30·00	8·50

142 Reaping

143 Nurse tending Baby

(Des P. Koroleff. Imp J. Saikali)

1963 (21 Mar). AIR. Freedom from Hunger. T **142** and similar design. P 13×13½ (15p., 20p.) or 13½×13 (others).

787	**142**	2p.50 yellow and blue	20	15
788		5p. yellow and grey-green	25	15
789		7p.50 yellow and reddish purple	50	20
790	–	15p. light yellow-green and brown-red	90	25
791	–	20p. light yellow-green and carmine-red	1·60	65
787/791 *Set of 5*			3·00	1·30

Design: Horiz—15p., 20p. Three ears of wheat within hand.

(Des P. Koroleff. Imp Cortbawi, Aley)

1963 (Mar). AIR. Arab League Week. Designs as T **133**, but inscr '1963'. P 12.

No.	Type	Description	Unused	Used
792		5p. violet and pale blue	20	15
793		10p. green and pale blue	50	40
794		15p. brown-purple and pale blue	80	50
795		20p. deep grey and pale blue	1·20	90
792/795		*Set of 4*	2·40	1·80

(De La Rue)

1963 (25 Sept). AIR. Centenary of Red Cross. T **143** and similar design. P 13.

No.	Type	Description	Unused	Used
796	–	5p. green and red	20	15
797	–	20p. light blue and red	50	25
798	**143**	35p. orange-red and black	90	50
799		40p. reddish violet and brown-red	1·60	80
796/799		*Set of 4*	3·00	1·50

Design: Horiz—5p., 20p. Blood transfusion.

144 Allegory of Music

145 Flag and Rising Sun

(De La Rue)

1963 (7 Nov). AIR. Baalbek Festival. P 13.

No.	Type	Description	Unused	Used
800	**144**	35p. orange and light blue	1·80	80

1963 (22 Nov). AIR. 20th Anniversary of Independence. Flag and Sun in red and yellow. P 13.

No.	Type	Description	Unused	Used
801	**145**	5p. turquoise-green	40	25
802		10p. yellow-green	80	65
803		25p. blue	1·00	90
804		40p. drab	1·70	1·40
801/804		*Set of 4*	3·50	3·00

146 Cycling

147 Hyacinth

1964 (23 Jan). Fourth Mediterranean Games, Naples (1963). T **146** and similar designs. P 13.

(a) POSTAGE

No.	Description	Unused	Used
805	2p.50 chestnut and reddish purple	40	15
806	5p. orange and blue	50	15
807	10p. light brown and reddish violet	85	25

(b) AIR. Inscr 'POSTE AERIENNE'

No.	Description	Unused	Used
808	15p. orange and deep green	1·00	40
809	17p.50 orange-brown and blue	1·30	50
810	30p. chestnut and turquoise-blue	2·00	80
805/810	*Set of 6*	5·50	2·00
MS810*a*	152×112 mm. Nos. 808/810. Imperf (*sold at* 100p.)	20·00	20·00

Designs: Vert—2p.50, T **146**; 5p. Basketball; 10p. Running; 15p. Tennis. Horiz—17p.50, Swimming; 30p. Skiing.

(De La Rue)

1964. Flowers. T **147** and similar designs. Multicoloured. P 13×13½ (50c. to 7p.50, postage) or 13 (others).

(a) POSTAGE

No.	Description	Unused	Used
811	0p.50 Type **147**	25	15
812	1p. As Type **147** (*different*)	35	15
813	2p.50 As Type **147** (*different*)	40	15
814	5p. Cyclamen	45	15
815	7p.50 Cyclamen (*different*)	65	15
816	10p. Poinsettia	90	20
817	17p.50 Anemone	1·70	35
818	30p. Iris	3·00	80
819	50p. Poppy	6·50	1·30

(b) AIR. Inscr 'POSTE AERIENNE'

No.	Description	Unused	Used
820	5p. Lily	50	40
821	10p. Ranunculus	90	40
822	20p. Anemone	1·20	45
823	40p. Tuberose	2·10	80
824	45p. Rhododendron	2·20	80
825	50p. Jasmine	2·50	90
826	70p. Yellow broom	4·00	1·30
811/826	*Set of 16*	25·00	7·50

Nos. 816/826 are vert, size 26½×37 mm.

148 Cedar of Lebanon

149 Cedar of Lebanon

(Des P. Koroleff. Imp Catholique (0p.50, (No. 827), 2p.50, 5p., 7p.50); Imp Slim (0p.50, (No. 828), 17p.50))

1964. P 13×13½.

No.	Type	Description	Unused	Used
827	**148**	0p.50 green	65	25
828	**149**	0p.50 green	65	25
829		2p.50 ultramarine	65	25
830		5p. magenta	80	25
831		7p.50 orange	1·60	25
832		17p.50 bright purple	2·50	35
827/832		*Set of 6*	6·25	1·40

150 Child on Rocking-horse

(Des P. Koroleff. Imp J. Saikali)

1964 (22 Mar). AIR. Children's Day. T **150** and similar design. P 13×13½ (5p., 10p.) or 13½×13 (others).

No.	Type	Description	Unused	Used
833	–	5p. red, yellow-orange and emerald	25	15
834	–	10p. red, yellow-orange and brown	40	25
835	**150**	20p. yellow-orange, pale blue and ultramarine	80	65
836		40p. yellow, pale blue and bright purple	1·60	1·00
833/836		*Set of 4*	2·75	1·80

Design: Horiz—5p., 10p. Children with skipping-rope.

151 League Session

(Des P. Koroleff. Imp Catholique)

1964 (20 Apr). AIR. Arab League Meeting. P 13×13½.

No.	Type	Description	Unused	Used
837	**151**	5p. buff, brown and black	80	40
838		10p. black	1·20	45
839		15p. bluish green	1·70	50
840		20p. mauve, brown and deep sepia	2·30	80
837/840		*Set of 4*	5·50	1·90

152 'Flame of Freedom'

(Des P. Koroleff. Imp Slim)

1964 (15 May). AIR. 15th Anniversary of Declaration of Human Rights. T **152** and similar vert design. P 13½×13.

841		20p. orange-red, salmon-pink and red-brown	40	25
842		40p. orange, grey-blue and light blue	90	40

Designs: 20p. T **152**; 40p. Flame on pedestal bearing UN emblem.

153 Sick Child

154 Clasped Wrists

(Des P. Koroleff. Imp J. Saikali)

1964 (30 June). AIR. 'Bal des Petits Lits Blancs' (Ball for children's charity). T **153** and another design. P 13½×13 (T **153**) or 13½ (others).

843	**153**	2p.50 multicoloured	20	15
844		5p. multicoloured	25	15
845		15p. multicoloured	45	25
846	–	17p.50 multicoloured	1·00	40
847	–	20p. multicoloured	1·30	45
848	–	40p. multicoloured	2·00	50
843/848 *Set of 6*			4·75	1·70

Design: Horiz (55×25½ *mm*)—17p.50 to 40p. Children in front of palace (venue of ball).

(Des Marck-Henry. Imp J. Saikali)

1964 (5 Oct). AIR. World Lebanese Union Congress, Beirut. P 13½×13.

849	**154**	20p. black, yellow and green	1·00	40
850		40p. black, yellow and slate-purple	1·80	90

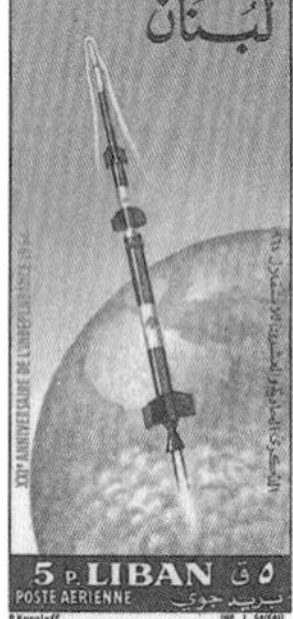

155 Rocket in Flight

156 Temple Columns

(Des P. Koroleff. Imp J. Saikali)

1964 (24 Nov). AIR. 21st Anniversary of Independence. T **155** and similar design. Wmk 'WATERTON' in sheet. P 13½.

851	**155**	5p. multicoloured	40	25
852		10p. multicoloured	40	25
853	–	40p. slate-blue and black	1·40	90
854	–	70p. brown-purple and black	2·50	2·00
851/854 *Set of 4*			4·25	3·00

Design: Horiz—40p., 70p. 'Struggle for Independence' (battle scene).

(Des Marck-Henry. Imp J. Saikali)

1965 (11 Jan). Baalbek Festival. T **156** and similar designs. Wmk 'WATERTON' in sheet.

(a) POSTAGE. P 13×13½

855	**156**	2p.50 black and red-orange	50	25
856		7p.50 black and light blue	1·00	40

(b) AIR. Inscr 'POSTE AERIENNE'. P 13½

857	–	10p. multicoloured	50	15
858	–	15p. multicoloured	1·00	20
859	–	25p. multicoloured	1·60	65
860	–	40p. multicoloured	2·30	80
855/860 *Set of 6*			6·25	2·20

Designs: Vert (28×55 *mm*)—10p., 15p. Man in costume; 25p., 40p. Woman in costume.

157 Swimming

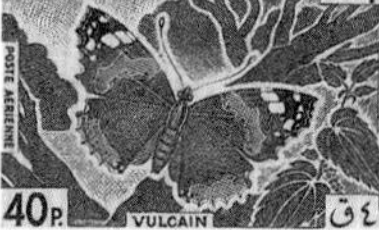

158 Red Admiral

(Des and eng J. Combet (postage), C. Durrens (air). Recess Govt Ptg Wks, Paris)

1965 (23 Jan). Olympic Games, Tokyo. T **157** and similar designs. P 13.

(a) POSTAGE

861		2p.50 black, turquoise-blue and magenta	40	15
862		7p.50 brown-purple, grey-green and sepia	1·60	90
863		10p. slate, brown and deep green	2·10	1·00

(b) AIR. Inscr 'POSTE AERIENNE'

864		15p. black and slate-green	1·30	40
865		25p. dull green and purple	2·00	65
866		40p. brown and indigo	2·30	1·00
861/866 *Set of 6*			8·75	3·75
MS866*a*		140×100 mm. Nos. 864/846. Imperf (*sold at* 100p.)	26·00	26·00

Designs: Horiz—2p.50, T **157**; 7p.50, Fencing; 15p. Horse-jumping; 40p. Gymnastics. Vert—10p. Basketball; 25p. Rifle-shooting.

(Des and eng P. Béquet (5, 15, 20p.), P. Gandon (40, 70, 85, 100p.). Des P. Lambert. Eng M. Monvoisin (10, 30, 45p.), Gauthier (17p.50, 32p.50), J. Miermont (35p.), R. Fenneteaux (200p.), A. Frères (300p.). Recess Govt Ptg Wks, Paris. 500p. Recess and litho State Ptg Wks, Vienna)

1965 (5 Feb–5 Oct). T **158** and similar horiz designs. P 13 or 12 (500p.).

(a) POSTAGE. Birds

867		5p. multicoloured (3.5)	2·30	25
868		10p. multicoloured (27.7)	2·00	35
869		15p. chocolate, orange and olive-brown (8.6)	5·75	50
870		17p.50 maroon, red and blue (15.3)	9·00	65
871		20p. black, orange-yellow and yellow-green (23.2)	11·50	80
872		32p.50 yellow, brown and emerald (9.8)	25·00	2·00

(b) AIR. Inscr 'POSTE AERIENNE'. Butterflies

873		30p. yellow, chocolate and vermilion (12.7)	2·20	25
874		35p. blue, red and bistre (9.2)	3·50	50
875		40p. bistre-brown, orange-red and deep bluish green (5.2)	4·25	65
876		45p. agate, yellow and greenish blue (29.6)	5·25	80
877		70p. multicoloured (6.8)	7·75	1·20
878		85p. black, orange and green (8.4)	9·00	1·40
879		100p. new blue and plum (18.5)	13·00	1·60
880		200p. blackish brown, blue and purple (22.2)	23·00	1·80
881		300p. sepia, yellow and deep bluish green (11.3)	34·00	5·50
882		500p. blackish, brown, blue and pale blue (5.10)	65·00	11·00
867/882 *Set of 16*			£200	26·00

Designs: As T **158**. Birds—5p. Northern Bullfinch; 10p. Eurasian Goldfinch; 15p. Hoopoe; 17p.50, Red-legged Partridge; 20p. Golden Oriole; 32p.50, European Bee-eater. Butterflies—30p. *Pericallia matronula*; 35p. *Heliconius erato*; 40p. *Vanessa atalanta*; 45p. *Hipparchia semele* (*Satyrus semele*); 70p. *Papilio machaon*; 85p. *Anthocharis cardamines*; 100p. *Morpho cypris*; 200p. *Amesia sanguiflua* (*Erasmia sanguiflua*); 300p. *Battus crassus* (*Papilio crassus*). 35½×25 mm—500p. *Charaxes ameliae*.

159 Pope Paul and President Helou

1965 (26 June). AIR. Pope Paul's Visit to Lebanon. Photo. P 12.

883	**159**	45p. reddish violet and gold	7·75	3·50
MS883*a*		100×81 mm. No. 883. Imperf (*sold at* 50p.)	80·00	80·00

160 Sheep

161 'Cedars of Friendship'

(Photo State Ptg Wks, Vienna)

1965 (10–30 Sept). T **160** and similar horiz designs. P 11½×12½.

884	0p.50 brown, orange-brown, red and lemon (10.9)	2·50	25
885	1p. deep grey, black and mauve (10.9)	2·50	25
886	2p.50 yellow, sepia and light yellow-green (30.9)	2·75	25
884/886	*Set of 3*	7·00	70

Designs: 0p.50, Cow and calf; 1p. Rabbit; 2p.50, T **160**.

(Photo State Ptg Wks, Vienna)

1965 (10 Oct). AIR. P 13×13½.

887	**161**	40p. multicoloured	2·20	40

162 Silk Manufacture

(Photo State Ptg Wks, Vienna)

1965 (14 Oct). AIR. World Silk Congress, Beirut. T **162** and similar vert design. Multicoloured. P 12½×13.

888	2p.50 Type **162**	90	25
889	5p. Type **162**	1·00	25
890	7p.50 Type **162**	1·20	25
891	15p. Weaver and loom	1·30	35
892	30p. Weaver and loom	3·50	50
893	40p. Weaver and loom	5·00	80
894	50p. Weaver and loom	6·50	1·20
888/894	*Set of 7*	17·00	3·25

163 Parliament Building

(Photo State Ptg Wks, Vienna)

1965 (26 Oct). AIR. Centenary of Lebanese Parliament. P 13×13½.

895	**163**	35p. deep brown, yellow-ochre and rose-red	90	50
896		40p. deep brown, yellow-ochre and yellow-green	1·30	80

164 UN Emblem and Headquarters

165 Playing-card 'King'

(Recess State Ptg Wks, Vienna)

1965 (10 Nov). AIR. 20th Anniversary of United Nations Organisation. P 12.

897	**164**	2p.50 greenish blue	20	15
898		10p. crimson	35	15
899		17p.50 violet	50	20
900		30p. green	1·00	40
901		40p. olive-brown	1·30	80
897/901		*Set of 5*	3·00	1·50
MS901*a*		101×80 mm. No. 901 in violet. Imperf (*sold at* 50p.)	22·00	22·00

(Photo State Ptg Office, Budapest)

1965 (15 Nov). AIR. World Bridge Championships, Beirut. P 12½×13.

902	**165**	2p.50 multicoloured	25	20
903		15p. multicoloured	1·20	25
904		17p.50 multicoloured	1·80	40
905		40p. multicoloured	3·75	1·60
902/905		*Set of 4*	6·00	2·20
MS905*a*		105×85 mm. Nos. 903 and 905. Imperf (*sold at* 75p.)	34·00	34·00

166 Dagger on Deir Yassin, Palestine

167 ITU Emblem and Symbols

(Photo State Ptg Office, Budapest)

1965 (12 Dec). AIR. Deir Yassin Massacre. P 12½×11½.

906	**166**	50p. red, blue, grey and black	6·50	1·70

1966 (13 Apr). AIR. Centenary (1965) of International Telecommunications Union. Photo. P 13×12½.

907	**167**	2p.50 multicoloured	15	15
908		15p. multicoloured	50	20
909		17p.50 multicoloured	80	25
910		25p. multicoloured	1·70	40
911		40p. multicoloured	2·30	65
907/911		*Set of 5*	5·00	1·50

PRINTERS. All the following issues until No. 1135 were printed by the State Printing Office, Budapest, *unless otherwise stated.*

168 Stage Performance

1966 (20 July). AIR. Baalbek Festival. T **168** and similar designs. Multicoloured. Photo. P 12.

912	2p.50 Type **168**	40	20
913	5p. Type **168**	50	20
914	7p.50 Ballet performance (*vert*)	65	20
915	15p. Ballet performance (*vert*)	90	25
916	30p. Concert	1·30	50
917	40p. Concert	1·70	65
912/917	*Set of 6*	5·00	1·80

169 Tabarja

170 WHO Building

1966 (28 July–25 Oct). Tourism. T **169** and similar horiz designs. Multicoloured. Photo. P 12×11½.

	(a) POSTAGE		
918	50c. Hippodrome, Beirut (29.7)	40	15
919	1p. Pigeon Grotto, Beirut (29.7)	50	15
920	2p.50 Type **169** (28.7)	80	15
921	5p. Ruins, Beit-Mery (25.10)	1·00	15
922	7p.50 Ruins, Anjar (25.10)	1·30	15
	(b) AIR. Inscr 'POSTE AERIENNE' (25 Oct)		
923	10p. Djezzine Falls	35	15
924	15p. Sidon Castle	40	15
925	20p. Amphitheatre, Byblos	50	15
926	30p. Sun Temple, Baalbek	90	20
927	50p. Palace, Beit ed-Dine	1·80	25
928	60p. Railway bridge, Nahr el-Kalb	2·30	45
929	75p. Tripoli	3·25	65
918/929	*Set of 12*	12·00	2·50

1966 (25 Aug). AIR. Inauguration of World Health Organisation Headquarters, Geneva. Recess. P 12.

930	**170**	7p.50 deep yellow-green	50	20
931		17p.50 rose-carmine	65	45
932		25p. greenish blue	1·30	65
930/932		*Set of 3*	2·20	1·20

171 Skiing

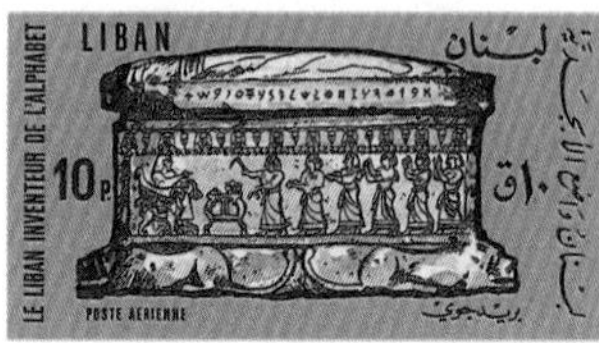

172 Inscribed Sarcophagus

1966 (15 Sept). AIR. International Cedars Festival. T **171** and similar horiz designs. Photo. P 12×11½.

933	2p.50 brown, red and light green	25	20
934	5p. brown, red, light green and light blue	40	20
935	17p.50 sepia, green, black and pale blue	65	40
936	25p. red, brown and light green	1·80	65
933/936	*Set of 4*	2·75	1·30

Designs: 2p.50, T **171**; 5p. Tobogganing; 17p.50, Cedar in snow; 25p. Ski-lift.

1966 (25 Sept). AIR. Phoenician Invention of the Alphabet. T **172** and similar horiz designs. Recess and photo. P 12.

937	10p. yellow-brown, black and bluish green	20	15
938	15p. brown, yellow-ochre and bright mauve	65	25
939	20p. deep sepia, light blue and ochre	1·00	40
940	30p. deep brown, orange and yellow	1·70	65
937/940	*Set of 4*	3·25	1·30

Designs: 10p. T **172**; 15p. Phoenician sailing ship; 20p. Mediterranean route map showing spread of Phoenician alphabet; 30p. Kadmus with alphabet tablet.

173 Child in Bath

1966 (15 Oct). AIR. International Children's Day. T **173** and similar designs. Multicoloured. Photo. P 11½×12 or imperf (50p.).

941	2p.50 Type **173**	20	15
942	5p. Boy and doll in rowing boat	25	15
943	7p.50 Girl skiing	50	20
944	15p. Girl giving food to bird	1·20	25
945	20p. Boy doing homework	1·70	65
941/945	*Set of 5*	3·50	1·30
MS946	100×69½ mm. 50p. Children of various races (*horiz*). Imperf	11·00	11·00

174 Decade Emblem

175 Rev Daniel Bliss(founder)

1966 (15 Nov). AIR. International Hydrological Decade. T **174** and similar vert design. Photo. P 12½.

947	**174**	5p. ultramarine, light blue and orange	20	15
948		10p. brown-red, light blue and orange	40	20
949	–	15p. sepia, yellow-green and orange	60	25
950	–	20p. greenish blue, yellow-green and orange	1·20	40
947/950		*Set of 4*	2·20	90

Design: 15p., 20p. Similar 'wave' pattern.

1966 (3 Dec). AIR. Centenary of American University, Beirut. T **175** and similar designs. Photo. P 12½×13.

951	20p. brown, yellow and green	65	35
952	30p. yellow-green, chestnut and light blue	80	45
MS953	125×85 mm. 50p. brown, orange-brown and green. Imperf	4·00	3·25

Designs: Vert—20p. T **175**; 30p. University Chapel. Horiz (59×37 *mm*)—50p. Rev Daniel Bliss, University and emblem.

Nos. 951/952 were each issued with *se-tenant* labels showing the University emblem.

176 ITY Emblem

177 Beit ed-Din Palace

1967 (28 July–25 Oct). International Tourist Year (1st issue). Photo.

(a) POSTAGE. T **176**. *P 11×12*

954	50c. multicoloured (29.7)	20	15
955	1p. multicoloured (29.7)	25	20
956	2p.50 multicoloured (28.7)	40	25
957	5p. multicoloured (25.10)	80	40
958	7p.50 multicoloured (25.10)	1·00	50

(b) AIR. T **177** *and similar horiz designs. Multicoloured. Inscr 'POSTE AERIENNE'. P 12×11½ (25 Oct)*

959	10p. Tabarja	1·30	50
960	15p. Pigeon Rock, Beirut	1·70	65
961	17p.50 Type **177**	2·00	65
962	20p. Sidon	2·10	65
963	25p. Tripoli	2·30	65
964	30p. Byblos	2·50	65
965	35p. Ruins, Tyre	3·00	65
966	40p. Temple, Baalbek	3·50	65
954/966	*Set of 13*	19·00	6·00

Nos. 954/966 were also used as definitives.

See also Nos. 977/**MS**980*a*.

D **178**

178 Signing Pact, and Flags

1967 (July). POSTAGE DUE. Photo. P 11.

D967	D **178**	1p. blue-green	50	25
D968		5p. mauve	65	40
D969		15p. bright blue	1·00	90
D967/D969		*Set of 3*	1·90	1·40

1967 (1 Aug). AIR. 22nd Anniversary of Arab League Pact. Photo. P 12×11½.

967	**178**	5p. multicoloured	20	15
968		10p. multicoloured	35	20
969		15p. multicoloured	65	40
970		20p. multicoloured	1·20	50
967/970		*Set of 4*	2·20	1·10

179 Veterans War Memorial Building, San Francisco

1967 (1 Sept). AIR. San Francisco Pact of 1945. T **179** and similar horiz design. Multicoloured. Photo. P 12½×11½.

971	2p.50 Type **179**	1·20	50
972	5p. As Type **179**	1·20	50
973	7p.50 As Type **179**	1·20	50
974	10p. Scroll and flags of UN and Lebanon	1·20	50
975	20p. As 10p.	1·20	50
976	30p. As 10p.	1·20	50
971/976	*Set of 6*	6·50	2·75

180 Temple Ruins, Baalbek

1967 (25 Sept). AIR. International Tourist Year (2nd issue). T **180** and similar horiz designs. Multicoloured. Photo. P 12½.

977	5p. Type **180**	25	15
978	10p. Ruins, Anjar	40	15
979	15p. Ancient bridge, Nahr-Ibrahim	80	20
980	20p. Grotto, Jeita	1·00	25
977/980	*Set of 4*	2·20	70
MS980*a*	112×90 mm. 50p. Beirut (plus flag and map of Lebanon). Imperf	33·00	33·00

181

1967 (30 Oct). AIR. India Day. Recess. P 12.

981	**181**	2p.50 vermilion	25	20
982		5p. claret	25	20
983		7p.50 brown	40	20
984		10p. blue	50	20
985		15p. emerald-green	1·00	25
981/985		*Set of 5*	2·20	95

182

1967 (25 Nov). AIR. 22nd Anniversary of Lebanon's Admission to United Nations Organisation. T **182** and similar horiz design. Recess. P 12.

986	**182**	2p.50 rose-red	15	15
987		5p. greenish blue	20	15
988		7p.50 emerald-green	25	20
989	–	10p. carmine-red	40	25
990	–	20p. ultramarine	65	35
991	–	30p. myrtle-green	1·00	40
986/991		*Set of 6*	2·40	1·40
MS991*a*		109×85 mm. 100p. red (Type **182**). Imperf	9·00	9·00

Design: 10, 20, 30p. UN emblem.

183 Goat and Kid

1968 (Jan). T **183** and similar horiz designs. Multicoloured. Photo. P 12×11½.

(a) POSTAGE. Animals

992	50c. Type **183**	65	20
993	1p. Cattle	65	20
994	2p.50 Sheep	65	20
995	5p. Dromedaries	65	20
996	10p. Donkey	1·30	25
997	15p. Horses	2·50	25

(b) AIR. Inscr 'POSTE AERIENNE'. Fish

998	20p. Basking Shark	2·50	25
999	30p. Garfish	3·00	25
1000	40p. Pollack	4·50	35
1001	50p. Cuckoo Wrasse	5·00	40
1002	70p. Red-striped Mullet	12·50	50
1003	100p. Rainbow Trout	16·00	65
992/1003	*Set of 12*	45·00	3·25

D **184** Emir Fakhreddine II

184 Ski Jumping

1968 (Jan). POSTAGE DUE. Litho. P 11.

D1004	D **184**	1p. deep slate and pale grey	20	15
D1005		2p. deep bluish green and pale green	25	15
D1006		3p. orange and pale yellow-orange	35	20
D1007		5p. bright purple and pale reddish purple	40	25
D1008		10p. olive and pale yellow-olive	65	35
D1009		15p. violet-blue and pale violet-blue	90	65
D1010		25p. new blue and pale blue	1·30	1·00
D1004/D1010		*Set of 7*	3·75	2·50

1968 (Feb). AIR. International Ski Congress, Beirut. T **184** and similar horiz designs. Photo. P 12½×11½.

1004	2p.50 multicoloured	25	15
1005	5p. multicoloured	45	15
1006	7p.50 multicoloured	65	20
1007	10p. multicoloured	80	25
1008	25p. multicoloured	1·30	40
1004/1008	*Set of 5*	3·00	1·00
MS1008*a*	121×91 mm. 50p. multicoloured. Imperf	10·50	10·50

Designs: 2p.50, T **184**; 5p. to 10p. Skiing (all different); 25p., 50p. Congress emblem of Cedar and skis.

185 Princess Khaskiah

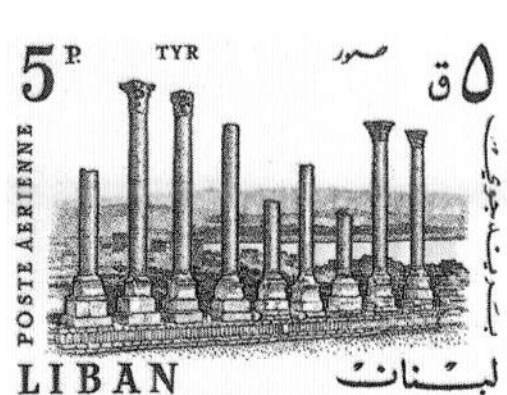

186 Colonnade

1968 (1 Mar). AIR. Emir Fakhreddine II Commemoration. T **185** and similar designs. Multicoloured. Litho. P 12.

1009	2p.50 Type **185**	25	20
1010	5p. Emir Fakhreddine II	40	20
1011	10p. Sidon Citadel (*horiz*)	50	20
1012	15p. Chekif Citadel (*horiz*)	80	25
1013	17p.50 Beirut Citadel (*horiz*)	1·30	35
1009/1013	*Set of 5*	3·00	1·10
MS1013*a*	120×86 mm. 50p. Battle of Anjar. Imperf	17·00	17·00

1968 (20 Mar). AIR. Tyre Antiquities. T **186** and similar designs. Recess and litho. P 12.

1014	2p.50 purple-brown, pale cream and light pink	25	15
1015	5p. purple-brown, pale blue and light yellow	40	15
1016	7p.50 purple-brown, buff and light blue-green	65	20

1017	10p. purple-brown, pale blue and light orange	1·00	40
1014/1017	*Set of 4*	2·10	80

MS1018 120×80 mm. 10p. blackish brown and pale blue. P 10½×11½ or imperf (*sold at* 50p.) 33·00 33·00

Designs: Vert—2p.50, Roman bust; 10p. Bas-relief. Horiz—5p. T **186**; 7p.50, Arch.

187 Justinian and Mediterranean Map

1968 (10 May). AIR. First Anniversary of Faculty of Law, Beirut. T **187** and similar multicoloured design. Photo. P 11½×12 (vert) or 12×11½ (horiz).

1019	5p. Justinian (*vert*)	25	15
1020	10p. Justinian (*vert*)	40	15
1021	15p. Type **187**	50	15
1022	20p. As Type **187**	90	25
1019/1022	*Set of 4*	1·80	65

188 Arab League Emblem

190 Jupiter's Temple Ruins, Baalbek

189 Cedar on Globe

1968 (10 June). AIR. Arab Appeal Week. Photo. P 12×11½.

1023	**188**	5p. multicoloured	25	15
1024		10p. multicoloured	40	15
1025		15p. multicoloured	50	15
1026		20p. multicoloured	90	25
1023/1026		*Set of 4*	1·80	65

1968 (10 July). AIR. Third World Lebanese Union Congress, Beirut. Photo. P 12×11½.

1027	**189**	2p.50 multicoloured	20	15
1028		5p. multicoloured	25	15
1029		7p.50 multicoloured	40	15
1030		10p. multicoloured	65	35
1027/1030		*Set of 4*	1·40	70

1968 (25 Sept). AIR. Baalbek Festival. T **190** and similar vert designs. Multicoloured. Photo. P 12½.

1031	5p. Type **190**	25	15
1032	10p. Bacchus's Temple	40	20
1033	15p. Corniche, Jupiter's Temple	65	25
1034	20p. Portal, Bacchus's Temple	1·00	40
1035	25p. Columns, Bacchus's Temple	1·30	65
1031/1035	*Set of 5*	3·25	1·50

191 Long Jumping and Atlantes

(Des M. Porada. Photo)

1968 (19 Oct). AIR. Olympic Games, Mexico. T **191** and similar horiz designs. P 12½×11½.

1036	5p. black, greenish yellow and blue	25	15
1037	10p. black, bright blue and bright purple	40	20
1038	15p. sepia, drab, yellow and yellow-olive	65	25
1039	20p. sepia, drab, yellow and red-orange	1·00	40
1040	25p. yellow-brown	1·30	65
1036/1040	*Set of 5*	3·25	1·50

Designs: (each incorporating Aztec relic)—5p. T **191**; 10p. High-jumping; 15p. Fencing; 20p. Weightlifting; 25p. Phoenician ship.

192 Lebanese driving Tractor (Work Protection)

193 Minshiya Stairs

(Des M. Bassili. Litho)

1968 (10 Dec). AIR. Human Rights Year. T **192** and similar vert designs. Multicoloured. P 11½.

1041	10p. Type **192**	25	15
1042	15p. Citizens (Social Security)	60	20
1043	25p. Young men of three races (Unity)	1·00	35
1041/1043	*Set of 3*	1·70	65

(Des M. Porada. Litho)

1968 (26 Dec). AIR. Centenary of First Municipal Council (Deir el-Kamar). T **193** and similar vert designs. Multicoloured. P 11½.

1044	10p. Type **193**	25	15
1045	15p. Serai kiosk	60	20
1046	25p. Ancient highway	1·00	45
1044/1046	*Set of 3*	1·70	70

194 Nurse and Child

1969 (20 Jan). AIR. United Nations Children's Fund. T **194** and similar horiz designs. Litho. P 12.

1047	5p. black, deep brown and pale blue	20	15
1048	10p. black, deep green and greenish yellow	35	15
1049	15p. black, vermilion and bright purple	50	15
1050	20p. black, greenish blue and pale olive-yellow	70	20
1051	25p. black, ochre and pale magenta	1·00	25
1047/1051	*Set of 5*	2·50	80

Designs: 5p. T **194**; 10p. Produce; 15p. Mother and child; 20p. Child with book; 25p. Children with flowers.

195 Ancient Coin

(Des M. Porada. Litho; gold inscriptions die-stamped)

1969 (20 Feb). AIR. 20th Anniversary of International Museums Council (ICOM). Exhibits in National Museum, Beirut. T **195** and similar horiz designs. Multicoloured. P 12.

1052	2p.50 Type **195**	25	15
1053	5p. Gold dagger, Byblos	40	15
1054	7p.50 Detail of Ahiram's sarcophagus	65	20
1055	30p. Jewelled pectoral	1·00	40
1056	40p. Khalde 'bird' vase	1·70	1·00
1052/1056	*Set of 5*	3·50	1·70

196 Water-skiing

1969 (20 Mar). AIR. Water Sports. T **196** and similar multicoloured designs. Litho. P 11½.

1057	2p.50 Type **196**	25	15
1058	5p. Water-skiing (group)	35	15
1059	7p.50 Paraskiing (*vert*)	45	20
1060	30p. Sailing (*vert*)	1·20	50
1061	40p. Dinghy racing	1·60	1·00
1057/1061	*Set of 5*	3·50	1·80

197 Frontier Guard

(Des M. Gebara. Photo)

1969 (1 Aug). AIR. 25th Anniversary of Independence. The Lebanese Army. T **197** and similar horiz designs. Multicoloured. P 12×11½.

1062	2p.50 Type **197**	15	15
1063	5p. Unknown Soldier's Tomb	25	15
1064	7p.50 Army foresters	40	15
1065	15p. Road-making	50	20
1066	30p. Land Rover 109 military ambulance and Sud Aviation SE 3160 Alouette III helicopter	1·00	50
1067	40p. Skiing patrol	1·60	65
1062/1067	*Set of 6*	3·50	1·60

198 Concentric Red Crosses

199 Foil and Flags of Arab States

(Des M. Porada. Photo)

1971 (6 Jan). AIR. 25th Anniversary of Lebanese Red Cross. T **198** and similar vert design. P 11½×12.

1068	15p. vermilion and black	65	25
1069	85p. vermilion and black	2·50	1·60

Designs: 15p. T **198**; 85p. Red cross in shape of cedar.

(Des M. Porada. Litho)

1971 (15 Jan). AIR. Tenth International Fencing Championships. T **199** and similar horiz designs. Multicoloured. P 12.

1070	10p. Type **199**	15	15
1071	15p. Foil and flags of foreign nations	25	20
1072	35p. Contest with foils	90	65
1073	40p. Epée contest	1·00	80
1074	50p. Contest with sabres	1·60	90
1070/1074	*Set of 5*	3·50	2·40

200 *Farmers at Work* (12th-century Arab painting)

(Des M. Gebara. Litho)

1971 (1 Feb). AIR. 50th Anniversary of International Labour Organisation (1969). P 12.

1075	**200**	10p. multicoloured	65	25
1076		40p. multicoloured	1·60	90

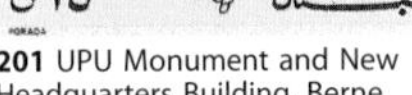

201 UPU Monument and New Headquarters Building, Berne

202 *Ravens setting fire to Owls* (14th-century painting)

(Des M. Porada. Litho)

1971 (15 Feb). AIR. Inauguration of New Universal Postal Union Headquarters Building, Berne. P 12.

1077	**201**	15p. orange-red, black and lemon	50	25
1078		35p. lemon, black and salmon	1·60	90

(Des M. Gebara. Photo)

1971 (1 Mar). AIR. Children's Day. T **202** and similar multicoloured painting. P 11 (15p.) or 12×11½ (85p.).

1079	15p. Type **202**	80	25
1080	85p. *The Lion and the Jackal* (13th-century) (*horiz, 39×29 mm*)	3·75	1·60

203 Arab League Flag and Map

204 Jamhour Electricity Sub-station

(Des M. Porada. Photo)

1971 (20 Mar). AIR. 25th Anniversary of Arab League. P 12×11½.

1081	**203**	30p. multicoloured	80	40
1082		70p. multicoloured	1·80	1·20

(Des M. Gebara. Litho)

1971 (25 Mar–June). AIR. T **204** and similar horiz designs. Multicoloured. P 12.

1083	5p. Type **204** (18.5)	40	20
1084	10p. Maameltein Bridge (1.6)	50	20
1085	15p. Hoteliers' School (1.6)	65	25
1086	20p. Litani Dam (1.6)	80	35
1087	25p. Interior of TV set	90	40
1088	35p. Bziza Temple (18.5)	1·20	45
1089	40p. Jounieh Harbour	1·60	50
1090	45p. Radar scanner, Beirut Airport (18.5)	1·80	60
1091	50p. Hibiscus (18.5)	2·30	65
1092	70p. School of Sciences Building (1.6)	3·50	90
1093	85p. Oranges (1.6)	4·00	1·00
1094	100p. Satellite Communications Station, Arbanieh	5·25	2·00
1083/1094	*Set of 12*	21·00	6·75

205 Insignia of Imam al Ouzai (theologian)

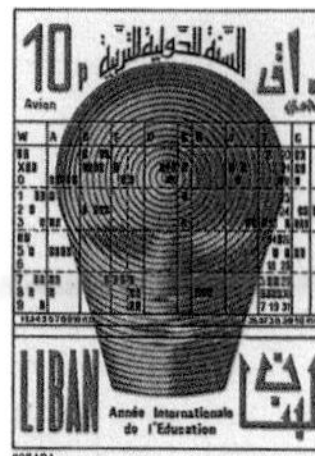
206 IEY Emblem and Computer Card

(Des M. Gebara. Photo)

1971 (10 Apr). AIR. Lebanese Celebrities. T **205** and similar horiz designs, but showing portraits. P 12×11½.

1095		25p. deep brown, gold and sage-green	50	35
1096		25p. chocolate, gold and yellow	50	35
1097		25p. chocolate, gold and yellow	50	35
1098		25p. deep brown, gold and sage-green	50	35
1095/1098		*Set of 4*	1·80	1·30

Portraits: No. 1095, T **205**; No. 1096, Bechara el Khoury (poet and writer); No. 1097, Hassan Kamel el Sabbah (scientist); No. 1098, Gibran Khalil Gibran (writer).

(Des M. Porada. Photo)

1971 (30 Apr). AIR. International Education Year. P 11½×12.

1099	**206**	10p. black, greenish blue and bluish violet	25	20
1100		40p. black, lemon and vermilion	1·20	65

207 Dahr el-Basheq Sanatorium

208 Solar Wheel Emblem

(Des M. Porada. Litho)

1971 (1 June). AIR. Tuberculosis Relief Campaign. T **207** and similar vert design, showing different view of the Sanatorium. P 12.

1101		50p. multicoloured	1·80	80
1102		100p. multicoloured	2·50	1·30

(Des M. Bassili. Photo)

1971 (1 July). AIR. 16th Baalbek Festival. T **208** and similar square design. P 11.

1103		15p. orange and ulramarine	25	20
1104		85p. black, blue and orange	1·80	1·20

Designs: 15p. T **208**; 85p. Corinthian capital.

209 Field-gun

210 Interior Decoration

1971 (1 Aug). AIR. Army Day. T **209** and similar horiz designs. Multicoloured. Photo. P 12×11½.

1105		15p. Type **209**	2·50	1·00
1106		25p. Dassault Mirage IIICJ jet fighters	4·00	2·00
1107		40p. Army Command Headquarters	6·50	3·25
1108		70p. *Tarablous* (naval patrol boat)	13·00	5·25
1105/1108		*Set of 4*	23·00	10·50

1971 (21 Aug). AIR. Second Anniversary of Burning of Al-Aqsa Mosque, Jerusalem. Litho. P 12.

1109	**210**	15p. yellow-brown and deep brown	90	25
1110		35p. yellow-brown and deep brown	2·10	90

211 Lenin

212 UN Emblem

(Des M. Porada. Photo)

1971 (1 Oct). AIR. Birth Centenary of Lenin. T **211** and similar portrait. Multicoloured. P 12×11½.

1111		30p. Type **211**	90	50
1112		70p. Lenin in profile	2·10	1·30

(Des M. Porada. Photo)

1971 (24 Oct). AIR. 25th Anniversary of United Nations. P 12½.

1113	**212**	15p. multicoloured	25	20
1114		85p. multicoloured	2·10	1·20

213 'Europa' Mosaic, Byblos

(Des M. Porada. Litho)

1971 (20 Nov). AIR. World Lebanese Union. P 12.

1115	**213**	10p. multicoloured	40	25
1116		40p. multicoloured	2·30	65

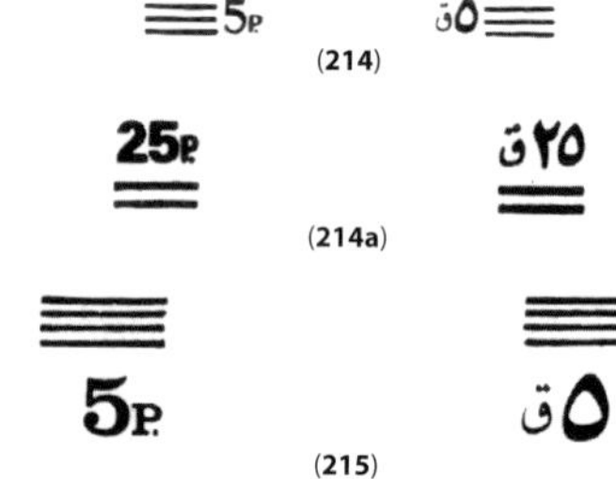
(**214**)

(**214a**)

(**215**)

(**216**)

1972 (24 Apr–20 May). Various stamps surch by typo locally.

*(a) POSTAGE. Surch as T **214** (No. 1118), **214a** (No. 1119) or similar surch (No. 1117) (20 May)*

1117	–	5p. on 7p.50 multicoloured (No. 922)	4·00	1·30
1118	**176**	5p. on 7p.50 multicoloured	4·00	1·30
1119	–	25p. on 32p.50 yellow, brown and emerald (No. 872)	10·50	4·00
		a. Surch double		

On No. 1117 the figures of value are as T **214** but the arrangement and number of bars are as T **214a**.

*(b) AIR. Surch as T **215** (No. 1120), **214** (Nos. 1121, 1123) or **216** (No. 1122)*

1120		5p. on 7p.50 purple-brown, buff and light blue-green (No. 1016) (20.5)	4·00	1·30
1121		100p. on 300p. sepia, yellow and deep bluish green (No. 881) (1.5)	13·00	5·75
1122		100p. on 500p. blackish brown, blue and pale blue (No. 882)	13·00	5·75
1123		200p. on 300p. sepia, yellow and deep bluish green (No. 881) (1.5)	23·00	13·00
1117/1123		*Set of 7*	65·00	29·00

Nos. 1117 and 1121/1123 exist with surcharge inverted but were not sold to the general public.

217 Morning Glory

218 Ornate Arches

1973 (15 Mar–1 June). AIR. T **217** and similar vert designs, showing flowers or fruit. Multicoloured. Litho. Phosphorescent paper. P 12.

1124	2p.50 Type **217**	25	20
1125	5p. Roses	40	25
1126	15p. Tulips	65	40
1127	25p. Lilies	90	45
1128	40p. Carnations	1·30	50
1129	50p. Iris	2·00	50
1130	70p. Apples	3·00	60
1131	75p. Grapes (1.6)	3·25	65
1132	100p. Peaches	4·75	1·60
1133	200p. Pears	7·75	1·30
1134	300p. Cherries (1.6)	10·50	2·30
1135	500p. Oranges	16·00	4·00
1124/1135	*Set of* 12	46·00	11·50

1973 (1 June–1 Aug). AIR. Lebanese Domestic Architecture, T **218** and similar horiz designs, showing types of Lebanese dwellings. Litho. Phosphorescent paper. P 14.

1136	35p. multicoloured	1·70	65
1137	50p. multicoloured (1.8)	2·50	1·30
1138	85p. multicoloured	4·25	2·00
1139	100p. multicoloured (1.8)	5·00	2·75
1136/1139	*Set of* 4	12·00	6·00

219 Girl with Lute

220 Swimming

1973 (1 Sept). AIR. Traditional Costumes. T **219** and similar vert designs. Multicoloured. Litho. Phosphorescent paper. P 14.

1140	5p. Woman with rose	1·30	65
1141	10p. Shepherd	2·00	1·00
1142	20p. Horseman	4·00	1·70
1143	25p. Type **219**	5·75	2·50
1140/1143	*Set of* 4	11·50	5·25

1973 (25 Sept). AIR. Fifth Pan-Arab Schools' Games, Beirut. T **220** and similar horiz designs. Multicoloured. Photo. P 11½×12.

1144	5p. Type **220**	45	15
1145	10p. Running	70	15
1146	15p. Gymnastics	90	15
1147	20p. Volleyball	1·20	20
1148	25p. Basketball	1·40	25
1149	50p. Table tennis	3·00	50
1150	75p. Handball	3·50	65
1151	100p. Football	4·00	2·00
1144/1151	*Set of* 8	13·50	3·75
MS1152	121×71 mm. No. 1151. Imperf	6·25	5·75

221 Brasilia

222 Marquetry

1973 (15 Nov). AIR. 150th Anniversary of Brazil's Independence. T **221** and similar horiz designs. Multicoloured. Litho. Phosphorescent paper. P 12.

1153	5p. Type **221**	60	25
1154	20p. Salvador (Bahia) in 1823	1·20	65
1155	25p. Map and Phoenician galley	1·70	90
1156	50p. Emperor Pedro I and Emir Fakhreddine II	2·75	2·00
1153/1156	*Set of* 4	5·75	3·50

1973 (1 Dec). AIR. Lebanese Handicrafts. T **222** and similar horiz designs. Multicoloured. Litho. Phosphorescent paper. P 12.

1157	10p. Type **222**	60	20
1158	20p. Weaving	1·20	35
1159	35p. Glass-blowing	1·70	40
1160	40p. Pottery	2·30	50
1161	50p. Metal-working	3·00	65
1162	70p. Cutlery-making	4·50	90
1163	85p. Lace-making	6·00	1·30
1164	100p. Handicrafts Museum	7·00	2·20
1157/1164	*Set of* 8	24·00	5·75

223 Cedar of Lebanon

224 Camp Site and Emblems

1974. Litho. P 11.

1165	**223**	50c. green, brown and red-orange	60	40

1974 (Oct). AIR. 11th Arab Scout Jamboree, Smar-Jubeil. T **224** and similar horiz designs. Multicoloured. Litho. P 12.

1166	2p.50 Type **224**	40	20
	a. Vert strip of 5. Nos. 1166/1170	3·25	
1167	5p. Scout badge and map	50	20
1168	7p.50 Map of Arab countries	70	25
1169	10p. Lord Baden-Powell and Baalbek	85	25
1170	15p. Guide and Camp	1·20	25
1171	20p. Lebanese Guide and Scout badges	1·40	25
	a. Vert strip of 5. Nos. 1171/1175	12·50	
1172	25p. Scouts around campfire	1·70	35
1173	30p. Globe and Scout badge	2·30	50
1174	35p. Flags of participating countries	3·50	60
1175	50p. Scout chopping wood for old man	5·25	90
1166/1175	*Set of* 10	16·00	3·50

Nos. 1166/1170 and 1171/1175 were issued together *se-tenant* in vertical strips of five within the sheet.

225 Mail Van

1974 (4 Nov). AIR. Centenary of Universal Postal Union. T **225** and similar horiz designs. Multicoloured. Photo. P 11½×12.

1176	5p. Type **225**	3·50	1·00
1177	20p. Container ship	2·30	80
1178	25p. Congress building, Lausanne, and UPU Headquarters, Berne	2·30	90
1179	50p. Mail plane	3·50	1·30
1176/1179	*Set of* 4	10·50	3·50

226 Congress Building, Sofar

227 *Mountain Road* (O. Onsi)

1974 (4 Dec). AIR. 25th Anniversary of Arab Postal Union. T **226** and similar vert designs. Multicoloured. Litho. P 13×12½.

1180	5p. Type **226**	60	25
1181	20p. View of Sofar	1·20	65
1182	25p. APU Headquarters, Cairo	1·70	65
1183	50p. Ministry of Posts, Beirut	3·50	2·00
1180/1183	*Set of* 4	6·25	3·25

1974 (6 Dec). AIR. Lebanese Paintings. T **227** and similar vert designs. Multicoloured. Litho. P 13×12½.

1184	50p. Type **227**	2·00	90

1185	50p. *Clouds* (M. Farroukh)	2·00	90
1186	50p. *Woman* (G. K. Gebran)	2·00	90
1187	50p. *Embrace* (C. Gemayel)	2·00	90
1188	50p. *Self-portrait* (H. Serour)	2·00	90
1189	50p. *Portrait* (D. Corm)	2·00	90
1184/1189	*Set of 6*	11·00	4·75

228 Hunter killing Lion

229 Book Year Emblems

1974 (13 Dec). AIR. Hermel Excavations T **228** and similar vert designs. Multicoloured. Litho. P 12½.

1190	5p. Type **228**	40	20
1191	10p. Astarte	65	25
1192	25p. Dogs hunting Bear	2·50	80
1193	35p. Greco-Roman tomb	5·75	2·75
1190/1193	*Set of 4*	8·50	3·50

1974 (16 Dec). AIR. International Book Year (1972). Litho. P 12½×13.

1194	**229** 5p. multicoloured	25	20
1195	10p. multicoloured	65	25
1196	25p. multicoloured	2·50	80
1197	35p. multicoloured	3·75	2·75
1194/1197	*Set of 4*	6·50	3·50

230 Magnifying Glass

231 Georgina Rizk in Lebanese Costume

1974 (20 Dec). AIR. Stamp Day. T **230** and similar vert designs. Multicoloured. Litho. P 12½.

1198	5p. Type **230**	40	20
1199	10p. Linked posthorns	50	20
1200	15p. Stamp printing	80	25
1201	20p. 'Stamp' in mount	1·20	50
1198/1201	*Set of 4*	2·50	1·00

1974 (21 Dec). AIR. Miss Universe 1971 (Georgina Rizk). T **231** and similar vert designs. Multicoloured. Litho. P 12½.

1202	5p. Type **231**	25	15
1203	20p. Head-and-shoulders portrait	1·00	40
1204	25p. As Type **231**	1·30	50
1205	50p. As 20p	2·50	1·70
1202/1205	*Set of 4*	4·50	2·50
MS1206	156×112 mm. Nos. 1202/1205. Imperf	12·00	11·50

232 Winds

233 UNICEF Emblem and Sikorsky S-55 Helicopter

1974 (23 Dec). AIR. UN Conference on Human Environment, Stockholm, 1972. T **232** and similar vert designs. Multi-coloured. Litho. P 13×12½.

1207	5p. Type **232**	15	15
1208	25p. Mountains and plain	85	20
1209	30p. Trees and flowers	90	40
1210	40p. Sea	1·20	90
1207/1210	*Set of 4*	2·75	1·50
MS1211	153×113 mm. Nos. 1207/1210. Imperf	10·50	10·50

1974 (28 Dec). AIR. 25th Anniversary of United Nations Children's Fund. T **233** and similar horiz designs. Multicoloured. Litho. P 12½×13.

1212	20p. Type **233**	1·00	25
1213	25p. Emblem and child welfare clinic	50	20
1214	35p. Emblem and kindergarten class	1·00	40
1215	70p. Emblem and schoolgirls in laboratory	2·00	50
1212/1215	*Set of 4*	4·00	1·20
MS1216	158×112 mm. Nos. 1212/1215. Imperf	8·75	8·50

234 Discus-throwing

235 Symbols of Archaeology

1974 (30 Dec). AIR. Olympic Games, Munich (1972). T **234** and similar vert designs. Multicoloured. Litho. P 12½.

1217	5p. Type **234**	40	25
1218	10p. Putting the shot	50	40
1219	15p. Weightlifting	65	50
1220	35p. Running	1·30	80
1221	50p. Wrestling	2·00	1·00
1222	85p. Javelin-throwing	3·75	1·60
1217/1222	*Set of 6*	7·75	4·00
MS1223	175×130 mm. Nos. 1217/1222. Imperf	13·00	11·50

1975 (20 Aug). AIR. Beirut–'University City'. T **235** and similar horiz designs. Multicoloured. Litho. P 12½×13.

1224	20p. Type **235**	1·30	25
1225	25p. Science and medicine	2·00	40
1226	35p. Justice and commerce	2·50	1·00
1227	70p. Industry and commerce	4·00	1·60
1224/1227	*Set of 4*	8·75	3·00

Following the outbreak of civil war in March 1975, the official postal service was frequently disrupted and from March to December 1976 suspended. From October to December 1976 overseas mail from the 'Western Zone', franked with Lebanese stamps, was forwarded via Damascus. The Phalangists, who occupied the 'Eastern Zone', organised their own postal service from April 1976. Overseas mail was sent by sea from Jounieh to Rhodes until September 1976, and after that to Larnaca; this mail was franked with Greek or Cypriot stamps respectively. This postal service continued to operate for a while after official postal services recommenced.

(236)

SECURITY OVERPRINTS. During the civil war so many stamps were looted from post offices that the authorities finally, in January 1977, declared all previous issues invalid. Cancellation by meter-franking continued and other mail was prepaid in cash, this being indicated by manuscript markings.

Following the return to normal conditions the Lebanese postal authorities decided to revalidate remaining stocks of stamps in their hands by applying various security overprints to them. These consist of various patterns but each includes the Cedar of Lebanon in its design. Most are rather faint and there is some difference in shade.

The various types of overprint are best described as follows:

- A – Interlocking quadrilaterals
- B – Small squares
- C – Interlocking hexagons
- D – 'Theatre curtain'
- E – Parallel lines
- F – Interlocking squares and vertical oblongs
- G – Diamonds
- H – 'Candelabra'

I	– 'Roof-ridge'
J	– Interlocking oblongs
K	– Intersecting broken lines
L	– Small triangles
M	– Small circles
N	– Chevrons
O	– 'Scallop shells'

1978 (1 Jan–Apr). AIR. Various issues overprinted with different patterns as T **236**. For key to types of security overprint, see notes above.

(a) Nos. 1090, 1092/1093

1228	A	45p. Radar scanner (P.)	2·50	90
1229	B	70p. School of Sciences (P.)	5·25	1·20
1230		85p. Oranges (Vermilion)	5·50	1·80

(b) Nos. 1124/1135

1231	C	2p.50 Type **217** (B.)	65	65
1232	D	5p. Roses (Vermilion)	65	65
1233		15p. Tulips (Vermilion)	1·30	65
1234	C	25p. Lilies (P.)	2·50	65
1235	E	40p. Carnations (Lilac)	2·50	90
1236	D	50p. Iris (P.)	3·75	90
1237	F	70p. Apples (P.)	5·25	1·20
1238	G	75p. Grapes (B.)	6·25	1·20
1239		100p. Peaches (O.)	6·50	2·30
1240		200p. Pears (O.)	14·50	7·25
1241	H	300p. Cherries (O.)	21·00	11·50
1242	I	500p. Oranges (O.)	31·00	18·00

(c) Nos. 1136/1139

1243	J	35p. multicoloured (Br.)	2·75	65
1244	K	50p. multicoloured (P.)	3·75	90
1245	J	85p. multicoloured (B.)	5·50	1·80
1246	L	100p. multicoloured (B.)	6·50	2·30

(d) Nos. 1140/1143

1247	J	5p. Woman with rose (B.)	65	65
1248		10p. Shepherd (B.)	80	65
1249		20p. Horseman (B.)	1·40	65
1250		25p. Type **219** (B.)	2·50	65

(e) Nos. 1157/1158, 1160/1164

1251	M	10p. Type **222** (Vermilion)	80	65
1252	J	20p. Weaving (B.)	1·40	65
1253	N	40p. Pottery (G.)	2·50	90
1254	O	50p. Metal-working (Br.)	4·25	90
1255	A	70p. Cutlery-making (B.)	5·25	1·20
1256	N	85p. Lace-making (G.)	5·50	1·80
1257	M	100p. Handicrafts Museum (Lilac)	6·50	2·30

237 Mikhail Naimy (poet) and View of al-Chakhroub Baskinta

(Des S. Ghantous. Litho Imp Catholique)

1978 (17 May). AIR. Mikhail Naimy Festival Week. T **237** and similar designs. Multicoloured. P 12.

1258	25p. Mikhail Naimy and Sannine mountains	80	15
1259	50p. Type **237**	1·80	50
1260	75p. Mikhail Naimy (*vert*)	3·25	90
1258/1260	*Set of 3*	5·25	1·40

238 Heart and Arrow　**239** Army Badge

(Des and photo State Ptg Wks, Budapest)

1978 (26 June). AIR. World Health Day. 'Down with Blood Pressure'. P 12.

1261	**238**	50p. new blue, vermilion and black	1·60	80

(Des S. Ghantous. Litho Imp Catholique)

1980 (28 Dec). Army Day. T **239** and similar multicoloured designs. P 11½.

(a) POSTAGE

1262	25p. Type **239**	1·00	65

(b) AIR. Inscr 'POSTE AERIENNE'

1263	50p. Statue of Emir Fakhr el Din on horseback	2·00	90
1264	75p. Soldiers with flag (*horiz*)	2·75	1·20
1262/1264	*Set of 3*	5·25	2·50

240 13th-century Danish King　**241** Congress, UPU and Lebanon Post Emblems

(Photo State Ptg Wks, Budapest)

1980 (28 Dec)–**81**. AIR. 50th Anniversary of International Chess Federation (1974). T **240** and similar multicoloured designs. P 12×11½ (50p.) or 11½×12 (others).

1265	50p. Rook, knight and Jubilee emblem (*horiz*) (22.1.81)	2·00	1·30
1266	75p. Type **240** (22.1.81)	3·25	2·50
1267	100p. Rook and Lebanese Chess Federation emblem	5·25	4·00
1268	150p. 18th-century French rook, king and knight	7·25	5·25
1269	200p. Painted faience rook, queen and bishop	9·00	6·50
1265/1269	*Set of 5*	24·00	18·00

(Des S. Ghantous. Photo State Ptg Wks, Budapest)

1981 (12 Feb). AIR. 18th Universal Postal Union Congress, Rio de Janeiro (1979). P 12×11½.

1270	**241**	25p. new blue, yellow-brown and black	2·00	90
1271		50p. bright rose, yellow-brown and black	3·25	1·70
1272		75p. bright green, yellow-brown and black	5·25	2·50
1270/1272		*Set of 3*	9·50	4·50

242 Children on Raft　**243** President Sarkis

(Des S. Ghantous. Litho State Ptg Wks, Budapest)

1981 (21 Mar). AIR. International Year of the Child (1979). P 12×11½.

1273	**242**	100p. multicoloured	6·50	4·00

(Photo Heraclio Fournier)

1981 (23 Sept). Fifth Anniversary of Election of President Sarkis. P 14×13½.

1274	**243**	125p. multicoloured	2·00	1·00
1275		300p. multicoloured	5·75	2·30
1276		500p. multicoloured	9·75	3·25
1274/1276		*Set of 3*	16·00	6·00

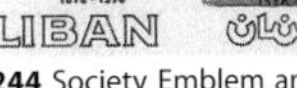

244 Society Emblem and Children　**245** Stork carrying Food

(Des S. Ghantous. Photo)

1981 (Dec). AIR. Centenary of Al-Makassed Islamic Welfare Society. T **244** and similar horiz designs. Multicoloured. P 13½×14.

No.	Description	Unused	Used
1277	50p. Type **244**	1·00	25
1278	75p. Institute building	1·60	40
1279	100p. Al-Makassed (founder)	2·00	65
1277/1279	*Set of 3*	4·25	1·20

(Des S. Ghantous. Photo)

1982 (23 Nov). World Food Day (1981). T **245** and similar horiz designs. Multicoloured. P 12×11½.

No.	Description	Unused	Used
1280	50p. Type **245**	1·60	50
1281	75p. Ear of wheat and globe	2·30	65
1282	100p. Fruit, fish and grain	3·25	1·20
1280/1282	*Set of 3*	6·50	2·10

246 WCY Emblem

247 Phoenician Galley flying Scout Flag

(Des S. Ghantous. Photo)

1983 (19 Dec). World Communications Year. P 14.

No.	Type	Description	Unused	Used
1283	**246**	300p. multicoloured	7·75	3·75

(Des S. Ghantous. Photo)

1983 (19 Dec). 75th Anniversary of Boy Scout Movement. T **247** and similar vert designs. Multicoloured. P 14.

No.	Description	Unused	Used
1284	200p. Type **247**	4·00	2·00
1285	300p. Scouts lowering flag and signalling by semaphore	5·25	2·50
1286	500p. Camp	9·75	4·00
1284/1286	*Set of 3*	17·00	7·75

248 *The Soul is Back*

249 Cedar of Lebanon

1983 (19 Dec). Birth Centenary of Gibran (poet and painter). T **248** and similar vert designs. Multicoloured. Photo. P 14.

No.	Description	Unused	Used
1287	200p. Type **248**	4·00	2·00
1288	300p. *The Family*	5·25	2·50
1289	500p. *Gibran*	9·75	4·00
1290	1000p. *The Prophet*	18·00	9·75
1287/1290	*Set of 4*	33·00	16·00
MS1291	130×151 mm. Nos. 1287/1290. Imperf (*sold at* L£25)	55·00	50·00

(Des S. Ghantous. Photo Heraclio Fournier)

1984 (Dec). P 14½×13½.

No.	Type	Description	Unused	Used
1292	**249**	5p. multicoloured	1·30	40

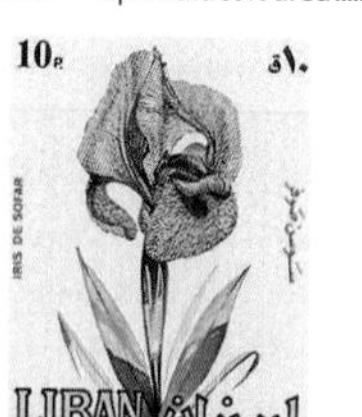

250 Iris

251 Dove with Laurel over Buildings

(Des S. Ghantous. Photo Heraclio Fournier)

1984 (Dec). Flowers. T **250** and similar vert designs. Multicoloured. P 14½×13½.

No.	Description	Unused	Used
1293	10p. Type **250**	90	40
1294	25p. Periwinkle	1·60	80
1295	50p. Barberry	2·50	1·30
1293/1295	*Set of 3*	4·50	2·30

(Des S. Ghantous. Photo Heraclio Fournier)

1984 (Dec). Lebanese Army. T **251** and similar vert designs. Multicoloured. P 14½×13½.

No.	Description	Unused	Used
1296	75p. Type **251**	2·30	90
1297	150p. Cedar and soldier holding rifle	4·50	2·10
1298	300p. Broken chain, hand holding Laurel wreath and cedar	11·00	4·50
1296/1298	*Set of 3*	16·00	6·75

252 Temple Ruins, Fakra

253 President taking Oath

(Des S. Ghantous. Photo Heraclio Fournier)

1984 (Dec). T **252** and similar horiz designs. Multicoloured. P 13½×14½.

No.	Description	Unused	Used
1299	100p. Type **252**	2·00	80
1300	200p. Temple ruins, Bziza	4·00	1·80
1301	500p. Roman arches and relief, Tyre	9·75	4·00
1299/1301	*Set of 3*	14·00	6·00

(Des S. Ghantous. Litho)

1988 (1 Feb). Installation of President Amin Gemayel. P 14½×13½.

No.	Type	Description	Unused	Used
1302	**253**	L£25 multicoloured	2·50	1·30

254 Map of South America and Cedar of Lebanon

255 Satellite, Flags and Earth

(Des S. Ghantous. Litho)

1988 (9 Mar). First World Festival of Lebanese Youth in Uruguay. P 13½×14½.

No.	Type	Description	Unused	Used
1303	**254**	L£5 multicoloured	1·60	65

(Des S. Ghantous. Litho)

1988 (9 Mar). *Arabsat* Telecommunications Satellite. P 13½×14½.

No.	Type	Description	Unused	Used
1304	**255**	L£10 multicoloured	1·30	65

256 Children

257 Arabic '75' and Scout Emblems

(Des S. Ghantous. Litho)

1988 (9 Mar). United Nations Childrens' Fund Child Survival Campaign. P 14½×13½.

No.	Type	Description	Unused	Used
1305	**256**	L£15 multicoloured	2·00	1·00

(Des S. Ghantous. Litho)

1988 (9 Mar). 75th Anniversary (1987) of Arab Scout Movement. P 13½×14½.

No.	Type	Description	Unused	Used
1306	**257**	L£20 multicoloured	3·25	1·30

258 President, Map and Dove

259 Red Cross and Figures

(Des S. Ghantous. Litho)

1988 (9 Mar). International Peace Year (1986). P 14.

1307	**258**	L£50 multicoloured	5·25	2·00

1988 (8 June). Red Cross. T **259** and similar horiz designs. Litho. P 14.

1308	L£10 +L£1 rosine, silver and black	2·00	1·00
1309	L£20 +L£2 multicoloured	2·50	1·60
1310	L£30 +L£3 silver, deep green and rosine	4·00	2·50
1308/1310 *Set of 3*		7·75	4·50

Designs: L£10, T **259**; L£20, Helmeted heads; L£30, Globe, flame, and dove holding map of Lebanon.

260 Cedar of Lebanon

261 Dining in the Open at Zahle, 1883

(Des S. Ghantous. Litho)

1989 (7 Dec). P 13.

1311	**260**	L£50 deep green and deep mauve	1·30	25
1312		L£70 deep green and reddish brown	2·00	50
1313		L£100 deep green and greenish yellow	2·30	80
1314		L£200 deep green and turquoise-blue	4·25	1·60
1315		L£500 deep green and apple green	10·50	4·00
1311/1315 *Set of 5*			18·00	6·50

1993 (22 Nov). 50th Anniversary of Independence. T **261** and similar multicoloured designs. Litho. P 14×13½.

1316	L£200 Type **261**	50·00	1·20
1317	L£300 Castle ruins, Saida (*vert*)	3·00	2·10
1318	L£500 Presidential Palace, Baabda	4·50	3·00
1319	L£1000 Sword ceremony (*vert*)	7·50	4·50
1320	L£3000 Model for the rebuilding of central Beirut	15·00	9·00
1321	L£5000 President Elias Hrawi and state flag (*vert*)	30·00	18·00
1316/1321 *Set of 6*		55·00	34·00
MS1322	130×149 mm. L£10000 As Nos. 1319/1324 but smaller and without face values. Imperf	£100	90·00

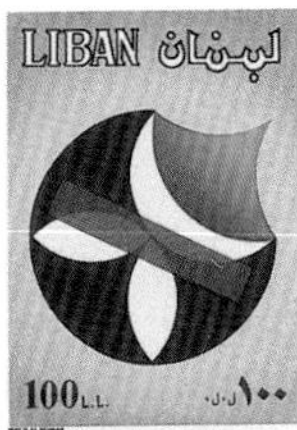

262 Protection of Plants

263 Martyrs' Monument, Beirut

(Des May al-Achkar. Litho)

1994 (7 May). Environmental Protection. T **262** and similar vert designs. Multicoloured. P 13½×13.

1323	L£100 Type **262**	1·10	45
1324	L£200 Protection against forest fires	1·50	75
1325	L£500 Reforesting with cedars	3·50	1·80
1326	L£1000 Creation of urban green zones	6·50	3·75
1327	L£2000 Trees	11·50	6·00
1328	L£5000 Green tree in town	36·00	18·00
1323/1328 *Set of 6*		55·00	28·00

(Des G. Ghali. Litho French Govt Ptg Wks, Paris)

1995 (6 May). Martyr's Day. P 13½×13.

1329	**263**	L£1500 multicoloured	9·00	8·75

FLUORESCENT SECURITY MARKINGS. These consist of a single Cedar of Lebanon, in various sizes.

264 Arabic Script under Magnifying Glass and Headquarters

265 Commemorative Medallion

(Des S. Ghantous (Nos. 1330, 1333, 1336), L. Ghaibeh (Nos. 1331, 1334/1335, 1337), N. Aoun (Nos. 1332, 1338). Litho)

1996 (21 Feb). Anniversaries and Events. T **264** and similar multicoloured designs. Fluorescent security markings (Nos. 1330, 1332/1333, 1336, 1338) or no markings (others). P 13½×13 (vert) or 14 (horiz).

1330	L£100 Type **264** (inauguration of Postal Museum, Arab League Headquarters, Cairo)	1·50	75
1331	L£500 Anniversary emblem (50th Anniversary of United Nations Children's Fund) (*horiz*)	6·00	3·75
1332	L£500 Ears of wheat and anniversary emblem (50th Anniversary (1995) of Food and Agriculture Organisation)	6·00	3·75
1333	L£1000 UN Building (New York) and anniversary emblem (50th Anniversary (1995) of United Nations Organisation)	12·00	7·50
1334	L£1000 Emblem (International Year of the Family (1994)) (*horiz*)	12·00	7·50
1335	L£2000 Anniversary emblem (75th Anniversary (1994) of International Labour Organisation) (*horiz*)	23·00	15·00
1336	L£2000 Emblem (50th Anniversary of Arab League)	23·00	15·00
1337	L£3000 Emblem (75th Anniversary (1994) of Lebanese Law Society)	30·00	23·00
1338	L£3000 René Moawad (former President, 70th birth Anniversary (1995))	30·00	23·00
1330/1338 *Set of 9*		£130	90·00

1997 (13 Oct). First Anniversary of Shelling of Cana Refugee Camp. Litho. P 14.

1339	**265**	L£1100 multicoloured	15·00	15·00

266 Pope John Paul II and President Hrawi

1998 (11 May). Papal Visit. Litho. P 13½.

1340	**266**	L£10000 multicoloured	£225	£170

(**267**)

268 Cedar of Lebanon

1999. Various stamps optd as T **267** in gold, values unchanged.

1341	L£100 multicoloured (No. 1330)	4·00	3·75
1342	L£200 multicoloured (No. 1316)	9·50	9·00

1343 L£500 multicoloured (No. 1318) 24·00 23·00
1344 L£500 multicoloured (No. 1325) 24·00 23·00
1345 L£500 multicoloured (No. 1331) 24·00 23·00
1346 L£500 multicoloured (No. 1332) 24·00 23·00
1347 L£1000 multicoloured (No. 1319) 48·00 45·00
1348 L£1000 multicoloured (No. 1326) 48·00 45·00
1349 L£1000 multicoloured (No. 1333) 48·00 45·00
1350 L£1100 multicoloured (No. 1339) £800 £750
1351 L£1500 multicoloured (No. 1329) 70·00 70·00
1352 L£2000 multicoloured (No. 1335) 80·00 75·00
1353 L£3000 multicoloured (No. 1337) £140 £140
1354 L£5000 multicoloured (No. 1328) £250 £225
1355 L£10000 multicoloured (No. 1340) £475 £450
1341/1355 *Set of 15* £1900 £1800

1999–2002. Litho.

(a) P 13 ×13½

(i) No watermark

1356 **268** L£100 dark red (2000) 95 45
1357 L£300 dark turquoise (2000) 1·60 1·20
1358 L£1000 ultramarine (2001) 4·75 3·75
1358a L£1500 violet 55·00 55·00

(ii) With watermark

1359 L£500 grey-green 2·40 2·00
a. Booklet pane. No. 1359×10 25·00
1360 L£1100 brown (2000) 6·50 4·25
a. Booklet pane. No. 1360×10 70·00
1361 L£1500 violet (2000) 8·00 5·75
a. Booklet pane. No. 1361×10 85·00

(b) P 11×11½

(i) No watermark

1362 L£1100 brown (2000) 6·50 4·25
1363 L£1500 violet (2001) 8·00 5·75

(ii) With watermark

1364 L£500 grey-green (7.02) 2·40 2·00
1365 L£1000 ultramarine (2000) 4·75 3·75
1366 L£1100 brown (2000) 5·50 4·25
1367 L£1500 violet (2000) 8·00 5·75
1356/1367 *Set of 12* £100 90·00

No. 1361 was re-issued in 2001.

Nos. 1359/1361 were only available from booklets.

100L.L. ل.ل١٠٠

(**269**)

1100 L L ل.ل١١٠٠

(**270**)

1999 (Mar). Nos. 1295/1296 and 1092 surch as T **269** (silver) or T **270** (black).

1368 L£100 on 50p. multicoloured (Type **269**) 1·60 90
1369 L£300 on 75p. multicoloured (Type **269**) 3·25 2·10
1370 L£1100 on 70p. multicoloured (Type **270**) 11·00 7·50
1368/1370 *Set of 3* 14·50 9·50

271 Emir Chehab's Palace, Hasbaya

272 Flag and Soldiers

1999 (15 Apr). Buildings. T **271** and similar multicoloured designs. Litho. P 12.

1371 L£100 Type **271** 1·60 75
1372 L£300 UN Economic and Social Commission for Western Asia, Beirut 3·25 1·50
1373 L£500 Emir Fakhreddine's Palace, Deir-el-Kamar (*horiz*) 4·75 3·00
1374 L£1100 Grand Serail, Beirut (*horiz*) 8·00 6·75
1371/1374 *Set of 4* 16·00 11·00

1999 (14 Aug). Various stamps optd as T **270**, in gold or silver.

1374*a* L£1500 multicoloured (gold) (No. 1329) 16·00 9·00
1375 L£2000 multicoloured (gold) (No. 1335) 24·00 18·00
1376 L£3000 multicoloured (silver) (No. 1338) 32·00 26·00
1376*a* L£5000 multicoloured (gold) (No. 1328) 40·00 36·00
1376*b* L£10000 multicoloured (gold) (No. 1340) 80·00 75·00
1374*a*/1376*b* *Set of 5* £170 £150

2001 (25 May). Return of South Lebanon (1st series). Litho. P 11½×11.

1377 **272** L£1100 multicoloured 5·75 5·00

See also No. **MS**1391.

273 Ibrahim Abd el Al

274 Hand and Bars

2001 (6 July). 93rd Birth Anniversary of Ibrahim Abd el Al (engineer). Litho. P 11 × 11½.

1378 **273** L£1000 multicoloured 5·00 5·50

2001 (14 July). Prisoners. Litho. P 11×11½.

1379 **274** L£500 multicoloured 3·25 2·30

275 Emblem

276 Hand holding '50'

2001 (26 Aug). SOS Children's Villages. Litho. P 11×11½.

1380 **275** L£300 multicoloured 1·80 1·40

2001 (31 Aug). 50th Anniversaries. T **276** and similar horiz designs. Litho. P 11×11½.

1381 L£500 brown-olive (Geneva Convention) 3·25 2·30
1382 L£1100 blackish lilac (Geneva Convention) 4·75 4·50
1383 L£1500 multicoloured (Red Cross and Red Crescent) 6·50 6·50
1381/1383 *Set of 3* 13·00 12·00

Designs:—L£500 T **276**; L£1100 Fist around bars and '50'; L£1500 Hand holding stylised people.

277 Ahas Abu Chabke

278 Father Monnot and Emblem

2001 (28 Sept). 97th Birth Anniversary of Ahas Abu Chabke (writer). Litho. P 11½×11.

1384 **277** L£1500 multicoloured 7·25 6·25

2001 (11 Oct). 125th Anniversary of Saint Joseph University, Beirut. P 11×11½.

1385 **278** L£5000 multicoloured 22·00 21·00

279 Abdallah Zakher

280 UN Emblem

2001 (20 Oct). 319th Birth Anniversary of Abdallah Zakher (first Arab printer). Litho. P 11×11½.

1386 **279** L£1000 multicoloured .... 4·75 4·50

2001 (9 Nov). 25th Anniversary of UN Economic and Social Commission for Western Asia. Litho. P 11×11½.

1387 **280** L£10000 dull ultramarine, new blue and magenta .... 48·00 44·00

281 Arabic Script

2002 (1 Feb). Day of the Arab Woman. Litho. P 13×13½.

1388 **281** L£1000 multicoloured .... 5·00 4·50

282 Emblem (*½-size illustration*)

2002 (27 Mar). Arab Summit Conference, Beirut. T **282** and similar horiz design. Multicoloured. Litho. P 13×13½.

1389 L£2000 Type **282** .... 9·25 8·75

1390 L£3000 Cedar tree and President Émile Lahoud .... 13·50 13·00

283 President Émile Lahoud

284 Judges, Scales and Cedar Tree

2002 (27 May). Return of Southern Lebanon (2nd series). Sheet 160×108 mm containing T **283** and similar vert designs. Multicoloured. Litho. P 13½.

MS1391 L£1100×4 Type **283**; President Lahoud with raised arm; President Lahoud and map; Sword ceremony .... 22·00 21·00

2002 (14 June). Martyrs. Sheet 120×90 mm. Litho. P 13×13½.

MS1392 **284** L£3000 multicoloured .... 13·50 13·00

285 UPU Emblem and Cedar Tree

286 Men seated at Table, Mikael Souk

2002 (11 Oct). 125th Anniversary of Universal Postal Union. Litho. P 13×13½.

1393 **285** L£2000 multicoloured .... 8·00 7·00

2002 (11 Oct–20 Dec). Souks. T **286** and similar vert designs. Multicoloured. Litho. P 13½.

1394 L£100 Type **286** 35 35

1395 L£300 Vendor with wheeled stall, Saida Souk .... 1·20 1·20

1396 L£500 Byblos (UNESCO world heritage site) (20.12) .... 2·10 2·10

1397 L£1000 Carpet mender, Tripoli (20.11) .... 4·25 4·25

1394/1397 *Set of 4* .... 7·00 7·00

287 Emblem and National Colours (*½-size illustration*)

2002 (23 Oct). Ninth Summit of French Speaking States, Beirut. T **287** and similar horiz designs. Multicoloured. Litho. P 13½.

1398 L£1500 Type **287** .... 6·50 5·25

1399 L£1500 President Lahoud .... 6·50 5·25

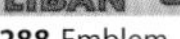

288 Emblem

289 Roman Temple, Bziza

2002 (13 Nov). Beirut, Arab Culture Capital, 2002. Litho. P 13½.

1400 **288** L£2000 multicoloured .... 7·25 7·00

2002 (20 Nov–20 Dec). Ruins. T **289** and similar vert designs. Multicoloured. Litho. P 13½.

1401 L£1100 Type **289** (20.12) .... 4·25 4·25

1402 L£1500 Arqa .... 6·00 6·00

1403 L£2000 Niha .... 8·50 8·50

1404 L£3000 Castle, Mousaïlaha .... 15·00 15·00

1401/1404 *Set of 4* .... 30·00 30·00

290 Lebanese Amber

2002 (20 Nov)–**03**. Fossils. T **290** and similar horiz design. Multicoloured. Litho. P 13½.

1405 L£5000 Type **290** (8.1.03) .... 25·00 25·00

1406 L£10000 *Nematonotus longispinus* .... 49·00 49·00

291 Tree, Signatures, Lebanese and French Leaders

292 Postal Building before Restoration, Riad El Solh-Beirut

2003 (22 Nov). 60th Anniversary of Independence. T **291** and similar horiz designs. Multicoloured. Litho. P 13.

1407 L£1250 Type **291** .... 4·75 3·25
1408 L£1250 Tree, signatures and parade .... 4·75 3·25
1409 L£1750 Tree, signatures of dignitaries .... 6·50 4·75
1410 L£1750 Tree and signatures .... 6·50 4·75
1407/1410 *Set of* 4 .... 20·00 14·50
MS1411 160×110 mm. L£6000 Nos. 1407/1410. Imperf .... 21·00 17·00

2004 (4 Mar). Restoration of Posts and Telecommunication Buildings. T **292** and similar vert design. Multicoloured. Litho. P 11½.

1412 L£100 Type **292** 65 30
1413 L£300 Restored building 95 50

293 Snow Scene, Faqra

294 Musical Score and Emblem

2004 (4 Mar). Tourism. Litho. P 11×12.

1414 **293** L£500 multicoloured .... 1·60 95

2004 (4 Mar). Al Bustan Music Festival, Riad El Solh-Beirut. Litho. P 11×11½.

1415 **294** L£1000 multicoloured .... 3·25 1·90

295 Kamouaa

296 Anniversary Emblem and Hospital

2004 (28 Oct–10 Dec). Tourism. Ski Resorts. T **295** and similar multicoloured designs. Litho. P 11½.

1416 L£100 Type **295** 50 30
1417 L£100 Aayoun Siman (10.10) 50 30
1418 L£250 Laklouk (*vert*) (26.11) 95 65
1419 L£300 Zaarour .... 1·30 70
1420 L£300 Kanat Bakish (10.12) .... 1·30 70
1421 L£1000 Cedres (10.12) .... 2·40 1·60
1416/1421 *Set of* 6 .... 6·25 3·75

2004 (28 Oct). 125th Anniversary of St Georges Hospital, Beirut. Litho. P 11×11½.

1422 **296** L£3000 multicoloured .... 8·00 6·50

297 Baalbeck International Festival

298 Rafic Hariri International Airport

2004 (26 Nov). Festivals. T **297** and similar multicoloured designs. Litho. P 11×11½.

1423 L£500 Type **297** .... 1·60 1·10
1424 L£1250 Tyre (*vert*) .... 4·00 2·75
1425 L£1400 Beiteddine (*vert*) .... 4·75 3·25
1426 L£1750 Byblos (*vert*) .... 6·50 4·75
1423/1426 *Set of* 4 .... 15·00 10·50

2005 (10 Oct–11 Nov). Buildings. T **298** and similar horiz designs. Multicoloured. Litho. P 13½.

1427 L£100 Type **298** 30 30
1428 L£250 Parliament (11.11) 80 80
1429 L£300 Camille Chamoun Sports Centre 95 95
1430 L£500 National Museum .... 1·60 1·60
1431 L£1000 Government Palace .... 3·25 3·25
1432 L£1250 National Bank (11.11) .... 4·00 4·00
1433 L£1400 St Paul Cathedral (11.11) .... 4·50 4·50
1434 L£1750 Bahaeddine Hariri Mosque (11.11) .... 5·50 5·50
1435 L£2000 Presidential Palace (11.11) .... 6·50 6·50
1427/1435 *Set of* 9 .... 25·00 25·00

299 Centenary Emblem (*Illustration further reduced. Actual size 26×59 mm*)

300 Rafic Hariri, Towers and Statue

2005 (23 Nov). Centenary of Rotary International. Litho. P 11½×11.

1436 **299** L£3000 multicoloured .... 8·00 6·50

2006 (13 Feb). Rafic Hariri (Prime Minister 1992–1998 and 2000–2004) Commemoration. T **300** and similar horiz designs. Multicoloured. Litho. P 13½×13.

1437 L£1250 Type **300** .... 5·50 4·50
1438 L£1250 Rafic Hariri and flag .... 5·50 4·50
1439 L£1750 Mosque .... 7·50 6·25
1440 L£1750 Child kissing portrait .... 7·50 6·25
1437/1440 *Set of* 4 .... 23·00 19·00
MS1441 160×110 mm. Nos. 1437/1440. Imperf .... 26·00 21·00

301 Pile of Books

2007. 50th Anniversary of Book Fair. Litho. P 13×13½.

1442 **301** L£1000 multicoloured .... 3·75 3·50

302 Basil Fuleihan

2007. Basil Fuleihan (Minister of Economy and Finance 2000–2003 (assassinated in 2005)) Commemoration. T **302** and similar horiz designs. Multicoloured. Litho. P 13½.

1443 L£500 Type **302** .... 1·90 1·80

1444 L£1500 Seated at desk, signing agreement and National and EU Flags .... 5·50 5·25
1445 L£2000 Head in hand and National Flag .... 7·50 7·00
1443/1445 *Set of* 3 .... 13·50 12·50
MS1445*a* 160×110 mm. Nos. 1443/1445 ....

303 President Chehab

2007 (4 June). President Fouad Chehab Commemoration. Litho. P 13½×13.
1446 **303** L£1400 multicoloured .... 4·50 4·25

304 Globe and Emblem

2007 (2 July). World Information Society Summit, Tunis. Litho. P 13×13½.
1447 **304** L£100 multicoloured 55 55

305 '125' (Arabic) enclosing Emblem

2007 (2 July). 125th Anniversary of Makassed Islamic Welfare Organisation in Beirut (2003) (Nos. 1448/1450 and 1453) and Saida (2004) (Nos. 1451/1452). T **305** and similar horiz design. Multicoloured. Litho. P 13½×13.
1448 L£250 Type **305** 95 90
1449 L£500 Saeb Salam (Prime Minister 1952, 1953, 1960–1961, 1970–1973) (Makassed chairman 1957–1982) .... 1·70 1·60
1450 L£1400 Rafic Hariri (Prime Minister 1992–1998, 2000–2004 (assassinated 2005)) .... 5·00 4·75
1451 L£1400 Rafic Hariri (*different*) .... 5·00 4·75
1452 L£1750 Riad El Solh (first Prime Minister) .... 6·00 5·75
1453 L£1750 Omar El Daouk .... 6·00 5·75
1448/1453 *Set of* 6 .... 22·00 21·00

306 Léopold Senghor

2007 (2 July). Birth Centenary of Léopold Sédar Senghor (poet and president of Senegal 1960–1980). La Francophonie (organisation of French speaking countries). Litho. P 13½×13.
1454 **306** L£300 multicoloured .... 1·30 1·20

307 Athlete (sculpture) **308** Names of Artistes

2007 (2 July). International Year of Sports and Sports Education (2005). Litho. P 13×13½.
1455 **307** L£500 multicoloured .... 2·20 2·10

2007 (2 July). 50th Anniversary of Baalbek International Festival. T **308** and similar horiz design. Multicoloured. Litho. P 13½×13.
1456 L£1000 Type **308** .... 3·25 3·25
1457 L£5000 Female artistes .... 11·00 10·50

309 '30' **310** Maxime Chaya and Flag on Summit

2007 (2 July). 30th Anniversary of OPEC Development Fund. Litho. P 13×13½.
1458 **309** L£1400 multicoloured .... 4·50 4·25

2007 (2 July). Maxime Chaya (First Lebanese climber to reach top of Mount Everest). Sheet 160×110 mm. Litho. P 13½×13.
MS1459 **310** L£3000 multicoloured .... 8·25 8·00

311 *Hills* (detail) (painting by Nizar Daher)

2007 (2 July). Sheet 160×110 mm. Litho. P 13½×13.
MS1460 **311** L£5000 multicoloured .... 13·00 12·50

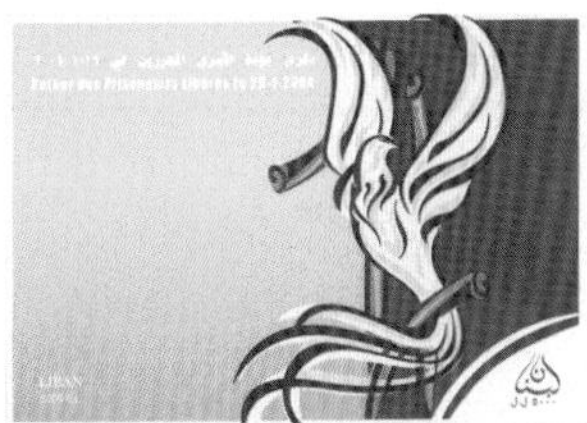

312 Dove and Broken Bars (*Illustration further reduced. Actual size 160×110 mm*)

2007 (2 July). Return of Prisoners. Sheet 160×110 mm. Litho. Imperf.
MS1461 **312** L£5000 multicoloured .... 13·00 12·50

313 *Mother and Child*

314 Flags as Rowers

2008 (30 Apr). 125th Birth Anniversary of Gibran Khalil Gibran (writer and artist). T **313** and similar vert designs. Multicoloured. P 13×13½.

1462	L£100 Type **313**	35	35
1463	L£500 *Sultana*	1·90	1·80
1464	L£1400 Gibran Museum	5·25	5·00
1465	L£2000 *Khalil Gibran*	7·50	7·00
1462/1465 *Set of 4*		13·50	12·50
MS1466 160×110 mm. L£4000 As Nos. 1462/1465. Imperf		15·00	14·50

2008 (30 Apr). Rotary International Conference, Beirut. P 13½×13.

1467	**314** L£2000 multicoloured	7·50	7·00

315 Pigeon

2008 (3 Aug). Arab Post Day. Sheet 170×60 mm containing T **315** and similar horiz design. Multicoloured. P 12×11½.

MS1468 L£5000 Type **315**; L£5000 Camels	19·00	18·00

316 Soldier, Flag and Moon

2008 (Aug). Army Day. T **316** and similar horiz designs. Multicoloured. P 13½×13.

1469	L£500 Type **316**	1·90	1·80
1470	L£1000 Script and tree	3·75	3·50
1471	L£1250 Hand holding grain	4·75	4·50
1472	L£1750 Eye enclosing emblem	6·50	6·25
1469/1472 *Set of 4*		15·00	14·50
MS1473 160×110 mm. L£4500 As Nos. 1469/1472. Imperf		17·00	16·00

317 Aircraft and Envelope

2008 (14 Dec). Tenth Anniversary of LIBANPOST. T **317** and similar horiz design. Multicoloured. P 13½×13.

1474	L£1250 Type **317**	4·75	4·50
1475	L£1750 '10th ANNIVERSARY'	6·50	6·25
MS1476 160×110 mm. L£3000 As Nos. 1474/1475. Imperf		11·50	11·00

318 Oak, Map of Mediterranean and Cedar Tree

(Des Jean-Paul Cousin. Photo)

2008 (14 Dec). Lebanon–France Relations. P 13½×13.

1477	**318** L£1750 multicoloured	6·50	6·25

A stamp of a similar design was issued by France.

319 François El Hajj

2008 (14 Dec). First Death Anniversary of General François El Hajj. P 13×13½.

1478	**319** L£1750 multicoloured	6·50	6·25

320 Charles Malik (member of Commission)

2008 (14 Dec). 60th Anniversary of Universal Declaration of Human Rights. P 13×13½.

1479	**320** L£2000 multicoloured	7·50	7·00

321 Emblem

(Des Khalid Fikri)

2009 (Aug). al-Quds–2009 Capital of Arab Culture. P 13½.

1480	**321** L£1000 multicoloured	4·00	3·75

322 Pierre Deschamps (founder)

2009 (Sept). Centenary of Mission Laïque Française (network of French schools abroad). P 13½.

1481	**322** L£500 multicoloured	2·00	1·90

323 Emblem

2009 (Sept). Beirut–Book Capital of the World. P 13½.
1482 **323** L£750 multicoloured .... 3·00 2·75

324 Emblem

2009 (Sept). Sixth Francophone Games. P 13½.
1483 **324** L£1000 multicoloured .... 4·00 3·75

325 Civil Defence Workers

2010 (2 Aug). Civil Defence. T **325** and similar horiz design. Multicoloured. P 13×13½.
1484 L£100 Type **325** 40 40
1485 L£250 Firefighters .... 1·00 95

326 Plants

2010 (2 Aug). Lebanon Nature Reserves. P 13×13½.
1486 **326** L£300 multicoloured .... 1·20 1·10

327 Building with Colonnade **328** Soaps

2010 (2 Aug). Traditional Buildings. T **327** and similar vert designs. Multicoloured. P 13½×13.
1487 L£500 Type **327** .... 2·00 1·90
1488 L£1000 Two storied building with white glazed door and blue shutters .... 4·00 3·75
1489 L£1250 Two storied building with blue door and shutters .... 5·00 4·75
1487/1489 *Set of* 3 .... 10·00 9·25

2010 (2 Aug). Traditional Industries. Soap. P 13×13½.
1490 **328** L£1400 multicoloured .... 5·50 5·25

329 Soldier carrying Map of Lebanon as Bag **330** Lungs full of Cigarette Butts

2010 (2 Aug). Lebanese Army. P 13×13½.
1491 **329** L£1750 multicoloured .... 7·00 6·75

2010 (2 Aug). Anti Drugs and Tobacco Awareness Campaign. T **330** and similar design. P 13×13½ (horiz) or 13½×13 (vert).
1492 L£2000 multicoloured .... 8·00 7·50
1493 L£5000 black and scarlet-vermilion (*vert*) .... 20·00 19·00
Designs: L£2000 T **330**; L£5000 Needle and emblem.

331 Al Imam Al Ouzai (inscr 'Al Imam Al Ouzaai')

2010 (2 Aug). Al Imam Al Ouzai Commemoration. P 13×13½.
1494 **331** L£1000 multicoloured .... 4·00 3·75

332 President-Elect Bachir Gemayel

2010 (9 Oct). Martyrs. T **332** and similar multicoloured designs. P 13×13½ (horiz) or 13½×13 (vert).
1495 L£1400 Type **332** .... 5·50 5·25
1496 L£1400 Kamal Jumblatt (politician) (inscr 'Kamal Joumblat') (*vert*) .... 5·50 5·25
1497 L£1400 Prime Minister Rashid Karame (*vert*) .... 5·50 5·25
1498 L£1400 Mufti Hassan Khaled .... 5·50 5·25
1499 L£1400 President Rene Mouawad (*vert*) .... 5·50 5·25
1500 L£1400 Musá aş-Şadr (*vert*) .... 5·50 5·25
1495/1500 *Set of* 6 .... 30·00 28·00

333 Woman and Globe **334** Dove and Flowers

2010 (9 Oct). World Tourism Day. 'An Open Door for Women'. P 13½×13.
1501 **333** L£2000 multicoloured .... 8·00 7·50

2010 (9 Oct). Peace. P 13½×13.
1502 **334** L£3000 multicoloured .... 12·00 11·50

335 Early Writing

336 Hand Holding Quill and Flag

2011 (23 May). Cradle of the Alphabet. P 13×13½.
1503 **335** L£250 multicoloured ... 1·00 95

2011 (23 May). Arab Permanent Postal Commission. P 13×13½.
1504 **336** L£500 multicoloured ... 2·00 1·90

337 Sabah

338 Nabih Abou El-Hossn

(Des Hiba Mikdashi)

2011 (23 May). Sabah (Jeanette Gergi Feghali) (singer and actress). P 13×13½.
1505 **337** L£1750 multicoloured ... 7·00 6·75

(Des Hiba Mikdashi)

2011 (23 May). Personalities. Nabih Abou El-Hossn (actor) Commemoration. P 13×13½.
1506 **338** L£2250 multicoloured ... 9·00 8·50

339 Hassan Alaa Eddine

340 Caracalla

(Des Hiba Mikdashi)

2011 (23 May). Personalities. Hassan Alaa Eddine ('Chouchou') (comedian) Commemoration. P 13×13½.
1507 **339** L£2750 multicoloured ... 11·00 10·50

(Des Hiba Mikdashi)

2011 (23 May). Caracalla (dance troupe). P 13×13½.
1508 **340** L£3000 multicoloured ... 12·00 11·50

341 Michel, Alfred, and Youssef Basbous

342 Said Akl

(Des Hiba Mikdashi)

2011 (23 May). Personalities. Basbous Brothers (sculptors). P 13×13½.
1509 **341** L£5000 multicoloured ... 20·00 19·00

(Des Hiba Mikdashi)

2011 (23 May). Personalities. Said Akl (poet) Commemoration. P 13×13½.
1510 **342** L£10000 multicoloured ... 40·00 38·00

343 Ehden Reserve

344 President Frangié

2011 (27 June). Ehden Reserve. P 13×13½.
1511 **343** L£750 multicoloured ... 3·00 2·75

2011 (27 June). President Sleiman Frangié (Suleiman Kabalan Frangieh) Commemoration. P 13½×13.
1512 **344** L£1000 multicoloured ... 4·00 3·75

345 Fayrouz (Fairuz)

346 Wadih El Safi

(Des Hiba Mikdashi)

2011 (27 June). Personalities. Fayrouz (Nouhad Wadi Haddad) (singer). P 13×13½.
1513 **345** L£1500 multicoloured ... 6·00 5·75

(Des Hiba Mikdashi)

2011 (27 June). Personalities. Wadih El Safi (Wadi' Francis) (singer, songwriter and actor) Commemoration. P 13×13½.
1514 **346** L£2000 multicoloured ... 8·00 7·50

347 President Suleiman

2011 (5 Nov). President Michel Suleiman. T **347** and similar horiz designs showing portrait of President Suleiman with different backgrounds. Multicoloured. P 13½.

1515	L£750 Type **347**	3·00	2·75
1516	L£1750 Children in background	7·00	6·75
1517	L£2500 Dove with flags as wings	10·00	9·50
1518	L£2750 United Nations emblem	11·00	10·50
1515/1518	*Set of* 4	28·00	27·00

348 Mother and Children

349 Cedar of Lebanon and Emblem

(Des Myrna Haddad Kalfayan)

2012 (12 Mar). Mothers' Day. P 13½.
1519 **348** L£2000 multicoloured ... £140 £130

(Des Leo Burnet)

2012 (2 Apr). 60th Anniversary of Lions International. P 13.
1520 **349** L£750 violet ... 3·00 2·75

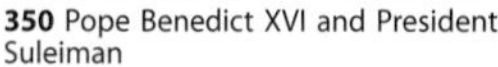

350 Pope Benedict XVI and President Suleiman

351 Emblem

(Des Mario Jad)

2012 (15 Sept). Pope Benedict XVI's visit to Lebanon. P 13.
1521 **350** L£1250 multicoloured .... 5·00 4·75

(Des Thérèse Karkafi)

2012 (12 Nov). Tenth Anniversary of Beirut Marathon. P 13.
1522 **351** L£750 multicoloured .... 3·00 2·75

352 Father Christmas

353 *The Lebanese Emigrant*

(Des Myrna Haddad Kalfayan)

2012 (12 Nov). Christmas. P 13.
1523 **352** L£2000 multicoloured .... 8·00 7·50

2012 (21 Nov). *The Lebanese Emigrant* (statue), Beirut. P 13.
1524 **353** L£500 multicoloured .... 2·00 1·90

354 Adel Osseiran

(Des Myrna Haddad Kalfayan)

2012 (21 Nov). Personalities. Adel Osseiran (politician) Commemoration. P 13.
1525 **354** L£1000 multicoloured .... 4·00 3·75

355 Areas of Research and Relief Map

(Des Hiba Mikdashi)

2012 (10 Dec). 50th Anniversary of Lebanese National Council for Scientific Research. P 13.
1526 **355** L£250 multicoloured .... 1·00 95

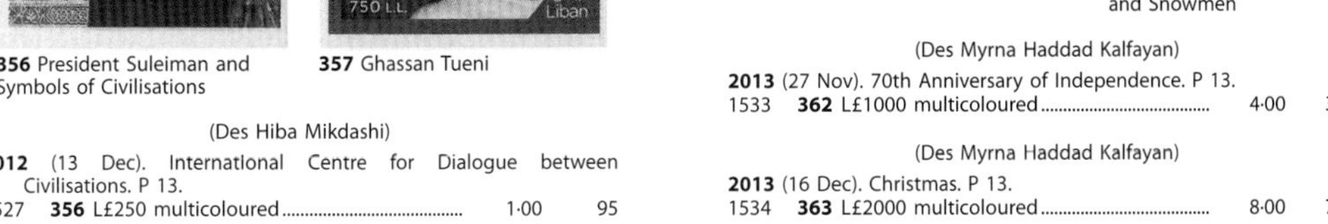

356 President Suleiman and Symbols of Civilisations

357 Ghassan Tueni

(Des Hiba Mikdashi)

2012 (13 Dec). International Centre for Dialogue between Civilisations. P 13.
1527 **356** L£250 multicoloured .... 1·00 95

(Des Myrna Haddad Kalfayan)

2012 (14 Dec). Personalities. Ghassan Tueni (politician) Commemoration. P 13.
1528 **357** L£750 multicoloured .... 3·00 2·75

358 Said Akl

2012 (26 Dec). Personalities. Birth Centenary of Said Akl (writer). P 13.
1529 **358** L£500 multicoloured .... 2·00 1·90

359 Birds

360 Anniversary Emblem

(Des Myrna Haddad Kalfayan)

2013 (20 Mar). Mothers' Day. P 13½.
1530 **359** L£2000 multicoloured .... 8·00 7·50

(Des Leo Burnett)

2013 (11 Nov). 15th Anniversary of Libanpost. P 13.
1531 **360** L£3000 multicoloured .... 12·00 11·50

361 Amin Maalouf

(Des Myrna Haddad Kalfayan)

2013 (19 Nov). Personalities. Amin Maalouf Member of the French Academy. P 13.
1532 **361** L£100 multicoloured 40 40

362 Flag

363 Father Christmas and Snowmen

(Des Myrna Haddad Kalfayan)

2013 (27 Nov). 70th Anniversary of Independence. P 13.
1533 **362** L£1000 multicoloured .... 4·00 3·75

(Des Myrna Haddad Kalfayan)

2013 (16 Dec). Christmas. P 13.
1534 **363** L£2000 multicoloured .... 8·00 7·50

364 Statue

365 Building Façade

(Des Myrna Haddad Kalfayan)

2014 (15 Apr). Armenian Genocide Memorial, Bikfaya, Lebanon. P 13.

1535	**364**	L£2000 multicoloured	8·00	7·50

(Des Carine Tohmé Haddad)

2014 (29 Apr). 300th Anniversary of St Joseph University. P 13½.

1536	**365**	L£500 multicoloured	2·00	1·90

366 Laure Moughaizel (Attorney and Women's Rights Advocate)

367 Banknotes

(Des Myrna Haddad Kalfayan)

2014 (22 May). Personalities. Prominent Women. T **366** and similar vert designs. Multicoloured. P 13½.

1537	L£2000 Type **366**	8·00	7·50
1538	L£2000 Alexandra Issa el Khoury (President of Lebanese Red Cross)	8·00	7·50
1539	L£2000 Mounira el Solh (one of first women in Lebanon and Middle East to run for parliament)	8·00	7·50
1540	L£2000 Anissa Najjar (founder of WILPF Lebanon)	8·00	7·50
1537/1540	*Set of 4*	29·00	27·00

(Des Myrna Haddad Kalfayan)

2014 (2 June). 50th Anniversary of Bank of Lebanon. P 13½.

1541	**367**	L£1750 multicoloured	7·00	6·75

368 Father and Children

(Des Myrna Haddad Kalfayan)

2014 (17 June). Fathers' Day. P 13½.

1542	**368**	L£1750 multicoloured	7·00	6·75

369 The Mediterranean

(Des Myrna Haddad Kalfayan)

2014 (9 July). EUROMED. Euromed 2014 Postal Conference. P 13.

1543	**369**	L£1000 multicoloured	4·00	3·75

370 Fuleco (mascot)

371 Germanos Mouakkad

(Des Myrna Haddad Kalfayan)

2014 (12 July). World Cup Football Championships–Brazil. T **370** and similar vert design. Multicoloured. P 13½.

1544	L£1750 Type **370**	7·00	6·75
1545	L£2000 Trophy	8·00	7·50

(Des Myrna Haddad Kalfayan)

2014 (5 Sept). Personalities. Germanos Mouakkad (founder of Missionary Society of St Paul, Harissa, Lebanon) Commemoration. P 13½×13.

1546	**371**	L£250 multicoloured	1·00	95

372 Ounsi El-Hage

(Des Myrna Haddad Kalfayan)

2014 (10 Nov). Personalities. Poets and Philosophers. T **372** and similar vert designs. Multicoloured. P 13.

1547	L£1750 Type **372**	7·00	6·75
1548	L£1750 Kamal Youssef El-Hage	7·00	6·75
1549	L£1750 Joseph Harb	7·00	6·75
1547/1549	*Set of 3*	19·00	18·00

373 Youssef Bey Karam

(Des Myrna Haddad Kalfayan)

2014 (10 Nov). Personalities. Youssef Bey Karam (Maronite notable who fought in civil war and led a rebellion against Ottoman Empire) Commemoration. P 13.

1550	**373**	L£1750 multicoloured	7·00	6·75

374 Flag as Map

375 '2015'

(Des Myrna Haddad Kalfayan)

2014 (25 Nov). Independence of Lebanon. P 13.

1551	**374**	L£2750 multicoloured	11·00	10·50

(Des Myrna Haddad Kalfayan)

2014 (16 Dec). Season's Greetings. P 13.

1552	**375**	L£5000 multicoloured	20·00	19·00

376 Saints Cyprien et Justine Convent, Kfifane   **377** Said Freiha

(Des Myrna Haddad Kalfayan)

2015 (15 Jan). Convents. T **376** and similar multicoloured designs. Multicoloured. P 13.

1553	L£250 Type **376**	1·00	95
1554	L£250 Saint Jean Al Kalaa Convent, Beit Mery (*vert*)	1·00	95
1555	L£250 Saint Sauveur Convent, Beit Mery	1·00	95
1553/1555	*Set of* 3	2·75	2·50

(Des Salim Sawaya and Dar Assayad)

2015 (20 Jan). Personalities. Said Freiha (journalist and founder of Dar Assayad) Commemoration. P 13.

1556	**377** L£1750 multicoloured	7·00	6·75

378 Internal Security Forces Emblem   **379** Mother and Daughter

(Des Myrna Haddad Kalfayan)

2015 (17 Mar). National Security Forces. T **378** and similar vert design. Multicoloured. P 13.

1557	L£1750 Type **378**	7·00	6·75
1558	L£1750 General Security Forces emblem	7·00	6·75

(Des Myrna Haddad Kalfayan)

2015 (20 Mar). Mothers' Day. P 13½.

1559	**379** L£2000 multicoloured	8·00	7·50

380 Pierre Sadek   **381** Leila Osserian

(Des Myrna Haddad Kalfayan)

2015 (26 May). Personalities. Second Death Anniversary of Pierre Sadek (caricaturist). P 13.

1560	**380** L£2250 multicoloured	9·00	8·50

(Des Myrna Haddad Kalfayan)

2015 (7 July). Personalities. Leila Osseiran and Amine El Hafez Commemoration. T **381** and similar vert design. Multicoloured. P 13.

1561	L£1750 Type **381**	7·00	6·75
1562	L£1750 Amine El Hafez	7·00	6·75

382 Boats   **383** Bechara El Khoury

(Des Myrna Haddad Kalfayan)

2015 (9 July). EUROMED. Boats of the Mediterranean. P 13.

1563	**382** L£5000 multicoloured	20·00	19·00

(Des Myrna Haddad Kalfayan)

2015 (14 July). Personalities. Politicians. T **383** and similar vert designs. Multicoloured. P 13½.

1564	L£1750 Type **383** (first President)	7·00	6·75
1565	L£1750 Riad El Solh (first Prime Minister)	7·00	6·75

384 *The Red Sunset* (Saliba Doughy)

(Des Myrna Haddad Kalfayan)

2015 (11 Aug). Paintings. P 13.

1566	**384** L£2000 multicoloured	8·00	7·50

385 Flag   **386** '2016'

(Des Myrna Haddad Kalfayan)

2015 (21 Nov). National Flag Day. P 13.

1567	**385** £L2000 multicoloured	8·00	7·50

(Des Impact BBDO)

2015 (30 Dec). Season's Greetings. P 13.

1568	**386** L£2000 multicoloured	8·00	7·50

387 Jawad Boulos   **388** Flags and Church of Saidet et Talleh

(Des Myrna Haddad Kalfayan)

2016 (17 Feb). Personalities. T **387** and similar vert design. Multicoloured. P 13.

1569	L£2000 Type **387** (politician)	8·00	7·50
1570	L£2000 Hani Fahs (Fahes) (founding member of Arab Committee for Islamic–Christian Dialogue)	8·00	7·50

2016 (2 Apr). Deir al-Qamar. P 13½.
1571 **388** L£250 multicoloured .... 1·00 95

389 Workers

2016 (30 Apr). International Labour Day. P 13.
1572 **389** L£2000 multicoloured .... 8·00 7·50

390 Monument

(Des Myrna Haddad Kalfayan)

2016 (5 May). Centenary of the Martyrs of 6 May. P 13.
1573 **390** L£2000 multicoloured .... 8·00 7·50

391 Fish

(Des Myrna Haddad Kalfayan)

2015 (9 July). EUROMED. Fish of the Mediterranean. P 13.
1574 **391** L£2250 multicoloured .... 9·00 8·50

392 Anniversary Emblem

(Des John Badr)

2016 (26 July). 60th Anniversary of Baalbeck Festival. P 13.
1575 **392** L£2000 multicoloured .... 8·00 7·50

393 Emblem as Medal **394** Elie Snaifer

(Des Myrna Haddad Kalfayan)

2016 (5 Aug). Lebanese Olympic Committee. P 13.
1576 **393** L£250 multicoloured .... 1·00 95

(Des Myrna Haddad Kalfayan)

2016 (6 Sept). Personalities. Elie Snaifer (comedian, actor and playwright) Commemoration. P 13×13½.
1577 **394** L£250 multicoloured .... 1·00 95

395 Emblem

(Des Myrna Haddad Kalfayan. Litho)

2016 (8 Oct). 70th Anniversary of UPU Membership. P 13.
1578 **395** L£2000 multicoloured .... 8·00 7·50

396 Building Façade

(Des Myrna Haddad Kalfayan. Litho)

2016 (22 Oct). 140th Anniversary of La Sagesse Academic Institute. P 13.
1579 **396** L£2000 multicoloured .... 8·00 7·50

397 Emblem, Globe and Envelopes

2016 (4 Nov). Arab Post Day. T **397** and similar horiz design. Multicoloured. P 13.
1580 L£10000 Type **397** .... 40·00 38·00
1581 L£10000 As Type **397** but with design reversed .... 40·00 38·00

398 Abdul Hamid Karami

(Des Ghassan Balesh. Litho)

2016 (18 Nov). Personalities in the Fight for Independence. T **398** and similar vert designs. Multicoloured. P 13.
1582 L£250 Type **398** .... 1·00 95
1583 L£250 Adnan Al Hakim .... 1·00 95
1584 L£250 Camile Chamoun .... 1·00 95
1585 L£250 Habib Abou Chahla .... 1·00 95
1586 L£250 Hamid Frangieh .... 1·00 95
1587 L£250 Henri Pharaon .... 1·00 95
1588 L£250 Majid Arslan .... 1·00 95
1589 L£250 Maroun Kanaan .... 1·00 95
1590 L£250 Mohamad El Fadl .... 1·00 95
1591 L£250 Pierre Gemayel .... 1·00 95
1592 L£250 Rashid Baydoun .... 1·00 95
1593 L£250 Saadi Al Mounla .... 1·00 95
1594 L£250 Sabri Hamadeh .... 1·00 95
1595 L£250 Saeb Salam .... 1·00 95
1596 L£250 Selim Takla .... 1·00 95
1582/1596 *Set of* 15 .... 13·50 13·00

399 Building and Emblem

(Litho)

2016 (3 Dec). 150th Anniversary of American University of Beirut. P 13.
1597 **399** L£2000 multicoloured .... 8·00 7·50

400 Zaki Nassif **401** '2017'

(Des Myrna Haddad Kalfayan. Litho)

2016 (15 Dec). Personalities. Zaki Nassif (songwriter) Commemoration. P 13.
1598 **400** L£2000 multicoloured .... 8·00 7·50

(Des Impact BBDO. Litho)

2016 (29 Dec). New Year. P 13.
1599 **401** L£5000 multicoloured .... 20·00 19·00

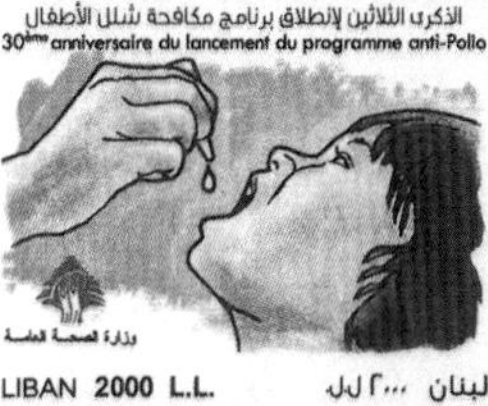

402 Child receiving Immunisation Drops **403** Woman's Face

(Des Myrna Haddad Kalfayan. Litho)

2017 (20 Jan). 30th Anniversary of Anti-Polio Programme. P 13.
1600 **402** L£2000 multicoloured .... 8·00 7·50

(Litho)

2017 (29 Mar). International Women's Day. Women in Power. P 13.
1601 **403** L£10000 multicoloured .... 40·00 38·00

404 Sursock Museum **405** Building

(Litho)

2017 (16 May). Museums. T **404** and similar horiz designs. Multicoloured. P 13.
1602 L£2000 Type **404** .... 8·00 7·50
1603 L£2000 Aquamarine (Mineral Museum, Beirut) 8·00 7·50
1604 L£2000 Phoenician sarcophagi (National Museum, Beirut (75th Anniversary) ...... 8·00 7·50
1602/1604 *Set of 3* .... 22·00 22·00

(Litho)

2017 (June). Centenary of the Islamic Orphanage. P 13.
1605 **405** L£2000 multicoloured .... 8·00 7·50

406 Instruments **407** Cedar of Lebanon

(Litho)

2017 (21 June). World Music Day. P 13½×13.
1606 **406** L£250 multicoloured .... 1·00 95

(Des Myrna Haddad Kalfayan. Litho)

2017 (9 July). EUROMED. Trees of the Mediterranean. P 13.
1607 **407** L£2250 multicoloured .... 9·00 8·50

408 Mikhail Naimy

(Litho)

2017 (22 July). Personalities. Mikhail Naimy (writer) Commemoration. P 13.
1608 **408** L£250 multicoloured .... 1·00 95

409 Shaking Hands

(Des Clementine. Litho)

2017 (1 Aug). Lebanese Army Day. P 13.
1609 **409** L£2000 multicoloured .... 8·00 7·50

410 Carlos Ghosn

(Des Myrna Haddad Kalfayan. Litho)

2017 (28 Aug). Personalities. Carlos Ghosn (business leader). P 13.
1610 **410** L£2000 multicoloured .... 8·00 7·50

411 Zalfa Chamoun

(Litho)

2017 (6 Oct). Personalities. Zalfa Tabet Chamoun (wife of President Camille Chamoun) Commemoration. P 13.

1611	**411** L£2000 multicoloured	8·00	7·50

412 Nasri Shamessedine

413 A Helping Hand

(Des Kamel Jaber. Litho)

2017 (19 Oct). Personalities. 90th Birth Anniversary of Nasri Shamessedine (singer and actor). P 13.

1612	**412** L£250 multicoloured	1·00	95

(Litho)

2017 (3 Nov). Caritas Lebanon. P 13.

1613	**413** L£2000 multicoloured	8·00	7·50

414 Mohamed Baalbaki

(Des Myrna Haddad Kalfayan. Litho)

2017 (28 Aug). Personalities. Mohamed Baalbaki (Press Federation President) Commemoration. P 13.

1614	**414** L£2000 multicoloured	8·00	7·50

415 President Aoun

(Litho)

2017 (6 Dec). President Michel Aoun. T **415** and similar horiz designs. Multicoloured. P 13.

1615	L£5000 Type **415**	20·00	19·00
1616	L£5000 Return of National Flag to the House of the People (*horiz*)	20·00	19·00
1617	L£5000 President Aoun and demonstrators (*horiz*)	20·00	19·00
1615/1617	*Set of* 3	55·00	50·00

CEDAR OF LEBANON DESIGNS (Actual Size)

5 Nos. 58/59, 61/63 and 69

20 Nos. 199/203

T **41** No. T289

46 Nos. 325/329

48 Nos. 333*a*/333*c*

56 Nos. 363/367 and 394/396

65 Nos. 407/410

73 Nos. 429/432

76 Nos. 444/447

78 Nos. 464/467 and 559/560

81 Nos. 481/484

86 Nos. 510/513, 552 and 582/585*b*

90 Nos. 530/533

99 Nos. 601/604

123 Nos. 686 and 695/697

148 No. 827

149 Nos. 828/832

223 No. 1165

249 No. 1292

260 Nos. 1311/1315

268 Nos. 1356/1367

STAMP BOOKLETS

Prices are for complete booklets

Booklet No.	*Date*	*Contents and Cover Price*	*Price*
SB1	1999	Cedar of Lebanon 3 panes. Nos. 1359a/1361a......................	£190

Palestine

1918. 10 Milliemes = 1 Piastre
100 Piastre = £1 Egyptian
1927. 1000 Milliemes = £1 Palestinian

The stamps of TURKEY were used in Palestine from 1865.

In addition various European Powers, and Egypt, maintained post offices at Jerusalem (Austria, France, Germany, Italy, Russia), Jaffa (Austria, Egypt, France, Germany, Russia) and Haifa (Austria, France) using their own stamps or issues specially prepared for Levant post offices. All foreign post offices had closed by the time of the British Occupation.

PRICES FOR STAMPS ON COVER TO 1945

No. 1/1*b*	*from* × 6
No. 2	*from* × 4
Nos. 3/4	*from* × 5
Nos. 5/15	*from* × 4
Nos. 16/29	*from* × 3
Nos. 30/42	*from* × 4
No. 43	—
No. 44	*from* × 10
No. 44*a*	—
Nos. 45/46	*from* × 10
Nos. 47/57	*from* × 3
Nos. 58/59	—
Nos. 60/68	*from* × 3
Nos. 69/70	—
Nos. 71/89	*from* × 3
Nos. 90/100	*from* × 4
No. 101	*from* × 15
Nos. 102/103	*from* × 10
Nos. 104/109	*from* × 10
Nos. 110/111	*from* × 100
Nos. D1/D5	*from* × 40
Nos. D6/D11	*from* × 100
Nos. D12/D20	*from* × 20

BRITISH MILITARY OCCUPATION

British and allied forces invaded Palestine in November 1917 capturing Gaza (7 November), Jaffa (16 November) and Jerusalem (9 December). The front line then stabilised until the second British offensive of September 1918.

Nos. 1/15 were issued by the British military authorities for use by the civilian population in areas they controlled, previously part of the Ottoman Empire. Before the issue of Nos. 1/2 in February 1918, civilian mail was carried free. In addition to Palestine the stamps were available from E.E.F. post offices in Syria (including what subsequently became Transjordan) from 23 September 1918 to 23 February 1922, Lebanon from 21 October 1918 to September 1920 and Cilicia from 2 September 1919 to 16 July 1920. Use in the following post offices outside Palestine is recorded in *British Empire Campaigns and Occupations in the Near East, 1914–1924* by John Firebrace:

Adana, Cilicia
Akkari ('Akkar'), Syria
Aleppo ('Alep, Halep'), Syria
Aleih ('Alie'), Lebanon
Alexandretta, Syria
Antakie, Syria
Ba'abda, Lebanon
Baalbek, Lebanon
Bab, Syria
Babitoma, Syria
Behamdoun, Lebanon
Beit ed Dine, Lebanon
Bekaa, Lebanon
Beyrouth, Lebanon
Beit Mery, Beyrouth, Lebanon
Bouzanti, Syria
Broumana, Lebanon
Damascus ('Damas'), Syria
Damour ('Damor'), Lebanon
Der'a ('Deraa'), Syria
Deurt-Yol, Syria
Djey Han, Syria
Djezzin ('Djezzine'), Lebanon
Djon, Lebanon
Djounie, Lebanon
Djubeil, Lebanon
Douma, Syria
Hajjin ('Hadjin'), Cilicia
Hama, Syria
Hasbaya, Lebanon
Hasine, Cilicia
Hommana, Lebanon
Homs, Syria
Kozan, Cilicia
Lattakia ('Laskie, Lattaquie'), Syria
Massel el Chouf ('Moussalc'), Lebanon
Merdjajoun, Lebanon
Mersina ('Mersine'), Cilicia
Mounboudje, Syria
Nabatti, Lebanon
Nebk ('Nebik'), Syria
Payass, Syria
Racheya, Lebanon
Safita, Syria
Savour, Tyre, Lebanon
Selimie, Syria
Sidan ('Saida (Echelle)'), Lebanon
Suweidiya ('Suvedie'), Syria
Talia, Syria
Tarsous, Cilicia
Tartous, Syria
Tibnin, Lebanon
Edleb, Syria
Feke, Turkey
Habib Souk, Syria
Tripoli, Syria
Zahle, Lebanon
Zebdani, Syria

This information is reproduced here by permission of the publishers, Robson Lowe Publications.

1

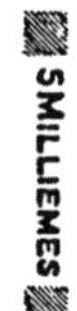

(2)

3

E.E.F. = Egyptian Expeditionary Force

W **100** of Great Britain

(Des G. Rowntree. Litho Typographical Dept, Survey of Egypt, Giza, Cairo)

1918 (10 Feb). Wmk Royal Cypher in column (W **100** of Great Britain). Ungummed. Roul 20.

1	**1**	1p. indigo	£200	£110
		a. Deep blue	£160	£100
		b. Blue	£160	£100
		s. Optd 'SPECIMEN'	£300	

Control: A 18 (*Prices, corner block of* 4; No. 1 £900. No. 1*a*, £800. No. 1*b*, £850).

1918 (16 Feb). As last (ungummed) surch with T **2**.

2	**1**	5m. on 1p. cobalt-blue	£110	£500
		a. 'MILLILMES' (R. 1/10)	£3750	£9500
		s. Optd 'SPECIMEN'	£300	
		w. Wmk inverted		

Control: B 18 A (*Corner block*, £1200).

1918 (5 Mar). As No. 1 but colour changed. With gum.

3	**1**	1p. ultramarine (*shades*)	2·00	2·00
		a. Crown missing from wmk	60·00	65·00
		b. Printed on the gummed side		
		w. Wmk inverted	£250	£300

Control: C 18. (*Corner block*, £85).

1918 (5 Mar–13 May). No. 3 surch with T **2**.

4	**1**	5m. on 1p. ultramarine	8·00	2·75
		a. Arabic surch wholly or partly missing (R. 1/11)	£375	£425
		b. Crown missing from wmk	95·00	
		w. Wmk inverted	£325	

Controls: C 18 B (Mar). (*Corner block*, £1000).
D 18 C (May). (*Corner block*, £225).

3b 4m. Arabic '40' (R. 10/3 and 18/3)

Typo Stamping Dept, Board of Inland Revenue, Somerset House, London)

1918 (16 July–27 Dec). Wmk Royal Cypher in column (W **100** of Great Britain). P 15×14.

5	**3**	1m. sepia	30	40
		a. Deep brown	60	40
6		2m. blue-green	30	45
		a. Deep green	2·00	1·00

No.		Description	Unused	Used
7		3m. yellow-brown (17.12)	50	35
		a. Chestnut	15·00	6·00
8		4m. scarlet	35	40
		a. Arabic '40'	12·00	13·00
9		5m. yellow-orange (25.9)	4·50	50
		a. Orange	65	30
		b. Crown missing from wmk	£180	
		w. Wmk inverted	†	£1600
10		1p. deep indigo (9.11)	50	25
		a. Crown missing from wmk	£150	£170
		w. Wmk inverted	£225	£250
11		2p. pale olive	3·50	60
		a. Olive	3·50	1·10
12		5p. purple	3·75	2·50
13		9p. ochre (17.12)	12·00	7·50
14		10p. ultramarine (17.12)	12·00	4·50
		w. Wmk inverted	£600	
15		20p. pale grey (27.12)	18·00	20·00
		a. *Slate-grey*	24·00	27·00
5/15 *Set of* 11			45·00	32·00

Nos. 5/15 exist imperforate, from imprimatur sheets sold by the National Postal Museum in 2013.

There are two sizes of the design of this issue:

19×23 mm. 1, 2 and 4m., and 2 and 5p.

18×21½ mm. 3 and 5m., and 1, 9, 10 and 20p.

There are numerous minor plate varieties in this issue, such as stops omitted in E.E.F., malformed Arabic characters, etc.

CIVIL ADMINISTRATION UNDER BRITISH HIGH COMMISSIONER

Palestine was placed under civil administration by a British High Commissioner on 1 July 1920.

(4) (5) (6)

Differences:—

T **5**. 20 mm vert and 7 mm between English and Hebrew.

T **6**. 19 mm and 6 mm respectively.

Two settings of T **4**:

Setting I (used for Nos. 16/26). This consisted of two horizontal rows of 12 of which the first setting row appeared on Rows 1, 3/7, 15, 17/18 and 20 of the sheet and the second on Rows 2, 8/14, 16 and 19.

On the first position in the top setting row the Arabic 't' (third character from the left) is incorrectly shown as an Arabic 'z' by the addition of a dot to its right. On the 11th position in the same row the first two letters in the Hebrew overprint were transposed so that ' character appears first. On row 12 stamp 1 the final 'E' of 'PALESTINE' appears as a 'B' on certain values. Once the errors were noticed vertical columns one and eleven were removed from the remaining sheets.

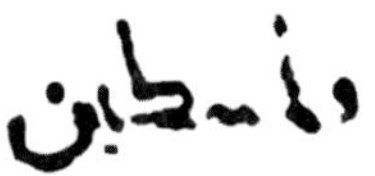

PALESTINB

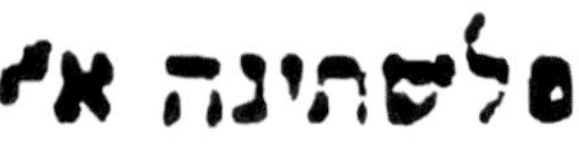

4a 'PALESTINB' (Setting I)

PALESTINB

4b 'PALESTINB' (Setting II)

Setting II (used for Nos. 16/29). This consisted of a single horizontal row of 12 reproduced to overprint the complete sheet of 240. The order in which the horizontal rows were used was changed several times during overprinting. During one such re-arrangement a damaged impression was replaced by one from Setting I showing the Arabic 'z' error. (R. 14/8 for 1, 2, 3, 4, 5 (P 14) 20p.). The 'B' error also occurs in the second setting, once in each sheet on either R. 17/8, 18/8 or 19/8.

(Optd at Greek Orthodox Convent, Jerusalem)

1920 (1 Sept). Optd with T **4** (Arabic 8 *mm* long).

(a) P 15×14

No.	Type	Description	Unused	Used
16	3	1m. sepia	9·50	1·90
		b. Arabic 'z' (Settings I and II)	£2750	
		c. Hebrew characters transposed (I)	£1400	
		d. 'PALESTINB' (II)	£130	
17		2m. blue-green	14·00	6·00
		b. 'Arabic 'z' (Settings I and II)	£1000	
		c. Hebrew characters transposed (I)	£1000	
		d. 'PALESTINB' (II)	£150	
18		3m. chestnut	18·00	8·50
		a. Opt inverted	£550	£700
		b. Arabic 'z' (Settings I and II)	£2250	
		c. Hebrew characters transposed (I)	£2250	
		d. 'PALESTINB' (II)	£100	
19		4m. scarlet	5·00	1·75
		b. Arabic 'z' (Settings I and II)	£2500	
		c. Hebrew characters transposed (I)	£2500	
		d. 'PALESTINB' (II)	80·00	
		e. Arabic '40'	48·00	38·00
20		5m. yellow-orange	25·00	4·25
		c. Hebrew characters transposed (I)	†	£5500
		d. 'PALESTINB' (II)	£160	
21		1p. deep indigo (Sil.)	5·50	1·00
		d. 'PALESTINB' (II)	60·00	
		w. Wmk inverted	£160	£170
22		2p. deep olive	7·00	2·50
		a. Crown missing from wmk	£600	
		b. Arabic 'z' (I)	£250	
		c. Hebrew characters transposed (I)	£250	£250
		d. 'PALESTINB' (Settings I and II)	£140	
23		5p. deep purple	27·00	30·00
		b. Arabic 'z' (I)	£1100	
		c. Hebrew characters transposed (I)	£650	
		d. 'PALESTINB' (Setting I and II)	£250	
24		9p. ochre	15·00	20·00
		b. Arabic 'z' (I)	£500	
		c. Hebrew characters transposed (I)	£600	
		d. 'PALESTINB' (Settings I and II)	£250	
25		10p. ultramarine	13·00	17·00
		b. Arabic 'z' (I)	£400	
		c. Hebrew characters transposed (I)	£500	
		d. 'PALESTINB' (Settings I and II)	£300	
26		20p. pale grey	35·00	50·00
		b. Arabic 'z' (Settings I and II)	£1000	
		c. Hebrew characters transposed (I)	£1000	
		d. 'PALESTINB' (Settings I and II)	£1900	
16/26 *Set of* 11			£150	£130

(b) P 14

No.	Type	Description	Unused	Used
27	3	2m. blue-green	4·50	1·75
		d. 'PALESTINB' (II)	60·00	

28		3m. chestnut	£130	65·00
29		5m. orange	8·00	75
		b. Arabic 'z' (I)	£300	£250
		d. 'PALESTINB' (II)	£150	

Faulty registration of the overprint in this issue has resulted in numerous misplaced overprints, either vertically or horizontally. All values exist with the overprint out of sequence, i.e. Hebrew/Arabic/English or English/Arabic/Hebrew. Also all values are known with Arabic/English or English/Hebrew only.

1920 (Dec)–**21**. Optd with T **5*** (Arabic 10 *mm* long).

(a) P 15×14

30	3	1m. sepia (27.12.20)	2·50	1·00
		a. Opt inverted	£450	†
31		2m. blue-green (27.12.20)	11·00	4·00
		a. Opt double		
32		3m. yellow-brown (27.12.20)	4·00	1·00
33		4m. scarlet (27.12.20)	6·00	1·50
		a. Arabic '40'	65·00	40·00
34		5m. yellow-orange	4·25	75
35		1p. deep indigo (Silver) (21.6.21)	£550	38·00
36		2p. olive (21.6.21)	85·00	40·00
37		5p. deep purple (21.6.21)	50·00	10·00

(b) P 14

38	3	1m. sepia	£850	£950
39		2m. blue-green	5·50	5·50
40		4m. scarlet	90·00	£120
		a. Arabic '40'	£375	£425
41		5m. orange	85·00	9·00
		a. Yellow-orange	11·00	1·25
42		1p. deep indigo (Silver)	65·00	1·75
43		5p. purple	£225	£500

* In this setting the Arabic and Hebrew characters are badly worn and blunted, the Arabic 'S' and 'T' are joined (i.e. there is no break in the position indicated by the arrow in our illustration); the letters of 'PALESTINE' are often irregular or broken; and the space between the two groups of Hebrew characters varies from 1 mm to over 1¾ mm. The " character in the left-hand Hebrew word extends above the remainder of the line (*For clear, sharp overprint, see Nos. 47/59.*).

The dates of issue given are irrespective of the perforations, i.e. one or both perfs could have been issued on the dates shown.

Nos. 31 and 39 exist with any one line of the overprint partly missing.

1920 (6 Dec). Optd with T **6**.

(a) P 15×14

44	3	3m. yellow-brown	60·00	32·00
44*a*		5m. yellow-orange	£15000	£12000

(b) P 14

45	3	1m. sepia	60·00	35·00
46		5m. orange	£450	30·00

PALESTINE PALESTINE PALESTINE

(**6a**) (**7**) (**8**)

1921 (29 May–4 Aug). Optd as T **6a**.

(a) P 15×14

47	3	1m. sepia (23.6)	20·00	4·00
48		2m. blue-green (18.6)	35·00	6·00
49		3m. yellow-brown (23.6)	48·00	3·00
50		4m. scarlet (23.6)	50·00	3·50
		a. Arabic '40'	£250	65·00
51		5m. yellow-orange	80·00	1·00
52		1p. deep indigo (Silver) (1.7)	32·00	1·50
53		2p. olive (4.8)	25·00	6·50
54		5p. purple (4.8)	25·00	8·00
55		9p. ochre (4.8)	75·00	£120
56		10p. ultramarine (4.8)	90·00	15·00
57		20p. pale grey (4.8)	£140	70·00
47/57 *Set of* 11			£550	£200

(b) P 14

58	3	1m. sepia	†	£2250
59		20p. pale grey	£12000	£2500

In this setting the Arabic and Hebrew characters are sharp and pointed and there is usually a break between the Arabic 'S' and 'T', though this is sometimes filled with ink. The space between the two groups of Hebrew characters is always 1¾ mm. The top of the " character in the Hebrew aligns with the remainder of the word.

The 3m. with 'PALESTINE' omitted is an essay (*Price* £2500 *unused*).

1921 (26 Sept)–**22**. Optd with T **7** ('PALESTINE' in sans-serif letters) by Stamping Dept, Board of Inland Revenue, Somerset House, London. Wmk Royal Cypher in column (W **100** of Great Britain). P 15×14.

60	3	1m. sepia (5.10.21)	2·00	30
61		2m. blue-green (11.10.21)	3·00	30
62		3m. yellow-brown (17.10.21)	3·25	30
63		4m. scarlet (15.10.21)	3·75	60
		a. Arabic '40'	50·00	14·00
64		5m. yellow-orange	3·50	20
65		1p. bright turquoise-blue (14.11.21)	2·75	35
		w. Wmk inverted	†	—
66		2p. olive (7.12.21)	4·75	50
67		5p. deep purple (11.12.21)	12·00	6·00
		a. Opt double, one albino	£1000	
68		9p. ochre (10.3.22)	25·00	14·00
69		10p. ultramarine (10.3.22)	28·00	£650
		w. Wmk inverted	†	—
70		20p. pale grey (10.3.22)	80·00	£1500
60/70 *Set of* 11			£150	

Dates quoted are of earliest known postmarks.

(Printed and optd by Waterlow & Sons from new plates)

1922 (Sept–Nov). T **3** (redrawn), optd with T **8**. Wmk Mult Script CA.

(a) P 14

71	3	1m. sepia	2·25	30
		a. Deep brown	2·75	30
		b. Opt inverted	†	£12000
		c. Opt double	£250	£450
		w. Wmk inverted	55·00	42·00
72		2m. yellow	3·00	30
		a. Orange-yellow	5·00	50
		b. Wmk sideways	†	£2000
		w. Wmk inverted	45·00	40·00
73		3m. greenish blue	3·25	15
		w. Wmk inverted	48·00	40·00
74		4m. carmine-pink	3·25	20
		w. Wmk inverted	70·00	55·00
75		5m. orange	3·50	20
		w. Wmk inverted	90·00	60·00
76		6m. blue-green	2·75	30
		w. Wmk inverted	65·00	70·00
77		7m. yellow-brown	2·75	30
		w. Wmk inverted	£325	£325
78		8m. scarlet	2·75	30
		w. Wmk inverted	75·00	80·00
79		1p. grey	3·25	30
		w. Wmk inverted	90·00	80·00
80		13m. ultramarine	4·00	15
		w. Wmk inverted	45·00	35·00
		x. Wmk reversed	†	£750
81		2p. olive	4·00	35
		a. Opt inverted	£325	£550
		b. Ochre	£130	6·50
		w. Wmk inverted	£325	£325
82		5p. deep purple	6·00	1·25
		aw. Wmk inverted	†	£750
82*b*		9p. ochre	£1100	£250
83		10p. light blue	90·00	17·00
		a. 'E.F.F.' for 'E.E.F.' in bottom panel (R. 10/3)	£2000	£550
84		20p. bright violet	£200	£120

(b) P 15×14

86	3	5p. deep purple	65·00	7·00
87		9p. ochre	10·00	9·00
88		10p. light blue	8·50	4·00
		a. 'E.F.F.' for 'E.E.F.' in bottom panel (R. 10/3)	£450	£300
		w. Wmk inverted	£550	£325
89		20p. bright violet	12·00	5·50
71s/89s Optd 'SPECIMEN' *Set of* 15			£450	

Most values can be found on thin paper.

All known examples of the 1m. with inverted opt (No. 71b) also have inverted wmk.

In this issue the design of all denominations is the same size, 18×21½ mm. Varieties may be found with one or other of the stops between 'E.E.F.' missing.

D **1**

(Typo Greek Orthodox Convent Press, Jerusalem)

1923 (1 Apr). P 11.

D1	D **1**	1m. yellow-brown	26·00	38·00
		a. Imperf (pair)	£325	
		b. Imperf between (horiz pair)	£1300	
D2		2m. blue-green	21·00	10·00
		a. Imperf (pair)	£450	
D3		4m. scarlet	10·00	13·00
D4		8m. mauve	7·50	7·00
		a. Imperf (pair)	£140	
		b. Imperf between (horiz pair)	†	£2250
D5		13m. steel blue	7·50	8·00
		a. Imperf between (horiz pair)	£1100	
D1/D5 *Set of 5*			65·00	70·00

Perfectly centred and perforated stamps of this issue are worth considerably more than the above prices, which are for average specimens.

BRITISH MANDATE TO THE LEAGUE OF NATIONS

The League of Nations granted a mandate to Great Britain for the administration of Palestine on 29 September 1923.

D **2** (MILLIEME)

(Typo D.L.R.)

1924 (3 Oct). Wmk Mult Script CA. P 14.

D6	D **2**	1m. deep brown	1·00	2·00
D7		2m. yellow	4·00	1·75
		w. Wmk inverted	†	£500
D8		4m. green	2·00	1·25
D9		8m. scarlet	3·00	90
D10		13m. ultramarine	3·25	2·50
D11		5p. violet	14·00	1·75
D6/D11 *Set of 6*			24·00	9·00
D6s/D11s Optd 'SPECIMEN' *Set of 6*			£300	

(New Currency. 1,000 mils = 1 Palestine pound)

9 Rachel's Tomb

10 Dome of the Rock

11 Citadel, Jerusalem

12 Sea of Galilee

(Des F. Taylor. Typo Harrison)

1927 (1 June)–**45**. Wmk Mult Script CA. P 13½×14½ (2m. to 20m.) or 14.

90	**9**	2m. greenish blue (14.8.27)	2·75	10
		w. Wmk inverted	†	£550
91		3m. yellow-green	1·75	10
		w. Wmk inverted	†	£325
92	**10**	4m. rose-pink (14.8.27)	9·00	1·50
93	**11**	5m. orange (14.8.27)	4·25	10
		a. From coils. Perf 14½×14 (1936)	16·00	20·00
		ac. Yellow. From coils. Perf 14½×14 (1945)	45·00	35·00
		aw. Wmk inverted	22·00	26·00
		b. Yellow (12.44)	3·00	15
		w. Wmk inverted	40·00	40·00
94	**10**	6m. pale green (14.8.27)	6·00	1·75
		a. Deep green	1·50	20
95	**11**	7m. scarlet (14.8.27)	11·00	60
96	**10**	8m. yellow-brown (14.8.27)	18·00	6·50
97	**9**	10m. slate (14.8.27)	2·00	10
		a. Grey. From coils. Perf 14½×14 (11.38)	20·00	27·00
		aw. Wmk inverted		
		b. Grey (1944)	2·25	10
98	**10**	13m. ultramarine	17·00	30
99	**11**	20m. dull olive-green (14.8.27)	3·50	15
		a. Bright olive-green (12.44)	2·25	15
		w. Wmk inverted	†	£550
100	**12**	50m. deep dull purple (14.8.27)	3·25	30
		a. Bright purple (12.44)	6·00	30
		x. Wmk reversed	†	£650
101		90m. bistre (14.8.27)	85·00	60·00
102		100m. turquoise-blue (14.8.27)	2·25	70
103		200m. deep violet (14.8.27)	8·00	5·00
		a. Bright violet (1928)	38·00	17·00
		b. Blackish violet (12.44)	13·00	3·75
90/103 *Set of 14*			£150	65·00
90s/103s Handstamped 'SPECIMEN' *Set of 14*			£450	

Three sets may be made of the above issue; one on thin paper, one on thicker paper with a ribbed appearance, and another on thick white paper without ribbing.

2m. stamps in the grey colour of the 10m., including an example postmarked in 1935, exist as do 50m. stamps in blue, but it has not been established whether they were issued.

Nos. 90/91 and 93 exist in coils, constructed from normal sheets.

D **3** (MIL)

(Typo D.L.R.)

1928 (1 Feb)–**45**. Wmk Mult Script CA. P 14.

D12	D **3**	1m. brown	2·50	85
		a. Perf 15×14 (1944)	42·00	80·00
D13		2m. yellow	3·50	60
		w. Wmk inverted	†	£550
D14		4m. green	4·00	1·60
		a. Perf 15×14 (1945)	75·00	£110
D15		6m. orange-brown (10.33)	18·00	5·00
D16		8m. carmine	2·75	1·75
D17		10m. pale grey	1·75	60
D18		13m. ultramarine	4·50	2·75
D19		20m. pale olive-green	4·50	1·25
D20		50m. violet	4·75	2·25
D12/D20 *Set of 9*			42·00	15·00
D12s/D20s Optd or Perf (6m.) 'SPECIMEN' *Set of 9*			£350	

Nos. D12a and D14a were printed and perforated by Harrison and Sons following bomb damage to the De La Rue works on 29 December 1940.

1932 (1 June)–**44**. New values and colours. Wmk Mult Script CA. P 13½×14½ (4m. to 15m.) or 14.

104	**10**	4m. purple (1.11.32)	3·00	10
		w. Wmk inverted	†	£650
105	**11**	7m. deep violet	1·50	10
106	**10**	8m. scarlet	1·75	20
		w. Wmk inverted	†	£800
107		13m. bistre (1.8.32)	3·75	10
108		15m. ultramarine (1.8.32)	6·50	10
		a. Grey-blue (12.44)	5·50	40
		b. Greenish blue	5·50	40
		w. Wmk inverted	†	£800
109	**12**	250m. brown (15.1.42)	7·50	3·50
110		500m. scarlet (15.1.42)	8·50	3·50
111		£P1 black (15.1.42)	12·00	3·50
104/111 *Set of 8*			40·00	10·00
104s/111s Perf 'SPECIMEN' *Set of 8*			£425	

No. 108 exists in coils, constructed from normal sheets.

POSTAL FISCALS

Type-set stamps inscribed 'O.P.D.A.' (= Ottoman Public Debt Administration) or 'H.J.Z.' (Hejaz Railway); British 1d. stamps of 1912–1924 and Palestine stamps overprinted with one or other of the above groups of letters, or with the word 'Devair', with or without surcharge of new value, are fiscal stamps. They are known used as postage stamps, alone, or with other stamps to make up the correct rates, and were passed by the postal authorities, although they were not definitely authorised for postal use.

STAMP BOOKLETS

The following checklist covers, in simplified form, booklets issued by the British Mandate in Palestine. It is intended that it should be used in conjunction with the main listing and details of stamps listed there are not repeated.

All booklets exist in more than one version, differing in the advertisements on the cover or interleavings. Such differences are not covered by this list, prices quoted being for the cheapest version.

Prices are for complete booklets

Booklet No.	*Date*	*Contents and Cover Price*	*Price*
SB1	1929	2 panes, No. 90×6; 2 panes, No. 91×6; 3 panes, No. 93×6 (150m.). Stitched	£2500
	a.	Stapled	£2500
SB2	1933	Contents as SB1 (150m.)	£3000
SB3	1937-38	1 pane, No. 90×6; 1 pane, No. 91×6; 1 pane, No. 93×6; 1 pane, No. 108×6 (150m.). Red cover	£2750
	a.	Blue cover (1938)	£2500
SB4	1937-38	2 panes, No. 93×6; 1 pane, No. 97×6 (120m.)	£2750

Palestinian Authority

Following negotiations in Oslo, during which the Israeli government recognised the Palestine Liberation Organisation as representing the Arab inhabitants of those areas occupied by Israel since 1967 and the PLO accepted Israel's right to exist within secure borders, an agreement was signed in Washington on 13 September 1993 under which there was to be limited Palestinian self-rule in the Gaza Strip and in an enclave around Jericho on the West Bank. Further talks followed, leading to the Cairo Agreement of 4 May 1994 which inaugurated Palestinian Authority rule in Gaza and Jericho. Under the Taba Accord of 28 September 1995 the Israeli army progressively withdrew from much of the remainder of the West Bank which was then placed under Palestinian Authority administration.

On the signing of the Cairo Agreement all Israeli stamps and postmarks were withdrawn from post offices in the Gaza Strip. The official handover date was 17 May when the Palestinian Authority took over the post offices, which however were only used initially for the distribution of incoming mail and the provision of banking services. From 1 August 1994 outgoing mail from Gaza was handled by the Israeli post office at Mevo Azza.

The handover date in Jericho was 9 May 1994, but an outgoing postal service via Jerusalem was maintained by the use of Israeli stamps available from the Palestinian Authority post office.

Under the terms of the initial agreement stamps of the Palestinian Authority were only valid within areas which it controlled and could not be used either internationally or on mail to the rest of Israel.

As agreed in the Taba Accord the Palestinian Authority took over the Israeli post offices on the West Bank on 8 November 1995 and from this date its issues became valid on mail to other parts of Israel and, via the Israeli postage authorities in Tel Aviv, on international mail also. The Israelis made certain stipulations concerning stamp designs, however, which resulted in a change from mils to fils as the unit of currency. They also insisted that stamps should not be inscribed 'Palestine' and that all designs should be 'in the spirit of the peace'.

CURRENCY. Israeli currency continues to be used in the Palestinian Authority areas. The first stamp issues had face values in mils, the currency of the Palestine Mandate period, but the Israeli authorities objected to this notional currency with the result that the face values were subsequently shown in the Jordanian currency of 1000 fils = 1 dinar.

PRINTER AND PROCESS. The following issues were printed in lithography by the German State Printing Works, Berlin.

PA **1** Monument from Hisham Palace, Jericho

PA **2** Arms of Palestinian Authority

1994 (Oct). T PA **1** and similar horiz designs. Multicoloured. P 14.

PA1	5m.	Type PA **1**	25	20
PA2	10m.	Type PA **1**	25	20
PA3	20m.	Type PA **1**	25	20
PA4	30m.	Church of the Holy Sepulchre, Jerusalem	25	20
PA5	40m.	As No. PA4	25	20
PA6	50m.	As No. PA4	30	25
PA7	75m.	As No. PA4	45	40
PA8	125m.	Flags of Palestinian Authority	70	65
PA9	150m.	As No. PA8	90	80
PA10	250m.	As No. PA8	1·50	1·40
PA11	300m.	As No. PA8	1·90	1·80
PA12	500m.	Flags of Palestinian Authority (51×29 *mm*)	3·00	2·75
PA13	1000m.	Dome of the Rock, Jerusalem (51×29 *mm*)	6·00	5·75
PA1/PA13		*Set of* 13	14·50	13·50

Nos. PA8/PA12 were released on 15 August 1994 and the remainder of the issue on 1 September by the philatelic agent acting for the Palestinian Authority in Europe. Supplies of these stamps, together with Nos. PA14/**MS**PA20, reached the post offices in Gaza and Jericho during October. No operational postmarks were available, however, until 10 January 1995, although special First Day of Issue cancellations were applied at Gaza and Jericho on 1 January 1995.

1994 (Oct). P 14.

PA14	PA **2**	50m. lemon	35	30
PA15		100m. emerald	45	40
PA16		125m. bright new blue	65	60
PA17		200m. dull orange	1·10	1·00
PA18		250m. olive-yellow	1·40	1·30
PA19		400m. dull claret	2·00	1·90
PA14/PA19 *Set of 6*			5·25	5·00

Nos. PA14/PA19 may have been intended for use as Official stamps but, as mail from the Palestinian Authority was sent without stamps, this issue was used for normal postal purposes.

Nos. PA14/PA19 were released on 15 August 1994 by the philatelic agent acting for the Palestinian Authority in Europe. For details of availability and use in Gaza and Jericho see note below No. PA13.

PA **3** Prime Minister Rabin of Israel and Chairman Arafat of PLO with President Clinton of USA

1994 (Oct). Gaza and Jericho Peace Agreement. Sheet 105×70 mm. P 14.

MSPA20 PA **3** 750m.+250m. multicoloured .... 8·00 7·75

No. **MS**PA20 was released on 7 October 1994 by the philatelic agent acting for the Palestinian Authority in Europe. For details of availability and use in Gaza and Jericho see note below Nos. PA13.

CURRENCY. From No. **MS**PA21 the face values are expressed as 1000 fils = 1 Jordanian dinar.

PA **4** *Land of My Dreams* (Ibrahim Hazimeh)

FILS ■ فلس ■

(PA **5**)

1995 (22 Mar). 50th Anniversary of Arab League. Sheet 105×70 mm. P 14.

MSPA21 PA **4** 750f.+250f. multicoloured .... 8·00 7·75

1995 (10 Apr). Award of Nobel Peace Prize to Yasser Arafat, Yitzhak Rabin and Shimon Peres. No. **MS**PA20 surch with T PA **5**.

MSPA22 PA **3** 750f.+250f. on 750m.+250m. multicoloured .... 8·00 7·75

No. **MS**PA22 also carries commemorative overprints on the sheet margins.

PA **6** Palestine Mandate 1927 2m. Stamp

PA **7** Woman in Embroidered Costume

1995 (17 May). Palestine Postal History. T PA **6** and similar vert designs showing stamps of the Palestine Mandate. P 14.

PA23	150f. deep grey-green and black	1·00	1·00
PA24	350f. dull orange and black	2·00	2·00
PA25	500f. carmine-red and black	2·75	2·50
PA23/PA25 *Set of 3*		5·25	5·00

Designs: 150f. T PA **6**; 350f. Palestine Mandate 1927 5m. stamp; 500f. Palestine Mandate 1932 8m. stamp.

The Israeli authorities objected to the design of these stamps and refused to process letters franked with them. Such envelopes were returned to the Palestinian Authority who covered the offending stamps with white adhesive labels struck with impressions of their 'Postage Paid' mark before resubmitting them.

1995 (31 May). Traditional Palestinian Women's Costumes. T PA **7** and similar vert designs. Multicoloured. P 14.

PA26	250f. Type PA **7**	1·40	1·30
PA27	300f. Woman carrying basket	1·70	1·60
PA28	550f. Woman in cloak	3·25	3·00
PA29	900f. Woman in veiled headdress	5·00	4·75
PA26/PA29 *Set of 4*		10·00	9·50

■ FILS فلس ■

(PA **8**)

1995 (7 June*). Nos. PA1/PA13 surch as T PA **8** ('FILS', both English and Arabic, in silver on 30, 40, 50 and 75f.).

PA30	PA **1**	5f. on 5m. multicoloured	15	15
PA31		10f. on 10m. multicoloured	15	15
PA32		20f. on 20m. multicoloured	15	15
PA33	–	30f. on 30m. multicoloured	20	20
PA34	–	40f. on 40m. multicoloured	20	20
PA35	–	50f. on 50m. multicoloured	25	25
PA36	–	75f. on 75m. multicoloured	40	40
PA37	–	125f. on 125m. multicoloured	55	50
PA38	–	150f. on 150m. multicoloured	70	65
PA39	–	250f. on 250m. multicoloured	1·40	1·30
PA40	–	300f. on 300m. multicoloured	1·80	1·70
PA41	–	500f. on 500m. multicoloured	2·40	2·30
PA42	–	1000f. on 1000m. multicoloured	5·50	5·25
PA30/PA42 *Set of 13*			12·50	12·00

* Earliest known postmark date.

The surcharges on 500 and 1000f. values are 47 mm wide.

(PA **9**)

1995 (14 June). Handstamped twice with T PA **9** ultramarine with one impression over each face value, at Jericho.

(a) On Nos. PA1/PA13

PA43	PA **1**	5f. on 5m. multicoloured	15	15
		a. Black surch	15	15
		b. Red surch	15	15
PA44		10f. on 10m. multicoloured	15	15
		a. Black surch	15	15
		b. Red surch	15	15
PA45		20f. on 20m. multicoloured	15	15
		a. Black surch	15	15
		b. Red surch	15	15
PA46	–	30f. on 30m. multicoloured	20	20
		a. Black surch	20	20
		b. Red surch	20	20
PA47	–	40f. on 40m. multicoloured	20	20
		a. Black surch	20	20
		b. Red surch	20	20
PA48	–	50f. on 50m. multicoloured	25	25
		a. Black surch	25	25
		b. Red surch	25	25
PA49	–	75f. on 75m. multicoloured	40	40
		a. Black surch	40	40
		b. Red surch	40	40
PA50	–	125f. on 125m. multicoloured	55	50
		a. Black surch	55	50
		b. Red surch	55	50
PA51	–	150f. on 150m. multicoloured	70	65
		a. Black surch	70	65
		b. Red surch	70	65
PA52	–	250f. on 250m. multicoloured	1·40	1·30
		a. Black surch	1·40	1·30
		b. Red surch	1·40	1·30
PA53	–	300f. on 300m. multicoloured	1·80	1·70
		a. Black surch	1·80	1·70
		b. Red surch	1·80	1·70
PA54	–	500f. on 500m. multicoloured	2·40	2·30
		a. Black surch	2·40	2·30
		b. Red surch	2·40	2·30
PA55	–	1000f. on 1000m. multicoloured	5·50	5·25
		a. Black surch	5·50	5·25
		b. Red surch	5·50	5·25

(b) On Nos. PA14/PA19

PA56	PA **2**	50f. on 50m. lemon	25	25
		a. Black surch	25	25
		b. Red surch	25	25
PA57		100f. on 100m. emerald	40	40
		a. Black surch	40	40
		b. Red surch	40	40

PA58	125f. on 125m. bright new blue	55	50
	a. Black surch	55	50
	b. Red surch	55	50
PA59	200f. on 200m. dull orange	1·10	1·00
	a. Black surch	1·10	1·00
	b. Red surch	1·10	1·00
PA60	250f. on 250m. olive-yellow	1·40	1·30
	a. Black surch	1·40	1·30
	b. Red surch	1·40	1·30
PA61	400f. on 400m. dull claret	2·00	2·00
	a. Black surch	2·00	2·00
	b. Red surch	2·00	2·00
PA43/PA61 *Set of* 19		18·00	17·00

(c) On No. ***MS****PA20*

MSPA62 PA **3** 750f.+250f. on 750m.+250m. multicoloured		6·75	6·50
	a. Black surch	6·75	6·50
	b. Red surch	6·75	6·50

PA **10** Bethlehem (old print)

PA **11** Yasser Arafat

1995 (18 Dec). Christmas. T PA **10** and similar multicoloured designs. P 14.

PA63	10f. Type PA **10**	20	20
PA64	20f. Manger Square, Bethlehem	25	20
PA65	50f. Entrance to Church of the Nativity (*vert*)	35	30
PA66	100f. Pope John Paul II with Yasser Arafat	85	80
PA67	1000f. Site of the Nativity	7·00	6·75
PA63/PA67 *Set of* 5		7·75	7·50

1996 (20 Mar). P 14.

PA68	PA **11** 10f. black and rose-lilac	15	15
PA69	20f. black and greenish yellow	25	20
PA70	50f. black and cobalt	30	30
PA71	100f. black and bright yellow-green	75	75
PA72	1000f. black and brown-ochre	6·75	6·50
PA68/PA72 *Set of* 5		7·50	7·00

PA **12** Summer Palace, Peking

1996 (18 May). International Stamp Exhibition and Fairs. T PA **12** and similar horiz designs. Multicoloured. P 14.

PA73	20f. Type PA **12** (China '96)	30	30
	a. Block of 4. Nos. PA73/PA76	9·25	
	b. Sheetlet. Nos. PA73/PA76, each×2, plus 2 labels	20·00	
PA74	50f. Hagia Sofia Mosque, Istanbul (Istanbul '96)	45	45
PA75	100f. Villa Hugel, Essen (Essen stamp fair)	75	75
PA76	1000f. Modern skyline, Toronto (Capex '96)	7·50	7·25
PA73/PA76 *Set of* 4		8·00	8·00

Nos. PA73/PA76 were issued together in *se-tenant* blocks of four stamps within sheetlets of eight stamps and two gutter labels.

PA **13** Crowd of Palestinians

PA **14** Boxing

1996 (20 May). First Palestinian Legislative and Presidential Elections. Sheet 105×70 mm. P 14.

MSPA77 PA **13** 1250f. multicoloured		9·00	8·75

1996 (19 July). Olympic Games, Atlanta. T PA **14** and similar square designs. Multicoloured. P 14.

PA78	30f. Type PA **14**	25	20
PA79	40f. Olympic medal of 1896	30	30
PA80	50f. Running	45	45
PA81	150f. Olympic flame and flag	1·10	1·00
PA82	1000f. Palestinian Olympic Committee emblem	7·75	7·50
PA78/PA82 *Set of* 5		8·75	8·50
MSPA83 140×105 mm. Nos. PA78 and PA80/PA81		6·00	5·75

PA **15** Poppy

PA **16** Three Wise Men

1996 (22 Nov). Flowers and Fruits. T PA **15** and similar square designs. Multicoloured. P 14.

PA84	10f. Type PA **15**	15	15
PA85	25f. Hibiscus	25	20
PA86	100f. Thyme	75	75
PA87	150f. Lemon	1·20	1·20
PA88	750f. Orange	6·00	5·75
PA84/PA88 *Set of* 5		7·50	7·25
MSPA89 105×70 mm. 1000f. Olive		7·50	7·25

1996 (14 Dec). Christmas. Sheet 165×105 mm containing T PA **16** and similar square designs. Multicoloured. P 14.

MSPA90 150f. Type PA **16**; 350f. Bethlehem; 500f. Shepherds: 750f. The Nativity		12·00	11·50

The four stamps in **MS**PA90 form a composite design.

PA **17** Great Tits

PA **18** Gaza

1997 (21 May). Birds. T PA **17** and similar vert designs. Multicoloured. P 14.

PA91	25f. Type PA **17**	45	45
PA92	75f. Blue Rock Thrushes	60	60
PA93	150f. Golden Orioles	1·40	1·30
PA94	350f. Hoopoes	2·75	2·75
PA95	600f. Peregrine Falcons	4·00	3·75
PA91/PA95 *Set of* 5		8·25	8·00

1997 (19 June). Palestinian Towns in 1839. T PA **18** and similar horiz design. Each sepia and black. P 14.

PA96	350f. Type PA **18**	2·30	2·20
PA97	600f. Hebron	3·75	3·75

PA **19** Chinese Junk

PA **21** *The Young Jesus in the Temple* (Anton Wollenek)

PA **20** Yasser Arafat and Wischnewski

1997 (1 July). Return of Hong Kong to China. Sheet 140×90 mm. P 14.

MSPA98 PA **19** 225f. multicoloured .... 1·80 1·70

1997 (24 July). Friends of Palestine (1st series). Hans-Jürgen Wischnewski (German politician). T PA **20** and similar horiz design. Multicoloured. P 14.

PA99	600f. Type PA **20**	3·00	3·00
	a. Vert pair or horiz strip plus label	6·25	6·25
PA100	600f. Wischnewski congratulating Yasser Arafat	3·00	3·00

Nos. PA99/PA100 were issued together in *se-tenant* sheetlets of four stamps arranged to give vertical pairs or horizontal strips of two stamps with intervening inscribed label.

See also Nos. PA103/PA104.

1997 (28 Nov). Christmas. P 14.

PA101	PA **21** 350f. multicoloured	1·80	1·70
	a. Pair. Nos. PA101/PA102	5·50	5·50
PA102	700f. multicoloured	3·50	3·50

Nos. PA101/PA102 were issued together in *se-tenant* pairs within sheets of six stamps.

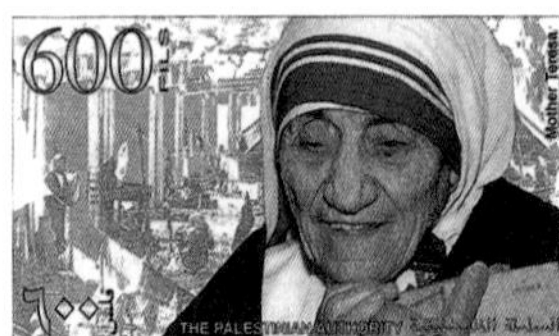

PA **22** Mother Teresa and Street Scene

1997 (17 Dec). Friends of Palestine (2nd series). Mother Teresa (founder of Missionaries of Charity). T PA **22** and similar horiz design. Multicoloured. P 14.

PA103	600f. Type PA **22**	3·00	3·00
	a. Vert pair or horiz strip plus label	6·25	6·25
PA104	600f. Mother Teresa with Yasser Arafat	3·00	3·00

Nos. PA103/PA104 were issued together in *se-tenant* sheetlets of four stamps arranged to give vertical pairs on horizontal strips of two stamps with intervening inscribed label.

PA **23** Baal, Tyre and Bull

1998 (15 June). Baal (Canaanite god). Sheet 72×101 mm. P 14.

MSPA105 PA **23** 600f. multicoloured .... 3·75 3·75

PA **24** Hare and Palm Tree

1998 (22 June). Mosaics from Jabalia. T PA **24** and similar square designs. Multicoloured. P 14.

PA106	50f. Type PA **24**	45	45
PA107	125f. Goat, Hare and Hound	1·10	1·00
PA108	200f. Lemon tree and baskets	1·70	1·60
PA109	400f. Lion	3·00	3·00
PA106/PA109 *Set of 4*		5·75	5·50

PA **25** Sea Onion (*Urginea maritima*)

PA **26** Emblem

1998 (30 Sept). Medicinal Plants. T PA **25** and similar vert designs. Multicoloured. P 14.

PA110	40f. Type PA **25**	25	20
PA111	80f. *Silybum marianum*	45	45
PA112	500f. *Foeniculum vulgare*	2·75	2·50
PA113	800f. *Inula viscosa*	4·50	4·25
PA110/PA113 *Set of 4*		7·25	6·75

1998 (12 Nov). Admission of Palestinian Authority as Non-voting Member to United Nations Organisation. Sheet 82×65 mm. P 14.

MSPA114 PA **26** 700f. multicoloured .... 4·50 4·25

PA **27** Bonelli's Eagle

1998 (12 Nov). Birds of Prey. T PA **27** and similar square designs. Multicoloured. P 14.

PA115	20f. Type PA **27**	15	15
PA116	60f. Hobby	30	30
PA117	340f. Verreaux's Eagle	1·80	1·70
PA118	600f. Bateleur Eagle	3·25	3·25
PA119	900f. Buzzard	5·00	4·75
PA115/PA119 *Set of 5*		9·50	9·25

PA **28** Southern Swallowtail (*Papilio alexanor*)

1998 (3 Dec). Butterflies. Sheet 106×84 mm containing T PA **28** and similar horiz designs. Multicoloured. P 14.

MSPA120 100f. Type PA **28**; 200f. African monarch (*Danaus chrysippus*); 300f. Cleopatra Butterfly (*Gonepteryx Cleopatra*); 400f. Levantine Marbled White (*Melanargia titea*) .... 7·50 7·25

PA **29** Ornamental Star

PA **30** Yasser Arafat and US President Clinton signing Agreement

1998 (3 Dec). Christmas. Sheet 90×140 mm. P 14.

MSPA121 PA **29** 1000f. multicoloured .... 6·00 5·75

1999 (8 Mar). Wye River Middle East Peace Agreement. Sheet 83×65 mm. P 14.

MSPA122 PA **30** 900f. multicoloured .... 5·00 4·75

PA **31** Control Tower   PA **32** Peking (China '99)

1999 (8 Apr). Inauguration of Gaza International Airport. T PA **31** and similar multicoloured designs. P 14.

PA123	80f. Type PA **31**	30	30
PA124	300f. Fokker F.27 Friendship airliner (*horiz*)	1·40	1·30
PA125	700f. Terminal building (*horiz*)	3·50	3·50
PA123/PA125	*Set of* 3	4·75	4·50

1999 (27 Apr). International Stamp Exhibition and UPU Anniversary. T PA **32** and similar horiz designs. Multicoloured. P 14.

PA126	20f. Type PA **32**	30	30
	a. Block of 6. Nos. PA126/PA131	9·50	
PA127	80f. Melbourne (Australia 99)	45	45
PA128	260f. Nuremberg (iBRA '99)	1·70	1·60
PA129	340f. Paris (Philexfrance 99)	2·10	2·00
PA130	400f. Emblem and landscape (face value at right) (125th Anniversary of Universal Postal Union)	2·30	2·20
PA131	400f. As No. PA130 but face value at left	2·30	2·20
PA126/PA131	*Set of* 6	8·25	8·00

Nos. PA126/PA131 were issued together in *se-tenant* blocks of six stamps within the sheet.

PA **33** Relief by Anton Wollenek   PA **34** Horse and Foal

1999 (20 Aug). Hebron. P 14.

PA132	PA **33** 400f. multicoloured	2·50	2·50
	a. Pair. Nos. PA132/PA133	6·25	6·00
PA133	500f. multicoloured	3·50	3·25

Nos. PA132/PA133 were issued together in *se-tenant* pairs within sheets of eight stamps.

1999 (31 Aug). Arabian Horses. T PA **34** and similar vert designs. Multicoloured. P 14.

PA134	25f. Type PA **34**	30	30
	a. Horiz strip of 5. Nos. PA134/PA138	9·50	
PA135	75f. Black horse	45	45
PA136	150f. Horse rearing	90	85
PA137	350f. Horse trotting	2·10	2·00
PA138	800f. Brown horse	5·50	5·25
PA134/PA138	*Set of* 5	8·25	8·00

Nos. PA134/PA138 were issued together in horizontal *se-tenant* strips of five stamps within sheetlets of ten.

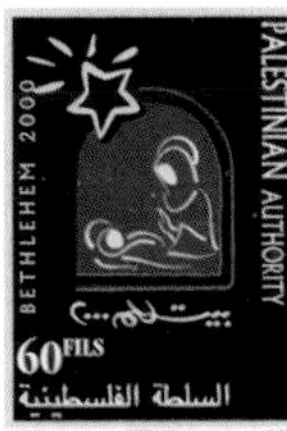

PA **35** Madonna and Child

(Litho Cartor)

1999 (15 Nov). Christmas (1st series). P 13½×13.

PA139	PA **35** 60f. royal blue, black and yellow-ochre	25	20
PA140	80f. multicoloured	30	30
PA141	100f. multicoloured	45	45
PA142	280f. multicoloured	1·20	1·20
PA143	300f. multicoloured	1·40	1·30
PA144	400f. multicoloured	1·80	1·70
PA145	500f. multicoloured	2·40	2·30
PA146	560f. multicoloured	2·75	2·50
PA139/PA146	*Set of* 8	9·50	9·00

PA **36** Nativity

(Litho Cartor (2000f. also embossed))

1999 (8–15 Dec). Christmas (2nd series). T PA **36** and similar vert designs with frames and face values in colours indicated. P 13½.

PA147	PA **36** 200f. multicoloured (black) (15.12)	45	45
	a. Pair. Nos. PA147/PA148	2·00	1·90
PA148	200f. multicoloured (silver) (15.12)	1·40	1·30
PA149	280f. multicoloured (white) (15.12)	60	60
	a. Pair. Nos. PA149/PA150	2·50	2·40
PA150	280f. multicoloured (silver) (15.12)	1·80	1·70
PA151	– 380f. multicoloured (black) (15.12)	75	75
	a. Pair. Nos. PA151/PA152	3·25	3·25
PA152	– 380f. multicoloured (silver) (15.12)	2·30	2·20
PA153	– 460f. multicoloured (white) (15.12)	1·00	95
	a. Pair. Nos. PA153/PA154	4·00	4·00
PA154	– 460f. multicoloured (silver) (15.12)	2·75	2·75
PA155	– 560f. multicoloured (lemon) (15.12)	1·20	1·20
	a. Pair. Nos. PA155/PA156	6·00	5·75
PA156	– 560f. multicoloured (silver) (15.12)	4·50	4·25
PA157	PA **36** 2000f. multicoloured	10·50	10·00
	a. Sheetlet of 4	43·00	
PA147/PA157	*Set of* 11	25·00	24·00

Designs: 380, 460f. Adoration of the Magi; 560f. Flight into Egypt.

Stamps of the same value were issued in *se-tenant* pairs within their sheets. No. PA157 was issued in *se-tenant* sheetlets of four stamps, with the haloes and decoration on Mary's dress embossed in gold foil.

PA **37** Palestine Sunbird

1999 (13 Dec). Sheet 105×70 mm. Litho. P 13½×14.

MSPA158	PA **37** 750f. multicoloured	4·75	4·75

PA **38** *The Last Supper*

(Litho and gold foil embossed (No. **MS**PA164) or litho (others))

2000 (23 Apr). Easter. T PA **38** and similar horiz designs showing paintings by Giotto di Bondone. Multicoloured. P 14.

PA159	150f. Type PA **38**	75	75
PA160	200f. As Type PA **38**	1·10	1·00

PA161 750f. *Lamentation* ... 1·40 1·30
PA162 800f. As No. PA161 ... 2·00 1·90
PA163 1000r. *Crucificion* ... 3·25 3·25
PA159/PA163 *Set of* 5 ... 7·75 6·75
MSPA164 155×98 mm. 2000f. As No. PA163 ... 9·50 9·00

No. **MS**PA164 has the outline of the cross embossed in gold foil.

PA **39** Landscape

PA **40** Pope John Paul II and Yassar Arafat

2000 (15 May). Children's Drawings. T PA **39** and similar square designs. Multicoloured. P 14.

PA165 50f. Type PA **39** ... 45 45
PA166 100f. Two boys ... 60 60
PA167 350f. Buildings ... 2·00 1·90
PA168 400f. Woman crying ... 2·50 2·50
PA165/PA168 *Set of* 4 ... 5·00 5·00

2000 (31 May). Papal Visit. T PA **40** and similar square designs. Multicoloured. P 14.

PA169 500f. Type PA **40** ... 2·30 2·20
PA170 600f. Pope John Paul II ... 2·75 2·50
PA171 750f. With hand on Yassar Arafat ... 3·25 3·25
PA172 800f. Looking at crib ... 3·75 3·75
PA173 1000r. Talking to Yassar Arafat ... 4·50 4·25
PA169/PA173 *Set of* 5 ... 15·00 14·50

(Litho and embossed Cartor)

2000 (29 June). Bethlehem 2000. Booklet Stamps. Multicoloured designs as T PA **36**. P 13½.

PA174 2000f. As No. PA157 but face value at top left ... 9·00 8·75
a. Booklet pane. No. PA174 ... 9·25
PA175 2000f. As No. **MS**PA164 but inscription in white (*horiz*) ... 9·00 8·75
a. Booklet pane. No. PA175 ... 9·25
PA176 2000f. *Madonna and Child* (Fra Angelico) ... 9·00 8·75
a. Booklet pane. No. PA176 ... 9·25
PA174/PA176 *Set of* 3 ... 24·00 24·00

PA **41** Yasser Arafat and Gerhard Schröder (German Chancellor)

2000 (4 Aug). Yasser Arafat's Visit to Germany. T PA **41** and similar horiz design. Multicoloured. Litho. P 14.

PA177 200f. Type PA **41** ... 1·50 1·50
PA178 300f. With President Johannes Rau ... 2·30 2·20

PA **42** Parrotfish

2000 (8 Nov). Marine Fauna. Sheet 175×105 mm containing T PA **42** and similar square designs. Multicoloured. Litho. P 13½.

MSPA179 700f.×8, Type PA **42**; Mauve Stinger; Ornate Wrasse; Rainbow Wrasse; Redstarfish; Common Octopus; Purple Sea Urchin; Striated Hermit Crab ... 26·00 25·00

The stamps and margins of No. **MS**PA179 form a composite design of the seabed.

PA **43** *Blue Madonna*

PA **44** *Nativity* (Gentile da Fabriano)

2000 (9 Dec). Sheet 70×110 mm. Litho. P 14.

MSPA180 PA **43** 950f. multicoloured ... 5·25 5·00

(Litho and gold foil embossed (No. **MS**PA187) or litho (others))

2000 (25 Dec). Christmas. T PA **44** and similar multicoloured designs. P 14.

PA181 100f. Type PA **44** ... 45 45
PA182 150f. *Adoration of the Magi* (Gentile da Fabriano) ... 90 85
PA183 250f. *Annunciation* (Fra Angelico) ... 1·50 1·50
PA184 350f. *Madonna and Child* (Fra Angelico) (As No. PA176) (*vert*) ... 2·10 2·00
PA185 500f. As Type PA **44** ... 2·50 2·50
PA186 1000f. As No. PA184 (*vert*) ... 4·50 4·25
PA181/PA186 *Set of* 6 ... 11·00 10·50
MSPA187 56×71 mm. As No. PA184 ... 10·50 10·00

No. **MS**PA187 has the halos and dress decoration embossed in gold foil.

PA **45** *Christ carrying the Cross* (Fra Angelico)

(Litho and gold foil embossed (No. **MS**PA164) or litho (others))

2001 (23 Apr). Easter. T PA **45** and similar horiz designs. Multicoloured. P 14.

PA188 150f. Type PA **45** ... 90 85
PA189 200f. As Type PA **45** ... 1·10 1·00
PA190 300f. *Removing Christ from the Cross* (Fra Angelico) ... 1·80 1·70
PA191 350f. As No. PA190 ... 2·30 2·20
PA188/PA191 *Set of* 4 ... 5·50 5·25
MSPA192 155×98 mm. 2000f. *Crucificion* (Giotto di Bondone) (*vert*) ... 10·50 10·00

No. **MS**PA192 has the figure of Christ embossed in gold foil.

PA **46** Palestinian Authority and Organisation for African Unity

2001 (3 May). International Co-operation. T PA **46** and similar square designs showing Palestine flag conjoined with other organisations. Multicoloured. P 14.

PA193 50f. Type PA **46** ... 30 30
PA194 100f. Organisation of the Islamic Conference ... 60 60
PA195 200f. European Union ... 1·10 1·00
PA196 500f. Arab League ... 2·30 2·20
PA193/PA196 *Set of* 4 ... 3·75 3·75

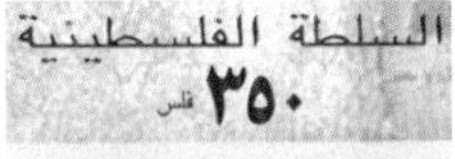

The Palestinian Authority 350 fils

PA **47** *Jerusalem after Rain*

(Litho German State Ptg Wks)

2001 (4 Aug). Art for Peace. Sheet 127×138 mm containing T PA **47** and similar vert designs showing paintings by Ibrahim Hazimeh. Multicoloured. P 14½×14.
MSPA197 350f. Type PA **47**; 550f. *Mysticism*; 850f. *Ramallah*; 900f. *Remembrance* .... 12·50 12·00

PA **48** Scene from *Aladdin and the Wonderful Lamp*

PA **49** Airship and Map of Route

2001 (18 Aug). *Tales from the Arabian Nights*. T PA **48** and similar horiz designs showing scenes from the stories. Multicoloured. P 14.

PA198	300f. Type PA **48**	1·20	1·20
PA199	450f. *Adventures of Sinbad*	2·00	1·90
PA200	650f. *The Enchanted Horse*	3·00	3·00
PA201	800f. *Ali Baba and the Forty Thieves*	3·50	3·50
PA198/PA201	*Set of 4*	8·75	8·75

2001 (17 Nov). 70th Anniversary of Flight of *Graf Zeppelin* (LZ-127) over Palestine. T PA **49** and similar square design. Multicoloured. P 14.

PA202	200f. Type PA **49**	1·20	1·20
PA203	600f. Airship over Palestine	3·25	3·25

PA **50** Male Displaying

2001 (24 Nov). Houbara Bustard (*Chlamydotis undulata*). T PA **50** and similar horiz designs. Multicoloured. P 14×14½.

PA204	350f. Type PA **50**	2·30	2·20
	a. Block of 4. Nos. PA204/PA207	14·00	
PA205	350f. Chick	2·30	2·20
PA206	750f. Female	4·50	4·25
PA207	750f. Male	4·50	4·25
PA204/PA207	*Set of 4*	12·00	11·50

Nos. PA204/PA207 were printed, *se-tenant*, in blocks of four stamps within the sheet.

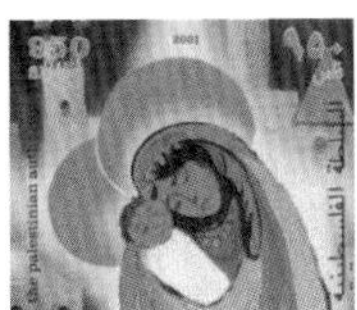

PA **51** Madonna and Child

PA **52** Woman

2001 (8 Dec). Peace for Bethlehem. Sheet 90×90 mm. P 14½×14.
MSPA208 PA **51** 950f. multicoloured .... 5·00 4·75

2002 (June). Traditional Costumes. T PA **52** and similar horiz designs showing women wearing traditional dress. Multicoloured. P 14½×14.

PA209	50f. Type PA **52**	60	60
PA210	100f. Wearing tall headdress and yellow skirt	90	85
PA211	500f. White head veil and panelled skirt	3·75	3·75
PA209/PA211	*Set of 3*	4·75	4·75

PA **53** Jerusalem

PA **54** Madonna and Child

2002 (21 Sept). Historic City Views. T PA **53** and similar square designs. Multicoloured. P 14×13½.

PA212	450f. Type PA **53**	2·50	2·50
PA213	650f. El-Eizariya	3·50	3·25
PA214	850f. Nablus	4·50	4·25
PA212/PA214	*Set of 3*	9·50	9·00

2002 (20 Dec). Christmas. Sheet 98×85 mm. P 14½×14.
MSPA215 PA **54** 1000f. multicoloured .... 5·75 5·50

PA **55** Prickly Pear

PA **56** Olive Tree

2003 (10 May). Flora. T PA **55** and similar vert designs. Multicoloured. P 14×14½.

PA216	550f. Type PA **55**	2·75	2·50
PA217	600f. Euphorbia	3·00	2·75
PA218	750f. Agave (Century Plant)	3·75	3·50
PA216/PA218	*Set of 3*	8·50	8·00
MSPA219	110×66 mm. Nos. PA216/PA218	9·75	9·50

2003 (12 July). Trees. T PA **56** and similar vert design. Multicoloured. P 14×14½.

PA220	300f. Type PA **56**	2·30	2·20
PA221	700f. Blessing Tree	4·00	3·75

PA **57** Al-Azhar University, Gaza

2003 (July). Universities. T PA **57** and similar horiz designs. Multicoloured. P 14×14½.

PA222	250f. Type PA **57**	1·20	1·20
PA223	650f. Hebron University	3·00	3·00
PA224	800f. Arab American University, Jenin	4·00	3·75
PA222/PA224	*Set of 3*	7·50	7·25

PA **58** Glass Necklace

PA **59** Madonna and Child

2003 (11 Oct). Handicrafts. T PA **58** and similar square designs. Multicoloured. P 14.

PA225	150f. Type PA **58**	95	85
PA226	200f. Headdress	1·10	1·00
PA227	450f. Embroidery	2·75	2·50
PA228	500f. Embroidery on costume	3·00	3·00
PA229	950f. Head veil	5·50	5·25
PA225/PA229	*Set of 5*	12·00	11·50

2004 (Dec). Christmas. Sheet 100×75 mm. P 14½×14.

MSPA230 PA **59** 1000f. multicoloured ..... 7·00 6·50

PA **60** Yasser Arafat and Jacques Chirac (French president 1995)

PA **61** Town

2004. Friends of Peace. Sheet 100×100 mm containing T PA **60** and similar horiz design. Multicoloured. P 14×14½.

MSPA231 200f.×2, Type PA **60**×2; 450f.×2, Jacques Chirac×2 ..... 9·00 8·25

2005 (July). 60th Anniversary of Arab League. Sheet 105×70 mm. P 14.

MSPA232 PA **61** 750f. multicoloured ..... 5·75 5·50

PA **62** Mahmoud Darwish

PA **63** Emblem and Skyline

2008 (29 July). Visit (2007) of Mahmoud Darwish (Palestinian writer). T PA **62** and similar horiz designs. P 13½.

PA233	PA **62** 150f. multicoloured	1·40	1·30
PA234	250f. multicoloured	2·30	2·20
PA235	250f. multicoloured	3·00	3·00
PA236	450f. multicoloured	4·00	3·75
PA233/PA236	*Set of 4*	9·50	9·25

Nos. PA234/PA236 are left for additions to Visit (2007) of Mahmoud Darwish (Palestinian writer).

2009 (Mar). Al Quds–Arab Capital of Culture. T PA **63** and similar vert designs. Multicoloured. P 11.

PA237	100f. Type PA **63**	1·20	1·20
	a. Strip of 3. Nos. PA237/PA239	10·00	
PA238	150f. As Type PA **63**	2·30	2·20
PA239	500f. Type PA **63**	6·25	5·75
PA240	1000f. Emblem (central, large)	12·50	11·50
PA237/PA240	*Set of 4*	20·00	19·00

PA **64** 'Jericho'

PA **65** 'Christmas for All'

2010 (26 Dec). 10000th Anniversary of Jericho. T PA **64** and similar vert designs. Multicoloured. P 13½×13.

PA241	50f. Type PA **64**	45	40
PA242	150f. Jericho in Arabic	1·30	1·20
PA243	350f. As Type PA **64**	3·00	2·75
PA244	1000f. As No. PA242	8·50	8·00
PA241/PA244	*Set of 4*	12·00	11·00

2010 (26 Dec). Christmas. P 13½×13.

PA245	PA **65** 100f. multicoloured	85	80
PA246	150f. multicoloured	1·30	1·20
PA247	250f. multicoloured	2·10	2·00
PA248	500f. multicoloured	4·25	4·00
PA245/PA248	*Set of 4*	7·75	7·25

PA **66** Camels

2011 (17 Mar). Arab Post Day. Sheet 180×60 mm containing T PA **66** and similar horiz design. Multicoloured. P 14×13½.

MSPA249 350f. Type PA **66**; 500f. Pigeon ..... 7·50 7·00

PA **67** Dome of the Rock

PA **68** Yasser Arafat

2011 (1 Aug). Ramadan Kareem. T PA **67** and similar horiz designs. Multicoloured. P 13×13½.

PA250	100f. Type PA **67**	45	40
PA251	150f. Lantern and mandala	85	80
PA252	250f. Hanging lantern and new moon	2·10	2·00
PA253	500f. Dome of the Rock (*different*)	4·25	4·00
PA250/PA253	*Set of 4*	7·00	6·50
MSPA254	150×100mm 1000f. Dome of the Rock	8·75	8·25
MSPA255	150×100mm 1000f. Script	8·75	8·25

2012 (6 June). Seventh Death Anniversary (2011) of Yasser Arafat. T PA **68** and similar vert designs. Multicoloured. P 14½.

PA256	50f. Type PA **68**	45	40
PA257	100f. Smiling facing front	85	80
PA258	150f. Facing left	1·30	1·20
PA259	250f. As young man wearing glasses	2·10	2·00
PA260	500f. Facing right	4·25	4·00
PA261	750f. Showing 'V' for victory sign	6·50	6·00
PA262	1000f. Wearing uniform	8·50	8·00
PA263	5000f. With hands raised	43·00	40·00
PA256/PA263	*Set of 8*	60·00	55·00

It is reported that Nos. PA260/PA262 were available both perf 14½ and perf 13½.

PA **69** Grapes

PA **70** Vehicles (Ministry of Transport)

2012 (6 June). Fruit. T PA **69** and similar horiz designs. Multicoloured. P 14.

PA264	150f. Type PA **69**	1·30	1·20
	a. Block of 4. Nos. PA264/PA267		
PA265	300f. Oranges	2·50	2·40
PA266	350f. Bananas	3·00	2·75
PA267	450f. Dates	3·75	3·50
PA264/PA267	*Set of 4*	9·50	8·75

Nos. PA264/PA267 were printed in sheets of eight with an enlarged illustrated margin.

2012 (6 June). In Pursuit of Excellence. Sheet 130×100 mm containing T PA **70** and similar horiz designs. Multicoloured. P 13½.

MSPA268 300f.×5, Type PA **70**; Road construction (Ministry of Public Works and Housing); Transmitters (Ministry of Telecommunications and Information Technology); Coins (Ministry of Finance); Passports (Ministry of the Interior) 13·50 12·50

PA **71** Football and Flag

2012 (6 June). Football. FIFA Recognises the Palestinian Home Game. Sheet 100×100 mm. P 13.

MSPA269 PA **71** 1000f. multicoloured 8·75 8·25

PA **72** Dove and Map

2012 (3 Aug). Arab Post Day. Multicoloured. P 13½.

PA270	PA **72**	150f. multicoloured	1·30	1·20
PA271		250f. multicoloured	2·10	2·00
PA272		350f. multicoloured	3·00	2·75
PA273		1000f. multicoloured	8·50	8·00
PA274		5000f. multicoloured	43·00	40·00
PA270/PA274		*Set of 5*	50·00	49·00

PA **73** Christmas Tree

2012 (24 Dec). Christmas. T PA **73** and similar vert designs. Multicoloured. P 14.

PA275	100f. Type PA **73**	15	15
PA276	150f. Red angular tree	2·10	2·00
PA277	250f. Decorated tree	5·00	4·75
PA275/PA277	*Set of 3*	6·50	6·25
MSPA278	150×100mm 1000f. Nativity	8·75	8·25

PA **74** Firemen tackling Fire

PA **75** White Iris

2013 (1 Mar). International Day of Civil Defence. T PA **74** and similar horiz designs. Multicoloured. P 14.

PA279	100f. Type PA **74**	1·70	1·60
PA280	150f. Firemen and appliances	2·10	2·00
PA281	250f. Firemen spraying building from long ladder	4·25	4·00
PA279/PA281	*Set of 3*	7·25	6·75
MSPA282	150×100mm 1000f. Firemen and fire appliance	8·75	8·25

2013 (3 June). Flora and Fauna. T PA **75** and similar multicoloured designs. P 14.

PA283	20f. Type PA **75**	15	15
PA284	100f. Caracal	85	80
PA285	200f. Little Green Bee-eater	1·70	1·60
PA286	480f. Poppies	4·00	3·75
PA287	720f. Turtle	5·75	5·50
PA288	1080f. Steinbock	8·75	8·25
PA283/PA288	*Set of 6*	19·00	18·00
MSPA289	150×100mm 1000f. Margerittes (*horiz*)	8·75	8·25
MSPA290	150×100mm 1000f. Short-toed Snake Eagle (*horiz*)	8·75	8·25

PA **76** Directing Traffic

PA **77** Football and Flag

2013 (1 July). Palestine Police Day. T PA **76** and similar multicoloured designs. P 14.

PA291	100f. Type PA **76**	85	80
PA292	200f. Policemen helping to pick olives	1·70	1·60
PA293	250f. Policemen working on hillside	2·10	2·00
PA291/PA293	*Set of 3*	4·25	4·00
MSPA294	150×100mm 500f. Helping and elderly woman (*vert*)	4·50	4·25

2013 (7 July). Fifth Anniversary of FIFA Recognition of Palestinian Home Ground. Sheet 100×100 mm. P 13.

MSPA295 PA **77** 1000m. multicoloured 8·75 8·25

No. **MS**PA295 is as No. **MS**PA269 but with different face value and FIFA emblem added to margin.

PA **78** A. Mahmoud

PA **79** UNESCO Emblem

2013 (13 July). Birth Centenary of Abdel Rahim Mahmoud (poet). P 14.

PA296	PA **78**	80f. multicoloured	65	60
PA297		200f. multicoloured	1·70	1·60
PA298		500f. multicoloured	4·25	4·00
PA296/PA298		*Set of 3*	6·00	5·50
MSPA299		100×100mm 1800f. As Type PA**78**	15·00	14·00

2013 (31 Oct). UNESCO Recognition of the State of Palestine. T PA **79** and similar multicolour designs. P 14.

PA300	100f. Type PA **79**	85	80
PA301	150f. As Type PA **79**	1·30	1·20
PA302	250f. As Type PA **79**	2·10	2·00
PA300/PA302	*Set of* 3	3·75	3·50
MSPA303	150×100mm 1000f. Palestine flag enclosing UNESCO emblem (*vert*)	8·75	8·25

PA **80** People with Arms Raised

PA **81** 'STOP Corruption'

2013 (29 Nov). First Anniversary of State of Palestine. Two sheets containing T PA **80** and similar horiz designs. Multicoloured. P 13½.

MSPA304	160×110mm 200m.×5, Type PA **80**; Music score 'An Asset of Sovereignty'; Woman and olive tree 'Palestine Olive Trees'; Buildings and emblem 'The Virtuous Holy Spirit of our Capital Jerusalem'; Sunbird and Anemone flower 'Sharing Peace and Love'	8·75	8·25
MSPA305	150×100mm 1000m. President Mahmoud Abbas holding document	8·75	8·25

2013 (9 Dec). International Anti Corruption Day. T PA **81** and similar multicoloured designs. P 14.

PA306	20f. Type PA **81**	1·70	1·60
PA307	100f. Hands held up against money	3·00	2·75
PA308	200f. Scales of justice	3·50	3·25
PA309	480f. Hand 'Let us Fight Corruption'	5·75	5·50
PA306/PA309	*Set of* 4	12·50	12·00
MSPA310	150×100mm 1000f. Hand held out for coins and STOP sign (*horiz*)	8·75	8·25

PA **82** Al-Aqsa Mosque, Jerusalem

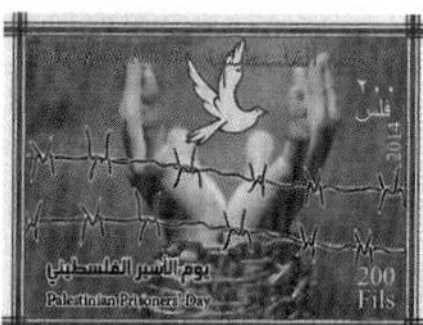

PA **83** Hands behind Barbed Wire releasing Dove

2014 (27 Feb). Shared History of Palestine and Turkey–Architecture. Sheet 120×70 mm containing T PA **82** and similar horiz design. Multicoloured. P 14.

MSPA311	1000f.×2, Type PA **82**; Sultan Ahmed Mosque, Istanbul	18·00	17·00

2014 (17 Apr). Palestinian Prisoners' Day. T PA **83** and similar horiz designs. Multicoloured. P 14.

PA312	200f. Type PA **83**	1·70	1·60
PA313	360f. Hands at window bars	3·00	2·75
PA314	600f. Blindfolded man and barbed wire	5·00	4·75
PA312/PA314	*Set of* 3	8·75	8·25
MSPA315	100×100mmm 1200f. Maysara Abu Hamdiya	10·00	9·50

PA **84** Emblem

PA **85** Bab Al-Shams

2014 (7 May). Centenary of Palestinian Scouts. T PA **84** and similar vert designs. Multicoloured. P 14.

PA316	100f. Type PA **84**	95	90
PA317	150f. As Type PA **84**	4·00	3·75
PA318	250f. As Type PA **84**	5·75	5·50
PA316/PA318	*Set of* 3	9·75	9·25
MSPA319	100×100mm 1500f. Scouting emblem	13·50	13·00

2014 (15 May). Popular Resistance. First Anniversary of the Camp at Bab Al-Shams. T PA **85** and similar multicoloured designs. P 14.

PA320	60m. Type PA **85**	50	50
PA321	920m. Encampment	7·50	7·00
MSPA322	105×70mm 1500m. Tent (*horiz*)	13·50	13·00

PA **86** Pope Francis, President Mahmoud Abbas, Patriarch Bartholomew and Church of Nativity, Jerusalem

PA **87** Mediterranean

2014 (25 May). Historic Visit of Pope Francis to Palestine. T PA **86** and similar vert designs. Multicoloured. P 14.

PA323	60m. Type PA **86**	2·10	2·00
PA324	920m. As Type PA **86** but with embroidery in key shape to left	4·00	3·75
MSPA325	71×105mm 1500m. Design as Type PA **86** but with Church of the Nativity, Bethlehem in background	13·50	13·00

(Des Helen Aposttolou)

2014 (9 July). EUROMED. Euromed 2014 Postal Conference. P 14.

PA326	PA **87** 600f. multicoloured	4·25	4·00

PA **88** Emblem

PA **89** Boy and Book

2014 (12 Aug). 70th Anniversary of Arab Lawyer's Union. Sheet 106×71 mm. P 14.

MSPA327	PA **88** 1200m. multicoloured	10·00	9·50

2014 (22 Oct). National Reading Campaign. T PA **89** and similar vert designs. Multicoloured. P 14.

PA328	60m. Type PA **89**	1·70	1·60
PA329	920m. Man reading to child	2·10	2·00
MSPA330	71×105mm 1000m. Tent forming book	8·75	8·25

PA **90** Solidarity

PA **91** Woman

2014 (29 Nov). International Year of Solidarity with the Palestinian People. P 14.

PA331	PA **90** 60m. multicoloured	1·70	1·60
PA332	920m. multicoloured	3·50	3·25
MSPA333	71×105mm 1800m. As Type PA **90**	15·00	14·50

2015 (8 Mar). International Women's Day. T PA **91** and similar vert designs. Multicoloured. P 14.

PA334 60m. Type PA **91** .... 2·10 2·00
PA335 920m. Drawing of woman carrying mattock.......... 5·00 4·75
MSPA336 71×105mm 1500m. Woman clinging to olive tree.......... 13·50 12·50

PA **92** Sister Maria Alfonsina Ghattas

PA **93** Boats in Harbour

2015 (17 May). Canonisation of Mariam Baouardy, 1846–1878 and Maria Alfonsina Ghattas, 1843–1927. Sheet 150×100mm containing T PA **92** and similar vert designs. Multicoloured. P 14.

MSPA337 Type PA **92**; 500m. Sister Mariam Baouardy; 750m. Sister Mariam Baouardy and Marie-Alphonsine Danil Ghattas; 750m. President Mahmoud Abbas and Pope Francis.......... 22·00 21·00

2015 (9 July). EUROMED. Boats of the Mediterranean. P 14.

PA338 PA **93** 500m. multicoloured.......... 4·25 4·00

PA **94** Emblem

PA **95** Figs and Olives

2015 (2 Oct). Al-Qudds (Jerusalem). Permanent Capital of Arab Culture. T PA **94** and similar vert designs. Multicoloured. P 14.

PA339 100m. Type PA **94**.......... 85 80
PA340 200m. As Type PA **94**.......... 1·70 1·60
PA341 500m. As Type PA **94**.......... 4·25 4·00
PA339/PA341 *Set of* 3.......... 6·00 5·75
MSPA342 105×71mm 1000f. As Type PA **94** but with cityscape as background.......... 8·75 8·25

2015 (10 Oct). Figs and Olives. T PA **95** and similar vert designs. Multicoloured. P 14.

PA343 480m. Type PA **95**.......... 4·00 3·75
PA344 920m. Fig and Olive leaves.......... 7·50 7·00
MSPA345 105×71mm 1200m. Figs.......... 10·00 9·50

PA **96** Camels

PA **97** President Mahmoud Abbas

2015 (15 Nov). Islamic New Year. T PA **96** and similar vert designs. Multicoloured. P 14.

PA346 60m. PA **96**.......... 1·70 1·60
PA347 920m. Setting sun and Dome of the Rock.......... 3·50 3·25
MSPA348 105×71mm 1500m. Setting sun and camel.......... 13·50 12·50

2015 (29 Nov). Presidential Speeches. Two sheets, each 105×71 mm containing T PA **97**. Multicoloured. P 14.

MSPA349 750m.×2, Type PA **97**; Yasser Arafat.......... 13·50 12·50
MSPA350 1500m. Yasser Arafat.......... 13·50 12·50

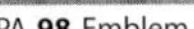
PA **98** Emblem

PA **99** Church of Nativity

2015 (3 Dec). International Day for People with Disabilities. P 14.

PA351 PA **98** 100m. multicoloured.......... 85 80

2016 (May). Church of the Nativity, Bethlehem. Self-adhesive. Die-cut perf 15.

PA352 PA **99** 250m. multicoloured.......... 2·10 2·00

No. PA352 was orignially planned for 27 March 2016.

PA **100** Worker enclosed in Cog

PA **101** Grey Mullet

2016 (May). International Workers' Day. T PA **100** and similar vert designs. Multicoloured. P 14.

PA353 60m. Type PA **100**.......... 2·10 2·00
PA354 920m. Worker and tools.......... 7·50 7·00
MSPA355 105×71mm 1500m. Brick worker.......... 13·50 12·50

Nos. PA353/**MS**PA355 were originally planned for 1 May 2016.

2016 (3 July). EUROMED. Fish of the Mediterranean. T PA **101** and similar horiz designs. Multicoloured. P 14.

PA356 500f. PA **101**.......... 4·25 4·00
a. Sheet of 10. Nos. PA356/PA365.......... 43·00
PA357 500f. Red Mullet.......... 4·25 4·00
PA358 500f. Grouper.......... 4·25 4·00
PA359 500f. Malabar Grouper.......... 4·25 4·00
PA360 500f. Sea Bass.......... 4·25 4·00
PA361 500f. Meagre.......... 4·25 4·00
PA362 500f. Sardine.......... 4·25 4·00
PA363 500f. Mackerel.......... 4·25 4·00
PA364 500f. Blue Runner.......... 4·25 4·00
PA365 500f. Albacore Tuna.......... 4·25 4·00
PA356/PA365 *Set of* 10.......... 38·00 36·00

Nos. PA356/PA365 were printed, *se-tenant*, in sheets of ten stamps.

PA **102** Pool

PA **103** Lake and 'No Water No Life'

2016 (8 Aug). Solomon's Pools. T PA **102** and similar multicoloured designs. P 14.

PA366 250m. Type PA **102**.......... 2·10 2·00
PA367 420m. Wall and pools.......... 3·50 3·25
MSPA368 105×70mm 1500m. Fireworks over pool (*vert*).......... 13·50 12·50

Nos. PA366/**MS**PA368 were originally planned for 21 May 2016.

2016 (8 Aug). Water is Life–Water in Palestine. T PA **103** and similar multicoloured designs. P 14.

PA369 100f. Type PA **103**.......... 3·50 3·25
a. Pair. Nos. PA369/PA370.......... 7.25· 6·75
PA370 150f. Fenced reservoir 'Water is a Human Right'.......... 3·50 3·25
PA371 250f. Droplet in barbed wire 'Our Water is our Right' (*vert*).......... 6·75 6·50
a. Pair. Nos. PA371/PA372.......... 14.50· 13·50

PA372 500f. Water droplet containing wheat and cog 'Water for Development' (*vert*) .... 6·75 6·50
PA369/PA372 *Set of 4* .... 18·00 18·00
MSPA373 105×71mm 1000f. Reaching for water droplet (*vert*) .... 10·00 9·50

PA **104** Globe surrounded by Envelopes

PA **105** Flag

2016 (17 Oct). Arab Post Day. T PA **104** and similar horiz design. Multicoloured. P 14.
PA374 10m. Type PA **104** 10 10
a. Pair. Nos. PA374/PA375 .... 4·25 4·00
PA375 480m. As No. PA374 but with design reversed 4·00 3·75
Nos. PA374/PA375 were printed, *se-tenant*, in horizontal pairs within the sheet, and were originally planned for 3 August 2016.

2016 (17 Oct). Palestinian Flag Day. T PA **105** and similar vert designs. Multicoloured. P 14.
PA376 250m. Flag and UN building .... 2·10 2·00
PA377 420m. Woman, olive tree and flag .... 3·50 3·25
MS378 105×71mm 1800m. Type PA **105** .... 15·00 14·00

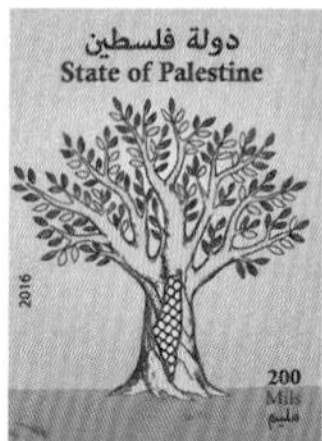

PA **106** Tree

PA **107** Script

2016 (15 Nov). Trees. P 14.
PA379 PA **106** 200m. multicoloured .... 1·70 1·60
PA380 1500m. multicoloured .... 11·00 10·50
PA381 4500m. multicoloured .... 36·00 34·00
PA379/PA381 *Set of 3* .... 44·00 41·00

2016 (18 Dec). Arab Calligraphy Day. T PA **107** and similar multicoloured designs. P 14.
PA382 250m. Type PA **107** .... 2·10 2·00
PA383 420m. Inscribed octagon .... 3·50 3·25
MS384 105×71mm 600m.×3, Script×2, Script (*different*) .... 15·00 14·00

PA **108** Fadwa Touqan

PA **109** Iris

2017 (1 Mar). Birth Centenary of Fadwa Touqan (Tuqan) (writer). T PA **108** and similar vert designs. Multicoloured. P 14.
PA385 150m. Type PA **108** .... 1·30 1·20
PA386 500m. As Type PA **108** .... 4·25 4·00
MSPA387 105×71mm 1800m. Fadwa Touqan (*different*) .... 15·00 14·00

2017 (5 Apr). National Flower–Iris. T PA **109** and similar vert design. Multicoloured. P 14.
PA388 500m. Type PA **109** .... 4·25 4·00
MSPA389 105×71mm 1500m. Group of Irises .... 13·50 12·50

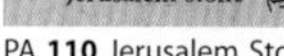

PA **110** Jerusalem Stone

PA **111** Dead Sea

(Litho)

2017 (1 June). National Industries. Stone. Sheet 160×110 mm containing T PA **110** and similar vert desings. Multicoloured. P 14.
MSPA390 100m. Type PA **110**; 200m. Nablus stone; 300m. Jenin stone; 400m. Ramallah stone; 500m. Hebron stone; 600m. Tulkarm stone; 700m. Bethlehem stone; 800m. Qalqilya stone .... 30·00 28·00

(Litho)

2017 (17 July). The Dead Sea. Sheet 150×100 mm containing T PA **111** and similar vert desings. Multicoloured. P 14.
MSPA391 150m. Type PA **111**; 280m. Dead Sea and coastline (bottom left); 420m. Dead Sea and coastline (upper right); 950m. Dead Sea and coastline (upper left) .... 15·00 14·00
The stamps and margins of **MS**PA391 form a composite design.

PA **112** Medjool Dates

PA **113** Emblem

(Litho)

2017 (25 Aug). Fruit. Dates. T PA **112** and similar vert designs. Multicoloured. P 14.
PA392 150m. Type PA **112** .... 1·30 1·20
PA393 200m. Berhi dates .... 1·70 1·60
PA394 500m. Hayani dates .... 4·25 4·00
PA392/PA394 *Set of 3* .... 6·50 6·00
MSPA395 105×70mm 1500m Palm trees .... 13·50 13·00

(Litho)

2017 (9 Oct). World Post Day. P 14.
PA396 PA **113** 500m. multicoloured .... 4·25 4·00

PA **114** Flag as Teacher

(Litho)

2017 (14 Dec). Palestinian Teacher' Day. P 14.
PA397 PA **114** 200m. multicoloured .... 1·70 1·60
PA398 400m. multicoloured .... 3·25 3·00
MSPA399 100×70mm 1500m. As Type PA **114** .... 13·50 13·00

STAMP BOOKLETS

Price is for complete booklet

Booklet No.	*Date*	*Contents and Cover Price*	*Price*
SBPA1	29.6.00	Bethleham 2000 3 panes. Nos. PA174a/PA176a (6000f.)	29·00

Syria

1919. 40 Paras = 10 Milliemes = 1 Piastre
1920. 100 Centimes (or Centiemes) = 1 Piastre
100 Piastres = 1 Syrian Pound

From 1516 to 1918 Syria was part of the Turkish Empire. The Turkish postal administration had an extensive network of offices in this region. In addition Egypt and France operated post offices in Latakia. The French office was open from June 1852 to August 1914, using unoverprinted stamps of France or stamps of the French Post Offices in the Turkish Empire see Stanley Gibbons *Central Asia* catalogue.

After the final British defeat of the Turks at Megiddo in Palestine in September 1918, Damascus, which had been entered by small Arab forces late on 30 September, was taken by an Australian Cavalry division early next day. French naval forces later landed at Beirut. For administrative purposes, Syria was divided in 1919 into a French zone of occupation, comprising a coastal strip with Beirut as chief town, and the interior, administered by Arabs.

From 23 September 1918 to 23 February 1922 E.E.F. stamps were available from their offices in Syria.

A. FRENCH MILITARY OCCUPATION

G.C. Paper. This is a cheaper paper, known as G.C. because the upper and lower margins of sheets bore these initials (= Grande Consommation), which was used for most French stamps printed between 1916 and 1920.

T E. O. 4MILLIEMES (1)

T. E. O. 1 MILLIEME (2)

T.E.O.—Territoires Ennemis Occupés

1919 (21 Nov). Issued at Beirut. Stamps of France, 1900–1917, surch as T **1**, by Gédéon Bros, Beirut.

No.	Type	Description	Unused	Used
1	**11**	1m. on 1c. grey	£275	£275
2		2m. on 2c. claret	£700	£700
		a. Small figure '2'	£3000	£3000
3		3m. on 3c. orange	£325	£325
		a. Small figure '3'	£1700	£1700
4	**15**	4m. on 15c. slate-green	75·00	75·00
5	**18**	5m. on 5c. blue-green	48·00	60·00
6		1p. on 10c. scarlet	65·00	49·00
7		2p. on 25c. blue	35·00	31·00
8	**13**	5p. on 40c. red and pale blue	48·00	55·00
		a. Small figure '5'	£160	£160
9		9p. on 50c. cinnamon and lavender	95·00	95·00
		a. Small figure '9'	£275	£275
10		10p. on 1f. lake and yellow	£130	£130
1/10 *Set of 10*			£1600	£1600

There are many minor surcharge varieties in this issue.
All the above are on G.C. paper except the 10c.

1919 (1 Dec). Stamps of French Post Offices in the Turkish Empire (French types inscr 'LEVANT') surch or optd only as T **2**, by Gédéon Bros, Beirut.

(a) Nos. 9/13 Surch

No.	Type	Description	Unused	Used
11	**11**	1m. on 1c. grey	3·75	4·00
		a. Surch inverted	40·00	40·00
12		2m. on 2c. claret	3·00	3·75
		a. Surch inverted	40·00	40·00
13		3m. on 3c. orange-red	5·00	5·25
14	**14**	4m. on 15c. pale red	2·50	3·25
		a. Surch inverted	40·00	40·00
15	**11**	5m. on 5c. green	2·10	1·90
11/15 *Set of 5*			14·50	16·00

(b) Nos. 19/23 optd 'T.E.O.' only

No.	Type	Description	Unused	Used
16	**14**	1p. on 25c. blue	1·80	1·50
		a. Opt inverted	40·00	40·00
17	**13**	2p. on 50c. brown and lavender	2·50	5·25
		a. Opt inverted	40·00	40·00
18		4p. on 1f. lake and yellow-green	5·75	7·00
19		8p. on 2f. deep lilac and buff	17·00	17·00
		a. Opt double	95·00	95·00
20		20p. on 5f. deep blue and buff	£350	£325
16/20 *Set of 5*			£350	£325

On Nos. 17/20 the overprint reads vertically upwards at the left of the stamp.
No. 11 is on G.C. paper and No. 12 exists on ordinary and G.C. paper; the rest are on ordinary paper.
Nos. 16/20 were also used in Cilicia from December 1919 to March 1920.

O. M. F. Syrie 1 MILLIEME (3)

O. M. F. Syrie 1 MILLIEME (4)

O.M.F. = Occupation Militaire Française

1920 (Feb–Mar). Stamps of France, 1900–1919, surch by Gédéon Bros, Beirut.

*(a) As T **3** ('O.M.F.' thin) (Feb)*

No.	Type	Description	Unused	Used
21	**11**	1m. on 1c. grey	5·50	10·00
		a. Surch inverted	80·00	80·00
22		2m. on 2c. claret	5·50	10·00
		a. Surch double	60·00	60·00
23	**18**	3m. on 5c. blue-green	19·00	26·00
		a. Surch double	85·00	85·00
24	**13**	20p. on 5f. deep blue and buff	£600	£600

*(b) As T **4** ('O.M.F.' thick) (Mar)*

No.	Type	Description	Unused	Used
25	**11**	1m. on 1c. grey	2·20	3·00
26		2m. on 2c. claret	5·75	7·00
27	**18**	3m. on 5c. blue-green	3·75	5·75
28		5m. on 10c. red	2·50	5·00
		a. Surch double	85·00	85·00
29	**13**	20p. on 5f. deep blue and buff	95·00	£140
30		20p. on 5f. deep blue and buff (R.)	£375	£375

Nos. 21/23 and 25/27 are on G.C. paper.

Syrian Currency

100 Syrian Piastres = 5 French Francs

O. M. F. Syrie 50 CENTIMES (5)

O. M. F. Syrie Ch. taxe 1 PIASTRE (D 6)

(Surch locally by Gédéon Bros, later by French High Commission, Beirut)

1920 (1 May–July). Stamps of France, 1900–1919, surch as T **5** (Nos. 31/33 value in CENTIMES).

No.	Type	Description	Unused	Used
31	**11**	25c. on 1c. grey	4·00	3·50
32		50c. on 2c. claret	3·50	3·50
33		75c. on 3c. orange	3·75	5·75
34	**18**	1p. on 5c. blue-green (R.)	2·75	5·00
35		1p. on 5c. blue-green (5.20)	3·50	1·00
		a. Surch inverted	35·00	35·00
36		2p. on 10c. scarlet	3·25	3·25
		a. Surch inverted	35·00	35·00
37		2p. on 25c. blue (R.) (5.20)	3·50	95
38		3p. on 25c. blue (R.)	3·75	3·75
		a. Surch inverted	35·00	35·00
39	**15**	5p. on 15c. slate-green	4·50	4·75
		a. Surch inverted	35·00	35·00
40	**13**	10p. on 40c. red and pale blue	7·00	7·50
41		25p. on 50c. cinnamon and lavender	7·75	8·50
42		50p. on 1f. lake and yellow	38·00	50·00
		a. 'PIASRTES'	£2000	£2000
43		100p. on 5f. deep blue and buff (6.20)	£350	£400
		a. 'PIASRTES'	£2000	£2000
44		100p. on 5f. deep blue and buff (R.) (6.20)	85·00	90·00
31/44 *Set of 14*			£475	£550

Value in CENTIEMES (July).

No.	Type	Description	Unused	Used
45	**11**	25c. on 1c. slate	2·00	1·10
		a. Slate-grey	4·75	2·30
		b. Error. 50c. on 1c. slate-grey	10·50	11·00
46		50c. on 2c. claret	1·60	90
		a. Surch inverted	35·00	35·00
47		75c. on 3c. orange	3·00	6·50
		a. Surch inverted	35·00	35·00
45/47 *Set of 3*			6·00	7·75

All are on G.C. paper except Nos. 36 and 43/44.

There were two printings by Gédéon Bros. In both there is a short 'y' and open 'e' in 'Syrie' but the second printing can be distinguished by the space between 'Syrie' and the figures of value which is only 1 mm instead of 2 mm.

The French High Commission made printings of Nos. 34, 37 and 39/43 which can be distinguished by the longer 'y' and almost closed 'e' in 'Syrie'. Nos. 42a and 43a occur on position 25 of this printing.

1920 (May). POSTAGE DUE. Nos. 14 and 16/18 of French Post Offices in the Turkish Empire (French types inscr 'LEVANT') surch as T D **6**, by Gédéon Bros, Beirut.

D48	**14**	1p. on 10c. carmine	£225	£225
D49		2p. on 20c. purple-brown	£225	£225
D50		3p. on 30c. deep lilac	£225	£225
D51	**13**	4p. on 40c. red and pale blue	£225	£225
		a. Thin '4'	£450	£450
D48/D51 *Set of 4*			£800	£800

Nos. D49/D50 are on G.C. paper.

(Surch by Gédéon Bros, from 1921 by French High Commission, Beirut)

1920 (June). POSTAGE DUE. Postage Due stamps of France surch as T **5**.

D52	D **11**	1p. on 10c. pale brown	4·75	8·25
D53		2p. on 20c. olive-green (R.)	4·75	8·25
		a. 'PIASTRE' ('S' omitted)	£1100	£1100
D54		3p. on 30c. pale carmine	4·75	7·00
D55		4p. on 50c. dull claret	7·50	19·00
		a. Error. 3p. on 50c. (in pair with normal)	£650	£650
D52/D55 *Set of 4*			20·00	38·00

No. D54 is on G.C. paper.

No. D55a has to be in pair with normal to distinguish it from No. D63.

See final note after No. 47 for distinguishing features of the French High Commission printings.

See also Nos. D60/D64.

(**5a**) (**6**)

1920 (Oct)–**21**. Aleppo Vilayet issue. Stamps of 1920–1921 (Gédéon printings), optd with rosette, T **5a**, at Aleppo.

A. In black

48A	**11**	25c. on 1c. (No. 45)	16·00	29·00
49A		50c. on 2c. (No. 46)	17·00	14·50
50A	**18**	1p. on 5c. (No. 35)	24·00	20·00
51A		2p. on 25c. (No. 37)	34·00	40·00
52A	**15**	5p. on 15c. (No. 39)	80·00	£100
53A	**13**	10p. on 40c. (No. 40)	£130	£140
54A		25p. on 50c. (No. 41)	£300	£300
55A		50p. on 1f. (No. 42)	£900	£900
56A		100p. on 5f. (No. 44)	£2750	£2750
48A/56A *Set of 9*			£3750	£3750

B. In red

48B	**11**	25c. on 1c. (No. 45)	19·00	18·00
49B		50c. on 2c. (No. 46)	19·00	15·00
50B	**18**	1p. on 5c. (No. 35)	25·00	15·00
51B		2p. on 25c. (No. 37)	16·00	16·00
52B	**15**	5p. on 15c. (No. 39)	70·00	£100
53B	**13**	10p. on 40c. (No. 40)	£130	£140
54B		25p. on 50c. (No. 41)	£275	£275
55B		50p. on 1f. (No. 42)	£600	£600
56B		100p. on 5f. (No. 44)	£2250	£2250
48B/56B *Set of 9*			£3000	£3000

Except for Nos. 56A and 56B all the above are on G.C. paper and No. 54B also exists on this paper.

All values exist with the rosette double in black, the 10p. to 100p. double in red and the 1p. to 100p. double, one in red and one in black. Nos. 48A/51A exist with final 'S' in the surcharge double.

Nos. 53/56 also exist overprinted in both colours on the French High Commission printings, but these were not issued.

1920 (14 Dec). AIR. Nos. 35 and 39/40 handstamped at Beirut with T **6**, in violet.

57	**18**	1p. on 5c. blue-green	£225	75·00
58	**15**	5p. on 15c. slate-green	£375	90·00
59	**13**	10p. on 40c. red and pale blue	£500	£140
57/59 *Set of 3*			£1000	£275

The above were for use on air services between Aleppo and Alexandria and between Aleppo and Déir-el-Zoor.

The handstamp was applied to the Gédéon and the High Commission printings, and there are many forgeries of it.

All values are on G.C. paper.

1921 (May)–**22**. POSTAGE DUE. Postage Due stamps of France surch as T **5** in 'CENTIEMES' or 'PIASTRES', by French High Commission, Beirut.

D60	D **11**	50c. on 10c. pale brown	1·40	2·30
		a. Error. 75c. on 10c.	£110	
		b. '50' omitted	£100	
		c. Thin '5'	£150	
		d. 'CENTIMES' for 'CENTIEMES'	16·00	16·00
D61		1p. on 20c. olive-green	1·80	2·30
D62		2p. on 30c. pale carmine	5·75	9·50
D63		3p. on 50c. dull claret	6·00	10·50
D64		5p. on 1f. claret/*straw* (2.22)	16·00	23·00
D60/D64 *Set of 5*			28·00	43·00

No. D63 is on G.C. paper.

Currency Revaluation

5 Syrian Piastres = 1 French Franc

Types of Arab Kingdom

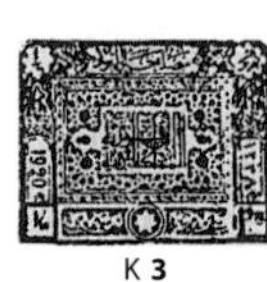

K **3**

K **4**

1921 (June–Nov). Damascus issue. Nos. K88/K95 of Arab Kingdom surch as T **5** (Nos. 60/61 in CENTIEMES), by French High Commission, Beirut.

60	K **3**	25c. on 1m. brown	7·00	5·25
61		50c. on $\frac{2}{10}$p. yellow-green	6·25	5·25
62		1p. on $\frac{3}{10}$p. orange-yellow	5·25	4·50
		a. Surch inverted	50·00	50·00
		b. Error '$\frac{2}{10}$' pi.	22·00	22·00
63	K **4**	1p. on 5m. carmine (13.11)	16·00	11·50
		a. Rose	10·00	11·50
		b. Do. *Tête-bêche* (pair)	£2750	
64		2p. on 5m. carmine	12·50	8·50
		a. Rose	9·00	8·50
		b. Do. *Tête-bêche* (pair)	£250	£250
		c. Surch inverted	50·00	50·00
65	K **3**	3p. on 1p. grey-blue	11·50	5·00
		a. Surch inverted	50·00	50·00
66		5p. on 2p. blue-green	12·00	23·00
		a. Surch inverted	50·00	50·00
67		10p. on 5p. brown-purple	11·00	14·00
68		25p. on 10p. grey	17·00	28·00
		a. Surch inverted	75·00	75·00
60/68 *Set of 9 (cheapest)*			80·00	95·00

O. M. F. Syrie Chiffre Taxe 50 CENTIEMES	O. M. F. Syrie 1 – PIASTRE	O. M. F. Syrie 2 PIASTRES
(D **7**)	(**6a**)	(**6b**)

1921 (July). POSTAGE DUE. Damascus issue. No. KD96 of Arab Kingdom surch as T D **7**, by French High Commission, Beirut.

D69	K **3**	50c. on 1p. black (R.)	6·25	12·50
D70		1p. on 1p. black (R.)	4·75	9·50

Both stamps exist with an inverted stop after 'F'.

Types of Turkey

60

65

74

75

1921 (7 July). Ain-Tab issue. Stamps of Turkey, 1916–1917, handstamped with T **6a** or T **6b**.

(a) In carmine

68*b*	**65**	1pi. on 10pa. on 20pa. rose (No. 915)	£225	£225
68*c*	**74**	1pi. on 20pa. carmine (No. 919)	£180	£180
68*d*	**60**	2pi. on 1pi. black and violet (No. 656)	£2000	£2000
68*e*	**75**	2pi. on 1pi. violet-blue (No. 920)	£120	£120
68*b*/68*e* *Set of 4*			£2250	£2250

(b) In black

68*f*	**65**	1pi. on 10pa. on 20pa. rose (No. 915)	£120	£120
68*g*	**74**	1pi. on 20pa. carmine (No. 919)	£120	£120
68*h*	**60**	2pi. on 1pi. black and violet (No. 656)	£1400	£1500
68*i*	**75**	2pi. on 1pi. violet-blue (No. 920)	£180	£180
68*f*/68*i* *Set of 4*			£1600	£1700

Nos. 68*b*/68*i* were authorised by the District Governor of Ain-Tab for mail to Aleppo and locally and were in use until 27 August 1921. Though Ain-Tab (now Gaziantep) was in Cilicia, 20 miles north of the Syrian border, in an area where French troops were fighting the Turkish Nationalists, the stamps were overprinted 'Syrie'.

1921 (July). Stamps of France surch as T **5** (Nos. 69/71, value in CENTIEMES), by French High Commission, Beirut.

69	**18**	25c. on 5c. green	4·00	1·80
70		50c. on 10c. scarlet	1·40	55
71	**15**	75c. on 15c. slate-green	1·40	1·80
72	**18**	1p. on 20c. brown-lake (*shades*)	4·00	40
73	**13**	2p. on 40c. red and pale blue	2·50	65
74		3p. on 60c. violet and blue	3·75	1·10
75		5p. on 1f. lake and yellow	7·25	7·00
76		10p. on 2f. orange and blue-green	11·00	9·00
77		25p. on 5f. deep blue and buff	£180	£180
		a. Surch in red	£9000	£9000
69/77 *Set of 9*			£190	£180

All are on G.C. paper except Nos. 70 and 76/77 and Nos. 71/72 and 75 also exist on ordinary paper.

See also Nos. 93/96*d*.

1921 (June). AIR. Nos. 72 and 75/76 handstamped with T **6**, in violet.

78	**18**	1p. on 20c. brown-lake (*shades*)	£160	65·00
79	**13**	5p. on 1f. lake and yellow	£550	£225
80		10p. on 2f. orange and blue-green	£550	£225
78/80 *Set of 3*			£1100	£475

The notes after No. 59 also apply here.

Nos. 79/80 are on G.C. paper and No. 80 also exists on ordinary paper.

O. M. F.
Syrie
2 PIASTRES
(7)

AVION
(8)

TAXE
(D 9)

(Surch by French High Commission, later by Capuchin Fathers, Beirut)

1921 (Oct). Stamps of France surch as T **7**.

81	**13**	2p. on 40c. red and pale blue	3·25	1·10
		a. Surch triple	£140	
82		3p. on 60c. violet and blue	3·25	1·10
83		5p. on 1f. lake and yellow	14·00	10·00
		a. '5' with serif at top and pointed tail	£250	£250
84		10p. on 2f. orange and blue-green	21·00	22·00
85		25p. on 5f. deep blue and buff	20·00	19·00
		a. '25 PIASTRES' omitted	£275	£275
81/85 *Set of 5*			55·00	48·00

From March 1922 the Capuchin Fathers took over the printing material from the French High Commission but it is difficult to distinguish their work apart from minor differences in spacing. Numerous minor varieties occurred, mainly in these printings.

The 2p. with '2 PIASTRES' in smaller letters is an essay.

1921 (Oct). AIR. Nos. 72 and 75/76 optd with T **8**, by French High Commission, Beirut.

86	**18**	1p. on 20c. brown-lake (*shades*)	£100	55·00
87	**13**	5p. on 1f. lake and yellow	£190	85·00
		a. Opt reading up	£500	£400
88		10p. on 2f. orange and blue-green	£250	90·00
		a. Opt double	£750	£700
86/88 *Set of 3*			£475	£200

1921 (13 Nov). POSTAGE DUE. Damascus issue. Nos. 64/65 optd with T D **9**, by French High Commission, Beirut.

D89	2p. on 5m. carmine	16·00	18·00
	a. 'A' inverted	£375	£375
D90	3p. on 1p. slate-blue	36·00	36·00

Poste par Avion
O. M. F.
Syrie
2 PIASTRES
(9)

1922 (May). AIR. Stamps of France surch as T **9**, by Capuchin Fathers, Beirut.

89	**13**	2p. on 40c. red and pale blue	31·00	65·00
90		3p. on 60c. violet and blue	31·00	65·00
91		5p. on 1f. lake and yellow	31·00	65·00
92		10p. on 2f. orange and blue-green	31·00	65·00
89/92 *Set of 4*			£110	£225

The overprint and surcharge were made by a single operation.

1922 (Nov)–**23**. Stamps of France surch as T **5** (Nos. 93/96 in CENTIEMES), by Capuchin Fathers, Beirut.

93	**11**	10c. on 2c. claret (8.23)	4·50	5·75
		a. Surch inverted	44·00	44·00
94	**18**	10c. on 5c. orange (R.) (7.23)	3·50	6·00
		a. Surch inverted	44·00	44·00
95		25c. on 5c. orange	2·50	1·00
		a. 'CENTIEMES' omitted	47·00	47·00
		b. 'N' inverted	44·00	44·00
		c. Surch inverted	44·00	44·00
		d. Surch double	47·00	47·00
		e. Surch double, one inverted	80·00	
96		50c. on 10c. green	4·00	1·60
		a. Surch double, one inverted	80·00	
96*b*		1,25p. on 25c. blue	3·50	1·00
		a. '5' omitted	75·00	
		b. '5' inserted by hand	£110	
96*c*		1,50p. on 30c. orange	4·75	1·90
		a. Thin, sloping '5'	£110	
96*d*	**13**	2p,50p. on 50c. brown and lavender	4·00	3·00
		a. '50' omitted	£140	95·00
96*e*	**15**	2,50p. on 50c. dark blue	4·50	1·40
		a. 'PIASTRE' ('S' omitted)	28·00	28·00
		b. '2' with thick straight foot	65·00	65·00
		c. Surch inverted	38·00	38·00
		d. Surch double	44·00	44·00
93/96*e* *Set of 8*			28·00	19·00

The above are all on ordinary paper but No. 96a also exists on G.C. paper.

B. ARAB KINGDOM

The Emir Faisal of the Hejaz, who with Colonel T. E. Lawrence had led the Arab forces against the Turks, organised an Arab State in the interior of Syria, with Damascus as capital. At Christmas 1919 fighting began between Arabs and the French, who aimed at control of all Syria. On 8 March 1920 a Syrian National Congress declared for complete independence and on 11 March the Emir Faisal was proclaimed King of Syria.

I. PROVISIONAL ISSUES FOR ALEPPO

1

2

1918 (Nov). Issued at Aleppo. Handstamped. Imperf.

A1 **1** (½pi.) greyish...

A2 **2** (½pi.) greyish...

Due to lack of availability of E.E.F. stamps the local Arab Authorities produced two stamps in the form of cut square vignettes with a handstamped greyish 26 mm diameter negative seal. The stamp having Arabic text translates to: 'The prescribed fee has been paid, 1337' whereas the other stamp shows a similar inscription in French: 'DROIT DE TAXE PERCU ALEP'. The stamps were in use for a few days at most and in Aleppo only.

II. ISSUES FOR WHOLE OF INTERIOR

Types of Turkey

15 21 22 23 28 30 31 32 33 34 36 37 38 39 41 45

47

48

D 49

60

62

63

64

65

69

73

74

75

76

1920 (Jan). Various stamps of Turkey handstamped with T K **1** (vert or horiz, according to shape), in black or violet or surch also with new values as shown. Nos. K31, K49, K77/K78 and KD18 are also optd in red.

A. Without Turkish Star and Crescent opt

(a) 1909 type

K1	**28**	20pa. rose-carmine	£180	£180

(b) Pictorial issue of 1914–1915 (Nos. K8 and K11 previously surch)

K2	**32**	1m. on 2pa. claret	2·10	2·10
K3	**33**	1m. on 4pa. sepia	2·10	2·10
K4	**34**	2m. on 5pa. dull carmine	3·00	3·00
K5	**36**	4m. on 10pa. green	13·00	13·00
K6	**37**	20pa. red	3·00	3·00
K7	**38**	1pi. bright blue	5·50	5·50
K8	**39**	1pi. on 1½pi. grey and rose (No. 521)	£750	£750
K9	**41**	2pi. black and green	£180	£180
K10	**45**	25pi. dull yellow-green	£700	£700
K11	**48**	25pi. on 200pi. black and green (No. 535)	£1000	£1000
K12	**47**	100pi. indigo	£900	£900

(c) As last, optd with small star

K13	**36**	4m. on 10pa. green (No. 516)	2·00	2·00
K14	**37**	20pa. red (No. 517)	£550	£550
K15	**38**	1pi. bright blue (No. 518)	£180	£180
K15*a*	**38**	1pi. on 1pi. blue		

(d) Postage Due stamps of 1914 (inscr 'CHIFFRE-TAXE')

KD16	D **49**	2m. on 5pa. purple	17·00	17·00
KD17	D **50**	20pa. carmine	17·00	17·00
KD18	D **51**	1pi. deep blue	17·00	17·00
KD19	D **52**	2pi. grey	17·00	17·00

*B. Optd with T **53***

(a) 1892 type

K20	**15**	2pi. orange-brown	3·75	3·75

(b) Surch '5 Cinq 5 Paras'

K21	**15**	2m. on 5pa. on 10pa. green (No. 536)	1·80	1·80

(c) 1901 type

K22	**21**	20pa. carmine	5·25	5·25
K23		1pi. dull blue	9·00	9·00
K24		25pi. deep brown	£750	£750

(d) 1905 type

K25	**23**	2m. on 5pa. yellow-buff	45·00	45·00
K26		1pi. blue	£110	£110
K27		2pi. slate	55·00	55·00
K28		2pi. slate (optd with Type **24**)	55·00	55·00
K29		5pi. brown	23·00	23·00

(e) 1909 type

K30	**28**	20pa. rose-carmine	5·25	5·25
K31		2pi. black	10·50	10·50

(f) 1913 type (GPO, Constantinople)

K32	**30**	4m. on 10pa. green	3·25	3·25
K33		20pa. rose	21·00	21·00
K34		1pi. ultramarine	11·50	11·50
K35		5pi. purple	45·00	45·00

*C. Optd with T **54***

(a) 1905 type

K36	**23**	10pi. dull orange	£700	£700

(b) 1909 type

K37	**28**	20pa. rose-carmine	5·25	5·25
K38		1pi. ultramarine	20·00	20·00
K39		5pi. slate-purple	£600	£600

(c) 1913 type (GPO, Constantinople)

K40	**30**	1pi. ultramarine	20·00	20·00

*D. Optd with T **55***

*(a) 1892 type surch with T **56***

K41	**15**	4m. on 10pa. on 20pa. dull rose	2·50	2·50

(b) 1901 type

K42	**21**	5pi. rosy mauve	90·00	90·00

(c) 1905 type

K43	**23**	1pi. blue	9·00	9·00
K44		1pi. blue (optd with Type **24**)	23·00	23·00

(d) 1913 type (GPO, Constantinople–horiz)

K45	**30**	20pa. rose	5·25	5·25
K46		20pa. rose (optd with Type **26**)	23·00	23·00
K47		1pi. ultramarine	26·00	26·00

(e) Postal Jubilee issue of 1916 (GPO, Constantinople–vert)

K48	**60**	4m. on 10pa. carmine	1·70	1·70
K49		20pa. blue	1·20	1·20
K50		1pi. black and violet	5·25	5·25
K51		5pi. black and brown	9·00	9·00

*E. Optd with T **57***

(a) 1901 type (internal)

K52	**21**	2pi. orange	9·75	9·75

*(b) 1901 type optd with T N **23***

K53	**21**	20pa. carmine (No. 732)	£550	£550

(c) 1901 type (foreign)

K54	**22**	20pa. magenta	21·00	21·00

*(d) 1901 type optd with T N **23***

K55	**22**	20pa. magenta (No. 737)	5·50	5·50

(e) 1905 type

K56	**23**	2m. on 5pa. yellow-buff	90·00	90·00
K57		20pa. rose	7·50	7·50
K58		1pi. blue (optd with Type **24**)	10·50	10·50

(f) Adrianople issue of 1913 (Selim Mosque)

K59	**31**	4m. on 10pa. green	14·50	14·50

(g) Postal Jubilee issue of 1916 (GPO, Constantinople)

K60	**60**	5pi. black and brown	9·00	9·00

*F. Occupation of Sinai Peninsula issue of 1916 (Optd with T **59**)*

K60*a*	**21**	2m. on 5pa. purple		
K61	**28**	20pa. rose-carmine	9·75	9·75
K62		1pi. ultramarine	20·00	20·00

G. Postal Jubilee issue of 1916 (Old GPO, Constantinople)

K63	**60**	2m. on 5pa. green	£550	£550
K64		4m. on 10pa. carmine	75·00	75·00
K65		20pa. blue	4·50	4·50
K66		1pi. black and violet	3·25	3·25
K67		5pi. black and brown	9·00	9·00

H. Pictorial issue of 1916–1917

K68	**62**	10pi. violet (Dolmabahçe Palace)	£200	£200
K69		10pi. deep green/*grey*	£250	£250
K70		10pi. brown	£700	£700
K71	**63**	25pi. carmine/*buff* (Sentry)	£180	£180
K72	**64**	50pi. indigo (Sultan Muhammad V)	£400	£400

I. War Charity stamp of 1917 (Soldier and family)

K73	**65**	4m. on 10pa. purple	4·75	4·75

*J. Provisional of 1917 (Surch with T **71**)*

K74	**65**	4m. on 10pa. on 20pa. rosine	4·75	4·75

K. Pictorial stamps of 1917–1918

K75	**73**	4m. on 10pa. green (Lighthouse), (vert)	3·00	3·00
K76	**74**	20pa. carmine (Martyrs' Column)	5·50	5·50
K77	**75**	1pi. violet-blue (Map of Gallipoli)	6·00	6·00
K78	**76**	1pi. on 50pa. blue (Map of Gallipoli)	2·50	2·50

*L. Provisional of 1918 (Howitzer) (Surch with T **70**)*

K79	**69**	5pi. on 2pa. greenish blue	5·50	5·50

*M. On Turkish Fiscal stamp (T **7** of Cilicia)*

K80	–	5m. on 5pa. red	1·80	1·80

(K **2**) ('Syrian Arab Government')   (2/10pi.)   (3/10pi.)

1920 (Mar). Handstamped with T K **2** and with values as shown in preceding issue and above for fractions, in black, green or violet.

*(a) On Turkish fiscal stamp, T **7** of Cilicia*

K81	1m. on 5pa. red	1·40	1·40
K82	2m. on 5pa. red	1·40	1·40
K83	2/10pi. on 5pa. red	75	75
K84	3/10pi. on 5pa. red	75	75
K85	1pi. on 5pa. red	2·50	1·50

*(b) T **34** of Turkey (Leander's Tower) handstamped only. Triangle and value in violet or triangle violet and value black*

K86	2m. on 5pa. dull purple	13·00	13·00

*(c) T **74** of Turkey (Martyr's Column) handstamped only and with triangle only. Violet or black*

K87	20pa. carmine	1·20	1·20

K 3

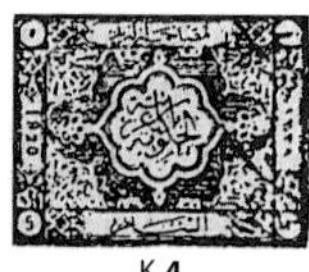
K 4

(Litho in Damascus)

1920 (Mar). P 11½.

		(a) Size 22×17 mm		
K88	K **3**	1m. brown	45	45
		(b) Size 27×21 mm		
K89	K **3**	²⁄₁₀pi. yellow-green	1·10	60
K90		³⁄₁₀pi. orange-yellow	60	45
		a. Error. ²⁄₁₀pi.	24·00	24·00
K91	K **4**	5m. carmine	45	45
		a. Rose	45	45
		b. Do. *Tête-bêche* (pair)	26·00	26·00
K92	K **3**	1pi. grey-blue	55	45
K93		2pi. blue-green	4·50	1·40
		(c) Size 32×25 mm		
K94	K **3**	5pi. brown-purple	6·00	3·00
K95		10pi. grey	6·00	4·50
K88/K95 *Set of 8*			18·00	10·00

1920 (Mar). POSTAGE DUE. P 11½.

KD96	K **3**	1pi. black	3·00	3·00

(Litho in Aleppo)

1920. Fine impression. P 11½.

K97	K **4**	5m. brown-red	45·00	2·30

تذكار
استقلال سوريه المتحده
٨ آذار ١٩٢٠
(K **5**)

('Commemoration of Syrian Independence, 8 March 1920')

1920. Optd with T K **5**.

K98	K **4**	5m. brown-red	£850	£450
		a. Opt inverted	£1000	£550

On 25 April 1920 the Supreme Council of the Allies offered to France the mandate to administer Syria under the League of Nations. On 25 July French troops took Damascus and King Faisal was dethroned. In 1921 he was made king of Iraq.

Arab Kingdom stamps were replaced by stamps of the French Military Occupation in the *Etat d'Alep*, north of the Hama-Deir as Zor line, from 1st October 1920. However, south of the line, in the *Etat de Damas*, the replacement did not occur until 1st June 1921.

C. FRENCH MANDATED TERRITORY

The League of Nations approved the French mandate on 24 July 1922 and it became effective on 29 September 1923.

I. ISSUES FOR LEBANON AND SYRIA

At the end of the military occupation period the stamps with 'O.M.F. Syrie' overprints were withdrawn. Great Lebanon, the Christian area, which had had a separate status from Syria since 1 September 1920, but where 'O.M.F. Syrie' stamps had been used, now had its name joined to that of Syria on the stamps in use.

Syrie
Grand Liban
25
CENTIEMES
(**10**)

Syrie - Grand Liban
10 PIASTRES
(**11**)

(Surch by Capuchin Fathers, Beirut)

1923 (Sept–Dec). Stamps of France, 1900–1921 surch.

		(a) As T **10**		
97	**11**	10c. on 2c. claret	55	90
98	**18**	25c. on 5c. orange (10.23)	2·00	3·50
99		50c. on 10c. green (10.23)	1·80	1·80
		a. '0,50' for '50'	£190	
		b. '25' for '50'	£400	£400
100	**15**	75p. on 15c. olive-green (11.23)	3·75	6·00
101	**18**	1p. on 20c. chocolate	3·25	2·30
102		1,25p. on 25c. blue (10.23)	3·25	2·75
103		1,50p. on 30c. orange (10.23)	2·30	4·00
104		1,50p. on 30c. scarlet (12.23)	1·90	5·00
105	**15**	2,50p. on 50c. blue (10.23)	1·60	90
97/105 *Set of 9*			18·00	24·00
		(b) As T **11**		
106	**13**	2p. on 40c. red and pale blue	3·00	90
		a. Pair, one without surch		
107		3p. on 60c. violet and blue (12.23)	4·75	6·50
108		5p. on 1f. lake and yellow (10.23)	5·75	7·25
109		10p. on 2f. orange and blue-green (12.23)	18·00	28·00
110		25p. on 5f. deep blue and buff (12.23)	65·00	75·00
106/110 *Set of 5*			85·00	£110
		(c) T **30** *(Pasteur) surch as T* **10** *(Dec)*		
111	**30**	50c. on 10c. green	3·50	5·75
112		1,50p. on 30c. red	3·25	5·25
113		2,50p. on 50c. blue	2·50	5·75
		a. '5' omitted	85·00	
111/113 *Set of 3*			8·25	15·00

Nos. 100, 102, 106 and 108 exist on G.C. paper.

Most values exist with surcharge inverted (*Price un £55 each*) or double (*Price un £60 each*).

Poste par Avion
Syrie - Grand Liban
2 PIASTRES
(**11a**)

(Surch by Capuchin Fathers, Beirut)

1923 (Nov). AIR. Stamps of France, 1900–1920, surch as T **11a**. 2¼ mm between second and third lines.

114	**13**	2p. on 40c. red and pale blue	65·00	65·00
		a. 3¾ mm between 2nd and 3rd lines	£120	£120
		b. Do. Error. 'Liabn'	£750	£750
115		3p. on 60c. violet and blue	65·00	65·00
		a. 3¾ mm between 2nd and 3rd lines	£120	£120
		b. Do. Error. 'Liabn'	£750	£750
116		5p. on 1f. lake and yellow	65·00	65·00
		a. 3¾ mm between 2nd and 3rd lines	£120	£110
		b. Do. Error. 'Liabn'	£750	£750
117		10p. on 2f. orange and blue-green	65·00	65·00
		a. Surch double	£200	
		b. 3¾ mm between 2nd and 3rd lines	£120	£120
		c. Do. Error. 'Liabn'	£750	£750
114/117 *Set of 4*			£225	£225

1923 (Nov–Dec). POSTAGE DUE. Postage Due stamps of France surch as T **10**.

D118	D **11**	50c. on 10c. pale brown	5·25	7·50
D119		1p. on 20c. olive-green	5·50	8·50
D120		2p. on 30c. carmine	3·50	7·75
D121		3p. on 50c. dull claret	3·50	7·75
		a. '2,50' for '3'	£250	
D122		5p. on 1f. claret/*straw*	7·00	12·00
D118/D122 *Set of 5*			22·00	39·00

No. D120 exists on G.C. paper.

II. ISSUES FOR SYRIA

From 1 January 1924 separate issues of stamps were made for Great Lebanon; these are listed under Lebanon. The following issues were made for Syria only.

SYRIE
1,25
PIASTRE
(**12**)

SYRIE
2 PIASTRES
(**13**)

(Surch by Capuchin Fathers, Beirut)

1924 (Jan–June). Stamps of France, 1900–1921, surch.

		(a) As T **12**		
118	**11**	10c. on 2c. claret	1·50	1·10
119	**18**	25c. on 5c. orange	1·90	1·30
		a. '25' omitted	24·00	
120		50c. on 10c. green	1·90	1·10
121	**15**	75c. on 15c. olive-green	3·75	3·00
		a. 'YSRIE'	28·00	
122	**18**	1p. on 20c. chocolate	2·50	65
		a. 'PIASTRES'	26·00	
123		1,25p. on 25c. blue	3·50	4·50
124		1,50p. on 30c. orange	4·50	6·00

125		1,50p. on 30c. scarlet (4.24)	3·25	5·25
126	15	2,50p. on 50c. blue	2·50	1·30
118/126 *Set of 9*			23·00	22·00

(b) As T **13**

127	13	2p. on 40c. red and pale blue	2·10	85
128		3p. on 60c. violet and blue	3·50	4·75
129		5p. on 1f. lake and yellow	6·25	5·25
130		10p. on 2f. orange and blue-green	7·50	9·75
131		25p. on 5f. deep blue and buff	11·00	16·00
127/131 *Set of 5*			27·00	33·00

(c) As T **12** *(June)*

132	30	50c. on 10c. green	2·50	3·50
133		1,50p. on 30c. red	3·25	6·50
134		2,50p. on 50c. blue	2·75	4·50
132/134 *Set of 3*			7·75	13·00

Nos. 121/123 exist on G.C. paper.

Poste par Avion
SYRIE
2 PIASTRES
(**13a**)

(Surch by Capuchin Fathers, Beirut)

1924 (Jan). AIR. Stamps of France, 1900–1920. surch as T **13a**.

135	13	2p. on 40c. red and pale blue	5·75	10·50
		a. Surch double	34·00	
136		3p. on 60c. violet and blue	5·75	10·50
		a. Surch inverted	£100	
137		5p. on 1f. lake and yellow	5·75	10·50
138		10p. on 2f. orange and blue-green	5·75	10·50
135/138 *Set of 4*			21·00	38·00

1924 (Jan). POSTAGE DUE. Postage Due stamps of France surch as T **12**.

D139	D 11	50c. on 10c. pale brown	1·40	6·50
D140		1p. on 20c. olive-green	2·50	6·50
D141		2p. on 30c. carmine	3·00	7·50
D142		3p. on 50c. dull claret	1·90	7·50
D143		5p. on 1f. claret/*straw*	2·75	7·75
		a. Surch inverted	£120	65·00
D139/D143 *Set of 5*			10·50	32·00

No. D141 exists on G.C. paper.

1924 (June). Olympic Games stamps of France T **31** surch as T **12**.

139	50c. on 10c. green and yellow-green	33·00	50·00
140	1,25p. on 25c. deep and dull carmine	33·00	55·00
141	1,50p. on 30c. red and black	33·00	70·00
142	2,50p. on 50c. ultramarine and blue	33·00	65·00
139/142 *Set of 4*		£120	£225

Designs: Horiz—10c. T **31**; 25c. Notre Dame. Vert—30c. Mllan de Crotone; 50c. The Victor.

Syrie
0, P. 50
سوريا
١/٢ الغرش
(**14**)

غرش ٢
(a) (singular)

غروش ٢
(b) (plural)

Fourth line of surcharge ('Piastres')

(Surch by Capuchin Fathers, Beirut)

1924 (July)–**25**. Stamps of France, surch as T **14**.

(a) Issues of 1900–1924

143	11	0,p.10 on 2c. claret	1·10	2·10
144	18	0,p.25 on 5c. orange	1·10	3·75
145		0,p.50 on 10c. green	1·50	5·25
146	15	0,p.75 on 15c. olive-green	2·50	6·00
		a. Comma omitted	5·00	7·50
147	18	1p. on 20c. chocolate	2·10	90
148		1,p.25 on 25c. blue	3·75	5·25
149		1p.50 on 30c. scarlet (no comma)	3·25	3·50
		a. With comma after '1'	4·50	4·50
150		1,p.50 on 30c. orange	26·00	26·00
151		2p. on 35c. violet (26.2.25)	3·25	6·25
152	13	2p. on 40c. red and pale blue (b)	3·75	1·40
		a. Arab surch in singular (a)	3·50	2·50
153		2p. on 45c. deep green and blue (26.2.25)	9·75	14·50
154		3p. on 60c. violet and blue	3·75	3·25
155	15	3p. on 60c. violet (26.2.25)	3·75	7·25
156		4p. on 85c. vermilion	2·10	4·50
157	13	5p. on 1f. lake and yellow	3·00	5·00
158		10p. on 2f. orange and blue-green	4·75	8·75
159		25p. on 5f. deep blue and buff	5·75	9·00
143/159 *Set of 17*			75·00	£100

Nos. 143/149, 152/152a, 154/155 exist with surcharge inverted (*Price un £45 each*).

Nos. 143/149 and 152/152a exist with surcharge double (*Price un £55 each*).

(b) T **30** *(Pasteur)*

160	30	0,p.50 on 10c. green	1·90	1·50
161		0p.75 on 15c. green (26.2.25)	4·00	6·50
162		1,p.50 on 30c. red	3·00	5·25
163		2p. on 45c. red (26.2.25)	3·50	6·25
164		2p.50 on 50c. blue	3·00	1·90
165		4p. on 75c. blue	4·75	7·00
160/165 *Set of 6*			18·00	26·00

Nos. 160/164 exist with surcharge inverted (*Price un £45 each*) or double (*Price un £55 each*).

(c) (Olympic Games) (26.9.24)

166	0,p.50 on 10c. green and yellow-green	23·00	65·00
167	1p.25 on 25c. deep and dull carmine	23·00	49·00
168	1p.50 on 30c. red and black	23·00	44·00
169	2p.50 on 50c. ultramarine and blue	23·00	44·00
166/169 *Set of 4*		85·00	£180

(d) T **35** *(Ronsard) (12.24)*

170	35	4p. on 75c. blue/*bluish*	1·50	6·50
		a. Surch inverted		

Syrie
2 Piastres
سوريا
غروش ٢
Avion
طيارة
(**15**)

(Surch by Capuchin Fathers, Beirut)

1924 (1 July). AIR. Stamps of France, 1900–1924, surch as T **15**.

171	13	2p. on 40c. red and pale blue	6·75	12·00
		a. Surch inverted	60·00	
172		3p. on 60c. violet and blue	6·75	23·00
		a. Surch inverted	60·00	
		b. '2' for '3'	70·00	
173		5p. on 1f. lake and yellow	6·75	23·00
		a. Surch inverted	60·00	
174		10p. on 2f. orange and blue-green	6·75	17·00
		a. Surch inverted	60·00	
		b. 'PIASTRSE'	£200	
171/174 *Set of 4*			24·00	70·00

1924 (1 July). POSTAGE DUE. Postage Due stamps of France surch as T **14**.

D175	D 11	0p.50 on 10c. pale brown	1·10	4·75
D176		1p. on 20c. olive-green	2·00	6·50
D177		2p. on 30c. carmine (b)	2·50	6·25
		a. Arab surch in singular (a)	10·50	15·00
D178		3p. on 50c. dull claret (b)	3·75	7·25
		a. Arab surch in singular (a)	10·50	15·00
D179		5p. on 1f. claret/*straw* (b)	4·75	9·00
		a. Arab surch in singular (a)	10·50	15·00
D175/D179 *Set of 5*			12·50	30·00

PRINTERS AND PROCESS. Nos. 175 to 270 were designed by J. de la Nézière and printed in photogravure by Vaugirard, Paris.

16 Hama

18 Damascus

17 Merkab

(**19**)

1925 (1 Mar). Types **16**, **18** and horiz views as T **17**. P 12½ (No. 175) or 13½ (others).

175 0p.10 violet .... 30 1·10
176 0p.25 olive-black .... 1·90 1·70
177 0p.50 yellow-green .... 1·20 50
178 0p.75 brown-red .... 1·60 2·40
179 1p. claret 90 40
180 1p.25 green .... 4·00 4·00
181 1p.50 bright rose 90 90
182 2p. sepia .... 3·75 70
183 2p.50 light blue .... 3·25 3·25
184 3p. brown .... 2·10 55
185 5p. bright violet .... 1·70 55
186 10p. plum .... 6·50 1·40
187 25p. bright blue .... 6·75 7·25
175/187 *Set of* 13 .... 31·00 22·00

Views: 0p.10 T **16**; 0p.25 T **17**; 0p.50, Alexandretta; 0p.75, Hama; 1p. T **18**; 1p.25, Latakia; 1p.50, Damascus; 2p., 25p. Palmyra (*different*); 2p.50, Kalat Yamoun; 3p. Bridge of Daphne; 5p., 10p. Aleppo (*different*).

1925 (1 Mar). AIR. Nos. 182 and 184/186 optd with T **19**.

188 2p. sepia (G.) .... 3·50 7·75
189 3p. brown (G.) .... 2·75 7·75
190 5p. bright violet (G.) .... 2·40 4·00
191 10p. plum (G.) .... 2·75 5·00
188/191 *Set of* 4 .... 10·50 22·00

D **20**

D **21**

D **22**

(**20**)

1925 (1 Mar)–**31**. POSTAGE DUE. T D **20** and similar views and Types D **21**/D **22**. P 13½.

D192 D **20** 0p.50 brown/*yellow* (Hama) .... 65 2·50
D193 1p. plum/*rose* (Antioch) (*vert*) 35 70
D194 2p. black/*blue* (Tarsus) .... 1·20 3·25
D195 3p. black/*red* (Banias) .... 1·90 2·30
D196 5p. black/*green* (Castle) .... 1·70 3·50
D197 D **21** 8p. black/*blue* (3.31) .... 10·50 12·00
D198 D **22** 15p. black/*rose* (3.31) .... 16·00 21·00
D192/D198 *Set of* 7 .... 29·00 41·00

1926 (Apr). AIR. Nos. 182 and 184/186 optd with T **20**.

192 2p. sepia (R.) .... 3·75 5·75
a. Opt inverted .... 60·00
193 3p. brown (R.) .... 2·75 3·75
a. Opt inverted ....
194 5p. bright violet (R.) .... 3·50 4·50
a. Opt inverted .... 60·00
195 10p. plum (R.) .... 3·50 7·50
a. Opt inverted .... 60·00
192/195 *Set of* 4 .... 12·00 19·00

Nos. 188/191 also exist overprinted with T **20** but there is some doubt as to whether they were issued (*Price per set un* £190).

See also Nos. 225/226 and 229.

Secours aux Réfugiés
Affᵗ 0P.50

(**21**)

Secours
aux
Réfugiés
Affᵗ 0P.50

(**22**)

1926 (Apr). War Refugees Fund.

(a) POSTAGE. Stamps of 1925 surch as T **21** *or with T* **22** *(No. 199)*

196 0p.25 on 0p.25 olive-black (R.) .... 3·50 7·25
197 0p.25 on 0p.50 yellow-green .... 3·50 8·25
a. Surch inverted .... 47·00
198 0p.25 on 0p.75 brown-red .... 3·00 6·50
a. Surch inverted .... 47·00
199 0p.50 on 1p. claret .... 3·50 6·25
a. Surch inverted .... 47·00
200 0p.50 on 1p.25 green (R.) .... 3·50 8·75
a. Surch inverted .... 47·00
201 0p.50 on 1p.50 bright rose .... 3·50 7·75
a. Surch inverted .... 47·00
202 0p.75 on 2p. sepia (R.) .... 3·50 8·75
203 0p.75 on 2p.50 light blue (R.) .... 3·50 8·25
204 1p. on 3p. brown (R.) .... 3·50 7·25
a. Surch inverted .... 47·00
205 1p. on 5p. bright violet .... 3·50 4·50
206 2p. on 10p. plum .... 3·50 7·75
a. 'au' for 'aux' .... 24·00
b. 't' of 'Afft' omitted .... 21·00
207 5p. on 25p. bright blue (R.) .... 3·50 9·00
196/207 *Set of* 12 .... 37·00 80·00

(b) AIR. Nos. 192/195 surch as T **21**

208 1p. on 2p. sepia (R.+Blk.) .... 4·50 9·50
209 2p. on 3p. brown (R.+Blk.) .... 4·25 9·50
a. '2' omitted £300
210 3p. on 5p. bright violet (R.+Blk.) .... 4·25 6·00
a. 'Secours aux Réfugiés' omitted £375
211 5p. on 10p. plum .... 4·25 8·25
a. 'au' for 'aux' £110
208/211 *Set of* 4 .... 16·00 30·00

On Nos. 208/210 the top two lines of T **21** are in black and the rest in red, on No. 211 the whole is in black.

The stamps were sold at face value plus the surcharge but had franking power only to the value of the surcharge, the original face value going to the war refugees fund.

05

(**22a**)

3P·50

(**23**)

4P·50

(**24**)

1926 (Sept–Dec). Pictorial stamps of 1925 surch as T **23** or T **24**.

212 **23** 3p.50 on 0p.75 brown-red .... 1·50 4·50
213 4p. on 0p.25 olive-black (8.10) .... 3·25 2·75
214 **24** 4p. on 0p.25 olive-black (12.26) .... 4·75 60
a. Surch double (Bk.+R.) £120
b. Surch double, one inverted £120
215 4p.50 on 0p.75 brown-red (12.26) .... 1·40 60
a. Surch double (Bk.+R.) £140
216 **23** 6p. on 2p.50 light blue .... 1·50 1·90
217 **24** 7p.50 on 2p.50 light blue (12.26) .... 1·40 80
a. Surch double (Bk.+R.) £190
218 **23** 12p. on 1p.25 green .... 3·25 5·00
219 **24** 15p. on 25p. bright blue (12.26) .... 3·00 1·10
220 **23** 20p. on 1p.25 green (8.10) .... 3·50 6·00
212/220 *Set of* 9 .... 21·00 21·00

In Nos. 214/215 the '4' has a slanting foot as in T **24**. In No. 213 it is normal.

Most of the above exist with surcharge inverted or double; also with surcharge on back and front.

For surcharges as Nos. 214 and 217 but in red, see Nos. 224/224*a*.

1928 (July)–**30**. Pictorial stamps of 1925 surch.

(a) With T **22a**

221 05 on 0p.10 violet (R.) (2.11.28) .... 75 1·20

(b) As T **23**

222 1p. on 3p. brown (6.30) .... 3·25 1·20

(c) As T **24**

223 2p. on 1p.25 green (R.) .... 4·50 75
224 4p. on 0p.25 olive-black (R.) .... 3·50 1·30
224*a* 7p.50 on 2p.50 light blue (R.) .... 4·50 70
221/224*a* *Set of* 5 .... 15·00 4·75

No. 224 has the '4' with slanting foot as in T **24**.

1929 (June)–**30**. AIR. Stamps of 1925 optd with T **20** or surch in addition as T **24**.

225 0p.50 yellow-green (R.) .... 1·80 2·00
a. Opt inverted £100
b. Opt double £100
c. Opt double, one inverted £140
226 1p. claret (opt vert down) .... 2·75 3·00
227 2p. on 1p.25 green (R.) (1.30) .... 5·00 5·50
a. Surch double £140
228 15p. on 25p. bright blue (R.) .... 6·00 8·25
a. Surch double £200
229 25p. bright blue (R.) .... 8·25 9·00
a. Surch inverted £190
225/229 *Set of* 5 .... 21·00 25·00

(25)

1929 (8 Sept). Damascus Industrial Exhibition.

(a) POSTAGE. Types **17**, **18** *and similar types, optd with T* **25**

230	0p.50 yellow-green (R.)	4·75	5·00
231	1p. claret (opt vert up) (B.)	4·75	5·00
232	1p.50 bright rose (B.)	4·75	5·00
233	3p. brown (B.)	4·75	5·00
	a. Opt double		
234	5p. bright violet (R.)	4·75	5·00
	a. Opt double		
235	10p. plum (B.)	4·75	5·00
236	25p. bright blue (R.)	4·75	5·00
230/236	*Set of 7*	30·00	32·00

(b) AIR. Nos. 225/226, 192/195 and 229 optd with T **25**

237	0p.50 yellow-green (R.)	4·50	8·25
238	1p. claret (opt vert up) (B.)	4·50	8·50
239	2p. sepia (V.)	4·50	5·75
240	3p. brown (B.)	4·50	5·75
241	5p. bright violet (R.)	4·50	8·50
242	10p. plum (B.)	4·50	6·00
243	25p. bright blue (R.)	4·50	6·00
237/243	*Set of 7*	28·00	44·00

26 Hama

I. II.

27 Damascus

28 River Euphrates

1930 (Sept)–**36**. Various views and frames.

(a) As T **26**. *Litho. P 12½*

244	0p.10 magenta (1.31)	90	70
244*a*	0p.10 purple (I) (5.32)	2·30	1·10
244*b*	0p.10 purple (II) (3.35)	55	1·60
245	0p.20 deep blue (1.31)	70	3·25
245*a*	0p.20 orange-red (7.33)	75	3·25
246	0p.25 grey-green (4.31)	3·25	2·30
246*a*	0p.25 deep violet (7.33)	2·50	4·50
244/246*a*	*Set of 7*	9·75	15·00

(b) As T **27**. *Photo. P 13½*

247	0p.50 bright violet (1.31)	2·00	45
247*a*	0p.75 orange-vermilion (8.32)	2·00	1·20
248	1p. green (1.31)	3·50	45
248*a*	1p. yellow-brown (1936)	4·00	60
249	1p.50 yellow-brown (1.31)	10·50	5·75
249*a*	1p.50 green (7.33)	14·50	4·50
250	2p. violet (1.31)	4·00	45
251	3p. apple-green (1.31)	4·50	4·75
252	4p. orange	2·10	45
253	4p.50 carmine (1.31)	3·50	1·20
254	6p. greenish black	3·25	1·30
255	7p.50 blue	3·75	1·00
256	10p. brown	4·50	80
257	15p. deep green	6·25	1·50
258	25p. maroon (1.31)	4·00	2·75
259	50p. sepia	65·00	48·00
260	100p. orange-vermilion (3.31)	70·00	70·00
247/260	*Set of 17*	£190	£130

Designs: As T **26**—0p.10 (T **26**), 0p.25, Hama (*different*); 0p.20, Aleppo. As T **27**—0p.50, Alexandretta; 0p.75, 4p.50, Homs; 1p., 7p.50, Aleppo (*different*); 1p.50, 4p. (T **27**), 100p. Damascus (*different*); 2p., 10p. Antioch (*different*), 3p. Bosra; 6p. Sednaya; 15p. Hama; 25p. St. Simeon; 50p. Palmyra.

The 1932–1936 colour changes of the 0p.10, 0p.20, 0p.25 and 1p. stamps are in redrawn designs, differing in several details from the original issues.

The word 'VAUGIRARD', forming part of the printer's imprint, is reversed on No. 247*a*.

1931 (Jan)–**33**. AIR. T **28** and similar horiz designs. P 13½.

261	0p.50 yellow (3.31)	1·60	1·70
261*a*	0p.50 sepia (1.7.33)	3·75	3·75
262	1p. red-brown (5.31)	3·50	2·40
263	2p. Prussian blue	4·25	3·75
264	3p. deep blue-green	2·75	2·00
265	5p. purple (3.31)	2·50	2·00
266	10p. greenish blue	2·40	2·00
267	15p. orange-vermilion (4.31)	3·25	2·75
268	25p. brown-orange	5·25	3·75
269	50p. black (5.31)	6·50	6·50
270	100p. magenta	7·75	5·50
261/270	*Set of 11*	39·00	32·00

Designs: Potez 29-4 biplane over—0p.50, Homs; 1p., 10p. Damascus (*different*); 2p. T **28**; 3p. Palmyra; 5p. Deir-el-Zor; 15p. Aleppo Citadel; 25p. Hama; 50p. Zebdani; 100p. Telebissé.

The designer's and printer's imprints on No. 261 measure 7½ mm and 8½ mm respectively and on 261*a*, 8 mm and 9 mm.

D. REPUBLIC UNDER FRENCH MANDATE

After a two-year insurrection of the Druses in 1925–1927 had been defeated, the French High Commissioner produced a constitution for Syria on 22 May 1930. Syria and Latakia were to be republics under French Mandate.

29 Parliament House, Damascus

31 Farman F.190 Aeroplane over Bloudan

30 Aboû l'Alâ al Ma'arri

30a President Mohammed Ali Bey el-Abed

30b Saladin

(Des M. Kurcheh (T **29**, T **30a**), Y. Cherif (T **30**, T **30b**) and S. Namani (T **31**). Recess (numerals typo) Institut de Gravure, Paris)

1934 (2 Aug). Establishment of Republic. P 12½.

(a) POSTAGE

271	**29**	0p.10 olive-green	2·75	2·50
272		0p.20 black	2·10	2·40
273		0p.25 vermilion	2·75	2·50
274		0p.50 ultramarine	2·50	2·50
275		0p.75 purple	2·75	2·50
276	**30**	1p. vermilion	4·50	5·25
277		1p.50 green	6·00	6·00
278		2p. lake-brown	6·25	6·25
279		3p. turquoise-blue	55·00	10·50
280		4p. violet	9·00	6·50
281		4p.50 carmine	11·50	9·00
282		5p. blue	7·50	9·00
283		6p. sepia	7·50	8·25
284		7p.50 ultramarine	11·50	12·50
285	**30a**	10p. sepia	15·00	15·00
286		15p. blue	18·00	13·00
287		25p. scarlet	36·00	48·00
288	**30b**	50p. sepia	65·00	65·00
289		100p. lake	70·00	70·00
271/289		*Set of 19*	£300	£275

(b) AIR

290	**31**	0p.50 brown	4·00	4·50
291		1p. green	3·75	3·50
292		2p. indigo	4·00	4·00
293		3p. scarlet	4·25	7·50
294		5p. purple	7·50	7·75
295		10p. violet	55·00	55·00
296		15p. orange-brown	50·00	45·00
297		25p. ultramarine	65·00	60·00
298		50p. black	75·00	75·00
299		100p. lake-brown	£120	£120
290/299		*Set of 10*	£350	£350

(32)

33 Exhibition Pavilion

1936 (15 Apr). Damascus Fair. Optd with T **32**.

(a) POSTAGE as T **27**

No.	Type	Description	Unused	Used
300		0p.50 bright violet (R.)	4·75	6·00
301		1p. yellow-brown	4·75	5·00
302		2p. violet (R.)	4·50	4·00
303		3p. apple-green	4·50	4·00
304		4p. orange	5·00	7·25
305		4p.50 carmine	5·00	7·00
306		6p. greenish black (R.)	5·25	5·25
307		7p.50 blue (R.)	5·75	5·50
308		10p. brown	6·50	6·25
300/308		*Set of 9*	41·00	45·00

(b) AIR as T **28**

No.	Type	Description	Unused	Used
309		0p.50 sepia (R.)	5·25	9·50
310		1p. red-brown	5·25	7·25
311		2p. Prussian blue (R.)	5·25	7·75
312		3p. deep blue-green (R.)	5·25	7·75
313		5p. purple	5·25	7·75
309/313		*Set of 5*	24·00	36·00

(Des M. Kurcheh. Photo Vaugirard, Paris)

1937 (1 July). AIR. Paris International Exhibition. P 13½.

No.	Type	Description	Unused	Used
314	**33**	½p. yellow-green	4·25	4·25
315		1p. green	4·25	4·50
316		2p. brown	4·25	4·25
317		3p. carmine	4·25	4·25
318		5p. orange	4·50	4·25
319		10p. blackish green	7·25	16·00
320		15p. blue	8·75	19·00
321		25p. violet	9·50	18·00
314/321		*Set of 8*	42·00	65·00

34 Savoia Marchetti S-73 over Aleppo

35 Potez 62 over Damascus

(Des M. Kurcheh. Eng Degorce (T **34**) and Hourriez (T **35**). Recess)

1937 (1 Sept). AIR. P 13.

No.	Type	Description	Unused	Used
322	**34**	½p. violet	1·00	1·00
323	**35**	1p. black	1·40	1·40
324	**34**	2p. green	2·10	1·90
325	**35**	3p. ultramarine	1·90	2·10
326	**34**	5p. magenta	3·25	2·30
327	**35**	10p. lake-brown	2·00	1·70
328	**34**	15p. purple-brown	5·25	3·50
329	**35**	25p. blue	6·75	8·00
322/329		*Set of 8*	21·00	18·00

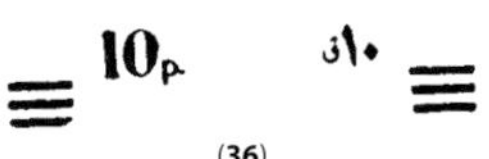
(36)

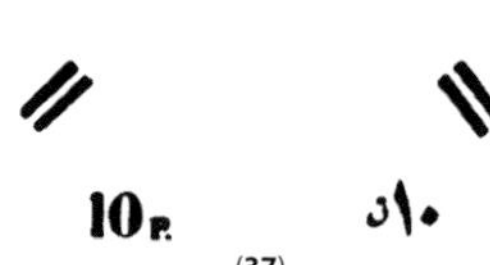
(37)

1938. Variously surch as Types **36** and **37**.

No.	Type	Description	Unused	Used
330	**36**	0p.25 on 0p.75 No. 247*a*	45	1·40
331		0p.50 on 1p.50 No. 249*a* (R.)	70	1·10
332		2p. on 7p.50 No. 255 (R.)	1·50	1·30
333	**37**	2p.50 on 4p. No. 252	1·50	75
334	**36**	5p. on 7p.50 No. 255 (R.)	2·50	1·20
335		10p. on 50p. No. 259	2·40	1·90
336	**37**	10p. on 100p. No. 260	2·00	1·50
330/336		*Set of 7*	10·00	8·25

38 CAMS 53H Flying Boat, Maurice Nogues and Flight Route

(Des G. Ricci. Photo. Vaugirard, Paris)

1938 (20 July). AIR. Tenth Anniversary of First Air Service Flight between France and Syria. P 11½.

No.	Type	Description	Unused	Used
337	**38**	10p. dull green	4·75	10·00
MS337*a*		160×120 mm. No. 337 in block of four. P 13½	70·00	95·00

No. **MS**337*a* exists imperforate from a limited printing (*Price* £1200).

39 President Atasi

12.50

(40)

1938. Surch with T **40**. P 13½.

No.	Type	Description	Unused	Used
338	**39**	12.50 on 10p. blue (R.)	3·00	1·10
		a. Surch inverted		

(Des S. Namani. Photo Vaugirard, Paris)

1938–42. P 13½.

No.	Type	Description	Unused	Used
339	**39**	10p. blue (1942)	3·50	1·40
339*a*		20p. sepia	3·75	1·20

41 Palmyra

(Litho Imp Catholique, Beirut)

1940. P 11½.

No.	Type	Description	Unused	Used
340	**41**	5p. pink	4·50	1·10

42 Damascus Museum

43 Hotel de Bloudan

44 Kasr-el-Heir

45 Potez 62 Aeroplane over Deir-el-Zor Bridge

(Des S. Namani. Eng G. Hourriez (T **42**), C. Dufresne (T **43**), E. Feltesse (T **44**) and A. Degorce (T **45**). Typo (T **42**) or recess (others) French Govt Ptg Wks)

1940 (15 May).

(a) POSTAGE

(i) P 13½×14

No.	Type	Description	Unused	Used
341	**42**	0p.10 carmine	30	80
342		0p.20 greenish blue	30	95
343		0p.25 chestnut	30	1·60
344		0p.50 bright blue	30	40
341/344		Set of 4	1·10	3·50

(ii) P 13

No.	Type	Description	Unused	Used
345	**43**	1p. blue	45	40
346		1p.50 brown	80	1·50

347		2p.50 green	75	55
348	**44**	5p. violet	1·00	60
349		7p.50 scarlet	1·30	1·10
350		50p. slate-purple	4·50	7·25
345/350 *Set of 6*			8·00	10·50
		(b) AIR. P 13		
351	**45**	0p.25 black	35	1·90
352		0p.50 greenish blue	35	1·60
353		1p. bright blue	45	2·10
354		2p. chestnut	75	2·10
355		5p. green	1·40	2·30
356		10p. carmine	2·10	1·50
357		50p. dull violet	6·25	7·50
351/357 *Set of 7*			10·50	17·00

E. SYRIAN REPUBLIC

A Franco-Syrian Treaty of 9 September 1936 provided for the termination of the mandate in three years, but the outbreak of war in September 1939 delayed its application. On 8 June 1941 British and Free French forces entered Syria and Lebanon and, after some fighting against the Vichy French, occupied the area. The independence of a Syrian Republic was proclaimed, with Free French agreement, on 16 September 1941.

The stamps issued for the Free French Forces are listed in this volume.

46 President Taj al-Din al-Hasani

(Des P. Koroleff. Litho Imp Catholique, Beirut)

1942 (6 Apr). Proclamation of National Independence. P 11½.

		(a) POSTAGE		
358	**46**	0p.50 green	6·25	6·00
359		1p.50 sepia	6·25	6·00
360		6p. red	6·25	6·00
361		15p. light blue	6·25	6·00
		(b) AIR. Inscr 'POSTE AERIENNE'		
362	–	10p. slate-blue	5·50	5·25
363	–	50p. purple	5·50	5·25
358/363 *Set of 6*			32·00	31·00
MS363*a* 205×138 mm. Nos 358/363. Imperf			£850	

Design: 10, 50p. As T **46** but showing aeroplane and another portrait of President.

47 President Taj al-Din al-Hasani

48 Syria and late President's Portrait

49 President Shukri Bey al-Quwatli

(Des P. Koroleff. Litho Imp Catholique, Beirut)

1942 (May). As T **47** and similar design. P 11½.

		(a) POSTAGE		
364	**47**	6p. claret and pink	4·00	3·75
365		15p. blue and pale blue	4·00	3·75
		(b) AIR. Inscr 'POSTE AERIENNE'		
366	–	10p. dull green and emerald	6·50	6·25
364/366 *Set of 3*			13·00	12·50

Design: 10p. As T **47**, but President bare-headed, in rectangular frame.

(Des Abousooud-Mousu. Litho Imp Catholique, Beirut)

1943 (1 Apr). Union of Latakia and Jebel Druze with Syrian Republic. T **48** and similar design inscr '20 JANVIER 1942'. P 11½.

		(a) POSTAGE. President bare-headed		
367	**48**	1p. green	4·00	3·50
368		4p. orange-brown	4·00	3·50
369		8p. violet	4·00	3·50
370		10p. red-orange	4·00	3·50
		a. 'JANVIFR'	£200	£190
371		20p. grey-blue	4·50	3·50
		(b) AIR. President wearing turban		
372	–	2p. chocolate	4·50	4·00
373	–	10p. purple	4·50	4·00
374	–	20p. turquoise-blue	4·50	4·00
375	–	50p. pink	5·25	4·00
367/375 *Set of 9*			35·00	30·00

Printed in sheets of 50, divided into two panes of 25. Nos. 370a and 379a occur on position 14 of the right-hand pane.

1943 (5 May). Death of President Taj al-Din al-Hasani. Nos. 367/375 optd with narrow black border.

		(a) POSTAGE. President bare-headed		
376	**48**	1p. green	4·00	3·50
377		4p. orange-brown	4·00	3·50
378		8p. violet	4·00	3·50
379		10p. red-orange	4·00	3·50
		a. 'JANVIFR'	£160	£150
380		20p. grey-blue	4·50	3·50
		(b) AIR. President wearing turban		
381	–	2p. chocolate	4·50	4·00
382	–	10p. purple	4·50	4·00
383	–	20p. turquoise-blue	4·50	4·00
384	–	50p. pink	5·25	4·00
376/384 *Set of 9*			35·00	30·00

(Des P. Koroleff. Litho Beirut)

1944 (19 May). AIR. P 11½.

385	**49**	200p. slate-purple	20·00	16·00
386		500p. blue	26·00	24·00

(**50**) *Trans* 'First Congress of Arab Lawyers, Damascus'

(**51**) *Trans* 'Aboulula-el-Maari. Commemoration of Millenary, 363–1363'

1944 (Oct). AIR. First Arab Lawyers' Congress. Nos. 327, 267/268, 270 and 385 optd with T **50**.

387	10p. lake-brown	5·50	5·00
388	15p. orange-vermilion (B.)	5·50	5·00
389	25p. brown-orange (B.)	5·50	5·00
390	100p. magenta (B.)	14·50	12·50
391	200p. slate-purple (R.)	23·00	21·00
387/391 *Set of 5*		49·00	44·00

1945 (13 Feb). Millenary of Aboulula-el-Maari (Arab poet and philosopher). Nos. 347, 349, 267/268 and 386 optd with T **51**.

	(a) POSTAGE		
392	2p.50 green (Hotel de Bloudan) (R.)	4·75	4·50
393	7p.50 scarlet (Kasr-el-Heir)	4·75	4·50
	a. Opt inverted	80·00	
	(b) AIR		
394	15p. orange-vermilion (Aleppo Citadel)	5·50	5·25
395	25p. brown-orange (Hama)	5·50	5·25
396	500p. blue (R.)	42·00	40·00
392/396 *Set of 5*		55·00	55·00

52 President Shukri Bey al-Quwatli

53 President Shukri Bey al-Quwatli

(Litho Beirut)

1945 (15 Mar). Resumption of Constitutional Government. P 11½.

		(a) POSTAGE		
397	**52**	4p. violet	65	65
398		6p. blue	80	75
399		10p. rose-red	90	90
400		15p. chocolate	1·70	1·60
401		20p. green	1·80	1·80
402		40p. red-orange	2·30	2·30
		(b) AIR		
403	**53**	5p. emerald-green	65	65
404		10p. rose-red	90	65
405		15p. red-orange	1·30	90

406	25p. light blue	2·30	1·40
407	50p. violet	3·50	1·40
408	100p. chocolate	6·25	2·40
409	200p. brown-lake	16·00	7·50
397/409	*Set of 13*	35·00	21·00

(**54**) (**55**) (**55a**)

1945. Various fiscal stamps inscr 'TIMBRE FISCAL' (as in Types T **57**/T **61**). Typo. P 11.

(a) Optd with T **54** *only (No. 411 surch also)*

410	25p. brown	8·50	8·25
411	50p. on 75p. red-brown	9·75	9·50
412	75p. red-brown	12·50	12·00
413	100p. pale yellow-green	18·00	18·00

(b) Surch with T **55**

414	12½p. on 15p. green	5·00	4·75

(c) Surch with T **55a**

415	25p. on 25s. brown-purple	5·00	4·75

(d) Optd with T **54** *and with additional Arabic inscription at top (No. 416 surch also)*

416	50p. on 75p. red-brown	5·50	5·25
417	50p. magenta	5·00	4·75
418	100p. pale yellow-green	6·25	6·00
410/418	*Set of 9*	70·00	65·00

(**56**)

1945. Fiscal stamp (32½×20½ *mm*) optd with T **56**. Arabic characters, at top, in black, remainder in red. Typo. P 11.

419	200p. light blue (Bk.+R.)	36·00	21·00

T **57** T **58** T **59**

T **60** T **61**

1945–49. OBLIGATORY TAX. Syrian Army Fund. Revenue stamps surch or optd as in Types T **57**/T **61**. P 11.

(a) As Type T **57**

T419	5p. on 25p. on 40p. rose	£225	38·00

(b) As Type T **57** *but with additional opt as top line of Type T* **61**

T420	5p. on 25p. on 40p. rose	£225	75·00

(c) As Type T **58**

T421	5p. on 25p. on 40p. pale rose	£225	50·00

(d) As Type T **59**

T422	5p. blue (R.)	£400	38·00

(e) As Type T **60**

T423	5p. blue (R.)	£225	31·00

(f) Top line of opt as Type T **59**, *other lines as Type T* **60**

T424	5p. blue (R.)	£250	25·00
	a. Black opt	£325	65·00
	b. Top line in black, other lines in red	£275	44·00

(g) As Type T **61**

T425	5p. blue (R.)	£250	41·00

(h) Top line of opt as Type T **61**, *other lines as Type T* **60**

T426	5p. blue (R.)	£275	44·00
	a. Black opt	—	95·00

57 Ear of Wheat

58 President Shukri Bey al-Quwatli

59 President Shukri Bey al-Quwatli

60 Arab Horse

61 Flock of Sheep

62 Kattineh Dam

63 Ruins of Corinthian Temple, Kanaouat

64 Sultan Ibrahim Mosque

(**65**)

(Des P. Koroleff. T **58** photo Cairo. Others litho Imp Catholique)

1946–47. P 13½.

(a) POSTAGE

420	**57**	0p.50 orange	25	15
421		1p. violet	90	25
422		2p.50 grey	1·00	25
423		5p. emerald-green	1·40	40
424	**58**	7p.50 sepia	40	15
425		10p. greenish blue	40	25
426		12p.50 violet	1·70	25
427	**59**	15p. scarlet (1947)	65	25
428		20p. violet (1947)	1·00	65
429		25p. ultramarine	1·70	65
430	**60**	50p. bistre-brown	8·50	1·40
431		100p. green (1947)	18·00	3·25
432		200p. deep reddish purple (1947)	£100	8·75
		a. Deep purple	£100	8·75

(b) AIR

433	**61**	3p. brown-lake (8.46)	90	25
434		5p. emerald-green (2.47)	90	25
435		6p. orange (2.47)	90	25
436	**62**	10p. grey (2.47)	65	25
437		15p. scarlet (2.47)	65	25
438		25p. blue (31.1.46)	80	40
439	**63**	50p. violet (31.1.46)	1·30	40
440		100p. greenish blue (31.1.46)	3·00	65
441		200p. bistre-brown (2.47)	6·50	1·90
442	**64**	300p. red-brown (2.47)	23·00	3·75
443		500p. olive-green (2.47)	26·00	5·75
420/443		*Set of 24 (cheapest)*	£180	28·00

1946 (17 Apr). Evacuation of Foreign Troops from Syria. Optd with T **65**.

(a) POSTAGE

444	**58**	10p. greenish blue	90	90
445		12p.50 violet	1·30	1·30
446	**60**	50p. bistre-brown (G.)	4·00	3·75

(b) AIR

447	**62**	25p. blue (R.)	3·25	1·90
444/447		*Set of 4*	8·50	7·00

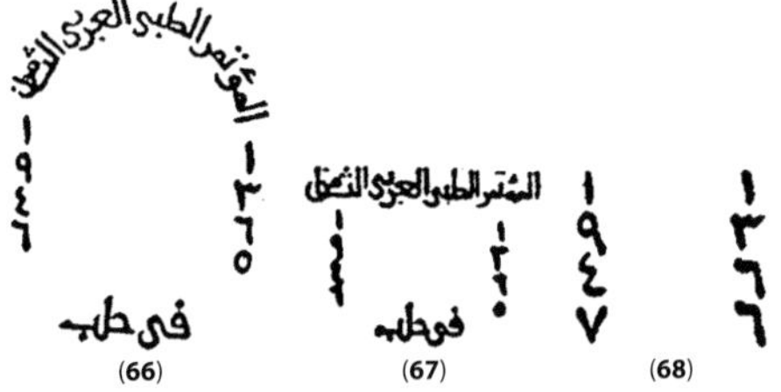

(**66**) (**67**) (**68**)

1946 (28 Aug). Eighth Arab Medical Congress, Aleppo.

*(a) POSTAGE. Optd with T **66***

448	**59**	25p. ultramarine (R.)	3·00	2·10

*(b) AIR. Optd with T **67***

449	**62**	25p. blue (R.)	3·50	1·90
450	**63**	50p. violet (R.)	4·25	2·50
451		100p. greenish blue (R.)	8·50	4·50
448/451		*Set of 4*	17·00	10·00

1947 (10 June). First Anniversary of Evacuation of Foreign Troops from Syria. Nos. 444/447 optd as T **68** ('1947' in two vert rows variously spaced).

(a) POSTAGE

452	**58**	10p. greenish blue (Blk.)	1·30	25
453		12p.50 violet (Blk.)	1·70	40
454	**60**	50p. bistre-brown (G.+Blk.)	3·75	1·30

(b) AIR

455	**62**	25p. blue (R.+Blk.)	4·00	1·90
452/455		*Set of 4*	9·75	3·50

69 Hercules and Lion

70 Mosaic at the Mosque of the Omayyades

(Des P. Koroleff. Litho Imp Catholique)

1947 (15 Nov). First Arab Archaeological Congress, Damascus. T **69** and horiz designs as T **70**. P 11½.

(a) POSTAGE

456	12p.50 grey-green (Type **69**)	1·70	1·00
457	25p. grey-blue (Type **70**)	4·00	1·60

(b) AIR. Inscr 'POSTE AERIENNE'

458	12p.50 grey-violet	3·00	1·00
459	50p. brown	8·00	3·00
456/459	*Set of 4*	15·00	6·00
MS459*a*	138×188 mm. Nos. 456/459	85·00	75·00

Designs: 12p.50 (Air), Window at Kasr El-Heir El-Gharbi; 50p. King Hazael's Throne.

71 Courtyard of Azem Palace

72 Congress Symbol

(Des P. Koroleff. Litho Imp Catholique)

1947 (15 Nov). Third Arab Engineers' Congress, Damascus. As T **71** (horiz designs) and T **72**. P 11½.

(a) POSTAGE

460	12p.50 purple (Type **71**)	1·20	1·00
461	25p. blue	2·30	1·60

(b) AIR. Inscr 'POSTE AERIENNE'

462	12p.50 grey-olive	1·70	1·00
463	50p. grey-violet (Type **72**)	5·75	3·00
460/463	*Set of 4*	9·75	6·00
MS463*a*	138×188 mm. Nos. 460/463	85·00	75·00

Designs: 25p. Telephone Exchange Building; 12p.50 (Air), Fortress at Kasr El-Heir El-Charqui.

73 Parliament Building

74 President Shukri Bey al-Quwatli

(Des P. Koroleff. Litho Imp Catholique)

1948 (23 June). Re-election of President Shukri Bey al-Quwatli. P 10½.

(a) POSTAGE. Inscr 'POSTES'

464	**73**	12p.50 brown and grey	1·20	40
465	**74**	25p. magenta	1·70	1·00

(b) AIR. Inscr 'POSTE AERIENNE'

466	**73**	12p.50 violet and blue	1·20	50
467	**74**	50p. purple and green	4·00	1·90
464/467		*Set of 4*	7·25	3·50
MS467*a*		139×186 mm. Nos. 464/467. Imperf	£375	£325

75 Syrian Arms

76 Soldier and Flag

(Des P. Koroleff. Litho Imp Catholique)

1948 (23 June). Obligatory Military Service. P 10½.

(a) POSTAGE

468	**75**	12p.50 brown and grey	1·20	65
		a. Brown (Eagle) printed double	£100	
469	**76**	25p. green, scarlet, black and blue	1·70	1·00
		a. Scarlet (stars) printed double	£100	

(b) AIR. Inscr 'POSTE AERIENNE'

470	**75**	12p.50 blue and light blue	1·20	65
		a. Blue (Eagle) printed double	£100	
471	**76**	50p. green, scarlet and black	5·75	1·50
468/471		*Set of 4*	8·75	3·50
MS471*a*		137×190 mm. Nos. 468/471. Imperf	£325	£275

(**77**)

1948 (19 Sept)–**50**. Various stamps surch as T **77**.

(a) POSTAGE. Nos. 247a and 431/432

472	–	0p.50 on 0p.75 orange-vermilion	45	15
472*a*	**60**	2p.50 on 200p. deep reddish purple (1950)	3·00	2·10
		ab. Deep purple	55	30
472*b*		10p. on 100p. green (1950)	90	40
473		25p. on 200p. deep purple	6·25	75

(b) AIR. Nos. 433, 435 and 440/443

474	**61**	2p.50 on 3p. brown-lake	15	15
475		2p.50 on 6p. orange	15	15
475*a*	**63**	2p.50 on 100p. greenish blue (1950)	25	15

No.	Type	Description	Unused	Used
476		25p. on 200p. bistre-brown (R.)	1·50	50
477	**64**	50p. on 300p. red-brown	28·00	1·30
478		50p. on 500p. olive-green	28·00	1·30
472/478		*Set of* 10 (*cheapest*)	60·00	5·75

78 Palmyra

79 President Husni al-Za'im and Lockheed L. 1049 Super Constellation Airliner over Damascus

(Des P. Koroleff. Litho Imp Catholique)

1949 (20 June). 75th Anniversary of Universal Postal Union. Types **78/79** and similar designs. P 11½.

(a) POSTAGE

No.	Type	Description	Unused	Used
479	–	12p.50 bluish violet	3·25	3·25
480	**78**	25p. blue	5·75	5·75

(b) AIR. Inscr 'POSTE AERIENNE'

No.	Type	Description	Unused	Used
481	–	12p.50 purple	12·50	12·50
482	**79**	50p. greenish black	31·00	23·00
479/482		*Set of* 4	47·00	40·00

Designs: Horiz—12p.50 (Postage) Ain-el-Arous; 12p.50 (Air), Globe and mountains.

An imperforate miniature sheet containing Nos. 479/482 exists from a limited printing.

80 President Husni al-Za'im

81 President Husni al-Za'im and Map

81a Multiple Eagles (upright)

(Des P. Koroleff. Litho Imp Catholique)

1949 (30 June). Revolution of 30th March, 1949. P 11½.

(a) POSTAGE. Inscr 'POSTES'

No.	Type	Description	Unused	Used
483	**80**	25p. light blue	1·40	1·00

(b) AIR. Inscr 'POSTE AERIENNE'

No.	Type	Description	Unused	Used
484	**80**	50p. brown	5·75	4·50

An imperforate miniature sheet containing Nos. 483/484 exists from a limited printing.

(Des Sh. Khadra. Litho Imp Catholique)

1949 (6 Aug). Election of President Husni al-Za'im. W **81a** (sideways). P 11½.

(a) POSTAGE. Inscr 'POSTES'

No.	Type	Description	Unused	Used
485	**81**	25p. brown and blue	5·75	3·75

(b) AIR. Inscr 'P. AERIENNE'

No.	Type	Description	Unused	Used
486	**81**	50p. blue-green and rose	7·00	5·00
MS486*a*		125×188 mm. Nos. 485/486. Imperf	£375	£375

82 Tel-Chehab

83 Damascus

(Litho. Imp Catholique, Beirut)

1949 (28 Sept). W **81a** (sideways on horiz design). P 11½.

No.	Type	Description	Unused	Used
487	**82**	5p. slate-grey	80	15
488		7p.50 grey-brown	90	25
489	**83**	12p.50 dull purple	1·20	25
490		25p. blue	2·30	65
487/490		*Set of* 4	4·75	1·20

See also No. 524.

84 Syrian Arms

85 GPO, Damascus

(Des P. Koroleff. Litho Imp Catholique, Beirut)

1950 (6 Nov)–**51**. Types **84/85** and similar design. P 11½.

No.	Type	Description	Unused	Used
491	**84**	0p.50 brown	25	15
492		2p.50 carmine-pink	25	25
493	–	10p. violet (5.1.51)	80	40
494	–	12p.50 grey-green	1·60	65
495	**85**	25p. light blue	2·20	40
496		50p. black	7·00	1·30
491/496		*Set of* 6	11·00	2·75

Design: Horiz—10p., 12p.50, Abous–Damascus road.

86 Port of Latakia

(Des P. Koroleff. Litho Imp Catholique, Beirut)

1950 (25 Dec). AIR. P 11½.

No.	Type	Description	Unused	Used
497	**86**	2p.50 dull violet	90	25
498		10p. turquoise-blue	2·00	25
499		15p. brown	4·50	40
500		25p. blue	9·00	65
497/500		*Set of* 4	15·00	1·40

See also No. 518 and No. 526.

87 Parliament Building

88 Book and Torch

(Des P. Koroleff. Litho Imp Catholique, Beirut)

1951 (16 Apr). New Constitution, 1950. P 11½.

(a) POSTAGE

No.	Type	Description	Unused	Used
501	**87**	12p.50 black	70	40
502		25p. blue	1·00	80

(b) AIR. Inscr 'POSTE AERIENNE'

No.	Type	Description	Unused	Used
503	**88**	12p.50 rose-carmine	80	40
504		50p. purple	2·10	2·00
501/504		*Set of* 4	4·25	3·25

89 Hama

(Des V. Pliss. Litho Imp J. Saikali)

1952 (22 Apr). T **89** and similar horiz designs. P 11½.

(a) POSTAGE

No.		Description	Unused	Used
505		0p.50 sepia	25	15
506		2p.50 slate-blue	35	15
507		5p. pale blue-green	45	15
508		10p. scarlet	60	20
509		12p.50 black	1·20	25
510		15p. claret	7·00	40
511		25p. deep blue	3·50	65
512		100p. bistre-brown	12·50	3·50

(b) AIR. Inscr 'POSTE AERIENNE'

No.		Description	Unused	Used
513		2p.50 red	30	15
514		5p. deep blue-green	60	15
515		15p. bluish violet	85	25
516		25p. blue	1·20	65
517		100p. bright purple	8·75	1·60
505/517		*Set of* 13	34·00	7·50

Designs: Postage—0p.50 to 10p. T **89**; 12p.50 to 100p. Palace of Justice, Damascus. Air—2p.50 to 15p. Palmyra; 25p., 100p. Citadel, Aleppo.

(**90**)

91 Qalaat el Hasn Fortress

1952 (8 Dec). AIR. United Nations Social Welfare Seminar, Damascus. Nos. 498, 515/516 and 439 optd with T **90**.

No.	Type	Description	Unused	Used
518	**86**	10p. turquoise blue	3·00	2·00
519	–	15p. bluish violet	3·00	2·00
520	–	25p. blue	5·25	2·75
521	**63**	50p. violet	12·50	4·25
518/521		*Set of* 4	21·00	10·00

(Des S. Namani. Photo Zeydoun, Damascus)

1953 (Oct). T **91** and similar designs. P 11½.

(a) POSTAGE

No.	Type	Description	Unused	Used
522	**91**	0p.50 scarlet	35	15
523	–	2p.50 deep brown	45	15
524	**82**	7p.50 green	70	20
525	**91**	12p.50 blue	3·00	25

(b) AIR. Inscr 'POSTE AERIENNE'

No.	Type	Description	Unused	Used
526	**86**	10p. dull violet-blue	90	25
527	–	50p. red-brown	2·50	40
522/527		*Set of* 6	7·00	1·30

Designs: Horiz—2p.50, As T **91** but taken from a photograph; 50p. GPO, Aleppo.

92 'Labour'

94 'Communications'

93 'Family'

(Des F. Buttgen. Photo Zeydoun, Damascus)

1954. Designs as Types **92/94**. P 11½.

(a) POSTAGE

No.	Type	Description	Unused	Used
528	**92**	1p. deep olive	25	15
529		2½p. brown-red	35	15
530		5p. blue	45	15
531	**93**	7½p. brown-red	60	15
532		10p. black	70	20
533		12½p. violet	90	25
534	–	20p. reddish purple	1·40	25
535	–	25p. violet	3·00	90
536	–	50p. deep green	6·25	1·60

Design: Horiz—As T **93**—20p. to 50p. 'Industry'.

(b) AIR

No.	Type	Description	Unused	Used
537	**94**	5p. violet	35	20
538		10p. chocolate	45	20
539		15p. deep green	70	25
540	–	30p. chocolate	60	35
541	–	35p. blue	1·20	40
542	–	40p. orange-red	2·50	65
543	–	50p. reddish purple	2·00	1·30
544	–	70p. violet	5·25	1·60
528/544		*Set of* 17	24·00	8·00

Design: Horiz—As T **93**—30p. to 70p. Syrian University.

95 Monument

(**96**)

(Des F. Buttgen. Photo Zeydoun, Damascus)

1954 (2 Sept). AIR. Damascus Fair. T **95** and similar design but vert. P 11½.

No.		Description	Unused	Used
545		40p. cerise	1·70	90
546		50p. green (Mosque and Syrian flag)	2·30	1·00

1954 (9 Oct). Cotton Festival, Aleppo. Nos. 532, 535, 527 and 517 optd with T **96**.

(a) POSTAGE

No.		Description	Unused	Used
547		10p. black (R.)	1·20	40
548		25p. violet (R.)	1·40	65

(b) AIR

No.		Description	Unused	Used
549		50p. red-brown (B.)	2·10	1·70
550		100p. bright purple	3·50	2·75
547/550		*Set of* 4	7·50	5·00

96a

97

98

(Photo Imp Catholique, Beirut)

1955 (1 Mar). Arab Postal Union. P 13½×13.

(a) POSTAGE

No.	Type	Description	Unused	Used
551	**96a**	12½p. green	90	40
552		25p. violet	1·60	65

(b) AIR. Inscr 'POSTES AER'

No.	Type	Description	Unused	Used
553	**96a**	5p. yellow-brown	60	40
551/553		*Set of* 3	2·75	1·30

(Des M. Kurcheh. Photo Zeydoun, Damascus)

1955 (26 Mar). AIR. Middle East Rotary Congress. P 11½.

No.	Type	Description	Unused	Used
554	**97**	35p. carmine	1·40	1·00
555		65p. green	3·00	2·00

(Des M. Kurcheh. Photo Zeydoun, Damascus)

1955 (27 Mar). AIR. 50th Anniversary of Rotary International. P 11½.

No.	Type	Description	Unused	Used
556	**98**	25p. deep reddish violet	90	80
557		75p. turquoise-blue	3·00	2·20

99 'Facing the Future'

100 Mother and Child

(Des P. Koroleff. Litho Imp Catholique, Beirut)

1955 (17 Apr). AIR. Ninth Anniversary of Evacuation of Foreign Troops from Syria. T **99** and similar horiz design. P 11½.

558	40p. deep magenta	90	90
559	60p. ultramarine	3·50	1·00

Designs: 40p. T **99**; 60p. Tank and infantry attack.
See also Nos. 847/849.

(Des Snip. Litho)

1955 (13 May). Mothers' Day. P 11½.

(a) POSTAGE

560	**100**	25p. vermilion	90	65

(b) AIR. Inscr 'POSTE AER.'

561	**100**	35p. bright violet	1·60	1·30
562		40p. black	2·75	2·00
560/562 *Set of 3*			4·75	3·50

101 Lockheed L. 1049 Super Constellation Airliner, Flag and Crowd

102 Syrian Pavilion

(Des N. Yafary. Litho Syrian Republic Ptg Wks)

1955 (26 July). AIR. Emigrants' Congress. T **101** and similar vert design. P 11½.

563	5p. deep magenta	90	40
564	15p. pale blue (Aeroplane over globe)	1·20	65

(Des Snip (No. 568), N. Yafary (others). Litho)

1955 (1 Sept). AIR. International Fair, Damascus. T **102** and similar horiz designs inscr 'FOIRE INTERNATIONALE DE DAMAS SEPT. 1955'. P 11½.

565	25p. +5p. black	90	90
566	35p. +5p. deep bright blue	1·40	1·30
567	40p. +10p. reddish purple	1·70	1·70
568	70p. +10p. deep bluish green	3·00	2·50
565/568 *Set of 4*		6·25	5·75

Designs: 25p. T **102**; 35p., 40p. Industry and Agriculture; 70p. Exhibition pavilions and flags.
See also Nos. 592/595.

103 Mother and Baby

104 UN Emblem and Torch

(Des G. Chury. Litho)

1955 (3 Oct). AIR. International Children's Day. P 11½.

569	**103**	25p. blue	1·20	65
570		50p. purple	2·10	90

(Des W. Eichel. Litho)

1955 (30 Oct). Tenth Anniversary of United Nations. T **104** and similar horiz design. P 11½.

(a) POSTAGE

571	**104**	7½p. scarlet	80	65
572		12½p. dull slate-green	1·50	1·00

(b) AIR. Inscr 'AER'

573	–	15p. bright blue	1·20	65
574	–	35p. sepia	2·30	1·00
571/574 *Set of 4*			5·25	3·00

Design: 15p., 35p. Globe, Dove and Scales of Justice.

105 Saracen Gate, Aleppo Citadel

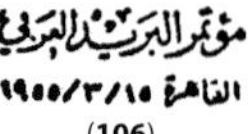
(**106**)

(Des N. Yafary. Litho State Ptg Works, Damascus)

1955 (21 Nov). Installation of Aleppo Water Supply from R. Euphrates. P 11½.

(a) POSTAGE

575	**105**	7p.50 reddish violet	45	15
576		12p.50 carmine	70	25

(b) AIR. Inscr 'AER.'

577	**105**	30p. deep grey-blue	3·00	2·00
575/577 *Set of 3*			3·75	2·20

1955 (29 Dec). Second Arab Postal Union Congress, Cairo. Nos. 551/553 optd with T **106**.

(a) POSTAGE

578	**96a**	12½p. green (B.)	70	65
579		25p. violet (G.)	2·30	1·00

(b) AIR

580	**96a**	5p. yellow-brown (B.)	90	25
578/580 *Set of 3*			3·50	1·70

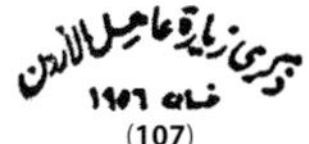
(**107**)

108 Monument

1956 (11 Apr). Visit of King Hussein of Jordan. Nos. 551/553 optd with T **107**.

(a) POSTAGE

581	**96a**	12½p. green	80	80
582		25p. violet	1·40	1·40

(b) AIR

583	**96a**	5p. yellow-brown	2·30	1·00
581/583 *Set of 3*			4·00	3·00

(Des Abandowitz. Litho)

1956 (17 Apr). AIR. Tenth Anniversary of Evacuation of Foreign Troops from Syria. T **108** and similar vert designs. P 11½.

584	35p. black-brown	90	80
585	65p. carmine-red	1·50	1·00
586	75p. deep greenish grey	3·00	1·70
584/586 *Set of 3*		4·75	3·25

Designs: 35p. T **108**; 65p. Winged female figure; 75p. President Shukri Bey al-Quwatli.

109 President Shukri Bey al-Quwatli

110 Cotton

111 Gate of Kasr al-Heir, Palmyra

(Des N. Yafary. Litho State Ptg Wks, Damascus)

1956 (7 July). AIR. P 11½.

587	**109**	100p. black	2·20	1·70
588		200p. violet	4·50	2·20
589		300p. rose-red	6·50	5·25
590		500p. deep bluish green	13·00	9·75
		a. Imperf (pair)		
587/590 *Set of 4*			24·00	17·00
MS590*a* 139×100 mm. Nos. 587/590. Imperf. Without gum			£120	£110

(Des Abandowitz. Litho State Ptg Wks, Damascus)

1956 (14 July). Aleppo Cotton Festival. P 11½.
591 **110** 2½p. deep blue-green 90 40

1956 (18 Aug). AIR. Nos. 565/568 with premiums obliterated by bars.
592 25p. black 90 40
593 35p. deep bright blue .... 1·00 65
594 40p. reddish purple .... 2·20 90
595 70p. deep bluish green .... 2·50 2·00
592/595 *Set of 4* .... 6·00 3·50

(Des M. Kurcheh (15p.), Abandowitz (20p., 30p.), W. Eichel (35p., 50p.). Litho Syrian Republic Ptg Works)

1956 (1 Sept). AIR. Third International Fair, Damascus. T **111** and similar vert designs inscr '3 EME. FOIRE INTERNATIONALE DAMAS 1956'. P 11½.
596 15p. brownish black 90 90
597 20p. ultramarine .... 1·00 1·00
598 30p. deep bluish green .... 1·40 1·40
599 35p. blue .... 1·60 1·60
600 50p. claret .... 2·00 2·00
596/600 *Set of 5* .... 6·25 6·25
MS600*a* 101×136 mm. Nos. 596/600. Imperf. Without gum .... 90·00 90·00

Designs: 15p. T **111**; 20p. Cotton mill; 30p. Tractor; 35p. Phoenician galley and cogwheels; 50p. Textiles, carpets and pottery.

112 Clay Alphabetical Tablet

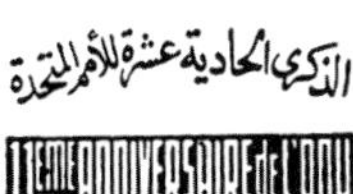

(**113**)

(Des W. Eichel. Litho State Ptg Wks, Damascus)

1956 (6 Oct). AIR. International Campaign for Museums. T **112** and similar designs. P 11½.
601 20p. grey-black .... 1·60 90
602 30p. crimson .... 1·70 90
603 50p. black-brown .... 3·25 1·70
601/603 *Set of 3* .... 6·00 3·25
MS603*a* 139×100 mm. Nos. 601/603. Imperf. Without gum .... £110 90·00

Designs: Vert—30p. Syrian legionary's helmet. Horiz—20p. T **112**; 50p. Lintel of Baalshamin Temple, Palmyra.

1956 (30 Oct). 11th Anniversary of United Nations. Nos. 571/574 optd with T **113**.

(a) POSTAGE
604 7½p. scarlet .... 1·00 65
605 12½p. dull slate-green .... 1·30 90

(b) AIR. Inscr 'AER.'
606 15p. bright blue (R.) .... 2·20 1·00
607 35p. sepia (G.) .... 4·25 2·50
604/607 *Set of 4* .... 8·00 4·50

114 Oaks and Mosque

115 Azem Palace, Damascus

(Des W. Eichel. Litho Syrian Republic Ptg Works)

1956 (27 Dec). AIR. Afforestation Day. P 11½.
608 **114** 10p. olive-brown 65 40
609 40p. deep olive-green .... 1·60 90

MINIATURE SHEETS issued in 1956 and 1957 exist in limited quantities.

(Des N. Yafary. Litho Syrian Republic Ptg Works)

1957 (13 Jan). P 11½.
610 **115** 12½p. purple 90 25
611 15p. black .... 1·00 25

116 'Resistance'

ذكرى الجلاء عن بورسعيد ٢٢/١٢/١٩٥٦
221256 EVACUATION PORT SAID
(**117**)

(Des Abandowitz. Litho Syrian Republic Ptg Works)

1957 (7 Feb). Syrian Defence Force. P 11½.
612 **116** 5p. deep magenta 80 25
613 20p. slate-green .... 1·80 65

1957. Evacuation of Port Said. Nos. 612/613 optd with T **117**.
614 **116** 5p. deep magenta 80 25
615 20p. slate-green (C.) .... 1·80 65

118 Mother and Child

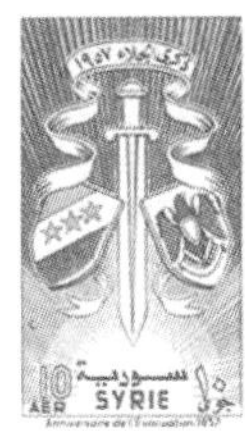

119 'Sword of Liberty'

120 *Latakia* (freighter) at Quay and Fair Emblem

(Des Abandowitz. Litho Syrian Republic Ptg Works)

1957 (21 Mar). AIR. Mothers' Day. T **118** and similar vert design. P 11½.
616 40p. bright blue (Mother fondling child) .... 1·40 1·40
617 60p. red .... 2·50 1·70

(Des Abandowitz. Litho Syrian Republic Ptg Works)

1957 (20 Apr). AIR. 11th Anniversary of Evacuation of Foreign Troops from Syria. T **119** and similar vert designs. W **81a**. P 11½.
618 10p. purple-brown 25 25
619 15p. deep bluish green 65 40
620 25p. bright violet 90 50
621 35p. magenta .... 1·30 90
622 40p. black .... 2·10 1·30
618/622 *Set of 5* .... 4·75 3·00

Designs: 10, 40p. T **119**; 15, 35p. Map and woman holding torch; 25p. President Shukri Bey al-Quwatli.

(Des H. Abandowitz. Litho Syrian Republic Ptg Works)

1957 (1 Sept). AIR. Fourth Damascus Fair. T **120** and similar designs inscr 'IV FOIRE INTERNATIONALE DE DAMAS'. P 11½.
623 **120** 25p. deep magenta 80 50
624 – 30p. red-brown 90 65
625 – 35p. blue .... 1·30 90
626 – 40p. blue-green .... 1·80 1·00
627 **120** 70p. olive .... 2·20 1·60
623/627 *Set of 5* .... 6·25 4·25

Designs: Vert—30, 40p. Girls harvesting and cotton-picking. Horiz—35p. Interior of processing plant.

121 Cotton

122 Children at Work and Play

(Des H. Abandowitz. Litho Syrian Republic Ptg Works)

1957 (3 Oct). Aleppo Cotton Festival. W **81a** (sideways). P 11½.

(a) POSTAGE
628 **121** 12½p. black and blue-green .... 1·00 40

(b) AIR. Inscr 'AER.'
629 **121** 17½p. black and orange .... 1·20 65
630 40p. black and pale blue .... 2·30 90
628/630 *Set of 3* .... 4·00 1·80

(Des Seyad. Litho Syrian Republic Ptg Works)

1957 (7 Oct). International Children's Day. W **81a** (sideways). P 11½.

(a) POSTAGE
631 **122** 12½p. yellow-olive .... 1·00 40

(b) AIR. Inscr 'AER.'
632 **122** 17½p. ultramarine .... 2·20 90
633 20p. red-brown .... 2·20 90
631/633 *Set of 3* .... 4·75 2·00

123 Letter and Postbox

(Des and litho Syrian Republic Ptg Works)

1957 (12 Oct). International Correspondence Week. T **123** and similar horiz design. P 11½.

(a) POSTAGE

634	**123**	5p. deep magenta	1·00	45

(b) AIR. Inscr 'AER.'

635	–	5p. emerald-green	1·00	35

Design: No. 635, Family writing letters.

اسبوع التحصين
١-٧ تشرين الثاني ١٩٥٧

(**124**)

125 Scales of Justice, Map and Damascus Silhouette

1957 (1 Nov). National Defence Week. Nos. 612/613 optd with T **124**.

636	**116**	5p. deep magenta	65	25
637		20p. slate-green (C.)	1·60	40

(Des Seyad. Litho Syrian Republic Ptg Works)

1957 (8 Nov). Third Arab Lawyers Union Congress, Damascus. W **81a** (sideways). P 11½.

(a) POSTAGE

638	**125**	12½p. emerald	65	40

(b) AIR. Inscr 'P.AER.'

639	**125**	17½p. scarlet	80	50
640		40p. black	1·60	90
638/640 *Set of 3*			2·75	1·60

126 Glider

(Des Eichel. Litho Syrian Republic Ptg Works)

1957 (8 Nov). AIR. Gliding Festival. W **81a**. P 11½.

641	**126**	25p. red-brown	2·00	40
642		35p. grey-green	2·50	65
643		40p. chalky blue	4·00	1·30
641/643 *Set of 3*			7·75	2·10

127 Torch and Map

128 Khaled Ibn el-Walid Mosque, Homs

(Des Seyad. Litho Syrian Republic Ptg Works)

1957 (8 Nov). Afro-Asian Jurists' Congress, Damascus. W **81a**. P 11½.

(a) POSTAGE

644	**127**	20p. olive-drab	90	50

(b) AIR. Inscr 'P.AER.'

645	**127**	30p. deep turquoise-green	90	65
646		50p. violet	1·30	90
644/646 *Set of 3*			2·75	1·80

1957 (27 Nov). Litho. P 12.

647	**128**	2½p. brown	50	15

UNITED ARAB REPUBLIC

Syria and Egypt united on 1 February 1958 to form the United Arab Republic.

> **NOTE.** Egyptian stamps, with values in milliemes, were also inscribed 'UAR' from 1958 to 1971. Some of these were in the same designs as the Syrian issues.

129 Telecommunications Building

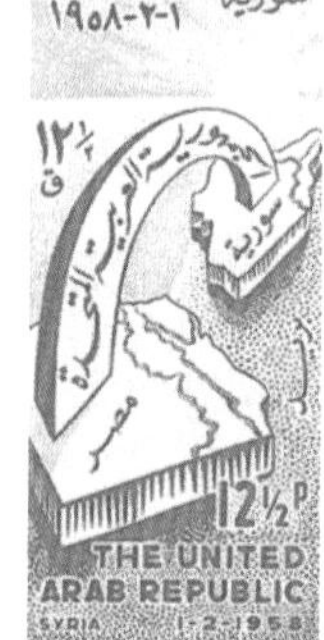

129a Union of Egypt and Syria

(Des N. Yafary. Litho Syrian Republic Ptg Works)

1958 (12 Feb). Five Year Plan. T **129** and vert design. W **81a** (sideways on T **129**). P 11½.

(a) POSTAGE

648	**129**	25p. ultramarine	1·00	40

(b) AIR. Inscr 'AER.'

649	**129**	10p. emerald	80	25
650	–	15p. brown	80	40
648/650 *Set of 3*			2·30	95

Design: 15p. Telephone, radio tower and telegraph pole.

> **PRINTERS.** The following issues were printed by lithography by the State Printing Works, Damascus, *unless otherwise stated.*

(Des W. Eichel)

1958 (2 Apr). United Arab Republic Commemoration. P 11½.

(a) POSTAGE

651	**129a**	12½p. green and yellow	40	25

(b) AIR. With aeroplane over horizon

652	**129a**	17½p. brown and cobalt	50	40
		a. Wmk **81a**	£100	

130 Eternal Flame

(Des Seyad)

1958 (15–17 May). 12th Anniversary of Evacuation of Foreign Troops from Syria. T **130** and similar horiz design. P 11½.

(a) POSTAGE

653	**130**	5p. violet and lemon	1·00	45
654		15p. Venetian red and yellow-green	1·50	1·00

(b) AIR. Inscr 'AER.' (17.5)

655	–	35p. black and carmine-red	2·50	1·00
656	–	45p. brown and blue	3·75	1·50
653/656 *Set of 4*			8·00	3·50

Design: 35p., 45p. Broken chain, Dove and olive branch.

131 Scout fixing Tent-peg

1958 (31 Aug). AIR. Third Pan-Arab Scout Jamboree. P 12.

657	**131**	35p. sepia	4·25	4·25
658		40p. blue	5·25	5·25

132 Mosque, Chimneys and Cogwheel

133 Bronze Rattle

1958 (1 Sept). AIR. Fifth International Fair, Damascus. T **132** and similar designs inscr '1.9.58'. P 11½.

659	25p. vermilion	1·90	1·30
660	30p. blue-green	3·00	1·90
661	45p. violet	3·25	2·50
659/661 *Set of 3*		7·25	5·25

MS661*a* 80×80 mm. 100p. black, red and green showing UAR flag and Fair Emblem. Imperf £225 £200

Designs: Horiz—25p. View of Fair. Vert—30p. Minaret, vase and emblem, 45p. T **132**.

1958 (14 Sept). Ancient Syrian Art. Vert designs as T **133** inscr 'COLLECTION MUSEES'. P 12.

662	10p. yellow-olive	30	20
663	15p. orange-brown	45	20
664	20p. purple	60	25
665	30p. sepia	75	30
666	40p. grey	85	45
667	60p. bluish green	1·50	75
668	75p. grey-blue	2·20	1·00
669	100p. claret	3·25	1·70
670	150p. dull purple	6·50	2·20
662/670 *Set of 9*		15·00	6·25

Designs: 10p. T **133**; 15p. Goddess of Spring; 20p. *Lamgi Mari* (statue); 30p. Mithras fighting bull; 40p. Aspasia; 60p. Minerva; 75p. Ancient gourd; 100p. Enamelled vase; 150p. Mosaic from Omayyad Mosque, Damascus.

الجمهورية العربية المتحدة
١٩٥٨/١٠/٦
RAU

(133a)

134 Cotton and Textiles

1958 (6 Oct). International Children's Day. Optd with T **133a**.

(a) POSTAGE

670*a*	**122**	12½p. yellow-olive	95·00	95·00

(b) AIR

670*b*	**122**	17½p. ultramarine	75·00	75·00
670*c*		20p. red-brown	75·00	75·00
670*a*/670*c* *Set of 3*			£225	£225

1958 (9 Oct). AIR. Aleppo Cotton Festival. P 12.

671	**134**	25p. greenish yellow and sepia	1·50	1·50
672		35p. orange-red and sepia	2·20	1·70

134a Hand holding Torch, and Iraqi Flag

135 Light Aeroplane and Children with Model Aeroplane

1958 (14 Oct). Republic of Iraq Commemoration. P 11½.

673	**134a**	12½p. carmine-red	60	45

1958 (28 Nov). AIR. Gliding Festival. P 12.

674	**135**	7½p. grey-green	1·90	1·20
675		12½p. yellow-olive	6·75	3·75

136 Damascus

137 UN Emblem and Charter

1958 (10 Dec). Fourth NE Regional Conference, Damascus. P 12.

(a) POSTAGE

676	**136**	12½p. green	85	45

(b) AIR

677	**136**	17½p. violet	85	75

1958 (10 Dec). AIR. Tenth Anniversary of Declaration of Human Rights. P 12.

678	**137**	25p. purple	75	60
679		35p. blue-grey	1·00	75
680		40p. red-brown	1·50	1·00
678/680 *Set of 3*			3·00	2·10

137a UAR Postal Emblem

137b

Wmk **161** of Egypt

1959 (2 Jan). Post Day and Postal Employees' Social Fund. W **161** of Egypt. P 13½×13.

681	**137a**	20p. +10p. red, black and bluish green	1·50	1·50

1959 (22 Feb). First Anniversary of United Arab Republic. W **161** of Egypt. P 12×11½.

682 **137b** 12½p. red, black and green 60 45

138 Secondary School, Damascus

1959 (26 Feb). P 12.

683 **138** 12½p. green 45 30

138a Telecommunications

1959 (1 Mar). AIR. Arab Telecommunications Union Commemoration. P 12.

684 **138a** 40p. black and emerald .... 1·50 85

(**139**) **139a** UAR and Yemeni Flags

1959 (1 Mar). AIR. Second Damascus Conference. No. 684 optd with T **139**.

685 **138a** 40p. black and emerald (C.) .... 1·60 1·00

(Photo Survey Dept, Cairo)

1959 (8 Mar). First Anniversary of Proclamation of United Arab States (UAR and Yemen). W **161** of Egypt. P 13×13½.

686 **139a** 12½p. scarlet and green 75 45

140 Mother with Children

1959 (21 Mar). Mothers' Day. W **81a**. P 12.

687 **140** 15p. carmine 60 45

688 25p. grey-green 85 60

(**141**)

142

1959 (6 Apr). No. 528 surch with T **141**.

689 **92** 2½p. on 1p. deep olive (R.) 30 30

1959 (17 Apr). AIR. 13th Anniversary of Evacuation of Foreign Troops from Syria. T **142** and similar design. P 12×11½.

690 15p. green and orange-yellow 45 30

691 35p. carmine-red and grey .... 1·00 60

Designs: 15p. T **142**; 35p. Broken chain and flame.

143 **144** Emigration

1959. Vert designs as T **143**. P 11½.

692 2½p. violet (10.6.59) 15 15

693 5p. olive-brown (6.10.59) 20 15

694 7½p. ultramarine (11.59) 30 15

695 10p. blue-green (12.59) 35 15

692/695 *Set of 4* 90 55

Designs: 2½p. T **143**; 5p., 7½p., 10p. Different styles of ornamental scrollwork.

1959 (4 Aug). AIR. Emigrants' Congress. P 11½×12.

696 **144** 80p. black, red and green .... 2·20 1·50

(**145**) **146** Oil Refinery

1959. Various issues optd as T **145**.

(a) POSTAGE

697 15p. black (No. 611) (R.) (11.59) 85 45

698 50p. deep green (No. 536) (R.) (10.59) .... 2·00 1·50

(b) AIR

699 5p. emerald-green (No. 635) (15.7.59) 30 30

700 50p. reddish purple (No. 543) (16.8.59) .... 1·20 60

701 70p. violet (No. 544) (16.8.59) .... 1·90 75

697/701 *Set of 5* .... 5·75 3·25

1959 (12 Aug). AIR. Inauguration of Oil Refinery. P 11½×12.

702 **146** 50p. carmine, black and blue .... 3·25 1·30

147 **148** **149** Child and Factory

1959 (30 Aug). Sixth Damascus Fair. P 11½.

703 **147** 35p. green, violet and grey .... 1·50 85

MS703*a* 80×80 mm. 30p. brownish yellow and green showing Fair Emblem and Globe. Imperf .... 3·75 3·75

1959 (1 Oct). AIR. Aleppo Cotton Festival. P 11½.

704 **148** 45p. slate-blue .... 1·20 75

705 50p. claret .... 1·20 1·00

1959 (5 Oct). AIR. Children's Day. P 11½.

706 **149** 25p. red, deep blue and lilac 85 45

150 Boys' College, Damascus

150a 'Shield against Agression'

Wmk **190** of Egypt

1959 (17 Oct)–**60**. T **150** and similar horiz design. P 11½.

707	25p. light blue	1·20	45
708	35p. brown (17.2.60)	1·60	75

Designs: 25p. T **150**; 35p. Girls' College, Damascus.

(Litho Survey Dept, Cairo)

1959 (20 Oct). Army Day. W **190** of Egypt. P 13½×13.

709	**150a**	50p. sepia	1·50	75

151 Ears of Corn, Cotton, Cogwheel and Factories

152 Mosque and Oaks

1959 (30 Oct). Industrial and Agricultural Production Fair, Aleppo. P 11½.

710	**151**	35p. yellow-brown, blue and blue-grey	1·50	75

1959 (31 Dec). Tree Day. P 11½.

711	**152**	12½p. yellow-brown and bronze-green	60	30

153 A. R. Kawakbi

153a

1960 (11 Jan). 50th Death Anniversary of A. R. Kawakbi (writer). P 12×11½.

712	**153**	15p. deep grey-green	60	45

(Photo Survey Dept, Cairo)

1960 (22 Feb). Second Anniversary of United Arab Republic. W **190** of Egypt. P 13½×13.

713	**153a**	12½p. blackish green and red	60	45

154 Diesel Train

1960 (15 Mar). Latakia–Aleppo Railway Project. P 11½.

714	**154**	12½p. chocolate, black and blue	4·25	1·60

154a Arab League Centre, Cairo

(Photo Survey Dept, Cairo)

1960 (22 Mar). Inauguration of Arab League Centre, Cairo. W **190** of Egypt. P 13×13½.

715	**154a**	12½p. black and green	60	45
		a. Black (value and inscr) omitted		

A sheet of No. 715a was found at Damascus. With the Arms and inscription omitted it would be identical with any of the corresponding issues for Egypt, Jordan, Libya, Sudan or Yemen having the black omitted.

يوم الأم العربية ١٩٦٠
ARAB MOTHERS DAY 1960

(**155**)

155a Mother, Child and Map of Palestine

1960 (3 Apr). Mothers' Day. Optd with T **155**.

716	**140**	15p. carmine	60	45
717		25p. grey-green (R.)	1·00	60

(Photo Survey Dept, Cairo)

1960 (7 Apr). World Refugee Year. W **190** of Egypt. P 13×13½.

718	**155a**	12½p. carmine	60	45
719		50p. deep green	1·50	1·00

156 Government Building and Inscription

1960 (12 May). 14th Anniversary of Evacuation of Foreign Troops from Syria. P 11½.

720	**156**	12½p. carmine, violet and green	85	30

157 Hittin School

١٩٦٠
1960

(**158**)

1960 (1 July). P 12.

721	**157**	17½p. bright reddish lilac	1·00	45

1960. Industrial and Agricultural Production Fair, Aleppo. No. 710 optd with T **158**, in red.

722	**151**	35p. yellow-brown, blue and blue-grey	85	75

159 Mobile Crane and Compasses

(**160**)

1960 (15 Aug). AIR. Seventh International Damascus Fair. P 11½×12.
723 **159** 50p. black, bistre and carmine .... 1·50 1·00
MS723*a* 70×160 mm. 100p. grey-green, light blue and brown (Fair emblem containing flags of all nations). Imperf .... 5·00 5·00

1960 (6 Sept). AIR. Aleppo Cotton Festival. Nos. 704/705 optd with T **160**.
724 **148** 45p. slate-blue (C.) .... 1·20 75
725 50p. claret (G.) .... 1·50 1·00

161

162 Basketball

1960 (3 Oct). Children's Day. P 11½.
726 **161** 35p. red-brown and green .... 1·50 85

1960 (27 Dec). AIR. Olympic Games. T **162** and similar vert designs. P 12.
727 15p. brown, black and blue 85 30
728 20p. orange-brown, black and blue .... 1·00 45
729 25p. violet, rose, black and yellow .... 1·00 45
730 40p. violet, rose and black .... 2·00 1·20
727/730 *Set of 4* .... 4·25 2·20
Designs: 15p. T **162**; 20p. Swimming; 25p. Fencing (Arab-style); 40p. Horse-jumping.

(**163**)

1960 (29 Dec). Tree Day. No. 711 optd with T **163**, in red.
731 **152** 12½p. yellow-brown and bronze-green 85 45

164 'UN' and Globe

165 Hanano

1960 (31 Dec). AIR. 15th Anniversary of United Nations. P 12.
732 **164** 35p. red, green and ultramarine .... 1·00 60
733 50p. blue, ochre and red .... 1·50 85

(Des Ziad)

1961 (20 Feb). AIR. 25th Death Anniversary (1960) of Ibrahim Hanano (patriot). P 12×11½.
734 **165** 50p. grey-green and drab .... 1·50 85

165a State Emblem

166 St Siméon's Monastery

(Photo Survey Dept, Cairo)

1961 (22 Feb). Third Anniversary of United Arab Republic. W **190** of Egypt. P 13½.
735 **165a** 12½p. reddish violet 60 45

1961 (1 Apr). P 11½.
736 **166** 12½p. blue 45 30

167 Raising the Flag

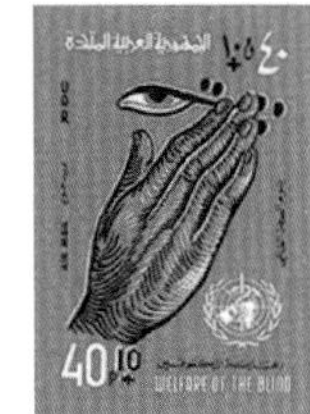

168 Eye, and Hand reading Braille

1961 (17 Apr). AIR. 15th Anniversary of Evacuation of Foreign Troops from Syria. W **81a** (sideways). P 11½.
737 **167** 40p. dull green .... 1·50 85

1961 (29 Apr). AIR. UN Campaign for Welfare of Blind. P 12×11½.
738 **168** 40p. +10p. black and deep grey-green. 1·20 1·00

169 Palestinian and Map

170 Cogwheel and Corn

(Des W. Eichel)

1961 (15 May). AIR. Palestine Day. P 12.
739 **169** 50p. blue and black .... 1·50 85

1961 (8 June). Industrial and Agricultural Production Fair, Aleppo. P 11½.
740 **170** 12½p. yellow, green, black and blue 60 45

171 Abou Tammam (796–846)

172 Damascus University, Discus-thrower and Lyre

(Des N. Yafary)

1961 (20 July). AIR. Abou Tammam (writer) Commemoration. P 12.
741 **171** 50p. sepia .... 1·20 60

(Des W. Eichel)

1961 (23 Aug). AIR. Fifth Universities Youth Festival. P 11½×12.
742 **172** 15p. black and carmine-red 60 30
743 35p. violet and blue-green .... 1·90 75
MS743*a* 100×63 mm. Nos. 742/743. Imperf .... 16·00 16·00

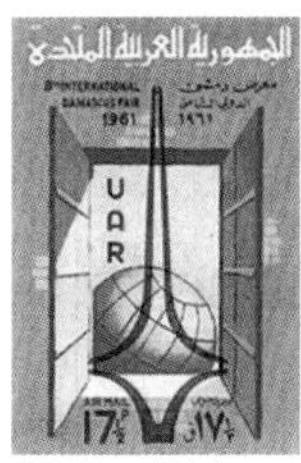
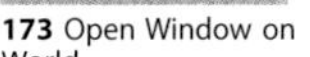

173 Open Window on World

174 St Simeon's Monastery

(Des M. Hammad)

1961 (25 Aug). AIR. Eighth International Damascus Fair. T **173** and similar vert design. P 12×11½.

744		17½p. bluish violet and deep green	45	30
745		50p. reddish violet and black	1·00	60
		a. Black (value and inscription omitted)	£100	

Designs: 17½p. T **173**; 50p. UAR Pavilion.

1961 (11 Oct). AIR. P 12.

746	**174**	200p. violet-blue	5·00	3·25

SYRIAN ARAB REPUBLIC

On 28 September 1961 Syrian troops revolted and proclaimed independence from the United Arab Republic. Syria took the name Syrian Arab Republic.

12½ and 50p. values as T **220** of Egypt (for UN Technical Co-operation Programme) were prepared but not issued.

175 Assembly Chamber

176 The Noria, Hama

177 Arch of Triumph, Latakia

177a *The Beauty of Palmyra* (statue)

(Des W. Eichel and M. Hammad)

1961 (2 Nov). Establishment of Syrian Arab Republic. P 12.

747	**175**	15p. lake	60	60
748		35p. olive	1·50	75
MS748*a*		80×80 mm. 50p. red, green, black and light blue (Syrian flag). Imperf	7·25	7·25

1961–63. Types **176/177a** and similar designs. P 11½ (2½p. to 10p.) or 12×11½ (others).

(a) POSTAGE

749	**176**	2½p. rose-red (17.12.61)	25	25
750		5p. greenish blue (10.1.62)	30	25
751	–	7½p. turquoise-green (24.1.62)	55	25
752	–	10p. orange (24.1 62)	80	25
753	**177**	12½p. drab (11.12.61)	1·40	15
754	**177a**	12½p. olive (3.10.62)	95	15
755		15p. ultramarine (11.10.62)	95	15
756		17½p. chocolate (15.10.62)	1·30	30
757		22½p. turquoise (18.10.62)	1·30	30
758	**177**	25p. red-brown (11.12.61)	2·10	30
749/758 *Set of* 10			9·00	2·10

Design: As T **176**—7½p., 10p. Khaled ibn el-Walid Mosque, Homs.

(b) AIR. Inscr 'AIR MAIL'

759	**177a**	45p. olive-yellow (17.12.61)	95	60
760		50p. orange-red (11.12.61)	1·30	75
761	–	85p. deep dull purple (17.12.61)	2·20	90
762	–	100p. purple (11.12.61)	3·00	1·10
763	–	200p. slate-green (12.11.62)	5·00	2·00
764	–	300p. deep blue (12.11.62)	6·75	2·10
764*a*	–	500p. purple (17.1.63)	10·50	5·00
764*b*	–	1000p. black (2.2.63)	22·00	9·00
759/764*b* *Set of* 8			47·00	19·00

Designs: Vert—85p., 100p. Archway and columns, Palmyra; 200p. to 1000p. King Zahir Bibar's tomb.

See also Nos. 799/800.

178 Arab League Emblem and Headquarters, Cairo

179 Campaign Emblem

(Des W. Eichel)

1962 (22 Mar). AIR. Arab League Week. P 12×11½.

765	**178**	17½p. deep bluish green and yellow-green	50	30
766		22½p. slate-violet and light blue	65	60
767		50p. sepia and salmon	1·80	1·10
765/767 *Set of* 3			2·75	1·80

(Des W. Eichel)

1962 (7 Apr). AIR. Malaria Eradication. P 12×11½.

768	**179**	12½p. violet, sepia and light blue	65	45
769		50p. blue-green, chocolate and pale yellow	1·60	1·10

180 Prancing Horse

(Des M. Hammad)

1962 (17 Apr). AIR. 16th Anniversary of Evacuation of Foreign Troops from Syria. T **180** and similar vert design. P 12×11½.

770		45p. orange and violet	95	45
771		55p. violet-blue and light blue	1·60	60

Designs: 45p. T **180**; 55p. Military commander.

181 Qalb Lozah Church

182 Martyrs' Memorial, Swaida

(Des W. Eichel)

1962 (28 May). P 11½×12.

772	**181**	17½p. olive	80	30
773		35p. deep bluish green	1·40	45

(Des Ziad)

1962 (11 June). Syrian Revolution Commemoration. P 12×11½.

774	**182**	12½p. black-brown and drab	50	15
775		35p. deep bluish green and turquoise-green	1·10	45

183 Jupiter Temple Gate

184 Globe, Monument and Handclasp

1962. P 11½.

776 **183** 2½p. dull turquoise (28.6.62) 50 15
777 5p. orange-brown (2.7.62) 65 15
778 7½p. sepia (4.7.62) 80 25
779 10p. reddish purple (8.7.62) 80 25
776/779 *Set of 4* .... 2·50 70

(Des M. Hammad)

1962 (25 Aug). AIR. Ninth International Fair, Damascus. T **184** and similar vert design. P 12×11½.

780 **184** 17½p. brown and reddish purple 50 30
781 22½p. magenta and rose-red 65 45
782 – 40p. deep dull purple and pale chocolate 80 60
783 – 45p. turquoise-blue and turquoise-green .... 1·60 75
780/783 *Set of 4* .... 3·25 1·90

Design: 40p., 45p. Fair entrance.

185 Festival, Emblem

186 President Kudsi

1962 (20 Sept). AIR. Aleppo Cotton Festival. P 12×11½.

784 **185** 12½p. yellow, brown-purple, black and bronze-green 65 40
785 50p. yellow, bronze-green, black and brown-purple .... 1·30 1·20

See also Nos. 820/821.

(Des Ziad)

1962 (14 Dec). Presidential Elections. P 12×11½.

(a) POSTAGE

786 **186** 12½p. chocolate and cobalt 65 15

(b) AIR Inscr 'AIR MAIL'

787 **186** 50p. indigo and buff .... 1·30 75

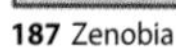

187 Zenobia

188 Saadallah el-Jabiri

(Des Ziad)

1962 (27 Dec). AIR. P 12×11½.

788 **187** 45p. bright violet .... 2·40 75
789 50p. carmine-red .... 2·40 75
790 85p. blue-green .... 2·40 1·10
791 100p. maroon .... 2·75 1·50
788/791 *Set of 4* .... 9·00 3·75

See also Nos. 801/804.

(Des Ziad)

1962 (29 Dec). AIR. 15th Anniversary of Death of Saadallah el-Jabiri (revolutionary). P 12×11½.

792 **188** 50p. deep grey-blue 95 60

189 Mohardé Woman

190 Ears of Wheat, Hand and Globe

(Des Ziad)

1963 (2 Jan–20 June). AIR. Women in Regional Costumes. T **189** and similar vert designs. Multicoloured. P 12.

793 40p. Marje Sultan (20.6) 95 75
794 45p. Kalamoun (20.6) .... 1·10 85
795 50p. Type **189** .... 1·30 90
796 55p. Jabal al-Arab (20.6) .... 1·60 1·10
797 60p. Afrine .... 1·80 1·10
798 65p. Hauran .... 2·40 1·50
793/798 *Set of 6* .... 8·25 5·50

(Des Ziad)

1963 (9–19 Feb). As Types **177a** and **187** but smaller (20×26 *mm*). P 11½.

799 **177a** 2½p. slate-violet 30 15
800 5p. bright purple 40 15
801 **187** 7½p. deep slate (19.2) 65 15
802 10p. olive-brown (19.2) .... 1·30 25
803 12½p. ultramarine (19.2) .... 1·90 25
804 15p. dull purple-brown (19.2) .... 3·25 30
799/804 *Set of 6* .... 7·00 1·10

(Des Ishel)

1963 (9 Apr). Freedom from Hunger. T **190** and similar vert design. P 12×11½.

(a) POSTAGE

805 12½p. black and ultramarine 50 30

(b) AIR. Inscr 'AIR MAIL'

806 50p. black and red 95 45
MS806*a* 90×65 mm. Nos. 805/806. Imperf .... 4·00 3·75

Designs: 12½p. T **190**; 50p. Bird feeding young in nest.

191 Faris el-Khouri (politician)

192 SAR Emblem

(Des Ziad)

1963 (17 Apr). AIR. 17th Anniversary of Evacuation of Foreign Troops from Syria. P 12×11½.

807 **191** 17½p. sepia 65 30
808 **192** 22½p. turquoise-green and black 95 45

193 Eagle

194 Aboû l'Alâ al-Ma'arri (bust)

(Des M. Hammad)

1963 (18 Apr). AIR. Baathist Revolution Commemoration. P 12×11½.

809 **193** 12½p. emerald 30 30
810 50p. magenta .... 1·10 60

(Des Ziad)

1963 (19 Aug). AIR. 990th Birth Anniversary of Aboû l'Alâ al-Ma'arri (poet). P 12×11½.

811 **194** 50p. slate-violet .... 1·30 90

195 Copper Water Jug **196** Central Bank

(Des Ziad)

1963 (25 Aug). AIR. Tenth International Fair, Damascus. P 12×11½.

812 **195** 37½p. yellow, red, black and ultramarine .... 1·10 60
813 50p. yellow, red, black and greenish blue .... 1·40 75

(Des Ishel)

1963. Damascus Buildings. T **196** and similar horiz designs. P 11½×12.

814 17½p. violet (28.11) .... 2·40 60
815 22½p. bluish violet (10.10) 65 45
816 25p. olive-brown (2.9) 50 30
817 35p. bright purple (23.11) 80 45
814/817 *Set of* 4 .... 4·00 1·60

Buildings: 17½p. Hejaz Railway Station; 22½p. Mouassat Hospital; 25p. T **196**; 35p. Post Office, Al-Jalaa.

197 Red Crescent and Centenary Emblem **198** Child with Ball

(Des Ishel)

1963 (9 Sept). AIR. Red Cross Centenary. T **197** and similar vert design. Crescent in red. P 12×11½.

818 15p. black and grey-blue 65 45
819 50p. black and yellow-green .... 1·30 75

Designs: 15p. T **196**; 50p. Red Crescent, globe and centenary emblem.

1963 (26 Sept). Aleppo Cotton Festival. Design as T **185** but with 'POSTAGE' and '1963' in place of 'AIRMAIL' and '1962'.

820 **185** 17½p. multicoloured 50 30
821 22½p. multicoloured 80 45

(Des Ziad)

1963 (24 Oct). Children's Day. P 12×11½.

822 **198** 12½p. deep green and light emerald 30 30
823 22½p. deep green and rose-red 80 40

199 Abou Feras al-Hamadani **200** Flame on Head

(Des Ziad)

1963 (13 Nov). AIR. Millenary of Death of Abou Feras al-Hamadani (poet). P 12×11½.

824 **199** 50p. sepia and bistre .... 1·30 90

(Des Ishel)

1963 (10 Dec). AIR. 15th Anniversary of Declaration of Human Rights. Flame in red. P 12×11½.

825 **200** 17½p. black and blue-grey 30 25
826 22½p. black and green 80 30
827 50p. black and violet .... 1·10 75
825/827 *Set of* 3 .... 2·00 1·20
MS827*a* 110×70 mm. Nos. 825/827. Imperf .... 3·25 3·00

201 Emblem and Flag

(Des Aeshille)

1964 (8 Mar). AIR. First Anniversary of Baathist Revolutions of 8 March 1963. Emblem and flag in red, black and green; inscr in black. P 11½.

828 **201** 15p. pale yellow-green 30 20
829 17½p. pink 50 30
830 22½p. light grey 80 45
828/830 *Set of* 3 .... 1·40 85

202 Ugharit Princess **203** Chahba, Thalassa, Mosaic

(T **203** des Ishel)

1964. P 11½ (T **202**) or 11½×12 (T **203**).

(a) POSTAGE

831 **202** 2½p. deep greenish grey (18.3) 15 15
832 5p. chocolate (5.8) 15 15
833 7½p. bright purple (23.5) 15 15
834 10p. emerald (25.8) 25 15
835 12½p. bright violet (5.4) 30 25
836 17½p. ultramarine (5.8) 50 30
837 20p. carmine-red (7.9) 95 30
838 25p. orange (7.9) .... 1·60 40

(b) AIR

839 **203** 27½p. carmine-red (8.6) 50 25
840 45p. deep purple-brown (15.7) 95 30
841 50p. emerald (8.7) .... 1·30 40
842 55p. bronze-green (15.7) .... 1·40 45
843 60p. blue (6.7) .... 1·60 60
831/843 *Set of* 13 .... 8·75 3·50

204 Kaaba, Mecca, and Mosque, Damascus **205** Abou al-Zahrawi

(Des Ishel)

1964 (30 Mar). AIR. First Arab Moslem Wakf Ministers' Conference. P 11½×12.

844 **204** 12½p. black and greenish blue 30 15
845 22½p. black and bright purple 50 30
846 50p. black and green .... 1·10 75
844/846 *Set of* 3 .... 1·70 1·10

1964 (17 Apr). AIR. 18th Anniversary of Evacuation of Foreign Troops from Syria. Design as T **99** but larger (38½×26 *mm*). Inscr '1964'. P 11½×12.

847 20p. blue 30 30
848 25p. claret 50 45
849 60p. emerald .... 1·10 75
847/849 *Set of* 3 .... 1·70 1·40

(Des Ziad Zoukari)

1964 (20 Apr). AIR. Fourth Dental and Oral Surgery Congress, Damascus. P 12×11½.

850 **205** 60p. bistre-brown .... 1·30 90

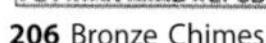

206 Bronze Chimes

207 Cotton Plant and Symbols

(**208**)

209 Aero Club Emblem

(Des Ziad and Ghiath)

1964 (25 Aug). AIR. 11th International Fair, Damascus. T **206** and similar vert design. P 12×11½.

851 20p. multicoloured 95 30
852 25p. magenta, black, green and yellow .... 1·10 45

Designs: 20p. T **206**; 25p. Fair emblem.

(Des Ishel)

1964 (17 Sept). AIR. Aleppo Cotton Festival. P 12×11½.

(a) T **207**

853 25p. yellow, green, black, blue and light blue 80 45

(b) T **207** *optd with T* **208**

854 25p. yellow, green, black, blue and light blue (R.) 80 45

(Des Ishel)

1964 (8 Oct). AIR. Tenth Anniversary of Syrian Aero Club. P 11½×12.

855 **209** 12½p. black and green 50 15
856 17½p. black and red 65 25
857 20p. black and blue .... 1·60 30
855/857 *Set of 3* .... 2·50 65

210 APU Emblem

211 Book within Hands

(Des G. Kilani)

1964 (11 Nov). AIR. Tenth Anniversary of Arab Postal Union's Permanent Office, Cairo. P 12×11½.

858 **210** 12½p. black and orange 50 15
859 20p. black and green 55 25
860 25p. black and magenta 65 30
858/860 *Set of 3* .... 1·50 65

(Des Ishel)

1964 (30 Nov). AIR. Burning of Algiers Library. P 12×11½.

861 **211** 12½p. black and green 50 15
862 17½p. black and carmine 55 25
863 20p. black and blue 65 30
861/863 *Set of 3* .... 1·50 65

212 Tennis

213 Flag, Map and Revolutionaries

1965 (7 Feb). AIR. Olympic Games, Tokyo. T **212** and similar vert designs. Multicoloured. P 12×11½.

864 12½p. Type **212** 30 20
865 17½p. Wrestling 80 25
866 20p. Weightlifting 95 30
864/866 *Set of 3* .... 1·80 70
MS866*a* 90×57 mm. 100p. Wrestlers and Drummer. Imperf .... 4·75 4·50

(Des A. Ismail)

1965 (8 Mar). Second Anniversary of Baathist Revolution of 8 March 1963. P 11½×12.

867 **213** 12½p. black, red, green and yellow-brown 30 15
868 17½p. black, red, green and blue 50 25
869 20p. black, red, green and grey 65 30
867/869 *Set of 3* .... 1·30 65

214 Rameses II in War Chariot, Abu Simbel

1965 (21 Mar). AIR. Nubian Monuments Preservation. T **214** and similar horiz design. P 11½×12.

870 22½p. black, blue and light emerald 65 30
871 50p. black, light emerald and blue .... 1·30 60

Designs: 22½p. T **214**; 50p. Heads of Rameses II.

215 Weather Instruments and Map

1965 (23 Mar). World Meteorological Day. P 11½×12.

872 **215** 12½p. black and dull purple 30 20
873 27½p. black and light blue 65 45

216 Al-Radi

217 Evacuation Symbol

(Des A. Ismail)

1965 (3 Apr). AIR. 950th Death Anniversary of Al-Sharif al-Radi (writer). P 12×11½.

874 **216** 50p. black .... 1·80 75

(Des M. Hammad)

1965 (17 Apr). 19th Anniversary of Evacuation of Foreign Troops from Syria. P 12×11½.

875 **217** 12½p. apple-green and turquoise-blue 30 25
876 27½p. lilac and red 65 30

218 Hippocrates and Avicenna

(Des A. Ismail)

1965 (19 Apr). AIR. 'Medical Days of the Near and Middle East'. P 11½.

877 **218** 60p. black and turquoise-green .... 2·50 1·10

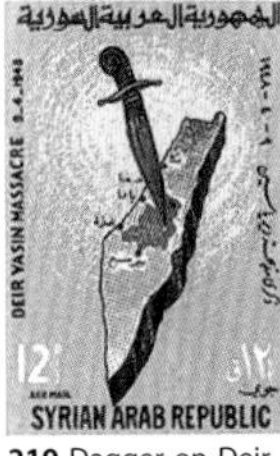

219 Dagger on Deir Yassin, Palestine

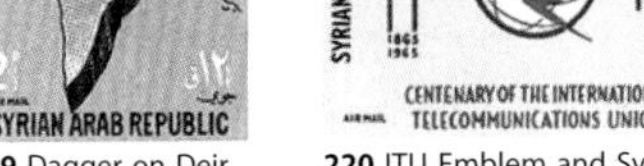

220 ITU Emblem and Symbols

(Des A. Ismail)

1965 (15 May). AIR. Deir Yassin Massacre on 9 April 1948. P 12×11½.

878 **219** 12½p. red, black, yellow and light grey-blue 50 15

879 60p. red, black, yellow and light reddish purple .... 1·30 60

(Des A. Ismail)

1965 (24 May). AIR. Centenary of International Telecommunications Union. P 11½×12.

880 **220** 12½p. red, ultramarine, black and pale blue 50 25

881 27½p. red, ultramarine, black and pale bistre 95 30

882 60p. red, ultramarine, black and pale turquoise .... 1·80 1·10

880/882 *Set of 3* .... 3·00 1·50

D **221**

221 Arab Family, Flags and Map

222 Hands holding Hoe and Pick

1965 (June). POSTAGE DUE. P 11½.

D883 D **221** 2½p. violet-blue 50 25

D884 5p. sepia 80 30

D885 10p. blue-green 90 40

D886 17½p. carmine .... 1·60 1·80

D887 25p. new blue .... 2·40 2·30

D883/D887 *Set of 5* .... 5·50 4·50

(Des A. Ismail)

1965 (12 June). Palestine Week. P 12×11½.

883 **221** 12½p. +5p. black, red, green and light orange-brown 65 40

884 25p. +5p. black, red, green and lilac 95 45

(Des M. Hammad)

1965 (11–28 Aug). Peasants' Union. P 11½×11.

885 **222** 2½p. blue-green 15 15

886 12½p. violet 30 15

887 15p. brown-purple (28.8) 50 15

885/887 *Set of 3* 85 40

The above stamps are inscribed 'RERUBLIC' for 'RE-PUBLIC'.

223 Welcoming Emigrant

224 Fair Entrance

(Des A Ismail)

1965 (23 Aug). AIR. 'Welcome Arab Emigrants'. P 12×11½.

888 **223** 25p. blue, brown, yellow-green and reddish violet 50 30

889 100p. blue, brown, yellow-green and deep olive-brown .... 2·10 1·20

(Des G. Rahmé)

1965 (25 Aug). AIR. 12th International Fair, Damascus. T **224** and similar vert designs. Multicoloured. P 12×11½.

890 12½p. Type **224** 15 15

891 27½p. Globe and compasses 65 30

892 60p. Syrian brassware .... 1·10 75

890/892 *Set of 3* .... 1·70 1·10

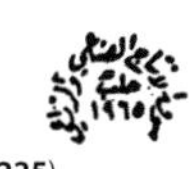

(**225**)

SYRIAN ARAB REPUBLIC

226 Cotton Boll and Shuttles

1965 (27 Sept). AIR. Aleppo Industrial and Agricultural Production Fair. No. 894 optd with T **225**, in red.

893 **226** 25p. multicoloured 95 30

(Des G. Rahmé)

1965 (30 Sept). AIR. Aleppo Cotton Festival. P 12×11½.

894 **226** 25p. multicoloured 95 30

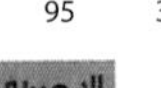

227 ICY Emblem and View of Damascus

228 Arabs, Torch and Map

(Des A. Ismail)

1965 (24 Oct). AIR. International Co-operation Year. P 11½×12.

895 **227** 25p. multicoloured 95 30

(Des M. Hammad)

1965 (23 Nov). National Revolution Council. P 12×11½.

896 **228** 12½p. deep emerald, red, black and new blue 30 25

897 25p. deep emerald, red, black and bistre 80 30

229 Industrial Workers

1966 (1 Feb). Labour Unions. P 11½.

898	**229**	12½p. greenish blue	15	15
899		15p. rose-carmine	30	20
900		20p. slate-lilac	50	25
901		25p. drab	65	30
898/901 *Set of 4*			1·40	80

230 Radio Aerial, Globe and Flag

(Des A. Ismail)

1966 (17 Feb). AIR. Arab Information Ministers' Conference, Damascus. P 12×11½.

902	**230**	25p. multicoloured	50	30
903		60p. multicoloured	1·10	75

231 Dove-shaped Hand holding Flower

232 Colossi, Abu Simbel

(Des K. Alwani and A. Jaffan)

1966 (8 Mar). AIR. Third Anniversary of Baathist Revolution of 8 March 1963. T **231** and similar multicoloured design. P 11½×12 (17½p.) or 12×11½ (others).

904	12½p. Type **231**	15	15
905	17½p. Revolutionaries (*horiz*)	30	20
906	50p. Type **231**	2·10	75
904/906 *Set of 3*		2·30	1·00

(Des A. Ismail)

1966 (15 Mar). AIR. Nubian Monuments Preservation Week. P 12×11½.

907	**232**	25p. deep blue	65	30
908		60p. olive-grey	1·30	45

233 Roman Lamp

234 UN Emblem and Headquarters

235 UN Flag

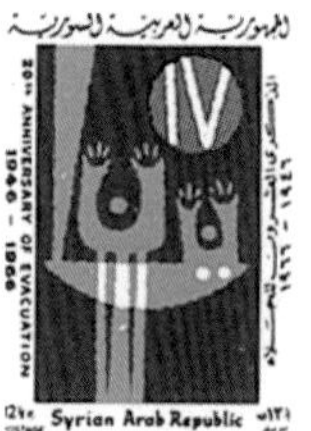

236 *Evacuation* (abstract)

(Des A. Ismail)

1966 (5 Apr–15 June). T **233** and similar vert design. P 11½.

909	**233**	2½p. grey-green	15	15
910		5p. reddish purple (15.6)	50	30
911	–	7½p. chocolate	30	25
912	–	10p. light reddish violet (15.6)	30	25
909/912 *Set of 4*			1·10	85

Design: 7½p., 10p. 12th-century Islamic vessel.

(Des M. Turkmani)

1966 (11 Apr). AIR. 20th Anniversary of United Nations Organisation. P 11½×12.

913	**234**	25p. black and light grey	30	30
914		50p. black and light emerald	95	75

MS915 90×70 mm. **235** 100p. yellow, bright blue and black. Imperf. 3·25 3·00

(Des K. Alwani)

1966 (17 Apr). 20th Anniversary of Evacuation of Foreign Troops from Syria. P 12×11½.

916	**236**	12½p. multicoloured	30	15
917		27½p. multicoloured	65	45

237 Workers marching across Globe

(Des A. Ismail)

1966 (1 May). AIR. Labour Day. P 11½×12.

918	**237**	60p. multicoloured	1·10	75

238 WHO Building

239 Traffic Signals and Map on Hand

(Des M. Turkmani)

1966 (3 May). AIR. Inauguration of World Health Organisation Headquarters, Geneva. P 11½×12.

919	**238**	60p. black, blue and greenish yellow	95	45

(Des G. Rahmé)

1966 (4 May). AIR. Traffic Day. P 12×11½.

920	**239**	25p. multicoloured	65	30

240 Astarte and Tyche (wrongly inscr 'ASTRATE')

241 Fair Emblem

(Des A. Ismail)

1966 (26 July). AIR. P 12×11½.

921	**240**	50p. light bistre-brown	95	45
922		60p. slate-grey	1·60	75

(Des G. Rahmé)

1966 (25 Aug). AIR. 13th International Fair, Damascus. P 12×11½.

923	**241**	12½p. multicoloured	30	15
924		60p. multicoloured	1·10	90

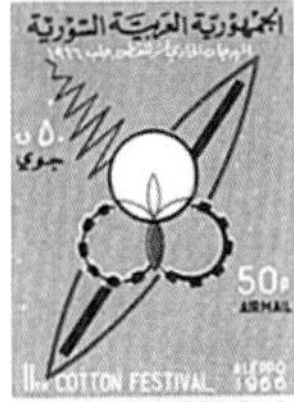
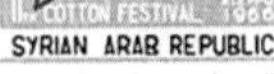
242 Shuttle (stylised)

243 Decade Emblem

(Des G. Rahmé)

1966 (9 Sept). AIR. Aleppo Cotton Festival. P 12×11½.

925	**242**	50p. black, carmine and silver-grey	1·10	75

(Des A. Ismail)

1966 (24 Oct). AIR. International Hydrological Decade. P 12×11½.

926	**243**	12½p. black, orange and yellow-green	30	15
927		60p. black, orange and blue	1·30	60

244 Emir Abd-el-Kader

(Des A. Ismail)

1966 (7 Nov). AIR. Return of Emir Abd-el-Kader's Remains to Algiers. P 12×11½.

928	**244**	12½p. black and light emerald	65	20
929		50p. red-brown and light emerald	95	60

245 UNRWA Emblem

(Des A. Ismail)

1966 (12 Dec). AIR. 21st Anniversary of United Nations Day, and Refugee Week. P 11½×12.

930	**245**	12½p. +2½p. black and violet-blue	30	30
931		50p. +5p. black and green	1·10	1·10

246 Handclasp and Map

247 Doves and Oil Pipelines

(Des A. Ismail)

1967 (8 Feb). AIR. Solidarity Congress, Damascus. P 12×11½.

932	**246**	20p. multicoloured	50	25
933		25p. multicoloured	65	30

(Des A. Ismail)

1967 (8 Feb). AIR. Fourth Anniversary of Baathist Revolution of 8 March 1963. P 12×11½.

934	**247**	17½p. multicoloured	50	25
935		25p. multicoloured	65	30
936		27½p. multicoloured	95	45
934/936 *Set of 3*			1·90	90

248 Soldier and Citizens with Banner

249 Workers' Monument, Damascus

(Des A. Ismail)

1967 (17 Apr). AIR. 21st Anniversary of Evacuation of Foreign Troops from Syria. P 12×11½.

937	**248**	17½p. emerald-green	30	20
938		25p. brown-purple	50	25
939		27½p. royal blue	65	30
937/939 *Set of 3*			1·30	70

(Des A. Ismail)

1967 (1 May). AIR. Labour Day. P 12×11½.

940	**249**	12½p. turquoise	30	15
941		50p. magenta	1·10	75

250 Core Bust

251 'African Woman' (vase)

252 Head of a Young Man from Amrith

(Des Ishel (T **250**), A. Ismail (others))

1967 (19 June–12 Dec).

(a) POSTAGE. P 11½

942	**250**	2½p. green	15	15
943		5p. rose-red (10.7)	25	15
944		10p. turquoise-blue (10.7)	30	15
945		12½p. brown	40	20
946	**251**	15p. bright purple (12.12)	50	25
947		20p. new blue (12.12)	55	25
948		25p. deep emerald (12.12)	65	30
949		27½p. ultramarine (12.12)	70	40

(b) AIR. P 12×12½ (7 Oct)

950	**252**	45p. vermilion	80	45
951		50p. magenta	1·10	55
952		60p. light turquoise-blue	1·30	75
953	–	100p. deep green	1·60	90
954	–	500p. brown-red	8·00	5·00
942/954 *Set of 13*			14·50	8·50

Design: Vert—100p., 500p. Bust of Princess (2nd-century bronze).

253 Flags and Fair Entrance

255 Cotton Boll and Cogwheel

254 Statue of Ur-Nina and Tourist Emblem

(Des A. Ismail)

1967 (25 Aug). AIR. 14th International Damascus Fair. P 12.

955 **253** 12½p. multicoloured ... 30 15
956 60p. multicoloured ... 1·10 75

(Des H. A. Ayash)

1967 (2 Sept). AIR. International Tourist Year. P 12.

957 **254** 12½p. bright purple, black and light blue ... 30 20
958 25p. red, black and light blue ... 40 25
959 27½p. royal blue, black and light blue ... 65 30
957/959 *Set of 3* ... 1·20 70
MS960 105×80 mm. **254** 60p. royal blue, black and light blue. Imperf ... 3·00 2·75

(Des A. Jaffan)

1967 (28 Sept). AIR. Aleppo Cotton Festival. P 12×12½.

961 **255** 12½p. black, light brown and orange-yellow ... 30 20
962 60p. black, light brown and light greenish yellow ... 1·10 75

(**256**)

257 Ibn el-Naphis (scientist)

1967 (28 Sept). AIR. Industrial and Agricultural Production Fair, Aleppo. Nos. 961/962 optd with T **256**, in red.

963 **255** 12½p. black, light brown and orange-yellow ... 30 20
964 60p. black, light brown and light greenish yellow ... 1·10 75

(Des A. Ismail)

1967 (28 Dec). AIR. Sciences Week. P 12×12½.

965 **257** 12½p. orange-red and green ... 30 25
966 27½p. bright magenta and deep blue ... 95 30

258 Acclaiming Human Rights

(Des M. Hammad)

1968 (21 Feb). AIR. Human Rights Year. T **258** and similar horiz design. P 12½×12.

967 **258** 12½p. black, turquoise and light blue ... 30 20
968 60p. black, brown-red and pink ... 1·10 90
MS969 105×80 mm. 100p. multicoloured (Human Rights emblem and outlines of faces). Imperf ... 3·25 2·75

259 Learning to Read

(Des A. Ismail (T **259**), H. A. Ayash (others))

1968 (3 Mar). AIR. Literacy Campaign. T **259** and similar vert design. Multicoloured, background colours given. P 12×12½.

970 **259** 12p. carmine ... 15 15
971 – 17½p. vermilion ... 30 20
972 **259** 25p. green ... 65 25
a. Black (value and inscr) omitted ...
973 – 45p. blue ... 95 60
970/973 *Set of 4* ... 1·80 1·10

Design: 17½p., 45p. Flaming torch and open book.

260 *The Arab Revolutionary* (Damascus statue)

261 Map of North Africa and Arabia

(Des Ziad Zoukari)

1968 (8 Mar). Fifth Anniversary of Baathist Revolution of 8 March 1963. P 12×12½.

974 **260** 12½p. brown, yellow and black ... 30 25
975 25p. magenta, pink and black ... 80 30
976 27½p. myrtle-green, light green and black ... 90 45
974/976 *Set of 3* ... 1·80 90

(Des A. Ismail)

1968 (7 Apr). 21st Anniversary of Baath Arab Socialist Party. P 12×12½.

977 **261** 12½p. multicoloured ... 30 20
978 60p. multicoloured ... 1·10 75

262 Euphrates Dam

(Des H. A. Ayash)

1968 (11 Apr). AIR. Euphrates Dam Project. P 12½×12.

979 **262** 12½p. multicoloured ... 30 20
980 17½p. multicoloured ... 50 25
981 25p. multicoloured ... 1·10 30
979/981 *Set of 3* ... 1·70 70

263 Hands holding Spanner, Rifle and Torch

264 Railway Track and Sun

(Des A. Jaffan)

1968 (13 Apr). 'Mobilisation Efforts'. P 12×12½.

982 **263** 12½p. multicoloured ... 25 15
983 17½p. multicoloured ... 30 25
984 25p. multicoloured ... 65 30
982/984 *Set of 3* ... 1·10 65

(Des A. Ismail)

1968 (17 Apr). 22nd Anniversary of Evacuation of Foreign Troops from Syria. P 12½×12.

985 **264** 12½p. multicoloured ... 1·60 30
986 27½p. multicoloured ... 3·50 45
a. Blue-grey (frame) omitted ... £150

The omission of the blue-grey on No. 986a gives a stamp with no face value.

265 Oil Pipeline Map

(Des H. A. Ayash)

1968 (1 May). Syrian Oil Exploration. P 12½×12.

987	**265**	12½p. new blue, green and light yellow-green	50	20
988		17½p. new blue, purple-brown and pink	1·10	30

266 Torch, Map and Laurel

267 Refugee Family

1968 (May). Palestine Day. P 12×12½.

989	**266**	12½p. multicoloured	50	15
990		25p. multicoloured	80	25
991		27½p. multicoloured	95	30
989/991		*Set of 3*	2·00	65

1968 (20 May). Red Crescent Refugees Fund. P 12½×12.

992	**267**	12½p. +2½p. black, bright purple and violet-blue	80	75
993		27½p. +7½p. black, carmine and light violet	95	75

268 Avenzoar (physician) and WHO Emblem

269 Ear of Corn, Cogwheel and Saracen Gate, Aleppo Citadel

(Des A. Ismail)

1968 (10 June). AIR. 20th Anniversary of World Health Organisation. T **268** and similar horiz designs. P 12½×12.

994	12½p. multicoloured	50	15
995	25p. multicoloured	65	30
996	60p. multicoloured	1·10	75
994/996	*Set of 3*	2·00	1·10

Designs: 12½p. T **268**. As T **268**, but with different portraits of Arab physicians—25p. Razi; 60p. Jabir.

(Des M. Hammad)

1968 (18 July). Industrial and Agricultural Production Fair, Aleppo. P 12×12½.

997	**269**	12½p. multicoloured	50	20
998		27½p. multicoloured	65	30

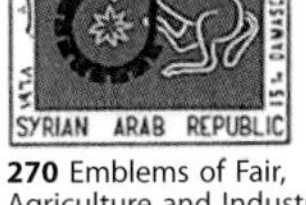

270 Emblems of Fair, Agriculture and Industry

271 Gathering Cotton

(Des G. Rahmé)

1968 (25 Aug). 15th International Damascus Fair. T **270** and similar design. P 12½×12 (27½p.) or 12×12½ (others).

999	**270**	12½p. black, bright green and chocolate	15	15
1000	–	27½p. black, red, emerald and light grey-blue	65	30
1001	**270**	60p. black, orange and slate-blue	1·10	75
999/1001		*Set of 3*	1·70	1·10

Design: Horiz—27½p. Flag, hand with torch and emblems.

(Des M. Hammad)

1968 (3 Oct). Aleppo Cotton Festival. P 12×12½.

1002	**271**	12½p. multicoloured	50	25
1003		27½p. multicoloured	65	30

272 Monastery of St Siméon the Stylite

273 Oil Derrick

1968 (10 Oct). AIR. Ancient Monuments (1st series). T **272** and similar designs. P 12½×12 (horiz) or 12×12½ (vert).

1004	15p. brown, sepia and light yellow-green	30	15
1005	17½p. deep purple-brown, red-brown and pale chocolate	50	25
1006	22½p. brown, light red, sepia and stone	65	30
1007	45p. brown, light red, sepia and light yellow	95	60
1008	50p. brown, sepia and pale grey-blue	1·10	75
1004/1008	*Set of 5*	3·25	1·80

Designs: Vert—17½p. El Tekkieh Mosque, Damascus; 22½p. Temple columns, Palmyra. Horiz—15p. T **272**; 45p. Chapel of St Paul, Bab Kisan; 50p. Amphitheatre, Bosra.

See also Nos. 1026/1030.

1968 (2–25 Nov). P 11½.

1009	**273**	2½p. green and blue (25.11)	15	15
1010		5p. ultramarine and blue-green	30	15
1011		7½p. new blue and light apple-green	40	15
1012		10p. emerald and light greenish yellow	50	15
1013		12½p. rose-red and light yellow	65	20
1014		15p. brown and bistre (25.11)	80	25
1015		27½p. brown and orange (25.11)	1·10	30
1009/1015		*Set of 7*	3·50	1·20

274 Al-Jahez (scientist)

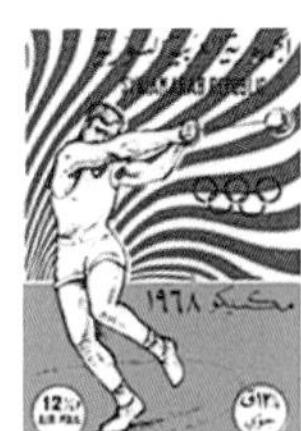
275 Throwing the Hammer

(Des Ziad Zoukari)

1968 (9 Nov). Ninth Science Week. P 12×12½.

1016	**274**	12½p. black and pale yellow-olive	50	30
1017		27½p. black and pale grey	1·10	45

(Des A. Qurabi (Nos. 1018/1021), Ismail (No. **MS**1022))

1968 (19 Dec). AIR. Olympic Games, Mexico. T **275** and similar designs. P 12×12½.

1018	12½p. black, magenta and emerald	30	25
1019	25p. black, red and emerald	50	30
1020	27½p. black, light grey and emerald	65	45
1021	60p. multicoloured	95	60
1018/1021	*Set of 4*	2·20	1·40
MS1022	105×80 mm. 50p. multicoloured. Imperf	4·75	4·50

Designs. Vert—12½p. T **275**; 25p. Throwing the discus; 27½p. Running; 60p. Basketball. Horiz (53×36 *mm*)—50p. Polo.

276 Aerial View of Airport

(Des H. A. Ayash)

1969 (20 Jan). AIR. Construction of Damascus International Airport. P 12½×12.

1023	**276** 12½p. deep bluish green, light blue and greenish yellow	50	20
1024	17½p. violet, vermilion and pale green	95	30
1025	60p. blue-black, magenta and light yellow	2·50	60
1023/1025	*Set of 3*	3·50	1·00

277 Baal-Shamin Temple, Palmyra

1969 (20 Jan). AIR. Ancient Monuments (2nd series). T **277** and similar designs. Multicoloured. Photo. P 12×11½ (horiz) or 11½×12 (vert).

1026	25p. Type **277**	50	30
1027	45p. Omayyad Mosque, Damascus (*vert*)	65	45
1028	50p. Amphitheatre, Palmyra	80	60
1029	60p. Khaled ibn el-Walid Mosque, Homs (*vert*)	95	70
1030	100p. St Siméon's Column, Jebel Samaan	1·60	1·20
1026/1030	*Set of 5*	4·00	3·00

278 'Sun' and Clenched Fists in Broken Handcuffs

279 Sun of Freedom

(Des M. Hammad)

1969 (8 Mar). Sixth Anniversary of Baathist Revolution of 8 March 1963. P 12½×12.

1031	**278** 12½p. red, yellow, black and chalky blue	30	20
1032	25p. red, yellow, black and grey	65	25
1033	27½p. red, yellow, black and bluish green	70	30
1031/1033	*Set of 3*	1·50	70

(Des A. Jaffan)

1969 (29 Mar). Fifth Youth Festival, Homs. P 12×12½.

1034	**279** 12½p. vermilion, yellow and greenish blue	30	25
1035	25p. vermilion, yellow and olive-green	50	30

280 Symbols of Progress

281 'Workers', Cogwheel and ILO Emblem

(Des H. A. Ayash)

1969 (17 Apr). 23rd Anniversary of Evacuation of Foreign Troops from Syria. P 12×12½.

1036	**280** 12½p. multicoloured	30	25
1037	27½p. multicoloured	50	30

(Des A. Jaffan (12½p., 27½p.), H. A. Ayash (60p.))

1969 (1 May). AIR. 50th Anniversary of International Labour Organisation. T **281** and similar miniature sheet. P 12½×12.

1038	**281** 12½p. multicoloured	30	25
1039	27½p. multicoloured	65	30
MS1040	76×54 mm. 60p. multicoloured. Imperf	3·25	3·00

Design: Larger (54×37 *mm*)—60p. ILO Emblem.

282 Russian Dancers

283 *Fortune* (statue)

(Des Ziad Zoukari)

1969 (25 Aug). AIR. 16th International Damascus Fair. T **282** and similar vert designs. Multicoloured. P 12½.

1041	12½p. Type **282**	50	15
	a. Strip of 5. Nos. 1041/1045	6·00	
1042	27½p. Ballet dancers	95	30
1043	45p. Lebanese dancers	1·10	60
1044	55p. Egyptian dancers	1·30	70
1045	60p. Bulgarian dancers	1·80	90
1041/1045	*Set of 5*	5·00	2·40

Nos 1041/1045 were issued in *se-tenant* strips within the sheet.

(Des A. Ismail)

1969 (1 Oct). AIR. Ninth International Archaeological Congress, Damascus. T **283** and similar vert designs. Multicoloured. P 12×12½.

1046	17½p. Type **283**	65	25
1047	25p. *Lady from Palmyra* (statue)	95	30
1048	60p. *Motherhood* (statue)	1·60	45
1046/1048	*Set of 3*	3·00	90

284 Children dancing

285 Mahatma Gandhi

(Des Ziad Zoukari)

1969 (6 Oct). AIR. Children's Day. P 12×12½.

1049	**284** 12½p. light green, deep blue and turquoise	30	20
1050	25p. light violet, deep blue and brown-red	65	25
1051	27½p. light grey, deep blue and bright blue	80	30
1049/1051	*Set of 3*	1·60	70

(Des Ziad Zoukari)

1969 (7 Oct). Birth Centenary of Mahatma Gandhi. P 12×12½.

1052	**285** 12½p. brown and light buff	80	30
1053	27½p. green and light greenish yellow	1·60	45

286 Cotton

287 'Arab World' (Sixth Arab Science Congress)

(Des H. A. Ayash)

1969 (10 Oct). Aleppo Cotton Festival. P 12×12½.

1054	**286** 12½p. multicoloured	30	15
1055	17½p. multicoloured	50	25
1056	25p. multicoloured	65	30
1054/1056	*Set of 3*	1·30	65

(Des Ziad Zoukari)

1969 (2 Nov). Tenth Science Week and similar events. T **287** and similar horiz designs. P 12½×12.

1057	12½p. ultramarine and pale turquoise-green	35	30
1058	25p. deep slate-violet and pink	55	50
1059	27½p. ochre and pale green	1·10	95
1057/1059	*Set of 3*	1·80	1·60

Designs: 12½p. T **287**; 25p. Arab Academy (50th anniversary); 27½p. Damascus University (50th anniversary of Faculty of Medicine).

288 Cockerel

(Des H. A. Ayash)

1969 (24 Dec). AIR. Damascus Agricultural Museum. T **288** and similar horiz designs. Multicoloured. P 12½.

1060	12½p. Type **288**	35	20
	a. Horiz strip of 4. Nos. 1060/1063 plus label	3·00	
1061	17½p. Cow	55	25
1062	20p. Maize	70	30
1063	50p. Olives	1·10	50
1060/1063	*Set of 4*	2·40	1·10

Nos. 1060/1063 were issued in *se-tenant* strips of four, together with a stamp-size commemorative label, in the horiz rows of the sheet.

289 Rising Sun, Hand and Book

290 Map of Arab World, League Emblem and Flag

(Des M. Hammad)

1970 (8 Mar). Seventh Anniversary of Baathist Revolution of 8 March 1963. P 12½×12.

1064	**289**	12½p. black, yellow-brown and new blue	35	25
1065		25p. black, blue and red	55	30
1066		27½p. black, light bistre-brown and light blue-green	1·10	50
1064/1066		*Set of 3*	1·80	95

(Des M. Hammad)

1970 (22 Mar). Silver Jubilee of Arab League. P 12½×12.

1067	**290**	12½p. black, red, green and bright lilac	35	25
1068		25p. black, red, green and light grey	55	30
1069		27½p. black, red, green and turquoise	1·10	50
1067/1069		*Set of 3*	1·80	95

291 Dish Aerial and Hand on Book

292 Lenin

(Des M. Hammad)

1970 (23 Mar). AIR. World Meteorological Day. P 12½×12.

1070	**291**	25p. black, olive-yellow and grey-green	1·20	30
1071		60p. black, olive-yellow and blue	1·90	1·10

(Des Ziad Zoukari)

1970 (15 Apr). AIR. Birth Centenary of Lenin. P 12×12½.

1072	**292**	15p. blackish brown and rose-red	35	20
1073		60p. myrtle-green and rose-red	1·40	95

293 Battle of Hattin

(Des Ziad Zoukari)

1970 (17 Apr). 24th Anniversary of Evacuation of Foreign Troops from Syria. P 12½×12.

1074	**293**	15p. deep chocolate and pale cream	55	30
1075		35p. reddish violet and pale cream	1·10	50

294 Emblem of Workers' Syndicate

295 Young Syrians and Map

(Des H. A. Ayash)

1970 (1 May). AIR. Labour Day. P 12½×12.

1076	**294**	15p. blackish brown and light blue-green	35	25
1077		60p. blackish brown and yellow-orange	1·80	1·10

(Des Ziad Zoukari)

1970 (7 May). Revolution's Youth Union, First Youth Week. P 12½×12.

1078	**295**	15p. dull green and ochre	35	15
1079		25p. brown and ochre	55	50

This issue is inscribed 'WEAK' in error.

296 Refugee Family

297 Dish Aerial and Open Book

(Des H. A. Ayash)

1970 (15 May). World Arab Refugee Week. P 12½×12.

1080	**296**	15p. multicoloured	35	30
1081		25p. multicoloured	90	30
1082		35p. multicoloured	95	50
1080/1082		*Set of 3*	2·00	1·00

(Des A. Ismail)

1970 (19 May). AIR. World Telecommunications Day. P 12½×12.

1083	**297**	15p. black and pale rose-lilac	35	30
1084		60p. black and turquoise-blue	1·80	1·10

298 New UPU Headquarters Building

(Des A. Ismail)

1970 (20 May). AIR. New Universal Postal Union Headquarters Building. P 12½×12.

1085	**298**	15p. multicoloured	25	15
1086		60p. multicoloured	1·40	95

299 Industry and Graph

300 Khaled ibn el-Walid

1970 (20 May)–**71**.

(a) POSTAGE. P 11½

1087	**299**	2½p. rose-red and red-brown (28.4.71)..	25	15
1088		5p. new blue and red-orange (6.70)....	35	30
1089		7½p. brownish grey and bright mauve (28.4.71)	25	15
1090		10p. grey-brown and yellow-brown (6.70)	45	15
1091		12½p. vermilion and new blue (28.4.71)..	35	15
1092		15p. deep mauve and blue-green	55	25
1093		20p. pale lake-brown and violet-blue (6.70)	60	30
1094		22½p. blackish green and lake-brown (21.2.71)	55	30
1095		25p. chalky blue and brownish grey (21.2.71)	55	30
1096		27½p. chocolate and turqouise-green (21.2.71)	60	40
1097		35p. emerald and bright rose-red (21.2.71)	70	50

(b) AIR. P 12×11½

1098	**300**	45p. magenta (11.70)	90	30
1099		50p. myrtle-green (11.70)	1·10	50
1100		60p. purple-brown (11.70)	1·40	65
1101		100p. deep blue (11.70)	1·90	80
1102		200p. grey-olive (21.2.71)	3·50	1·80
1103		300p. bright violet (21.2.71)	5·25	3·25
1104		500p. deep brownish grey (21.2.71)	8·75	6·50
1087/1104 *Set of* 18			25·00	15·00

301 Mediaeval Warriors

(Des A. Ismail)

1970 (12 Aug). AIR. Folk Tales and Legends. T **301** and similar horiz designs showing different scenes. P 12×12½.

1105	5p. multicoloured	20	25
	a. Horiz strip of 5. Nos. 1105/1109	2·75	
1106	10p. multicoloured	25	30
1107	15p. multicoloured	35	40
1108	20p. multicoloured	55	50
1109	60p. multicoloured	1·30	1·10
1105/1109 *Set of* 5		2·40	2·30

Nos. 1105/1109 were issued together *se-tenant* in horizontal strips.

302 Cotton

(Des H. A. Ayash)

1970 (18 Aug). Aleppo Agricultural and Industrial Fair. T **302** and similar horiz designs. Multicoloured. P 12×12½.

1110	5p. Type **302**	25	25
	a. Horiz strip of 5. Nos. 1110/1114	3·00	
1111	10p. Tomatoes	35	25
1112	15p. Tobacco	45	25
1113	20p. Sugar beet	55	30
1114	35p. Wheat	1·10	80
1110/1114 *Set of* 5		2·40	1·70

Nos. 1110/1114 were issued together *se-tenant* in horizontal strips.

303 Mosque in Flames

(Des M. Hammad)

1970 (21 Aug). AIR. First Anniversary of Burning of Al-Aqsa Mosque, Jerusalem. P 12½×12.

1115	**303**	15p. multicoloured	55	30
1116		60p. multicoloured	1·60	65

304 Wood-carving

(Des Z. Zoukari)

1970 (25 Aug). AIR. 17th Damascus International Fair. T **304** and similar horiz designs. Multicoloured. P 12×12½.

1117	15p. Type **304**	35	25
	a. Horiz strip of 5. Nos. 1117/1121	5·00	
1118	20p. Jewellery	45	30
1119	25p. Glass-making	55	40
1120	30p. Copper-engraving	1·10	50
1121	60p. Shell-work	2·30	80
1117/1121 *Set of* 5		4·25	2·00

Nos. 1117/1121 were issued together *se-tenant* in horizontal strips.

305 Scout, Encampment and Badge

1970 (2 Sept). Ninth Pan-Arab Scout Jamboree, Damascus. P 12½×12.

1122	**305**	15p. light grey-green	1·10	65

306 Olive Tree and Emblem

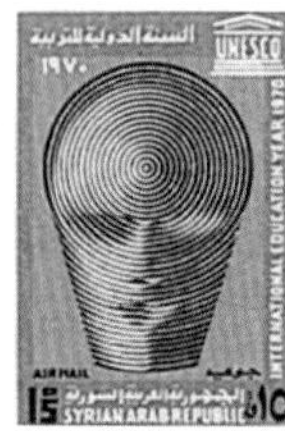

307 IEY Emblem

(Des H. A. Ayash)

1970 (28 Sept). World Year of Olive-oil Production. P 11½×12.

1123	**306**	15p. multicoloured	35	25
1124		25p. multicoloured	90	30

(Des A. Ismail)

1970 (2 Nov). AIR. International Education Year. P 12½×12.

1125	**307**	15p. chocolate, grey-green and black....	35	30
1126		60p. chocolate, violet-blue and black....	1·80	1·10

308 UN Emblems

309 Protective Shield

(Des M. Hammad)

1970 (3 Nov). AIR. 25th Anniversary of United Nations. P 12½×12.
1127 **308** 15p. multicoloured 35 30
1128 60p. multicoloured .... 1·80 1·10

(Des Z. Zoukari)

1971 (8 Mar). Eighth Anniversary of Baathist Revolution of 8 March 1963. P 12½×12.
1129 **309** 15p. chalky blue, olive-yellow and yellow-olive 25 15
1130 22½p. yellow-olive, olive-yellow and orange-brown 35 30
1131 27½p. orange-brown, olive-yellow and chalky blue 70 50
1129/1131 *Set of 3* .... 1·20 85

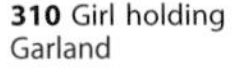

310 Girl holding Garland

311 Globe and World Races

(Des B. Maoulaoui)

1971 (17 Apr). AIR. 25th Anniversary of Evacuation of Foreign Troops from Syria. P 12×12½.
1132 **310** 15p. multicoloured 35 15
1133 60p. multicoloured .... 1·20 65

(Des B. Maoulaoui)

1971 (28 Apr). AIR. Racial Equality Year. P 12½×12.
1134 **311** 15p. multicoloured 25 15
1135 60p. multicoloured .... 1·20 80

312 Soldier, Worker and Labour Emblems

313 Hailing Traffic and Traffic Lights

(Des M. Hammad)

1971 (1 May). Labour Day. P 12½×12.
1136 **312** 15p. dull claret, new blue and greenish yellow 35 25
1137 25p. grey-blue, new blue and greenish yellow 70 30

(Des G. Rahmé (25p.), M. Hammad (others))

1971 (4 May). World Traffic Day. T **313** and similar design. P 12×11½ (25p.) or 11½×12 (others).
1138 **313** 15p. dull scarlet, greenish blue and black 35 15
1139 – 25p. multicoloured 55 30
1140 **313** 45p. dull scarlet, greenish yellow and black .... 1·10 65
1138/1140 *Set of 3* .... 1·80 1·00

Design: Vert—25p. Traffic signs and signal lights.

314 Cotton, Cogwheel and Factories

315 APU Emblem

(Des M. Hammad)

1971 (15 July). Aleppo Agricultural and Industrial Fair. P 12½×12.
1141 **314** 15p. black, greenish blue and light green 35 15
1142 30p. black, bright scarlet and rose-red.. 75 70

(Des G. Rahmé)

1971 (13 Aug). 25th Anniversary of Solar Conference and Founding of Arab Postal Union. P 12×11½.
1143 **315** 15p. multicoloured 35 25
1144 20p. multicoloured 95 35

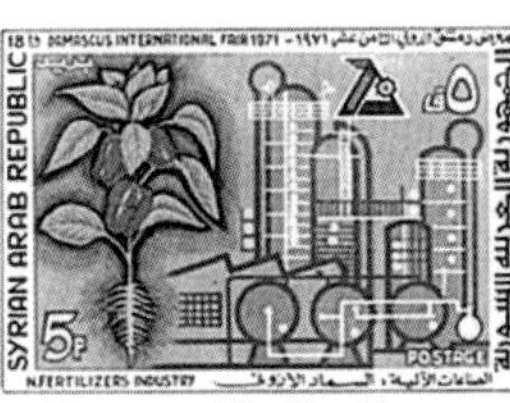

316 Peppers and Fertiliser Plant

317 Flag and Federation Map

(Des Z. Zoukari)

1971 (25 Aug). 18th Damascus International Fair. Industries. T **316** and similar horiz designs. Multicoloured. P 12×12½.
1145 5p. Type **316** 35 15
1146 15p. TV set and telephone ('Electronics') 95 25
1147 35p. Oil lamp and dish ('Glassware') .... 1·50 70
1148 50p. Part of carpet ('Carpets') .... 2·20 1·00
1145/1148 *Set of 4* .... 4·50 1·90

(Des M. Hammad)

1971 (1 Sept). Arab Federation Referendum. P 12×11½.
1149 **317** 15p. dull green, black and bright carmine 75 15

318 President Hafez al-Assad and People's Council Chamber

319 President Nasser

(Des A. Ismail)

1971 (30 Sept). AIR. People's Council and Presidential Election. P 12½×12.
1150 **318** 15p. multicoloured 35 35
1151 65p. multicoloured .... 1·90 1·00

(Des Z. Zoukari)

1971 (17 Oct). AIR. First Death Anniversary of President Nasser of Egypt. P 12×12½.
1152 **319** 15p. brown and yellow-green 55 15
1153 20p. brown and pale brownish grey 95 35

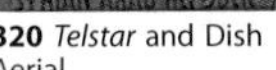

320 *Telstar* and Dish Aerial

321 Flaming Torch

(Des A. Ismail)

1971 (8 Dec). 25th Anniversary of United Nations Educational, Scientific and Cultural Organisation. P 12×12½.
1154 **320** 15p. multicoloured 55 15
1155 50p. multicoloured .... 1·30 70

1971 (9 Dec). Movement of 16 November 1970. P 12×12½.

1156	**321**	15p. multicoloured	35	15
1157		20p. multicoloured	55	50

322 Quill-pen and Open Book

323 Children with Ball

1971 (11 Dec). Eighth Writers' Congress. P 12½×12.

1158	**322**	15p. deep chocolate, orange and light turquoise-green	75	15

(Des M. Hammad)

1971 (21 Dec). 25th Anniversary of United Nations Children's Fund. P 12×12½.

1159	**323**	15p. bright carmine, violet-blue and deep violet-blue	35	15
1160		25p. brown-ochre, light turquoise-green and deep violet-blue	75	50

324 Book Year Emblem

325 Emblems of Reconstruction

(Des Z. Zoukari)

1972 (2 Jan). International Book Year. P 12½×12.

1161	**324**	15p. violet, pale greenish blue and cinnamon	35	15
1162		20p. dull blue-green, pale green and chestnut	75	50

(Des M. Hammad)

1972 (8 Mar). Ninth Anniversary of Baathist Revolution of 8 March 1963. P 12×12½.

1163	**325**	15p. bluish violet and blue-green	20	15
1164		20p. rose-carmine and olive-bistre	55	35

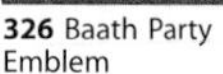

326 Baath Party Emblem

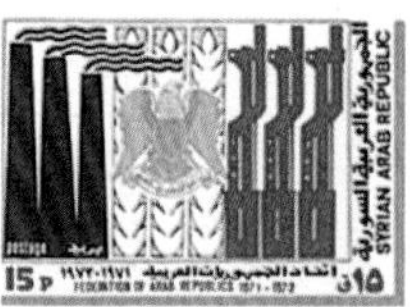

327 Eagle, Factory Chimneys and Rifles

(Des M. Hammad)

1972 (7 Apr). 25th Anniversary of Baath Party. P 12×12½.

1165	**326**	15p. multicoloured	20	15
1166		20p. multicoloured	55	35

(Des H. A. Ayash)

1972 (17 Apr). First Anniversary of Arab Republics Federation. P 12½×12.

1167	**327**	15p. gold, black and bright carmine	55	15

328 Flowers and Broken Chain

329 Hand with Spanner

(Des M. Hammad)

1972 (17 Apr). 26th Anniversary of Evacuation of Foreign Troops from Syria. P 12½×11.

1168	**328**	15p. silver-grey and bright rose-red	35	15
1169		50p. silver-grey and light turquoise-green	1·10	70

(Des M. Hammad)

1972 (1 May). Labour Day. P 12×11½.

1170	**329**	15p. multicoloured	35	35
1171		50p. multicoloured	1·50	1·20

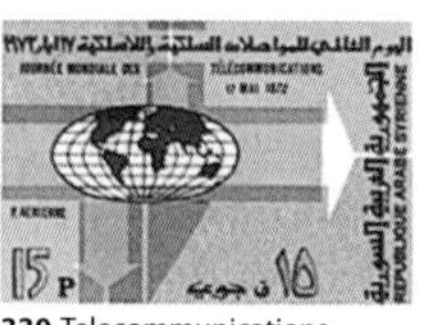

330 Telecommunications Emblem

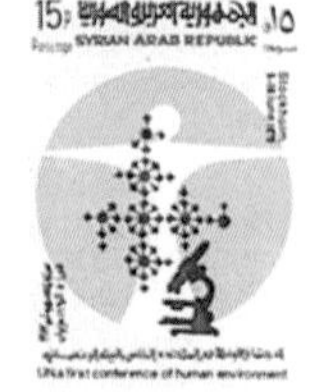

331 Environment Emblem

(Des H. A. Ayash)

1972 (17 May). AIR. World Telecommunications Day. P 11½×12.

1172	**330**	15p. multicoloured	35	15
1173		50p. multicoloured	1·50	50

(Des A. al-Jaffan)

1972 (5 June). UN Environmental Conservation Conference, Stockholm. P 12×11½.

1174	**331**	15p. ultramarine, azure and pale rose	35	15
1175		50p. slate-purple, yellow-orange and greenish yellow	1·50	70

332 Discus, Football and Swimming

333 Horsemen

1972 (15 July). Olympic Games, Munich. Types **332/333** and similar horiz design. P 12½×12.

1176	15p. violet, black and olive-bistre	75	35
1177	60p. dull orange, black and pale violet blue	2·75	1·20
MS1178	100×81 mm. **333** 75p. multicoloured. Imperf.	4·50	4·25

Designs: 15p. T **332**; 60p. Running, gymnastics and fencing.

334 Dove and Factory

335 President Hafez al-Assad

(Des A. al-Jaffan)

1972 (17 July). Aleppo Agricultural and Industrial Fair. P 12×11½.

1179 **334** 15p. multicoloured 35 15
1180 20p. multicoloured 55 35

1972 (17 July). AIR. P 12×11½.

1181 **335** 100p. deep bluish green .... 2·75 1·20
1182 500p. bistre-brown .... 13·00 5·00

336 Women's Dance

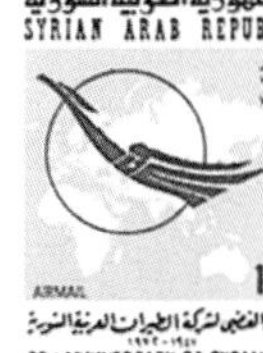

337 Airline Emblem

1972 (25 Aug). 19th Damascus International Fair. T **336** and similar horiz designs. Multicoloured. P 12½×12.

1183 15p. Type **336** 35 15
1184 20p. Tambourine dance 45 35
1185 50p. Men's drum dance .... 1·50 70
1183/1185 *Set of 3* .... 2·10 1·10

(Des A. al-Jaffan)

1972 (16 Sept). AIR. 25th Anniversary of Syrianair Airline. P 12×11½.

1186 **337** 15p. deep turquoise-blue, pale blue and black 55 15
1187 50p. deep turquoise-blue, pale grey and black .... 1·70 50

338 Emblem of Revolution

1973 (8 Mar). Tenth Anniversary of Baathist Revolution of 8 March 1963. P 11½×12.

1188 **338** 15p. light emerald, rosine and black 20 15
1189 20p. pale orange, rosine and black 35 25
1190 25p. pale turquoise-blue, rosine and black 55 35
1188/1190 *Set of 3* .... 1·00 70

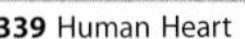

339 Human Heart

340 Emblems of Agriculture and Industry

1973 (21 Mar). 25th Anniversary of World Health Organisation. P 11½×12.

1191 **339** 15p. greenish blue, claret and brownish grey 55 15
1192 50p. greenish blue, claret and olive-sepia .... 1·30 50

1973 (17 Apr). 27th Anniversary of Evacuation of Foreign Troops from Syria. P 12×12½.

1193 **340** 15p. multicoloured 35 15
1194 20p. multicoloured 45 25

341 Globe and Workers

342 Family and Emblems

1973 (1 May). Labour Day. P 11½×12.

1195 **341** 15p. black, pale claret and deep stone 20 15
1196 50p. black, pale turquoise-blue and buff .... 1·10 70

1973 (7 May). Tenth Anniversary of World Food Programme. P 12×11½.

1197 **342** 15p. brown-red and turquoise-green 35 15
1198 50p. blue and bright lilac .... 1·30 70

343 Three Heads

344 Stock

1973 (May)–**74**. T **343** and similar designs. P 11½.

1199 2½p. yellow-olive (3.74) 20 15
1200 5p. yellow-orange (3.74) 20 15
1201 7½p. red-brown (3.74) 30 15
1202 10p. bright rose-red (3.74) 30 15
1203 15p. bright blue 35 25
1204 25p. pale slate-blue (3.74) 45 25
1205 35p. new blue (3.74) 55 35
1206 55p. deep bluish green 75 45
1207 70p. reddish purple .... 1·10 50
1199/1207 *Set of 9* .... 3·75 2·20

Designs: Horiz—2½p., 5p. As T **343**; 7½p., 10p., 55p. As T **343** but with one head above the other two. 15p. T **343**. Vert—25p., 35p., 70p. Similar to T **343**, but with heads in vertical arrangement.

1973 (15 May). International Flower Show, Damascus. T **344** and similar horiz designs. Multicoloured. P 12×11½.

1208 5p. Type **344** 35 25
a. Horiz strip of 5. Nos. 1208/1212 .... 4·00
1209 10p. Gardenia 55 25
a. Rose (background) omitted £190
1210 15p. Jasmine 75 25
a. Light orange (background) omitted £190
1211 20p. Rose 95 25
a. Green (background) omitted £190
1212 25p. Narcissus .... 1·10 35
1208/1212 *Set of 5* .... 3·25 1·20

Nos. 1208/1212 were issued together *se-tenant* in horizontal strips.

As the values and inscriptions are in white on the background, Nos. 1209a and 1210a show only the central flower motif.

345 Cogs and Flowers

1973 (17 June). Aleppo Agricultural and Industrial Fair. P 11½×12.

1213 **345** 15p. multicoloured 75 15

346 Euphrates Dam

1973 (5 July). Euphrates Dam Project. Diversion of the River. P 12½×13.

1214	**346**	15p. multicoloured	55	35
1215		50p. multicoloured	1·30	50

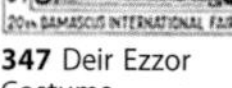

347 Deir Ezzor Costume

348 Anniversary Emblem

1973 (25 July). 20th Damascus International Fair. Costumes. T **347** and similar vert designs. Multicoloured. P 12.

1216	5p. Type **347**	35	25
	a. Horiz strip of 5. Nos. 1216/1220	4·25	
1217	10p. Hassake	55	25
1218	20p. As Sahel	75	35
1219	25p. Zakie	95	45
1220	50p. Sarakeb	1·50	50
1216/1220	*Set of 5*	3·75	1·60

Nos. 1216/1220 were issued together *se-tenant* in horizontal strips.

1973 (20 Aug). 25th Anniversary of Declaration of Human Rights. P 12×11½.

1221	**348**	15p. black, rose-red and pale turqoise-green	20	15
1222		50p. black, rose-red and pale blue	95	50

349 Citadel of Ja'abar

350 WMO Emblem

1973 (5 Sept). Save the Euphrates Monuments Campaign. T **349** and similar multicoloured designs. P 11½×12 (10p.) or 12×11½ (others).

1223	10p. Type **349**	30	15
1224	15p. Meskeneh Minaret (*vert*)	35	25
1225	25p. Psyche, Anab al-Safinah (*vert*)	55	35
1223/1225	*Set of 3*	1·10	70

1973 (12 Sept). Centenary of World Meteorological Organisation. P 12×11½.

1226	**350**	70p. multicoloured	1·10	50

351 Ancient City of Maalula

1973 (22 Oct). Arab Emigrants' Congress, Buenos Aires. T **351** and similar horiz design. P 11½×12.

1227	15p. black and slate-blue	35	15
1228	50p. black and red-brown	1·10	50

Designs: 15p. T **351**; 50p. Ruins of Afamia.

352 Soldier and Workers

353 Copernicus

1973 (16 Nov). Third Anniversary of November 16th Revolution. P 12½×12.

1229	**352**	15p. ultramarine and olive-bistre	35	25
1230		25p. bluish violet and Venetian red	75	35

1973 (15 Dec). 14th Science Week. T **353** and similar vert design. P 12×11½.

1231	15p. black and gold	95	35
1232	25p. black and gold (Al-Biruni)	1·70	50

354 National Symbols

355 UPU Monument, Berne

(Des M. Hammad)

1974 (8 Mar). 11th Anniversary of Baathist Revolution of 8 March 1963. P 11½×12.

1233	**354**	20p. greenish blue and pale grey-green	35	15
1234		25p. dull violet-blue and turquoise-green	45	35

(Des A. Ismail and A. R. Hreitani)

1974 (15 Mar). Centenary of the Universal Postal Union. T **355** and similar multicoloured designs. P 11½×12 (20p.) or 12×11½ (others).

1235	15p. Type **355**	35	25
1236	20p. Emblem on airmail letter (*horiz*)	45	35
1237	70p. Type **355**	1·50	1·20
1235/1237	*Set of 3*	2·10	1·60

356 Postal Institute

1974 (10 Apr). Inauguration of Higher Arab Postal Institute, Damascus. P 11½×12.

1238	**356**	15p. multicoloured	45	15

357 Sun and Monument

358 Machine Fitter

1974 (10 Apr). 28th Anniversary of Evacuation of Foreign Troops from Syria. P 11½×12.

1239	**357**	15p. multicoloured	35	25
1240		20p. multicoloured	45	35

1974 (1 May). Labour Day. P 12×11½.

1241	**358**	15p. multicoloured	45	35
1242		50p. multicoloured	1·10	70

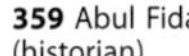

359 Abul Fida (historian)

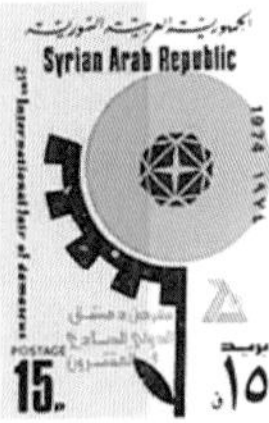

360 Diamond and Part of Cogwheel

1974 (1 May). Famous Arabs. T **359** and similar vert design. P 11½.

1243	100p. blue-green	1·90	1·00
1244	200p. light brown (Al-Farabi (philosopher and encyclopedist))	4·00	2·00

(Des A. al-Jaffan)

1974 (25 July). 21st Damascus International Fair. T **360** and similar vert design. Multicoloured. P 12×12½.

1245	15p. Type **360**	35	25
1246	25p. 'Sun' within cogwheel	45	35

361 Figs

362 Flowers within Drop of Blood

(Des A. Ismail)

1974 (21 Aug). Aleppo Agricultural and Industrial Fair. Fruits. T **361** and similar vert designs. Multicoloured. P 12×12½.

1247	5p. Type **361**	30	25
	a. Horiz strip of 5. Nos. 1247/1251	4·00	
1248	15p. Grapes	55	25
1249	20p. Pomegranates	75	35
1250	25p. Cherries	95	45
1251	35p. Rose-hips	1·10	50
1247/1251	*Set of 5*	3·25	1·60

Nos. 1247/1251 were issued together in *se-tenant* horizontal strips within the sheet.

(Des A. al-Jaffan)

1974 (6 Oct). Frist Anniversary of October Liberation War. T **362** and similar vert design. Multicoloured. P 12×12½.

1252	15p. Type **362**	75	35
1253	20p. Flower and stars	1·10	45

363 Knight and Rook

364 Symbolic Figure, Globe and Emblem

(Des A. al-Jaffan)

1974 (23 Nov). 50th Anniversary of International Chess Federation. T **363** and similar vert design. P 12×12½.

1254	15p. greenish blue, light blue and black	1·50	35
1255	50p. multicoloured	4·75	2·75

Designs: 15p. T **363**; 50p. Knight on chessboard.

(Des A. al-Jaffan)

1974 (4 Dec). World Population Year. P 12×12½.

1256	**364**	50p. multicoloured	1·10	70

365 Ishtup-ilum

366 Oil Rig and Crowd

1974 (12 Dec). Statuettes. T **365** and similar vert designs. P 11½.

1257	20p. bright emerald (Type **365**)	55	25
1258	55p. red-brown (Woman with vase)	1·10	35
1259	70p. ultramarine (Ur-nina)	1·70	70
1257/1259	*Set of 3*	3·00	1·20

1975 (17 Mar). 12th Anniversary of Baathist Revolution of 8 March 1963. P 12×11½.

1260	**366**	15p. multicoloured	55	15

367 Savings Emblem and Family ('Savings Certificates')

368 Dove Emblem

1975 (17 Mar). Savings Campaign. T **367** and similar vert design. P 12×11½.

1261	15p. black, red-orange and blue-green	35	15
1262	20p. blackish brown, black and salmon	55	25

Designs: 15p. T **367**; 20p. Family with savings box and letter ('Postal Savings Bank').

1975 (17 Apr). 29th Anniversary of Evacuation of Foreign Troops from Syria. Litho. P 12×11½.

1263	**368**	15p. multicoloured	35	25
1264		25p. multicoloured	35	25

369 Worker supporting Cog

370 Camomile

1975 (1 May). Labour Day. Litho. P 12×11½.

1265	**369**	15p. multicoloured	35	25
1266		25p. multicoloured	35	25

1975 (27 May). International Flower Show, Damascus. T **370** and similar vert designs. Multicoloured. P 12×11½.

1267	5p. Type **370**	35	25
	a. Horiz strip of 5. Nos. 1267/1271	4·00	
1268	10p. Chincherinchi	55	25
1269	15p. Carnations	75	25
1270	20p. Poppy	95	35
1271	25p. Honeysuckle	1·10	45
1267/1271	*Set of 5*	3·25	1·40

Nos. 1267/1271 were issued together *se-tenant* in horizontal strips of five within the sheet.

371 'Destruction and Reconstruction'

1975 (5 June). Syrian Reoccupation of Qneitra. P 12½.

1272	**371**	50p. multicoloured	1·10	70

372 Apples

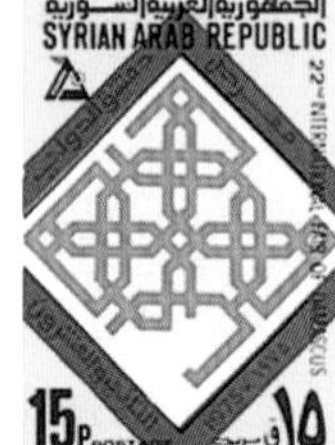

373 Arabesque Pattern

1975 (21 Aug). Aleppo Agricultural and Industrial Fair. Fruits. T **372** and similar vert designs. Multicoloured. Litho. P 12½.

1273	5p. Type **372**	30	25
	a. Horiz strip of 5. Nos. 1273/1277	2·75	
1274	10p. Quinces	35	25
1275	15p. Apricots	45	25
1276	20p. Grapes	55	35
1277	25p. Figs	95	45
1273/1277	*Set of 5*	2·30	1·40

Nos. 1273/1277 were issued together *se-tenant* in horizontal strips of five within the sheet.

1975 (Aug). 22nd International Damascus Fair. Litho. P 12×11½.

1278	**373**	15p. multicoloured	35	25
1279		35p. multicoloured	95	35

374 President Hafez al-Assad

1975 (29 Nov). Fifth Anniversary of Movement of 16 November 1970. Litho. P 11½×12.

1280	**374**	15p. multicoloured	35	35
1281		50p. multicoloured	1·30	70

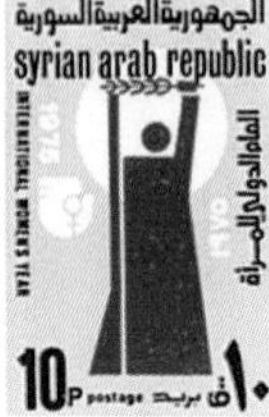

375 Symbolic Woman

376 Bronze 'Horse' Lamp

1975 (29 Nov). International Women's year. T **375** and similar vert designs. Multicoloured. P 12×11½.

1282	10p. Type **375**	20	15
1283	15p. Motherhood	30	25
1284	25p. Education	35	35
1285	50p. Science	75	50
1282/1285	*Set of 4*	1·40	1·10

1976 (13 Jan)–**78**. T **376** and similar designs showing exhibits from National Museum, Damascus. P 11½.

1286	5p. deep dull green (22.1.78)	20	15
1287	10p. turquoise-green	30	15
1288	10p. dull ultramarine (22.1.78)	30	15
1289	15p. bistre-brown (22.1.78)	30	15
1290	20p. carmine	35	25
1291	25p. bright blue	45	25
1292	30p. reddish brown	55	25
1293	35p. yellow-olive	65	25
1294	40p. salmon (13.7.78)	75	35
1295	50p. greenish blue	1·10	50
1296	55p. magenta (22.1.78)	95	35
1297	60p. violet (7.12.76)	1·00	45
1298	70p. rose-red (22.1.78)	1·10	50
1299	75p. yellow-orange	1·30	70
1300	80p. yellowish green (13.7.78)	1·50	75
1301	100p. dull magenta (10.2.77)	1·90	85
1302	200p. new blue (13.7.78)	4·50	1·20
1303	300p. deep mauve (1.7.78)	6·00	2·00
1304	500p. olive-grey	10·00	6·50
1305	1000p. deep grey-green	19·00	10·00
1286/1305	*Set of 20*	47·00	23·00

Designs: Horiz—10p. (No. 1287), 20p., 25p. T **376**; 15p. Wall-painting showing figures; 300p. Coin from Palmyra, Herodian period. Vert—5p. Wall-painting showing figure of a man; 10p. (No. 1288) Flying goddess with wreath; 30p., 35p., 40p. Man's head inkstand; 50p., 55p., 60p. Statue of Nike; 70p., 75p., 80p. Statue of Hera; 100p. Imdugub-Mari (bird-goddess); 200p. Arab astrolabe; 500p. Coin from Palmyra, Valabathus period; 1000p. Abraxas stone.

See also Nos. 1403/1411.

377 National Theatre, Damascus

378 Nurse and Emblem

1976 (8 Mar). 13th Anniversary of Baathist Revolution of 8 March 1963. P 11½×12.

1306	**377**	25p. emerald, black and silver	55	35
1307		35p. yellow-olive, black and silver	75	50

1976 (8 Apr). Eighth Arab Red Crescent Societies' Conference, Damascus. P 12×11½.

1308	**378**	25p. new blue, black and red	75	35
1309		100p. bluish violet, black and red	1·90	1·20

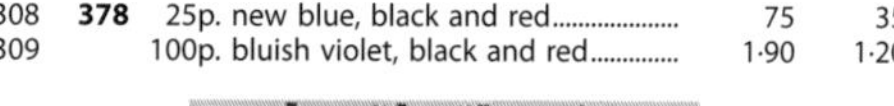

379 Syrian 5m. Stamp of 1920

1976 (12 Apr). Arab Post Day. P 12×12½.

1310	**379**	25p. multicoloured	75	35
1311		35p. multicoloured	95	70

380 Eagle and Stars

381 Hand gripping Spanner

1976 (17 Apr). 30th Anniversary of Evacuation of Foreign Troops from Syria. P 12×11½.

1312	**380**	25p. multicoloured	75	35
1313		35p. multicoloured	95	70

1976 (1 May). Labour Day. T **381** and similar vert design. P 12×11½.

1314	25p. new blue and black	75	35
1315	60p. multicoloured	1·10	70

Designs: 25p. T **381**; 60p. Hand supporting globe.

382 Cotton Boll

383 Tulips

1976 (1 July). Aleppo Agricultural and Industrial Fair. P 12×11½.

1316	**382**	25p. multicoloured	75	35
1317		35p. multicoloured	95	70

1976 (26 July). International Flower Show, Damascus. T **383** and similar vert designs. Multicoloured. P 12×11½.

1318	5p. Type **383**	35	15
	a. Horiz strip of 5. Nos. 1318/1322	4·00	
1319	15p. Yellow Daisies	55	25
1320	20p. Turk's-cap Lilies	75	35
1321	25p. Irises	95	45
1322	35p. Honeysuckle	1·10	50
1318/1322	*Set of 5*	3·25	1·50

Nos. 1318/1322 were issued together *se-tenant* in horizontal strips of five within the sheet.

384 Pottery

1976 (23 Aug). AIR. 23rd International Damascus Fair. T **384** and similar horiz designs. Multicoloured. P 12×12½.

1323	10p. Type **384**	55	35
	a. Horiz strip of 5. Nos. 1323/1327	5·75	
1324	25p. Rug-making	75	50
1325	30p. Metalware	95	75
1326	35p. Wickerware	1·10	85
1327	100p. Wood-carving	2·20	1·50
1323/1327	*Set of 5*	5·00	3·50

Nos. 1323/1327 were issued together *se-tenant* in horizontal strips of five within the sheet.

385 People supporting Olive Branch

386 Football

1976 (2 Sept). Non-aligned Countries Summit Conference, Colombo, Sri Lanka. T **385** and similar horiz design. Multicoloured. P 11½×12.

1328	40p. Type **385**	95	85
1329	60p. Symbolic arrow penetrating grey curtain	1·30	1·00

1976 (6 Oct). Fifth Pan-Arab Games. T **386** and similar square designs. Multicoloured. P 12½.

1330	5p. Type **386**	55	25
	a. Horiz strip of 5. Nos. 1330/1334	6·25	
1331	10p. Swimming	95	35
1332	25p. Running	1·10	45
1333	35p. Basketball	1·50	50
1334	50p. Throwing the javelin	1·90	85
1330/1334	*Set of 5*	5·50	2·20
MS1335	75×56 mm. 100p. Horse-jumping (56×36 *mm*). Imperf	4·75	4·50
	a. Scarlet (bottom inscription) omitted		

Nos 1330/1334 were issued together *se-tenant* in horizontal strips within the sheet.

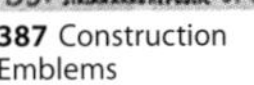

387 Construction Emblems

388 *The Fox and the Crow*

1976 (16 Nov). Sixth Anniversary of November 16th Revolution. P 12×12½.

1336	**387**	35p. multicoloured	75	35

1976 (7 Dec). Fairy Tales. T **388** and similar designs. Multicoloured. P 12.

1337	10p. Type **388**	55	25
	a. Strip of 5. Nos. 1337/1341	5·00	
	ab. Black (inscr) omitted. Strip of 5	£375	
1338	15p. *The Hare and the Tortoise* (*horiz*)	75	35
1339	20p. *Little Red Riding Hood*	95	45
1340	25p. *The Wolf and the Goats* (*horiz*)	1·10	50
1341	35p. *The Wolf and the Lamb*	1·30	85
1337/1341	*Set of 5*	4·25	2·20

Nos. 1337/1341 were issued in *se-tenant* strips of five within the sheet.

389 Muhammad Kurd-ali (philosopher)

391 Woman hoisting Flag

390 Boeing 747SP

1976 (30 Dec). Birth Centenary of Muhammad Kurd-ali. P 12×12½.

1342	**389**	25p. multicoloured	75	35

1976 (30 Dec). Civil Aviation Day. P 12½×12.

1343	**390**	35p. multicoloured	2·20	70

1977 (8 Mar). 14th Anniversary of Baathist Revolution of 8 March 1963. Litho. P 12×12½.

1344	**391**	35p. multicoloured	1·10	70

392 APU Emblem

393 Mounted Horseman

1977 (12 Apr). 25th Anniversary of Arab Postal Union. P 12×12½.

1345	**392**	35p. multicoloured	95	35

1977 (17 Apr). 31st Anniversary of Evacuation of Foreign Troops from Syria. P 12½.

1346	**393**	100p. multicoloured	2·20	1·20

394 Industrial Scene and Tools

1977 (1 May). Labour Day. P 12½×12.

1347	**394**	60p. multicoloured	1·10	85

395 ICAO Emblem, Boeing 747SP and Globe

396 Lemon

1977 (11 May). 30th Anniversary of International Civil Aviation Organisation. P 12½×12.

1348	**395**	100p. multicoloured	3·00	2·00

1977 (1 Aug). International Agricultural Fair, Aleppo. T **396** and similar vert designs. Multicoloured. P 12.

1349	10p. Type **396**	55	25
	a. Strip of 5. Nos. 1349/1353	5·50	
1350	20p. Lime	75	25
1351	25p. Grapefruit	95	35
1352	35p. Oranges	1·30	45
1353	60p. Tangerine	1·70	85
	a. Grey (blackground) omitted	£190	
1349/1353 *Set of 5*		4·75	1·90

Nos 1349/1353 were issued in *se-tenant* strips of five within the sheet.

397 Mallows

398 Young Pioneers and Emblem

1977 (6 Aug). International Flower Show, Damascus. T **397** and similar vert designs. Multicoloured. P 12½.

1354	10p. Type **397**	55	25
	a. Strip of 5. Nos. 1354/1358	5·50	
1355	20p. Cockscomb	75	45
1356	25p. Convolvulus	95	50
1357	35p. Balsam	1·30	60
1358	60p. Lilac	1·70	1·00
1354/1358 *Set of 5*		4·75	2·50

Nos. 1354/1358 were issued in *se-tenant* strips of five within the sheet.

1977 (15 Aug). Al Baath Pioneer Organisation. P 12.

1359	**398**	35p. multicoloured	95	70

399 Arabesque Pattern and Coffee Pot

400 Globe and Measures

1977 (10 Sept). 24th International Damascus Fair. P 12×12½.

1360	**399**	25p. red, blue and black	35	35
1361		60p. brown, green and black	1·10	85

1977 (5 Nov). World Standards Day. P 12×12½.

1362	**400**	15p. multicoloured	55	15

401 Microscope, Book and Lyre

402 Shield, Surgeon and Crab

1977 (5 Nov). 30th Anniversary of United Nations Educational, Scientific and Cultural Organisation. P 12×12½.

1363	**401**	25p. multicoloured	75	25

1977 (17 Nov). Cancer Fighting Week. P 12×12½.

1364	**402**	100p. multicoloured	1·90	70

403 Archbishop Capucci and Map of Palestine

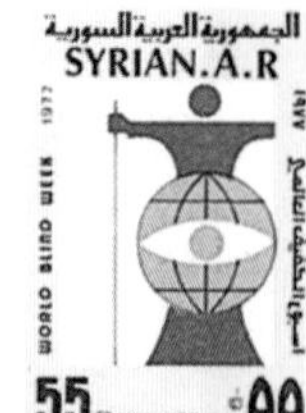

404 Blind Man, Eye and Globe

1977 (17 Nov). Third Anniversary of Archbishop Capucci's Arrest. P 12×12½.

1365	**403**	60p. multicoloured	1·10	35

1977 (17 Nov). World Blind Week. P 12×12½.

1366	**404**	55p. multicoloured	75	25
1367		70p. multicoloured	1·10	35

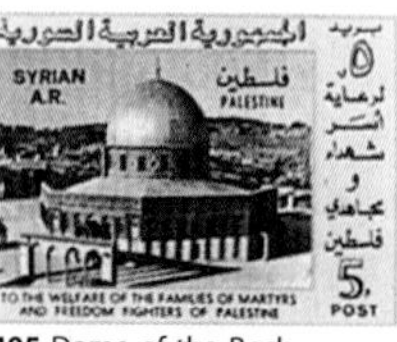

405 Dome of the Rock, Jerusalem

406 President Hafez al-Assad and Government Palace, Damascus

1977 (6 Dec). Palestinian Welfare. P 12.

1368	**405**	5p. multicoloured	35	25
1369		10p. multicoloured	55	35

1977 (31 Dec). Seventh Anniversary of Movement of 16 November 1970. P 12×11½.

1370	**406**	50p. multicoloured	95	35

407 Eurasian Goldfinch

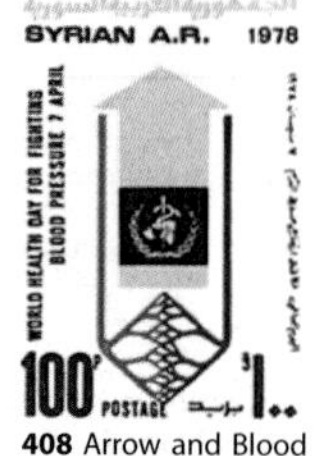

408 Arrow and Blood Circulation

1978 (18 Apr). Birds. T **407** and similar horiz designs. Multicoloured. P 11½×12.
1371 10p. Type **407** ... 3·25 1·70
a. Vert strip of 5. Nos. 1371/1375 ... 33·00
1372 20p. Peregrine Falcon ... 3·75 2·00
1373 25p. Feral Rock Dove ... 4·75 2·00
1374 35p. Hoopoe ... 9·25 2·50
1375 60p. Chukar Partridge ... 11·00 4·75
1371/1375 *Set of 5* ... 29·00 11·50
Nos. 1371/1375 were issued together *se-tenant* in vertical strips of five within the sheet.

1978 (22 Apr). World Health Day. 'Fighting Blood Pressure'. P 12×11½.
1376 **408** 100p. multicoloured ... 1·50 70

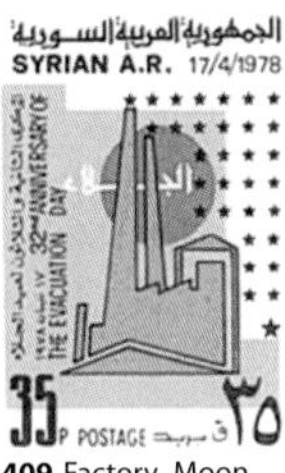

409 Factory, Moon and Stars

410 Geometric Design

1978 (22 Apr). 32nd Anniversary of Evacuation of Foreign Troops from Syria. P 12×11½.
1377 **409** 35p. turquoise-green, orange and black ... 75 35

1978 (22 Apr). 14th Arab Engineering Conference, Damascus. P 12×11½.
1378 **410** 25p. yellowish green and black ... 55 25

411 Map of Arab Countries, Eye and Police

412 Brown Trout

1978 (22 Apr). Sixth Arab Conference of Police Commanders. P 12×11½.
1379 **411** 35p. multicoloured ... 75 35

1978 (10 June). Fish. T **412** and similar horiz designs. Multicoloured. P 11½×12.
1380 10p. Type **412** ... 1·30 35
a. Vert strip of 5. Nos. 1380/1384 ... 9·00
1381 20p. Sea-bream ... 1·60 45
1382 25p. Grouper ... 1·70 50
1383 35p. Striped Red Mullet ... 2·00 70
1384 60p. Wels ... 2·20 85
1380/1384 *Set of 5* ... 8·00 2·50
Nos. 1380/1384 were issued together *se-tenant* in vertical strips of five within the sheet.

413 President Assad

414 *Lobivia* sp.

1978 (28 Aug). AIR. Re-election of President Hafez al-Assad. P 12½×12.
1385 **413** 25p. multicoloured ... 75 25
1386 35p. multicoloured ... 95 35
1387 60p. multicoloured ... 1·10 45
1385/1387 *Set of 3* ... 2·50 95
MS1388 79×105 mm. **413** 100p. multicoloured. Imperf ... 3·00 2·75

1978 (1 Nov). International Flower Show, Damascus. T **414** and similar vert designs showing flowering cacti. Multicoloured. P 12½×12.
1389 25p. Type **414** ... 75 25
a. Horiz strip of 5. Nos. 1389/1393 ... 5·75
1390 30p. *Mamillaria* sp. ... 95 30
1391 35p. *Opuntia* sp. ... 1·10 35
1392 50p. *Chamaecereus* sp. ... 1·30 50
1393 60p. *Mamillaria* sp. (*different*) ... 1·50 85
1389/1393 *Set of 5* ... 5·00 2·00
Nos. 1389/1393 were issued together *se-tenant* in horizontal strips of five within the sheet.
See also Nos. 1440/1445.

415 President Hafez al-Assad

417 Fair Emblem

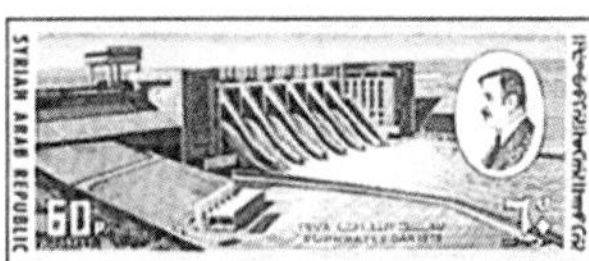

416 Euphrates Dam

1978 (16 Nov). Eighth Anniversary of Movement of 16 November 1970. P 12×12½.
1394 **415** 60p. multicoloured ... 1·10 85

1978 (10 Dec). Inauguration of Euphrates Dam. P 12½×12.
1395 **416** 60p. multicoloured ... 1·90 85

1978 (10 Dec). 25th International Damascus Fair. T **417** and similar design. P 12×12½.
1396 **417** 25p. multicoloured ... 35 15
1397 35p. black, bright violet and silver ... 55 35
MS1398 105×80 mm. 100p. multicoloured. Imperf ... 3·00 2·75
Design: **MS**1398, Arabesque pattern.

418 Averroes (philosopher)

419 Standing Figures within a Globe

1979 (7 Mar). Averroes Commemoration. P 12×12½.
1399 **418** 100p. multicoloured ... 3·00 1·70

1979 (7 Mar). International Year to Combat Racism. P 12½.
1400 **419** 35p. multicoloured ... 75 35

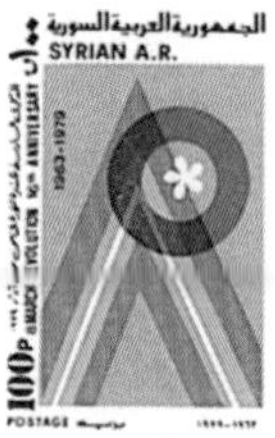
420 Pyramid and Flower

421 Hands supporting Globe

1979 (20 Mar). 16th Anniversary of Baathist Revolution of 8 March 1963. P 12×12½.

1401	**420**	100p. multicoloured	2·00	35

1979 (20 Mar). 30th Anniversary of Declaration of Human Rights. P 12×12½.

1402	**421**	60p. multicoloured	1·10	85

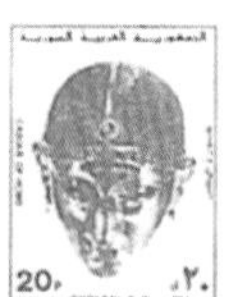
422 Helmet of Homs

1979 (Apr)–**81**. T **422** and similar designs showing exhibits from National Museum, Damascus. P 11½.

1403	5p. bright scarlet (23.5.81)	30	15
1404	10p. light green (2.9.81)	55	15
1405	15p. deep mauve (23.5.81)	55	25
1406	20p. deep dull green (19.8.79)	35	15
1407	25p. carmine	35	15
1408	35p. sepia (19.8.79)	55	25
1409	75p. deep ultramarine (2.9.81)	1·10	50
1410	160p. deep green (23.5.81)	2·20	85
1411	500p. deep brown (23.5.81)	8·25	3·00
1403/1411	*Set of 9*	13·00	5·00

Designs: Vert—5p., 160p. Umayyad window; 10p. Figurine; 15p. Rakka horseman (Abbcid ceramic); 20p. T **422**; 25p. Head of Clipeata (Cleopatra); 35p. Seated statue of Ishtar (Astarte). Horiz—75p. Abdul Malik gold coin; 500p. Umar B. Abdul Aziz gold coin.

Nos. 1412/1415 are vacant.

423 Geometric Design and Flame

1979 (25 June). 33rd Anniversary of Evacuation of Foreign Troops from Syria. P 12×11½.

1416	**423**	35p. multicoloured	75	35

424 Ibn Assaker

425 Tooth, Emblem and Mosque

1979 (25 June). 900th Anniversary of Ibn Assaker (historian and biographer). P 11½×12.

1417	**424**	75p. light brown, greenish blue and olive-green	1·10	50

1979 (25 June). International Middle East Dental Congress. P 11½×12.

1418	**425**	35p. multicoloured	1·10	35

426 Welder working on Power Pylon

427 Girl holding Emblem with Flowers

1979 (26 July). Labour Day. P 12×11½.

1419	**426**	50p. multicoloured	95	70
1420		75p. multicoloured	1·30	85

1979 (26 July). International Year of the Child. T **427** and similar vert design. Multicoloured. P 12×11½.

1421	10p. Type **427**	35	15
1422	15p. Boy and Globe	55	25

428 Wright Type A

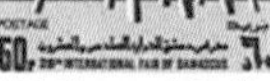
429 Power Station

1979 (26 July). 75th Anniversary of First Powered Flight. T **428** and similar horiz designs. Multicoloured. P 11½×12.

1423	50p. Type **428**	2·20	50
1424	75p. Blériot's XI plane crossing English Channel	3·00	85
1425	100p. Lindbergh's *Spirit of St Louis*	4·00	1·00
1423/1425	*Set of 3*	8·25	2·10

1979 (19 Aug). P 11½.

1426	**429**	5p. new blue	25	15
1427		10p. magenta	30	20
1428		15p. dull green	35	25
1426/1428		*Set of 3*	80	55

430 Flags and Pavilion

431 Running

1979 (2 Oct). 26th International Damascus Fair. T **430** and similar vert design. Multicoloured. P 12×11½.

1429	60p. Type **430**	75	25
1430	75p. Lamp post and flags	95	35

1979 (2 Oct). Eighth Mediterranean Games, Split. T **431** and similar horiz designs. Multicoloured. P 11½×12.

1431	25p. Type **431**	35	25
1432	35p. Swimmer on starting-block	55	35
1433	50p. Football	95	50
1431/1433	*Set of 3*	1·70	1·00

432 President Assad with Symbols of Agriculture and Industry

433 *Papilio machaon*

1979 (16 Nov). Ninth Anniversary of Movement of 16 Nov 1970. P 11½×12.

1434 **432** 100p. multicoloured .... 2·00 50

1979 (18 Dec). Butterflies. T **433** and similar vert designs. Multicoloured. P 12×11½.

1435 20p. Type **433** .... 2·50 25
1436 25p. *Inachis io* .... 3·25 35
1437 30p. *Limenitis camilla* .... 4·00 45
1438 35p. *Morpho cypris* .... 4·75 50
1439 50p. *Parnassius apollo* .... 6·75 1·00
1435/1439 *Set of 5* .... 19·00 2·30

1980 (9 Jan). International Flower Show, Damascus. Vert designs similar to T **414** showing varieties of rose. P 12½×12.

1440 5p. multicoloured 30 15
1441 10p. multicoloured 35 15
1442 15p. multicoloured 55 25
1443 50p. multicoloured 75 35
1444 75p. multicoloured .... 1·10 50
1445 100p. multicoloured .... 1·70 70
1440/1445 *Set of 6* .... 4·25 1·90

434 Astrolabe

435 '8' over Buildings

1980 (15 Mar). Second International Symposium on History of Arab Science. P 12½.

1446 **434** 50p. bluish violet 75 35
1447 100p. bistre-brown .... 1·30 70
1448 1000p. bronze-green .... 14·00 7·25
1446/1448 *Set of 3* .... 14·50 7·50

1980 (25 Mar). 17th Anniversary of Baathist Revolution of 8 March 1963. P 12×11½.

1449 **435** 40p. multicoloured 75 35

436 Smoker

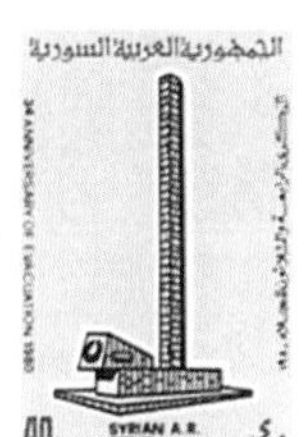

437 Monument

1980 (26 June). World Health Day. Anti-smoking Campaign. T **436** and similar vert design. P 12×11½.

1450 60p. orange-brown, light green and black .... 1·30 50
1451 100p. multicoloured .... 2·40 70

Designs: 60p. T **436**; 100p. Skull and cigarette.

1980 (26 June). 34th Anniversary of Evacuation of Foreign Troops from Syria. P 12×11½.

1452 **437** 40p. multicoloured 75 35
1453 60p. multicoloured 95 50

438 Wrestling

439 'Savings'

1980 (17 Aug). Olympic Games, Moscow. T **438** and similar horiz designs. Multicoloured. P 11½×12.

1454 15p. Type **438** 55 15
a. Strip of 5. Nos. 1454/1458 .... 5·00
1455 25p. Fencing 75 20
1456 35p. Weightlifting 95 25
1457 50p. Judo .... 1·10 30
1458 75p. Boxing .... 1·50 35
1454/1458 *Set of 5* .... 4·25 1·10
MS1459 105×80 mm. 300p. Discus thrower, Games emblem and runner. Imperf .... 33·00 31·00

Nos. 1454/1458 were issued together in *se-tenant* strips of five within the sheet.

1980 (14 Oct). Savings Certificates. P 11½×12.

1460 **439** 25p. violet, rosine and turquoise-blue ... 75 15

440 *Aladdin and the Magic Lamp*

1980 (5 Nov). Folk Tales. T **440** and similar horiz designs. P 11½×12.

1461 15p. *Sinbad the Sailor* 55 15
a. Strip of 5. Nos. 1461/1465 .... 7·75
1462 25p. *Shahrazad and Shahrayar* 95 25
1463 35p. *Ali Baba and the Forty Thieves* .... 1·30 35
1464 50p. *Hassan the Clever* .... 1·70 85
1465 100p. Type **440** .... 3·00 1·20
1461/1465 *Set of 5* .... 6·75 2·50

Nos. 1461/1465 were issued together in *se-tenant* strips of five within the sheet.

441 Kaaba and Mosque, Mecca

1980 (5 Nov). 1400th Anniversary of Hegira. P 12½×12.

1466 **441** 35p. multicoloured 75 35

442 Daffodils

443 Industry

1980 (5 Nov). International Flower Show, Damascus. T **442** and similar vert designs. Multicoloured. P 12×11½.

1467 20p. Type **442** 55 50
a. Strip of 5. Nos. 1467/1471 .... 5·25
1468 30p. Dahlias 75 70
1469 40p. Bergamòt 95 85
1470 60p. Globe flowers .... 1·10 1·00
1471 100p. Cornflowers .... 1·70 1·40
1467/1471 *Set of 5* .... 4·50 4·00

Nos. 1467/1471 were issued together in *se-tenant* strips of five within the sheet.

1980 (16 Nov). Tenth Anniversary of Movement of 16 November 1970. P 11½×12.

1472 **443** 100p. multicoloured .... 1·90 85

444 Construction Worker

445 Children encircling Globe

1980 (30 Dec). Labour Day. P 12×11½.

1473	**444**	35p. multicoloured	75	35

1980 (30 Dec). International Children's Day. P 12×11½.

1474	**445**	25p. yellow-olive, black and bistre yellow	75	15

446 Goldsworthy Gurney Steam powered Passenger Wagon (1830)

1980 (30 Dec). Cars. T **446** and similar horiz designs. Multicoloured. P 11½×12.

1475	25p. Type **446**	75	70
	a. Strip of 5. Nos. 1475/1479	5·50	
1476	35p. Benz vis-a-vis (1899)	85	75
1477	40p. Rolls-Royce tourer (1903)	95	85
1478	50p. Mercedes tourer (1906)	1·10	1·00
1479	60p. Austin tourer (1915)	1·50	1·20
1475/1479 *Set of 5*		4·75	4·00

Nos. 1475/1479 were issued together in *se-tenant* strips of five within the sheet.

447 Mother's Arms round Child

448 Fair Emblem

1980 (30 Dec). Mothers' Day. T **447** and similar vert design. Multicoloured. P 12×11½.

1480	40p. Type **447**	75	35
1481	100p. Faces of mother and child	1·50	85

(Des H. A. Ayash)

1981 (24 Jan). 27th International Damascus Fair. T **448** and similar horiz design. Multicoloured. P 11½×12.

1482	50p. Type **448**	95	35
1483	100p. As T **448** but with different motif on right	1·90	85

449 Armed Forces

(Des H. A. Ayash)

1981 (24 Jan). Army Day. P 12½×12.

1484	**449**	50p. multicoloured	2·40	70

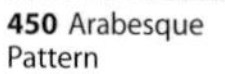

450 Arabesque Pattern

451 Geometric Design, Laurel and Hand holding Torch

(Des A. Ismail)

1981 (8 Mar). 18th Anniversary of Baathist Revolution of 8 March 1963. P 12×11½.

1485	**450**	50p. multicoloured	1·10	35

(Des H. A. Ayash)

1981 (17 Apr). 35th Anniversary of Evacuation of Foreign Troops from Syria. P 12×11½.

1486	**451**	50p. multicoloured	1·10	35

452 Mosque and Script

(Des A. Khorzom)

1981 (30 May). History of Arab-Islamic Civilisation World Conference, Damascus. P 12½×12.

1487	**452**	100p. dull deep green, deep grey-green and black	2·00	1·00

453 Marching Workers and Emblem

454 Human Figure and House on Graph

(Des A. Ismail)

1981 (30 May). Labour Day. P 12×11½.

1488	**453**	100p. multicoloured	1·90	85

(Des A. al-Jaffan)

1991 (1 June). Housing and Population Census. P 12×11½.

1489	**454**	50p. multicoloured	1·10	35

455 Family and Savings Emblem

456 Dove and Map on Globe

(Des A. al-Jaffan)

1981 (22 June). Savings Certificates. P 12×11½.

1490	**455**	50p. black and ochre	1·10	35

(Des O. el-Kourdi)

1981 (22 June). International Syrian and Palestinian Solidarity Conference, Damascus. P 12×11½.

1491	**456**	160p. multicoloured	5·50	2·50

457 Avicenna

458 Glass Lamp

1981 (13 July). Birth Millenary of Avicenna (philosopher and physician). P 12×11½.

1492	**457**	100p. multicoloured	1·90	70

1981 (13 July). Damascus Museum Exhibits. T **458** and similar horiz designs. P 12×12½.

1493	50p. crimson	1·50	50
1494	180p. multicoloured	4·00	1·70

1495 180p. multicoloured .... 4·00 1·70
1493/1495 *Set of 3* .... 8·50 3·50
Designs: No. 1493, T **458**; No. 1494, *Grand Mosque, Damascus* (painting); No. 1495, Hunter (tapestry).

459 Festival Emblem

460 Decorative Pattern

1981 (15 Aug). Youth Festival. P 12½.
1496 **459** 60p. multicoloured .... 1·10 35

1981 (22 Aug). 28th International Damascus Fair. T **460** and similar vert design. P 12×11½.
1497 50p. deep mauve, royal blue and pale green 75 25
1498 160p. purple-brown, orange-yellow and lilac. 2·20 1·00
Designs: 50p. T **460**; 160p. Globe encircled by wheat and cogwheel.

461 Palestinians and Dome of the Rock

462 FAO Emblem

1981 (2 Sept). Palestinian Solidarity. P 12×11½.
1499 **461** 100p. multicoloured .... 1·90 70

1981 (2 Sept). World Food Day. P 11½×12.
1500 **462** 180p. blue, green and black .... 3·75 1·90

463 Tobacco Flowers

464 Hands releasing Dove and Horseman

1981 (2 Sept). International Flower Show, Damascus. T **463** and similar vert design. Multicoloured. P 12×11½.
1501 25p. Type **463** .... 1·30 85
a. Strip of 5. Nos. 1501/1505 .... 11·00
1502 40p. Mimosa .... 1·70 1·00
1503 50p. *Ixias* .... 2·20 1·10
1504 60p. Passion Flower .... 2·40 1·20
1505 100p. Dendrobium .... 2·75 1·70
1501/1505 *Set of 5* .... 9·25 5·25
Nos. 1501/1505 were issued together in *se-tenant* strips of five within the sheet.

1981 (30 Sept). 1300th Anniversary of Bulgarian State. P 11½×12.
1506 **464** 380p. multicoloured .... 5·50 2·00

465 Classroom

1981 (30 Sept). International Children's Day. P 11½×12.
1507 **465** 180p. black, dull vermilion and deep green .... 3·75 1·90

466 Reading the Koran and President Assad (*half-size illustration*)

1981 (31 Oct). Koran Reading Competition. Sheet 105×80 mm. Imperf.
MS1508 **466** 500p. multicoloured .... 19·00 17·00

467 President Assad and Diesel Train

468 Symbols of Development

1981 (16 Nov). 11th Anniversary of Movement of 16 Nov 1970. P 12×11½.
1509 **467** 60p. cobalt, black and orange-brown.... 4·75 1·50

(Des S. Haqi)

1982 (8 Mar). 19th Anniversary of Baathist Revolution of 8 March 1963. P 12×11½.
1510 **468** 50p. grey, brown-red and black .... 1·10 35

469 Robert Koch and Microscope

470 Pattern and Hand holding Rifle

(Des M. Turukmani)

1982 (23 Mar). Centenary of Discovery of Tubercle Bacillus. P 11½×12.
1511 **469** 180p. new blue, reddish brown and black .... 4·50 1·50

(Des S. Haqi)

1982 (17 Apr). 36th Anniversary of Evacuation of Foreign Troops from Syria. P 12×11½.
1512 **470** 70p. vermilion and steel blue .... 1·10 50

471 Disabled People and Emblem

472 APU Emblem

(Des A. Ismail)

1982 (17 Apr). International Year of Disabled Persons. P 12×11½.

1513 **471** 90p. black, deep bright blue and bistre-yellow .... 1·90 70

(Des A. Ismail)

1982 (22 Apr). 30th Anniversary of Arab Postal Union. P 12×11½.

1514 **472** 60p. orange-vermilion, bronze green and greenish yellow .... 1·50 50

473 Traffic Lights

474 Geometric Pattern

(Des S. Haqi)

1982 (22 Apr). World Traffic Day. P 12×11½.

1515 **473** 180p. black, bright scarlet and light new blue .... 3·75 1·40

(Des A. R. Hreitani)

1982 (1 May). World Telecommunications Day. P 12.

1516 **474** 180p. green-yellow, reddish brown and yellow .... 3·00 1·40

475 Oil Rig, Factory Chimneys and Hand holding Torch

476 Mother and Children

(Des F. Bennouh)

1982 (1 May). Labour Day. P 12×11½.

1517 **475** 180p. bright carmine, royal blue and light new blue .... 3·00 1·40

1982 (3 July). Mothers' Day. P 11½.

1518	**476**	40p. deep dull green	55	15
1519		75p. reddish brown	1·10	50

477 Olives

478 President Assad

1982 (3 July). Types **477**/**478** and similar vert design. P 11½.

1520	**477**	50p. olive-green	75	25
1521		60p. deep greenish slate	95	35
1522	–	100p. deep mauve	1·30	70
1523	**478**	150p. deep ultramarine	1·90	1·00
1524	–	180p. vermilion	2·75	1·20
1520/1524 *Set of 5*		....	7·00	3·25

Design: As T **477**—100, 180p. Harbour.

479 Footballer

480 Policeman

(Des H. A. Ayash and F. Bennouh)

1982 (15 July). World Cup Football Championship, Spain. T **479** and similar horiz designs. Multicoloured. P 12½.

1525	40p. Type **479**	95	35
1526	60p. Two footballers	1·30	50
1527	100p. Two footballers (*different*)	2·40	1·70
1525/1527 *Set of 3*	....	4·25	2·30
MS1528 73×34 mm. 300p. World Cup emblem. Imperf	....	31·00	29·00

(Des A. Ismail)

1982 (19 Aug). Police Day. P 12×11½.

1529 **480** 50p. black, carmine-vermilion and light green .... 1·40 35

481 Government Building

482 Communications Emblem and Map

1982 (4 Nov). T **481** and similar designs. P 11½.

1530	30p. deep brown	55	15
1531	70p. dull blue-green	1·30	50
1532	200p. rose-carmine	3·75	1·50
1530/1532 *Set of 3*	....	5·00	1·90

Designs: Vert—70p. Arched Wall. Horiz—30p. T **481**; 200p. Ruins.

(Des A. Ismail)

1982 (4 Nov). Arab Telecommunications Day. P 11½×12.

1533 **482** 50p. light new blue, ultramarine and scarlet .... 1·10 35

483 Scout pitching Tent

484 Dish Aerial and Map

(Des O. el-Kourdi)

1982 (4 Nov). 75th Anniversary of Boy Scout Movement. P 11½×12.

1534 **483** 160p. green .... 3·25 1·40

(Des F. Bennouh)

1982 (4 Nov). International Telecommunications Union Delegates' Conference, Nairobi. P 11½×12.

1535 **484** 180p. light new blue, ultramarine and scarlet .... 3·75 1·70

485 President Assad

486 Water-wheel, Hama

(Des A. Khorzom)

1982 (16 Nov). 12th Anniversary of Movement of 16 November. P 11½×12.

1536 **485** 50p. indigo and pale grey .... 1·10 35

(Des A. Khorzom)

1982 (25 Nov)–**84**. P 11½×12.

1537	**486**	5p. reddish brown (15.1.84)	35	15
1538		10p. violet (15.1.84)	55	15
1539		20p. rosine (15.1.84)	75	25
1540		50p. deep turquoise	1·10	35
1537/1540 *Set of 4*		....	2·50	80

487 Dragonfly

488 Honeysuckle

(Des A. Ismail)

1982 (25 Nov). Insects. T **487** and similar square designs. Multicoloured. P 12½.

1541	5p. Type **487**	75	50
	a. Strip of 5. Nos. 1541/1545	8·75	
1542	10p. Stag Beetle	95	70
1543	20p. Seven-spotted Ladybird	1·30	1·00
1544	40p. Desert Locust	2·50	2·00
1545	50p. Honey Bee	3·00	2·20
1541/1545	*Set of 5*	7·75	5·75

Nos. 1541/1545 were issued together in *se-tenant* strips of five within the sheet.

(Des A. Ismail)

1982 (25 Nov). International Flower Show, Damascus. T **488** and similar vert design. Multicoloured. P 12×11½.

1546	50p. Type **488**	1·30	50
1547	60p. Geranium	1·50	85

489 Satellites within Dove

490 Dove on Gun

(Des M. Jarâd)

1983 (5 Feb). United Nations Conference on Exploration and Peaceful Uses of Outer Space, Vienna. P 12×11½.

1548	**489**	50p. multicoloured	1·10	35

(Des S. Haqi)

1983 (5 Feb). International Palestine Day. P 12×11½.

1549	**490**	50p. multicoloured	1·90	70

491 Damascus Airport

(Des A. Ismail)

1983 (21 Mar). 20th Anniversary of Baathist Revolution of 8 March 1963. P 12½×12.

1550	**491**	60p. multicoloured	3·00	1·20

492 Communications Emblems

(Des A. Khorzom)

1983 (21 Mar). World Communications Year. P 12½×12.

1551	**492**	180p. multicoloured	3·75	1·50

493 Figurine

494 Pharmacist

1983 (21 May). P 11½×12.

1552	**493**	380p. deep yellow-brown and grey-green	9·25	3·50

(Des F. Bennouh)

1983 (6 July). Arab Pharmacists' Day. P 11½×12.

1553	**494**	100p. multicoloured	2·40	85

495 Liberation Monument, Qneitra

496 Wave within Ship's Wheel

1983 (6 July). Ninth Anniversary of Liberation of Qneitra. T **495** and similar vert design. P 11½.

1554	50p. grey-green	2·20	85
1555	100p. dull chocolate	4·75	1·20

Designs: 50p. T **495**; 100p. Ruined buildings.

(Des I. Intabi)

1983 (6 July). 25th Anniversary of International Maritime Organisation. P 12×11½.

1556	**496**	180p. multicoloured	4·00	1·40

497 Flame on Map

498 ISO Emblem and Factory

(Des F. Bennouh)

1983 (6 July). Namibia Day. P 11½×12.

1557	**497**	180p. azure, magenta and black	3·25	1·40

(Des A. al-Jaffan and A. Khorzom)

1983 (14 Oct). World Standards Day. T **498** and similar vert design. P 12×11½.

1558	50p. multicoloured	1·10	50
1559	100p. violet, deep green and black	2·40	1·40

Designs: 50p. T **498**; 100p. International Standards Organisation emblem and measuring equipment.

499 Gateway, Bosra

500 Flowers

(Des F. Bennouh)

1983 (14 Oct). Tenth Anniversary of World Heritage Agreement. P 12×11½.

1560	**499**	60p. reddish brown	1·30	50

(Des A. Ismail)

1983 (14 Oct). International Flower Show, Damascus. T **500** and similar vert design. Multicoloured. P 12×11½.

1561	50p. Type **500**	1·30	50
1562	60p. Hibiscus	1·50	1·00

501 Farmland

502 Factory

(Des A. Khorzom)

1983 (16 Oct). World Food Day. P 11½×12.

1563	**501**	180p. apple green, greenish cream and deep green	3·75	1·70

(Des A. Khorzom)

1983 (16 Nov). P 12×11½.

1564	**502**	50p. bottle green	1·10	50

503 Statuette

504 Aleppo

(Des F. Bennouh)

1984 (15 Jan). International Deir Ez-Zor History and Archaeology Symposium. P 12.

1565	**503**	225p. reddish brown	5·50	2·50

(Des A. R. Hreitani)

1984 (15 Jan). International Symposium for the Conservation of Aleppo. P 12×12½.

1566	**504**	245p. multicoloured	5·50	2·50

505 Alassad Library

(Des A. Ismail)

1984 (24 Mar). 21st Anniversary of Baathist Revolution of 8 March 1963. P 12½×12.

1567	**505**	60p. multicoloured	1·90	85

506 Bodies and Mourning Woman with Child

507 Mother and Child

(Des F. Bennouh)

1984 (2 June). Sabra and Shatila (refugee camps in Lebanon) Massacres. P 11½×12.

1568	**506**	225p. multicoloured	4·75	2·20

(Des A. Ismail)

1984 (2 June). Mothers' Day. P 12½.

1569	**507**	245p. sepia and deep dull green	4·75	2·50

508 Dam, Emblem and Pioneers

509 Swimming

(Des F. Bennouh and A. Khorzom)

1984 (14 June). Ninth Regional Festival of Al Baath Pioneers. T **508** and similar horiz design. Multicoloured. P 11½×12.

1570	50p. Type **508**	1·30	85
1571	60p. Pioneers, ruins and emblem	1·90	1·00

(Des A. Ismail and M. Jarâd. Litho)

1984 (14 June). Olympic Games, Los Angeles. T **509** and similar vert designs. Multicoloured. P 12×11½.

1572	30p. Type **509**	1·10	85
	a. Strip of 5. Nos. 1572/1576	8·00	
1573	50p. Wrestling	1·30	1·00
1574	60p. Running	1·50	1·20
1575	70p. Boxing	1·70	1·40
1576	90p. Football	2·20	1·90
1572/1576	*Set of 5*	7·00	5·75
MS1577	77×55 mm. 200p. Footballer within football. Imperf	20·00	19·00

Nos. 1572/1576 were issued together in *se-tenant* strips of five within the sheet.

510 Flowers

511 President Assad and Text

(Des A. Ismail)

1984 (14 June). International Flower Show, Damascus. T **510** and similar vert design. Multicoloured. P 12×11½.

1578	245p. Type **510**	5·50	2·50
1579	285p. Flowers (*different*)	6·50	3·50

(Des A. Khorzom)

1984 (2 Oct). Fourth Revolutionary Youth Union Congress. T **511** and similar horiz design. P 12½ (50p.) or 11½×12 (60p.).

1580	50p. orange-brown, deep bistre-brown and deep blue-green	1·10	50
1581	60p. multicoloured	1·20	85

Designs: 50p. T **511**. 37×25 mm—60p. President Assad and saluting youth.

512 Emblem and Administration Building, Damascus

(Des A. Ismail)

1984 (2 Oct). Arab Postal Union Day. P 12½.

1582	**512**	60p. multicoloured	1·10	70

513 Globe, Dish Aerial and Telephone

514 Arabesque Pattern

(Des F. Bennouh)

1984 (2 Oct). World Telecommunications Day. P 12½.

1583 **513** 245p. multicoloured .... 5·50 3·00

(Des A. Ismail. Litho)

1984 (27 Oct). 31st International Damascus Fair. T **514** and similar vert design. Multicoloured. P 12×11½.

1584 45p. Type **514** .... 1·10 35

1585 100p. Ornate gold decoration .... 3·25 1·20

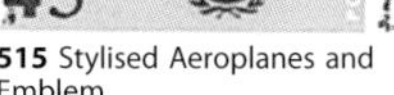

515 Stylised Aeroplanes and Emblem

516 Text, Flag and President Assad

(Des A. Khorzom)

1984 (27 Oct). 40th Anniversary of International Civil Aviation Organisation. T **515** and similar horiz designs. P 11½×12.

1586 45p. light new blue and deep new blue........ 1·30 50

1587 245p. light new blue, deep ultramarine and deep new blue.. 5·50 3·00

Designs: 45p. T **515**; 245p. Emblem and stylised building.

(Des A. Khorzom)

1984 (3 Dec). 14th Anniversary of Movement of 16 Nov 1970. P 12½×12.

1588 **516** 65p. yellow-orange, black and reddish brown .... 1·50 1·70

517 Palmyra Roman Arch and Colonnades

518 Wooded Landscape

(Des A. Khorzom)

1984 (3 Dec). International Tourism Day. P 12½×12.

1589 **517** 100p. cinnamon, black and pale blue...... 2·20 1·00

1985 (23 Feb). Woodland Conservation. P 12½×12.

1590 **518** 45p. multicoloured .... 1·90 50

519 University and Students

520 Oil Lamp

1985 (23 Feb). 26th Anniversary (1984) of Aleppo University. P 12½×12.

1591 **519** 45p. black, blue and cinnamon .... 1·30 50

1985 (23 Feb). 26th Anniversary (1984) of Supreme Council of Science. P 12½×12.

1592 **520** 65p. apple green, scarlet and black........ 1·90 85

521 Soldier holding Flag

522 President Assad

1985 (23 Feb). Army Day. P 12½×12.

1593 **521** 65p. reddish brown and bistre.................. 1·90 85

1985 (12 Mar). Re-election of President Assad. P 12½.

1594 **522** 200p. multicoloured .... 4·75 3·00

1595 300p. multicoloured .... 6·00 3·50

1596 500p. multicoloured .... 11·00 5·00

1594/1596 *Set of* 3 .... 20·00 10·50

MS1597 140×85 mm. Nos. 1594/1596. Imperf .... 28·00 26·00

a. Black (value and inscr on stamps) omitted ....

523 Flag and Party Emblem

524 Torch and '22'

1985 (27 Apr). Eighth Baath Arab Socialist Party Congress. P 12½×12.

1598 **523** 50p. multicoloured .... 1·30 50

1985 (27 Apr). 22nd Anniversary of Baathist Revolution of 8 March 1963. P 12×12½.

1599 **524** 60p. multicoloured .... 1·30 50

525 Tractor and Cow

526 Liberation Monument, Qneitra

1985 (27 Apr). Aleppo Industrial and Agricultural Fair (1984). T **525** and similar vert design. Multicoloured. P 12½×12 (65p.) or 12×12½ (150p.).

1600 65p. Type **525** .... 1·50 50

1601 150p. Fort and carrots.. 4·00 2·00

1985 (27 Apr). Tenth Anniversary (1984) of Liberation of Qneitra. P 12½×12.

1602 **526** 70p. multicoloured .... 3·25 85

527 Parliament Building

1985 (27 Apr). Tenth Anniversary of Arab Parliamentary Union. P 12½×12.

1603 **527** 245p. multicoloured .... 6·00 3·00

528 UPU Emblem and Pigeon with Letter

529 APU Emblem

1985 (27 Apr). World Post Day. P 12×12½.
1604 **528** 285p. multicoloured .... 7·75 2·00

1985 (12 Aug). 12th Arab Postal Union Conference, Damascus. P 12×12½.
1605 **529** 60p. multicoloured .... 1·30 85

530 Medal

532 Emblem and Child with empty Bowl

531 Steam and Diesel Locomotives

1985 (12 Aug). Labour Day. P 12½.
1606 **530** 60p. multicoloured .... 1·30 85

1985 (16 Nov). Second Scientific Symposium. P 12½.
1607 **531** 60p. indigo .... 3·75 1·00

1985 (16 Nov). United Nations Child Survival Campaign. P 12½×12.
1608 **532** 60p. black, turquoise-green and flesh ... 1·30 85

533 President Assad and Road

1985 (16 Nov). 15th Anniversary of Movement of 16 November 1970. P 12½.
1609 **533** 60p. multicoloured .... 1·30 85

534 Emblem and '40'

1985 (16 Nov). 40th Anniversary of United Nations Organisation. P 12×12½.
1610 **534** 245p. multicoloured .... 4·75 3·00

535 Lily-flowered Tulip

536 Flask

(Des A. Ismail)

1986 (1 Feb). International Flower Show, Damascus (1985). T **535** and similar vert design. Multicoloured. P 12×12½.
1611 30p. Type **535** 95 45
1612 60p. Tulip .... 1·90 1·40
a. Black (inscr) omitted ....
b. Magenta omitted ....

(Des A. Ismail)

1986 (1 Feb). 32nd International Damascus Fair (1985). P 12½.
1613 **536** 60p. multicoloured .... 1·50 85

537 Abd-al-Rahman I

538 President Hafez al-Assad

(Des T. Shabân)

1986 (1 Feb). 1200th Anniversary of Abd-al-Rahman I ad Dakhil, Emir of Cordoba. P 12½×12.
1614 **537** 60p. reddish brown, pale cinnamon and light brown .... 1·50 85

1986 (16 Apr)–**90**. P 12×11½.
1615 **538** 10p. bright rose-red 20 15
1616 30p. blue 30 15
1616*a* 50p. brown-lilac (30.10.90) 75 25
1617 100p. new blue .... 1·30 85
a. Imperf (pair) ....
1618 150p. chocolate (2.2.88) .... 1·90 70
a. Imperf (pair) ....
1619 175p. dull violet (2.2.88) .... 2·20 85
1620 200p. red-brown .... 2·50 1·50
1621 300p. deep mauve .... 3·75 2·20
1622 500p. yellow-orange (9.8.86) .... 6·50 3·75
1623 550p. bright rose (2.2.88) .... 7·50 3·50
1624 600p. grey-olive (2.2.88) .... 9·25 3·75
1625 1000p. bright magenta (9.8.86) .... 15·00 7·75
1626 2000p. blue-green (9.8.86) .... 31·00 15·00
1615/1626 *Set of* 13 .... 75·00 36·00

For similar designs but with full-face portrait see Nos. 1774/1780.

539 Tooth and Map

540 Tower Blocks, Ear of Wheat and Kangaroo

(Des F. Bennouh)

1986 (16 Apr). 19th Arab Dentists' Union Congress, Damascus. P 12½×12.
1627 **539** 110p. multicoloured .... 3·75 2·00

(Des F. Bennouh)

1986 (20 May). 15th Anniversary of Syrian Investment Certificates. P 12×11½.
1628 **540** 100p. multicoloured .... 2·75 1·20

541 Traffic Policewoman, Globe and Traffic Lights

542 Policeman and Building in Laurel Wreath

(Des A. al-Jaffan)

1986 (20 May). World Traffic Day. P 12×12½.
1629 **541** 330p. multicoloured .... 6·75 3·75

(Des A. al-Jaffan)

1986 (21 June). Police Day. P 12×11½.
1630 **542** 110p. multicoloured .... 2·20 70

543 Industrial Symbols and Hand holding Spanner

544 Building

(Des A. al-Jaffan)

1986 (21 June). Labour Day. P 12×11½.
1631 **543** 330p. rose-red, black and cobalt .... 6·00 4·25

(Des F. Bennouh)

1986 (26 June). 12th Anniversary of Liberation of Qneitra. P 11½×12.
1632 **544** 110p. multicoloured .... 2·00 70

545 Pictogram and Ball

546 Mother and Children

(Des F. Bennouh)

1986 (7 July). World Cup Football Championship, Mexico. T **545** and similar horiz design. P 12×11½.
1633 **545** 330p. multicoloured .... 5·50 3·00
1634 370p. multicoloured .... 6·00 3·50
MS1635 105×80 mm. 500p. multicoloured (Ball and hemispheres). Imperf .... 13·00 12·00

(Des F. Bennouh)

1986 (9 Aug). Mothers' Day. P 12×11½.
1636 **546** 100p. multicoloured .... 1·90 70

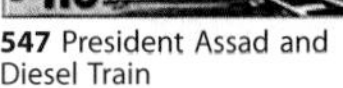

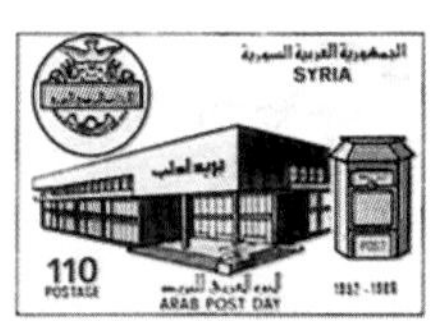

547 President Assad and Diesel Train

548 APU Emblem, Post Office and Box

(Des F. Bennouh)

1986 (9 Aug). 23rd Anniversary of Baathist Revolution of 8 March 1963. P 11½×12.
1637 **547** 110p. multicoloured .... 3·75 1·70

(Des T. Shabân)

1986 (9 Aug). Arab Post Day. P 11½×12.
1638 **548** 110p. multicoloured .... 1·90 70

549 Fists. Map and Globe

550 Tulips

(Des F. Bennouh)

1986 (9 Aug). International Palestine Day. P 12×11½.
1639 **549** 110p. multicoloured .... 1·90 70

(Des A. Ismail)

1986 (11 Oct). International Flower Show, Damascus. T **550** and similar vert designs. Multicoloured. P 12½.
1640 10p. Type **550** 35 35
a. Strip of 5. Nos. 1640/1644 .... 12·00
1641 50p. Mauve flowers 95 85
1642 100p. Yellow flowers .... 2·00 1·50
1643 110p. Pink flowers .... 2·20 1·70
1644 330p. Yellow flowers (*different*) .... 6·00 3·75
1640/1644 *Set of* 5 .... 10·50 7·25

Nos. 1640/1644 were issued together in *se-tenant* strips of five within the sheet.

551 President Assad and Tishreen Palace

552 Rocket and Flags

(Des Z. Zakari)

1986 (16 Nov). 16th Anniversary of Movement of 16 November 1970. P 12½.
1645 **551** 110p. multicoloured .... 1·90 70

(Des F. Bennouh)

1986 (16 Nov). First Anniversary of Announcement of Syrian–Soviet Space Flight. P 12×12½.
1646 **552** 330p. multicoloured .... 6·50 3·50
a. Black (value, inscr and frame) omitted .... 65·00

553 Jug and Star

554 Girls and National Flag

(Des T. Shabân and F. Bennouh)

1986 (9 Dec). 33rd International Damascus Fair. T **553** and similar horiz design. P 11½×12.
1647 110p. multicoloured .... 2·75 1·70
1648 330p. black, grey-green and lake-brown .... 6·50 3·50

Designs: 110p. T **553**; 330p. Coffee pot.

1987 (28 Jan). International Children's Art Exhibition. P 11½×12.
1649 **554** 330p. multicoloured .... 4·75 2·50

555 UPU Emblem and Airmail Envelope

1987 (28 Jan). World Post Day. P 12½×12.
1650 **555** 330p. multicoloured .... 4·75 2·50

556 Children in Balloon

1987 (28 Jan). International Children's Day. P 12×12½.
1651 **556** 330p. multicoloured .... 4·75 2·50

557 Citadel, Aleppo

1987 (28 Jan). International Tourism Day. T **557** and similar horiz design. P 12½×12.
1652 330p. Type **557** .... 4·75 2·50
1653 370p. Water-wheel, Hama .... 5·50 3·00

558 Industrial Symbols

1987 (8 Mar). 24th Anniversary of Baathist Revolution of 8 March 1963. P 12½×12.
1654 **558** 100p. multicoloured .... 1·50 50

559 Doves flying from Globe

560 Party Emblem

1987 (8 Mar). International Peace Year. P 12×11½.
1655 **559** 370p. multicoloured .... 4·75 3·00

1987 (7 Apr). 40th Anniversary of Baath Arab Socialist Party. P 12½.
1656 **560** 100p. multicoloured .... 1·50 50

561 Stars

562 Draughtsman

1987 (17 Apr). 41st Anniversary of Evacuation of Foreign Troops from Syria. P 12½×12.
1657 **561** 100p. multicoloured .... 1·50 50

1987 (21 Apr). Sixth Arab Ministers of Culture Conference. P 12½.
1658 **562** 330p. light blue, deep bluish green and black .... 6·00 3·00

563 Map of Arab Postal Union Members

564 Couple within Cogwheel

1987 (1 May). Arab Post Day. P 11½×12.
1659 **563** 110p. multicoloured .... 1·50 50

1987 (1 May). Labour Day. P 12×11½.
1660 **564** 330p. multicoloured .... 4·75 3·00

565 Statue

566 President Assad with Children and Nurse

1987 (25 June). 13th Anniversary of Liberation of Qneitra. P 12×11½.
1661 **565** 100p. multicoloured .... 1·50 70

1987 (25 June). Child Vaccination Campaign. P 11½×12.
1662 **566** 100p. multicoloured .... 2·20 1·20
1663 330p. multicoloured .... 5·50 3·00

567 Dome of the Rock, Battle Scene and Saladin

1987 (25 June). 800th Anniversary of Battle of Hattin. P 12½×12.
1664 **567** 110p. multicoloured .... 1·90 70

568 Rocket Launch and National Flags

1987 (22 July). Syrian–Soviet Space Flight. T **568** and similar vert designs. Multicoloured. P 12½×12 (No. 1665), 11½×12 (No. 1666) or 12×11½ (No. 1667).

1665 330p. Type **568** .... 4·75 3·00
1666 330p. Spacecraft docking with *Mir* space station (37×25 *mm*) .... 4·75 3·00
1667 330p. Space capsule re-entering Earth's atmosphere and group of cosmonauts (25×37 *mm*) .... 4·75 3·00
a. Imperf (pair) £120
1665/1667 *Set of* 3 .... 13·00 8·00
MS1668 150×110 mm. 300p. Rocket launch; 300p. Space capsule re-entering atmosphere; 300p. Spacecraft docked with space station; 300p. Stylised Syrian and Soviet cosmonauts. Imperf .... 30·00 27·00

569 Flags, Cosmonauts and President Assad

1987 (12 Aug). President's Space Conversation with Lt.-Col. Mohammed Faris (Syrian cosmonaut). P 12½×12.

1669 **569** 500p. multicoloured .... 9·25 3·75

570 Stylised Flowers

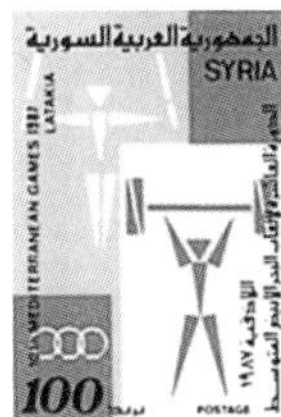

571 Sports Pictograms

1987 (16 Aug). 34th International Damascus Fair. P 12×11½.

1670 **570** 330p. multicoloured .... 4·75 3·00

1987 (10 Sept). Tenth Mediterranean Games, Latakia. T **571** and other designs. P 12×11½ (100p.), 11½×12 (110p.) or 12½×12 (others).

1671 100p. bright purple and black .... 1·30 85
1672 110p. multicoloured .... 1·90 1·00
1673 330p. multicoloured .... 4·75 2·50
1674 370p. multicoloured .... 5·50 3·50
1671/1674 *Set of* 4 .... 12·00 7·00
MS1675 151×112 mm. 300p.×4, multicoloured. Imperf .... 24·00 22·00

Designs: As T **571**. Horiz—110p. Swimming bird and emblem. Vert—100p. T **571**; **MS**1675: Gymnastics, Weightlifting, Tennis, Football. 52×23 mm—330p. Phoenician galley (Games emblem); 370p. Flags forming 'SYRIA'.

572 Soldier, Mikoyan Gurevich MiG-21D Fighter, Ship and Tank

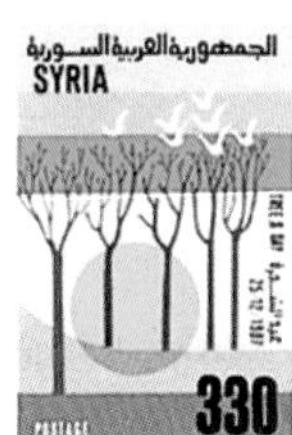

573 Trees, Sun and Birds

1987 (15 Oct). Army Day. P 12×11½.

1676 **572** 100p. multicoloured .... 2·40 85

1987 (15 Oct). Tree Day. P 12×11½.

1677 **573** 330p. multicoloured .... 4·75 2·50

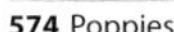

574 Poppies

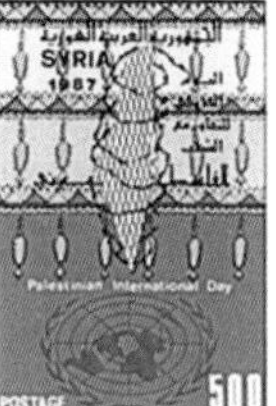

576 Barbed Wire around Map of Israel

575 President Assad acknowledging Applause

1987 (15 Oct). International Flower Show, Damascus. T **574** and similar horiz design. P 11½×12.

1678 330p. Type **574** .... 5·50 2·00
1679 370p. Mauve flower .... 6·00 2·20

1987 (16 Nov). 17th Anniversary of Corrective Movement of 16 November 1970. P 12½.

1680 **575** 150p. multicoloured .... 2·20 1·20

1987 (16 Nov). International Palestine Day. P 12×11½.

1681 **576** 500p. multicoloured .... 7·75 3·75
a. Black (inscr and barbed wire) omitted .... 85·00

577 UPU and UN Emblems

1988 (25 Feb). World Post Day. P 12½×12.

1682 **577** 500p. multicoloured .... 8·25 4·25

578 Bosra Amphitheatre

1988 (25 Feb). International Tourism Day. T **578** and similar horiz design. Multicoloured. P 11½×12.

1683 500p. Type **578** .... 7·75 3·50
1684 500p. Palmyra ruins .... 7·75 3·50

579 Children as Cosmonauts

1988 (27 Feb). International Children's Day. P 12½×12.

1685 **579** 500p. multicoloured .... 7·75 3·50

580 Hand holding Torch

581 Woman cradling Baby, Children and Adults

1988 (8 Mar). 25th Anniversary of Baathist Revolution of 8 March 1963. T **580** and similar horiz design. Multicoloured. P 12×11½.

1686 **580** 150p. multicoloured ... 2·00 1·20

MS1687 110×81 mm. 500p. No. 1686, map and flag. Imperf ... 9·25 8·50

1988 (12 Apr). Mothers' Day. P 12×12½.

1688 **581** 500p. multicoloured ... 7·75 3·50

582 Arms, Cogwheel, Laurel Branch and Book

583 Dove, Airmail Envelope and Map

1988 (17 Apr). 42nd Anniversary of Evacuation of Foreign Troops from Syria. P 12×12½.

1689 **582** 150p. multicoloured ... 2·00 1·00

1988 (17 Apr). Arab Post Day. P 12½×12.

1690 **583** 150p. multicoloured ... 2·00 1·00

584 Spanner, Chimney, Cogwheel and Scroll

585 Modern Buildings

1988 (1 May). Labour Day. P 12×12½.

1691 **584** 550p. multicoloured ... 7·50 3·50

1988 (25 May). Arab Engineers' Union. P 12×11½.

1692 **585** 150p. multicoloured ... 2·00 1·00

586 Lily

587 Clay Tablet

1988 (25 May). International Flower Show, Damascus. T **586** and similar vert design. Multicoloured. P 12×11½.

1693 550p. Type **586** ... 7·75 3·50

1694 600p. Carnations ... 9·25 4·25

1988 (28 Aug). International Symposium on Archaeology of Ebla. T **587** and similar horiz designs. P 12½.

1695 175p. brownish black and yellow-brown ... 2·75 1·20

1696 550p. orange-brown, new blue and black ... 7·75 3·50

1697 600p. multicoloured ... 8·25 3·75

1695/1697 *Set of 3* ... 17·00 7·50

Designs: 175p. T **587**; 550p. King making offering (carving from stone votive basin); 600p. Golden statue of goddess Ishtar.

588 Old City

589 Emblem

1988 (28 Aug). Preservation of Sana'a, Yemen. P 12½.

1698 **588** 550p. multicoloured ... 8·25 3·50

1988 (28 Aug). Children's Day. P 12×11½.

1699 **589** 600p. black, yellow-olive and emerald ... 8·25 3·75

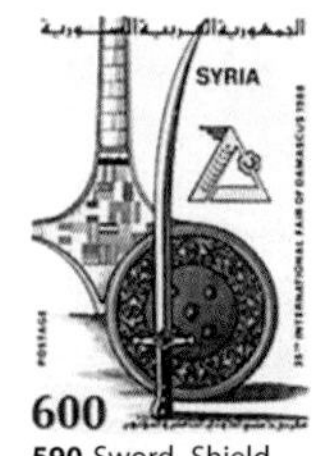
590 Sword, Shield and Emblems

591 Emblem and People

1988 (28 Aug). 35th International Damascus Fair. P 12×11½.

1700 **590** 600p. multicoloured ... 8·25 3·75

1988 (28 Aug). 40th Anniversary of World Health Organisation. P 12×11½.

1701 **591** 600p. multicoloured ... 8·25 3·75

592 Emblems and Map

1988 (17 Sept). 50th Anniversary of Arab Scout Movement. P 12½×12.

1702 **592** 150p. multicoloured ... 3·25 1·00

593 Cycling

1988 (17 Sept). Olympic Games, Seoul. T **593** and similar horiz designs. Multicoloured. P 11½×12.

1703 550p. Type **593** ... 9·25 3·50

1704 600p. Football ... 9·50 3·75

MS1705 80×60 mm. 1200p. Emblem and Hodori (mascot). Imperf ... 30·00 27·00

594 Old Houses and Modern Flats

1988 (18 Oct)–**89**. Housing. T **594** and similar horiz designs. Multicoloured. P 12½×12.

1706	150p. Type **594** (Arab Housing Day)	2·50	1·40
1707	175p. House and makeshift shelter (International Year of Shelter for the Homeless (1987)) (6.2.89)	2·75	1·20
1708	550p. Types of housing (World Housing Day)	7·00	3·50
1709	600p. As No. 1707 but inscr for International Day for Housing the Homeless	7·50	3·75
1706/1709	*Set of* 4	18·00	8·75

595 Euphrates Bridge, Deir el Zor

596 Ear of Wheat and Globe

1988 (18 Oct). International Tourism Day. T **595** and similar horiz design. Multicoloured. P 12½×12.

1710	550p. Type **595**	7·50	3·50
1711	600p. Tetrapylon of Latakia	7·75	3·75

No. 1711 is erroneously inscribed 'INTEPNATIONAL'.

1988 (18 Oct). World Food Day. P 12×12½.

1712	**596** 550p. multicoloured	7·75	3·00

597 Al-Assad University Hospital

1988 (16 Nov). 18th Anniversary of Corrective Movement of 16 November 1970. P 12½×12.

1713	**597** 150p. multicoloured	2·20	1·00

598 Tree and Flowers

599 Dove with Envelope over Globe

1988 (16 Nov). Tree Day. P 12×12½.

1714	**598** 600p. multicoloured	8·25	3·50

1988 (7 Dec). World Post Day. P 12×12½.

1715	**599** 600p. multicoloured	7·75	3·50

600 Emblem and Doctor within Stethoscope

601 Symbols of Agriculture and Industry

1989 (6 Feb). Tenth Anniversary of Arab Board for Medical Specialisations. P 12½.

1716	**600** 175p. multicoloured	2·40	1·00

1989 (8 Mar). 26th Anniversary of Baathist Revolution of 8 March 1963. P 11½×12.

1717	**601** 150p. multicoloured	95	50

602 President Assad and Women

603 Candle and Books

1989 (8 Mar). Fifth General Congress of Union of Women. P 12½.

1718	**602** 150p. multicoloured	95	50

1989 (8 Mar). Arab Teachers' Day. P 11½×12.

1719	**603** 175p. multicoloured	1·10	70

604 Nehru

605 Mother and Children

1989 (8 Mar). Birth Centenary of Jawaharlal Nehru (Indian statesman). P 12½.

1720	**604** 550p. brown and light brown	3·50	2·00

1989 (21 Mar). Mothers' Day. P 12½.

1721	**605** 550p. multicoloured	3·50	2·00

606 Eurasian Goldfinch

607 State Arms on Map

1989 (21 Mar). Birds. T **606** and similar horiz designs. Multicoloured. P 11½×12.

1722	600p. Type **606**	5·50	2·50
1723	600p. European Bee-eater	5·50	2·50
1724	600p. Turtle Dove	5·50	2·50
1722/1724	*Set of* 3	15·00	6·75

1989 (17 Apr). 43rd Anniversary of Evacuation of Foreign Troops from Syria. P 11½×12.

1725	**607** 150p. multicoloured	95	50

608 Workers

609 Snapdragons

1989 (1 May). Labour Day. P 12×11½.

1726	**608** 850p. turquoise-green and black	5·25	3·25

1989 (3 June). International Flower Show, Damascus. T **609** and similar square designs. Multicoloured. P 12½.

1727 150p. Type **609** 95 50
a. Strip of 5. Nos. 1727/1731 .... 16·00
1728 150p. *Canaria* 95 50
1729 450p. Cornflowers .... 2·75 1·70
1730 850p. *Clematis sackmani* .... 5·25 3·25
1731 900p. *Gesneriaceae* .... 5·50 3·50
1727/1731 *Set of 5* .... 14·00 8·50

Nos. 1727/1731 were printed together in *se-tenant* strips of five stamps within the sheet.

610 Girl and Envelope

611 Emblem and Map

1989 (6 June). Arab Post Day. P 12×11½.

1732 **610** 175p. multicoloured .... 1·10 70

1989 (6 June). 13th Arab Teachers' Union General Congress. P 12×11½.

1733 **611** 175p. multicoloured .... 1·10 70

612 *Cynthia cardui*

613 Symbols of International Co-operation

1989 (6 June). Butterflies. T **612** and similar square designs. Multicoloured. P 12½.

1734 550p. Type **612** .... 4·00 2·20
1735 550p. *Colias crocea* .... 4·00 2·20
1736 550p. *Pieris brassicae* .... 4·00 2·20
a. Green and yellow omitted ....
1734/1736 *Set of 3* .... 11·00 6·00

1989 (6 June). World Telecommunications Day. P 11½×12.

1737 **613** 550p. multicoloured .... 3·50 2·00

614 Emblem and Map

615 Monument and Al-Baath Pioneers

1989 (19 June). 17th Arab Lawyers' Union Congress. P 11½×12.

1738 **614** 175p. multicoloured .... 1·10 70

1989 (26 June). 15th Anniversary of Liberation of Qneitra. P 12×11½.

1739 **615** 450p. multicoloured .... 2·75 1·70

616 Globe and Envelopes

1989 (26 June). World Post Day. P 11½×12.

1740 **616** 550p. multicoloured .... 3·50 2·00

617 Parliament Building

1989 (12 July). Centenary of Interparliamentary Union. P 12½.

1741 **617** 900p. multicoloured .... 5·50 3·50

618 Emblem and Monument

619 Jaabar Castle, Raqqa

1989 (16 Oct). 36th International Damascus Fair. P 12×11½.

1742 **618** 450p. multicoloured .... 2·50 1·00

1989 (16 Oct). International Tourism Day. T **619** and similar horiz design. Multicoloured. P 11½×12.

1743 550p. Type **619** .... 3·75 2·00
1744 600p. Baal-Shamin Temple, Palmyra .... 4·00 2·20

620 Child's View of 'Intifida'

621 Common Carp

1989 (24 Oct). Palestinian Intifida Movement. P 12×11½.

1745 **620** 550p. multicoloured .... 3·00 1·00

1989 (24 Oct). Fish. T **621** and similar horiz design. Multicoloured. P 11½×12.

1746 550p. Type **621** .... 3·75 1·90
1747 600p. Brown Trout .... 4·00 2·00
a. Imperf (pair) ....

622 Omayyad Palace, President Assad and Ebla Hotel

1989 (16 Nov). 19th Anniversary of Corrective Movement of 16 November 1970. P 12½×12.

1748 **622** 150p. multicoloured 95 50

623 Children of Different Races taking Food from Large Bowl

624 Dove, Globe and Children of Different Races

1990 (13 Feb). World Food Day (1989). P 11½×12.
1749 **623** 850p. multicoloured .... 4·75 2·20

1990 (13 Feb). International Children's Day. P 12×11½.
1750 **624** 850p. multicoloured .... 4·75 2·20

625 Flag, Emblem and Ear of Wheat

626 Tree-lined Road

1990 (8 Mar). Fifth Revolutionary Youth Union Congress. P 12½.
1751 **625** 150p. multicoloured 95 35
a. Black and magenta (inscr etc) omitted ....

1990 (8 Mar). 27th Anniversary of Baathist Revolution of 8 March 1963. P 12×11½.
1752 **626** 600p. multicoloured .... 3·00 1·00

627 Flag and Arab Fighters

628 Woman carrying Child

1990 (17 Apr). 44th Anniversary of Evacuation of Foreign Troops from Syria. P 12×11½.
1753 **627** 175p. multicoloured 95 35

1990 (17 Apr). Mothers' Day. P 12½.
1754 **628** 550p. multicoloured .... 3·00 1·00

629 Globe and Couple

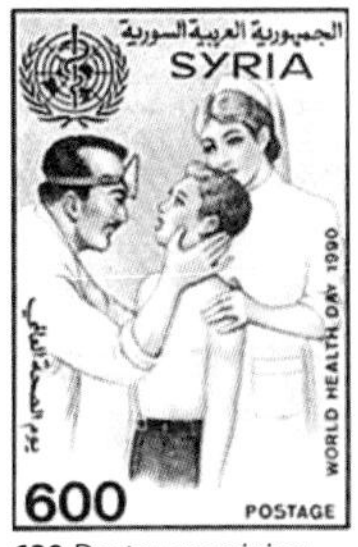

630 Doctor examining Boy

1990 (1 May). Labour Day. P 12×11½.
1755 **629** 550p. multicoloured .... 2·75 1·40

1990 (1 May). World Health Day. P 12½.
1756 **630** 600p. multicoloured .... 3·00 1·50

631 Lilies

632 Goalkeeper saving Goal

1990 (27 May). International Flower Show, Damascus. T **631** and similar vert designs. Multicoloured. P 12×11½.
1757 600p. Type **631** .... 3·00 1·50
a. Strip of five. Nos. 1757/1761 .... 16·00
1758 600p. Cyclamen .... 3·00 1·50
1759 600p. Marigolds .... 3·00 1·50
1760 600p. *Viburnum opulus* .... 3·00 1·50
1761 600p. Swan River Daisies .... 3·00 1·50
1757/1761 *Set of 5* .... 13·50 6·75

Nos. 1757/1761 were issued together in *se-tenant* strips of five within the sheet.

1990 (8 June). World Cup Football Championship, Italy. T **632** and similar multicoloured designs. P 12×11½ (600p.) or 11½×12 (others).
1762 550p. Type **632** .... 2·75 1·40
1763 550p. Players marking opponent .... 2·75 1·40
1764 600p. Map of Italy and ball (*vert*) .... 3·00 1·50
1762/1764 *Set of 3* .... 7·75 3·75
MS1765 74×55 mm. 1300p. Floodlit stadium and mascot. Imperf .... 20·00 19·00

633 Flag, Tree and City

634 Man and Book

1990 (26 June). 16th Anniversary of Liberation of Qneitra. P 12×11½.
1766 **633** 550p. multicoloured .... 2·75 1·40

1990 (26 June). International Literacy Year. P 12×11½.
1767 **634** 550p. multicoloured .... 2·75 1·40

635 Weather Map

636 Emblem

1990 (28 Aug). World Meteorology Day. P 11½×12.
1768 **635** 450p. multicoloured .... 2·20 1·00

1990 (28 Aug). 37th International Damascus Fair. P 12×11½.
1769 **636** 550p. multicoloured .... 2·75 1·40

637 Old and Modern Methods of Ploughing

638 Boy watering Young Tree

1990 (7 Oct). United Nations Conference on Least Developed Countries. P 11½×12.
1770 **637** 600p. multicoloured ... 3·00 1·40

1990 (30 Oct). Tree Day. P 12×11½.
1771 **638** 550p. multicoloured ... 3·00 1·40

639 Children with Bread and Water in Wheat Field

640 Al-Maqdisi and Map

1990 (30 Oct). World Food Day. P 12½.
1772 **639** 850p. multicoloured ... 4·75 1·70

1990 (5 Nov). Death Millenary of Al-Maqdisi (geographer). P 12×11½.
1773 **640** 550p. multicoloured ... 3·00 1·40

641 President Hafez al-Assad

642 President Assad with Scouts

1990 (16 Nov)–**92**.

(a) As T **538** *but with full-face portrait. P 11½*

1774	50p. brown-lilac	20	15
1775	70p. brownish grey	30	15
1776	100p. new blue	35	15
1777	150p. chocolate	55	25
1778	150p. chocolate (19.5.92)	55	25
1779	300p. bright mauve (19.5.92)	1·10	50
1780	350p. greenish slate (19.5.92)	1·50	70
1781	400p. dull vermilion (19.5.92)	1·60	75

(b) T **641**. *P 12×11½*

1782	175p. multicoloured	75	25
1783	300p. multicoloured	1·30	35
1784	550p. multicoloured	2·20	50
1785	600p. multicoloured	3·00	1·00

(c) Horiz design with portrait as T **641** *within decorative frame. P 11½×12*

1786	1000p. multicoloured	4·75	1·40
1787	1500p. multicoloured	6·50	2·00
1788	2000p. multicoloured	9·25	2·75
1789	2500p. multicoloured	11·00	3·50
1774/1789	*Set of* 16	40·00	13·00

No. 1777 has 'POSTAGE' in chocolate and is dated 1990. No. 1777*a* has 'POSTAGE' in white and is undated.

Nos. 1778/1780 are as No. 1777*a*.

Nos. 1790/1794 are vacant.

1990 (16 Nov). 20th Anniversary of Corrective Movement of 16 November 1970. Sheet 120×95 mm. Imperf.
MS1795 550p. Type **642**; 550p. President Assad and cheering crowd; 550p. President Assad in uniform and Liberation Monument, Qneitra; 550p. President Assad and Euphrates Dam ... 12·00 11·00

643 Control Tower, Douglas DC-9-80 Super 80 Airliner and Emblem

644 Emblem, Open Book, Cogwheel and Ear of Wheat

1990 (11 Dec). Arab Civil Aviation Day. P 11½×12.
1796 **643** 175p. multicoloured ... 1·50 50

1990 (11 Dec). 40th Anniversary of United Nations Development Programme. P 11½×12.
1797 **644** 550p. multicoloured ... 2·75 1·20

645 UPU Emblem and Girl posting Letter

646 Leapfrog

1990 (11 Dec). World Post Day. P 12×11½.
1798 **645** 550p. multicoloured ... 2·75 1·20

1990 (11 Dec). World Children's Day. P 12×11½.
1799 **646** 550p. multicoloured ... 2·75 1·50

647 Emblem, Flames and Open Book

648 Paths to and away from AIDS

1990 (24 Dec). Arab–Spanish Cultural Symposium. P 12×11½.
1800 **647** 550p. multicoloured ... 3·25 1·70

1990 (24 Dec). World AIDS Day. P 12×11½.
1801 **648** 550p. multicoloured ... 3·25 1·70

649 Modern Roads and Buildings

650 *Apatura iris*

1991 (8 Mar). 28th Anniversary of Baathist Revolution of 8 March 1963. P 11½×12.
1802 **649** 150p. multicoloured ... 1·90 35

1991 (17 Mar). Butterflies. T **650** and similar square designs. Multicoloured. P 12½.

1803	550p. Type **650** (inscr 'Change Ful Great Mars')	5·50	1·90
1804	550p. *Aglais urticae*	5·50	1·90
1805	550p. *Papilio machaon*	5·50	1·90
1803/1805	*Set of* 3	15·00	5·25

No. 1805 is wrongly inscr 'Papillion'.

651 Golden Orioles

652 Three Generations

1991 (17 Mar). Birds. T **651** and similar vert designs. Multicoloured. P 12×11½.

1806	600p. Type **651**	4·50	1·90
1807	600p. House Sparrows	4·50	1·90
1808	600p. European Roller	4·50	1·90
1806/1808	*Set of* 3	12·00	5·25

1991 (21 Mar). Mothers' Day. P 12×11½.

1809	**652** 550p. multicoloured	3·25	1·40

653 Statue

1991 (17 Apr). 45th Anniversary of Evacuation of Foreign Troops from Syria. P 11½×12.

1810	**653** 150p. multicoloured	95	35

654 Dividers and Spanner

655 Daffodils

1991 (1 May). Labour Day. P 11½×12.

1811	**654** 550p. multicoloured	3·25	1·40

1991 (8 July). International Flower Show, Damascus. T **655** and similar vert design. Multicoloured. P 12×12½.

1812	550p. Type **655**	3·25	1·40
1813	600p. Bee Balm (*Monarda didyma*)	3·75	1·50

656 City and Ruins

657 Running

1991 (22 July). 17th Anniversary of Liberation of Qneitra. P 11½×12.

1814	**656** 550p. multicoloured	3·25	1·20

1991 (22 July). 11th Mediterranean Games, Athens. T **657** and similar horiz designs. Multicoloured. P 11½×12.

1815	550p. Type **657**	3·25	1·40
1816	550p. Football	3·25	1·40
1817	600p. Show jumping	3·75	1·70
1815/1817	*Set of* 3	9·25	4·00
MS1818	80×65 mm. 1300p. Dolphins playing water polo. Imperf	9·25	8·50

658 Hall

659 Courtyard, Azem Palace, Damascus

1991 (28 Aug). 38th International Damascus Fair. P 12×12½.

1819	**658** 550p. multicoloured	3·50	1·50

1991 (27 Sept). International Tourism Day. T **659** and similar horiz design. Multicoloured. P 11½×12.

1820	450p. Type **659**	2·75	1·20
1821	550p. Castle, Arwad Island	3·50	1·50

660 People encircling Block of Flats

661 Roller Skating

1991 (7 Oct). Housing Day. P 12×11½.

1822	**660** 175p. multicoloured	1·10	50

1991 (16 Oct). International Children's Day. P 12×11½.

1823	**661** 600p. multicoloured	3·75	1·50

662 Rhazes treating Patient

1991 (2 Nov). Science Week. P 12½×12.

1824	**662** 550p. multicoloured	3·50	1·50

663 Envelopes and Globe

1991 (12 Nov). World Post Day. P 12½×12.

1825	**663** 550p. multicoloured	3·50	1·50

664 Globe, Produce and Livestock

665 Tomb of the Unknown Soldier, Damascus

1991 (12 Nov). World Food Day. P 12½×12.

1826	**664** 550p. multicoloured	3·50	1·50

1991 (16 Nov). P 12½.

1827	**665** 600p. multicoloured	3·75	1·60
MS1828	65×80 mm. 1000p. Tomb. Imperf	6·50	6·00

666 President Hafez al-Assad

1991 (16 Nov). 21st Anniversary of Corrective Movement of 16 November 1970. Sheet 77×89 mm. Imperf.
MS1829 **666** 2500p. multicoloured .... 16·00 14·50

667 Polluted and Clean Environments

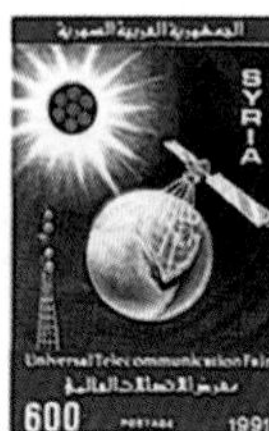

668 Transmission Mast, Globe and Satellite

1991 (20 Nov). Environmental Protection. P 12½×12.
1830 **667** 175p. multicoloured .... 1·30 70

1991 (20 Nov). International Telecommunications Fair. P 12×12½.
1831 **668** 600p. multicoloured .... 3·75 1·50

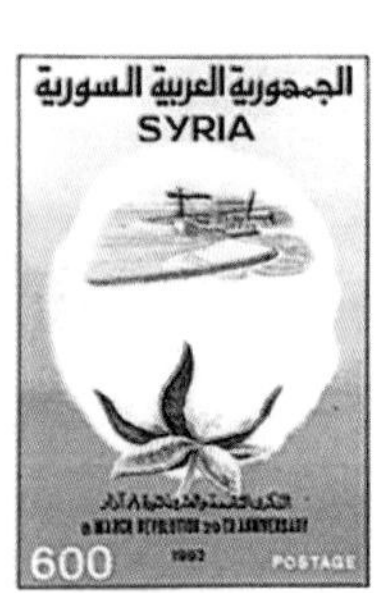

669 Leaf and Port

670 President Assad

1992 (8 Mar). 29th Anniversary of Baathist Revolution of 8 March 1963. P 12½.
1832 **669** 600p. multicoloured .... 2·75 1·20

1992 (12 Mar). Re-election of President Hafez al-Assad. Multicoloured. Imperf.
MS1833 Two sheets. (a) 65×95 mm. 5000p. Type **670**; (b) 100×85 mm. 5000p. Stamp portraits of President Assad as in Type **670** but with State Arms and inscriptions in right-hand margin .... 22·00 20·00

671 Chimneys, Gun-barrel, Ear of Wheat, Dove and Flag

672 Crane and Mason building Wall

1992 (7 Apr). 45th Anniversary of Baath Arab Socialist Party. P 12½×12.
1834 **671** 850p. multicoloured .... 3·75 1·70

1992 (1 May). Labour Day. P 12×12½.
1835 **672** 900p. black, greenish blue and deep mauve .... 4·00 1·90

673 Girls at Pedestrian Crossing

674 Girl listening to Mother's Stomach

1992 (19 May). Road Safety Campaign. P 12×12½.
1836 **673** 850p. multicoloured .... 3·75 1·70

1992 (19 May). Mothers' Day. P 12×12½.
1837 **674** 900p. multicoloured .... 4·00 1·90

675 Memorial

676 Flax (*Linum mucronatum*)

1992 (19 May). 46th Anniversary of Evacuation of Foreign Troops from Syria. P 12½×12.
1838 **675** 900p. multicoloured .... 4·00 1·90

1992 (5 July). International Flower Show, Damascus. T **676** and similar multicoloured designs. P 12½×12 (300p.), 12×12½ (800p.) or 12×11½ (900p.).
1839 300p. Type **676** .... 1·30 50
1840 800p. *Yucca filamentosa (vert)* .... 3·50 1·50
1841 900p. *Zinnia elegans (vert)* .... 4·00 1·90
1839/1841 *Set of 3* .... 8·00 3·50

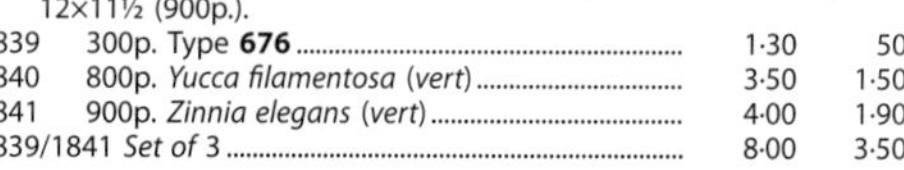

677 Football

678 Smoker standing in Ashtray

1992 (25 July). Olympic Games, Barcelona. T **677** and similar vert designs. Multicoloured. P 12×11½.
1842 150p. Type **677** 95 35
a. Strip of 4. Nos. 1842/1845 .... 7·75
1843 150p. Running 95 35
1844 450p. Swimming .... 1·90 85
1845 750p. Wrestling .... 3·75 1·40
1842/1845 *Set of 4* .... 6·75 2·75
MS1846 80×125 mm. 5000p. As Nos. 1842/1845 but without face values. Imperf. .... 11·00 10·00

Nos. 1842/1845 were issued together in *se-tenant* strips of four within the sheet.

1992 (28 Aug). Anti-smoking Campaign. P 12×12½.
1847 **678** 750p. multicoloured .... 3·25 1·40

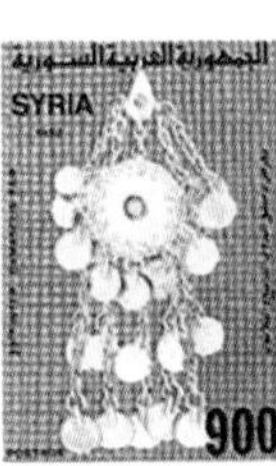

679 Pendant

680 Football

1992 (28 Aug). 39th International Damascus Fair. P 12×12½.
1848 **679** 900p. multicoloured .... 3·75 1·70

1992 (4 Sept). Seventh Pan-Arab Games, Damascus. T **680** and similar diamond-shaped designs. Multicoloured. P 12½.
1849 750p. Type **680** .... 3·25 1·40
a. Strip of 3. Nos. 1849/1851 .... 12·00
1850 850p. Gymnastics .... 3·75 1·70
1851 900p. Pole vaulting .... 4·25 1·90
1849/1851 *Set of 3* .... 10·00 4·50

Nos. 1849/1851 were issued together in *se-tenant* strips of three within the sheet.

681 Envelopes, Dove and Globe

682 Boy blowing Dandelion Clock

1992 (9 Oct). World Post Day. P 12×12½.
1852 **681** 600p. multicoloured .... 2·75 1·20

1992 (7 Nov). International Children's Day. P 12×11½.
1853 **682** 850p. multicoloured .... 3·75 1·70

683 Sebtt al-Mardini (astronomer)

684 Table Tennis

1992 (7 Nov). Science Week. P 12×11½.
1854 **683** 850p. multicoloured .... 4·50 1·90

1992 (7 Nov). Paralympic Games for Mentally Disabled, Madrid. P 12½.
1855 **684** 850p. multicoloured .... 3·75 1·70

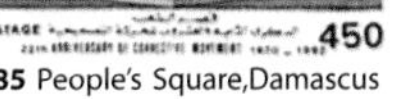

685 People's Square,Damascus

686 Tree

1992 (16 Nov). 22nd Anniversary of Corrective Movement of 16 November 1970. P 11½×12.
1856 **685** 450p. multicoloured .... 2·00 85

1992 (31 Dec). Tree Day. P 12×12½.
1857 **686** 600p. multicoloured .... 2·75 1·20

687 Statue of President Assad, Damascus

688 Common Blue

1993 (8 Mar). 30th Anniversary of Baathist Revolution of 8 March 1963. P 11½×12.
1858 **687** 1100p. multicoloured .... 2·75 1·20

1993 (13 Mar). Butterflies. T **688** and similar horiz designs. Multicoloured. P 11½×12.
1859 1000p. Type **688** .... 2·75 1·20
a. Strip of 3. Nos. 1859/1861 .... 13·50
1860 1500p. Silver-washed fritillary .... 3·75 1·50
1861 2500p. Blue argus (*Precis orithya*) .... 6·50 2·75
1859/1861 *Set of 3* .... 11·50 5·00

Nos. 1859/1861 were issued together in *se-tenant* strips of three within the sheet.

689 Family

690 Saladin Monument, Damascus

1993 (17 Apr). Mothers' Day. P 12×11½.
1862 **689** 1100p. multicoloured .... 2·75 1·20

1993 (17 Apr). 47th Anniversary of Evacuation of Foreign Troops from Syria. P 11½×12.
1863 **690** 1100p. multicoloured .... 2·75 1·20

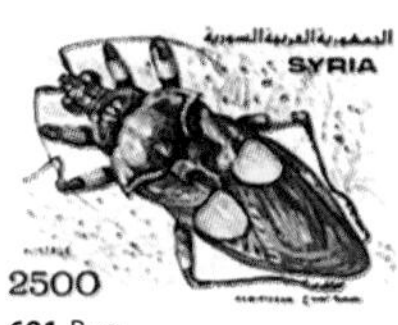

691 Bug

692 Tractor in Field of Crops

1993 (17 Apr). P 11½×12.
1864 **691** 2500p. multicoloured .... 6·25 2·75

1993 (20 Apr). 25th Anniversary of Arab Agrarian Union. P 11½×12.
1865 **692** 1150p. multicoloured .... 2·75 1·20

693 Oil Workers

694 Eye and Eye-chart

1993 (1 May). Labour Day. P 12×11½.
1866 **693** 1100p. multicoloured .... 2·75 1·20

1993 (12 May). Second Pan-Arab Ophthalmology International Council Congress. P 12.
1867 **694** 1100p. multicoloured .... 2·75 1·20

695 Landscapes and Eye

696 *Alcea setosa*

1993 (12 May). 25th Anniversary of National Ophthalmological Association. P 11½×12.
1868 **695** 1150p. multicoloured .... 2·75 1·20

1993 (17 June). 21st International Flower Show, Damascus. T **696** and similar vert designs. Multicoloured. P 12×11½.
1869 1000p. Type **696** .... 2·75 1·00
a. Strip of 3. Nos. 1869/1871 .... 9·25
1870 1100p. Primulas .... 3·00 1·20
1871 1150p. Gesnerias .... 3·25 1·30
1869/1871 *Set of 3* .... 8·00 3·25
Nos. 1869/1871 were issued together in *se-tenant* strips of three within the sheet.

697 Prism Tomb

698 Hand posting Letter and Globe

1993 (27 Sept). International Tourism Day. P 11½×12.
1872 **697** 1000p. multicoloured .... 2·75 1·20

1993 (9 Oct). World Post Day. P 12½×12.
1873 **698** 1000p. multicoloured .... 2·75 1·20

699 Boys playing Football

700 Ibn al-Bittar (chemist)

1993 (6 Nov). International Children's Day. P 11½×12.
1874 **699** 1150p. multicoloured .... 2·75 1·20

1993 (6 Nov). Science Week. P 12×11½.
1875 **700** 1150p. multicoloured .... 2·75 1·20

701 President Assad

1993 (16 Nov). 23rd Anniversary of Corrective Movement of 16 November 1970. Sheet 76×88 mm. Imperf.
MS1876 **701** 2500p. multicoloured .... 5·50 5·00

702 White Horse

703 Orchard in Blossom

1993 (30 Dec). Arab Horses. T **702** and similar square designs. Multicoloured. P 12½.
1877 1000p. Type **702** .... 2·75 1·00
a. Strip of 4. Nos. 1877/1880 .... 13·50
1878 1000p. Horse with white feet .... 2·75 1·00
1879 1500p. Black horse .... 3·75 1·40
1880 1500p. White horse with brown mane .... 3·75 1·40
1877/1880 *Set of 4* .... 11·50 4·25
Nos. 1877/1880 were issued together in *se-tenant* strips of four stamps within the sheet.

1993 (30 Dec). Tree Day. P 12½×12.
1881 **703** 1100p. multicoloured .... 2·75 1·20

704 Flags outside Venue

705 Basel al-Assad

1993 (30 Dec). 40th International Damascus Fair. P 12½×12.
1882 **704** 1100p. multicoloured .... 2·75 1·20

1994 (1 Mar). Basel al-Assad (President's son) Commemoration. P 12×12½.
1883 **705** 2500p. multicoloured .... 5·50 2·50

706 Oranges

707 Flags, Flame, Laurel and Dates

1994 (8 Mar). 31st Anniversary of Baathist Revolution of 8 March 1963. T **706** and similar horiz designs. Multicoloured. P 12½×12.
1884 1500p. Type **706** .... 3·25 1·40
a. Strip of 3. Nos. 1884/1886 .... 10·00
1885 1500p. Mandarins .... 3·25 1·40
1886 1500p. Lemons .... 3·25 1·40
1884/1886 *Set of 3* .... 8·75 3·75
Nos. 1884/1886 were issued together in *se-tenant* strips of three stamps within the sheet.

1994 (17 Apr). 48th Anniversary of Evacuation of Foreign Troops from Syria. P 12½×12.
1887 **707** 1800p. multicoloured .... 3·75 1·70

708 Mechanical Digger loading Dump Truck

709 Mother and Child at Different Ages

1994 (1 May). Labour Day. P 12½×12.
1888 **708** 1700p. multicoloured .... 3·75 1·70

1994 (1 May). Mothers' Day. P 12½×12.
1889 **709** 1800p. multicoloured .... 3·75 1·70

710 Emblem, '50' and '75'

711 Match Scene

1994 (1 June). 75th Anniversary of International Labour Organisation and 50th Anniversary of Philadelphia Declaration (social charter). P 12½×12.
1890 **710** 1700p. multicoloured .... 3·25 1·40

1994 (17 June). World Cup Football Championship, USA T **711** and similar square design. Multicoloured. P 12½.
1891 1700p. Type **711** .... 3·25 1·40
a. Pair. Nos. 1891/1892 .... 6·75 3·00
1892 1700p. Match scene (*different*) .... 3·25 1·40
MS1893 80×80 mm. 4000p. Match scene (*different*). Imperf .... 8·25 7·75
Nos. 1891/1892 were issued together in *se-tenant* pairs within the sheet.

712 Olympic Flag, Greek Temple and '100'

713 Flags, Lanterns and Fountain

1994 (3 Aug). Centenary of International Olympic Committee. P 11½×12.
1894 **712** 1700p. multicoloured .... 2·75 1·40

1994 (3 Aug). 41st International Damascus Fair. P 12×12½.
1895 **713** 1800p. multicoloured .... 3·25 1·40

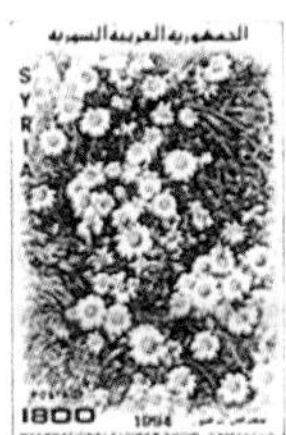

714 Camomile

715 Apollo

1994 (3 Aug). International Flower Show, Damascus. T **714** and similar vert designs. Multicoloured. P 12×11½.
1896 1800p. Type **714** .... 3·25 1·40
a. Strip of 3. Nos. 1896/1898 .... 10·00
1897 1800p. Gloxinia .... 3·25 1·40
1898 1800p. Mimosa .... 3·25 1·40
1896/1898 *Set of 3* .... 8·75 3·75
Nos. 1896/1898 were issued together in *se-tenant* strips of three within the sheet.

1994 (9 Aug). Butterflies. T **715** and similar horiz designs. Multicoloured. P 11½×12.
1899 1700p. Type **715** .... 3·25 1·40
a. Strip of 3. Nos. 1899/1901 .... 10·00
1900 1700p. Purple emperor (value at right) .... 3·25 1·40
1901 1700p. Birdwing (value at left) .... 3·25 1·40
1899/1901 *Set of 3* .... 8·75 3·75
Nos. 1899/1901 were issued together in *se-tenant* strips of three within the sheet.

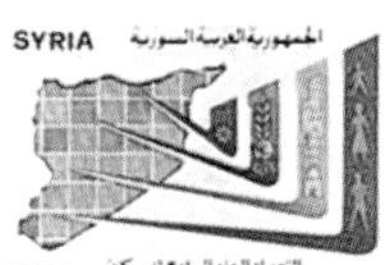

716 Symbols and Map

717 Al-Kindi (philosopher)

1994 (15 Aug). Fourth Population Census. P 11½×12.
1902 **716** 1000p. multicoloured .... 1·70 70

1994 (5 Nov). Science Week. P 12½.
1903 **717** £S10 multicoloured .... 1·90 85

718 President Assad

1994 (16 Nov). 24th Anniversary of Corrective Movement of 16 November 1970. Sheet 76×88 mm. Imperf.
MS1904 **718** £S25 multicoloured .... 4·75 4·25

719 Airport

1994 (7 Dec). 50th Anniversary of International Civil Aviation Organisation. P 12½.
1905 **719** £S17 multicoloured .... 2·75 1·40

720 Al-Marjeh Square

721 Child with Tennis Racquet

1994 (7 Dec). P 11½×12.
1906 **720** £S50 deep mauve .... 8·25 3·75
See also Nos. 2063/2065 and 2122.

1994 (19 Dec). International Children's Day. P 12×11½.
1907 **721** £S10 multicoloured .... 1·90 85

722 **Girl watching Birds with Envelopes**

723 Palmyra Roman Arch

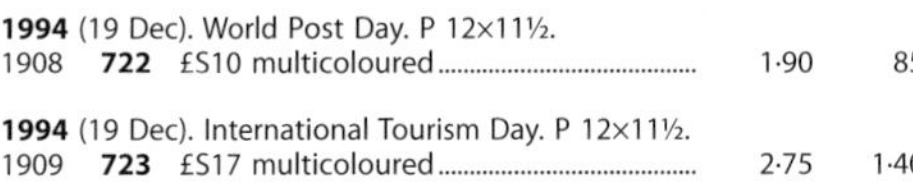

1994 (19 Dec). World Post Day. P 12×11½.

1908	**722**	£S10 multicoloured	1·90	85

1994 (19 Dec). International Tourism Day. P 12×11½.

1909	**723**	£S17 multicoloured	2·75	1·40

724 Modern Building

725 League Emblem and Map

1995 (8 Mar). 32nd Anniversary of Baathist Revolution of 8 March 1963. P 11½×12.

1910	**724**	£S18 multicoloured	2·40	1·50

1995 (22 Mar). 50th Anniversary of Arab League. P 12½.

1911	**725**	£S17 multicoloured	2·40	1·40

726 Water Pump

727 Woman sheltering Figures

1995 (9 Apr). World Water Day. P 12×12½.

1912	**726**	£S17 multicoloured	2·40	1·40

1995 (9 Apr). Mothers' Day. P 12½×12.

1913	**727**	£S17 multicoloured	2·40	1·40

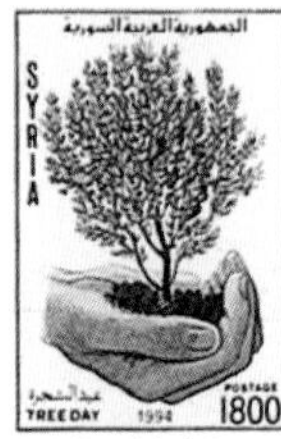

728 Hand holding Tree

729 Family

1995 (9 Apr). Tree Day. P 12×12½.

1914	**728**	1800p. multicoloured	3·00	1·50

1995 (30 Apr). International Year of the Family (1994). P 12×11½.

1915	**729**	1700p. multicoloured	2·40	1·40

730 Statue and Flag

731 Honey Bees on Flowers

1995 (30 Apr). 49th Anniversary of Evacuation of Foreign Troops from Syria. P 12×11½.

1916	**730**	£S17 multicoloured	2·40	1·40

1995 (30 Apr). First Anniversary of Arab Apiculturalists Union. P 12×11½.

1917	**731**	£S17 multicoloured	4·00	1·50

Nos. 1918/1919 are vacant.

732 President Assad

733 Welder

1995 (3 May–31 Dec). P 12×11½.

1920	**732**	£S10 bright purple	1·90	85
1921		£S17 brown-lilac (31.12.95)	2·40	1·40
1922		£S18 deep bluish green (31.12.95)	2·50	1·50
1923		£S100 new blue (31.12.95)	20	15
1924		£S500 orange-yellow (31.12.95)	55	35
1920/1924		*Set of 5*	6·75	3·75

1995 (25 June). Labour Day. P 12×12½.

1925	**733**	£S10 multicoloured	1·90	85

734 Anniversary Emblem

735 Desert Festival

1995 (25 June). 50th Anniversary of Food and Agriculture Organisation. P 12½×12.

1926	**734**	£S15 multicoloured	2·00	1·20

1995 (25 June). Tourism Day. P 12½×12.

1927	**735**	£S18 multicoloured	2·40	1·50

736 Astilbe

737 Anniversary Emblem on UN Headquarters

1995 (30 July). 23rd International Flower Show, Damascus. T **736** and similar square designs. Multicoloured. P 12½.

1928	£S10 Type **736**	1·90	1·20
	a. Horiz strip of 3. Nos. 1928/1930	6·00	
1929	£S10 Evening primrose	1·90	1·20
1930	£S10 Campanula (blue carpet)	1·90	1·20
1928/1930	*Set of 3*	5·25	3·25

Nos. 1928/1930 were issued together in *se-tenant* strips of three stamps within the sheet.

1995 (13 Aug). 50th Anniversary of United Nations Organisation. P 12×11½.
1931 **737** £S18 multicoloured .... 2·40 1·50

738 Woman holding Globe

739 Fair Entrance

1995 (21 Aug). Fourth World Conference of Women, Beijing. P 12×11½.
1932 **738** £S18 multicoloured .... 2·40 1·50

1995 (28 Aug). 42nd International Damascus Fair. P 11½×12.
1933 **739** £S15 multicoloured .... 2·20 1·20

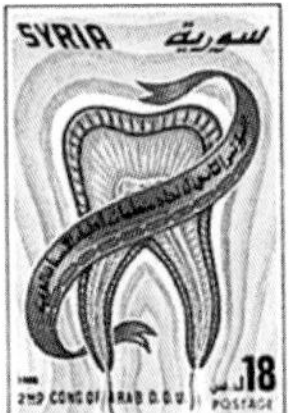

740 Tooth and Ribbon

741 Writing Letters and Air Mail Colours around Globe

1995 (16 Sept). Second Congress of Arab Dentists' Association. P 12×11½.
1934 **740** £S18 multicoloured .... 2·40 1·50

1995 (2 Oct). World Post Day. P 11½×12.
1935 **741** £S15 multicoloured .... 2·20 1·20

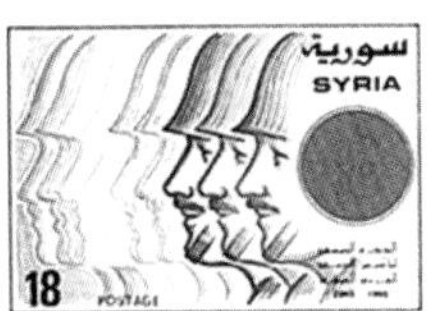

742 Children playing on Beach

743 Soldiers

1995 (2 Oct). World Children's Day. P 12×11½.
1936 **742** £S18 multicoloured .... 2·40 1·50

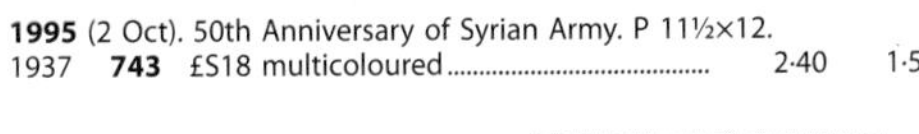

1995 (2 Oct). 50th Anniversary of Syrian Army. P 11½×12.
1937 **743** £S18 multicoloured .... 2·40 1·50

744 Ahmed ben Maged

745 President Assad

1995 (4 Nov). 500th Death Anniversary of Ahmed ben Maged (cartographer). P 11½×12.
1938 **744** £S18 multicoloured .... 2·40 1·50

1995 (11 Nov). 25th Anniversary of Corrective Movement of 16 November 1970. T **745** and similar multicoloured design. P 12½.
1939 £S10 Type **745** .... 1·70 85
MS1940 111×75 mm. £S50, Assad and 1975, 1980, 1985 and 1990 stamps. Imperf .... 7·00 6·50

746 Mother and Chicks

1995 (5 Dec). Birds. T **746** and similar square designs. Multicoloured. P 12½.
1941 £S18 Type **746** .... 2·75 1·90
a. Strip of 3. Nos. 1941/1943 .... 8·50
1942 £S18 Robin in snow .... 2·75 1·90
1943 £S18 Bird on post .... 2·75 1·90
1941/1943 *Set of 3* .... 7·50 5·25

Nos. 1941/1943 were issued together in *se-tenant* strips of three stamps within the sheet.

747 Pasteur and Laboratory

1995 (21 Dec). Death Centenary of Louis Pasteur (chemist). P 12½×12.
1944 **747** £S18 multicoloured .... 2·40 1·50

748 Olive Tree

749 Pumping Station, Kudairan

1996 (8 Mar). Tree Day. P 12×12½.
1945 **748** £S17 multicoloured .... 2·40 1·40

1996 (8 Mar). 33rd Anniversary of Baathist Revolution of 8 March 1963. P 11½×12.
1946 **749** £S25 multicoloured .... 3·75 2·20

750 Woman and Horsemen

751 Woman and Baby

1996 (17 Apr). 50th Anniversary of Evacuation of Foreign Troops from Syria. P 12½.
1947 **750** £S10 multicoloured .... 1·30 85
1948 £S25 multicoloured .... 3·75 2·20
MS1949 80×60 mm. **750** £S25 multicoloured. Imperf... 5·50 5·00

1996 (1 May). Mothers' Day. P 12×11½.
1950 **751** £S10 multicoloured .... 1·30 85

752 Textile Factory Workers

1996 (1 May). Labour Day. P 12½.
1951 **752** £S15 multicoloured .... 2·20 1·20

753 Memorial

1996 (26 June). 22nd Anniversary of Liberation of Qneitra. P 11½×12.
1952 **753** £S10 multicoloured .... 1·50 85

754 Map, Palestinian Flag and Arabic Script

755 *Mammilaria erythosperma*

1996 (1 July). 50th Anniversary of *Al-Baath* (newspaper). P 12½×12.
1953 **754** £S18 multicoloured .... 2·50 1·50

1996 (1 July). 24th International Flower Show, Damascus. Cacti. T **755** and similar square design. Multicoloured. P 12½.
1954 £S18 Type **755** .... 2·50 1·50
1955 £S18 *Notocactus graessnerii* .... 2·50 1·50

756 Wrestling

1996 (19 July). Olympic Games, Atlanta. T **756** and similar horiz designs. Multicoloured. P 11½×12.
1956 £S17 Type **756** .... 2·50 1·40
a. Vert strip of 3. Nos. 1956/1958 .... 7·75
1957 £S17 Swimming .... 2·50 1·40
1958 £S17 Running .... 2·50 1·40
1956/1958 *Set of 3* .... 6·75 3·75
MS1959 80×59 mm. £S25 Football. Imperf. .... 5·50 5·00
Nos. 1956/1958 were issued together in vertical *se-tenant* strips of stamps.

757 Guglielmo Marconi and Transmitter

758 Family protected from burning 'AIDS'

1996 (18 Aug). Centenary (1995) of First Radio Transmissions. P 12½.
1960 **757** £S17 multicoloured .... 2·75 1·50

1996 (18 Aug). World AIDS Day. P 12×11½.
1961 **758** £S17 multicoloured .... 2·75 1·50

759 Fair Emblem, Pattern and Globe

760 Computer, Emblem and Globe

1996 (28 Aug). 43rd International Damascus Fair. P 12×11½.
1962 **759** £S17 multicoloured .... 2·75 1·50

1996 (5 Sept). Fifth Anniversary of National Information Centre. P 11½×12.
1963 **760** £S18 multicoloured .... 2·75 1·70

761 Girls playing

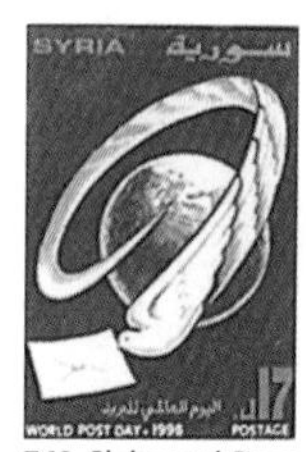
762 Globe and Dove with Letter

1996 (9 Oct). World Children's Day. P 12×11½.
1964 **761** £S10 multicoloured .... 2·00 95

1996 (9 Oct). World Post Day. P 12×11½.
1965 **762** £S17 multicoloured .... 2·75 1·50

763 Sons of Musa ibn Shaker

1996 (2 Nov). Science Week. P 12½×12.
1966 **763** £S10 multicoloured .... 1·90 95

764 President Assad

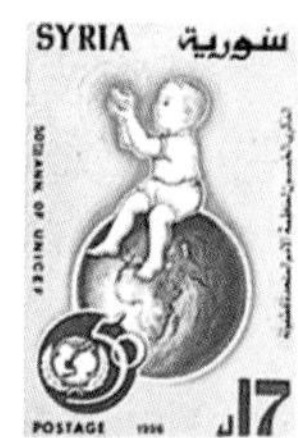
765 Child sitting on Globe

1996 (16 Nov). 26th Anniversary of Corrective Movement of 16 November 1970. P 12½.
1967 **764** £S10 multicoloured .... 1·90 95
MS1968 65×90 mm. **764** £S50 multicoloured. Imperf... 7·50 7·00

1996 (20 Nov). 50th Anniversary of United Nations Children's Fund. P 12×11½.
1969 **765** £S17 multicoloured .... 2·75 1·50

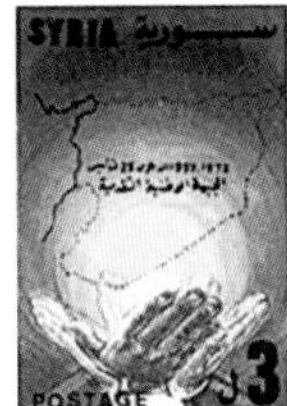

766 Hands and Map

767 Grain Silos and Wheat

1997 (7 Mar). 25th Anniversary of National Progressive Front. P 12×11½.
1970 **766** £S3 multicoloured 95 20

1997 (8 Mar). 34th Anniversary of Baathist Revolution of 8 March 1963. P 12×11½.
1971 **767** £S15 multicoloured .... 2·75 1·50

768 Party Emblem

769 Apple Trees

1997 (3 Apr). 50th Anniversary of Baath Arab Socialist Party. P 12½.
1972 **768** £S25 multicoloured .... 4·75 2·75
MS1973 91×66 mm. No. 1972. Imperf .... 7·00 6·50

1997 (8 Apr). Tree Day. P 12×12½.
1974 **769** £S10 multicoloured .... 1·90 95

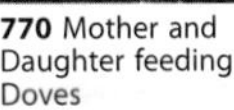

770 Mother and Daughter feeding Doves

771 *Beautiful Woman from Palmyra* (relief)

1997 (8 Apr). Mothers' Day. P 12×11½.
1975 **770** £S15 multicoloured .... 2·75 1·50

1997 (8 Apr). World Tourism Day (1996). P 12×11½.
1976 **771** £S17 multicoloured .... 2·75 1·50

772 Fish

1997 (8 Apr). Fish. T **772** and similar horiz design. Multicoloured. P 12½×12.
1977 £S17 Type **772** .... 3·25 1·70
a. Pair. Nos. 1977/1978 .... 6·75 3·75
1978 £S17 Fish (country inscr at top) .... 3·25 1·70
Nos. 1977/1978 were issued together in *se-tenant* pairs within the sheet.

773 Horsemen

774 Building Pipeline

1997 (17 Apr). 51st Anniversary of Evacuation of Foreign Troops from Syria. P 11½×12.
1979 **773** £S15 multicoloured .... 2·75 1·50

1997 (1 May). Labour Day. P 12×11½.
1980 **774** £S15 multicoloured .... 2·75 1·50

775 Library and Books

776 Smoker's Diseased Lungs and Cigarettes

1997 (16 June). World Book Day. P 12½.
1981 **775** £S10 multicoloured .... 1·90 95

1997 (16 June). World No Smoking Day. P 12×11½.
1982 **776** £S18 multicoloured .... 2·75 1·70

777 *Echinoereus purporeus*

778 Emblem

1997 (21 June). International Flower Show, Damascus. T **777** and similar vert design. Multicoloured. P 12×11½.
1983 £S18 Type **777** .... 2·75 1·70
a. Pair. Nos. 1983/1984 .... 5·75 3·75
1984 £S18 Irises .... 2·75 1·70
Nos. 1983/1984 were issued together in *se-tenant* pairs within the sheet.

1997 (4 Sept). Fourth Arab Union of Dentists' Association Congress. P 12×11½.
1985 **778** £S10 multicoloured .... 1·90 95

779 Flags and Monument

780 Child reaching for Landmine

1997 (4 Sept). 44th International Damascus Fair. P 12×11½.
1986 **779** £S17 multicoloured .... 2·75 1·50

1997 (27 Sept). International Children's Day. P 11½×12.
1987 **780** £S17 multicoloured .... 2·75 1·50

781 Post Rider and Dove

782 Tourists on Flying Carpet

1997 (27 Sept). World Post Day. P 11½ × 12.
1988 **781** £S17 multicoloured .... 2·75 1·50

1997 (27 Sept). International Tourism Day. P 11½ × 12.
1989 **782** £S17 multicoloured .... 2·75 1·50

783 Jabir ibn Haijan (alchemist)

784 President Assad

1997 (1 Nov). Science Week. P 12×11½.
1990 **783** £S17 multicoloured .... 2·75 1·50

1997 (16 Nov). 27th Anniversary of Corrective Movement of 16 November 1970. T **784** and similar multicoloured design. P 12½.
1991 £S10 Type **784** .... 1·90 95
MS1992 101×85 mm. £S50 Portrait as in T **784** with inscriptions arranged beside it. Imperf .... 7·50 7·00

785 Emblem, Minarets and Banner

1997 (9 Dec). 30th Anniversary of Organisation of the Islamic Conference. P 11½×12.
1993 **785** £S10 multicoloured .... 1·90 95

786 Sewage Works

1998 (8 Mar). 35th Anniversary of Baathist Revolution of 8 March 1963. P 12½×12.
1994 **786** £S17 multicoloured .... 2·75 1·50

787 Mother with Children

788 Warrior with Raised Sword

1998 (21 Mar). Mothers' Day. P 11½×12.
1995 **787** £S10 multicoloured .... 1·90 95

1998 (17 Apr). 52nd Anniversary of Evacuation of Foreign Troops from Syria. P 12×11½.
1996 **788** £S10 multicoloured .... 1·90 95

789 Computer and Industrial Sites

790 Players challenging for Ball

1998 (1 May). Labour Day. P 12×11½.
1997 **789** £S18 multicoloured .... 2·75 1·70

1998 (22 June). World Cup Football Championship, France. P 12×12½.
1998 **790** £S10 multicoloured .... 1·90 95
MS1999 80×75 mm. £S25 Match scene. Imperf .... 4·25 3·75

791 *Bougainvillea glabra*

793 Mother Teresa

795 Cigarette piercing Heart

792 Bust of Princess of Banias

1998 (22 June). International Flower Show, Damascus. T **791** and similar vert design. Multicoloured. P 12×11½.
2000 £S17 Type **791** .... 2·75 1·50
a. Pair. Nos. 2000/2001 .... 5·75 3·25
2001 £S17 *Hibiscus rosa-sinensis* .... 2·75 1·50
Nos. 2000/2001 were issued together in *se-tenant* pairs within the sheet.

1998 (22 July). International Tourist Day. P 12×11½.
2002 **792** £S17 multicoloured .... 2·75 1·50

794 Post Office

1998 (22 July). Death Commemoration of Mother Teresa (founder of Missionaries of Charity). P 12×11½.
2003 **793** £S18 multicoloured .... 2·75 1·70

1998 (26 Sept). Arab Post Day. P 12½.
2004 **794** £S10 multicoloured .... 1·90 95

1998 (26 Sept). World 'No Smoking' Day. P 12×11½.
2005 **795** £S15 multicoloured .... 2·50 1·30

796 Doves and World Map

1998 (26 Sept). World Post Day. P 11½×12.
2006 **796** £S18 multicoloured .... 2·75 1·70

797 Child on Globe and Doves
798 Fish Fountain and Fair Venue

1998 (26 Sept). International Children's Day. P 12×11½.
2007 **797** £S18 multicoloured .... 2·75 1·70

1998 (26 Sept). 45th International Damascus Fair. P 11½×12.
2008 **798** £S18 multicoloured .... 2·75 1·70

799 President Assad and Combat Scenes (*½ size illustration*)

1999 (26 Sept). 25th Anniversary of October Offensive against Israel. Sheet 110×75 mm. Imperf.
MS2009 **799** £S25 multicoloured .... 4·75 3·75

800 Ibn ad-Duraihim (mathematician)
801 President Assad

1998 (3 Nov). Science Week. P 11½×12.
2010 **800** £S10 multicoloured .... 1·90 95

1998 (16 Nov). 28th Anniversary of Corrective Movement of 16 November 1970. T **801** and similar multicoloured design. P 12½.
2011 10p. Type **801** .... 1·90 95
MS2012 110×75 mm. £S25 Portrait as in T **801** and State Flag. Imperf .... 4·75 3·75

802 Dome of the Rock and Old City

1998 (25 Nov). Jerusalem. P 12½×12.
2013 **802** £S10 multicoloured .... 1·90 95

803 Dromedaries
804 President Assad

1998 (25 Nov). P 12½.
2014 **803** £S17 multicoloured .... 3·75 1·90

1999 (11 Feb). Re-election of President Hafez al-Assad to Fifth Term. P 12½.
2015 **804** £S10 multicoloured .... 1·50 95
2016 £S17 multicoloured .... 2·75 1·50
2017 £S18 multicoloured .... 3·25 1·70
2015/2017 *Set of* 3 .... 6·75 3·75
MS2018 149×119 mm. £S50 multicoloured (Portrait as in Type **804** and stamps of 1971, 1978, 1985 and 1992). Imperf .... 7·50 6·75

805 New Communications Office Building

1999 (8 Mar). 36th Anniversary of Baathist Revolution of 8 March 1963. T **805** and similar multicoloured design. P 12½.
2019 £S25 Type **805** .... 3·75 2·20
MS2020 75×110 mm. £S25 Communications Office and statue of President Assad. Imperf .... 4·25 3·50

806 Fig Tree
807 Mother breastfeeding Baby

1999 (29 Apr). Tree Day. P 12½.
2021 **806** £S17 multicoloured .... 2·75 1·90

1999 (29 Apr). Mothers' Day. P 12×11½.
2022 **807** £S17 multicoloured .... 2·75 1·90

808 Woman in Baath Party Colours and Man with Rifle

809 16 November Workers' Further Education Institute

1999 (29 Apr). 53rd Anniversary of Evacuation of Foreign Troops from Syria. P 12×11½.
2023 **808** £S18 multicoloured .... 2·75 1·70

1999 (5 June). Labour Day. P 12×11½.
2024 **809** £S10 multicoloured .... 1·50 95

810 Crowd with Human Rights Banner

811 Jasmin

1999 (5 June). 50th Anniversary (1998) of Universal Declaration of Human Rights. P 11½×12.
2025 **810** £S18 multicoloured .... 2·40 1·70

1999 (20 June). International Flower Show, Damascus. T **811** and similar vert design. Multicoloured. P 12×11½.
2026 £S10 Type **811** .... 1·90 1·30
a. Pair. Nos. 2026/2027 .... 4·00 2·75
2027 £S10 Acanthus .... 1·90 1·30

Nos. 2026/2027 were issued together in *se-tenant* pairs within the sheet.

812 Show Jumping and Crowd with Lighted Crowns

813 Globes and Emblem

1999 (1 Aug). Tenth Friendship Festival, Al Basel. P 11½×12.
2028 **812** £S10 multicoloured .... 1·90 1·10

1999 (28 Aug). 46th International Damascus Fair. P 11½×12.
2029 **813** £S15 multicoloured .... 2·75 1·30

814 Patient receiving Treatment and Emblem

815 Postman and Map of Arab States

1999 (21 Sept). Seventh Arab Union of Dentists' Associations Congress. P 12×11½.
2030 **814** £S17 multicoloured .... 2·75 1·50

1999 (12 Oct). Arab Post Day. P 12×11½.
2031 **815** £S10 multicoloured .... 1·90 95

816 Abu Hanifah al Deilouri (botanist)

817 Postal Transport, Emblem and Headquarters, Berne

1999 (12 Oct). Science Week. P 11½×12.
2032 **816** £S17 multicoloured .... 2·75 1·50

1999 (12 Oct). 125th Anniversary of Universal Postal Union. P 12×11½.
2033 **817** £S17 multicoloured .... 2·75 1·50

818 Umayyad Mosque and Our Lady of Saydnaya Convent, Damascus

1999 (16 Nov). 2000 Years of Religious Co-existence. P 12½×12.
2034 **818** £S17 multicoloured .... 2·75 1·50

819 October 1973 Liberation War Monument and President Assad (statues)

1999 (16 Nov). 29th Anniversary of Corrective Movement of 16 November 1970. T **819** and similar multicoloured designs. P 12½.
2035 £S17 Type **819** .... 2·50 2·20
2036 £S17 Close up detail of statue (*vert*) .... 2·50 2·20
MS2037 110×76 mm. £S25 October 1973 Liberation War Monument and Fountains before statue. Imperf .... 4·75 3·75

820 Children holding Hands around Globe

821 Factories, Corn and Family

1999 (16 Nov). International Children's Day. P 12×11½.
2038 **820** £S18 multicoloured .... 2·75 1·50

2000 (8 Mar). 37th Anniversary of Baathist Revolution of 8 March 1963. P 12½.
2039 **821** £S18 multicoloured .... 3·00 2·75

822 Mother holding Child

2000 (21 Mar). Mothers' Day. P 12½.
2040 **822** £S17 multicoloured .... 3·00 2·50

823 Battle Scene (*⅔ size illustration*)

2000 (17 Apr). 54th Anniversary of Evacuation of Foreign Troops from Syria. Sheet 95×80 mm. Imperf.
MS2041 **823** £S25 multicoloured .... 4·75 3·75

824 Rose and Cog

825 Foxy Charaxes (*Charaxes jasius*)

2000 (1 May). Labour Day. P 12×11½.
2042 **824** £S10 multicoloured .... 1·90 1·50

2000 (15 May). Butterflies. T **825** and similar square design. Multicoloured. P 12½.
2043 £S17 Type **825** .... 3·25 2·75
a. Pair. Nos. 2043/2044 .... 7·00 6·00
2044 £S18 *Apatura iris* .... 3·50 3·00
Nos. 2043/2044 were issued together in *se-tenant* pairs within the sheet.

826 Tree and Fruit

827 President Basher Al-Assad

2000 (15 May). Tree Day. P 12×11½.
2045 **826** £S18 multicoloured .... 3·00 2·75

2000 (17 July). Election of President Basher Al-Assad. T **827** and similar vert designs. P 12½.
2046 **827** £S3 multicoloured 55 35
a. Horiz strip of 4. Nos. 2046/2049 .... 9·50
2047 £S10 multicoloured .... 1·90 1·70
2048 £S17 multicoloured .... 3·25 2·75
2049 £S18 multicoloured .... 3·50 3·00
2046/2049 *Set of 4* .... 8·25 7·00
MS2050 109×75 mm. £S50 President Al-Assad. Imperf.. 10·50 9·25
Nos. 2046/2049 were issued together in *se-tenant* strips of four stamps within the sheet.

828 Child with Balloons

829 Flags, Exhibition Building and Crowd

2000 (20 Aug). P 12×11½.
2051 **828** £S10 multicoloured .... 1·90 1·70

2000 (20 Aug). 47th International Damascus Fair. P 11½×12.
2052 **829** £S15 multicoloured .... 3·00 2·40

830 UPU Emblem, Envelope and Globe

2000 (20 Aug). World Post Day. P 11½×12.
2053 **830** £S18 multicoloured .... 3·50 3·00

831 Map and Emblem

832 Weightlifting

2000 (20 Aug). Arab Post Day. P 11½×12.
2054 **831** £S18 multicoloured .... 3·50 3·00

2000 (1 Oct). Olympic Games, Sydney. T **832** and similar vert design. Multicoloured. P 12×11½.
2055 £S17 Type **832** .... 3·25 3·00
a. Pair. Nos. 2055/2056 .... 7·00 6·50
2056 £S18 Shot-put .... 3·50 3·25
MS2057 81×75 mm. £S25 Javelin. Imperf .... 5·25 4·75
Nos. 2055/2056 were issued together in *se-tenant* pairs within the sheet.

833 Nasir Al-din al-Tusi (scientist)

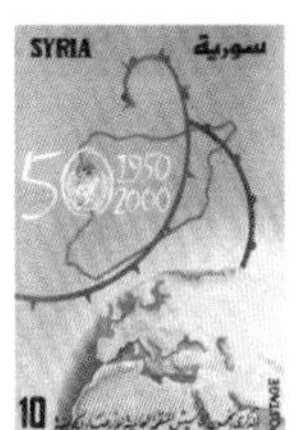

834 Emblem and Globe

2000 (1 Nov). Science Week. P 12½.
2058 **833** £S15 multicoloured.. 3·50 3·25

2000 (6 Dec). 50th Anniversary of World Meteorological Organisation. P 12×11½.
2059 **834** £S10 multicoloured.. 1·90 1·70

835 Cherubs in Rowing Boat and City (mosaic)

2000 (6 Dec). World Tourism Day. Sheet 111×85 mm. Imperf.
MS2060 **835** £S50 multicoloured.. 9·00 8·25

836 Dam and Emblem

837 Computers

2001 (2 Jan). 50th Anniversary of Engineer Syndicate. T **836** and similar square design. Multicoloured. P 12½.
2061 £S17 Type **836**.. 2·75 2·75
MS2062 85×95 mm. £S25 As No. 2061 but with design enlarged. Imperf.. 5·25 4·75

2001 (1 Mar). Al-Marjeh Square. Horiz designs as T **720**. P 11½×12.
2063 **720** 100p. light blue-green.. 95 55
2064 £S10 brown red.. 1·90 1·70
2065 £S50 deep blue.. 7·50 7·50
2063/2065 *Set of 3*.. 9·25 8·75

2001 (8 Mar). 38th Anniversary of Baathist Revolution of 8 March 1963. P 12×11½.
2066 **837** £S25 multicoloured.. 4·50 4·00

838 President al-Assad and Agricultural Painting

839 Statue of Mother and Baby

2001 (8 Mar). Ninth Agricultural Congress. P 12½.
2067 **838** £S25 multicoloured.. 4·50 4·00

2001 (21 Mar). Mother's Day. P 12×11½.
2068 **839** £S10 multicoloured.. 1·90 1·70

840 Horse's Head

841 Hand, Quill and Emblem

2001 (17 Apr). 55th Anniversary of Evacuation of Foreign Troops from Syria. P 12×11½.
2069 **840** £S25 multicoloured.. 4·50 4·00

2001 (23 Apr). Book and Copyright Day. P 12×11½.
2070 **841** £S10 multicoloured.. 1·90 1·70

842 Statue of Man holding Spade and Globe

843 Weigela

2001 (1 May). Labour Day. P 12×11½.
2071 **842** £S18 multicoloured.. 3·25 3·00

2001 (28 May). International Flower Show, Damascus. T **843** and similar vert design. Multicoloured. P 12×11½.
2072 £S10 Type **843**.. 2·10 1·70
a. Pair. Nos. 2072/2073.. 4·50 3·75
2073 £S10 Mertensia.. 2·10 1·70

Nos. 2072/2073 were issued in horizontal *se-tenant* pairs within the sheet.

844 Ruined Building

845 President Bashar Al-Assad

2001 (24 June). 27th Anniversary of Liberation of Qneitra. P 11½×12.
2074 **844** £S17 multicoloured.. 2·75 2·40

2001 (17 July). First Anniversary of Election of President Bashar Al-Assad. P 12½.
2075 **845** £S10 multicoloured.. 2·10 1·70
a. Pair. Nos. 2075/2075*b*.. 5·00 3·25
2075*b* £S17 multicoloured.. 2·75 2·40

Nos. 2075/2075*b* were issued together in *se-tenant* pairs within the sheet.

846 People climbing Globe and UNHCR Emblem

847 Postman and Van

2001 (28 July). 50th Anniversary of United Nations High Commissioner for Refugees. P 11½×12.
2076 **846** £S17 multicoloured .... 2·75 2·40

2001 (3 Aug). Arab Post Day. P 11½×12.
2077 **847** £S18 multicoloured .... 2·75 2·40

848 Aerial View of Damascus surrounded by Flags

849 Skull, Cigarettes and Ash Tray

2001 (18 Aug). 48th International Damascus Fair. P 12×11½.
2078 **848** £S10 multicoloured .... 1·90 1·70

2001 (9 Sept). World No Smoking Day. P 11½×12.
2079 **849** £S18 multicoloured .... 3·25 3·00

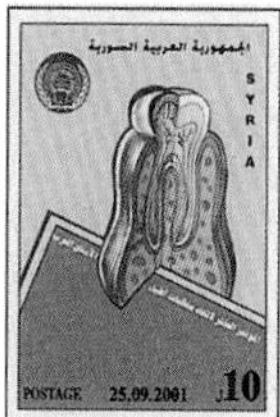

850 Cross Section of Tooth

851 Bust of Princess of Banias

2001 (25 Sept). Tenth Arab Union of Dentists' Association Congress. P 12×11½.
2080 **850** £S10 multicoloured .... 1·90 1·70

2001 (27 Sept). World Tourism Day. P 12½.
2081 **851** £S17 multicoloured .... 3·25 2·75

852 Globe, Envelope and UPU Emblem

853 Boy

2001 (9 Oct). World Post Day. P 11½×12.
2082 **852** £S10 multicoloured .... 1·90 1·70

2001 (16 Oct). International Children's Day. P 12×11½.
2083 **853** £S18 multicoloured .... 3·25 3·00

854 Inscribed Scroll

855 The Citadel, Aleppo

2001 (17 Oct). Arab Document Day. T **854** and similar vert design. Multicoloured. P 12×11½.
2084 £S10 Type **854** .... 1·90 1·70
MS2085 84×110 mm. £S25 As No. 2084 but with design enlarged. Imperf. .... 5·25 4·75

2001 (16 Nov). The Aga Khan Award for Architecture Presentation Ceremony, Aleppo. T **855** and similar horiz designs. P 11½×12.
2086 £S10 Type **855** .... 1·90 1·70
2087 £S17 The Citadel from below .... 3·25 2·75
2088 £S18 As No. 2087 .... 3·50 3·00
2086/2088 *Set of 3* .... 7·75 6·75

856 Planning Commission Building, Damascus

857 Youth Stoning Tank

2001 (16 Nov). 31st Anniversary of Corrective Movement of 16 November 1970. P 11½×12.
2089 **856** £S5 multicoloured 75 75
2090 £S15 multicoloured .... 2·30 2·20

2001 (17 Dec). Al Aqsa Intifada. P 11½×12.
2091 **857** £S17 multicoloured .... 2·75 2·40

858 Flowering Tree

859 Gazelle

2001 (27 Dec). Tree Day. P 12×11½.
2092 **858** £S5 multicoloured .... 1·50 1·10

2002 (8 Mar). P 12½.
2093 **859** £S15 multicoloured .... 2·50 2·20

860 Cement Factory

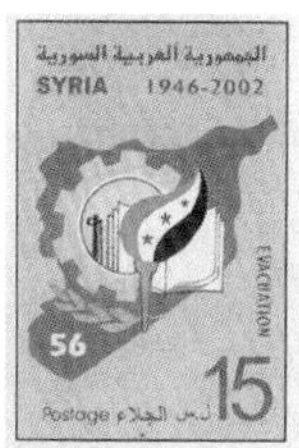

861 Mother holding Child

2002 (8 Mar). 39th Anniversary of Baathist Revolution of 8 March 1963. P 11½×12.
2094 **860** £S15 multicoloured .... 2·50 2·00

2002 (21 Mar). Mothers' Day. P 12×11½.
2095 **861** £S25 multicoloured .... 3·50 3·25

862 Party Headquarters

863 Map and Emblem

2002 (7 Apr). 55th Anniversary of Al-Baath Party. P 11½×12.
2096 **862** £S15 multicoloured .... 2·30 2·00

2002 (17 Apr). 56th Anniversary of Evacuation of Foreign Troops from Syria. P 12×11½.
2097 **863** £S15 multicoloured .... 2·30 2·00

864 UNESCO Emblem **865** Players

2002 (1 May). Labour Day. P 12×11½.
2098 **864** £S10 multicoloured .... 1·70 1·50

2002 (31 May). World Cup Football Championship, Japan and South Korea. T **865** and similar multicoloured designs. P 12.
2099 £S5 Type **865** 95 75
a. Pair. Nos. 2099/2100 .... 3·00 2·40
2100 £S10 Player chasing ball .... 1·90 1·50
MS2101 79×65 mm. £S25 Player jumping for ball. Imperf .... 5·25 3·75
Nos. 2099/2100 were issued in horizontal *se-tenant* pairs within the sheet.

866 Wallflower **867** Envelopes circling Map of Arab States

2002 (15 June). International Flower Show, Damascus. T **866** and similar vert design. Multicoloured. P 12×11½.
2102 £S15 Type **866** .... 2·75 2·00
a. Pair. Nos. 2102/2103 .... 6·00 4·50
2103 £S17 Narcissus .... 3·00 2·20
Nos. 2102/2103 were issued in horizontal *se-tenant* pairs within the sheet.

2002 (3 Aug). Arab Post Day. T **867** and similar horiz design. P 11½×12.
2104 **867** £S5 multicoloured 95 75
2105 (£S10) multicoloured .... 1·90 1·50

868 Abdul-Rahman Al-Kawakibi **869** Emblem

2002 (13 Aug). Death Centenary of Abdul-Rahman Al-Kawakibi (writer). P 12×11½.
2106 **868** £S10 multicoloured .... 1·90 1·50

2002 (18 Aug). 49th International Damascus Fair. T **869** and similar vert design. Multicoloured. P 12×11½.
2107 £S5 Type **869** .... 1·10 75
a. Pair. Nos. 2107/2108 .... 3·25 2·40
2108 £S10 Mosaic .... 1·90 1·50
Nos. 2107/2108 were issued in horizontal *se-tenant* pairs within the sheet.

870 Map, Bridge and Train **871** Sea Goddess, Shahba (mosaic)

2002 (9 Sept). Centenary of First Syrian Railway. P 12.
2109 **870** £S10 multicoloured .... 2·30 2·20

2002 (27 Sept). World Tourism Day. P 12.
2110 **871** £S10 multicoloured .... 1·90 1·50

872 Protesters and Tank **873** Dove holding Letter

2002 (28 Sept). Second Anniversary of Al Aqsa Intifada. T **872** and similar vert design. Multicoloured. P 12×11½.
2111 £S10 Type **872** .... 1·90 1·50
MS2112 64×80 mm. £S25 As No. 2111 but with design enlarged. Imperf .... 3·75 3·25

2002 (9 Oct). World Post Day. T **873** and similar multicoloured design. P 12×11½ (vert) or 11½×12 (horiz).
2113 £S10 Type **873** .... 1·90 1·50
a. Pair. Nos. 2113/2114 .... 4·00 3·25
2114 £S10 Envelope and UPU emblem (*horiz*) .... 1·90 1·50
Nos. 2113/2114 were issued in *se-tenant* pairs within the sheet, No. 2113 laid vertically.

874 Children **875** Techrin Thermal Power Plant

2002 (16 Oct). International Children's Day. P 12.
2115 **874** £S10 multicoloured .... 1·90 1·50

2002 (16 Nov). 32nd Anniversary of Corrective Movement of 16 November 1970. P 12×11½.
2116 **875** £S10 multicoloured .... 1·90 1·50

876 Sand Grouse **877** Pine Tree

2002 (15 Dec). Birds. T **876** and similar horiz designs. Multicoloured. P 11½×12.
2117 £S3 Type **876** 65 50
a. Strip of 4. Nos. 2117/2120 .... 7·25
2118 £S5 Francolin .... 1·10 75

2119 £S10 Mallard .... 2·10 1·40
2120 £S15 Goose .... 3·25 2·10
2117/2120 *Set of 4* .... 6·50 4·25

Nos. 2117/2120 were issued in vertical and horizontal *se-tenant* strips within the sheet.

2002 (26 Dec). Tree Day. P 11½×12.
2121 **877** £S10 multicoloured .... 1·90 1·50

2003 (5 Mar). Al-Marjeh Square. Horiz design as T **720**. P 11½×12.
2122 **720** 300p. orange brown .... 1·10 55

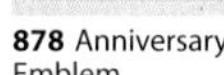

878 Anniversary Emblem

879 Stylised Classroom

2003 (8 Mar). 40th Anniversary of Baathist Revolution of 8 March 1963. P 11½×12.
2123 **878** £S15 multicoloured .... 2·50 1·70

2003 (8 Mar). Teachers' Day. P 12×11½.
2124 **879** £S17 multicoloured .... 2·75 1·90

880 Mother holding Sleeping Child

881 Soldier

2003 (21 Mar). Mothers' Day. P 12×11½.
2125 **880** £S32 multicoloured .... 5·00 3·75

2003 (17 Apr). 57th Anniversary of Evacuation of Foreign Troops from Syria. P 12×11½.
2126 **881** £S15 multicoloured .... 2·75 1·70

882 Man and Machine

883 Flower Border (inscr 'Damask rose-violet')

2003 (1 May). Labour Day. P 12×11½.
2127 **882** £S10 multicoloured .... 3·25 2·75

2003 (15 June). International Flower Show, Damascus. T **883** and similar vert design. Multicoloured. P 12½.
2128 £S10 Type **883** .... 1·50 1·10
a. Strip of 5. Nos. 2128/2132 .... 7·75
2129 £S10 Red flowers (inscr 'Anemone') .... 1·50 1·10
2130 £S10 White flowers (inscr 'Daisy') .... 1·50 1·10
2131 £S10 Flower border (inscr 'Damask rose-gillyflower') .... 1·50 1·10
2132 £S10 Sunflowers .... 1·50 1·10
2128/2132 *Set of 5* .... 6·75 5·00

Nos. 2128/2132 were issued in horizontal *se-tenant* strips of five stamps within the sheet.

884 Flags and Anniversary Emblem

885 Al Hamidieh Souk

2003 (3 Sept). 50th International Damascus Fair. T **884** and similar multicoloured design. P 12×11½.
2133 £S32 Type **884** .... 4·25 3·50
MS2134 90×65 mm. £S50 Jewelled spheres. Imperf .... 8·50 7·25

2003 (27 Sept). World Tourism Day. P 12½.
2135 **885** £S32 multicoloured .... 4·75 3·75

886 Flags and Globe

887 Children Playing

2003 (9 Oct). World Post Day. P 11½×12.
2136 **886** £S10 multicoloured .... 2·10 1·30

2003 (16 Oct). International Children's Day. P 11½×12.
2137 **887** £S15 multicoloured .... 2·75 1·70

888 Building Façade and Pope John Paul II (⅔ *size illustration*)

889 Flower, Map and '33'

2003 (16 Oct). 25th Anniversary of the Pontificate of Pope John Paul II. P 12½.
2138 **888** £S32 multicoloured .... 4·75 3·50

2003 (16 Nov). 33rd Anniversary of Corrective Movement of 16 November 1970. P 12×11½.
2139 **889** £S15 multicoloured .... 2·75 1·70

890 President Bashar Al-Assad

891 Binaries, Globe, Figures and Computers

2003 (8 Dec). P 12×11½.

2140 **890** £S15 turquoise-green ..... 2·10 1·70
2141 £S25 blue ..... 3·25 2·75
2142 £S50 magenta ..... 7·25 6·00
2140/2142 *Set of 3* ..... 11·50 9·50

See also No. 2301.

2003 (10 Dec). World Information Technology Summit, Geneva. P 12×11½.

2143 **891** £S15 multicoloured ..... 2·75 1·70

892 Woodcock (⅔ *size illustration*)

893 Pomegranate

2003 (15 Dec). Birds. T **892** and similar vert designs. Multicoloured. P 12½.

2144 £S5 Type **892** 85 55
a. Strip of 5. Nos. 2144/2148 ..... 10·00
2145 £S10 Lapwing ..... 1·50 1·10
2146 £S15 European Roller ..... 2·10 1·70
2147 £S17 Teal ..... 2·50 1·90
2148 £S18 Bustard ..... 2·75 2·10
2144/2148 *Set of 5* ..... 8·75 6·50

Nos. 2144/2148 were issued in *se-tenant* strips of five stamps within the sheet.

2003 (25 Dec). Tree Day. P 11½×12.

2149 **893** £S25 multicoloured ..... 3·25 2·75

894 Euphrates River Dam (⅔ *size illustration*)

2004 (8 Mar). 41st Anniversary of Baathist Revolution of 8 March 1963. P 12½.

2150 **894** £S10 multicoloured ..... 2·10 1·30

895 Teacher and Pupil

896 Mother holding Baby

2004 (11 Mar). Teachers' Day. P 12×11½.

2151 **895** £S5 multicoloured ..... 1·30 95

2004 (21 Mar). Mothers' Day. P 11½×12.

2152 **896** £S15 multicoloured ..... 3·00 1·70

897 Map and '58'

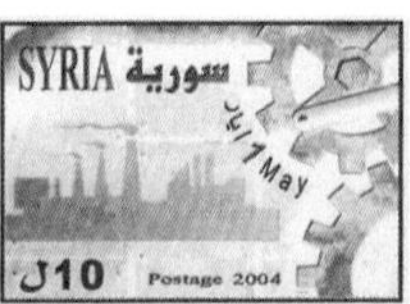

898 Factory and Cogs

2004 (17 Apr). 58th Anniversary of Evacuation of Foreign Troops from Syria. P 12×11½.

2153 **897** £S10 multicoloured ..... 2·10 1·10

2004 (1 May). Labour Day. P 12×11½.

2154 **898** £S10 multicoloured ..... 2·10 1·10

899 Emblem and Players

900 Inscr 'Gladiola lavender'

2004 (21 May). Centenary of FIFA (Fédération Internationale de Football Association). (1st issue) T **899** and similar horiz designs. Multicoloured. P 11½×12.

2155 £S10 Type **899** ..... 1·10 55
2156 £S10 Two players and emblem ..... 2·10 1·30
MS2157 81×66 mm. £S10 Emblem, players and ball. Imperf ..... 5·25 3·75

See also Nos. 2167/2168.

2004 (15 June). International Flower Show, Damascus. T **900** and similar vert designs. Multicoloured. P 12½.

2158 £S5 Type **900** ..... 1·10 55
a. Horiz strip of 5. Nos. 2158/2162 ..... 5·75
2159 £S5 Inscr 'The Jasmine' ..... 1·10 55
2160 £S5 Inscr 'Iris' ..... 1·10 55
2161 £S5 Inscr 'Orange Nesrien' ..... 1·10 55
2162 £S5 Tulips ..... 1·10 55
2158/2162 *Set of 5* ..... 5·00 2·50

Nos. 2158/2162 were issued in horizontal *se-tenant* strips of five stamps within the sheet.

901 Emblem

2004 (17 June). International Red Cross Committee Campaign to protect Children in War. P 12½.

2163 **901** £S32 rosine and black ..... 4·50 3·75

902 Runners

903 Anniversary Emblem

2004 (13 Aug). Olympic Games, Athens. T **902** and similar multicoloured designs. P 12½×11½.

2164 £S5 Type **902** 85 55
2165 £S10 Boxers (*horiz*) ..... 1·70 1·10
2166 £S25 Swimmer (*horiz*) ..... 3·75 2·75
2164/2166 *Set of 3* ..... 5·75 4·00

2004 (Sept). Centenary of FIFA (Fédération Internationale de Football Association) (2nd issue). Multicoloured designs as T **899**. P 12½.

2167 £S15 Emblem (*vert*) ..... 2·75 1·90
2168 £S32 Emblem and '100' ..... 5·25 4·25

2004 (3 Sept). 51st International Damascus Fair. P 12×11½.

2169 **903** £S25 multicoloured ..... 3·25 2·75

904 Family on Map   **905** Locomotive

2004 (14 Sept). Census. P 12.
2170 **904** £S10 multicoloured.. 1·50 1·10

2004 (27 Sept). World Tourism Day. T **905** and similar horiz designs. Multicoloured. P 11½×12.
2171 £S5 Type **905**.. 1·10 55
2172 £S10 Building façade.. 2·10 1·10
2173 £S10 Locomotive with short funnel.. 2·10 1·10
2171/2173 *Set of* 3.. 4·75 2·50

906 Envelopes

2004 (9 Oct). World Post Day. P 12×11½.
2174 **906** £S17 multicoloured.. 3·00 2·30

907 Babies

2004 (16 Oct). International Children's Day. P 11½×12.
2175 **907** £S18 multicoloured.. 3·25 1·90

908 Building and '34'

2004 (16 Nov). 34th Anniversary of Corrective Movement of 16 November 1970. P 13×12½.
2176 **908** £S25 multicoloured.. 4·25 3·25

909 Shami Goat

2004 (30 Dec). Domestic Animals. T **909** and similar horiz designs. Multicoloured. P 12.
2177 £S5 Type **909**.. 1·10 55
a. Vert strip of 4. Nos. 2177/2180.. 8·75
2178 £S15 Awassi Sheep.. 2·10 1·70
2179 £S17 Buffalo.. 2·50 1·90
2180 £S18 Shami Cow.. 2·75 2·10
2177/2180 *Set of* 4.. 7·50 5·75

Nos. 2177/2180 were issued in vertical *se-tenant* strips of four stamps within the sheet.

910 Walnut   **911** Northern Bald Ibis

2004 (30 Dec). Tree Day. P 12×11½.
2181 **910** £S10 multicoloured.. 1·70 1·10

2004 (30 Dec). P 12½.
2182 **911** £S10 multicoloured.. 1·70 1·10

912 Port

2005 (8 Mar). 42nd Anniversary of Baathist Revolution of 8 March 1963. P 12½.
2183 **912** £S17 multicoloured.. 3·00 1·90

913 Teacher and Pupil   **914** Mother bathing Child

2005 (13 Mar). Teachers' Day. P 11½×12.
2184 **913** £S25 multicoloured.. 3·50 2·75

2005 (21 Mar). Mothers' Day. P 12×11½.
2185 **914** £S18 multicoloured.. 3·25 2·10

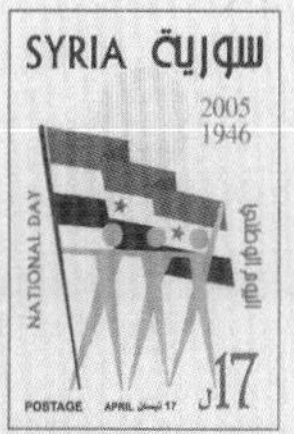

915 Emblem   **916** Figures holding Flag

2005 (22 Mar). 60th Anniversary of Arab League. P 12×11½.
2186 **915** £S10 multicoloured.. 1·70 95

2005 (17 Apr). 59th Anniversary of Evacuation of Foreign Troops from Syria. P 12×11½.
2187 **916** £S17 multicoloured.. 3·00 1·90

917 New Road

918 Hyacinth (inscr 'Jacinthe')

2005 (1 May). May Day. P 12×11½.

2188 **917** £S15 multicoloured .... 2·75 1·50

2005 (15 June). International Flower Show, Damascus. T **918** and similar vert designs. Multicoloured. P 12½×11½.

2189 £S5 Type **918** .... 1·10 75
a. Horiz strip of 5. Nos. 2189/2193 .... 11·00
2190 £S10 *Sternbergia clusiana* .... 1·50 1·10
2191 £S15 *Primula obconica* .... 2·10 1·70
2192 £S17 *Primula malacoides* .... 2·75 2·30
2193 £S18 Inscr 'Canaria' .... 3·25 2·50
2189/2193 *Set of 5* .... 9·75 7·50

Nos. 2189/2193 were issued in horizontal *se-tenant* strips of five stamps within the sheet.

919 Inscr 'Papilio Ulysses'

920 Emblem

2005 (7 Aug). Butterflies. T **919** and similar horiz designs. Multicoloured. P 12½.

2194 £S10 Type **919** .... 1·90 1·30
a. Horiz strip of 5. Nos. 2194/2198 .... 9·75
2195 £S10 Monarch .... 1·90 1·30
2196 £S10 *Baeotus baeotus* .... 1·90 1·30
2197 £S10 Inscr 'Lace wing' .... 1·90 1·30
2198 £S10 Inscr 'Tiger swallowtail' .... 1·90 1·30
2194/2198 *Set of 5* .... 8·50 5·75

Nos. 2194/2198 were issued in horizontal *se-tenant* strips of five stamps within the sheet.

2005 (3 Sept). 52nd International Damascus Fair. P 12×11½.

2199 **920** £S15 multicoloured .... 2·75 2·40

921 Arwad Island

922 Rumi

2005 (27 Sept). World Tourism Day. P 11½×12.

2200 **921** £S17 multicoloured .... 3·00 2·50

2005 (30 Sept). Mawlana Jalal Eddin Al-Rumi (Jalal al-Din Muhammad Rumi) (writer) Commemoration. P 12½.

2201 **922** £S25 multicoloured .... 4·50 4·00

Stamps of a similar design were issued by Afghanistan, Iran and Turkey.

923 Envelopes and Globe

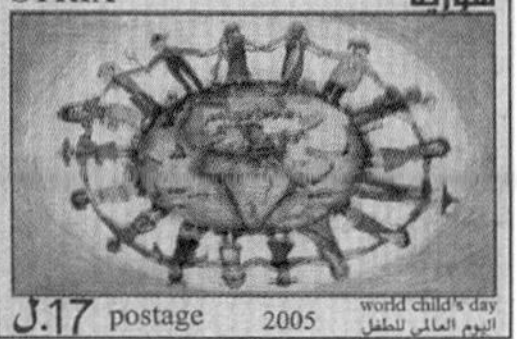

924 Children encircling Globe

2005 (9 Oct). World Post Day. P 12½×11½.

2202 **923** £S18 multicoloured .... 3·00 2·50

2005 (16 Oct). International Day of the Child. P 12½.

2203 **924** £S17 multicoloured .... 2·50 2·20

925 Emblem and Stone Tablet

2005 (16 Nov). World Information Society Summit, Tunis. P 12½.

2204 **925** £S17 multicoloured .... 2·30 2·00

926 Teshreen Dam

2005 (16 Nov). 35th Anniversary of Corrective Movement of 16 November 1970. P 11½×12½.

2205 **926** £S25 multicoloured .... 3·50 3·00

927 Nizar Kabbani

928 Palm

2005 (26 Dec). Writers Commemoration. P 13.

2206 £S10 Type **927** .... 1·60 1·40
a. Strip of 3. Nos. 2206/2208 .... 6·75
2207 £S17 Sadalah Wannous .... 2·30 2·00
2208 £S18 Omar Abu Reisheh .... 2·50 2·20
2206/2208 *Set of 4* .... 5·75 5·00

Nos. 2206/2208 were issued in horizontal *se-tenant* strips of three stamps within the sheet.

2005 (30 Dec). Tree Day. P 12½.

2209 **928** £S17 multicoloured .... 2·30 2·00

NOTE. From No. 2210 the stamps were printed on thicker paper with sheet watermark. The watermark shows as dark lines *when viewed through the back of the stamp.*

929 Flags and Dove **930** Mosque, Aleppo

2006 (8 Mar). 43rd Anniversary of Baathist Revolution of 8 March 1963. P 12×11½.

2210 **929** £S18 multicoloured .... 2·50 2·20

2006 (16 Mar). Aleppo–Capital of Islamic Culture. T **930** and similar multicoloured designs. P 12½×11½ (vert) or 11½×12½ (horiz).

2211 £S17 Aleppo castle (*horiz*) .... 2·30 2·00
a. Pair. Nos. 2211/2212 .... 5·00 4·50
2212 £S18 Type **930** .... 2·50 2·20
MS2213 80×60 mm. £S25 Script and buildings. Imperf .... 5·00 4·00

Nos. 2211/2212 were issued in horizontal *se-tenant* pairs within the sheet, No. 2211 laid at right-angles giving the appearance of two vertical stamps.

2006 (19 Mar–June). Thicker paper and sheet watermark. P 12×11½.

2213*a* **890** £S1 pale greenish blue (8.06) 25 20
2213*b* £S3 pale magenta (8.06) 45 40
2213*c* £S5 bistre brown (8.06) 70 60
2213*d* £S10 reddish lilac .... 1·40 1·20
2214 £S15 turquoise-green .... 2·10 1·80
2214*a* £S17 salmon .... 2·30 2·00
2214*b* £S18 deep grey blue (8.06) .... 2·50 2·20
2215 £S25 blue .... 3·50 3·00
2216 £S50 magenta .... 7·25 6·50
2216*a* £S100 grey-olive (8.06) .... 14·00 12·00
2213*a*/2216*a* *Set of* 10 .... 31·00 27·00

931 Mother and Child **932** Sultan Pasha al Atrach

2006 (21 Mar). Mothers' Day. P 12×11½.

2217 **931** £S17 multicoloured .... 2·30 2·00

2006 (17 Apr). National Day. Personalities. T **932** and similar vert designs. Multicoloured. P 12×11½.

2218 £S10 Type **932** .... 1·60 1·40
a. Horiz strip of 5. Nos. 2218/2222 .... 8·25
2219 £S10 Yousef al Azmeh .... 1·60 1·40
2220 £S10 Sheikh Saleh al Ali .... 1·60 1·40
2221 £S10 Ibrahim Hanano .... 1·60 1·40
2222 £S10 Ahmad Moraiwed .... 1·60 1·40
2218/2222 *Set of* 5 .... 7·25 6·25

Nos. 2218/2222 were issued in horizontal *se-tenant* strips of five stamps within the sheet.

933 Figures and Emblem **934** *Hyoscyamus aureus*

2006 (1 May). May Day. P 12×11½.

2223 **933** £S17 multicoloured .... 2·30 2·00

2006 (15 June). International Flower Show, Damascus. T **934** and similar horiz design. Multicoloured. P 11½×12.

2224 £S5 Type **934** 90 60
a. Pair. Nos. 2224/2225 .... 2·75 1·90
2225 £S10 *Cistus salviaefolius* .... 1·60 1·20

Nos. 2224/2225 were issued in vertical *se-tenant* pairs within the sheet.

935 Two Players

2006 (25 June). World Cup Football Championship, Germany. T **935** and multicoloured designs. P 12×11½.

2226 £S17 Type **935** .... 2·50 2·00
a. Pair. Nos. 2226/2227 .... 5·50 4·50
2227 £S18 Two players (*different*) .... 2·75 2·20
MS2228 60×82 mm. £S50 Players and trophy. Imperf... 10·50 8·00

Nos. 2226/2227 were issued in vertical *se-tenant* pairs within the sheet.

936 Great Walls and Ruins, Palmyra
(*Illustration reduced. Actual size 68×28 mm*)

2006 (1 Aug). 50th Anniversary of China–Syria Diplomatic Relations. P 12½.

2229 **936** £S10 multicoloured .... 1·80 1·60

937 Living and Dead Tree **938** '53'

2006 (13 Aug). International Year of Deserts and Desertification. P 12½.

2230 **937** £S10 multicoloured .... 1·80 1·60

2006 (3 Sept). 53rd International Fair, Damascus. P 12½×11½.

2231 **938** £S10 multicoloured .... 1·80 1·60

939 Storyteller **940** Symbols of Postal Delivery

2006 (27 Sept). World Tourism Day. T **939** and multicoloured design. P 12½.

2232 £S10 Type **939** .... 1·80 1·60
2233 £S10 Baptism basin (28×58 *mm*) .... 1·80 1·60

2006 (9 Oct). World Post Day. P 12×11½.

2234 **940** £S17 multicoloured .... 2·30 2·00

941 Building (*Illustration reduced. Actual size 68×28 mm*)

2006 (16 Nov). 36th Anniversary of Corrective Movement of 16 November 1970. P 11½×12½.

2235	**941**	£S15 multicoloured	2·30	1·80

942 Fateh Almudarres

2006 (Nov). Artists. T **942** and similar horiz designs. Multicoloured. P 12½.

2236	£S10 Type **942**	1·60	1·40
	a. Strip of 5. Nos. 2236/2240	8·25	
2237	£S10 Adham Ismail	1·60	1·40
2238	£S10 Saeed Makhlouf	1·60	1·40
2239	£S10 Burhan Karkutli	1·60	1·40
2240	£S10 Michael Kirsheh	1·60	1·40
2236/2240 *Set of 5*		7·25	6·25

Nos. 2236/2240 were issued together in *se-tenant* strips of five stamps within the sheet.

943 *Pistacia atlantica*

2006 (26 Dec). Tree Day. P 12½.

2241	**943**	£S15 multicoloured	2·00	1·80

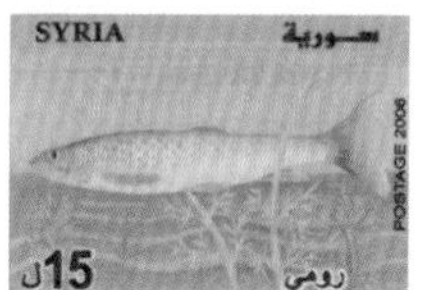

944 Shabut (barb)

2006 (26 Dec). Fish. T **944** and similar horiz designs. Multicoloured. P 12½.

2242	£S15 Type **944**	2·00	1·80
	a. Vertical strip of 3. Nos. 2242/2244	6·25	
2243	£S15 Catfish	2·00	1·80
2244	£S15 Mullet	2·00	1·80
2242/2244 *Set of 3*		5·50	4·75

Nos. 2242/2244 were issued together in *se-tenant* strips of three stamps within the sheet.

945 Emblems

2007 (8 Mar). 44th Anniversary of Baathist Revolution of 8 March 1963. P 12½.

2245	**945**	£S17 multicoloured	2·00	1·80

946 *Mother and Child* (statue)

947 Torch and Map

2007 (21 Mar). Mother's Day. P 12½.

2246	**946**	£S15 multicoloured	1·80	1·60

2007 (7 Apr). 60th Anniversary of Baath Party. P 12½.

2247	**947**	£S25 multicoloured	3·00	2·75

948 Man holding Banner

949 Workers holding Emblem

2007 (17 Apr). National Day. P 12½.

2248	**948**	£S15 multicoloured	1·80	1·60

2007 (1 May). May Day. P 12½.

2249	**949**	£S10 multicoloured	1·40	1·30

950 Freesia

951 President Assad

2007 (27 June). International Flower Show, Damascus. T **950** and similar horiz design. Multicoloured. P 12½.

2250	£S15 Type **950**	1·80	1·60
	a. Strip of 3. Nos. 2250/2252	5·75	
2251	£S15 *Ipomea purpurea*	1·80	1·60
2252	£S15 *Plumbago capensis*	1·80	1·60
2250/2252 *Set of 3*		4·75	4·25

Nos. 2250/2252 were issued in vertical *se-tenant* strips of three stamps within the sheet.

2007 (17 July). Second Term of President Bashar al-Assad. T **951** and similar multicoloured designs. P 12½.

2253	£S10 Type **951**	1·40	1·30
	a. Pair. Nos. 2253/2254	3·75	3·25
2254	£S15 President Assad (*different*)	2·00	1·80
MS2255	84×70 mm. £S25 President and assembly. Imperf	3·50	3·00

Nos. 2253/2254 were issued in *se-tenant* pairs within the sheet.

951a Emblems

952 St Paul's Church, Bab Kissan, Damascus

2007 (15 Aug). 54th International Fair, Damascus. P 12½×11½.
2255*a* **951a** £S15 multicoloured .... 2·00 1·80

2007 (27 Sept). World Tourism Day. P 12½.
2256 **952** £S10 multicoloured .... 1·40 1·30

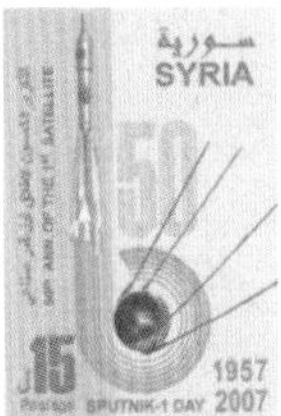
953 '50' and *Sputnik I*

954 Globe enclosed in Envelope

2007 (4 Oct). 50th Anniversary of Space Exploration. T **953** and similar vert design. Multicoloured. P 12½.
2257 £S15 Type **953** .... 2·00 1·80
a. Pair. Nos. 2257/2258 .... 5·50 5·00
2258 £S25 Spacecraft and *Sputnik I* .... 3·25 3·00
Nos. 2257/2258 were issued in *se-tenant* pairs within the sheet.

2007 (9 Oct). World Post Day. P 12½.
2259 **954** £S25 multicoloured .... 3·25 3·00

955 Industrial Structure

2007 (16 Nov). 37th Anniversary of Corrective Movement of 16 November 1970. P 11½×12½.
2260 **955** £S15 multicoloured .... 2·00 1·80

956 *Juniperus excelsa* (inscr 'Juniperu excelsa')

957 Hussny Sabah

2007 (27 Dec). Tree Day. P 12½.
2261 **956** £S18 multicoloured .... 2·40 2·20

2007 (30 Dec). Personalities. T **957** and similar vert designs. Multicoloured. P 12½.
2262 £S10 Type **957** .... 1·40 1·30
a. Strip of 5. Nos. 2262/2266 .... 7·25
2263 £S10 Wajieh al Barudy .... 1·40 1·30
2264 £S10 Nadim Shoman .... 1·40 1·30
2265 £S10 Tawfik Izzeddin .... 1·40 1·30
2266 £S10 Abdussalam Al Ojaily .... 1·40 1·30
2262/2266 *Set of 5* .... 6·25 5·75
Nos. 2262/2266 were issued in horizontal *se-tenant* strips of five stamps within the sheet.

958 White Stork

959 Symbols of Industry and Culture

2007 (30 Dec). Birds. T **958** and similar vert designs. Multicoloured. P 12½.
2267 £S10 Type **958** .... 1·40 1·30
a. Strip of 5. Nos. 2267/2271 .... 7·25
2268 £S10 Woodpecker (inscr 'Syrian woodpecker') .... 1·40 1·30
2269 £S10 Shoveler .... 1·40 1·30
2270 £S10 Bee-eater .... 1·40 1·30
2271 £S10 Turtle Dove .... 1·40 1·30
2267/2271 *Set of 5* .... 6·25 5·75
Nos. 2267/2271 were issued in horizontal *se-tenant* strips of five stamps within the sheet.

2008 (8 Mar). 45th Anniversary of Baathist Revolution of 8 March 1963. P 12½.
2272 **959** £S15 multicoloured .... 2·00 1·80

960 Mother and Child

961 Emblem and Flags of Members

2008 (21 Mar). Mothers' Day. P 12½.
2273 **960** £S10 multicoloured .... 1·40 1·30

2008 (29 Mar). Arab Summit, Damascus. T **961** and similar vert design. P 12½.
2274 £S10 Type **961** .... 1·40 1·30
MS2275 70×85 mm. £S25 Emblem and rider. Imperf .... 3·50 3·25

962 Al-Shamieh School

2008 (30 Mar). Damascus-Arab Capital of Culture 2008. T **962** and similar multicoloured designs. P 12½.
2276 £S10 Type **962** .... 1·40 1·30
2277 £S15 Al Thaheria Library .... 2·00 1·80
MS2278 70×85 mm. £S25 Damascus University. Imperf .... 3·50 3·25

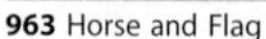

963 Horse and Flag

964 Figures, Emblem and Cog Outline

2008 (17 Apr). 62nd National Day. P 12½.

2279	**963**	£S10 multicoloured	1·40	1·30

2008 (1 May). May Day. P 12½.

2280	**964**	£S20 multicoloured	2·50	2·30

965 Anniversary Emblem

966 Roses

2008 (4 May). 50th Anniversary of Aleppo University. P 12½×11½ .

2281	**965**	£S15 multicoloured	2·00	1·80

2008 (30 May). International Flower Show, Damascus. T **966** and similar vert designs. Multicoloured. P 12½.

2282	£S10 Type **966**	1·40	1·30
	a. Strip of 5. Nos. 2282/2286	7·25	
2283	£S10 Cacti	1·40	1·30
2284	£S10 Dahlias	1·40	1·30
2285	£S10 Primula (inscr 'wallflower')	1·40	1·30
2286	£S10 Marguerites	1·40	1·30
2282/2286	*Set of 5*	6·25	5·75

Nos. 2282/2286 were issued in horizontal *se-tenant* strips of five stamps within the sheet.

967 Camels

2008 (3 Aug). Arab Post Day. Sheet 170×60 mm containing T **967** and similar horiz design. Multicoloured. P 12×11½.

MS2287	£S15 Type **967**; £S20 Pigeon	4·75	4·50

968 Weightlifting

2008 (8 Aug). Olympic Games, Beijing. T **968** and similar multicoloured designs. P 12½.

2288	£S5 Type **968**	70	65
2289	£S10 Long jump (*vert*)	1·40	1·30
MS2290	85×62 mm. £S25 Swimming. Imperf	3·50	3·25

969 Emblem

969a Steam Locomotive

2008 (15 Aug). 55th International Fair, Damascus. P 12½×11½.

2291	**969**	£S25 multicoloured	3·25	3·00

2008 (19 Aug). Centenary of Hijaz Railway. T **969a** and similar multicoloured design. P 12½.

2291*a*	£S25 Type **969a**	3·25	3·00
MS2291*b*	70×85 mm. £S50 Route and locomotive emerging from tunnel. Imperf	6·75	6·00

970 Vase

971 Dove, Envelope and Globe

2008 (27 Sept). World Tourism Day. T **970** and similar multicoloured design. P 12×11½ (vert) or 12½ (square).

2292	£S10 Type **970**	1·40	1·30
2293	£S15 Dish (37×37 *mm*)	2·00	1·80

2008 (9 Oct). World Post Day. P 12×11½.

2294	**971**	£S18 multicoloured	2·40	2·20

972 Sham (First Syrian produced car)

2008 (16 Nov). 38th Anniversary of Corrective Movement of 16 November 1970. P 11½×12½.

2295	**972**	£S10 multicoloured	1·40	1·30

973 Hawthorn (inscr 'Howthorn')

974 Inscr 'Golan Snake'

2008 (25 Dec). Tree Day. P 12½.

2296	**973**	£S17 multicoloured	2·20	2·00

2008 (Dec). Snakes. T **974** and similar square designs. Multicoloured. P 12½.

2297	£S20 Type **974**	2·50	2·30
	a. Strip of 3. Nos. 2297/2299	7·75	
2298	£S20 *Eryx jaculus*	2·50	2·30
2299	£S20 *Colubridae*	2·50	2·30
2297/2299	*Set of 3*	6·75	6·25

Nos. 2297/2299 were issued in horizontal *se-tenant* strips of three stamps within the sheet.

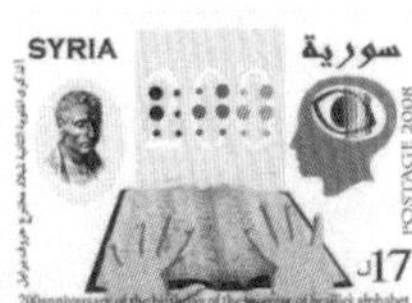

975 Louis Braille and Hands 'Reading'

976 Moustapha Akkad

2009 (4 Jan). Birth Bicentenary of Louis Braille (inventor of Braille writing for the blind). P 11½×12.

2300 **975** £S17 multicoloured .... 2·20 2·00

2009 (Jan). President Assad. P 12×11½.

2301 **890** £S10 reddish lilac .... 1·40 1·30

2009 (Jan). Personalities. T **976** and similar vert designs. Multicoloured. P 12½.

2302 £S20 Type **976** (Syrian American film producer and director) .... 2·50 2·30
a. Strip of 5. Nos. 2302/2306 .... 13·00
2303 £S20 Nihad Kalaai (actor) .... 2·50 2·30
2304 £S20 Maha al-Saleh (actress) .... 2·50 2·30
2305 £S20 Abd al-Latiff Fathy (actor) .... 2·50 2·30
2306 £S20 Inscr 'Fahd Kaaekati' .... 2·50 2·30
2302/2306 *Set of 5* .... 11·00 10·50

Nos. 2302/2306 were printed, *se-tenant*, in horizontal strips of five stamps within the sheet.

977 Emblem

978 Mother and Child

2009 (8 Mar). 46th Anniversary of Baathist Revolution. P 12×11½.

2307 **977** £S10 multicoloured .... 1·40 1·30

2009 (21 Mar). Mothers' Day. P 12½.

2308 **978** £S18 multicoloured .... 2·40 2·20

979 Soldier, Woman, Dove and Flag

2009 (17 Apr). 63rd National Day. P 12½.

2309 **979** £S17 multicoloured .... 2·20 2·00

980 Symbols of Labour

981 Wallflowers

2009 (1 May). May Day. P 11½×12.

2310 **980** £S15 multicoloured .... 2·00 1·80

2009 (15 June). International Flower Show, Damascus. T **981** and similar vert designs. Multicoloured. P 12½.

2311 £S20 Type **981** .... 2·50 2·30
a. Strip of 5. Nos. 2311/2315 .... 13·00
2312 £S20 Inscr 'Maemoza' .... 2·50 2·30
2313 £S20 Iris .... 2·50 2·30
2314 £S20 Inscr 'Lily' .... 2·50 2·30
2315 £S20 Inscr 'Adalia' .... 2·50 2·30
2311/2315 *Set of 5* .... 11·00 10·50

Nos. 2311/2315 were printed, *se-tenant*, in horizontal strips of five stamps within the sheet.

982 Emblem

983 Emblem

2009 (15 Aug). 56th Damascus Fair. P 12×11½.

2316 **982** £S15 multicoloured .... 2·00 1·80

2009 (8 Sept). al-Quds–2009 Capital of Arab Culture. P 13½.

2317 **983** £S10 multicoloured .... 1·40 1·30

984 Bab Al-Hawa

2009 (27 Sept). Tourism. T **984** and similar horiz designs. Multicoloured. P 12.

2318 £S25 Type **984** .... 3·25 3·00
a. Strip of 3. Nos. 2318/2320 .... 10·00
2319 £S25 Mabrak al Naqa Mosque .... 3·25 3·00
2320 £S25 Amphitheatre, Bosra .... 3·25 3·00
2318/2320 *Set of 3* .... 8·75 8·00

Nos. 2318/2320 was printed, *se-tenant*, in vertical strips of three stamps within the sheet.

985 Dove, Flower and Envelope

2009 (9 Oct). World Post Day. P 12½.

2321 **985** £S50 multicoloured .... 6·50 5·75

986 New Prime Ministry Headquarters

2009 (16 Nov). 39th Anniversary of Correctionist Movement of 16 November 1970. P 12.
2322 **986** £S10 multicoloured .... 1·40 1·30

987 Trees in Blossom

2009 (31 Dec). Tree Day. P 12½.
2323 **987** £S15 multicoloured .... 2·00 1·80

988 Thrasher

2009 (31 Dec). Birds. T **988** and similar horiz designs. Multicoloured. P 12.

2324	£S20 Type **988**	2·50	2·30
	a. Strip of 5. Nos. 2324/2328	13·00	
2325	£S20 Redstart	2·50	2·30
2326	£S20 Blue Headed Yellow Wagtail	2·50	2·30
2327	£S20 Honeyeater	2·50	2·30
2328	£S20 Syrian Serin	2·50	2·30
2324/2328	*Set of 5*	11·00	10·50

Nos. 2324/2328 were printed, *se-tenant*, in vertical strips of five stamps within the sheet.

989 Emblem

990 Hand holding Rose

2010 (8 Mar). 47th Anniversary of Baathist Revolution. P 12½.
2329 **989** £S25 multicoloured .... 3·25 3·00

2010 (21 Mar). Mothers' Day. P 12.
2330 **990** £S10 multicoloured .... 1·40 1·30

991 Flag, '64' and Outline of Prancing Horse

992 Metal Workers

2010 (17 Apr). 64th National Day. P 12.
2331 **991** £S50 multicoloured .... 6·50 5·75

2010 (1 May). Labour Day. P 12½.
2332 **992** £S25 multicoloured .... 3·25 3·00

993 Inscr 'Calendula'

994 Four Players

2010 (May). International Flower Show, Damascus. T **993** and similar vert designs. Multicoloured. P 12½.

2333	£S25 Type **993**	3·25	3·00
	a. Strip. Nos. 2333/2337	17·00	
2334	£S25 Inscr 'Cyeclamen'	3·25	3·00
2335	£S25 Rose	3·25	3·00
2336	£S25 Inscr 'Fuschia'	3·25	3·00
2337	£S25 Inscr 'Roza bracteata'	3·25	3·00
2333/2337	*Set of 5*	14·50	13·50

Nos. 2333/2337 were printed, *se-tenant*, in horizontal strips of five stamps within the sheet.

2010 (June). World Cup Football Championships, South Africa. T **994** and similar horiz designs. Multicoloured. P 12½.

2338	£S25 Type **994**	3·25	3·00
	a. Pair. Nos. 2338/2339	6·75	6·25
2339	£S25 No. 3, No.10 and No. 11 players tackling for ball	3·25	3·00
MS2340	85×63 mm. £S50 Championship emblem and trophy. Imperf	6·75	6·25

Nos. 2338/2339 were issued together in *se-tenant* pairs within the sheet.

995 '2010' containing Symbols of Biodiversity

996 Anniversary Emblem

2010 (6 June). International Year of Biodiversity. P 12½.
2341 **995** £S50 multicoloured .... 6·50 5·75

2010 (24 June). 50th Anniversary of Aleppo Industrial and Agricultural Production Fair. P 12.
2342 **996** £S15 multicoloured .... 2·00 1·80

997 Rio de Janeiro, Brazil and Maalula, Syria

998 '57'

(Des Luciomar de Jesus)

2010 (28 June). Syria–Brazil Diplomatic Relationships. P 12½.
2343 **997** £S50 muticoloured .... 6·50 5·75
A stamp of a similar design was issued by Brazil.

2010 (14 July). 57th Damascus Fair. P 12×11½.
2344 **998** £S50 multicoloured .... 6·50 5·75

999 Clasped Hands **1000** Square

2010 (23 Sept). Syria–Chile Diplomatic Relationships. P 12½.
2345 **999** £S25 multicoloured .... 3·25 3·00

2010 (23 Sept). World Tourism Day. T **1000** and similar vert design. Multicoloured. P 12.
2346 £S25 Type **1000** .... 3·25 3·00
a. Pair. Nos. 2346/2347 .... 6·75 6·25
2347 £S25 Dancers .... 3·25 3·00

Nos. 2346/2347 were issued together in *se-tenant* pairs within the sheet.

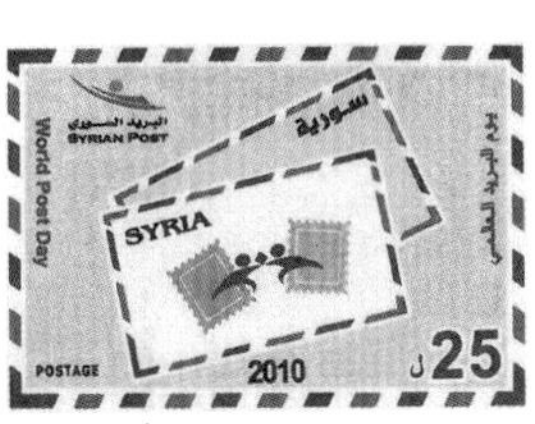

1001 Envelopes **1002** President Assad

2010 (9 Oct). World Post Day. P 12½.
2348 **1001** £S25 multicoloured .... 3·25 3·00

2010 (16 Nov). 40th Anniversary of Correctionist Movement of 16 November 1970. P 12.
2349 **1002** £S25 multicoloured .... 3·25 3·00

Nos. 2350 and T **1003** are vacant.

1004 Squirrel

2010 (21 Dec). Fauna. T **1004** and similar horiz designs. Multicoloured. P 12.
2351 £S30 Type **1004** .... 4·00 3·50
a. Strip. Nos. 2351/2353 .... 13·50
2352 £S30 Hedgehog .... 4·00 3·50
2353 £S40 Egyptian Mongoose (inscr 'Ichnewmon') .... 5·25 4·75
2351/2353 *Set of* 3 .... 12·00 10·50

Nos. 2351/2353 were printed, *se-tenant*, in horizontal strips of three stamps within the sheet.

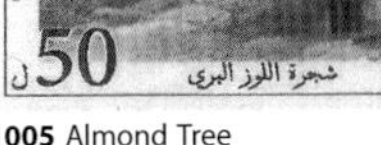

1005 Almond Tree **1006** Fathullah Al-Sakal

2010 (29 Dec). Tree Day. P 12.
2354 **1005** £S50 multicoloured .... 6·50 5·75

2010 (31 Dec). Lawyers. T **1006** and similar vert designs. Multicoloured. P 12.
2355 £S25 Type **1006** .... 3·25 3·00
a. Block of 6. Nos. 2355/2360 .... 21·00
2356 £S25 Faris Al-Khouri .... 3·25 3·00
2357 £S25 Saeed Al-Gazi .... 3·25 3·00
2358 £S25 Abd-El-Salam Al-Tirmanini .... 3·25 3·00
2359 £S25 Mohammad Al-Fadel .... 3·25 3·00
2360 £S25 Ahmad Fouad Al-Koudmani .... 3·25 3·00
2355/2360 *Set of* 6 .... 18·00 16·00

1007 Symbols of Progress **1008** Child's Hand holding Mother's Hand

2011 (8 Mar). 48th Anniversary of Baathist Revolution. P 12×11½.
2361 **1007** £S25 multicoloured .... 3·25 3·00

2011 (21 Mar). Mothers' Day. P 12×11½.
2362 **1008** £S25 multicoloured .... 3·25 3·00

1009 Arm holding Flag **1010** Baker

2011 (17 Apr). 65th National Day. P 11½×12.
2363 **1009** £S25 multicoloured .... 3·25 3·00

2011 (1 May). Labour Day. P 11½×12.
2364 **1010** £S50 multicoloured .... 6·50 5·75

1011 Male and Female Outlines and AIDS Ribbon **1012** *Nerium oleander*

2011 (1 June). 30th Anniversary of AIDS Prevention Campaign. P 12×11½.
2365 **1011** £S25 multicoloured .... 3·25 3·00

2011 (22 June). International Flower Show, Damascus. T **1012** and similar vert designs. Multicoloured. P 12½.
2366 £S50 Type **1012** .... 6·50 5·75
a. Strip of 5. Nos. 2366/2370 .... 34·00
2367 £S50 Lily-of-the-Valley .... 6·50 5·75
2368 £S50 Lotus flower .... 6·50 5·75
2369 £S50 Bird of Paradise .... 6·50 5·75
2370 £S50 Dahlia .... 6·50 5·75
2366/2370 *Set of* 5 .... 29·00 26·00

Nos. 2366/2370 were printed, *se-tenant*, in horizontal strips of five stamps within the sheet.

1013 Emblem

2011 (13 July). 58th Damascus Fair. P 12×11½.
2371 **1013** £S15 multicoloured .... 2·00 1·90

No. 2372 and T **1014** are vacant.

1015 Sultan Ibrahim Mosque, Jableh

2011 (27 Sept). World Tourism Day. P 12½.
2373 **1015** £S20 multicoloured .... 2·50 2·40

1016 Globe encircled by Envelopes

1017 Ariba–Latakia Highway (inscr 'Lattakia')

2011 (9 Oct). World Post Day. P 12.
2374 **1016** £S20 multicoloured .... 2·50 2·40

2011 (16 Nov). 41st Anniversary of Correctionist Movement of 16 November 1970. P 11½×12.
2375 **1017** £S15 multicoloured .... 2·00 1·90

1018 Olive Tree

2011 (29 Dec). Tree Day. P 12.
2376 **1018** £S15 multicoloured .... 2·00 1·90

1019 *Physeter macrocephalus* (Sperm Whale)

1020 Nazek Al-Abed

2011. Agreement on Conservation of Cetaceans of Mediterranean Sea. T **1019** and similar horiz designs. P 12.
2377 £S25 Type **1019** .... 3·25 3·00
a. Block of 6. Nos. 2377/2382 .... 21·00
2378 £S25 *Globicephalus melas* (Long-finned Pilot Whale) .... 3·25 3·00
2379 £S25 *Stenella coeruleoalba* (Striped Dolphin). 3·25 3·00
2380 £S25 *Grampus griscus* (Risso's Dolphin) .... 3·25 3·00
2381 £S25 *Tursiops truncatus* (Bottlenose Dolphin) 3·25 3·00
2382 £S25 *Orcinus orca* (Killer Whale) .... 3·25 3·00
2377/2382 *Set of 6* .... 18·00 16·00

Nos. 2377/2382 were printed, *se-tenant*, in blocks of six stamps within the sheet.

2011. Pioneering Arab Women. T **1020** and similar vert designs. Multicoloured. P 12½×11½.
2383 £S20 Type **1020** (campaigner for women's rights, volunteered for Syrian Army, and fought in Battle of Maysaloun, 1920) (inscr 'Abid') .... 2·50 2·40
a. Block of 6. Nos. 2383/2388 .... 16·00
2384 £S20 Inscr 'Fateema Solyman al-Ahmed' .... 2·50 2·40
2385 £S20 Adleh Bayhum Aljazairi (established 'Awakening of Shami Women' Society, 1927, founded the College of 'Dawhet Aaladab' and founded the nucleus for Syrian Women's Union, 1933) (inscr 'Adila Byham al-Jazairy') .... 2·50 2·40
2386 £S20 Thuraya al-Hafiz (feminist pioneer) (inscr 'Thorya') .... 2·50 2·40
2387 £S20 Mary Ajamy (writer, poet, and journalist) (inscr 'Marry Ajami') .... 2·50 2·40
2388 £S20 Inscr 'Souad Abdullah' .... 2·50 2·40
2383/2388 *Set of 6* .... 13·50 13·00

Nos. 2383/2388 were printed, *se-tenant*, in blocks of six stamps within the sheet.

1021 '8'

1022 Mother and Child

2012 (8 Mar). 49th Anniversary of Baathist Revolution. P 12½.
2389 **1021** £S20 multicoloured .... 2·50 2·40

2012 (21 Mar). Mothers' Day. P 12½.
2390 **1022** £S30 multicoloured .... 4·00 3·75

1023 Flowers and Flags

1024 Symbols of Work

2011 (17 Apr). 66th National Day. P 12½×11½.
2391 **1023** £S50 multicoloured .... 6·50 6·00

2012 (1 May). Labour Day. P 12×11½.
2392 **1024** £S50 multicoloured .... 6·50 6·00

1025 Dahlia

2012 (20 June). International Flower Show, Damascus. T **1025** and similar vert designs. Multicoloured. P 12½.
2393 £S10 Type **1025** .... 1·40 1·30
a. Strip. Nos. 2393/2397 .... 7·25
2394 £S10 Hydrangea .... 1·40 1·30

2395	£S10 Hemerocallis	1·40	1·30
2396	£S10 Inscr 'Primevere'	1·40	1·30
2397	£S10 Lantana	1·40	1·30
2393/2397 *Set of 5*		6·25	5·75

Nos. 2393/2397 were printed, *se-tenant*, in horizontal strips of five stamps within the sheet.

1026 Syrian Eagle

2012 (26 July). The Syrian Eagle. T **1026** and similar horiz designs. Multicoloured. P 12½.

2398	£S50 Type **1026**	6·50	6·00
	a. Block of 4. Nos. 2398/2401	27·00	
2399	£S50 In flight	6·50	6·00
2400	£S50 Perched on rock	6·50	6·00
2401	£S50 Head	6·50	6·00
2398/2401 *Set of 4*		23·00	22·00

Nos. 2398/2401 were printed, *se-tenant*, in blocks of four stamps within the sheet.

1027 Wine Seller

1028 Globe and Envelopes as Doves

2012 (27 Sept). World Tourism Day. P 12½.

2402	**1027**	£S50 multicoloured	6·50	6·00

2012 (9 Oct). World Post Day. P 12.

2403	**1028**	£S15 multicoloured	2·00	1·90

1029 Dam

2012 (16 Nov). 42nd Anniversary of Correctionist Movement of 16 November 1970. P 12½×12.

2404	**1029**	£S15 multicoloured	2·00	1·90

1030 Abed Alkareem Alyafy

1031 Cherry Tree

2012 (25 Dec). Syrian Writers. T **1030** and simlar vert designs. Multicoloured. P 12×11½.

2405	£S50 Type **1030**	6·50	6·00
	a. Block of 6. Nos. 2405/2410	40·00	
2406	£S50 Kamar Kaellany	6·50	6·00
2407	£S50 Kostaky Al Houmsy	6·50	6·00
2408	£S50 Sedky Ismail	6·50	6·00
2409	£S50 Alfat Al Edelby	6·50	6·00
2410	£S50 Midhat Akash	6·50	6·00
2405/2410 *Set of 6*		35·00	32·00

Nos. 2405/2410 were printed, *se-tenant*, in blocks of six stamps within the sheet.

2012 (31 Dec). Tree Day. P 11½×12.

2411	**1031**	£S40 multicoloured	5·25	4·75

1032 *Serinus syriacus*

1033 Mustapha Al Shehabi

2013 (1 Jan). Syrian Birds. T **1032** and similar vert designs. Multicoloured. P 12×11½.

2412	£S75 Type **1032**	9·75	9·00
	a. Block of 6. Nos. 2412/2417	65·00	
	b. Sheet of 6. Nos.2412/2417		
2413	£S75 Starling	9·75	9·00
2414	£S75 *Erithacus rubecula* (Robin)	9·75	9·00
2415	£S75 Yellow-breasted Chat	9·75	9·00
2416	£S75 *Megarhynchos luscinia* (Nightingale)	9·75	9·00
2417	£S75 Cinereous Bunting	9·75	9·00
2412/2417 *Set of 6*		55·00	49·00

Nos. 2412/2417 were printed, *se-tenant*, in blocks of six stamps within large sheets and, together in small sheets of six stamps.

2013 (1 Jan). Syrian Writers. T **1033** and simlar vert designs. Multicoloured. P 12×11½.

2418	£S100 Type **1033**	13·00	12·00
	a. Block of 6. Nos. 2418/2423	85·00	
2419	£S100 Khalil Mardam Beyk	13·00	12·00
2420	£S100 Mohammed Kurd Ali	13·00	12·00
2421	£S100 Marwan Al Mahasseni	13·00	12·00
2422	£S100 Shaker Al Fahham	13·00	12·00
2423	£S100 Husni Sabah	13·00	12·00
2418/2423 *Set of 6*		70·00	65·00

Nos. 2418/2423 were printed, *se-tenant*, in blocks of six stamps within the sheet.

1034 'Forgotten Cities'

1035 Anniversary Emblem

2013 (20 Jan)–**16**. Cultural Heritage. T **1034** and similar vert designs

2424	£S5 orange-brown	70	65
2425	£S5 pale orange (25.1.14)	70	65
2426	£S5 pale brown (1.9.16)	70	65
2427	£S10 rose	1·40	1·30
2428	£S10 pale carmine (25.1.14)	1·40	1·30
2429	£S10 rose (1.9.16)	1·40	1·30
2430	£S25 sepia (14.11.16)	3·25	3·00
2424/2430 *Set of 7*		8·50	8·00

Nos. 2431/2433 have been left for this continuing series.

2013 (8 Mar). 50th Anniversary of Baathist Revolution. P 12½.

2436	**1035**	£S25 multicoloured	3·25	3·00

1036 Mother and Child

1037 Soldier and Flag

2013 (21 Mar). Mothers' Day. P 12.
2437 **1036** £S25 multicoloured ... 3·25 3·00

2013 (17 Apr). 67th National Day. P 12½×11½.
2438 **1037** £S25 multicoloured ... 3·25 3·00

1038 Workers and Emblem

2013 (1 May). Labour Day. P 12½×12.
2439 **1038** £S25 multicoloured ... 3·25 3·00

1039 Wooden Overshoes

1040 UPU Emblem and Globe

2013 (27 Sept). World Tourism Day. P 12½.
2440 **1039** £S100 multicoloured ... 13·00 12·00

2013 (9 Oct). World Post Day. P 12.
2441 **1040** £S100 multicoloured ... 13·00 12·00

1041 People of Many Trades

2013 (16 Nov). 43rd Anniversary of Correctionist Movement of 16 November 1970. P 12½×12.
2442 **1041** £S50 multicoloured ... 6·50 6·00

1042 Orange Tree

2013 (26 Dec). Tree Day. P 11½×12.
2443 **1042** £S150 multicoloured ... 19·00 18·00

1043 *Mustela frenata* (Long-tailed Weasel)

1044 Script

2014 (1 Jan). Fauna. T **1043** and similar horiz designs. Multicoloured. P 11½×12.

2444	£S75 Type **1043**	9·75	9·00
	a. Strip of 3. Nos. 2444/2446	43·00	
2445	£S80 Fox	10·50	9·50
2446	£S170 Jackal	22·00	20·00
2444/2446	*Set of 3*	38·00	35·00

Nos. 2444/2446 were printed, *se-tenant*, in horizontal strips of three stamps within the sheet.

2014 (1 Mar). Arab Language Day. P 13.
2447 **1044** £S180 multicoloured ... 23·00 21·00

No. 2447 was perforated in a circle contained in an outer perforated square.

1045 '2014'

1046 Mother and Child

2014 (8 Mar). 51st Anniversary of Baathist Revolution. P 12½.
2448 **1045** £S80 multicoloured ... 10·50 9·50

2014 (21 Mar). Mothers' Day. P 12.
2449 **1046** £S100 multicoloured ... 13·00 12·00

1047 Eagle, Map and Flag

2014 (14 Apr). 68th National Day. P 12½×11½.
2450 **1047** £S180 multicoloured ... 23·00 21·00

1048 Emblem

2014 (1 May). Labour Day. P 12½×12.

2451	**1048**	£S75 multicoloured	9·75	9·00

1049 Players

2014 (12 June). World Cup Football Championships, Brazil. T **1049** and similar horiz design. Multicoloured. P 12½.

2452	£S100 Type **1049**	13·00	12·00
	a. Pair. Nos. 2452/2453	33·00	31·00
2453	£S100 Players tackling	19·00	18·00

Nos. 2452/2453 were printed, *se-tenant*, in horizontal and vertical pairs within the sheet.

1050 President Assad

2014 (22 July). Re-Election of President Bashar al-Assad. T **1050** and similar multicoloured designs. P 14.

2454	£S60 Type **1050**	7·75	7·25
2455	£S90 President Assad and workers	11·50	10·50
2456	£S150 President Assad (32×63 *mm*)	19·00	18·00
2454/2456 *Set of 3*		34·00	32·00

1051 Soldier and Flag

2014 (1 Aug). Army Day. P 12½.

2457	**1051**	£S250 multicoloured	32·00	30·00

1052 Emblems

2014 (16 Aug). Nanjing 2014. Youth Olympic Games. P 12½.

2458	**1052**	£S200 multicoloured	26·00	24·00

1053 Glass Blower

2014 (27 Sept). World Tourism Day. P 12½.

2459	**1053**	£S80 multicoloured	10·50	9·50

1054 Emblem

2014 (9 Oct). World Post Day. P 12.

2460	**1054**	£S80 multicoloured	10·50	9·50

1055 Figures and '44'

2014 (16 Nov). 44th Anniversary of Correctionist Movement of 16 November 1970. P 12½×12.

2461	**1055**	£S60 multicoloured	7·75	7·25

1056 Pistachio Tree

2014 (25 Dec). Tree Day. P 11½×12.

2462	**1056**	£S245 multicoloured	32·00	30·00

1057 Lynx

1058 Faud Ghazi

2015 (1 Jan). Fauna. T **1057** and similar horiz designs. Multicoloured. P 11½×12.

2463	£S110 Type **1057**	14·00	13·00
	a. Strip of 3. Nos. 2463/2465	43·00	
2464	£S110 Oryx (Inscr 'Arab Deer')	14·00	13·00
2465	£S110 Syrian Bear	14·00	13·00

2463/2465 *Set of 4* .... 38·00 35·00

Nos. 2463/2465 were printed, *se-tenant*, in horizontal and vertical strips of three stamps within the sheet.

2015 (1 Jan). Syrian Musical Artists. T **1058** and similar vert designs. Multicoloured. P 12×11½.

2466 £S100 Type **1058** .... 13·00 12·00
a. Strip of 5. Nos. 2466/2470 .... 70·00
2467 £S100 Abd Al Fattah Sukar .... 13·00 12·00
2468 £S100 Sameer Hilmi .... 13·00 12·00
2469 £S100 Adnan Abi Al Shamat .... 13·00 12·00
2470 £S100 Fahed Ballan .... 13·00 12·00
2466/2470 *Set of 5* .... 60·00 55·00

Nos. 2466/2470 were printed, *se-tenant*, in horizontal strips of five stamps within the sheet.

1059 Symbols of Industry

2015 (8 Mar). 52nd Anniversary of Baathist Revolution. P 12½.

2471 **1059** £S300 multicoloured .... 39·00 36·00

1060 Mother and Embryo

2015 (21 Mar). Mothers' Day. P 12.

2472 **1060** £S110 multicoloured .... 14·00 13·00

1061 Flag and Statue

2015 (17 Apr). 69th National Day. P 12½.

2473 **1061** £S60 multicoloured .... 7·75 7·25

1062 Steeplejack **1063** Martyrs' Star

2015 (1 May). Labour Day. P 12½×12.

2474 **1062** £S235 multicoloured .... 30·00 28·00

2015 (6 May). Martyrs' Star. P 12.

2475 **1063** £S260 multicoloured .... 34·00 31·00

1064 Soldiers, Map and Flag **1065** 'Tambourine Beater from Ugharit'

2015 (1 Aug). Army Day. P 12½.

2476 **1064** £S110 multicoloured .... 14·00 13·00

2015 (27 Sept). World Tourism Day. T **1065** and similar vert design. Multicoloured. P 12½.

2477 £S150 Type **1065** .... 19·00 18·00
a. Pair. Nos. 2477/2478 .... 39·00 37·00
2478 £S150 Male bust, Palmyra .... 19·00 18·00

Nos. 2477/2478 were printed, *se-tenant*, in horizontal pairs within the sheet.

1066 Emblems

2015 (9 Oct). World Post Day. P 12.

2479 **1066** £S60 multicoloured .... 7·75 7·25

1067 Stylised Symbols of Syria

2015 (16 Nov). 45th Anniversary of Correctionist Movement of 16 November 1970. P 12½×12.

2480 **1067** £S60 multicoloured .... 7·75 7·25

1068 Tree, Face and Globe

2015 (25 Nov). National Environment Day. P 12.

2481 **1068** £S100 multicoloured .... 13·00 12·00

1069 Oak Tree

2015 (31 Dec). Tree Day. P 11½×12.
2482 **1069** £S250 multicoloured .... 32·00 30·00

1070 Woman as Tree

1071 Doves and Ears of Corn

2016 (8 Mar). International Women's Day. P 12½.
2483 **1070** £S100 multicoloured .... 13·00 12·00

2016 (8 Mar). 53rd Anniversary of Baathist Revolution. P 12½.
2484 **1071** £S200 multicoloured .... 26·00 24·00

1072 Mother and Child reading

2016 (21 Mar). Mothers' Day. P 12.
2485 **1072** £S150 multicoloured .... 19·00 18·00

1073 Industry

1074 Weightlifting

2016 (1 May). Labour Day. P 12½×12.
2486 **1073** £S300 multicoloured .... 39·00 36·00

2016 (6 Aug). Rio 2016. Olympic Games, Brazil. T **1074** and similar vert designs. Multicoloured. P 12½×11½.
2487 £S200 Type **1074** .... 26·00 24·00
a. Strip of 5. Nos. 2487/2491 .... £140
2488 £S200 Athletics .... 26·00 24·00
2489 £S200 Swimming .... 26·00 24·00
2490 £S200 Tennis .... 26·00 24·00
2491 £S200 Judo .... 26·00 24·00
2487/2491 *Set of 5* .... £120 11·00

Nos. 2487/2491 were printed, *se-tenant*, in horizontal strips of five stamps within the sheet.

1075 Emblem

1076 Clay Jug

2016 (9 Oct). World Post Day. P 12.
2492 **1075** £S250 multicoloured .... 32·00 30·00

(Litho)

2017 (Jan). Cultural Heritage. T **1076** and similar multicoloured designs. P 12½.
2494 £S25 Type **1076** .... 3·25 3·00
a. Strip of 5. Nos. 2494/2498 .... 60·00
2495 £S50 Marble bowl (*horiz*) .... 6·50 6·00
2496 £S75 Necklace, *c.* 100 BC (*horiz*) .... 9·75 9·00
2497 £S100 Hawk statuette .... 13·00 12·00
2498 £S155 Female fertility symbol .... 20·00 18·00
2494/2498 *Set of 5* .... 47·00 43·00

Nos. 2494/2498 were printed, *se-tenant*, in vertical strips of five stamps within the sheet, No. 2495/2496, laid at right-angles, giving the appearance of vertical stamps.

1077 Emblem

(Litho)

2017 (17 Aug). 59th Damascus Fair. P 12½.
2499 **1077** £S200 multicoloured .... 26·00 24·00
2500 £S300 multicoloured .... 39·00 36·00
MS2501 63×85 mm. £S500 As Type **1077**. Imperf. .... 70·00 65·00

ALAOUITES

(STATE OF THE)

The Alawis (or Alaouites, as the French call them) are members of the Shi'ite division of Islam who inhabit the coastal region of Syria between Hatay and Lebanon. On 1 September 1920 Syria was divided by the French into the autonomous states of Aleppo, Damascus and the Alaouites. After the mandate for Syria had been given to France, an administrative reorganisation was made on 1 January 1925. The mandated territory was divided into the state of Syria (consisting of the former states of Damascus and Aleppo) and the state of the Alaouites, and separate issues of stamps were made for each state.

PRINTERS. All the overprints and surcharges of Alaouites were made by the Capuchin Fathers, Beirut.

ALAOUITES
1 PIASTRE
العلويين
غرش ١
(1)

3
(I)

3
(II)

1925 (1 Jan–26 Feb). Stamps of France surch as T **1**.
1 **11** 0p.10 on 2c. claret .... 2·50 10·50
2 **18** 0p.25 on 5c. orange .... 3·00 9·00
3 **15** 0p.75 on 15c. olive green .... 5·50 11·50
a. Figures '75' spaced apart .... 37·00 37·00
4 **18** 1p. on 20c. chocolate .... 2·75 9·00
5 1p.25 on 25c. blue .... 3·25 11·50
6 1p.50 on 30c. scarlet .... 10·00 32·00
7 2p. on 35c. violet (26.2) .... 3·50 9·75
8 **13** 2p. on 40c. red and pale blue .... 4·75 12·50
9 2p. on 45c. deep green and blue (26.2) .... 12·00 32·00

No.	Type	Description	Unused	Used
10		3p. on 60c. violet and blue (I)	4·75	17·00
11	15	3p. on 60c. violet (I) (26.2)	19·00	30·00
		a. Surch double	£160	£160
		b. Type II	£150	£150
12		4p. on 85c. vermilion (2.2)	2·50	8·25
13	13	5p. on 1f. lake and yellow	4·75	22·00
14		10p. on 2f. orange and blue-green	7·25	25·00
		a. Figures '10' spaced apart	55·00	55·00
15		25p. on 5f. deep blue and buff	11·00	36·00
1/15		*Set of 15*	85·00	£250

Nos. 1 and 8 exist on G.C. paper.

Nos. 7/9 and 12/13 exist with surcharge inverted (*Price un £33 each*).

T **30** *(Pasteur) with similar surch*

No.	Type	Description	Unused	Used
16	30	0p.50 on 10c. green	2·50	9·00
17		0p.75 on 15c. green (26.2)	3·00	9·25
18		1p.50 on 30c. scarlet	2·50	10·00
19		2p. on 45c. red (26.2)	3·00	10·50
20		2p.50 on 50c. blue	4·50	11·50
21		4p. on 75c. blue	5·00	13·50
16/21		*Set of 6*	18·00	55·00

Nos. 17/20 exist with surcharge inverted (*Price un £20 each*).

(**2**)

1925 (1 Jan). AIR. Stamps of France surch as T **2**.

No.	Type	Description	Unused	Used
22	13	2p. on 40c. red and pale blue	8·50	27·00
		a. Surch inverted		
23		3p. on 60c. violet and blue (I)	10·00	42·00
		a. Surch inverted	£130	£130
		b. Type II	£180	£190
24		5p. on 1f. lake and yellow	7·25	24·00
25		10p. on 2f. orange and blue-green	7·25	28·00
22/25		*Set of 4*	30·00	£110

No. 22 exists on G.C. paper.

1925 (1 Jan). POSTAGE DUE. Stamps of France, surch as T **1**.

No.	Type	Description	Unused	Used
D26	D 11	0p.50 on 10c. pale brown	3·75	13·00
D27		1p. on 20c. olive-green	3·75	13·00
D28		2p. on 30c. carmine	3·75	13·00
		a. Opt double		
D29		3p. on 50c. dull claret (I)	3·75	13·00
		a. Type II	£170	£170
D30		5p. on 1f. lake-brown/*straw*	3·75	13·00
D26/D30		*Set of 5*	17·00	60·00

(**3**) (**4**)

1925 (1 Mar)–**30**. As Types **16** to **18** of Syria, optd as T **3** or T **4**.

No.	Type	Description	Unused	Used
26	3	0p.10 violet (R.)	60	4·25
		a. Surch inverted	35·00	35·00
		b. Surch double	47·00	47·00
		c. Pair, one without surch	£200	
		d. Surch in black	48·00	55·00
		e. Surch vertical	70·00	80·00
27	4	0p.25 olive-black (R.)	1·30	7·75
		a. Surch inverted	40·00	40·00
		b. Surch in blue	65·00	65·00
28		0p.50 yellow-green	1·50	2·00
		a. Surch inverted	40·00	40·00
		b. 'S' omitted	48·00	48·00
		c. Surch in blue	65·00	65·00
		d. Surch in red	65·00	65·00
		e. Pair, one without surch	£325	
29		0p.75 brown-red	2·20	6·75
		a. Surch double		90·00
		b. Surch in red	65·00	75·00
30	3	1p. claret	1·90	2·75
		a. Surch inverted	50·00	50·00
		b. 'ALACUITES'	44·00	44·00
		c. 'ALAUCITES'	50·00	50·00
31	4	1p.25 green	3·00	8·00
		a. Surch in red	65·00	65·00
32		1p.50 bright rose (B.)	2·30	5·00
		a. Surch inverted	45·00	45·00
		b. Surch in black (1930)	45·00	55·00
33		2p. sepia (R.)	2·30	3·75
		a. Surch inverted	44·00	44·00
		b. Surch in blue	80·00	90·00
34		2p.50 light blue (R.)	3·75	7·75
		a. Surch in black	80·00	90·00
35		3p. brown	2·10	3·75
		a. Surch in blue	75·00	75·00
36		5p. bright violet	3·00	3·75
		a. Surch in red	75·00	75·00
37		10p. plum	4·25	5·50
38		25p. bright blue (R.)	5·50	13·00
26/38		*Set of 13*	30·00	65·00

Views: 0p.10 Hama; 0p.25 Merkab; 0p.50, Alexandretta; 0p.75, Hama; 1p. Damascus; 1p.25, Latakia; 1p.50, Damascus; 2p., 25p. Palmyra (*different*); 2p.50, Kalat Yamoun; 3p. Bridge of Daphne; 5p., 10p. Aleppo (*different*).

(**5**)

1925 (1 Mar). AIR. Nos. 33 and 35/37 additionally optd with T **5**, in green.

No.	Type	Description	Unused	Used
40	3	2p. sepia	4·00	10·00
		a. Opt inverted	50·00	50·00
41		3p. brown	4·00	8·75
		a. Opt inverted	50·00	50·00
42		5p. bright violet	4·00	7·50
		a. Opt inverted	50·00	50·00
		b. Error. On 5p. of Lebanon	£350	
43		10p. plum	4·00	7·50
		a. Opt inverted	45·00	50·00
40/43		*Set of 4*	14·50	30·00

Stamps with 'AVION' overprint in red, either normal or inverted, are probably colour trials.

1925 (1 Mar). POSTAGE DUE. As T D **20** of Syria and similar views, optd as T **3** or T **4**.

No.	Type	Description	Unused	Used
D44	4	0p.50 brown/*yellow* (Hama)	1·70	8·00
		a. Opt inverted	38·00	38·00
D45	3	1p. plum/*rose* (Antioch) (B.)	2·20	8·25
		a. Opt inverted	44·00	44·00
		b. Opt in black	55·00	65·00
		c. Opt double (Blk.+B.)	£140	£140
D46	4	2p. black/*blue* (Tarsus) (R.)	2·75	9·75
		a. Surch in blue	50·00	
D47		3p. black/*red* (Banias) (B.)	3·75	12·50
D48		5p. black/*green* (Castle) (R.)	5·00	15·00
D44/D48		*Set of 5*	14·00	48·00

1926 (1 May). AIR. Nos. 192/195 of Syria (as Types **16**/**18**) optd with T **4**.

No.	Type	Description	Unused	Used
44		2p. sepia	3·75	12·00
45		3p. brown	3·75	12·00
46		5p. bright violet	4·50	12·00
47		10p. plum	4·50	12·00
44/47		*Set of 4*	11·50	43·00

(**6**)

(**7**)

1926 (Sept–8 Oct). Postage stamps of Alaouites of March 1925 further surch as T **6**.

No.	Type	Description	Unused	Used
48	4	3p.50 on 0p.75 brown-red	1·80	5·25
		a. Surch back and front	25·00	25·00
		b. Surch inverted	39·00	39·00
49		4p. on 0p.25 olive-black (C.)	2·50	5·50
		a. Surch inverted	55·00	55·00
		b. Surch with Type **7** (R.) (8.10)	75·00	75·00
50		6p. on 2p.50 light blue (R.)	3·00	6·00
		a. Surch inverted	55·00	55·00
51		12p. on 1p.25 green	3·50	8·25
		a. Surch inverted	55·00	55·00
52		20p. on 1p.25 green	4·00	11·00
48/52		*Set of 5*	13·50	32·00

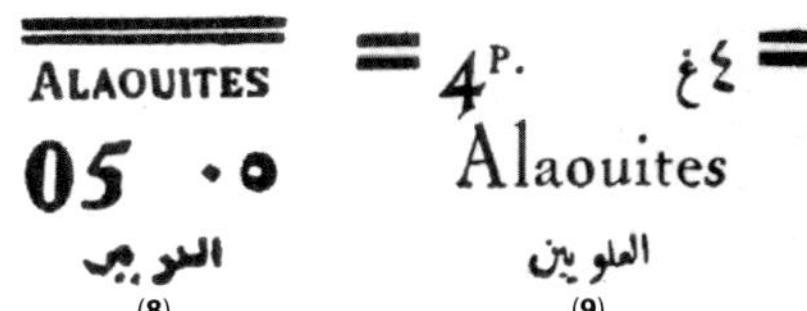

(8) (9)

1926 (Dec)–**28**. Stamps of Syria (Types **16/17**) surch at one operation as T **8** or T **9**.

No.	Type	Description	Unused	Used
53	**8**	5c. on 0p.10 violet (R.) (2.11.28)	75	5·00
		a. Surch double	44·00	
54	**9**	2p. on 1p.25 green (R.) (7.28)	16·00	10·50
		a. Surch inverted	55·00	
55		4p. on 0p.25 olive-black (R.) (7.28)	10·00	7·00
		a. Surch inverted	55·00	
		b. Surch double	55·00	
56		4p.50 on 0p.75 brown-red	5·50	7·00
		a. Surch inverted	65·00	
		b. Surch double	60·00	
		c. Arabic fraction omitted	28·00	
57		7p.50 on 2p.50 light blue	5·00	3·25
		a. Surch inverted	65·00	
58		15p. on 25p. bright blue	8·25	12·00
		a. Surch inverted	65·00	
53/58		*Set of 6*	41·00	40·00

(10)

1929 (June)–**30**. AIR.

*(a) Pictorial stamps of Syria (as Types **16/18**) surch with T **10***

No.	Description	Unused	Used
59	0p.50 yellow-green (R.)	2·75	9·50
	a. Opt inverted	90·00	
	b. Opt double	£180	
	c. Aeroplane only inverted	£275	
60	1p. claret (opt sideways, reading up)	6·50	16·00
61	25p. bright blue (R.)	37·00	60·00
	a. Opt inverted	£140	

(b) Nos. 54 and 58 of Alaouites optd with aeroplane

No.	Description	Unused	Used
62	2p. on 1p.25 green (R.) (1.30)	4·25	12·00
	a. Surch inverted	55·00	
63	15p. on 25p. bright blue (R.)	46·00	50·00
	a. Aeroplane only inverted	£250	
59/63	*Set of 5*	85·00	£130

LATAKIA

On 22 May 1930 the State of the Alaouites was made a republic, which on 22 September was given the name of Latakia.

LATTAQUIE LATTAQUIE

(11) (12)

1931 (July)–**33**. Views as Types **26** and **27** of Syria, optd with Types **11** and **12** respectively.

No.	Description	Unused	Used
64	0p.10 magenta	1·10	3·00
65	0p.10 purple (I) (8.33)	2·00	4·25
66	0p.20 deep blue (R.)	85	2·50
67	0p.20 orange-red (8.33)	1·80	6·50
68	0p.25 grey-green (R.)	1·40	4·00
69	0p.25 deep violet (R.) (8.33)	3·25	6·25
70	0p.50 bright violet	2·50	5·75
71	0p.75 orange-vermilion (8.32)	3·50	8·00
72	1p. green (R.)	2·75	3·00
73	1p.50 yellow-brown (R.)	5·00	9·00
74	1p.50 green (8.33)	10·00	10·00
75	2p. violet (R.)	4·50	3·75
76	3p. yellow-green (R.)	9·00	7·75
77	4p. orange	5·75	5·00
78	4p.50 carmine (11.31)	7·75	13·00
79	6p. blackish green (R.)	7·75	13·00
80	7p.50 blue (R.)	7·25	6·25
	a. Opt inverted	£700	
81	10p. chocolate (R.)	9·25	16·00
	a. Opt inverted	£700	
82	15p. deep green (R.)	12·50	26·00
83	25p. maroon (11.31)	30·00	50·00
84	50p. sepia (R.)	32·00	50·00
	a. Opt inverted	£700	
85	100p. orange-vermilion (11.31)	70·00	£110
64/85	*Set of 22*	£200	£325

Designs: As T **26**—0p.10, 0p.25, Hama (*different*); 0p.20, Aleppo. As T **27**—0p.50, Alexandretta; 0p.75, 4p.50, Homs; 1p., 7p.50, Aleppo (*different*); 1p.50, 4p., 100p. Damascus (*different*); 2p., 10p. Antioch (*different*); 3p. Bosra; 6p. Sednaya; 15p. Hama; 25p. St. Simeon; 50p. Palmyra.

1931. POSTAGE DUE. Nos. D197/D198 of Syria (Types D **21**/D **22**) optd with T **12**.

No.	Type	Description	Unused	Used
D86	D **21**	8p. black/*blue* (R.) (11.31)	33·00	55·00
D87		15p. black/*rose* (R.) (7.31)	26·00	34·00

LATTAQUIE

(13)

1931 (Nov)–**33**. AIR. Nos. 261/270 of Syria, optd with T **13**.

No.	Description	Unused	Used
86	0p.50 yellow	1·60	3·75
	a. Surch inverted	£1300	
87	0p.50 sepia (R.) (8.33)	2·75	6·00
88	1p. red-brown	2·75	3·25
89	2p. Prussian blue (R.)	5·00	7·25
90	3p. deep blue-green (R.)	6·00	7·75
91	5p. purple	7·75	18·00
92	10p. greenish blue (R.)	10·00	14·50
93	15p. orange-vermilion	14·00	24·00
94	25p. brown-orange	30·00	55·00
95	50p. black (R.)	44·00	55·00
96	100p. magenta	45·00	55·00
86/96	*Set of 11*	£150	£225

Designs: Potez 29-4 biplane over—0p.50, Homs; 1p., 10p. Damascus (*different*); 3p. Palmyra; 5p. Deir-el-Zor; 15p. Aleppo Citadel; 25p. Hama; 50p. Zebdani; 100p. Telebissé.

The designer's and printer's imprints on No. 86 measure 7½ mm and 8½ mm respectively and on 87, 8 mm and 9 mm.

By the Franco-Syrian Treaty of 9 September 1936, Latakia was merged with Syria, under a decree made on 5 December. At the end of February 1937, Latakian stamps were withdrawn and replaced by those of Syria.

ROUAD ISLAND (ARWAD)

(FRENCH OCCUPATION)

The island of Arwad (called Rouad by the French) lies off the coast of Syria, south of Latakia. During the First World War it was occupied in 1916 by French naval forces and used as a base from which to supply provisions and arms to the Maronite Christians of Syria, who were hostile to the Turks.

25 Centimes = 1 Piastre

ILE ROUAD ILE ROUAD ILE ROUAD

(1) (2) (3)

Stamps of the French Post Offices in the Turkish Empire of 1902–1920, overprinted

1916 (12 Jan). Handstamped locally with T **1**.

No.	Type	Description	Unused	Used
1	**11**	5c. green	£550	£275
2	**14**	10c. carmine	£550	£275
3		1p. on 25c. blue	£550	£275

The 40c. and 2p. on 50c. values were also handstamped but were not issued and used copies have been cancelled by favour.

1916 (Dec)–**20**. Optd with Types **2** or **3** (T **13**).

No.	Type	Description	Unused	Used
4	**11**	1c. grey	1·30	5·25
		a. Slate (1920)	3·50	4·50
5		2c. claret	1·40	6·50
6		3c. orange-red	1·60	6·25
		a. Surch double	£250	
7		5c. green	2·20	5·00
8	**14**	10c. carmine	2·75	8·50

9		15c. pale red	2·20	8·00
10		20c. chocolate	4·75	9·00
11		1p. on 25c. blue	5·00	9·50
12		30c. deep lilac	3·50	11·00
13	**13**	40c. carmine and blue	6·25	16·00
14		2p. on 50c. brown and lavender	8·50	17·00
		a. Background colour omitted	£250	£250
15		4p. on 1f. lake and yellow	16·00	36·00
16		20p. on 5f. deep blue and buff	50·00	75·00
4/16 *Set of* 13			95·00	£190

The 1, 2, 3, 20 and 30c. exist on G.C. paper.

After France received the mandate for Syria, Arwad became part of the State of the Alaouites. It was used by the French as a place of detention for recalcitrant Syrian politicians.

FREE FRENCH FORCES IN THE LEVANT

(SYRIA AND LEBANON)

After British and Free French troops had occupied Syria and Lebanon in June 1941, the following stamps were issued for the use of Free French forces in those areas.

100 Centimes = 1 Franc

(**1**)

1942. No. 252 of Syria surch with T **1**.

1	50c. on 4p. orange	7·75	19·00
	a. Surch inverted	£850	

1942. Nos. 251 and 208 of Lebanon surch as T **1**, in red.

2	1f. on 5p. greenish blue	7·75	19·00
3	2f.50 on 12½p. ultramarine	7·75	18·00

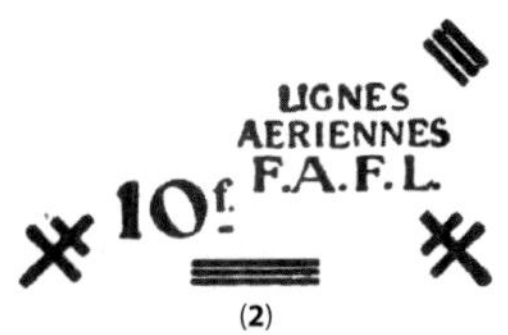

(**2**)

1942. AIR. Nos. 269/270 of Syria surch as T **2**.

4	4f. on 50p. black (R.)	7·25	16·00
5	6f.50 on 50p. black (R.)	7·25	12·50
6	8f. on 50p. black (O.)	7·25	12·50
7	10f. on 100p. magenta	7·25	18·00
4/7 *Set of* 4		26·00	55·00

3 Camelry and Ruins at Palmyra

4 Wings bearing Lorraine Crosses

(Des R. Soriano. Litho Beirut)

1942. P 11½.

(a) POSTAGE. Buff background

8	**3**	1f. lake	1·70	3·00
9		1f.50 violet	1·40	4·25
10		2f. orange	1·30	4·25
11		2f.50 sepia	1·50	5·75
12		3f. blue	1·70	6·50
13		4f. green	2·10	6·25
14		5f. claret	2·10	5·75
		a. Imperf	20·00	39·00

(b) AIR

15	**4**	6f.50 rose-carmine	3·25	6·50
16		10f. purple and blue	3·50	7·00
8/16 *Set of* 9			17·00	44·00
MS16*a* 106×16 mm. Nos. 15/16. No gum			33·00	65·00
		ab. Imperf	26·00	50·00

(**5**)

1942. AIR. No. 15 surch with T **5** in the colour of the stamp.

17	**4**	4f. on 6f.50 rose-carmine	3·00	8·50

RÉSISTANCE

(**6**)

RÉSISTANCE

(**7**)

1943.

*(a) POSTAGE. Surch as T **6** with premium*

18	**3**	1f. +9f. lake	11·00	13·50
19		5f. +20f. claret	11·00	13·50

*(b) AIR. Surch as T **7** with premium*

20	**4**	6f.50 +48f.50 rose-carmine	55·00	75·00
21		10f. +100f. purple and blue	60·00	75·00
18/21 *Set of* 4			£120	£160

4F

(**8**)

1943. AIR. No. 12 surch with T **8**.

22	**3**	4f. on 3f. blue and buff	3·00	4·25

By an Anglo-French agreement of 13 December, 1945 all British and French troops left Syria and Lebanon by 15 April 1946.

DESIGN INDEX

Where the same design, or subject, appears more than once in a set only the first number is given. Scenes and buildings are listed under the town or geographical area in which they are situated. Portraits are listed under surnames only. In cases of difficulty part of the inscription has been used to identify the stamp.

Early stamps of Syria are overprinted French or Turkish stamps.

Dear Catalogue User,

As a collector and Stanley Gibbons catalogue user for many years myself, I am only too aware of the need to provide you with the information you seek in an accurate, timely and easily accessible manner. Naturally, I have my own views on where changes could be made, but one thing I learned long ago is that we all have different opinions and requirements.

I would therefore be most grateful if you would complete the form overleaf and return it to me. Please contact Lorraine Holcombe (lholcombe@stanleygibbons.com) if you would like to be emailed the questionnaire.

Very many thanks for your help.

Yours sincerely,

Hugh Jefferies,
Editor.

Questionnaire

2018 Middle East

1. Level of detail

   Do you feel that the level of detail in this catalogue is:

   a. too specialised O
   b. about right O
   c. inadequate O

2. Frequency of issue

   How often would you purchase a new edition of this catalogue?

   a. Annually O
   b. Every two years O
   c. Every three to five years O
   d. Less frequently O

3. Design and Quality

   How would you describe the layout and appearance of this catalogue?

   a. Excellent O
   b. Good O
   c. Adequate O
   d. Poor O

4. How important to you are the prices given in the catalogue:

   a. Important O
   b. Quite important O
   c. Of little interest O
   d. Of no interest O

5. Would you be interested in an online version of this catalogue?

   a. Yes O
   b. No O

6. Do you like the new format?

   a. Yes O
   b. No O

7. What changes would you suggest to improve the catalogue? E.g. Which other indices would you like to see included?

   ....

   ....

   ....

   ....

8. Which other Stanley Gibbons Catalogues do you buy?

   ....

   ....

   ....

   ....

9. Would you like us to let you know when the next edition of this catalogue is due to be published?

   a. Yes O
   b. No O

   If so please give your contact details below.

   Name: ....

   Address:..

   ....

   ....

   ....

   Email: ....

   Telephone:...

10. Which other Stanley Gibbons Catalogues are you interested in?

    a. ....

    b. ....

    c. ....

Many thanks for your comments.

Please complete and return it to: Hugh Jefferies (Catalogue Editor)
Stanley Gibbons Limited, 7 Parkside, Ringwood, Hampshire BH24 3SH, United Kingdom
or email: lholcombe@stanleygibbons.com to request a soft copy

Middle East Order Form

YOUR ORDER

Stanley Gibbons account number

Condition (mint/UM/ used)	Country	SG No.	Description	Price	Office use only
			POSTAGE & PACKING	£3.60	
			TOTAL		

The lowest price charged for individual stamps or sets purchased from Stanley Gibbons Ltd, is £1.

Payment & address details

Name

Address (We cannot deliver to PO Boxes)

Postcode

Tel No.

Email

PLEASE NOTE Overseas customers MUST quote a telephone number or the order cannot be dispatched. Please complete ALL sections of this form to allow us to process the order.

☐ Cheque (made payable to Stanley Gibbons Ltd)

☐ I authorise you to charge my

☐ Mastercard ☐ Visa ☐ Diners ☐ Amex ☐ Maestro

Card No. (Maestro only)

Valid from Expiry date Issue No. (Maestro only) CVC No. (4 if Amex)

CVC No. is the last three digits on the back of your card (4 if Amex)

Signature Date

4 EASY WAYS TO ORDER

Post to
Mark Pegg, Stamp Mail Order Department, Stanley Gibbons Ltd, 399 Strand, London, WC2R 0LX, England

Call
020 7836 8444
+44 (0)20 7836 8444

Fax
020 7557 4499
+44 (0)20 7557 4499

Click
mpegg@stanleygibbons.com

"This is My Promise to YOU"
"Massive Philatelic Choice in a Unique Reducing Estimate System Delivering VAL-YOU, with Absolutely NO Buyer's Premium PLUS ALL Lots Guaranteed"
Andrew McGavin,
Managing Director Universal Philatelic Auctions
Shield Yourself & Save
I SUPPORT NO BP
SUPPORT NO BUYER'S PREMIUM
1st £55 FREE WINNINGS
THE COLLECTORS' SECRET WEAPON
Lot 19609
Ex archive, see back cover
CLOSING DATE:
REQUEST YOUR FREE CATALOGUE NOW
CATALOGUE £20
Discover the Difference
UNIVERSAL PHILATELIC AUCTIONS
Philately Understood
ALL LOTS · 100% NO QUIBBLE · GUARANTEED